Gallant Creoles

A History of the Donaldsonville Canonniers

GALLANT CREOLES

A History of the Donaldsonville Canonniers

by

MICHAEL MARSHALL

2013
University of Louisiana at Lafayette Press

ISBN 13 (paper): 978-1-935754-21-3

http://ulpress.org
University of Louisiana at Lafayette Press
P.O. Box 40831
Lafayette, LA 70504-0831

Printed on acid-free paper.

Library of Congress Cataloging-in-Publication Data

Marshall, Michael, 1954-
Gallant creoles : a history of the Donaldsonville Canonniers / by Michael Marshall.
p. cm.
Includes bibliographical references and index.
ISBN 978-1-935754-21-3
1. Confederate States of America. Army. Donaldsonville Artillery. 2. Louisiana--History--Civil War, 1861-1865--Regimental histories. 3. United States--History--Civil War, 1861-1865--Regimental histories. 4. United States--History--Civil War, 1861-1865--Artillery operations, Confederate. I. Title.
E565.8.D66M37 2012
973.7'463--dc23
2012031614

Cover Images:

Front: A uniform button of "Le Canonniers de Donaldsonville," which was recovered during a 1996 archeological dig at the site of Fort Butler in Donaldsonville, La. Courtesy of Dr. Charles "Chip" McGimsey. Photograph by Andrew Capone.

Front: Sons of Confederate Veteran's gun detachment posed in front of the Donaldsonville Courthouse, September 18, 1891, celebrating the 30th anniversary of the Donaldsonville Canonniers departure for Richmond, Virginia. Courtesy of Confederate Memorial Hall, New Orleans.

Spine: First Confederate National Flag of Dreaux/Rightor 1st Louisiana Infantry Battalion—probably very much similar to the bellum flag of the Donaldsonville Canonniers as twenty-three members of Dreaux/Rightor's Battalion joined the Donaldsonville Artillery at the end of their enlistment. Courtesy of Confederate Memorial Hall, New Orleans.

Rear: Canonnier veteran Henri Gamotis. Coutesy of Beverly Gamotis Hardy and Joe Hardy.

Art thou of those, the sons of generous valor,
such as stands between country and her foes,
Defenders of her rights, avengers of her wrongs,
And guardians of her sacred honor.

Aye, thou shalt be a hero.

"My Little Grandson"
by Mrs. Louisia H. Nicholls,
Poems (New York, New York; 1857)

This book is lovingly dedicated to my grandchildren.

Table of Contents

"Ah, friends there are memories which should be perpetuated and which it is criminal to forget. Then let us hand down to our children and our children's children, to unborn generations, the pathetic story of a land of brave men who fought for constitutional rights against might, against invasion, against incendiarism; who fought to protect their wives and mothers, their sons and daughters and themselves from wrong and oppression. Traitors and rebels they never were, and it is a slander so to call them. But as secessionist, as revolutionist they stand side by side upon the same plane in history with George Washington, father of his country, founder of a great nation of free people, who likewise seceded from England and fought against tyranny and wrong."

~ Mrs. Amelia Landry,
a witness to the Donaldsonville Canonniers departure on September 18, 1861,
in a speech given on June 6, 1909, in honor of Confederate Memorial Day.
Donaldsonville Chief, June 12, 1909.

"The day is coming when . . . our children and their children's children will glory in the exploits of Americans, no matter who led or where they fought . . . our prosaic mountains and rivers and villages will be full of ennobling legend and poetic tradition to the coming generations, because of the men in blue and the men in gray who struggled in them. And this we know, and it thrills our hearts to know it, that the rivers by which our heroes sleep will be drained and the sea and the battle-mountains on which they rest will be leveled with the plains before the story of their valor dies out or the record of their heroism ceases to ennoble mankind."

~ Eugene H. Levy,
Donaldsonville Artillery, A. P. Hill's Corps,
Army of Northern Virginia, April 15, 1897.
New York Tribune, April 28, 1897.

"Everything I have to say about the writing of history was summoned up by John Keats in ten words in a letter . . . nearly two hundred years ago. He said, 'A fact is not a truth until you love it.' You have to become attached to the thing you're writing about—in other words, 'love it'—for it to have any real meaning."

~ Shelby Foote,
"Interviews," *The Paris Review*, Summer 1999, No. 151.

PREFACE

How did I come to write this history? My mother, Gloria Templet Marshall, dabbled in genealogy and one summer day in 1985 asked me, "Did you know that your grandfather's grandfather Camille Templet (who we knew from family lore had fought in 'The Late Unpleasantness') and his brother Hypolite surrendered with the Donaldsonville Artillery and General Lee's army at Appomattox?" This piece of noteworthy news set me off to read about his exploits and those of his comrades.

I was somewhat familiar with the armies, leaders, and battles of the so-called War Between the States having been a youngster during the Civil War Centennial commemoration. Throughout the 1960s I read as much as I could (with a lot of gazing and gaping at the drawings and pictures) of numerous publications about the war. During this time my family visited many of the Virginia battlefields and coastal forts on vacations; family photographs and home movies show me wearing a coonskin cap, of Davy Crockett fame, posing and climbing on cannons with my brother Bobby and sister Gail. These fond memories and excursions into history whetted my appetite to learn more. As I grew older I continued to read about the Blue and Gray, along with other histories and military books. I did a two year stint in the United States Marine Corps during which time I made sure my field pack, containing mostly olive drab socks stuffed with C-rations, had space for a paperback history book.

It soon became apparent to me that there were no complete or comprehensive chronicles of the Gunners of Donaldson, "Creoles all and gallant soldiers," just bits and pieces of stories and information. That they were "the oldest" and "finest artillery" company in Louisiana when "The War of Secession" came was virtually unknown. I even located a newspaper article about the forgotten command, written thirty years after the conflict, which noted: "Pen and press have neglected its gallant career."

I started out to read of my heritage and after twenty-seven years of research and ongoing composition ended up with *Gallant Creoles: A History of the Donaldsonville Canonniers.* My ambition with this book is that the veterans of the *Canonniers de Donaldson* will no longer be forgotten, but rather their service and sacrifice will be memorialized. May their descendants glory in their exploits and perpetuate their memory so their story of audacity and courage will never die out.

One of the most important accounts of the Donaldsonville Artillery that started me out and guided me on this journey was a typescript paper, "The Diary of a Donaldsonville Cannoneer—Romain Octave Landry—Confederate States of America, 1861-1865, copied and edited by Evans J. Casso." With Mr. Casso's encouragement I met the great-grandniece of the diary's author, Yvonne Landry of Donaldsonville, and she graciously allowed me to examine the original little booklet. I was now captivated by the *Canonniers de Donaldson* and determined to move *en avant* (forward).

My quest through the years led me to great friends and historians whose contributions to this endeavor have been immeasurable. As it happens, we became a loose-knit historical research association and are proud of our discoveries, contributions, and understanding of past people, places, and events in Louisiana and elsewhere. This amazing group of confidants include Andrew Capone of Capone Plantation, Labadieville, founder and president of Donaldsonville's Fort Butler Foundation, a nonprofit historical and preservation organization; Glenn Falgoust of French Settlement; Louise "Pie" Lanoux of Gonzales; and private investigator extraordinaire Denise "DeeDee" DiBenedetto Sanders of Lake Martin.

To the following two curators I owe a tremendous debt of gratitude for their able assistance and time: Patricia Ricci of Confederate Memorial Hall, New Orleans, and Sherrie Pugh of the Library of the Adjutant General of Louisiana, Jackson Barracks, New Orleans. Thank you.

I must also give thanks and appreciation for the kind assistance and sharing of their extensive knowledge to U.S. National Park Service historians Christopher Calkins, retired from Petersburg National Battlefield Park and currently managing Sailor's Creek Battlefield Historical State Park; Robert K. "Bob" Krick, retired from Fredericksburg & Spotsylvania National Military Park; and Robert E. L. "Bobby" Krick of the Richmond National Battlefield Park.

I would like to thank the numerous archivists and librarians who assisted me in my research and all the universities and organizations visited, which are duly acknowledged in the appropriate footnotes and bibliography. Of special note are the staff of the Louisiana Division at the New Orleans Public Library; Dr. Wilbur Meneray (retired) and Leon Cahill Miller, along with the staff of Howard-Tilton Memorial Library, Special Collections, Tulane University, New Orleans; Dr. Charles R. "Chip" McGimsey, Louisiana State Division of Archaeology, Baton Rouge; Amanda Knippers Marshall, Troy H. Middleton Library, Louisiana State University; Eve A. Cassat, Special Collections, Marlene and Nathan Addlestone Library, College of Charleston, South Carolina; and James D. Wilson Jr., Associate Director, University of Louisiana at Lafayette Press.

On research trips I met a number of very kind Virginians who invited me into their homes and shared their stories and insight. To them I am most grateful, especially to Harold E. Howard, publisher of the Virginia Regimental Histories Series, for graciously allowing me into his Lynchburg office and on a later trip into his home near Appomattox Court House National Historical Park; Charles and Barbara Bourne of Mechanicsville; William B. Gates III of Colonial Heights; Raymond Shaw of Inglewood Farm near Gordonsville; Eugene Zimmerman of Fredericksburg (near United States Ford); and Donald E. and Virginia Austin, longtime residents of Fredericksburg. I would also like to thank Thomas G. Ledford, the museum administrator of the Lynchburg, Virginia Museum System for his kind assistance. I would be remiss if I did not mention my father Robert C. Marshall who cheerfully accompanied me on a few of these journeys.

Many individuals took time to make contributions. Of special note are Dr. Keith Cangelosi of Abita Springs; Joseph William "Bill" Carmena of Baton Rouge; Arthur M. Colomb of San Francisco, California; Sylvia Degruy of Gonzales; Beverly Gamotis Hardy and her son Joseph Thomas Hardy of New Orleans; John S. Hilbert of Los Angeles; Shirley Keen Jackson of Greenville, South Carolina; Chandler L. Klotz Jr. of McComb, Mississippi; Charles M. Lanier Jr. of New Orleans; Ken Legendre of Gretna; Paul Marchand of Donaldsonville; Lee Victor Maurin of Metairie; John H. McClellan of Waynesboro, Pennsylvania; Doris Melancon of Gonzales; Nathalie G. Nelson of Metairie; Robert Pugh of Thibodaux; Joseph Ricci of Metairie; John and Mary Bangs of Metairie; R. Hughes Simmons of Paoli, Delaware; David Wright of Petersburg, Virginia; and Julissa Guerrero Marshall of Ponchatoula.

I would like to give notice to and thank Russell Desmond of *La Librarie d' Arcadie* (Arcadian Books), New Orleans, for his French translations; S. Lorraine Toerner of Baton Rouge and her daughter Karen Dodds of Chatom, Alabama, for sharing the original François Bienvenue Cire memorandum book; John J. Hennessey, formerly historian at Manassas National Battlefield Park and now historian at Fredericksburg & Spotsylvania National Military Park; and the late Kirk P. Landry for the use and information about his superb Donaldsonville postcard collection.

I must give special appreciation and thanks for the enthusiastic encouragement and support to "Keep those caissons a rolling along" to Charles H. Coates Jr., of Baton Rouge, a 1957 West Point graduate (like his father, Class of 1924) and the maternal great-great-grandson of Major Victor Maurin.

Thanks again to all. Your assistance and camaraderie is greatly appreciated and my gratitude is immeasurable

Finally, the biggest and most heartfelt thanks goes to Debra, *ma très chère épouse*, who has graciously allowed me through two decades and several years to spend an inordinate amount of time with those of another age. Additionally, I want to convey my appreciation and gratitude to my two sons Michael Jr. and Christopher for their understanding in allowing me to pursue our heritage.

Michael Marshall
Hammond, Louisiana

Chapter One

Canonniers de Donaldsonville d'ante-bellum
(The Antebellum Canonniers of Donaldsonville)

"Shining with snow-white plumes, large flocks of pelicans waded.
Level the landscape grew, and along the shores of the river,
Shaded by china trees, in the midst of luxuriant gardens,
Stood the houses of planters, with negro-cabins and dovecots.
They were approaching the region where reigns perpetual summer,
Where through the Golden Coast, and groves of orange and citron,
Sweeps with majestic curve the river away to the eastward."

So Longfellow describes the Acadian or Golden Coast of Ascension Parish, Louisiana, in his classic work *Evangeline.*[1] The seat of justice for Ascension Parish is the town of Donaldsonville, at the point where Bayou Lafourche diverges from the Mississippi River. The settlement was originally called *La Fourche des Chetimaches* after the Indian tribe that dwelt at the fork of the river and bayou. It began as a trading post established by a few French and Spanish settlers before 1750. The arrival between the years 1757 and 1790 of French Acadian exiles made an affecting increase in the region's population.

Louisiana came under Spanish rule in 1763, and that government augmented the population ostensibly for military defenses by recruiting immigrant-soldiers and their families from the Canary Islands. A number of these Isleños settled on Bayou Lafourche near *La Fourche des Chetimaches* and called it *Valenzuela de la Fourche.*[2] On August 15, 1772,[3] Father Angelus de Revillagodos by order of the Catholic Bishop of Toledo and Charles III, King of Spain, established a church to minister to the spiritual welfare of the community. The Capuchin friar named his parish l'Ascension, dedicating it to "the Ascension of Our Lord."[4]

In 1775 the Spanish governor granted the land just below the entrance to Bayou Lafourche to an Acadian exile named Pierre Landry. In 1806 William Donaldson acquired the farm from the widow of Landry and subdivided it into city lots, naming the town *Ville de Donaldson.* Eleven months after Louisiana was admitted into the Union, the State Legislature on March 25, 1813, incorporated the thriving town located approximately seventy five miles upriver from New Orleans. This handsomely built "old French"[5] town, with its "tiled and turreted buildings of French and Spanish times,"[6] became a center of Creole culture and civilization known for its hospitality and politeness to strangers. The population of the "good society"[7] in 1830 was 492, of whom 261 were white and almost exclusively Creole, 76 were free persons of color, and 155 were slaves. Donaldsonville was ideally situated as a commercial center for the many small farmers, *les petits habitants*,[8] who flourished along both sides of the river and bayou. It was not uncommon to meet Creole, French Acadian, and Isleños families of twelve to eighteen children.[9]

During the boom period of the late 1820s and 1830s, an influx of Anglo-American planters from the eastern United States bought much of Ascension's alluvial lands from small proprietors and converted these farms into large plantations of the most valuable sugar-growing lands. This resulted in their bringing in many more slaves to cultivate the land, thus causing a rapid increase of slave labor, though the vast majority of the free population of Ascension remained non-slaveholding.[10] This sugar country became a favored and colorful part of the Old South of "ample cane plantations interspersed with narrow sugar farms, of white-columned mansions contrasting with humble dwellings, of tall-chimneyed sugarhouses in juxtaposition with primitive mule-drawn cane mills, of Anglo-American planters among Creole proprietors, of Irish and 'Cajun'[11] laborers in the midst of a multitude of Negro slaves, and of affluent and graceful living in the presence of rural simplicity and back-breaking toil."[12]

In May 1837 a national financial panic resulted in a severe crisis for Louisiana's economy. Ascension Parish planters additionally suffered from a new tariff that depreciated the value of American sugar. Ruin and desolation was reported while agriculture languished from want of stimulation. It was during these tough economic times that an increased anxiety surrounding the question of slavery occurred.[13] A newspaper report out of Donaldsonville stated that it was "ready to believe that the last maneuvers of the northern abolitionist have scattered some germ of insurrection among the slaves of [Ascension] parish. For some time different circumstances are found and seem to be the precursor of silently plotted agitation."[14]

Much excitement was caused in Donaldsonville that year when an overseer was "found barbarously murdered"[15] by "negros"[16] in neighboring Assumption Parish. The Donaldsonville and New Orleans newspapers editorialized, "God forbid that our intention is to throw alarm among the planters," adding, this "should arouse our citizens to a sense of the danger to which they are exposed by the internal spirit of abolition; and should put them more upon their guard!"[17]

Ever-present in the mind of the slaveholder and his non-slave owning neighbors was the fear of servile insurrection. Of course, among the slaves, as among the whites, there was a criminal element against whose depredations society had to be defended.[18] Increasingly persistent rumors of potential bank failings across the region, which almost assuredly would result in violence, further elevated social tensions. In this time of economic unrest and civil distress a group of young men from Donaldsonville with "patriotic spirit"[19] founded a military association. They called themselves *Canonniers de Donaldson*.[20]

On August 8, 1837, these men adopted eighteen regulations and seven general provisions under the title, "*Reglemens de la Compagnie des Canonniers de Donaldson*" and committed themselves to "*l'honneur à obeir strictment aux . . . reglements*" (the honor to obey the rules and regulations). Articles stipulated the number of rank, including a fife and drummer, in the company; a description of "*L'Uniforme*" (the uniform); and that "*la compagnie prendra les armes pour être passée en revue et inspectée par l'Officier commandant*" (the company with weapons will be reviewed and inspected by the Captain) every first Sunday of the month and perform "*exercices pour l'instruction des Canonniers*" (exercises for instruction of gunners) every Thursday. Most important, Provision Four of the regulations specified the location to rendezvous in case of public calamities, such as insurrection, riot, or fire, or to protect the properties of citizens.[21]

The company's leading organizer and first captain was Joseph Numa Augustin, a twenty-five-year-old Creole gentleman with thick, jet-black facial hair. A New Orleans native, Numa, as he was called, moved to Donaldsonville after obtaining employment as a cashier in the Ascension branch of the Canal and Banking Company of New Orleans. When the financial crash occurred on May 13, 1837, fourteen of the eighteen banks in New Orleans suspended specie payment with the Canal Bank being one of four that came through the calamity unhurt.[22]

Augustin's father had previously escaped the disorder bred in France from their revolution by moving his family to a plantation he purchased on Saint Domingue in 1789. The Augustins were residents of the island when the black insurrection began and during the long and bloody rebellion the family abandoned their adopted home. They were able to make their escape through the agency of a slave named Circé who accompanied them on their flight. In 1811 Jean Augustin brought his family to New Orleans and settled there. Numa was his fifth child, the only one born in Louisiana. The organizer and captain of the Donaldsonville military association had received his education in New Orleans from the College d'Orleans, whose first head master was Jules D'Avezac, a native of Saint Domingue. Augustin and the other pupils of D'Avezac were made well aware of the history of Saint Domingue and the potential for similar unrest in Louisiana.[23]

Another of the founders of the *Compagnie d'Artillerie* was Victor Auguste Maurin. Just eighteen years old in 1837, he rose from grade to grade until he became captain and would always be remembered as one of the company's most zealous members. He was the son of Victor Marie Maurin, who along with his brother Joseph Maurin, were officers in the army of Napoleon Bonaparte. Joseph obtained the rank of brigadier general, officer of the Legion of Honor, Knight of St. Louis, and Baron,[24] and served as the French army commander guarding the Algarve Coast in Faro, Portugal.[25] Victor Marie (born in 1784) served in the Saint Domingue campaign. In 1803, after the French forces were defeated (the army suffered more casualties than at Waterloo, mostly from disease) the massacre of French citizens ensued.[26] The nineteen-year-old Maurin survived by hiding under a bridge for three months with the help of an African who provided food. He finally escaped from the island by swimming three miles to an American vessel bound for New York. He then served his adopted country, the United States, in the War of 1812 and was a participant in the Battle of New Orleans under Andrew Jackson. He married Elizabeth Ann Slattery of Johnstown, New York, and in 1813 settled in Donaldsonville, where Victor Marie became sheriff. His son Victor Auguste Maurin was born in 1818 and later obviously learned the history of Saint Domingue, too.[27]

One member would later describe the beginning of this "gallant body of young Creoles"[28] by saying: "With the single hope, and laudable ambition to be useful to their fellow citizens, they rallied forth, [this] little band of brave men, and trusting to the unknown future, they unfurled to the breeze a young flag which bore these two short words: '*En Avant*!'"[29] The volunteers served as firemen, "ever ready to save the hearth" and "to risk their own lives to save the life of a human being."[30] Their organization also acted as a "charitable association."[31] A local newspaper wrote, "Each member of this corps deserves a portion of the praise which we give for their patriotism and the enthusiasm with which they responded to the call that we made to them," adding, "who knows if, later, the state will not have need of their services."[32] Before that need would arise in 1861, it was said, "While the cannoneers existed as a body, no riot, no mob ever disturbed the peace of the Parish or violated the laws of the land."[33]

At the time of the company's formation Donaldsonville had an old arsenal that was equipped by the state in 1833 with muskets, swords, and pistols. Now a new arsenal was under construction, a brick armory on the Court House Square at Opelousas Street, which would be called *l'Arsenal.*

Joseph Numa Augustin, 1812-1872; first Captain (1837-1845) of *Le Canonniers de Donaldson*.
Courtesy of the Historic New Orleans Collection.

Victor Auguste Maurin in regulation Confederate officer's artillery frock coat of gray with red trim and gold piping of a captain. The photograph was taken probably in October or November 1861 at Rees' Photographic Gallery, 145 Main Street (over West and Johnson's Bookstore) Richmond, Virginia.
Courtesy of Lee Victor Maurin, Metairie, La.

In February 1837, Louisiana Governor Edward Douglas White, who previously lived and practiced law in Donaldsonville before being appointed to a judgeship in New Orleans, authorized the purchase of a brass twelve-pounder artillery fieldpiece for each militia brigade in the state. The *Canonniers de Donaldson* were hopeful of obtaining a fieldpiece from the government, but in December 1837, the state decided it did not want to incur the expense of purchasing artillery pieces that might not come within the class and description ascertained by the United States Ordnance Department, which was conducting experiments on which guns were most efficient. Organized with the ambition to serve as an artillery company, the *Compagnie d'Artillerie* at the time of its formation lacked one essential element to compliment its identity—cannons![34]

Undaunted, Captain Augustin in the same month sent a committee to the Church of the Ascension of Our Lord in Donaldsonville asking to assist in the Mass, "In military style in honor of their patroness, St. Barbara, and to have the *Te Deum* sung for them."[35] At this Catholic service on the eve of St. Barbara's Day, December 3, 1837, a Donaldsonville resident by the name of Hinkley sang in French and in English, in equal parts, a song he had composed for "*les canonniers de Donaldson.*"[36]

In January 1838, with the assistance of the governor and with backing from the state's Senate and House of Representatives, Louisiana formally requested of the U.S. secretary of war, "[t]he gift or loan of two field pieces (six pounders) for the use of an organized volunteer cannoneer company, in the Parish of Ascension."[37] The request was not fulfilled, and the cannons were not forthcoming. However the *Compagnie d'Artillerie* continued to be a military presence in and around Donaldsonville with events such as a *Tir à la Cible* (Target Practice) that took place in April 1838. This became an annual event and brought some recognition.

Considerations for government support and the furnishing of arms to militia companies were especially noted when volunteers, at their own expense, bought uniforms and equipment for themselves.[38] The *Canonniers de Donaldson* were a uniformed company with their attire "very tasty"[39] and characterized as "*les brillants uniforms de nos . . . Canonniers*"[40] (the brilliant uniforms of our . . . Cannoneers) consisting of a head dress (shako) with a red plume, dark blue coat with red trimming, trousers of blue in winter and white in summer, boots, complete equipment, and a knapsack.[41]

The sought after recognition by the *Compagnie d'Artillerie* was finally obtained in 1839 when the state granted the sum of $250.00 annually for five years. The *Canonniers de Donaldson* were to use this money to buy "powder and balls to be used to perfect them in the science of gunnery."[42] By 1841 the company boasted an enlistment of sixty-seven members, making it one of the largest volunteer units in the state. In 1843 the annual appropriation of $250.00 was continued for an additional five years by the state.[43]

1840 uniform of the Donaldsonville Canonniers.
Courtesy of the Library of the Adjutant General of La. (hereafter cited as LAGL).

Throughout the antebellum period the *Canonniers de Donaldson* received orders once a month to "*Rendez-vous a l'Arsenal*" (rendezvous at the Arsenal) where they attended soldier school and drilled. Besides the monthly gatherings, the captain assembled the company to fire salutes in celebration of holidays such as the Battle of New Orleans (January 8, 1815); Washington's Birthday (February 22); the Feast of the Ascension (the Thursday, forty days after Easter); Independence Day (July 4); and Saint Barbara's Day (December 4); and to honor and attend the funeral of any deceased member of the company.[44]

For St. Barbara's celebration the Canonniers customarily invited the Orleans Artillery and presented a banquet, or traveled to New Orleans, where the artillery corps would celebrate together in commemoration of their patron. These festivities were described as pleasing affairs that usually began at an early hour when the artillerists attended a solemn mass. Afterwards they would march through the main streets of the city full of enthusiasm and *esprit d'corps*.[45]

One noteworthy celebration occurred in Donaldsonville in 1850 and was attended by Louisiana Governor Joseph Walker and State Adjutant General Charles N. Rowley. After a splendid collation, the Canonniers, about fifty strong, formed and marched to the courthouse for a presentation of *du drapeau* (the colors) by Aimé Bercegeay, a lieutenant colonel of the militia and formerly sergeant major of the *Canonniers de Donaldson*.[46] The flag was described as simply the Stars and Stripes, but it was made of a rich material and beautifully ornamented. After the presentation, Captain Maurice Grivot, commander of the Orleans Artillery, fastened a wreath to the top of the flagstaff, and the company moved off to the town square,[47] where a large number of ladies graced the surroundings with fair faces and bright eyes. Military marches were performed by the *Compagnie d'Artillerie de Donaldson* to the stirring strains of martial music. The scene was described as one of much animation and excitement. On this occasion, as on others, the evening concluded with a sumptuous repast, after which the host commander gave the first of many toasts. In turn, each distinguished guest followed with a tribute or compliment of their own, like this sublime one: "The grand and noble feeling, which makes a citizen a soldier, and a soldier a citizen."[48] Accolades were also received, such as the one from Grivot (later to become Adjutant General of Louisiana), who declared, "The Canonniers of Donaldsonville, citizens and soldiers, who, when occasion calls, are ever ready to seize the musket to enforce obedience to the laws."[49] In the end, the ringing of glasses ceased, a final adieu was given, and a grand salute was fired in honor of St. Barbara.[50]

The annual target shoot and encampment was exercised each April, when sugar estates in the vicinity of Donaldsonville were cleared of cane. In a festival-like atmosphere, the day began with the *Compagnie d'Artillerie* assembling at *l'Arsenal*, knapsacks filled. They then marched out of town to the sound of fife-and-drum war music provided by their Field Band made up of "splendid musicians"[51] that were "colored."[52] The company's flapping flag would lead the way to the location of the event. The customary place was two miles below Donaldsonville on the grounds of Madame (widow) Louis Mollere in a beautiful meadow shaded by green oak trees, although in certain years the event was held across the Mississippi River on the edge of Bayou Conway, or five miles above Donaldsonville on the plantation of Narcisse Landry. After arriving at the given locality, tents were arranged and set up while provisions of all kinds arrived, the voluntary donations of planters and friends. Supper was then prepared and consumed at a grand party. Early the next morning all the Canonniers, armed with muskets, met on the target range. The target was usually nothing more than a plank on which was drawn a mannequin. After the mass shoot the first and second place finishers were given a medal or a pompon, plus a chicken respectively. After the match, the *Compagnie d'Artillerie* took up its arms and paid its respects to local residents by performing military maneuvers, followed by a parade around Donaldsonville. The greater part of the population turned out for these events to cheer the citizen-soldiers and show their appreciation and admiration.[53]

In February 1845, Captain Augustin and the *Compagnie d'Artillerie* traveled to New Orleans to participate in a Grand Military Spectacle, a mimic battle in celebration of George Washington's birthday. Major General John L. Lewis's First Division of Louisiana Militia participated, as did four companies of U.S. troops from the Baton Rouge garrison, two from the barracks below New Orleans (present day Jackson Barracks), and one each from Fort Pike and Fort Wood, along with volunteer companies of the Louisiana Legion, Regiment of Louisiana Volunteers, Washington Regiment, Captain Todd's Company of State Artillery from Mobile, Alabama, and the *Canonniers de Donaldson*. This sham battle with 2,500 to 3,000 troops took place on the Oak Plains three miles above the city with the Louisiana Volunteers of Militia attacking the Louisiana Legion positioned along Bayou St. John. The *Compagnie d'Artillerie* was assigned to and maneuvered with the Louisiana Legion, with whom Major J. B. Donatien Augustin, Captain Numa Augustin's brother, served. Thousands of citizens came to witness this grand and imposing battle, which began at ten o'clock in the morning.[54]

A newspaper reporter described it:

> The military array—the rattling drums—the shrill fife and spirit stirring trumpet, the flaunting banners, the dazzling arms, the rush of cavalry and fierce charge of columns of infantry, half veiled by dense smoke of the cannon and musketry, the hoarse voices of the officers sounding loud amidst the din, the advance, the conflict—and the retreat . . . gave a perfect idea of the "pomp and circumstances of glorious war."[55]

A second reporter wrote: "We heard noise in abundance, and saw any quantity of smoke; but after the final discharge of artillery, that was all we could see."[56] After the suspension of mock hostilities and the smoke of the conflict floated away, the troops passed in review before the governor and other field officers. A bountiful feast was then partaken of by the citizen-soldiers and invited guests in an adjacent field.[57]

Ten months after their participation in the sham fight and celebration in New Orleans, the *Canonniers de Donaldson* lost their organizer and first officer, Captain Joseph Numa Augustin. His brother, J. B. Donatien Augustin, was elected and commissioned brigadier general to command the Legion of Louisiana by the governor on December 31, 1845. Having joined the Legion at age fifteen when it was first organized in 1818, J. B. rose through the ranks to lieutenant of artillery, then aide-de-camp before becoming its commander and issuing Special Order No. 1 appointing his younger brother, Numa—the Canonnier Captain—to one of six aide-de-camp positions. This prompted Numa Augustin to move with his family back to New Orleans, where he became a commission merchant and later entered the brokerage business.[58] After leaving Donaldsonville, the name Numa Augustin remained "agreeably in the heart of the citizens and was never forgotten."[59]

Replacing Augustin as captain of the *Canonniers de Donaldson* was Sergeant Major Joseph M. Vidal, who had affixed his name to the *Reglement* (Regulations) at the organizational meeting on August 8, 1837. A forty-five-year-old native of Spain, recording secretary of the town council, and school teacher at Donaldsonville's only public school, Vidal was characterized as *bon et honnete* (good and honest)[60] and *son digne* (worthy).[61] Vidal commanded from 1846 to 1849, and the *Compagnie d'Artillerie* under his leadership continued with *fêtes*, drill, and ceremonies to celebrate holidays and anniversaries.

One such event took place in December 1847. Soon-to-be U.S. President and Mexican War hero Zachary Taylor visited Donaldsonville on his way home after leaving New Orleans. A city newspaper reported:

> At half past 4 P. M., the [steamboat] *Missouri* came within sight of Donaldsonville. The display which had been for the general's reception at this beautiful and public-spirited little town . . . was really . . . beautiful and interesting. Our national flag waved to the breeze from every place where a staff could be erected. The steamboats and vessels at the entrance to the Lafourche, were covered with gay bunting and crowded with eager persons. The balconies and windows of the houses were filled with the lovely fair of Donaldsonville and of the neighboring parishes, and the levee was crowded with an immense concourse of citizens, who flocked to Donaldsonville from the interior . . . .
>
> In the meantime as the boat neared the wharf, the battery of that splendid volunteer corps, the Donaldsonville Artillery, kept up a constant blaze of fire and 'deep-toned thunder.' As soon as the boat was made fast . . . the mayor delivered a very neat and appropriate welcome address, to which the general responded in a few brief and fervent words.
>
> On arriving at the house [called Bustle Hall[62]] of Judge [Thomas C.] Nicholls, the general entered the parlor to be introduced to the brilliant array of beauty which had been assembled to greet him. There were two large rooms filled with lovely Creoles, whose dark eyes, beaming faces and cherry lips were lit up with joy and delight at the sight of the brave old hero.
>
> As the old hero came into the room, there was a general rush—or, as an old campaigner styled it, a regular stampede—towards him, to get hold of his hand, or to snatch the long-to-be-remembered kiss from his weather-beaten cheeks. Having passed this severe ordeal, and made his obeisance . . . the general was escorted by the military to the ballroom, where a splendid collation had been prepared.
>
> Towards dark, after much hilarity, and many toasts and speeches, the procession was reformed and marched back to the boat . . . and bidding adieu to the crowd, the *Missouri* resumed her upward course, amid the loud buzzas of the vast assemblage. In the evening, the whole town was brilliantly illuminated with "the market-house in the centre, and the large mansions . . . surrounding it . . . a most beautiful appearance."[63]

During Vidal's reign, the Mexican War drew individual Canonniers into the fight along with other volunteers from Donaldsonville. The most notable Gunners of Donaldson were veteran and original members, brothers and sons of Judge Nicholls, Canonnier 1st Lieutenant Robert W. Nicholls and Canonnier Sergeant Major Edward F. Nicholls. For their gallantry and daring on the field of battle in Mexico the people of Ascension Parish rewarded the brothers with a presentation of swords before a vast Donaldsonville assembly on July 4, 1848, where each of the other Ascension volunteers were presented with an inscribed silver medal. All the veterans were received in triumph upon their return from Mexico with a warm reception.[64]

Captain Vidal's tenure also saw the election in 1846 of Ascension's Representative, Trasimon Landry, to lieutenant governor and president of the Louisiana Senate. During his term in office Landry presented the memorial of the volunteer corps of *Le Canonniers de Donaldsonville,* "praying for relief."[65] Landry's motion was referred to the Committee on Militia and resulted in the continued appropriation of five hundred dollars (one-half paid in 1849 and one-half paid in 1850) for their benefit.[66]

Vidal's commission expired[67] in 1849, and he relinquished command of the *Compagnie d'Artillerie de Donaldson*. Vidal also retired from teaching the next year. He did continue on with his town council duties and assumed the additional role of town treasurer as he championed the Canonniers' new leader as his security. Vidal considered the company not only his "true comrades" but "veritable friends."[68] During his years of leadership it was said the *Canonniers de Donaldson* "were never more gay, happy and brother-like."[69] The company had a *fête* to commemorate their retiring captain and each member in turn gave praise. After four hours the cry goodbye was given along with: "*Vive le Capitaine Vidal!*" (Long Live Captain Vidal!).[70]

On Saturday, April 20, 1849, between 9:00 a.m. and 2:00 p.m. at *l'Arsenal* in Donaldsonville an election was held to name the new captain of the *Canonniers de Donaldson*. Elected one week before his thirty-fourth birthday was Andrew Jackson Powell, a former militia cavalry officer and the chief clerk and deputy surveyor employed by the U.S. Surveyor General's Office in Donaldsonville. Such personages as ex-Governor André B. Roman, State Senator Duncan F. Kenner, and others employed him as a surveyor. Born in Adams County, Mississippi, and a resident of Louisiana since 1824, Powell moved into Vidal's office on the second floor of *l'Arsenal* in September 1849.

Powell was described as having *la probite* (honesty and integrity)[71] and *politesse exquise et d'une amabilité charmante* (exquisite politeness and amicable charm),[72] and under his leadership the *Compagnie d'Artillerie's* enlistment increased by one-third from the fifty volunteers who answered the roll call at the commencement of his command. In May 1850, Powell obtained from the Adjutant and Inspector General of Louisiana Charles N. Rowley, sixty muskets, sixty artillery sabers with cross belts, and ten thousand cartridges, balls, and caps, besides the money already appropriated by the legislature. The day when the new steamboat *Gipsy* made her cruise from Baton Rouge to Donaldsonville to deliver this military material was described as one of the most wonderful in the town's history.[73] When St. Barbara's Day arrived in December of 1850, a New Orleans newspaper reported the *Canonniers de Donaldson* "are a gallant body of young Creoles, and from Capt. Powell, down to the last private, every member is a gentleman and a soldier."[74]

Yet the *Compagnie d'Artillerie* remained without a cannon. Powell made note of this fact as early as December 1849 at the feast and celebration of St. Barbara, at which the visiting Artillery of Orleans presented to the *Canonniers de Donaldson* a magnificent centerpiece for their banquet table, a bouquet of a castle with a raising gate, turrets, towers, and artillery guns. After eating an extensive meal, Powell made a "bit cynical but happy illusion" to the castle—"Voila," he said, "the only castle that the Cannoneers of Donaldson can pretend to demolish with the cannons they now possessed."[75]

In 1848 Captain Powell's name was submitted to the Democratic Convention as a nominee for representative to the state legislature, but he declined giving the reason that he supported Zachary Taylor, the Whig Party candidate, for the United States presidency. Powell, who had been a Democrat, soon switched political parties and became a Whig delegate to the Taylor Convention held in New Orleans on February 22, 1848. There he joined twenty-five other Ascension Whigsters including: Senator Duncan F. Kenner, the state's Whig Party leader; Edward F. Nicholls; J. Narcisse Terrio, editor of the Donaldsonville newspaper *Le Vigilant*; Pierre G. Dannequin, treasurer and clerk of the Church of the Ascension, and later promoted to sergeant major of the *Compagnie d'Artillerie* under Powell's command; prominent attorney William C. Lawes; and Canonnier officer Victor Maurin.[76] Powell was named a delegate to the Whig Congressional Convention meeting at Donaldsonville on September 10, 1850, where, with the backing of personal and political friends, the "esteemed citizen A. Jackson Powell"[77] was nominated the Whig candidate to represent the Parish of Ascension in the lower house of the state legislature in August of 1851. Thanks to the Donaldsonville voters, Powell won the November election by a slim majority of six votes.[78]

After his election, Captain and Representative Powell traveled to the state capitol in Baton Rouge where the Legislature met on January 19, 1852, and adjourned just sixty days later. To the pleasure of the Whigs, an act was passed that provided for sounding the people on the

Model 1841 6-pounder field cannon.
Courtesy of Library of Congress.

call of a convention to revise the constitution of the state. To the pleasure of the Ascension representative and Canonnier captain, Powell obtained for the *Compagnie d'Artillerie* what they had always wanted, "A couple of well mounted field [artillery] pieces to complete their equipment and render them fit for any service."[79] It seems that Powell's old acquaintance and respected comrade, Adjutant and Inspector General Charles N. Rowley, after six years of service was leaving office, but before doing so issued to Powell two bronze, Model 1841, 6-pounder cannons valued at $1,760.00, along with their carriages worth $1,405.00, and one 6-pounder caisson costing $340.00. In lieu of the state receiving its militia quota of muskets from the federal government, the adjutant general accepted the two artillery pieces that included two sets of horse's harnesses and all the implements and equipment for a total value of $3,905.46.[80]

On Tuesday morning, April 13, 1852, the *Canonniers de Donaldson* were agreeably awaken to again await the much-anticipated arrival from Baton Rouge of the *Gipsy.* After the ship's appearance and docking, the "magnificent"[81] pieces of artillery were off loaded into a festival-like atmosphere of the curious population of Donaldsonville. The sight of these two cannons provoked a "thousand and one commentaries"[82] from the crowd on their beauty and elegance. Two hours after the pieces were disembarked and gazed upon they were brought in a procession to the new room of *l'Arsenal,* a long, low frame building called Armory Hall, which had just been completed that very day. Finally, after fifteen years, the desire of *La Compagnie d'Artillerie de Donaldson* was accomplished. Captain Powell received praise for his perseverance and zeal in obtaining the cannons.[83]

A week after the arrival of the guns, dubbed *Honoré* and *Fidélité,*[84] the *Canonniers de Donaldson* along with friends of Powell met at the new Armory Hall now decorated and transformed into a ballroom. It was a gala celebration of the captain's birthday while also inaugurating the new room. At least three hundred people attended, and all were eager to give by their presence a testimony of the esteem they had for Powell. The local newspaper complimented him for "the intelligent manner and devotion with which he commanded his company."[85]

In Decemeber 1851, Powell led the *Canonniers de Donaldson* to New Orleans, where the city's artillery corps escorted the bishop of New Orleans as he consecrated the St. Louis Cathedral after its restoration. After the ceremonies the militia companies marched through the principal streets of the *Vieux Carré* before having a banquet at the Orleans Saloon next to the French Opera House. "Substantial refreshments" and "general hilarity"[86] occupied the remainder of the day. The *Compagnie d'Artillerie* were "united"[87] with the Orleans Battalion of Artillery of the Louisiana Legion, one of the city's "elite units,"[88] and became its Seventh Company. The dark blue uniforms and appendages of the *Canonniers de Donaldson* at this time were entirely similar to the city battalion.[89]

During this time Donaldsonville boasted a population of 1,056, with 763 born in Louisiana, 134 French citizens, 8 Spaniards, 27 Irishmen, 13 born in other states, 16 born in other foreign lands, 74 free men of color with 62 of them born in Louisiana, and 482 slaves. Sixteen slaves were legally freed during 1850 while there were a total of five runaway slave advertisements during the same year. The town had 219 homes and 29 stores, a courthouse, the armory, an Opera House, a post office, a market, an engine house, 5 schools, and 2 churches (one Catholic and one Protestant) with the main streets being Mississippi and Cabahanosse (present-day Railroad Avenue). Each of the two thoroughfares were sixty-five feet wide and lined with commercial hotels that offered every comfort, including cigars and liqueurs, cafés that catered to the thirsty, with bourbon and anisette being popular, and restaurants that made every meal a Parisian banquet. For entertainment horse races were held every Sunday and each hotel had a cockpit. Fancy dress and costume balls were held often, with Donaldsonville's entrancing ladies showing off Parisian gowns and New Orleans styles. It was noted that even black residents hosted their own balls. Most of Donaldsonville and Ascension Parish's citizens had some formal education, which showed in their love of books, whether novels or the latest nonfiction. Books were available by subscription at Rougeau's Bookbinding (at the rate of $3.00 per year). The biweekly *Le Vigilant* newspaper provided front page stories of French Romanticism, novels and novelettes, with many having a Louisiana background. The local citizens additionally had a keen interest in the stage and with a zest attended the Donaldsonville Opera House performances of *Robert le Diable,*[90] *La Fille du Regiment,*[91] *Le Barbier de Seville,*[92] and *Le Domino Noir,*[93] or theatricals titled *The Wife Won as a Lottery Prize, Les Pirates du Bayou Lafourche*, and *I Love Only Creoles Now.*[94] The Canonniers and the people of Donaldsonville in the 1850s preserved the French cult of the *panache*, which entailed according to a learned recipient of the *Chevalier de la Legion d'Honneur*, "The art of making life worth living and of enjoying it to be the highest measure within self-imposed bounds."[95]

In politics the population seemed to be imbued with the French mysticism of the revolutionary trinity: Liberty, Equality, and Fraternity, which produced a majority for the Whigs over Democrats. The Whigs originally espoused a belief that the Union and property rights must be preserved and maintained, however, during the 1856 presidential election the party fell apart over the slavery issue. Donaldsonville's *Le Vigilant* newspaper reported the "Old Line Whigs" (Victor Maurin, A. J. Powell, L. D. Nicholls, William C. Lawes, and Prosper Landry)[96] supported former President Millard Fillmore as the American Party candidate and passed the following resolution:

> That in the present dangerous state of the country on the slavery question it becomes our duty as true citizens to co-operate in the election of a tried and faithful chief magistrate: that in Millard Fillmore we recognized an enlightened statesman and a pure patriot—a public servant who has proved honest and capable entirely devoted to the Union and during agitation and sectional strife, firm and impartial in the discharge of his duties.[97]

Throughout the state in the early 1850s the militia deteriorated to a "baleful"[98] condition from indifference, lack of desire, or weakening military ardor. Apathy toward preparedness was so bad that even the famed Washington Artillery of New Orleans in 1857 "languished until but thirteen members answered the roll call."[99] The strength of many militia companies was meager but the Powell-led *Canonniers de Donaldson* remained a veteran and disciplined corps with seventy-five members in 1857. The adjutant general that year was another familiar friend and comrade of the *Compagnie d'Artillerie*, the competent and former Captain of the Orleans Artillery, Maurice Grivot, who wrote in his annual report to the governor: "The

Donaldsonville Cannoneers, under the command of Captain A. J. Powell, is deserving of the highest praise and can compete in its efficiency with any corps in the Union."[100] With this high acclamation came the continued support of the state, which by legislative acts continued the appropriations of $500.00 just about every year throughout the decade for the maintenance of the company. The *Compagnie d'Artillerie* also received support through the Donaldsonville town council, which appropriated $27.00 for each occasion the guns fired a national or holiday salute and $22.50 quarterly for the upkeep of the arsenal.[101]

Under Powell's "goodwill and devotion,"[102] the *Canonniers de Donaldson* went from a cannon-less volunteer company who's motto was: "*le vin, le jeu, l'amour et Sainte Barbe*"[103] (wine, games, love, and Saint Barbara) to an "efficiency of discipline."[104] The company was not only uniformed and equipped with Mississippi rifles,[105] they also possessed two 6-pounder guns and were considered a "truly admirable corps."[106] Brilliant feasts and grand balls were not neglected under Powell and it was boasted, "The Canonniers of Donaldsonville—if they are as good at fighting as getting up dinners, they are hard to beat."[107]

Three noteworthy banquets occurred during Powell's reign. The first when former Captain Augustin visited Donaldsonville. He and Powell and the *Compagnie d'Artillerie* (after taking up their arms) marched to former Captain Vidal's home and

> with enthusiastic hurrahs the three captains took to the head of the company and paraded through the streets of Donaldsonville. Everyone . . . went to l'Arsenal where a magnificent collation awaited the celebrants. Frequent toasts . . . were made, the number of glasses which were broken, and the unfortunate mess which was made on the table filled with desserts, wines, and plates of food, indicated a joyous and charming evening was had by all.[108]

In the second instance, *Le Vigilant*'s reporter noted another banquet's centerpiece, an enormous cake with figures attending a cannon-piece on top:

> Especially admired, as perfect as it was original . . . this squadron attending a cannon, one giving the command, another placing a finger on the lantern, another setting fire and another recharging. At first glance, the observer remains struck with astonishment and the explanation for this anomaly is alone capable of removing the surprise which you feel despite yourself. Certainly nothing less than the intervention of [its creator] was necessary to explain the mystery. Then we learned that these new animated artillerymen were quite simply beetles which he had put into military dress and removed their unnecessary legs.[109]

The third banquet of note occurred on January 2, 1859, when the "Canonniers of Donaldsonville, a company composed of many of the best citizens of [Ascension] parish and [Donaldsonville] town, celebrated twenty-two years of service and Saint Barbe."[110] This event was chronicled by a New Orleans correspondent who reported:

> "Early in the morning the usually quiet little town was aroused by the booming of cannon, and the stirring notes of the fife and drum. About nine o'clock, the company, some forty muskets in strength, met at their arsenal, and after organizing, marched out into the large square in front, where they were put through the military evolutions, both as infantry and artillery. Their exercises were gone through with all the ease and precision of old veterans, and in such a matter as reflected great credit on officers and men. After this they marched all around town and returned to their arsenal, where a mid-day salute of thirty-four guns was fired. At two o'clock the company again left their arsenal, and, headed by their band and some ten or twelve invited guests, paraded through town on their way to . . . a sumptuous feast. Upon entering the large and spacious room, the eye was struck with the neatness and taste with which everything was arranged; the room was fancifully decorated with flags and boughs, while the long rows of tables presented

> a sight well calculated to please . . . a dinner that was set out with a taste and elegance . . . At the head of the table presided the gallant commander of the company Capt. A. J. Powell, who as nobly looked the soldier and gracefully played the host. On his right sat the much loved curate of this place, the Rev. [Charles] Boglioli. After all had appeased that hunger which the day's exercises had accelerated, the corks began to fly and the regular toast commenced . . . "The Governor of the State," "General Grivot of New Orleans," . . . and "Capt. Numa Augustin, the founder of the company." In answer to this last sentiment, Capt. Powell read a letter of apology from Capt. Augustin, regretting his being unable to be present, and closing with a sentiment which put the table in a roar . . . here followed many excellent toasts and witty remarks . . . a number of songs were sung, out of the number of which I would particularize one by Gus [Conway], the leader of their band . . . who has marched at the head of the company in the capacity of first fifer . . . the evening was wound up by escorting their captain to his home, and the compliments of a serenade to each of the officers of the company; after which all retired.[111]

Later in 1859 the commander's position, by state law limitations, became vacant and Powell, like Augustin, relocated with his family to New Orleans. One citizen reported, "Donaldson is quite in a state of excitement and grief. We are . . . losing one of the most respectable families. The Powells are going!!!"[112]

An election to replace Powell was held on February 12, 1859, at which time First Lieutenant Victor Maurin's rise through the ranks culminated. He was elected captain to command *Le Canonniers de Donaldson* for five years. Taking the Oath of Acceptance on February 15, Maurin, a fellow student with Powell at the Academy of Donaldson when they were boys, was one of the company's better marksmen and a successful merchant with a remarkable business ability who had just recently took office as Mayor of Donaldsonville. Maurin was characterized as a gentleman with propriety and reserve, but he was also a disciplinarian, and he continued the efficient discipline and able leadership of his predecessor to the extent that Adjutant General Grivot reported in January 1860 that Maurin's *Compagnie d'Artillerie* still "can challenge any artillery corps in the Union."[113]

Military preparedness by the *Canonniers de Donaldson* seemed to replace gala feasts under Maurin, though there were two outings worth mentioning in 1860. The first was the Baton Rouge State or Industrial Fair in March, with a grand review and competition where the best drilled of several volunteer companies from different parts of the state and the U.S. troops garrisoned in Baton Rouge competed for prizes. During the fair the local newspaper especially noticed the Donaldsonville Canonniers for their "military display"[114] and their "excellent band."[115] Maurin's company defeated the Pelican Rifles of East Baton Rouge Parish "fair and square" for first prize as the best drilled company.[116]

A month later the Donaldsonville volunteers went to New Orleans for the celebration and unveiling of a bronze statue to the statesman known as the Great Pacificator, Henry Clay. For this ceremony the *Compagnie d'Artillerie* marched during the military procession with their comrades in the Louisiana Legion. This event marked the last peacetime antebellum excursion by the Donaldsonville Canonniers.[117]

The year 1860 was politically active in Louisiana and Donaldsonville particularly as the presidential election approached. In June a "Donaldsonville Douglas Convention" met with 141 delegates attending from twenty-one of the forty-nine parishes. A resolution backing Stephen A. Douglas for president was offered, but after a very warm debate the motion was withdrawn. Participants of this convention were looked upon by the regular Democrat Party of the state as betrayers of Southern rights, but Ascension Parish, having a strong Union sentiment and being conservative, especially among the Acadian population, remained supportive of Douglas because he upheld individual responsibility and honor, and he had a better chance of defeating the Republican nominee. In the November presidential election Douglas garnered a majority of votes in just three Louisiana parishes: Ascension, Assumption, and Lafourche. John C. Breckenridge, the Guardian of Southern Rights, received the majority of votes cast in the state.[118]

With the election of Abraham Lincoln to the presidency of the United States (his name was not on the Louisiana ballot) the people of the South became apprehensive that a Republican-controlled federal government meant aggression and interference with the sovereignty of the southern states. The debate in Louisiana turned to "secessionists," those that stood for immediate, separate state action, and "co-operationists," those who advocated waiting for the collective southern action or questioned the wisdom of leaving the Union so suddenly and with so little real cause, though most of the citizenry favored resistance to the perceived aggression of the non-slave-holding states.

Soon after the election, Louisiana Governor Thomas O. Moore issued a call for the Louisiana legislature to meet in an extra session to consider the question of secession and the possibility of war. The legislature met on December 10, 1860, and passed bills calling for a state secession convention and an election for delegates on January 7, 1861. Secession was not very popular in Ascension Parish and the residents in the election overwhelmingly voted for cooperation, sending delegates Thomas Cottman (422 votes) and Edward Duffel (348 votes) to the state convention over the two secession delegates, Canonnier Lieutenant Lawrence D. Nicholls (258 votes) and Duncan F. Kenner (234 votes). Ascension's delegates gathered in Baton Rouge on January 23 with other state delegates to consider the condition of Louisiana with regard to the rest of the Union.[119] The result is best described by historian John D. Winters:

> On January 26, 1861, the fateful, irrevocable decision was made. On that day, Saturday, in the drafty halls of the ornate state house at Baton Rouge, the secession convention severed Louisiana's connections with the United States. Voices had been raised in protest; delaying tactics had been introduced; compromises and plans had been offered to keep Louisiana a part of the Union; but in the face of overwhelming pro-secessionist power, one by one the opposition had been won over, discouraged, overridden, or ignored. By a vote of 113 to 17 the delegates of the convention declared Louisiana to be a "free" and "independent power."[120]

Chapter Two

Le Siège de la guerre
(To the Seat of War)

Two weeks before Louisiana became self-governing, Governor Thomas O. Moore, urged upon by leading men of the secession movement, ordered the state volunteers to make a military display and seize the U.S. Arsenal in Baton Rouge. Subsequent orders were issued by the governor in which seven New Orleans militia companies under command of the Washington Artillery's Captain James B. Walton boarded the steamboat *National*, bound for the state capital. On their mission up the Mississippi River the *National* stopped in Donaldsonville for the *Compagnie d'Artillerie de Donaldsonville,* where for some time Walton met with the Canonnier Captain Victor Maurin. Not included in Walton's orders issued by the governor, Maurin and *Canonniers de Donaldson* did not participate in this successful expedition.[1]

Louisiana remained a free and independent power from January 26 to March 21, 1861, when the state ratified the Confederate Constitution and became a member of the Confederate States of America. During her fifty-four days of independence the Louisiana National Congress appropriated $1,500,000 for the state's defenses. Five hundred dollars went to the support of the Donaldsonville gunners by an act approved by the governor on March 8, 1861. That day Moore noted, "The war spirit is very active all over the state, having extended to the lower parishes, [Ascension, Assumption, and Lafourche] where until very recently it was quite quiescent."[2] From relatively quiet to "the war feeling getting up"[3] by those who were opposed to secession, along with the faithful, honest, and devoted citizens, all now disapproved of and were disgusted with the Federal government, "for the base and deceitful manner in which they had treated the loyal and law-abiding people in the South."[4] A majority of Louisianians believe that the United States government would not assert its authority by maintaining laws and protecting citizens from the dominance of unprincipled politicians. This majority then decided that the Federal authorities were no longer entitled to their respect or allegiance.[5]

At 4:30 a.m. on the morning of April 12, 1861, the Civil War commenced when Confederate batteries and mortars under command of Brigadier General Pierre Gustave Toutant Beauregard opened fire on Fort Sumter in Charleston Harbor, South Carolina. Beauregard, a Louisiana native, resigned his commission in the United States army and joined, as a private, the Battalion of Orleans Guards composed of the elite of the Creole population of New Orleans. This command was recently organized by the original founder of the *Canonniers de Donaldson*, Numa Augustin, of "whom no better citizen soldier was known, in the volunteer service of the state."[6] After the fall of Fort Sumter (on April 14) Beauregard sent a piece of the flagstaff of the fort to Augustin to be used as the staff of the Orleans Guards' colors.[7]

When news of a shooting war was received, the Louisiana governor issued General Order No. 81. This commanded the state's volunteer troops, including *Le Compagnie d'Artillerie de Donaldson,* to "assemble fully armed and equipped at their respective armories on receipt of this order and hold themselves in readiness for immediate active service" while awaiting "further orders from headquarters."[8] Maurin's Canonniers gloried in the fact that it was the oldest and best-equipped battery in the state, and with the first cannon shot fired at Fort Sumter the company began preparing for their departure to *le siege de la guerre* (the seat of war) in Virginia.[9] Nine days after the fall of Fort Sumter—days filled with "the greatest excitement and jubilation" along with "frequent blunders and falsities" of news[10]—Captain Maurin received the following order:

> Headquarters Louisiana Militia,
> Adjutant General's Office.
> Order No. 105. New Orleans, April 23, 1861.
>
> Four Regiments of Infantry will be received and mustered into the service of the Confederate Army, under the requisition, by Companies, as soon as presented.
>
> Companies or Battalions will rendezvous at the City of New Orleans, without delay, and report to the Adjutant General.
>
> By order of,
>
> Thomas O. Moore,
> Governor and Commander-in-Chief.
>
> M. Grivot,
> Adjutant and Inspector Gen'l Louisiana.[11]

The Ascension gunners, like other companies, read Abraham Lincoln's war proclamation issued immediately after the bloodless bombardment of Fort Sumter. Lincoln called upon the South to lay down its arms and submit unconditionally to Federal authority before the invasion of 75,000 Union men.[12] Also read was a call by the Confederate Government for volunteers to serve for one year to resist this invasion. A foreign correspondent in the South observed the sentiments and expectations around him and wrote, "The land is on fire, the earth is shaking with the tramp of armed men, and the very air is hot with passion."[13] He also noted there is an "immense energy, great resolution, and fixed principles of action."[14]

Father Aegidius Smulders, a hardworking, dependable Catholic priest who later ministered to Louisiana troops in Virginia, reported, "A universal, patriotic enthusiasm pervaded the whole of the southern States, in which even the Negroes took a lively part; and many a fervent prayer arose from the heart of the Catholic slave that God may not allow Lincoln to deprive them of the masters they loved and of the home of their childhood."[15] A young Donaldsonville Canonnier described his feelings when he informed his father upon joining the *Compagnie d'Artillerie*, "I believe that it is a holy and glorious cause fighting for ones [*sic*] country, ones [*sic*] hearth, and all that one has dearest in the world."[16] Another volunteer wrote, "Many had before them the question of 'States Rights' *versus* 'Federal authority,' but the greatest number were animated only by a determination to resist Lincoln's proclamation."[17]

In response to the governor's order, troops began rapidly arriving in New Orleans. Many firmly believed the war would not last a year.[18] *Le Canonniers de Donaldsonville*, under the command of Maurin, with Lieutenants Villeor Dugas, Lestang Fortier, and Michel Cazaré, eight non-commissioned officers, four artificers, one surgeon, five black musicians, and seventy-two privates, all fully uniformed in dark blue cloth coat with unique brass buttons similar to those of the French Artillery with crossed cannon and flaming shell bearing the inscription "*Le Canonniers de Donaldsonville,*"[19] immediately prepared to leave for the rendezvous.[20] Equipped with knapsacks and armed with forty muskets and the cannons *Honoré* and *Fidélité*, they boarded the regularly scheduled and popular river passenger packet *Mary T* during the late evening of April 30, 1861. The elegant and fast *Mary T,* along with other steamers, continued along the swift flowing muddy Mississippi River carrying the volunteers who were characteristically in a high glee. Many danced and sang while others lounged and slept, piled all about in the steamer's cabins on chairs and sofas and under tables. The New Orleans bound steamboats made their scheduled calls to discharge commissariat stores, parcels, and passengers; at these short layovers, the population along the levee banks greeted and gave many hearty cheers to the soldiers.

The nearly eight hour voyage ended for Maurin's company on the morning of May 1 when the *Mary T* docked in New Orleans at the foot of St. Louis Street. On the edge of the *Vieux Carré* the *Mary T* floated on the springtime-swollen river nine feet above the land on the other side of the levee that stretched for miles protecting the Crescent City. Here the Canonniers leaned against the steamer's rails and looked down along the brick paved streets crowded with horses, mules, drays and wagons, and men in assorted uniforms that generally followed the taste of France. In the distance, the domes and spires of churches, houses, and public buildings flew the newly adopted Confederate "Stars and Bars" flag.

The city docks were also crowded with piles of boxes of muskets, ammunition, accoutrements, and heavy gun carriages, all lining the wharfs where produce formerly had been. During the time the *Mary T* remained docked, other steamers arrived with troops from the state's interior, and upon each arrival banners were displayed and bands of martial music struck up spirited airs as the crowds on the levee greeted each company with cheers.[21] The *Canonniers de Donaldson* disembarked from the *Mary T* to a pair of newspaper reporter's accolades of "a fine body of troops, belonging to the effective arm of the service"[22] and "this handsome body of men . . . from LaFourche."[23]

On the levee, Adjutant General Maurice Grivot, the long time friend and admirer of the Donaldsonville company, greeted the troops as they came ashore. A boy observing the troops would later write:

> Down on the steamboat landing, our famous Levee, a superb body of Creoles . . . paraded in dark-blue uniform. The orders were given in French; the manual was French; the movements were quick, short, nervy. Their 'about march' was four sharp stamps of their neatly shod feet—*un, deux, trois, quatre*—that brought them face about and sent them back, tramp, tramp, tramp, over the smooth white pavement of powdered oyster shells.[24]

Maurin led the "Gunners of Donaldson"[25] off into the hazy atmosphere of summer warmth in New Orleans, which presented a very warlike and military appearance. Baggage wagons filled with tents, camp utensils, muskets, knapsacks, and provisions rolled along the city streets. Company after company left the levee and marched to Canal Street, the main thoroughfare, keeping step to fife and drum. The companies from outside the city marched three miles along wide and spacious Canal Street through the city center, then along the oyster-shell road leading to the Metairie Race Course where a military encampment named Camp Walker was set up.[26]

Surrounded by swamps teeming with rank vegetation and ditches filled with drainage from the city, the race course camp (oval-shaped and about a mile and a half in circumference) was enclosed by a close board wall about twelve feet high with several gates and doors for admission. Inside the track, canvas tents with board floors were laid out over soft, marshy black soil with mud and pools of water here and there. The non-commissioned officers and privates of Donaldsonville, when not drilling or on guard duty, lounged about in groups, reading, smoking, chatting, singing, sleeping, whittling, and tinkering in a hundred ways, with jokes and banter keeping up their spirits. The patriotic songs were sung chiefly in French by the Creoles, including the *Marseillaise* (French national anthem).[27]

One witness described Camp Walker to a Baton Rouge newspaper:

> It is a somewhat strange spectacle . . . to see young men reared amid the comforts and luxuries of home-life, doing soldier duty, bending over the camp fire, preparing meals or boiling coffee; tears streaming from their eyes caused by villainous smoke from these same camp-fires; carry wood and water; and when the day's duties are ended, lying down upon a board or the bare ground, with a knapsack or stick of wood for a pillow and single blanket for a covering. . . . It is a fine spectacle when night has its dark mantle over the earth, to see the numerous camp-fires, surrounded by groups of men or the regular rows of the city of tents, all lighted up from within, while the laugh and song and jest mingled with the strains of instrumental music, and the roll of the drum are borne on the evening breeze.[28]

The *Compagnie d'Artillerie*'s arrival in the Crescent City meant all the Ascension Canonniers were prepared to offer their services to the Confederacy through the mediation of Governor Moore. Unfortunately, the governor received a message on May 3 from Confederate Secretary of War Leroy Pope Walker that there was no necessity to rendezvous troops at New Orleans.[29] In response, two days later Moore issued Order No. 251, which stated that no more companies would be mustered for Confederate duty until the secretary of war made a further requisition.[30] In consequence, the governor proposed to Maurin and his officers to enroll the company in the service of the state for one year, but Maurin let it be known that they had no other ambition but to go immediately to Virginia and would accept no other commitment. The unpleasant response received from the governor *"mortifies"* (mortified)[31] the members of the *Compagnie d'Artillerie*, and they marched away from Camp Walker. On Monday, May 6, at twelve noon, the Canonniers departed New Orleans aboard the *Mary T* for the Lafourche district and Donaldsonville.[32]

On May 10 Governor Moore sent orders for Maurin to return the "two old Iron 6# Guns and the forty old Muskets which are now in your possession and take a receipt for the same."[33] A week later after "commendable consideration"[34] the governor allowed the two state pieces and rifles to remain in possession of the Ascension gunners. Meanwhile the governor telegraphed the secretary of war in response to an inquiry, "I think I can get for twelve months the Donaldsonville Cannoneers, a uniform company with two 6-pounders, to go to Ship Island" (off the Mississippi Gulf Coast along the water route to the mouth of the Mississippi River).[35] Of course Maurin and the Canonniers were not aware of the governor's offer, but no matter, Walker telegraphed Moore back: "I do not well see what necessity there is for a light battery on this island."[36]

After the *Compagnie d'Artillerie* returned to Donaldsonville, many of its patriotic and gallant members threatened to disband, with a large number of its members proposing to join other units forming in the town and neighboring parishes. Maurin's brother-in-law and former Canonnier officer Lawrence (Larry) D. Nicholls was recruiting in Ascension Parish along with his brother Francis T. Nicholls, who was doing the same in Assumption Parish, to organize an infantry company. After receiving a sufficient number of enlistments, the Nicholls brothers formed the United Guards and, like the Canonniers, became dissatisfied over the "unpardonable line of conduct by the government."[37] This caused the break-up of the Guards, but the remnants of their infantry company remained in Donaldsonville. After adding more recruits this group successfully reformed as the Phoenix Company and was mustered into Confederate service.[38]

"There [*sic*] departure . . . took place among some hard feeling and malicious gossip attributed by friends of the 'Phoenix Company' to the bad conscience of men who had not re-enlisted and to jealousy on the part of the 'Donaldsonville Cannoneers', one of the oldest and proudest companies in the state," wrote a bystander.[39] The zealous rivalry among the young citizen soldiers for enrollment for active service was written about in the newspapers, with one noting, "In many instances it has led to momentary alienation among brothers, all being willing to go."[40]

The local antagonism continued when the Donaldsonville newspaper *Le Drapeau* published a June 15, 1861, article by someone with the moniker "J. De C." in Nicholls's company now bivouacked at Camp Moore in Tangipahoa Parish, who asked if the "Cannoniers of notoriety"[41] concluded to join Lieutenant Colonel Edmonson's battalion in New Orleans. "J. De C." added, "To the Cannoniers to whom we owe the disorganization of our [United Guards] company once, I will tell them that if they wish to join Col. Edmonson's Battalion to take care. This is QUANTUM SUFFICIT."[42]

Edmonson was a prominent Englishman of New Orleans, extremely pro-Confederate, who was attempting at this time to raise a battalion of infantry. An auxiliary detachment was assembled in Donaldsonville for recruitment with former Canonnier Captain A. J. Powell, at his office in New Orleans, taking subscriptions for Edmonson's Battalion. It is also interesting that one newspaper reported Nicholls's Phoenix Company would muster into Edmonson's Battalion at New Orleans.[43]

Maurin requested *Le Drapeau* to publish his response to the insinuations he judged insulting to the Canonnier company. The newspaper did on June 29, 1861, "I find it strange," wrote Maurin, "that Mr. J. De C. should avail himself of his absence from [Donaldsonville] to make such a false statement [in reference to the break up of the United Guards]. It would have been more honorable on his part to have expressed himself when here and not at a distance." Maurin added, "In regard to his admonition to the Cannoneers not to join Lieut. Col. Edmonson's battalion, J. De C. may rest assured that should they need any advise [*sic*] they will not take in consideration any suggestion on his part to that effect. Yours respectfully, V. Maurin, Capt. Cannrs. of Donaldson."[44]

Not discouraged by the obstacles or disparaging remarks, Maurin drew a promise from the members of the *Compagnie d'Artillerie* that they would direct their efforts immediately to preparing for a departure to Virginia. With characteristic determination, Maurin, along with the indefatigable First Lieutenant Lestang Fortier[45] redoubled their energy and activities to attain the Canonniers' goal.

Their efforts were not soon enough as the newspaper headlines for July 19, 1861, proclaimed, "BATTLE AT BULL'S RUN, The Washington Artillery Distinguished Themselves."[46] It was a source of much regret that the *Canonniers de Donaldson* were not able to stand side-by-side with the Washington Battalion on the day of the First Battle of Manassas. Some poorly informed people were even pleased to attribute to the company a feeling of cowardice.[47] Larry Nicholls called the Canonniers a "set of ninnies," adding, "They have been driven to the war by public opinion and why after having been insulted, hooted at and ridiculed."[48]

No matter what some said or wrote, the ranks swelled, with Maurin and his officers continuing their efforts not to be "behindhand in seeking to share in the glories and dangers

Man and Horse.
Alfred R. Waud illustration (hereafter cited as ARW); courtesy of Library of Congress (hereafter cited as ARW).

of our defensive war."[49] Former Lieutenant Governor, and then current parish leader, Trasimon Landry, headed the Ascension Parish Police Jury appropriations which funded materials the soldiers needed for campaign duty. Citizens of Ascension and Assumption Parishes and private subscriptions also supported and furnished the volunteers with liberal supplies. In the first week of August the state continued its support, through Adjutant General Grivot, when it issued quartermaster stores for the ninety-five members of the *Compagnie d'Artillerie*.[50] In the meantime members of the company went from Donaldsonville "looking out for horses to fit themselves for the war."[51]

The next difficulty the *Compagnie d'Artillerie* had to overcome was the fact it had only two cannons, though they numbered a force to efficiently manage six field pieces. That they did not have the full number of guns for an artillery battery was now the sole cause of the company being kept out of the service. To overcome this the police jury again lent its assistance by voting the *Canonniers de Donaldson* an additional sum of ten thousand dollars. Maurin, along with Fortier, then traveled to New Orleans on August 19, 1861, and procured from the John Clark and Company foundry a Model 1841, bronze, 6-pounder Field Gun. Described as very light and weighing much less than other 6-pounders, it was engraved on top between the neck and vent with the words *Liberté et Égalité* (Liberty and Equality), a maxim from the French Revolution.[52]

Maurin also learned that the Congress of Confederate States passed an act allowing the president authorization to accept the services of volunteers directly through the Confederate Secretary of War, meaning that a volunteer unit no longer had to muster into service through the governor of its state. The day after acquiring *Liberté et Égalité,* Maurin, on behalf of *Le Compagnie d'Artillerie de Donaldson,* and through former Captain Andrew Jackson Powell in New Orleans, sent a dispatch to Richmond for the Honorable Duncan F. Kenner, now serving as a representative from Louisiana's Third Congressional District (which included Donaldsonville) in the Confederate Congress. This dispatch related how the *Canonniers de Donaldson* now had three pieces of artillery and eighty-five horses in their possession and requested acceptance into Confederate service. The dispatch was shown by Kenner to Confederate Secretary of War Walker, and on August 26, 1861, Powell received the following reply from the secretary:

> Company of Cannoniers . . . will be received for the war . . . when you are ready to move, orders will be given.[53]

Just four days later (on August 30) Powell wrote a letter to the secretary informing him the *Compagnie d'Artillerie* under the command of Captain Maurin were ready to receive their orders. The order came in less than a week, on September 5, and read:

> The 'Cannoniers of Donaldson' will be accepted for the War, and the Commandant at New Orleans is authorized to have them mustered into service. The company will then proceed at once to [Richmond], bringing their equipments, horses, caissons, forges and where upon their arrival, such other equipments, as may [be] necessary, will be furnished.
>
> Respectfully,
> L. P. Walker, Scty. of War.[54]

When the mustering officer came to Donaldsonville on September 13, 1861, Maurin's gunners numbered 103 members. Since their return in May from New Orleans, the company's enrollment was augmented by the creation of another officer, three sergeants, eight corporals, and two artificer positions.[55]

At the outbreak of hostilities the respected Jean Reynaud Jacques Prosper Landry joined the *Compagnie d'Artillerie* as a private and, after an election, assumed the new position of junior second lieutenant. Prosper Landry, as he was called, was the son of Valery Landry, a large land owner and distinguished citizen who took an active part in public affairs, and a grandson of Joseph Landry, one of the area's first settlers who was appointed post commandant of the Lafourche District. Prosper graduated in 1846 from Georgetown College in Washington, D.C., then traveled for two years through Europe before returning to study law at the State (now Tulane) University in New Orleans. Upon graduation in 1854, Landry returned to Donaldsonville to practice law. Described as "just and upright, warmhearted and sympathetic, a man of highest integrity and exceptionally engaging personality, he earned the regard and affection of his intimates and respect and esteem of all who knew him . . . and those who knew him best loved him most."[56] The thirty-five-year-old Landry had "manifold virtues and numerous lovable traits"[57] and liked to carry "a most elaborate toilet"[58] that kept his facial hair and clothing meticulously groomed no matter what the circumstances or conditions. Able to speak French and English fluently, he would serve the command with distinction and fearlessness and with an exalted sense of duty. He left behind a pregnant wife and two small children.[59]

Prosper Landry. Photographed taken circa 1875, about the time of the reorganization of the company. Landry is wearing the dark blue uniform similar to that of the antebellum Canonniers with a gold and blue trim on red kepi cap instead of a shako with red plume. From Sydney A. Marchand, *Marchand's on the Mississippi and the St. Lawrence.*

Senior First Lieutenant Villeor Dugas, who went from flag bearer to an officer during antebellum times, resigned his commission on September 3, 1861, to remain sheriff of Donaldsonville (the office he was elected to, coincidentally, on September 3, 1859). Dugas was replaced by the election of former State Senator and District Judge William Conway "Billy" Lawes. Described as having a "quiet, gentle, and amicable disposition . . . warmhearted and kind . . . modest and retiring in his habits, he was beloved and esteemed by all who knew him."[60] Lawes was considered the guardian in Donaldsonville of a large population of free men of color and it was said he was "incapable of a dishonorable act."[61] During the days of secession he was well-known as an outspoken and unflinching Union man.[62] Now in defense of his home and state, he resigned his commission as major in the Ascension Regiment of Louisiana Militia to accept the first lieutenant's position in the *Canonniers de Donaldson* and fight for his homeland and new government.[63]

Another change in the company's command structure during the summer of 1861 was the addition of a quartermaster sergeant whose duties chiefly consisted of obtaining and supplying rations for the company and subsistence for the horses. Jonathan Scheuer, a forty-year-old German Hebrew whose parents still lived in Mayence, Germany, ably filled this position with his executive abilities. Having married a twenty-year-old bride from Germany in New York City two years earlier, Scheuer was a trusted and efficient merchant who managed a hardware store in partnership with fellow Canonnier enlistee Jean Trasimond "John" Landry. He also cared for property in Donaldsonville belonging to Jacob Lemann, a New York resident who moved with his family to Paris to avoid confiscation of his Ascension Parish property by Confederate authorities. Scheuer had many friends in the Canonniers and joined the *Compagnie d'Artillerie* with Landry. Scheuer's first order of business was likely to charter the fast-running river packet *Prince of Wales* whose accommodations for travelers were unsurpassed.[64]

Reverend Charles Boglioli, C. M.
From Dorothy Dawes and Charles Nolan, eds. *Religious Pioneers, Building the Faith in the Archdiocese of New Orleans.*

One of the few documented members who left the battery was Sergeant Major Charles H. Illsley who decided to enlist on July 3, 1861, in the Point Coupee Artillery with the rank of second lieutenant.[65] Replacing him was Clement B. Israel, a Donaldsonville youth of twenty-one and married just that past May to a niece of Mrs. Victor Maurin. He performed the mainly executive duties of taking all general or special roll calls and overseeing the stable duties and details of men under the direction of the officers. He would be serving in distant Virginia when his daughter was born in March of 1862.

Another notable departure was that of Dr. Auguste Thibaut, the battery's distinguished surgeon. Replacing him was forty-six-year-old Father Charles Boglioli, a Vincentian brother not only known for his spiritual zeal, but endowed with intellectual gifts and extraordinary physical strength and endurance. He was 5'11", 205 pounds, erect, with a military bearing, muscular and strong, and a healthy man whom no danger could intimidate, though he had a gentle disposition, was pious and affable, and courteous to all. Known as a philosopher, he was the master of about twelve languages. Said to be a courageous priest, the auspicious Reverend Boglioli, while serving at Donaldsonville as the Catholic administrator to the Church of the Ascension, and an associate of the *Canonniers de Donaldson*, sought and received permission of the bishop to join the *Compagnie d'Artillerie* and "share their hardships" while trying "to save their souls as he could not save their bodies."[66]

Other Canonnier veterans were promoted along with notable citizens to fill the available sergeant and corporal positions. The two most significant corporal enlistees were Jean Trasimond "John" Landry, a trusted and true friend of Schreuer. Landry was the son of the distinguished and wealthy parish leader Trasimon Landry and first cousin to Canonniers Adolphe Landry and Prosper Landry.[67] New Hope Plantation where John was born, raised, and married, and which he helped manage with his father, was also called Home, a "sacred and holy spot" of the Landry family, and worth defending.[68] The other corporal position was filled by Louis Aristide "Tip" Landry, John's second cousin. Tip's father, Aristide Joseph Landry, had been a sergeant in the antebellum *Chasseurs de l'Ascension* cavalry, and served as a congressman, state representative, and president of the Ascension Parish Police Jury. About the two new Landry corporals it was said their "participation in the 'doings'" and "presence" was enough to bring a *"hearty enjoyment"* to any occasion.[69]

Not wanting to stay behind, the *Compagnie d'Artillerie* drew citizens of various backgrounds as privates. There were Creoles and Cajuns from Donaldsonville with "volatile spirits and lightheartedness,"[70] like twenty-two-year-old cooper Jean Marie Mathieula Richard who signed the muster roll "John"; the bookkeeper "Sabin" Braud, who turned out to be "brave and faithful" while never losing his "buoyant spirits and genial disposition";[71] "Bienvenue" (St.) Cire, a handyman and student—appointed artificer, he continued his learned ways by keeping a memorandum book; Lubin Guedry and Gontrand Dugas, an overseer and a clerk, both nineteen-years-old, and both enlisted ready for action. All made preparations to go. Then there was A. J. Gautreaux, a clerk in Donaldsonville who became not only a *compagnon d'armes* (brother-in-arms) but later a *beau-frere* (brother-in-law) to six Canonniers. The "highly esteemed"[72] Herman Landry, an eighteen-year-old Ascension planter, suffered from chronic diarrhea for months after enlisting but lived well into the next century and became the last surviving Canonnier war veteran.[73]

The Cajuns from the interior of the parish and across the river from Donaldsonville were represented by eighteen-year-old farmer Octave Boudreau, a genuine Acadian, unchanged in character and mode of living and comfortable with his own kind; he put his pending marriage to Olivia Babin on hold in order to serve. Cajuns from down the bayou in Assumption Parish eagerly volunteered with a "cheerful countenance,"[74] like the "extremely popular"[75] Severin Blanchard, of whom it was said as a soldier he had "no superior";[76] teenage laborers Gustave Evariste Aucoin, just five feet tall—he later noted it was a "hard Struggle"[77]—and Clairville Savoy, nine inches taller and "greatly esteemed by every one";[78] the Paincourtville student, James Landry, whose older sister was the stepmother of the three Canonnier Newchurch brothers; and the "exemplary"[79] Cleophus Landry, a clerk in Paincourtville, though his father was one of the wealthiest Assumption Parish sugar planters. Other sons of Assumption Parish were the brave twenty-year-old Gustave Charlet, his father a *Soldat de Napoleon I*, and Claudius Auguste Linossier, named after his father, who marched off with the *Compagnie d'Artillerie* soon after his father's death while his brother Julien (one year older) joined and left with Nicholls's Phoenix Company. At twenty-three years of age the "good and brave"[80] Claudius worked as a coffee house keeper, experience that would make him popular around the campfire; plus having grown up knowing Father Boglioli, he likely could hold his own around the campfire *raconteurs* (storytellers).[81]

The Spanish settlers of Ascension and Assumption Parishes were from the Canary Islands. All were descendants of immigrant-soldiers. Of the twelve *Canarian Isleños* to enlist in the *Compagnie d'Artillerie*, one of the first was "Arthur" Echavaria, who served with "credit and distinction."[82] Versatile thirty-three-year-old John Hernandez, mustered in on his birthday, was one of the first Canonniers wounded in battle. "Esteve" Hildalgo, at nineteen-years-old and five-feet-five-inches tall, became an entrusted private. Other Isleños joining were the bachelor Suarez brothers, nineteen-year-old *hacendado* (farmer) Antoine André and John Sebastien, a "respected"[83] eighteen-year-old—they went by the nicknames Tony and John and both were looked after by their wedded twenty-seven-year-old cousin, Raphael Hilaire Suarez. Hypolite Acosta, twenty-three, proved worthy of promotion. Then there was fellow *Isleño* Narcisse Villeneuve Corneil Plesencia, a farmer who despite his imposing name enrolled by signing the muster roll with his mark of "X."

The Catholic Irish laborers working on the Donaldsonville riverfront gave their measure for the most part by joining what was later designated Company F, Seventh Louisiana Infantry Regiment. Few exerted control over the old hands from the Emerald Isle like thirty-year-old Timothy Boham, said to be "nobel of spirit";[84] thirty-six-year-old Alex McCullet; thirty-one-year-old carpenter John Murphy, whose wife gave birth to a daughter nine months after he enlisted; and thirty-year-old Michael "Hick" Flannigahn. Both "Murph" and "Hick," who could be bossy, would later show their anarchic side. Six Irish in all joined no doubt because of the reputation of the *Compagnie d'Artillerie* and because each was a reliable hard worker they were accepted into the mostly Catholic Creole company.

French immigrants drawn to the company included Gabriel Kling, living in Ascension Parish at Dutchtown, and the peddler Abraham Klotz; both learned enough about horses during the conflict to buy and sell them after the war. Peter Hauplin was a shoemaker, a vocation that would be put to good use. Enlistee Jean Oleziphore Delmere was of German-Acadian extraction. German immigrants who joined included the two Heim brothers from Donaldsonville—Martin, blue-eyed with red hair and later labeled by the Canonnier captain as "one of the bravest of the brave,"[85] and younger brother Jacob, dubbed "Jacko," who was more of an absconder. Although both Heim brothers supported the Confederate cause during the war, each would subsequently marry African American women and father several biracial children. Arthur Comstock, just seventeen when he enlisted, showed his English "bulldog tenacity"[86] when, years later, he proudly proclaimed that he was "never captured" though he "engaged in all battles."[87] The three Newchurch brothers, "gallant"[88] John, "good and worthy"[89] Henry, both carpenters, and Bill, at nineteen the youngest and an apprentice mason, enlisted. Their parents were of English/German stock from North Carolina and settled the family along Bayou Lafourche in Paincourtville, where their children were raised among the French Creoles and Acadians. Interestingly enough, also enlisting was Pierre Caesar Rybiski, an eighteen-year-old Louisiana-born sugar maker whose father, a cigar maker, came from Poland. Rybiski's name would appear under the "Present Column" on every Donaldsonville muster roll during the war.[90]

There was a devastating fire in Donaldsonville on June 21, 1861, which burned down a number of businesses, including Paul Humbert's jewelry store and Lion's dry goods. In consequence, two of the fire victims (and possibly others) joined the Gunners of Donaldson. The twenty-three-year-old Humbert, from Germany, was steadfast and later earned a promotion. The French native Sylvain Lion could no longer work for his father's destroyed dry goods store so he enlisted for the war.[91]

Le Compagnie d'Artillerie de Donaldson had 103 members mustered into Confederate service for three years or the duration of the war. Sixty-three of them lived in Donaldsonville, with another fifteen living in other parts of Ascension Parish. Twenty-two were from Assumption Parish, with eight of those being from Paincourtville. Two were from New Orleans and one from St. James Parish. The "dramatic flavor"[92] of the *Compagnie d'Artillerie* was decidedly French Creole and Cajun with fifty-one members, the Spanish Isleños contributed twelve men, nine were of English origin, with six French and eight German immigrants, six Irishmen, four descendants of Spain, two Italians (one immigrant, one descendent), one from Portugal, one from Canada, with a descendent each from Poland, Scotland, and Sweden.

The Canonniers average age was twenty-five, with the median for the seventy-two privates being 22.5 years; the twenty-four non-commissioned officers averaged thirty years, while the five officers averaged thirty-five years. Captain Victor Maurin was the oldest officer at forty-two years, while the honorable First Sergeant Pierre "Peter" Ramirez, married with four sons, was the oldest member at forty-three years of age. Of the volunteers, twenty-five were married with eighteen of them having children.

The occupations of the Canonniers reflected Donaldsonville's location as a commercial and agricultural center prospering along the river and bayou with nineteen members listed as clerks or bookkeepers, sixteen as laborers, nine as coopers (to make or repair wooden casks) five as carpenters, and one stave maker. There were four merchants, a trader, and a peddler, while one noted he was a sailor. The six farmers, eight planters, one sugar maker, and four overseers personified the agricultural interests in the battery, while skilled workers were signified by three shoemakers, three butchers, a tailor, a blacksmith, a saddle maker, a jeweler, and three masons. A district judge, an attorney, and a notary, along with a coffee house keeper, a schoolmaster, and three students made up the *savoir faire* (know how) of the *Compagnie d'Artillerie.* Only nine members were not literate enough to write their name when signing the muster roll. In the whole company a total of five members owned slaves with the most possessed being eleven, two members owned but one slave each while four widowed mothers of Canonniers and the parents or guardians of another four members had slaves. Of the last eight, four had a substantial number.[93]

Father Boglioli departed with the *Canonniers de Donaldsonville*, as did their field band of five pieces led by Frederick "Gus" Conway. The band included his brother Prosper Conway, John and Lanlee Barré, and Sosthene Braud, the bass drummer. Gus, the band's fifer, was described as "a tall yellow boy, who weighs three hundred pounds and has been attached to the company . . . [since its organization]; the drummer his brother; the two are splendid musicians."[94] All were black men who furnished abundant and moving music that Donaldsonville and the Canonniers were "very proud of."[95]

Louis G. Lefort.
Courtesy of the Donaldsonville Public Library.

One of the few servants or cooks leaving with the battery was a volunteer valet, cook, and aide to Captain Maurin, Louis G. Lefort, a twenty-six-year-old *homme de couleur libre* (free man of color). Born in Haiti, he came to Louisiana at the age of two and lived in Donaldsonville working as an artistic painter. Lefort was described as brave, honest, dependable, and one of the leading free men, who along with the musician Prosper Conway, were considered thinking men of their race.[96] Another personal servant was a slave by the name of Titus, owned by Lietenant Prosper Landry who wrote: "Titus has gone up a grade, like his master, [when Landry was promoted to Captain] from cook he has become *valet de chambre.* But when I return to the army [from sick furlough] it will be necessary that Titus go back to the kitchen because in the army you can't undress to go to bed, and I would hardly have need of a *valet de chambre.*"[97]

With orders to report to headquarters at Memphis, Tennessee—though they were destined for Richmond—the day determined upon for the departure of the *Compagnie d'Artillerie* from Donaldsonville was September 18, 1861. This was just two days after the resignation of Confederate Secretary of War Walker, who had accepted the battery for Confederate service, and the evacuation of Confederate forces from Ship Island, where it had been discussed sending Maurin's Canonniers just a few months earlier.

Wednesday, September 18, 1861, arrived with a beautiful morning. It turned into a day many would never forget. *Le Compagnie d'Artillerie de Donaldsonville* started the morning off by going to the massive gray moss-grown Catholic Church with its prominent towers "to implore the blessing of One who is more powerful than all armies."[98] The women of Donaldsonville, mothers and sweethearts, bestowed upon the Canonniers a flag for them to bear to Virginia. Tears flowed in the shade of the church.[99] The large side-wheeler *Prince of Wales,* hauling freight and a fair load of passengers from New Orleans, arrived at eight o'clock in the morning at Donaldsonville's large and superbly constructed wharf. In a short time the state cannons *Honoré, Fidélité,* and the Clark Foundry-cast *Libertié et Égalité,* with three caissons, eighty horses and twelve mules, complete harnesses, one ambulance wagon, equipment, and tents, were loaded and secured aboard this "new and magnificent"[100] steamboat. About an hour after docking and being loaded, the *Compagnie d'Artillerie* prepared to set forth from *l'Arsenal* at Louisiana Square with banners unfurled, escorted by Bonlanger's recently organized French Militia Company and the Landry Guards, recently raised by the vener-

The Donaldsonville Catholic Church at the time of the war.
Courtesy of Kirk Landry, Donaldsonville, La.

able Trasimon Landry. The neatly uniformed *Compagnie d'Artillerie* with the "finest looking young men"[101] paraded about a quarter of a mile along Houmas Street towards the river, past the brick market building in the middle of Crescent Park, then across Mississippi Street and onto the levee that was thronged with people.[102]

It was estimated that upwards of three thousand people from Donaldsonville and the adjoining parishes were present to take leave of these young men who had enlisted for the war. As the companies approached the river, a band announced their arrival and the crowd gave hurrahs and shouted cheers as never before heard in the city. The kepi-covered Canonniers themselves gave "shouts of patriotic fervor in response to the waving and fluttering of handkerchiefs to silent signals of farewell, amid the sobs and wailing of uncontrollable emotion."[103] The wharf was crowded to suffocation, and the two escorting companies formed a lane for the splendidly attired *Compagnie d'Artillerie* to pass through. After exchanging salutes, Captain Maurin led the Canonniers aboard.[104]

It was a gala day, saving only the pain experienced by parents and relatives in seeing those so dear to them going off to war. An aching was also felt by the artillerymen too. Canonnier Sergeant Hubert "Pousse" Treille reminisced, "I left a wife and two children and as I bade them good bye and stood ready to board the steamer I was crying. A young man back of me punched me in the back and asked 'What the Dickens are you crying about?' Because I am leaving my wife and family I replied. 'Why I am not crying,' responded the young man, 'for I am going for glory!'"[105] Just twelve days before this moment that Treille would never forget, his second daughter, fittingly named "Virginie" had been born.

The boarding was an intensely wretched scene with crying women and children bidding farewell, but the women of Ascension met with resignation the sacrifice of their husbands and their children because they understood that the country came before the family. It was recorded that "many of the women, in emulating the Spartans, hide their tears to their parents and friends who are leaving, but at the moment the boat gives the final clap of the bell, that mournfully resonates . . . bitter tears flow."[106]

Paddling up the winding Mississippi River that had nearly reached the low water mark of the season, the *Prince of Wales* stopped in Baton Rouge before continuing its journey past the ornate turrets of the Gothic Revival state capitol building, situated on a high bluff overlooking the river. Within a day the steamer stopped at Natchez, Mississippi, "where," Canonnier Corporal John O'Hara recorded in his diary, "There was a crowd on the wharf to receive us."[107] The following day, September 20, the boat arrived in Vicksburg, Mississippi, where, O'Hara wrote, "We got . . . to stretch legs as all well and enjoying themselves well."[108] O'Hara made note of why some were enjoying themselves and hoped to continue the gratification. He jotted in his tattered notebook, "Edward Terrio invented a new plan for getting whiskey by the sentinels easily."[109] The "witty"[110] Private Terrio, just five feet tall with blue eyes, dark hair, and a light complexion, would later be promoted to bugler. According to friends "he was noted for his happy disposition, strict performance of duty and disregard of privations or danger."[111] No word was written by O'Hara on if the plan succeeded but that might be an indication it did.

It was an agreeable trip for the *Compagnie d'Artillerie*, with or without "the juse of corn,"[112] for the *Prince of Wales* was "sumptuously furnished and possessed [of] every accommodation for passengers."[113] The scenery became wilder and less cultivated the farther upriver the boat paddled. It was noted that listening to the beat of the ship's steam drums and blowing of whistles became "extremely tiresome."[114]

The wearisome but amiable river journey ended on the fifth day as the *Prince of Wales* docked at Memphis on September 22 at eleven o'clock on a very cool morning. Maurin received orders for the battery to camp at the Memphis Fair Grounds for a few days to await transportation by rail to Richmond. Finished disembarking at three o'clock in the afternoon, the *Compagnie d'Artillerie*, minus one mule that strayed during the unloading, marched five miles through the city and arrived at the campgrounds near five o'clock in the evening.[115] After pitching tents and taking care of the horses and mules, the Canonniers, recorded O'Hara, at "7 o'clock had . . . supper. Every fellow reached his peace."[116]

The next day Maurin dispatched the following message:

> Memphis, Sept. 23, 1861
>
> Capt. A. J. Powell, N. O.:
> Arrived yesterday safely; pleasant trip; all well.
> Leave Thursday for Richmond.
>
> Maurin.[117]

The trip so far had indeed been affable, and Maurin and the officers of the battery publicly thanked the captain and clerk of the *Prince of Wales* for the "kind treatment and polite attention bestowed upon [the officers] and every member of the company."[118] The Memphis newspaper correspondents that observed the Gunners of Donaldson reported, "Among the many fine companies which have passed through Memphis, none surpassed in appearance and respectability the Donaldsonville Cannoneers."[119] Another wrote that they were a "splendid company"[120] and "one of the finest artillery companies we have ever seen since the war commenced."[121] The newspapers likewise informed the citizens, "The officers of the *Prince of Wales* speak in the highest terms of the gallant and gentlemanly bearing of all the members . . . and commend them to the hospitalities of our citizens."[122]

The day the *Compagnie d'Artillerie* landed in Memphis one newspaper took note of the levee along the river where twenty-four 6-pounder cannons cast at the Richmond Tredegar Iron Works sat awaiting allocation. The article compared these guns for beauty and general appearance with those cast in Memphis by the Quinby and Robinson Company, and proclaimed that the Memphis cast guns "cannot be excelled by any in the world."[123] In the same newspaper column immediately above the "Memphis Manufactured Cannon" article was a story entitled "Interesting Relic." This story informed its readers:

> Among the pieces brought to this city by the Donaldsonville Cannoneers yesterday, is a brass six pounder cannon captured from the English at the battle of New Orleans. It had been captured from the French in 1792. Upon top the piece are the words 'Liberty and Equality,' in French. What service it did for the republic and how it was obtained by the English would no doubt be a very interesting history, and we regret that we are unable [to] narrate it.[124]

Another of the Memphis tabloids gave the same account but clarified, "It was taken by General [Andrew] Jackson at the battle of New Orleans."[125]

It is unknown if the newspaper journalists interviewed a Canonnier officer, or one of the privates, or if the entire *Compagnie d'Artillerie* were in on the *'tit mensonge* (a small story or fib.) It was such a good tale that the New Orleans newspaper *Daily True Delta* reprinted the article for its readers on September 26, 1861.[126]

Memphis presented thousands of temptations to the Canonniers who went into the city. One could find ladies on the street corners or in houses of ill repute, saloons with billiard tables like the ones in Donaldsonville, ten pin alleys, and card tables that were visited two and three times a day. The Lafourche boys liked nothing more than *la tite partie* (a little game) for stakes. A more moderate public amusement was the theatre, which presented such plays as *Richard III*, *Romeo and Juliet*, *Merchant of Venice*, and *Hidden Hand*.[127] Canonnier Private

Albert Schmidt wrote home, "All well . . . and feel fresh and hardy as ever."[128]

The *Canonniers de Donaldsonville* in Confederate service came to be identified as Maurin's Battery and, according to O'Hara, had "the expectation of leaving on Thursday for Richmond." He also noted "it is the opinion of several gentlemen that we will remain in this place."[129] O'Hara's conviction was on the mark when the *Compagnie d'Artillerie* left the hospitalities of Memphis by the Memphis & Charleston train on Thursday, September 26, 1861.

Most Confederate volunteers had never ridden a train. The majority of the Donaldsonville Canonniers, not only had never been on a train, "many of them had never journeyed twenty miles from their homes."[130] The wood-burning locomotive was noisy, hot, smelly, and mysterious, and there was an apprehension by first-time passengers to board the thirteen to fifteen assorted cars pulled by the iron horse. The artillery battery was hauled on three platform cars with the cannons, caissons, and ambulance, plus a car for the saddles and equipment. Six stock or boxcars with about fifteen animals in each was the standard, followed by three wooden passenger cars that accommodated thirty to forty people on two-seated wooden benches with a thin wicker padding. Going by rail was anything but pleasant with tiring discomforts and boredom. The train traveled between fifteen and twenty miles per hour, but with frequent stops for wood, water, and at sidings, the average distance made was eight or ten miles per hour. To relieve the stuffy cars meant opening the windows and that allowed dust, hot cinders, and pungent smoke from the engine's pinewood fuel to come in. The most serious discomfort, though, was the lack of suitable eating accommodations.[131]

The train hauling the *Compagnie d'Artillerie* arrived in the evening of September 27 at Chattanooga, Tennessee, which served as a hub for several railroad lines. The Canonnier battery switched trains as O'Hara noted in his diary, "Chattanooga is a beautiful town 2 miles from Lookout mountain."[132] Unable to enjoy the city's hospitality, Donaldsonville Artificer François "Bienvenue" Cire recorded in his memorandum book, "we left the same evening."[133] Neither O'Hara nor Cire mention their new accommodations on the East Tennessee & Virginia but young Canonnier Schmidt did. He wrote that on the new train they were transported in baggage cars "packed up like sardines."[134]

The journey continued 113 miles to Knoxville, Tennessee, where the Canonniers remained overnight. The next day, September 29, the company still rode in baggage cars; the soldiers knocking holes in the sides for ventilation and sightseeing. With their heads sticking out, it made them look like chickens in a poultry wagon. Traveling along they sang and yelled to onlookers as they went through a beautiful, fertile, and picturesque region.[135] The train crossed the Virginia-Tennessee border at Bristol, where they awaited a swap to the Virginia & Tennessee Railroad. O'Hara described the small but pleasant town, its neat houses and shops ranged along slightly sloped hills with mountains standing out sharply against the sky, as "a beautiful place."[136] Maurin sent off another dispatch to Powell in New Orleans that the *Compagnie d'Artillerie* "had arrived, all well in Bristol."[137]

The trek continued the following day, September 30, along the Virginia and Tennessee tracks. The Blue Ridge Mountains towered high on the right and the Cumberland Mountains sometimes on the left. One rider exclaimed, "Oh! The beautiful scenes and scenery."[138] After 188 miles and crossing the Blue Ridge Mountains from Roanoke to Bedford, Virginia, an unexpected stoppage occurred at Goode's Junction. Schmidt wrote, "We have been detained here, nearly two days, on account, as I have understood, of several bridges, on the [rail] road, that have been washed away, the river having risen considerably."[139] With the tracks open on October 4 the *Compagnie d'Artillerie* travelled another sixteen miles before reaching Lynchburg, Virginia.

At Lynchburg the train unloaded armaments, horses, saddles, bridles, halters, picket rope, girths, blankets, and forage, before boarding another train. Following this transfer to the South Side Railroad, Maurin's Battery left Lynchburg at three o'clock in the evening and passed through country that was "quite beautiful."[140] One of the short stops made along the line was at a railway station described as "silent and destitute"[141] and located near a placid little village with nothing especially interesting in it and "where nothing epochal had ever occurred."[142] Its name was Appomattox Court House.

From there the train continued on through Farmville, which lay south of and alongside the Appomattox River. After chugging along for another four miles, the engine greatly reduced speed to cross the Appomattox River over High Bridge. This "railway viaduct"[143] was a wooden trestle supported by twenty brick piers varying in height from 60 to 125 feet that spanned the river's valley for half a mile, from a bluff in Cumberland County to a bluff in Prince Edward County. The crossing gave passengers a feeling of suspension since the bridge was not visible from inside the coach and afforded a scenic view of the beautifully cultivated fields of tobacco and corn, the river valley delicious in the color of autumn sunlight, and the distant mountains. The crossing also reportedly conferred to travelers the "shivers."[144]

The locomotive steamed on from the bridge pulling its cars for another thirteen miles before the train arrived at Burkeville Junction, approximately eight hours after leaving Lynchburg. Here the *Compagnie d'Artillerie* disembarked and spent the night under the stars before swapping trains. This time they loaded onto the Richmond and Danville railroad and rode in swaying cars clacking over rough and uneven iron rails past pine forest and cornfields. The train puffed northeast for a final fifty-four miles before the Canonniers saw their destination, the picturesque outlines of the hill-city, the Capital of the Confederacy—Richmond, Virginia.[145]

One hundred and seventy-seven days after the bombardment of Fort Sumter began, and after enduring an eighteen-day journey from Donaldsonville, the last ten days traveling 880 miles by rail, *Le Compagnie d'Artillerie de Donaldson* under the command of Captain Victor Maurin arrived at *le siege de la guerre* (the seat of war). In summarizing the trip, one *Donaldsonville* Canonnier wrote, "So far, we have fared remarkably well. We have had some hard times of course . . . but that is the lot of the soldier, and he has no reason for complaint."[146]

High Bridge with a train headed east towards Petersburg; painted by Edward Beyer from *Album of Virginia* (Plate 4) circa 1857. Courtesy of Virginia State Library.

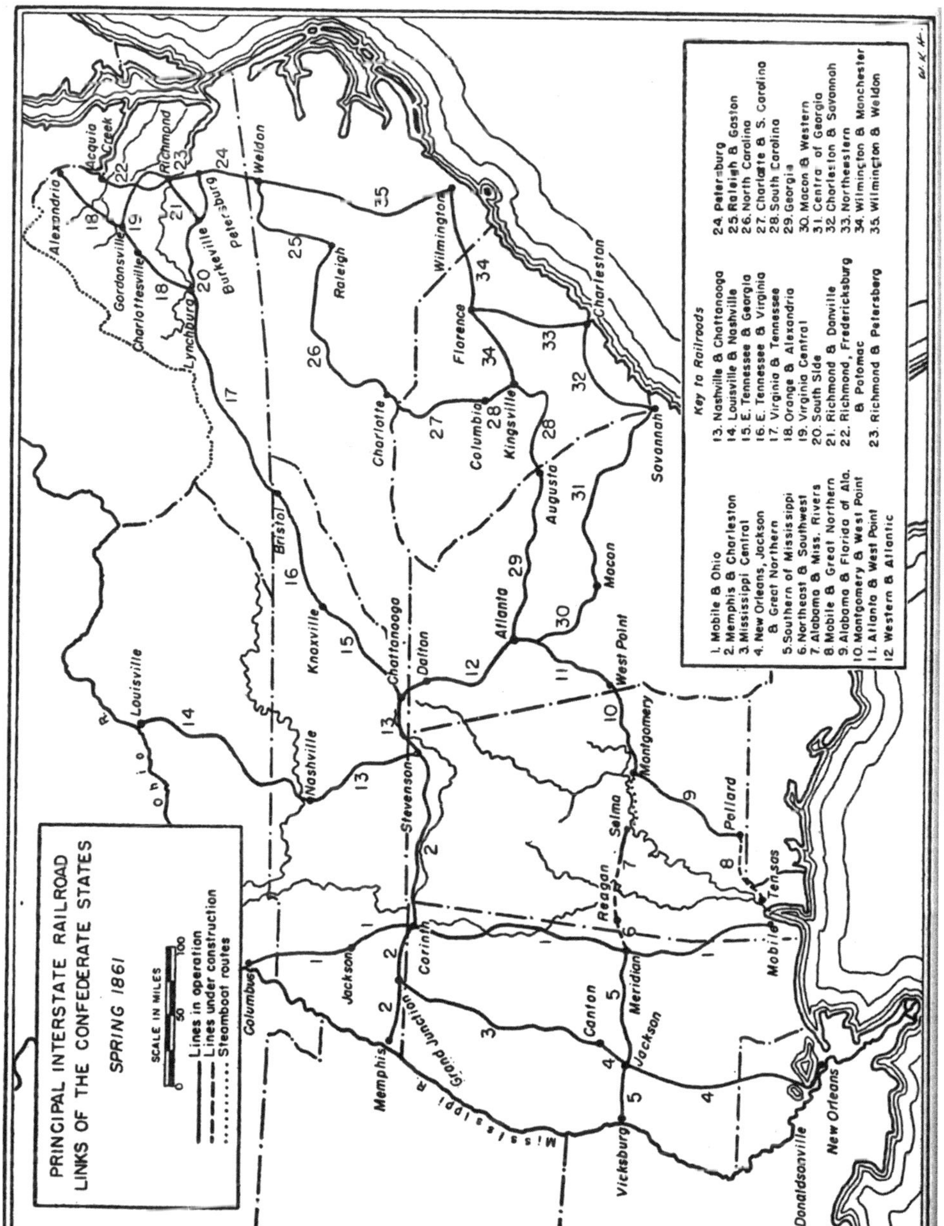

The route that the Canonniers took from Donaldsonville to Richmond can be traced up the Mississippi River by steamboat to Memphis, then by railroad following the numbers 2, 13, 15, 16, 17, 20, and 21.

From Robert C. Black, III, *The Railroads of the Confederacy.*

Chapter Three

En avant
(Forward, to the Front)

On Saturday, October 5, 1861, *Le Compagnie d'Artillerie de Donaldsonville* rode the Richmond and Danville train across a long wooden railroad bridge spanning the James River, its muddy yellowish-red waters below flowing past jutting rocks and splashing over boulders of granite that encumber its bed, past numerous foliaged islands covered with birch and willow trees coated in white frost. The train moved slowly, affording its riders the most picturesque sights. The scene ahead was the Confederacy's capital city—Richmond, scattered prominently up and on several verdant hills with many steeples and towers and the Greek temple-like capitol with its lofty portico and rectangular mass dominating the skyline. Stopping at the depot located near Fourteenth Street at the terminus of Mayo's Bridge, next to the river, the Canonniers unloaded their cannons, caissons, horses, and equipment from the train.[1] A correspondent for the Richmond *Dispatch* newspaper evidently did not see the artillery pieces or equipment amongst the many horses being unloaded for he unknowingly reported, "ARRIVAL OF TROOPS—A fine body of cavalry, from Louisiana, arrived . . . by the Danville railroad."[2]

In the meantime Captain Victor Maurin, per orders, reported to Brigadier General John H. Winder, the provost marshal of Richmond, at Broad and Ninth Streets in a commodious but mucky first floor hall.[3] Upon returning with orders Maurin likely announced, "*Messieurs,*

Entering Richmond.

From R.U. Johnson and C.C. Buel (editors), *Battles and Leaders of the Civil War* (hereafter cited as *Battles and Leaders*).

nous marchons—au Rocketts"[4] (Gentlemen, we march on—to Rocketts). Rocketts was a dilapidated suburb on the river immediately south of Richmond where the *Compagnie d'Artillerie* was directed to set up camp. The place already had large troop encampments with numerous tents that whitened the hillsides, along with a hospital.

The Confederate government augmented Maurin's Battery and furnished them with three 12-pounder Blakely rifle guns of English manufacture. They were short, light, accurate, and when fired, they kicked like a mule besides making a distinctive sound.[5] The battery also received from the government a traveling forge (for fixing ironwork and horseshoeing), and four wagons. Each individual Canonnier received an artillery sword to complete the battery's armaments.[6] On October 8, a day before the weather became "about as disagreeable as any misanthropic individual could desire,"[7] Maurin received by special requisition from the assistant quartermaster in Richmond three wall tents for himself and his subalterns, four "Bell" or "Sibley" soldier tents, and a storeroom tent to supplement the ones brought from Donaldsonville.[8]

In Camp Rocketts the Canonniers, like other batteries awaiting assignments, were employed in camp duties and drill, and for the next thirty-six days the *Compagnie d'Artillerie* lived and drilled in the soft red clay that was impossible to keep out of clothing, tents, guns, or anything else. They trained daily in unusually fine autumn weather on the summit of a hill with an extended plateau that overlooked the James River and Rocketts' wharfs and warehouses. From here too they could see a large part of Richmond, the oldest part, with its broad streets rising and dipping over the city's hills and the capitol building with tree-embowered terraces descending the hill, along with dwellings densely arrayed to the river.[9]

Although the Canonniers would not receive their initial pay for months, Richmond was visited for its innumerable whiskey dram shops, lager beer houses, billiard rooms, faro banks, oyster cellars, and *fille soumise* (promiscuous women). Many of those in uniform who, as it was, had a little money, soon became penniless. The billiard rooms of Richmond were a favorite spot for many of the Canonniers. Perhaps the oaken bar rooms flanked by billiard tables reminded the men of the "café billards"[10] that they had frequented back at home on the main streets of Donaldsonville.

Several members of the company visited photographic studios and got their likeness taken, including Maurin in his regulation officer's artillery frock coat of gray with the red trim and gold piping of a captain. It cost $4.00 or more at Rees's "extensive Gallery"[11] on Richmond's Main Street where Maurin had the photograph taken without being "detained more than ten minutes." Rees's studio advertised each photograph produced was "a gem every pop."[12]

One pastime that didn't cost anything was strolling about in the maze of city streets or standing about on the Capitol Square, "the gathering place of all Richmond."[13] A Louisiana Creole described it in his journal:

> This square is magnificent. I think it is on the highest hill. From that point you look down on five-story houses. On this square are the statehouses and the home of the governor of Virginia. There are also two monuments. On one gigantic pedestal there is the equestrian statue of Washington, which is very high. It also has statues of Patrick Henry, Madison, and Jefferson and several other pedestals without statues. . . .There is another smaller monument, a statue of Henry Clay, the same model that is on Canal Street in New Orleans only smaller, and it is surrounded by a gallery with a roof and a small colonnade.[14]

Another favorite haunt of the Creole soldiers to hang out at was the Columbian Hotel, where the kitchen was capable of feeding a battery's contingent of men for breakfast and

At right: Blakely cannons and tubes in the Charleston Arsenal Yard [courtesy of Library of Congress]; bottom right: "Antoine" Sanchez (on the right) and an unidentified comrade. Their likeness was probably taken when the Donaldsonville Artillery was camped near Richmond in October or November 1861, after being issued the artillery sabers that were soon discarded. Private Sanchez, who was promoted to lieutenant in March 1863, appears to be wearing a gray shell jacket with shoulder straps, possibly a Richmond Depot Type I, over a flannel or cotton shirt. The kepi cap was either gray (with a red band) or red (with a dark blue band) and a cross-cannon insignia in front. Pants were a plain gray or grayish-blue in color with a rectangle buckle [at right center] depicting the state seal of Louisiana, a pelican feeding her young, which was likely made in New Orleans near the beginning of the war. A bursting French cannon ball insignia and inscribed Le Canonnier de Donaldsonville buttons or Louisiana State seal pelican buttons adorn their jackets or a combination thereof. [Courtesy Joseph William "Bill" Carmena. Baton Rouge, La.]; bottom left: a Louisiana Pelican and Gallant Creole [from *Battles and Leaders*].

supper. "The fare," noted a soldier about the hotel food, "was plentiful and well served."[15] In Richmond many soldiers and artillerymen just stood on the thoroughfares where their activity was best described by the comment of one to his friends, "Goodness gracious, there's a lady. See the condition of that form, the elegant expansiveness of that crinoline skirt, that labyrinth of flounce, that foot fit for a Dutchess, and that eye which has caught and held the sunbeams. Bless my soul, boys, feast your eyes." Then the speaker "stood still in silent wonder."[16]

One of the adolescents from the bayou country in a gray uniform remembered, "I was a very lonely little boy in Richmond," adding, "Louisiana was farther away in those days . . . and somehow I was made to feel as though I was a foreigner. I suppose that was on account of our accent being different from that of other Southerners."[17]

Many of the artillerymen, when not employed in their duties or training, lounged about in or near the camp in the shade of fragrant pine trees. Here they played chess or checkers, cards and games, read newspapers and books that were plentiful, chatted, smoked, sang, and ate.[18] For those on guard and sentinel duty the post most coveted was the storeroom tent because they could spend their midnight vigils around a blazing fire with comrades as opposed to promenading on a lonely post. "With a pot of coffee, a canteen of liquor, cigars, and perhaps a deck of cards," wrote a Louisiana artillerist with experience watching over the storeroom tent, "the night passes more like a pleasant dissipation than ordinary guard duty. Thus whiling away the dull hours, comrades who have been little intimate grow social, old friends more friendly, and secrets are told, and confidence reposed which would never be communicated in any other situation."[19]

For the Canonniers the *veillées* (an evening spent in company) around the campfire was not only expended recounting tales and adventures, but each *raconteur* (storyteller) in turn related the various trials with which fortune had favored them. In these hours, especially for the Cajuns, the "usual topic of conversation was not politics or agriculture but folktales."[20] There was always music and singing, and the Creoles were quite fond of reading books aloud. Political principles and affairs, along with other deliberations on varied topics, certainly took place at the officers' campfire with Maurin the commander, the distinguished Lieutenant Lestang Fortier, the amiable William "Billy" Lawes, who before secession was an "Old Line Whig"[21] who had been appointed judge by a Democratic governor and confirmed by a Democratic senate, Lieutenant Prosper Landry, well-traveled with a Georgetown education, and the Catholic Father, Charles Boglioli, whom the renowned philosopher-writer Orestes A. Brownson singled out "to be the only philosopher he had ever met in America."[22]

In the Donaldsonville camp food was well served as it was recorded that Maurin's cook Louis Lefort was "a noted chef and could prepare the best Creole dishes."[23] Titus, Prosper Landry's slave, was a *cuisine cook de la bonne bouffe* (kitchen cook of good food) to the soldiery, too. A favorite dish of the Lafourche artillerymen was *un bon gombo* (a good gumbo), which could be cooked in vast quantities in the large camp kettle with just a pinch of filé (made by pounding the sassafras leaf into a very fine dull grayish-green powder) and adding whatever else was on hand such as turkey, chicken, ham, oysters, or sausage. The gumbo was usually prepared with a combination of central ingredients—chicken and oysters being a favorite.[24]

Frolic occurred around the campfires as the Louisianians were passionately fond of dancing. The French Creoles exhibited their "lightheartedness"[25] by stag dancing, while the Acadians exhibited "remarkable dexterity and grace"[26] in the cotillions and round dances. These dances were performed to the "inspiring"[27] violin notes of Donaldsonville Canonnier Pierre "Turiaffe" Babin, who was credited as being the "most popular, efficient, honest, kindly, reliable, thoughtful man."[28] Artificer Aimé Richard was another highly esteemed Canonnier and normally quiet, but he played melodies on a wooden flute that he carried throughout the war. Most of the music enjoyed in camp was provided by the five-piece Canonnier field band, which included the crooning of the band's leader Gus Conway, who was exalted not only for his fife playing, but his voice as well. A glee club was also formed; the rich bass voice of Tomasso Morelli led the troupe in "gay songs of a foreign tongue."[29] Private songs were also belted out by *la société des amis* (the society of friends) who assisted each other in emptying a few canteens of "Oh! Be Joyful."[30] Nights continued to be whiled away with liquid cheer, speech making, and toast drinking, interspersed with instrumental music, chin music, mirth, and jollity galore.[31]

During the day, and every day, over and over again, the cannoneers and drivers trained in their respective duties. Each also drilled in the duties of every other man. The tiresome exercise was alleviated with field practice that was "animated and apparently confused" with horses and men flying in all directions but, "in a moment the guns are seen unlimbered in line, the cannoneers at their post, and the piece-limbers and caissons aligned at their respective distances in the rear." The maneuvers continued with the rattle and roar of the "six cannons, with their accompanying six caissons, sped by seventy-two horses across the plain at a lively pace, the cannoneers either mounted or in hot pursuit [on foot], suddenly halt at the bugle signal, and in a moment after appear 'In Battery' belching forth mimic thunder in blank cartridge at a rapid rate, and the next minute 'limbered up' and away again to another part of the field."[32]

The training of the horses required as much drilling as that of the men and was extremely grueling. The horses were first practiced in their harness, next with the caisson, and then with the gun itself, and finally they were adapted to the close discharge of artillery volleys. The only casualty during this time in the *Compagnie d'Artillerie* was one horse, which died from disease.[33]

On Wednesday, November 6, 1861, the same day voters went to the polls and elected, without opposition, Jefferson Davis as President of the Confederate States of America, *Le Compagnie d'Artillerie de Donaldsonville* received the following order:

> SPECIAL ORDERS, } Adjt. And Insp. General's Office,
> No. 208. } *Richmond, November 6, 1861.*
>
> * * * * * * *
>
> VI. Captain Maurin will immediately proceed with his light battery of Louisiana artillery to Yorktown, Va., and report for duty to Major-General Magruder, Commanding.
>
> * * * * * * *
>
> By command of the Secretary of War:
>
> JNO. WITHERS,
> Assistant Adjutant-General[34]

The *Compagnie d'Artillerie* was now *en avant* (forward, to the front) and "from this time," wrote one of the Canonniers, "holiday soldiering was over."[35] On November 11 half the battery, with the three 6-pounders, left Rocketts for the trip down the James River on the steamboat *North Hampton*. The balance of the company following the next day. After boarding, one Louisianian described how "the woods that border on the river are very thick, so thick that it looks like a painting. There are magnificent views. The water of the river is red . . . but it is nothing when you have seen the Mississippi."[36] After a six-hour journey down the James River, which another of the Louisiana artillerist described as "m-e-a-n-d-e-r-i-n-g,"[37] the two detachments reunited a few miles below Jamestown Island at Kingsmill Wharf.[38]

Maurin's Battery of eighty-seven horses and eleven mules, pulling six guns with caissons, a forge, an ambulance, and four wagons, and hauling "sacks of grain and bales of hay, or whatever may have fed a horse, or stopped the bray of the musical mule . . . ammunition . . . tent and kettle; all the traps for 'shoulder-straps,'"[39] meaning their knapsacks, began the march in column. The battery of 114 men,[40] with canteens filled with river water, though a few canteens no doubt had liquid cheer, moved about twelve miles across the flat and sparsely settled Virginia Peninsula. The column went through vast stretches of pine woods and ground covered with broom sedge. The road, which had recently been flooded, made the going difficult and a tired, hungry lot of Canonniers reached Yorktown at five o'clock in the evening of November 13, 1861. Marching on crackers and a slice of raw bacon, which was normally issued on the boat before debarking, the *Compagnie d'Artillerie* at Yorktown found plenty of water, fresh beef, and more crackers, also called hardtack.[41] "Notoriously poor eating," remembered an artilleryman about the hardtack, although, "when there was leisure to do it . . . soaked well and then fried in bacon grease . . . it was a dish which no Confederate had the weakness or the strength to refuse."[42]

Yorktown, quaint and historic, with tree-lined streets and neat, impressive houses was located along a fifty-foot bluff on the south bank of the York River. England's Lord Cornwallis surrendered here to George Washington in 1781 and now Southern forces under Major General John B. Magruder extended the old forts and redoubts around Yorktown, which enclosed a much larger area than the British Army defended.

Maurin learned that Magruder's headquarters were temporarily located eleven miles away at Big Bethel Church and therefore reported to Magruder's chief of artillery in Yorktown. Here Maurin's company came under the immediate control of Brigadier General Gabriel J. Rains, commander of the Peninsula Army's First Division, which was composed of troops stationed in and around Yorktown. The *Compagnie d'Artillerie* remained here for four days, which coincided with the arrival of frosty mornings and very cold weather.[43]

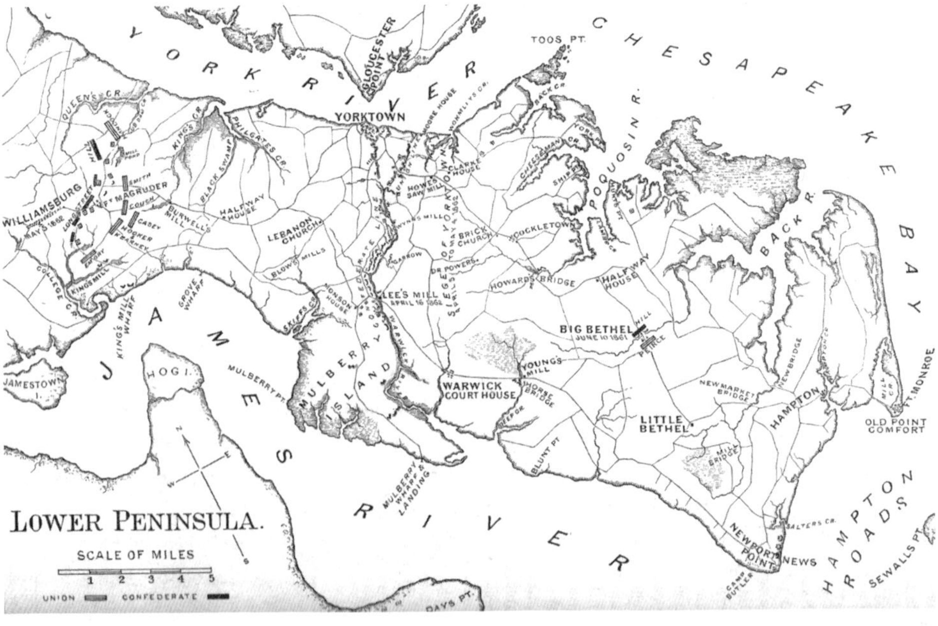

Lower Peninsula.
From *Battles and Leaders*.

In preparing for field duty, the days encompassed: "Roll-call, drill, watering the horses, greasing caissons and gun-carriages; cleaning, repairing, and greasing harness; cleaning the chests of the limbers and caissons; storing and arranging ammunition; and many little duties."[44] When night came the Canonniers in their little social groups closed around the fire and divided into several *ordinaire* (company messes) composed of eight to twelve men. Each Canonnier was drawn together by similar tastes and associations. "Likes and dislikes," remembered a veteran, "but soon one found that his best friend was not inclined to cut wood, fetch water, make a fire or do his share of washing the tin plates. Others who had been foppish in dress at home, became careless and dirty, and others used much profanity and vulgarity. So these messes . . . became greatly changed . . . by weeding out objectionable fellows."[45]

Lineage played but a small part in the *Compagnie d'Artillerie.* Documentation on two of the *ordinaire* reveals that five French Creoles or Cajuns, one Spanish Creole, one English, and one Italian descendant, comprised one mess, while another had four Irishmen, two Isleños, two English, and two French Creoles or Cajuns, along with one Spanish Creole and a French immigrant.[46] It could be truly said that each mess was "separated into distinct circles, as indifferent to each other, save in the common cause."[47]

For cooking and warmth the different *ordinaire* of the *Compagnie d'Artillerie* in the first five days at Yorktown burned four and three quarters cords of wood[48] as in:

> The camp fire blazed, the ample kettle swung,
> On two cross poles, all dark and sooty hung,
> While jovially the cook sang out his lay,
> The song of Dixieland, so far away.[49]

The horses were the most important asset of an artillery battery because without them, the guns could not get to where they were needed. Success depended on taking good care of them, though some called it "the drudgery of the service."[50] In feed and water a battery horse on average needed fourteen pounds of hay and twelve pounds of oats, barley, or corn each day plus four gallons of water. To feed their animals, wagons of the *Compagnie d'Artillerie* now hauled forage of 5,880 pounds of corn and 6,860 pounds of fodder—five days' rations for the battery's eighty-seven horses and eleven mules. Everyday the animals had to be fed and watered, rubbed down, and their horseshoes inspected, not to mention the hauling away of twelve to fifteen pounds of manure each horse and mule produced. The fact that Maurin and many of the Canonniers were *homme de cheval* (thorough horseman, lover of horses) would greatly benefit the efficiency and service of the battery.[51]

On November 18 Maurin led the Gunners of Donaldson on an eleven mile "expedition"[52] over the flat country to Big Bethel, a town of a dozen ordinary houses scattered over a third of a mile with a wooden church that looked very little like one. Here the Canonnier guns were deployed into breastworks located midway between Yorktown and the Yankee strong point at Fortress Monroe, the same works used to defeat the Yankees in the first land battle of the war on June 10, 1861.[53] This was the most advanced position in Magruder's defense of the Virginia Peninsula and an attack was now expected. Maurin's guns were positioned near the Tenth Louisiana Infantry Regiment. Both waited impatiently for the attack.

Here at Magruder's spear point a Creole infantrymen wrote of the artillery battery in their support, "The men were neatly uniformed and the entire corps gave evidence of the best of discipline and training. On inquiry, it gave me pride to learn that they were Louisianians. That they were the Cannoneers of Donaldsonville, commanded by Captain Maurin."[54] The same Creole later wrote, "The company of Donaldsonville gunners was at our side and thought that if they should ever fight they would not shame the Washington Artillery."[55]

Big Bethel and its earthworks with houses scattered over a third of a mile and a wooden church that looked very little like one was the most advanced Confederate position on the Virginia Peninsula. From November 18 to December 9, 1861, the guns of the *Canonniers de Donaldson* and Creole soldiers of the 10th Louisiana Infantry Regiment occupied breastworks as a strong picket force. From *Battles and Leaders*.

Morning arrived without the enemy showing themselves. From November 18 to December 9 the *Compagnie d'Artillerie* supported the infantry in the breastworks of Big Bethel as a strong picket force. Different detachments of Maurin's Battery went out on expeditions with the infantry who were ordered to gather forage within reach of the Yankees. Over the terrible and tough clay roads, and amongst a small number of houses on the Virginia Peninsula, they traveled past immense pines, arising to great heights without branches until near the upper half where limbs spread out like parasols.[56]

A Donaldsonville Canonnier articulated: "It was no child's play to march at short intervals to all portions of the line . . . across the . . . Peninsula, and . . . attest [to] the arduous service of this company. Amid snow and ice the agile Creoles, enduring for the first time such extreme temperature, cheerfully performed the duties assigned them to the complete satisfaction of their superior officers."[57] A member of the Tenth Louisiana added, "We set out each morning from [Big] Bethel and returned in the evening to pass the night there, lying in our blankets around a fire."[58]

Smoke Ring. From *Battles and Leaders*.

On November 25, while on another expedition, the *Compagnie d'Artillerie's* fourth detachment fired a shot with a Blakely gun at a company of Yankees in the distance.[59] Magruder, their commanding general and known in the army as "Prince John,"[60] reported, "The enemy made an unsuccessful attempt at ambuscade . . . within a few miles of Hampton. [The] party was flushed by a discharge of one of the rifle pieces of Maurin's Louisiana Battery."[61] After being in existence for twenty-four years this was the first shot ever fired in battle by members of *Le Compagnie d'Artillerie de Donaldsonville.*

Maurin received orders to withdraw to Wynn's Mill on December 9 with the belief that the enemy was disembarking a large number of men at Newport News. After a week without any Federal landings or attacks—and "hunting old hares" while, according to a Louisiana diarist, "having Jolly times as usual"[62]—Magruder ordered most of the artillery in from different points to strengthen the works in Yorktown.[63] The *Compagnie d'Artillerie* subsequently left Wynn's Mill and on the evening of December 15 arrived near Yorktown, where the Canonniers bivouacked and called the place "Camp Randall."[64]

For an artillery company in the field on the Peninsula a newspaper correspondent noted, "How great were the changes which a few weeks had wrought."[65] Refitting was called for and kept the artificers and drivers busy. Horses continued to receive their normal ration day after day, but new halters replaced old ones, fifty pounds of wagon grease was used for the gun carriages, and two hundred pounds of coal was burned to make repairs and shoe the horses.[66]

At Camp Randall the Creoles of the *Compagnie d'Artillerie* probably celebrated Christmas Eve in the usual fashion—with a long and elaborate preparation of hot eggnog made with just the right amount of whiskey and exactly enough sweetening. It was consumed during a *réveillons* (all night party that ended at daylight), but with the dawn of December 25 there came the spiritual silence of the *religieuse.*[67] An officer expressed the feelings of most when he penned in his journal, "Christmas—and how different from any . . . most of us ever saw before! No family reunions, no happy children, no Santa Claus."[68]

On Christmas Day, Magruder announced through General Orders: "The troops will winter where they now are" and, "if the enemy attacks we will defeat him, and after the victory we will have better quarters."[69] Better quarters than their tents were coming, but not by defeating the Yankees.

New Years day was bright, balmy, and beautiful as spring, and many of the Louisianians again celebrated with an "Egg Nog party."[70] From that first day of January 1862 to the middle of March, there were not two consecutive days of fine weather, but alternate snow and sunshine, rain, hail, sleet, and mud, and all things disagreeable in the weather of winter. On the third day of the year the army's quartermaster in Yorktown issued to Maurin lumber and tools for the Canonniers to begin building log cabins for winter quarters.[71] Forty-year-old First Artificer[72] Philippe Comstock, serving with the company since 1850, and twenty-two-year-old Second Artificer Aimé Richard, highly esteemed but very quiet and an unpretentious character,[73] were both carpenters by trade and directed the construction. In the building of billets near Yorktown a Louisianian wrote that "many a one then learned to wield an ax, and mix clay to daub the chinks of the cabins, who never dreamed of such experiences."[74] The weather turned very cold, with ice on the ground, a day after the tools and wood were received.

While the cabins were being built, on January 6, 1862, Magruder issued Special Order No. 580, which assigned Colonel Valery Sulakowski of the Fourteenth Louisiana Infantry Regiment command of the left flank of the Army of the Peninsula, from the mouth of Wormley's Creek to Ship Point and the immediate neighborhood. Sulakowski was known as a tough and efficient commander who took good care of his soldiers, but his men feared and did not care for him though they respected him. He was a civil engineer in New Orleans before the war and influenced Magruder's construction of fortifications across the Peninsula, which were called remarkable and exceedingly formidable.[75]

Sulakowski's command consisted of Maurin's Donaldsonville Artillery, Captain William Southall's Albemarle Everett (Virginia) battery, the Fourteenth Louisiana Regiment, the Fifty-third Virginia Regiment, the Second Florida Regiment, and two of the largest companies of the Fifth North Carolina Regiment. Magruder's order specified that Sulakowski "will make immediate arrangements to attack and defeat if possible the enemy in the act of landing to prevent his farther advance."[76] With these arrangements Maurin's guns moved in support of Sulakowski's infantry on an expedition that very day. It returned to camp without incident the next day.

Stables for the horses were constructed at camp of which a veteran wrote, "This building of horse-shelters was at times no mean or trivial enterprise, and sometimes employed a great many men a great many days."[77] The completion of the stables and the winter quarters (the last built for Maurin and his officers) occurred in mid-January with five inches of snow on the ground. For the remainder of the month and into February 1862 the Donaldsonville Canonniers remained inactive with many of the troops on the Peninsula claiming it was "miserably dull"[78] with "oppressive monotony."[79]

Irrespective of being Creole, Cajun, Isleño, Irish, English, French, or German, the Gunners of Donaldson enjoyed the jokes, jests, quips, and songs of their fellows around the campfire, and many an hour sped away delightfully in camp listening to witty *commentaire* (annotations), *anecdotes* (anecdotes), and *galejer* (tall tales). Every now and then "John Barleycorn" made his appearance, the intoxicating spirits being sold by older gentlemen of the neighborhood and elderly ladies, ostensibly for medicinal purposes. The cold Canonniers no doubt enjoyed *un tit cou* (a draught of intoxicating beverage that in proper French is spelled *un petit coup*).[80]

Living in winter quarters through the chilling rains and frequent snows rendered the season unhealthy, and by the end of March two Canonniers received medical discharges, and another two, including Lieutenant Michel Cazaré, received sick furlough back to Louisiana. Several more members required hospitalization, usually for diarrhea and fever, while others remained in camp ill.[81]

The battery also lost Private Felix Le Besque in February when he was discharged after appealing to the secretary of war and received a captain's commission, after which he was placed in command of a company of artillerists composed of New Orleanians in Degournay's Independent Heavy Artillery Regiment.[82] The secretary of war also granted permission for Sergeant Richard Winchester to recruit and organize a company of infantry.[83]

In response to these endorsements Maurin wrote to Magruder's aide-de-camp, "I beg have to call your attention to two authorizations granted within a few days by the Secretary of War . . . These authorizations are obtained I suppose . . . without taking in consideration the agreements [they] have towards me by those applicants. I would therefore respectfully submit that measures be taken to prevent a continuance of such actions and thereby in sure the full effectiveness of my company."[84] No similar authorizations were granted out of the company after Maurin's appeal.[85]

Though the *Compagnie d'Artillerie* lost men to sickness, discharges, and transfers, the strength of the battery increased when nineteen soldiers from Dreux/Rightor's First Louisiana Infantry Battalion and nine men of Coppen's First Louisiana Zouave Infantry Battalion, attracted by the *Compagnie d'Artillerie*'s "brilliant reputation,"[86] joined Maurin's Battery at the end of their twelve-month enlistments between February 1 and April 1, 1862.[87]

Additional new troops were the result of recruitment efforts in New Orleans by former Donaldsonville Canonnier Captain A. J. Powell during March and April 1862. Romain Octave Landry enlisted on March 21, 1862. Eighteen-years-old and called "Octave" by parents and friends, he returned home after attending Spring Hill College in Mobile, Alabama, to join. It was later said, "Young Landry's devotion to the cause made him respected by his officers and loved by his comrades."[88] Brothers Edouard and Mathieu Morin later "served valiantly"[89] after having enlisted in New Orleans with their father, Michel Morin, a forty-seven-year-old house carpenter. The elder Morin left behind three married daughters and one younger daughter, as well as his wife of many years, in order to follow his two sons into the field of strife. Called "Calabasse," Michel Morin was born in New Orleans, was well thought of in Creole society, and had a renowned reputation as a repairman. Known before the war by Lieutenant Prosper Landry, Morin was soon promoted to artificer in the battery that at the end of March 1862 had a total enrollment of 134 men rank and file.[90]

Michel Celicour "Calabasse" Morin
Courtesy Sylvia Degruy and Doris Melancon, Gonzales, La.

In April Powell continued to forward recruits to the *Compagnie d'Artillerie.* A contingent of six friends and neighbors from the Napoleonville vicinity enlisted at New Orleans on April 16, 1862. They were led by school teacher William Marks, a former captain in the Assumption militia's Hope Guards. He joined two days after his thirty-seventh birthday and left behind a wife, five daughters, and a son. Hypolite Templet was twenty-eight-years-old at the time of his enlistment. "Genial" and "kind,"[91] Templet was previously a lieutenant in the Hope Guards. He left behind three daughters and a son. Ernest Monnot was the son of a veteran from Napoleon's army, and he had recently married (in January 1861) the niece of Hypolite "Hip" Templet. Widowed nine months later, Monnot's martial spirit was now ready to *en avant.* The other new enlistments were Désiré Carmouche, twenty-one, who became "another one of our good soldiers,"[92] Duffosard Mollere, nineteen, a cousin of Canonnier Camille Mollere, and Maurice Landry, seventeen, an orphan raised by the Templet family. Two others from Ascension Parish also joined on April 16, 1862: Gustave Boudreau, twenty-one, joined his older brother, who was already with the battery in Virginia, and Olibert Hebert, thirty-one, a "most estimable gentleman."[93]

Eighteen-year-old Oscar Schmidt signed up with Powell at New Orleans on April 15 to join his twenty-nine-year-old half-brother Albert Schmidt, another Ascension gunner already serving in Virginia. Enlisting on April 21, 1862, were the "indefatigable"[94] William Ely, a twenty-four-year-old Virginian who was working in Donaldsonville as an overseer, and Jules Guedry, a twenty-six-year-old cooper in Donaldsonville. Guedry left a wife (Victorine) and two young daughters to join his Canonnier brother-in-law Alfred Melancon.

During March and April 1862, as active campaigning was about to begin, the discipline, instruction, and military appearance of the Donaldsonville Artillery, as they were now identified, was rated good. Their armaments and accoutrements, upon inspection, were considered in good order, but normal camp wear and tear had damaged the Canonniers' wardrobe, which was listed "not very good."[95] A Donaldsonville gunner in the field noticed, "How rapidly even boys grew bronzed and aged and desperately thoughtful."[96]

Maurin received orders on March 2, 1862, for the battery to move across the Peninsula to Young's Mill to the line of fortifications near Warwick Court House. Slogging through rain and mud, the Donaldsonville guns arrived in the late afternoon. The artillerymen spent a wet night where the not uncommon stories of misery were those of lying down upon as dry spot of earth as could be found and awakening to discover oneself almost submerged in water.

The next day Canonnier diarist François "Bienvenue" Cire wrote, "Left Young's Mill for our camp at Yorktown *still in the rain*."[97] The Canonniers slogged back to Yorktown.[98]

After three days in Yorktown, where the most significant event reported by Maurin was Private Augustin Albares's arm fracture, the guns were again ordered out. Cire recorded in his memorandum book: "March 6th Left camp again and arrived at Ship Point at 4 p.m. Snow in the night. Camped near the 14th Louisiana Regiment."[99] At Ship Point, located at the confluence of Poquoson River and Cheeseman's Creek, Maurin was instructed to place his guns in positions assigned by the commander of the Fourteenth Louisiana, Lieutenant Colonel Richard W. Jones.[100] After three days there, Maurin's Battery was again ordered, along with the Fourteenth Louisiana, to Bethel Church. The men believing the Yankees were advancing since Magruder, at 3 a.m. on March 9, issued Special Order No. 657. This order required all the troops on the Peninsula to occupy the most advanced post as a show of force and was given in conjunction with the second naval attack of the ironclad *C. S. S. Virginia* in Hampton Roads off the Peninsula coast.[101]

Resting for an hour after their arrival at Bethel Church, Maurin's guns were ordered forward at three o'clock in the evening. After progressing about four miles on the New Market Bridge Road, horsemen were seen approaching. The guns were immediately placed in battery, but as soon as it was done the cavalry waved and signaled not to fire. "We found that they were our own men," wrote Cire for the disappointed Canonniers, adding, "The Battery then went back to Bethel, arriving there at 7 p.m. At 3:00 a.m. an order came to hitch up to go and meet the enemy, but as soon as we were ready a counter order came."[102]

It was another boring day on March 11. A Louisianian in the Fourteenth Regiment noted there was "no item of interest to relate, or any account of such incidents, to give as would be liable to interest anyone."[103] Cire's lone diary entry for the day was, "A false alarm."[104] Exposure to the awful rain and elements, fatigue, loss of sleep, and hunger were constant inconveniences.

On March 12 orders to return to Ship Point were received. "Sometimes it is a little uncomfortable," wrote the member of the Fourteenth Louisiana about their distress, "but the knowledge of being almost in sight of an enemy, makes the feeling somewhat agreeable."[105] Maurin chronicled this expedition of the Donaldsonville Artillery with, "We returned . . . without anything of importance to report."[106]

At Ship Point, the weather became more agreeable, with one soldier observing that it was a delightful place with "bright sunshine, the fine breeze and the rippling water."[107] The Canonniers were again quartered near the 14th Louisiana, whose camp was described as a neat little village of whitewashed cabins, a log church, and an opera house, all built near small groups of fifty-foot high pine trees. The commissary rations of salt meat and hard bread were supplemented by the men who caught crabs, harvested oysters, and went fishing everyday, generally catching plenty enough for each detachment's dinner. This rural setting gave the men a chance to lounge about lazily and gaze out at the sea. Ship Point was considered one of the healthiest and most pleasant places on the Peninsula, unfortunately, the Donaldsonville Artillery remained only one week.[108]

On March 18 at eight o'clock in the morning Maurin's Battery made a two-hour march to Howard's Mill, located between Yorktown and Bethel Church. There the Canonniers spent the night. They once again continued in the morning to Bethel Church, where they sheltered themselves from the weather by sleeping in the church. Orders were received the next day, March 20, to return to Yorktown and Camp Randall. Upon arriving at noon they found their camp used by another company; Cire noted the Canonniers "took possession of it."[109]

A few days after being back in Camp Randall, forty-seven-year-old Father Boglioli made known his intention to leave the *Compagnie d'Artillerie* and return to Louisiana. There would be trials and difficulties with the Canonniers in war, but the priest knew there was even more severe troubles for the population back home. The Reverend Father, who had endeared himself to all by his gentle disposition, purity of character, affability, and courteousness, left for Donaldsonville the next day, March 24, with an affectionate *adieu*.[110]

From their arrival on the Peninsula through the winter months, the Donaldsonville Artillery lost the services of only a few animals. The horses and mules generally remained in good condition. The main reason, besides having stables for shelter and tending to their needs, were that the animals exceeded their daily allowance of rations per day through February and March with twelve pounds of corn, ten pounds of bran, and fourteen pounds of fodder.[111] On March 26, 1862, from Camp Randall, Maurin, wrote to Major J. Thompson Brown, commander of the artillery at Yorktown, that he had:

> the honor to report that I have on hand eighty horses and ten mules, in that number are included officers and non-commission officers horses; and also the horses and mules used for the waggons. Ten of the number which are used at the pieces, are for the present unfit for service, and they are now under treatment, two of the ten I think will never be serviceable. I am expecting from Richmond this week 30 horses and 10 mules, with the necessary harness to use six horses to each piece and caisson.[112]

Magruder was aware of the lack of horses in a number of artillery batteries and wrote on April 7, 1862, to the recently appointed military advisor to President Davis, General Robert E. Lee: "I am also short of horses for the artillery. I made a requisition some time ago, and it was neither filled nor noticed. I beg to earnestly call your attention to this fact. This deficiency is serious and its being provided for is an absolute necessity."[113] The quartermaster general was then made aware of the situation and the horses and mules were delivered. On April 16 Maurin's Battery received twenty horses and ten mules, and on April 26 an additional nine mules and two horses.[114]

By April, the Federal army, commanded by Major General George B. McClellan, was moving methodically up the Peninsula towards Yorktown with two corps numbering 60,000 men and a third corps following as reinforcements. Magruder held the Yorktown (Warwick River) defensive line of eight miles with not more than 17,000 Confederates. From his headquarters now located at Lee's Farm (near Lee's Mill on the Warwick River), Magruder issued General Order No. 168 on March 28, 1862. This order gave a few general directions to the troops and notified the Army of the Peninsula:

> The enemy is at length advancing. We shall fight him on the line of Warick [*sic*] river. . . . The men are reminded that, our forces not being equal to the enemy's, it will be necessary to remove them from the front to the rear and from the right to the left, withdrawing them from battle in one place to engage them in battle at another, and therefore their movements in withdrawing from battle should be deliberate and calm, holding themselves in readiness to repel any attack that may be made upon them while withdrawing to the rear, marching to the front, or moving to the right or left.[115]

Magruder later informed Lee, "I have made arrangements to fight with my small force, but without the slightest hope of success."[116]

Continuing their advance, the enemy skirmished with Confederate forces at nearby Cockletown on April 4, the same day Maurin received orders to place two of the Canonnier rifle guns in the Yorktown defensive works known as Redoubt Number 5. Located between the Warwick River and Yorktown were two redoubts, No. 4 and No. 5, which were connected by a curtain (a wall or parapet connecting two bastions) with wings or lateral breastworks

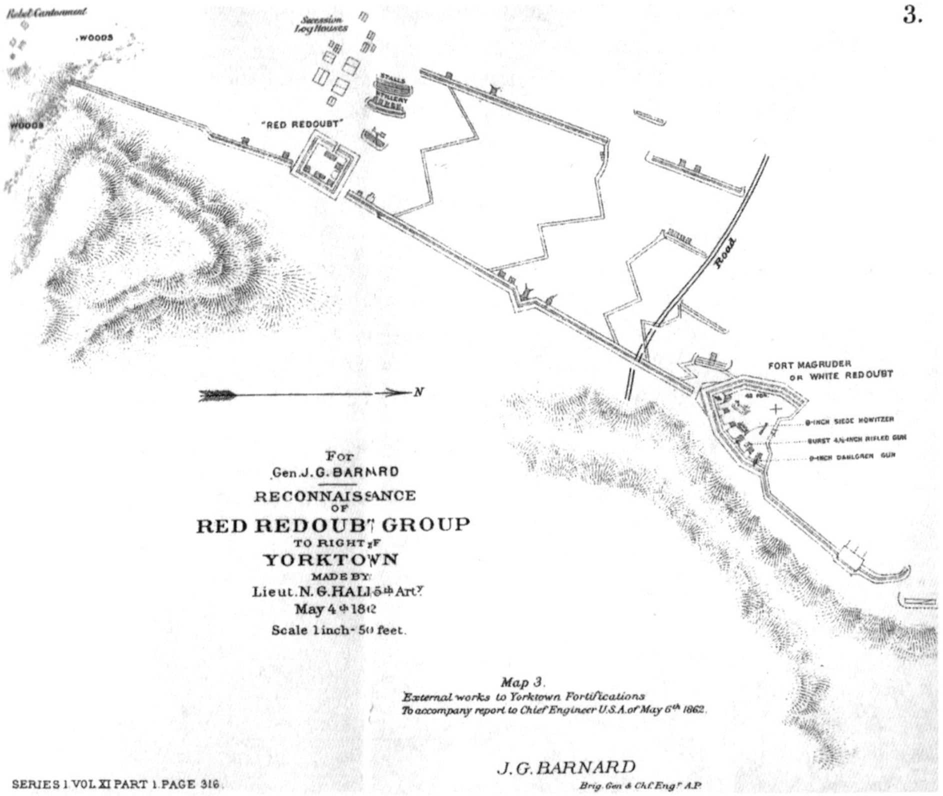

Red & White redoubts at Yorktown.
From *The Atlas to Accompany the Official Records of the Union and Confederate Armies* (hereafter cited as *Atlas to Official Records*).

extending to the Warwick River on one side, and the head of a deep ravine between Redoubt No. 4 and Yorktown on the other. Maurin's other rifle gun and the three 6-pounder smoothbore guns were positioned along the curtain to the left of redoubt No. 5. The earthworks were defended by Colonel George T. Ward's Second Florida Infantry Regiment along with other artillery under command of Captain William H. Southall. The artillery units were:

	AMMUNITION ON HAND			
	Spherical	Shell	Solid	Canister
Donaldsonville Artillery Capt. Victor Maurin	160	177	481	155
86 men manning 3 12-pounder rifles and 3 6-pounder smooth bore guns.				
James City Artillery Capt. Lucien W. Richardson	0	80	16	41
49 men manning 1 32-pounder.				
Hanover Artillery (Capt. William Nelson) Sgt. John McP. Cooke	25	4	73	22
19 men manning 1 12-pounder field piece.				
Albemarle Everett Artillery Capt. William H. Southall	112	82	152	116
75 men manning 2 24-pounder howitzers and 2 12-pounder field pieces.				

Magruder Light Artillery	Spherical	Shell	Solid	Canister
Capt. Thomas Jefferson Page	120	149	0	55

49 men manning 1 6-pounder rifle and 2 12-pounder howitzers.[117]

Out of the mist and rain the Federal army approached Yorktown the next day, April 5, 1862. The Canonniers and other Confederates crowded the ramparts to get a look at the blue-clad Yankees who made their appearance in front of the redoubts at ten o'clock in the morning. When they first appeared, a Louisiana artilleryman recollected, they were all "more or less excited as we were confident that [the Yankees] would attack us at once, and hustle and bustle; and vigilance, was the order of the day and night."[118]

Shortly after their appearance the Federal artillery opened a brisk fire to which the two Donaldsonville rifle guns in Redoubt No. 5, along with other Confederate batteries, quickly responded and warmly returned. Magruder believed the enemy would soon attempt an assault with heavy columns of troops and sent word to the batteries, which he depended on to repel the enemy, to be supplied with sufficient canister shot.[119] The artillery practice was exceedingly severe on both sides but after a short time it slackened to an occasional shelling. Canonnier Corporal John O'Hara recorded in his diary, "The fight commenced at Yorktown, the Donaldson Artillery opened the battle, cannonading lasted 4 hours."[120]

Magruder considered the redoubts a very important position in the defense of Yorktown. Unfortunately both Redoubts (4 and 5) with their curtain and lateral works out of necessity were constructed on ground sloping towards the enemy, making the interior and rear of the works exposed to the enemy's fire. Zigzag trenches had been dug that enabled the men to pass into and from the works with as little exposure as possible, but the enemy sharpshooters, reported Magruder, "found a protected position, which they have constantly occupied, in a peach orchard about 600 yards in front of Redoubt No. 5, and having ascertained the range, they made it dangerous for our men to expose their persons. Three men (none mortally) and five horses were wounded at this position."[121] Two of the wounded horses belonged to the Donaldsonville Artillery. Of the Canonniers, Maurin reported, "None of my command during the different engagements was injured."[122] The Federals reported the Confederate artillery fire was good, but casualties after the day's shelling were minimal, largely due to the fact that many of the shells fired bore deep into the soft ground before exploding.[123]

Maurin's gun positions continued to receive annoying fire from the Yankee sharpshooters (now in rifle pits) throughout April 6 as skirmishing continued along the whole line. This was also the day Southern troops first saw a Yankee balloon in the air attempting to reconnoiter their positions. Canonnier Cire noted the balloon's flight in his diary and added that the sharpshooters "were . . . firing on everyone who showed his head."[124] Most of the infantry supports for the redoubts were armed with smoothbore muskets and couldn't compete with the sharpshooter's rifle, while the artillery ammunition was too scarce to permit its use against the enemy's individual riflemen.

For the next five days Canonnier O'Hara briefly jotted in his diary, "6 and 7th and 8th heavy firing and 9 raining hard, sum skirmishing. April the 10th snowing hard, no fighting this morning and no general fight yet."[125] Despite no general battle the shooting continued as Maurin reported, "Occasional firing has taken place" by the Canonnier guns in the redoubt.[126]

One of the Louisiana artillerymen in the redoubts recalled the attack: "We were lolling around chatting and joking as was our wont. When Crack! Almost over our heads . . . burst one of these pesky . . . shells. Startled? Of course we were. We jumped to our stations and prepared for action."[127] Another of the Louisiana soldiers in the earthworks near Yorktown described the artillery fire, "They get to us some seconds before the report of the powder that sent them so that the first thing we know of them a shrill whistle unlike anything you or I ever heard, before, then the sharp bell-like crack of the bomb—the whistle of the little balls like bumble-bees—then the report of the Gun—but it all comes so nearly at the same time that it takes a very *fine ear* to distinguish which is first."[128]

On April 8 orders were issued that regulated conduct at the redoubts. Officers and sentinels were stationed at each gun, with not less than five men to be stationed at each post during the day and night. No gun was to be fired except by order of a commissioned officer, which meant no general firing at enemy's batteries. Care was to be taken that each shot fired was effective, and men were specifically forbidden from firing on any small body of troops.[129]

The redoubts and curtain continued to receive incoming fire without replying until, finally, on April 11 at three-thirty in the afternoon, with the weather clear and pleasant, Magruder ordered sorties to be made from the main parts of the line to skirmish with and determine the position of the enemy. The Second Florida Regiment and the Second Mississippi Battalion went out from the right and left of Redoubt No. 5, the artillery firing in support, and drove the enemy from their rifle pits. This force advanced through the pink and white blossoming peach orchard in front and to the main road, driving an enemy battery from its earthwork alongside the road to enthusiastic cheering from the artillerymen and soldiers observing along the lines. The troops returned, according to orders, when a large force of the enemy's infantry approached. When moving back they purposely set fire to a house that was in front of the Confederate works.[130] "It was a sad sight to witness the changes wrought in a few minutes," remembered one of the Louisianians, "the blossoming trees lying prone . . . the destroyed fences and the smoke of conflagration, and here and there the field dotted by dead and wounded men."[131]

On the night following this sortie, the Twenty-fourth Virginia Regiment moved to the front of the redoubts and cut down more of the peach orchard and burned the rest of the houses that afforded the enemy shelter. Canonnier Cire noted the above action in his diary and recorded that their Fifth detachment with a Blakely gun rejoined the battery along the curtain, leaving just Maurin's Sixth detachment's Blakely gun inside the redoubt.[132]

The Fifth North Carolina Regiment ventured out the following night, April 13, and moved farther to the front and cut down some cedar trees along the main road that partially screened the enemy's movements. After this the enemy sharpshooters no longer bothered Redoubt No. 5 and the curtain.[133]

The Army of Northern Virginia's commander, General Joseph E. Johnston, took over command of the defenses on the Peninsula on April 12, 1862, as his army began arriving from the Rappahannock Line to reinforce Magruder's Peninsula Army. Six days later Johnston issued General Order No. 1 of the Department of Northern Virginia designating that Redoubts 4 and 5 and Yorktown were under the immediate command of Major General Daniel H. Hill. He in turn assigned command of Redoubt No. 5, including the Donaldsonville Artillery's Sixth detachment, to Brigidier General Robert E. Rodes. Redoubt 4 and the curtain connecting the two redoubts (with Maurin's five other guns) were assigned to Brigidier General Jubal A. Early's command.

Magruder's Army of the Peninsula no longer existed after being absorbed into Johnston's Army of Northern Virginia. Magruder was assigned to command the right of the Warwick River Line, Hill assumed command of the left, Major General James Longstreet was charged with the center, and Major General Gustavus W. Smith the reserves. Supervision of the artillery was delegated to Brigadier General William N. Pendleton. Magruder issued a statement to the old Army of the Peninsula on April 19, 1862, publicly expressing "the approval with

Yorktown redoubts as seen from the Union line.
ARW; courtesy of Library of Congress.

which their uniform good conduct has inspired him."[134]

The Union army continued its siege work and building approaches and occasionally fired on working parties and the redoubts with their artillery. When not in the front line trenches, the Confederate artillerists and soldiers, along with a force of blacks under the command of an engineer, were kept employed by strengthening the traverses and epaulements of the redoubts. These duties were rigorous and exhausting and worse, "We," wrote a private, "have the worst water to drink you ever saw."[135] Their rations were bad, too, and very limited and consisted of the plainest and roughest food, usually raw meat such as pickled pork or salted meat. Uncooked flour was issued and the food cooked by details in the rear before being brought to the front lines. There was no coffee or sugar, but rain and mud in abundance. Here they had their "first experience with body lice, that pertinacious pest of all armies," wrote a Confederate.[136]

Between April 5 and April 15 rain fell nearly every day. A Confederate soldier noted how "very disagreeable" the water filled trenches were. Of the works and firing he added,

> We're well covered . . . and we can see the flash of their cannon some time before the shells reach us, and all we have to do is to fall down till they pass over us. We . . . stay 48 hours longer in the trenches and then we get a rest for a while, but our men are all better satisfied in the trenches than in camp, as we always know better what is going on, where as in camp we are always uneasy, whenever we hear guns firing.[137]

On April 16, an unusually pleasant day, the Yankee artillery opened a heavy fire against the redoubts. This barrage continued on for four days with an incessant roar. Cire wrote in his Canonnier memorandum book that several skirmishes took place, resulting in "nothing of importance."[138]

Referring to the bombardment, one Confederate jotted, "They keep firing cannons at our men all the time but seldom hurt any of us."[139] Another gray soldier wrote in his journal, "If our friends across the field knew to what inconvenience they are putting us, they would certainly stop," adding, "they haven't given us fifteen minutes rest at any one time."[140] There was amusement in the trenches when a third Confederate described how, "Many were the laughs indulged in about the manner in which this or that man ducked or dodged."[141]

With "some rain" on the nineteenth, "weather moist" on the twentieth, and "rain" every day from the twenty-first to twenty-seventh, except for a "pleasant" April 24,"[142] the artillery fire of the Yankees lightened up. On April 21 Cire noted, "We fired on the breast works they had erected during the night."[143]

The Federal gunboats on the York River fired a good deal and conducted an almost daily shelling. Describing the 120-pound gunboat shells, a Confederate artilleryman wrote, "When they exploded, it seemed as if they would destroy all of us." Surprisingly he added, "No one was hurt. I do not see how we escaped, for we were cooped up here . . . and the place was crowded with men."[144]

With the expectation of an assault, Maurin's five guns remained for the entire month along the curtain between the redoubts with the Sixth detachment in Redoubt No. 5. At the end of April 1862, McClellan's Union Army, now reinforced, numbered 112,000 troops against Johnston's 60,000 Confederates. The Donaldsonville Artillery numbered: "Present for Duty . . . 4 officers, 116 enlisted men with another 6 present but sick; Enlisted men gained . . . 34 (18 recruits from Louisiana, 16 re-enlisted); Absent Sick . . . 1 officer, 7 enlisted men (2 in Louisiana, 4 in Yorktown and 2 in Richmond Hospitals), 6 Field Pieces, 95 Serviceable Horses, 26 Mules."[145]

Without tents, shelter, or fires in the trenches (none could be kindled day or night without it becoming the focus of heavy shell fire), the Canonniers and the army, their uniforms threadbare and in rags, suffered from the cold and rainy weather. The suffering got worse for the Canonniers and other Louisiana troops as the Richmond press reported with bitterness and surprise on April 28, 1862, that New Orleans had fallen to Union troops. The news was as "unexpected as mortifying and discouraging."[146] It conveyed anxiety to those who pondered the consequences of the capture of New Orleans and its effect on Donaldsonville, now in range of the Federal navy. The arrival of eleven *Compagnie d'Artillerie* recruits from Louisiana two days later, undoubtedly with several letters and news of home, must have buoyed some spirits.

On May 1 there was heavy firing all along the line, particularly from Redoubt No. 5.[147] Word was passed that Johnston was ordering "a retrograde movement"[148] back to Richmond. In preparing to abandon the line Maurin received orders to leave the company's three wall tents standing while their six wagons (the battery received two additional wagons on April 23) were loaded with all the baggage, ammunition, and army stores. On May 2 Cire wrote, "Orders to prepare to march given when all ready that night the march was put off . . . heavy firing all day and night from our side."[149]

General orders were received on May 2 to evacuate the Yorktown Line after sunset. D. H. Hill would keep up an active fire from his heavy guns until after midnight. Other portions of Hill's command would move at dark for Williamsburg by the direct road, with Hill's Division being the last to leave the Yorktown Line. The Donaldsonville Artillery was assigned to the Reserve Artillery, organized for use wherever needed under Pendleton, but was still attached to the command of Early's Brigade in Hill's Division with the Second Florida Regiment and Second Mississippi Battalion at Redoubt No. 5. For the movement, Maurin was instructed to march with Early's troops composed of the Fifth North Carolina, Twenty-third North Carolina, Twenty-fourth Virginia, and Thirty-eighth Virginia Infantry Regiments.[150]

On May 3 Cire recorded that the Donaldsonville Artillery, "Began the evacuation of Yorktown at 8 p.m., the night was very dark; the roads very bad and traveling very slowly the guns and caissons constantly sticking in the mud."[151] Not only were the guns and caissons sticking in the muddy road but the men too, and in pulling their feet out many left their shoes in the muck. Cire later wrote, "At daylight still on the march, a tremendous explosion heard . . . at Yorktown. Kept on marching and in the afternoon reached Williamsburg and halted for the night."[152]

Early's Brigade of 3,270 men was the rear guard on the thirteen mile march from Yorktown to Williamsburg. The general remembered: "Our progress was very slow . . . my command passed through Williamsburg after sunrise on the morning of Sunday, May 4 and bivouacked about two miles west of that place."[153] The last regiment in Early's line of march was the Twenty-fourth Virginia of whom an officer wrote, "The mud and water were ankle and sometimes knee deep, and the weary infantry had often to help the struggling horses, drag wagons and guns, from holes and ruts, whose wheels had sunk to the very axle. So the march was tedious and slow. Men fell asleep on the wet wayside at every halt, and sometimes not a mile was made in an hour."[154]

While another officer recalled:

> It could hardly be called marching; it was wading in mud & slush from one to three feet deep . . . cut into bottomless sloughs by the tremendous traffic of army trains & artillery. . . . It was a dark night, & there was no picking one's way, & the whole width of the road was filled with either wagons, ambulances, artillery, or infantry plunging & laboring through the mud, with frequent long halts when some gun, or wagon, stalled in some deep spot, & men from the ranks marching near had to swarm in & help the jaded horses pull them out, while everything behind . . . had to come to a stop & wait. And so it went on all night—march or wade two minutes and halt ten or longer.[155]

After getting to Williamsburg a private inscribed in his small pocket booklet:

> A very nice though quite old looking place. The Country surrounding for miles being all cleared up rendered the view magnificently beautiful. The whole plain being cov[ere]d with Troops[,] artillery[,] cavalry. Wagons [and] ambulances & all moving in the same direction extending as far as the eye can see. In passing through Williamsb'g all the eligible places in the buildings were crowded with men, women & children all of whom wore a countenance of Sadness & deep regret.[156]

Of the troops, the officer in the Twenty-fourth Virginia added, "Supper less and without sleep, in a pelting rain they lay upon the ground that night, and without breakfast, jaded, wet and hungry . . . they fell in next morning to resume the march.[157]

Early's command with the Donaldsonville Canonniers received orders to be ready to march at three o'clock in the morning, but the rain during the night made it very difficult for the wagons and artillery in front to make headway. This delayed the following brigades from moving off and caused Early's infantry and artillery, and Maurin's Battery, to wait in their same position. Later in the morning word passed around of a skirmish in the rear and Cire noted, "That night our forces had a fight with the enemy who had followed us up."[158]

Longstreet's Division had taken over responsibility of the rear guard the day before and was now occupying the field works in front of Williamsburg. Early's Brigade and attachments were just about to move off at noon when orders were received from Hill to halt for a time. Early soon received another order to move back to Williamsburg and report to Longstreet. After splashing their way back through the mud and rain, Early reported to Longstreet, who instructed him to halt his command in the open space in the rear of the buildings on the campus of William and Mary College. There the Canonniers and infantrymen waited, dripping wet in the cold, drizzling rain, which continued to fall. To escape the rain, officers and crowds of soldiers from different units filled the halls, corridors, and lecture rooms, of the old college.[159] "While we waited at the college the

Wren building, College of William and Mary.
From the author's collection.

music of the battle sounded continually in our . . . ears, and wounded friends and ambulances, and squads of prisoners passed frequently by," wrote a Virginian. "Everyone looked for orders 'to the front!' each moment."[160]

The dark evening drew slowly on. Suddenly, between three and four o'clock, the expected courier came dashing up to Early with orders: "Move quickly Longstreet's support."[161] The rapid rolling of the drums indicated a hasty move, and Early's regiments and artillery, along with the Donaldsonville guns, moved off as rapidly as the condition of the streets of old historic Williamsburg permitted. They headed towards an earthen fortification called Fort Magruder, about two miles east of Williamsburg, with the sound of battle plainly audible and getting louder from the front. Forward went the Canonnier horses pulling their guns, galloping and rattling down the middle of the long, straight, narrow main street, past long lines of wet gray-clad infantry moving on the sidewalks. In going through, an officer wrote there were "cheers and tears of the women and maidens, whose pallid faces appear at every window and door, waiving adieu . . . as they pass quickly by."[162] A foot soldier observed:

> the cannoneers holding on to the limber and caisson boxes with all their strength. The broken down men and horses of an hour ago were pushing on with renewed strength and flaming eyes . . . not an eye was turned to right or left. The battery horses with their nostrils distended, every sinew in their bodies worked to full tension, went flying by. The gait was so rapid the men could scarcely retain their places on the boxes . . . time seemed and age, and yet it was but a moment.[163]

As Early's Brigade neared Fort Magruder, Longstreet rode up and ordered him to move to a position on a ridge in a wheat field to the left and rear of the fort and await further orders. Maurin received orders to send half his battery to Fort Magruder, where Colonel Micah Jenkins of the South Carolina Regiment of Palmetto Sharpshooters (from Brigadier General Richard H. Anderson's Brigade, Longstreet's Division) and six companies of the Fifth South Carolina Regiment, along with a few artillery pieces, kept up a "constant *pounding*" and where "here and there a puff of smoke among the tree-tops denotes the bursting of a Federal shell."[164]

Longtime Canonnier Lieutenant François Lestang Fortier, Creole, thirty-five years old, energetic, exact, loyal in character, and upright in every exploit and who had spent most of his time the last couple of months sick in camp with "bad health,"[165] led the Donaldsonville Artillery's First, Second, and Third detachments of smoothbore guns—*Honoré, Fidélité,* and *Libertié et Égalité*—towards Fort Magruder. They moved through the cold rain and what one Donaldsonville Canonnier described as "the deepest kind of mud."[166] A Frenchman in the battle wrote, "What a tumult! The whole edge of the woods on fire, the musketry rolling uninterruptedly."[167]

At Fort Magruder, Jenkins reported, "Prompt re-enforcements having been sent by the commanding general, I . . . placed Captain [James] Dearing's[Lynchburg Artillery, two guns] and [Capt. Robert M.] Stribling's [Fauquier Artillery, two guns] and three pieces of Donaldsonville Artillery, under Lieutenant Fortier, in position to answer the heavy fire."[168] Of the Canonnier actions Fortier submitted his brief report five days later: "Sir: I have the honor to report that three brass 6-pounders were engaged in Fort Magruder. I reported at 5 p.m. and took position in said fort. Thirty-three rounds of shell and solid shot were fired during the engagement. No casualties of importance to report."[169]

Regarding the fight Dearing reported,

> About this time, between 4 and 5 o'clock, I think, the enemy again began their musketry from the woods. I opened on them from the fort, and soon after I changed my fire to a solitary piece of artillery of the enemy . . . after nearly twenty minutes' firing

> . . . it ceased firing and fired no more . . . I was ordered by Captain [G. Moxley] Sorrel, of General Longstreet's staff, to open upon the enemy's infantry in the wood, whose position he pointed out to me. I did so, and continued to fire until nearly dark, when all of my ammunition was completely exhausted. While firing the latter part of the evening from the fort my men were exposed to a most annoying fire from the enemy's sharpshooters, but by adopting the precaution of making my men load kneeling, all of the guns being mounted in barbette, fortunately none were hurt. I had one horse shot here at that time by a minie-ball in the shoulder, and had to leave him. I had only twenty-two men engaged with the two guns, officers and men.[170]

Stribling reported, "I was ordered to take two guns to . the fort and open upon a line of the enemy's skirmishers. A fire was kept up on them."[171] He added that it was "an almost continuous fire until dark when it [the battery] was drawn off, having done excellent work."[172] Jenkins reported that he too "must speak in the highest terms of the conduct of the batteries."[173] Lieutenant Colonel J. Thompson Brown of the artillery wrote of the guns in Fort Magruder: "These pieces were used with the greatest effect under a galling fire from sharpshooters."[174]

Fortier's health remained bad, and he tendered his resignation, which was accepted in August 1862. Upon receiving it Brown replied, "I take great pleasure in testifying to the energy and faithfulness which Lieutenant Fortier has displayed in the discharge of his duties, and would exceedingly regret to lose the services of so valuable an officer."[175]

Near five o'clock in the evening, Hill with Early's Brigade prepared to attack the enemy on the extreme left of Fort Magruder through a dense wood, where they heard the loud echoes of enemy artillery firing. At this time Hill posted some pieces of the Second Company Richmond Howitzer Battery (assigned to Pendleton's Artillery Reserve) to cover the retreat of Early's Brigade in case it had to fall back. The remaining guns—Maurin's three Blakely's and the Jeff Davis (Alabama) Artillery's—remained standing by in reserve along the road.

The attack by Early's Brigade resulted in it retiring to its previous position with heavy losses. Early was severely wounded, and the brigade's wounded were brought out as darkness ended the conflict. The weather was nasty with Hill's Division remaining in line of battle all night in the cold and wet with the batteries and artillerists standing at their guns in the pouring rain.[176]

Without any fires the men gathered in little groups and discussed the incidents of the day, one of them remembering that on this occasion it

> was inexpressibly somber and depressing. The twilight deepened into a solemn darkness, with nothing audible save the ceaseless patter of the rain, the moaning of the wounded in the thickets, the voices of the litter bearers hunting comrades that had been left in the heat of battle, the crackling of the underbrush as an officer came in from the out pickets—or the far-off cry of some poor wretch beseeching 'water, water, water!'—How long the hours seemed after the excitement of the day! How strangely still and solemn seemed the vast forest after all the uproar and clamor of an hour before. And so we waited,—waited,—waited;—a long grey-clad line of men . . . waiting to begin a dismal, fatiguing night march![177]

After a night of almost unparalleled suffering, Hill's Division formed the rear guard on May 6 that dawned with a clear sky, the day after the battle being bright and sunny. "Every one was glad to get in motion, glad to stir his blood, and shake the dripping rain from his clothes," remembered a Southern soldier. The march however wasn't pleasant in that they moved over roads "literally knee-deep in soft mud and slush—and with artillery, wagons, ambulances and footmen all jumbled together in the narrow roads—was almost appalling!"[178] Donaldsonville Canonnier Eugene Levy remembered that Maurin's Battery, "Quietly fell into line."[179]

Hill reported and described the retreat: "Thousands of soldiers had sought shelter from the storm of the night before in barns and outhouses, and it was with the utmost difficulty they could be driven out. Cold, tired, hungry, and jaded, many seemed indifferent alike to life or capture. The roads were in a truly horrible condition. Horses could with difficulty wade through the mud and slush, and to footmen the task seemed almost impossible. The straggling was enormous, but more especially on this the first day after leaving Williamsburg."[180] The road, recorded a private in his booklet, for five miles "was strewn with Blankets, over coats, clothing, knapSacks, Cooking utensils, Sick men &c &c." He added it was "awful muddy & wagons & artillery continually bogging down."[181] Passing again through Williamsburg the streets were again filled with soldiers "but now," noted one of them, "there were no signs of inhabitants . . . the houses and everything as quiet and desolate as a country village."[182]

Maurin's Battery kept on, but the march from Williamsburg to "within sight of the spires of Richmond" was, as Canonnier Levy said, "distinguished by the utmost hardships. The roads, rendered soft by many rains, had been cut up by the wagon trains and artillery of the entire army, and on many occasions we were forced to chop a road through the woods. The men subsisted for three days on parched corn and roots, and yet bore all with a patient and patriotic spirit."[183] One soldier sorrowfully remembered he was "tired of stealing corn from the horses [knowing] they can't well do without it."[184] Another exclaimed, "The men were so hungry that they ate corn, collard stalks, Turnips, beets or any thing they could get hands on."[185]

On May 7 Cire recorded that the Donaldsonville guns and caissons were "on the march [and] made about 2 miles and halted, marched at night again lost our way and got stuck in the mud and stayed stuck until daylight." The next day, he continued, "After getting our pieces & caissons out of the mud we camped for a while on the Chickahominey River. After having cooked rations we resumed the march and camped at night."[186] After being much of the time without food "our long fast," wrote a soldier, "was broken by the slaughter of some cattle, which . . . had to be roasted on coals, and eaten without salt or bread. Tough beef, served up in that style, was not a palatable dish, even to men as hungry as we were."[187]

The Donaldsonville Artillery resumed the march at noon on May 9 and traveled in fine weather for about five miles before camping at dark. The next morning Cire recorded, "In the same camp, sent two of our pieces to Richmond for repairs, weather fine."[188] Another of the ragged gray soldiers wrote, "All seem to be cheerful . . . all in fine spirits today having met the provision train, and had a good breakfast, with the prospect of a good rest and a sleep which we need very much."[189]

Now with Longstreet's Division, Maurin's Battery remained in bivouac, where for a few days "supplies were still very scarce, and sometimes the men had to content themselves with one cracker and a very small piece of bacon."[190] Here they remained for the next week on the Chickahominey River at Bottom's Bridge, about thirty-eight miles from Williamsburg on the road to Richmond. There the Donaldsonville Canonniers and their horses received a much-needed rest.

Dragging Guns.
ARW; courtesy of Library of Congress.

Chapter Four

En Defense de la capitale
(In Defense of the Capital)

Having rested from the tiresome services in the trenches near Yorktown and the laborious march made while half dead from fatigue and loss of sleep, the *Compagnie d'Artillerie de Donaldsonville* welcomed the abundant supplies that began to arrive from Richmond fourteen miles away. In bivouac near Bottom's Bridge on the Chickahominey River, the gray uniformed men in the hot and muggy weather found themselves "the dirtiest and most miserable looking . . . it is possible to imagine."[1] After sleeping on soft beds of pine needles along the river with water moccasins and copperheads about and the Magnolia trees in full fragrant bloom, "We," remembered a Louisiana artilleryman, "had acquired quite a contingent of wood ticks in addition to . . . other vermin we brought from Yorktown and of which we had been unable to rid ourselves."[2] Another wrote, "It was common around the camp fires to see men holding their shirts above the fire to rid them of the annoying enemy."[3]

On May 15, 1861, news was received of an attack at Drewry's Bluff on the James River and of confusion and panic in Richmond, but the army and the Canonniers were in fine spirits *en defense de la Capitale* (in defense of the Capital). They were anxious and ready to prove themselves as valiant as those in P. G. T. Beauregard's army.[4] Orders were issued during the night of May 15 for the divisions of Longstreet and Hill to cross the Chickahominey River and move closer to Richmond.

Donaldsonville Canonnier François "Bienvenue" Cire recorded in his memorandum book that Captain Victor Maurin's battery had "orders to leave at 3 a.m. but only left at 3 p.m. It having rained since morning. After having marched 7-miles halted and camped, raining."[5] Another in the column also recorded in his diary, "All hands roused up this morning out of our comfortable Bunks an hour before day-light & dident take up the line of march until ½ past 3 O'clk . . . had a muddy wet & disagreeable march . . . Commenced traveling again."[6] The next day that same diarist wrote, "Continued until after dark. Roads very bad & all quite hungry. Truly is the life of a soldier hard."[7]

Under an overcast sky with light rains, Cire added that Maurin's Battery "left again at 3 p.m. and camped about 3-miles from Richmond (Stern [*sic*] farm.)"[8] The next day, May 18, Cire recorded the Gunners of Donaldson were "at the same place (fine weather)."[9] Still another diarist recorded that thousands of troops were in the ponds and streams of the bottom lands at Stearns's Tree Hill farm and "had a glorious wash . . . Bathing & having a jolly time of it."[10] Living in the open air and on hard crackers and bacon, the Canonniers remained on Tree Hill farm near Almond Creek for one week.

The Donaldsonville artillerymen were able, as Private Eugene Levy put it, "To relieve the monotony of every-day camp life" by making "occasional surreptitious visits to Richmond, and [having] a few tame adventures."[11] Another Louisiana artillerist wrote, "We enjoyed promenading the Main street, gazing into the shop-windows, and lounging about."[12]

The Canonniers must have been a sight in Richmond in their *haillonneé uniformes* (tattered uniforms) before Maurin, on May 21, sent a Special Requisition for clothing to the quartermaster department apprising them that the clothing was "absolutely requisite—for the use of my company."[13] Along with their deplorable clothing, the earlier stay on the Peninsula affected the health of the Canonniers in that the number confined to the hospital doubled in May 1862 with most, like other commands, "Debilitated by the 'soldier's scourge,' camp diarrhoea."[14] Of the five officers, only Maurin and Lieutenant William "Billy" Lawes were well enough to take the field. Hospitalized and soon back in Louisiana was Lieutenant Lestang Fortier, while Lieutenant Prosper Landry was hospitalized and went to Amelia Springs on a thirty-day sick furlough. Lieutenant Michel Cazaré remained on sick leave in Louisiana. Cire also noted on May 24 that the "able and affable"[15] Canonnier Sergeant "Dick" Winchester after having been discharged from the service left for Louisiana.[16]

The battery's horses needed rest and forage too, and grazing the five hundred-plus fertile acres of Tree Hill no doubt invigorated the animals. The only incident of note documented by Cire during this time was the battery's wagons going near the James River for forage and returning after seeing a gunboat in the river.

On May 25 the Gunners of Donaldson broke camp after receiving additional mounts. One hundred and four horses and sixteen mules pulled their guns, caissons, and wagons. Cire recorded that they "left camp marched through Richmond and camped at about 2-miles in rear of the city."[17] After passing through the northeast suburbs of Richmond near Oakwood Cemetery, Maurin's Battery bivouacked near the Fairfield Race Course. It was located along the Nine Mile Road, one and one half miles northeast of Capitol Square, about midway to the Mechanicsville Turnpike. A large part of Longstreet's Division was encamped there.

On May 27 Maurin visited the Canonniers confined in the Louisiana Hospital in Richmond. The next day Maurin placed the following newspaper advertisement in the *Richmond Dispatch:*

> $50 REWARD.-Strayed or stolen from the yard of the Louisiana Hospital on Sunday night, May 25th, between the hours of 10 and 2 o'clock A. M., a large iron-gray HORSE, about 6 ½ hands high; another in the same yard and at the same time, a small sorrel HORSE, a natural pacer, branded "S. H." on the left shoulder and left thigh. A liberal reward will be given for their recovery.
>
> Address, at "Louisiana Hospital," or
>
> Capt. V. Maurin
Donaldsonville Artillery, near
Richmond, Va.[18]

The Donaldsonville Artillery remained here in camp while McClellan's Union Army slowly approached the Confederate capital. Cire recorded in his memorandum book: "May 26th—Heavy cannonading in the direction of New Bridge Road. May 27th—Cannonading heard in the distance. May 28th—Cannonading still heard—fine weather. May 29th—No change. May 30th—No change [rain]."[19]

On a warm and sultry May 30, ten days after Maurin submitted the clothing requisition, he went into Richmond and acknowledged receipt of two boxes containing 100 cotton under

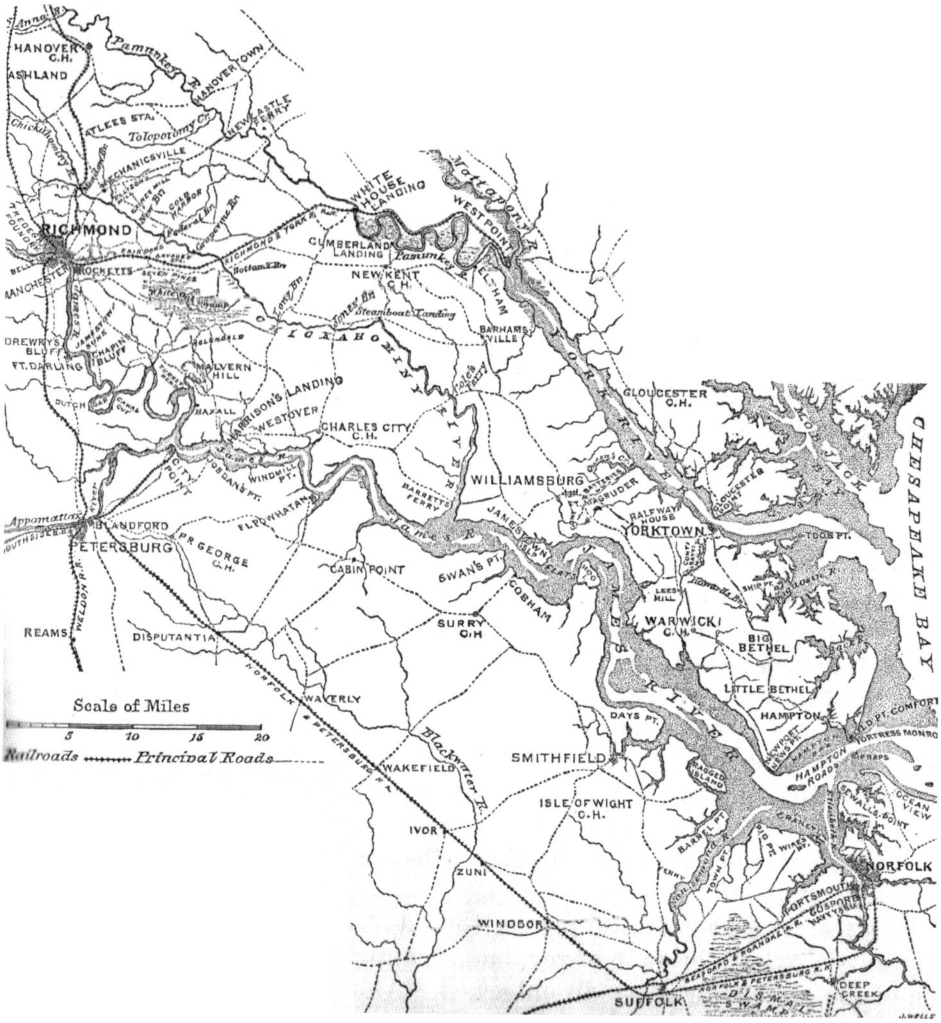

Richmond and the Peninsula.
From *Battles and Leaders*.

shirts, 150 pairs of cotton underwear, 29 shirts, 100 pairs of shoes, and 200 pairs of socks. The battery's accoutrements were in good order, and now it could be reported that the clothing and military appearance of the Donaldsonville Artillery was good.[20]

The evening after receiving their clothing, a Louisiana cannoneer wrote, "A most terrific thunderstorm swept over the vicinity commencing at 5 p.m. and continuing with unabated fury until 11 p.m."[21] During the night an officer also reported, "The men were poorly sheltered, many with little fly tents, others with only a single blanket on a pole . . . this dreadful night . . . its sheets of lightening and torrents of rain, its sharp and deafening thunder."[22]

In the early morning of May 31, after the storm passed, and with the air fresh and cool, Maurin received marching orders. He instructed the Canonniers to get ready to move by daylight with three days' provisions in haversacks and filled canteens. The artillerymen, along with Longstreet's Division, cooked rations and busily broke camp and loaded their wagons with knapsacks and equipage.

The Donaldsonville Artillery was attached to Longstreet's Division that moved out at six-thirty in the morning; Maurin's guns followed and moved out a half hour later. They traveled from the Nine Mile Road towards the Williamsburg Road on what Cire described as horrid roads deep with mud and water until the division halted two and one-half hours later. They stopped on the side of the Williamsburg Road opposite the point where the Charles City Road forked. Although the distance between the lateral running Nine Mile and Williamsburg Road in this area is no more than two and a quarter miles apart, delays occurred in the passage of Gillies Creek, which was raging from the previous night's rainfall. Longstreet's command waited for five or six hours under dull and cloudy skies in fields with water ankle deep, along the roadside where everything appeared unusually quiet.[23] Parked just one and a half miles from Richmond, Maurin with his battery awaited further orders in an open field. The Canonniers watched as large bodies of troops from Longstreet's Division started moving and went by "with bands in full blast, colors flying, and men hilarious with delight, supposing, as was the case, that the enemy were to retreat or surrender."[24]

Some time between one and two o'clock in the afternoon, the rattle of musketry and sounds of battle could be heard along the Williamsburg Road in the direction of Seven Pines. The Canonniers waited through the evening with the roar of artillery and musketry distinctly heard, while trains of ambulances and wounded on foot passed by them. At five o'clock in the evening Maurin received orders to move his guns up the Williamsburg Road to the battlefield of Seven Pines and report to Brigadier General D. H. Hill, the belief being that the fight would be renewed in the morning.[25]

Before starting out, Canonnier Corporal John O'Hara penciled in his notebook: "May the 31st, 1862 we are expecting to meet the Yankees, should I fall I'm requesting that my remains be buried in Donaldsonville. John O'Hara, Donaldsonville Artillery, tell all my friends good by."[26]

Maurin's Battery started forward. It rained again during the night, which made it almost impossible to move through the continuous mud-puddles. In going six or so miles towards the battlefield, the horses pulling the guns were "almost goaded to death."[27] The Canonniers travelled past stalled and wrecked wagons, caissons, and other vehicles. Not only was their progress slow and irksome, contending with the muddy road (it was impassable off the route with the forest and boggy conditions) there was the approaching darkness. They also had to contend with other troops going forward along with the returning wounded and squads of prisoners who "scowl upon their captors ominously, while others whistle and joke along the road as if infinitely gratified at being captured."[28]

When darkness arrived, the movement was slowed even more as the Canonniers, not being able to see the holes and ruts in the muddy road, stumbled and fell down. Finally they reached the battlefield, which was marked by blazing fires of pine-knots with men trying to dry out. Hill's command was on the battlefield located at the captured entrenchments of Federal Brigadier General Silas Casey where they crossed over the Williamsburg Road. Captain Robert M. Stribling's Fauquier Artillery and Captain David Watson's Second Company, Richmond Howitzers, were already on the field, having been earlier sent forward and engaged. Maurin's guns arrived to augment these two Virginia batteries some time around eleven o'clock that night. To Canonnier Private Eugene Levy it seemed like they had been "traveling all the night."[29]

Maurin's six guns went into battery and occupied a plateau in the swamp where the headquarters of General Casey had been the day before.[30] The Canonniers and other artillery batteries readied their guns while the drivers unhitched their teams of horses so they could have some breathing time. The Yankee entrenchments around Casey's headquarters were described by a member of Watson's Battery: "One solid mass almost of dead horses and men . . . there were some places pools of blood and the horses were actually piled up on each other."[31] A Donaldsonville combatant noted, "The fields and woods through which we passed were strewed with stiffened carcasses, broken wagons, dead and dying horses and dead and wounded Yankees."[32] Cire too wrote in his memorandum the terrible battlefield was covered with the dead and stores strewn about in profusion.[33]

During the night the artillerymen left their guns and, according to two Louisianians, "Got plenty . . . provisions"[34] and "supped on Their rations, drank Their fine brandy, [and] dressed our ragged bodies in Their fine clothes."[35] Baggage, blankets, guns, and army rations were scattered far and near with the artillerymen picking up "splendid India rubber clothes [rain ponchos] and knapsacks and overcoats and blankets . . . barrels of Sugar and Coffee and . . . filled their knapsacks with nice clean Yankee clothes."[36] One soldier gleefully noted they "got canteens & many other little tricks from the Yankees."[37] Even General D. H. Hill at the captured works reported, "We all fared well that night."[38]

It wasn't easy to plunder the camps with the wounded and dying who, wrote the artillerist from Watson's Battery, "Were all around us, uttering the most hideous and painful groans all night."[39] On seeing this ghastly reality a southern correspondent reported, "Friend and foe [were] scattered far and wide, in death, or in last agonies . . . All crave water, and crawling through mud, lap the blood-stained and slimy flood. Some curse, some moan and turn their eyes toward heaven sadly. Rebels hand around water to their late foes, and eyes glisten in thankfulness."[40] Some of the Southerners got their first Yankee canteen and filled it with whiskey from a captured barrel and gave it to the wounded Yankees. A Confederate soldier noted, "Some drank it like water." This Confederate Samaritan returned to his command after "refilling" his own canteen.[41]

At daylight on June 1 the enemy made a bold endeavor to retake the lost ground and made a furious attack on five Confederate brigades in front of the captured earthworks. These assaults were repulsed after which the Confederate brigades were withdrawn. Hill concentrated his own and the remaining brigades of Longstreet and Huger's divisions, plus the guns of Maurin, Stribling, and Watson, along the entrenchments.[42]

Watson's artillerist wrote, "We remained there all day and were . . . subjected to a hot fire from the enemy's artillery, but hadn't an opportunity of returning it."[43] Cire recorded that the Canonniers, "At 9:00 a.m . . . are in a hot place."[44] Another of the Donaldsonville men noted that about a quarter of a mile away, "The volleys of musketry were almost deafening and we c[oul]d see the boys loading and firing at the enemy."[45] Cire added, "The Yankees again attacked us and they were repulsed at 11:00 a.m. the 4th & 5th [detachments of Blakely] guns were sent off and opened on the enemy."[46] O'Hara recorded in his diary that the Donaldsonville "4th and 5th pieces checked the enemy in the center, 5th piece fired 37 rounds."[47] Maurin personally commanded and led these two guns during the fight. Hill for the balance of the day reported there was "a desultory fire of artillery."[48]

The remaining four Canonnier guns stayed put in position to defend the entrenchments under the command of Lieutenant William "Billy" Lawes. During the evening Captain Lawrence "Larry" Nicholls, the antebellum Canonnier and former mayor of Donaldsonville, came across Lawes and the four Donaldsonville guns whose members were "delighted to meet with an old acquaintance."[49] The next day Nicholls wrote his wife, Maurin's sister, "I saw Lawes who was well and was told that Victor was also well. They had fired their guns three times [in battle] but had lost no men."[50]

Of the battery's actions Maurin reported, "On the 1st of June at Seven Pines one section took part in the engagement. Nothing of importance to mention on this occasion."[51] After the morning's action Hill reported, "The day was spent in removing . . . muskets and rifles . . . ordnance, commissary, and medical stores," adding that the fire of the enemy's artillery had "the gratifying result of stampeding the amateur fighters and the camp plunderers from Richmond."[52] The day was also spent burying the Confederate dead. The artillerist from Watson's Battery wrote, "The sun was shining very hot and it certainly was the most sickening offensive place I ever saw."[53]

In the twilight of the battle on May 31 General Joseph E. Johnston, the Confederate commander, was severely wounded near Fair Oaks Station. Confederate President Jefferson Davis informed General Robert E. Lee that he would command the Army of Northern Virginia. Upon taking command Lee, in the evening of June 1, 1862, ordered the whole army back to the lines it had occupied before the disjointed affair of the previous day.[54]

Major General James Longstreet received the orders and passed them on to Hill who reported, "The thirteen brigades [of Hill, Longstreet, and Huger] were not got together until near midnight, and the delicate operation of withdrawing 30,000 men in the presence of a superior force of the enemy had to be performed before daylight. The artillery and wagons had to pass through the slushes and mud-holes over their axles, and the whole road was almost impassable for infantry. Nevertheless, we regained our own entrenchments by sunrise without leaving behind a gun, caisson, wagon, or even a straggling soldier."[55]

"At night our battery," briefly noted Cire, "retreated and came nearer to Richmond."[56] Upon reaching the Confederate defensive line, the Donaldsonville guns were again placed in the entrenchments. "We expected an attack today but were not, remained on picket on the line," wrote Cire.[57]

During the next several days: "There was rain on June 3, a heavy storm during the night of June 3-4, a downfall on the 4th, no sunshine on the 5th, showers during the night of the 5th-6th, and a near-deluge on the morning of the 6th."[58] O'Hara noted that the Canonniers were still on duty at this time, while another Louisiana artillerist bemoaned, "Just drenched to the skin and no opportunity for drying as the rain is incessant."[59] It was noted too that the nights were terrible from being under wet blankets, but genuine coffee was had twice a day. Throughout a cloudy June 6, Maurin's guns remained on picket duty until, an assuaged Cire jotted down, "At 5 p.m. the battery was relieved and came and camped near Richmond."[60]

In bivouac on Harrison's farm[61] the Donaldsonville Artillery had 112 horses. The drivers devoted their time "to the refreshment of our jaded battery horses," remembered Levy.[62] Not pulling guns or caissons during this interval helped their recuperation, but each of the animals was receiving just five pounds of hay and twelve pounds of corn from the quartermaster (seven pounds short of their daily hay average) though grazing made up some of the deficiency. Having a "reputation"[63] and "famous for their 'classy horses,'"[64] the Donaldsonville men under Maurin's charge kept the battery in as efficient condition as possible, but the difficulty of maintaining artillery horses was for an artillery commander a cause of "much anxiety & trouble."[65]

The Canonniers themselves were able to make frequent trips into Richmond and along the way visited comrades confined in Louisiana Hospital. They also visited a quite popular German beer garden next door to the hospital called the Belleville Garden, "where the shooting at target and bowling alley was indulged in."[66] The Louisianians enjoyed "very bad" beer and "bad whiskey"[67] there. Back in the hospital a sick Larry Nicholls wrote his wife, "I have met here quite a number of friends from La. troops . . . the Donaldsonville Artillery is encamped near here and almost everyday I meet some members of the company. They report Victor & Lawes both well. A member of the company [Kellet] died here a day or so ago."[68]

Donaldsonville Canonnier Corporal James Kellet, a native of Ireland, was sick at the

Louisiana Hospital with erysipelas, and on June 4, 1862, became the first member of *Le Compagnie d'Artillerie de Donaldsonville* to die during the war. It could be imagined that the Gunners of Donaldson had a Louisiana Irish wake for Kellet with "plenty of drinking and smoking out of those . . . clay pipes with shag tobacco"[69] before and after his comrades buried him in the Masonic Burying Grounds of Hollywood Cemetery in Richmond.[70]

Since the fall of New Orleans in late April 1862, those from Donaldsonville heard news of home only by "some casual chance."[71] The word from there was usually disheartening as "everything is unsettled."[72] Other Louisiana troops in Richmond noted "The difficulty if not the impossibility of getting a letter to Louisiana by the usual course."[73] Consequently many Louisianians visited Richmond's Columbian Hotel or the Spotswood Hotel[74] for intelligence, and to send by private hands letters home.

Not receiving mail from home was a problem. "In fact," noted a Louisianian in camp near Richmond, "I have long since given up all hope of hearing again by letter from my beloved family."[75] Nicholls wrote to his wife on June 9: "My patience is surely tested at not hearing from you."[76] From Donaldsonville to Virginia the word was eventually conveyed to, "Please when you write . . . or when anyone does, mention as many names of different acquaintances as you can, for we will depend upon hearing through each other."[77] Passed back to the families in Ascension Parish from Virginia was the suggestion: "Do not be alarmed sh[ould you] not hear from anybody at long intervals."[78]

The Canonniers, through Nicholls, learned the disturbing news conveyed in a letter from Maurin's sister at Donaldsonville that in part read,

> Yesterday three gun boats & a ship passed up the river—the levee & wharf were lined with people . . . & see them pass so securely by—we could see the soldiers . . . they had two flags displayed-the stars & stripes & a blue flag with stars in front. They got out a spy-glass & gazed at the crowd. I do hope they read on the countenances of those they saw—defiance & hatred—they made no stop here.[79]

The tracks of the Richmond & York River Railroad ran from the peninsula into Richmond parallel with and in between the Williamsburg and Nine Mile Road. On June 11, Cire recorded that the Canonniers "changed camp to [the] York River Rail Road,"[80] adding, "nothing could exceed the desolation of the countryside, with its depressing ensemble of fences torn down, wheat fields trodden underfoot, and abandoned farm houses."[81] Cire made no other entries in his memorandum book for the next couple of days, as duty was comparatively light while in camp. Another Louisianian described the beginning of a typical day in a June 14 letter: "Some of the mess are stretching blankets in a cool place preparatory to another little nap before breakfast while others are helping or rather imagining they are helping in the culinary department. This would be a perfectly fair picture of our appearance at this time almost every morning."[82]

There was little protection during the day from the very warm weather, and the men sheltered themselves from exposure with their blankets or other contrivance. Here their rations were good and the troops nearly well fed with fresh beef or bacon and flour. They even got a whiskey ration when it was deemed essential to their health because of the inclemency of the weather or exposure. There were rumors and hints of an assault by the Yankees, and the atmosphere in camp was one of expectancy.[83] The thoughts expressed by one Louisianan was, "There is perfect stagnation here along the lines—apparently a fight being imminent every day and yet day after day passes and nothing is done."[84]

In the middle of June 1862 Cire recorded the proceedings of the Donaldsonville Artillery: "14th Orders to keep ready and have the horses harnessed. 15th In the morning left for an expedition on the lines, at 3 p.m. ordered to return to camp, rain. 16th Ordered to march, hitched up but received counter orders—P.M. drill. 17th 18th Horses harnessed—drill & drill. 19th drill—after drill ordered to prepare to march received counter orders. 20th Orders to be ready to move at a moment's notice—21st drill."[85]

On June 22, the Donaldsonville guns went back to the entrenchments on picket duty, immediately to the right of the Williamsburg Road. The following day there was infantry skirmishing and rain during the night. The twenty-fourth was quiet with Cire recording the rain falling in the evening. On the morning of the twenty-fifth a section of Captain Frank Huger's Norfolk (Virginia) Battery arrived and relieved a portion of the Donaldsonville guns from the front line. While placing two guns into position, heavy musket firing started in the woods in front that killed one of Huger's horses. Maurin's gunners pulled back along the Williamsburg Road and returned to camp without any casualties. The other Donaldsonville guns stayed in the entrenchments with the infantry who skirmished in front for the remainder of the day.[86]

Brigadier General Roger Atkinson Pryor.
From Mrs. Roger A. Pryor, *Reminiscences of Peace and War.*

On June 26, Cire recorded that "The other part of the battery was relieved and left for camp but before arriving received orders . . . both parts of the battery joined on the road."[87] After leaving the entrenchments and reuniting, Maurin's Battery moved nearer Richmond along the Williamsburg Road, where Pryor's Fifth Brigade of Longstreet's division camped. General Order No. 71 had been recently implemented; it stated: "A battery duly assigned to a brigade will . . . report to and be controlled by the brigade commander."[88] The Donaldsonville Artillery having been thus assigned to this brigade reported to Brigadier General Roger A. Pryor, a thirty-three-year-old "politician-general"[89] from Petersburg, Virginia. He was described as "tall and straight, with the elastic step of an Indian"[90] and "graceful, of a fascinating manner and irresistibly charming in speech . . . and in his well-tuned voice."[91] A lawyer, newspaper editor, and Congressman at the outbreak of the war, Pryor was elected to the Provisional Confederate Congress but resigned to enter the army as colonel of the Third Virginia Infantry. Pryor was promoted to brigadier general on April 16, 1862.[92]

On the morning of June 26, Longstreet's Division, including Pryor's Brigade and Maurin's Battery, received orders to move to the Mechanicsville Turnpike. Pryor was sick and listless upon his bed at the Spotswood Hotel in Richmond when he received the following note: "Dear General, put yourself *at once* at the head of your brigade. In thirty-six hours it will all be over. LONGSTREET."[93] After reading the note Pryor got out of bed and rejoined his command.

Donaldsonville Canonnier Lieutenant Prosper Landry had been out on sick furlough for the preceeding month. He was at Amelia Court House, about forty miles southwest of Richmond, when word came. He later wrote his wife, "I left Amelia Springs, before the expiration of my leave and when I was still very weak, but it was to participate in the battle of Richmond. But to be truthful, I was afraid that the war would end before I had the chance to participate in a battle. How naive! How vain! It is true that I had already smelled the gunpowder of Yorktown and at Williamsburg, but Yorktown seemed too much like a siege and at Williamsburg we arrived practically at the end." Landry arrived in time to command his Gunners of Donaldson section.[94]

At Pryor's camp in the early morning hours "all was hurry and confusion." A witness wrote, "Ambulances were hitching up, troops forming in line, servants running hither and thither, horses standing to be saddled, light army wagons loading."[95] Maurin's guns and caissons were made ready along with two wagons that were allowed to go with the battery, one to haul the battery ammunition and the other two days' forage for the horses. The Canonniers and soldiers were instructed to be ready in light marching order, taking only one blanket and leaving behind their knapsacks with the sick men in camp. Several days' rations of hard bread were issued, ordered cooked, and placed in haversacks.[96]

The stern command, "Fall in! Fall in!" passed from company to company, and when it reached the Donaldsonville Artillery, "*Former les rangs! Former les rangs!*" could be heard along with the bugle call "Boots and Saddles." When the brigade was formed Pryor exited his tent, mounted his horse and drawing his sword, gave the order to advance, "Head of column to the right!"[97] and with a steady tramp company after company, stretching far down the road, began to march. When the bilingual Captain Maurin gave the order to his battery it was repeated and cried out through the detachments: "*'tention!*" ("attention!") "*Rouliers, prets à monter. Montez!*" ("Drivers, prepare to mount. Mount!") "*Canonniers, montez!*" ("Cannoneers, mount!") "*Colonne*" ("Column"), and then the command every Donaldsonville Canonnier knew—the one that sent the blood of the Creole artillerymen coursing more rapidly through the veins, "*En Avan-n-n-ce!*" ("Forward!").[98]

Elated to be moving, for the flies were thick and tormented the nervous horses, the Gunners of Donaldson, with six guns, caissons, and two wagons, moved out. When they reached Pryor's tent, the general's wife and another woman cheered and blessed the Canonniers as they filed past. The column marched down the muddy Williamsburg Road through Richmond and took the Mechanicsville Turnpike. By eight o'clock in the morning Longstreet's Division was halted and stretched along the road leading up to the Mechanicsville Bridge, masked behind the crest of hills overlooking the Chickahominey River.[99]

It was a cloudless day, and as the sun got higher in the sky it grew warmer. To escape the heat the soldiers and artillerists ranged along the woods in the shade parallel to the turnpike. At first all the artillerymen could do was fuss around their pieces, adjust the horses' harnesses, and inspect the ammunition boxes on the caissons as the hours dragged by. "We," wrote one, "lounged on the side of the road with perfect indifference. The sun reached its zenith, and yet we knew nothing, but as the shadows grew long a distant, but distinct, musketry was heard."[100]

At three o'clock in the afternoon there was a great stir as staff officers dashed along the lines of divisions, up and down the roads, carrying orders to brigade commanders. The loud voices of the officers could be heard calling, "'tention! 'tention! Fall in, men, fall in!" The lounging soldiers sprang up, and the gunners stood to their pieces, anxiously awaiting the word of command. "The columns," remembered a Louisiana artillerist, "were quickly formed and moved forward, the canteens rattling and the company officers crying, 'Close up! Close up!'"[101]

After moving closer to the many channels of the Chickahominey River, the long column halted. The sound of musketry and artillery was distinctly heard across the water that meandered through a low swamp covered by impenetrable undergrowth. The firing continued as Longstreet's Division gradually moved forward following Hill's Division along

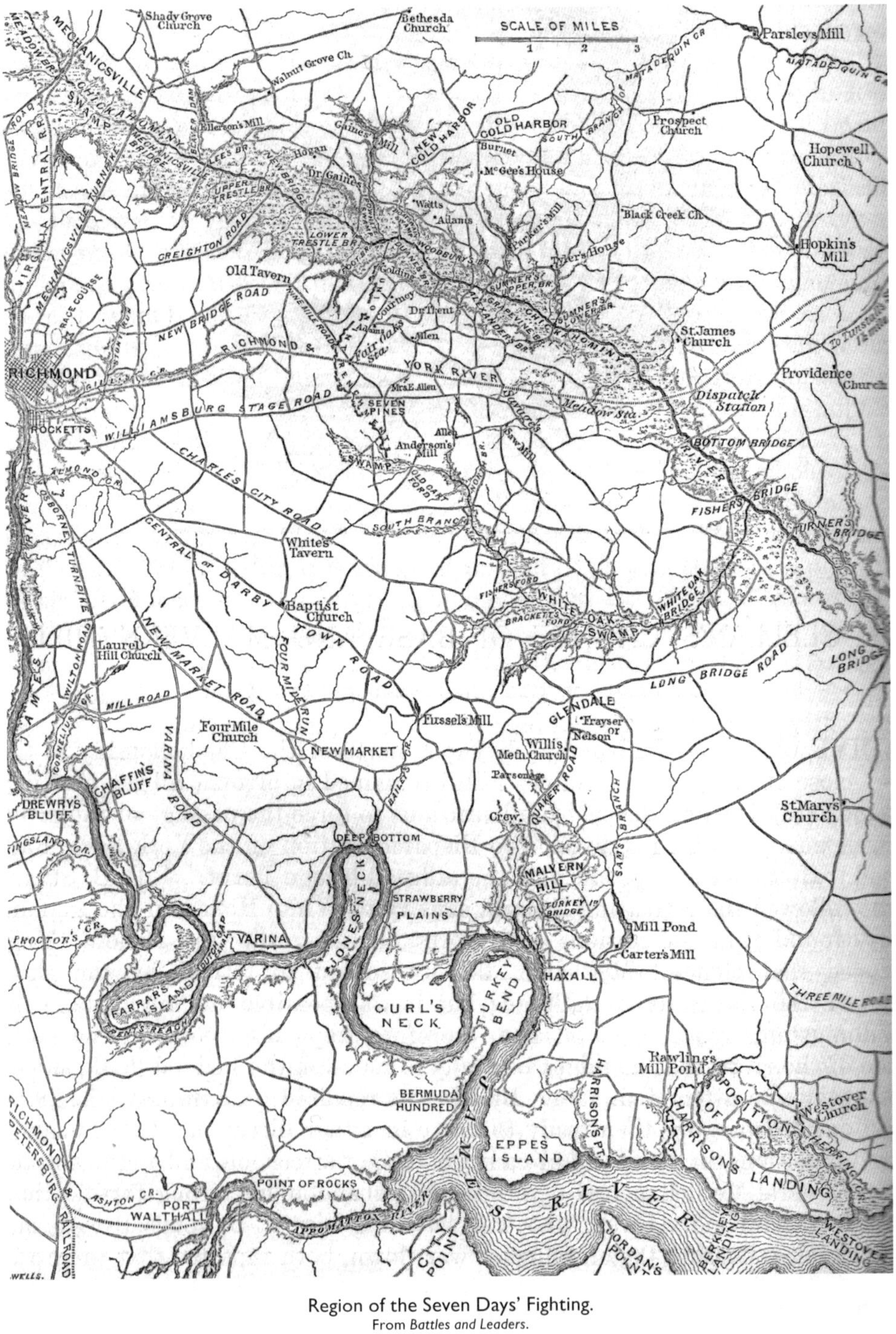

Region of the Seven Days' Fighting.
From *Battles and Leaders*.

the turnpike. They moved across the nasty, muddy river over one bridge, then another, both having been repaired by planks. It was sometime after dark before Longstreet's Division completed the crossing, and after a half mile march, stopped on a hill at the little village of Mechanicsville.

From the bridge it was slow going for Maurin's guns and caissons that moved over a slightly rolling plain on a road deep in sand. Burning houses, barns, and stacks of hay and straw lit up the countryside. The night was hot and stifling, with a full moon rising.[102] "As the night closed," remembered Major David Zable of the Fourteenth Louisiana in Pryor's Brigade, "the situation had assumed a serious aspect, we felt that a great struggle was impending on the morning, our men were eager . . . they felt sanguine of their ability to overpower, and dislodge [the enemy] from in front of our capitol."[103]

The Donaldsonville Artillery had not stopped for long near the village when at about eleven o'clock that night Longstreet directed Pryor's Brigade to relieve a brigade of Colonel Alfred H. Colquitt in its advanced position on the field of that day's fight. Longstreet also sent Brigadier General Winfield S. Featherston's Brigade of Mississippians in relief of Brigadier General Roswell S. Ripley's Brigade near Colquitt's. The Donaldsonville guns followed Pryor's Brigade for one half to three quarters of a mile, the way lighted by a solemn moon. Shortly after three o'clock in the morning, Pryor's infantry took position in a field not far in the rear of Featherston's Brigade, which was located on an edge of woodland fronting Beaver Dam Creek. Pryor posted Maurin's guns on an elevation in the rear of his brigade and later reported that he positioned the battery "Whence it might fire without affecting our men and yet attain the enemy, who occupied another eminence across Beaver Dam Creek."[104]

Immediately after Pryor finished his arrangements and by the light of the earliest dawn on the morning of June 27, 1862, the enemy opened a very brisk fire. Featherston's Brigade receiving the first shock. With daylight, Maurin gave the order to fire—and all six of his guns became engaged. Shortly thereafter Pryor sent a note to Longstreet for reinforcements and rapidly hurried his troops forward to assist Featherston. A heavy fog lay over the twelve foot wide and waist deep Beaver Dam Creek, and as the firing intensified, the smoke from the muskets made the fog heavier.

The Donaldsonville guns continued firing from their position on the hill, behind the 14th Louisiana Regiment, which was enveloped in the fog and smoke. The regiment had a number of men wounded by fragments of shells falling in their ranks. From the way the men had been struck and knowing that Confederate smoothbore shells very frequently exploded prematurely, it was

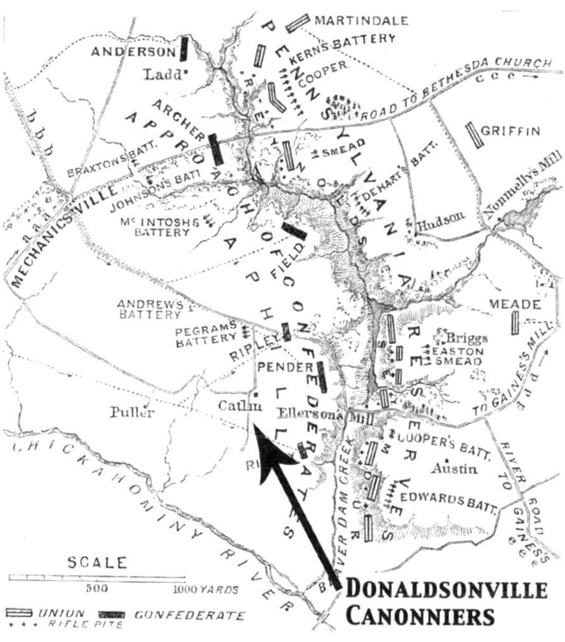

Beaver Dam Creek
From *Battles and Leaders*.

realized that the fire came from the battery on the hill to their rear.[105]

Major Zable wrote:

> A courier was sent to the battery to inform the officer in command of the fact, but as the shells were still being exploded over our heads, I determined to go and see why the firing did not cease. I found that the courier had been wounded before carrying out his orders, also learned that our command was in a ravine, that we were, and had been firing into the side of a hill; from the position of the battery could be seen above the fog and smoke that hung over our troops in the ravine the position of the enemy on the hill opposite to us. I asked the officer [Maurin] commanding the battery to open fire on a house on the hill in our front as the enemy's sharp shooters might be firing from it, just as the command was to be given to fire, I said to the officer don't fire, may be woman and children are taking refuge there; we learned afterwards it was so.[106]

Major David Zable, Fourteenth Louisiana Infantry Regiment. Courtesy of the Confederate Memorial Hall Museum, New Orleans, La..

For the time being, the Donaldsonville guns ceased firing.

At sunrise Featherston ordered his brigade artillery, Captain Benjamin Smith's Third Company, Richmond Howitzers, in position two hundred yards from the left wing of the brigades. Two guns were placed in the front yard and two in the rear of the William Catlin House[107] with orders to return the fire of the enemy's artillery, which was then playing sharply on the troops. The "long-bodied, eagle-faced"[108] and carelessly dressed Featherston ordered Maurin's guns moved too, along with a section of Captain R. Snowden Andrews's First Maryland Flying Artillery.[109] They were placed near Smith's in the Catlin yard, where they could shell the enemy near Ellison's Mill on the creek.

As the sun rose brilliantly over the treetops, Featherston anxiously watched the artillery as they covered the infantry with accurate and deliberate fire, the shots and shells chipping the embrasures and slicing off chunks of the enemy's parapets. The Donaldsonville guns and the others sent in such a hot fire that the Union gunners found it impossible to stand up to load their pieces.[110] A Richmond newspaper correspondent, evidently with Featherston's staff, reported they "played upon the enemy's position magnificently."[111] The very blunt Featherston exultantly exclaimed: "By Jupiter, that beats all! Just look at our boys tumbling the breastworks about! Who would of ever believed it of raw volunteers? Why, sir, the 'regulars' could not beat them! Gentlemen, I must confess, I entertained poor opinions of our artillery till now, and looked upon them as fit for little else but to waste ammunition, but the manner in which they fought . . . convinces me that we are a superior stock altogether."[112]

Featherston later wrote in his operations report: "Both companies [six guns of the Donaldsonville Artillery and four guns of the Third Company Richmond Howitzers, plus the two guns from Andrews's Maryland section] behaved with great gallantry and coolness, and displayed a skill in the use of their guns highly creditable to that arm of the service. The two [batteries and section] played very handsomely on the enemy's lines, keeping up a constant and well directed fire."[113]

"This view is taken from the left of the Union position on the east slope, looking up-stream, the ruins of Ellerson's Mill being shown in the middle ground. The house at left is Dr. Catlin's. . . . The Union position at this point was held . . . with artillery entrenchments, rifle-pits, and abatis. The Confederates came across the open hills and down the slope and along the road. . . . Their loss . . . frightful. Dr. Catlin's son says that the slope of the hill was fairly covered with dead and wounded." The second position where the Donaldsonville Artillery guns fired was from the yard of the Catlin house. From *Battles and Leaders*. No. 12, p. 356.

The Richmond correspondent recorded, "The Generals speak in high terms of the execution of our field pieces in this attack, the Third Richmond Howitzers, some of the [First Maryland Flying Artillery], Donaldsonville, and Thomas artillery, having caused great destruction among the enemy, and with slight loss to themselves. The rapidity of their fire quite astonished the Yankees."[114] An artillery staff officer observing the battle wrote, "The boys deserved such praise, for the constancy with which they served their pieces."[115]

The Canonniers, Howitzers, and Maryland section worked their guns with coolness, precision, and determination, and the enemy's artillery soon ceased firing. It was evident the Federals were drawing in their lines. "We," wrote a member of the Howitzers, "were now fighting only a heavy rear guard. Nevertheless their sharp-shooters were swarming like bees on the opposite hills, across the Beaver Dam, and they made it uncomfortably warm where we were."[116]

Brigadier General William D. Pender, in bringing his brigade to the creek in front of Ellison's Mill, on the left of Featherston and Pryor's brigades, observed Maurin's Donaldsonville Artillery and reported that they "shelled [the enemy] with spirit and effect, his men being exposed to a galling fire from the enemy's sharpshooters, not 200 yards off in the rifle pits."[117] Many of the Yankee sharpshooters were stationed up tall pine trees and, according to the Howitzer gunner, "Had many advantages over our men, we fighting in an open field all the time."[118]

Longstreet ordered Brigadier General Cadmus M. Wilcox's Alabama Brigade forward from Mechanicsville at sunrise to assist Featherston and Pryor, and upon arriving Wilcox placed his battery, the Thomas Artillery, with Maurin's guns and the others. Wilcox reported they "fired a few well directed shots at the retreating foe."[119]

Lieutenant Edwin J. Anderson commanded the Thomas Battery from Virginia and arrived near the end of the engagement. Although only firing 150 rounds, the battery had a man killed by the enemy's sharpshooters. A member of the Richmond Howitzers wrote, "Strange to say none of my company were hurt."[120] The section of Andrews's Maryland Battery also reported no casualties, but in the infantry Featherston advised that his brigade-losses in killed and wounded was "comparatively heavy."[121] Pryor reported his regiments "sustained a considerable loss."[122] Here at Beaver Dam Creek the Donaldsonville Artillery sustained its first combat casualty when Canonnier Artificer Joseph S. Stanley, a native of Ohio but longtime resident of Ascension Parish, was "instantly killed."[123]

With the enemy abandoning their entrenchments and retiring, the batteries were ordered to cease firing between seven and eight o'clock that morning. The guns had been at it for three hours. Longstreet sent orders to Wilcox, Featherston, and Pryor to advance eastward along the Chickahominey River. Wilcox, being the senior brigadier general, sent one of his regiments along Beaver Dam Creek to the right of the brigades to find a place to cross. Some distance down the creek, or deep ditch as some described it, the remnants of an old bridge destroyed by the enemy was found by the regiment. The Louisianians of the Fourteenth Regiment, rebuilt the bridge using axes, spades, and nails (likely supplied by Maurin's Battery), along with soldiers of the Nineteenth Mississippi Regiment and planks obtained from an abandoned enemy camp. The process took less than thirty minutes. Longstreet rode up while the rebuilding was in progress, gave directions on the coming movements, and ordered the advance in line of battle when the bridge was made passable.[124]

The scene around them was somber. A Confederate artillery officer at Beaver Dam Creek near Ellison's Mill recalled years later "the shocking impression made . . . by large numbers of our men who had fallen the evening before in assaulting the works. Most of them from their butternut suits I took to be North Carolinians, and they still lay just as they fell, some with their arms still in their hands, and in every variety of posture."[125]

Upon completion of the bridge, Wilcox's Brigade crossed the creek. The Canonniers and Pryor's Brigade followed with their guns, caissons, and wagons. Well under way by nine o'clock in the morning, the brigades passed Yankee bivouacs in flames, the enemy retreating and burning everything they could not carry away. This included a number of wagons.[126] "The road then," remembered an artilleryman, "was lined on either side with piles of knapsacks, and the fields were great deserted camps with abandoned stores and accoutrements of every sort, much of it burning."[127] Another veteran in the advance wrote, "We saw great piles of army stores of every description which had been fired, and great red flames, high as the trees, consumed everything in reach, and great volumes of smoke floated skyward."[128] Past the burning camps the brigades continued on with Wilcox's regiments deploying on the right, nearest the river, and Pryor's on the left. The rest of Longstreet's Division followed in support.

Maurin's Battery moved on farm roads, the horses pulling through deep and heavy sand while accompanying Pryor's regiments in the pursuit. The infantry in line of battle moved slowly over the hills and valleys of open farmland and through woods, the line intact and presenting, wrote a witness, "A beautiful appearance, as we advanced with banners rippling in the morning breeze."[129] Continuing on for a few miles before halting, unidentified troops were seen over on the left front and after a few minutes of resting, word was passed along the line that it was part of "Stonewall" Jackson's forces. Ordered forward again, the command inclined toward the river through woods and exited into an open field where the enemy's fieldworks in an orchard were abandoned. Here the advance stopped on the Hogan Farm, where the dusty men, their once gray uniforms now turned a sandy brown, rested a few minutes under the oppressively hot sun.[130]

During the movement and now while resting, many of the artillerists rummaged through the abandoned Yankee camps. One member of the Howitzers battery attached to Wilcox's Brigade related, "I was securing a very plump looking bag of oats, a body of our cavalry dashed in at the other end of the [deserted] camp, and . . . one of them was about to shoot me for a Yankee—remembering I had on a Yankee jacket, I cried out lustily, that I was a

Confederate soldier, whereupon they rode swiftly on, leaving me to carry off my booty."[131]

Lee made his temporary quarters at the shot and shattered two-story Hogan house called "Selwyn."[132] It was situated on a knoll in a grove of old oak and hickory trees. The whole yard and orchard became overrun with general officers, aids, couriers, and prisoners. An artillery staff officer related how Wilcox, Pryor, and Featherston were there for orders, "conversing freely and gaily, as if about to start upon some pleasant 'pic-nic.'"[133] After receiving orders they rode off at a gallop with "some prophesy that the advance will soon begin again."[134] Pryor was directed by Longstreet to lead his brigade as the advance guard, which now moved cautiously forward. Maurin's Donaldsonville guns went with them in support, followed by Wilcox and Featherston's Brigades close behind.

Continuing along a road through a heavy pine forest, the brigade cleared the woods where Pryor reported, "I had not proceeded more than a mile when the enemy were observed in the woods on Dr. Gaines' farm. I detached a few companies to drive in his nearest skirmishers and to dislodge his sharpshooters from their cover. This was effected without much difficulty.

Dr. Gaines' Powhite home.
From the author's collection.

A line of skirmishers extending along the entire front of the woods in rear of Dr. Gaines' house discovered to me the position in which the enemy had resolved to offer battle."[135]

Emerging from the woods the road led to the left and then to the right, round Gaines's house, where for some two miles the land was open tableland with an unbroken succession of undulating hills beyond. To the east the land sloped gradually for one mile before suddenly dipping to Boatswain's Creek. In front, to the left, were orchards and gullies running gradually to the wood-covered creek, and beyond stood a timbered-covered hill where one of Wilcox's Alabamians reported, "We could plainly see three lines of Federal infantry—one at the base, one about midway up, and one near the top of the opposite hillside from where we lay. Each one of their lines was protected by an abatis of heavy timber, which had been felled for their protection."[136]

After the enemy skirmishers withdrew, Pryor ordered Maurin's Battery forward to the knoll where Dr. Gaines's home Powhite was located. The front of the home faced north and was located amongst many fine old oaks with a beautiful terrace garden of "magnificent" flowers

Brigadier General Cadmus Marcellus Wilcox
Courtesy of the Library of Congress.

in the rear. Around the house were choice fruit and ornamental trees with storehouses. A barn stood nearby.[137] When the Canonniers approached, they passed along the roadside one or two dead Union soldiers and the guns of an abandoned Federal battery.[138] Upon reaching an orchard near the front of Gaines's house, Maurin halted and unlimbered the guns that started firing northeast across the wheat and open fields. The distance to where the enemy was seen in the woods was about a mile.[139]

The First Michigan Infantry and the Twenty-second Massachusetts Infantry (positioned behind the Michigan riflemen) received the fire from the Donaldsonville guns. At about twelve o'clock noon the commander of the First Michigan reported, "The enemy commenced firing shot and shell, which fell and burst among and near the men, costing us a few lives."[140] A captain of the Twenty-second Massachusetts reported, "The enemy opened a well-directed fire from a battery on this position . . . for they rained metal enough into this piece of woods . . . their effort was furious and full of determination."[141]

The Union infantry did not return the fire, but Federal batteries on an eminence across the Chickahominey River were soon brought into action and began to reply to the fire of Maurin's guns. A Donaldsonville Canonnier later wrote, "The federal batteries on the opposite side of the Chickahominey [gave] us a great deal of annoyance."[142]

Maurin's guns received a converging fire from across the river by three batteries of the First Battalion New York Light Artillery equipped with 20-pounder Parrott rifled-guns. Eight of the guns belonged to Captain John Knieriem and Captain Otto Diederich who fired from in front of a redoubt near Goldring's house. Captain Adolph Voegelee had four guns in position 2,000 yards away near Woodbury's Bridge. The Yankee artillery easily outranged the Donaldsonville guns.[143]

Brigadier General Cadmus Wilcox went forward to the high ground to have a look and dismounted before approaching an officer behind a large tree and asking, "Can I get a view of the enemy from your position?" The officer told him he could, and scarcely had Wilcox got in position when a shot from a Federal gun struck the tree. "General Wilcox," recounted the officer, "appeared to be suddenly satisfied as he tumbled from his position to a safer place below." The officer asked him if he got a good view to which Wilcox replied, "Too good for me."[144]

Wilcox reported the enemy's batteries beyond the river were "of heavy rifled guns, and beyond range of the pieces of [Maurin's] battery, which was now withdrawn."[145] The Canonnier gunners limbered up their guns and moved out of the orchard and back to the woods, the shot and shell falling and bursting nearby.

Longstreet's entire division was now stationed in the thick woods west of Gaines's house and awaiting orders. "The enemy soon found out our position in this wood and commenced

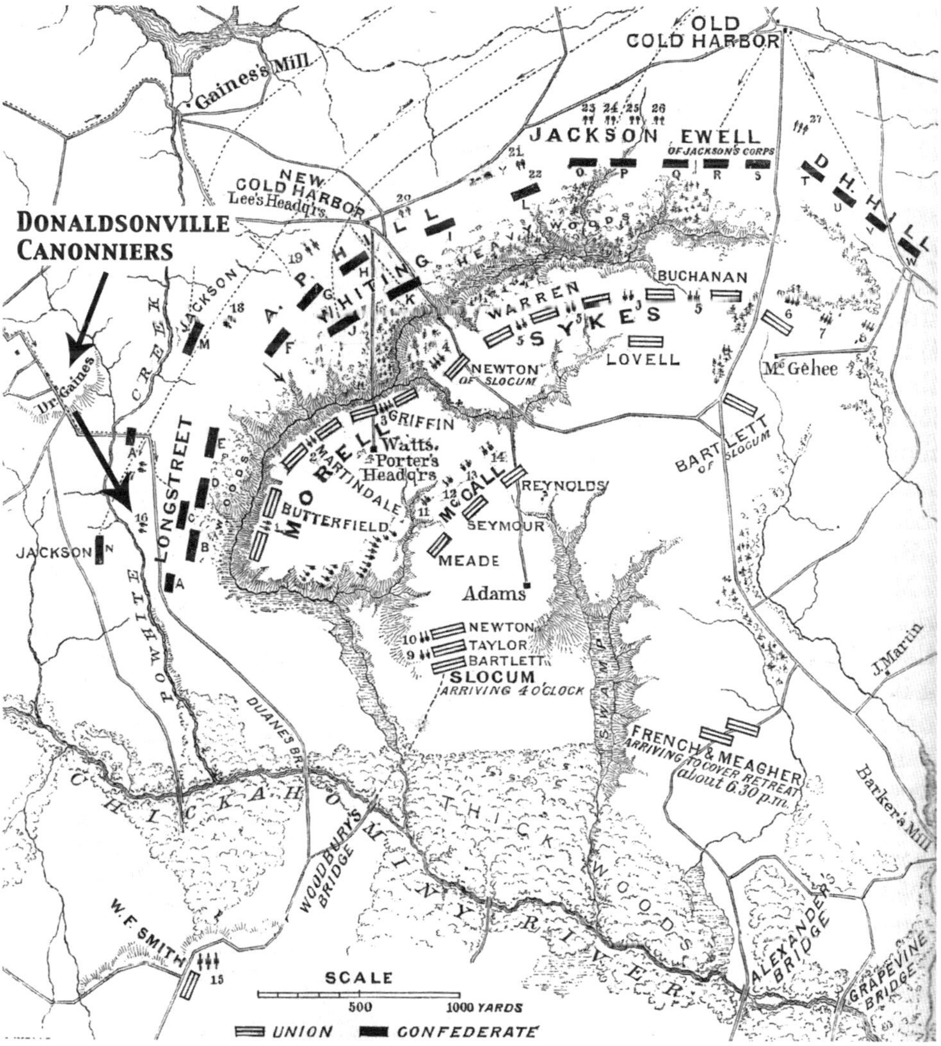

The Donaldsonville Artillery's first position at Gaines' Mill was near the front of Dr. Gaines' house; their second position was on the plateau below the house, in support of Longstreet's attack. From *Battles and Leaders*.

shelling us at a terrific rate," wrote one of the artillerymen, adding, "Their guns were well aimed for their shots skim'd above and around us in no very pleasant manner."[146] Here the Canonniers remained with the division, the men lying on the ground. It "seemed," according to one, "to be an age."[147] The only consolation was the trees protecting them from the glaring sun, but "none who were there," wrote an artillerist, "will ever forget the meridian sun nor the agonizing thirst of that day."[148]

Shortly after three o'clock in the afternoon the sound of musketry was heard on the left. Receiving orders to make a demonstration on the right of the fight, Longstreet wrote, "I threw my three brigades opposite the Federal left and engaged them in a severe skirmish with infantry and artillery. The battle then raged with great fierceness."[149] Wilcox, Pryor, and Featherston's Brigades led the demonstration in support of an attack by Major General A. P. Hill's Division and "Stonewall" Jackson's troops on Hill's left. Longstreet then put in the brigades of Brigadier General Richard H. Anderson and Brigadier General George E. Pickett, along with Brigadier General John B. Hood's and Colonel Evander M. Law's of Brigadier General William H. C. Whiting's Division, making this the heaviest of the attacks.

"Our entire line advances in splendid style," remembered a Richmond Howitzer, "our infantry moving across an open field, subjected to a terrific fire poured into them by the enemy, who were strongly entrenched."[150] Pryor reported his brigade, on "ascending the hill in front of his position . . . were staggered by a terrific volley at the same time that they suffered from the battery across the Chickahominy. . . . In these assaults I sustained a very great loss—as much almost from the enemy's artillery as from his infantry fire. A single shell killed and disabled 11 of my men."[151] Levy, with Maurin's guns, later recalled, "The charge of our division on this occasion . . . was the most superb fighting which fell under my observation during the entire war."[152]

Maurin's Gunners of Donaldson likewise advanced with orders to open fire on the enemy while the division charged the enemy works. After moving within range on a naked plateau on Gaines's Farm, the six Donaldsonville guns were soon again at work firing at the Federal infantry around the ravine as the shot and shell of the Yankee cannons were striking and ricocheting in and around their pieces. It was reported, "The noise of the musketry was not rattling, as ordinarily, but one intense metallic din. The sound of the artillery was sublime."[153] An artilleryman added that there were "clouds of dust, woods smoking on every hand, long lines of musketry fire, the deafening roar of artillery, and piercing yells" along with "the bursting of caissons, and the explosion of ammunition wagons."[154] Another soldier-diarist recorded, "The cannonading was heavy and the musketry was a complete thunder."[155] A Donaldsonville Canonnier uttered, "Our work was very heavy."[156]

The Third Company Richmond Howitzers took position near Maurin's guns close to the barn on the brow of the knoll and opened fire. The enemy diverted some of its heavy artillery fire from the infantry to the Confederate guns. A Howitzer wrote, "We were also under a galling fire from their infantry directly in our front."[157] The Donaldsonville guns were a target for the Federal sharpshooters too, but the Canonniers continued to work their field pieces as the conflict was raging and shot and shells "with that peculiar 'Whar is you?' sound . . . falling thick and fast and shrieking through the air."[158]

Within a few minutes of being exposed on the knoll, Canonnier Privates John Hernandez and William Taylor, along with Bugler Louis Meminger and three of the Donaldsonville horses, went down with wounds. Pierre "Turiaffe" Babin, the violin playing private, reported receiving "but a slight flesh wound"[159] in the calf of his leg while the action continued.

The smoke of battle became so thick it became impossible to distinguish anything in front except the dim outline of the wooded ravine from which the volleys of musketry continued until "the sun had set looking through dust and smoke and fire of the battlefield, of a blood red color."[160] The Donaldsonville Artillery finally ceased firing with night coming on. A Richmond Howitzer nearby wrote, "Our field of observation is so extremely limited, we can learn little . . . of the battle or of the specific results. The wounded stragglers all pass through our battery and tell the same old tale of being *'cut up,' 'badly whipped,'* etc., so that for a long time we were really in doubt whether we or the Yankees had been successful."[161]

Finally, a Louisianian in Pryor's Brigade reported, "We soon learned that our Army have won the day."[162] After hearing the news a jubilant artilleryman recorded, "Thus at eight p.m., Friday, June twenty-seventh, the Battle of Gaines' Mill was over, and the victory was ours!" adding, "in a few hours . . . most of the troops lay fast asleep where they had halted."[163] For the Donaldsonville Canonniers, Levy noted, "Night put a stop to the engagement, and allowed us a term of much-needed repose."[164]

The next morning, June 28, the Donaldsonville Artillery moved to the position occupied by the Yankees the day before. An Ascension Parish soldier observed, "All around this knoll of battle were the debris of the struggle, dead men, gray and blue intermingled, broken and uninjured guns, thousands of muskets, heaps of horses, showed the bloody eddies and tide lines of the combat."[165] Except for working parties burying the dead and caring for the wounded, and gathering up arms and sutler's stores left on the field, the Canonniers remained idle throughout the day. The victorious soldiers ate a hearty breakfast with "beneficial" tin cups of whiskey being passed around.[166] "Nearly all the canteens of the slain and captured Yankees," noted a Southerner, "contained *whiskey*."[167]

The removal of the wounded began during the darkness after the battle and continued into the next evening. One soldier remarked, "I presume that every ambulance in the army is flying to and fro carrying the wounded to Richmond. . . . The gaping, bleeding wounds of the wounded and dying are pitiful, but not more heartrending than will be the agony of breaking hearts at home."[168]

After daylight, troops in large numbers were detailed in burying the dead. "The smell," wrote a soldier, "was very disagreeable."[169] Another veteran wrote, "The dead and wounded horses presented a horrible spectacle and one never to be forgotten . . . some with a leg shot entirely away and others with a great gap ripped in their sides, with their entrails dragging on the ground, were peacefully grazing on the young, tender clover as if there was nothing the matter with them. Poor creatures! They all had to be shot to put an end to their misery. How cruel is war?"[170]

The Federal units in the area where Maurin's Battery rested and where Pryor's Brigade fought reported losing "Knapsacks, blankets, and shelter-tents, &c.,"[171] "all the effects available to a soldier,"[172] and "haversacks . . . even tin cups, plates, knives and forks, and spoons."[173] Donaldsonville Canonnier Cire remembered the field was covered with "everything."[174] Another Louisiana artillery diarist noted, "We found plenty of provisions and every convenience a soldier requires."[175] A different soldier wrote, "The spoils of the field were a source of joy to many a poor fellow, who . . . enjoyed a feast of genuine coffee, sugar, pickles, canned fruit, oranges, etc., etc."[176] A Confederate correspondent reported, "We have captured large quantities of army wagons, tents, equipments, shoes. Clothing in abundance was scattered about, and immense piles of new uniforms were found untouched. Every conceivable article of clothing was found . . . and came quite apropos to our needy soldiery, scores of whom took a cool bath, and changed old for new under-clothing."[177]

Depending upon their needs, some members of the Donaldsonville Artillery would wear blue Yankee uniforms to the end of the war. So many of the Confederate soldiers wore Federal uniforms that three days later an officer of the Nineteenth Massachusetts Regiment recorded, "We met a line clothed in Union blue, and thinking it was . . . of our brigade . . . we were mistaken, and that the line was composed of rebels in our uniforms."[178]

During the long hot day clouds of smoke from the burning plunder in the Federal camps and the frequent explosions of magazines could be seen and heard south of the Chickahominy River. In the afternoon clouds of dust showed that the Federal Army was in motion.

Bright and early the next morning, June 29, Longstreet and A. P. Hill's men made preparations for an immediate movement. Longstreet commanded his own and Hill's division by order of Lee as the Army of Northern Virginia would attempt to intercept the Federal army as it retreated to the James River. After orders were received the sound of "Boots and Saddles" sent the Canonniers in motion and the Donaldsonville Battery on the march.

Under cloudy skies, though it was still an awfully hot day, Maurin's six guns and two wagons rolled along with Pryor's Brigade and Longstreet's Division from Dr. Gaines's farm.

They again traversed the Chickahominey River over the new bridge and moved down the dust-covered Nine Mile Road across the Richmond & York River Railroad. Here the air was redolent with the smell of burnt coffee, and for miles along the tracks the Canonniers saw boxes of crackers, barrels of rice, pork, dried fruit, along with overcoats, muskets, cartridge boxes, drums, bayonets, and such.[179] The column turned towards Richmond on the Williamsburg Road after having passed the enemy's camps where "havoc and destruction"[180] was everywhere. The column then headed away from the city on the Darbytown Road.[181]

It was a hard and miserable march under a broiling sun, and according to Canonnier Cire, it lasted "the whole day."[182] Of this movement one of Pryor's Louisianians described the scenes: "In almost any direction you might look you could see large columns of smoke, showing that the enemy was destroying his quartermaster and commissary stores, and, not satisfied with that, burning up farm-houses, barns, haystacks, fences—everything that would burn. . . . The fields over which we passed were strewn with all sorts of military accoutrements, guns and swords thrown away, abandoned wagons, ambulances, and all sorts of things that belong to an army."[183]

In this column, marching along the Darbytown Road, another dust-covered Rebel remembered how strange and careless men can become.

He wrote:

> *Now*, the boys are chatting away as gaily as though on a pleasure excursion, and one would not think that only two days had passed since they witnessed such terrible scenes, and saw their comrades fall by their sides. . . . We laugh and play cards, and make arrangements and calculations for the future although we know that it cannot be many days before we go into battle again. . . . One would think that a life of danger would influence men to prepare for death, but it has a directly contrary influence.[184]

Having marched some ten or twelve miles through the heat and ankle deep dust that rose in clouds, Longstreet's Division at long last encamped in the fields just along the Darbytown Road before sundown. With a creek close by to water the horses and men, the Canonniers pulled in and parked their guns for the night near a little pinewood chapel called the Pioneer Baptist Church.[185] In a short time the open fields all around were covered with camp fires and men frying meat, baking bread, and making coffee, all compliments of the Yankees. Not long after going into camp, torrential rain showers began to fall and lasted far into the night.

When the army awoke on the morning of June 30, the weather was calm and the skies clear. Many of the soldiers were confident this would be the day that McClellan's invading army would be destroyed. Shortly after eight o'clock in the morning, while Maurin and the Canonniers awaited orders in the yard of the chapel, they observed and greeted their old comrades from New Orleans, the Washington Artillery, moving slowly along the Darbytown Road. Colonel J. B. Walton, mounted on a black stallion, along with two other riders and the guidon-bearer carrying the scarlet banner with its blue cross led the battalion of nearly three hundred men and two hundred horses drawing sixteen guns and caissons.[186]

Shortly after, Pryor's Brigade, with Wilcox and Featherston's, also started down the Darbytown Road. The six Donaldsonville guns and their contingent moved out into the dirt road around noon. Longstreet's column continued on with frequent stops, for what, one supposed, was to await "further development of the enemy."[187] Within a mile of starting, Maurin's Battery bypassed the Washington Artillery who were stopped alongside the road in a cornfield. Later during the march deafening cheers arose from the rear and accompanied a group of riders forward as they continued through the long line of soldiers. A member of the Fourteenth Louisiana, Pryor's Brigade, remembered: "Our division was joined by President Davis and staff, and, together with our general officers, made a body of such fine looking men that I will never forget the picture."[188] A soldier in Wilcox's Brigade expressed his feelings as President Davis and Longstreet passed: "Each felt new stimulus . . . in the fact that we would fight under the immediate eye of our President," adding, "We always like to see Longstreet about too . . . and has won the name of the old 'war horse.'"[189]

The advance of Longstreet's Division approached the junction with Long Bridge Road, it being now evident that the enemy was in front and not far distant. Wilcox, Pryor, and Featherston's Brigades were ordered to take positions in line of battle on the left of the road. Wilcox reported they "formed in line . . . in the edge of the woods, with a field in front of us. . . . We remained in this position for two or three hours. Skirmishers were thrown out to the front, and some firing ensued between them and those of the opposing forces."[190]

The men lay over ground covered with scrubby pines and underbrush; from the north the sound of light artillery fire was heard. One of the soldiers lounging on the soft carpet of pine tags and leaves remembered, "They laughed and chatted one would not have imagined that they had been fighting . . . and about to renew the strife."[191]

Near three o'clock in the afternoon Longstreet ordered several batteries hurriedly forward. Maurin's Canonniers, with guns rumbling and horse harnesses rattling, galloped into a field on the left of Pryor's Brigade. Canonnier Levy noted they were "occupying a position on the extreme left of our [Longstreet's] division, and under the eye of General Longstreet himself."[192] Heavy woods obscured the enemy in front, though their batteries

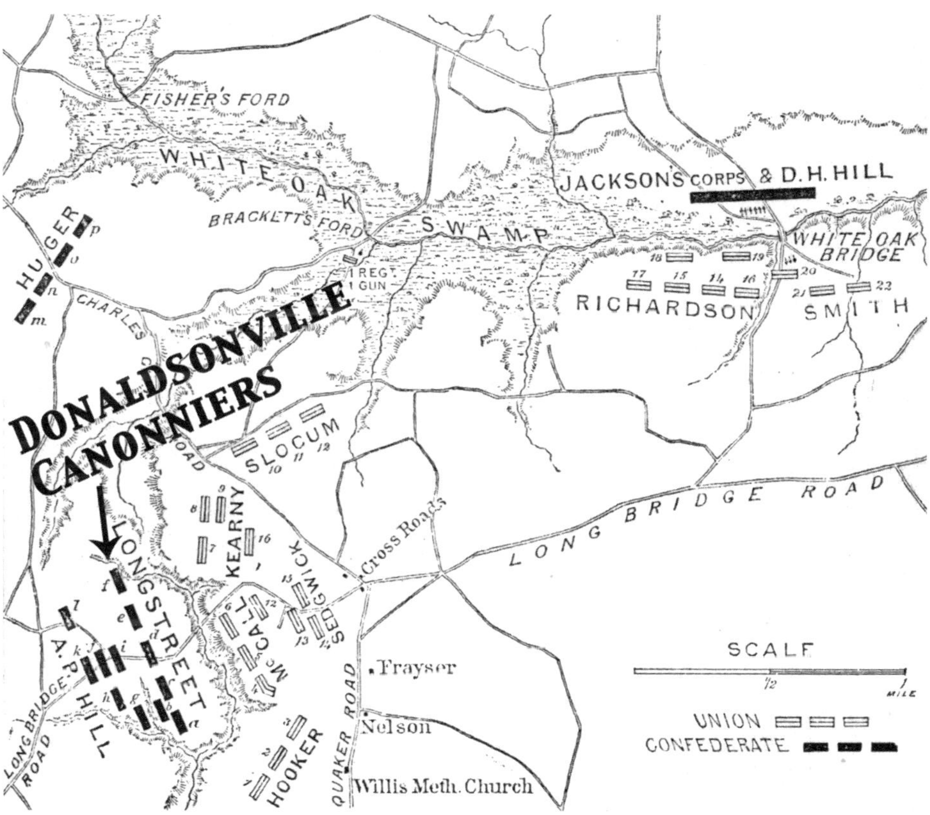

At Frayser's Farm, "Longstreet" (f) is the position of Pryor's Brigade and the Donaldsonville Artillery. Their opponents were the Federal Brigades of "Kearny" with (7) representing Robinson's, (8) being Birney's, (9) Berry's, and (16) Caldwell's brigades. From *Battles and Leaders.*

nonetheless were firing with great rapidity. The woods also did not shield the Canonniers from the shot and shell that hurdled through "cutting off treetops, crashing here, there, and everywhere."[193] Canonnier Cire recorded their "battery was placed in position on a hill where we were exposed to terrible fire of shells."[194]

On the skirmish line during the artillery fire, Pryor's horse lost a leg to a shell burst, but the general was unscathed. For almost an hour the enemy artillery fired before Pryor's Brigade, still lying in the woods, received orders to advance. Because of the thick woods and underbrush, Pryor changed the brigade advance from in-line to columns and sent the regiments forward successively.[195] Maurin's guns hitched up and followed through the woods, which became less dense. Finding a position to shell the enemy, the Donaldsonville guns went into action, and wrote Cire, "We were exposed to their minie balls and shells."[196]

Going through and exiting the woods, Pryor's Brigade boldly charged the enemy across an open field where they were exposed to a destructive fire on the flank as well as in front. Compelled to fall back to the edge of the woods, Pryor called for reinforcements. During the battle and in holding the line, Maurin's guns shifted position five different times. An appreciative member of the Fourteenth Louisiana related how, "At a critical moment in the battle the Donaldsonville Artillery came up on our right, and in a few moments made things very lively in the enemy's lines."[197] One Yankee would recollect, "One loud-sounding battery, the roar of which would burst out and echo in the forest with an almost gloomy sound followed by the long, horrid shriek of its shell."[198]

Featherston's Brigade was held in reserve until five o'clock when it marched forward on the left in support of Pryor's Brigade. Featherston reported that, "The contest was becoming very hot."[199] Near sunset Brigadier General Maxcy Gregg's Brigade of A. P. Hill's Division reinforced Pryor and Featherston's hard-pressed troops. The Fourteenth South Carolina of Gregg's Brigade found Featherston lying wounded in the woods when they went in. A member of the brigade wrote, "The battle . . . was one of the most complicated affairs . . . owning principally . . . to the dense, tangled nature of the woods in which we fought."[200]

In the confusion the brigades would regroup and charge twice more while the Yankees counter charged, after which both sides stood their ground and poured a steady fire into the obscurity of the smoke that covered the field. The artillery continued to blaze away, shot and shell going thick and fast through the trees while the roar of musketry and cannon was deafening, the air filled with missiles, and every moment its peculiar sound of terror.

Into the night Maurin's guns, wrote Levy, "Kept up the action by moonlight until the enemy retired from this most stubbornly-contested field."[201] In the dimness of the night the last Southern brigade in reserve raised the rebel yell, moved down the road on a wide front, and delivered a volley on the Donaldsonville Artillery's right, ending the Federal defense as they broke and ran. The artillery continued a blind fire until nine o'clock that night.[202]

In the Battle of Frayser's Farm, Pryor's Brigade suffered "uncommonly heavy"[203] losses. The Fourteenth Louisiana, for instance, reported one hundred killed and wounded. Yet, miraculously, the Donaldsonville Artillery had no casualties. The Canonniers spent the night on the field, and one Louisianian who couldn't sleep later spoke about it: "From the blue and gray alike came piteous calls for water or help, so I and others arose and did all we could to alleviate their suffering. Save these piteous cries, the flickering lights about the dead or wounded were all there was to tell that we were upon a battle-field, so ominous had grown the stillness and so thick the darkness."[204] A Richmond Howitzer wrote of the night, "'Twas almost a matter of impossibility to sleep, but nature must at length claim its own, and so we slept at last as only broken down soldiers can."[205]

The next morning the men awoke to the sound of heavy firing. Cire noted, "The gunboats [on the James River] also opened fire."[206] Though it was the first day of July, the weather was cool and through the intermittent rain it was observed, "Thousands of round shot and unexploded shell lay upon the surface . . . among the latter were many of the enormous shells thrown by the gunboats. They were eight inches in width by twenty-three in length. The ravages of these monsters were every where discernible through the forest. In some places long avenues were cut through tree-tops, and here and there great trees, three and four feet in thickness were burst open and split to very shreds."[207]

During the morning the weather cleared and a bright sun came out. Levy recorded:

> Having worked our horses terribly without proper food or rest . . . was ordered in reserve during the battle of Malvern Hill, but, being within range of the enemy's rifled guns, the high shots made our position anything but enviable. To be passive and under fire is the most terrible position for a soldier. On this occasion while the drivers were busy with the horses, the [Donaldsonville] artillerist[s] performed the duty of assisting the wounded and burying our dead comrades.[208]

On July 29, 1862, Pryor submitted his report of the operations of the Fifth Brigade in Longstreet's Division concerning the battles of Gaines's Mill and Frayser's Farm, part of the Seven Days' Battles that ended at Malvern Hill and raised the siege of Richmond. He wrote, "I crossed the Chickahominey [River] on the 26th with 1,400 men. In the fights that followed I suffered a loss of 849 killed and wounded and 11 missing." Pryor distinguished the officers who he "thought worthy of promotion," noting, "Capt. V. Maurin, of the Donaldsonville Artillery, attached to my brigade, exhibited himself a most courageous and capable officer."[209]

As for the Canonniers and soldiers of the Army of Northern Virginia, a Richmond Howitzer explained: "In marching and fighting through the tangled belt along the Chickahominey, trying hardships and privations, hunger, loss of sleep, fatigue, pain and sorrow as well as joy and victorious shouts fell to the lot . . . they emerged from these famous fields as full-fledged veterans."[210]

Loathsome Horror.
ARW; courtesy of Library of Congress.

Chapter Five

Une Deuxième Rivière "Taureau"
(A Second Bull Run)

After a night of "copious showers,"[1] July 2, 1862, dawned with a morning mist. Captain Victor Maurin's Canonniers awoke soaking wet. They remained all day camped in the same spot. "We went with our horses to get Yankee caissons as one of ours was damaged in the engagement yesterday, the Yankees are still retreating—Rain,"[2] wrote Donaldsonville Artificer François "Bienvenu" Cire in his memorandum book.

Upon entering the nearby battlefield at Malvern Hill one artilleryman observed, "Such scenes of horror as baffles all description" and the "disabled caissons, with their many dead horses lay thick."[3] The loathsome horrors of the bloody field were further disconcerting with the great numbers of disfigured horse carcasses and their stench.[4]

The rain came down so hard that a wet soldier said it felt, "as if it had a great deal of raining to do and only a little time to do it in."[5] The artillerymen that remained in camp built fires to cook and dry clothes while the occasional boom of a heavy gun was heard. In finding warmth and rest around a fire, an Ascension Parish soldier mused:

> I have never seen it otherwise in my experience, that the survivors of a battle, however great may be the loss, when sitting around a camp fire undergo a reaction from the stress, grief and fatigue of the march and battle, which is manifested in jest and anecdote, and while the comrades who have fallen are not forgotten, yet the reaction carries the spirit from the extreme of depression of a campaign so bloody that each one of us realized that it was a special mercy that he had escaped the countless perils which had swept away thousands of our comrades.[6]

Donaldsonville Canonnier Corporal John O'Hara, with the help of a captured Yankee canteen, scribbled in his diary, "July the 2nd, Donaldsonville all drunk and raining like Hell."[7] During the night it continued to rain very hard, but being so nearly broken down (or otherwise) an artilleryman wrote about sleeping, the rain "did not even arouse me."[8]

The Army of Northern Virginia's commander General Robert E. Lee issued a congratulatory order on July 5 and followed two days later with an order thanking the army:

> The immediate fruits of our success are the relief of Richmond from a state of siege; the rout of the great [Northern] army that so long menaced its safety; many thousand prisoners, including officers of high rank; the capture or destruction of stores to the value of millions; and the acquisition of thousands of arms and forty pieces of superior artillery.

> The service rendered to the country in this short but eventful period can scarcely be estimated, and the general commanding cannot adequately express his admiration of the courage, endurance, and soldierly conduct of the officers and men engaged. These brilliant results have cost us many brave men; but while we mourn the loss of our gallant dead let us not forget that they died nobly in defense of their country's freedom, and have linked their memory with an event that will live forever in the hearts of a grateful people. Soldiers, your country will thank you for the heroic conduct you have displayed—conduct worthy of men engaged in a cause so just and sacred, and deserving a nation's gratitude and praise.[9]

General Robert E. Lee on his favorite horse, Traveller.
From Mrs. Roger A. Pryor, *Reminiscences of Peace and War.*

After this first campaign the army's faith in Lee was unbounded, and the troops believed "their lives and their cause were safe in his hands."[10] One confident soldier wrote, "Richmond was safe. We knew we had an army of soldiers and a general worthy of the men he commanded."[11] The *Compagnie d'artillerie de Donaldsonville*'s feelings toward Lee were apparent when Canonnier Private Eugene Levy wrote, "The men, inspired by success, and confident in our noble leader, never for a moment despaired of the ultimate triumph of our cause."[12]

After resting and collecting arms and other property abandoned by the enemy, the Gunners of Donaldson left camp at four o'clock in the morning on July 5 and marched through reedy bottomlands and past bluffs covered with oak, holly, and wild cherry interspersed with underbrush and magnolia trees growing along a swampy base. For about ten miles the Canonniers followed the Northern army's route. Cire recorded, "The Yankees are still retreating. Burning what they cannot carry."[13] One remarkable aspect of the area was noted by another correspondent who wrote it "differed in appearance from any of the preceeding days. In the track of the enemy's flight there were no cast-away blue great-coats, no blankets, tents, nor stores. He had evidently, before reaching this point, thrown away every thing that could retard his hasty retreat."[14]

Maurin's guns moved with other Confederate troops along clay roads that had now dried into a gray crust. At midday the Donaldsonville guns halted and remained in the same location on picket duty not far from the Yankee-held Harrison's Landing on the James River. Here they remained for the next few days with hot but pleasant weather.[15]

Having been relieved from picket duty on the morning of July 10, the Donaldsonville Artillery packed up. The Canonniers traveled under a cloudy and rainy sky along the New Market Road (also called the River Road) that passed through a dreary waste of a once beautiful country. That evening Maurin's gunners camped in sight of Richmond; it again rained during the night. They remained here alongside the road for another day, and on July 12, with the rain continuing to fall, the battery moved nearer Richmond where they again bivouacked at Stearn farm, Tree Hill. Their camp was near the Washington Artillery and other batteries of Longstreet's artillery who were again massed along Almond Creek, just three-fourths of a mile from the James River. The artillery park was dubbed Camp Longstreet.[16]

The bivouac was laid out with sinks conveniently arranged for the men in consideration of decency, cleanliness, and health, and after details were formed to clean the area, tents were brought up from Richmond and pitched.[17] After these work details the artillerists were given speeches upon "discipline"[18] and then paid two months pay ($24.00 a private) after which, many of the artillerymen with money in their pockets went to Richmond and again enjoyed the cheery society of a relieved citizenry. "We would go up into the city everyday or two . . . and enjoy ourselves as best we could." wrote one Louisianian. "[19]

To others back in bivouac, "The quiet of the camp was very acceptable and pleasant after such hardships as we passed through."[20] Many of the privates however, "Indulged very much in 'poker,' and other games."[21] The Canonniers had decent rations, and after receiving their pay one Louisiana artillerist noted in his diary, "Went around the country purchasing provisions for the Mess, Irish Potatoes $2.00 Pick Tomatoes .75¢ a dozen . . . a very good dinner [with] Meat. Irish Potatoes an uncommon thing and Tomatoes, this was an extraordinary Dinner."[22] There were plenty of dried vegetables and poultry too for soups, or gumbo thickened with *filé*.

A more important reason why camp was acceptable and pleasant was that many ladies and their escorts from Richmond visited Camp Longstreet daily for "serenading"[23] by the Louisianians. The Creole Canonniers were special favorites of the young damsels who took pleasure in listening to their singing and speaking French. [24]

Most of the men were anxious for news from home. July 22 was an especially noteworthy day: Camille Leblanc, the long time antebellum corporal discharged two months earlier, returned to Virginia on a visit and delivered letters. Unfortunately the news from Louisiana was now a source of further anxiety for many Canonniers. They learned a Yankee gunboat had on May 31, 1862, ventured a short distance down Bayou Lafourche from Donaldsonville. Additionally, recent crevasses on the Mississippi River caused much of Ascension and Assumption parishes to be inundated with water. This made food scarce, and *famille* (the folks) suffered privations and discomforts. It was estimated that three-fifths of the Lafourche District soldier families were now in a destitute condition. In an attempt to relieve fears one wife wrote on July 1, 1862, "The Bayou within its banks" and "the Yankees all gone."[25]

The day after Leblanc's arrival he was charged with a bundle of letters from the Donaldsonville gunners and left for Louisiana by railroad in company with recently discharged Canonnier artificers Louis Lanoix (a light-haired forty-one year old discharged July 13 because of kidney disease and impaired motion of the knee caused by a fractured leg) and Adolphe Landry (a gray-haired forty-four year old who received a certificate of disability on July 14 due to a hernia and old age). It took the three, after reaching Lynchburg, Virginia, eight days to make it to Donaldsonville. Misfortune struck along the way as Leblanc lost the package of papers.[26]

The return of the three former Canonniers did little to boost morale in the public mind. Just a week after their arrival the population of Donaldsonville was given a warning of three days to evacuate by Federal Rear Admiral David G. Farragut. All the families took heed and soon filled the roads with lines of wagons. On August 9, 1862, two United States sloops of war and a gunboat under Farragut's command anchored immediately in front of Donaldsonville and bombarded it with guns and mortars. According to one resident the Federals fired about ninety shells into the town. The only casualty was a free man of color by the name of Zenon.[27] The Yankees then landed a force that set fires in the town and across the bayou in Port Barrow, turning two-thirds of Donaldsonville into smoke-blackened ruins with a few chimneys and brick walls remaining. It was reported, "All the tiled and turreted buildings of French and Spanish times were leveled with the dust, except for the venerable church, whose antique towers were spared the visitation of the iron ball."[28] Port Barrow was completely ruined except for Canonnier Sergeant Hubert Treille's house, the only one left standing.[29] A total of seventy-one families had their homes eaten up by the flames as the people of Donaldsonville retired upon the bayou where each farm or plantation received two or three families. Many were later burned out a second time. Then the women and children, black and white, moved to the *brules*[30] along the bayous and in the interior of the parishes.[31]

Lise Vives Maurin, wife of the Donaldsonville Canonnier captain, left with her children and moved to the home of her sister at *Ville de Bois* in Brule Maurin, Assumption Parish. More than fifty years after these affaris it was still said: "The heroism, self-sacrifice, and devotion to duty of Mrs. Maurin in those trying days is a part of the tradition of the country."[32] Most of the women of the bayou country drew comfort from their religious faith and "bore the trials of war with admirable fortitude."[33]

The bombardment of Donaldsonville remained unknown to the Canonniers for some time. The stay in their July bivouac for several days was an easy life in comparison to those of the past months, and they spent the time reflecting upon their "great idea" of "foreign intervention, peace, and home."[34] Maurin conducted inspections and regular roll calls and held daily drills. The battery's artificers were kept busy as harnesses and equipment were repaired or replaced. Guns in need of repairs or inferior pieces were replaced in the batteries

Burned ruins of the Donaldsonville courthouse.
From Francis T. Miller (editor), *The Photographic History of the Civil War in Ten Volumes.*

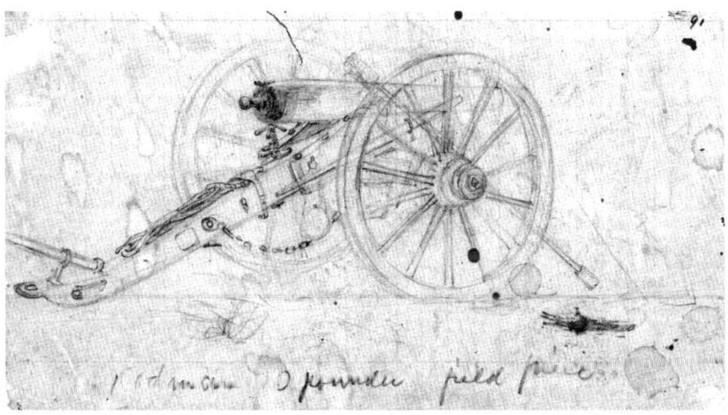

3-inch ordnance rifle.
ARW; courtesy of Library of Congress.

with some of the captured ordnance. The Donaldsonville Artillery exchanged their fifth piece (one of the Blakely guns) for a United States 3-inch Ordnance Rifle that, "Still bore, written on its stock, the name of General George A. McCall."[35]

Maurin reported that the battery had 126 animals, although eighteen were unserviceable and three had been wounded in the recent battles. The forage allowance at this time was twelve pounds of corn and five pounds of fodder, but an assistant quartermaster reported a greater allowance of forage was needed to fatten and prepare them for service. When brought to his attention, Major General James Longstreet replied the allowance was "one of necessity, not of choice."[36] It was suggested that the batteries pasture the horses if the corn or fodder allotment was not increased. The horses received constant attention. Nearly every day squads of artillerymen were sent into Richmond with horses to be shod.[37]

The muster roll for the Donaldsonville Artillery in July/August 1862 listed 114 Canonniers present for duty with their clothing in good shape, even if much of it was blue. The roster also indicated twenty-three Canonniers were absent sick and another six were on sick furlough in Louisiana during this time. Lieutenant Prosper Landry, though still weak from his sickness, remained with the battery, but popular Lieutenant William "Billy" Lawes, "beloved and esteemed by all who knew him,"[38] took sick and went into the hospital. He soon received a sick furlough to Louisiana and because of his health never returned to Virginia.[39]

Rest and refitting ended for the Donaldsonville Artillery and the Second and Third companies of the Washington Artillery on a hot but pleasant July 25. Orders arrived at noon. The three batteries prepared for a march with instructions to report to and support Colonel George T. Anderson and his Georgia Brigade. Maurin's Canonniers moved from their bivouac with another brigade from A. P. Hill's division to outpost duty on New Market Heights, where the Federals would be "watched and restrained."[40] Leaving one and a half hours after receiving the order, Maurin's six guns and the two companies of the Washington Artillery, along with Hill's infantry brigade, arrived to support Anderson's troops camped in positions under cover of woods along the heights, on the crest of hills between the Darbytown and New Market roads.

Here, when not on picket duty, the soldiers entrenched and threw up fortifications. "It was dig, dig, dig—lift and throw—until the bank reached the height of the embrasures and platforms for the field pieces; then the work was varied for some who were to fill grain-bags with earth, which, piled in tiers, were to constitute the sides of the embrasures," wrote one soldier.[41] In the usual routine of camp duty, rations of flour and bacon were issued, but here "blackberries and huckleberries," noted another Southerner, "constitute our luxuries."[42]

"While resting by the roadside," a Georgia soldier on the heights wrote, "I saw, for the first time . . . no less a personage than Robert E. Lee. . . . He was mounted on his famous horse Traveller, a very dark iron gray. The horse might have passed without much notice had it not been for his rider, who could have been picked out of his army at the first glance. He was tall and well formed, sitting his horse with a grace acquired by but few men. . . . His beard covers his face, is closely trimmed and of a dark gray color. His eyes, well an eagle would flinch before them."[43]

Each one of Anderson's Georgia regiments were required to take a turn doing picket duty at Malvern Hill along with one of eight batteries that were constantly on duty along New Market Heights. On July 29 the Canonnier guns left the fortifications and spent their time on picket duty at Malvern Hill where Maurin reported, "Nothing of importance transpired."[44] On the afternoon of August 4 Captain Robert M. Stribling's Fauquier (Virginia) Artillery relieved Maurin's guns and Canonniers. Walton ordered them back to the fortifications.

The enemy attacked Malvern Hill with a strong force the very next morning at sunrise. Stribling's Battery suffered three dead and some wounded who fell into the hands of the enemy. The outnumbered Confederate forces fell back slowly to the fortifications at New Market Heights while the enemy occupied Malvern Hill. Lee consequently ordered four divisions, including Longstreet's, to march against the Federals, but before the troops could be posted, and before daylight on August 6, the enemy had moved back to their camp at Harrison's Landing. After the retaking of the abandoned Malvern Hill, Maurin's Battery, along with the two companies of Washington Artillery, were sent there on picket duty on August 7.[45]

After two days of standing watch in the very warm and almost suffocating heat, the two companies of Washington Artillery returned to Camp Longstreet at Tree Hill on the evening of August 9. The Donaldsonville Artillery spent one more night on Malvern Hill. The next morning, Maurin's Battery was relieved. It arrived at ten o'clock in Camp Longstreet along Almond Creek. The Canonniers hardly had time to set up their three-legged kettles for cooking when orders came for them to prepare four days' rations, put themselves in light marching order, and be ready to move the next morning at daylight. The Donaldsonville camp soon bustled with cooking while the drivers cared for the 112 horses and mules and the gunners attended to their pieces and caissons. Others struck down the tents and loaded the wagons for traveling.[46] The excess baggage was sent to a warehouse in Richmond with twenty-nine-year-old "rotund, smiling, and serene" Canonnier Private Henry Loeb, detailed to guard the trunks and baggage.[47]

It was another hot day on August 10, 1862. Rumors circulated that the Canonniers were heading for "Stonewall" Jackson's army in the Shenandoah Valley. But "no one," noted a Louisiana artillerist, "knew where" they were going.[48] In truth, Lee ordered Longstreet, with ten brigades dubbed the "Right Wing" of the Army of Northern Virginia, to arrive by train on August 13 in Gordonsville to aid Jackson's command. When Pryor received orders to move his brigade, he was informed that the Donaldsonville Artillery (as Pryor's brigade battery) had separate orders from Longstreet's Headquarters. The artillery was not going by rail, but moving to Gordonsville by road in two artillery columns. One column was to be led by the Washington Artillery's Walton and the other by Major John J. Garnett, Chief of Artillery on the staff of Brigadier General David R. Jones. The columns were to follow the same route and were instructed to move as rapidly as practicable with due regard to the condition of the animals.[49]

Maurin received orders to report to Garnett's column, which left on August 10 at five o'clock in the evening.[50] The next day, under cloudy skies, assembly was sounded, and at five o'clock in the afternoon Garnett's column left Stearns's Farm. Maurin led the Donaldsonville

Artillery's 115 Canonniers riding and marching with *Honoré, Fidélité,* and *Libertié et Égalité* (their three 6-pounder guns) plus the two Blakely 12-pounder guns, and the 3-inch "McCall" ordnance rifle, six caissons, an ambulance, six wagons, and a traveling forge. The artillery column moved in single file with each gun followed by its caisson, then the wagons and forge. All rattled up Richmond's Main Street before turning north onto Brook Avenue. The column headed out the city, crossing Brook Run Bridge. From there the guns, caissons, and wagons continued on to the Chickahominey River (about thirteen miles) on the Mountain Road and the Louisa Court House plank road.[51]

The movement halted in the night around eleven o'clock. After being unhitched and rubbed down, the horses drank while their legs were washed down by their drivers near the river's ford. The artillerists meanwhile checked the carriages and ammunition in the caissons while others prepared supper around the campfires that lit up the darkness. After completion of these tasks, all except the posted sentinels settled down to rest. They had made what is considered an ordinary day's march for field artillery, traveling about two and one half miles per hour.[52]

To avoid marching in the heat the next day, August 12, Cire recorded that the battery, "At 3 p.m. resumed the march and camped at 9 p.m. We had rain during the march."[53] The artillerists and horses rested that night under "a glorious full moon."[54] Cire did not mention passing the few houses of Montpelier (twenty-seven miles from Richmond), but he did note that at about the time they camped a message was received from Richmond relating that Canonnier Private Valentin Hebert had become the second member of the battery to die of illness in Louisiana Hospital.[55]

Cire's Canonnier memorandum continued on August 13: "Resumed the march at 5 a.m. and halted at 12 N, left again at 2 o'clock and halted at 5 p.m. to camp."[56] The road to Louisa Court House made for a smooth, if uninteresting, journey as the column ascended westward though well wooded meadows and teeming fields of grain. "Left at 5 a.m.," wrote Cire on August 14, "passed through Louisa Court House at 8 a.m."[57] This was a very neat little town with a courthouse near an ordinary (tavern) and some very fine homes. There were four or five hundred inhabitants, and it was a place where some very good apple brandy was obtainable with little trouble.[58] After leaving Louisa Court House on a clear and pleasant day, and after traveling another thirteen miles, Cire happily noted that they "arrived near Gordonsville at 2 p.m."[59]

The *Historical Memoranda* of the Donaldsonville Artillery described their sixty-nine mile journey with a matter-of-fact, "Nothing of importance transpiring on the march."[60] Their bivouac was made into an artillery park near Gordonsville, a town described as an uninteresting village with two small groups of buildings about two-thirds of a mile apart along a macadamized road. There was a railroad station, the Exchange Hotel[61] (lately converted to a Receiving Hospital), and a stage stable located at the southern end of town. In all there were about thirty frame houses. Gordonsville was located in lovely country with fine scenery at the foot of the Blue Ridge Mountains where the Canonniers enjoyed the pine air in open fields. They camped with Longstreet's Division that was spread out from the eastern corner of the town in a southwestern direction across Negro Run into Louisa County.[62]

Some of the Louisiana artillerymen noted that the weather was "cool"[63] and the nights "very chilly."[64] This caused the men to huddle around the flickering campfires listening to the "crooking frogs" and the "cries of the whip-poor-will."[65] Laying on the ground at night the Louisianians used fences and rails for pillows under the "brilliant lustre"[66] of the moon and stars that shone brightly down upon them. The region was bountiful, and the troops would bemoan the fact that their pleasant stay would be "short and sweet."[67]

A Virginia soldier at this time described Gordonsville as a "village of hard boiled eggs and chicken bones,"[68] but the men camped all about were reveling as they had not done for the many months when their rations consisted of nothing other than beef and flour. Here the troops had the opportunity to obtain from local farms eggs and chickens, apples, corn, vegetables, and apple brandy that filled many a canteen. The animals in the artillery batteries received an abundance of forage too.

Orders on August 15 to cook three days' rations of bread and meat to be carried in haversacks meant an advance was immediately in prospect. This made everyone on edge but, they were "in excellent spirits" and "confident."[69] In light marching order the Donaldsonville Artillery left camp at noon on August 16and joined with Walton's column of guns, caissons, and wagons under a burning hot sun. The artillery didn't get far before being detained at four o'clock in the afternoon by columns of infantry passing. When they did move (the artillery batteries of Longstreet's "Right Wing" passed through Gordonsville) it was very slow over a very hilly and bad road that was constantly blocked by wagons. The tedious ten-mile march ended at two o'clock in the morning on another chilly night near the beautiful, steep hillside town of Orange Court House, a railroad and turnpike transportation hub.[70]

Awaking on a clear and pleasant August 17, Maurin received orders to hitch up the battery, but the Canonniers in the hurry-up-and-wait style of the military remained in bivouac the whole day. There they watched as Longstreet's infantry and wagons went by. Counter orders to unharness and camp in the same spot for the night arrived at three o'clock in the afternoon. It was another very cold night.[71]

The smoky haze of morning dawned on August 18, and it seemed like everything was in motion towards the Rapidan River. Maurin received instructions from Walton that the Donaldsonville Artillery's six guns were again assigned to Brigadier General Roger A. Pryor's brigade and ordered to report immediately for duty to him during the present campaign.[72] "Boots and Saddles" was sounded at ten o'clock in the morning, and within the hour the Canonniers were on the march. After just two miles they halted yet again to let another large force of infantry pass before joining Pryor's Brigade.

In the middle of the day the weather became very warm, and when the march was resumed their progress was again slow, trudging along the old red dirt roads. During the move a Louisianian wrote, "We indulged in friendly jest, and harmless badinage passed down the line at those whose dress was out of the usual order, or who's [*sic*] feet began to hurt."[73] At two o'clock in the afternoon the battery again camped, and this gave the Canonnier foragers (those "who were constantly seeking from the hospitable Virginia people something better to eat than our army rations")[74] an opportunity to scavenge about. From these forays some were able to fill up their haversacks with green apples and peaches. When darkness came (the moon rose about midnight but was obscured by thick clouds)[75] it was another very cold night, made colder by not being allowed to light a campfire.

The next morning, August 19, it was again smoky and hazy at daylight. Orders arrived to put everything in light marching order with each Canonnier instructed to take just one blanket and cook three days' rations of flour and bacon. The guns and caissons were also lightened and prepared for battle. Cire recorded, "We resumed the march and camped at 3 p.m. received orders to hitch up, marched a short time made about a mile and received counter orders—then we received orders to be ready to march next morning at 3 o'clock."[76]

Camped in rich clover fields along the road, an artilleryman noted, "Upwards of 50,000 men, with proportionate cannon and bulky wagon trains, lie scattered within four miles of this spot. The enemy is reported to be moving & we eat, drink, and sleep in momentary expectation of an attack by us or by them. . . . It is strange to see how little affected are

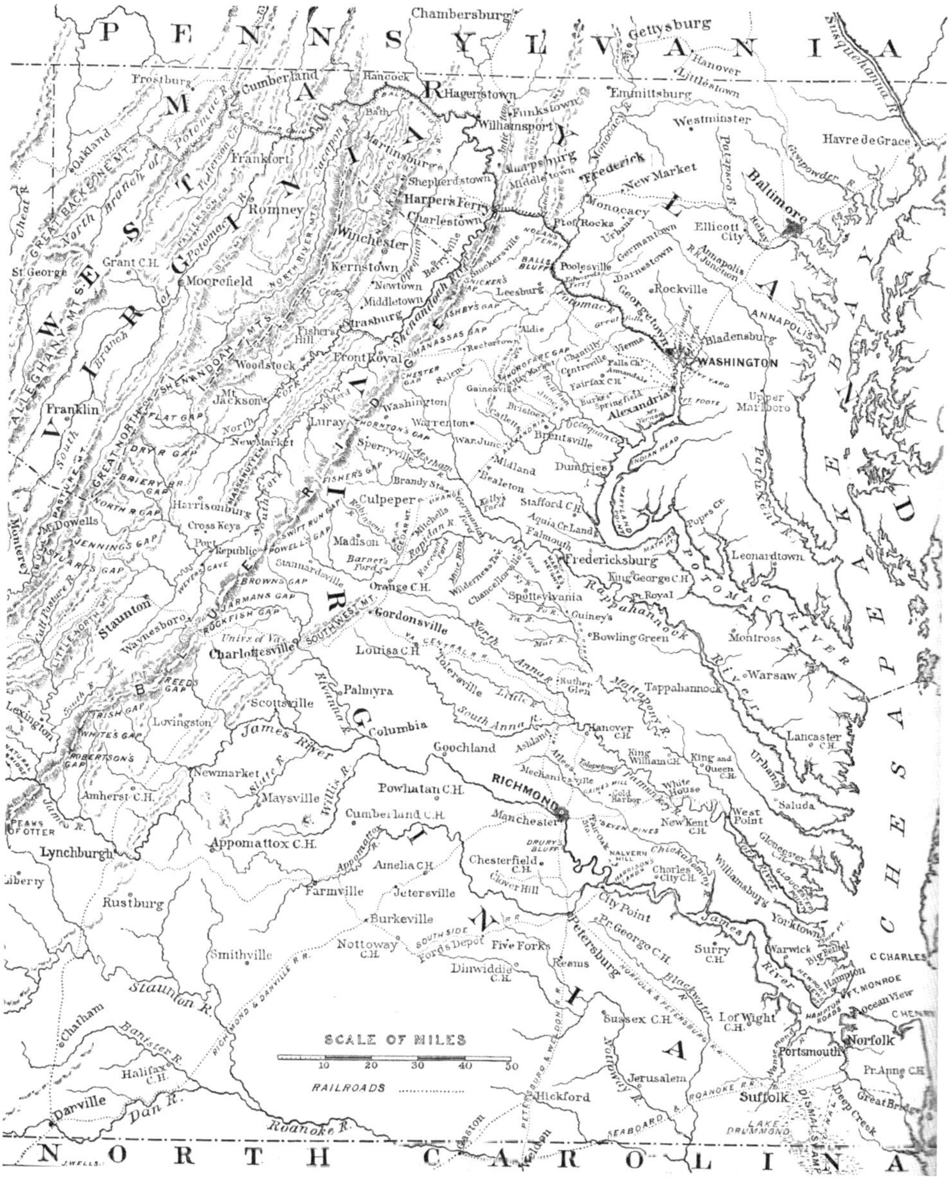

Map of the Virginia campaigns.
From *Battles and Leaders.*

the soldiers by eminency of action; the nearer we are to the enemy the greater seems the inclination to jest and merriment."[77]

Reveille was sounded at two o'clock in the morning on August 20, and an hour later with the rising moon the line of march was taken up over a very rough road. Lee's army at day light crossed the Rapidan River at the thigh-deep Raccoon Ford where the scene was described as "exciting and amusing."[78] After crossing the ford where there was a "little hamlet of a few houses"[79] the road became dusty and the day very warm. Maurin's Battery, after traveling slowly with many halts, made camp in the evening after a movement of about fifteen miles.

Riding along with Wilcox, Pryor, and Featherston's Brigades and artillery was newspaper correspondent Felix Gregory de Fontaine, an intellectual reporter who wrote under the sobriquet *Personne.*[80] His father was French and therefore he had something in common with many of the Canonnier artillerists. Fontaine, or *Personne,* would later particularize Maurin's guns in battle and even sent letters to Louisiana for some of the Pelican State gunners.[81] From a hill alongside the Rapidan River, Fontaine could see for miles:

> Three columns—long, black winding lines of men, their muskets gleaming in the sunshine like silver spears, are in sight, moving . . . Good many stragglers by the wayside, but they are generally broken down soldiers, and trudge slowly along in the tracks of their comrades. An attractive part of the procession is the baggage trains, wending their way in the rear of the army. Thousands of wagons are in sight, and between the stalling trains, the shouting of drivers and the chaotic confusion which emanates from the motley mess, no man can complain of the *ennui* of a march.[82]

After this day's march Fontaine wrote:

> Nothing can be more picturesquely beautiful than the bivouac at night. Thousands of troops line the woods on both sides of the road for miles. Camp-fires are glimmering in the trees, muskets are stacked along the edge of the forest, and the men are disposed in every conceivable manner. Some are sitting around camp-fires watching the roasting [corn] ears, and discussing the 'coming events which cast their shadows before,' and some are among the trees, moving to and fro in the grey film of smoke that has risen from the myriad fires and rests upon the earth. Between the dusty figures of the soldiers, the various occupations in which they are engaged, the road filled with wagons and guns, the appearance of the illuminated trees and bushes, forming against the deep gloom of the night a fantastic background . . . We live on what we can get—now and then an ear of corn, fried green apples, or a bit of ham broiled on a stick, but quite as frequently do without either from morning until night. We sleep on the ground without any covering than a blanket, and consider ourselves fortunate if we are not frozen stiff before morning. The nights are both damp and cold.[83]

Daylight on August 21 presented another busy scene as the advance was resumed. Wilcox's three brigades led the movement along a much-traveled road towards Jennings Place, an old one-and-a-half-story house built of hewn logs bolted at the corners.[84] From there the divisions headed west towards Stevensburg while the weather turned warm and cloudy. The dust was kicked up by the moving column of feet, hoofs, and wheels, causing all to suffocate upon the powdery cloud before it rose up above the trees. Upon reaching a road that bore off to the right, the command was directed to take it towards Kelly's Ford on the Rappahannock River. The column turned, now led by Featherston's Brigade under command of Colonel Carnot Posey (Featherston was still recovering from his Frayser's Farm wound.) They were followed by Pryor's Brigade and Maurin's Battery, then Wilcox's Brigade and artillery. The advance continued along a hilly country road, and after having marched about a mile and a half, the Donaldsonville guns splashed across a beautiful, shaded, and small rocky stream called Mountain Run. There the men and horses obtained a gulp or two of cold water under

Reveille
From *Battles and Leaders.*

Felix Gregory de Fontaine
From J. Cutler Andrews, *The South Reports the Civil War.*

Going into bivouac.
By Edwin Austin Forbes (hereafter cited as EAF); courtesy of the Library of Congress].

fine shade trees before hurriedly moving on. The brigades and artillery went a short distance farther, following the road up a hill where Confederate cavalry pickets approached. They galloped in with the news that a large Yankee cavalry force had crossed at Kelly's Ford about two miles away and were advancing on this road.[85]

Two of Featherston's Mississippi Regiments were immediately formed in lines of battle on each side of the dirt road with the others drawing up behind them. Pryor's infantry moved in support. Word spread quickly through the ranks "that we are in a trap."[86] The reporter Fontaine recorded that Wilcox came forward and "was riding in advance . . . attended by a single trooper, when the latter discovered one of the Yankee pickets peeping over the top of a bulder. [*sic*] 'Shall I bring him down?' said the soldier. 'No,' replied the General, 'better not waste your powder, the distance is too great.' Hardly were the words out of his mouth, before 'whiz'—a Minnie ball flew within three inches of the General's ear, and lodged in the bank behind him."[87]

After his regiments got into position, Wilcox ordered the lines to move forward. Not long after, a shot was heard, and then firing became quite brisk along the whole line as it advanced. Entering a field descending to the river, which was about a thousand yards away, the enemy's camp across the river could be seen covering a considerable space on much higher ground. The skirmishers continued to fire at each other until Longstreet directed Wilcox to withdraw his command back across Mountain Run. Maurin's Battery was ordered back across the stream. There the Canonniers unlimbered their guns on a high hill overlooking the fields towards the river.

Upon seeing the Confederate infantry withdraw the enemy cavalry made a spirited dash but were driven off by a covering force of two Mississippi companies positioned at the junction of two roads leading to the ford. The two covering companies then fell back towards its regiment posted in a cornfield about three or four hundred yards back. The other companies of Mississippians raced back, barely reaching the regiment's position before the Yankee cavalry again came down in line at full speed. A Mississippi foot soldier described the scene:

> The cavalry appeared at the summit of the long slope in front of us. They bore down on us in a gallop, four lines deep. With the sun behind us, their shining sabers and polished accouterments flashed brilliantly. The order was passed along our line: 'Hold your fire.' This was a tense moment. The enemy huzzahed. The front line was only about fifty yards off . . . when the order 'Fire!' rang out. A sheet of flame leaped out from the whole front of our brigade. In an instant, that well ordered body of cavalry was converted into a jumble of plunging and falling horses and men. The horses quailed before the fire, wheeled and bolted into the lines behind.[88]

Fontaine recounted, "Thirty or forty saddles were emptied in less time than you can tell it . . . the regiment took to its heel, and amid the cheers and jeers of the boys got out of sight in the most industrious manner possible."[89]

Wilcox reported the cavalry was scattered with utmost confusion over the field for more than a mile with some thirty saddles emptied. He also wrote,

> At length they reformed far off from the infantry that had just punished them so severely; but they were in full view of where my own and General Pryor's Brigades were resting, on high ground in an open field on the far side of the Mountain Run. I directed Captain [Edwin J.] Anderson (Thomas Artillery) to come into battery on high ground under cover of some pine with his Parrott gun and to fire upon them. . . . This artillery fire drove them entirely out of view, and nothing more was seen of them until about 5 p.m., when the cavalry reappeared. Three rifled pieces were now placed in position and after a few rounds the cavalry fled again in confusion.[90]

The three rifle pieces, positioned behind the Mississippians were operated by the Canonniers of the Donaldsonville Artillery.

"My command," continued Wilcox, "was now (near sundown) put in march in rear of the column for Stevensburg. Just at this time the enemy reappeared on the ground where his cavalry had been twice repulsed by our artillery. This time he came with four pieces of rifled artillery and began to fire upon us as we were moving off."[91] Fontaine detailed how,

> At Mountain Run, a small branch which joins the Rappahannock, a Federal battery of six pieces commenced this afternoon to throw shells by way of diversion, but were promptly engaged by the Donaldsonville battery, (Louisiana,) Capt. M[aurin], and soon after retired. In this affair General Roger Pryor had a narrow escape. While sitting on a fence by the roadside, a shell burst immediately over his head, and the fragments dashed into the ground around him on every side, but . . . without doing injury. As he wears a light felt hat, and was plainly in sight of the artillerist, the presumption is that he was made their mark.[92]

During the exchange of cannon fire the Mississippians moved back to the cover of the road as the artillery rounds went over their heads. A member of the Fourth Company Washington Artillery (attached to Pickett's Brigade) later wrote in his diary that the Yankees "fired Parrott shells that passed over us some burst within 25 yards of us. We . . . could not reply to them on account of having short range Guns, but . . . the La. Donaldsonville Artillery did reply and silenced their battery."[93] Cire simply recorded that Maurin's guns "were shelled by the Yankees and we shelled them back in return."[94] The Donaldsonville Artillery's *Historical Memoranda* documented that Wilcox's command had "taken the wrong road, led to do so by a fictitious order brought by a Yankee spy, came very near falling into an ambush, but which fortunately ended in an artillery duel."[95]

After the duel Maurin's guns joined the rear of the column. During the march a slight rain shower occurred that laid the dust, making the movement more tolerable but it was a very dark night. A Louisiana artillerist on foot bemoaned it was "dangerous to us poor miserable pedestrians."[96] Wilcox concluded his report of this affair by writing, "Pursuing our march, we bivouacked at Stevensburg at 1 o'clock at night."[97]

Soon after sunrise on August 22, rations for two days were given out, after which the camps were in a state of bustle, some cooking and some getting the horses, guns, and caissons ready to resume the march. At ten o'clock in the morning "Boots and Saddles" was sounded, but no order came to move and the Canonniers remained at Stevensburg. Fontaine described the town as being, "Once a fine old sober Virginia village, but now deserted, dilapidated, and as rough as . . . second-hand rubbish." He noted the place was now "alive with a cosmopolitan humanity."[98]

From their camp on a hill, a Louisiana artilleryman wrote, "A sublime scene was presented to our view" and "afforded a scene delightful to behold."[99] Fontaine put pen to paper and wrote at Stevensburg: "We have one of the handsomest views in the country. Around the edge of the horizon is the Blue Ridge, hanging like a misty veil dropped from the clouds, the huge tops illuminated by the sunlight. Between here and there spreads out a broad plan, broken at intervals by hills and patches of woods . . . miles to the left of our line of travel is Culpeper Court House. Four miles ahead is Brandy Station . . . and already there is filing away in that direction a train of a thousand wagons. In the meadows at your feet are camps of other wagon trains, containing ordnance, quartermaster and commissary stores for the use . . . of the army. Several brigades are also bivouacked here, while others are in motion, filing across the country."[100]

Leaving Stevensburg during the day, Maurin's Battery resumed its movement with

Pryor's Brigade and after a couple of hours camped near Brandy Station. Cire noted that they heard artillery fire a short distance ahead, adding, "We believe it is Jackson."[101] In any case orders did not come, though they were expected. The horses were taken care of while many of the Canonniers settled down, resting in camp until a thunderstorm with heavy rain fell to disturb their sleep.

At sunrise on August 23 a heavy cannonading again commenced and continued on for several hours. Maurin received orders to send a section of long-range guns forward.[102] Lieutenant Prosper Landry led his section with the two Blakely rifle guns in tow and reported to the Washington Artillery's First Company commander Captain Charles W. Squires. He was in charge of ten guns located on a hill opposite to Rappahannock Station, which was west and northwest of a Yankee lodgment (a small redoubt on the Confederate side of the river) at Rappahannock Bridge. At about seven o'clock in the morning Squires reported that the enemy had placed a battery on the extreme left and had partly succeeded in enfilading his batteries. He then withdrew Lieutenant John M. Galbraith's section of two guns to engage these.[103] After relocating, Galbraith's guns received a heavy fire and were partly forced from their first position.

Immediately upon the arrival of Landry's two Donaldsonville guns, Squires sent them to Galbraith's assistance, where they took position to the right of the two Washington Artillery guns and fought side by side. Squires reported, "The four guns . . . managed to keep a heavy enfilading fire from [Squire's other] batteries by the[ir] coolness and bravery."[104] The cannon fire was rapid and the guns hotly engaged with the oppressively hot air fairly rent with the shrieks of the cannon balls and shells bursting, and covering the sweaty Gunners of Donaldson and Washington Artillery men with dirt and smoke. The artillery battle continued for some time as the enemy placed more guns in position, but in a while their fire slackened and only occasionally replied to the Confederate guns.

The Federal troops retreated from the lodgment back across the river while setting fire to the railroad bridge and private dwellings nearby. The correspondent Fontaine came forward at twelve noon to observe and reported "the flames are in full view, spitefully licking the timbers of the trestle work."[105] The bridge soon collapsed into the swift flowing Rappahannock River waters.

At about two in the afternoon Major John J. Garnett rode up and requested Squires to send four rifle guns to the right and report to Colonel Stephen D. Lee. Landry's Canonnier section, along with a section of Washington Artillery under Lieutenant Edward Owen, were disengaged for this purpose and, with another gun or two from Captain William Parker's Virginia Battery, moved down the hill and across the railroad tracks to the cover of woods. Meanwhile Colonel Lee selected a position for the guns. At about three o'clock the artillery moved to their assigned position as a terrific thunderstorm, with plenty of lightning, swept over the land rendering it impossible to fire as the rainfall hid from view all objects more than a few yards away.

A half hour later, with the rain slackening, the gunners observed flames burst forth from the foremost houses in the town. At this time Landry's Blakely guns along with Owen and Parker's pieces started firing and, noted a Louisianian, caused the enemy "to desist from their infamous work and skedaddle."[106] They fired for about a half hour and it was said the guns got in "some good practice."[107] The guns then advanced to the enemy's deserted lodgment and subsequently moved to positions on the banks of the river alongside the burnt railroad bridge where they "sent a few shots after their straggled and retreating cavalry."[108]

The artillery horses then took their evening drink undisturbed in the waters of the river before the guns limbered to the rear around five-thirty under orders from Squires to report back to their respective commands. Before leaving, the Louisiana artillerists and Canonniers spent a half hour examining the abandoned Yankee encampment on the fortified hill and gathered coffee, biscuits, and clothing. Landry and his gun section, completely exhausted, then returned to the Donaldsonville bivouac near Brandy Station.[109]

Two days after the battle, Walton reported,

> The combat on the right was gallantly fought by the batteries there. . . . The object sought to be attained by this engagement . . . was fully accomplished, by driving the enemy from all his positions before night-fall and causing him to withdraw from our front entirely during the night. . . . The officers and men in all the batteries engaged are deserving the highest praise for their gallantry upon the field. . . . Too much praise cannot be awarded . . . to Captain Squires, Stribling, and Lieutenants Landry and Chapman on the right.[110]

In the engagement at Rappahannock Station, Squires's guns expended 400 rounds and lost four men killed and five wounded, along with one horse killed and one wounded. The bursting of their Richmond-made 10-pounder Parrott gun near the end of the engagement caused the death of one man and wounded two. The Donaldsonville Artillery's two guns fired 119 rounds in the duel and received no casualties in men or horses. Prosper Landry later remarked about the lack of casualties, "Some may call this chance, but we give it a better and a holier name."[111]

Maurin's Battery resumed the march with Pryor's Brigade early on the morning of August 24 under cloudy skies. Cire noted that they changed direction with Longstreet's gray regiments but still moved slowly over the green hills "much delayed by troops and trains on the road."[112] During the day and into the night, the column moved unhurriedly on for seven or eight miles before stopping at two o'clock in the morning near the Hazel River, where the air was raw and chilling. This caused all the men to hug the campfires while sleeping on

Artillery Duel near Rappahannock Station, August 23, 1862.
From William Miller Owen, *In Camp and Battle with the Washington Artillery.*

the wet grass with a heavy dew. Most went without eating, but some of the lucky Louisiana artillery foragers were able to get a supper along the route at the "hospitable mansion" of North Cliff.[113]

The morning of August 25 opened fair and cool. The movement continued around daylight and progressed through a beautiful day, though the tramping of men and horses stirred up a cloud of dust along the generally narrow road. With the wagon trains mixed up among the infantry and artillery, the day's movements were again "greatly impeded as usual."[114] The column passed Little Fork Church, of which a Louisiana artillerist noted, "On our route we see signs of the Yankee Ravages, churches completely destroyed, all the benches and fixtures inside broken up and Yankee names written in prominent places."[115] Continuing on past the church, around noon, the Canonniers went through a small place with a few stores and several houses known as Jeffersonton, a "poor deserted hamlet"[116] that the war made into a dilapidated, broken-down place.[117]

After marching about nine miles for the day, Cire wrote, "We heard shelling going on not far from us. We went about a mile further and camped. The Yankees shelled us but did no harm, they were at too great a distance."[118] The Canonniers bivouacked in very warm weather within a mile or two of the Rappahannock River. "The surrounding scenery," wrote Fontaine, "is *magnificent*. We are among the mountains, and from the tall summits the eye embraces a vista covering miles in extent. Not the least interesting portion of the spectacle is the moving trains and troops of the enemy, three or four miles distant, across the Rappahannock."[119] At night from the Confederate bivouac Fontaine wrote, "The Federal camp fires were gleaming on the hill sides until nearly midnight, and everyone looked forward with various emotions to a desperate contest on the morrow . . . the men were excited, but quiet and subdued, awaiting with calm patience the hour which was to decide their destinies."[120]

Early on the morning of August 26 not a vestige of the Federal army was visible. It had moved off during the night. Three days' rations of crackers and sparing pieces of bacon were issued to the Confederates along with forage for the artillery horses. Besides feeding and caring for the animals, the Canonniers spent most of the warm day resting. They hardly noticed the cannon fire in the distance. There Cire recorded, "We left at 3 p.m. and marched until midnight, we lost our Brigade by taking the wrong road."[121] It was an exhausting march over a difficult and rough road through thickly wooded foothills. Many of the Canonniers were now barefooted, and in the darkness, "I think I must have fallen down a dozen times" wrote a Louisiana artillerist.[122]

At daylight on August 27 Maurin's Battery "came back"[123] and rejoined the long column of men and wagons strung out for miles on a bad road between Jeffersonton and Amissville, six miles apart. After passing the latter place—a quaint little village with a few homes, general store, blacksmith shop, two-room school house, and church (located on the Sperryville-Rappahannock Turnpike that was foremost in moving agricultural goods to other points by four and six horse wagons)—the troops turned to cross the river.[124]

The column moved along an old narrow road full of holes to the Rappahannock River, where they passed the two-story Henson home and store and crossed slightly downstream from Henson's Mill, dam, and raceway.[125] On the other side the road wended along the brows of steep hills and through the shadows of woods under a hot cloudless sky. The dust burned the eyes of the Canonniers and parched their throats while blistered, weary feet dragged on, one foot moving after another. The gray horde, wrote one, were too exhausted "to bestow a glance of admiration to the beautiful scenery through which we were passing."[126] Upon reaching Orlean, with its store and a few houses, and where, if one had the money, honey and bread could be bought, the fatigued Canonniers halted amongst "a great many straggling soldiers that had fallen out."[127]

During the day's advance a soldier wrote that the troops along the column were "almost too tired even to respond, with a cheer, to the grateful salutations of the bevies of ladies fair who at the little towns on our route stood on the streets to encourage us by their approving smiles."[128] After an hours rest in Orlean, Maurin's tired horses and sleepy Canonniers resumed the march, stiff and sore, and plodded along into the night, finally coming to a halt some time around four o'clock in the morning near Big Cobbler Mountain, four miles from the town of Salem. Here the men stopped and fell asleep in open fields fragrant with mint and pennyroyal. An exhausted Cire, before closing his eyes noted that the battery had "caught up with our Brigade (Pryor's.)"[129] A member of Featherston's Brigade wrote, "We never make much progress after night. Bad crossings & bad roads makes our progress so little that the distance gained is a poor compensation for our fatigue & lack of sleep."[130]

Fontaine noted the people along the route were appreciative of the army being there, and the farmers and women gave out food to the passing hoard, but by the time the latter half of the column passed (with the Gunners of Donaldson) they were almost "eaten out of house and home."[131] Fontaine also noticed there was not a murmur of complaint heard from the tired and hungry men although many, especially those without shoes, had blistered feet and "it became a trite remark among the troops, that 'all a Yankee is now worth is his shoes.'"[132] The correspondent also commented on how few stragglers there were from Hood's Texas Brigade and Pryor's Brigade. "I might say, further," wrote Fontaine, "that if there are any heroes in this war, the men of these commands deserve the name" as they "have never faltered in their duty."[133]

After a short night's broken slumber the Canonniers awoke about daylight on August 28 to a light rain and the news that they would soon be going in support of "Stonewall" Jackson's "Left Wing" at Manassas. After awakening, the drivers fed and cared for the animals while many others huddled around campfires for warmth. For a few fortunate soldiers there was warm coffee that was sure to bring shouts of, "I'll take the grounds after you!" and, "After you" and, "Next after you," so that, "it seemed the coffee-grounds had to do service half-a-dozen times round."[134] Also heated over the fires were the roasting ears of green corn of which the men had now to subsist on, along with apples out of the fields, for the commissary wagons were lagging far back. The commanders made a determined effort to restrain the men from stripping the gardens, poultry houses, and pigpens along the route. Fontaine reported, "Gen. Pryor deliberately shot at one of these fellows, whom he caught coming out of a field, loaded down, and made him return and pay for his spoils."[135]

The route was taken up at eight o'clock in the morning with a warm but pleasant breeze, in a beautiful country near the mountains where along the line of march there was picturesque scenery of foothills and broad beautiful valleys dotted with farms and elegant mansions. The progress was again slow as the column literally traveled over hills and dales. Maurin's Battery with Pryor's Brigade went through the pretty little country town of Salem stretching along the hilly road with several stores, one hotel, about 150 houses, and "many young ladies."[136]

Five miles further the guns passed through the Plains, a place of about thirty houses where the road followed the railroad tracks through Thoroughfare Gap. The leading troops of Longstreet's command reached Thoroughfare Gap about three o'clock in the afternoon with Wilcox's command halting two miles back as skirmishing was heard at the mountain pass. Wilcox received orders to detach his three brigades and force his way across the Bull Run Mountains at Hopewell Gap, located three miles to the north. After a three hour rest Wilcox led his brigade, with two artillery batteries following. Featherston's Brigade went next with three artillery batteries, then Pryor's Brigade with the Donaldsonville Artillery.[137]

The detached column traveled over a rough and hilly road of which Wilcox reported, "After a tedious, fatiguing, and rather difficult march, the Gap was reached at 10 p.m. Halting the column, a regiment was detached, preceded by a company, both under . . . Brigadier-General Pryor. . . . In one-half or three-quarters of an hour General Pryor reported that he had threaded his way through the pass as far as Antioch Church, near 1 mile beyond. The troops were then moved forward through the pass, and after posting pickets . . . the command at 12 o'clock bivouacked for the night."[138] The troops slept in an old field covered with stones under bright constellations sparkling in the night sky. Here Corporal Jules Vegue, a twenty-four-year-old French Creole clerk from New Orleans, got lost from his First Louisiana (Coppen's) Zouave Battalion and joined the Donaldsonville Canonniers on the march at Hopewell Gap.[139]

The Gunners of Donaldson, along with the soldiers of Wilcox's command, awoke early on the morning of August 29 on the east side of the Bull Run Mountains. "We could hear Jackson's guns and we knew he must be sorely pressed," wrote a Louisiana artilleryman, adding, "From our elevated position we could see for miles around and what a sight there was . . . so off we go at a rapid pace down the hill side."[140] Soon the horses were sweating, snorting, and foaming while the clanking of chains accompanied the rumbling wheels of the rolling guns and caissons. The artillerymen, with perspiration pouring off, "evinced the anxiety which possessed all to be pushing to the front."[141]

By nine-thirty in the morning, Wilcox's command rejoined Longstreet's Division at the intersection where the red-clay roads from Thoroughfare Gap and Hopewell Gap met just before the deserted village of Haymarket, a place with thirty houses along the railroad tracks. With the roar of cannon and small arms coming from the fields along Bull Run, where Jackson was supposed to be, Wilcox's command joined the line and followed in the rear of Longstreet's troops. The tramping men raised a red cloud of dust with their feet. They passed through dreary rolling plains some times covered with woods, but mostly with high,

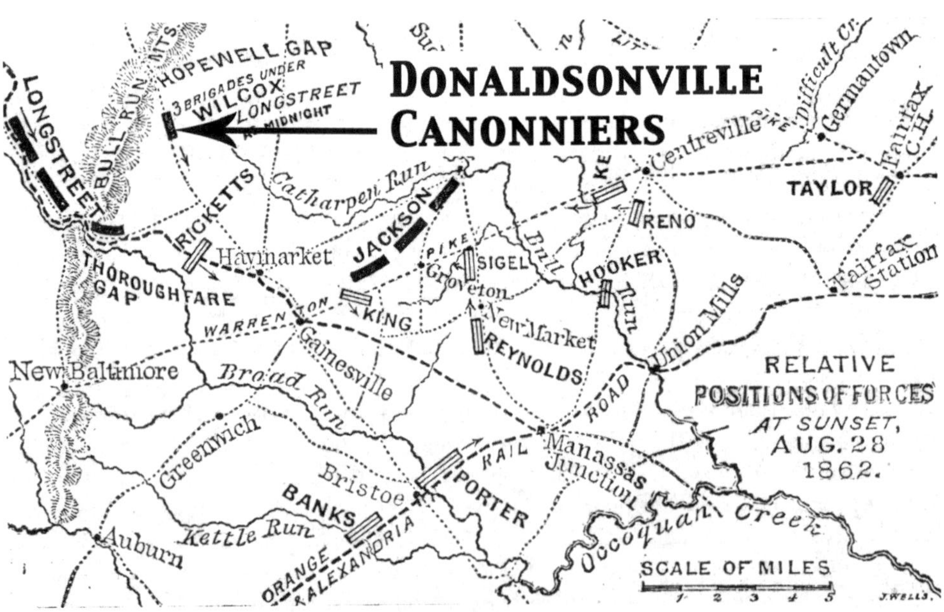

Hopewell Gap heading toward Manassas.
From *Battles and Leaders*.

coarse weeds and rank grass. "The heat and dust," wrote the adjutant of the Washington Artillery, "are something terrible, and the men suffer much for water, some stooping down and drinking from the pools of dirty water by the road-side and from the cow tracks."[142]

Pursuing the line of march along the well-worn road through Gainesville (five houses and a station on the railroad) Wilcox's brigades advanced some two or three miles beyond where they passed through woods on the left of the Warrenton Turnpike. They then deployed in line of battle in a field at right angles to the road. The battle line of infantry advanced nearly three-fourths of a mile further before halting, the enemy in front and not far distant on the plains of Manassas. The artillery turned off into the same piece of woods, but halted in the shade of the trees.

Around noon Longstreet sent for Walton, his artillery commander, who along with Adjutant Owen found the General and his staff with Wilcox in a field dismounted and standing behind their horses. The sharpshooters were popping away vigorously. The adjutant recorded Longstreet directed, "All the long-range guns that can be gotten up to occupy the hill just abandoned by the enemy, and to open upon the enemy's left."[143] Squires's and Miller's companies of Washington Artillery were sent for at once.

Squires remembered, "In going into position I had to deviate from a straight course, making it zig-zag, that I might not run over the bodies of the enemy's dead."[144] The guns were among putrefying corpses of Federals killed the previous day by Jackson's troops. Much to the disgust of Wilcox, the guns also had to pass through his infantry in line of battle. The Washington Artillery positioned itself on a centrally located hill, fringed on the right and left with heavy masses of timber and a broad slightly undulating plain spread in front. The Artillery guns opened fire upon Federal batteries located less than a mile away on hills near Groveton House.[145]

In less than an hour Miller's guns exhausted their ammunition and retired from the field. Under a broiling sun and a heavy fire the Donaldsonville Artillery's two Blakely guns,

Going in.
EAF; courtesy of the Library of Congress.

commanded by Prosper Landry replaced Miller's on a clear ridge about two hundred yards northeast of the Brawner House. For the second time in as many battles Landry's Canonniers again "fought side by side"[146] with Squires's Washington Artillery men.

Joining these guns on the hill was Captain James Reilly's Rowan (North Carolina) Artillery of which, "every horse in the battery carried a rider and the caissons and gun carriages were covered with red caps [of the artillerymen] holding on like monkeys as they thundered over gullies, rocks, even over dead and wounded soldiers."[147] Reilly's guns whirled into position immediately on the left of Squires's two guns where they began to bellow and roar.[148] One rifled-gun of Anderson's Thomas Artillery and one Napoleon gun of Chapman's Dixie Artillery came up on the right of the Donaldsonville Blakely's that were shooting as fast as they could. Landry, field glasses to his eyes, directed their fire by *appelez ordonners* (singing out orders) to his Canonniers.

The Rowan Artillery kept up their fire of shot and shell until, wrote their captain, "The guns grew so hot that the gunners could not touch them, and the left gun of the right section fired a charge without a primer. Although we were under a hot fire, the battery ceased firing and the men raised the muzzles of the guns and emptied all the canteens in them to cool them off. In a few minutes the guns were again in action, and all were well served until the last shot in the chest was fired . . . six hundred and fifty-five rounds of ammunition."[149]

Captain William K. Bachman's German (South Carolina) Artillery later joined the sharp fight and was compelled to pass the line of guns, the captain saying after, "On we passed through a rain of shot and shell and shrapnel! We were all covered with dirt from the shell, as they threw it up near us. . . . At last, we came into position. . . . For two and a half hours we poured it into them."[150] These fourteen guns continued a terrific fire upon the enemy's batteries, except when the gunners and loaders had to beat down the flames of the high and dry grass around them that were frequently set ablaze from the sparks, both from their own guns and the enemy's bursting shells.[151]

Near three o'clock in the afternoon the Federal infantry began an attack on Jackson's troops positioned behind an unfinished railroad cut and embankment, but the fourteen Confederate guns on the hill were positioned at right angles to Jackson's line and commanded the extensive ground over which the enemy was advancing. In twenty minutes the attack was repulsed with the artillery pouring a destructive fire into the panicked ranks of the enemy.

Coming forward and observing the retreat, Fontaine reported, "As they ran, our artillery opened upon the flying mass with shell and round shot. Every ball could be seen taking effect. The enemy fell by scores, until finally the . . . line melted confusedly into the woods. . . . Again they renewed the attack, and gradually the fight became general along nearly the entire column of Jackson. The enemy made tremendous efforts, but the old 'Stonewall' withstood every shock."[152] An artilleryman working with Thomas's gun on the right of the Donaldsonville Blakelys wrote, "Our guns did some good execution."[153]

Near four o'clock in the afternoon, after the infantry assaults on Jackson's line were broken up, the enemy's artillery withdrew out of range. Walton at this time ordered the artillery from the field to refill their ammunition chest from the ordnance wagons that had just come up. After replenishing the caissons in an open field about a mile to the rear, Walton sent word that the gun crews could rest. For a while there were occasional shots from the front and an hour or so before dark a fierce and general engagement took place on the right after which Lee's army bivouacked in line of battle.

Landry's section rejoined Maurin's four guns camped about a mile from Gainesville. With water sparse in camp there was "much suffering . . . experienced in consequence."[154] Many were terribly fatigued, others discomforted by the deprivations, and with the enemy's

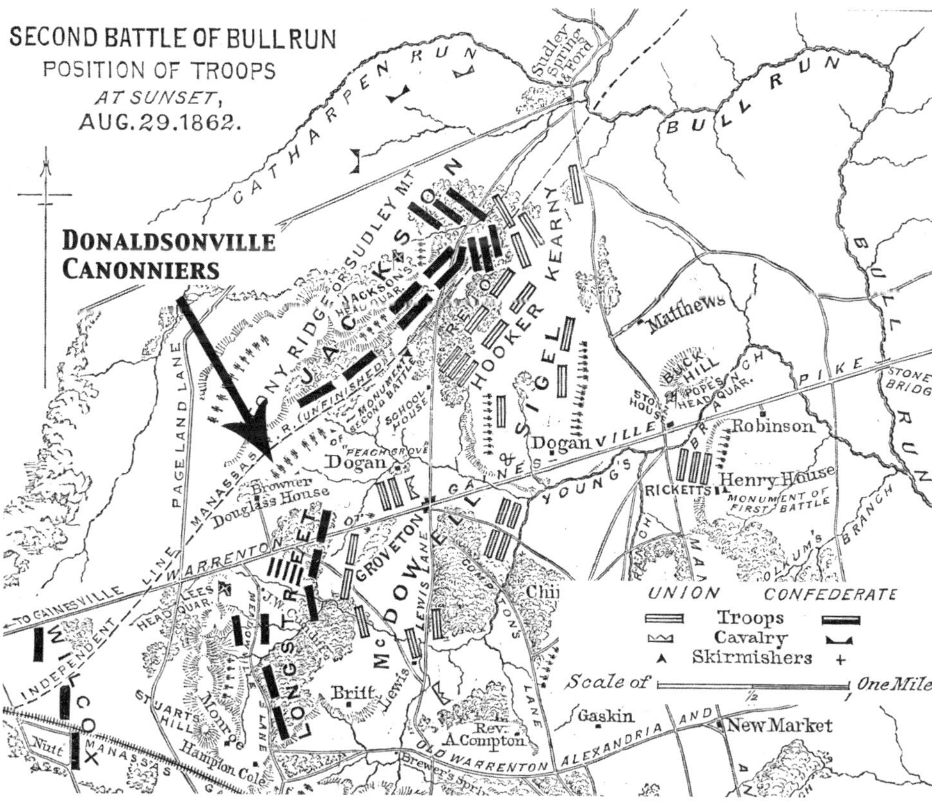

At 2nd Manassas, Walton's Confederate guns, with Lieutenant Prosper Landry commanding two guns of the Donaldsonville Artillery, were located near the Brawner House (Browner Douglas House on map). From *Battles and Leaders*.

campfires visible and extending far off to the left, front, and right, the weary went to sleep expecting the battle to resume at daylight.

Again providence protected the Donaldsonville Artillery with no casualties in men or horses even though they were located in the same position on the hill, and for a much longer time, than Captain Miller's Washington Artillery, which lost three men wounded and five horses. On Landry's immediate left, Squires's had no men injured though they lost one horse killed and two wounded. On Squires's left Reilly's Battery had one man wounded and five horses killed, four by one shot, and on Reilly's left, Bachman's Battery had one man wounded. Anderson's one gun immediately to the right of Landry's had two men wounded by shell fragments. Chapman's Dixie Artillery, the last in line on the right, reported no casualties.

During the evening Walton sent Adjutant Owen to report the condition of affairs to Longstreet, then with Lee and Jackson. Owen later recorded, "Gen. Jackson paid a compliment to our artillery, saying, after having observed the practice of the . . . guns, 'Gen. Longstreet, your artillery is superior to mine.' Our timely arrival probably caused him to look most favorably upon the batteries engaged."[155]

The only disturbances during the night were the movements of the ambulance corps and the groans of the wounded and dying. The next morning before the sun was seen picket firing was heard along the entire front line. With the first streak of daylight, the men sprang up. They prepared for the onset; the drivers doing their usual duties with the animals and the Canonniers checking the guns and ammunition boxes. The hungry men also roamed the nearby cornfields to find for themselves the rations the commissary could not deliver.

By seven o'clock in the morning the Donaldsonville guns and the batteries of Longstreet's division had moved a short distance to positions alongside the Warrenton Turnpike, behind the infantry. There they waited limbered up. Orders passed down the line of guns that warned all to economize with the ammunition, as it could not be replaced immediately. At dawn Steven D. Lee's battalion of reserve artillery, eighteen guns, was sent to the commanding ridge occupied by Walton's guns on the previous day. Throughout the morning Maurin, Landry, and the Gunners of Donaldson observed clouds of dust from the moving columns of troops and heard unremitting small arms and artillery fire that increased in intensity as noon approached. At midday all firing ceased and an ominous silence prevailed, followed by occasional shots. During this time the Canonniers sought some tolerably comfortable positions on the gun and caisson carriages or the ground to doze.

At about three o'clock in the afternoon there was a crash of musketry heard rolling in heavily from Jackson's front, and shortly after, Longstreet, accompanied by his staff and orderlies, passed along the turnpike to the front. Maurin and the other officers of the batteries, thinking that the battle was at hand, ordered the men to stand to their guns and horses. Hardly five minutes had elapsed before a courier came back at full speed saying Longstreet wanted a few batteries. Chapman's, Boyce's, and Reilly's, the nearest, sped forward towards the action. Maurin's guns, along with Squires's and Miller's, and the other batteries, remained in reserve while the battle raged in front with whirls of smoke drifting and the roar of the guns shaking the hills.[156]

In another half hour the charge was ordered by Longstreet, who later wrote, "My troops leaped forward with exultant yells, and all along the line we pushed forward. Farther and still farther back we pressed them."[157] Owen, with the artillery reserve along the turnpike recalled, "Forward sweeps the line, steadily, determinedly; no halting, but 'Forward!' 'Forward!' always 'Forward!' No other order is necessary. The reserve batteries . . . follow, but so rapid is the advance that they cannot get a shot."[158] Landry's two guns joined with Squires's and Miller's as they doubled quick to hold a hill in the immediate vicinity of Groveton. The enemy having fled, they didn't fire their guns. Of the other four Donaldsonville guns under Maurin it was simply recorded: "August 30th Battle of Manassas (battery engaged)."[159]

A staff officer of Longstreet remembered, "The easy, rounded ridges ran at right angles to the turnpike, and over these infantry and artillery poured in pursuit. The artillery would gallop furiously to the nearest ridge, limber to the front, deliver a few rounds until the enemy were out of range, and then gallop again to the next ridge."[160]

During the attack Fontaine viewed a considerable portion of the field from an elevated position and reported,

> Between the armies, the ground is already covered with the dead and wounded, for a distance lengthwise of nearly a mile. Our own artillery are likewise upon commanding positions and you hear the heavy rush of shot, the terrible thumps into the ground, and the crash of trees through which they tear with resistless force. . . . Meanwhile the grand chorus of battle is thundering along our front as if every atom of space had its peculiar echo. . . . The battle raged . . . until after dark, and when . . . the heavens were lit up by the still continued flashes of the artillery, and the meteor flight of shells scattering their iron spray. By this time the enemy had been forced across Bull Run, and their dead covered every acre from the starting point of the fight to the Stone Bridge.[161]

An overcast sky and approaching storm brought on an early darkness with low visibility, causing the battle and the pursuit by Confederate forces to finally end after a mile and a half advance. The retreating Federals hastened to the heights at Centreville. The rainfall soon began and Maurin's guns rejoined Landry's and the reserve artillery about a mile beyond Groveton, where the exhausted artillerymen camped. Except for the snorting horses, nothing was heard except the patter of rainfall that very dark night.

The rain came down all night and into the morning, with a sharp wind blowing and making everyone uncomfortable. While the batteries awaited orders, the traveling forges were kept busy repairing damages and shoeing the horses. Besides being drenched, the Canonniers and Lee's army had to endure the pains of an empty stomach until morning when, by way of captured Yankee haversacks, coffee, salt pork, boiled beef, cracker-bread, and canned vegetables were retrieved. Regardless of the stormy and excessively disagreeable weather, that morning Cire recorded the Canonniers shared "large quantities"[162] of supplies with shoes, after food, being in most demand. For the horses large bundles of hay and bags of corn were also found.

"I do not know whether you would call the act disgraceful or not," wrote Fontaine, "but there is not a dead Yankee in all that broad field who has not been stripped of his shoes or stockings, had his pockets turned inside out, and in numerous cases been left as naked as the hour he was born. If you could see our bare-footed and ragged men, you might think there was even a virtue in stealing from a defeated enemy."[163] Virtue or not, groups of Confederate soldiers dressed in blue sat about the campfires on the soggy wet ground boiling, stewing, frying, sharing, and eating "off and on all night."[164]

On Sunday, August 31, Lee ordered Jackson to take his entire command and cross the Bull Run stream at Sudley Springs, then move north to the Little River Turnpike, and turning southeast, strike the enemy's line of retreat. To aid Jackson, Brigadier General J. E. B. "Jeb" Stuart's cavalry, supported by Pryor's Brigade, were to pass over Bull Run at the destroyed Stone Bridge and create a diversion. The rest of Longstreet's command was to remain on the battlefield until Jackson had a good start, then follow. Maurin, with his six guns, was ordered to rejoin Pryor's Brigade who, at about noon, received his orders from Longstreet to occupy the heights between the streams of Bull Run and Cub Run.

Maurin's Battery, with Pryor's Brigade, moved on the muddy Warrenton Turnpike, which was obstructed by overturned and abandoned wagons, and passed downtrodden meadows with hundreds of bodies. The most sickening were the ones ridden over and crushed by the artillery or cavalry. There were numerous dead horses scattered about along with caissons overturned. The Canonniers passed broken, riddled, or blown down trees, destroyed fences knocked into splinters or houses in undistinguishable heaps of brick, with the dead everywhere, and when they crossed the rising water of Bull Run the wounded and dying of both armies lined the banks. One artillery officer recorded it as a sight he would "never wish to witness again."[165]

The Donaldsonville guns and Pryor's Brigade stopped along the Warrenton Turnpike amidst a wooded plain about four miles east of the battlefield. Cire recorded, "We fired a few shots at the retreating Yankees—we stayed on picket duty until 3 o'clock next morning, there we were ordered to join the main body of the army which had taken the line of march on another road, we caught up with them at daylight."[166]

Maurin's guns slowly followed Pryor's Brigade on the turnpike and back across Bull Run. From there, they headed for Sudley Springs along a narrow and muddy road. The wheels of the gun carriages and caissons made deep cuts through the quicksand and mud. The rain had finally stopped during the morning (September 1), but it was still an awful march that wore out men and horses. The worn road made it worse as the feet of the men, the hoofs of the horses, and the weight of the wheels, sloughed through the muck and mire. In passing houses along the route a Confederate wrote, "The soldiers were very bad, stealing everything eatable they could lay their hands on, after trying to buy it. They were nearly famished, our wagons being still behind. They were also very thirsty, water being very scarce."[167]

Pryor's Brigade and Maurin's Battery moved through an oak forest to the Little River Turnpike where a fatigued Cire wrote, "We marched all day until late in the evening and arrived near Fairfax (Chantilly) Genl. Jackson had a fight and defeated the Yankees, took many prisoners, the Yankee Genl. Kerney was killed."[168] No fires were allowed in camp. "In the wet, showery, drowning rain, we had to spend the night," wrote a high private. "[169]

On September 2 the artillery stirred in the cold and rain at four o'clock in the morning when Longstreet ordered forward a line of battle. It was reported that the Yankees were in force and approaching. By dawn it was clear, cool, and windy with reports the enemy had now gone and fallen back. For the day Cire wrote, "We marched a short distance and camped to cook rations."[170] After the movement of the guns things remained quiet the balance of the day. The sun's warm beams darted through the gaps in the clouds and dried the wet clothes of the Canonniers. The whole army rested here near Chantilly where the provision trains reached the troops, who were ordered to cook three days' rations of meat and bacon.

Though it had been a source of much regret that *Le Compagnie d'artillerie de Donaldsonville* was not able to stand side-by-side with the Battalion Washington Artillery at the First Battle of Manassas, the Donaldsonville Artillery was there for *une deuxième rivière "taureau"* (a Second Bull Run). With the Second Manassas Campaign ended, Lee reported, "The history of the achievements of the army from the time it advanced from Gordonsville leaves nothing to be said in commendation of the courage, fortitude and good conduct of both officers and men"[171]

Chapter Six

Enfers d'artillerie
(Artillery Hell)

Unlike prior campaigns, the one embarked upon on September 3, 1862, would advance into Maryland, as General Robert E. Lee decided to lead the Army of Northern Virginia into the "Old Line State." Lee admitted his army was "not properly equipped for invasion, lacking much of the material of war, feeble in transportation, the troops poorly provided with clothing, and thousands of them destitute of shoes."[1] Yet he believed his army was "strong enough to detain the enemy on the northern frontier until the approach of winter should render his advance into Virginia difficult, if not impracticable."[2]

Douglas Southall Freeman, the Army of Northern Virginia's ablest and highly authoritative historian reasoned "destiny beckoned northward,"[3] and after Lee considered "necessity, advantage, and risk,"[4] he set the army in motion to take advantage of an invasion of the North. An artillery officer writing later about this campaign recounted how Lee's army now "had acquired that magnificent morale which made them equal to twice their numbers."[5] That wonderful self-esteem remained with Captain Victor Maurin's Canonniers long after the war and was characterized by Donaldsonville Private Hypolite Templet, eulogized decades later: "To have belonged to the Army of Northern Virginia to him was a pride greater than any other."[6]

The army moved at daylight, with the Donaldsonville battery again following Brigadier General Roger Pryor's Brigade from the Little River Turnpike to Frying Pan Road, where a small frame clapboard church of the same name was passed. While going by, a private mused it was "suggestive of some hot gospels, and a place where doubtless the doctrine of total damnation of man was preached."[7]

Canonnier Artificer François "Bienvenu" Cire related that on September 3, 1862, the Donaldsonville Artillery moved all day with their smoke covered caissons groaning, rickety wagons rattling, and the worn wheels carrying the guns creaking.[8] The column continued on the Dranesville Road through rolling wooded country to Dranesville, an indistinct community of houses and the junction with the Alexandria-Leesburg Turnpike. There the Canonniers and other artillerists with their batteries moved onto the turnpike. According to one diarist in the column they were "not aware where we are going."[9] A Louisiana artillerist noted it was a clear day with pleasant weather, and though the troops were never in better spirits, not a mouthful of food was had. There was not even a sign of any commissary wagons. The day's march ended near five o'clock in the afternoon about a mile or so past Dranesville.[10]

Before starting out on September 4 Donaldsonville Corporal John O'Hara noted in his memo book that Canonnier Quartermaster Sergeant Jonathan Scheuer delivered fourteen ounces of salt meat and flour per man that constituted four days' worth of rations. O'Hara gladly wrote that he took responsibility for issuing out the fourteen ounces per man to the squads.[11] The artillerists cooked their scanty rations and then, as usual, ate them in one sitting while waiting for the infantry in large numbers to move along the turnpike.

After their rest, Cire recorded, "We left in the evening and marched all night, and after having crossed Goose Creek—we camped."[12] In actuality Maurin's Battery was on the road all night, but didn't move much owing to the crowded state of the dusty road. When they did move it was very slow with constant stopping. "The road," according to another battery gunner, "was crowded with wagons and consequently we made slow progress. We were detained three hours at Goose Creek, a small stream two miles from Leesburg, where the ford was deep and miry, and the water came near running over our guns."[13] The creek was twenty-five yards wide with wooded bluffs. The bridge across it had been burnt.

Cire's September 5 entry reads: "We marched and halted on the south side of Leesburg, one mile from town."[14] Thousands of soldiers camped around the fine old town and Major General James Longstreet remembered, "As our columns approached Leesburg, 'Maryland, my Maryland' was in the air, and on the lips of every man from General Lee down to the youngest drummer boy."[15] All seemed to be in a cheerful mood and expected brilliant results in crossing the Potomac River and entering Maryland. "Many a youthful hero," wrote a veteran, "looked forward to his triumphant entry into the Federal capitol, or to a joyous reception at the hands of the fair women of Baltimore."[16]

On September 5 and 6, Longstreet's column of five divisions moved from the picturesque environs of Leesburg over pleasantly variegated hills to the crossings of the Potomac River at the not too distant fords.[17] The Donaldsonville Artillery and other batteries on September 6 stopped to feed their horses in Leesburg, a city of square blocks filled generally with small and mostly red brick or stone houses, along with some handsome mansions. In passing through the town of about 1,500 inhabitants a Louisiana artillerist noted how "the ladies greeted us and how much it reminded [him] of home."[18] Of the demonstrative ladies standing on the curbstones lining the narrow streets, another of the Louisiana gunners happily jotted in his diary, "Saw a fine array of beauty."[19] After feeding the horses, the Canonniers moved on about two miles from town to a field near a large spring along Nolan's Ferry Road.[20] A Confederate wrote at the time, "The pond constituting the spring-head is 25 feet across and from two to six feet deep, furnishing pure sparkling water of icy coldness, sufficient to supply a hundred thousand men, and half as many animals."[21]

For the remainder of the day and the next, September 7, the Donaldsonville Canonniers camped with other batteries and spent their time snoozing on the green turf and allowing stragglers to catch up. The unfortunate drivers taking care of the worn horses, and the artificers busy repairing and putting into shape broken and worn equipment, had no time to rest. Scheuer was busy too and delivered another day's ration of fresh meat and flour. It still was not enough food, and artillerymen from the different batteries went about looking to find a meal, but food was almost impossible to obtain as the whole army had passed through and eaten the town out. A Leesburg resident took note of the soldiers "running over the country, hunting something to eat."[22]

The artillery now showed the effects of the long marches and severe fighting. During the stop in Leesburg, Longstreet sent orders to Colonel J. B. Walton: "To proceed at once to a thorough inspection of the Batteries . . . condemning all unserviceable horses and batteries found. From the batteries thus found with useless animals the good horses will be taken to supply Batteries that may be in comparative good order. The Batteries thus found unserviceable will be left behind and the good horses taken from them ought to put the remaining batteries in excellent order."[23]

Maurin's Battery of 113 men and 112 horses was inspected and considered to be in relative good order. The Canonniers' assiduity towards their horses and mules forestalled many of the animals from being too much reduced by the service, but there were weak ones and these were exchanged, per instructions, with Captain Robert Stribling's Fauquier (Virginia) Artillery. In the inspection the Donaldsonville guns and accoutrements were rated in good order, but Maurin was instructed to exchange his two English-made Blakely guns with a depleted battery and in return received two of the tough, practical, and accurate 10-pounder Parrott rifles.[24]

Maurin's leadership, discipline, intrepidness, and determination maintained the efficiency of the Donaldsonville Artillery despite the long and rapid marches with insufficient supplies of food and the want of shoes. No account or document mentions any Canonnier stragglers during the campaign, though there must have been at least a few in that "all the roads of northern Virginia were livid with soldiers, comprehensively denominated 'stragglers;' but the great majority of these men had fallen out from the advancing column from physical inability to keep up with it . . . they had no shoes, and their bleeding feet could carry them no further, or the heavy march without rations had broken them down."[25] How ever many Canonnier stragglers there were, it did not affect the efficiency of the Donaldsonville Artillery. They were judged to be well disciplined.[26]

On the march the men had become exhausted, dirty, lean, and unshaven. Their caps had lost their color. No two dressed alike and their clothes were foul and raggedy. Many of them were barefooted.[27] It is understandable that during the inspection the Canonnier clothing, even with Yankee blue, was rated not very good. The men had bathed in the nearby icy coldness of Big Spring's limestone water, and their military appearance during the inspection was deemed, surprisingly, "Good."[28]

Since Maurin and Lieutenant Prosper Landry were the only commission officers present for duty, an election to fill the battery's officer vacancy was authorized and held in camp on Sunday, September 7. The vote resulted in the promotion of twenty-three-year-old, hazel-eyed Corporal Jean Baptiste Camille Mollere to Second Lieutenant. Mollere was known for his "faithful performance of duty and the exhibition of soldierly qualities of the highest order."[29] This new position placed him in charge of the three smoothbore guns while assuming Prosper Landry's tedious duty of certifying and witnessing the completion of the four copies of the battery's bimonthly muster roll. Landry continued in charge of the three rifle pieces.[30]

The many batteries with the divisions were much depleted in personnel and horses, and of the six batteries assigned to Longstreet's brigades only the Donaldsonville Artillery rejoined its command (Pryor's) in the Maryland Campaign. The others, Captain A. L. Rogers's Loudoun (Virginia) Artillery of Kemper's Brigade, Captain Robert M. Stribling's Fauquier (Virginia) Artillery of Jenkin's Brigade, and Captain Edwin J. Anderson's Thomas (Virginia) Battery of Wilcox's Brigade, were all considered depleted after the inspection and, with ten other batteries from the army, ordered detained at Leesburg. The Dixie (Virginia) Artillery, Captain William H. Chapman, previously assigned to Featherston's Brigade was attached to the Battalion of Washington Artillery and later disbanded. Captain James Dearing's Lynchburg (Viriginia) Artillery, assigned to Pickett's Brigade, remained in Richmond it seems, for the want of horses when the campaign began. The battery assigned to Pickett's Brigade at Gordonsville was the Fourth Company from the Washington Artillery Battalion.

After receiving the two Parrott guns, ammunition, and serviceable horses, Maurin received orders on September 8 for his six-gun battery to rejoin Pryor's Brigade now camped about Frederick, Maryland, with Longstreet's command and the Army of Northern Virginia. Owing to the army being stripped of all encumbrances and many wagons left at the Manassas battlefield to supplement the ambulances in evacuating the wounded, Maurin's Battery was apt to have just two wagons to carry the animals forage and haul the gun's ammunition not carried in the caissons. Without the extra wagons the Gunners of Donaldson now bore the burden of their own *petit equipements* (kits) and *musettes* (haversacks) that were by this time reduced to "the simplest elements and smallest dimensions."[31]

After departing Big Springs, Cire recorded, "We left camp at 3 p.m. . . . crossed the Potomac at White's Ford."[32] Like those who had gone before, the Canonniers "halted, stripped, or pulled frayed trouser legs high . . . and plunged into the shallow water of the boundary river."[33] All the artillerymen, due to the care of the horses on the march, were "positively prohibited from riding on the ammunition chest or guns."[34] In wading into the wide and very clear blue river there was "splashing, slipping over smooth boulders, playfully wrestling, shouting, yelling, singing . . . and general noise, confusion and jollification, like a mob of school boys bantering."[35]

After crossing Cire reported they "marched along the canal to the [aqueduct] Bridge, then crossed and after marching about a mile further, we halted and camped for the balance of the night."[36] The Chesapeake and Ohio Canal parallels the course of the Potomac River on the Maryland side, and Maurin's Battery followed the river and canal to the Monocacy River, where an aqueduct over 500 feet in length spans the river. An artilleryman years later would remember a "distinct impression of the dripping nasty passage under the canal."[37]

The days lately had been hot, but it was noted that this evening felt like a fall afternoon. After crossing the aqueduct and camping, the artillerists were expected to cut green corn from the stalks in the field for their first meal in Maryland. Provender transactions from local farmers also supplied feed to the horses.[38]

On the morning of September 9 Maurin's Battery rolled past the country people lining the road who were "gazing in open-eyed wonder upon . . . ragged Rebels."[39] A few of these civilians gave food for their haversacks, even as they passed their fields that had been flourishing crops of grain but were now unsightly after being trodden down by the feet of Lee's passing army before. The Donaldsonville battery, like Lee's army, traveled "clad in fluttering rags" of gray (and sometimes blue) jackets as "the groves and green fields of Maryland made vocal with laughter."[40] Cire wrote they "passed through Bucktown, and we halted about 3 miles from Frederick City."[41] Actually the town's name is Buckeystown, and Cire probably had difficulty finding out the name considering "the houses were all shut up & nearly all the people we saw looked as if they lost a dear friend."[42]

The Army of Northern Virginia was camped about the city of Frederick, described as quite a large place and pleasantly situated in the center of a beautiful valley with perhaps 10,000 to 12,000 inhabitants. Here the Donaldsonville Artillery rejoined Pryor's Brigade, bivouacking on the bank of the Monocacy River, close to the remains of the double track iron railroad bridge that had been blown up the day before.

The army awaited orders on this pleasant and clear day, and with nothing transpiring, Lee's troops bathed and cleaned their clothes in the nearby river. For at least a mile the river was full of splashing and washing men. Though the soldiers had helped themselves to roasting ears of corn and green apples around Buckeystown, the quartermaster and commissary officers were now supplying the army with provisions like bread and meat from Frederick. The men were also paid here, but by the time the Canonnier contingent could reach the city it had pretty much been swept clean of consumables.

The horses and mules fared better on this day as Maurin, through a requisition, acquired a near normal day's ration for the animals with 1,152 pounds of oats and 112 pounds of corn. This was better than the husk and stalks of corn they were fed when the Canonniers themselves ate roasted ears.[43]

Lee's army was up early on September 10, with reveille at three o'clock in the morning. Two hours later the Canonniers of Donaldsonville were ready and awaiting their position to join Longstreet's long column on the march. It dawned bright and beautiful, with Maurin's Battery finally starting out with Pryor's Brigade after three hours of waiting. By now it was "horribly dusty"[44] with the troops, artillery, and wagons moving, but with bands playing and colors flying. The Louisianians filed through the long avenue of Frederick City and, wrote a Private,

> We were rather disappointed at our reception, which was decidedly cool. . . . . It was true the streets were generally well filled with citizens, and the balconies and porches too, but there was positively no enthusiasm, no cheers, no waving handkerchiefs and flags—instead a death-like silence—some houses were closed tight . . . there were many friendly people in the windows and doors, but they seemed afraid to make any manifestation of their feelings—only smiling covertly.
>
> The marching soldiery did not imitate the cautious silence of the Frederick citizens; they had full haversacks, and therefore light hearts, jokes, witticisms, and badinage flew from lip to lip, and some one striking up a song, it was chanted . . . and in that way we went through the most loyal city in Maryland.[45]

One of the Louisianians noted the army passed through in good order with the artillery boys marching in front of their batteries and singing their choruses. All were in

> the merriest and jolliest mood possible, indulging occasionally in good-natured chaff. . . . Any peculiarity of costume or surroundings of any person was sure to bring out some remark that would set whole regiments in a roar. On a small gallery stood a buxom young lady, with laughing black eyes, watching the scene before her; on her breast she had pinned a small flag, the 'stars and stripes.' This was observed, and some soldier sang out, 'look h'yar, miss, better take that flag down; we're awful fond of charging breast-works!' This was carried down the line amid shouts of laughter.[46]

Upon reaching the Canonniers it would have been said amongst them, "*En avant à la parapets!*" while excitedly looking upon the little lady standing by her colors. Longstreet too noted, "It was a rollicking march, the Confederates playing and singing, as they marched through the streets."[47]

After leaving the city, Longstreet's column and the Gunners of Donaldson marched along the narrow and winding National Turnpike, a macadamized roadway. They passed over the Catoctin Mountains at Braddock Heights, where the peak is 950 feet high and the pass 250 feet wide. Moving into Middletown Valley the troops in the column were struck with the beautiful scenery. A sergeant wrote, "Not a mile have we passed over but there has been something to attract the eye. The houses and barns all have a thrifty appearance. The orchards are weighted down with the best of apples, with a rich flavor than any I have ever ate. . . . Scattered along the road is flour mills . . . while every inch of space is filled with wheat or flour. Don't look much like starvation in this land of plenty. The corn is just in roasting ear and caused . . . a large number of roasting ear thieves."[48]

Regarding foraging another soldier recorded,

> The great horde of Negro cooks and servants that usually followed the army were allowed to roam at will over the surrounding country, just the same as down in Virginia.

> The Negroes foraged . . . wherever they went, and . . . they were quite an adjunct to the Commissary Department, gathering chickens, butter, flour, etc. Even now, when so near the Free States, with nothing to prevent them from making their escape, the Negroes showed no disposition to take advantage of their situation and conditions . . . some few were lost . . . but they were lost like many of the soldiers—captured by foraging parties or left broken down along the roadside.[49]

It was reported by a northern diarist in Maryland that "Negroes . . . were clad in all kinds of uniforms, not only castoff or captured United States uniforms, but in coats with Southern buttons, State buttons, etc. These were shabby, but not shabbier or seedier than those worn by white men in the rebel ranks. . . . They were supplied . . . with knapsacks, haversacks, canteens, etc.; and . . . were seen riding horses and mules, driving wagons, *riding on caissons* . . . mixed up with all the rebel horde."[50]

The day became warm, and a gray clad diarist thought the march "would never halt."[51] After about twelve miles, Cire recorded that the Canonniers camped on the other side of Middletown, just outside the town in fields along the turnpike. In passing through the town, with its solidly built and well-appointed houses, air of modest wealth and comfort, and about nine hundred inhabitants, it was found to be almost deserted except for women. "It is a real Union place" wrote a Louisiana artillerist. "[52] Another soldier noted, "Middletown was entirely Union, and some of the Ladies expressed their opinion quite freely."[53] The talk that night by many a soldier and artilleryman around the campfire as they cooked up their "little balls of cornmeal, covered with ashes in which they had been baked"[54] was "speculation as to our destination."[55]

The Donaldsonville Artillery's destiny was now directly linked to Major General Lafayette McLaws's command. His four brigades and five batteries,[56] along with Anderson's Division of some 8,000 men that included Pryor's Brigade and Maurin's Battery, were detached from Longstreet's command. At daylight on the morning of a very warm September 11, McLaws led his brigade and Anderson's from Middleton, following the road toward Burkittsville. Lee's orders were read at the first rest. McLaws reported they were "to take possession of Maryland Heights, and endeavor to capture the enemy at Harper's Ferry and vicinity."[57] Lee's orders were issued in Special Order No. 191 and, according to the Southern army's preeminent historian Douglas Southall Freeman, McLaws had "the most difficult tactical operation in the effort to capture Harpers Ferry."[58]

The march continued on. As they approached Burkittsville, a church steeple was seen above the trees and upon reaching and passing through the town's one street, the command was met with a "warm reception from some few people in the village."[59] A little further on, camp was made in a field where Canonnier Private Octave Landry bemoaned, "We have nothing to eat but green apples and corn."[60] Confederates generally complained about the commissary department's lack of rations, and the Canonniers no doubt grumbled about *la nourriture* (the food), especially as dining well was considered "a pleasure" by Louisiana's Creoles and Cajuns.[61] The enjoyment also included "its preparation" along with "eating, one of life's genuine delights."[62] Of their *culinaire* (culinary) skills one private remembered, "We were hungry . . . and our *menu* consisted of apples and corn. We toasted, we burned, we stewed, we boiled, we roasted these two together, and singly, until there was not a man whose form had not caved in, and who had not a bad attack of diarrhea."[63]

The lack of sanitation made things worse. The same private wrote, "The situation . . . was deplorable . . . they were dirty, tattered and infested with vermin . . . these insects, which in camp parlance were called graybacks [*le pou* by the Cajuns]. . . Every evening . . . when the army halted and bivouacked for the night, hundreds of the soldiers could be seen, sitting on the roads or fields, half denuded with their clothes in their laps busily cracking, between the two thumb-nails, these creeping nuisances . . . to have a daily examination and execution was a habit just as regularly and naturally indulged in as washing our faces and hands."[64] During this campaign particularly, a Louisiana artillerist recorded, "It was an hourly scene for the men to congregate, take off clothing and inspect the seams. It was reported that . . . mites were found branded '(I. F. W.) In for the War.'"[65]

On September 12, the Donaldsonville Artillery took up the march with Anderson's Division on a difficult movement as they hauled the guns, caissons, and wagons up and over the shingly side of South Mountain at Brownsville Gap, an elevation a little over one thousand feet. Their trek up went through a panorama of autumn landscape. Upon reaching the gap, which was gilded by the rays of the September sun, a member of Pryor's Brigade wrote, "From the top . . . you had a fine view of the most beautiful, undulating valley, stretching out for many miles to the north and south, thickly dotted with neat farm houses and fine fields almost ready for harvest."[66] Cire noted they could "see the country for 25 miles around, it is a beautiful scene."[67]

The slog down was on a steep path of dirt and rocks. Keeping the horses under control was tedious until they reached the Brownsville settlement of a few houses. From there they continued towards the Potomac River along the South Mountain Road, which ran beside the "grandeur and loveliness"[68] of broad Pleasant Valley. Although the men were short on rations, their thirst was satisfied along the route. "It was a valley of nice running water. There were more good gushing small springs than I ever saw along a valley road," wrote a soldier in Pryor's Brigade.[69]

McLaws detached the brigades of Kershaw and Barksdale with orders to carry the formidable Maryland Heights across the valley while Cobb's Brigade supported Kershaw's at the base of the Heights. Wright's Brigade moved along South Mountain to overlook the Weverton Pass, situated alongside the Potomac River. The brigades of Semmes and Mahone were left on the valley road opposite Brownsville Gap to guard the other passes over South Mountain. The four remaining brigades of Wilcox, Pryor, Featherston, and Armistead moved along the South Mountain Road, keeping up with the advance of Kershaw's Brigade on Maryland Heights. Wright's troops gained a position on South Mountain overlooking Weverton without opposition, and at sundown Anderson pushed forward Pryor's Brigade toward Weverton, where he positioned his troops to defend the pass between the mountain and the Potomac River, guarding the main road from Frederick to Harpers Ferry.[70]

Upon arriving in support of Pryor's Brigade at Weverton,[71] Maurin's guns went into battery. Cire recorded they "opened fire on the Yankee's cavalry near the gap, and we slept that night on the rocks near the gap."[72] A few booming rounds from the Donaldsonville guns echoed and reverberated throughout the distant mountain ravines. When firing ceased, it was described how, "The objects and scenery of this place present on a calm evening by a clear moonlight, many of the most grand and sublime prospects in nature. The beautiful Potomac and the 'silver mantle' cast on the waters, mountains, rocks and trees by the reflected rays of the full moon . . . an assemblage of the most picturesque and gorgeous scenery, and . . . is truly enchanting."[73]

Enchanting or not, on the morning of September 13 Cire recorded, "We hear the fighting that is going on Maryland Heights."[74] During the day the weather was excessively warm, and though there were a number of springs of the purest mountain water, the soldier's thoughts turned to a "longing for the meat and bread diet."[75] Unfortunately there was no bread to be had, but there was cattle around. "There we got some of the best beef of the whole war," wrote one of the guardians of Weverton Pass.[76]

During the day some men from Washington were captured. Pryor escorted them to McLaws's headquarters where it was said the enemy was advancing and skirmishing up the river, by way of Frederick. The troops, wrote one, "Expect the enemy to come up the river."[77] Pryor's Brigade with Maurin's guns moved into a better position, deployed, and prepared to defend the pass, while Wright's Brigade formed a line of battle on the steep side of the mountain overlooking Weverton. By the end of the day, with the men resting on their arms, the expectant soldier added the enemy "did not come."[78]

On September 14 Maurin was instructed to move his guns forward, towards the east where the adjoining village of Knoxville was located along the river with the B. & O. Railroad and C. & O. Canal. This "dirty, desolate"[79] little village with its small industries was situated on an easy slope, from which the view north extended for many miles up the fertile Middletown Valley over undulating fields. In the distance to the west Harpers Ferry Gap and the waters of the Potomac and Shenandoah could be seen. Towering above were Elk Ridge, Blue Ridge, and South Mountain, all standing in clear sight. Three of Maurin's guns were positioned along the railroad tracks near the river. The other three stood on an adjoining hill covering the valley road. During the day the Donaldsonville artillerists could hear the booming of cannons over towards Harpers Ferry.

"Startling news" came during the chilly night as an officer on McLaws's staff related "that the enemy had carried the Pass & were in the valley!" The officer recorded in his diary that this was "very sad news for us . . . so we are here between two fires. . . . A very anxious predicament . . . anxious feeling in all our bosoms—sat up late consulting. All feel that tomorrow will be a bloody day."[80] The two fires mentioned were the 13,000 Federals still occupying Harpers Ferry and the Federal Sixth Army Corps of 12,000 men now in possession of Crampton's Gap (one mile north of the Brownsville Gap) with access to Pleasant Valley. McLaws's ten brigades were now in great danger between the two forces.

"His one chance of safety," wrote an artillery officer, "was in an early surrender of Harper's [*sic*] Ferry to afford him an outlet for escape."[81] An officer in Pryor's Brigade wrote, "Our salvation depended upon the fall of [Harpers Ferry]; every officer and private knew it, and the suspense was awful."[82]

Around three o'clock in the morning on September 15 Pryor and Wright went to McLaws's headquarters to get instructions. Within half an hour every soldier, including the Gunners of Donaldson were up and awake, huddled together and trying to keep warm as their "teeth chattered."[83] McLaws's staff officer recorded, "I pray to God that he," referring to Jackson's forces besieging Harpers Ferry, "may take the place and thus give us a fair fight with the enemy in our present front." At six o'clock in the morning a terrible fire was heard from Harpers Ferry and the continuous roar that echoed through the hills told the men that the siege was on. Three hours later the firing ceased.

"The joyful tidings thrilled along our line like an electric flash that Harper's Ferry with all its garrison, stores, and supplies, had surrendered," wrote the officer in Pryor's Brigade.[84] Pryor's troops and the Canonniers standing by their guns celebrated as there was "all the cheering you never heard."[85]

Official confirmation was received at ten o'clock in the morning. The enemy showed no disposition to advance into Pleasant Valley from Crampton's Gap. McLaws went to see Jackson and left directions for Anderson to push the wagon train across the river to Harpers Ferry as fast as possible and follow with the infantry. Pryor and Wright's brigades with Maurin's Battery remained to guard the rear at Weverton Pass.[86]

McLaws returned and rode to Weverton to give instructions to Pryor and Wright. Upon seeing the C. & O. Canal full of water, he directed Pryor "to cut the canal just above a culvert near the place, which he did, and . . . also broke the canal lock."[87] The two brigades and Maurin's Battery were then withdrawn towards Sandy Hook leading to Harpers Ferry along a narrow, winding road with the C. & O. Canal on one side and the perpendicular rocks of Maryland Heights on the other. Cire simply recorded, "That night we left our position and slept on the road."[88] McLaws reported the troops slept as they waited in line to pass over the river on the crowded pontoon bridge into Harpers Ferry.

On the morning of September 16, Cire recorded in his Canonnier memorandum: "We left in the morning passed through Sandy Hook and crossed the Potomac on a pontoon at Harpers Ferry. We marched through the town in front of the prisoners, drawn up in line . . . we continued our march towards Shepardstown."[89] It was after two o'clock in the morning when McLaws and Anderson's commands crossed, followed by Pryor and Wright's Brigades around eleven o'clock in the morning. Cire didn't mention it, but it was a terribly hot day during the morning hours with a burning sun and no breeze, though it did become overcast with a little air stirring from time to time later. Along the route there was "tedious waiting"[90] as the river crossing was very much impeded by many of the paroled prisoners passing over the bridge and frequent accidents that caused temporary halts to the wagon train and batteries. The streets of Harpers Ferry were also crowded with Yankee prisoners and wagons. While marching through, "the ragged, forlorn appearance" of the Southern men "excited the combined merriment and admiration" of the Federal prisoners.[91]

Many of McLaws and Anderson's men received a day's ration of bread or five hard-tacks each while going through the town. Others got nothing. This caused much grumbling, and the men complained bitterly because most of the booty had been devoured or appropriated by Jackson's troops.[92]

Continuing on past Harpers Ferry along a choking, dusty road, Maurin's gunners, exhausted and with sore feet, went over and around numerous hills until McLaws and Anderson's divisions finally halted, the column scattered for two miles along the route. After stopping, the troops rested among the deep deposit of leaves in the woods along the roadside near Halltown,[93] with its few houses along Flowering Springs Run and fork in the road that turned to the right toward Shepardstown. McLaws reported, "The entire command was very much fatigued."[94] Octave Landry recorded that the Donaldsonville battery camped at midday but "late in the afternoon resumed the march and at midnight stopped at camp; about ½ hour after received orders to resume the march immediately and started towards Shepherdstown."[95]

McLaws had ordered the march to continue again at three o'clock in the afternoon and the column moved on, even after it got dark. Within two miles of Shepardstown, the scattered command halted around midnight. Soon after stopping, instructions to hasten forward were received from Lee. McLaws ordered his and Anderson's men to move again. During this stop many of the men were content to fall upon the bare ground and snatch a few moments of rest. It was reported that many, after falling asleep, did not wake when the order came urging them forward.[96]

Straggling was a problem, and one witness noted how the men were very bad off for shoes. The ranks were greatly reduced as a result of the hard and incessant marching over Maryland's graveled turnpike roads, which cut up feet terribly, and caused bleeding and soreness. Many had rags tied around their feet for protection as they tried to keep up. Their diet too had much to do with men lagging behind. The artillery's lean Confederate stock struggled as well, the horses worked hard on short rations, pulling the guns and caissons through daylight and darkness.

The night was very dark as McLaws's Division, followed by Anderson's, moved on along a narrow road through wooded country. A steady drizzle of rain started to fall shortly after midnight, and the men became soaked to their skins when it turned into a downpour. An officer in McLaws's command managed to scribble in his diary, "So tired and cold."[97] Another officer later wrote, "It was tramp, tramp, the whole night long; mounted officers dozed on their horses, and the men fell asleep as they stood at every one of the momentary halts caused by the temporary and vexatious stoppings of the jaded teams [of horses pulling artillery and wagons] that intervened along the line."[98] The column's pace quickened at times, but it was still a hard, slow, and straggling march with fatigued men falling out by the wayside. The overexertion reduced many to the state of sleepwalking, and "not a sound could be heard except the din of the moving artillery."[99]

A comparison of units in the column of Anderson's Division struggling along with the Donaldsonville Artillery reveals how hard the march was. A member of the Third Virginia Regiment of Pryor's Brigade recorded on the morning of September 17, 1862, "the march was so severe that when the roll was called only thirty-seven men out of about four hundred were present."[100] The Eighth Alabama Regiment, Wilcox's Brigade, had "only 120"[101] men, while the Twenty-second Georgia Regiment, Wright's Brigade, had "about 60."[102] The whole of Mahone's Brigade "mustered only eighty-two officers and men."[103]

It was the same in McLaws's Division with "only forty-five men"[104] present in the 8th South Carolina, Kershaw's Brigade. In Company C, Eighteenth Mississippi Regiment of Barksdale's Brigade, it was recorded they "left Harpers Ferry with over sixty men and three officers, but . . . sixteen men and one officer" remained in the morning.[105] One of these Mississippians wrote, "Other companies, of course, suffered similar diminution. The march was one of the severest . . . about thirty miles in fourteen hours."[106]

Through the night Maurin, Prosper Landry, and Mollere led their sections of Canonniers and horses hauling their six guns and caissons. Though some fell by the wayside or fell behind, it seems the majority of the Donaldsonville men were able to keep up.[107] Their *Historical Memoranda* indicates that only two members of the battery at Harpers Ferry did not make it to Sharpsburg, old Michel Morin, who later caught up, and Adam Schriver, suffering from chronic diarrhea. Private Cyrille Decoux (another twenty-four-year-old French Creole clerk from New Orleans) of Company A, Seventh Louisiana Battalion, the St. Paul's Foot Rifles, became "*en avant*" and joined the Donaldsonville Artillery on this campaign.[108]

The rain stopped in the predawn hours of September 17. The sky lightened, revealing a heavy overcast and foggy mist covering the fields. The leading surviving elements of McLaws's column reached the vicinity of Lee's headquarters near Sharpsburg at about sunrise with the column's long, drenched, and raggedy gray line following and stretching back four miles. During the rainy night they had traveled nearly twelve miles between Harpers Ferry and Sharpsburg.

With day dawning, the Gunners of Donaldson went through quaint Shepherdstown, with its rows of gabled-roofed old houses flush with the street and crowds of hungry, sick, lean, and straggling soldiers. After exiting the town, Maurin's wet guns and caissons and tired men and horses moved over a narrow and stony road that in one spot was very steep and difficult for vehicles. They traveled less than a mile on this route that lay partly along the face of a rocky and precipitous cliff on one side and the Potomac River on the other. Finally, the guns reached the ford called Boteler's.[109] Here the stalwart but exhausted Canonniers entered the water with the sun rising, their hunger gnawing mightily on their stomachs. The Donaldsonville artillerymen probably took no notice as they passed the eighty-foot high bluffs on their right hand side, which were now left behind when they and their horses, pulling guns and caissons, negotiated the somewhat hazardous and stony three hundred yard wide and three-foot deep, swift-flowing Potomac.

After reaching the Maryland side of the river and the willow-fringed towpath along the C. & O. Canal, Maurin's Battery followed the column over gentle and rounded hills along stiff red clay roads to the outskirts of the village named Sharpsburg. There, near Lee's headquarters, the infantry was allowed to rest in a high grassy field along the main road.

"The cannonading," wrote one of the resting soldiers, "was an indication of trouble awaiting us."[110] An additional warning was the groans of the wounded that passed them in ambulances. Another of Anderson's soldiers observed, "It was often difficult to tell which was the worst off, many of the broken down soldiers, or the wounded."[111]

Up Hill
From *Battles and Leaders.*

Between nine and ten o'clock in the morning, the Donaldsonville Artillery arrived before Sharpsburg. They were ordered at once to the scene of action. Octave Landry recorded, "As soon as we arrived in the road near where the battle was going on, received news to go and relieve a battery whose ammunition was short and on going to relieve them, a terrible fire opened on us from the enemy batteries."[112] Canonnier Private Eugene Levy remembered the guns "moved at a trot through the town" then "northward by the Hagerstown Turnpike, and took . . . position on crest of a hill [west] of the road."[113]

At about the time the Donaldsonville guns were going in, around ten o'clock in the morning, Colonel Stephen D. Lee's badly damaged artillery battalion was moving away from the ridge of hills on the westside of the Hagerstown Turnpike near Piper's Lane to refit and replenish their ammunition. The Federal guns on the other side of Antietam Creek and beyond the Sunken Road had Maurin's guns under a cross fire while they and Anderson's three divisional batteries attempted to cover the advance of Anderson's four thousand foot soldiers moving across fields towards Piper's farm. Amidst a deafening roar of artillery and musketry, and a deadly and withering fire, Anderson's men moved to reinforce Major General D. H. Hill's riflemen located in a sunken road known thereafter as "Bloody Lane."[114]

Under command of Captain Carey F. Grimes, Anderson's three batteries moved into position at nearly the same time as the Donaldsonville Artillery. Grimes's Portsmouth (Virginia) Light Artillery guns went into position on a ridge on the immediate right of the

Sharpsburg's Main Street. In the distant background is St. Paul's Church and beyond, near the left-hand edge of the woods on the horizon, the location of Lee's headquarters during the battle. The Donaldsonville Artillery moved on this road towards the camera, then turned to their left at the Hagerstown Turnpike located a few house down on the right near the tree.
Alexander Gardner photograph; courtesy of the Library of Congress.

Hagerstown Turnpike and north of Piper's Lane. There the battery soon had two men killed and two others wounded. Grimes was mortally wounded in the fighting. On Grimes's right, the guns of Captain Marcellus Moorman's Lynchburg (Virginia) Beauregard Battery went in, but before firing a shot had two men killed and three wounded. One man was shot through the body while in the act of unlimbering his gun. Three others were soon wounded, and the battery in a short time was "badly used up."[115] Captain Frank Huger's Norfolk (Virginia) Battery, commanded by Lieutenant James D. Gale, was immediately west of the pike and had one man killed and two wounded. In less than twenty minutes the three batteries were withdrawn two miles from the field towards Shepardstown by the battalion commander Major John S. Saunders, who arrived after the guns went into action. While retiring, Huger's Battery—following Moorman and Grimes's—abandoned a 6-pounder gun along the pike a few yards south of Piper's Lane due to its horses being killed.[116]

Shortly after the withdrawal of the three batteries, the division of D. H. Hill, after a savage struggle (along with Anderson's troops) were driven in some confusion from the sunken road and into the cornfield and apple orchard of Piper's Farm. When the Yankees followed, the confusion was increased and disorder prevailed. Most of the Confederates were subjected to a severe fire of artillery and musketry. Many fell back towards Piper's barn and out buildings, while others rallied and made a stand behind a small stonewall skirting the Hagerstown Turnpike.[117]

Huger's abandoned 6-pounder gun was now placed in action on the turnpike and used with effect by Lieutenant William W. Chamberlaine of the Sixth Virginia Infantry, Mahone's Brigade, with the assistance of other volunteer infantrymen. They fired until the ammunition was exhausted. Chamberlaine wrote about firing the gun: "I discovered that there were no more friction primers in the limber chest and requested one of the crew to go to a Battery on the elevation to the left and rear of our position and ask for a supply of primers. He did so and soon returned with them."[118]

To Chamberlaine's left and rear were the Donaldsonville Artillery's six "hotly engaged" guns.[119] Landry and Mollere's cannons fired at canister range (up to 400 yards) from the ridge crest overlooking the turnpike and sunken road. Near Maurin's guns were those of Captain Robert Hardaway's Alabama Battery of two 3-inch Rifles and one 12-pounder Whitworth and Captain Miles C. Macon's Richmond Fayette Artillery with two 10-pounder Parrotts.[120] The Canonnier position was a good one on the ridge, near haystacks, with their caissons in a nearby depression in the rear. Their canister shot was extremely effective against the ranks of Union infantry pushing forward beyond the sunken road into Piper's cornfield following

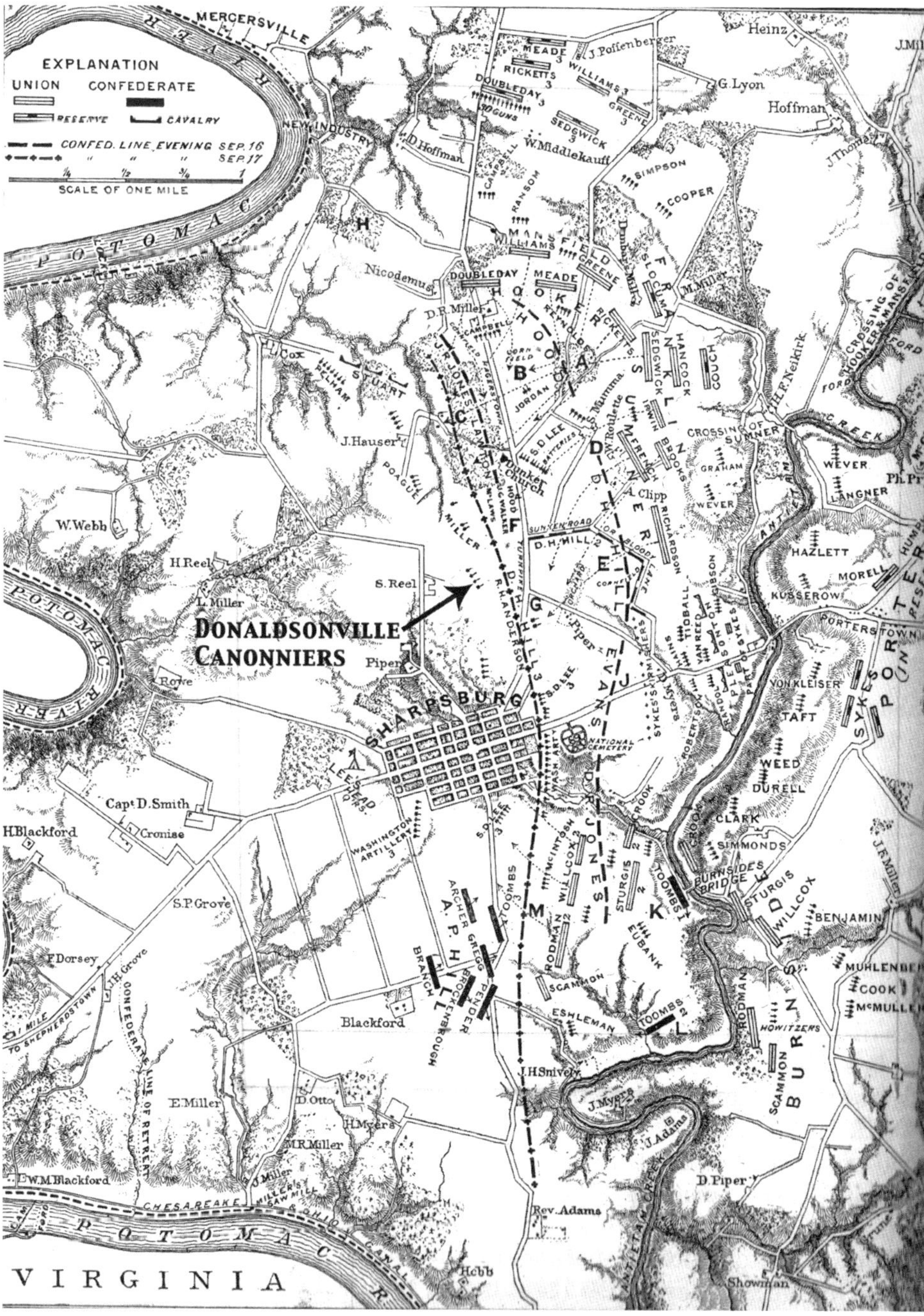

Between nine and ten o'clock the Donaldsonville Artillery arrived at Sharpsburg with their six guns and immediately went to relieve a battery short of ammunition at Colonel Lee's second position. Maurin's six guns battled and remained in this position throughout the day. From *Battles and Leaders*.

D. H. Hill's troops falling back. The Donaldsonville guns sent a destructive fire into the Union infantry heading for two guns of Captain Merritt B. "Buck" Miller's Third Company Washington Artillery, which had gone into action immediately in the rear of Hill's line in Piper's apple orchard.[121]

"Our men," wrote one of Miller's Louisianians, "worked that day desperately, almost despairingly, because it looked for a time as if we would not stop the blue wave from coming forward, although we were tearing it to pieces with canister and shell."[122] Miller's pieces, along with two guns of Captain Robert Boyce's Macbeth (South Carolina) Light Artillery on Miller's left—plus Maurin's, Hardaway's, and Macon's guns on the ridge—kept up a "galling"[123] and "vigorous"[124] fire, "pouring"[125] in shell, grape, and spherical-case shot.

"In battle," remembered Donaldsonville Canonnier Levy, "nothing can be more inspiriting than when Morel, the crack gunner of the battery, with his rich bass voice starts up the 'Marseillaise.' At the invocation *'Allons enfants de la patrie'* the blood seems to course through the veins with fever heat, and the nervous feeling with which one invariably goes into the fray gives way under the influence of the inspired words of Roget de Lisle."[126] The Gunners of Donaldson after their tiring and tedious march, joined the struggle with a renewed vigor that allowed them to slog away at their six guns with a sublime spirit in a hellish atmosphere.

The correspondent Fontaine witnessed the battle and penned, "The air was filled with the white fantastic shapes that floated away from bursted shells. Men were leaping to and fro, loading, firing and handling the artillery, and now and then a hearty yell would reach the ear, amid the tumult, that spoke of death or disaster from some well aimed ball."[127] Four members of the Donaldsonville Artillery were struck down with wounds: Felicité "Felicien" Hebert, Alexander McCullet, the Zouave infantryman Jules Vegue, and Alfred Melancon, who had his leg cut off by a shell. Fifteen of the Donaldsonville horses went down with wounds too. A veteran wrote, "The artillery horses were standing near, and . . . under fire. They looked tired, hungry, and sleepy, with their heads down, ears drooped, and eyes closed. I could not but pity them, knowing they, like myself, were suffering from the pangs of hunger. Through the neck of one a cannon ball had passed, but he was still walking about."[128]

"The constant booming of cannon, the ceaseless rattle and roar of musketry, the glimpses of galloping horsemen and marching infantry, now seen, now lost in the smoke,

"Battle of Sharpsburg" by W. L. Sheppard.
Courtesy of the Confederate Memorial Hall.

adding weirdness to terror, all together make up a combination of sights and sounds wholly indescribable," wrote one Confederate.[129] "Everything in front was obscured from view by the dense smoke" recorded a soldier in Pryor's Brigade, "only waiting for the smoke to clear away, the vivid flash from the cannon of the enemy informed our men of the whereabouts of the enemy. A volley of musketry followed, again obscuring everything from view."[130] The smoke, along with the haystacks, screened and almost certainly prevented the Federal cannons and sharpshooters from inflicting more casualties on the Canonniers, though the enemy artillery continued to rain in a heavy fire. The smoke did not prevent Maurin's, Hardaway's, and Macon's gunners from delivering an effective enfilading fire upon the approaching Federal infantry. The guns "mowed them down with grape and canister," wrote an Alabamian.[131]

Shortly after midday a Yankee battery of six 12-pounder Napoleon Guns under Captain William M. Graham (Battery K, First United States Artillery) came into position fronting the Bloody Lane. Maurin's two Parrott guns, along with other Confederate rifle guns, then delivered a "very sharp fire of shot"[132] upon the Federal artillerymen that at times were covered with the dust and smoke of bursting shells. Captain Thomas H. Carter's King William (Virginia) Artillery, with one Parrott piece and four smoothbores, reported he "received an order from [Brigadier] General [Robert E.] Rodes to plant my battery . . . near the Donaldsonville Artillery. With the consent of General Lee, I at once moved my battery to this point. On reaching it, I found several batteries[133] engaged in driving off a Yankee battery. My battery at once took part . . . and continued firing until the battery was withdrawn."[134]

Within twenty-five minutes Graham's Yankee guns were driven off, but not before a Federal division commander, Major General Israel Richardson, rode up to Graham and was mortally wounded by a ball of a spherical case shot from one of the enfilading Confederate guns on the ridge beyond the Hagerstown Turnpike.[135] With Richardson struck down, casualties mounting, and what a modern historian calls, "A dauntless stand . . . by a handful of Confederates . . . and determined stands by several batteries,"[136] the Federal infantry halted and fell back. A pause in the battle followed for about two hours though there was an occasional discharge of artillery as the exhausted combatants, according to Fontaine, "Stood silently eyeing each other."[137]

After this lull, between three and four o'clock in the evening, the Canonniers could hear the battle over on the right. The fighting ended there with the final charge of Major General A. P. Hill's troops from Harpers Ferry.

A half hour later, at about five o'clock, the Yankee's Seventh Maine Regiment made an attack across Bloody Lane, heading towards Piper's barn. A small force of Southern troops from D. H. Hill and Anderson's division behind the stonewall along the pike rose suddenly and poured musketry volleys into them as Maurin's guns, and others, fired over their comrades' heads into the advancing Federals. Mollere's guns and Captain Jefferson Peyton's Richmond "Orange" Battery, each with three 6-pounder guns, were dreadfully effective with case and canister shot. Only half of the Yankee regiment reached the vicinity of Piper's barn through the canister barrage and musketry before they retreated back through the orchard and cornfield to their original position. This last attack lasted about twenty minutes.[138]

During the day at the Sunken Road/Bloody Lane, Richardson's First Division and Brigadier General William H. French's Third Division of the Army of the Potomac's Second Corps attacked with 10,000 men. Opposing them were the divisions of D. H. Hill and Anderson, the two having a total of 7,200 Confederates. Casualties suffered by the Federals were 2,920 and by the Confederates 2,574.[139]

"On the roads and across the fields, borne in gory litters, or leaning upon the arms of comrades, the wounded were returning by hundreds to the farm houses, barns and sheds along the road [that] had been appropriated by the surgeons . . . and hundreds of poor fellows, maimed and suffering, were lying on the ground, waiting to take their turn under the knife, saw and probe," observed Fontaine.[140]

Among the wounded in the Donaldsonville Artillery were "Felicien" Hebert and the infantry Corporal Jules Vegue, who were later admitted to Richmond's Receiving and Wayside Hospital and afterward transferred to Richmond's General Hospital Number 10. The thirty-seven-year-old Irishman "Alex" McCullet was not seriously wounded and remained with the battery. Alfred Melancon's wound, the loss of a leg, was life threatening.[141]

"The day had closed, but what a scene presented itself to our view!" exclaimed a Confederate, adding, "The dead lay in every direction—in numerous places piled on each other."[142] An artillery officer wrote, "When the sun sank, all felt infinite relief from the fatigue and dangers of the day."[143]

With sunset and darkness covering the battlefield, Mollere moved his section of Donaldsonville 6-pounder guns to a bivouac about two miles in the rear of the battle line. Prosper Landry's rifle section remained in the same position on the ridge, overlooking the turnpike and sunken road where the battlefield took on an eerie sight. The lanterns of the ambulance corps flashed about across the fields and along the turnpike searching for and bringing in the wounded, while help was given to the dying. All were not assisting the wounded though. Many were exhausted and "dropped down where they were."[144] Others, according to a Southern artilleryman, "Prowled about, picking up various articles from the Federal dead."[145]

The correspondent Fontaine reported, "For two days many of the men had not tasted a morsel of food and detachments were now busy around the wagons cooking rations for the respective commands. Several ordnance trains had also arrived, and the caissons of various batteries were around them, being filled with fresh messengers of death."[146] When cooked rations of hardtack and tough beef were brought up, it was still difficult to awaken many of the worn out men. The night, wrote an artilleryman, "Passed wearily by."[147] Despite the innumerable watch fires the night was also described as "Dark and lowering and the air heavy and dull."[148]

Lee would later write in his battle report about Sharpsburg: "Our artillery, though much inferior to that of the enemy in the number of guns and weight of metal, rendered most efficient and gallant service throughout the day, and contributed greatly to the repulse of the attacks on every part of the line."[149] Longstreet in his report called attention to and made particular mention of the courage and good conduct of Miller and Boyce's batteries during the battle. Regrettably Maurin, Hardaway, and Macon's guns were not extolled or even mentioned in official reports.[150]

"Early the next morning," a soldier in Pryor's Brigade wrote, "our pickets and those of the enemy began firing; but both sides seemed to have done enough already."[151] Washington Artillery Adjutant William Owen observed, "The day passed away with nothing done except a little firing now and then between skirmishers and sharpshooters."[152] Prosper Landry's section stayed in position and unlimbered throughout the day while Mollere's section remained in the bivouac. Maurin's Canonniers laid about with many a thought of home. It was exactly one year since the *Le Compagnie d'Artillerie* had departed Donaldsonville on its journey to Richmond.

The day passed without a renewal of the conflict, and at dark all received orders to move to the rear at once. Maurin reunited the battery's two sections and prepared to move everything along. The wounded that could be taken were placed in wagons and went back with the army while those who could not move, such as Canonnier Melancon, were left behind and later taken care of by the Union army. Because of the seriousness of Melancon's wound the Yankees paroled him on September 30, 1862. He died days later. After receiving the news of her son, Melancon's mother passed away in Donaldsonville before the war ended at "age 50 plus a few years."[153]

The Donaldsonville drivers, with their horses pulling guns and caissons, and the Canonniers joined an immense mass of troops and wagons of all descriptions at eight o'clock in the evening. The main body of Lee's army moved slowly towards Boteler's Ford, crossing over to the south side of the Potomac River. There was dense fog and campfires burning on the side of the road, and only with great difficulty the army moved along. The way seemed constantly blocked by wagons. The exhausting march took all night. The driver of one gun, like many others, was "overcome with sleep" and "fell sprawling from his horse, rousing those about him from a similar condition."[154]

The river crossing, a Louisiana wagoner with the artillery noted "rivaled Bedlam." He added,

> The wagon train had to go down a very high and almost perpendicular bank, and except for the still greater danger from behind, was such a descent as no prudent wagoner would ever have attempted to make . . . the teamsters had to make an elbow half way down, at the imminent risk of an overturn—some of the wagons actually meeting with such a calamity. These were set on fire to [*sic*], partly for warmth, partly for the purpose of seeing; and these and the flaring torches held by different hands, gave a weird Rembrandt touch to the scene. . . . Some who were mounted went to sleep in their saddles. All of this time there would be a confused shouting among the wagoners, and the cry of 'Pull around to the right and then swing to the left,' was to be heard with each descent.[155]

The immense fires blazing on the banks, a Louisiana artilleryman wrote, created "the effect of blinding both men and animals."[156] In crossing the Potomac River there appeared an "inextricable confusion"[157] with the mix of artillery, infantry, ambulances, and wagons. "Staff-officers stood on either bank," added the Louisianian, "shouting to the drivers of vehicles and artillery where they should land. Drivers were whipping their animals, and loudly urching [*sic*] them on. Altogether there was a terrible racket."[158] The Canonniers traveling on foot stripped off most of their clothes, and like others, went shuddering and shivering into the cold water.

While crossing, General Lee was observed sitting on his horse in the river watching the wagons and artillery passing. Maurin, on riding his horse across received instructions to report to Brigadier General William N. Pendleton. Upon doing so, he received orders to have his battery take position "to protect the retreat."[159] The Gunners of Donaldson were ordered to move on the same eighty-foot bluffs that the Canonniers probably took no notice of when they forded the river going towards Sharpsburg forty-eight hours earlier. Moving through the dense morning fog to the heights a couple of hundred yards from the river, Maurin's six guns unlimbered and took position on Pendleton's right-hand flank overlooking the ford.[160]

Circ recorded: "We then went into position on the extreme right . . . at about 9 a.m. the Yankees appeared on the opposite hills, they placed their artillery in position and an artillery duel took place which lasted all day."[161] Prosper Landry's two Parrott guns exchanged fire with the Federal batteries,[162] but Mollere's three smoothbore 6-pounders, because of their short range, were of no service, and the 3-inch rifle gun was not used because it had no long-range fuses.

While the two Donaldsonville Parrott guns continued to fire, the last of the Confederate cavalry, (led by Colonel Thomas T. Munford), crossed the river. Munford later remarked his mounted troops were "shielded by a fierce fire from the Virginia hills, just above the ford, which attracted to these hills the whole Federal fire, diverting it from the Cavalry, and that after safely crossing, [Munford] rode up to the hill, and found there a little Louisiana Battery."[163]

Amid a terrific fire and roar of artillery Munford observed the Donaldsonville artillerists cheering and working their guns in what Canonnier Private Ernest Monnot remembered as "a lively artillery duel."[164] No doubt Canonnier Corporal Morelli was again aiming his Parrott gun to the tune of the "Marseillaise." Munford wrote:

> There I saw Capt. [Maurin], his face was beaming with animation, watching and directing the fire of his Cannoneers, his deportment seemed to give inspiration to his splendid men. They moved to & fore with an interest indicating that time & well filled limber chest was all that they asked for! A centre shot was made blowing up a caisson of the enemy while I was near & a shout went up from the battery that could only be given by Anglo French hearts in perfect accord. It seemed to set the whole Battery ablaze. 'Steady Cannoneers! Give them another loosening your guns & bear them more to the right,' said the Captain. Turning to me he said, 'we are giving them some of their 'own medicine' pointing to the ammunition which was captured and had been theirs, as well as to his guns I believe. The enemy's battery he had engaged now moved off but he was at another at once, and as long as I staid there (which was not very long for it was too hot for Comfort; having to get back to my Command).

"I do not speak French," continued Munford,

> and of course I did not appreciate all that was said, but it really seemed more a Frolic than battle, to the brave men engaged at that point. Shot and shell was shrieking and bursting all along the line and plowing up the ground and tearing through his lines, but the Battery seemed more interested in the effect of their shots upon the enemy than any damage they might sustain, though I saw many dead and wounded horses struggling nearby. One of my Couriers laughed and said 'Them Frenchmen are either crazy or they love that kind of work better than I do.' The Captain's eye sparkled like a diamond & his men seemed to understand every thing he wanted before he said it. I will never forget the splendid spirit that Battery exhibited.[165]

Colonel Thomas Taylor Munford.
From *The Civil War: The Bloodiest Day, Battle of Antietam, 1862.*

Of that spirit New Orleanian and Donaldsonville Canonnier Private Eugene Levy had already taken note after he joined the battery five months before. Levy related: "The gayety of the Creoles displayed [in battle] in contrast with the serious demeanor of the Virginia artillerymen, whose best thoughts are then fixed on God and the eternal life beyond the grave; tis but the difference in temperament."[166]

The Donaldsonville gunners' supply of ammunition was not endless, and care had to be taken not to expend the rounds to soon. To prevent this, Maurin had the guns firing at intervals throughout the remainder of the day. During the morning the enemy's fire was furious. Although it slackened for a time, it became fiercer than before when the Federals brought up more batteries in the afternoon. During the whole conflict the Canonniers were exposed to an intense cross fire. A member of a nearby battery remembered "it seemed the whole artillery force of the Yankee army came up and occupied the heights on the Maryland side of the river, and . . . they poured shot and shell into us. . . . At times a solid shot would strike the ground, ricochet, and throw dirt and gravel in our faces."[167]

Along with the cannon fire, the enemy's skirmishers and sharpshooters lined the banks of the river and laid in the bed of the C. & O. Canal alongside the river. From this position they "exceedingly annoyed"[168] the Southern artillerymen with rifle fire that "was coming too fast and close."[169] According to one artillerist, the Federal artillery on the heights across the river "had the advantage of position, but failed to lower their guns sufficiently. Thus, "most of their shots went over our heads."[170]

Landing behind the front line guns, these shells blew up one of the Donaldsonville 6-pounder caissons. Other shots took their toll on the animals in the rear, striking down ten horses. One explosion seriously wounded Canonnier Private Arnold Wiedemere on this, his twenty-fourth birthday. His arm was later amputated at the shoulder joint. The Switzerland native, like the wounded Melancon, was left at Shepherdstown, where he was captured and paroled on September 30, 1862.[171] Private Frederick Wagner, also twenty-four-years-old and a German immigrant and butcher from New Orleans, who had previously served as a hospital steward, became the second Canonnier of the war to be killed in action. The third and last casualty of the day was Sergeant Hubert Treille, who received a contused wound to the shoulder from a shell fragment.[172] "Strange to say," wrote a veteran of this all-day artillery battle, "our casualties were but few."[173]

Late in the evening Pendleton authorized permission to retire any guns that could do so without being seen by the enemy and sent instructions "to retire in specified order, as dusk deepened to conceal them."[174] The three 6-pounders and 3-inch rifle gun, being of no service, Maurin sent to the rear about four o'clock in the evening with orders for them to join Pryor's Brigade, which was resting in woods two miles back from the river. Cire recorded, "At dusk left amidst showers of shells and minie balls . . . through fields . . . we marched the whole night."[175]

Maurin also reported,

> The two Parrott guns remained in position until dark, and, when ordered to move back, could no longer pass through the road, it being commanded by the enemy's artillery. I was, therefore, obliged to cut across fields and fences and a country entirely unknown to me, without a guide, and, in the darkness of the night, the rear piece, with worn-out horses, lagged behind. Lieutenant Landry returned to bring it up, but lost his way, and having come before a thick wood which could not be crossed, it was there abandoned and spiked, the enemy shouting in the rear, and, as he believed, gaining upon him.[176]

Other batteries on the bluff "were mixed in [a] helter-skelter race for the road, the whole field and road being crowded with men, guns, horses, limber chests without the guns, caissons, officers on horseback and on foot, all in a confused mass and all making the best time possible to where they expected to find the rear of General Lee's army."[177] The night was "interminable,"[178] but the Creole Canonniers "having joyfully returned to Dixie land"[179] long remembered *Maryland, My Maryland* as an *Artillerie les Enfers* (Artillery Hell).[180]

Chapter Seven

Le Geste audacieux
(The Daring Deed)

On September 20, 1862, the Donaldsonville Artillery traveled over a rough but firm road to join the remnants of Pryor's Brigade six miles from Shepardstown. Donaldsonville Canonnier Artificer François "Bienvenu" Cire recorded in his memorandum book, "In the morning we joined the main body of the army and camped all day, and at dusk we left and marched a short distance and camped."[1] Captain Victor Maurin sent a detachment back for the Donaldsonville gun and caisson left behind on the retreat from Boteler's Ford and reported, "Only the caisson was recovered, the piece having been taken away."[2] The abandoned Parrott gun was found by troops from the Fourth Michigan Infantry and recovered by Battery D (West Point Battery) Fifth U.S. Artillery which, by coincidence, lost that very gun at the First Bull Run battle in July 1861.[3]

With Major General James Longstreet's Right Wing Corps, the Donaldsonville Artillery for the next five days camped in open rolling country along the banks of Opequon Creek near the town of Martinsburg, resting both men and horses and "waiting for stragglers to catch up."[4] There was "universal bathing"[5] in the flashing and rushing waters of the creek and a determined effort to rid themselves of the "abominable vermin."[6] A Confederate in bivouac with Gen. Robert E. Lee's army wrote,

> It is difficult to describe the condition of the troops at this time, so great and various was their wretchedness. They were sunburnt, gaunt, ragged, scarcely at all shod . . . they had worn out their clothing and shoes, and received nothing but what they could pick up on the battlefield . . . and lastly, they were covered with vermin. They now stood, an emaciated, limping, ragged, filthy mass, whom no stranger to their valiant exploits could have believed capable of anything the least worthy.[7]

Not only were the Canonniers tired, they, like the rest of the troops, were also hungry and desirous to find something to eat since the wagon trains could provide only the meager fare of hardtack and tough beef. At one point they received just three days' rations of flour. Some were fortunate enough to forage for and find stray chickens, or a shoat, or a half grown turkey, but most of the men supplemented their rations in the cornfields. Maurin's weary battery horses, instead of just grazing on clover or corncobs from the field like they had been, finally received twenty-five bushels of corn the same day the men got flour. The horses received an additional 940 pounds of corn the next day.[8]

While the Canonniers foraged or procured rations, Maurin and other battery commanders received notice of General Orders from Lee that stated: "Field Returns will be sent in promptly today or tomorrow in accordance to orders."[9] Upon completion, the Donaldsonville returns were sent to Colonel J. B. Walton of the Washington Artillery, who communicated to Longstreet:

"Report of Batteries, Right Wing Dept. of N. Va.- their condition, losses, requirements & etc."[10]

BATTERIES-GUNS	MEN		FOR DUTY		HORSES	
	Killed	Wounded	Officers	Men	Killed	Required
Squires's (FIRST CO. W. A.)-3	5	18	3	59	21	9
Richardson's (SECOND CO. W.A.)-4	2	8	3	67	13	14
Miller's (THIRD CO. W. A.)-4	6	23	2	49	55	25
Eshelman's (FOURTH CO. W. A.)-4	0	3	4	69	3	7
Reilly's ROWAN (N.C.) Artillery-6	2	8	5	110	8	20
Bachman's GERMAN (S. C.) Arty-4	0	4	3	74	8	21
Garden's PALMETTO (S.C.) Lt. Batty-3	0	11	4	68	14	20
Maurin's DONALDSONVILLE (La.) Arty-5	1	6	3	98	25	50
Chapman's DIXIE (Va.) Artillery-3	1	1	4	32	4	33
Boyce's MACBETH (S.C.) Artillery-4	2	17	4	32	16	20

Maurin's Battery was the only one of those listed that was detached with McLaws's command on the Harpers Ferry expedition, which explains the loss of as many horses to fatigue and lameness as in combat. One fact the Canonniers could be justly proud of was the Donaldsonville Artillery had more men present for duty on September 24, 1862, (the date of the report) than all but one of the other nine batteries. In combat casualties six other batteries had more men killed and wounded than Maurin's Battery, though none of them took part in the artillery battle at Boteler's Ford."[11]

The five days in camp came with pleasant weather and beautiful days, although it was very dry and dusty. An artilleryman described how, once again, "the jest, the practical joke, the ready laugh passed around; and for a time the whole army seemed to be in extravagant spirits, cheering upon the least provocation, like a party of boys, and permitting no occasion for indulging in laughter to escape them."[12] In a letter home, another wrote, "The soldiers are grouped around laughing and conversing gaily, some eating, others cooking, and many otherwise occupied."[13] Many wrote to obtain news and to relieve the uncertainty of their own fate to family and friends, and a Louisiana artillerist in the hope of getting word home noted that he "remained all day occupied with letter writing."[14]

"We get most of our news from Richmond," wrote another letter writer, "and since we have no access to the daily newspaper, our store of news must consequently be quite limited."[15] A dearth of news, which meant no bad news, was conceivably why a Louisiana chaplain with the troops reported at the time "the boys were in the best of spirits."[16] The army's mail had been withheld from it since their departure from Richmond on August 11, 1862, and now letters began arriving in camp from Louisiana. An artilleryman from New Orleans recorded on September 24 that he "received a letter . . . dated August 18th."[17]

The Canonnier spirits consequently plummeted when they learned the news that Donaldsonville had been bombarded, burned, and "literally left a heap of shapeless ruins" on August 9.[18] One letter from Donaldsonville written on August 13 reported "71 families have been cast upon the world, they have had their homes eaten up by the flames, and themselves and little ones . . . without a roof to cover their heads."[19] Another described how "Fire has reduced [Donaldsonville], to a few scattering huts and stray ghostlike chimneys."[20] Canonnier Corporal John O'Hara, a cooper by trade, learned his property was destroyed with a loss of "100,000 staves, 50,000 hoop-poles, one shop, two warehouses and one dwelling house."[21] Many others faced losses too, including Maurin, whose merchandising business and "old home" were destroyed.[22]

"The nights," wrote a soldier in Virginia on September 24, 1862, "now are becoming very cool for the . . . [few] blankets among us."[23] Upon awakening on September 26, a Louisiana artillerist noted "white frost, the first of the season, discovered this morning."[24] In the evening of the twenty-sixth orders were received for the artillerymen "to cook 2 days' rations and prepare to move at daylight."[25] Preparation for the move occupied the time on a pleasant day. Though he requested fifty horses for the battery, Maurin received only six from the quartermaster department.[26] The next morning at daybreak the Canonniers, with their guns, caissons, and wagons pulled by the animals on hand, marched with Major General Richard H. Anderson's Division that temporarily was commanded by Brigadier General Cadmus M. Wilcox.[27] They marched with Longstreet's Right Wing that was headed by Walton and Alexanders's Reserve Artillery Battalions. They were followed by Hood, Walker, Wilcox (with Maurin's Battery), Pickett, Jones, McLaws, and Evans' divisions.[28]

A diarist in the Washington Artillery wrote, "At 6 took up the line of march, Generals Lee and Longstreet at the head. Moved by crossroads over a circuitous route until we arrived at Bunker Hill, where took Martinsburg and Winchester tpke. Proceeded to within 6 miles of Winchester . . . and bivouacked."[29] Cire recorded the Canonniers "left camp and marched all day. We passed through Mills [Creek] and camped at 10 o'clock pm."[30] The men of the Donaldsonville Artillery, in the middle of Longstreet's column, probably took little notice that their route was through one of the most highly cultivated sections of the Shenandoah Valley, with "gorgeous scenery to the right and left."[31] The column arrived near Bunker Hill where, wrote a soldier, "There was no town, nothing but a large spring surrounded by a beautiful level, fertile land."[32]

Maurin's Battery rested during the morning of September 28. That evening it "resumed the march and camped 5 miles north of Winchester."[33] Longstreet's troops were ordered to select campsites on waters flowing into Opequon Creek and on parallel roads from the Martinsburg Pike. The camps stretched for miles on both sides of the road, with Walton and Alexander's reserve artillery battalions (along with the Donaldsonville Artillery) bivouacking near Stephenson's Station (or Depot), which was close to a spring that was described by the

Washington Artillery's Adjutant William Owen as "the finest and largest we had seen in Virginia."[34] Lee and his headquarters camp of a few small tents were also near Stephenson's Depot, a few hundred yards from the station to the northeast and near the artillery in a meadow.[35]

After having survived on squirrels and rabbits for a while, one noted about the local wildlife, "nothing survives before them."[36] The artillery batteries finally began to receive rations of fresh beef and flour, which were "ample, if not abundant."[37] On October 5 the army's rations of beef, flour, and water constituting breakfast, lunch, and dinner were increased and, wrote a Confederate, "poor as our fare is I manage to fatten on it."[38]

The troops remained in untroubled camps in a beautiful country of wooded hills and rich fields in "autumnal tinges."[39] The Donaldsonville Artillery's encampment was convenient for wood and water. A soldier wrote in his diary, "Enjoying camp life" and "the sweets of camp."[40] There was monotonous inactivity with jokes and songs helping them to forget the "fatigues and hardships of the recent campaign."[41]

Cire went ten days here without making a memorandum entry. According to another Louisiana artillerist much of the time was devoted to getting plenty of rest and "reading books aloud, or telling camp-fire stories, and generally enjoying the superb climate."[42] There were few tents in the camps, and "most of the men," wrote another artillerist, "ensconce themselves in bush built shelters of various shapes, in fence corners, under gun-blankets, eked out by cedar boughs, or burrow semi-subteraneously."[43]

As the Federals were slow to cross the Potomac River and renew the campaign, Lee allowed his army to rest with food and refitting. Disciplinary measures were also undertaken along with a reorganization, of which the most important step was the assignment of troops into two corps under Longstreet and "Stonewall" Jackson with both being promoted to lieutenant general.[44]

The "determined valor"[45] of the artillery service did not keep it exempt from reorganization, and Lee instructed Brigadier General William N. Pendleton to diligently examine the condition of the numerous batteries and report his findings. As a result, orders were issued on October 4, 1862, reducing the army's artillery by nineteen batteries with the small and weak companies being consolidated, the belief being they encumbered the service with their enormous consumption of horses. The Donaldsonville Artillery remained in their present assignment, attached to Pryor's Brigade with Anderson's Division.[46]

Lee also desired from Pendleton a statement of captains of batteries who had distinguished themselves in the recent battles, and Pendleton listed fourteen artillery commanders by a "relative grade of distinction recently earned."[47] The Donaldsonville Artillery's Captain appeared fourth on this list with the observation that Maurin was "an officer of tried merit."[48]

To inspire the army "anew,"[49] Lee on October 2 issued General Orders to compliment and hearten the army. These read: "In reviewing the achievements of the army during the present campaign, the commanding general cannot withhold the expression of his admiration of the indomitable courage it has displayed in battle and its cheerful endurance of privation and hardships on the march."[50] The order then recounts the army's campaign since leaving Richmond and finishes with,

> History records few examples of greater fortitude and endurance than this army has exhibited, and I am commissioned by the President to thank you in the name of the Confederate States for the undying fame you have won for their arms. Much as you have done, much more remains to be accomplished. The enemy again threatens with invasion, and to your tried valor and patriotism the country looks with confidence for

deliverance and safety. Your past exploits give assurance that this confidence is not misplaced.[51]

During this time frequent inspections by company commanders were held along with a "Dress Parade everyday,"[52] which was a sight, with the "war-worn appearance"[53] of the troops in their tattered uniforms. "Barring the guard and fatigue duty necessary to preserve order and keep the camp cleanly, and occasional short drills, the men had little to do," wrote a veteran.[54] Under abundant gigantic oaks and near walnut, chestnut, locust, and hickory trees, rest and quiet was enjoyed by the troops as was congregating by the thousands at nearby streams to refresh themselves. Some, however, thought this camp life was not good, for "it gives them time to think of home, and . . . sad thoughts would arise when we looked back to home and loved ones, and knew, while our sufferings were great to feel, that those we loved were, perchance, suffering more than we."[55]

"Here, in this then land of plenty," wrote a Confederate, "the men reveled in the best of fresh beef, vegetables, fruits, not forgetting the honey, needing nothing for the stomach's sake."[56] The abundance of the neighborhood did cause a problem for the unit commanders in bivouac as private property was destroyed or injured by the troops, especially the burning of wood and the foraging for food on local farms. Commensurate with foraging the Louisianians were usually successful when they went "on a '*piroute*'" (slang for *pirater*; meaning to practice piracy).[57]

On October 9 Longstreet issued a Special Order to the quartermaster department that they were to pay "promptly"[58] these property owners who suffered damage or losses. The same day, Maurin received instructions to move the battery's camp and relocated the battery near the farm of Warner McKarne. The Canonniers had hardly settled down when the next day, wrote Cire, "We had rain all day and all night."[59]

Lack of forage for the animals was most likely the reason for the camp move.[60] O'Hara noted the Donaldsonville battery was paying $8.00 for a load of hay, as opposed to $2.75 six months earlier, and $20.00 for corn that had cost $5.50 a barrel. The deficiency of horses, not only in the artillery, but also in the army had become a major concern of the commanding general, so much so that on October 1 Lee issued orders "to impress upon all officers in charge of horses . . . the urgent necessity of energetic and unwearied care of their animals, and of preventing their neglect and abuse."[61] The order goes on to say, "Artillery horses especially must be kept in good condition . . . with sufficient and suitable food, sparing no effort or reasonable expense."[62] Division commanders were likewise reminded "of their responsibility for the condition of their artillery, and especially of its horses."[63]

On October 13 Cire recorded, "We had a grand review by Gnl. Longstreet."[64] It seems Wilcox's Division with Maurin's Battery and the Washington Artillery (Second and Fourth Companies with one section each from the First and Third Companies) were reviewed by Longstreet out of compliment to Colonel Sir Garnet Wolseley of the British Army, and two or three members of the English Parliament who were visiting the army. Owen of the Washington Artillery described the troop's appearance as "war-worn"[65] and "hard-looking."[66] Another in the reviewing column of about ten to twelve thousand men said it was "a grand sight."[67] Rain cut short the ceremonies, though Owen recorded that,"The review went off creditably."[68]

There was a bustle in camp at one-thirty on the morning of October 17 when Maurin gave orders to hitch up and be ready to move at a moment's notice. "The enemy," reported Owen, "came out of Harper's [*sic*] Ferry in force, and we were under arms all day."[69] Nothing came of it, and in the evening a counter-order was received to unhitch and unharness the horses. The next day Cire recorded that the Donaldsonville guns were still in camp as it was reported the enemy had retreated back across the Potomac River and "all was quiet again."[70]

It remained that way for another two weeks. The diaries of the Louisiana artillerymen were mostly concerned with the recording of the weather, which turned out to be clear, cool, windy, pleasant, or rain.[71] On October 20 Maurin was instructed to answer inquiries from Lieutenant Colonel Edward P. Alexander, Chief of Ordnance, concerning the loss of the Parrott gun on September 19 at Boteler's Ford. Alexander found no fault with the battery, and Maurin received another 10-pounder Parrott gun from the Ordnance Department along with horses from the quartermaster department.[72] Other than the rainy days, the only significant entry made by Cire in his memorandum book during this time was on October 21 with, "A grand review by Genl R. E. Lee."[73]

With the cool weather and lack of clothing the Louisianians kept up in the woods large fires constantly burning day and night. Though supplies of shoes and clothing were being daily received, most of the Donaldsonville contingent were poorly clad and "getting used to that."[74] According to an October 25 consolidated report, of the quantity of clothing and shoes required by the four companies of the Washington Artillery, the average per battery and greatly needed was 25 overcoats, 18 jackets, 141 flannel shirts, 3 pairs of pants, 155 wool drawers, 200 pairs of socks, 73 pairs of shoes, and 71 blankets, and this was two weeks after a distribution of light gray jackets, pants, and red or pink shirts.[75] The Donaldsonville Artillery likely received some clothing during the month, but not nearly enough, as their clothing situation at the end of October was reported as "not very good."[76]

On a hazy, rainy autumn day (October 29) Maurin received orders to have his two lieutenants, four sergeants, five corporals, two buglers, six artificers, and seventy-eight privates cook three days' rations. They were about to move. The next day, on a cold midmorning, the six guns, caissons, wagons, and ambulance, pulled by one hundred serviceable horses and mules set out. The battery exited camp in company with Anderson's Division and Longstreet's corps. "We left camp and passed through Winchester. We marched 25 miles & camped on the Front Royal road," recorded Cire.[77]

It was a very fatiguing march through Winchester[78] and thereafter throughout a poor and thinly settled country. The artillerymen were not allowed to ride or load their baggage on the guns and caissons, and each detachment was instructed to keep with its own gun and not wander off. That evening one of Longstreet's soldiers recorded, "A great many apples near the camp, most the boys went out in the country and got their supper. We had one days ration of Beef too [*sic*] cook, so we were up quite late, the night was quite cold."[79]

On October 31, another very cold morning with heavy frost, the Donaldsonville Artillery resumed their movement. Cire noted, "In the morning we resumed the march and forded the Shenandoah river and marched through Front Royal, and took the Gaines Cross road turnpike and marched until night. We marched about 14 miles and crossed the Blue Ridge [mountains] at Chester gap and camped a short distanced from Flint."[80] A Confederate in the column later wrote,

> The march was a hard one in more respects than in distance & in this respect it was very unusually hard. We had the two branches of the Shenandoah River—both quite broad streams—to cross—the first one a little over knee deep, the second one fully waist deep & of all the excruciating pain which I ever suffered none can compare to that I endured from the first five minutes or so after getting into the water at both places. They are both mountain streams & the thermometer was considerably below freezing point the morning we crossed.[81]

Shortly after passing through deserted-looking Front Royal (the seat of Warren County), described by one passing artillerist as being "stagnant as a Quaker settlement,"[82] the column halted along the road a few hours. Upon resuming the march they moved over Chester Gap, where the Donaldsonville boys observed a picturesque and sublime view of the lofty mountain peaks and fast flowing Shenandoah River. A mounted Confederate noted, "The forest skirting the course of the Shenandoah were now glowing with gorgeous hues of . . . autumn. . . . The light saffron of the chestnut-trees was in effective contrast with the rich crimson of the oaks and maples, while the trailing vines and parasites displayed every tint from the palest pink to the deepest purple."[83]

After camping for the night in woods near Flint, the extended column of Longstreet's corps, with its many stragglers, continued down the thickly forested Blue Ridge Mountains early on the morning of November 1. Cire reported, "We marched the whole day, we passed through Flint Hills and Washington and camped at night."[84] Traveling over large hills on a rough country road through "a poor and rigid"[85] Rappahannock County, the column went through "little" Washington. A Louisiana artilleryman described it as a "handsome Country village of about 500 inhabitants."[86]

Continuing the next morning with Anderson's Division, Maurin's Battery passed through Sperryville, which by the time the division went through was "eaten out."[87] Next passed was deserted old Woodville, and, after having "marched 21 miles," Cire noted that the Canonniers "reached Culpeper Court House at 3 p.m. and camped one mile [north] of it."[88] According to a member of the infantry, "That march . . . will long be remembered by the men of the Army of Northern Virginia, or that part of it to which I was attached—R. H. Anderson's division." He added, "It was . . . very cold . . . when we forded the Shenandoah River . . . the ice was one-half inch thick."[89]

Two days after arriving near Culpeper, another of Anderson's men wrote, "I have not yet recovered from the effects of my march from Winchester; my feet are quite sore," adding, "we were out of provisions for two days on our march, but have plenty now, I mean plenty of tough beef, and raw bread without salt, as usual."[90] Still another infantryman recorded, "Marched leisurely & camped in evening near C[ulpeper] C[ourt] H[ouse] . . . not half the army has kept up. . . . The stragglers will range thro the country in the wake of the army & sometimes ahead of it, living off the citizens, plundering & pillaging & . . . they come back to their commands . . . relating their exploits."[91]

Anderson's Division camped one and one-half mile north of Culpeper Court House while Maurin's Battery joined Longstreet's artillery battalions near the edge of large oak woods and pine thickets, a mile northeast of the town along the Warrenton Turnpike that passed over rolling grain fields and pasture land amid patches of woods. Here there was grazing land and large quantities of corn stored in barrels for the animals. "The waters there," wrote a soldier, "are so impregnated with sulphur that the odor of over ripe eggs is smelled afar."[92] The troops were paid two months salary and able to buy tobacco, flour, coffee, honey, preserves, molasses, apples, and whiskey, though the goods were "sold in camp at any price one chooses to ask for them."[93]

In passing through Longstreet's camps an artilleryman described how the troops now "were certainly hard looking ones, dirty, unwashed, uncombed, with their clothes in rags and many without shoes."[94] For the next few days they rested with the weather uncommonly fine and nothing of importance happening except a rumor in camp that "Longstreet's Corps is to be sent to Beauregard."[95]

With the weather getting colder Longstreet issued General Orders on November 7, 1862: "The inclement season having set in, commanders will take every method of protecting and quartering their men from the weather in their present exposed situation. To this end company and regimental commanders will take care that warm fires are kept burning during the entire day, and will at night see that the men can make their bivouacs on the earth thus warmed during the day."[96]

Cire recorded that on the day Longstreet issued the order, "We had snow all day."[97] Not only did it snow to the point that the limbs of the trees were loaded down nearly to breaking, but a cold biting wind blew through the camps. About the wind and cold an officer wrote, "Through a person [it blows] and nearly chills the blood in ones veins."[98] Another noted that when the wind blew "the smoke is very disagreeable,"[99] and they "could scarcely keep warm by large comfortable fires."[100] To keep their body heat at night the troops snuggled and covered up with blankets while the horses were protected from the harsh winds by brushwood in sheltered localities.[101]

With dawn on November 8, the snow of the previous day had mostly disappeared and the weather was "milder and sunshiny."[102] Orders from Longstreet's Assistant Adjutant General G. Moxley Sorrel informed battery commanders at seven o'clock in the morning to be in readiness to move at a moment's warning and, in separate orders, to send at once to Culpeper Court House for the mail "as by a sudden movement from this point it might be lost."[103]

While the Canonniers stood around their campfires with horses hitched and harnessed to their guns and caissons, the joy of any letters received was offset by news that came with the recent arrival from Ascension Parish of nineteen-year-old student Henry Duffel, oldest son of District Judge Henry L. Duffel and owner of Woodstock Plantation, and a cousin to Prosper Landry and "John" Trasimond Landry. A week later Eugene Cooley, a former officer in the 14th Louisiana Infantry who "labored and fought faithfully"[104] and was described as "a friend to his country and a believer in Christ"[105] joined the battery. Duffel and Cooley brought the latest news of home and no doubt the word that the Yankees had landed in Donaldsonville on October 25, 1862, and of the "confusion and dismay"[106] occurring along Bayou Lafourche. About the enemy's arrival in Donaldsonville an Assumption Parish citizen wrote, "Our hearts were heavy with the tidings just received."[107] The news of invasion down the bayou and letters from Donaldsonville leading off with "Such is the chaos"[108] likely struck the Canonnier camp the same as the chilling snow storm that fell the night of November 8 on the Gunners of Donaldson.

It was a cloudy, cool, and quiet day on November 9, and the artillery batteries were informed that they would not move. It was the Sabbath and many of the Louisiana artillerymen had the opportunity to attend church in Culpeper. Many prayers and thoughts were of home and families, particularly after the near termination of communications between the Canonniers and home as a result of the Federal invasion of the Lafourche District. There Helene Dupuy, a diarist living just outside Donaldsonville along the bayou with relatives in the Donaldsonville Artillery scrawled in French nearly a year later: "But we do not even know what has become of them. We have not had a single word from any of them for the last ten months."[109] After the information and letters received at Culpeper Court House, it would not be until September of 1863 before the Donaldsonville Canonniers received more than snippets of news from home.

Maurin's gunners awoke on November 10 to all day heavy firing coming from the direction of the Hazel River to the north. Longstreet's artillery was ordered to cook rations and be ready to move at a moment's notice, but at four o'clock in the afternoon the order was countermanded when the firing ceased. It was learned by the Louisianians in camp that "The firing proved to be upon the advance of the enemy endeavoring to cross the Hazel River but were repulsed."[110]

Special Orders on this day also announced that Brigadier General Roger A. Pryor was relieved from duty as brigade commander, and Colonel Edward A. Perry, having been appointed brigadier general, was assigned to command the brigade that Maurin's guns were attached to. The brigade was now composed of the Second, Fifth, and Eighth Florida Regiments. Perry was described by one of his veteran Floridians as "a brave, generous, and cool commander . . . a good officer and he enjoys the full confidence of his entire command."[111]

No reason was given for Pryor being relieved of duty with the Army of Northern Virginia. There had been criticism of Pryor at the battle of Second Manassas and after Anderson was wounded at Sharpsburg where the command passed to Pryor, the senior brigadier. From the moment Pryor assumed command at Sharpsburg it was noted the division ceased to act as a unit. Additionally on the night of September 19 during the artillery battle at Boteler's Ford, a retreating Pendleton confronted Pryor and asked for infantry support for the artillery still defending the river crossing. Pryor simply referred him to the nearest divisional commander, who was not found. Brigadier General Cadmus Wilcox described Pryor as "rather wild and inaccurate,"[112] and as Pryor was a politician-general with no military training, Lee made no effort to keep him with the army.[113]

Major General Richard Herron Anderson
From *Battles and Leaders*.

The Donaldsonville Artillery remained assigned to Perry's Brigade of Anderson's Division. From recent inspections it was communicated to Pendleton, chief of artillery, through the following correspondence the effectiveness of the attached artillery:

> Head Quarters Anderson's Division
> Culpeper C. H. VA
> Nov 11th 1862
>
> General
>
> I have the honor to submit the accompanying reports of the commanders of batteries in my division. The relative efficiency of the batteries is as follows:
>
> First- Captain Maurin's Donaldsonville Artillery
> Second- Captain Huger's battery
> Third- Captain Moorman's battery
>
> My opinion of the relative merit of the commanders of batteries would place them in the same order as that of the relative efficiency of batteries...
>
> I am your obedient servant,
> R. H. Anderson
> Major General Commanding
>
> To W N Pendleton[114]

Within a few months Captain Frank Huger was promoted to major and appointed second in command of Alexander's Battalion. Of Huger being recommended for promotion Pendleton wrote, "I am told . . . his battery now evinces peculiar care and efficiency on the part of its commander."[115] Anderson's note to Pendleton listed Maurin's Donaldsonville

Artillery above Huger's battery in attention to detail and capabilities, and listed Maurin ahead of Huger as a qualified and worthy commander. Nevertheless Huger was promoted, possibly because he was "the only West Point captain not yet promoted."[116] Lee's adjutant, a friend of Huger, wrote, "He is a good fellow and deserves it."[117] A Georgia artilleryman in 1864 recorded, "Promotion in this [the artillery] branch of service is of low grade and comes slowly, especially to any but Virginians."[118] Huger was a Virginian and a West Pointer. Maurin remained the captain of the Donaldsonville Artillery, and it was later said, "He . . . declined all promotions so that he could keep his word with the parents of the young men that he took away with him, that he would ever remain with and watch over them."[119]

On November 10 Maurin received orders to send two of the Donaldsonville guns the next day to support Confederate cavalry doing picket duty on the banks of the Hazel River. The pair of Canonnier guns went on picket duty at the river near Rixeyville. Upon observing the enemy's advance cavalry pickets on the road of the opposite bank, the Gunners of Donaldson fired their guns.[120] Maurin described it as simply an "occasion at skirmishing."[121] No casualties were suffered in the battery, and the two guns remained on picket duty, supporting the cavalry with "nothing of importance transpiring."[122] On November 19 the two Donaldsonville guns were ordered back to camp from picket duty. For the remainder of the Canonniers in their bivouac with Longstreet's corps around Culpeper the "times are now very dull."[123]

On November 16 Longstreet issued another General Order informing the troops to be "in readiness for battle upon a moment's notice. Commanders will see that provisions, ammunition, and transportation are at hand."[124] Maurin's Battery made their preparations. One horse was unfit for service and turned in to the quartermaster department. The Canonnier guns in the Culpeper camp remained until the evening of November 19 when half-rations for three days were received along with orders for "special care . . . in grooming the horses" since they were about to march through muddy roads. The men were also instructed to "aid at the wheels" of the guns, caissons, and wagons and have "no straggling."[125]

"The section that was on picket was ordered to join [Perry's] Brigade which had left Culpeper with the other [Donaldsonville] section and the whole army for Fredericksburg," wrote Cire. He added "We had rain all day & all night, roads are very muddy."[126] On the move after reuniting, Maurin's six gun battery, Perry's Florida Brigade, and Anderson's Division passed through Culpeper Court House and "marched through a continuous, drenching and very cold rain, over roads shoe-top deep with mud and badly cut up by wagon trains & artillery."[127] The column stopped at night around eight o'clock, a few miles from Culpeper on the Raccoon Ford Road with it "being too dark to march."[128] They camped along the road "in a pine thicket where there was no wood to dry with-or keep warm," and the troops "slept in drenching wet clothes, on drenching wet ground, under drenching wet blankets and the rain still pouring."[129]

Reveille was at four o'clock in the morning but the march didn't resume until daybreak. When they moved it was "over if possible worse roads, the rain falling harder than before-all day."[130] Near nine o'clock in the morning the Donaldsonville guns forded the Rapidan River at Raccoon Ford where there was difficulty in getting the pieces and caissons through the mud-holes and up the high muddy banks on the south side. It was even difficult for the men to cross. One exclaimed "the water over knee deep & cold—whew!!!"[131]

After marching all day with the men frequently having to assist the horses in pulling the guns and caissons through mudholes and up hills, then locking the wheels in other places, the tired, wet Canonniers made camp at night along the road in pine thickets near Mine Run Creek. The rain still came "down in torrents."[132]

The next morning Lee's army and the Canonniers again awoke in the rain "a more drenched and disgusted set."[133] The movement continued near nine o'clock that morning through the sticky and thick Virginia mud and into the gloomy "Wilderness of Spotsylvania"[134] County where the army reached the Orange Turnpike around midday. The rain continued falling, and the horses plunged along and spattered mud in showers until the column was literally smothered in ooze. Clouds of steam arose from the heated bodies of the animals as they tugged at the harnesses while everything, including the uniforms of the men, partook of the clay color of the road. Along the turnpike the guns and caissons traveled until five o'clock in the evening. They halted near a place called Chancellorsville.

The march continued the next morning, November 22, and though the deluge finally stopped, it remained cloudy and cold. Near eleven o'clock that morning Anderson's Division and the Donaldsonville Artillery slowly approached the western outskirts of Fredericksburg, Virginia.[135]

In advancing, great excitement went through the division as word was passed that "the Yankees had ordered our forces to surrender the town or they would shell it at 12 o'clock. As we advanced the excitement increased."[136] Maurin's guns, along with Huger's Virginia Battery, were ordered up. They dashed by the columns of marching troops, but were halted at the hills back of Fredericksburg. There the artillerymen met and watched the "dolorous procession"[137] of women, children, and old people walking and riding in carts, and carrying their household goods with them as they left the city on crowded and muddy roads. While the women passed they repeatedly addressed the soldiers watching the exodus with a stouthearted "God bless you." They sought shelter in the woods and farmhouses behind the Confederate lines. "Such sights," wrote an officer, "tend to exasperate our brave boys, and the Yankees will doubtless feel the effects someday."[138] Many of the Canonniers forgot the cold and dampness and, "with a thought of the sufferings and deprivations . . . at home,"[139] were determined to defend and, like Donaldsonville Private Edward Severin Terrio, willing to die "without a murmur . . . in the defense of the rights and firesides of fellow citizens."[140]

Upon arriving, the rest of the army's artillery and infantry filed to the left of the Plank Road and camped in a line of battle. The Canonniers in a short time unhitched and fed their horses but did not unharness them while awaiting orders. During the wait a soldier noticed "the sun shone out this evening, for the first time in a week."[141] Without further orders the men lay down and went to sleep on the ground as darkness came on with a steady drizzle. The night turned into another miserable one.

The Canonniers awoke on November 23 and although there was no rain, a snapping cold wind from the north set in. It was dark and cloudy all day. Maurin had the wagons sheltered while the guns were readied for action, after which many of the artillerists took the opportunity (before provost guards were posted on the roads) to go into deserted Fredericksburg. In heading towards the town the Yankee tents on the heights across the Rappahannock River could be seen and, wrote one soldier, "An innumerable number they seemed to be-in full view," adding it made "a very picturesque scene though they are Yankee tents."[142]

While the gunners visited one of the oldest towns in Virginia, the Yankee pickets were seen across the riverbanks and at times some of the Louisianians "conversed with them."[143] The following days passed off quietly with nothing of interest occurring except for the Yankee camps perceptibly increasing. The men, wrote an artillery officer, remained "cheerful almost to recklessness, used to hardship, veterans in action & in camp life."[144]

Regarding the army and the Donaldsonville Artillery's clothing and food needs, "The government," reported a soldier, "has issued things needful very liberally . . . and in this way most of the absolute want has been met."[145] One Louisianian noted however, "Some of the boys are still without shoes and consequently have to keep themselves about the fire. Most of them have good clothes and none of them are without a good blanket."[146] In Anderson's Division there were those still barefooted and badly clad. The axes rang ceaselessly in the woods as the soldiers chopped firewood to stay warm and cook.

"Our fare is very bad; nothing but beef and flour," added the Louisianian, "and no chance to buy anything in the country."[147] An efficient forager from another mess wrote that they "scour the country for ten miles around for provisions, such as we cannot get in camps. We get gingercakes, and gingernuts by the barrel from Richmond; the cakes sell at 35 cents a piece, and the nuts at $1 per quart. We get a few sweet potatoes occasionally at $6 a bushel, but our regular diet is fresh beef, hard crackers, and cold water. We also use large quantities of smoking tobacco."[148]

Anderson's Division bivouacked on the hills in back of Fredericksburg. On November 30 Maurin's Battery moved from near the Orange Plank Road to Dunman's farm, where they camped about a mile back of the battle line and near pine thickets.[149] Maurin was instructed to have his battery held in readiness to cooperate with Anderson's division "or for any other service that might be required of them."[150]

While in readiness the Canonniers resorted to every expedient to keep themselves warm with the most practical way being quartered in dug outs described as "two feet deep, with a fire place in one end, and a turf chimney, the hole covered with a little fly tent, the ends closed in with cedar brush."[151] For those without captured fly tents, a blanket covered their dug out. Said one, "We slept, cooked and ate in those holes, what little we could get to cook."[152] Though rations were issued almost daily it was noted, "one man could eat at one meal all the rations drawn by a mess of six or seven men for a day."[153] An artilleryman unable to get a good night's sleep because of the cold and damp ground related how his mess "Fixed up our bed off the ground on some pine poles, put little pine twigs a foot deep on top of the poles and some hen's nest grass on the top of the twigs. This made a very good and comfortable bed, and we slept first rate."[154]

On the hills overlooking Fredericksburg, artillery positions were selected on December 1. Longstreet ordered the batteries of the Washington Artillery and Alexander's Reserve Battalion to occupy the earthworks. Alexander, acting chief of artillery for Longstreet's corps,[155] was informed that if the two battalions were not sufficient to occupy the redoubts on the line he was to "call on any suitable brigade battery near."[156] Maurin was subsequently summoned and the Donaldsonville Artillery assigned to occupy four bastions,[157] the first being immediately on the left of the Plank Road and the three others in extended order to the left, along the ridge where Captain Charles Grandy's Norfolk Light Artillery Blues continued the defensive line. To the Canonniers' immediate right, across the Plank Road would be nine guns of the Washington Artillery with a 10-pounder Parrott rifle under Lieutenant John M. Galbraith of the First Company Washington Artillery next to the road, then two 3-inch rifles of the First Company (Captain Charles W. Squires) and two 12-pounder Napoleons of the Third Company (Captain Merritt B. "Buck" Miller) in the center, and two 12-pounder Napoleons and two 12-pounder howitzers of the Fourth Company (Captain B. F. Eshleman) on the extreme right, extending to the Telegraph Road.

Describing their position on Marye's Hill, the Washington Artillery's adjutant wrote

> [It] juts out towards the town, forming a sort of salient, and nearer to it than any of the other fortifications. Behind it rises Guest's Hill, and on the right, looking towards the town, is Lee's Hill. The plank road passes over the former, and the telegraph road to Richmond over the latter.
>
> At the foot of Marye's Hill the telegraph road runs, and then turns abruptly at right

> angles and branches off into the town. In front of Marye's Hill it is a sunken road, and on the side towards town is a stone wall about breast high.The field beyond is flush with the top of the wall.
>
> Before Marye's Hill is an open plain, with a few cottages and market-gardens, and divided up into lots by board fences until the outskirts are reached.
>
> In front of the town flows the Rappahannock, and opposite are the Stafford Heights, upon which the enemy has posted more than a hundred pieces of artillery, commanding the town. Thus, between our position on Marye's Hill and the enemy on Stafford lies the old-fashioned revolutionary town of Fredericksburg.

For the first time," noted Owen, "our army will fight behind dirt."[158]

Maurin and Lieutenants Prosper Landry and Camille Mollere were instructed to acquaint themselves with the position and bridges as Longstreet issued orders to examine all lines of approach so cannon ranges could be set from the parapets along the front. The engineers laid out their works though the infantrymen built them. After the works were occupied and inspected by the artillerymen, they improved them to their own satisfaction. The distance between the first and last pit assigned to the Donaldsonville guns on the line were, according to Landry, "About four hundred yards."[159]

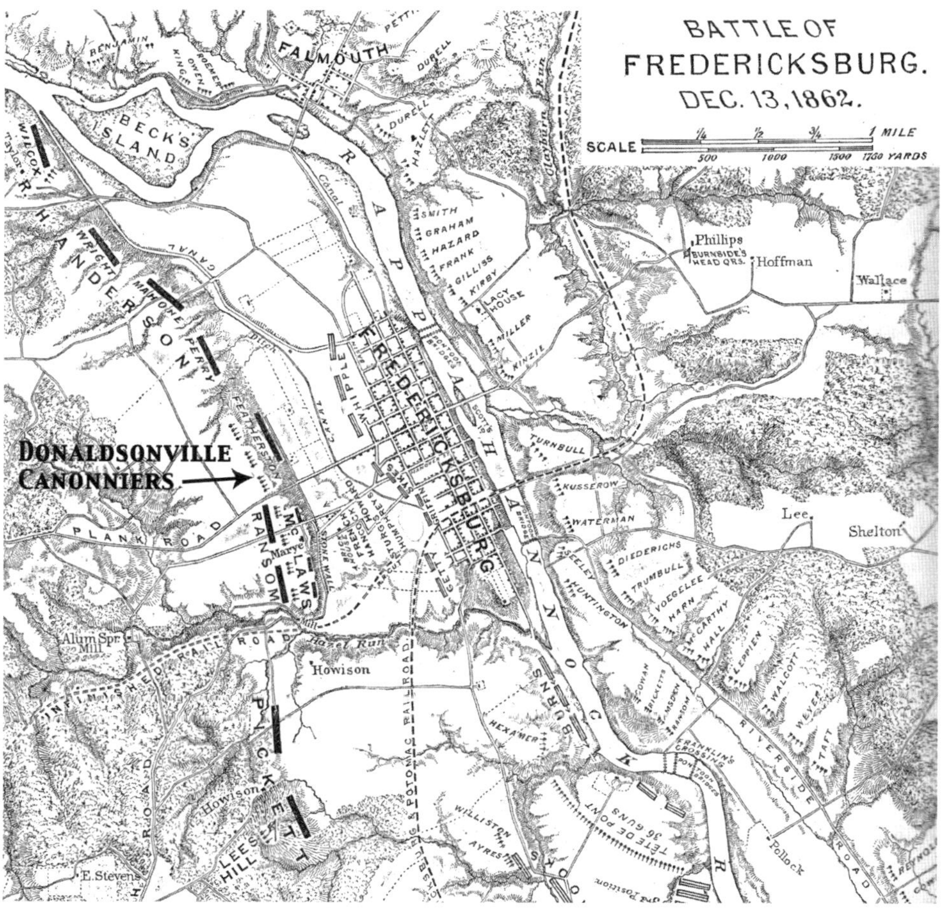

The Donaldsonville Artillery's four lunettes were on the northside of the Plank Road where Featherston's command is marked on the map. From *Battles and Leaders*.

On the night of December 1 Maurin's two 10-pounder Parrott rifles were placed on picket duty under Landry, who occupied the first two lunettes nearest the Plank Road. Mollere's detachment would occupy the other two lunettes with a 6-pounder smoothbore and the 3-inch rifle. Landry and Mollere's orders were to "move to these positions, but not to go there until the alarm, which will be the firing of two guns in rapid secession."[160] Maurin was ordered to have the other two 6-pounders in reserve under cover of the hills, and to have all his Canonniers issued "three days' rations, to be kept on hand for sudden moves, in addition to the supplies for daily consumption."[161] The great bulk of the commissary issue was fresh beef, cornmeal, and black-eyed peas.[162]

While Maurin's Battery and the Army of Northern Virginia waited with every expectation of a battle, ten days passed in cold and freezing weather with the ground "wet and slushy and the bivouac grounds . . . any thing but inviting."[163] December 5 turned out to be one of the more disagreeable days, as a Louisiana artillerist wrote, "It commenced raining at 10 am. Soon after turned to hail and sleet continuing with unabated fury during the entire day. Towards night it commenced snowing continuing until about midnight. The entire day was passed inside the tent reading and writing letters."[164] It was so cold that many of Longstreet's troops stood "shivering around their log fires."[165] A soldier in Anderson's Division noted he had not been more than a hundred yards "from his little fire."[166] "Everything," wrote another, "presents a lovely appearance covered in a mantle of white snow."[167] Even with the severe weather it was noticed, "Genl Lee visits the works often."[168]

Unusual activity prevailed on the Yankee side of the river at Stafford Heights on December 9 and 10 with the outpost bringing word that during the night heavy wagon trains were heard moving. Longstreet issued orders for his batteries to be hitched up at daylight on December 11 and at every campfire afterward, wrote the army's imminent historian, "The questions were argued, would the attack come with the dawn?"[169] The thoughts "were still vaguely ranging in the sleeping minds of the soldiers when, about 4:45 o'clock on the morning of December 11 there came from Marye's Heights, behind the town, the roar of a cannon, then another, and then silence. Two guns . . . signal guns . . . the agreed warning that the enemy was attempting to force a crossing of the Rappahannock."[170]

With the alert of the signal guns one of Anderson's soldiers recorded, "The long roll began to beat in our camp . . . and extended down the River as far as one could hear. Then the artillery bugles, then came the picket firing, then the booming of the heavy cannon, the trampling of horses on the frozen ground, the melting wagons, then orders, fall in. The men fell in. It could be heard on every hill and bottom near Fredericksburg, men, horses, wagons, all moving in double quick time." It "presented a picture almost indescribable."[171]

Though it was intensely cold, Canonnier Bugler Numa Braud joined in the sounding of "Boots and Saddles," which "sent the blood of artillerymen . . . coursing more rapidly through the veins."[172] All were instantly astir in the raw air and darkness. They picked up blankets and hurriedly packed haversacks, and harnessed and hitched horses to guns and caissons before hastening to their positions in the heavy, gray chilling fog. "At the same time," Prosper Landry reported, "the enemy opened a brisk cannonade, which lasted only a few minutes."[173] Up the hill they went on a frozen and slippery road with the cannons and their Canonniers going to their assigned gun pits. After the ammunition chest had been taken off the limbers and placed behind the parapets, and the horses brought to the rear, Maurin reported he "found every man to his post."[174]

The dense fog and smoky mist covered them and the surrounding country. It limited the view to less than a hundred yards and completely hid Fredericksburg from their view, except its steeples. Some time between six-thirty and seven o'clock in the morning the Federal artillery opened a tremendous fire upon the town to cover their infantry's river crossing. The firing was very rapid and almost incessant. When the fog lifted from the Donaldsonville positions around nine o'clock, the weather became pleasant and clear. The Gunners of Donaldson could now see the bright flashes of the Yankee guns and round white clouds of bursting shells and "the infernal bellow of the artillery drowned all other sounds."[175]

"The enemy," reported Maurin, "opened fire on me from his numerous field batteries and heavy guns on the opposite bank of the river, his shots falling around, some striking the works, but none doing any injury."[176] A Washington artilleryman in his lunette remembered,

> Thin white puffs of smoke float out from the long range guns planted high upon the crest of Stafford Heights . . . the continued roaring of these guns and the mad screech of their projectiles . . . did not curb the enthusiasm nor did it weaken the equilibrium of the gallant fighters of the army of Northern Virginia. . . . When the heavy shot and shell rained down mercilessly . . . and beat heavily against their rude earthworks, throwing sand and gravel in their faces and zig zagging with a shrill whir . . . one might have supposed . . . a shadow of a chance against such thundering artillery.[177]

The bombardment gradually subsided around ten o'clock in the morning with an occasional five minutes of rapid firing and flying shells "shrieking through the air, sounding like a wail of agony from some lost spirit."[178] This was repeated at intervals. Maurin added, "But with no better result for him or none worse for me."[179]

"The worst ordeal the soldier has to encounter," wrote an artilleryman, "is to lie still, and do nothing under heavy fire. It will get on his nerves . . . these hours of bombardment were trying. The only relief, if such it was, was trying to pierce the mist in front, and interpreting the meaning of the various sounds which floated up to us, and when the mist lifted, gazing with mingled curiosity and awe upon the glittering spectacle below us."[180]

Near midday it seemed every Federal gun was now firing into the town with "an earth-shaking cannonade."[181] The Confederate gunners looked silently on. Dense black columns of smoke began to rise from several houses that had caught on fire from the explosions. While the Donaldsonville gunners peered out over their mud lunettes, Colonel Edward P. Alexander, commander of the reserve artillery battalion, came forward to Marye's Hill to watch the events and remembered "few more magnificent spectacles."[182] He reported,

> The whole federal army had broken up their camps, packed their wagons and moved out on the hills, ready to cross the river as soon as the bridges were completed. Over 100,000 infantry were visible, standing apparently in great solid squares upon the hilltops, for a space of three miles, scattered all over the slopes were endless parks of ambulances, ordnance, commissary, quartermaster and regimental white-topped wagons, also parked in close squares and rectangles, and very impressive in the sense of order and system which they conveyed. And still more impressive to military eyes though less conspicuous and showy were the dark colored parks of batteries of artillery scattered here and there among them. Then, in front, was the three mile line of angry blazing guns firing through white clouds of smoke and almost shaking the earth with their roar. Over and in the town the white winkings of the bursting shells reminded one of a countless swarm of fire-flies. Several buildings were set on fire, and their black smoke rose in remarkably slender, straight, and tall columns for two hundred feet, perhaps, before they began to spread horizontally and unite in a great black canopy. And over the whole scene there hung, high in the air, above the rear of the Federal lines, two immense black, captive balloons, like two great spirits of the air attendant on the coming struggle.[183]

"To all this cannonade," added Alexander, "not one of our guns replied with a single shot!"[184] Orders had been issued that every battery officer "was to fire with great deliberation, and to fire only upon large bodies of troops."[185] Maurin was in acknowledgement and reported, "According to orders, I withheld my fire until late in the evening, when the enemy came down to cross, but the increasing darkness preventing me from seeing the effects of my shots, I ceased firing."[186] A member of Grandy's Battery to the left of Mollere's guns related their rifled section opened and "after firing some forty rounds they ceased, and shortly after the enemy also stopped as it was becoming too dark to sight the guns."[187] After dark all remained quiet.[188]

The different commands bivouacked for the night in the works beside their guns. The bleak winds and bitter cold made the hours long and the men shivered through the night. While the Canonniers huddled in their bastions the enemy's bugles and drums were almost constantly heard playing reveille and "Long Roll" from three-thirty in the morning to daylight. "I shall never forget . . . that night," wrote a Washington artilleryman in his lunette, "bands played, drums beat, horns blew and every known character of noise conceivable was resorted to . . . reminding one of a boisterous carnival night in the 'Crescent City.'"[189]

At four-thirty in the morning the rumbling of Federal artillery trains moving across the pontoon bridges could be heard, and shortly after six o'clock, December 12, Maurin received the same instructions as given to the Washington Artillery's commander: "As soon as the enemy's infantry comes in range of your long-range guns Gen. Longstreet wishes you to open upon them with effect. Be particular in acquiring the bearing and range of the streets of the town. The enemy passing through them will give you an opportunity to rake him, which you will, of course, take."[190]

At seven o'clock in the morning a good view of the town was had before the fog settled down and limited the Canonniers' view to three or four hundred yards. "At 8:30 a.m.," wrote a Washington artilleryman, "skirmishing began gradually."[191] Shortly after, at about twenty minutes past nine o'clock, Maurin reported, "A company of sharpshooters advanced on my left, but a few well-directed shots from Mollere's section drove them back into the town."[192] This drew an immediate and very rapid reply from the numerous Federal batteries and heavy guns, despite an exceedingly heavy fog, but after half an hour the firing gradually ceased.

Skirmishing then began in front of the Washington Artillery's guns "with no important result," according to one of the artillerymen.[193] The fog did not lift until two o'clock in the afternoon, at which time the Confederate artillerists could "discern the hills opposite the city densely covered with the enemy's infantry and artillery."[194] Alexander also noted the continued crossing of the Federal army, which "Occupied nearly the whole day" as "the fog completely hid the Federal movements . . . and no fighting occurred, except a liberal shelling of the Confederate batteries, from the opposite shore, and a little practice by the latter at infantry columns when exposed in easy range."[195]

Of this "little practice," Maurin reported,

> The enemy was now seen coming down in force from the opposite hills in order to cross. The distance was rather too great for much accuracy, yet a shell from my 10-pounder Parrott proved effective, bursting in the midst of an advancing column, causing it to stagger, making some run, and sending the mounted officers to arrest the flight of the fugitives. That this shot effected more than a mere panic was attested, a short time after, by the arrival in that spot of four ambulances, which returned with their load of killed and wounded.[196]

While waiting near the riverbank a Yankee noted this same evening "a little affair" opposite Maurin's guns and wrote, "A brigade of infantry came marching gaily over the hill by the Lacy House, with a full band playing 'Bully for You,' when a rebel battery on the high land opposite Falmouth dropped a percussion shell into the midst of the band, and promptly followed it up with two or three more which took effect among the troops. The defiant music instantly ceased, and band and infantry broke ranks and ran for shelter amidst cries of derision from our men."[197]

By four o'clock in the afternoon all was quiet again. With the gloom of night approaching and no campfires, details came up to the heights with rations of cornbread and a little piece of bacon. The Canonniers ate in the dark. Beside their guns the Donaldsonville Artillery and Lee's army passed another cold bitter night, and "as we lay on the cold ground," wrote a veteran, "we could see smoke and even the flames ascending from the burning city."[198]

During the night the wind died down and the freezing fog rose, making the early morning of December 13, 1862, "Dark and much obscured."[199] The Confederate artillerists along the heights were unable to see but could again very distinctly hear the rumbling of wagons and artillery. At daybreak the bugles and drum corps of both armies sounded reveille, after which the troops began to stir and prepare their early meal of the customary cornbread and bacon.

With the air fresh and nipping, Maurin's four gun crews anxiously waited in their pits "for all knew," remembered the Washington Artillery's adjutant, "we should have a battle to-day and a great one, for the enemy had crossed the river in immense force, upon his pontoons during the night."[200] Another indication of the coming conflict was the visit along the line by Longstreet before daylight and later of Pendleton, who reported the works "occupied by Maurin's and other batteries . . . all were ready."[201]

While thick fog still enveloped the plain and made everything invisible beyond fifty or sixty yards, Colonel Walton, Adjutant Owen, and the Washington Artillery's bugler, inspected their gun pits. While visiting the First Company's gun near the plank road, Owen recorded, "We found Galbraith and his boys wide-awake and ready for business. Across the plank road, in an earthwork, was the battery of Donaldsonville Cannoneers, of Louisiana, all Creoles and gallant soldiers."[202] In recognition Prosper Landry noted too, "Our old friends, the Washington Artillery."[203]

The Louisiana artillerists on Marye's Heights waited, shivering, excited, and gazing into the muffled valley. At an early hour the Federal batteries across the river "began to play"[204] and fired blindly through the fog at Longstreet's dug-in artillery positions. After nine o'clock in the morning the fighting began on the far right. Although the roar was incessant, the intervening fog obstructed the Canonniers' view. For the next hour or so the Louisianians chatted with each other and ate a lunch of hard crackers. The fog began to dissipate near ten o'clock in the morning, and soon the white steeples of Fredericksburg's churches were visible above the gray mist. At ten-thirty in the morning, Lee ordered Longstreet's guns to test the ranges and soon a quick blaze of fire swept from Marye's Heights northward.[205]

A half-hour later Longstreet sent word that the batteries were to open fire through the streets or at any points where blue troops were seen about the city. Maurin reported that his gun in the first pit near the Plank Road fired a few shots at a column of the enemy seen crossing the street of which the Plank Road is a prolongation and "forced it to take another line of march behind the brow of the hills."[206]

Before opening fire an artillerist wrote, "What an awful suspense these last moments are. The gun is charged, lanyard in hand, the gunner at the trail, ammunition heaped in piles nearby, waiting for the order to fire."[207]

A diarist in the Washington Artillery recorded, "We could plainly see the enemy in strong force moving through the town and about noon we saw them advancing, amid the ringing of all the bells and music in the town."[208]

Of the Northern regimental bands' music a Confederate officer noted it "could be distinctly heard along the whole line."[209] One Yankee brass band that came across the pontoon bridge with its column occupied a house where they began to play the spirited tune "Yankee

Doodle." Being within range, Maurin personally sighted one of his field pieces at the house but missed it. After the crew reloaded, Maurin again took aim and this time when the gun was fired the second shot "hit it straight." The music from that band, like the day before, ceased at once![210]

Between eleven and eleven-thirty in the morning a brisk skirmish fire was heard toward the town. Confederate skirmishers fired and fell back as the head of a Federal column emerged from one of the city streets. More Yankees followed, pouring out from the streets in their strong columns as the mist rolled away under a bright noonday sun. The Yanks headed straight for Marye's Heights. When the enemy's "heavy column's debauched from the town and were marching across the valley in line of battle to attack our lines," reported Maurin, "the second and third pieces were the only [Donaldsonville] guns that could be brought to bear on them."[211] With the Canonniers of the second piece, Landry noted, "Until we saw them advancing, we had no idea of the splendid position of that gun. It could enfilade them as easy as rolling off a log—and it did it with a hearty good will."[212]

Still observing, Alexander recorded, "No sooner did their columns appear than the eleven guns of Walton and Maurin, which bore upon their advance, opened a murderous fire on them, in the face of which, however, they crossed the canal and took shelter behind the rising ground between it and Marye's hills."[213] Of this advance Owen observed, "They came on at the double-quick, with loud cries of 'Hi! Hi! Hi!' which we could distinctly hear. Their arms were carried at 'right shoulder shift,' and their colors were aslant the shoulders of the color-sergeants. They crossed the canal at the bridge, and getting behind the bank to low ground to deploy, were almost concealed from our sight. It was 12:30 p.m., and it was evident that we were now going to have it hot and heavy."[214]

For a while the Yankee regiments remained hidden from the Confederate view while the Louisiana guns in disclosing their positions again received a furious fire from the Union

Artillery on Marye's Hill
From *Battles and Leaders*.

heavy batteries across the river. The enemy infantry soon "showed himself above the crest of the ridge and advanced in columns of brigades, and at once," wrote Owen, "our guns began their deadly work with shell and solid shot." He noted "their bright bayonets glistening in the sunlight made the line look like a huge serpent of blue and steel."[215]

Now plainly visible, "On they came . . . completing their deployment as they advanced. They planted three standards defiantly, but in the very act received the full blast of the artillery. . . . So intense was the fire and so perfectly laid that the ranks thinned at the very first round and soon were melting back to the ditch in blue and blood. The Confederate infantry had scarcely anything to do in repulsing their first advance. Shellfire sufficed."[216]

So effectively did the Donaldsonville guns fire, Maurin reported, "The enemy brought forward, immediately in front, on the edge of the town, eight pieces, which opened on me so furiously that they succeeded in diverting my fire, but not before I had fired more than 200 rounds."[217] Landry did not count the enemy's batteries that "sallied forth from the town, and appearing in our front, began to play on us. We let it play on, preferring the enfilading game, which was more interesting and more profitable."[218]

Of these several batteries that advanced to the edge of the city, Alexander wrote they "opened a severe cannonade to aid those on the Stafford side in extinguishing the Marye's Hill guns."[219] Landry added, "If only one of their shells had fallen in our pit it would have silenced many a voice besides that of our gun. Fortunately for us none did, but unfortunately for the infantry supporting us, some did fall among them, as usual, and killed many."[220]

The second Federal attack pushed beyond the point of the first before it struck a storm of canister shot from the artillery and deadly infantry fire from the base and crest of Marye's Heights.[221] A Yankee infantryman described the scene,

> As we took position for the charge . . . their artillery opened on us; before we had dressed our line the head of tall Warren Webster, of Company I, flew from his shoulders, and while the horrid red fountain was still spouting from the neck, our well-ordered line was sweeping forward on the double-quick, under the best directed artillery fire that we had ever suffered or seen, and soon came within range of canister and the deadly fire of well-covered infantry . . . and the men, looking only to the front, went pluckily on through that hell of countless projectiles which shrieked, burst, and hissed through the air, or tore the ground around us. Our colors fell again and again . . . coming to halt within two hundred yards of the rebel infantry, our line opened fire . . . making no further attempt to advance, we passed the rest of the afternoon lying flat upon the ground, firing slowly, whenever a covered rebel showed his head.[222]

After the second attack was stopped, a third attack began. Others came at intervals of scarcely more than a quarter of an hour. Behind each attack was the might of all the guns the Federals could bring to bear, and before three o'clock in the afternoon, one attack with much vigor pushed even closer to the stone wall from behind which the infantry fired. Landry wrote,

> We then beheld a grand spectacle. Instead of falling back, like all its predecessors . . . one regiment kept on advancing in the face of this storm of lead and iron.
>
> It kept on advancing until it had reached a declivity at the foot of Marye's Hill, where the men squatted in comparative security. . . Having rested a moment, the commanding officer ascended that declivity, followed by his color-bearer, and within pistol-shot of the star-spangled cross the star-spangled banner waved defiantly. Raising his sword, he called aloud, urging his men to follow their flag. But the flag had gone too far and they did not follow. Before so much bravery anger seemed to give way to admiration, and of those thousand muskets still warm with the fire which had thinned his ranks, there was but one that had the courage to fire—and the color-bearer fell.

A view of Fredericksburg. The Donaldsonville Artillery's position would be on the horizon above the artist signature's initial "A." ARW; courtesy of the Library of Congress.

> He was, doubtless, killed in conformity with the usages of civilized warfare. Nevertheless we were sorry to see him fall...The flag did not remain long on the ground. A man stepped forward and raised it. For several minutes these two men stood on the hill, looking defiantly in the very eyes of death which glared at them from every muzzle of a thousand guns. Despairing to bring his men to the assault, the officer and his solitary companion finally returned to the shelter offered by the declivity at the foot of the hill, and the threatened charge was not attempted again.[223]

The Federals with their overmastering artillery continued "plastering the whole front."[224] Maurin reported that the enemy's "shots were so well directed that I could only occasionally give a round to the infantry whenever the opportunity occurred. What harm I did them their smoke, as well as mine, prevented me from seeing, yet I saw one shell burst fairly among one of his detachments."[225] Landry also recorded a "number of sharpshooters from many windows before us began to send us those little bullets which kill more men than your big cannon balls. These guns soon got the range on us to such a fine point that almost every shot hit the epaulment of our pit and ricocheted over our heads. We had now to load and fire kneeling."[226]

The Gunners of Donaldson took casualties as Maurin reported, "Of the first piece Cannoneers Adolph[e] Grilhe and F[elix] Babin were wounded, the former severely and the latter slightly."[227] Jean Batiste Adolphe Grilhe, a five-foot five inch, twenty-two-year-old Donaldsonville native and "good hearted man"[228] was finally admitted to General Hospital Number 11 (Globe Hospital) in Richmond a week later. He returned to duty on Christmas, four days before his birthday.[229] The twenty-year-old Babin's injury was so slight that he remained with the battery.[230]

Brigadier General Winfield S. Featherston's Mississippi Brigade had, around ten o'clock that morning, moved from the left to a position about one hundred yards behind the Donaldsonville gun emplacements. Mollere's far left lunette with the smoothbore six-pounder gun faced Mary Washington's tomb. During the Federal charges against Marye's Heights many Yanks seeking shelter crawled out of the canal up to the Mary Washington tomb, and into the graveyard near it. In response to their fire, a message was sent to Mollere's Canonniers "asking them to direct fire on the tomb and the graveyard and flush the covey of blue bellies" so "we could take them on the wing," wrote a Mississippian. He added that,

> The request to shell the grave of the mother of the 'Father of His Country' was refused, but they consented to fire a few shots into the cemetery. Soon a great noise of bursting marble was heard and double results obtained, as a fragment of marble was as good for killing purposes as a shell. Many a Yank doubtless had this inscription on his tomb, 'Killed by a tombstone that broke loose at Fredericksburg.' When the artillery flushed

> them we got in some deadly work with our rifles. . . . In a short time the Yanks ceased fire and cleared the graveyard.[231]

From their position on the hillside the Mississippians saw that Mollere's gun threw "a hot fire into the Yanks . . . the enemy having the protection of the canal bank and cemetery."[232] In his report Maurin simply noted, "A regiment . . . was driven back by Lieutenant Mollere's section."[233]

Freeman wrote, "Along the sunken road the volleys flashed; down the hillside roared the echo of the guns." He noted that during the next two attacks "against the enemy the full weight of lead and iron was hurled. The repulse was swift, easy, ghastly. Dead men were piling up now between the ditch and the wall."[234]

The gallant crews of the two enfilading Donaldsonville guns had to load and fire at the attacking columns while kneeling. The crew had to replenish their caissons three times, which was made difficult by the loss of three horses killed and two wounded.[235] The popular Assumption Parish lad Antoine Sobral, just eighteen years old with big brown eyes and the nickname "La Fortune," received a slight wound to the head by a piece of exploding shell. The fortunate youngster was not hospitalized.[236] Eugene Cooley who had just recently joined the battery, received a wound through the right leg below the knee, sending him to the General Hospital in Staunton, Virginia. Cooley rejoined the battery in March 1863.[237]

After three-thirty in the afternoon and during a lull before the sixth enemy attack, an aide of Longstreet's, Captain Osman Latrobe, decided he wanted "to go over and play the deuce with the enemy."[238] Latrobe rode over to the Washington Artillery's position to see how they were doing. "We tell him," wrote their adjutant, "'All right, except we are running short of ammunition,' and . . . he promises to see about it, and, as our place is 'too hot for him,' he gallops away, only to get into a hotter one; for he rode over to Maurin's battery."[239]

Maurin stated Latrobe "came and suggested the propriety of dislodging two or three regiments standing behind a steep hill, which not only protected, but also concealed them from our men, on whom they were evidently preparing to make a charge." Landry explained however, "To execute this order, it was necessary . . . to move the gun out of the pit, because it could not be depressed within range of the objective point without bringing the muzzle below the epaulement and against the wall of the pit." Maurin reported the 10-pounder Parrott "could not be brought to bear on them without taking it out of the bastion, and, to do this, were to meet certain death from the guns in front, which by this time obtained a perfect range." Not only was the aim of the Federal guns on target, Landry noted the enemy's "shots were following each other so rapidly that they shut us down, as it were, under solid bars of iron projectiles."[240]

General Longstreet's aide, Captain Osman Latrobe, who "suggested the propriety" of moving Lieutenant Prosper Landry's gun out of its lunette.
Courtesy of the Confederate Memorial Hall.

On riding to Landry's gun pit, one shot struck Latrobe's horse in the right hind leg, very badly wounding the animal while Latrobe was on it. He continued on foot and made "the suggestion" to Landry. It "was no sooner made" said Maurin, "than Lieutenant Landry ordered it out, and, together with Captain Latrobe, helped the men to pull and put [the gun] in position." Landry later remembered,

> It was simple justice to say there was not a man who went out of that pit without believing he was going out to die—and yet they went without hesitation. And they succeeded in getting that gun out; but, alas! they did not succeed in getting out between shots, for as they emerged above ground the next shot came and, bursting in their midst, killed as good and brave a man as ever lived—Claudius Linossier.[241]

Maurin reported, "It was scarcely out, and not yet in position, when Cannoneer Linossier fell, dead, pierced to the heart by a piece of shell."[242]

"The fate of their comrade seemed to inspire my men with renewed determination, and, undaunted by the shots of the guns and bullets of the sharpshooters, which were flying thick and fast around them, they behaved with the calm courage which deserves the highest praise," wrote Maurin.[243] About the deadly explosion, Landry added, "Wonderful to relate, it killed no other, wounded none, and left our gun uninjured and ready to do its duty. . . . By taking that gun on the open hill it had been raised about three feet above and moved some twenty feet to the right of its former position."[244]

The 126th Pennsylvania Infantry was one of the regiments that lay massed on the right of the Plank Road in a meadow, their left near the tan yard of Hurkamp's Tannery. "While there," wrote one, "we noticed unusual activity about a battery of the enemy planted on a hill about ½ mile distant—we distinctly saw an officer ride up—the cannoniers come out from their cover and load and train the gun—we knew it was intended for us. The next moment they opened fire on us—with shell."[245] The first shot struck amidst the resting Ninety-first Pennsylvania Infantry Regiment; it left one lieutenant mortally wounded, six men killed, and one wounded. Their colonel reported, "We were immediately removed."[246] The next shell landed amongst the 126th Pennsylvania, a member of which wrote, "Our brigade was crowded up close to each other as we possibly could get—we all laid down in the mud never thinking what a dangerous position we were in until we saw 4 or 5 Rebels push a cannon out from behind a large earth work and fire a shell at us."[247] The second explosion killed three and wounded two. One "poor" Yankee had his head torn off. "It was the most horrible thing that ever I saw," wrote the Pennsylvanian, adding, "They fired 2 or 3 rounds more, we had to get out of that as quick as we could. We crossed the pike to get out of range of the guns, but in crossing the sharp shooters commenced to pick our men off."[248]

After Maurin's men relocated the gun from the lunette, the Federal artillery had to alter its aim accordingly. "Before they recovered it," wrote Landry, "our men had time to fire five rounds, giving their undivided attention to the task assigned them, not noticing the ten guns, the sharpshooters, and the heavy guns, whose shots were plowing the ground around them."[249] Observing the action, Maurin wrote, "The piece was loaded and fired with such precision that not one shot was lost, but every one telling with frightful effect."[250] The gun was loaded for the sixth time when the first shot that struck it knocked it down by breaking a wheel in two pieces and wounding nearly every man. "It was loaded ready to fire," clarified Maurin, "when it was disabled by a shell, which broke a wheel, and at the same time wounded 3 men."[251]

Of the seven men who put a shoulder to the wheel to take the gun out, three were not injured: Latrobe, who stood by the gun all the while cheering; a Canonnier who was getting the seventh round from an ammunition chest in the pit; and Prosper Landry. "Of all the wounded," reported Landry, "Dernon Leblanc was the only one who could not walk. We carried him back to our pit, which we found quite comfortable. One of his heels had been shot off. With a face all bloody from a wound in the head, Morelli recollected that the gun was loaded. He went out and fired it. If it was no longer well aimed it was at least pointing in the right direction."[252]

Of the three wounded Donaldsonville artillerymen, Corporal Tomasso Morelli (who went by the pseudonym of Thomas Morel) with the rich bass voice was described as a "good, honest, and brave man" and "ever willing to serve."[253] Maurin reported his "skill as a gunner cannot be too highly prized."[254] Landry wrote, "His services were very valuable,"[256] but not solely as a gunner. Being the best "Printer" in the company, he was utilized in writing out the four copies of the bi-monthly Muster Rolls and other paperwork for the battery. Morelli was sent to Richmond on December 15 and admitted into Louisiana Hospital where he was treated for his head wound. Released on January 2, 1863, he returned to the battery that day.

Arriving in Richmond a day later on December 16, 1862, was the rather tall, hazel-eyed, twenty-six-year-old Ascension planter, Private Louis-Dernaud "Dernon" Leblanc, brother of fellow Canonnier Private Narcisse Leblanc. Dernon was admitted into Louisiana Hospital after having his foot amputated because of his heel being shot off. He remained in Richmond and was discharged on November 24, 1863, on a surgeon's certificate from Jackson Hospital. He returned to the Louisiana Hospital where for the next year his attentiveness to fellow sick and wounded Canonniers and Louisianians was exceedingly appreciated.[257]

The third seriously wounded Canonnier was Private François Perez, thirty-five, who was hit in three different places. He reached Richmond on December 19 and was admitted into the Globe, or General Hospital Number 11. Perez transferred to the Louisiana Hospital on January 8, 1863, and some time in March 1863 returned to the battery. On April 2, 1863, suffering from his wounds received at Fredericksburg, Perez went back to Richmond's Receiving and Wayside Hospital before being transferred to Henningsen Hospital. He eventually succumbed to his wounds there on May 5, 1863. A bachelor and native of France, he lived and worked as a stave maker in Donaldsonville when the war broke out. He left $26.50 in effects.[258]

Prosper Landry would later remember the affair of trying to dislodge the enemy and wrote, "If we did not succeed, we had the satisfaction of having tried."[259] Maurin reported, "But the object was accomplished; some fled, some were killed, and the remainder dared not leave their cover."[260] It was recorded: "For this action" the Donaldsonville Canonniers "received the compliments and thanks of Lieut. Genl. Longstreet on the field."[261]

La Audacieux Fait or the daring deed of Lieutenant Prosper Landry's gun was "seen by hundreds of Confederate soldiers"[262] and "cheered lustily by many throats," which "inspired them in a way that nothing but such heroic actions on the field of battle can do."[263]

This depiction of Lieutenant Prosper Landry's gun crew at the Battle of Fredericksburg, December 13, 1862, was drawn by Leon Fremaux, considered one of the war's great topographical engineers because of his maps and drawings. Courtesy Mrs. W. C. "Nathalie G." Nelson, Metairie, La., and a special thanks to Ken Lejeune, Gretna, La.

Chapter Eight

Un Adversaire demi-nu, demi-affamé, à moitié-armé
(A Half-Naked, Half-Starved, Half-Armed Foe)

On December 13, 1862, the last Federal attack from Fredericksburg against Marye's Heights began after twilight had already begun to obscure the scene. Earlier in the evening, between four and five o'clock, and before this last attack, nine guns from Lieutenant Colonel Edward P. Alexander's artillery battalion rode in and replaced the guns of the Washington Artillery next to the Donaldsonville Artillery's lunettes.

"Through the smoke and twilight," remembered Alexander, "the assaulting column was scarcely seen in its dark uniform."[1] The Confederate fire, including the lone Donaldsonville gun that could be brought to bear, did all that could be done and ceased firing only when the flashes of the Federal guns no longer gave targets. This attack, like the others before, faltered, and after dark, at about six o'clock, the firing gradually died out on both sides. A combatant near the Canonniers and their guns wrote, "Night closed on the bloody scene, oh, what a blessing to the weary soldier is night; none can appreciate it who have not been in battle."[2]

> Soon after darkness fell over the battlefield there rose a glow on the Confederate left, far up the Rappahannock. It was a dim, ghostly light beyond the horizon that grew in brightness until it covered a wide arc of the horizon. Then the sky flushed and grew dark again. Now shining white, it reddened and dimmed and blazed once more till it lighted the faces of the marveling soldiers. It could be nothing less than that of which Southern boys often had heard, though never had they seen.

So wrote Douglas Southall Freeman. The fantastic sky painting was called by the Creoles *L'aurore,* the Aurora Borealis. It was around this time the Canonniers replaced the broken wheel and removed Lieutenant Prosper Landry's disabled gun, it being relieved by another gun from Alexander's Battalion.[3]

The three remaining Donaldsonville guns remained in their lunettes with everyone expecting another attack in the morning. In the darkened field in front of the Confederate lines a number of Yankees were still alive and lying where they fell wounded, their piteous groans and cries for water plainly audible to the Confederates throughout the night. Lieutenant General James Longstreet issued orders during the night to be prepared for a renewal of the battle at daylight. Ammunition for the artillery was replenished during the miserably cold and damp night while the Southern wounded were cared for.[4]

After the night passed off quietly, the morning was again obscured by a smoky mist and fog. At dawn three guns from Alexander's Battalion relieved the three remaining Donaldsonville guns from their lunettes. The Canonniers returned to camp near Dunman's Farm. It turned out to be a clear day. Though another assault was expected on this day, December 14, the time passed with little firing from the enemy batteries and only an occasional skirmish along the front line.

For the Gunners of Donaldson the time was spent in camp talking and listening as the day was filled with "nothing but flying rumors."[5] Captain Victor Maurin reported for the day, "Nothing worth mentioning was done on Sunday."[6] When night came the Donaldsonville captain received orders to send two guns to the works on the left of the front line. Maurin subsequently ordered Lieutenant Camille Mollere's two old 6-pounders that had been in reserve during the battle sent to Brigadier General Cadmus Wilcox's Alabama Brigade that was on guard near the dam of the Rappahannock River towards Marye's Heights.

"On the 15th," reported General Robert E. Lee, "the enemy still retained his position, apparently ready for battle, but the day passed as the preceding."[7] For the Donaldsonville Artillery and other batteries of Anderson's Division in camp, Private John Walters of Grandy's Norfolk Blues Battery noted, "Very little was done by us today." Rumors were again received in the camps "but none," added Walters, "are worth recording owing to their indefiniteness."[8] The two Donaldsonville 6-pounder guns with Wilcox's pickets on the extreme left of the lines were joined by the First, Third, and Fourth Companies of the Washington Artillery, who took position in the works on their right nearby.

"The night of the 15th was dark, windy, and rainy, and the morning of the 16th foggy," reported Wilcox. "When the fog disappeared it revealed the fact that the enemy had recrossed the river, nothing remaining on this side but a few of the wounded, the unburied dead, and a few of the infantry pickets whom they had failed to relieve. These delivered themselves up to my command as prisoners."[9]

On the southern side of the river, Donaldsonville Canonnier Artificer François "Bienvenu" Cire scribbled in his memorandum: "All quiet."[10] A Washington artilleryman observed the enemy on the northern side of the river "moving from our front all day," adding, they "withdrew their forces from the river, the smoke from their camp fires distinctly seen in the woods."[11] While the Federals moved away the Gunners of Donaldson and the soldiers of the Army of Northern Virginia were this day unaware of a northern newspaper's report of the Battle of Fredericksburg that read, "The finest army that ever trod the earth has suffered a decided repulse at the hand of a *half-naked, half-starved, half-armed foe*."[12]

A soldier in Wright's Georgia Brigade that had been positioned near the lunettes occupied by Maurin's guns during the battle wrote, "We discovered to our great surprise that the enemy was entirely gone from this side of the river. Wishing to see where they had gone and to get some relics, I ventured out through the battlefield, and . . . picked up several little articles on the field, among which were a nice Yankee uniform coat, several pipes, a pocket knife, fork, etc." He added, "The battlefield like all others . . . presented a horrible sight." That did not stop him from noticing, "There were a good many soldiers moving over the field."[13]

Many Canonniers were likely part of those visiting the town and field, and unquestionably had experiences similar to Walters from Grandy's Battery which fought and camped here alongside the Donaldsonville Artillery. On December 16, 1862, Walters wrote in his diary:

> Wishing to see in what condition they had left the city, in company with some of our boys, I went there and knowing very well that sentinels had been posted, we executed a flank movement and entered it in the rear of the lines of sentinels. I found the city a wretched sight, three or four squares burned to the ground, churches and dwellings riddled by shot and shell and many of the latter entirely demolished, while the streets were full of destroyed furniture, books, papers, and dead horses. While in many of the

> gardens, lanes, and house porches were lying dead soldiers in every conceivable shape and position, some recently dead, while many, possibly those slain the first day of the fight, were far gone towards decomposition, the whole presenting an appearance such as I never care to see again. . . . After looking around for some time I went to the field from which the troops charged our batteries, and here the sight was horrible. 'Tis true the wounded had been removed . . . but six or seven hundred lay strewn around, from whom our men were busily engaged in removing the clothing and other articles of value. I did a little in that line myself and got an excellent knapsack (empty), a haversack, a canteen, and four one pound bars of yellow soap. While looking about I saw a good pair of boots on a man's feet and as they looked to be about my size, I concluded to appropriate them, to which I began to pull at them, but while tugging away . . . the leg came off with it just above the knee. As this was more than I bargained for, I left the boots.[14]

Many in Lee's army needed a new outfit of clothing to keep warm in. "The blue," wrote a veteran, "had been transferred from the forms of the dead to those of living Confederates. They had just drawn their winter clothing, the blues."[15] An officer reported, "Nearly all the dead were stripped," adding, "A woman who lived in one of the houses near the stone-wall has related that 'the morning after the battle the field was blue; but the morning after the Federals withdrew the field was white.'"[16] Longstreet's Confederates took numerous blankets and overcoats, knapsacks, haversacks, canteens, and fly-tents. Among the Louisiana artillerymen there were "big jollifications"[17] over the captured supplies.

For ten days (December 17-27, 1862) the Canonniers camped on Dunman's Farm, except the two guns at the front, and all tried to keep warm while talking of home. Most lounged about in the bivouac and had undisturbed slumbers at night in troughs that were covered with the little tents taken from the battlefield. These were used as a lean-to over the troughs and covered with a layer of pine poles, leaves, brush, and dirt with the open ends closed with cedar brush and a campfire. These quarters kept out the wind blast but not the cold, though with three to a tent and using blankets in common the men slept "tolerably comfortably."[18]

Maurin's Battery along with Anderson's Division cooked and ate in their holes wrote one, as they "settled in camp with all the conveniences possible for Confederate soldiers, except rations and clothes, which were scant."[19] The dominant compulsion of the men "was to find more food than the commissary could provide,"[20] and the obtaining of firewood for cooking and warmth was just as prevailing. It was commemorated in verse:

> *wander to and fro,*
> *seeking wood to kindle*
> *Fires amidst the snow.*[21]

These few lines speak of the importance of and how scarce firewood had become around the camps.

Of these December nights about the campfire one veteran artillerist remembered, "There was a bugler in Colonel Walton's [Washington Artillery] battalion who . . . excelled. . . . Never can I forget the dreamy beauty of 'taps' (lights out) as he played it in the pine-woods back of Fredericksburg. . . . As soft as the notes of a flute . . . the 'wooing music of this 'sleep call,' as it floated in soothing wavelets out into the quiet woods."[22]

The most arduous task during the day for the Canonniers was procuring feed for the battery's horses that for the most part were gaunt and jaded. The country immediately around the army had been so completely swept of fodder that the battery's wagons had to travel thirty miles for forage. Adding to the Donaldsonville battery's commissary troubles was the fact that Canonnier Quartermaster Sergeant Jonathan Scheuer, whose duty it was to look after the forage, fuel, and provisions for the battery, took sick and died at forty-one years old in camp on December 24, 1862.[23]

On December 18 Maurin submitted his report on "the part taken by my battery in the engagements before Fredericksburg" to Brigadier General Edward A. Perry. In closing the report Maurin wrote, "I can but render praise to Lieutenants Landry and Mollere for their gallant conduct, and to my cannoneers and drivers."[24] On the same day, Perry submitted his brigade report to Major General Richard H. Anderson and wrote, "I respectfully call to the attention of the general the gallant conduct of the Donaldsonville Battery throughout the engagement. Both officers and men stood bravely and faithfully at their posts, and, while exposed to an unusually heavy fire, the guns were handled with masterly skill and with great effect."[25] Anderson completed his division report on January 3, 1863, noting, "The commanders of batteries Captains Maurin, Huger, and Lewis, and Lieutenant Peet, commanding Grandy's battery, merit especial notice for their skills, courage, and good management throughout the five days. Their batteries were subjected to a very heavy fire from those of the enemy. None of their shot, however, were spent in an artillery duel, but were reserved for those opportunities which the advancing and retiring columns of the enemy gave them."[26]

Brigadier General Robert Ransom Jr. commanded infantry at the crest of Marye's Hill and submitted his divisional report. He made mention of the Donaldsonville Artillery by writing: "Lieutenant Landry, of Captain Maurin's battery . . . by direction of Captain Latrobe, acting adjutant and inspector general, took his piece from behind the epaulment in order to dislodge a body of the enemy upon whom the battery could not play. Most effectually he performed this service, but in doing so lost several of his men, and had his piece disabled. His conduct was admirable, for during the time he was exposed to a direct fire of six and an enfilade fire of four guns."[27]

On December 18, 1862, Lieutenant General James Longstreet issued General Orders stating, "The General commanding the First Corps desires to express his gratitude for the good conduct of his troops in the late encounter with the enemy. They had so often attested their valor upon the battle-fields . . . yet, notwithstanding he knew them to be steadfast veterans, they still kindle in him a new admiration by the remarkable firmness with which they defended Marye's Hill."[28]

In summarizing the December 13 battle, Lee reported, "Six times did the enemy, notwithstanding the havoc caused by our batteries, press on with great determination to within 100 yards of the foot of the hill, but here encountered the deadly fire of our infantry, his columns were broken and fled in confusion to the town."[29] Lee added, "The artillery rendered efficient service on every part of the field, and greatly assisted in the defeat of the enemy. The batteries were exposed to an unusually heavy fire of artillery and infantry, which officers and men sustained with a coolness and courage worthy of the highest praise."[30] Alexander later estimated the nine guns of the Washington Artillery and his relieving nine guns, plus the Donaldsonville Artillery's two guns on Marye's Hill "fired about twenty-four hundred rounds from eleven pits."[31]

In *The Long Arm of Lee,* the classic work on Lee's artillery, Jennings C. Wise wrote,

> The *esprit de corps* of many of the batteries was superb. . . the *entente cordiale* existing between the sister arms [infantry and artillery] was the natural consequence of services rendered. It could never [have] arisen from mere theoretical potency. What soldier of Jackson's army could suppress his admiration for Pelham and his men, who under the very eyes of the whole corps had with dauntless courage assailed, unaided, a Federal division? What soldier of Longstreet's corps whose heart failed to respond to the

> emotions which such deed as those of Landry . . . are wont to generate?
>
> Verily the plain of Fredericksburg was an amphitheater upon which the Confederate Artillery won the proud acclaims of a martial race, the leaders of which, whether friend or foe, have echoed their applause through the pages of history. Gens. Lee, Longstreet, Jackson, A. P. Hill, McLaws, in fact all Confederate commanders, in their reports of the battle of Fredericksburg, speak again and again of the 'rapid,' 'destructive,' 'well-directed,' 'demoralizing,' 'murderous,' 'accurate,' 'efficacious,' fire and 'extraordinary' effect of their guns at all points, and of the 'unflinching' courage, 'unshaken steadiness,' 'animation and spirit' with which they were 'admirably served,' and repeatedly mention with high commendation individual commanders and batteries.
>
> The tribute paid the Confederate Artillery by the Federal commanders is even more emphatic as to the important and preeminent part it played in the repulse of Burnside's army. Their reports—from those of Gen[eral]s . . . to those of officers commanding brigades, regiments, companies, and especially batteries,—characterize the fire of opposing artillery as murderous, deadly, terrific, destructive, continuous, severe, galling, vigorous, furious, heavy, enfilading, cross, and concentrated. In some instances special reference is made to the effect of individual batteries or guns, which unless exceptionally well served would have made no particular individual impression.[32]

The Gunners of Donaldson evidently made a "particular impression," for the historian Wise wrote the Donaldsonville Canonniers "are worthy of the best traditions of their ancestors who fought with the great Napoleon."[33]

On Christmas Eve, Special Orders from Lee were issued directing all the army's artillery batteries except twelve to move to more convenient positions because of the difficulty in obtaining forage. The batteries of Longstreet's Corps were ordered to a point on the Telegraph Road about midway between the Mattapony and North Anna Rivers and within about five miles of Chilesburg in Caroline County. The last paragraph of this order referenced the army's worn horses and stated, "The commanding officer of each camp is required to give particular and earnest attention to the proper care of the horses, seeing that they are placed in position as much sheltered as possible, and that they are properly groomed and fed . . . and every effort will be made to resuscitate and restore them to proper condition for the spring campaign."[34]

Although the artillery was about to change campsites, Maurin's Battery remained on Dunman's Farm, where they celebrated Christmas and awaited relief for the two guns still on picket duty. Christmas left many of the men in the Army of Northern Virginia in a pensive mood. One Southerner took up the pen in the hope of getting a letter home. He wrote, "The sun shines feebly through a thin cloud, the air is mild and pleasant, a gentle breeze is making music through the leaves of the lofty pines that stand near our bivouac. All is quiet and still, and that very stillness recalls some sad and painful thoughts."[35] Others used the holiday more pragmatically by "washing and mending clothes." Wrote one judicious cannoneer, it was "a pleasant pastime for this hallowed day."[36]

A holiday dinner was for many the only way to celebrate, and they made do with a little brown sugar and a little fresh meat and the seemingly inexhaustible camp biscuit issued by the commissary. Various messmates were able to supplement their Christmas meals with purchases made in Richmond. Members of the Canonniers had that opportunity with the sad duty of transporting Scheuer's body for burial. With the return to duty of Corporal Adolphe Grilhe on Christmas Day it would seem the battery's ambulance was making regular trips to the capital and no doubt supplementing their rations. When luxuries from Richmond arrived back in camp or were bought from sutlers, the men indulged. Turkeys were had for four dollars each, chickens a dollar-fifty apiece, a dozen apples (for dumplings) cost three-fifty, butter was a dollar a pound, molasses six dollars a gallon, and coffee four dollars a pound. Whiskey for making sauce was also obtained for five dollars a pint from the country around.[37] All the whiskey was not used for sauce though, as Anderson's aid noted; "During Christmas the men would smuggle processed whiskey into camp and sell it at five dollars a drink and surprising as it is the privates who only get eleven dollars a month are the men who buy."[38]

A recently promoted ex-private reported on Christmas, "Everything is very quiet now-a-days. . . . I will have a leetle drop of the crathur and have egg-nog."[39] One would imagine Corporal John O'Hara who took on the quartermaster duties, and his fellow Canonniers celebrated in a like style. Before receiving their feast, one messmate said it was a "dull Christmas," but after indulging reported, "we have been living in style."[40] In this regard another of the Louisianians wrote, "So it may be seen that our Christmas dinner though in camp was none the worse."[41]

Christmas Night of '62 became etched in many a Southern soldier's mind as a veteran artilleryman later penned:

The wintry blast goes wailing by,
The snow is falling overhead;
I hear the lonely sentry's tread,
And distant watch-fires light the sky.

Dim forms go flitting through the gloom;
The soldiers cluster round the blaze
To talk of other Christmas days,
And softly speak of home and home.[42]

During the morning of December 27 some twelve or fourteen batteries, including the Donaldsonville Artillery, received their orders to prepare to leave. In preparation Maurin submitted to Perry a Special Requisition for material, "Indispensable for my battery," which included wagon grease that was especially needed for the carriages and caissons whose axles were in dire need. Out of the five items requested—fifty pounds of wagon grease, five gallons neat's-foot oil (for the harnesses and other leather gear) seventy-five halters, seventy-five sets horseshoes, and fifty pounds of horseshoe nails, only the halters and horseshoes were received on the day of the requisition. In conjunction with the orders to move, the two Donaldsonville guns on picket duty were relieved after dark and rejoined the battery.

At an early hour on December 28 the Donaldsonville Artillery and the Norfolk Light Artillery Blues were called up and with the artillery column of Longstreet's Corps were soon underway. Maurin's Canonniers and Grandy's Blues moved by road from Fredericksburg towards Richmond through a flat, sand-clay land of small farms with vast reaches of pine and cedar forest alongside the road. For the most part the march was very good, except at the fords of the Massaponax Creek, Ni River, and Po River. There it was muddy, rocky, and very hilly. The column traveled a total of thirteen miles before halting within two miles of the ford on the Matta River, near the crossroads of Thornburg (formerly called Mud Tavern).[43]

At daybreak on December 29 the batteries started out and crossed the Matta River. After traveling nineteen miles for the day, the weary Canonniers, with their 105 tired horses and sixteen mules, and with Grandy's Battery, camped late at night within a few miles of Chesterfield Station on the Richmond, Fredericksburg, and Potomac Railroad tracks.

The next morning the artillerymen cut roads through the dense pinewoods where locations protecting the horses and men from the wind were found. They then started building winter quarters of pine and cedar brush while the officers put up their wall tents.[44]

Within a half mile of the Donaldsonville Artillery, the Washington Artillery set up camp. Their adjutant wrote:

> Here each mess is thrown upon its own resources and ingenuity to make themselves as comfortable as they can. Some dig a deep square hole or cellar, with a fireplace and chimney at one end. Over the hole is stretched a tent 'fly,' and then, by covering the floor with clean straw, a comfortable dwelling-place is made. Others are in Sibley tents, with large mud fireplaces and chimneys; and, as wood is plenty, all hands are enjoying a much-needed rest. Head-quarters are in tents, and the whole camp is in a large pine woods.[45]

As soon as their quarters were finished the Canonniers started cleaning up the woods, cutting down bushes, and constructing the stables, which took until January 9, 1863, to finish. The poles used for building the shelters had to be carried over half a mile on the shoulders of the men. The animals, no matter what the weather, were fed and watered everyday, and needed to be shod. This kept the battery's brightly glowing forge constantly busy by those with blacksmithing experience, such as Canonnier Artificer Olibert Hebert, "a most estimable gentleman"[46] who was considered an "engineer,"[47] and Privates Octave Dupas, just nineteen from Paincourtville, or Leopold Keroll, a French immigrant who often was detailed during the war as a blacksmith. All made "the flying sparks" and "ringing of blacksmith's hammer" a common sight and sound in the bivouac.[48]

For others, camp duties were light and consisted of maintenance and repairs on equipment, accoutrements, and leather goods, guarding horses and guns, and feeding and caring for the animals. Forage requisitions for the quartermaster department were being signed every other day by Maurin for 5,808 pounds of corn (twelve pounds for each animal per day) at Hanover Junction where the railroad was shipping it in to a very active Chesterfield Station. From there, the wagons hauled it to camp.[49]

With the horses sheltered and the men as comfortable as circumstances permitted, and abundant fuel for their campfires, the Louisianians enjoyed a much-needed rest. The weather cooperated too; a Louisiana artilleryman recorded it was "clear," "pleasant," or "beautiful" for eleven of the first fifteen days of 1863.[50] Rations for the men, according to another artillerist, were "sufficient, if not abundant."[51] It was also noted how cornbread was the most constant item in the diet along with fresh and salt meat. This made the Cajun Canonniers *satisfait* (content) as cornbread was the *piece de resistance,* while *la couche-couche* (Cajun corn cereal) made with fresh milk meant they were getting an enjoyable and healthy meal.

There were a few peddlers in the vicinity of the camps who made a regular business of peddling whiskey and ginger cakes out of barrels from their wagons and so, on some nights, along with the dancing and singing around the campfire there no doubt was some *la soulrie* (drunkeness.)[52] Even the Donaldsonville officers and sergeants like Prosper, John, and "Tip" Landry liked to partake of liquid cheer, interspersed with music and toasts, and all heartily enjoyed the "doings."[53]

Music not only added its cheer, it was a favorite recreation, with one nearby camp having a string band of which a veteran wrote, "'Oft in the silly night,' when the winds were gentle, and the moonlight shimmered through the leafless trees, did the sweet strains of this band beguile the earlier hours, reminding us of sweethearts and the 'old folks at home.' Then, again, we would perpetrate a desperate masculine dance to the time of merrier strains."[54] "Richmond is a Hard Road to Travel" was an enormously popular tune in these artillery camps.[55]

The Confederate artillerists and Canonniers occupied themselves not only with music, humor, and the use of spirits, tobacco, and religion, they also chased hares and squirrels and yelled at every citizen seen. They played card games—the Euchre game was the most popular, especially with the French Creoles.[56] Another favored diversion in camp was the whittling of wood, a favorite pastime of the Cajuns and many other Confederates. Naturally the men were cheerful with few complaints. An artillery officer noted the "general feeling is that after one or two more defeats the enemy would surely give it up."[57]

A rain fell on the night of January 15/16, 1863, and in the morning, very unexpectedly, orders came. Maurin and Grandy were instructed to have their batteries ready to move at a moment's notice. Walters of Grandy's Battery wrote, "While the bustle incident to such an order and the eager 'What's the meaning of this?' were circulating about, the order came to hitch up and take the road . . . without delay."[58]

Cire later recorded that the Donaldsonville Artillery, with some twenty or twenty-five other batteries, received orders to go to Fredericksburg while leaving a few men and eight horses behind to guard the camps and baggage. The artillery column marched all day in weather that was intensely cold with a keen wind and horrendous mud causing the guns to get stuck often. At dark the column halted for the night and soon campfires with cheerful blazes dispelled the cold and wind, which died down about ten o'clock that night.

The artillery column started again at an early hour the next morning and struggled all day to move through the mud. Cire recorded the "roads are very bad, and it is very cold."[59] Many of the artillerists on foot took to the fields to walk where the roads were bad. On the night of January 17/18, 1863, the column bivouacked in large-oak woods in the vicinity of Massaponax Church, nine miles from Fredericksburg.[60]

"We left at 10-a.m.," continued Cire on January 18, "and camped for the night at 5 miles from Fredericksburg."[61] The Canonniers spent another night trying to stay warm around the campfire and awoke the next morning with Maurin receiving orders. The battery was to take its guns on picket duty at United States Ford on the Rappahannock River in support of Brigadier General Ambrose "Rans" Wright's Georgia Brigade which arrived there two days earlier. Maurin's Battery, in the evening of this "splendid day"[62] and with the roads "firm,"[63] reached Wright's brigade camp located about two miles back from the river. The Georgia troops guarded the ford on the river and at the same time built breastworks. A Georgia soldier said, "The river is the dividing line between ours and the Yankee pickets. The pickets are in plain view of each other, but neither side is allowed to fire on the other, or to speak to each other."[64]

For the next two days, January 20 and 21, Cire recorded, "We began making breast works, it rained in the night," and, "Rain again, we were ordered to work on the breast works in the day and at night."[65] The orders were no doubt as a result of the Yankees attempting to flank Lee's army by the upper river fords, but with the inclement weather turning the roads into bottomless quagmires the Federal army floundered and returned to its camps. This movement of the Army of the Potomac became known as the "Mud March."[66]

About five hundred yards below the ford the Canonniers began building their fortifications with a "total insufficiency"[67] of entrenching tools. With few shovels and picks, along with bad weather, the work was dawdling. Conditions were described as being "intensely disagreeable"[68] with rain coming down in torrents nearly the whole time, which brought mud and water a foot deep for the first week of work. In the second week the rain turned to snow with Cire on January 27 recording, "It rained all day." On the twenty-eighth he added, "Snow all day."[69]

Another nearby artillerist recorded, "At an early hour this morning it began to snow, which continued all day without intermission; clothing everything in winter's garb. The picture presented was beautiful in the extreme, covered as the ground and bushes were with snow, while the trees bent and broke with the weight of their burden. All afternoon and night could be heard the crash of falling pines, some of them huge old fellows, while limbs of cedars bent to the ground, all their thousand little sprigs and limbs pointing downward."[70] Although it was stunning scenery, "We had a rough time in the snow," wrote a Georgian, and "it was very cold going to and from work."[71]

In the Donaldsonville and Georgia brigade camp along the road, the troops slept under pine shrubbery covered with a fly tent or blanket on top of the bushes put up in "wagoners style."[72] All were buried under the snow, and to keep the fires burning, firewood had to be cut and carried about two hundred yards. The Canonniers finally finished their "strong breastworks"[73] on February 3. The guns remained in camp until February 8 at which time they were brought into the finished redoubts. "We were ordered to make other breast works," noted Cire.[74] Works for two additional guns were built nearer the ford along the riverbank.

The waters of the Rappahannock rushed noisily over the rocks as either snow or rain fell three days in the week. The Canonniers, like others guarding the ford, tried to forget their misery while they worked on or occupied the works and did picket duty. The country around United States Ford was "poor and miserable,"[75] and during the winter it was "a horrible place." An officer noted, "The road approaching it was almost impassable and rations reached our soldiers less frequently than biting necessity demanded."[76] Another later wrote, "It was all one monotonous mess," adding, "the only redeeming feature about that camp was plentiful wild onion and chives."[77] This allowed the messmates to manufacture a garlic, or wild onion stew. What else went into the stew can only be conjecture, as Maurin reported, "During our stay at United States Ford we lost three horses & two mules from exposure, want of food & exhaustion."[78]

In acknowledgement of their stay and for the record of the Georgia infantrymen and the Gunners of Donaldson it was written, "The sufferings . . . at United States Ford, from cold, short rations, and a scanty supply of clothing, could scarcely have been excelled by those which so severely tried the fortitude and patriotism of our forefathers, when quartered in the historic Valley Forge." "Our sufferings were greater than men can usually endure," it was concluded.[79]

On February 22 the Donaldsonville Artillery and Wright's Brigade received orders to send off their baggage and move the next day for Hamilton's Crossing near Fredericksburg. "That night," wrote one of Wright's Georgians, "there came a very severe snow storm, the severest we ever witnessed. It was extremely cold; the wind seemed to come the near way from the North pole. We were so cold, owing to the keen wind and drifting snow, covering us where we lay, trying to sleep, that we are compelled to 'retreat,' from our pleasant beds, build fires and stand around them until morning, to prevent freezing."[80]

The Donaldsonville Artillery started out for the Orange Plank Road from their camp about midday on the Spotswood Road. The snow was about eighteen inches deep and in traveling over the very bad roads through the nasty snow they covered about nine miles. "We camped after dark, making holes in the snow so as to lie down," recorded Cire. The next day the Canonnier artificer scribbled in his memorandum that the battery remained in the same place on the Plank Road about three miles from Fredericksburg. He added that it was "awfully cold."[81]

The following day, February 25, Cire wrote, "We left and marched through Fredericksburg to Hamilton's Crossing and there camped. We were lucky for we found log cabins already made."[82] The Donaldsonville camp of log huts with clay-filled interstices was situated on the sides of two hills, sheltered from the cold north winds and, though not very regularly laid out, presented a cozy, comfortable appearance. Everything was quiet along the lines even though the Yankees were in plain view on the heights across the river. One of the Louisianians noted they saw on the other side of the river "thousands of snow-white tents and hundreds of waggons parked . . . the camps were swarming with our blue-coated enemies, some engaged in playing games, some in drilling, and others ranged in long, dark lines going through 'dress parade' or 'inspection.'"[83]

With very wet and miry ground rendering the maneuverability of cannon "quite difficult if not impossible"[84] the Donaldsonville Artillery remained bivouacked at Hamilton's Crossing for thirty-seven days. During this time of idleness, their days were employed in two important purposes. The first was to again try and get more to eat than the scanty rations issued, which was eighteen ounces of flour, four ounces of an indifferent quality of bacon, and an occasional supply of rice, sugar, or molasses. Daily details were sent out into the woods to gather sassafras buds, wild onions, garlic, lamb's quarter, and poke sprouts to supplement the rations. "Our fare here," reported an artilleryman, "was greatly improved by the addition of fresh fish, so abundant . . . in the Rappahannock and adjacent creeks . . . of the herring and shad left by the hundreds in the grass and shallows as the tide receded, the soldiers had only to wade in and with stick or bare hand to secure all they could carry."[85] During the battery's time at Hamilton's Crossing trout, shad, bass, and rock herring fish were all frequently caught. "One apiece," wrote a veteran, "makes us a good meal."[86]

In the middle of March 1863 two months pay was issued to the Canonniers, most of which probably went straight to the sutlers who, wrote a Louisianian from Hamilton's Crossing, "Have a few beans & peas which we buy and have a feast of liquor about once a week." He also noted, "We can procure Oysters here at from five to ten Dollars per gallon of which we are all passionately fond."[87]

The second aim of Maurin's Battery was having the horses cared for. Browsing and grazing of the horses when possible lessened the want of forage that was now futile to procure in sufficient quantity. The Donaldsonville Battery's ninety-seven horses on March 12, 1863, were given constant personal attention, however the lack of forage along with the previous hard service reduced their efficiency and brought their numbers down to eighty-one within a month. The mules who generally were better able to stand hard usage, bad feed, or no feed, suffered too as their numbers dropped from twenty-one to thirteen.[88]

On the muster roll for March 12, 1863, Maurin reported ninety-seven privates present for duty with the battery's total number being well over one hundred men, an indication that sickness prevalent among many other batteries did not strike the Donaldsonville Artillery. Interestingly enough Canonnier Private Ernest Monnot kept a recipe, "For dysentery," possibly handed down by his father who had been a major and health officer of the Ninety-third Regiment of the Line in Napoleon Bonaparte's army[89] that stated, "2 oz. simaruba, 1 oz. buck horn, 1 oz. Carb. Of Iron, 1 bottle white wine, 1 bottle water. Mix and boil the whole, until reduces to half the quantity, Dose a table spoon 3 times a day & reduce the dose as soon as effects are beneficial."[90] The general health of the Donaldsonville camp for whatever reason was better than most.

Maurin reported the battery's discipline, instruction, and military appearance were good, though their clothing was not.[91] During this winter one veteran would later write, "A fellow sometimes don't get a chance to change his rags more than once per month, and when such is the case the lice get so numerous that they tote a fellow clean away."[92]

On March 3 Cire recorded that Brigadier General Harry T. Hays's First Louisiana Brigade, with two familiar compatriot companies, the Irish Volunteers from Donaldsonville of the Seventh Louisiana Regiment and the Eighth Louisiana Regiment's Phoenix Guards from Ascension and Assumption Parishes, "came and camped near us."[93] The Canonniers and the Louisiana Brigade bivouacked within a few hundred yards of each other and for the next month they visited with each other like *amis et parents* (kith and kin) and spent the inclement evenings "in playing cards, singing and jovial conversation."[94] When it was not raining or snowing, "We frequently amuse ourselves at leisure times by a game of ball. This is quite a show sometimes. As many as one hundred are engaged at once," wrote one of Hays's Louisianians.[95]

In early April Maurin received orders to have his battery report back to the artillery camps around Chesterfield Station. On April 3 the guns were brought to the railroad station to await a train to transport them as the roads were impassable and the weather still very cold. On the morning of April 4 the battery's horses were walked cross-country from Hamilton's Crossing through fields and woods of thick Loblolly Pine, Evergreen Holly bushes, and Sweet Juniper trees before arriving in the afternoon at the Camp Caroline artillery camps along the Telegraph Road near Carmel Church and Chesterfield Station. The battery's six guns, three caissons, one forge, three wagons, and one ambulance were loaded onto cars and left in the evening of April 4 by rail. Despite the snowfall through the night, the train arrived early the next morning. The horses hauled the guns from the station and parked them in an open field.

The men camped in woods full of large oak and hickory trees while the horses were sheltered in the pine thickets.[96] There was barely enough work to keep the Canonniers and animals employed. One mule, evidently not liking the idle times, was "distempered and unserviceable"[97] and turned in. Maurin's battery remained in camp near Chesterfield Station up to the thirtieth of April with the Captain reporting, "Nothing of importance transpired during that time."[98]

In April there was nothing of importance concerning military maneuvers, but there were significant transformations taking place within the organization of the artillery in the Army of Northern Virginia. The attaching of a battery to a brigade was abolished, and in its place artillery battalions were formed. The battalions would be comprised for the most part of four batteries and each particular battalion would ordinarily attend to a certain division, and report to and receive orders from the division commander, though they were liable to be divided or detached. On April 16, 1863, Special Orders No. 106 announced the new organization. Maurin's Donaldsonville Artillery was assigned to and designated Company B of Battalion A, under command of Lieutenant Colonel John J. Garnett. This battalion included Captain John W. Lewis's Pittsylvania (Virginia) Battery as Company A, Captain Charles R. Grandy's Norfolk (Virginia) Light Artillery Blues as Company C, and Captain Joseph D. Moore's (formerly Huger's) Norfolk (Virginia) Battery as Company D. The battalion was assigned to Major General Richard H. Anderson's Division of Longstreet's First Corps.[99]

John J. Garnett late in life.
From R.A. Brock (editor), *Gen. Robert Edward Lee: Soldier, Citizen, and Christian Patriot.*

The handsome and martial looking Garnett, with "magnificent black eyes and hair,"[100] was deemed an efficient officer, well liked, with a great deal of dry humor. Just twenty-four years of age, he was well-known and highly appreciated by Longstreet, having been an inspector of ordnance and artillery in his corps since November 14, 1862. He attended the Military Academy at West Point but resigned a couple of months before graduating when hostilities broke out in 1861. Garnett did not assume command of the new battalion until May 1, 1863. His battalion flag was white satin with the battle flag in the corner and in heavy gilt on the white field the words "Garnett's Battalion," under which was the letter "A" and the words "Light Artillery."[101]

Retained as the second field officer of the battalion was Major Charles Richardson, Anderson's divisional artillery chief since November 1862. Though ambitious, Richardson was later described by a private in the battalion as "a fine gentleman and a good soldier who pays more attention to the comfort and welfare of his men and horses than to his own ease."[102]

Maurin reported the discipline of the Gunners of Donaldson at this time was good, although their military appearance was only satisfactory since their clothing, with an additional two months wear, was still not very good. It appears the Canonniers, like other batteries in the artillery camps, were issued on average per company eight jackets, nineteen shirts, two pants, ten drawers, and four pairs of socks, when thirty to forty more pants and socks were needed. As to the jackets, shirts, and drawers supplied, this was just a third or a quarter of that requisite, plus canteens, haversacks, and caps needed by a couple of dozen artillerymen. Half the men in the artillery companies needed shoes to replace worn ones.[103]

The artillerists, regardless of inadequate clothing, shoes, and provisions had what was described as "that distinctive mien so characteristic of the field artillery." Along with "élan" and "morale" came promotions in the Donaldsonville Artillery.[104] Prosper Landry was officially made senior first lieutenant of the battery after Fredericksburg. Camille Mollere was advanced to junior first lieutenant on March 22, 1863. Sergeant François Hubert "Pousse" Treille and Private Antonio Raymond Rufin "Anthony"/"Antoine" Sanchez were promoted to the second lieutenant positions. The respected and sentimental Treille, who was twenty-eight years old, stood five-feet six-inches tall with hazel eyes and a *pousse* (growth of hair) on his chin, had shed a tear when he left his wife and two children on that gala day in 1861. In 1862, a year and a day after leaving Donaldsonville, he received a contused battle wound to the shoulder from a shell fragment at Boteler's Ford and now was a veteran who led "with soldier feeling" and "patriotism."[105] Sanchez was from Assumption Parish and of Isleños heritage. His ancestors were soldiers recruited for service in Louisiana by the Spanish Crown in the preceeding century. He was two months older than Treille but two inches shorter with dark eyes, dark hair, and a beard. Like Treille he was a gallant soldier who served "with distinction in the company"[106] and "commanded unqualified popular esteem."[107]

Promoted to sergeant positions from first, second, third, and fifth corporal were the eminent Oscar Demesme, a French born laborer twenty-six-years-old; Pierre Theophile Blouin, a young twenty-two-year-old Ascension veteran with gray-eyes who stood five feet eleven inches and was a *spiritali amicitia* (spiritual friend) of Prosper Landry;[108] Jean Trasimond "John" Landry, the thirty-two-year-old son of Donaldsonville's leading citizen who (irregardless of his high position in Creole society) was willing on the march to carry the baggage of an exhausted Canonnier;[109] and Louis Aristide "Tip" Landry, another twenty-two-year-old Creole veteran and son of a former Ascension congressman. The two Landry's, John and Tip, were not only cousins and brothers-in-arms but *meilleur ami (*best friends) though almost ten years apart in age. Of the Donaldsonville Artillery's twelve original corporals in September 1861 only one now remained a corporal after these promotions.[110]

Accordingly, eleven privates were now advanced to the rank of corporal. Promoted were Hypolite Eugene Acosta, a twenty-fiver-year-old Isleños from Donaldsonville; Thomas Burns, from Houma, Terrebonne Parish, a hard-working twenty-one-year-old Irishman and veteran of Drieux's First Louisiana Infantry Battalion; William F. "Buck" Chase, a Hebrew veteran of Drieux's Battalion who was twenty-two-years-old and later said he was proud to have "shared the distinguished service"[111] of the Creole gunners; Joseph Arthur Comstock, twenty-years-old from Donaldsonville, "widely known" and a participant "in every major engagement";[112] Jean Arture "Arthur" Eschavaria, son of an Assumption Parish *docteur*, twenty-two-years-old, five-feet six-inches tall with blue eyes and dark hair that "served with credit and distinction";[113]Jean Baptiste Adolphe Grilhe, age twenty-three, "good hearted"[114] and "inspiriting;"[115] and Tomasso Morelli, age twenty-eight (both Grilhe and Morelli were now recovered from their Fredericksburg wounds); Paul Humbert, a twenty-five-year-old Donaldsonville citizen and the last of this respected German family that had settled on the Lafourche;[116] Ygnace Louis Rougeau, age twenty-three, another brave gunner who "always faithfully fulfilled all his duties";[117] and finally, Antoine Sobral, "La Fortune,"[118] who at age eighteen was the youngest of the new corporals and probably the most encouraging.

Through a requisition, the battery on April 10 received eight sets of harnesses, sixteen horse leads, thirty pairs of spurs and straps, thirty-four pounds of nail rod, and one pair of wheel harnesses. After overhauling old harnesses and equipment, Maurin now reported a greater portion of the battery's accoutrements in good order, though the carriages and caissons to the guns after extended service were listed as bad.[119] The next day, April 11, Maurin was ordered to send the three 6-pounder guns *Honoré, Fidélité*, and *Liberté et Égalité* to the Tredegar Iron Works in Richmond, where they would be melted down and recast into, ironically, Napoleons, the 12-pounder bronze field gun that was now the most effective weapon in field artillery. The three inferior 6-pounders were promptly turned in and sent to Richmond.[120]

On March 2, 1863, Lee wrote to President Jefferson Davis that seventy Napoleons were required to replace the obsolete 6-pounder smoothbores in the army and requested the manufacture of Napoleons be accelerated, as they would increase the efficiency of the artillery. Tredegar could produce only forty-one of the seventy Napoleons needed between March 7 and May 1, 1863. The Donaldsonville Artillery received only two Napoleon guns, and those it seems, did not reach the battery until the first week of May 1863. Lee noted, "More delays . . . occurred than . . . anticipated in replacing our 6-pounders with Napoleons."[121]

Through April 28 the Donaldsonville and artillery camps along the Telegraph Road near Carmel Church and Chesterfield Station were undisturbed. The area was idyllic, with large clusters of pine woods "with only one or two farm houses of very poor people therein."[122] The artillerists did occasional guard duty at the artillery depot and train station while others assisted in the loading and unloading of the thirty-two artillery wagons coming and going as supplies and forage from expeditions were hauled in. For the nearby rural inhabitants the foraging by the artillerymen made the times "very lively."[123] The government compensated the owners of nearby properties after Pendleton ordered "a just appraisement of damages" as a result of the several artillery camps.[124]

While the horses browsed and grazed and chewed bark off the trees, "rumors" circulated in camp amongst the Louisiana artillerists that were soon followed by the words "no news."[125] During this interim of idle time the Canonniers attended Catholic Mass and made their Easter Communion from the priest of the 14th Louisiana Infantry, Reverend James B. Sheeran, who visited on a raining and very disagreeable April 15 morning.[126]

A nearby young Washington artilleryman recalled,

> Some of the boys . . . had dug a hole in the ground about 12 x 14 built a chimney and covered the shack with boards . . . dirt had been excavated to the depth of four feet, a plank was thrown around the center and leading to the fireplace on either side, planks for seats had been placed. This made a cozy and comfortable rest room and dining room. Pine knots were used for lights and the boys played all kinds of games with cards for money, so-called, and amusement. I remember in camp . . . drilling, answering roll calls, playing cards, for fun playing chess.[127]

The quiet and enjoyment of winter quarters ended on a cloudy and rainy April 29, when news was received that the enemy was throwing a pontoon bridge across the Rappahannock River below Fredericksburg. Pendleton was ordered to bring all the artillery near Chesterfield Station towards Fredericksburg in what was the beginning of the Battle of Chancellorsville. The artillery column was composed of Alexander's Battalion, along with Captain Henry H. Carlton's Troup (Georgia) and Captain Basil C. Manly's Ellis (North Carolina) batteries of Cabell's Battalion, and Moore's Norfolk Battery from Anderson's Division. The column took up the line of march at one o'clock in the afternoon under command of Frank Huger, the recently promoted major whose merit along with his battery's effectiveness did not exceed, according to his division commander, that of Maurin's merit or the Donaldsonville Artillery's efficiency.

Canonnier Private Octave Landry wrote, "Two different batteries took our three rifle guns to go on the line."[128] Huger's old battery was armed with just one 10-pounder Parrott rifle and one 3-inch Ordnance Rifle and probably received one of the Donaldsonville Artillery's rifle pieces. Carlton's Battery was armed with two 10-pounder Parrott rifles and a 12-pounder Howitzer and received an additional Parrott gun at the artillery camp. Not only short of guns, these two batteries also required sixteen and eighteen horses each.[129] All the batteries short of guns were awaiting the arrival of Napoleons from Richmond. The four companies of Washington Artillery under Captain B. F. Eshleman were ordered to move with efficiency that afternoon but, "We did not have enough horses, so we received orders to be ready to move in the morning," explained a Washington artilleryman.[130]

Pendleton instructed Eshleman to "borrow the best horses from Captain Maurin and the section of Grandy's battery. If your detail sent for horses reduces you much in men, get Captain Maurin to lend a few of his; they will be willing, I hope."[131] The Donaldsonville Artillery had eighty-one horses on hand, with another thirty-nine in Grandy's section. With Huger and Carlton's Batteries' needs, and the four companies of the Washington Artillery requiring sixty-five horses, there were only enough able horses left for Eshleman to lead ten of the Washington Artillery's sixteen guns towards Fredericksburg. There was no need to borrow any men, and except for a detail sent to Richmond for more horses, the Donaldsonville Artillery and section of Grandy's Norfolk Blues—along with the remaining Washington artillerymen—waited in camp.[132]

The Canonniers and other artillerists from their bivouac could only wait. Recorded one of the Louisianians:

> May 1st clear day, firing heard in direction of Fredericksburg.
> " 2nd clear & warm day, firing distinctly heard.
> " 3rd clear day, Ten pieces of [Washington Artillery] Battn. that went to the front were engaged today & six pieces were captured by the enemy . . . some members of the . . . companies were taken prisoners.
> " 4th clear day, some of the [Washington Artillery] boys who had lost their guns and escaped capture arrived in camp.[133]

Cire's memorandum on May 3 and 4 simply recorded, "Fighting is going on at

Chancellorsville, the enemy routed."[134] On May 5 Cire made no comments in his memorandum, perhaps for the reason that the detail that went to Richmond returned with horses and two Napoleon 12-pounder guns for the Donaldsonville Artillery.

Napoleon 12-pounder light field gun.
EAF; courtesy of the Library of Congress.

The very next day, May 6, Grandy's two rifle guns that had taken part in the first two days of battle and the Donaldsonville section with its two new "Napoleons were sent to Hanover Junction to protect the Bridge."[135] With large enemy cavalry forces in the area, Brigadier General James J. Pettigrew ordered the guns from the artillery camps to move three miles south to Chesterfield Bridge, where the Telegraph Road crossed the North Anna River. From there, the railroad span was located half a mile away to the east of the turnpike. Joined by a regiment of Pettigrew's Brigade, the Norfolk Blues and Donaldsonville Artillery gun sections spent the next four days in small earthen redoubts with the bridges fully guarded.[136]

Meanwhile back in Camp Caroline the remaining Canonniers awaited the return of their rifle pieces. Moore's Battery returned to camp on May 6. Carlton's Battery, with his extra Parrott rifle arrived on May 9.[137] The next day Cire recorded, "We came back to our camp and received orders to be ready to move at a moments notice."[138]

That evening Cire also recorded, "Genl. T. J. Jackson died of his wounds."[139] Thomas "Stonewall" Jackson, commander of the Army of Northern Virginia's Second Corps, was mortally wounded by accidental fire of his own men during the night of May 2, 1863, during the battle of Chancellorsville. Though the fight was another Confederate triumph, it was a "Pyrrhic victory"[140] because of Jackson's death on May 10, 1863. It was officially announced "with deep grief" to the army on May 11 by Lee.[141]

On the day of Lee's announcement about Jackson, orders attaching Maurin's Battery to Garnett's Battalion were received, and the Canonniers "raised camp."[142] They marched sixteen miles towards Fredericksburg and stopped on a small sluggish stream named the Po River near Stanard's Mill. The Donaldsonville Artillery bivouacked here near the Washington Artillery on Mrs. Stanard's farm in a splendid camp where the other three batteries of Garnett's Battalion soon joined them. They dubbed the place Camp Anderson. The Gunners of Donaldson and the battalion remained here for twenty-three days under mostly clear skies. One Louisiana artillerist simply noted they were "resting themselves."[143]

The artillerymen were "paid off"[144] on May 22, and they were "getting tolerable plenty of rations"[145] and "some nice milk every other day."[146] A Pelican State artillerist, in the Louisiana sportsman tradition, recorded during this time he and others "went fishing down the creek at day light, at 10 returned with 2 fish and 3 eels." On another day he went "to Po River . . . fished up one side and down the other for several miles—with meager success . . . 2 cats and a perch. Gave them to a Negro man ploughing in cropfield."[147] There was even sports as a Washington artilleryman noted on the day they were paid, "Match game of BaseBall between cannoneers and drivers, the cannoneers beat them 12 points."[148]

Walters from Garnett's camp wrote, "Nothing worth recording has taken place."[149] Another of the Louisiana artillerymen thought this was worth recording though, "Plenty of good whiskey selling for only 30c gallon."[150]

A Washington artilleryman also wrote, "Nights passed off quietly and no Boots and Saddles broke the stillness of our slumbering camp . . . nights beginning to be bright with newlight from a half moon . . . Heard Whipperwills."[151] After a week in Camp Anderson another of the Pelican artillerymen recorded, "Boys all in a good humor on account of our Rations being increased from a quarter to a half pound of Bacon and also giving us Peas."[152]

While one hundred horses allocated to the Donaldsonville Artillery grazed in fields with a grass springing, Captain Maurin requisitioned and received forage (twelve pounds of corn, per horse, per day) at Guinea Station, eight miles from camp on the R. F. & P. Railroad. Within two weeks Garnett's quartermaster was handling the forage requisitions for the battalion and receiving weekly at Guinea's a seven day supply of 26,124 pounds of corn for the four batteries with their 397 animals. Still, the majority of horses were thin and their condition generally bad.[153] The Donaldsonville guns were again in good order with two Napoleons, two Parrott rifles, and one 3-inch Ordnance Rifle, with caissons to each piece.

On June 1 a diarist in the Washington Artillery recorded, "Went down to wash our Pieces today, in the River. Some of the young men from New Orleans exiled by Gen. Banks joined our Battalion."[154] Two of those enlistees were natives of Ascension Parish who had been working as clerks in New Orleans, Louis Marcellin Comes, age twenty-seven, the son of a former mayor of Donaldsonville,[155] and Achilles Désiré Dupuy, age twenty-three and respectable, were now *en avant* (forward, to the front) with the Canonnier battery.

General Robert E. Lee reorganized the Army of Northern Virginia after the death of Jackson and on May 30, 1863, formally announced the establishment of a Third Corps under command of Lieutenant General Ambrose P. Hill. Major General Richard H. Anderson's division from Longstreet's First Corps was detached and assigned with two newly organized divisions (these being commanded by Major General Henry Heth and Major General William D. Pender) to comprise Hill's new command.

Pendleton was instructed to designate which battalions of artillery would serve in this new corps. On June 2 the adjustment of artillery battalions occurred with Garnett's Battalion of seventeen guns (Maurin's five, with, Grandy, Lewis, and Moore each having four) assigned to Major General Henry "Harry" Heth's Division. There was no formal announcement made to the troops in camp about the reorganization, so they could only speculate, pass rumors, and "feel pretty confident"[156] they had been transferred to Hill's Corps.[157] "The new Third Corps was not stinted" in regards to its artillery, wrote historian Douglas Southall Freeman. "Every one of the five battalions designated for it was good. Quick as Hill was to take offense at any alleged slight, he seems to have been entirely satisfied with the batteries allotted him."[158]

The Canonniers didn't have much time to ponder the new arrangement. The next day, "Orders were given to send heavy baggage to the rear and get ready to move at daylight next morning," wrote a Louisiana artillerist.[159] The following day, June 4, Cire recorded, "We have raised camp and marched to Fredericksburg and arrived there early in the evening and camped near the plank road—The Yankees have two balloons up."[160] Having moved to within about a mile of Fredericksburg, another of Garnett's artillerymen observed: "From the way our troops are moving I am inclined to think that our present idle life will soon be exchanged for a more stirring one."[161]

Chapter Nine

Destin dependent
(Fate Hung)

On June 5, 1863, Lieutenant General Ambrose P. Hill's Third Corps of the Army of Northern Virginia, with the divisions of Anderson, Heth, and Pender, began defending the entire Fredericksburg defensive line after the withdrawal of Lieutenant General Richard Ewell's Second Corps. One of five artillery battalions assigned to Hill's Corps was Colonel John J. Garnett's that included Captain Victor Maurin's Donaldsonville Artillery. Maurin functioned additionally as the second in command of the battalion while Major Charles Richardson was on leave in Richmond. Garnett's Battalion was composed of Maurin's five guns, plus four guns each from the batteries of Grandy's Norfolk Light Artillery Blues, Lewis's Pittsylvania (Virginia) Artillery, and Moore's Norfolk (Virginia) Battery, plus caissons and limbers, thirteen four-horse wagons carrying forage and commissary supplies plus baggage, one two-horse wagon for the medical department, and four traveling forges for repairs by the artificers.[1] The drivers and teamsters for the Donadsonville Artillery's three wagons were Privates Severin Blanchard, George Eppinger, Cleophus Landry, the brothers John and Henry Newchurch, and Adolphe Rougeau. Detailed as blacksmiths with the forge were Olibert Hebert and Leopold Keroll. Artificer Pierre Oubre was detailed to Gordonsville as a saddler.[2]

With the wagons parked near the plank road leading into Fredericksburg, a soldier wrote, "The impression in camp was that the enemy was moving up the [Rappahannock] river to confront Longstreet and Ewell's corps, which were said to have crossed above. All the troops that had been stationed here had gone towards Culpepper, and Hill's corps was now in charge of this position."[3] Scarcely had the last of Ewell's regiments wound their way over the hills when the Federals began to lay a pontoon bridge over the river on the old site opposite Deep Run. Donaldsonville Canonnier Artificer François "Bienvenu" Cire noted in his memorandum book on June 5, "We marched to the front—the Yankees have crossed the river."[4]Another member of Garnett's Battalion wrote of the day's events, "This afternoon . . . two guns were fired from the direction of the river below the city, and a minute or two after, the artillery from both sides opened on each other and continued until dark. The firing was very heavy. During its continuance we received orders to hitch up and prepare to move . . . at ten o'clock at night we received orders and moved to the old Telegraph road near Marye's Heights, where we awaited daylight in the confident anticipation of having a fight."[5]

Cire recorded the next day, "We are in position in the breast works on Lee's heights firing now and then."[6] Private John Walters of Grandy's Norfolk Light Artillery Blues battery noted, "Contrary to expectation, no fight took place today and but little firing, though the enemy are on our side of the river with quite a large force."[7]

Hill's Corps remained at Fredericksburg, where a member recorded, "We lay behind our works, expecting the enemy, until Sunday, June 14. But they, not indulging in anything more hostile than music and cheering, or, on one or two occasions, such a bold display of pickets as to require a few shells at our hands."[8] The Donaldsonville guns on June 9 and 10 "Opened fire on both sides," recounted Cire, adding, "We are having an artillery duel." After this and for the next few days it remained relatively quiet as the opponents eyed each other.

On June 14 Cire recorded, "The Yankees have recrossed the river."[9] Walters added,

> Up to this time, nothing of importance has occurred. Occasionally there has been a little firing from one side or the other, with no apparent results on either side. The enemy during the past week has thrown up some two or three miles of artillery and infantry breastworks, but judge our surprise this morning to learn that they had recrossed the river during last night and in such haste as to leave a large quantity of stores and arms behind, besides all their advance pickets who were taken prisoners. Further observation during the day showed that they have not only left their position on this side of the river, but the whole army has gone from the other side also.[10]

On the morning of June 15· Colonel and Chief of Artillery Reuben Lindsay Walker,[11] the new commander of the Third Corps' five artillery battalions and their eighty-six cannons,[12] ordered Garnett to withdraw his battalion from its position on Lee's Hill and move immediately to the rear on the Telegraph Road. Garnett's Battalion was ordered to report to Major General Henry Heth's Division.[13] This division contained four brigades numbering about seven thousand muskets and a long train of wagons that now included an additional twenty-five wagons from Garnett's Artillery. Each brigade of the division had roughly twenty wagons that, noted an onlooker, "Were marked U.S." It was also recorded that "in the rear of each regiment were from twenty to thirty Negro slaves, and a certain number of unarmed men carrying stretchers and wearing in their hats the red badges of the ambulance corps."[14]

With the weather intensely hot, Garnett's Battalion moved out on June 15 at eleven o'clock in the morning. Heth's infantry followed two hours later. Cire recorded, "We left our position, and marched in the direction of Culpeper. We have slept on the old Chancellors battle field."[15] The division's wagon train continued on after dark and finally stopped after going through Chancellorsville. The artillery battalion camped on the recent battleground. The infantry brigades were spread back along the road for a mile.

In camping here "our noses," wrote one, "received indisputable evidence of [the battle] in the effluvia arising from the many dead horses along the road. It was a curious fact . . . that horses killed in battle would swell into very large proportions from the gases generated internally and would lie in that state for months and no buzzards were ever seen to feed on them."[16]

Walters, Grandy's artilleryman, recorded, "Having walked about twenty miles today and it being very hot, I was pretty well used up at night."[17] All the troops were very tired and sleepy and spread their blankets under the sheltering trees as the disturbed whippoorwill's notes floated around. Stopping on a battlefield restrained many from mirth and jesting, but new enlistees arriving in camp, "*especially from home,*" brought out "our folly" and caused many to act "so much like children."[18] Donaldsonville Private Octave Landry jotted down on this night, "Camille Templet and others arrived from Louisiana and joined our company."[19]

Camille, the brother of amiable Canonnier Private Hypolite Templet, was a paroled prisoner of war cavalry corporal described as a "worthy and esteemed comrade" who was "not only a soldier in name but a soldier in deed."[20] He arrived with his brother-in-law Alcide Giroir and neighbor Armas Triche, both "good"[21] citizens. All were from near Napoleonville on Bayou Lafourche, Assumption Parish, and all three were veterans of the Second Louisiana Cavalry and the recent battles in the Lafourche District. The three brought salutations and news of home. Such an event, wrote a veteran, "Raises excitement among us."[22]

Octave Landry also recorded that night in camp, "Orders to cook 3 days rations, the only water to be had, in a well near where they had a hospital at the battle of Chancellorsville."[23] Walters wrote, "Near where we [camped] is a house that the enemy used as a hospital during the last battle, and I did not learn until it was to late that they had thrown the amputated arms and limbs of their wounded in the well. It is true that while drinking I thought the water had a peculiar smell and flavor, but I did not attribute that to the right cause until I saw an arm fished up. However I must confess that as thirsty as I was and not knowing what other water was to be obtained, a full knowledge of what was in the well would not have deterred me from drinking the water."[24] Early the next morning, June 16, having been aroused at four o'clock and told to get ready and march, Octave Landry recorded, "This morning in drawing water from the well a human foot was pulled up in a bucket."[25]

Garnett's Battalion of nine rifle guns, eight smoothbore guns, and seventeen caissons pulled by paltry horses moved off at sunrise. They followed Pettigrew's North Carolina Brigade, dressed in "splendid uniforms."[26] The weather again was very hot and the sweaty artillerymen wore their clothing in the usual utter absence of uniformity as to color and shape, with felt hats prevailing that soon became the same tint of a yellowish-brown color as "the dust which once puffed and puddle[d] under a single foot-fall, now billowed up in buff, choking clouds."[27] The very good but exceedingly dusty road soon became lined with discarded blankets and jackets as the dust strangled and blinded men and horses that traveled about fourteen miles before stopping near two o'clock in the evening. Cire simply documented the Canonnier movement for the day in his memorandum book, but another noted that when the troops camped they were "all in good spirits."[28]

The next morning, June 17, the division again rose at four in the morning with Maurin's Battery, and the battalion again following Pettigrew's infantry at sunrise. Marching in the most oppressive heat was very tiresome. Cire noted they went through Stevensburg, then at about eleven o'clock in the morning passed through Culpeper Plain with the infantry encamping a mile beyond the town of Culpeper. The artillery and wagons, having traveled some ten miles, stopped about midday and parked just outside the town. At Culpeper an officer noted, "Troops are continually passing in every direction & going it appears in the most opposite directions & yet they all have one common aim one common destination."[29]

After making camp some of the artillerymen from Garnett's Battalion went into town, which was filled with rumors received at no cost. Grandy's artillerist Walters paid two dollars for a meal and six dollars for a pint of "very poor quality" whiskey.[30] Others of the battalion remained in camp where they, like other soldiers, "Lie down at night upon a single blanket & have a biscuit or two & piece of ham for each meal."[31]

Heth's infantry left at three o'clock on the morning of June 18 with the artillery leaving four hours later at about seven o'clock. "In the early morning hours it was very cool and pleasant and we did not object to the rule of leaving camp by or before daylight, but as the sun got up in the sky, his rays beat down with fearful power. On this day it was particularly hot and as we trudged along we passed a number of men who had fallen out on account of the excessive heat," wrote a member of the Twenty-sixth North Carolina's Regimental Band, J. A. Lineback.[32] The Twenty-sixth along with the Eleventh, Forty-seventh, and Fifty-second North Carolina regiments of Pettigrew's Brigade, Heth's Division, marched just ahead of

Garnett's four artillery batteries with the long train of wagons following nearly every day.[33] Walters noted on this day, "The heat was so intense that it was almost impossible to go any further."[34] Landry and Cire jotted basically the same entry, that the Canonnier battery left in the morning, crossed the Hazel River, and later camped somewhere between the deserted town of Woodville and Sperryville, having made almost twenty miles. "In the course of the evening a heavy shower of rain fell, which was very grateful," noted Walters.[35] Just before dark the rain again came down and continued to fall during the night, but those who stretched out their blanket for a shelter "slept dry and comfortable all night."[36]

"Did not start until 5 o'clock," wrote Lineback on June 19, "it was cloudy nearly all the morning, but very warm and sultry. Soon we began ascending the mountain and had some very fine views of the low country."[37] The column went through Sperryville and Washington, and passed a profusion of lovely flowers over the fields, lawns of clover, and woods and groves clad in green. Cire for the day recorded the Donaldsonville Battery, "Resumed the march passing at Flint Hill and took the Gaines Cross Road and camped near the [Chester] gap."[38] Having again moved close to twenty miles for the day, Walters noted,

> Owing to the rain of last night, marching was a little more tolerable today...passed through the village of Flint Hill . . . . where I saw quite a number of very fine looking young ladies and also a couple of mustachioed highbreds, who dressed in broadcloth and played agreeable to the ladies, and seemed to have no ambition beyond that. Tired, foot-sore, and muddy as I was, I could not but pity them, and I replied to their looks of pity with those of scorn at their want of manhood in being content to stay at home in these times of war.[39]

Along the Gaines Cross Road between Flint Hill and Chester Gap, the column and Canonniers halted. The troops drew rations of crackers, bacon, and dried beef while the horses grazed in clover fields. Since leaving Culpeper the horses had been "sufficiently supplied throughout the march with provender."[40] With it dark as pitch during the night, a heavy storm brought wind and rain pouring down in torrents that left Heth's tired division drenched. "Yet," wrote Lineback, "we laid down in our wet clothes on the wet ground and covering with wet blankets and slept well."[41]

The command and Maurin's Battery again started at sunrise on June 20, but the march was very heavy owing to the road being "one mud hole."[42] The column moved up the gentle rise past fine farms and over the Blue Ridge Mountains at Chester Gap, where the column was enveloped in a dense fog that, complained Walters, "Shut out all those fine views on which I anticipated feasting."[43] It was a horrid, muddy, march though at the gap's summit the men were able to quench their thirst "from a cool spring pouring out of a crevice in the ponderous rocks piled on side of the highway."[44] In going through the mist at the gap a tired Confederate noted that General Lee "has marched us everywhere and has even taken us above the clouds."[45] They moved down the mountain from Chester Gap towards torpid Front Royal. The marching was difficult, wrote Walters, "The heavy rain of last night filled the road with mud which, in many places, was over our shoe tops."[46]

A woman in Front Royal recorded in her diary, "At ten o'clock A. P. Hill's Corps commenced marching through town and there was an immense sensation. Children all went over to see troops—bad to worse."[47] A South Carolinian wrote, "As we marched through Front Royal . . . the people were in ecstasies and our bands played lively airs for them."[48] The musician Lineback added, "Many ladies threw us big bouquets but as we were playing we could not pick them up but the men behind us did."[49] The ladies were out of flowers by the time the artillery guns came along, but "many a pretty face showered sweet smiles upon us, and many a Confederate flag fluttered in the breeze," wrote Walters.[50]

Just beyond the town at the two fords of the North and South Shenandoah River, the batteries were greatly delayed by the bottleneck of infantry and brigade wagons. A youngster from Front Royal later remembered, "At this confluence a pontoon bridge had been placed, and the men, and wagons, and artillery had to cross in a narrow file. The passage . . . over the bridge was slow, and the marching columns were often delayed and had to rest by the roadside until the line of march could be continued. For miles the road was often blocked, and while the men were waiting for the order to march they had a merry time by the way."[51] After the Donaldsonville Artillery finally crossed the bridge, the battery moved about four miles past the river as darkness settled in. Garnett's Battalion made camp for the night. After a trying day, Cire simply recorded, "Heavy rain."[52] Lineback noted too, "Several thunder showers passing over us."[53]

"Off again at sunrise, and when within about ten miles from Winchester where we thought we were going, our column turned to the right," noted Walters on June 21.[54] Cire recorded, "We resumed the march and went 8 miles towards Winchester and took the cross road. We went through White Post and camped 2 miles from Berryville."[55] Of the slow hard day's march, another wrote, "You cannot imagine how delighted the valley people are at our appearance. The ladies wave their handkerchiefs from every little farmhouse we pass and cheer us onward."[56] In passing through the beautiful village of White Post, Walters spoke to some citizens about the origins of the tall white post surmounted by an old fashion lantern located in the middle of the intersection. Others passing through preferred seeing the "many ladies . . . decorated with stars and bars."[57]

After White Post it was a hard road to travel—rocky and muddy—but along the day's route of about sixteen miles there was an "abundance of blackberries . . . that did us much good," remembered a ragged veteran.[58] "After we had settled down in camp," Lineback recorded, "the 11th Mississippi, 11th, 55th, and 26th N. C. bands played in succession until dark."[59] That night a foreign observer of Hill's Corps wrote the army "looked very picturesque" in its encampment, "illuminated with innumerable campfires."[60]

"We were up again at 4 o'clock," wrote Lineback on June 22, "expecting to be on the march, but were agreeably disappointed; therefore we had nothing to do but lie about and rest all day."[61] Cire's memorandum merely noted the Canonniers were "Still in the same place."[62] Besides lounging about so both men and horses could rest sore feet, the animals received a little corn and plenty of time to graze in the clover and timothy that was knee high and thick. Aid and care was also rendered at the same time. An artilleryman recorded, "The shoulders of the horses and all other parts in contact with the collars needed frequent rubbing with wisp of straw to restore the circulation of blood."[63] Even with the attention, Garnett reported their "condition was generally bad, in consequence of the hardships they encountered during the past winter."[64]

While the men rested in the woods and fields near Berryville, they ate dewberries and green apples, smoked their tobacco, and conversed. "As a matter of course, there were rumors and guesses as to our destination and the object to be sought by our expedition. A pretty generally accepted one was that General Lee intended crossing over into Maryland, dividing his forces thus compelling the enemy to do the same, and then defeat him in detail," gossiped Lineback.[65] In contrast, a Floridian from Heth's Division didn't speculate when he wrote, "We are entirely in the dark as to general Lee's object of this move, and more so (if possible) as to his future plans and operations."[66] An old hand remarked, "One thing is certain, we are marching in the direction of the enemy's lines."[67] The Louisianians on this campaign talked of "an unfaltering faith in the righteousness of our cause" and a belief that "we could surmount every obstacle," and they expected that "our great Lee would lead us to full victory."[68]

The Gunners of Donaldson, along with their horses, carriages, and caissons, were on the road shortly after sunrise on June 23 but were ordered back to camp, where rations of fresh beef and crackers were issued. The delay was also due to Pender's Brigade having joined up, which extended the column. In a short time the bugle sounded the hitch call, and, wrote Walters, "we were again ready."[69] It was a bright and beautiful day. The battalion with Maurin's Battery followed in close proximity to Colonel Henry K. Burgwyn's Twenty-sixth North Carolina Regiment. They passed batches of attractive houses interspersed with old trees and lawns before entering the modest colonial crossroads community of Berryville, with its little main street, nondescript commercial buildings, and red brick rectangle courthouse. In "passing thru" the town of 3,000, Lineback noted, "A lady wearing the stars and bars came running up a side street shouting at the top of her voice, 'Hurrah for the rebels.' As she reached the street we were on she exclaimed, 'I never was in such a fix in my life; whoop, I'm all out of breath.' She was well cheered by the men."[70]

The trek continued six miles to the north. Walters wrote, "Passing on our way through the scattered village of Rippon, everyone turned out to see the soldiers, which they could do only at the expense of a vast amount of patience, as one column consist[ed] of the divisions of Heth and Pender, numbering some eighteen thousand men, and three battalions of artillery having about fifty pieces and about two hundred wagons. The people are ardent secessionist[s], and greeted us with many a pleasant smile and kindly word."[71] For eighteen miles the officers, gun, caisson, and wagon drivers rode, while the innumerable soldiers and artillerymen marched. That afternoon they passed over rolling fertile grounds with fine residences with "the road side in many places adorned by the 'Fair ones,' apparently glad to see the 'boys in gray.'"[72] The long column stopped for the night four miles before Charles Town. Before falling asleep an exhausted Cire spent a few moments jotting the battery's movements in his memorandum.

An official proclamation was issued this day to the Third Corps by its commander that stated, "We will move . . . to cross the Potomac [River] and conquer a glorious peace on their own soil!"[73] In the evening an order "forbidding trespassing and enjoining respect for the rights of private property while in the enemy's country"[74] was read as well. "Some of the boys," wrote a soldier, "who have fully realized the effects of the war at their own homes are fairly itching to retaliate, but Gen'l Lee's order issued . . . is to [*sic*] strict."[75] In camp there was also "the most extravagant rumors of Confederate success . . . circulated among the men."[76]

Roused up and on the march at four in the morning of June 24, Lineback bemoaned the fact that, "We had no time to prepare breakfast these mornings, but ate whatever we might happen to have cold as we trudged along."[77] On trudging along, another soldier wrote,

> What a difference there is between the beginning and the end of such a journey! For the first five miles one gets on quite cheerfully. At the end of the *tenth* mile he has become extremely heated, a little footsore, very dusty, quite dry, and a good deal discouraged at finding it only 9 o'clock in the morning! It is nearly noon before the fifteenth mile is numbered; and his sufferings from heat, dust, thirst and fatigue give him a haggard woebegone look, which is not lessened by the numerous streaks of pasty grime that the minglings of dust and perspiration have left on his face. The next two miles require a full hour's time. Then . . . halt for rest and dinner.
>
> The nearest spring is half a mile across a sunny field; the only shade is the clump of chinquapin bushes, or a few dwarf cedars on the roadside. So the men lie down in the broad glare, and pulling a greasy haversack 'to the "fore"' proceed to crunch a couple of dry 'hardtack,' as tough as sole leather, and the best things in the world to provoke intense thirst. Here and there a soldier has a morsel of boiled beef or rusty bacon; but generally we eat up all our day's ration of meat *at breakfast time.*[78]

Early on this morning Garnett's Battalion passed through tree-shaded streets and by aged homes in battered Charles Town where one Rebel described how they "were received with every evidence of joy by the inhabitants. The doors and windows of the houses were thrown wide open, handkerchiefs were waiving, and the porches were filled with ladies looking as fresh as roses, and cheering us with their sweet smiles."[79] Walters noticed that "Charles Town is without exception the rankest rebel hold in this section of the state. There seemed to be none but old men there, and the ladies, of whom there are many and handsome at that, are perfectly enthusiastic."[80] Lineback noted, "We moved rapidly, and soon after leaving town could see Maryland Heights opposite Harper's Ferry, the United States flag floating on top."[81] Maurin's guns now moved over steeper dips and rises as they headed nearer the mountains that changed from blue to green, from hazy smoothness to the shaggy reality of rocks and trees. Cire took notice: "We were in sight of Harper's Ferry all day."[82]

The day's march covered approximately twenty-three miles over hills and a splendid country that impressed many with its beauty. The command passed through the crossroads of Halltown before it. "Camped one mile from Shepardstown," that night, recorded Cire.[83] According to Walters, who visited the town, it was "a very poor place indeed, and though in Virginia and but a few miles from Charles Town, yet it is full of Unionist."[84]

An early start was again made on June 25 and "soon," wrote Lineback, "we came to the Potomac River, which was pretty wide and halfthigh deep. Taking off our shoes, socks, pants and drawers, we made a comical looking set of men. Many did not take the trouble of undressing even partially."[85] Men—many halfway stripped naked—waded across, shouting and hurrahing. "It was quite a sight," according to Walters.[86]

In wading across, did the Donaldsonville Canonniers take fleeting glances at the bluffs overlooking Boteler's Ford? Did the memory of crossing in September of '62 remind them of how they were almost starved on that campaign? If it did, it was probably just a brief recollection that did not overshadow the troops' much improved outlook. "We have had plenty of meat and bread to eat since we started," and "our troops are in fine health and I have never before seen them get along half so well on a march. Not a man has given out," wrote a campaigner.[87]

The Canonniers continued on across the river in columns while the Twenty-sixth North Carolina band played "Maryland, My Maryland," which reverberated along the shores and "woke the echo of the hills, far and wide."[88] For the day, Cire wrote, "We marched through Shepardstown to the Potomac and crossed, and marched to Sharpsburg and took the Hagerstown Turnpike, and camped one mile from Hagerstown."[89]

In passing through Sharpsburg, Walters noted, "Many houses . . . still bear the marks of last year's battle . . . Saw many a long face and frowning brow and heard many an insulting remark from [the women] to all of which, when addressed to myself, I made no other reply than a pleasant smile while raising my cap."[90]

Turning onto the Hagerstown Turnpike the Canonniers soon approached the sunken road or "Bloody Lane" where it intersected with the turnpike. On the high ground to their left as they passed was the position where the Donaldsonville guns participated in "Artillery Hell." In going by, though the battle took place nine months before, signs of the conflict were still visible, with low mounds that covered the bodies of those who fell, the rutted ground and scarred trees, the fresh wood rails that replaced the fences that were destroyed. All the indications of the past conflict were readily visible. Passing old battlefields an artillery officer reflected: "Our memory . . . was forcibly refreshed."[91]

The gray multitude continued on another five miles through the crossroad settlements of

Tilghmanton and, a little over a mile further, Jones Crossroads, both of which Walters called "small affairs."[92] Moving another six miles, everything from the road "looks strange to us" wrote a soldier, "coming as we do from desolate fields of Virginia. Here we see houses, barns filled with grain, fine stock, etc."[93] The troops on the move were able to feed themselves as they went: "cherries were ripe and the trees bending with delicious fruit."[94] Since crossing the Potomac River there was an abundance of very delicious cherries that were filling but not very sustaining. Heth's men filled up several times a day. "We never enjoyed fruit more," wrote one.[95]

This hard day's march ended outside Hagerstown when, around five o'clock in the evening, Garnett's Battalion moved off the road into a clover field. Provisions were abundant and a number of men got permission to go into town and, wrote Walters, take a look at the

> very fine town (or city?) of some five or six thousand people. It contains many fine residences, churches, hotels, and other buildings. From what I could learn the people are divided; about half being Union while the other half are Secessionist, though there are many of the latter who dare not express themselves openly. I never was in a place where there was such a mania for soldier's buttons. Nearly every boy you meet in the street would ask, 'Please, Mister, give me a brass button,' and sometimes ladies sitting in their doors or by their windows would ask for them, in an indirect but perfectly plain matter.[96]

Other soldiers in town and especially those with money "patronized the barber shop, hotel, and saloon, and . . . laid in a supply of the 'needful'"[97] that made up the content of a canteen. "But money of every kind was so scarce that we," wrote an officer in Hill's Corps, "were compelled to rely for our extras on the charity of the citizens, or the lightness of our fingers."[98]

The three divisions of Hill's Third Corps had marched on successive days from Fredericksburg—first Anderson's, then Heth's, then Pender's. The latter caught up with Heth's at Berryville, and then at Hagerstown the three commands were united. With the resonance of martial music the Donaldsonville Artillery with Garnett's Battalion and Heth's Division resumed the march in conjunction with the whole corps on the morning of June 26.

This first morning in Maryland, as the musician Lineback recorded, "was a very disagreeable one, cold, rainy, and the roads muddy. Getting a rather late start at 7:30 we played as we marched thru the town . . . quite a number of ladies had Confederate flags, which they waived at us as we passed."[99] The Canonniers went through Hagerstown, and a wet Cire dispassionately jotted, "We had rain."[100] Walters gave a more revelatory view: "After dark last night it began to rain and has continued to do so all day in no gentle shower, which has made marching very unpleasant."[101]

In fair conditions, the turnpike was excellent to travel on, as it passed deep groves of hickory trees, woods of oak and walnut, and rail fences alongside fields. For several miles through rain and mud, there was the constant slow suck of the wheels out of the mud and clanking of artillery carriages as hoofs and feet slogged along. The column came to and crossed the rushing white waters of the rain-swollen Antietam Creek, where the sycamore trees grew on the banks and their outmost branches touched at midstream. Past the creek, the Canonniers plodded on with the column through Leitersburg, a place of some four hundred people. After going another two miles, Maurin's guns crossed the state line into Pennsylvania at four o'clock in the afternoon. "The ladies of the Keystone state received us with waving Union flags, the men with silent contempt, and the Dutch women with horrid imprecations."[102]

It didn't help the fears of the civilians that the sunburned and war-worn veterans of the gray column would "hoop and yell on all occasions"[103] and call out, "Och, mine contree!"[104] Shortly before the day's soggy march ended, Garnett's batteries again reached the Antietam and crossed at the confluence of the east and west branches of the creek on a substantially built covered bridge that, but for the rain, normally would have kept the Canonniers and horses dry on crossing. On the bridge Walters noted, "The word commissioners is spelled 'Comisoners'. As there is a well built school house within two hundred yards of the bridge, comment is unnecessary."[105]

Camp was made a half mile past the Pennsylvania State line and two miles shy of Waynesboro. There was great rejoicing at being on Federal soil and rations being drawn plentifully and regularly, even an uncommon liquor ration was issued this night.[106]

Up at four o'clock on the morning of June 27 and soon on the road, Hill's Corps made an early start. The weather was cool and pleasant. After a couple of miles, the Confederate troops reached prosperous and attractive Waynesboro, set in a natural hollow and surrounded by hills. Here Walters noticed the town was "quite a large place of about a thousand people." He added, "The ladies expressed many a kind wish for our complete overthrow."[107] Another in the column noted, "We are in Yankeedom this time, for certain, and a beautiful and magnificent country it is too."[108]

After leaving Waynesboro, the Canonniers and corps passed through the rich lands of the Blue Ridge region with Quincy and Funkstown, both described as "small but rather neat villages."[109] A gray clad chronicler added, "In every direction yellow fields of grain extended themselves; on every farm were droves of the largest, fattest cattle; gardens thronged with inviting vegetables; orchards gave promise of a bounteous fruit yield, and . . . the most delicious cherries; full dairies, flocks of sheep, and poultry were almost monotonously frequent."[110]

As the Confederate army moved deeper into Pennsylvania it was further noted, "The people whom we saw looked glum and even sorrowful. Some were badly frightened; for, to persons unfamiliar with armies, a few divisions look like a countless host, and as for an army wagon train, it looks endless."[111] That did not stop the Pennsylvanians all along the road from selling apple-butter and other edibles even though "they had no use for Confederate money, but they took it for whatever the boys wanted to eat."[112] Lineback wrote, "It was impossible for the officers to keep the men from 'flanking' to some extent, but upon the whole there was less depredating than might have been expected."[113]

An officer wrote that the foraging "was not as extensive as one would have expected. It was true that numbers of men flanked patrols and slipped through to capture what they needed to eat . . . that nothing was wantonly destroyed, that no man or woman was insulted. The citizens were amazed at our moderation. Many of them bade us help ourselves to poultry, milk, vegetables, fruit, honey, bread, whatever we wanted to eat, provided we spared more valuable property."[114]

On the subject of pressing chickens, vegetables, and other foods, Garnett chronicled, "We, who had commands, exerted ourselves diligently in trying to restrain our men from violating [Lee's General Order 72] but found it at times a difficult matter to control troops who had been subjected to many hardships through the depredations of their opponents in their own territory, and who now had an excellent chance to illustrate the gospel of retaliation." On trying to make "amends" to a victim Garnett related,

> I leaped the fence with my horse and rode up to where the old man . . . calmly sat on the porch and watched.
>
> 'At what do you value your loss?' I asked.

> 'It is of no consequence,' he answered. 'The town Council has given you permission to take all you find, and if they don't pay me Abe Lincoln will. Don't trouble yourself, sir.'
>
> This philosophical view of the matter seemed to be shared by all of the residents, and it proved very agreeable to the tired and hungry throng that had arrived among them.[115]

Whether the residents were agreeable or not, the French and German speaking Canonniers were apt to benefit after getting "on the good side . . . by talking German."[116] In foraging the Donaldsonville gunners had leverage over other Johnny Rebs simply because many of the Pennsylvanisch Deutsch[117] inhabitants "can speak no English."[118] The bilingual Canonniers got plenty to eat. "We had a fine time on our advance march into Pennsylvania," wrote one Louisianian. "Cherries were ripe and the Dutch people gave us plenty of onions, light bread, milk, and butter, with apple sauce to spread on our bread."[119] The only ones who seemed to be having a hard time were the artillery drivers, especially if they messed together, because at the end of a day's march, as an artillerist wrote, "They had to unhitch and unharness their horses, go . . . for water, groom, feed, and cut clover for them. By the time all this was accomplished . . . they were too wearied to cook anything for themselves to eat."[120]

The movement continued another six miles in a thickly settled country with fields of wheat and clover, until they reached the Baltimore and Chambersburg Turnpike near Fayetteville. It was "the longest little town I ever saw," wrote one Louisiana artillerist, adding, "All the houses [were] on one street, the main road."[121] Garnett's Battalion with Heth's Division turned east and halted a mile beyond the town at about one o'clock in the evening. They stopped near Greenwood, described as a "one horse place."[122] The troops and horses bivouacked in splendid grass and clover along the turnpike. The camps, recorded a soldier diarist, were "the most delightful . . . the woods were ample and shady, and water abundant and convenient. The surrounding country abounded in provisions of every kind."[123]

The troops were ordered to clean themselves up and wash their clothes, and soon the waters of nearby Conococheague Creek was hazy and cloudy like the overcast sky. The battery's horses had to be washed as well, with scores of the animals practically exhausted and many suffering severely for want of horseshoes. Traveling over the rocky roads and limestone turnpikes took its toll, and many animals were lost because of their lameness. A lack of horseshoes and nails was a persistent problem in the Third Corps artillery battalions.[124]

Encamped here the men were in excellent health and full of confidence. "Our rations," wrote the diarist, "were increased, and more of improved quality; we got half pound of good bacon, or a pound of excellent beef a day. The vegetables which we picked up were very grateful."[125]

A foreign military observer of Lee's army versed in French noted, "They seemed in high spirits."[126] For the French-speaking Creoles, "skilled in the fine art of having a good time,"[127] and their brethren the "fun-loving"[128] Acadians, high morale manifested that the Donaldsonville Artillery's bivouac was no doubt vivacious. Describing such an encampment of Louisianians on this campaign was a Virginia artillerist who wrote "If there was anything . . . Creoles did and loved to do better than to fight, it was to dance; and their camp stag dances, sandwiched in between a big march and a big fight, were said to be the most 'utterly utter' performances in the way of faun-like pranks, that grown and sane men ever indulged in."[129]

The next morning, June 28, the Canonniers received the good news that they would remain camped for a rest. Repose was not for everyone, however, and some took advantage to hunt around a little. They again found an abundance of things to eat and drink such as bread, butter, milk, apple butter, honey, fowls, pigs, mutton, lard, cherries, and whiskey, all at little cost. Walters recorded, "The people do not care to have us about their houses, and give us what we asked for to get rid of us, a very reasonable proceeding, as who wishes to remain after getting what he wants?"[130] For the Creoles and Acadians everything seemed to revolve around food and music, and with the artillery camps full of eatables the day was spent cooking, eating, and "living splendidly."[131] Even the run down horses indulged in the high grass and clover.

Cire recorded, "Scouts are sent out to get horses and a good many brought in."[132] "It seemed," wrote another artilleryman, "almost an absolute necessity that fresh animals be secured from the farmers of the surrounding country. These, however, were not to be taken without remuneration. Specific values were to be fixed and quartermaster receipts given in exchange, redeemable in gold at the close of the war."[133] Walters wrote, "The horses which we get here are excellent drought . . . well adapted for artillery service, that is as a general thing."[134] A different view however was given by an artillery officer who recorded, "It was my ill fortune to have to go frequently in charge of one of these expeditions . . . it appeared . . . that every other animal seized be the especial favorite of the woman and children of the family, who with 'wailing and crying,' begged that their 'pets' might be spared. Moreover, these horses turned out to be utterly useless. They were big, fat and clumsy, totally unfit for the quick movement and long, forced marches of the Confederate artillery service, and most of them had to be abandoned before we again reached Virginia."[135]

The day of rest, foraging, and getting of horses ended with an evening of drizzling rain and orders to cook three days' rations and move at four o'clock the next morning. On June 29 the Canonniers were up at three in the morning to cook breakfast. The weather remained inclement. Maurin received word that their marching orders had been countermanded and after eating they remained around the campfire *tirer sa flemme* (to lounge about). The Donaldsonville Artillery with Garnett's Battalion in Heth's column moved out between midday and one o'clock and wended its way up the steep west side of South Mountain. "The scene around us," wrote a campaigner, "was very different from what we had just passed through. Instead of the enticing field and lovely landscape, we had now around us that which was rugged, grand and towering."[136]

Heth's long column with its artillery and wagon train passed through Caledonia and the smoking ruins of the Caledonia iron works.[137] Slowly they continued on through the 1,440-foot high gap on the pike between Mt. Newman and Mt. Graeffenburg (alt. 1,770 feet) where, upon reaching the eastern heights, a good view of the country was presented. The spires of a town called Gettysburg could just be seen. Continuing down the road, Heth's Division passed in the shadow of the mountain called Rock Top and through Cashtown (alt. 745 feet), which Walters noted was "of little account."[138] With it nearly sunset, Heth's command bivouacked less than a mile farther down the pike. The division's wagon camp was established a quarter mile closer to Cashtown, from which the men were employed in foraging and gathering provisions amongst the farmers thereabout.

A northern civilian wrote, "They seized beef-cattle, flour, and grain" by the "old farce of professing to pay for what they took, by offering freely their worthless 'Confederate' scrip; which, they said, would, in a few days, be better than our own currency."[139] The quartermaster and commissary departments bought up practically everything as they went along. As a result, soldiers in the column, like Lineback complained, "We could buy nothing along the road."[140] Many of the Canonniers had no complaints, for men mounted on horses from the artillery or wagon train actually did the best foraging.

A northern civilian observed soldiers and artillerymen from Heth's Division, "Resting, and feeding themselves and their animals, and placing themselves in readiness for an encounter

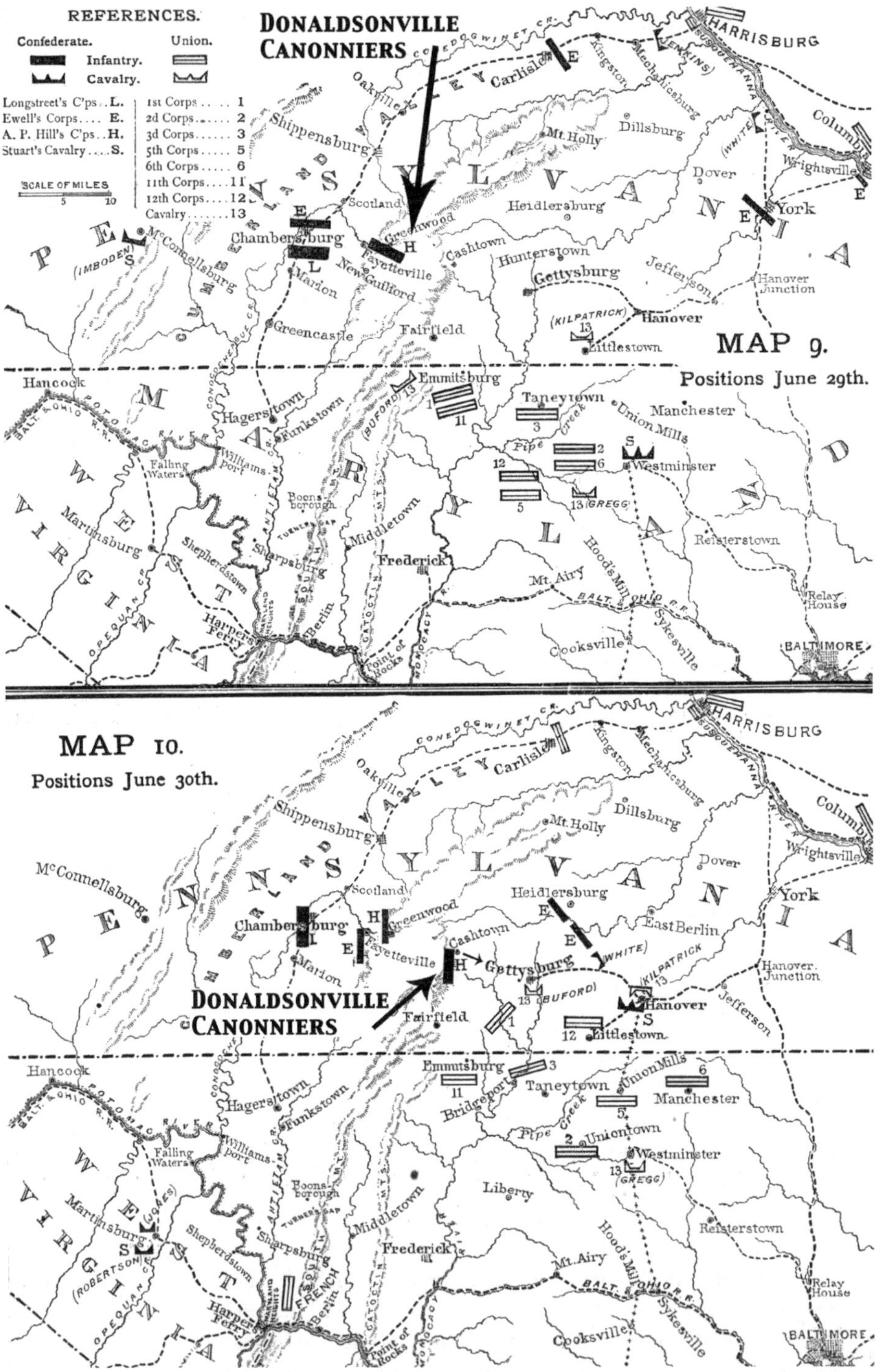

On June 30 from Cashtown, Captain Maurin and three guns of the Donaldsonville Artillery, with Brigadier General J. Johnston Pettigrew's Eleventh, Twety-sixth, and Forty-seventh North Carolina regiments and the Fifty-fifth Virginia Infantry Regiment, along with a number of wagons, headed for Gettysburg, Pennsylvania, to search the town for supplies. From *Battles and Leaders*.

with our forces."[141] Many of the dirty gray-clad troops had the chance to wash clothes and take baths in the north branch of Marsh Creek, which flows past Cashtown. Of course, after turning in, more rain came during the night.[142]

June 30 turned out to be a "cloudy and drizzly day."[143] Early in the morning Maurin received instructions to have three field pieces of the Donaldsonville Artillery ready to accompany three regiments of Pettigrew's Brigade who, with a number of wagons, were ordered by Heth to Gettysburg to search the town for supplies (shoes especially) and return the same day.[144] North Carolina First Lieutenant and aid-de-camp Louis G. Young recorded, "It was told to General Pettigrew that he might find the town in possession of a home guard, which he would have no difficulty in driving away; but if, contrary to expectations, he should find any organized troops capable of making resistance, or any portion of the Army of the Potomac, he should not attack it. The orders to him were peremptory, not to precipitate a fight."[145]

After the Canonnier drivers groomed, watered, harnessed, and hitched-up their horses to the three Donaldsonville guns, they and their rain-drenched crews joined with the Eleventh, Twenty-sixth, and Forty-seventh North Carolina regiments and fifteen wagons and departed camp at six-thirty in the morning towards Gettysburg. Moving a mile and one half along the pike, the column reached a broad intersection next to a fair-size cemetery,[146] where the Fifty-fifth Virginia Infantry of Brockenbrough's Brigade were cooking breakfast after spending the night on picket duty. Pettigrew, on his beautiful dappled gray horse, requested Colonel W. S. Christian, commanding the veteran Virginia regiment, to accompany his command on the expedition. Christian agreed and his 284 riflemen joined the line of march that extended at least a mile and a half in length. Pettigrew's force continued rapidly on for six miles over rolling hills with many gentle swells of ground covered in timber. In their progress they passed a spy for General Longstreet who informed Pettigrew that three thousand Union cavalry had arrived that day and were holding the town.[147]

According to Cire, the Donaldsonville guns "Marched as advance guard to the outskirts of Gettysburg."[148] The front of Pettigrew's procession reached the top of a hill overlooking the town on the Chambersburg Turnpike between nine-thirty and ten-thirty in the morning and halted. The three guns of the Donaldsonville Artillery exited the column and readied for action. A Gettysburg resident observed, "We had a good view of them from our house, and every moment we expected to hear the booming of cannon, and thought they might shell the town."[149] The guns remained in battery without firing a shot as two-dozen skirmishers went forward about 300 yards east of the ridge. Meanwhile several southern officers on horseback advanced, reconnoitered with field glasses, and engaged in conversation with people living near the road.

Captain John H. Thorp, back in the column with the Forty-seventh North Carolina wrote, "We were almost at our destination when a person in citizen's dress, on a farm horse, rode leisurely from the adjacent woods up to the fence, on the other side of which we were moving, inquired for our commander, and paced up to the head of our column. On his arrival there the command 'Halt!' rang down our line. Was this a spy? 'About face—quick time march!' and back we went; but not without several shots at long range being fired at us from both sides of the road."[150]

This civilian, protected by an umbrella, confirmed that Yankee cavalry were ahead. The Donaldsonville guns, under orders, "fell back one mile and . . . were placed on picket duty," according to Cire.[151] Here, along Marsh Creek, the infantry and Donaldsonville Canonniers waited, hoping to ambush Union cavalry from the town.[152]

Pettigrew meanwhile immediately sent a report to Heth about what he had learned and ask for further instructions. The reply by courier from Heth to Pettigrew arrived in the evening and was simply a repetition of the orders previously given, coupled with an expression of disbelief as to the presence of any portion of the Army of the Potomac. As he had no cavalry to ascertain the strength of the force in Gettysburg and was not willing to hazard an attack on his force, Pettigrew ordered his command back towards Cashtown where he could report to Heth in person. As he and his men moved away, blue-clad Yankee cavalry scouts followed at some distance.[153]

After returning to Cashtown, Pettigrew met with Heth, who recorded,

> There was evidently a cavalry force occupying the town, the strength of which he could not tell; that some of his men reported the beat of drums (indicating infantry) on the further side of the town; that if he entered the town his men when searching for shoes would have become scattered, and if there was a large force there, it might have proved disastrous to his command. Under the circumstances he deemed it prudent to return and not carry out my orders. General Hill rode up just then, and I directed General Pettigrew to repeat to Hill what he had told me.[154]

Douglas Southall Freeman wrote that Hill's poised reply to Pettigrew's story was,

> "The only force at Gettysburg is cavalry, probably a detachment of observation. I am just from General Lee, and the information he has from his scouts corroborates that I have received from mine—that is, the enemy are still at Middleburg, and have not struck their tents."
>
> "If there is no objection," Heth answered immediately, "I will take my Division tomorrow and go to Gettysburg and get those shoes."
>
> "None in the world," was the reply by Hill.

"On those four words," added Freeman, "fate hung." Or as the Creoles would say, "*destin dependent.*"[155]

Chapter Ten

Un Jour triste
(A Sad Day)

On the morning of July 1, 1863, Lieutenant Colonel John J. Garnett, commander of the Artillery Battalion "A" in the Army of Northern Virginia's Third Corps that included Captain Victor Maurin's Donaldsonville Artillery, remembered, "In the Confederate camp the night had passed without incident of special note. The pickets had been warned to be alert and vigilant . . . and those of the troops who sought their . . . rest lay down with the consciousness that this day was to be one of importance. The rank and file knew that a great battle was inevitable." Garnett added, "The reckless soldiers of the contending armies sang ribald and patriotic songs, played cards and cracked jokes, enjoying themselves in any and every way their fancies led, unmindful of the fearful fate impending over them."[1]

Regardless of sleep or jocularity, wrote Private John Walters in Captain Charles Grandy's Norfolk Blues Battery of Garnett's Battalion, "we were called up at four o'clock and everything made ready."[2] As the sun cast its first beams across the hilltops on this first morning of July 1863, Maurin's Battery along with its sister batteries were placed "on the line"[3] and readied to move.

Third Corps Chief of Artillery Lindsey Walker removed Garnett and his battalion as artillery support for Heth's Division early in the morning and placed it in reserve, directly subject to Walker's orders.[4] In their place, Major William J. Pegram's Reserve Artillery Battalion was ordered to support Heth's Division in its advance to Gettysburg. Pegram had been home in Virginia sick with a fever but upon hearing the army was in motion, left to rejoin his command. He reached his battalion the day after it crossed the Potomac River and was seen by General Robert E. Lee, who informed Major General A. P. Hill a few moments after, "General Hill, I have good news for you. Major Pegram is up." Hill replied, "Yes, that *is* good news." Clearly Pegram was highly thought of by Lee and Hill.[5]

Of the unusual swap of artillery Pegram said, "We happened to be in front that day." However, he was known to beg to take his battalion into a fight and had solicited permission from Hill to lead the way.[6] Heth thought highly of Pegram too, and would say, "When I was going into battle, I always applied for Colonel Pegram's battalion of artillery to accompany me."[7] A member of the battalion wrote that Pegram "sought and obtained for his command, intended for reserve, 'a place in the picture near the flashing of the guns.'"[8]

A disagreement may have also occurred between Garnett and his superiors over an occurrence the previous day when one of his Virginia batteries became disorganized because the men were plundering. Garnett had not helped his cause, as he recorded: "Calling my adjutant, I ordered him to have the men brought into battery at once, and to compel them to quit their plundering . . . and my adjutant succeeded poorly in the errand on which I dispatched him."[9]

Maurin and the Donaldsonville Canonniers could only standby and watch when at five o'clock in the morning, Heth's command started its march on the Chambersburg Turnpike with Pegram's guns and caissons rolling behind the division. Following them were Major General William D. Pender's Division and Major David G. McIntosh, who was described as having a "dauntless character" and who later married Pegram's sister.[10] McIntosh's reserve artillery battalion took the place of Major William T. Pougue's Battalion, which was previously assigned to Pender's Division. Like Garnett, Pougue was instructed to remain in camp near Cashtown with his battalion as a reserve "and await orders."[11]

Later in the morning with the sun shining through showery clouds and the sky in the east spanned by a rainbow, Garnett recorded:

> My command was . . . on the Chambersburg pike, and, not expecting the battle to open so soon, I had ordered my horses to be taken into a large field of clover, taking the opportunity to allow them a chance to graze, giving orders, however, that they be kept in harness and under charge of the drivers, who must be ready to hitch up and move forward at a moment's notice. A short time had elapsed when I heard the roar of musketry at the front. It came to me with the peculiar sound not unlike the rumble of a train of cars approaching at a distance, and I realized that the battle of Gettysburg was on. Louder and fiercer grew the sound of musketry, and my men began to grow impatient to take part in the strife. Looking up the turnpike some considerable time after the engagement had begun, I saw a courier dashing madly along past the bodies of troops that were moving forward. Coming up to where I sat on a rail fence, he handed me an order from General Hill to move my command at once . . . in less time than it can be imagined the command was galloping down the road to the front.[12]

This was about eleven o'clock in the morning. "We were ordered forward and went up the road at a double quick, the horses in a lively trot for about six miles, where we halted," wrote Walters.[13] The Donaldsonville Canonniers with the battalion stopped on the pike near the W. H. Wierman farm where they not only could hear the sound of battle but could see smoke swept by the breeze into a long cloud.[14]

After having moved nearer the conflict, Garnett reported that, "I halted my battalion in column on the side of the road, and awaited further orders. After a delay of about an hour, I received a message from Major Pegram, requesting that I relieve one of his batteries, whose ammunition had become exhausted. I accordingly sent him Capt. V[ictor] Maurin, of the Donaldsonville Battery, with six of my rifled pieces."[15]

The teams of horses pulling Maurin's three Donaldsonville guns and the other three pieces (two guns from Moore's Norfolk Battery and one from Lewis's Pittsylvania Artillery) moved up the pike and promptly reached Herr Ridge. There the six guns took position "about 350 to 400 yards southwest of Herr Tavern on the crest of the hill"[16] after Pegram's guns without ammunition were withdrawn. Pegram's remaining guns on the ridge continued to fire and "played . . . with telling effect."[17]

Maurin's order for *"Action Front!"* was immediately given and repeated by the screaming section chiefs. The Canonniers and Garnett's artillerists ran to their post and:

Whirling the Parrotts like children's toys,
The horses strain to the rushing noise;
To right and to left, so fast and free,

They carry the light artillery.
'Drive on!'

The gunner cries with a tug and a jerk,
The limbers fly, and we bend to our work;
The handspike in, and the implements out—
We wait for the word, and it comes with a shout—
'Load!'[18]

After being unlimbered and wheeled about by hand the guns were loaded as the gunners took aim and the limbers dashed off to the rear. When they were ready, Maurin's six guns "immediately opened upon the enemy and with apparent effect" and "kept up a slow and steady fire."[19] The midday heat was oppressive causing the artillery fire to slow on both sides while "perspiration poured from our bodies," wrote a southern combatant.[20]

Pegram's remaining guns and Maurin's six fired on the Federal infantry[21] with effective results by aiming at the Federal flags. McIntosh reported the Yankee's were "entirely discomforted."[22] Northern regimental commanders reported their men were "subjected to"[23] and "under a heavy fire of artillery"[24] while their Yankee artillery support received a "galling fire."[25]

Soon after the arrival of Maurin's guns two Confederate batteries, Captain William P. Carter's King William (Virginia) Artillery and Captain C. W. Fry's Orange (Virginia) Artillery, assigned to Colonel Thomas H. Carter's Battalion with Major General Robert E.

Battery in action—"the gunner cries with a tug and a jerk . . . and we bend to our work; the handspike in."
From *Battles and Leaders.*

Rodes's Division from Lieutenant General Richard S. Ewell's Second Corps, arrived on the Federal right flank and opened fire on the enemy batteries posted near the pike. From the crest of Oak Hill, these eight guns caused Pegram's, Maurin's, and McIntosh's "to increase their rate of fire from their position . . . so catching the Union guns in a wicked crossfire."[26] The result was the reposition or withdrawal of Yankee guns "in haste"[27] and further opportunities to fire on the enemy infantry which they did "with marked effect."[28]

Behind the guns on Herr Ridge, Brigadier General William N. Pendleton and Lee overlooked the field and observed that the enemy was "handsomely enfiladed by the batteries of McIntosh and Pegram."[29] Meanwhile, Ewell's Second Corps was marching under orders to join Lee at Gettysburg. Having heard the sound of battle, they hurried Rodes's Division in advance against the Federal right flank. During this attack and another by Major General Jubal A. Early's Division, Lee ordered an assault with Heth's and Pender's infantry. The charge took place at about two-thirty in the afternoon.

Douglas Southall Freeman described the scene: "With a rebel yell that echoed weirdly over the Pennsylvania hills, Heth's brigades swept eastward. . . . Pender's troops moved across the ridge, joined with Heth, and charged irresistibly over Willoughby Run. Rodes pressed on; Early swept everything before him."[30] One of Pender's men wrote, "As we advanced the cannonading increased in fury. It was Heth's Division, ahead of ours, fighting . . . we could see Heth's cannon arranged and booming away at the Yankees, who were replying with considerable briskness, and we could also see the infantry of Heth's Division advancing in line of battle."[31]

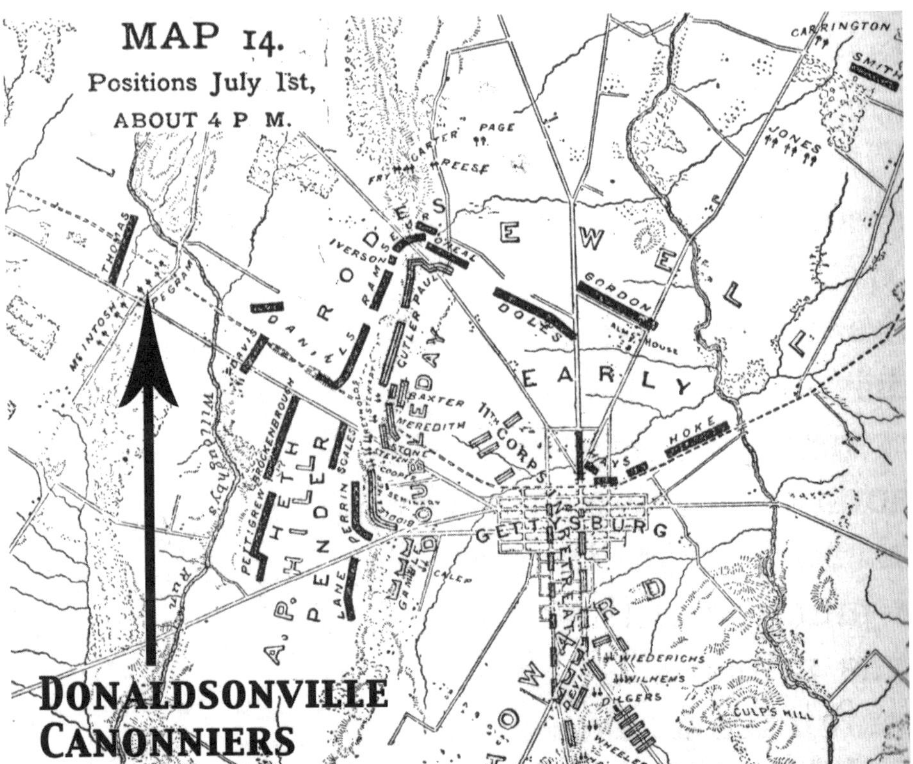

Gettysburg, July 1, 4 p.m.—Captain Maurin commanded the Donaldsonville Artillery's three rifle pieces and an additional three rifle pieces of Garnett's Battalion when they relieved some of Pegram's guns along the Chambersburg Pike. From *Battles and Leaders*.

Garnett recorded,

> The Confederates went into the attack with fury, indifferent to the terrible whirlwind of death that impeded their progress. On they rushed over the bodies of their fallen comrades, heedless of whatever fate awaited them. Their only thought was victory, and it inspired them with a valor that was almost superhuman; and as they saw the enemy slowly waver before their terrific onslaught, the famed rebel yell went up in a mighty paean of triumph above the thunder of artillery and musketry, which seemed to make the very air tremble with its burden of sound.[32]

Of the conflict Donaldsonville Canonnier Artificer François "Bienvenue" Cire as usual made a *franche element* (straightforward entry) in his memorandum: "Our rifle pieces went into action & the Yankees were compelled to give way."[33]

"In forty-five minutes," according to Freeman, "the battle was over. The Federals were routed and had been hurled back toward the ridges south and east of Gettysburg. The town was in Early's hands. Nearly 5,000 bewildered prisoners were being herded on the field. Almost as many dead and wounded lay on the ground."[34]

Casualties in Pegram's Battalion came to two men killed and eight wounded with six horses killed; McIntosh suffered one man killed and one wounded by a premature explosion from their own gun, with several horses disabled.[35] Cire recorded that Canonnier Private Octave Boudreau was "slightly wounded."[36]

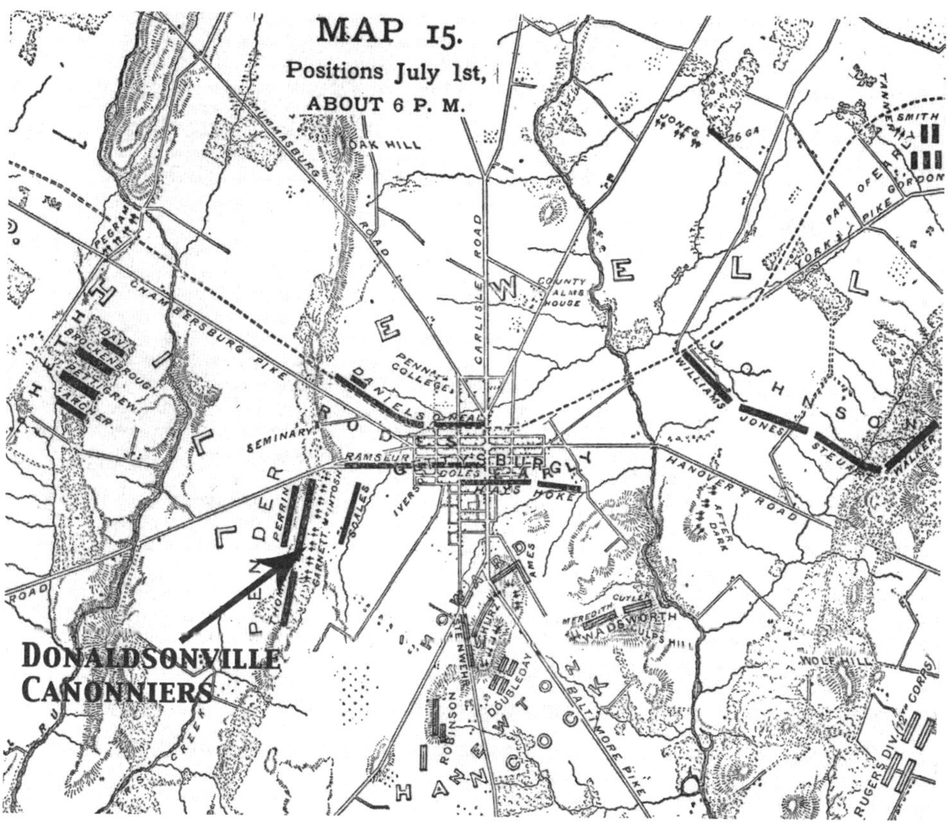

Gettysburg, July 1, 6 p.m.—Garnett's rifle guns under Captain Maurin relocated to their second position of the first day's battle, south of the Hagerstown Road and Gettysburg Seminary along Seminary Ridge, when the Federals retreated to Cemetery Hill. From *Battles and Leaders*.

Gettysburg Seminary
ARW; courtesy of the Library of Congress.

General Lee addressing Garnett as Maurin's six guns with the battalion advance to the front.
From R.A. Brock (editor), *Gen. Robert Edward Lee; Soldier, Citizen, and Christian Patriot.*

The enemy retreated in great confusion and out of range of the artillery. The guns then replenished their caissons, after which Garnett's Battalion moved to the lane in back of the brick Theological Seminary.[37] Garnett reported Maurin's six guns, along with the other pieces of the battalion, were then "advanced to the front, in the rear of the line of battle nearly opposite Cemetery Hill."[38] Many years later Garnett wrote,

> As I was moving to the front with my command . . . I saw General Lee with his staff at a point to the right of the Chambersburg turnpike, and on a range of hills just to the rear of Seminary Ridge. He sent an officer with an order to me to report to him at once in person. Riding up to where he stood, I dismounted and, having saluted him, asked his pleasure. Pointing away beyond Seminary ridge and calling my attention to what seemed to be a large body of troops, with wagons and ambulances, he handed me his field-glass, and asked if my guns would reach them from the Seminary. I replied that they would, and he said: 'They seemed to be moving towards the Emmettsburg Road, do they not?' and added: 'Place your batteries on Seminary Ridge and either disperse them or develop the purpose of their movement.'[39]

Garnett deployed his rifle guns under the charge of Maurin and as a result, likely caused "an amusing incident" that, according to a Yankee staff officer,

> occurred soon after our forces had concentrated on Cemetery Hill. The enemy opened quite a brisk artillery fire upon our position, causing some confusion among our troops. About the first shell fired exploded directly under the kettle which the servant had on boiling our dinner and supper, for we had had neither that day. He had brought up 'old shave-tail,' our pack horse, and left him feeding a few feet east of the fire while he was busy about six feet north of it. The shell came from the west, and while it tore 'old shave-tail' all to pieces, the man did not receive a scratch, but was so badly frightened that he stood like a statue for some moments as if paralyzed and as white as a corpse. It was the most laughable sight I ever saw in battle. We dined and supped on hardtack that night as our provisions went up with the kettle.[40]

"Having complied with the order and drawn the fire of several batteries on Cemetery Hill upon me," recorded Garnett, "I discovered that the troops which General Lee had alluded to were in full retreat, and the general coming up about that time had the satisfaction of seeing the plain intervening between the two ridges filled with flying Federals. These retreating troops were, however, concentrating on that 'rock-ribbed hill that served as a burial ground for the village.'"[41]

Pendleton reported, "Garnett's battalion moved to the front, slightly participating in the fight, and then, under cover of a hill near the brick seminary, awaited orders."[42] He added, "General Ramseur coming up from the town, which his command had just occupied, met me at this point, and requested that our batteries might not then open, as they would draw a concentrated fire upon his men, much exposed. . . . Captain [V.] Maurin . . . in command of several batteries, was therefore directed to post his guns, and be ready, but to keep his horses under cover, and not to fire till further orders."[43]

Garnett later wrote, "I remember a conversation with the gallant General Ramseur . . . which took place near the Seminary, and while the Federal batteries were shelling us, in which he said, while pointing to the hill: 'Garnett, we must get that hill to-night or never.'"[44]

Pendleton reported, "No further attack, however, was made, and night closed upon the scene."[45] Garnett's Battalion and Maurin's guns, "Remained in park until the following morning, protected from the enemy's fire by a high hill."[46]

During the night a Southern artillerist noted that when the moon rose over the battlefield with her pale light "sad sights are witnessed."[47] For a span of time many of the men from Garnett's Battalion assisted the wounded on the field while the drivers went for water and feed and took care of the horses. Others, as usual used the opportunity to get battle plunder, especially clothing and shoes. The Union dead were left "stripped to almost nakedness."[48] The haversacks of the slain enemy were rifled through for hardtack and bacon with a Gettysburg civilian observing that the "tired rebels . . . found recreation and amusement in opening the knapsacks of the soldiers who had retreated, taking out and reading the letters they contained."[49]

Concerning citizens and food, a South Carolina officer whose regiment received artillery fire from Cemetery Hill while resting near Garnett's guns wrote,

> No violence was offered to the citizens by our troops. With the exception of the wheat trampled, and one or two houses fired on the outskirts of the town, by our shells, to dislodge sharpshooters, they were uninjured. They were so badly frightened, that they contributed many articles of food, to pacify us, but . . . some light-fingered persons helped themselves secretly to fowls and other dainties, but even these things were done gently . . . there was a general uprooting of gardens and depopulation of henhouses. But there no insult was offered, nor was there any wanton destruction whatever.

He added, "Servants were more difficult to restrain than soldiers. They insisted on universal pillage."[50] Titus, Prosper Landry's servant and cook, no doubt gathered enough rations for Canonnier kettles to even keep the artillery drivers rapturous. All the artillerymen went to sleep "in the very best of spirits."[51]

"At two o'clock this morning [July 2] we were called up," wrote Walters, "and at four the rifled pieces of our battalion went forward to take position in a piece of woods in front of us."[52] During the night Walker had assigned positions to the Third Corps artillery along

Dinner at Gettysburg.
From *Battles and Leaders.*

Seminary Ridge. Garnett reported, "Having received an order to send all my rifles to the position immediately opposite Cemetery Hill, and to the right of the Fairfield turnpike, I accordingly dispatched Major Richardson with the nine rifle pieces of the battalion to the hill indicated."[53]

Some time in the night the battalion's second in command, Charles Richardson, having been on leave in Virginia, arrived in camp and, supplanting Maurin, was given command of the gun detachment on the line. The three Donaldsonville rifle guns along with two from Lewis's battery were positioned next to the northern side of the McMillan home. Four rifle pieces from Moore and Grandy's batteries were located on the other side of the square, one and one half story frame house with a chimney. Garnett's rifle guns were afforded some protection by a stone wall, numerous oak, honey locust, and mulberry trees, and orchards of apple, peach, pear, plum, and cherry trees, which covered acres around the house.[54]

"The morning was pleasant," wrote Garnett, "the air calm, and the sun shone mildly through the smoky atmosphere."[55] Another described it as, "A heavy vapor hanging over the terrain between the armies."[56] A third witness simply said there was "a cloudy sky" but, by ten o'clock on this July 2 morning, described how "the threatening clouds vanished and the green meadows were bathed in sunlight, with here and there the shadow of transient clouds flitting across the sunlit valley and hills. Cattle were grazing in the fields . . . the shrill crowing of [roosters] was heard . . . pigeons cooed on the hillside, and birds sang among the trees. The crest, as far as the eye could see, glittered with . . . burnished brass pieces of artillery and the glittering bayonets of the infantry."[57] A Confederate artilleryman along the line wrote, "Yet everything is unusually quiet—men move about carelessly . . . the merry laugh still wreaths in smiles the lips of many . . . and the joyous tale is told with the same merriment, as if they stood around their cheerful camp fires with danger far, far away."[58]

An instance that no doubt caused glee and cheerfulness in the Donaldsonville camp this second day of a decisive battle was the arrival of four recruits with dauntless spirit from Mobile, Alabama. The four, all of whom had previously been studying in New Orleans, were Ernest Lynd, age eighteen, Henri Gamotis, age seventeen, and the Mioton brothers, Seymore and John, ages eighteen and seventeen.[59]

A young Confederate artillerist with a sense of humor recorded,

> The recruit—our latest acquisition—was *so* interesting. His nice clean clothes, new hat, new shoes, trimming on his front shirt, letters and cross-guns on his hat, new knife for all the fellows to borrow, nice comb for general use, nice little glass to shave by, good smoking tobacco, money in his pocket to lend out, oh, what a great convenience he was! How *many* things he had that a fellow could borrow, and how willing he was to go on guard, and . . . give away his rations, and bring water, and cut wood, and ride horses to water! And he was so clean . . . all the fellows wanted to bunk with him under his nice new blanket, and impart to him some of their numerous and energetic 'tormentors' [lice].
>
> And then it was so *interesting* to hear him talk. He knew *so much* about war, arms, tents, knapsacks, ammunition, marching, fighting, camping, cooking, shooting, and everything a soldier is and does. It is remarkable how much a recruit and how little an old soldier knows about such things. After a while the recruit forgets all, and is as ignorant as any veteran.[60]

Of the new, young Donaldsonville Artillery volunteers, Gamotis would soon win "the encomiums from his comrades for the . . . brave deportment displayed by him in action."[61] The five-foot five-inch "Johnee" Mioton, described as "fond and petit,"[62] quickly became a popular and "ignorant" veteran that in later years saw him elected as commander of the United

John Stephen "Johnee" Mioton, photograph taken at Petersburg, Virginia, in February 1865.
Courtesy of the Confederate Memorial Hall.

Confederate Veterans Camp No. 1.[63] The older Mioton brother, Seymore, before the year was out would spend close to four months sick in a hospital while Lynd, who suffered inflammation of the eyes, wound up in Richmond's Louisiana Hospital for six months. Both *garçons* (lads), when well, returned to the battery and served honorably.[64]

Richardson, commanding the nine rifle guns that included the three Donaldsonville cannons, received orders early in the morning "to retain our fire until Longstreet opens from our extreme right—then we are to open, but fire slowly and carefully."[65] During the early part of the day there was some brisk skirmishing along the picket line and in the evening desultory firing, but Richardson's guns remained silent. During the lull the Canonniers rested in the shade of the trees. Garnett, Richardson, and Maurin, along with other officers, likely took their leisure in the McMillan house and waited, watching the enemy and the minutes, for standing on a shelf over the fireplace was an eight-day mantle clock keeping time. Found days later by its owner still ticking, the clock certainly was wound by one of the men in gray.[66]

In the shade of the trees a waiting artilleryman recorded, "Hour after hour rolls on, until we begin to think that Longstreet has deferred the attack until to-morrow, it being understood that he will make the attack on the far right sometime in the afternoon."[67] Those positioned on the McMillan property soon began to cut down post and rail fencing and used it to throw up hasty earthworks and burn in campfires. They also dug defensive holes in the ground throughout the woods along the ridge. Other members of the battalion were employed in details sent to gather food and water.

With the wells speedily exhausted and no water fit to drink within a mile, men were sent with dozens of canteens a considerable distance on horseback amid the arid hills in an attempt to find a brook or creek with clear water.[68] Garnett's second-in-command, Major Charles Richardson later wrote in *Tales of a Warrior*, "A man with a string of canteens around his shoulders returns; his canteens are all empty; he was sent to fetch water for our thirsty men, but brings none. The few springs and wells the country afford are guarded. General Lee's orders are that only wounded and the sick shall be allowed water, and there is scarce sufficient for them. I was never thirsty until now; how I long for a gourd of water from the old spring at home!"[69] Perhaps during one of these forays for water or on a foraging expedition this day, Canonnier Privates Benjamin "Sebastion" Treshe, a German born Zouave veteran, and the sickly Oscar Schmidt were captured and sent to Fort Delaware, Delaware, as prisoners of war, ending their service with the battery.[70]

Skirmishing became heavy and continuous around two o'clock in the afternoon on July

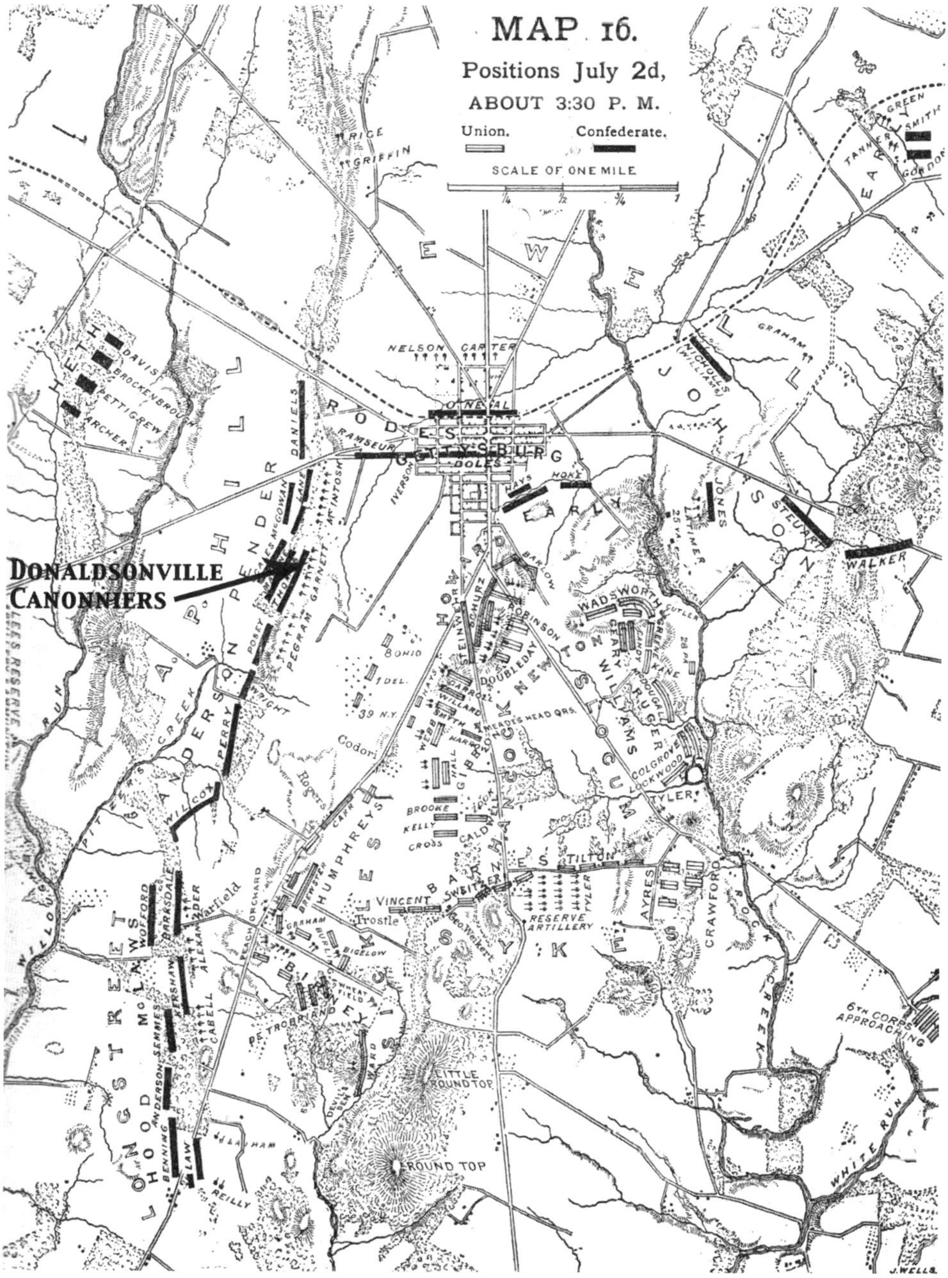

Gettysburg, July 2.
From *Battles and Leaders.*

2 and lasted for two hours before Longstreet's artillery on the right opened fire. "Our line followed," recorded Walters, "and soon Ewell on our left . . . joined in. To this, the enemy replied most vigorously, and soon the noise and din of battle became truly infernal."[71] Garnett reported, "When the engagement became general, [Richardson's] pieces opened fire upon the enemy's batteries opposite, which kept up without cessation until about thirty minutes before sunset."[72]

An artilleryman near the Donaldsonville guns along the ridge observed,

> One by one the artillery on [Longstreet's] left joins in . . . and our line becomes a living sheet of flame. A puff of white smoke is seen on the enemy's line—another and another—his line is clouded with the smoke . . . and the deadly cannon balls come hurtling and screaming through the air . . . the roar of the artillery is sublimely terrific . . . the plunging, rolling musketry fire of the infantry can be heard sweeping down the valley, and the earth shakes and trembles 'neath the continued shock. The birds of the air flap their dusky wings and fly far away . . . the beast of the field gaze in affright . . . then snuffing the sulphurous air...betake themselves to headlong flight; even the mighty war-horses . . . paws the earth in fear.[73]

The batteries of the Third Corps, from their position in the center of the army, occupied the attention of the enemy by a deliberate fire during the whole afternoon, with Richardson's guns firing and recoiling five to six feet with every shot and the crews working "as fast as men could work their guns."[74] The Donaldsonville Parrotts and 3-inch rifle were "actively engaged"[75] with the Canonniers rolling the pieces forward and realigning them while the gunners aimed and others sponged the barrels and loaded the next shot. Canonnier Artificer Cire recorded it was "the greatest and most terrible artillery duel."[76] Canonnier Private Octave

Gettysburg artillery duel.
From *Battles and Leaders*.

Landry said it was "the heaviest cannonading ever heard."[77]

Walters, assigned to a smoothbore gun in reserve, wrote, "The shouts of the enemy and yells of our own men, and the groans of the wounded as they were bourne past where I sat and the whole made up a scene such as I never before heard."[78] The Federals from Cemetery Hill "with good effect"[79] returned the heavy discharge of shot, shell, and musketry from the Confederate guns.[80] Garnett recorded, "The Federal shot and shell flew around us and over our heads into the country back of us at least two miles."[81] Astoundingly the lone Donaldsonville Canonnier casualty was the wounding of Private Emile Barras, employed as a teamster and probably struck from an over shot that landed in the rear near the horses.[82]

The Confederate attack was made by two divisions of Longstreet's Corps towards the Federal left at the Round Tops, two hills on the southern end of Cemetery Ridge. In support was Anderson's Division from Hill's Third Corps, with Ewell's Second Corps making a secondary attack about six o'clock in the evening on the Federal right at Cemetery and Culp's Hill. "Just as the sun had disappeared behind the horizon," reported Garnett, "the enemy's guns were observed to be turned upon a portion of General Ewell's forces, which attacked them in the rear, when Major Richardson, by opening upon them with his nine rifles, succeeded in diverting their fire."[83]

Another watchful diarist in the artillery recorded, "By six o'clock all the atmosphere had become filled with smoke, like a thick fog, and I could only see the flashes of the artillery through this thick smoke. After dark, the fighting appeared grand and sublime in the extreme."[84] Richardson's guns continued firing in the dark until all firing gradually ceased. Cire recorded it "lasted until 9 p.m."[85]

Richardson later penned:

The cannons' smoke drifts gently on the wind,
The moon refulgent, lights the reeking vale;
The silent stars look sadly on the scene,
While Death stalks horrid o'er the bleeding plain.[86]

The exhausted crews needed a chance to get a little sleep, but an artillery officer remembered,

> How much there was to do! . . . Our poor horses needed to be taken off somewhere & watered & brought back & fed, the crippled ones killed, & harness taken from the dead, & fresh ones scuffled for with the quartermasters. Then limbers & caissons of all guns rendezvous with ordnance wagons containing the particular kind & caliber of ammunition which its gun needs, & the boxes must be opened & cartridges, shells, fuses, primers, etc. be packed in the ammunition chests replacing all expenditures of the afternoon. The men must get something to eat—not only for tonight but tomorrow too. And then the scattered batteries & battalions must all be . . . fit & ready to resume action at dawn.[87]

The situation with the horses was dealt with when Stuart's cavalry sent in a large train of captured horses and mules. The state of affairs with food was not so good as many of the Louisiana artillerists "had nothing to eat, and very often [were] without water."[88] The hungry troops and many of the "Negro servants"[89] foraged that night across the luminous moonlit landscape. As to sleep, an artilleryman near the Donaldsonville guns wrote, "Who can rest upon a battle-field? One may sleep, indeed, but it is not the gentle sleep that brings *rest* to the weary body."[90]

At a very early hour during the morning of July 3 Pendleton, under orders from Lee, visited Walker's Third Corps artillery line for what Pendleton described as "securing readiness."[91] Walker's sixty-three guns were retained in the same position as the previous day, including Garnett's nine rifle pieces, who received orders to be "prepared for opening, as early as possible on the morning . . . a concentrated and destructive fire, consequent upon which a general advance was to be made."[92]

Specific instructions were received by battalion and battery commanders that at the given signal of two guns fired in quick succession by the Washington Artillery, located at a peach orchard, all the guns on the line of the First and Third Corps were to open simultaneously on the enemy batteries. After they were silenced, Pickett's Division, supported by Heth and Wilcox, ten brigades in all, was to advance and pierce the enemy's line "who we hoped would be demoralized by our fire," noted the Washington Artillery's Adjutant William Owen.[93]

Before daylight a mild cannonade on the right "recommenced"[94] and awoke those Louisiana artillerists who were sleeping. "Daylight had just appeared when the commanders began to rectify and strengthen the lines," Garnett remembered.[95] The Canonniers and others built up the small stone fence that ran along their front with furniture, books, and bedding taken out of the McMillan house and piled it into "hastily thrownup 'earthworks.'"[96] The day dawned sultry and became oppressively hot, the sun shining fitfully through the broken clouds by the time the Gunners of Donaldson finished fortifying their position.

The increasing heat rendered the need for water, but not without a toll by those seeking it. Canonnier Private Simon Thibodeaux, a steady veteran, while looking for water, suffered capture and later interment at Fort Delaware, on this day. Others on this third day of July faired better, as a wounded Yankee prisoner sitting on the steps of a Gettysburg church (used as a hospital) later wrote in his diary:

> Two rebel soldiers came along loaded down with things that they had confiscated from a drug store. Each had a large basket filled to the overflowing with things obtained there, besides pockets were filled. One had a large jug in his hand, and the other a large open mouthed jar under his arm.
>
> On seeing us they stopped and bade us good evening. . . . I wished them a good evening, at the same time rising. They sat their bundles down, and we commenced to talk . . . they were very intelligent fellows and . . . being familiar with drugs and medicine, had come into the village to replenish their stock that they were in need of. After talking a few moments they asked if we wished to have something to drink. They said they had some that could not be beat, in the army at least . . . they . . . took the large mouthed jar up and drank our health in a good draught therefrom, then they passed it to me with the request that I would not disappoint them but drink their health as hearty as they had ours.
>
> As they had not told what kind of liquor the jar contained I drank rather sparingly at first but still without fear, and passed it to my comrade, who followed my example. Then we sat down and talked as only soldiers can; they passed the jar, and we talked on until they were rested, when they rose to go, and—wishing to empty the jar—they passed it again for a final pledge, and we, knowing it was our last chance, took a good long pull, and after [our] shaking hands and bidding each other good [bye, they] took up their things and departed. They were young men from New Orleans and had worked in a drug store. They said the liquor was French brandy.[97]

The soldiers were possibly Donaldsonville Canonnier comrades John "Eck" Eckleburg and "Charley" Fuhri, both twenty-five, both druggist that settled before the war in the Crescent City, and both, apparently given to enjoying *consommation excessive* (excessive consumption).

Through the morning there was a calm and quiet on the field. "In our army," wrote Garnett, "the thought was uppermost that the day would establish the Confederacy. That defeat awaited our troops was never entertained."[98] Some hours after sunrise nine guns from Dance's Battalion were moved and placed in position amongst Walker's guns with Captain B. H. Smith's Third Richmond Howitzers moving in on the immediate left of the three Donaldsonville rifle guns. Garnett's eight smoothbore guns, including Maurin's two Napoleons, were again in reserve "in readiness whenever they should be called upon."[99]

After visiting Walker's line, Pendleton met with Colonel Edward P. Alexander who was in charge of Longstreet's seventy-four guns on the right of Walker's, and who, wrote Alexander, "Looked over & approved my dispositions." Alexander added, "As I rode with him & talked over matters he told me that Col. R. L. Walker . . . had nine 12 pr. Howitzers for which he had no special use as their range was too short. Gen. Pendleton asked me if I could make use of them. I jumped at the idea, & thanked him & said, 'yes, I had the very place for them.' And I rode on with him immediately, and had them turned over to me, under command of a Maj. Richardson."[100]

Garnett reported, "Richardson was ordered to the position held by Major General Anderson's Division, and to the right of Major Pegram's Battalion."[101] This detachment of nine 12-pounder smoothbore guns was made up of two Napoleon guns from the Donaldsonville Artillery, two Napoleons and four howitzers of Captain George M. Patterson's Company B, and one howitzer of Captain Hugh M. Ross's Company A, both from Lieutenant Colonel Allen S. Cutts's Sumter (Georgia) Battalion temporarily commanded by Major John Lane.[102]

In reference to Richardson's nine guns, Alexander noted,

> I intended not to let them fire a shot in the preliminary cannonade, & to keep them under cover & out of view, so that with fresh men, & uninjured horses, & full chest of ammunition, these 9 light howitzers might follow Pickett's infantry in the charge, more promptly, & also, perhaps more *safely* than guns out of the firing line could do. . . . So I led Maj. Richardson & his 9 howitzers to the best protected little hollow I could find behind a piece of woods & left him there with orders simply to wait until I sent for him. As I intended to take personal charge of him, when the time came, no further orders were necessary.[103]

Although the Confederate artillery along Seminary Ridge was prepared to fire at an early hour, a delay of several hours took place before the expected attack. During this time Maurin, back with Garnett and the nine rifle guns on both sides of the McMillan house, prepared themselves for action, carefully noticing distances as every gunner had his target selected. It was, according to one soldier, "Long hours of breathless anxiety."[104]

"Between eleven & twelve o'clock there was a severe artillery duel, between Hill's guns & the enemy, which seemed to me to begin in a fight between the skirmishers over a barn . . . & the barn was set on fire," wrote Alexander. "At last, at least 100 guns, on the two sides, got into a duel which lasted nearly a half hour & then finally died out. . . . This duel made a great deal of noise while it lasted, and . . . there was about an hour . . . in which there was scarcely a shot anywhere, except among the sharpshooters

The McMillan House, photographed by William H. Tipton.
Courtesy of the Gettysburg National Military Park.

between the lines."[105]

After this action Alexander decided to change his plan: "I got afraid that Richardson might get in trouble bringing his guns through some open, but rocky woods he had to pass. So, just to be sure, I decided to bring him beforehand & get him . . . ready & to move him out in front of Pickett instead of behind him . . . & at the best location I could find in advance, short of their infantry fire, I would unlimber & fire a few rounds before Pickett's men passed on forward in between my guns."

Alexander then sent a courier to bring up Richardson's detachment, but the courier returned after some time and reported he could not locate Richardson and the guns. Believing his courier had gone to the wrong place, Alexander stated, "He would not dare to leave there without orders. You go again & find him & don't you come back without him." The courier was again gone a long time and, wrote Alexander, "After our cannonade opened, he returned & said that Richardson was certainly gone, & that he had looked all around but could not find him."

"After the battle," wrote Alexander, "I found that Gen. Pendleton, himself, had sent & taken four or five of the guns, & disposed of them elsewhere without any notice to me. The remainder Maj. R. admitted having moved 'a short distance' because he said he found himself in the range of shell from the enemy, thrown at some of A. P. Hill's guns."[106]

Richardson in his *Tales of a Warrior* wrote:

> Under cover of a friendly hill, July 3 . . . waiting for orders, while shells scream and Minies whiz over us; but not always over us—a shrapnel bursts and the two lead horses of our Number Two gun rear and fall; one dead, the right fore leg of the other is shot off below the knee. He is unharnessed and led apart; but when we move he hobbles on three legs and takes his place at the gun as if nothing had happened. Poor creature! We pistol him to end his misery. Think we will not have horses in Heaven![107]

The four or five guns moved and arrayed in other positions by Pendleton were likely the two Napoleons of the Donaldsonville Artillery and two Napoleons of Patterson's Battery with the remaining five howitzers, being of short range and useless on the Seminary Ridge line, staying with Richardson. The location of Maurin's Napoleon's on the line is not recorded, but the *Record of Events* documents they "were ordered to different points and engaged."[108]

"At seven minutes past one, to be precise—I remember looking at my watch—we heard the ominous booming of a cannon fired by the Washington Artillery on the right center of the Confederate line," wrote Garnett. "The echoes of that discharge had scarcely died away over the field when 150 guns on each side opened fire. The combined roar was deafening. It seemed to benumb every sense but that of fear. It was terrible. The air filled with deadly lines of whizzing, screaming, bursting shells and solid shot."[109]

About a hundred yards or so to the left of the Donaldsonville Artillery's booming rifle guns were the cannons of the Third Richmond Howitzer Company. Private William White of this company, who manned a gun alongside Maurin's Canonniers during the Beaver Dam Creek fight of June 27, 1862, was again working his gun nearby and remembered, "We received orders to 'commence firing,' and briskly our men step to the guns . . . pour into the enemy a closely concentrated fire, and hotly is it returned . . . slowly . . . we pour into it a storm of shot and shell . . . immediately in front of our guns there was a stone fence, and when our boys were not actively engaged they nestled down pretty close to it. The firing on both sides was incessant, and the smoke was almost suffocating."[110]

A member of Heth's Division not far from Maurin's guns wrote, "The artillery commenced firing, and . . . we had pandemonium . . . artillery firing as fast as the men could load them coupled with the bursting of shells, and . . . the noise. The air seemed to be in a state of vibration, and produced a very strange feeling in one's head."[111] Other soldiers behind the guns recorded, "The shot and shell made the air hideous with their shrieks"[112] and "the noise and din were so furious and overwhelming as well as continuous that one had to scream to his neighbor lying beside him to be heard."[113] Others enduring the fire wrote, "The very ground seemed to quiver under our feet from the awful concussion from the many guns and the bursting bombs,"[114] and "the very earth shook as from a mighty quake. So intense were its vibrations that loose grass, leaves, and twigs arose from six to eight inches above the ground, hovered and quivered as birds about to drop."[115]

The infantry behind the guns not only sought protection in their holes and makeshift breastworks but also had to deal with the wounded artillery horses that began to come back into their lines. "One large horse, with his mouth shot off," wrote a Mississippian in Anderson's Division, "clambered over our breastwork and fell down lengthwise in the ditch . . . the horse was on his back and his legs were waving in the air." With pieces of wooden rails the soldiers managed to pry the horse up "and dragged him back of the ditch about ten feet." After this, the men received orders "to shoot every badly wounded horse that came back from the batteries in our front."[116] During the cannonade two of the Donaldsonville Artillery horses were killed.

Amid the foliage on Seminary Ridge the Yankee shells crashed through the woods like a fierce hailstorm with wicked violence, cutting limbs and bringing down great portions of the trees. An artilleryman along the firing line wrote, "The tops of the trees near us were cut off, the limbs broken and the leaves fairly covered us. The noise was like the blast of a trumpet on a mountain side. I was completely dazed but still held to the sponge staff . . . about the ninetieth round I was nearly exhausted, covered with wet powder . . . the firing continued. It seemed to me as if our gun would spring at each discharge, high in the air . . . not a word was said only . . . 'Stand by your guns, Load, Fire.'"[117]

Garnett recounted, "Along Seminary Ridge was a thick growth of saplings, among the sturdy trees, and many fell before the leaden rain as if they had been assailed by a tornado. There was no thought of flinching along our line from the galling fire we were receiving."[118] One oak tree near the stone wall was pierced by a shell through the center of the trunk. The shell forced its way out, splintering the outer layer of bark, and landed about six feet from the ground.[119]

White recalled that while working his gun, "An enemy's shell came whirling over . . . and, cutting down a tree directly in front of my gun, bursted . . . the tree falling across the fence in such a manner as to completely obstruct my line of sight, I was compelled to mount the fence and cut the tree down." As White "worked like a beaver all up and down the line the cannon are busily engaged in hurling shot and shell over into the Federal ranks, and they reply gun for gun—the smoke is so intense and the distance so great, that we cannot see the effect of our shots . . . though we cannot hope to break their line with artillery, we may open a way for our infantry to break through."[120]

Another artillerist in the center of the front line who had an excellent view recorded, "It was a hellish scene. The air was dotted with clouds of smoke where shells burst, and the fragments of shells and the solid shot were screaming and shrieking in every direction."[121] In the Federal lines the Confederate artillery fire "was extremely galling"[122] and caused an unusually large number of caissons and limbers to explode, only adding to the mayhem. The McMillan house received nineteen gaping shell holes in the walls and roof, and everywhere, inside and outside the house, shattered cannon shells, round shot and long shells, with some unexploded, lay where they had landed.[123]

Walker reported that the Third Corps artillery, "Kept up an incessant fire from 1 p.m.

to the time of the advance of the infantry," adding, the barrage "continued so long and with such rapidity, the ammunition was almost exhausted."[124] The bombardment lasted about two hours. Garnett wrote, "I take natural pride in saying that our troops exhibited no timidity in facing the frightful ordeal to which they were being subjected. Man to man they stood, shoulder to shoulder at the guns as if each felt himself the bulwark of the Confederacy's hopes . . . the cannonading continued with unabated force from start to finish, and then gradually diminished in its intensity until it ceased along both lines."[125]

The Canonniers suffered no casualties during the bombardment. On the Donaldsonville Battery's left the four guns of the Third Company Richmond Howitzer's lost two men killed, both by the same shot, and further left, the Salem Artillery's two guns had just one man very slightly wounded. The other three batteries of Garnett's Battalion to the right of Maurin's guns miraculously had only one casualty, a man wounded in Moore's Norfolk Battery.[126] The few casualties amongst these batteries might be explained by a comment made by the Federal artillery commander opposing them, Major T. W. Osborn. He noted that the guns on Seminary Ridge, "Held a fine crest for the protection of artillery, at a distance of 1,000 to 1,400 yards from us."[127]

White continued his narrative: with the order,

> Cease firing! Our infantry is about to charge, and we anxiously gather in squads upon the brow of the hill to witness that charge . . . boldly do troops of Hill and Longstreet advance across the intervening space, and the infantry fight commences—nearer and nearer do they advance towards the enemy's works, and a fire such as man never stood is poured into their devoted ranks. Some waver and fall back . . . pell mell our brave boys are driven back—the enemy leaves his works and with banners flying, rapidly advances upon our troops; our artillery opens to cover the retreat of our troops, but for some unaccountable reason is ordered to 'cease firing.' Quickly our infantry are rallied . . . and with a yell turn upon the enemy who break and take cover under their works. Again and again this is repeated—sometimes our men would actually be in their works, but . . . the enemy would regain them, and drive our men away . . . and our troops gradually fall back to our former lines, *not pursued by the enemy.*[128]

Regarding what became known as Pickett's Charge, Lee reported,

> The troops moved steadily on, under a heavy fire of musketry and artillery, the main attack being directed against the enemy's left center. His batteries reopened as soon as they appeared. Our own having nearly exhausted their ammunition in the protracted cannonade that preceded the advance of the infantry, were unable to reply, or render the necessary support to the attacking party. Owing to this fact . . . the enemy was enabled to throw a strong force of infantry against our left, already wavering under a concentrated fire of artillery from the ridge in front, and from Cemetery Hill, on the left. It finally gave way, and the right, after penetrating the enemy's lines, entering his advance works, and capturing some of his artillery, was attacked simultaneously in front and on both flanks, and driven back with heavy loss. The troops were rallied and reformed, but the enemy did not pursue.[129]

The Union artillery commander reported,

> The enemy advanced magnificently, unshaken by the shot and shell which tore through his ranks . . . [they] approached in three lines . . . they advanced gallantly until they reached the stone wall behind which our troops lay. Here ensued a desperate conflict, the enemy succeeding in passing the wall and entering our lines, causing great destruction of life, especially among the batteries. Infantry troops were, however, advanced from our right; the rear line of the enemy broke, and the others, who had fought with a gallantry that excited the admiration of our troops, found themselves cut off and compelled to surrender.[130]

The exhausted remnants of the Confederate brigades came staggering back through the smoke singly or in small groups and reformed immediately in the rear of the artillery. With brave spirits, the Donaldsonville Canonniers and other artillerists again poised themselves for an attack. "A counter assault was confidently expected by the Confederate officers, and active preparations were made to meet it. Along the line of artillery the drivers stood to their horses and the cannoneers stood ready at their respective posts. These men were prepared to use their scant supplies of ammunition to the greatest advantage," wrote a gunner.[131] Garnett recorded, "In anticipation of such an attack our lines were reformed along the Seminary Ridge, and everything put in readiness for defense. We watched with intense anxiety every movement of the troops in our front."[132]

The Confederates' confidence in Lee was exemplified by the words of an artillery sergeant at the front, who told a foreign military observer, "We've not lost confidence in the old man: this day's work won't do him no harm. 'Uncle Robert' will get us into Washington yet; you bet he will!"[133]

Lee, on the field and with no trace of emotion in his calm and self-possessed bearing, rallied and encouraged the broken troops. With shells bursting around, he informed the observer, "This has been a sad day for us, Colonel—a sad day; but we can't expect always to gain victories."[134] For the Donaldsonville Canonniers, it too was *un jour triste* (a sad day), despite having suffered no casualties.

Chapter Eleven

N'Oublier jamais cette campagne
(Never Forget This Campaign)

It was a warm summer's night with few campfires after the third day of the Gettysburg battle. The weary Donaldsonville Canonniers laid and sat under a bright, silvery moon. Some slept, others discussed the events of the day, the drivers watched the horses so they did not straggle off. The night passed, and on the morning of July 4, 1863, "The rising sun shone on the thousands of dead and wounded men lying between the lines of the two contending armies," noted a Louisiana artillerist.[1]

Everything was comparatively quiet along the opposing lines. The exhausted antagonists spent the day quietly watching each other.[2] Though the battlefield was quiet, Private John Walters wrote, "At an early hour a very heavy shower of rain fell which lasted a couple of hours. When it cleared off, the sky gave promise to more [before] long."[3]

Major Charles Richardson, second in command under Garnett, reported, "About 7 o'clock on the morning . . . I received orders from Brigadier-General [William N.] Pendleton to proceed at once to Cashtown with the rifled guns of Captains [Victor] Maurin and [J. D.] Moore, and report to [Brigadier] General [John D.] Imboden, for duty with his command."[4] Imboden was ordered by General Robert E. Lee to guard and escort the army's vast wagon train of wounded back to Virginia. Canonnier Lieutenant Prosper Landry commanded the three Donaldsonville rifle guns and their caissons assigned to Richardson's detachment that included two guns of the Norfolk Battery. All left at nine o'clock in the morning.

The Donaldsonville wagons and forge also left with the battalion's vehicles to join Imboden's wagon train. This contingent moved slowly along the Chambersburg Turnpike alongside thousands of the army's wagons and ambulances "assembling in the fields along the road from Gettysburg to Cashtown, in one confused and apparently inextricable mass."[5]

Some time between noon and one o'clock, the rain began falling in blinding sheets and caused further delays so that Richardson's detachment did not arrive in Cashtown until about two o'clock that afternoon. Richardson immediately went to Imboden, and

> The general informed me that his command would act as a convoy to the great wagon train of our army then passing through the town, and that he would at the proper time designate the positions in the column to be occupied by my guns. Having waited several hours without receiving any order from General Imboden, during which time I frequently presented myself to the general and conversed with him, I at length, having informed the general where my artillery was, with his consent returned to my command, which was on the Gettysburg to Cashtown road, about 300 yards from where I left the

Retreat From Gettysburg.
From *Battles and Leaders*.

> general and his staff. Here I remained until about sunset, when, having received no orders from the general, I returned to the point in Cashtown where I had left him, and learned that he and his staff had gone forward on the line of march. Deeming it necessary that I should communicate with him as soon as possible, in order that I might receive his orders, I turned over the command of my artillery to Captain Moore, and at once hastened to overtake General Imboden.[6]

In the darkness, Richardson set off looking for Imboden while the guns with Landry's Canonniers and Moore's artillerymen waited as the motley procession of wagons, ambulances, and wounded men on foot splashed along, passing them in the rain and mud. They waited for what seemed like an immeasurable amount of time amidst thunder and lightning and great torrents of cold rain that caused the fields to overflow and raging streams to run across the road in every depression of ground. Everything was drenched and the men became "very chilly."[7] The horses and mules, blinded and maddened by the wind and water, became "almost unmanageable."[8] The sounds of the storm were augmented by the horrible groans of maimed, wounded, and dying coming from the wagons in the immense train, its length estimated at anywere from seventeen to thirty miles.

The head of the column started moving at about four o'clock in the afternoon and began the ascent of South Mountain, but it wasn't until some time after two o'clock in the morning when a sergeant from one of the wagons of Garnett's Battalion brought word from Richardson that he desired Moore and Landry to join the wagon convoy "and move forward without unnecessary delay."[9] After receiving word from Richardson, who had not been able to overtake Imboden, Moore and Landry's guns finally joined near the end of the irretrievably mixed procession of wagons, ambulances, cavalry, stragglers, walking wounded, and Yankee prisoners and their guards.[10] Canonnier François "Bienvenue" Cire recorded, "We have nothing to eat and are compelled to march . . . without stopping and it is raining all the time."[11]

While the vast and crowded wagon train of woe slowly and painfully toiled up and over the winding pass from Cashtown, Imboden wrote,

> After dark I set out . . . to gain the head of the column during the night. My orders had been peremptory that there should be no halt for any cause whatever. If an accident should happen to any vehicle, it was immediately to be put out of the road and abandoned. The column moved rapidly, considering the rough roads and the darkness, and from almost every wagon for many miles issued heart rending wails of agony. For four hours I hurried forward on my way to the front, and in all that time I was never out of hearing of the groans and cries of the wounded and dying . . . very few of the wagons had even a layer of straw in them, and all were without springs. The road was rough and rocky from the heavy washings of the preceding day . . . from nearly every wagon as the teams trotted on, urged by whip and shout, came such cries and shrieks as these:
>
> 'O God! Why can't I die?' 'My God! Will no one have mercy and kill me?' 'Stop!' 'Oh! For God's sake, stop just for one minute; take me out and leave me to die on the roadside.' 'I am dying! I am dying! My poor wife, my dear children, what will become of you?'
>
> Some were simply moaning; some were praying, and others uttering the most fearful oaths and execrations that despair and agony could wring from them; while a majority, with a stoicism sustained by sublime devotion to the cause they fought for, endured without complaint unspeakable tortures, and even spoke words of cheer and comfort to their unhappy comrades of less will or more acute nerves. Occasionally a wagon would be passed from which only low, deep moans could be heard. No help could be rendered to any of the sufferers. No heed could be given to any of their appeals. Mercy and duty to many forbade the loss of a moment in the vain effort then and there to comply with the prayers of the few. On! On! we *must* move on. The storm continued, and the darkness was appalling. There was no time even to fill a canteen with water for a dying man; for, except the drivers and the guards, all were wounded and utterly helpless in that vast procession of misery.[12]

A sick Donaldsonville Canonnier Private Octave Landry moving with the wagons and traveling forge, recorded, "Raining very hard all day and night. Never stopped, not even to water our horses."[13] In the dark there were momentary halts that were followed by rapid trots of a hundred yards, and then another halt, resulting from the breaking down of a wagon, or difficulty in passing mud holes. When descending the mountains the wagons and ambulances rushed along side by side, and one could see sheets of sparks as the iron horse hoofs of the animals struck the stony surface of the pike.[14]

Napier Bartlett of the Washington Artillery (their guns also assigned to protect the wagon train) wrote, "So important was our movement that no halt for bivouac, though we marched scarcely two miles an hour, was made . . . the men and officers on horseback would go to sleep without knowing it, and at one time there was a halt occasioned by all of the drivers—or at least those whose business was to attend to it, being asleep in their saddles. In fact the whole of the army was dozing while marching and moved as if under enchantment or a spell—were asleep and at the same time walking."[15]

Imboden's column of fatigued men and horses pulling wagons and guns simply followed the vehicle ahead of them. Upon reaching Greenwood, instead of going on through to Chambersburg, Imboden decided to leave the main road and take "a near cut" across the country.[16] Troopers of the vanguard directed the drivers of the lead wagons to turn left onto Pine Stump Road. By the time the Donaldsonville guns turned off of the solid based, though bumpy Chambersburg Pike, the country road had turned into a rut-filled quagmire with broken wagons and dead and dying horses strewed along the route.

At New Guilford and its crossroads the column moved back onto a hard surfaced road. The clattering of horses' feet and rumbling of wagons made a great deal of noise. New Franklin was passed next, where, wrote a citizen, "Daylight at length dawned, and revealed to the farmers along the road that their fences were torn down and ambulances and wagons, together with hundreds of cavalry, were making their way through their fields and their wheat, corn and grass were being ruined. The narrow road in many places was so badly cut up that the wagons could scarcely get along, and many had to take the fields. Broken down wagons and caissons, yet containing large amounts of ammunition were strewn all along the route. Oh, what a sight!"[17]

A young witness at New Franklin would later write, "Rebel soldiers, wounded, were left all along the route of retreat. Many died and were buried by the roadside. I shall never forget those ghastly wounds, those thousands of faces dusky with powder, and the battery of black and horrid field pieces they had sent."[18]

A little over an hour later, Marion was reached. Here the column turned south on the Williamsport Turnpike, though "many of the teamsters did not attempt to keep the road, but took the nearest route across the fields, the wheels cutting in the soft ground up to the axles."[19]

After Marion there was another five miles of the road deep with gritty mud until the town of Greencastle was reached. Here in the somnolent town of red brick and white paint, with a central square, a civilian observed the passage and recorded, "A more crestfallen, woe-begone mob may never have been seen. Hurry was the order of the day. They seemed almost to be pushing each other forward."[20] Another observer recorded, "Many persons threw taunts at the retreating foe, such as, 'How are you Gettysburg?' 'Have you been to Philadelphia already?' and 'Did you meet the Pennsylvania militia down there?' An officer rode up to a pump and asked for water. A citizen standing by said, 'Did you get enough of *Meade* over there?' The officer grew furious and called him an impudent puppy."[21]

Octave Landry with the Donaldsonville wagon contingent recorded in his diary on July 5,

> After having traveled all night without stopping and after daylight it ceased raining and we watered our horses in going through a creek. Passed Greencastle and after having made about two miles, the Yankee cavalry made a dash on our wagon train and captured many prisoners, several from our company. And after having made us double-quick through oat fields, to a crop road, our cavalry made a charge and we were exposed to their fire as well as of the enemy's. We were recaptured and came back to the main road where our wagons had been left and four spokes in the wheel of the wagon, battery wagon and forge cut (by citizens), but managed to pull them and resumed our march. . . . Jean Baptiste Gaudet was wounded in the head after having been taken prisoner with the wagon train and only one of the company Duffosard Mollere was not recaptured by our cavalry.[22]

Here too it was reported that Canonnier Private Abraham Klotz was "taken prisoner . . . while left in the care of Octave Landry, who was ill, he managed to make his escape, and carried back to the Confederate lines some artillery [caisson & horses?] which was supposed to be so damaged as to be unfit for further use."[23] On making his escape, Klotz, known for his "soldierly bearing in camp, on the march and on the battlefield [that] won commendation from his comrades,"[24] simply said he was "rescued by General Imboden's command."[25] Both fearless and bighearted, Klotz became "known for his charitable disposition towards brother-Confederates."[26]

In this attack south of Greencastle near Cunningham's Crossroad,[27] where the Williamsport Pike route traverses flat rocky country, one hundred Yankee cavalry troopers from Captain Ulrich Dahlgren's Sixth Pennsylvania Cavalry and a group of local partisans (citizens) remained hidden nearby until over 300 wagons had passed. They then charged a section of the wagon train at opposite ends, with the ax wielding partisans going into the road jammed full of wagons and smashing and cutting their wooden wheels.

Imboden wrote, "The citizens to the number of thirty or forty attacked the train with axes, cutting the spokes out of ten or a dozen wheels and dropping the wagons in the street. The moment I heard of it I sent back a detachment of cavalry to capture every citizen who had been engaged in this work, and treat them as prisoners of war."[28]

The relieving cavalry soldiers were members of companies F and I, Eighteenth Virginia Cavalry. One wrote, "We struck the Yankees in both flanks and drove them away, getting back all they had taken, together with some prisoners."[29] Ten of the Yankee cavalrymen and some of the civilian partisans were captured while many of the freed Confederates returned to the wagon train "delighted at being recaptured."[30] At least one captured Donaldsonville Canonnier, Private Edward Morin, "Escaped and made his way back to Confederate lines."[31] Morin along with his father Michel and brother Mathieu served "valiantly" during this campaign and "took a daring and conspicuous part."[32] However, it must have taken a toll in Edward's life as evidenced by his epitaph: "Rest Soldier, Rest—Thy Warfare is O'er."[33]

Richardson, who was still looking for Imboden, met the brigadier general's adjutant in Greencastle and reported, "I had received no orders to march. I did not see the general then, but learned that he had gone forward. Riding forward . . . our train was attacked by a body of the enemy's cavalry, and I was captured, but was soon rescued by a company of our cavalry. I, however, did not recover my horse, which had been taken by the enemy. I therefore had to proceed as best I could, part of the way on foot, and arrived at Williamsport during the afternoon of the 5th ultimo."[34]

The Donaldsonville wagons arrived in Williamsport along with the enormous train and came to a dead halt at the Potomac River. The still sick Octave Landry recorded, "And about 12 noon arrived on the banks of the Potomac at Williamsport. The river being too high to ford, we camped on the bank of the river."[35] Wagons were jammed in close order along the banks of the surging river or on nearby level meadows below the town. Wagons and their drivers also jammed into the town's streets. Throughout the day horses and mules pulling the white canvas-covered wagons rolled in and joined the immense concourse of parked wagons. Imboden wrote that the Union cavalry "began to swarm down upon us from the fields and cross-roads, making their attacks in small bodies, and striking the column where there were few or no guards, and thus creating great confusion."[36]

At Williamsport, Richardson finally met with Imboden during the evening

> and informed him again as I had done at Cashtown the previous day, that my [artillery] horses were in bad condition, and asked him if he could furnish me with more horses, as I thought I might need assistance. He said he had already directed . . . a regiment of infantry belonging to his command, and then not far from the rear of the wagon train, to take charge of and turn over to the artillery and wagons all the serviceable led horses in the train. The horses in the wagon train of [Garnett's] battalion which had arrived were not in condition . . . to assist in bringing up the artillery.[37]

Richardson spent the night at Williamsport, where campfires blazed between the wagons and big chunks of fat meat were supplied, cooked, and eaten with crackers. Some were even lucky enough to get their canteen filled with whiskey.[38] The food was provided by Imboden who wrote, "Our supply of provisions consisted of a few wagon-loads of flour in my own brigade train, a small lot of fine fat cattle which I had collected in Pennsylvania . . . and some sugar and coffee procured in the same way."[39]

Upon awakening on the morning of July 6, Richardson noticed that neither Moore nor Landry were in camp with their guns, and he "directed that all serviceable horses in camp should be at once sent to aid in bringing up the artillery."[40] Meanwhile Imboden recorded, "Early on the morning . . . I received intelligence of the approach . . . of a large body of cavalry with three full batteries of six rifle guns . . . and ordered as many of the wagoners to be formed as could be armed with the guns of the wounded . . . by noon 700 wagoners were organized into companies of 100 each and officered by wounded line-officers and commissaries and quartermaster—about 250 of these were . . . on the right next to the river—about as many . . . on the left, and the residue were used as skirmishers. My own command proper was held well in hand in the center."[41]

A Catholic priest with the wounded Louisiana troops, Father James Sheeran, described how the drivers were armed with guns from the ordnance wagons: "many of whom mounted on horses and mules acted with the cavalry, while the dismounted drivers acted with the sharpshooters."[42]

While the defensive line at Williamsport was being prepared, Prosper Landry's Canonniers with the three Donaldsonville guns and caissons, continued on through another night amongst the last of the moving wagons. At daylight they struggled along and passed the "terrible evidences"[43] and broken wagons along the route between Marion and Greencastle. The end of the column went through Greencastle at eleven o'clock in the morning and moved along without sleep, rest, or subsistence, though some of the Louisiana artillerymen stopped at farmhouses for food.[44]

Many of the horses were entirely worn-out and unable to go on. They had to be abandoned while those that were too much broken down to be of any use or those that suffered from not being shod, causing their hoofs to be worn off to the quick, were turned over to Imboden's infantry. The lack of serviceable horses compelled both Landry and Moore to abandon their caissons. Landry also had to turn over to Captain James F. Hart's South Carolina Battery two of the three Donaldsonville guns that were unable to go farther when their reduced teams had one too many *cheval claque* (broken-down horse).[45]

Fatigue affected all and, wrote a Louisiania atilleryman, "Never had the men and horses been so jaded, and stove up . . . battery horses would drop down dead."[46] The men too, observed another Louisiana gunner, were "all dead on their feet."[47] Landry's doughty Donaldsonville Canonniers continued on. The lone Donaldsonville gun, a Parrott rifle, struggled on over the macadam and plank road towards Williamsport following Moore's two Norfolk guns.[48]

Richardson reported,

> General Imboden ordered me, the morning of July 6, to ride around the line of battle that he had formed, and select positions to be occupied by my artillery as soon as it should arrive. This order I obeyed, and, on returning to camp, found Captain Moore with his two guns, the caissons having been unavoidably abandoned. I lost no time in placing Captain Moore's battery in position, and had just done so when Lieutenant Landry arrived with one 10-pounder Parrott...as the enemy was then threatening us, I lost no time in placing Lieutenant Landry's piece in position, and this had just been done when Captain Moore opened upon a battery of the enemy's guns which appeared in range on the Sharpsburg road.[49]

Moore's two guns were placed between the Hagerstown and Boonsboro Roads, while Landry's gun was posted on the Greencastle Road that they had come in on.

Imboden wrote, "As we could not retreat further, it was at once frankly made known to the troops that unless we could repel the threatened attack we should all become prisoners, and that the loss of his whole transportation would probably ruin General Lee . . . so far from repressing the ardor of the troops, this frank announcement of our peril inspired all with the utmost enthusiasm. Men and officers alike, forgetting the sufferings of the past few days, proclaimed their determination to drive back the attacking force or perish in the attempt."[50]

Imboden had over twenty pieces of artillery on hand. Without earthworks of any kind they were posted in a semi-circle defensive line on a summit of a slight rising ground half a mile to one mile outside the town. The country was open and almost level.[51] Imboden remembered,

> The enemy appeared in our front about half-past one o'clock on both the Hagerstown and Boonsboro roads, and the fight began . . . with artillery on both sides. The firing from our side was very rapid, and seemed to make the enemy hesitate about advancing. In a half hour J. D. Moore's battery ran out of ammunition, but as an ordnance train had arrived from Winchester, two wagon-loads of ammunition were ferried across the river and run upon the field behind the guns, and the boxes tumbled out, to be broke open with axes. With this fresh supply our guns were all soon in full play again. As the enemy could not see the supports of our batteries from the hill-tops, I moved the whole line forward to his full view, in single ranks, to show a long front . . . my line passed our guns fifty or one hundred yards, where they were halted awhile, and then were withdrawn behind the hill-top again, slowly and steadily.[52]

During this time Richardson reported Landry's Donaldsonville cannon and Moore's two guns "were worked carefully."[53]"

It was an awful hot, sultry day," wrote one of Imboden's Confederate cavalrymen, leading to "our clothes [being] soaked with perspiration."[54] The tired and sweat-covered Gunners of Donaldson on the Greencastle Road worked their gun. It, along with the other cannon shots, "shook the earth, and reverberated among the hills. Another, and still another and then the musketry began to rattle," wrote a witness.[55]

The artillery rounds in the distance made "small white knots of smoke in the blue sky,"[56] and soon the smoke of the musketry covered over the battlefield and obscured everything, friend and foe alike. Still the action of the wagoners and artillery on the left of the line (in the area of Landry's gun) was so resolute that the Federal commander reported his dismounted cavalry soldiers "could not dislodge them without too much sacrifice."[57]

In the meantime Imboden's command moved rapidly to the right and charged and repelled the dismounted advancing enemy, who fell back grimly to their horses. A description of the fight was given by Father Sheeran, who wrote, "Our artillery opened on the enemy with telling effect, while our cavalry and drivers charge them with a tremendous yell. The Yankees fly in every direction, leaving many fine horses behind. Our drivers fought like heroes. It is said to be a most laughable sight to see them mounted on their mules and in full pursuit of the flying enemy."[58]

"Night was rapidly approaching," recorded Imboden,

> when a messenger from Fitzhugh Lee arrived to urge me to 'hold my own,' as he would be up in a half hour with three thousand fresh men. The news was sent along our whole line, and was received with a wild and exultant yell. We knew then that the field was won, and slowly pressed forward. Almost at the same moment we heard distant guns on the enemy's rear and right on the Hagerstown road. They were Stuart's, who was approaching on that road, while Fitzhugh Lee was coming on the Greencastle road. That settled the contest. The enemy broke to the left and fled by the Boonsboro' road. It was too dark to follow.[59]

A short time before the enemy withdrew, the Donaldsonville gun had exhausted its ammunition and Richardson "ordered . . . Lieutenant Landry to retire."[60]

"During the day," Octave Landry recorded, "the enemy's cavalry tried to capture our wagon train—the whole army's wagon train near the ford—but was repulsed by the wagon drivers, one of our men, Miles Joyner, was wounded in the engagement."[61] Richardson later reported Moore had four men wounded and two horses killed, with Prosper Landry having two horses killed. Joyner was the lone Donaldsonville Cannonier casualty during the battle. Imboden recorded he could never ascertain the loss on either side, but estimated Confederate casualties at about 125 while noting the capture of 125 of the enemy who failed to reach their horses to escape.[62]

"The wagoners fought so well that this came to be known as 'the wagoners' fight,'" and, recorded Imboden, "by extraordinary good fortune we had thus saved all of General Lee's trains. A bold charge at anytime before sunset would have broken our feeble lines, and then we should all have fallen an easy prey to the Federals."[63]

That night, having relocated to their wagon camp, Landry's crew ate their first meal in some time while not on the move and conversed with 'the wagoners' of the day's action. After, the Canonnier contingent and almost everyone else went to sleep. A tired combatant noted that during the night "the rain came down like cloud bursts and drenched us."[64] The next day, July 7, the army arrived at Williamsport from Gettysburg.

Lee's army had remained in position at Gettysburg back on July 4, where Walters of Garnett's Battalion noted, "We all expected this to be the heaviest day's fighting of the battle, notwithstanding the terrible work that has already been done, but in this we were, I must say pleasingly, disappointed."[65] After Richardson's detachment had left with Imboden's wagon train, Garnett, at about eleven o'clock in the morning, placed the battalion's eight smoothbore guns (including Maurin's two Napoleons) in position with the remaining four rifle pieces on the line. When the great downpour of rain occurred to break the quiet monotony that prevailed, the Canonniers and soldiers of both armies tried in vain to keep up their smoldering fires.[66]

Garnett remembered, "The gloomy day was drawing to a close when General A. P. Hill stopped to warm himself by my bivouac fire. I saw plainly that his spirit was gone, and that he made no effort to hide the fact. Presently, without a word of comment upon the result, he turned sorrowfully toward me and said: 'Colonel, we must return to Virginia and prepare to try it again.'"[67]

Lee issued orders to vacate their position that evening. The news of a "retrograde movement for the Potomac"[68] came as a shock to some. Walters recorded, "At dark, great was our surprise to see all the troops in motion, and all taking the back track. We were wondering what this movement meant."[69] Garnett simply reported, "When darkness had fully set in the troops were quietly put on the march."[70] The two Donaldsonville Napoleons, caissons, and a mule-pulled wagon containing rations and provender led by Maurin, along with Garnett's other guns and few wagons, withdrew from Seminary Ridge with the Third Corps artillery.

When the army withdrew from its lines, Lee and A. P. Hill rode in front of the Third Corps troops, followed by Longstreet's Corps, then Ewell's Second Corps, and behind Ewell's infantry, his train of ambulances and wagons. Moving away from Gettysburg along the Fairfield Road, which was very crowded with men and horses greatly worn down by hard service and fatigue, the column moved "at a snail's pace."[71] Walters wrote, "We marched all of that night over one of the worst roads that I ever saw and at five o'clock in the morning, packed at the foot of South Mountain, having passed through the small but rather neat village of Fairfield. . . . I had eaten nothing for twenty-four hours."[72]

An extract from a Louisiana artilleryman's notebook revealed, "The night was very bad—thunder and lightening, torrents of rain—the road knee deep in mud and water, and often blocked up with wagons 'come to grief.' I pitied the wretched plight of the unfortunate soldiers who were to follow us. Our progress was naturally very slow indeed, and we took eight hours to go as many miles."[73]

The wheels of the guns and caissons cut up the muddy road so much that Maurin's Canonniers could hardly get along on foot. With the rain "in about the right proportions and the tramping troops acted as a sort of mud mill, working the mud into the right consistency to make brick. It clung to our feet and to our clothes. When one stepped into a rut, he found it a hard matter to pull out his feet," described a soldier.[74] Many left the road in the inky darkness and marched through the soggy fields tramping down the almost ripe wheat as the men "halloo out the names of their comrades in order to keep together."[75]

It was a grueling and wearisome march and "what sorry specimens of humanity we 'rebels' must have appeared," speculated a southern artillerist, "standing in the muddy road with our 'Confederate grey' drenched to our skins, our slouched hats drawn down over our faces, and our forms trembling and shaking with cold!"[76] Another later wrote in a letter, "It rained nearly all night, and such a sight as our troops were next day! They were all wet and many of them muddy all over from having fallen down during the night."[77] Regarding the movement, still another noted, "We lacked rations and some of us lacked shoes, but there was no grumbling."[78] Lee reported, "Little progress was made that night owing to a severe storm, which greatly embarrassed our movements."[79]

At the foot of South Mountain near the entrance to the mountain pass, the twelve guns of Garnett's Battalion remained in the same location for ten hours. There the men rested and ate what they had, two biscuits and no meat for some, others, without flour, ate broiled beef or mutton chops. Either way it was "meager rations"[80] with "very few blackberries along that road."[81] Garnett's assistant quartermaster also reported ninety bushels of grain were "unavoidably lost or destroyed" because of the condition of the horses and for want of transportation.[82] While they rested, the horses were given a respite and "unhooked from the guns and caisson carriages, and, harness remaining on them, they were given their provender."[83]

Maurin's Canonniers and others tried to dry their clothing before a log or rail fire and rested or slept on the rain-saturated ground, under caissons, or in fence corners. At three o'clock in the afternoon on July 5 the two Donaldsonville Napoleons and caissons, with their one wagon, finally moved slowly over a horrible road up and through the mountains by way of Fairfield Gap.[84] It was a rough go with the vehicle's wheels caked with mud and the labor of men and animals multiplied four-fold in moving them. An artillery officer wrote, "Travel a little ways, & stopped by the thing in front of you stopping—it may be for a few seconds, it may be a half hour. Nothing is more wearying. Our carriages were light of ammunition, but we had lost enormously in horses."[85]

The day's respite had its renewed effect on the men though, and a Louisiana artillerist noted, "The road was full of soldiers marching in a particularly lively manner—the wet and mud seemed to have produced no effect whatever on their spirits, which were as boisterous as ever. The same old chaff was going on of 'Come out of that hat—I know you're in it—I see your legs a-dangling down,' &c."[86]

When night set in, Walters later wrote, "I have seen bad roads, but this was without exception the worst that I have ever seen. One moment we were up to our knees in mud, and the next, lying full length in the mud, having tripped over a rock which we could not shun, owing to the total darkness in which we were enveloped."[87] The battery's movement and the Louisianians' banter continued on even with the mishaps as "the soldiers were so completely covered with mud that the color of their clothing could not be distinguished."[88]

At four o'clock on the morning of July 6 Garnett's Battalion emerged from the mountain gap along the Mercersburg, Greencastle, and Waynesboro Turnpike. A short distance further on they reached a string of houses along the wet but well maintained thoroughfare where the deafening chorus of frogs and toads was heard from the adjacent widespread marsh. Halting at this village called Frogtown, which Walters described as "a mean affair,"[89] the battalion waited. "While here," added Walters, "some seven or eight thousand prisoners passed on their way to Richmond . . . shortly after, General Lee passed, who was saluted in that silent, respectful manner which the glorious old man so much admires. After him passed Extra Billy, our [Virginian] Governor elect, who received hearty and prolonged cheering to which he did not seem at all adverse."[90]

Garnett's Battalion with Hill's Corps remained awaiting the army's other two corps who were following across the mountain route. Maurin's Canonniers and twelve guns of the battalion again got under way at three o'clock in the afternoon and headed west, re-passing through Waynesboro then south to Leitersburg. "In both places," wrote Walters, "the people seem jubilant over what they suppose to be our defeat." He added, "Now it is true we did not gain a victory, but we are far from being defeated."[91] The slow movement continued, with the troops "very much fatigue[d] and wearied from loss of sleep."[92]

After traveling twelve hours, Garnett's Battalion stopped three miles from Hagerstown and rested for one hour. Walters wrote that the twelve guns "were again called up and in a short time passed through Hagerstown and camped a mile on this side of it, where it is likely that we will be for some days."[93] Artillery and infantry units filed into wheat fields to rest. "We," wrote another soldier, "slept comfortably, having made us good beds of wheat."[94]

Back at Williamsport Lieutenant Prosper Landry obtained additional horses but was unable to retrieve the two Donaldsonville guns from Hart's Battery. Landry, with the lone Parrott rifle and Moore's two guns under Richardson, rejoined Garnett's Battalion and the main body of the army near Hagerstown. The battalion's wagons remained at Williamsport waiting to cross the river.[95]

"On reaching Hagerstown," Garnett reported, "the battalion was reunited under Major Richardson, who continued in command."[96] This one sentence is the only source to indicate that Garnett was not in charge at this time. He did resume command after a week, but in another few weeks he received a sick furlough suggesting that his absence here was a precursor to an illness. The muster rolls and official reports give no indication as to the fact. Since the move from Gettysburg the Donaldsonville captain acted in Richardson's place with the battalion, and now Maurin continued as second in command with Richardson leading the battalion. Prosper Landry was temporarily assigned the command of the Donaldsonville Artillery, now armed with just two Napoleon guns and one Parrott rifle.

Upon awakening on July 7 the artillery and infantry of Lee's army were placed in line of battle behind hastily thrown up entrenchments after which there was a brush with the enemy. The Sixth New York Cavalry made a dash for the Confederate line and suffered four casualties. Canonnier Octave Landry recorded, "One of our Parrotts and one Napoleon in the engagement."[97] This was the only "demonstration"[98] of the day by the enemy. Octave Landry also noted in his diary, "This morning and all night, rain."[99]

For the next few days the Confederate Army laid drawn up in line of battle and, wrote an artilleryman, "Wishing the Yankees to give us battle."[100] Another Southern soldier commented, "The stillness doesn't seem natural. You don't feel right unless you hear cannonading going on."[101] All enjoyed the rest, but an artilleryman also took note that they were "decidedly in a bad way for something to eat and wear."[102] The only food around was "fine ripe cherries &

raspberries which grew everywhere."[103] From day to day "very slender"[104] rations began to be issued by Heth's divisional commissary wagons.

On July 7 Prosper Landry made a Special Requisition for nine pair of shoes for the Canonniers who "are absolutely in need of them."[105] Richardson approved the requisition, which normally included a price tag with the item so that the recipient could have it deducted from his clothing allowance. This one didn't, possibly because captured Yankee shoes had no cost.

On July 9 another artilleryman's diary entry simply read, "Nothing of importance has occurred."[106] Meanwhile a foot soldier's diary noted, "Many unfounded rumors in circulation."[107]

On July 10 there were two significant events. The first was the arrival of artillery ammunition opposite Williamsport, after which battalion commanders were directed to send their caissons immediately so they could be loaded with the ammunition brought across the river. After the batteries were supplied a Louisianian recorded, "We are thankful."[108] The second recorded event, appreciated by all was "Today we drew fresh beef, for a rarity."[109]

Lee reported, "The rains that had prevailed almost without intermission since our entrance into Maryland, and greatly interfered with our movements, had made the Potomac unfordable, and the pontoon bridge left at Falling Waters had been partially destroyed by the enemy. The wounded and prisoners were sent over the river as rapidly as possible in a few ferry-boats, while the trains awaited the subsiding of the waters and the construction of a new pontoon bridge."[110]

In Williamsport Canonnier Cire wrote on July 7, "We are still at the ford. . . . The Yankees taken prisoner were sent across the river in boats."[111] Another diarist with the wagons recorded on July 8, "The river began rising again, and the whole flat, on which the wagons were parked, was almost like a pond."[112]

Williamsport by this time had turned into an awful place with "green flies . . . around us all the time," wrote a mounted Confederate, adding, "the dead horses and offal of the great number of beeves, etc., killed for the army packed around the little town made it very unpleasant."[113] Not only was it unpleasant, it was also unhealthy. On July 11 Garnett's Battalion Assistant Quartermaster, Captain Thomas M. Hewitt, was too sick to perform his duties, and Lieutenant Prosper Landry from the Donaldsonville Battery was now detached to act as the battalion's quartermaster. Returning to Williamsport Landry received in the field under his charge two wagons, four mules, and two horses containing rations of 1,120 pounds of grain plus the battalion's forage totaling 10,586 pounds of corn and 12,520 pounds of hay (four days of full rations for the battalion's animals).[114] Another quartermaster observed, "We cannot subsist long here. Our space is so contracted to forage our horses in. We feed together on wheat, and clover, and timothy hay. At present there seems plenty of that."[115]

Private Octave Landry that day recorded, "This morning the battery's wagon went back 2 miles from the ford on the Hagerstown Road and reported to Captain Scott, the guns on the line."[116] It seems Maurin was obliged to turnover to the quartermaster department one unserviceable horse, one wagon, four sets of harnesses, and four mules, while Prosper Landry in his new quartermaster position of purchasing and supplying documented that he received from Hewitt, one wall tent and one fly tent, one table, one desk, one chest, one ink stand, one ink bottle, one blank book, and twenty-four quarrels of paper. The government allowed Prosper Landry an extra twenty dollars in pay to perform these tasks of which it was written, "this is a hard world" and "grab is the game."[117] Being a quartermaster was a calling that probably didn't suit the "just and upright, warmhearted and sympathetic"[118] Canonnier lieutenant. A month later Prosper Landry went back to the battery after being relieved from these duties when Hewitt returned.[119]

At this time the Donaldsonville horses were broken down and worn out, but they were feeding better than they had been—one reason being there were less horses to feed, with Maurin reporting only forty-four serviceable horses on his muster roll after Gettysburg. In comparison, a little more than a month before the campaign started the battery had eighty-seven horses and thirteen mules. The entire battalion had 397 horses and mules before Gettysburg. After, Garnett reported just 159 (an average of nearly forty animals per battery). The battalion's transportation was in a deplorable state and insufficient.[120]

The countryside had already been foraged empty and there were now few supplies that could be collected. The means of obtaining subsistence was becoming precarious too, but Lee's army was in fine spirits and confident of success. The soldiers of the Army of Northern Virginia were more than eager to fight at Hagerstown.

While waiting to be attacked in their entrenchments and with some somberness about the drizzly atmosphere and leaden sky, the soldiers renewed their jest as the bands and minstrel ensembles began to play "Dixie" (over and over) "Maryland, my Maryland," the "Bonnie Blue Flag," and "The Girl I Left Behind Me," along with comic songs, folk melodies, and other popular musical favorites of the army.[121] The commanding general stated, "He didn't know how they would get along without bands," adding that "they cheered up the men so much."[122]

One incident of marvel on July 9 was recorded by an artillerist from the Richmond Howitzer Third Company: "A few of our negro cooks, who were with our wagon when it was captured by the enemy, escaped and returned to camp today. Certainly they were the happiest fellows I ever saw and was [*sic*] greeted with loud cheers by our men. A chance for *freedom* they had, but they preferred life and *slavery* in Dixie to liberty at the north."[123] However another Confederate on the same day recorded, "A great many negroes have gone to the Yankees."[124]

There were other instances of note on this campaign regarding the service and dedication of slaves and free men of color who chose to stay with Lee's army. One such story told was: "The housewife, questioning a Negro . . . on the march, tested his loyalty by asking him if he was treated well, and she got a careful answer. 'I live as I wish,' he told her, 'and if I did not, I think I couldn't better myself by stopping here. This is beautiful country, but it doesn't come up to home in my eyes.'"[125] A Confederate soldier wrote about his servant, "As the darkies passed" in Maryland on the return from Gettysburg, "broad-mouthed abolition dutch gals would stop them and entreat them to . . . desert their masters, and remain with them . . . and offered . . . money, lots to eat, and . . . freedom to run away." His servant preferred to remain loyal, and the soldier noted he rejoined his company after telling the gals "nary time."[126] The servants of the Donaldsonville Artillery it seems remained with their command, and it was related that Captain Maurin's servant, Louis Lefort, "Often participated in battle" and his "bravery and courage was well known."[127]

Lee issued General Orders, Number 76, on July 11:

> After long and trying marches, endured with the fortitude that has ever characterized the soldiers of the Army of Northern Virginia, you have penetrated the country of our enemies, and recalled to the defense of their own soil those who were engaged in the invasion of ours.
>
> You have fought a fierce and sanguinary battle, which, if not attended with the success that has hitherto crowned your efforts, was marked by the same heroic spirit that has commanded the respect of your enemies, the gratitude of your country, and the admiration of mankind.

> Once more you are called upon to meet the army from which you have won on so many fields a name that will never die.
>
> Once more the eyes of your countrymen are turned upon you, and again do wives and sisters, fathers, mothers, and helpless children lean for defense on your strong arms and brave hearts.
>
> Let every soldier remember that on his courage and fidelity depends all that makes life worth having—the freedom of his country, the honor of his people, and the security of his home. Let each heart grow strong in the remembrance of our glorious past, and in the thought of the inestimable blessings for which we contend, and, invoking the assistance of that Divine Power which has so signally blessed our former efforts, let us go forth in confidence to secure the peace and safety of our country.
>
> Soldiers! your old enemy is before you! Win from him honors worthy of your righteous cause—worthy of your comrades dead on so many illustrious fields.[128]

"A great battle is daily expected, and General Lee has issued an order to our troops, exhorting them to contend valiantly for the victory," wrote an artilleryman from the line, "We will not disappoint our great leader's expectations—in no sense is the Army of Northern Virginia whipped, discouraged, or demoralized."[129]

Confederate cannon and troops began moving all day between Williamsport and Hagerstown, and Garnett's Battalion, still under Richardson's command, "Hitched up and moved to within a short distance of the Sharpsburg Turnpike, where our troops are drawn up in line of battle on a splendid range of hills," related Walters.[130] Part of the battalion was placed in position, including the "whole battery"[131] of the Donaldsonville Artillery. The remainder of the battalion guns were "held at hand ready for orders."[132] Richardson's guns, including Maurin's three, went into position with Heth's Division in front of the College of St. James's brick schoolhouse.[133]

The whole of the Third Corps Artillery was located in front and on the right and left of St. James College with Richardson's guns supporting Heth's Division.[134] Here the Canonniers diligently strengthened their position by digging entrenchments and throwing up breastworks. All the guns on the line received a large supply of ammunition from which a few shots were occasionally fired to scatter such of the enemy as showed themselves.[135]

The Donaldsonville guns remained in position through July 12 and 13 with no action, the men enduring the discomfort of hunger and mosquitoes while trying to protect themselves as well as possible from the rain that came steadily down.[136] "Some slight skirmishing is going on in front," recorded an artillery diarist positioned to the left of Maurin's guns on July 13, "but the enemy are chary of us, and make no attempt to advance, seemingly intent upon worrying us if we attempt the crossing of the Potomac, the which 'tis thought we will accomplish to-night."[137]

During the morning of July 13 a still sick Octave Landry recorded the Donaldsonville Battery's "wagons and forge left, crossed the Potomac . . . the river high to axle of wagons and at 10 p.m. camped . . . rain all day and night."[138] The battalion's wagons crossed at Williamsport under Prosper Landry's command at about five o'clock in the afternoon. Crossing too was the army's artillery caissons, which were ordered back from the front lines.

"As we expected," wrote an artillery diarist, "at dark, we left our position [in the front lines] and moved in the direction of Falling Waters."[139] Richardson and Maurin had the battalion batteries limbered up and ready to move at dark and just as they started, it began to rain. Hill's Corps was the last to leave the line; Heth's Division and Garnett's Artillery served as the rear guard. The Canonniers trekked for about an hour through woods where an artilleryman noted "the blackness of the night was phenomenal."[140] Walters recorded, "We had hard work to get along . . . we were compelled to light some port-fires to enable our drivers to see where to drive."[141] With heavy rains, the guiding fires, made out of piles of burning fence rails, and torches were at times dimmed as they moved along the route over a small farm road. "They were already bad from the previous rains," wrote an artilleryman about the roads, "and now under the long procession of wheeled vehicles, stirring the interminable mud, they became channels of mud, and often they were so deep that the slush ran over the shoe tops of the men."[142]

The column of infantry moved with and on either side of the wagons and artillery that seldom went more than a few yards at a time before stopping. When they did move it was very slow going through muck and slush. An artilleryman described how, in the darkness, he held his hand "repeatedly" before his eyes and couldn't see it, which explained why "many of the men fell headlong into ditches of varying depth, where they were almost covered with slime; many had more than a single such experience."[143] One sanguine marcher noted, "One Consolation we have got, it is raining so hard that the mud is washed off our clothing."[144] Yet another artilleryman added, "It was a terrible time for all of us and not soon to be forgotten—we were completely drenched and mudded over—Our poor fellows suffered very much."[145] During the times when the column moved alongside the Canonniers, the men on foot repeatably called to the drivers and other mounted men to identify their commands to keep up with each other.

It was still dark when Garnett's Battalion reached Williamsport (where Ewell's Corps was crossing) and turned to the left. The march continued south on the road to Downsville, where Hill's Corps followed Longstreet's towards the west on the Falling Waters Road. The artillery moved slowly and tediously as the horses drawing the guns and caissons were in an enfeebled condition. Many were so completely worn out that they died from exhaustion. Two rifle guns from Lewis's Battery of Garnett's Battalion were abandoned during the night because the horses "had given out."[146]

On the morning of July 14, Garnett resumed command of his battalion at Falling Waters. About Lewis's two lost guns, Garnett reported, "Every effort was made to bring them off, but being the rear of the artillery, and before my arrangements could be completed, which were made with all possible dispatch, the enemy's cavalry charged and took them, together with 6 men and spare horses which had been sent back for the purpose of bringing them off."[147]

The rain finally ceased with the arrival of daylight, and though it was still misty, the column was able to increase its speed. Some batteries still stalled in the puddled roadway where the mud was halfway to the knee. Maurin's three guns along with the others of the battalion passed waiting infantry and crossed the Potomac River on a pontoon bridge between nine and ten o'clock in the morning. This shaky bridge swayed to and fro from the current as the guns crossed on planks covered with bushes that prevented the wheels from rumbling.[148] Garnett reported, "On reaching the Virginia shore, I was ordered to place six of my pieces (two Napoleons and four rifled guns) in position on the hills to the left of the turnpike . . . commanding the pontoon bridge, which I accordingly did."[149]

Maurin contributed one Napoleon and the 10-pounder Parrott rifle gun for this defense while the remainder of the Canonniers and the other Napoleon gun continued on with the army. The gunners were so exhausted that "they all fell asleep as soon as they were halted."[150]

Four batteries from Lieutenant Colonel Thomas H. Carter's Battalion[151] were assigned to protect the crossing on a hill just below the bridge, with Garnett's six guns just upriver. Major John Lane's 20-pounder Parrott guns from the Sumter (Georgia) Battalion were some distance farther down, and a breech-loading Whitworth rifle from the Alabama Battery of

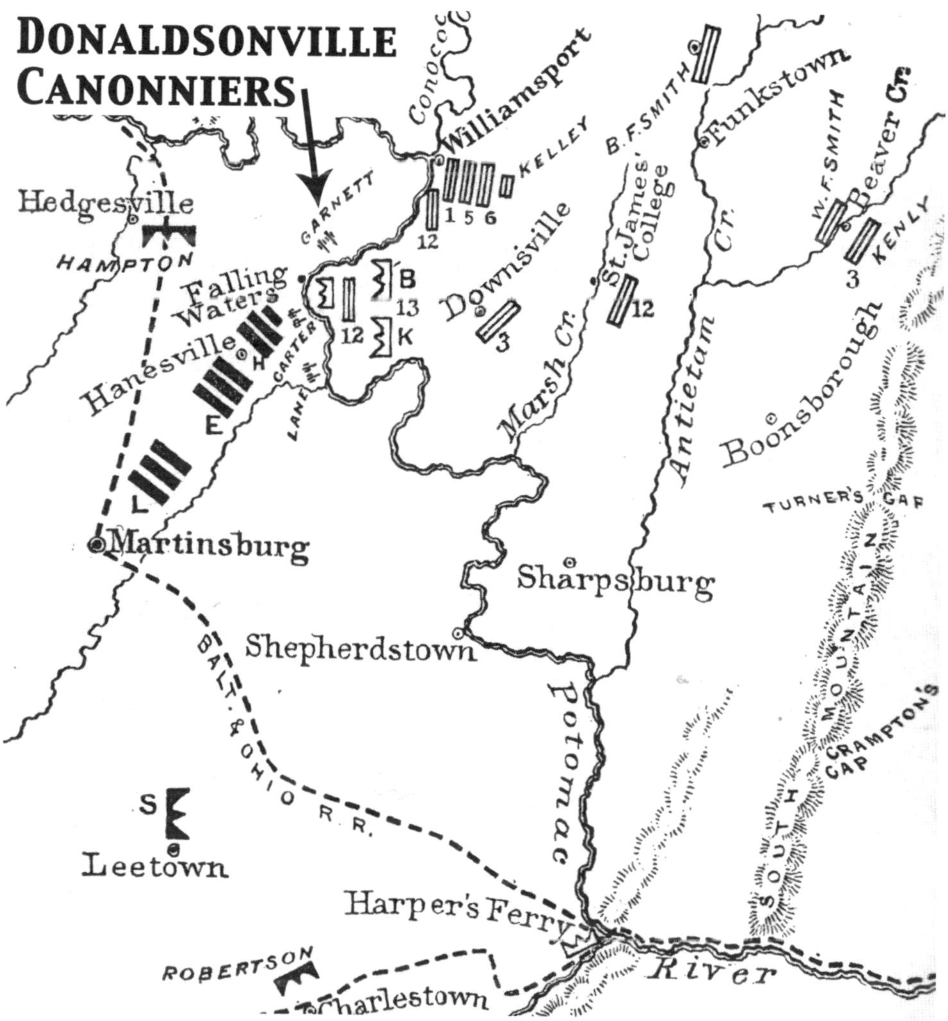

Position of Garnett's six guns, including two of the Donaldsonville Artillery under Captain Maurin, which protected the Potomac River crossing of General Lee's Army of Northern Virginia. From *Battles and Leaders*.

Captain William B. Hurt was higher up.[152]

While the Canonniers with the two Donaldsonville guns likely paid no attention to the foot soldiers crossing the pontoon bridge, another of the artillerymen whose gun was assigned to the defense overlooking the bridge wrote, "I immediately threw myself on the ground in rear of the limber chest of my gun, first spreading my Yankee gum cloth down to protect my body from the wet ground. When my eyes closed it was but a moment till I lost sensibility to the passing throng."[153] The soundly sleeping artilleryman was soon called to get up and send a charge to his gun as he noted, "The popping of small arms was plainly heard behind the hill, which was perhaps a mile beyond the river, but the contestants had not approached a point to be seen. After some delay, some horseman . . . galloped to the top of the ridge. This seemed to be the signal for the artillery to fire, and more than twenty guns fired as if one almost and the missiles threw up the loose earth. The formation disappeared, but a battery beyond the hill threw a few shells, but took care to keep out of sight."[154]

Brigadier General William N. Pendleton was present with Garnett and Maurin looking on at Falling Waters where Garnett, after waking the artillerists, reported, "They opened on the enemy's skirmishers, and checked their advance upon the bridge."[155] Carter reported, "A few rounds were fired at the enemy's line of sharpshooters as they attempted to press our skirmishers approaching the bridge."[156]

One of the Confederate skirmishers would later reminisce, "We had arrived in sight of the Virginia Bluffs, a half or three-quarters of a mile away, when . . . two pieces of artillery planted on the bluff . . . open fire on the enemy. The boom of the first gun, the shriek of the shell high over our heads from a friendly direction, the bursting of the shell's in the enemy lines, followed rapidly by other shots, stopped their advance. To this little band, so seriously pressed and overcome with fatigue, the sound of these guns was to us the sweetest music that ever fell upon our ears."[157]

The passage of the river was completed by one o'clock in the afternoon with the crossing of Heth's rear guard, though many stragglers were left behind when the pontoon bridge was cut loose and swung into the river where it broke up.[158]

During the brief engagement to protect the crossing of Lee's army the two Donaldsonville guns expended about thirty rounds apiece.[159] Garnett reported, "These pieces kept up an irregular fire until evening, when I ordered them to cease firing, the enemy evincing no intention of attempting to cross, and their formations not being sufficiently large to warrant the further expenditure of ammunition."[160] Walters, with the rear guard, recorded,

> The pieces of our battalion remained all night, where we were entirely unsupported by infantry and almost by cavalry, there being but one hundred of the latter on picket. . . . We have had but little to eat, nothing in fact but four ounces of bread and about two pounds of beef with no salt. I am very hungry, and the attempt to fill up with unripe apples I find to be a miserable future. If they do not give us something soon, I do not know what I shall do. This is not the case with our battalion alone, it is so with the whole army . . . during the afternoon we had a very heavy shower of rain which lasted about two hours.[161]

Cire too reported it rained while many of the exhausted Canonniers slept in the mud.[162]

Although hungry, wet, footsore, and weary the sentiments of Lee's soldiers were made plain by one who wrote, "We are now, thank God, on Confederate soil, but oh . . . we can never forget this campaign."[163] In the hope of sending a letter home another later wrote, "I shall never forget much that I have seen, heard and felt since we crossed the river."[164] For *Le Compagnie d' Artillerie de Donaldsonville,* they too would *n'oublier jamais cette campanie* (never forget this campaign).

Chapter Twelve

En Toutes Circonstances
(Under All Circumstances)

Early on the morning of July 15, 1863, Lieutenant Colonel John J. Garnett's six guns, including one Napoleon and one 10-pounder Parrott rifle from Captain Victor Maurin's Donaldsonville Artillery, left their position on the hill overlooking Falling Waters and rejoined (on the Shenandoah Valley Turnpike) the battalion comprised of Maurin's other Napoleon gun, Grandy's four guns, Lewis's remaining two guns, and the four guns of Moore's Battery. The artillery moved at a sluggish pace with the horses "breaking down by the score."[1] Garnett's Battalion followed the battered Army of Northern Virginia on its grueling march back to Virginia from Pennsylvania with the Canonniers "worn out"[2] over the "wearisome"[3] traveling. Their only rations during this time were blackberries gathered up alongside the road.

Private John Walters of Grandy's Battery recorded in his diary on July 15, "The turnpike road all the way [for eight miles] was very good but we were greatly delayed by the passing of divisions and their wagon trains, so that it was four o'clock in the afternoon before we got to Martinsburg."[4] The town was described as quite a large place with a bank, several churches and mills, and a large, ruined railroad depot. To many in the passing horde, the town looked "gloomy and sullen."[5] The place had few Confederate sympathizers. "In consequence of which we could not get anything to eat there, though we stand in great need of it," wrote Walters.[6]

After passing through Martinsburg and making another six miles, more or less, the battalion's guns caught up with their quartermaster wagons in camp at the small town of Darkesville.[7] The wagons, under temporary command of Donaldsonville Canonnier Lieutenant Prosper Landry, had crossed the river at Williamsport and traveled twenty miles before stopping. Here the battalion's artillerists and drivers procured, cooked, and ate food for the first time in quite a while. Walters recorded, "During the latter part of the afternoon, the Major . . . succeeded in getting a barrel of flour. He exchanged sixty pounds . . . for thirty loaves of bread, which gave us nearly a third of a loaf for each man. He was also enabled to secure a small quantity of ham and middlings sufficient to give every man about three ounces. Hungry as we were, this was insufficient to supply us, but with the flour we did very well."[8]

After eating, the battalion moved along the pike for a couple of more miles, where it reached Lieutenant General A. P. Hill's Third Corps bivouac along the waters of Mill Creek, just west of Bunker Hill. The whole army took shelter and rested in the shade of huge hickory

Supper after a hard march.
From *Battles and Leaders*.

and oak trees in the surrounding woods on elevated ridges along the creek, where country roads meandered from and to seemingly nowhere.[9]

General Robert E. Lee contrived to give a sufficient ration of captured beef and ground wheat to his army while groups from the different companies were also sent out in different directions to forage for provisions. In the depleted country, proof of the army's hunger was evinced when it was noted that beehives were not even safe; when brought in, "many crowded around for a taste of honey."[10] Most of the foraging parties returned to camp with "indifferent success,"[11] and "they seldom make good hauls."[12] A few were lucky in as much as one diarist noted they killed three turkeys and only "the bones . . . were left behind."[13]

On July 16 two days' rations were issued, and the men, besides resting their feet, spent the day cooking. On this day Lee reported that the army "is a little foot-sore, and in much need of shoes for men and horses. . . . I expect a supply of shoes of both kinds to-day, which will afford some relief, but not enough. Clothing is also required. The labors of the march have been increased by the constant rains, muddy roads, etc."[14] Walters gave credence to Lee's concerns by writing, "My feet are becoming very sore, owing to my shoes being nearly worn out. They both have holes in the bottoms which cause my toes to touch the ground and let in rocks and gravel. These have ground the skin off my feet in several places, and makes walking very hard indeed."[15] Another soldier asserted, "One third of the men are barefooted or almost destitute of necessary clothing."[16] It took a couple of days after the army received a shipment of shoes for the Canonniers to benefit, but on July 21 Landry requisitioned twenty-six pairs of shoes at $8.75 and forty-four pairs of shoes at $6.00, the amount deducted from each recipients clothing allowance.[17]

Of the five battalions of artillery in the Third Corps immediately after Gettysburg,

Garnett's had the least number of serviceable horses with 159, compared with McIntosh's 206, Cutts's 205, Pogue's 187, and Pegram's 184. Garnett reported thirteen animals killed in action, forty abandoned on the march, and forty-four turned in to the quartermaster. At a time when field batteries were averaging about fifty horses per battery, Garnett's four batteries averaged less than 40. Maurin reported that the Donaldsonville Artillery had forty-four serviceable horses with five lost to wounds in action, seven unserviceable, and thirty-three turned over to the quartermaster. Of particular note, none of Maurin's horses were abandoned on the march. Of the forty-four horses turned over to the quartermaster by Garnett's Battalion, three-quarters were from the Donaldsonville Artillery.[18]

Besides having the fewest horses, Garnett's Battalion had the fewest casualties during the campaign. A tabulation of men lost in Garnett's Battalion were:

	Maurin's	Grandy's	Lewis's	Moore's
Seriously wounded	1	0	0	1
Lightly wounded	3	0	0	0
In hands of the enemy	4	3	5	2

A comparison of casualties of all five Third Corps Artillery Battalion's reveals:[19]

	Garnett's	Cutts's	McIntosh's	Pegram's	Poague's
Killed	0	3	7	10	2
Wounded	5	21	25	37	24
Captured/Missing	14	6	0	1	6
Aggregate	19	30	32	48	32[20]

The loss of horses, casualties, and other factors all brought the competency of Garnett towards the artillery service in question and reverberated up to headquarters, where Lee's adjutant wrote of Garnett's Battalion, "The batteries have been unfortunate, their commander does not appear to have realized the anticipations formed of his ability. The battalion . . . is said to be in a worse condition than any other in the army."[21]

There were rumors Garnett's Batteries were to be divided up, and on July 18 Walters wrote, "Our battalion has been considerably exercised for the last day or two by the report that it was to be broken up and perhaps merged into other battalions. Should this be so, it will be owing to the fact of our having lost several guns and horses, and men since leaving Gettysburg. The reason of our losing them being the breaking down of our horses which have not been sufficiently fed for the last three weeks. In fact, you see horses lying by the side of the road dying from exhaustion and literal starvation."[22] Regardless of the rumors, the battalion at length remained together, and Garnett continued in command.

During this lull the batteries did what they could to refit. On July 17 Prosper Landry received $800.00 in funds to buy forage for the battalion's batteries, while the army "collected horseshoes as rapidly as practicable, reduced transportation once more, procured corn for animals that had not tasted it since Gettysburg, and [Lee] did what he could at so great a distance from Richmond to refit the troops."[23]

Most of Garnett's artillerymen were fairing very poorly in the clothing and ration realm when Walters wrote, "For the last eight days we received nothing but four pounds of flour, three pounds of fresh beef, and one pound of fresh mutton. This we were obliged to eat without salt, as none of that article is to be obtained. There are but few farm houses around here and they have nothing to sell."[24]

Sassafras roots were used to concoct a tea and to supplement the scanty rations.[25] The men also scattered over the big open briar fields below the ridges and picked and feasted on blackberries. The berries were so plentiful the wagon drivers would come back to camp with horse buckets full and using their flour ration made unsweetened blackberry pies.[26] So many pies were made and gobbled up that a Confederate later confessed, "It made me sick."[27]

The artillerymen continued their rest, lying idle during the hot days and in the evening blackberry hunting. An artilleryman in Pegram's Battalion recorded, "News came—how, I know not—that the Confederacy had been recognized by France, and that other European powers were ready to do the same—that our ports were to be opened to the world and our independence was soon to be an assured fact. How joyous was this news, with what delight and pleasure was it told and retold by the men!"[28]

This no doubt was splendid news to all, but especially to the French-speaking *Canonniers de Donaldsonville.* "But," continued the artilleryman, "it soon became noised about that this unexpected joy was like the morning dew, to be dissipated by the first rays of the sun, and we soon learned that the report was untrue, which had, of course, the effect of causing the men to express their opinion on this very important subject in no uncertain way."[29] About this time also came the sad news of the capture of Vicksburg, Mississippi, and the tidings of unconditional surrender at Port Hudson, Louisiana.[30] Upon learning the news many of the men became "gloomy"[31] and "despondent."[32] One of Pegram's artillerymen recorded: "Although our troops were still sanguine of the ultimate success of our arms, it was a dark hour for the Confederacy."[33]

Indications of a move came on July 19 when the artillerists were ordered to cook two days' rations. Nevertheless they remained in camp. "Some would gather wood for the night, some take the canteens and get water, and with the cheerful blazes, would arise the shouts of laughter and the hum of conversation. The meal . . . being over, the old campaigners would bathe his feet in cold water, rub the bottoms . . . and toast them before the fire in order to harden them for the next day's tramp," wrote a veteran.[34]

The horses of the artillery were still in a very bad condition owing to the want of forage, but irrespective of their robustness the expected orders to hitch up were received at eleven o'clock on the morning of July 21. The Donaldsonville Artillery with Garnett's Battalion moved out onto the Valley Turnpike in a southerly direction with the four other battalions of the Third Corps Artillery. All the guns and caissons moved ahead of the infantry divisions and traveled slowly, even though they moved on a road that was in splendid condition and smooth.

The horses lathered in sweat while straining at the harnesses of guns and caissons; the gray and ragged Canonniers walked and talked, smoked together, and journeyed over gently rolling ridges near the northern entrance to the Shenandoah Valley. The long file of cannons and caissons passed through Winchester, the old Virginia town again crowded with sick and wounded soldiers. From there the grimy, sweaty Canonniers continued alongside beautiful woods with noble trees, the blue, misty mountains in the background, past farm homes that had been burnt or past curious people and beautiful women who looked out of the verandas of old houses that were still standing while children played by the road.[35]

After seven miles, the town of Newton was reached and characterized by Walters: "A singular looking village of seven or eight hundred people, and is nearly a mile long, all the houses being on the main street. There are no side or back streets in the place. It contains two churches, one built by the Methodists (the fish on the steeple tells us) in 1825. The other is a Lutheran Church. It also contains a hotel where I obtained an excellent supper for a dollar."[36]

About a mile beyond Newton, along the turnpike, the artillery battalions at about seven o'clock in the evening finally made camp near Grand View, a four-story brick house on the west side of the turnpike in open fields and across the road from a marshy pond where the horses could water.[37] It was near sundown, and Donaldsonville Canonnier François "Bienvenu" Cire, after the day's twenty-two mile journey, wearily noted in his memorandum book: "Left camp passed through Winchester and Newton and took the Staunton turnpike and camped at P.M."[38]

Early on the morning of July 22 a flour ration was issued to the troops, but there was no time to bake it before the column moved on.[39] "We started at daylight," wrote Walters, "and going back to Newton, turned to the right and made for the Winchester Turnpike on which we expected to go to Front Royal, but when within about six miles of that place (after traveling nine miles) received orders . . . to make for Gordonsville by the nearest route. To do this we were again obliged to take the Staunton Turnpike, which we did after traveling seven or eight miles more. We struck the pike at Middletown, which is just five miles from where we stopped last night."[40]

Of the day's movement, Cire wrote, "Left in the morning marched all day went through Middletown and camped."[41] Located on a low plateau with the hills and mountains always in view, Middletown, Virginia was, according to Walters, "A long line of houses, all pointing on the principle street which forms a portion of the Turnpike."[42]

Marching sixteen or seventeen miles and stopping only five miles from where they started did not bode well for Garnett, who either did not receive the day's marching orders—which Walters (a private) asserted: "Should have reached us last night"[43]—or misunderstood his orders. Either way it brought on further discontent with his performance by his immediate commander, of which an indication was now evident when he received instructions to move his battalion to Gordonsville, marching a day in advance of Lieutenant General Richard Ewell's Second Corps. Garnett's Battalion was thus detached from A. P. Hill's Third Corps, whose divisions and artillery battalions continued moving by way of Front Royal to Culpeper Court House.[44]

The worn down men and horses of the Donaldsonville Artillery and three other batteries of the battalion, marching at least a dozen extra miles for the day, were met with ready food at almost every house along the route. Walters wrote that the charges for food "were in nearly all cases very reasonable."[45] The citizens along the pike would sometimes invite a few soldiers into their home for a meal but more often would sell food to them as they went by. Those without money obtained food in the usual way, by foraging, and virtually no civilian henhouse, garden, turnip or onion patch was safe, though blackberries remained principally what the traveling throng lived on.

The movement through the valley over the hot, dry, and dusty, though macadamized, turnpike caused the horses to produce a foaming sweat and the men to drip perspiration from under their caps and down their noses and chins. A Louisiana artillerist going through the Shenandoah Valley noted he "endured more than I thought myself capable of enduring."[46] As they repeatedly wiped themselves with their sleeves they caused the sides of their faces to be covered with muddy streaks. Cire wrote brief memorandum entries on these hot July days, such as the one on the twenty-third, "Left in the morning went through Strasburg, Woodstock & camped."[47]

It was nearly six miles from Middletown to the neat town of Strasburg, where in the distance one got a breathtaking view of a regular unbroken ridge on one side of the town and on the other the bold, precipitous bluffs that marked the end of nearby Massanutten Mountain. In Strasburg the Valley Pike turned at a right angle from South Massanutten

Street onto West King Street, where the moving column passed the brick two-story Hotel Spengler on the southwest corner.[48]

The march continued in the sultry heat with the artillerists' canteens clattering at their sides, the dust covering everything including the powder-and-smoked-blackened cannon muzzles, limbers, caissons, and wagons, plus blankets and other traps fastened to the vehicles. Here and there a bag of oats or bundle of hay lay for the horses.[49] Garnett's Artillery continued along the Valley Pike over rolling pastures and past broad expanses of forest and fields dotted with farmhouses and punctuated by the numerous curves of the nearby Shenandoah River. The most conspicuous feature on the march was the picturesque and lofty Massanutten Mountain that was always in view on their left as they moved eleven and a half miles south. They passed through Woodstock, the seat of Shenandoah County, where the drooping and spiritless horses, bathed in perspiration and tortured by flies, dragged the guns, caissons, and wagons past the high-ceilinged limestone courthouse designed by Thomas Jefferson, still looking much as it did when it was built in 1791-92.[50]

A number of Garnett's artillerymen for various reasons were unable to keep up with their batteries. One of them was Walters who, on July 23 recorded, "Just before lying down for the night we learned from a wagon that our battalion was still some five miles ahead. During the day, the road led us through some of the finest scenery of this most beautiful section, frequently giving us views from an elevated position of the winding Shenandoah [river], but the pain attendant upon my locomotion blunted my perception of the grand or beautiful."[51]

"Left passed through Edenburg [sic] and Mount Jackson and camped," was Cire's curt July 24 diary entry.[52] "As the men tired," wrote a young artilleryman, "there was less and less talking, until the whole mass became quiet and serious. Each man was occupied with his own thoughts. For miles nothing could be heard but the steady tramp of the men, the rattling and jingling of canteens and accoutrements, and the occasional 'Close up, men,—close up!' of the officers."[53]

The day's approximately twelve mile march over the pike brought the guns through Edinburg, where the frame houses were in line and flush with the street between a graveyard and a gully, with Stony Creek running through the town. The women of Edinburg were known to feed Confederate soldiers as they passed by "taking bread right out the hot oven and [the troops] eating it on the spot."[54] Walters wrote of Edinburg, "In this village of about five hundred inhabitants, the houses are not quite so much confined to one street . . . though it has nothing to distinguish it from the average country village beyond a fine, large flour mill."[55]

After a day's jaunt a young artilleryman reminisced: "The most refreshing incidents of the march occurred when the column entered some . . . village where the people loved the troops. Matron and maid vied with each other . . . their scanty larders poured out the last morsel, and their bravest words were spoken, as the column moved by."[56]

Mount Jackson, the next town passed, appeared to have gathered accidentally around a group of shops, it being the southern terminus of the valley's railroad and where a large number of Confederate sick and wounded were treated. "The buildings used for the purpose," according to Walters, "are two large wooden ones, full of windows and therefore well adapted. Everything about the buildings looked clean and tidy, and . . . a hundred or more ambulances were unpacked close by the village."[57]

The tiresome trek continued on July 25 with Cire writing, "Left in the morning passed New Market and crossed the Shenandoah Mountains and camped, 10-miles to go up and down. We had rain in the night."[58] Still trailing the battalion, Walters added, "New Market is the finest village I have yet seen on this road and contains some four or five churches. From the number of stores here, I should judge that it was quite a business place."[59]

At New Market, where two or three rows of houses were built along the road, the battalion left the Valley Turnpike at the old town pump (where canteens where filled with pure limestone water) and turned sharply off to the left on the road that ran east to Luray. A mile or so after leaving New Market the road passed through marshes and woodlands where Smith Creek, a small stream, was crossed before ascending the road up Massanutten Mountain. The artillery column moved upward with the air growing perceptibly thinner and purer, and the Canonniers had a last view of the valley spread out beneath them. Here they could see numerous farm houses and villages that dotted the valley, and behind them in the distance more lofty mountains and blue skies. After marching four miles past forest filled with faint rose and the glossy green of rhododendrons and laurel, the battalion went through Massanutten Pass. This was the highest point on the road at 1,850 feet and where the jagged crest was laid out along an old Native American trail. Upon reaching the top of the mountain, and before descending, there was a house with a water well close by where the artillerymen quenched their thirst on water as cold as ice and crystal clear. The battalion moved down and bivouacked at the base of Massanutten Mountain in the central Shenandoah Valley.[60]

"We left in the morning," wrote Cire the next day, July 26, "crossed the south fork of the [Shenandoah] river and camped at the foot of the Blue Ridge Mountains."[61] The scenery was described by a somewhat wearied artilleryman as "romantically wild and beautiful,"[62] with the mountain's lush forest towering about and the blue waters of the river flowing noiselessly by. The fording of the beautiful south fork of the Shenandoah River at midday was no easy task with the water waist deep, but the brown-faced and begrimed Canonniers drank and washed off and again filled their canteens. After reaching the other bank they squeezed and wrung the water out of their tatty uniforms that by now were diminished and toned to a butternut brown. The horses loitered in the cool water until "the sharp cracking of the long black-snake whips in the hands of the drivers . . . urge[d] them along." "With much reluctance" they splashed out with guns, caissons, and wagons in tow.[63]

The day's travel from the eastern base of Massanutten Mountain over what seemed like an endless series of knolls and across several streams was an arduous task for the Canonniers, whether they were on horseback or foot. Cire didn't mention the town, possibly because the toil in walking blunted awareness, but the battalion went past and moved four miles beyond the village of Luray with its several mercantile stores and two or three churches; Hawksbill

Watering horses.
From *Battles and Leaders.*

Creek flowed through the village of about 500 people. The battalion camped near Pumpkin Hill at the western base of the Blue Ridge Mountains. Under the stars, the whippoorwills called from peak to peak as the weary artillerymen slept.[64]

At dawn we wake and hear it still,—
Thy ceaseless song,—oh, whip-poor-will![65]

After awakening on July 27 the battalion's fifteen guns, wrote Cire, "Left in the morning crossed the Blue Ridge 18-miles to go up and down and camped. (Rain.)"[66] Octave Landry jotted in his diary it was, "25 miles up and down."[67] Walters recorded it was "at least twenty-four miles," adding, "in reality we did not make more than sixteen or eighteen miles . . . owing to the steepness of the mountain which causes the road to wind in one continuous string of S's."[68]

Going through the oak and hickory forest with its "riotous profusion"[69] of wild flowers, the men crossed the Blue Ridge summit at Thornton's Gap (2,300 alt.) on a smooth but steep and narrow road in a series of curves and hairpin turns. In many places the battalion moved on the edge of the precipice that gave an impressive open view of mountain peaks to the north and south and deep valleys with sparkling streams along with the twisting road below.

After descending the mountain the artillery column turned south at Estes Mill (before reaching Sperryville), crossed Thornton Creek, and headed south along the mountains and over the foothills of the Blue Ridge. They moved up and down hollows for another twelve miles or so before camping on the cascading Robinson River about a mile from Criglersville, which Walters described as a "small six house affair."[70] During the latter part of this afternoon a very heavy shower of rain fell on the batteries. "We were obliged to take it all. At night . . . and as the night was warm, we suffered but little from our clothes being wet," continued Walters, who had now caught up with the battalion.[71]

Grand though the views were during the day's march, especially for flat-land Louisianians, the travel was especially difficult for the animals. An artillerist in another battery in going through the gap noted, "The condition of our horses is really terrible; but few of them shod, most of them lame, and they get nothing to eat except grass, and very little of that—light food for mountain pulling!"[72] For the men blackberries picked in fields alongside the road were the usual fare and though some food, usually butter and bread, was obtained through the kindness of the few inhabitants they now passed along the way. For those who earned the name of "forager" and left the column, they often found enticing things for their appetite and often would return with their canteen "filled with pure old 'Mountain Corn' or 'Apple Jack.'"[73]

Washing and resting along the gushing and clear cool waters of the stony Robinson River was the activity for most of July 28. The battalion got underway at four o'clock in the evening and made about eight miles. After passing gently rolling fields and beautiful woods, the battalion went through Madison Court House, situated along a ridge and strung out along one street. Walters described Madison as, "A bright, thriving looking place of perhaps five hundred inhabitants, having a couple of churches and a Masonic Hall, besides the courthouse and other public buildings."[74] About a mile outside the town the battalion camped at dark where a tired Cire simply wrote: "We left and passed through Madison court house and camped."[75]

On July 29 the battalion moved off shortly after daylight and traveled about fifteen miles. Cire recorded, "Left in the morning and in the evening arrived at Gordonsville and camped, we drew corn for the horses they not having had any to eat since June."[76] The next day Maurin's Battery remained in camp and the following evening (July 31) the battalion moved three miles from Gordonsville to a new camp site in a field along the Charlottesville Road. This area once had prosperous estates, but now they were despoiled. Here the horses and men rested while "suffering some little from pain in the feet, caused by hard marching."[77] Garnett's Battalion remained here from August 1 to August 26, 1863. Their comrades in the Third Corps and the Army of Northern Virginia in the meantime occupied a defensive line miles away along the Rapidan River.

On August 2, 1863, Garnett reported on the role of his battalion during the Gettysburg Campaign and concluded it with, "I regret to state the losses which my battalion has incurred during the recent campaign are especially heavy in horses, those now remaining being for the present almost totally unserviceable. It is my opinion, however, that with a short respite I will soon be able to report them as serviceable."[78] The worn and feeble horses while grazing in the fields received little grain in the beginning of August and recovered slowly, so slowly that Lee wrote on August 24, 1863, to President Jefferson Davis about the army's animals, "Nothing prevents my advancing now but the fear of killing our artillery horses. They are much reduced, and the hot weather and scarce forage keeps them so."[79]

In this camp Maurin also directed a correspondence to Pendleton that read:

> Garnetts Battalion Light Artillery
> Camp near Gordansville, Va
>
> Dear Sir
>
> On the 4th July last part of my Battery then stationed in the Front line at Gettysburg, Penn., under command of Major Richardson was ordered to report to Gen'l Imboden at Cashtown to serve as escort to ambulance and wagon trains on their way to Williamsport.
>
> On the way thither the exhausted and reduced number of horses belonging to that part of my Battery, and the forced march combined, rendered it necessary to abandon three caissons, and seeing the necessity of abandoning two three inch U.S. regulation guns Lieut. P. R. Landry, then in command turned them over to Capt'n Hart of [the] Hampton Legion.
>
> I respectfully solicit that an order to return said guns be sent to me in order to render my Battery effective as soon as possible.
>
> I am Respectfully
> your obedient Servant,
> V. Maurin
> Capt Commanding Co. B[80]
>
> Brig. Gen. Wm. N. Pendleton
> Chief of Artillery
> Army Northern Virginia

It would be over a month before the Donaldsonville Artillery received their guns and were again a six-gun battery.

At first, rations for the artillerymen in camp were meager. "Our fare," wrote a soldier on August 8, "is pretty hard since blackberries are gone."[81] Just two days later, however, it was reported by another, "We get plenty to eat now . . . beef, bacon and flour, and sometimes sugar and potatoes, are issued to us."[82] Donaldsonville's sixty horses (up from forty-four a couple of weeks earlier) likewise received a bonanza on August 11 with the wagons bringing in from the railroad in Gordonsville a twenty-day supply of corn, sheaf, hay, and fodder for the battery. Water was obtained from a "splendid spring"[83] located about four hundred yards from camp that was dug by members of the battalion when they had first bivouacked.[84]

Almost everyone had a tent, but some of the Louisianians had lost theirs on the trip back and they slept in the open air or under a tree. In this camp the Canonniers pitched the small Yankee fly tents in rows or stretched the canvas under oak trees where "time passed, as usual," wrote an artillerist, "quietly in camp."[85] A Louisiana artilleryman recorded in his diary it was quiet but so "intensely warm" that in the middle of the day (on August 10) around the Gordonsville camps it was ninety-two degrees in the shade. [86] The August days were "very hot"[87] and "exceedingly warm and unpleasant,"[88] but "clear day"[89] more often than not was the scribbled diary entry of another Louisiana artillerist. Octave Landry's Canonnier diary mostly accounted for the rainy days in camp (August 5, 6, 8, 16, 24, 25) while Cire made no entry except to mark the date. Walters likewise didn't bother to write at this time and made only one entry for the entire month of August 1863.

Spending quiet time in camp and recording the weather were not the only activities partaken by the Donaldsonville Canonniers. At least two sentinels were normally always "kept on post—one to see after the guns and ammunition, the other to catch and tie loose horses or extricate them when tangled in their halters, and the like."[90] To relieve the boredom of camp life, the age-old diversion of shooting the bull and complaining of the scantiness of clothing, the inadequacy of rations, the multiplicity of pests and numerous other trials and tendencies towards amusement mollified the privates. Their complaints, as noted by a scholar, had little depth, and cheerfulness outweighed dejection as they invented all sorts of escapes from the pall.[91] The soothing power of a pipe filled with Virginia tobacco made life in camp tolerable and was highly cherished not only by the Confederate army, but also by the officers and men of the Donaldsonville Artillery. Camp life became much like "ordinary life," though tendencies "to amusement" were "far more prevalent."[92] In these scanty pleasures of the bivouac a soldier with the Louisianians wrote, "We partially forgot the trials of the past and prepared ourselves for those of the future."[93]

Foraging by men and the wagons was naturally another fundamental, though difficult, day-to-day operation in this devastated country. Towards the end of August rations were again "menacingly short."[94] The batteries now had to depend on the commissary department which alternately issued bacon and fresh beef. An officer grudgingly reported, "Our rations were sufficient, though plain, and partaking somewhat too largely of the cornmeal element."[95] Octave Landry noted as much, when on August 21, when he wrote "They gave us corn meal for rations instead of flour."[96]

On August 16 Lee issued General Order No. 84 that granted furloughs at the rate of two for every one hundred men present for duty, "in order to allow as many of our brave soldiers to visit their families and friends . . . and at the same time to give some reward for meritorious conduct."[97] One stipulation of the order that adversely affected practically every Donaldsonville artilleryman was that "In no case will these furloughs carry permission to go within the enemy's lines or pass through them."[98] Sergeant "John" Trasimon Landry, son of the *Compagnie d'Artillerie* benefactor Trasimond Landry, was given a furlough and in all likelihood, as he was wont to do, went to Richmond where a number of prominent Creoles lived as refugees in 1863. Landry would have met with friends living in the capital city and often visited the Secession Club, a billiard hall where the men from Louisiana usually met and where the latest news from Louisiana was obtained. Additionally, the brothers Eugene and Julian Levy were granted thirty-day furloughs to visit with friends and family in Mobile, Alabama, where there was another large number of Louisiana exiles.[99]

In the middle of August Garnett took sick and went on leave in Richmond, whereupon the command of the battalion again devolved on Richardson. The Donaldsonville captain again became second in command and signed the bi-monthly muster roll as acting inspector and mustering officer. With the men cared for and the letter written to Pendleton about their guns, the horses were foremost in Maurin's efforts to refit, but with the weather hot and the animals suffering with sore legs he could only remark in a requisition on August 24 "that my

Shoeing the horses.
From *Battles and Leaders*.

battery is very much in need of horses."[100]

Eighty pounds of badly needed horseshoes and seven pounds of shoe nails were procured, and these were immediately used for the animals on hand. The battalion moved on a clear and cool August 26. Cire recorded, "Changed camp to the Orange Court House road—pretty cold."[101] The new battalion camp was located in a field south of McMullen's farmhouse[102] less than a mile northeast of Gordonsville, where the obtaining and transportation of supplies from the railroad depot and commissary was more expedient. Lee's army was now almost entirely dependent on the Virginia Central Railroad for its supplies.

At the new bivouac site the Donaldsonville Canonniers, along with the other three batteries of the battalion, again settled into the drabness of camp routine with clear sunny days, although it was beginning to get chilly at night. Ear shattering shrieks of the steam-pipe were a daily occurrence as the trains rolled in and out of an "uninteresting"[103] Gordonsville that now had extensive storehouses and many neat little frame hospitals on the side of a hill under a grove of oaks and shade trees.

Except for a religious spirit that arose in Lee's army, there was nothing much to write about for the diarists in camp. The repeated entries scrawled by one Louisiana artilleryman from August 27 through the middle of September of, "Nothing new," "d[itt]o," "In bivouac, no news," "In bivouac, no news of importance," "d[itt]o," "no news today,"[104] and the single missive by another artillerist of, "Dusty & warm. . . Every thing quiet,"[105] explicitly disclosed how, "days come and go, and with them nothing to relieve the dullness of the times."[106]

As to the religious spirit, on the first two days of September the Catholic priest from the First Louisiana Brigade, Aegidius Smulders,[107] visited the Donaldsonville Artillery camp. Smulders would later report, "In all the divisions of the army, we always met the greatest politeness and respect from the officers and men; and generally the colonel or major would give up his tent to us for confessions and holy Mass."[108] A Louisianian in camp noted there was a considerable revival going on in the army lately and that thousands of men were joining the church. An officer also recorded that scarcely a day passed without a sermon being preached and not a night without the sounds of prayer and hymn singing.[109] Canonnier Private Eugene Levy, a Jew, remarked: "Army chaplains come to visit us occasionally, and are received with respectful attention, but the majority of the men of the Donaldsonville artillery, being Catholic, are wont to count the beads of their rosaries and offer up supplications to the God of battles in a private matter. The Norfolk (Virginia) Blues . . . is composed of a model and fervently religious set of men, who enjoy preaching and prayer meetings at frequent intervals."[110]

Muster rolls were also completed and revealed that in the beginning of September 1863 the Donaldsonville Artillery had:

PRESENT	ABSENT
5 Officers	3 With Leave
7 Sergeants	5 Without Leave
12 Corporals	4 In Hands of the Enemy
2 Buglers	
4 Artificers	
2 Farriers & Blacksmiths	
75 Privates	
5 On Extra or Daily Duty	
13 Sick	
1 In Arrest or Confinement	

Maurin rated his battery's discipline "Good." Its arms were "in Good Order," while the greater portion of the accoutrements were also noted "in Good Order." Military appearance was surprisingly "Satisfactory" even though the Canonnier clothing was "Very Bad." This situation was somewhat rectified on September 5 as a result of a requisition by Maurin; the Canonniers received 100 pairs of pants, 100 shirts, 100 pairs of drawers, 130 pairs of socks, and 40 pairs of shoes, all coming in one large box. After the apparel was disbursed the ranks no doubt looked decidedly better.[111] The men also alleviated themselves of every sign of the "greybacks" and itch, and with crisp nights their new outfits, still supplemented by the appropriated blue jacket (turned butternut brown on the road) and U.S. blanket. For those Louisiana artillerymen and soldiers who had only the stars to cover their pile of leaves that constituted a bed, they now received new tents with Maurin getting one of the very few large Confederate flies that were issued to officers.[112]

Along with the completion of the bi-monthly muster roll the men were paid. The Donaldsonville privates received two months wages of $24.00. "The bills," reported one Confederate, "were large and showy, but they had small purchasing power, and, when spent, got mighty little for the money."[113] Another private recalled, "The occasional old darkey with his cider cart or basket of pies and cakes—so called—and it was marvelous to see how quick the old contraband's stock would be cleaned out."[114] Local farmers also sold their produce. Apples about the size of a walnut went for $1.00 a dozen, Irish potatoes for $12.00 or $16.00 a bushel, onions at twenty-five cents a head, small chickens at $1.50 to $2.50, green peas $2.00 a quart, and whiskey and brandy were obtainable at a price "wholly fabulous."[115] It was not long before the Canonniers were again dependent on the commissary department's issuance of meat and flour or the cornmeal ration.[116] "A man was lucky," added a private, "if he had any of the good things left after a few days enjoyment."[117]

A thirty-day allowance of edibles for the sixty animals serving the Donaldsonville Artillery on September 1 was the last requisition signed for and approved by Maurin at this time as Garnett returned from sick leave in the beginning of September. The horses were slowly recuperating and the Canonnier captain was able to add ten serviceable horses to the Donaldsonville contingent in mid-September and another three later in the month. Garnett's

An old soldier.
EAF; courtesy of the Library of Congress.

Battalion by the end of September had a total of 234 horses on hand with the Donaldsonville Artillery possessing the most out of the battalion's four batteries with seventy-three horses.[118]

The horses (without a stable) stood tethered to a long picket rope and at almost any hour could be seen munching their corn or hay, stomping, or showing some signs of wakefulness until early in the morning when it was generally quiet and they slept in position, some resting on three legs, the toe of the other foot just touching the ground. As to the mules, they stood flapping their ears lazily, indifferent to their surroundings as they brayed and kicked, and "each one seemed to delight in aggressively kicking his neighbor, who in turn would repay the favor a hundred-fold, or pass it along the line, like boys at play."[119] Garnett reported three of the battalion's mules died in September with one being kicked, one breaking a leg, and one from an unknown disease.[120]

Shortly after reveille each day the bugler sounded forth the shrill notes of Stable Call, to which the drivers would say:

Go to the stable, as quick as you're able,
And groom off your horses, and give them some corn;
For if you don't do it the captain will know it,
And then you will rue it, as sure as you're born.[121]

The doldrums of this camp ended on September 16, when Maurin received orders to move his battery between Orange Court House and the Rapidan River. While cooking one day's ration for the move, some may have thought this gave credence to the latest rumors circulating through the battalion's bivouac of "a supposed advance of the enemy."[122] Regardless, the Gunners of Donaldson marched over the rocky and very dusty turnpike near Orange Court House and camped for two days in the rain. An officer at Orange Court House described the scene: "All nature seems to be refreshed by the bath. We had a great quantity of dust before and now, as is usual in this country of mud and dust, we have oceans of mud."[123]

The second day in the camp was September 18. That date marked exactly two years since *Le Compagnie d'Artillerie de Donaldson* embarked from Donaldsonville for Richmond. Of the 103 original members, seventy-one were still present for duty, along with fifty others who had joined later.[124]

On September 19, with the morning very cold, Cire recorded, "We raised camp and marched to within 3-miles of the Rapidan Bridge."[125] The four batteries of Garnett's Battalion marched through Orange Court House, where Moore's Battery and Penick's Battery remained "stationed" and "in camp" at the farm of John H. Lee, near Madison Mills and Barnett's Ford on the Rapidan River. Hill's Third Corps Artillery bivouacked along the river.[126]

The Donaldsonville Artillery and Grandy's Norfolk Blues Battery continued a few miles farther along the river road and bivouacked about two miles northeast of Rapid Ann Station (the nearest town) on the summit of a steep hill in a pine grove next to an old field. Northeast of their camp, at the base of this hill, sat Willis Mill and a small creek dammed at the river. The Donaldsonville Artillery's earthworks and camp was located on a spur of the 1,100-foot high Clark Mountain and overlooked the Rapidan River at the mill where Willis or Horse Ford crossed the river.[127]

Here the two batteries were assigned picket duty on the approximately twenty-mile Confederate defensive line along the Rapidan River, across from the enemy in force on the opposite bank. On the Yankee side of Willis Ford was an abandoned cottage fronting the road that came down to the river. North of the ford, a couple of miles away, striking twin mountains stood out of the flat terrain. The soldiers called the pair the "Bubbies," "Bubby," "Twin Sisters," "Maiden's Hearts," and "Maiden's Breast," because, wrote a Confederate, "of their marked resemblance to that interesting and important portion of the female anatomy."[128]

The Gunners of Donaldson were kept busy clearing off and arranging camp in the pinewoods, contriving to make themselves comfortable by erecting good chimneys to their Yankee tents, and chinking and daubing the sidewalls. With it cool and autumn like during the day and chilly and frosty at night, blankets were "coming into active demand for comfortable sleeping."[129] Meanwhile the earthworks were continuously strengthened and occupied with "heavy details for fatigue & guard duty."[130]

On the fourth day in position here, with all quiet, the Canonniers received the mark visit in camp of "old Eloi" Brunette from Donaldsonville, and the next "fine day,"[131] September 24, the stopover of General Andrew Jackson Powell, former captain of the antebellum *Canonniers de Donaldson* and Louisiana State militia general.[132] Brunette, whom Octave Landry last recorded visited the battery at the Yorktown defenses in April 1862 and the "well known"[133] Powell brought word and possibly letters from home for some favored Canonniers. Little news and few letters if any, were received of late from the Lafourche area, and now both Brunette and Powell likely brought the calamitous intelligence of the battle at Donaldsonville, where more houses were burned in recent fighting and the roads overflowed with refugees of women and children.[134] There was also the "curse of blue coated soldiers" at Donaldsonville who, when ordered out from recently built Fort Butler, "ride night and day [and] steal chickens, hogs, and every thing they can eat or carry off."[135]

For Maurin's Canonniers and other Louisianians in Lee's army, nothing could have been more depressing than the knowledge that wives, children, and parents were deprived of their home, sufficient food, and clothing, and it made them more determined than ever to carry on the struggle for "their rights, honor, and freedom."[136] With Powell leaving and Brunette returning to Louisiana on the morning of September 25 another opportunity presented itself to send word home and like others, they probably left with pockets filled with letters. Exhibiting his determination, a Louisianian wrote his father, "We will never give over the struggle. . . . No, as long as there is one man left of Lee's noble army the enemy will never possess themselves of our soil."[137]

The same morning the Canonniers bid farewell to old Eloi, Maurin's three guns (the two Napoleon guns and Landry's Parrott gun) were sent on picket at nearby Robertson's

Ford. Located north of Willis Ford between Clark Mountain and the twin mountains, the Donaldsonville horses had quite a hard time pulling the guns to the location because a portion of the road was recently cut through the woods on the side of and along spurs of Clark Mountain. Once in position high up behind the pickets and defensive line, on a sort of plateau, the guns commanded the ford and gave the Canonniers a beautiful view.

Here they could glimpse the twisting Rapidan River covered by forest and wearing the colors of autumn foliage along its banks. Beyond the level plain there were, here and there, manors surrounded by barns, houses, and slave quarters, yellow cornfields surrounded by deep green meadowlands and shade trees, and in the distance, spurs of the Blue Ridge Mountains. Along the path of the river as far as the eye could see were groups of three and four men at intervals of fifteen or twenty yards in Confederate uniforms on one side of the river. Not more than a thousand yards on the other were similar groups of men in blue uniforms. Both sides were their army's advance pickets.[138]

The duties of the Canonniers overlooking Robertson Ford during the day were now light, and throughout the chilly nights only a small guard was in effect (the men overlooking Robertson Ford slept near the guns in huts built along the ridge facing the river) and this provided plenty of time to go about the neighborhood around Clark Mountain. A Mississippian camped next to the Donaldsonville Artillery bivouac that overlooked Willis Ford wrote there were "numerous cabins of mountain folk who constituted a distinct class and had some notions that seemed queer to us."[139] He added, "They were unlike . . . any of the planters or town folk. They had numerous parties to which we were invited, after we had made their acquaintance . . . the girls were all Baptist and models of propriety . . . no refreshments were served, and the music . . . generally they sang as they danced."[140]

The Donaldsonville Louisianians always had a number of parties "in the way of amusement."[141] The Creoles love their folk songs and the Acadians their music, and so with a Cajun traditionally presenting a pleasant figure on an accordion (the Mississippi rebel saying it was "an old wheezy accordion")[142] they no doubt made a *fais do-do*, combined with a shindig, an entertaining gathering.[143] The French and English-speaking Creole and Cajun gunners would have serenaded too, and it must have been interesting to hear their *aimer le discours* (love talk) to the mountain-folk ladies and their niceties.

On September 26 Maurin received orders to move out of the pinewoods with the section of the battery that did not have guns and relocate to the Corps' artillery camp on Lee's farm. The Canonnier contingent moved through Orange Court House by the Madison Turnpike for a couple of miles to near Madison Mills and Barnett's Ford where they joined Moore and Penick's Battery at the battalion's bivouac.[144] The area was described as a very pretty place even though the land was dotted with thousands of captured white tents in Southern infantry and artillery camps. This section of Donaldsonville gunners remained for eleven days with little to do, sufficient rations, and beautiful weather.[145]

The three guns of the Donaldsonville Artillery remained on picket at Robertson's Ford with all quiet on the Rapidan. Horses during this time were rested, and it was hoped the animals would be invigorated when Garnett's four batteries received a three-week allotment of forage on October 1. The feeding of horses in an artillery battalion took much work and was exemplified by the amount of this three-week allotment of feed that totaled 89,662 pounds. The seventy-three horses of the Donaldsonville Artillery received 14,879 pounds of corn (half of it new corn), 576 pounds of oats, and 12,920 pounds of fodder. On average for Maurin's horses it equaled out to nineteen pounds for a daily ration, a pound more than the previous month and two and one half pounds more than they received in August.[146]

The ordnance of the battalion was also refitted. Maurin signed for the battery's newly cast 12-pounder Napoleon Smoothbore (bronze) gun, serial number 1814, along with its carriage, one 12-pounder caisson, the gun's implements, plus twelve horses in good condition. The Donaldsonville Artillery after having turned in their three 6-pounder guns to be melted down and recast in April, and having received in return only two Napoleons, now received this third Napoleon. Ironically the gun just obtained was cast in Richmond on April 16, 1863, just five days after the three 6-pounder guns *Honoré, Fidelité,* and *Libertié et Égalité* were turned in.

With rain falling all day on October 2, a wet detachment of Canonniers went in the evening from the Lee farm to Orange Court House and retrieved the new Napoleon gun and caisson.[147] Penick's (formerly Lewis's) Pittsylvania Artillery also received at this time one Napoleon and one 12-pounder bronze Howitzer with two caissons and equipment to replace its two guns lost on the Gettysburg campaign. Moore's Battery also exchanged two of its guns and caissons for new Richmond-made Parrott rifles while receiving twenty-four horses. Maurin evidently received a pair of rifle guns at this time too, possibly their own two or Moore's old two, replacing the ones turned over by Landry during the Gettysburg campaign.[148] Their armament for the first time since April 1863 was back to six guns, three Napoleons, and three rifle pieces.

An artillery sergeant in quarters near Orange Court House on October 5 gave a fair description of what camp life was like at this time: "At daylight we have roll-call, curry horses an hour, feed stock and cook breakfast, then graze horses, police [cleaning and putting into order] camp and drill; at 12 o'clock, roll-call; at 3 o'clock, another drill; at 4 o'clock, 'catch up' horses, water, groom and feed; roll-call at 6, another at 8, and from that time until bedtime we devote ourselves to 'cussin out' the whole business."[149]

Early on the morning of their twelfth day in camp, October 8, the contingent of three Donaldsonville pieces returned from picket duty near Robertson's Ford and rejoined the battery's three newly aquired guns on the Lee farm. Upon returning to camp it was observed at daylight that the numerous infantry regiments around were breaking camp and marching. Soon Garnett's Battalion also received orders to hitch up and be ready to move. In preparation and continuing to refit, Maurin turned over to the ordnance officer of the battalion one of the battery's three wagons and the forge with its tools, along with other worn and unserviceable equipment and leather gear. Besides the ammunition on hand, Maurin received for the three Napoleons 104 rounds of 12-pounder spherical case shot, thirty-two rounds of canister, and thirty-two rounds of shell, with 504 friction primers, 425 fuses, five yards of slow match, and six sets of artillery harnesses. Like everyone else the Canonniers also baked up their flour ration and loaded into the wagon two days' worth of forage for the animals. All indications gave evidence that a new campaign was about to begin.[150]

The Donaldsonville Artillery's six guns, caissons, and two four-horse wagons (for forage and commissary supplies) left camp at twelve noon marching with Moore and Penick's guns, caissons, and wagons under Garnett's command. The column moved on very muddy roads, it having rained the day before, and went through Orange Court House where the narrow, irregular main street had too many mudholes to be avoided. Passing the courthouse with its square's central tower, then attractive homes on hills at the end of the street, Garnett's Battalion with Hill's Corps headed west out of town. After four miles the red mud splattered Canonniers marched past the pillared entrance to Montpelier, once the home of President James Madison, the "Father of the Constitution."[151] They moved all day although there were some stops to let infantry pass by. Cire recorded the battery and battalion "Camped one mile from Liberty Mill[s] on the Rapidan."[152] Another marcher noted, "It seemed to be a pretty general move of a good portion of the army," adding, "we had no knowledge as to our destination," and "it was reported that Ewell's Corps was crossing the river lower down, while we [Hill's Corps] are to cross above somewhere. . . . Indications seemed to point toward a fight."[153]

This was the beginning of what was later called the Bristoe Station Campaign—Lee's attempt to outflank the Union army from the west. It was believed that this would force the Federals to retreat and allow Lee to intercept them. Hill's Third Corps, taking a longer route, was on the left flank of Ewell's Second Corps, with the immediate objective of both being the town of Warrenton. The Third Corps artillery battalion assignments were Poague's with Heth's Division, McIntosh's with Anderson's Division, Cutts's with Wilcox's Division; the corps reserve being Pegram's, Garnett's, and Haskell's, which remained from Longstreet's First Corps that was still detached. Grandy's Battery had remained on picket duty and now marched with Brigadier General Henry H. Walker's Brigade to Warrenton where it would rejoin the battalion.[154]

During the night some did not sleep well because of the cold. They instead sat by the campfires until morning, at which time the Canonniers, according to Cire on October 9, "Left at daylight crossed the Rapidan at Liberty Mill[s] and camped near Madison Court House."[155] It was a long day as Hill's column, after crossing the Rapidan River, tramped quietly along. Many stumbled and fell into holes along the very muddy path. The column avoided the main road, which was bad, and moved over hills, through woods and fields, and along country roads. The pace was rapid, but they stopped often and took long rests. Garnett's Battalion was next to last in the line of Third Corps artillery reserve battalions that followed Hill's three divisions and attached artillery batteries, with thousands of soldiers marching four men aside.[156]

Cire documented the Donaldsonville Artillery's move on October 10 with an entry of, "Left at 3-a.m. passed through Madison C. H. and crossed the [Robinson] river and camped."[157] It was another long day's march "winding thro . . . the country"[158] and interrupted by long stops throughout the day when the pioneer corps built bridges across nearly every stream (about seven) they came to. When waiting, the men were able to get plenty of persimmons to eat. While moving they were constantly presented with striking and beautiful sights of landscape containing clumps and groves of rich, dark green pine trees along and among the hills, and contrasting with the woods in their autumn colors. The Canonniers camped about six o'clock in the evening close to the woods with orders to have very small campfires.[159]

On October 11 Cire continued his memorandum, "Sounded Reveille at 3-a.m. crossed the [Hughes] & Hazel Rivers and when within 6 miles of Culpeper . . . traveling north east—at night we camped and we were ordered to cook 3-days rations."[160] The march this day was unhurried though without singing or making of any noise. Hill's Corps moved north over the splendid Madison-Sperryville Turnpike through the foothills of the Blue Ridge Mountains, where from the rises one could see for miles without seeing either end of the long column. After crossing the Hughes River the line of march turned east and continued over terrible country roads that followed the river to its junction with the Hazel River where, according to orders, everyone wading across had to take off shoes and pants. "It was very cold," wrote a soldier, though very soon after crossing the river camp was made and fires were started.[161] During the night wagons from the supply train came up, and rations were issued, which meant a member of each mess spent the night baking bread.[162]

On October 12 an exhausted Cire simply wrote, "Left and camped near Amissville." The movement started at eight o'clock in the morning by easy stages that were exceedingly rapid on comfortable, dry, and well-heeled roads. The air was cool and invigorating. Their route brought the Donaldsonville Battery over the rolling hills through Woodville, Sperryville, and Washington, but before arriving near Amissville that night, artillery fire was heard some distance away. Rations were eaten in the bivouac amidst much discussion about the current campaign.[163]

The army's flanking movement continued with Cire hurriedly writing on October 13, "We left early Genl. Stuart's cavalry fighting ahead, marched through Amissville on the Waterloo Turnpike the yankees had been there the night before, we forded the Rappahannock [River] at Glen Mills these mills had been burnt by the Yankees and we camped near Warrenton under order to be ready to move at a moments warning."[164] According to a soldier in gray the preceding day and a half 's movement by Hill's column was "over the worst roads on earth."[165] The Third Corps encamped about a mile outside of Warrenton, where Walters (whose battery here rejoined Garnett's Battalion) wrote, "The whole country around here is one scene of desolation and destruction. The land is overrun with weeds and pine brush springing up all around, and chimneys stand lonely and gaunt to mark the place where houses once stood."[166]

At their encampment the troops and Canonniers received two days' rations of beef and flour, and some were able to enliven their supper with boiled white cabbages. During the day artillery fire was again heard. "We were convinced that Meade was unwilling to face us, and we, therefore, anticipated a pleasant affair, if we should succeed in catching him," wrote an officer.[167]

On the sixth day of the campaign, October 14, Cire recorded, "We left early and at double quick all day . . . we went through Warrenton and New Baltimore."[168] Maurin's six guns were called up before daylight, but did not move until six o'clock in the morning. Garnett's Battalion with Hill's Corps passed through Warrenton where there was nothing but sad sights to see with the buildings and large hotel in ruins. The Canonniers' scrutiny in passing through no doubt struck a nerve with the Donaldsonville gunners, whose hometown had suffered a similar or worst fate. Notwithstanding the devastation, a marcher described how "the ladies and children gathered to the roadside to see . . . they were cheering us by waving their handkerchiefs and giving 'Huzzas' for the 'Rebels' and telling us to go and kill all the Yankees and throw them into the Potomac."[169]

The pace of the march was fast and after six miles Hill's Corps passed the "decayed hamlet"[170] of New Baltimore, described by Walters as "a mean insignificant affair, but just beyond it we passed by a group of some ten or a dozen ladies who were viewing the passing troops and uttering those pleasant nothings, with which the dear sex know so well how to cheer weary soldiers."[171]

Shortly after passing these women a sudden shout of orders set the column of artillery flying down the road as fast as the horses could draw guns and caissons. The Canonniers on foot alongside their pieces attempted to keep up as Maurin and his lieutenants, Landry, Mollere, Treille, and Sanchez all urged greater speed. It was a hard run of five miles when the captain gave the order for the Donaldsonville Canonniers (those that were able to keep pace) to mount up.

"Up at last!" wrote Walters, "And such a scene . . . about a hundred guns, all thundering over the road while conjecture runs riot as to the meaning of it all, though we feel sure that battle is not far distant. On we go, through the sweet little village of Greenwich, all around which last night's campfires of the Yankees are still burning. On still, over roads and through fields, catching every now and then the sound of cannon . . . far off on our right. At last after keeping up this mad race for ten or twelve miles, the artillery column comes to a halt, while the sound of cannon not far ahead tells that the head of the column is engaged."[172]

Canonnier Octave Landry too noted the "fighting ahead."[173] Added an officer, "We heard artillery and the rattle of small arms, and it was announced to us that Heth's division had struck the enemy."[174] After two hours of resting by the roadside Garnett's Battalion moved about a mile ahead and turned into a field on the right of the road and parked. Here the Donaldsonville Artillery and other batteries remained in the field until dark when the firing in front ceased. The horses were then unhitched and fed, but there were no rations for the men. This did not discourage the troops because the field was made up of briars and broom sedge with stunted pines and other small, scrubby trees, and all about the artillery camp were old hares in great numbers. The Canonniers and other soldiers began chasing and catching rabbits, and killing great numbers with sticks.[175] The troops had a great deal of fun and good eating as "we feasted on hare," wrote a soldier.[176]

The advance of Hill's Third Corps had reached Greenwich at about ten o'clock in the morning, when its commander sent two brigades of Heth's Division forward to cut off the Federal V Corps at crossings of Broad Run. About mid-afternoon, intent on pursuing the troops across the run, Heth's Brigades were surprised by a devastating fire on their flank. In his haste to attack, Hill overlooked the Federal II Corps in strong positions behind a railroad embankment, and they inflicted heavy casualties that caused the falling back of the attacking two brigades. McIntosh's Artillery Battalion in support lost five guns in the process. Before reinforcements could be brought into position, the battle (with night falling) was ended and the enemy continued its retreat beyond Bull Run where it entrenched.[177]

During the night Garnett was instructed to report to Major General Richard H. Anderson. Accordingly Canonniers with Garnett's Battalion were called up at two-thirty in the morning with orders to hitch up the horses to guns and caissons and prepare to move. The battalion was still waiting when just before daylight on October 15 it began to rain. It very soon started falling in torrents on the exposed batteries. About ten o'clock in the morning, word was brought that the enemy had fallen back. Soon after, rations were brought up by the supply wagons and served out with orders to cook up two-day's worth. Six hours after being ordered to cook, Garnett's Battalion was sent into position near the railroad bridge over Broad Run, a short distance from Bristoe Station. Cire simply recorded that the Donaldsonville Artillery, "In the evening took position at Bristoe."[178] While here on picket duty, Octave Landry also noted in his diary that the infantry began tearing up the railroad tracks.[179]

"We are in the same place—Rain again,"[180] recorded Cire the next day, October 16. The country all around was devastated and deserted with not a livable house, a fence, or a citizen seen, and making it worse was an almost blinding rain pouring down incessantly all day, thoroughly drenching everyone and everything. Garnett's Batteries remained on guard while the foot soldiers continued the hard work of destroying the railroad. Octave Landry recorded, "Heavy rain, army in motion. Still tearing the railroad, burning all crossties to Rappahannock River."[181]

After remaining in the same position for most of the day on October 17, the Donaldsonville Artillery with Garnett's Battalion followed the army southwest. Cire recorded, "In the evening left and camped at Warrenton Junction tearing and burning the Railroad as we returned."[182] Walters wrote, "At half past three this afternoon we were suddenly ordered to hitch-up, which we did, and took the back track toward the Rappahannock."[183] The battalion moved about ten miles beside the torn up railroad on a very good wagon road even if, because of the mud, it was "extremely disagreeable."[184] While Garnett's Batteries plodded along, the infantry continued tearing up tracks and tearing down bridges and embankments and, added Walters, "Far as the eye could stretch in front or to the rear, there fires were burning brightly ten or fifteen yards apart, while at each, men were at work keeping up the fires or bending the rails."[185]

Garnett's Battalion made an early start on October 18 as the movement continued past woods and fields and across numerous creeks and runs. The weather was now beautiful, though there were "lines in the sky."[186] Cire documented, "Left and camped near the Rappahannock [River] on the Yankees camping ground."[187] Camp was made about four o'clock in the afternoon, after which some made a few visits and "rummaged thru the old camp which was strewn with empty cans, bottles, etc. . . . and found some potatoes, soap, etc.," wrote a Confederate.[188] Another soldier describe how, "The whole country around here is bright with tin cans used by the Yanks for vegetables, condensed milk, lobster, oysters, fruit & everything else while broken bottles in vast quantities attest their prevalence of 'Spirits.'"[189]

At the river troops were busy putting down a pontoon bridge because the waters were too high to ford. "At dark," wrote a soldier, "we received orders to be ready to move in a few hours, so we laid down at once to get what sleep we could."[190] Walters recorded, "We were called up at half past twelve this morning for no earthly reason . . . than to be ready to move by sunrise, a thing we generally do in half and hour. About five o'clock a cold, drenching shower fell from which we had no protection, as our fires were put out by it. It ceased and cleared off finely about eight, and shortly after the wagons having all crossed, the artillery [crossed and] moved to about two miles from Brandy Station where we packed."[191] Cire's entry for this October 19 was, "Left and crossed the Rappahannock and camped near Brandy Station. We had heavy rain in the morning."[192]

For days the weather continued dark and gloomy overhead with pelting rain and bleak winds blowing across the gently rolling, open country around Brandy Station. "Our camps are a sad looking spectacle . . . our men lounging about on the ground . . . and it rained . . . the earth is covered with mire, making it disagreeable," was the way an officer described this bivouac.[193] The howling winds continued after the rains ceased, and for days it was very cold, but great hilarity also prevailed in the Confederate camps as they enjoyed themselves around blazing campfires.

"No one," wrote a soldier, "who has not camped out can fully appreciate the luxury good warm fires are to the soldier. We pitched our tents, build our chimneys, make our beds off the ground & consider ourselves lusciously appointed."[194] The food supplied was simply hardtack, bread, and meat, and an artilleryman wrote,

> Our rations are *short* and our appetites *long,* consequently we are compelled to fill up with persimmons, haws, or anything get-at-a-ble. If an old hare or a squirrel dares to perambulate anywhere within the confines of our camp they are gobbled up in a minute, and even a quail has to quail before our 'rebel yell.' Well, I would not be surprised if we had to make soup out of *old shoes,* fence-rails, or oak leaves before we wind up this little difficulty . . . but we are not yet starved out . . . at night we build rousing log fires and sing ourselves warm; if we are very hungry, we take a big drink of water and go to bed.[195]

While here Octave Landry simply recorded the weather, Cire noted the rainy days, and Walters entirely neglected his diary.

On October 23 the battalion's quartermaster again took sick. This time he was replaced by Lieutenant William T. Peet of Grandy's Norfolk Blues Battery instead of Donaldsonville's Lieutenant Prosper Landry, with the reason being that headquarters surprisingly allowed Richardson, the battalion's second in command, to again go on a leave of absence beginning October 26 for thirty days. Subsequently Maurin again tended to the duties of the battalion's executive officer while Prosper Landry took charge of the six guns, 118 men, and seventy-three serviceable horses of the Donaldsonville Artillery.[196]

It was the usual routine of business for the Canonniers towards the horses by grazing them and looking for forage. Having turned over seventeen horses unfit and unserviceable, the battalion was only able to obtain twelve horses as replacements. The Donaldsonville guns got three of them.

On November 4 Maurin submitted a special clothing requisition, emphasizing it was "absolutely requisite" for his men. As a consequence those Donaldsonville Canonniers most in need received seventeen overcoats, two blankets, eleven jackets, and fifteen pairs of shoes.[197] The United States government inadvertently furnished the Gunners of Donaldson with needed articles when the Federal army in its rapid retreat left knapsacks, blankets, and other items strewn along the road near Greenwich.

Two days after this requisition, Octave Landry recorded, "Inspection this morning."[198] Garnett reported the Donaldsonville Artillery's discipline, instruction, military appearance, arms, and accoutrements were all good. Their clothing was "Tolerably good."[199]

The Bristoe Station Campaign ended with the army camped around Brandy Station and the Donaldsonville Artillery with Garnett's Battalion and Hill's Third Corps, "In good health and cheerful as can be expected *under all circumstances.*"[200]

Chapter Thirteen

Notre Travail, notre loisir
(Our Work, and Our Play)

On November 7, 1863, Captain Victor Maurin's Donaldsonville Artillery, temporarily commanded by Lieutenant Prosper Landry (the Canonnier captain was again acting second in command of the battalion) were camped with three other batteries of their battalion under command of Lieutenant Colonel John J. Garnett. They camped north of the railroad town of Brandy Station, Virginia, near Lieutenant General A. P. Hill's Third Corps Confederate defensive positions along the Rappahannock River. The Army of Northern Virginia led by General Robert E. Lee was positioned in a defensive line fronting the Rappahannock River with the Orange and Alexander Railroad intersecting the center. Hill's Corps was located on the left of the railroad tracks while Lieutenant General Richard S. Ewell's Second Corps was to the right, with cavalry covering each flank.

For the past twenty days the Donaldsonville Canonniers had spent their time doing nothing beyond the ordinary camp routine. The previous few days had brought beautiful Indian summer weather. Many thought the year's bitter fighting had at last ended. However on this day, "Our camp," wrote Private John Walters of Grandy's Battery with Garnett's Battalion, "was disturbed by the sound of artillery firing across the river to the left of Brandy Station."[1] To Garnett's artillerists word was passed to be on alert and prepared to move, and to the Gunners of Donaldson a day's rations were issued and ordered cooked.

Brigadier General Harry T. Hays's Louisiana Brigade (with the Seventh and Eighth Louisiana regiments, each with a company organized in Donaldsonville) of Major General Jubal A. Early's Division of Ewell's Second Corps was entrenched and defended a bridgehead at a pontoon bridge across the Rappahannock River. Around noon the Federal artillery bombarded the position. Just at dusk (about five o'clock) the Federals attacked and almost immediately overwhelmed the works, advanced to the bridge, and cut off the Louisiana troops' only route of retreat. This news shocked everyone, and consequently Hill's infantry and artillery were called up at midnight with orders to strike tents, load wagons, and be ready to move in an hour.[2]

The Donaldsonville guns and the entire Third Corps artillery under command of Colonel Lindsey Walker accompanied Anderson's Division as it advanced to defensive positions along the Rappahannock River. François "Bienvenu" Cire, in keeping up his Donaldsonville Artillery memorandum book, wrote, "We left camp at 3-p.m. and moved ahead and again camped at 9-p.m. Sounded reveille at 12-midnight the yankees have attacked our pickets forced them back and captured the 1st Louisiana brigade."[3]

With their battalion and the four others that comprised Hill's Third Corps artillery, the Donaldsonville Artillery left their defensive positions along the river and moved to the rear promptly at one o'clock in the morning. The guns under Prosper Landry's command moved slowly to within a couple of miles of Culpeper Court House and halted at daylight. There the artillery again formed a defensive line of battle with timber breastworks hurriedly thrown up to the northeast of town. The infantry fell back to the artillery line shortly after. "The enemy apparently was not far off as our men were thrown into line of battle in a large open space, skirmishers were thrown forward and every preparation made for a fight," wrote a man from Anderson's Division.[4]

The weather was somewhat threatening but cleared off. As all remained quiet on the line, it gave the men time to rest and enjoy the warmth of a fire in woods to the rear of the breastworks. During the afternoon heavy artillery fire could be heard on the left towards the Hazel River, and at about four o'clock in the evening, Walters wrote, "All the artillery was ordered to move to the rear to make the Rapidan [River] at the nearest crossing points."[5] About moving back Walters added, "This retrograde movement is no evidence of Lee's weakness for while I feel satisfied we could whip the enemy here, yet the position to which we are going is so much superior to this, that it would be criminal in General Lee not to take it in preference."[6] Garnett's Battalion and the Canonniers prepared to move as Walters finished his diary entry for November 8 with, "The bugles are just sounding the drivers' mount call, and we have all night before us."[7] Cire for the day wrote, "Our battalion placed in position, our wagons keeping on."[8]

At about five o'clock in the evening the Donaldsonville guns and caissons began the night march. Garnett's Battalion soon passed through an apparently deserted and darkened Culpeper, with every house closed up. Donaldsonville Artillery Private Octave Landry noted that as they moved it was "very cold."[9] Another marcher in the column wrote, "We came to fires built all along the pike, where we could warm ourselves. These fires had been built by the pioneer corps . . . it was bitterly cold, and the ground was frozen as hard as iron, and a brisk wind was blowing . . . but we protected ourselves against the wind with our blankets, and no one was injured or frozen."[10] Walters described it as, "A long, cold, dark, and dreary march."[11]

Lee's infantry and artillery progressed through the night without halting to rest. "Much of our way," said a soldier, was "across fields & thro-woods without any roads."[12] The moving column of men could see in the distance "the beautiful twin mountains, the Bubbies," which according to another of Lee's soldiers, "had camp fires all around them, and over them, as if the army had gone into camp. These fires had been built by the cavalry, and kept burning, to deceive the enemy, and enabled Gen. Lee to remove everything south of the Rapidan. They looked beautiful indeed, and very enticing to cold soldiers."[13]

The column crossed the Robinson River at about two o'clock in the morning and the Rapidan River at about eight o'clock that morning over improvised and hastily built pontoon bridges. When the Confederate columns finally ascended the hills beyond the river the men cheered lustily.[14]

Garnett's Battalion then moved to their old campsites at the Lee farm near Madison Mills and Barnett's Ford on the Rapidan River from where a wearisome Cire rambled on in his memorandum: "We left our position at night and marched all night passed Culpeper Court House at day light on the 9th kept on marching and crossed the Rapidan [River] the Battalion at one ford and the wagons at another and journeyed toward Orange Court House when we reached near the place we went back to our old camp site."[15]

There were no rations for the Canonniers, and all were very tired and hungry. A flurry of snow soon came that covered the ground in a few minutes causing the horses to be quickly picketed near woods to protect them from the weather. Under hastily set up fly tents "we slept," wrote one, "huddled together like pigs and so tired we would willingly have slept with pigs had it been necessary."[16] Very meager commissary rations were finally received; some messes were able to supplement their rations from the locals. Some bought turnips and some sweet potatoes at $5.00 for just a few. Cooking and eating a vegetable supper revitalized several of the men, but most had that general broken down feeling and were "thoroly [*sic*] tired."[17] The Donaldsonville chroniclers were worn out too as neither Cire nor Octave Landry made memorandum or diary notations for November 10-12, 1863.

On November 13 Prosper Landry received orders for the six guns of the Donaldsonville Artillery to go back on picket duty. The usual orders to prepare two days' rations (what little there was) and be ready to move and to harness the horses followed. In due course the Canonniers, on a fresh, crisp morning, left the battalion bivouac with their guns, caissons, and wagons filled with all the movable camp property. Cire recorded, "We left camp for the line near Rapidan Station."[18] Prosper Landry led the Donaldsonville guns back to their old camp in the pine grove next to an old field overlooking the bend in the Rapidan River at Willis or Horse Ford, where the wind now blew like winter over the strongly fortified hills.[19]

The Canonniers again cut timber and erected tents and chimneys, and chinked and daubed the sidewalls over their old foundations. It remained perfectly quiet along the Rapidan, except for the rush of the river and the rustle of the wind. Rations that had been short before now ceased to be delivered altogether. "Fortunately," wrote the Mississippi infantryman again camped next to the Donaldsonville artillerymen, "brown wood rats invaded the camp. They came like the quail did to the children of Israel in the wilderness. We set the skillet with a figure four trigger every night and rarely failed to make a catch."[20] After a few days of rodent meat, scanty rations were again received. The picketed horses remained almost without forage. Lee's army was suffering because it was almost entirely dependent on supplies being delivered by the Virginia Central Railroad that was at this time in poor condition with frequent accidents of cars running off the tracks.

During a whole day of rain at the camp near Rapid Ann Station a Donaldsonville Canonnier private wrote a letter to his father in New Orleans:

> We are now camped within four miles of Orange Court House, the boys are all in perfect health and I myself, have always, thank Heaven! Enjoyed good health . . . I have no reason to complain, for I am with two very good messmates and we manage remarkably well. If I could receive, one good blanket, some clothes and a little money from home; I would have nothing to wish for. If you could send me those things, dear father, you would oblige me exceedingly and would probably save me from sickness, this winter. Of news, there are none, except that I hardly think there will be any fight this winter, and it is very probable that the army will go into winterquarters, by the latter end of next month. . . . John Landry, and all your acquaintances, in the company send you their complimcnts. Kiss Mother, Charles and all the children for me and my love to all parents, friends and acquaintances. Your very affectionate and devoted son [signed] Albert J. Schmidt.[21]

Though Schmidt believed there would not be another campaign until spring, Canonniers prone to anxiety might have interpreted Maurin signing for and the battery receiving "ordnance stores"[22] on November 24 as a portent of a movement against the Yankees, instead of going into winter quarters. By the next day many rumors were being passed about an enemy advance. Throughout this day and during the night the Canonniers remained in their breastworks manning the guns and annoyed by the constant alarms. Cire noted, "The enemy is in motion," adding, "it is very cold."[23]

With dawn on November 26 came a heavy fog, but after it lifted the day became clear and pleasant. Yankee pickets across the river could still be observed. Prosper Landry nonetheless received orders during the day to have the Canonniers "ready to move at a moment's notice."[24] While all remained quiet in the immediate front the soldiers drew two days' rations of crackers and cooked up all the flour on hand. They were ordered to take down their tents too. Afterwards, they did nothing but sit around for the remainder of the day.[25]

Three companies of Cutts's Georgia Artillery Battalion were with the Donaldsonville Artillery along the picket line near Rapid Ann Station. Hill's other three Third Corps artillery battalions remained in camp near Madison Mills until November 27. On that day Lee, from Orange Court House, sent the following message to President Jefferson Davis in Richmond: "General Meade's army crossing the Rapidan at Germanna, Ely's Ford, &c., and moving on Chancellorsville. I am concentrating this army upon its right flank with a view to bring him to battle."[26] Hill's Third Corps infantry and artillery was then ordered to move by the Orange Plank Road towards Chancellorsville.

Prosper Landry received orders to have the Donaldsonville guns hitch up and join the artillery corps moving through Orange Springs to Verdiersville.[27] While the Canonniers were preparing to move it was so intensely cold that "all around one's mouth innumerable icicles hung appendant from moustache and whiskers," noted an observant officer.[28]

The Donaldsonville Artillery's movements were reported by Cire, "We left at 2-a.m. took the plank road and then the Pamunky road to Orange Springs and camped at 10 ½ p.m."[29] The Canonniers marched for twenty and one-half hours from the Rapidan River position over the River Road to Rapid Ann Station Road, then on the newer Orange Plank Road to Pamunky Road, before finally stopping near Orange Springs, a resort hotel.[30] Owing to the hard frozen and very slippery roads, the Gunners of Donaldson made but fifteen miles. It was noted, "Many a laugh is occasioned at the expense of some unfortunate fallen slipping down."[31]

Cire later recorded that, after four and a half hours of trying to rest while keeping warm by a fire "We left again at 3-a.m. we were ordered to turn back and go on to Madairaville [New Verdiersville] on the Orange Plank road and arrived there at 12 midnight the roads are very bad almost impracticable. Rain all day."[32] Prosper Landry led the battery as it backtracked on the Pamunky Road where they, for the second time, passed the "lovely brick" Macedonia Church.[33] Shortly after, they reached Jackson's Shop. Here the Donaldsonville guns headed northeast on the road to New Verdiersville. When the rain finally stopped late in the evening, the wind rose and the temperature dropped to an extreme chill though the thick pine forest along the muddy roads gave some protection to the column. It was still "a great wonder," wrote a Louisiana officer, "that these men do not freeze to death these terribly cold nights."[34]

After moving for another twenty-one hours to make about ten miles, the Canonniers halted in the middle of the frigid night. The only sound was the sighing of pine branches from the wind. Soon the cackling of fires was also heard, and the Donaldsonville men slumped and fell asleep around the warmth and eerie glow of flickering flames along the plank road near New Verdiersville, a small town the locals called "My-Dear's-ville."[35]

At daylight on the morning of November 29, with the weather clear but still very cold, Garnett's Battalion moved forward about two miles and parked along the plank road. Here the battalion and the Donaldsonville Artillery merged with numerous other batteries. The "shivering graycoats"[36] waited for orders. It was impossible for commanders to handle the masses of artillery in the tangled terrain of this area. Later in the day, for an hour or so, there

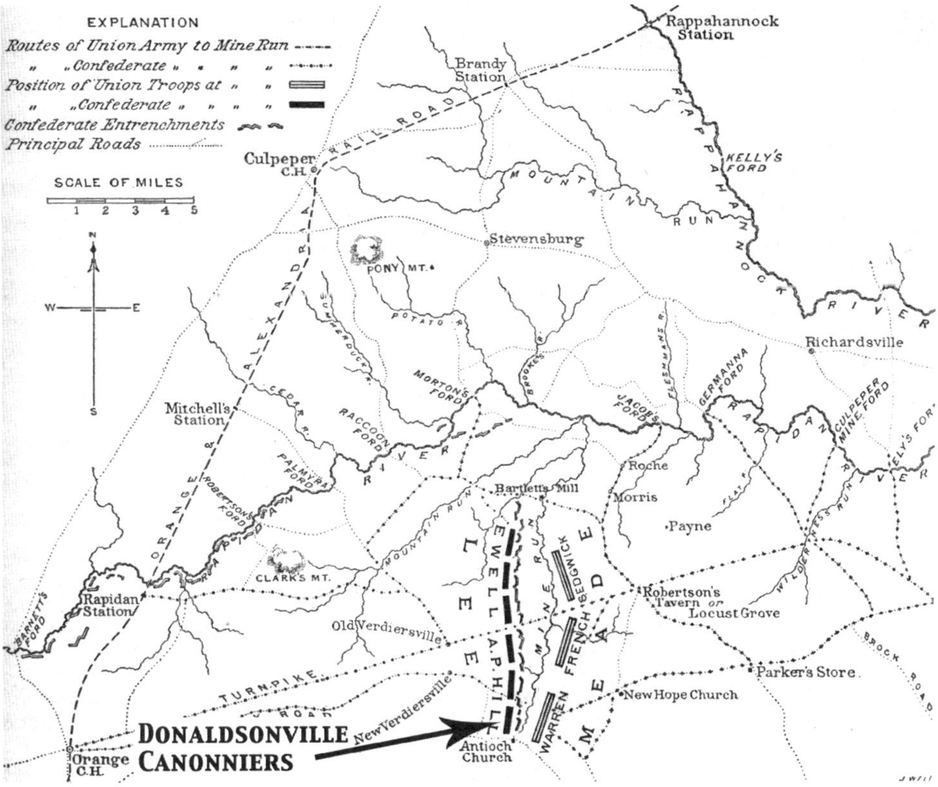

Mine Run.
From *Battles and Leaders.*

was considerable infantry fire on the extreme left of the front line along Mine Run.

In the evening Prosper Landry was directed to send two of the Donaldsonville guns to a position towards the right of the front line, where the infantry had thrown up an extended line of earthworks along a series of hills. The Canonniers and two guns moved three or four miles through densely wooded terrain and joined other artillery spread out along the line.

Here the Canonnier section started building redoubts for each gun. An artilleryman reported that it was "slow and tedious work, for we are badly supplied with working implements."[37] At one point General Lee with his adjutant and A. P. Hill with his staff and others rode together along the line at a pretty fair gait viewing "the parapet . . . crowded with men—here and there at proper intervals waved the battle flag and from many dozen embrasures frowned the silent artillery."[38] Cire again noted it was "very cold."[39] That night all the Canonniers, whether they were with the two guns in the embrasures or the four guns parked along the plank road, endured not only another wintry night but also the hardship of a lack of rations.[40]

Early in the morning of November 30 the whole of Garnett's Battalion, along with the balance of Donaldsonville guns were sent from the plank road to the extreme right of the Mine Run line in support of Wilcox's Division. Cire recorded, "Heavy firing began early."[41] Walters wrote, "Our position is not a very enviable one as our guns are on a hill, at the foot of which is a dense woods. The enemy's skirmish line is in position not more than five hundred yards off . . . shortly after placing the guns . . . we were ordered to throw up breastworks for our guns, which are so well advanced already that we expect to finish them early tomorrow morning. The weather is intensely cold and we have nothing but pine to burn."[42]

For the most part the day passed without incident, though an occasional stray shot went whizzing overhead. When not working on the earthworks, the men gathered about big fires. When darkness came it was another bitterly cold night with icy winds blowing away the heat of the flames.[43]

Before daybreak on December 1 Garnett's artillerists were ordered to their post as two of Wilcox's Brigades moved, extending and strengthening the line on the right. The battalion's breastworks under the eyes of Garnett and Maurin were finished at an early hour. "We all expected the fight to begin with the first approach of day, but . . . hardly a gun was heard during the day," wrote Walters.[44]

Having nothing to do while on the line the soldiers and artillerymen lay around and "suffered intensely"[45] from the cold. At eight o'clock in the evening the Gunners of Donaldson and the battalion moved back from the line and tried to get warm around campfires. It was so cold that after dark the water froze in their canteens. A veteran of this campaign remembered, "Much of the wonderful morale of Lee's army was due to the fact that the men carried on under great hardships by jesting and finding a laugh or joke in their difficulty."[46]

At two o'clock on the morning of December 2 the Donaldsonville Artillery, along with the other guns supporting Wilcox's Division, withdrew and moved to New Verdiersville. The infantry in the meantime began moving farther down the line to the right in preparation for a charge. Cire simply recorded, "During the night we retired with our pieces."[47]

With no sign of the Federals planning to attack, Lee determined to take the initiative. He directed Hill to move Anderson and Wilcox's Divisions to the extreme right and sweep down on the enemy's left flank while the Second Corps and Heth's Division held the defensive line near Mine Run creek. Late in the evening of December 1, the Yankees had withdrawn undetected. The movement wasn't discovered until the next morning, when it was too late for Lee's army to pursue.[48]

Before daybreak on December 2 Garnett's Battalion remained idle while "a rumor began to circulate that the enemy had fallen back, which was shortly after confirmed by a prisoner who was brought in, who reported that Meade had made a hurried retrograde movement."[49] Walters added, "Anderson and Wilcox were immediately sent in pursuit at a double quick . . . learning that the enemy had recrossed the Rapidan [River], they halted."[50]

This ended the Mine Run Campaign. Lee reported, "The conduct of both officers and men throughout these operations deserves the highest commendation. The promptness with which they marched to meet the enemy, their uncomplaining fortitude while lying in line of battle for five days exposed without shelter to a drenching storm, followed by intense cold, and their steadiness and cheerful resolution in anticipation of an attack, could not have been excelled."[51]

The *Historical Memoranda* of the Donaldsonville Artillery simply recorded that after the Donaldsonville guns went into position the "Yankees decamped."[52] The only apparent Canonnier casualty of the campaign was Private Jean Gustave Judice, a twenty-seven-year-old who had enlisted in June 1863. After being under the weather, Judice was sent to Pratt Hospital in Lynchburg, where he died of a fever on December 4, 1863.[53]

On December 3 Garnett's Battalion was instructed to return to its previous camps. After the batteries hitched up their horses, they moved back towards Orange Court House along the plank road which was by this time "completely ruined by wheels of artillery which broke two-inch thick pine cross planks."[54] Many of the men were aptly thinking of winter quarters that was "hailed," wrote one, "by the soldiers with joy and delight. First, because it brought a period of rest and comparative comfort after the arduous trials and struggles of the . . . campaign. Then too, it was the season to get furloughs home, and write home letters giving an account of our trials, joys and sorrows to the loved ones there. A time for reflection and thankfulness."[55]

If Cire had these thoughts, and no doubt every artilleryman and soldier in Lee's army did, he did not convey them in his memorandum book and simply wrote: "We left and went back to our same camp near Rapidan Station."[56] Finding things much as they left them, many again put up their tents and fly on the old foundations overlooking Willis Ford. "We felt at home once more," wrote a camper.[57] Upon arriving at the old campground another wrote, "A certain home feeling possessed me as we reentered our old camp and I felt very thankful that we were all safely back."[58]

From December 4 through the twelfth there was little to do, but the men were "in fine heart notwithstanding the bitter cold."[59] Cire's only notation during this time was on the twelfth: "We are still in the same place, it rained all night."[60] Rations had lately been increased in quantity, and for entertainment the troops in camp built a big fire and danced and sang every night. The horses' daily supply of corn feed continually declined, and sometimes they got only a little hay or unthreshed wheat or dry straw.

On December 13 Brigadier General William N. Pendleton (also an Episcopal minister) came to the Donaldsonville Artillery camp and officiated "Devine" service for the Louisiana artillerymen. A nearby Mississippi infantryman reported,

> We heard a band playing a hymn about a half mile from camp. Somebody said it was Sunday, so some of us went over to the band and asked what was going on. An artilleryman said that General Pendleton . . . was going to preach . . . the general had no robes nor prayer book, but he had his boots blackened, his spurs rubbed up, his hair trimmed, and his suit brushed . . . he opened up in proper style from memory and went through the morning service. He preached a manly sermon, the gist of which was 'Stand by your guns.'[61]

Another attendee wrote that Pendleton gave "A very plain, sensible sermon."[62]

Lee had now to implement drastic relief measures for all the horses and mules in the army. To more easily supply the batteries, artillery officers were instructed to retire their commands along the line of the Virginia Central Railroad for winter quarters.[63] Ensuing orders were issued, and on December 14 Cire recorded, "Reveille sounded at 3-a.m. left & marched through Orange Court House and Gordonsville and then halted to camp on the Charlottesville road. It is very cold."[64]

It was a leisurely and steady movement with "anticipated pleasures . . . of . . . enjoyment"[65] increasing as the column neared the appointed camp. Garnett's four batteries stopped two or three miles from Gordonsville on the Charlottesville Road, where Major Charles Richardson finally rejoined the battalion after his leave of absence that began a month before. Richardson's return allowed Maurin to again command "the boys of his home."[66] The Donaldsonville Artillery now numbered 109 subalterns, non-commissioned officers, musicians (servants), and privates.[67]

Walters wrote about Garnett's Battalion on December 15:

> We moved about three miles this morning and halted at the place where we expect to spend the winter. The place is a good one, as wood and water are abundant, and we are only about one mile from Lindsey's Turnout; a station on the Virginia Central Railroad from which we get our rations and forage. On our arrival the order was published that stables for all the horses should be built before the men would be allowed to build their quarters. This is hard as the nights are very cold and it will take some time to build the

> stables, as we are obliged to cut and hew all the timber and rive out boards for the roofs, but it is perhaps best that the horses should be sheltered as soon as possible, from the fact that they are becoming scarce, and they will require the best of care to render them serviceable in the spring.[68]

The guns were parked and snugly stowed under tarpaulins while the animals were turned over to the horse sergeant for care. The hard labor and lack of provender cost Maurin's command five unserviceable horses that were immediately turned in, leaving sixty-nine animals in the Donaldsonville Artillery.[69]

It was another very cold night on December 16 when Octave Landry noted in his diary, "This morning commenced to build stables and houses . . . Rain all night."[70] A young artilleryman related, "The woods soon resound with the ring of the axe; trees rush down, crashing and snapping, to the ground; fires start here and there till the woods are illuminated, and . . . around each fire gathers the little group who . . . make . . . hasty plans for comfort and convenience are eagerly discussed till late into the night, and await only the dawn of another day for execution."[71] The encampment was named Camp Taylor.

The next day Cire recorded it continued to rain "all day and all night."[72] The young artilleryman added,

> "Roll-call over and breakfast eaten, the work of the day commences . . . a pine wood of heavy original growth furnishes the ground and the timber. Each company is to have two rows of houses, with a street between, and each street is to end on the main road to the railroad depot. The width of the street is decided; it is staked off; each 'mess' selects its site for a house, and the work commences. The old pines fall rapidly . . . the logs are cut into lengths, notched and fitted one upon another, and the structure begins to rise. The builders stagger about here and there, under the weight of the huge logs . . . they shout and whistle and sing, and are as merry as children at play.

Winter Quarters of Garnett's Battalion Light Artillery, Camp Taylor at Lindsey's Turnout near Gordonsville, Va. Courtesy of the Confederate Memorial Hall.

> At last the topmost log is rolled into place and the artistic work commences,—the 'riving' of slabs. Short logs of oak are to be split into huge shingles for the roof . . . it is done; the roof is covered in . . . now the 'bunks,' which are simply broad shelves one above another, wide enough to accommodate two men 'spoon fashion,' are built . . . the chimney, built like the house, of notched sticks or small logs, rises rapidly, till it reaches the apex of the roof and is crowned with a nail keg or flour barrel.
>
> Next, a pit is dug deep enough to reach the clay; water is poured in and the clay well mixed, and the whole mess takes in hand the 'daubing' of the 'chinks.' Every crack and crevice of house and chimney receives attention . . . and when the sun goes down the house is proof against the most searching winter wind. Now the most skillful man contrives a door and swings it on its hinges; another makes a shelf for the old water bucket; a short bench or two appear, like magicians' work, before the fire.[73]

The days went by with the "very busy"[74] labor of building stables and huts. The young artilleryman recorded, "The whole battalion did the work, and the poor old shivering and groaning horses are under cover. And the guard-house, another joint production, open wide its door every day to receive the unhappy men whose time for detail has at last arrived."[75]

Rations drawn during this time were very poor and usually consisted of just a pound and a half of bacon for each man during the week. On December 16 rations were so bad an artilleryman camped at Lindsey's wrote he was eating tripe.[76] Cire and Walters did not mention the lack of food, although neither of them wrote much during this time. Walters's last diary entry was on December 18. He did not write again until Christmas day. Cire's next notation was December 23: "We had snow for a change."[77]

"It was getting near Christmas time," wrote another Confederate from the bivouac, "and every man wanted to do something or get something that was out of the ordinary to show his perfect appreciation of the festive season. With some men, that something was to get drunk. But General Lee saw to it that the opportunity was wholly lacking."[78] Lee had all the stores near the camps closed, but there was a little foraging in the country around. A soldier wrote, "There was some brandy running around loose, however, and we had some funny scenes which had best not be described."[79]

One incident was decribed years after, however. It involved Prosper Landry and illustrated the Donaldsonville artilleryman's sense of good cheer during the holiday season. He commanded a friend,

> to appear . . . for trial, to answer the charge of being thirsty on Christmas day: At 7 P.M., he made his appearance before the Courtmartial and plead guilty to the charge, and was condemned to be shot . . . the sentence was enough to make any thing . . . afraid, but seeing the weapons (four glasses of eggnog) brought to bear upon him, he exclaimed . . . 'I'm not afraid!' and with that the order to fire was given, the contents of the four glasses all entered the head and took effect on his brain. Thinking he was about to die, he said he had a few remarks to make, which he did in broken sentences and as follows:
>
> *'To the Cannoneers—may the shooting-stick of the printer—may the printer shoot the stick—may the stick shoot the printer—may the printer stick the shooter—Hold on gentlemen I've got it now!'*
>
> *'To the Cannoneers—may the shooting-stick of the printer render obsolete the shooting-stick of the soldier.'*
>
> After making the above toast . . . [he] asked that he be shot again, where upon that obliging gentleman . . . loaded another glass and fired this shot; [it] proved too much for the thirsty individual, by causing his feet to get tangled and making it difficult for him to find his way home.[80]

Christmas and New Year's came and went and in between, on December 28, Cire noted, "Rain all day. We have finished our Winter Quarters." Of the two holidays Octave Landry, wrote undivided entries for both: "Very Cold."[81] Besides being intensely cold with biting winds, ice was very abundant around camp. Those who were on guard, caring for the horses, working on corduroy roads from camp to the railroad, or the wagoners hauling forage, suffered severely out in the frigid weather.

Clothing in the army was not plentiful. Nor were blankets, or shoes. Richardson, on inspecting the Donaldsonville Artillery on December 31, reported the scarcity of clothing and added that their military appearance was "not good in consequence of bad condition of clothes."[82] Within a month their clothing was described as "indifferent, many of the men being almost without and destitute of under clothing, also of pants."[83] For the most part the Gunners of Donaldson had jackets, overcoats, and blankets, though many were United States blue and the blankets marked U.S. Maurin issued just five blankets to men in want of them

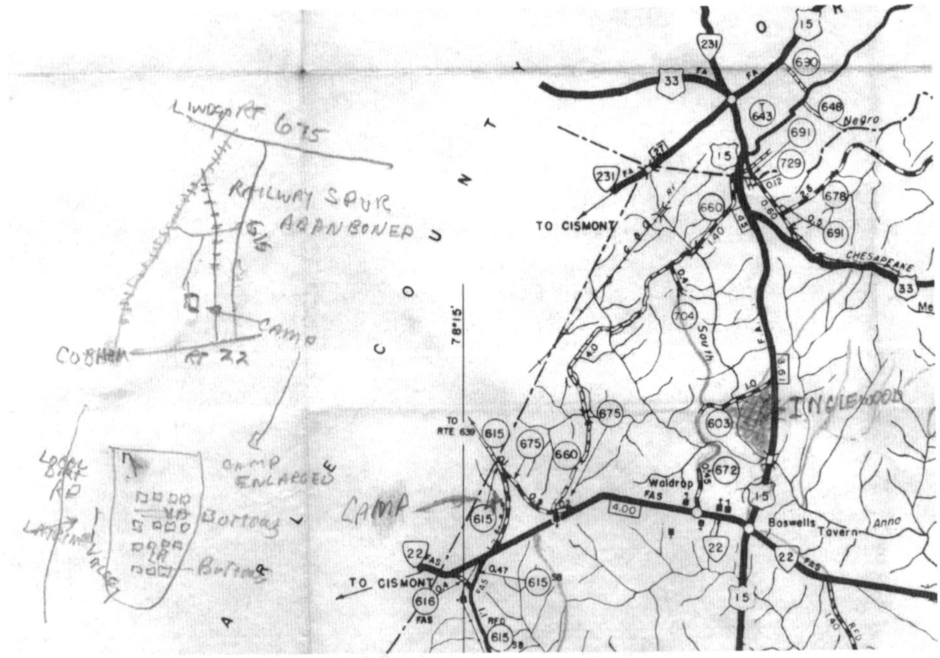

Top: Location of the 1864 Lindsey camp site of Garnett's Battalion marked by Raymond Shaw on a 1965 highway map of "Louisa County, Virginia. . . ." Gordonsville is at the point where the five roads meet. The camp was located between the now abandoned railroad spur and the tracks of the Virginia Central railroad between Lindsey's and Cobham Stations. Courtesy of Raymond Shaw, Gordonsville, Va.

Bottom: The Louisiana "Pelican" button was found in the southern end of the camp, while "A" artillery and Virginia buttons were found on the northern end. Federal Infantry buttons were found throughout the camp. The latrine and garbage dump were located in a low area or valley on the western side of the camp. Photographed buttons are similar to those found. Courtesy of Harry Ridgeway, Winchester, Va.

from a January 31 requisition.[84]

A greater hardship for the artillerymen to bear in the new year of 1864 was the lack of food. Rations continued to diminish. In early January, four ounces of salt meat and twelve ounces of fresh meat, some lard and flour, along with an issue of fruit and half rations of sugar and coffee were issued daily, but by mid-January it was reduced to one pint of cornmeal and four ounces of bacon or salt meat.[85] In time, rations became "scarce as Hen's teeth."[86] Wrote an officer, "there was rather too much cornmeal and far too little bacon (beef was a thing of the past, now) but still we did not starve."[87]

As early as January 11, Lee was pestering President Jefferson Davis[88] and Secretary of War James A. Seddon about the army's crying need for food. "Short rations are having a bad effect upon the men, both morally and physically. Desertions . . . are becoming more frequent, and the men cannot continue healthy and vigorous if confined to this spare diet for any length of time," Lee wrote.[89] Rations became so scarce that Lee believed he owed an explanation to the army and issued General Orders No. 7 on January 22, 1864: "The temporary reduction of rations has been caused by circumstances beyond the control of those charged with its support." He counseled "patriotic devotion."[90]

One partial solution to alleviating the supply problem was the granting of furloughs. This policy resulted in twelve Donaldsonville Canonniers (eight privates, two sergeants, one corporal, and one artificer) leaving with a furlough of indulgence. These were approved and signed by Maurin and Richardson, since Garnett was on a fifteen-day furlough that started December 31, 1863. The furloughed Canonniers were permitted to go only as far as Woodville, Mississippi, after having pledged not to go beyond the Confederate lines or run the risk of being captured. If so caught, they would be considered a deserter. Of the twelve who left in January and early February, only five, Sergeant Louis Aristide "Tip" Landry who was "promoted to Sergeant at Fredericksburg";[91] Philogene "Philo" Viala, the battery's first corporal; Artificer François "Bienvenue" Cire, the memoranda writer; and Privates Julian "Doc" Levy and Asbury Overby, returned to the battery. Of the seven who did not, one joined the Trans-Mississippi Cavalry, four remained absent without leave, and two surrendered and took the United States Oath of Allegiance.[92]

Over forty years later Prosper Landry related, "I can only depend upon my memory—which, of course, does not retain every thing, but there are certain things which I remember now as well as if they had happened yesterday. For instance: I can call the names of every man of the company who went wrong and the circumstances of their going wrong . . . unpleasant recollections."[93]

On January 10, 1864, the day after the first group of Canonniers left on furlough, Maurin submitted for approval his resignation to Lee's headquarters. It seems Maurin's health was deteriorating at this time (he was eligible to join the Invalid Corps), and his status as intermittent battalion executive officer had taken him away from his battery command continually. He was now serving in that capacity with Garnett gone yet again on furlough. He didn't want to leave the boys from home to whose parents he gave his word that he would remain and watch over them, but his health and the latest news from the war-torn Louisiana sugar country were not good. Food was scarce too in the Lafourche region, and the Federals for the past year had officially confiscated agricultural products and unofficially encouraged plunder as "a grate miny negroes . . . from Donilsonville"[94] followed the Yankee army and often participated in the pillaging. Even more distressing for the captain was the news of the capture and detainment in October 1863 of his brother Robert Maurin, formerly a captain of Louisiana militia who transferred to the Confederate engineering department. This meant Maurin's wife, Lisa, and their children staying with Robert's wife, Malvina, (who was Lisa's sister) were now isolated at Robert's Assumption Parish home of *Ville de Bois* at Brule Maurin. Forty-five-year-old Maurin believed that if he were entirely free from military duty he would be able to render assistance to his family and recover his health.[95]

A similar situation involved the forty-nine-year-old Canonnier Artificer Michel Morin in that his "old" wife and daughter now "needed and asked his protection and support."[96] At Lee's headquarters, Major Walter Taylor, with the assistance of only five clerks, handled the burden of the army's paperwork. Consequently, Maurin's resignation matter and Morin's discharge would not be addressed for some time.

"January," recorded a private in the Army of Northern Virginia, "proved a most miserable month, the mud worse than cold and snow. When everything was frozen hard the going was good, and we danced every night . . . but when a thaw came, and the rain wet us all up, the mud balled up on our feet . . . sticky red clay commenced to accumulate whenever one stepped out of his shack, and the further he went the more mud he had to tote. It made the gathering of firewood a burden and a snare."[97]

At the end of January the strength of the Donaldsonville Artillery remained significant with a reported 101 men, but the battery's horse situation worsened with the loss of five more animals during the month. Like December, the horses' provisions only totaled twelve pounds of rations per day per animal. It was so bad that at times "the horses would eat the bark off trees, would gnaw through trunks of the smaller forest growth and would devour empty bags, scraps of papers and all the small debris of the camp."[98]

On January 26 there was an inspection by Lee's chief of staff and the army's Inspector and Adjutant General, Robert H. Chilton. Though the state of affairs with the horses in Garnett's Battalion was not good, the horses of Pegram's Battalion, also camped near Lindsey's, seemed to be worse off. Major William R. J. Pegram wrote,

> I don't believe that any command in the army causes as much anxiety and trouble as a battalion of artillery. This is chiefly owing to the large number of horses you have, and the difficulty you have in keeping them up. I don't mind the trouble, provided the horses are kept in good condition. Mine unfortunately, are at this time in low order and I have lost many owing to the prevalence of an epidemic amongst them. This is exceedingly discouraging—particularly as I believe that Genl. Lee regards the horses above everything else.[99]

In an attempt to combat the epidemic in Garnett's Battalion, Richardson placed a man in charge of the sick horses and made a special requisition in January for flour sulfur, salt petre, blue stone, cuprous, spirits nitre, asafetida, spirits of turpentine, and alum "for the use of the sick horses in the Battalion."[100] Ten pounds of tobacco and seventy pounds of salt for the use of the horses were issued later to each battery.[101]

The insufferable (for some) camp routine was brought to a standstill on January 30 when Cire recorded, "We have received orders for us to be ready to move at a moment's notice." [102] No follow up orders were received however. Continued Cire in the beginning of February, "We have had rain during the night 1st & 2nd Rain—and rain during the night."[103] The camp routine returned for a few days until February 7, when Walters wrote, "Last night our camp was greatly disturbed by the sudden order to make ready to leave in a moment as the enemy were advancing. We received no further orders till about two o'clock this morning, when we were ordered to hitch up. In about twenty minutes we were ready and the companies ordered off in different directions."[104]

The Donaldsonville Artillery in due course sent four of their six guns to Lindsey's Station on guard. Meanwhile members of McIntosh's Battalion arrived in camp with orders to procure the remaining two of Maurin's guns (a Parrott rifle and the 3-inch Ordnance rifle) and four other pieces from Garnett's Battalion. The next day, February 8, with "all quiet,"[105] orders were received, and the four Donaldsonville guns returned to camp "as the enemy had recrossed the Rapidan, being somewhat closely pushed by Lee's boys."[106]

McIntosh's Battalion needed replacements for their five guns lost at Bristoe Station and thus retained the two Donaldsonville pieces. Lee preferred to have all battalions and batteries "equalized" and "adjusted to the standard of four guns."[107] This standardization left the Donaldsonville Artillery armed with three Napoleons and one 10-pounder Parrott, Moore's Battery with four 10-pounder Parrotts, Grandy's Battery with just three pieces, a Napoleon, a 3-inch Ordnance Rifle, and a 10-pounder Parrott, and Penick's Battery with only three pieces, a Napoleon and two 3-inch Rifles.

With the change of armament the horses in Garnett's batteries for February numbered foty-five with Maurin, fifty-three with Grandy, forty-seven with Moore, and forty-two with Penick. A positive for the horses was that with fewer of them, and with trains running forage supplies "pretty regularly,"[108] rations for the animals improved by one-third in February. During that month the Donaldsonville horses received a little more than eight pounds of corn, four pounds of hay, three pounds of straw, and two and a half pounds of oats and fodder per day, totaling an acceptable winter ration of eighteen pounds each day.[109]

"Where everything has been very quiet, and the usual routine of camp life gone through with," a young artilleryman wrote in late January, "artillerist[s], generally speaking have a much easier time than infantry."[110] While it was an unusually severe winter that passed through Camp Taylor, the artillerymen around Lindsey's lived in "tolerable comfort."[111]

From camp there was a call for a renewal of enlistment and allegiance to the Confederacy and to continue in arms until independence was achieved. Consequently, every unit's voluntary reenlistment for the war was commended by Lee in "general orders."[112] On February 12 the Donaldsonville Artillery reenlisted for the duration of the war and after. The following commendation was sent forth:

> Received at Richmond, Va., March 5th 1864.
> By Telegraph from Orange C. H. March 5th.
> To General S. Cooper,
> A. & I. General.
>
> The following troops have reenlisted for the war since my announcement of 19th Feby. Most of them before the law retaining all men in the service was made known. Phillip's Legion Cavalry, Carrington's Battery, Garbers' Battery, Jeff. Davis' Legion, 1st South Carolina Cavalry, 44th. Virginia, Louisiana Battery, Carpenter's Battery, 1st. North Carolina Regiment, 13th. Virginia Infantry, 58th. Virginia Infantry, 12th.Virginia Cavalry, Stafford's Brigade, 2d. North Carolina Cavalry, 10th. Virginia Infantry.
>
> [signed] R. E. Lee
> Genl.
>
> Official copy of telegram received March 6th, 1864 and respectfully submitted to Genl. B. Bragg.
>
> John W. Riley
> Capt. & A. A. G.
>
> [Endorsed]
> Orange C. H.
> 5th March 1864.
> R. E. Lee
> Genl.
> Announcing reenlistments.
> R. B. 41
> Recd. 7th. March 64.[113]

All four of Garnett's Batteries made the pledge. From headquarters at Orange Court House on February 15, Lee notified the adjutant and inspector general: "The following troops have re-enlisted for the war . . . Garnett's, Poague's, Haskell's, and Pegram's battalions of artillery. The following . . . have reiterated their determination to continue in service: Cutts's battalion of artillery."[114]

Three months earlier, on November 20, 1863, Brigadier General and Chief of Artillery William N. Pendleton acted upon instructions from Lee to carefully reconsider all recommendations for promotion in the artillery service and concluded, with the collaboration of the Third Corps artillery commander Colonel Lindsey Walker, that Garnett "may with advantage to the service be relieved of his command and assigned to other duty. He has proved less efficient in the field than was expected of so well trained and capable a soldier. It is believed he can be more useful on conscript service than in his present position. Such change for him is therefore respectfully recommended."[115]

Some time in January, Walker made an application to have Garnett relieved from his battalion command based on "such carelessness and in attention in the discharge of his duties as to disqualify him from his position," wrote Lee's biographer.[116] When Lee removed someone from command "he did so as tactfully and as quietly as possible. Not once during the whole war did he initiate court-martial proceedings against an officer, and only in the rarest instances did he call for courts of inquiry."[117] On Walker and Pendleton's recommendation Lee uncharacteristically arranged to have Garnett and Richardson "tried before an examining board for incompetency."[118] In the meantime Lee instructed Pendleton to assign a field officer from one of the other Third Corps Battalions to temporarily command Garnett's Battalion. Major David G. McIntosh was so assigned.

After Garnett returned from furlough, a Board of Examiners was convened. Three days after his battalion was applauded for their reenlistment, Garnett on February 18 was found incompetent for his position because of negligence and inattention. Lee suspended Garnett from command and granted him a leave of absence to Richmond.[119]

During the battalion's evening roll call of February 23, Garnett "Bade us his adieus," noted Donaldsonville Canonnier Octave Landry.[120] The following letter was read to the artillerymen of Maurin's, Grandy's, Moore's, and Penick's Batteries:

> To the officers and men of Garnett's Battalion
>
> It is with feeling of no ordinary sorrow and regret that I bid you good-by. After a companionship with you for nearly a year during which time I have been with you in your trials on the march, on the battlefield, and in your camp, I have been proud of the honor of commanding such men, and sharing in their trials and privations. I would do injustice to my own feelings were I to leave you without a parting word--it is to you that I look for a justification of my course, it is to you who have witnessed the interest and untiring zeal in your behalf and in behalf of the cause of our country, to whom I look to vindicate my character as an officer--your interests have been mine; your hardships mine; your dangers mine; if I have failed in any particular to gain for you all the comforts and to place your organization upon an equality with those of the army, it has not been from want of desire, or from want of energy or activity on my part, but from the inability of the government to supply them.
>
> In leaving you I ask you to accept from me as a token of my high regard and esteem the flag which was presented to me last summer. I shall always entertain toward you the liveliest emotions of friendships and regard.
>
> (signed) Jno. J. Garnett
> Liet. Co. Commanding[121]

"On the reading of this letter," wrote Walters, "a committee of three from each of the companies were appointed to draft a suitable address in reply."[122] After having about an hour to compose it, the reply was presented in camp to Garnett at the tattoo (nine o'clock roll call). It read:

> Beloved and Respected Sir:
>
> It is with feelings of sincere and deep regret that we, the members of Garnett's Battalion, hear of your departure from us, and listen to the reading of your farewell. Your regret at leaving us, however painful, is equaled by our own distress at parting from one on whom we have ever looked with feelings of friendship and perfect satisfaction, and in whom, independent of the man we recognize and acknowledge, the able and kind commander.
>
> Without flattery to ourselves we feel well assured that were your feelings only consulted, you would not be called upon to utter the word farewell, but in our parting we can readily trace the malign influence of those who possibly can trace their feelings to a source of base envy.
>
> With unfeigned pleasure we accept at your hands that noble flag, fully understanding and appreciating the motive that entrusts to our keeping the glorious emblem of our present hour and future freedom and greatness. Our hearts being all fixed in the same purpose and our sympathies being similar, we can truly say that it shall live while we live, and fall only with us, and that whatever our trials or triumphs, the name inscribed upon it shall ever be held in dear remembrance as that of a perfect gentleman and pure patriot, however ruthlessly or maliciously it may have been assailed. Be assured sir, that in the future on many a long march, or by the cheerful light of the campfire, your name will often be mentioned by us and many a kindly wish will be wafted toward you wherever you may be and that your lines may be cast in as pleasant places as we feel that you richly merit.
>
> In conclusion we earnestly and sincerely wish that your separation from us will at least accrue to your own advantage, and that the evil genius which at present seems to preside over your destiny will ere long be ignominiously put to flight by the Angel of Truth, and like the diamond from the hands of the lapidary, your fortune may shine the better and brighter for its past rough treatment.
>
> (signed) by the committee from all companies.[123]

Some members of the battalion remained hopeful of Garnett's staying, but the next day he left for Richmond. Walters recorded, "This separation between ourselves and our Colonel whom we all respect highly and greatly admire is due to the sentences adjudged against Col. Garnett by a Court-Martial [Board of Examiners] before which he lately appeared, on charges made against him by a person of superior rank, but of largely inferior abilities, and who was possibly afraid of Col. Garnett's influence."[124]

The same order that directed Garnett to appear before the examining board insructed Richardson also to do so. Richardson was not relieved of his position, but on the day Garnett left, February 24, Richardson was placed in arrest "on charges of making use of false statements reflecting on Comdg Officer."[125] One of the last duties that Richardson performed before his arrest was the approval of a requisition for stationary submitted by Prosper Landry so that the paperwork of the army pertaining to the Donaldsonville Artillery could continue to be performed.[126]

The next day McIntosh inspected his temporary command. The monotony of camp routine for the men continued for a few more days, albeit with numerous discussions regarding the past week and future concerns. On February 28 Maurin and the other battery commanders under McIntosh received orders "to be ready to move at a moments notice."[127] The next day, February 29, the Canonniers were mustered and, along with guns and ammunition, inspected in camp. The Donaldsonville men this day were issued seventy-five haversacks, fifty knapsacks, fifty canteens and straps, and nine pairs of spurs and straps. The battery received ordnance stores of four felling axes, three pick axes, three long handle shovels, thirty-six curry combs, two spare wheels, and four prolonges. Maurin turned over to the battalion's ordnance officer twenty-one rounds of Parrott and eighteen rounds of Napoleon ammunition, which was probably bad.[128]

Orders arrived just before dark. With the words "Fall in!" by Donaldsonville Orderly Sergeant William Vincent Parks, "a good soldier all through the war,"[129] the usual "Orders to move! Where? when? what for?—are the eager questions of the men as they begin their preparations to march."[130] During the bustle in camp word was passed that "the enemy are making another raid, and there is some fear that they may pay the artillery camps a visit."[131]

The horses were soon hitched up, and the battalion's fourteen guns moved out at six o'clock in the evening towards Gordonsville, though some few artillerymen were left behind to guard the camp. The Canonniers—dressed in assorted jackets and overcoats with new haversacks and canteens and with their Yankee rubber cloth on the outside and blanket rolled up on the inside looking like a horseshoe collar, the ends tied together with the loop placed over one shoulder and the tied ends under the other arm—marched with their pieces under a dark sky.

"Shortly after we started," wrote Walters, "it began to rain and continued to do so during the night which made our situation extremely interesting, especially as we have no tents with us." Upon arriving at Gordonsville, added Walters, "We were halted for the night in a field adjoining the government hospital sheds, under which we crawled and went to sleep, and though it was very cold under there, it was at least dry."[132]

The next day, March 1, Walters recorded,

> The rain poured down incessantly all day from which we had no shelter. At eight o'clock pm all the artillery was ordered off in different directions. Our battalion took the road to Liberty Mills on the Rapidan [River], and arrived and packed about half a mile from that place between twelve and one o'clock at night. The march there was a very severe one, as shortly after dark the rain changed first to snow and then to sleet. The night was an intensely dark one and the mud deep. A short time after we packed the sleet ceased falling and the stars came out, so that by daylight with the aid of good fires, we had our clothes and blankets dried out and all hands went to sleep to make up for lost time.[133]

Upon awakening on March 2, Cire recorded, "We are in the same place with orders to be ready to move at a moments notice."[134] They did not move. Early in the morning the battalion received orders to have their battery horses hitched up because, noted Walters, "It was reported that the enemy intended to attempt to force their way out of our line at this place. We remained in readiness all day and by dark, learned that they were all going by another route."[135] The next day, March 4, was also spent in the same position. Walters again noted, "Nothing doing today. We have heard that the enemy had made their way out of our lines, having done but very little damage."[136]

On March 5 Walters recorded, "Early this morning we received orders to hitch up and return to quarters, where we arrived about four o'clock pm."[137] Regarding the Donaldsonville guns, Cire recorded, "We have left and arrived at our camp at Lindsay [*sic*]."[138] Another artilleryman noted it was "a dark rainy march to Gordonsville—oh how pleasant it is to get back under shelters and comfortable fires."[139]

At Camp Taylor, the battalion now under the charge of McIntosh resumed life in winter quarters with the weather cold and wet, and although the snows were not as heavy or as frequent as the previous winter, the rain seemed constant. The Canonniers were comfortably fixed with their duties being light guard duty, plus watering and caring for the horses. There was little else to do but forage and make culinary preparations with the rations on hand. Cooking was done in two camp kettles and who knows what went into making the Louisianians' famous, "'*Gombo'*—compounded of many odds and ends."[140]

The Cajun Canonniers no doubt took up their favorite pastime of whittling and, according to a young artilleryman, it was

> a good time to make and carve beautiful pipes of hard wood with horn mouth-pieces, very comfortable chairs, bread trays, haversacks, and a thousand other conveniences. At night the visiting commences, and soon in many huts are little social groups close around the fire. The various incidents of the campaign pass in review, and pealing laughter rings out upon the crisp winter air. Then a soft, sweet melody floats out of that cabin door as the favorite singer yields to the entreaty of his little circle of friends; or a swelling chorus of manly voices, chanting a grand and solemn anthem, stirs every heart for half a mile around.[141]

Smoking and chewing tobacco was another favorite pastime that the young artilleryman wrote about:

> Some poor fellows, after eating, could only sleep. They were incapable of the noble satisfaction of 'a good smoke.' But there were some good men and true, thoughtful men, quietly disposed men, gentle and kind, who, next to a good 'square' meal prized a smoke . . . who can find words to tell the story of the soldier's affection for his faithful briar-root pipe! As the cloudy incense of the [tobacco] weed rises in circling wreaths about his head, as he hears the murmuring of the fire, and watches the glowing and fading embers, and feels the comfort of the hour pervading his mortal frame, what bliss!
>
> But yonder sits a man who scorns the pipe—and why? He is a chewer of the [tobacco] weed. To him, the sweetness of it seems not to be drawn out by the fiery test, but rather the persuasion of moisture and pressure. But he, too, is under the spell.[142]

Canonnier Lieutenant Prosper Landry very much appreciated his pipe and tobacco but willingly shared and gave away "much" of his rolls of tobacco to comrades.[143]

Inspections of the batteries were conducted, one on March 14 and two on March 18, the first couple by McIntosh and the last one by Brigadier General Armistead L. Long. The inspections obviously reflected well on Maurin and the 104 Canonniers present, for their discipline and instruction were rated "very good," and their guns, carriages, caissons, accoutrements, and military appearance, despite their clothing, "good."[144]

During March of 1864 the policy of issuing leaves continued unabated, and seven more Canonniers received furloughs of indulgence, including Lieutenants Prosper Landry and Antoine Sanchez, along with Privates Charles Alba, Octave Boudreau, Esteve Hildago, Thomas Love, and Clarville Savoy. Of the seven who left only one did not return, having been captured by Federal cavalry in Ascension Parish on April 21, 1864.[145]

After the battalion's return from Liberty Mills little of interest took place, and Walters made no further diary entries for the month of March. Cire made a few weather notations, while Octave Landry made thirteen entries in his diary, the most notable being, "March 16. Orders to detail fifteen men to drill as infantry."[146] This order came about because of the four-gun battery rule, of which Pendleton wrote it "is deemed best; the surplus men to be armed with muskets, and used on occasions as guards, etc."[147] In consequence, on March 31 the battalion received thirty-two .58 caliber rifles and eighteen .69 caliber muskets with bayonets along with their accoutrements (fifty cartridge boxes, fifty cap pouches, fifty belts, and fifty bayonet scabbards), and a box of ammunition.[148]

Other entries of note by Octave Landry occurred on consecutive days (March 22-24) with, "Heavy snow, the heaviest of the season. P.M.—Heavy rain. Two of our men arrested and delivered by the Provost Marshal; they are accused of stealing hides from one tannery and selling them at another—Another of our men arrested for stealing hides."[149] After being in the hands of the civil authorities Privates Michael "Hick" Flannigahn, John Murphy, and Joseph "Willie" Newchurch were returned to the battery. Their underhanded business practice measured up to the lawless reputation of the Louisiana Tiger commands, but there were few documented arrests from the Donaldsonville Artillery owing to Maurin's discipline.[150]

Morale did not decline in Lee's army during the winter months. This was attributed to the previous record of victories, the men's ingenuity and adaptability in the face of hardships, and their invincible good cheer. Only the most incurable pessimist failed to contribute to the merriment of camp, which often seemed much like the manner of boys who were "showing off."[151] Religion was another factor in sustaining their spirit through the long, blusterous months as Lee ordered the "proper observance of the Sabbath."[152] To this end it was directed that on Sundays all labor of both men and animals were suspended and only duties that were strictly necessary would be carried out. The usual inspections were to be held on Sundays, though at a time when it did not interfere with the attendance of the men at divine service at the customary hour in the morning.

At Camp Taylor a log church was built and Presbyterian, Episcopal, and Baptist chaplains visited to preach and hold prayer meetings.[153] For the Catholic Canonniers, Father Smulders visited on April 17 and remained a few days, saying Mass, giving communion, and taking confessions. Smulders recorded, "Not only did our Catholics attend, but also a large number of Protestants attended divine services" and "as usual . . . tried to hear all the Easter confessions of Lee's army."[154] One Confederate soldier wrote, "We had more church services . . . than we had had during the whole war put together. The only way we could tell when Sunday came was when we heard the band play hymns on some hill near camp . . . and go over . . . some fellow was sure to ask, 'What day is this?'"[155]

On March 26 Richardson was relieved from arrest (Pendleton in the past favored Richardson and probably had something to do with the favorable adjudication) and ordered to assume command of Garnett's Battalion. Born in Richmond in 1831, Richardson had served as an adjutant on Pendleton's staff in early 1861 and was assigned by Pendleton in September 1862 the arduous task of moving the broken down horses and surplus artillery from Leesburg to Winchester, Virginia, after the battle of Second Manassas. The army's commander was guided largely by Pendleton when it came to promotions in the artillery, and now Pendleton recommended Richardson for promotion and battalion command saying "the best men are believed to be advanced."[156] On April 19 Octave Landry recorded, "Our battalion takes the name of Richardson's Battalion."[157]

Maurin was under the impression he would be entirely free from military service when he submitted his resignation in January, however a law soon decreed that all persons between the ages of forty-five and fifty in the military service shall be retained during the present war. Not wanting to take advantage and enter the Reserve Corps or wanting to join the Invalid Corps, Maurin requested on March 24 the withdrawal of his resignation. He received an answer one week later:

> Hd-qts: 31 Mar '64
>
> I rejected Captain Maurin's resignation, I recommend it be not accepted—I now

recommend he be allowed to withdraw it.

[signed] R. E. Lee
Genl.[158]

Before Maurin submitted the withdrawal of his resignation request, and while Richardson was still under arrest, Captain Merritt B. "Buck" Miller of the Third Company Washington Artillery was ordered to Garnett's Battalion as second in command to assist McIntosh. When Richardson later assumed command of the battalion, Miller was promoted to major and retained as second in command "in place of . . . Maurin,"[159] who evidently was absent sick.[160]

In the latter part of April the weather became much warmer, and the rains slackened. Cire and Octave Landry both recorded the precipitation for the month: "1st (rain), 2nd (snow), 4th (snow, sleet & rain, very cold), 5th, 9th, 10th, & 16th (rain), 17th (snow), & 25th (rain)." On April 12 the weather was good enough to allow one gun from each company of the battalion to go out and target shoot. These and one or two other notations were the few diary entries by the Canonnier chroniclers. With little of interest occurring at Lindsay's, Walters disregarded his diary for the month.

Octave Landry made a noteworthy entry on April 3 when he wrote, "Old Michel Morin, having been discharged from the army (old age) left for Louisiana." Leaving his sons Edward and Mathieu with the battery, the elder Morin bade a solemn goodbye to them and his comrades and left Virginia for home to protect and provide for his wife and youngest daughter. Concerning his two years of service with the Donaldsonville Artillery, Prosper Landry in 1902 wrote an endorsement letter for Morin that read in part, "He is probably the oldest veteran in the state and probably one of the most deserving."[161]

A report of the companies of artillery in the Third Corps for April 1864 listed the strength of Richardson's battalion:

	NON-COMMISSION OFFICERS	OFFICERS	ENLISTED MEN	SICK	EXTRA DUTY
Co. A, Penick's	3	12	64	10	7
Co. B, Maurin's	3	18	69	4	5
Co. C, Grandy's	3	12	76	9	9
Co. D, Moore's	3	12	64	2	10

In regards to the artillery horses, disease took its toll and the numbers reveal how appalling the situation was:

	SERVICEABLE HORSES	UNSERVICEABLE	TOTAL
Co. A, Penick's	26	11	37
Co. B, Maurin's	37	7	44
Co. C, Grandy's	28	12	40
Co. D, Moore's	24	12	36[162]

This was the state of affairs when, on April 28, Octave Landry recorded, "Left our winter quarters and went and camped near Cobham Station."[163] The four batteries of Richardson's Battalion in the morning bade adieu to their camp in the woods. Before leaving Walters wrote,

> A glaring evidence of what some might call insubordination was exhibited this morning. Our Major in command had heard that it was the intention of the men to burn their cabins before leaving, as the person on whose land we were camped had on several occasions acted in a very ungentlemanly manner toward us. To prevent this, he had issued orders that nothing should be destroyed, but early this morning one of the cabins in Company D was discovered on fire and as everything was very dry, the fire spread with the greatest rapidity and soon communicated to the cabins of our company. Here we had a striking evidence of how very active an element fire is, for while some of the men under order from officers would endeavor to extinguish the fire of one cabin, it would soon break out in a fresh place several cabins off, and soon all the intermediate ones would be in a bright blaze and at last, after much useless labor, it was allowed to burn itself out.[164]

Richardson's Battalion camped in a grove of oak trees near Cobham Station, which was only about three miles from Lindsay's on the Orange and Alexandria Railroad. With spring coming on, wrote an artillerist, "We knew that our stay here could not last much longer," adding, "we take no anxious thought for the morrow; we go on with *our work, and our play.*"[165]

CHAPTER FOURTEEN

Du Cote du Sud
(To the South Side)

On May 1, 1864, Donaldsonville Canonnier Private Eugene H. Levy started the last of his war diaries: "The month of flowers was ushered in with gentle zephyrs and bright sunshine. The snow has totally disappeared from the mountain tops, and the graceful Blue ridge is being robed in the lovely garments of spring. In the gladness of their hearts, the birds send up their great Gladstone notes. . . . Nature smiles."[1] This was written from a field camp near Cobham Station, with its small two-story depot building and a few houses along the Orange and Alexandria Railroad tracks.[2] Here Lieutenant Colonel Charles Richardson's Artillery Battalion, composed of Batteries A, B, C, and D, Penick's Pittsylvania Battery, Maurin's Donaldsonville Artillery, Grandy's Norfolk Light Artillery Blues, and Moore's Norfolk Light Artillery, had bivouacked since April 29, 1864. The batteries were actively refitting (packing ammunition, friction primers, and fuses, and oiling new bridle reins and harnesses) and turning over to the quartermaster one wagon and two traveling forges while waiting "for horses in order to move nearer the lines."[3]

For most of the Canonniers, thoughts turned not to the surrounding beauty or approaching battle but to food. Rations now consisted of a little bacon and a quarter pound of cornmeal, plus a little rice, sugar, and coffee. Their daily menu consisted of "corn bread and bacon with an occasional change to bacon and corn bread." Some times "we go into the fields" wrote a Confederate, "and dig up a handful of wild onions which we fry in our bacon gravy, making a most welcome addition to our standard dish."[4] Among the Gunners of Donaldson's refreshments, Levy reported "Sassafras tea is now the favorite beverage in camp."[5]

On May 2 Donaldsonville Lieutenant Antoine Sanchez arrived in camp from Mobile, Alabama, bearing "satisfactory news"[6] of families and home, but he was also placed under arrest by General Orders for overstaying his furlough. He would not be the only one.

At about four o'clock that afternoon Levy recorded that a "terrific tornado" passed over the Cobham Station encampment. Hard winds and heavy rain began soon after. It was nearly dark, noted Levy, "Before we could rebuild the camp fire and shout for joy."[7]

The next day, May 3, the Gunners of Donaldson learned their commander Captain Victor Maurin was promoted to major "in the Provisional Army in the service of the Confederate States."[8] Upon receiving his commission Maurin was ordered to report to General Robert E. Lee for a new assignment. Command of the battery in Maurin's absence was held by

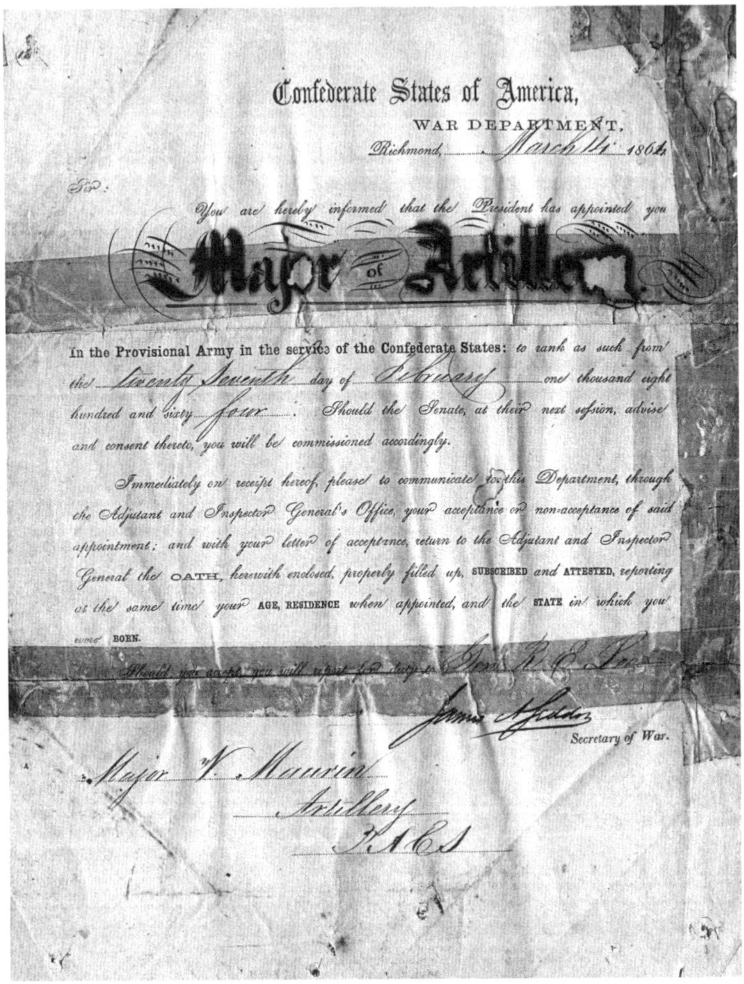

Confederate States of America,

WAR DEPARTMENT,

Richmond, March 14 1864.

Sir:

You are hereby informed that the President has appointed you

Major of Artillery

In the Provisional Army in the service of the Confederate States: to rank as such from the Twenty Seventh day of February one thousand eight hundred and sixty four. Should the Senate, at their next session, advise and consent thereto, you will be commissioned accordingly.

Immediately on receipt hereof, please to communicate to this Department, through the Adjutant and Inspector General's Office, your acceptance or non-acceptance of said appointment; and with your letter of acceptance, return to the Adjutant and Inspector General the OATH, herewith enclosed, properly filled up, SUBSCRIBED and ATTESTED, reporting at the same time your AGE, RESIDENCE when appointed, and the STATE in which you were BORN.

Should you accept you will report for duty to

Secretary of War.

Major V. Maurin
Artillery
P.A.C.S.

Victor Maurin's certificate of promotion to Major of Artillery in the Provisional Army in the service of the Confederate States. Courtesy of Arthur M. Colomb, San Francisco, Ca.

Lieutenant Camille Mollere because Lieutenants Prosper Landry and Hubert Treille were still absent on furlough and Sanchez was under arrest.

On the sixth day in camp at Cobham Station the Donaldsonville Canonniers received orders (in conjunction with Richardson's Battalion) "to be ready to move at a moment's notice."[9] Later during the day news arrived of the forward movement of the Yankee army, and at four o'clock in the evening orders arrived from Lieutenant General A. P. Hill's Third Corps artillery commander Lieutenant Colonel Lindsay Walker. On May 4 Private John Walters of Grandy's Battery recorded, "This afternoon (little expecting it) we received orders to send as many guns as we could to the front, and as our battalion had not been fitted up yet, [Moore's] Battery and ours took all the horses that were fit for service and all the Napoleon guns were ordered off. All that we could fit up was six guns, of which [Moore's] had three Napoleons, while we had the remaining two and a ten-pounder Parrott."[10]

Levy wrote, "As we possessed but one officer it was decided that the guns and horses of this battery should be turned over to Capt. Moore. This decision was received by the boys with evidence of dissatisfaction."[11] Donaldsonville Private Octave Landry added with disgust, "Moore's and Grandy's battery left and took our horses and those of [Penick's] battery."[12] An hour after the order was received, Richardson led the six guns and caissons out of camp towards Gordonsville and the Spotsylvania County Wilderness.[13]

Major Merritt B. "Buck" Miller
Courtesy of Dr. Keith Cangelosi, Abita Springs, La.

The Donaldsonville Artillery, now armed with four 10-pounder Parrotts, and the Pittsylvania Battery, armed with three 3-inch ordnance rifles, remained under command of Major Merritt B. "Buck" Miller at Cobham Station for want of horses. "We are consoled," noted Levy, "by the assertion of Maj. Miller that horses will probably be furnished tomorrow when we will join the rest of the battalion on the line of battle."[14]

The next day, May 5, Prosper Landry arrived in camp from Louisiana and passed out letters and money sent from home. He too met with a predicament of which he wrote, "At my return from Louisiana I found myself under arrest, by general orders, for having prolonged the time of my leave." Being four days late, Landry, in a letter, informed his wife,

> The order which put me under arrest demanded that each soldier who was late to report should send immediately in writing the reason of his delay. What could I say? Certainly I had the best reason in the world and if it had been necessary to plead my cause in front of a military court, I would have challenged them to condemn me, but the honorable General Lee, who was brought up and aged in military life and who would not recognize anything except the regulations; would he have accepted them? The fact is I shirked my duty—I was at fault. But we were going into battle and this was not the moment to write, and therefore . . . I then obtained the permission to go see my Lieut. Col. Richardson, who had already left with the other half of the battalion.[15]

Landry continued, "While we were eating we heard cannon fire in the distance. The battle had already begun and I was not there."[16] He met with the "generous and genial"[17] and "open handed"[18] "Buck" Miller[19] and "instead of sending the written reason of his delay, as required, he obtained of Major Miller permission to report in person to . . . Richardson."[20]

After marching all day, Landry reached the battlefield and rejoined Richardson's six guns in the Wilderness, Spotsylvania County, around twilight as "Boots and Saddles" was sounding. Landry noted the battalion's guns had "not yet . . . been engaged in battle"[21] and were just going into the line to relieve McIntosh's Battalion. Noted a thankful Landry, "I had arrived in time for the first battle."[22] Richardson referred the matter to Walker, in charge of the Third Corps Artillery, and he consented to having Landry assigned to Moore's Battery and given the section of an absent lieutenant.

Back at the Donaldsonville camp Levy recorded on May 6, "Heavy cannonading commenced this morning at dawn—The boys are very much discouraged at the idea of our guns being engaged and not ourselves."[23] For the next five days, as the battle raged in the Wilderness, the Canonniers under Mollere could only stand by and listen to the conflict. For three days Octave Landry recorded in his diary, "Fighting going on between Orange Court House and Chancellorsville"; "Fighting still going on"; "Still fighting."[24]

The Gunners of Donaldson and Pittsylvania artillerymen remained idle with the monotony of camp life (except to go out on food foraging expeditions) until shortly after noon on May 10, when orders were received "to strike tents and prepare to march."[25] Levy noted, "The boys never displayed more alacrity than in obedience to this command. At six o'clock, the mules of our ordnance train arrived at camp and were hitched to the guns and caissons."[26] Cire wrote, "We left camp and went near the Rail Road depot at Gordonsville."[27] Octave Landry recorded they left Cobham Station at 8:30 p.m. with Penick's command and after a quick march along the dusty road arrived in Gordonsville. The two batteries parked their guns and wagons in a field adjoining the railroad station, where the men slept under the night sky with rumors being passed. Octave Landry took note and believed, "The enemy's cavalry [is] in our lines."[28]

On the morning of May 11 camp was established. "The Major (Miller)," wrote Levy, "indicated a contemptible spirit by authorizing the guard to arrest all of his men who might be caught in town without a pass."[29] Most of the day was spent in camp watching the coming and going of locomotives pulling their cars. Many of the cars were filled with wounded heading for Lynchburg since a Yankee cavalry raid had cut the tracks and intercepted communications with Richmond.[30] Levy noted that one train arrived loaded with wounded and prisoners, "among the latter a Negro of the 1st New Jersey Reg't." "The rascal," wrote Levy, "contended that he was acting only in the capacity of cook but the story would not digest. Our guard shot him through the neck as he attempted to escape by jumping from the train."[31] Levy closed his journal for the day: "Rain fell in the afternoon."[32]

A few days after the battle of Spotsylvania Court House, Prosper Landry "was sent to get the rest of the battalion with horses captured."[33] The Donaldsonville lieutenant wrote, "Having received some horses which were taken from the enemy, Richardson sent me to Gordonsville to bring back the battery. But I had to give half of them to [Penick's] company."[34] Octave Landry, besides noting the rain, finished this day's diary entry: "Our company received 74 horses which have just been captured from the enemy's cavalry."[35]

With a heavy rain falling throughout the next day, May 12, Miller's command remained in camp awaiting further orders. Levy meanwhile was able to procure a pass to go to the depot where rumors circulated by the thousand. Upon returning to camp, Levy entertained Mr. Walker of the Crescent Rifles, Seventh Louisiana Regiment, who arrived without rations in charge of prisoners.[36]

Sergeant Walker and Prosper Landry's Canonniers remained sheltered in camp the next day, except to make a raid on a train containing commissary stores. Each man's share of the plunder was ten pounds of rice, two pounds of sugar, and half a gallon of beans. The rain continued to fall for twenty-four hours with Levy observing, "There is no immediate prospect for a clearing up."[37]

The rain continued into the morning of May 14 with the Canonniers, besides cooking and eating, still watching the trains. One came through from Richmond for the first time in a week, but there was still no news of importance as the newspapers reported little about military affairs.

Octave Landry recorded, "This morning went out a few miles with horses hitched to limbers to graze and break to harness our new horses and during the afternoon on coming back to camp the caisson of the 4th piece busted and the tongue driver William Kuhn was mortally wounded."[38] Levy added, "A terrible accident occurred at 4 p.m. when the limber chest . . . exploded . . . and hurried poor Kuhn into eternity. Two fine horses were also killed!

Kuhn lingered until 10 p.m. Thus departed a brave, true hearted, amicable soldier."[39] When the rains again fell during the night it was heavy drops that thumped against the canvas tents over the solemn Canonniers. The deluge stopped at seven o'clock in the morning when his comrades buried William Kuhn's body.[40]

After the burial and while preparing breakfast, orders arrived for the Donaldsonville and Pittsylvania guns to move to the front at Spotsylvania Court House. There were not enough horses for the Donaldsonville Artillery to move, and Prosper Landry, now in charge of the battery, recorded, "When it was decided that only half of the company would go . . . everyone wanted to come. I was obliged to refuse half of them."[41] Just one Donaldsonville section of two guns and caissons under Lieutenants Hubert Treille and Antoine Sanchez joined with Penick's three guns and caissons on the march to the front. All three Donaldsonville officers had arrived late from their furloughs and were "affected" with anxious fears of being placed under arrest. They did not know what would become of them because of their predicament, but they were ready to go and join Lee's army to do their duty.[42]

The two other Donaldsonville guns, with forty-one Canonniers under command of Lieutenant Camille Mollere and Sergeants Oscar Demesme and William V. Parks, remained in the Gordonsville camp to await further orders.

Miller put the five-gun command, with their accompanying wagons hauling nothing but cooking utensils, in motion before nine o'clock in the morning. Prosper Landry led the Donaldsonville section with "parental solicitude."[43] As the diminutive Levy recorded,

> Major Miller proved to be a very attentive officer, nothing escaped his notice, there was no straggling. A rest of ten minutes occurred each hour. Showers fell occasionally, blankets and clothing wet through. [Sergeant] Tip Landry carried my rations and [Private] Fuhri my blanket roll, very heavy. Bought a snack of bread and milk at noon and on reaching the sweet village of Louisa C[ourt] H[ouse] was presented with a lunch of ham and light bread. We made twenty-three miles by 9 p.m. and went into park about half a mile north of Tolersville. Having no shelter, [Private] Seymour [Mioton] and myself went to the nearest house and after a long engagement were allowed to spread our blanket on the floor.[44]

"Made an excellent breakfast of rice, sugar with coffee," wrote Levy on the morning of May 16, adding, "the column moved promptly at 8 a.m. by the road to Spotsylvania C[ourt] H[ouse]. Heavy rains in the afternoon. Halted for three hours in order to rest the horses, then proceeded over a lousy road to Dr. Gibson's farm where the guns parked for the night. Twenty miles were accomplished by dark. It was very uncomfortable to lay upon the cold, wet ground and rheumatism tortured me."[45]

The next day, May 17, Levy documented,

> Cloudy—left bivouac at 6 a.m. our route lay through a densely wooded country very thinly settled by farmers in poor circumstances. The road was very lousy until we reached the vicinity of the old Spotsylvania C[ourt] H[ouse] where the sappers and minors had been busy at corduroying. The C[ourt] H[ouse] presented a dismal appearance with its edifices amid innumerable field hospitals. Parked on the farm of Mr. Addison McKenney[46] about a mile south of the centre of our lines of battle. Col. Richardson paid us a visit in the course of the afternoon and spoke in glowing terms of the condition of affairs in the front. The Blues [Grandy's Battery] and Moore's [Battery] have done heavy duty losing about eighteen men killed and wounded. Matters have been comparatively quiet in our front . . . On guard, thus finding an opportunity to enjoy until a late hour the delicious strains discoursed by brass bands.[47]

Canonnier Levy continued his diary on May 18:

> The noise of combat in a northeasterly direction roused me from sweet slumbers. From 6 to 7 a.m. the affair sounded quite loud . . . half an hour later we were ordered to report in front and with merry hearts did we set out. Col. Walker whom we met at the inner line of fortifications ordered [Prosper] Landry to report to Col. Pogue [*sic*] whom was in charge of the guns on the left of the new [Spotsylvania] C[ourt] H[ouse].[48] We ran the gauntlet of very brisk shelling from six Yankee guns, and on reporting as directed, we ascertained that our services were not required as the batteries along the lines refused to be relieved. We were forced to return to the bivouac which we had left in the morning, all the boys cursing and grumbling. Cloudy weather—At six o'clock we were again ordered to the front and after a march of less than a mile were conducted to a position by Major Miller. It became necessary to build a traverse in order to protect our guns from enfilade fire, also to construct a floor. Spades were trumps and it was past midnight before we could rest with needed repose. Rain began to fall just as I was about to retire, but rolling myself in my blanket I laid down under a majestic oak a few feet from the breast works and fell into a profound slumber.[49]

The artillery of A. P. Hill's Third Corps arrived at the front on May 9, 1864, during the Spotsylvania Campaign (May 7-20), which followed the Wilderness Campaign. These campaigns were General Ulysses S. Grant's attempt to envelop General Robert E. Lee's flank and advance towards Richmond. Hill's artillery was posted to the right of Spotsylvania Court House with Poague's Battalion, then Pegram's, (crossing the Fredericksburg Road a few hundred yards from the courthouse) and Cutts's on the extreme right before the road to Massaponax Church. Richardson's Battalion was held in reserve for a day and on May 10, with an additional battery from Pegram, accompanied Heth's Division in a flank movement led by Major General Jubal A. Early, who was temporarily commanding in place of an ill A. P. Hill. After this expedition Richardson's Battalion occupied the line to the right of Cutts's three batteries with the First Corps Artillery to their right. Miller's command of Richardson's six guns was the last of Walker's artillery reserve.

During the evening of May 18, Landry's guns were positioned due to an expected attack the next morning. "The enemy," reported Brigadier General William N. Pendleton, "will probably open fiercely with artillery very early."[50] During the night one-third of each command was required to be awake, with everyone expected up at four o'clock in the morning.

On May 19 Levy recorded,

> Contrary to universal expectation, the day broke undisturbed by the roar of cannon; picket firing, which had been suspended during the night was resumed at dawn. Gen'l Lee, who by the way acts rashly in exposing himself, made a reconnaissance near our position this morning. We are in position about five hundred yards to the right (SE) of the new Spotsylvania Court House. The enemy in our front can be easily distinguished employed at throwing up formidable looking earthworks. We are entertained almost hourly by the Yankee bands which discourse excellent music. At 5 o'clock p.m. a brisk attack was made by our brigade under Early on the enemy's right . . . it was clearly demonstrated on this occasion that there is no charge left in the Yanks.[51]

At first light on the morning of May 20, the Canonniers observed about a hundred yards away, a new line of Yankee redoubts that had been built during the night. A worried Levy scribbled some time during this excessively hot day, "All is well thus far."[52] Private John Walters of Grandy's Battery with Richardson's Battalion noted in his diary, "Nothing done today beyond brisk sharpshooting along the whole line."[53] Pendleton reported, "The enemy, apparently satisfied with his fruitless efforts near Spotsylvania Court-House, made no further attempt."[54]

On May 21 Levy recorded,

> Reveille at 3 o'clock A. M. instead of 4 as heretofore. Wilcox's old brigade of Alabamians[55]

> moved toward the right last night and Davis' Mississippians became our support. Enjoyed the . . . music dispensed by the band of the 55th N[orth] C[arolina].[56] Received orders to limber near about 5 o'clock P. M. in the midst of a drenching shower and had just retired a hundred yards when an engagement took place between Wilcox's Division and the enemy's rear guard and we double quicked back to the redoubt. The affair took place in the woods just in front of our position and lasted about an hour. The shells and Minnie balls whistled around us in rather exciting proximity and although charged with canister our guns could not open on account of the position of the combatants. By night fall everything was quiet and it was evident that Grant had withdrawn his forces from our left and extended his lines towards Richmond. At 7 o'clock the battalion was withdrawn from the front and its redoubts occupied by Pegram's guns.[57]

Lee learned the enemy was shifting its position towards the southeast and consequently ordered Hill's Corps to withdraw from the Spotsylvania defensive line and move across the North Anna River, about twenty miles to the south.[58] Captain John T. Wingfield of Cutts's Battalion, Company C, Irvin (Georgia) Artillery, reported, "Left the lines about dark. About midnight halted 2 miles [past] Mt. Pleasant."[59]

"In marching with Cutts' battalion," Canonnier Levy wrote, "we took the road to the old Spotsylvania C[ourt] H[ouse] and struck out thence in a southeasterly direction and went into bivouac on Mrs. Herndon's farm about twelve miles distant from our starting point at half after one o'clock a.m."[60]

Hill's three divisions and artillery, along with the army's supply trains and heavy baggage wagons, moved west of and parallel to the route of Ewell and Anderson's Corps. Moving from the earthworks by the New Court-House Road, across the Po and Ta Rivers through Mount Pleasant, then across the Mat River through New Market to Chilesburg, Hill's column was scattered along the entire route. Heth's Division was at the head of the column and drudged into Chilesburg near midnight, while Mahone's Division, bringing up the rear, was just starting out at about the same time from Spotsylvania Court House. Cutts's and Richardson's guns were strung out along the road near the center of the corps, the dust-caked artillerymen and beasts shuffling along. "Many noticed an uncanny silence . . . everybody was so tired . . . that the usual conversation on the march ceased," wrote one soldier.[61]

The rolling of the gun, caisson, and wagon wheels were drowned out for a short time when a marcher finally broke into song and, with others joining in, the music engulfed the column.[62] "As far in front and rear as the ear could hear came welling up the stanzas of . . . 'When I was Seeing Sweet Nellie Home,'" remembered one of the weary soldiers.[63] In the middle of the night, with the dark star-studded sky, the Gunners of Donaldson finally halted for a rest. A tired Confederate declared, "Most of us were too weary to spend much time in spreading down blankets, but lay down and slept." [64]

"On Sunday, May 22, resumed our march at sunrise," continued the Canonnier diarist Levy, "No food for the animals. Hot weather, dusty road. We forded the North Anna River at Anderson's Mill. Took a refreshing bath in the stream. A march of two miles brought us to the [Virginia] Central R[ail] R[oad] about a mile below 'Beaver Dam' Station. Parked in a field alongside of the R[ail] R[oad] and awaited further orders."[65]

From Chilesburg it appears the artillery left the main column, probably to avoid crowding,[66] and crossed at Anderson's Ford, while the infantry and wagon train crossed four miles to the east at Butler's Bridge and Island Ford. The wagons and infantry moved a mile or so after crossing the river and camped around Hewlett's Station east of Beaver Dam Station.[67]

While Richardson's batteries with the Gunners of Donaldson waited from noon to midnight for orders, time was at hand to allow the worn horses to graze in the fields under the hot sun, though there was a pleasant breeze. During the evening the artillerymen took their ease as some of the tattered gray clad men scattered over adjoining fields to gather polk-salad and wild garlic to boil over campfires.[68] Some particularly lucky Donaldsonville Canonniers met and dined with a very hospitable and agreeable matron of the neighborhood.[69]

"We were called up in the greatest haste at twelve o'clock [midnight], hitched up, moved off," recorded Walters in Richardson's Battalion.[70] Prosper Landry led the two Donaldsonville guns with alacrity as the battalion headed east on the road beside the railroad tracks. After moving four miles near Hewlett's Station, the guns were parked, and the horses picketed. It was two o'clock in the morning, and the men soon fell asleep. Following sunrise on the morning of May 23 the Canonniers were issued rations that, per day, equaled five crackers and a quarter pound of bacon. Orders also came to get ready to move, and with a breeze again blowing, Richardson's Battalion and Donaldsonville guns marched at eight o'clock that morning. They later parked on the farm of E. M. Anderson, located south of the railroad tracks between Noel's and Anderson's Stations.[71]

At two o'clock that afternoon, the battalion and Prosper Landry received orders to take position in the center of the line of breastworks running parallel with and protecting the railroad near Hewlett's. In an hour, the guns were in position and ready for action. The enemy had crossed the river at Jericho Mills and was advancing through densely wooded country. Upon their discovery, Hill ordered Wilcox's Division to attack from Noel's Station. The attack took place at six o'clock in the evening and was badly managed, leaving a Yankee corps entrenched on the south bank of the North Anna River.[72]

Levy wrote, "Having no spades we made some of plank and worked hard at the redoubt until past midnight when we were ordered to accompany Pegram's battalion to the rear. They parked amid Anderson's wheat field and we were sent farther down the road to rejoin [Richardson's] command [at Anderson's Station]. By this time the entire wagon train of the army was moving to the rear and we were forced to crawl along with the vast column until six o'clock A.M."[73]

The army's train started rolling at seven o'clock that morning. The wagon train headed east along the dirt road, paralleling the railroad tracks from Hewlett's to Hanover Junction, where it turned south for the South Anna River five miles away.[74] The Donaldsonville guns remained on the parallel dirt road for the entire day and night.

On May 24 the sun rose like a disc of molten brass,[75] and, wrote Levy, "found us up with the battalion. 'Boots and Saddle' sounded as we entered the [artillery] park and ten minutes later found the battalion again <u>in route</u> for the front. Found that a new line was being established and a short march brought us to J. T. Anderson's farm in whose barn yard my piece was posted. Without food or rest we went again to work at the breastworks."[76]

The batteries of Richardson's Battalion stood interspersed on a defensive line with Mahone's Division, the two 10-pounder Parrott guns of the Donaldsonville Artillery positioned in the immediate vicinity of the Twelfth Virginia Regiment ("composed of an intelligent set of men," noted Levy)[77] from Mahone's old Virginia Brigade, now commanded by Colonel David A. Weisiger.[78] Located in an open field on a ridge made for defense the Virginia riflemen and Gunners of Donaldson dug entrenchments and earthworks using "every available instrument that would throw up an ounce of earth . . . knives, iron forks, tin plates, spoons and pieces of broken canteens were used as spades."[79] With artillery positions well entrenched at strategic intervals these entrenchments were "among the most formidable constructed during the war."[80]

Mahone's Division and Richardson's Battalion were part of Lee's defensive position that was said to be "a novel system,"[81] wherein the entrenched line formed a very wide inverted V

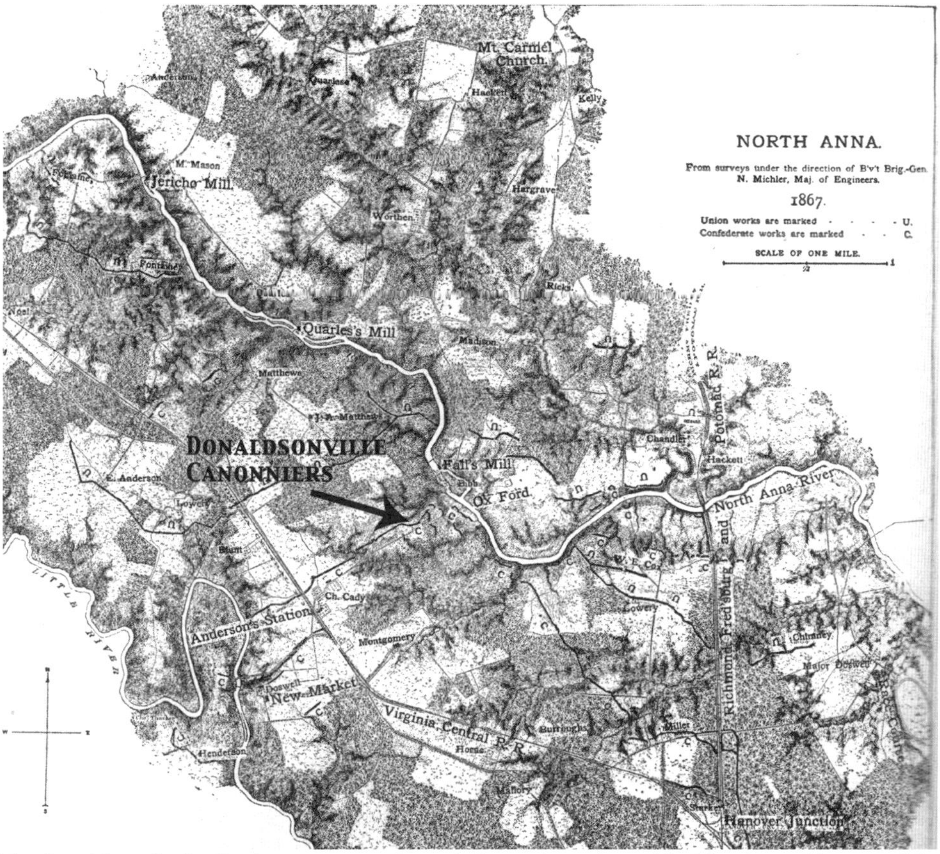

The Donaldsonville Artillery's position was located about where the middle (c) is located between "Ox Ford" and "Anderson's Station," their guns facing Northwest. From *Battles and Leaders*.

with its apex at Ox Ford. The line began with Heth's Division and Poague's artillery battalion on the banks of the Little River that extended northeastward to Wilcox's Division, whose position, with Pegram's artillery battalion, ran through Anderson's Station. Continuing northeastward was Mahone's Division and Richardson's guns, whose line ended on the high bluffs at Ox Ford, where McIntosh's Artillery Battalion and six guns from Cutts's Battalion were located. The lines of Anderson's First Corps, then Ewell's Second Corps, overlooked the river and ran from Ox Ford along the defensible high ground southeastward. The line ended on the swampy ground east of Hanover Junction.[82]

Later during this sweltering hot May 24, Levy recorded,

> An artillery duel between heavy field pieces continued on our right during the day. At 4 o'clock P.M. a very heavy skirmish in our front relieved the tedious work of the hot trenches. A Whitworth gun posted on a commanding imminence across the river enfiladed our line and the shells kept the infantry very low in the ditches while the minies[83] bothered us considerably. The skirmish line when reinforced by an entire brigade, Wilcox's [now Colonel John C. C. Sander's Alabama Brigade], made a beautiful charge and drove the enemy clear through the woods to the river. Seventy prisoners and a stand of colors were brought in as trophies of the affair.[84]

Federal Brigadier General James H. Ledlie, commanding the First Brigade of the First

Division in Major General Ambrose E. Burnside's Fourth Army Corps, was intoxicated from whiskey and ordered and led his small brigade (1,500 men) in a rash charge against Mahone's Division in their earthworks. The hopeless attack, though supported by Federal artillery from the north bank, failed. During the charge Ledlie's flanks were exposed and two regiments of Sanders's and one from Harris's Mississippi Brigade raised the rebel yell and sprinted for the open flanks. With this counter attack the entire Yankee brigade broke and ran pell mell with the Rebels in pursuit. The unequal fight cost the Federal Brigade 450 casualties with about 150 captured. Sander's Eighth and Eleventh Alabama and Harris's Twelfth Mississippi regiments lost fifty-eight and seventeen men respectively.[85] A thunderstorm began as the remnants of Ledlie's troops fell back. The pouring rain fell well into the night.

As at Spotsylvania Court House one-third of the Canonniers remained on guard and awake throughout the night. Almost every Confederate on the line was protected from the weather with items captured in the recent fighting. "I have often thought," wrote a Virginian, "how great a task it is on 'Uncle Sam' to furnish both our army and his own with tents and oilcloths."[86]

It was not a long night, as Levy wrote on May 25: "Up at three o'clock A.M. building traverses and digging pits for ammunition chest. Heavy skirmishing along the line which continued without intermission until 5 P.M. when a Yankee battery . . . opened upon our position at a distance of 500 yards."[87]

The guns lobbing these shells were six Coehorn mortars under the command of Union Second Corps artillery commander Colonel John C. Tidball, who reported that, "The effect was magical, even the fire of the sharpshooters was stopped, and the enemy sought new ways of covering himself from this strange fire."[88] Levy added, "For nearly an hour the missles [*sic*] flew around us thick and fast. One solid shot being buried in our earthwork two feet from the muzzle of my gun. We were not allowed to respond."[89] Around the Donaldsonville guns "other shell bursts emptied [the nearby] barn full of sleeping Confederates, who ran very quickly for the safety of the trench line. Colonel Weisiger . . . also broke for the trench line, 'uttering as he jumped in an 'ugh,' that brought forth a suppressed titter from the boys."[90] The enemy continued their "brisk"[91] fire for another hour. Levy ended the day's entry with, "Cheering and affectionate letters from home arrived today. Rain prevailed towards dark."[92] Levy's father was now in nearby Richmond.

The armies remained facing each other on May 26. Vigorous skirmishing resulted in an incessant fire from both sides, despite a heavy rain that fell from dawn to dark. With the rain the trenches filled up in knee-deep and chilling rainwater that caused the Canonniers to spend the day working to maintain the earthworks. It was a miserable day with the night no better.

"Our scouts are in this morning confirming our suspicions concerning the movements of the enemy," recorded Levy on May 27, adding, "Several squads of prisoners were brought in by our skirmishers this morning."[93] The North Anna River Campaign (May 23-27) was another turning movement by Grant and interpreted correctly by Lee. Entrenched across Grant's path, Lee's position was too strong to assault, and Grant withdrew on the night of May 26-27 toward Hanover on the Pamunkey River.[94]

Richardson's Battalion and the Donaldsonville guns were withdrawn at ten o'clock in the morning and again joined with Cutts's Georgia Battalion moving south. With the sun coming out from the clouds, the men began to sweat as they jostled along. "Being in the rear the journey became very irksome," noted Levy, "we proceeded at a snail's pace and made long halts at frequent intervals."[95]

Hill's Third Corps formed the rear guard of Lee's army, and just a few miles after starting, the batteries of Richardson and Cutts were halted for several hours at Hanover Academy, where the clapboard buildings sat on a wide lawn shaded by oaks.[96] Slow progress continued along on the Telegraph Road. Richardson's guns and caissons, and very tired and very hungry Canonniers, followed in the rear of seven or eight miles of wagon trains. The group crossed the Little River and then the South Anna River before camping at Stoney Creek. Levy recorded, "The battalion went into park at midnight three miles below Ashland having accomplished a distance of ten miles in fourteen hours."[97] Before settling in, Prosper Landry and the other battery commanders received orders to be ready to move at five o'clock in the morning.

Reveille sounded at dawn on May 28, and the Donaldsonville guns moved out at seven o'clock in the morning. "Our route," wrote Levy, "lay by the 'Mountain Road' through a country remarkable for picturesque scenery. Very fine sand roads."[98] From the rolling country of hazy distances Lee's army moved into the flat sand-clay outer fringes of the Coastal Plain past vast forest and scattered farm houses where the women waved their handkerchiefs at the passing troops, artillery, and wagons.[99] "We crossed the Central R[ailroad] at Atlee's Station," continued Levy, "at which point the wounded of Fitzhugh Lee's command were being conveyed. . . . Our bivouac was established on the Mechanicsville road 6 ½ miles N[orth] E[ast] of Richmond. During the night the weather turned very cool."[100]

Hill's Corps was now positioned near Shady Grove Church where Levy agreeably wrote, "To the surprise of all hands today [Sunday, May 29] proved a day of rest. The horses were refreshed with plenty of corn and grass while we were busy cleaning up and cooking rations. Half a pound of meat issued this morning together with rice and molasses. At six P.M. orders came to move towards the front and by nine o'clock we were again in bivouac about a mile north of the last."[101]

Walters noted too that when the wagons came up it was "the first time in ten days [they] got enough to eat."[102] Hill's Corps was the extreme left of the army, and Lee on this day shifted the defensive line somewhat northeast and closer to the Totopotomoy River. Hill's Corps covered the point where the road from Shady Grove to Hanover Court House crossed the river.[103]

"Reveille at 3 o'clock A.M.," recorded Levy on May 30,

> The battalion moved at dawn and an hour later we were posted on the line building breast works for the third time since the campaign opened. We are located on Mr. James Carter, 1¼ mile east of Atlee Station.[104] At noon just as we were giving the finishing touches to our redoubt orders came from Col. Cutts commanding the reserve art[illery] directing us to move about two hundred yards to the left [north]. Again did we have to labor at building traverses' ditches and a platform. It was dark before my gun was established in its new location. In the morning Kirkland's brigade[105] was our support. In the afternoon Brig. Gen. Cook's [*sic*] command of dirty "tarheels"[106] constituted our defenses . . . weather cool and pleasant. The section of my battery was concealed by a dense forest of pines so that we hope to give the Yanks an agreeable surprise should they have the tenacity to charge the left of the line . . . brisk cannonading on the extreme right which did not cease until 9 o'clock P.M.[107]

Lee again blocked Grant's movement south between May 26-30 at Totopotomoy Creek. Though a number of skirmishes occurred, Lee's position was again considered too strong to assault.[108]

"All quiet in our front," continued Levy on May 31, "the fighting seems to be confined to the extreme right. . . . At about one o'clock the line was extended towards the right and the battalion withdrew to the bivouac on the Mechanicsville road whilst which we had left on Sunday morning."[109]

Levy's father was in nearby Richmond at this time. At midday he visited the Donaldsonville camp. He brought with him a fine lunch snack of light bread and cold ham for his sons and a bottle of spirits that, "was speedily discovered by the boys." Levy obtained permission to go to Richmond for the mail so he could escort his father back to the city. At dawn on June 1 they rode in a wagon to the city's outer defenses on the Mechanicsville Turnpike. From there they walked into the capital, of which Levy wrote, "The city is dull as all the merchants are serving in the militia. Few ladies were visible on the street, even the 'Spottswood' [hotel] did not exhibit the usual gay groups of soldiers and travelers." Levy was busy all morning "in executing commissions" (getting supplies) for his comrades and, after spending the rest of the day visiting friends, he took leave of his father and "wended" his way back towards camp.[110]

"On nearing the point at which I left the battalion" wrote Levy, "met the guns advancing up the road. After a march of five miles Col. Richardson went into position on Nelson Gardner's farm, near Hanover C[ourt] H[ouse] eight miles east of Ashland. The position is a very commanding one, almost impregnable . . . on our portion of the line everything was quiet."[111]

The quietness continued through June 2, when Levy wrote,

> I visited the mansion of Mr. Gardner, which is situated just on the picket line and found it profusely riddled by solid shot.[112] Of course our men were busy completing the destruction which the Yankees had commenced . . . moved at 10:20 A.M. [after waiting for the infantry to pass] southward by Mechanicsville road. On reaching the village of Mechanicsville our route lay eastward by the Gaines Mill road. A few minutes march brought us to Ellyson's Mill where poor Stanley was killed two years ago. The land over which we passed is classic and there comes vividly to my mine the remembrance of those horrible scenes which accompanied the battles around our devoted capitol. A most distressing march was this to man and horse. The dust arose in dense volumes and not a breath of air stirred. In the course of the afternoon a thunder storm arose which cooled the atmosphere. The sounds of action became plainer as we advanced, the musketry was continuous and sounding very heavy . . . the battalion went into park within about a mile of the front and three hundred yards north of Dr. Gaines' farm where we fought during the afternoon of the 27th June 1862. The troops in our front fought fiercely until nine o'clock and heavy skirmishing continued throughout the night, notwithstanding the heavy rain which prevailed. Passed a miserable night having retired perfectly drenched through.[113]

Hill's Corps arrived in the area of Cold Harbor during the evening of June 2, 1864. Lee had Breckenridge's Division and two brigades from Wilcox's Division "thrown forward."[114] They pushed the enemy from the dominant ground at Turkey Hill, which secured Lee's right flank and extended the line to within half a mile of the Chickahominey River.

"The grand roar of the battle coming upon the stillness of the early dawn was something terrific to hear," wrote an artillery officer on the morning of June 3.[115] Levy recorded,

> A heavy engagement commenced directly east of our bivouac shortly after daylight. . . . The musketry was terrific and as our advance line of battle was less than a mile distant we could frequently distinguish amid the din of battle the shout of the Yankees as they advanced in <u>drunken</u> array to charge the earthworks which our men had erected during the night. By eight o'clock the combat appeared to have become less severe and at nine the most obstinate fighting was to our left in the direction of Cold Harbor. Gen'l. Lee has just passed the battalion conveyed by a light Jersey wagon. The old patriot looks as calm and pleasant as if Grant's defeat has been already consummated.[116]

Lee's health was still fragile as a result of "violent intestinal complaint"[117] that occurred on May 24. He still had to ride in a (soon to be discarded) carriage. Lee's uniform worn at this time was unpretentious and described as "blue military breeches with boots, a short linen sack coat . . . a soft felt hat and buff gauntlets," and he "carried neither sword, pistol, nor fieldglasses."[118]

At ten o'clock in the morning—after Lee passed—a light drizzling rain began to fall. Orders arrived to send two of Moore's Napoleon guns to the front. "The heavy fighting ceased before noon," continued Levy, "the result has been a . . . repulse of the Yankees along the entire line. Their dead and wounded cover acres of ground in solid bloody phalanx."[119]

This was the Second Battle of Cold Harbor, of which Lee reported, "Our loss to-day had been small, and our success, under the blessing of God, all that we could expect."[120] On a six-mile front the attacking Federal army was repulsed with 7,000 casualties while the defending Confederates lost 1,500.[121]

"In the afternoon, all the Napoleons of [Richardson's] battalion were put in position about two miles to the left of the new bridge over the Chickahominey," according to Walters.[122] Levy noted that after the fighting the remainder of the battalion and the Canonniers received "satisfactory quantities" of sugar, coffee, and tobacco, but, "three times in the course of the afternoon . . . the battalion [was] forced to change position on account of the visits of 'commissary searchers' as the boys termed those shells which are shot far to the rear. This night we went into bivouac in Dr. Gaines' oatfield 500 yards S[outh] W[est] of his elegant mansion."[123]

The lines remained steadfast for over a week, and during that time Levy continued his chronicle:

> Saturday, 4th June. Reveille at 1 o'clock A.M. Only five guns left in the park this morning, the balance having gone into position during the night. I suppose that our section of Richmond Parrotts will be the last pieces required for. It was seven o'clock before the sun had dissipated the heavy fog which hung heavily around us. The pickets and sharpshooters have been busy at their bloody work since dawn. Pretty sharp cannonading in our front between eleven o'clock and noon. The day wore away quietly. Just after dark as Finnegan's [Florida] brigade [of Mahone's Division] moved forward to relieve the picket line the enemy made an advance. The Floridians were ordered to fall back to the earthworks and as the Yankees persisted in the charge the rattle of musketry and roar of the Napoleon guns told plainly that another harvest of death was being reaped. Rain set in at 4 P.M. and continued throughout the night. . . .
>
> Sunday–5th June. The heavens continued overcast with threatening clouds and light showers fell until ten o'clock. Our line of battle now extends from a point one and a half mile's east of Mechanicsville to the upper edge of [Gaines's] farm. The demonstrations this morning which are quite feeble are against our left flank. Rations of one onion per man distributed for the first time since I have been in the service. A brisk little affair occurred near Cold Harbor at 8 o'clock P.M. when we were about to relieve the pickets. The enemy withdrew with considerable loss.
>
> Monday, 6th June. A bright sunny day. Save the usual picket firing all was quiet in front . . . just about noon as I was seated on the lower branch of a magnificent oak enjoying the cool breeze and reading Miss Evans' last novel, "Macaria,"[124] the hoarse clangorous of the bugle proclaimed a move. Joyfully did the boys strike tents when it was intimated that we were about to assume a position on the line. A march of less than a mile brought us to our destination and after the usual delays we were set at work with spades and picks to fortify the guns. We were located on McGee's farm, a mile east of Dr. Gaines' house.[125] The range of hills which is occupied by Hill's Corps is called "Turkey Ridge." It is here that the lamented [Stonewall] Jackson struck the flank of McClellan's army in the brilliant campaign of June, 1862. In front of the earthworks which are occupied by our support (Lane's Brigade, Wilcox's division)[126] is an intricate abatis of pointed stakes, while at the foot of the hill on which my gun is planted is a swamp covered with a dense undergrowth. The roads which McClellen built [during the 1862 campaign]

> through this "swamp" are of great assistance to us, thus is the engineer hoist by his own petard. The gun detachment was kept hard at work until dark erecting traverses, a platform, and planting three ammunition chest. In the course of the afternoon I paid a visit to Mahone's old brigade which occupies the works at and to the north of McGee's house.[127] Here it is impossible to look over the breastworks without being shot at while in our front the pickets have established amicable relations and traffic [trade] with each other. A brisk affair of the pickets in front of Mahone's took place at nine o'clock P.M. which caused a general vigilance along the line. The Minnie balls, coming in a left oblique direction flew all around us without harming a single man.
>
> Tuesday- 7th June, 1864. Reveille at 3 A.M. We finished our defenses by five. Sharp skirmishing to the left while all is quiet in front. At 5 P.M. a flag of truce was sent in by Grant with the request that he might be allowed to bury his dead, which was granted. The cessation of hostilities existed from 6 to 8 P.M. Having prepared a letter to Grandma. I had an interview with some Pennsylvanians of Hancock's Corps and by means of a swathe of tobacco procured some Federal postage stamps and got my communication mailed. The fellows whom I met seemed quite confident of capturing Richmond although they did not explain by what "modus operandi" the act was to be accomplished. Tobacco was very much in demand among the Yanks, but they were not willing to exchange food for it, a pretty good indication that rations are short with them. One fellow had the impertinence to ask me to desert, and my indignant answer seemed to please his comrades. After the truce had expired there was no more picket firing during the night.
>
> Wednesday- June 8th. A quiet day in front of our position with the exception of a short artillery duel between two guns of our battalion and a Yankee rifled piece in the woods to our right. . .
>
> Saturday, 11th June. Grant's "impetuous rush" to Richmond seems to have degenerated into an advance by the usual siege process. His army has assumed what the Northern papers style a defiant attitude. . . . Matters have been remarkably quiet along our lines of late. McIntosh's [artillery battalion] has planted a 24-pounder howitzer at an angle of 40 [degrees] just in the rear of Mahone's brigade and has thrown shells in mortar style to prevent the enemy from entrenching. The Yankees have mounted a mortar in opposition but their practice is very imperfect when compared with ours. Visited [members] of the Purcell battery[128] yesterday and enjoyed a game of whist in the trenches; the enemy sharpshooters keep heads down at this portion of the lines. Fuhri brought from Richmond a few cakes and herrings which were demolished for supper.[129]

Another artilleryman wrote at this time, "This is a most terrible country, you can't find water for 3 or 4 miles at a time, and now on the bank of the Chickahominey we have to drink the most miserable swamp water, that tastes as if [it] were greasy; and the other day I went to the river to bathe, and found the river so filthy with a grease scum on it from the mass of human bodies bathing that I was disgusted & went back. My clothes were so dirty that to get rid of the virmin I took them off and boiled them. . . . This is the most terrible ordeal in a soldier's life."[130] During the nights there was "the oder of the dewy grass and the foliage of the swamps mingled with the cries of night birds."[131]

"Monday. 13th June," penciled the Donaldsonville Canonnier Levy,

> It has been ascertain[ed] that the enemy had disappeared from our front and moved in the direction of the South side. By six o'clock our corps was streaming by every road toward the Chickahominey [river]. Having joined the balance of the battalion our line of march led through dense swamp over which McClellan had constructed a substantial road. We crossed the Chickahominey, now an insignificant creek at "Federal" or "5th Cavalry" bridge two miles above "Grape Vine" bridge [to the Nine Mile Road]. Half an hours march amidst volumes of dust brought us to "Fair Oaks Station" on the [Richmond and] York River R[ail] R[oad] where we halted to wait orders. Near this

> point the right wing of the enemy rested during the battle of Seven Pines. Moved by the "Nine mile" road to its intersection with the Williamsburg road where a halt of two hours ordered for the refreshment of the horses. While here I could view five hundred yards to westward the position held by my gun during the bloody Sunday's fight of Seven Pines. By eight o'clock P.M. the line of march was resumed and after a pleasant tramp (for the night was quite cool) the bivouac was established at Williams' farm on the Charles City road,[132] 15 miles S[outh East] of Richmond at two o'clock on the morning of Tuesday- 14th June.
>
> This days rations have been donated to the poor of Richmond by unanimous consent of our section. Grant's new line extends from Malvern Hill on the James [River] to the Chickahominey [River] (about the long bridge). The enemy's gunboats thundered forth several times during the day. It is the general impression that Grant is changing his base to the south side. Mint tea was fashionable in camp today. Doc [Levy's brother] and myself enjoyed some [tea]with pork and beans for supper. Very cool night, heavy dew, rested badly.[133]

Near the Donaldsonville Canonnier bivouac an infantry private on June 15 wrote in a letter home, "Grant still slides to the left, I think we'll keep it up until he lays siege to Petersburg instead of Richmond. He held us mighty uncomfortable at Cold Harbor, gave us a taste of what a siege would be—It was unsafe to shit in a half mile of the line—both sides sharpshooting, throwing mortar shells nearly all the time."[134] Historian Douglas S. Freeman politely chronicled that this day "opened one of the most difficult periods in the history of the Army of Northern Virginia."[135] Having been repeatedly blocked on the advance to Richmond, Grant did indeed shift his line of operation to the south side of the James River or *du côte du sud* as the Creole Canonniers called it.

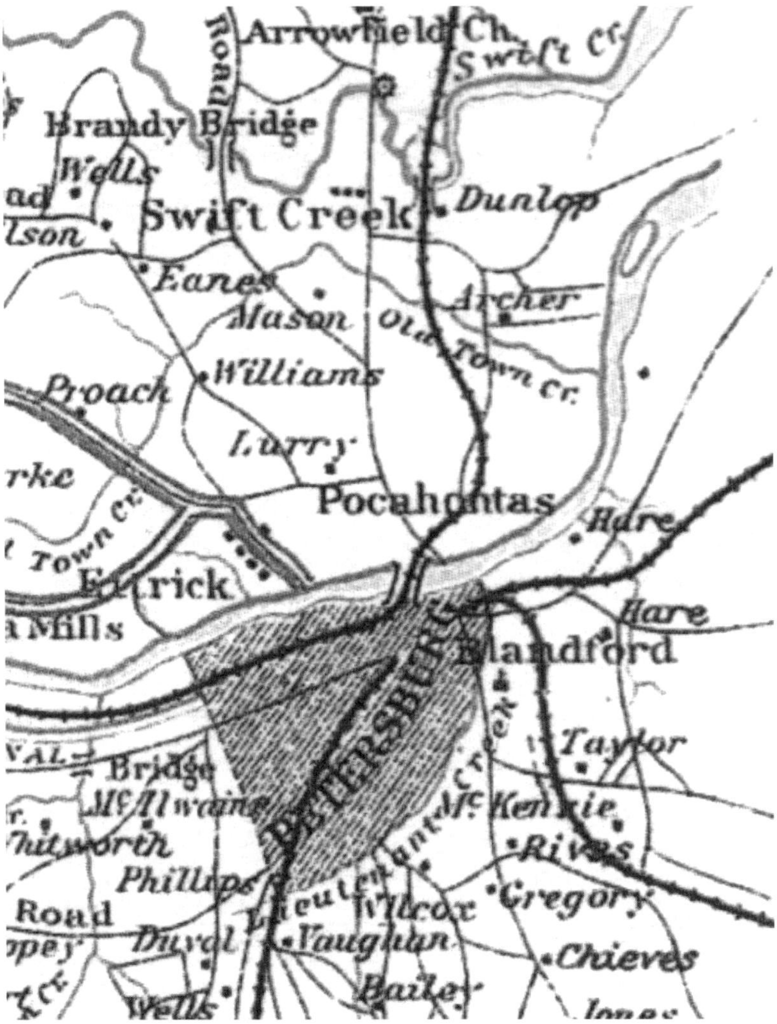

Siege of Petersburg — the Canonniers initial location was at the point designated Archer;
they subsequently rested for three days at Dunlop on Swift Creek before proceeding to Rives's (Salient).
From *Atlas to Official Records.*

Chapter Fifteen

Assiéger Petersburg
(To Lay Siege to Petersburg)

"I think the enemy must be preparing to move South of James River." So wrote General Robert E. Lee to Confederate States President Jefferson Davis on June 14, 1864.[1] He advised: "We ought therefore to be extremely watchful and guarded."[2] Lee placed Lieutenant General A. P. Hill's Third Corps on standby for protection of the capital on a defensive line from Malvern Hill to Ridell's Shop.

Part of Hill's command on June 15, 1864, was his artillery reserve, commanded by Colonel Allen S. Cutts and composed of his own and Lieutenant Colonel Charles Richardson's battalions.[3] A component of Richardson's Battalion was Lieutenant Prosper Landry's Donaldsonville Artillery section of two Richmond-made 10-pounder Parrott guns operated by seventy-one Donaldsonville Canonniers. One member was Private Eugene H. Levy who kept a journal and documented his and the Creole artillerists' activities during the time the Federal forces began *assiéger Petersburg* (to lay siege to Petersburg).

On June 15 Prosper Landry's Gunners of Donaldson had "Reveille at 2 o'clock A.M. Moved promptly at 3. A steady march of one and a half hours duration brought us to Jacob S. Atlee's farm[4] on the Darbytown road 6 miles south of Richmond. Here we halted until 7 o'clock to prepare breakfast and graze the animals, then moved about a quarter of a mile up the Darby Road and settled for the balance of the day. Bathed [in Cornelius Creek] and changed clothing. As this point is but four miles distant from Drury's [*sic*] Bluff, the growling of the gun boats was heard quite plainly."[5]

The artillerists of the combined battalions of the reserve artillery caught up on much needed sleep and remained for two days "quiet in camp."[6] One officer of the Third Corps recorded, "Our health was very bad. The constant exposure to sun and rain, the rancid bacon and half-raw corn bread . . . issued us, the filth[y] . . . vile water of this section of the country . . . the want of rest at night, (for we had still to keep one-third always awake at night, and to rouse all at 3 o'clock in the morning) and . . . the constant, excited anxiety, had produced and aggravated diarrhea, dysentery, dyspepsia, and slow fevers, which were wasting men surely away."[7] Not surprisingly, Levy, a prolific writer, did not make a journal entry for the days spent here on June 16 and 17.

By the evening of June 17 Lee was still not sure what Federal troops remained on the north side of the James River, but he deemed that the situation on the south side of the river at Petersburg was serious. Lee now prepared the army for a movement and a shift southward. Hill's Third Corps was ordered to Chaffin's Bluff on the river and at ten o'clock at night ordered to cross the pontoon bridge over the James River and move to the Petersburg Turnpike, where Hill was to wait for orders.[8]

In the early morning hours of June 18, recorded Levy, the Gunners of Donaldson had

> Reveille at half past one o'clock A. M. as orders to move had been received during the night. At daylight found the Darbytown Road crowded with infantry marching northwards. Heavy firing in the direction of Chaffin's farm. The reserve artillery followed a tortuous route across the country to the "River" road which we met near Stern's [*sic*] farm, a former camp ground of the battery in 1862. Here (the boys stripped an orchard)[9] I gathered cherries and green apples and had a refreshing lunch. The battalion crossed the James River at Col. Knights' farm[10] by means of a bridge partly made of wooded piers and the balance over large luggers and flat boats. The view from the bridge was delightful including Richmond on the right and Drury's [*sic*] Bluff to the left.[11] Midway between the bridge and the bluff are placed some formidable river obstructions.[12] On reaching the Chesterfield [County] bank we traversed the plantation of W[illia]m Watkins; one of the wealthiest estates in Virginia.[13] On emerging from the plantation land we struck the "Richmond & Petersburg Turnpike" at a point 5 miles below the Capitol. The dust, which on the north bank of the river had been quite disagreeable now became intolerable, and taken in connection with the intense heat of the sun rendered this march memorable for discomfort. Moving in the rear of the corps wagons, our march was necessarily slow and accompanied by annoying halts, but the prospect of fighting under our own Beauregard[14] and in defense of the dear old "Cockade City—"[15] made us forget fatigue. When opposite Port Whalthall Junction the sound of musketry was quite plan, proceeding from the direction of the river, while the booming of light artillery could be distinguished in the neighborhood of the besieged city. During a halt of the column in the rear of Drury's [*sic*] Bluff, a kind lady with whom I entered into conversation furnished me with a delicious draught of milk. From the flank fortifications of the bluff to the city breastworks the road is lined with graves and the debris of the battle of the 16th ult. At six o'clock P.M. the guns went into park on Dunn's Hill overlooking Petersburg and to the north of the city.[16]

Lee had arrived at Petersburg at about eleven o'clock in the morning with the leading troops of Hill's exhausted corps. Marching as fast as possible, the Third Corps was spread out along the Petersburg Turnpike. Upon arriving in the afternoon most were placed in position on the extreme right of the line. The numerically superior Federals were in a strong position. Lee notified the president, "I fear he will not attack us but advance by regular approaches."[17] On Sunday, June 19, Lee went to church in Petersburg, despite his military problems.

The Gunners of Donaldson with the other batteries of the reserve artillery remained in park with the artillerists washing and mending their worn and ragged uniforms and taking their ease during the day. Levy noted,

> The head quarters of Gen[era]l Beauregard being but a hundred yards distant from my gun I had the pleasure to see our beloved chief several times in the course of the day. Time has played sad havoc with him and sure has worn deep furrows in his brow. His hair and mustache have become quite gray and his eye has lost that merry expression which was wont to distinguish it in the good old times.
>
> Desultory skirmishing to the north and east of the city continued from dawn until the moon had set. The enemy threw a few shells into town today. At seven o'clock P.M. our section was detached from the battalion and joined in the line of march with ten other "Parrots" under command of Col. Cutts.[18]

During the morning Levy and the Donaldsonville artillerymen observed Beauregard with Lee's chief of artillery, Brigadier General William N. Pendleton, the two being on a reconnaissance and inspection of the terrain along the bank of the Appomattox River. As a result of this survey, Cutts was instructed to detach the rifle guns from his battalion (including Landry's two guns and Penick's Battery) and fortify the commanding eminence at the Archer House, which overlooked the river and entire right wing of the Union army occupying the old Confederate works on the other side of the Appomattox River, north of the city. Cutts's instructions were to "check the enemy's fire."[19]

Levy wrote that after Landry's section received orders they went

> proceeding down the R[ichmond] & P[etersburg] Turnpike about half a mile, took the Clifton's road leading eastward and by nine o'clock were assigned to a position in the garden of Mme. [Mrs.] Archer's house on the west bank of the Appomattox [river] about two miles north of Petersburg. The Col. [Cutts] commanding laid out a breastwork for our piece in the shape of an obtuse angle (V') the longer side of which being designed as a protection against an enfilading battery. The work had a base of sixteen feet with a four feet slope and although we labored incessantly throughout the night and at daylight found us with the work but half accomplished. A cup of strong coffee (the precious berry of Arabia having been filched from one of our box cars)[20] made just after dawn [Monday June 20] helped my drooping spirits (at dawn. We crept down to the river's bank to enjoy a wash, and felt decidedly refreshed ere the sun rose.)[21] A heavy fog which shrouded the city until seven o'clock proved our good friend as we were enabled to finish the earthwork and open fire with the rest of the guns as soon as the mist had disappeared. Our position, which was partially masked on the left by the thick foliage of the trees which line the river commanded full view of Battery 5 of the city defenses which the enemy had captured last week. As the twelve guns opened simultaneously, we made lively music for men and horses. The Yankees were not slow to reply but the experience found that neither party was able to harm the other to any extreme. The Richmond "Parrot" gun on which I acted No. 3 proved to be less effective and accurate than any gun that I ever stood behind.[22]

An officer in one of Cutts's batteries nearby noted that two of their guns were "shooting badly" due to "inferior ammunition."[23] About the Confederate cannon fire one Yankee recorded,

> There was great diversity in the sound of the various missiles which our considerate friends hurled at us. The shriek of a Whitworth, seeming to cry, "Which one, which one, which one?" the whir-r of a round shot, and the scream of a conical shell, were readily distinguished. Some good, honest shells flew over, with a professional directness which insured respect. Occasionally one appeared, as it were, to stumble along with a sideling motion and a swaggering noise, which was often interpreted as saying, "Where's that nigger? Where's that nigger?"[24]

Pendleton reported, "On the morning of the 20th these guns opened upon the enemy with such power—from their number and from the direction in which they struck flank and reverse—as to produce much confusion in their ranks and compel him to effect a sudden change of position."[25] Levy's statement of damage was more accurate than Pendleton's if inference is made from Yankee Captain William B. Rhodes's report of the action that involved Battery E of the First Rhode Island Light Artillery opposite Archer's Hill. Rhodes wrote, "I discovered the enemy throwing up a work . . . in my rear on a bend of the river, in consequence . . . the men worked all night, throwing up a traverse in rear of the guns. June 20, the enemy opened on my position at daylight with . . . a brisk fire for four hours, when . . . they ceased firing. They would have undoubtedly ruined the battery were it not for the strength of my works. . . . I lost four horses killed."[26] No matter what the damage wrote a witness, the artillery shells "Made a fluttering sound as they traversed the air, descending with a frightful hiss, to explode in midair . . . a puff of smoke, white as an angel's wing, would drift away, and the particles would patter down like hail."[27]

"Every thing being quiet by 11 o'clock," noted Levy, "I paid my respects to Mme. [Mrs.] Archer's cherries and raspberries. Doc [Levy's brother] stewed gooseberries with sugar and made quite a palatable addition to our bill of fare. A duck was found in the parlor of Mrs. James Archer's house, in consideration of good manners and the articles of war and met with an appropriate end being made to serve our purpose at supper and breakfast."[28] Years later Levy reminiscenced about the "old drake" and wrote, "We cooked the ancient bird fourteen different ways, but could only enjoy soup seasoned by his carcass, as the flesh could not be separated from the bone."[29]

"At five o'clock P.M.," continued Levy,

> The enemy moved a column of infantry towards our left and as the troops filed past all our guns opened on them with shell (5" fuses). At the first volley the cowards ran away not stopping to care for there [*sic*] wounded whom we distinguished dragging themselves along long after their comrades had disappeared. The episode was very pleasant and the excitement was heightened by the opening of the enemy's guns upon our position. At dark another earthwork was laid out for us by which the two guns of our section were connected. The accomplishment of this labor occupied all the night. My comrades worked until midnight and my watch extended until sun up. More guns were planted on the hills near us in the course of the night.[30]

"Additional guns," reported Pendleton,

> among them several 30-pounder Parrotts and 12-pounder Whitworths, were subsequently posted near the Archer house to enable the armament there to hold its ground against tremendous efforts of the enemy to silence it. These guns were opened upon the enemy whenever his infantry appeared and when his shells were thrown into the city. Batteries erected in every available position on the opposite side and armed with their most formidable guns and mortars were plied with fierceness and constancy against this armament—a sufficient proof of the efficiency with which it disturbed the enemy's operations and frustrated his plans.[31]

The Confederate artillery line of about fifty guns was now almost a mile long. Pendleton's opposite, Federal Brigadier General Henry J. Hunt, countered against the Southern guns with a siege train organized of heavy formidable guns and mortars placed in greatly strengthened earthworks.[32]

For the next week the two Donaldsonville guns remained on this line. Levy documented in detail his activities. In due course the actions of the Gunners of Donaldson began on June 21:

> At ten o'clock our guns provoked a duel, the enemy using ten and twenty pounder rifles from the river bank on our right. Beasley's farm[33] was to the left and Battery 4 (Petersburg City defenses) beyond the City Point Road and immediately opposite my gun.[34] The affair lasted until noon, the Yankees indicating in an unpleasant manner that they had got the exact range of our works. Capt. Penick, whose position was immediately to the left of my gun, lost five men of which only one was dangerously wounded.
>
> The enemy sent shells wherever working parties appeared in front of our lines, aside from this nothing happened to disturb the quiet of the afternoon. As my blanket had been carried to the rear with the limber of the piece I was forced to sleep without covering until fortune favored me by throwing in my path an old boat sail with which I made myself quite comfortable at night.
>
> Wednesday. 22nd June. While cooking breakfast this morning the Yanks opened from Battery 4 with a rifled 32-pounder. Simultaneously the guns from their river and the Beasley batteries raked us in enfilade. This continued for an hour eliciting no response

> from our line . . . a gunner in the Irvin Artillery (Cutts' Battalion) had charge of a rifled gun on the left of our work. Having noticed some man straggling about the yard of Capt. Page's house, which is on the east bank of the Appomattox immediately opposite my gun, he threw a shell into the house and discovered a hornet's nest. The pickets streamed out and as they passed along the road leading from Page's to Battery 5 we put into their ranks five effective shells.
>
> At dark I ran the blockade into Petersburg arriving just in time to receive the first news of a beautiful flank movement by portions of Wilcox and Anderson's divisions. We captured four guns and 1500 prisoners. All Petersburg was on Sycamore street discussing a thousand rumors and straining for a look at the prisoners.[35]

After this Levy recorded he traded his

> accumulated rations of coffee for the same quantity of sugar and proceeded toward camp. In passing through a dense forest I lost my way and after having wandered about until eleven o'clock concluded to camp out.
>
> Thursday 23rd June. Found Archer's farm by 4 o'clock with ease. The enemy opened fire just as I was preparing breakfast. As I left the fire with a fine pot of pork and beans a shell struck the place which I had just vacated. A new battery of powerful guns situated east of Beasley's house paid its compliments to us this morning. So accurate in firing have the Yankees become, through long practice at our position, that our boys were forced to keep close to the traverse of the work for safety. A shell knocked a spoke from the wheel of my gun (exploding beyond the works)[36] and a solid shot tore to fragments a blanket and oil cloth which was placed on the top of the right hand traverse. Weather excessively hot, half of us are forced to take refuge on Mrs. Archer's lawn to prevent being melted. At ten o'clock the sixth piece was struck and a portion of the felloe[37] of a wheel carried away. Half an hour later one of Cutts's Parrots immediately south of our section was disabled by a twenty-four pounder solid shot. The fire from the new enfilading was inordinate and excessively annoying. The boys were not at all pleased at being forced to lay low and submit to a bombardment without answering. The result proved how futile are artillery duels or, thanks to a merciful Providence, not a man on Pleasant Hill was struck.[38]

Levy added, "Despite the continuous iron compliments of the enemy, not one of the men of my battery has been seriously wounded, so the boys think Pleasant Hill a lucky spot to fight from. While off duty the boys found time to bathe in the river at the base of the hill, and thus kept fresh and cheerful."[39] He also noted,

> Bathing and fishing in the Appomattox [River] have become fashionable amusements. For dinner today I enjoyed a mess of excellent fish.[40]
>
> Friday 24th June. My gun detachment was aroused at 1½ A.M. and ordered to assist in moving to another portion of the line as it had been decided that the guns on Pleasant Hill were too close together. The new position which my gun occupies is about seventy yards to the right of its former location and opposite Capt. Page's house. By command of Gen'l Pendleton, who delivered the order in person, we commenced a demonstration the object of which was to attract the attention of the enemy from a movement of our troops on the extreme left. From eight until ten o'clock the cannonading continued along our entire line making a truly terrible concert. The enemy fired at my gun from the Beasley battery, Battery No. 4 and Battery No. 1, the last mentioned is located on Rowlett's Farm[41] which lies on the east bank of the river about a mile south of us.[42]
>
> The lighted fuses looked like huge fireflies as they whizzed just over our heads and cut the limbs from the beautiful trees in the rear of our position.[43]
>
> Many were the "hairbreadth escapes" which the boys related when we congregated on the cool lawn to fight the battle over again. Two shells buried themselves in the traverse

which protected Ely[44] and myself (Nos. 1 and 3). My gun fired 90 rounds in the course of the action.

The weather was intensely hot and I could only find relief in the afternoon by bathing and resting quietly on board of the old scow which is aground in the middle of the river. At dark the enemy, guided by our camp fires, opened upon our position with two new guns from Battery 5. The lighted fuses indicating the course of the missles and there was no difficulty in avoiding danger.

Saturday 25th June. 1864. At ten o'clock the enemy opened on the city with a 'Blakely' 32 p[oun]der [siege gun] and the order from Beauregard was transmitted by means of signal flags to "fire on the heavy gun." As our guns could not reach Battery 4 the Parotts and three inch rifles to the right and left of Archer's House commenced a rapid fire. In five minutes the existence of a new opposing battery was developed in front of my gun on Capt. Page's farm midway between ourselves and Battery 5. Our new opponent consisted of four ten p[oun]der Parrotts which were admirably worked. An hour's firing convinced us that the enemy could shell the city at their pleasure and the artillery duel ceased. We were glad enough to be allowed to leave the trenches and roll on the lawn of Mrs. Archer's house enjoying cold water at the expense of her ice house. Boiled (beans formed our dinner, the bacon having been consumed yesterday, but we find that beans fill "the empty, aching void" effectually).[45] At four o'clock "Battery 2 ½" (so the boys dubbed the latest discovered guns) opened a terrific fire upon my gun. More beautiful practice was never seen by "the oldest artilleryman"; every shot struck some object in the immediate vicinity of the gun. The little shade trees which we had planted were cut down, every minute a shower of dirt overwhelmed us, the earthworks were repeatedly bored, and a shot which was directed at our left hand neighbor penetrated thirteen feet of earth and mortally wounded Lieut. James of Cutts' Battalion.[46] No one was permitted to show himself without being made a target of. This state of affairs continued until dark, after which a few shots were thrown in the direction of our camp fire by our vindictive adversary. At nine o'clock all the short range pieces were withdrawn from Chesterfield heights and their places supplied by guns of heavy caliber. Our section went into bivouac in one of Mrs. Archer's fields on the Fort Clifton road about a mile to the rear of Pleasant Hill.[47]

Regarding Cutts's command that included Prosper Landry's two Donaldsonville Artillery guns, a contemporary source wrote:

With inferior guns, and far inferior ammunition, [they] fought the enemy more or less everyday or night, with unyielding tenacity. "The iron watchdogs" on Archer's Hill belched forth their thunders in its defence, forcing the Vandals to turn from the shelling of women and children to defend himself. The Petersburg Press was loud in its praise of "our strong batteries on the Chesterfield side." Finally after in vain attempting to silence our guns, a sort of tacit truce prevailed. Whenever the enemy attempted to shell the town, a few shots from the Archer's House would produce perfect silence; the enemy ceasing their fire to prevent our guns from enfilading their infantry line. Under this arrangement the Federal batteries on our front became comparatively useless and were moved further to their left. Subsequently Major Lane with all the guns of his Battalion [and Prosper Landry's and Penick's] . . . were ordered to the more immediate Petersburg front.[48]

Years later Levy remembered,

Those were hot days on the Chesterfield heights, when passions of men turned a paradise into a hell. Along the line of earthworks stood the gunners, half naked, working like fiends, shouting words of encouragement or chanting the refrain of some patriotic song, while above the hoarse roar of the cannon rose the shrieks of the wounded, as the hot fragments of iron shells tore ragged furrows in their tender flesh. The summer sun shone down fiercely on the green, hot metal monsters that hurled death and destruction to hundreds, while sulfurous smoke settled down on the terrible scene as if to blot

> out the horror of the picture . . . strong men, although inspired by the excitement . . . frequently fell, fainting from fatigue, at their post, and were dragged away by detailed stretcher-bearers, to be placed under the shade of the trees. With lungs full of smoke, almost to the point of strangulation, the brave fellows swabbed the hot guns, stood like statues with thumbs on vent, and as the command "Fire!" rang out, fell back of the axle, and there, with brawny arms, hurled the heavy gun back from its recoil, and shouted with the strange joy of action.[49]

In his Donaldsonville Artillery war diary Levy wrote,

> Sunday, June 26th/64. Rose early and went with Deles[50] in search of milk which was procured at the very reasonable price of a dollar per quart. (By the way, the lacteal fluid was almost as much debased as the currency of the realm. After *au 'al fresco'* breakfast the cannoniers and horses enjoyed a bath in)[51] a beautiful limpid stream called Swift's Run, but the weather has become so intensely hot that the exercise incidental to the return to the bivouac destroyed all the good effects of the bath. I felt this morning that the only method of keeping cool was to "get out of one's flesh and sit down in his bones" as Sydney Smith so graphically expresses it.[52] The steady pounding of light field pieces on the left of our line, and an occasional bellow from the guns which were wantonly throwing shells into the city, continued until "night threw her sable mantle o'er the earth and pinned it with a star."

> Monday. 27th June . . . Bathed at dawn. Adjacent to the field in which our temporary camp has been established and bordering on the romantic Swift Run lies the beautiful estate of Mr. Dunlop.[53] Here amidst majest groves of oak, or in sweet summer houses, which are located so as to command the best views of the surrounding country, we lay and idle away time. Having become quite refreshed the boys are yearning for the excitement of battle and I believe that the most fervent prayers are offered up that we may be able to procure better guns and be again placed in the front.

> Tuesday. 28th June . . . A few drops of rain fell yesterday evening and the lightening had the effect of cooling and purifying the atmosphere. Feeling quite unwell I consulted Dr. Hill at the corps hospital and (he ascribed to too much salt food, and jestingly suggested a trip to the south of France).[54] On returning to the bivouac found that we had been ordered to report to Richardson on the right by nightfall. The guns went around town crossing the river at Campbell's Bridge.[55] I passed through the city in order to purchase a tooth brush and attend to some few commissions for the boys. Found that the damage done by the enemy's shells was inconsiderable, although the inhabitants appeared very much depressed in spirits at the sight of a few breaches in roofs and brick walls. The streets were almost deserted except in that portion of the city which had not been subjected to cannonading. There appeared to be a vast deal of sufferings among the poor, and as I awaited the appearance of the guns at the bridge, the opportunity presented itself for studying human nature. Sitting at a public pump to which a large number of persons resorted for water, I could not help being impressed by the faces of the women. They bore that quiet expression of intense suffering which is more indicative than the wails of agony. . . . By eight o'clock the guns were in park on a hill at the intersection of the Baylor Road and Halifax Street; here we remained during the night.[56]

When Prosper Landry and Penick's guns had been detached with Cutts's rifles and sent to Archer's Hill on June 19, the remainder of Richardson's Battalion passed through Petersburg and was assigned to a position on the defensive line near the right of the First Corps. Richardson, with Grandy and Moore's guns, occupied a salient at a junction of the new line with the old Dimmock works known as Rives's Salient. The position was, according to Private John Walters of Grandy's Battery, "A horrid one owing to the incessant shower of bullets that the enemy are constantly sending over, and to which the night gives us but little sleep."[57] In the eight days Grandy's guns were in position, despite the extensive earthworks, the battery suffered casualties of one killed and six wounded with several more being slightly wounded.

On reporting to Richardson on June 29, Prosper Landry was ordered to take the two Donaldsonville guns to the defensive salient after dark and replace Grandy's Norfolk artillerists, giving them some relief from the hazards and tedium of their position.

Levy recorded, "Pleasant weather after a very cool night. . . . No firing along the front this morning, even the miserable practice of sharpshooting had ceased by mutual consent. At dark we proceeded without our guns to Timothy Rives' farm by order of Col. Richardson in order to relieve the "Norfolk Blues" but Grandy very properly refused to withdraw from the line of battle unless his guns went with him. We had then the pleasure to return to camp after a fruitless walk of four miles."[58] Walters recorded that the Donaldsonville detachment was "not at all dissatisfied with the stand taken by our company."[59]

Before going to the defensive line Levy remarked that he "protested in the presence of the officers and company against being separated from my gun, a bad feeling was engendered in the breast of our stupid commander towards me."[60] Surely Private Levy's actions and comments did not make his commanding officer fond of him, and the next day, June 30, Levy noted, "At noon I was one of a party of ten men detailed for fatigue duty. We repaired to a pine grove near the front and cut and carried thirty logs for the purpose of building traverses."[61] If there was any animosity with his commander, it did not last for Levy would later characterize Prosper Landry as "an upright, honest gentlemen [*sic*]."[62]

Landry's section remained idle with its two guns in park on the hill at Baylors Lane and Halifax Street. Levy wrote,

> Friday. 1st July. The enemy increased their fire on the city this morning, several buildings were set on fire by the shells. Deles and myself took a walk into Petersburg this afternoon and . . . we found [many citizens] badly "bung stung" and on the point of leaving for Richmond. (Passes from our commanding officer allows us to visit the town for two hours at a stretch. The vivandiere is very much in evidence on these occasion, and her name is legion. Well! Eat, drink and be merry, for tomorrow.)[63]
>
> Saturday. 2nd July. As regards military affairs the programme was about as usual, there was desultory firing on the city resulting in some smashing up of buildings in the lower portions of the corporation. Deles and myself spent a couple of hours after dark in conversation with two Misses Scribner whose acquaintances we had accidentally formed. Innocent pastime, but not improving morally or mentally as the females were not well bred or dignified.[64]
>
> Sunday. 3rd July. Bathed and dressed early in the morning in order that I might run the blockade and attend church . . . met Willie Keiley,[65] now a member of Martin's battery, who asked me to accompany him to church, and afterwards to dinner, both very reasonable requests I acceded to. After service (which, by the way, was quite flat without sacred music), I escorted Miss Ellen Keiley[66] home where I met with a cordial reception on the part of Mrs. K. and Major Jack.[67] Enjoyed an excellent dinner and the pleasing conversation of the ladies during the afternoon.[68]
>
> On returning to camp found that marching orders had been received and by sun down the guns were in motion towards the front. My piece was planted on Tim Rives' farm on the Jerusalem Plank Road about 2 ½ miles distant from town. At this point the line of battle is formed about fifty yards in advance of Battery 27 of the regular city defenses.[69] The gun detachment worked until midnight and retired anticipating the enactment of a bloody drama on the morrow.[70]

Walters of Grandy's Battery noted in his diary, "Orders had been received along the line for great vigilance to be observed, as a charge is anticipated."[71]

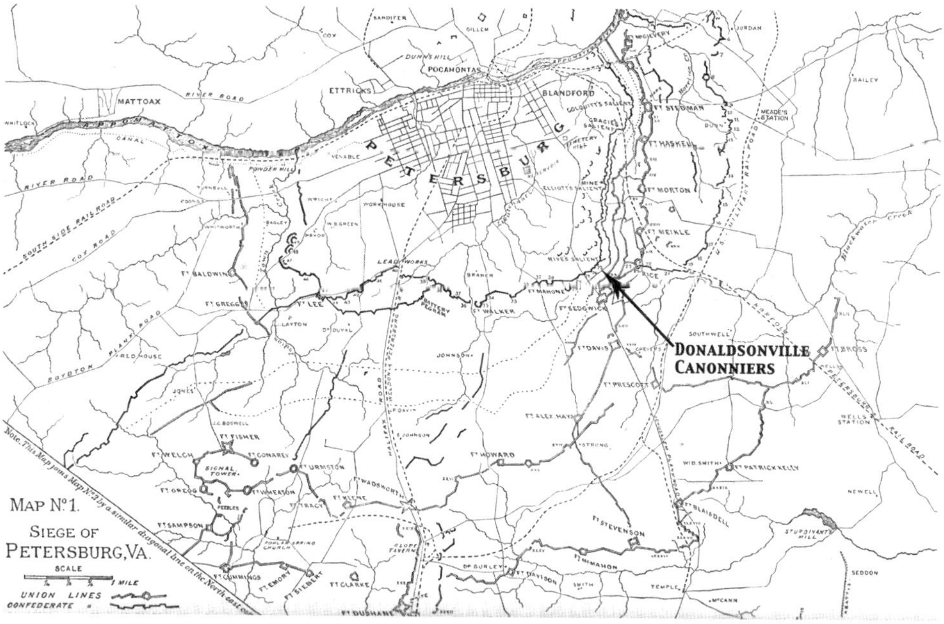

The Donaldsonville Artillery's position is located at Battery 25, Rives's Salient.
From *Battles and Leaders.*

The Fourth of July arrived after a night of being "vigilant" with "no sleep,"[72] wrote a soldier from Rives's Salient. With the weather hot and the dust intolerable in the trenches Levy recorded, "Contrary to universal expectations the once 'glorious fourth' was ushered in without the discharge of cannon. When the sun rose the Yankee bands favored us with a perfect hurricane of national airs, while the 'star spangled banner' floated from a thousand flag staffs. Seven standards were visible in front of my gun at a distance of six hundred yards. As a truce has been established between Wright's skirmishers[73] and the opposing pickets, the earthworks were lined with spectators and with the aid of Lt. Landry's glass I found myself confronted by a '<u>distinque</u>' looking group of officers who were also making use of field glasses."[74]

Levy added:

> Blue jays . . . shouted at and jeered their opponents in ludicrous style. The "hip, hip, hurrah!" of the Yankees sounded right hearty, founded, as the cry is, on plenty of good grub and whiskey galore; on our side the half-famished soldier would tighten his belt, so as to keep down the pangs of hunger, and give a sharp yell of defiance that sounded uncanning [*sic*] in that balmy Virginia air.[75]
>
> After sun down our brass bands and those of the enemy indulged in a musical duel. The Yanks played "Dixie" which we cheered; then followed "Yankee Doodle" which elicited groans and cat calls from our boys. At eight o'clock a pretty exhibition of fire works was visible in our front.[76]

A Mississippi infantryman at Rives's Salient this day recorded, "The enemy's line of battle and pickets are over 150 yards from us, but no shooting. Some of the boys exchanged papers, Tobacco &c with the Yankees, contrary to orders."[77]

"Life in the trenches has fairly begun," recorded Levy,

> The more is the pity of it. Our men have been, to a certain extent, demoralized by fighting under cover. They now betray a sort of nervousness as indicated by dodging

> shells, an involuntary motion in wondrous contrast to the reckless bravery displayed when fighting in the open. . . . The horrors of our daily life is beyond description . . . our shelters consist of two sheets of canvass or rubber cloth stretched over a cross-pole to protect us from the heavy dew; rain we can scarcely provide against. The dust of the inner ditch is intolerable, and, we take off our valuable shoes and try to drain the water down towards the covered way.
>
> Water is brought from an old well on the farm, and is so precious that half a canteen is considered a full allowance for the morning ablutions. Our simple breakfast of corn bread, rusty bacon and such other articles of prime necessity as our scant purses will permit is prepared in a frying pan over a small open fire; the boiling process is done in a tin cup. As the sharpshooters are comfortably lodged in trees opposite our position, every incautious movement away from the shelter of the earthworks is attended with peril.
>
> Forty yards in front of the works are the rifle pits, occupied by the ever-gallant pickets. All night long these tireless heroes are straining their eyes through the darkness to prevent a surprise, or firing at working parties of the enemy as the parallel approach creep towards us. At dawn a white cloth is elevated on a ramrod by one of the men on picket, as a sign of truce during the day, and this truce is held inviolate.
>
> Supplies are sent us by the covered way (a long, deep and wide ditch with a log and dirt roof that could protect and hide a man or a column of men) from the wagon camp, some miles in the rear; while the people of Petersburg, forced to trade on the necessities of the army, bring cakes, pies, fried chicken and other delicacies of the season for sale to the men. Whiskey is smuggled in that way . . . our amusements consist of reading, playing chess, checkers or cards. . . . On occasion when firing has ceased in our front by mutual consent, we scramble over the earthwork with haversack on shoulder and gather pieces of shell, solid shot and flattened lead bullets, which had been fired at us . . . this metal we "tote" to town when on leave of absence and sell to the ordnance department at 10 cents per pound. Thus fragments of shell are recast at Tredegar Iron Works at Richmond and shot back at their original owners within a week. The hard-earned money obtained from this source avails but little in buying the necessities of life, as salt and sugar are worth a dollar a pound, peas sixty dollars a bushel and a pair of red russet shoes cost a hundred dollars.[78]

In their redan at Rives's Salient, Levy continued to record in his journal the daily events in the trenches: "Tuesday. 5th July. We opened early this morning with six inch mortars which were promptly responded to; the firing took place on the left of our position. The bomb shells shrieking through the darkness of the night formed a magnificent spectacle."[79] Another combatant wrote, "Often, in the darkness, we were treated to brilliant displays, interesting in direct ratio to their distance. The mortar-firing always attracted attention. A flash at some distance . . . was followed by the hollow boom of the mortar, and a little spark of fire could be seen rising slowly into the air, describing a beautiful curve as it reached its height. Beginning to descend, it moved more and more rapidly, the hissing of the fuse sounding louder and louder as it came nearer. Suddenly, coincident with the explosion, came a flash that illumined the whole landscape, and the ensuing darkness could almost be felt."[80]

Levy wrote:

> Wednesday. July 6th. Visited the 12th V[irgini]a [Regiment] of Mahone's Brigade which holds a position on Wilcox's Farm, a mile to our right. Weather clear and windy. At dark we moved a hundred yards to the right to make room for one of Moore's guns. This placed my gun directly on the ruins of Tim Rives' house.[81] The operation of transferring the ammunition and altering the new earthwork kept the gun detachment up until past midnight. Rations decreased to a pound of meal and four ounces of meat.
>
> Thursday. 7th July. During the night the enemy in our front advanced a hundred yards

> and an immense earthwork greeted our eyes in the midst of the wheat field of old Rives' where none had appeared at the setting of the sun. It is evident that Grant has inaugurated the siege of Petersburg by parallel approaches in Vicksburg style. Harry Marks of the W. A. paid a visit and dined with me.[82] The guns on our right and left opened at different periods of the day and the enemy responded with alacrity and indicated great accuracy in gunnery."[83]

Walters observed that the new Yankee earthwork was a short distance to the left of his gun and added, "Our artillery opened a slow fire on them which, though it was returned at the rate of three shots to our one, put an end to their digging for the day.[84]

On July 8 Levy was happy to note,

> Borrowed Shakespeare from Miss Scribner and enjoyed my favorite play "Othello" during the morning. . . . At five o'clock P.M. in accordance with special instructions from Gen[era]l Mahone, each gun along the line opened fire (with "three rounds")[85] in order to develop the position of the Yankee artillery. There was a grand war chorus for about half and hour (the enemy "giving a very hot fire in return")[86] when, the object of the demonstration having been accomplished, quiet reigned along the line except on Longstreet's front. On our left the lines are so near each other that an incessant fusillade is kept up during the day and night. The shelling of Petersburg continues, the damage affected in some portions of the city is apparent; several fires have ignited from incendiary missiles, and, as yet, the brutal Grant has not notified the authorities to move non-combatants.
>
> Saturday. July 9th Within twenty yards of my gun stands a solitary locust tree, the sole representative of a once noble grove which graced the graceful lawn. Charred from the burning of the mansion, and torn by relentless cannon balls, truly "grand, gloomy, and peculiar," its glory has not all departed. Amidst a tuft of foliage which graces the topmost bough, there daily sits a mockingbird, which, with the rising of the sun, carols forth its superb madrigal until the first gun fires. What a subject for contemplation, this "glean of heaven," in the midst of the "pomp, pride, and circumstance" of glorious war! How painfully am I reminded by the winged messenger of peace of my once happy home in the far South!
>
> The gun detachment worked all day at the breast work which Major Miller had thought proper to remodel. Weather hot as blazes. In the afternoon we threw a few shells at the working parties whenever they appeared in our front. Repaired our embrasures with bags of sand. The cool nights and hot days which prevail at this season of the year conspire to make the low country in our front extremely unhealthy.
>
> Sunday, 10th July. A scouting party of Mississippians drew the fire of the Yankee line of battle at three o'clock this morning and caused all of us to get to our posts at a double quick. The affair lasted but a few minutes.[87]

Petersburg artillery.
From Battles and Leaders.

Walters clarified, "At early daylight our pickets, who had formed the foolish idea that during the night the enemy had left our front, advanced, but soon found out that they were mistaken by coming on the enemy's picket line. They however continued to advance until they had driven the enemy back to their main line, when they fell back to their old position."[88] One of the Mississippi pickets elucidated, "We all formed the opinion that the enemy made some kind of a movement . . . we heard trains rumbling in our front. Some thought we would find empty works before us in the morning, but were mistaken. A few shots from our pickets before day, called forth quite a volley from Yankeedom. Some exchanging of papers during the day. Relieved & returned to trenches after dark."[89]

After this affair Levy recorded,

> This being my day of recreation (two from each gun detachment being allowed to go to the rear each day) I visited Petersburg. Saw Gen[era]l Braxton Bragg at Jarratt's hotel.[90] He has become very haggard, gray, and careworn since last we met. His presence so near our line made me feel quite uncomfortable for he is a bird of ill omen in the sight of all soldiers. As success is the only criterion among warriors, Gen[era]l Bragg is unpopular in proportion to his misfortune[91] . . . Bought a nice snack at an eating house for $5 (that consisted of a plate of hash (no questions allowed as to ingredients) and pone of corn bread . . . but 25 cents silver is accepted as the equivalent of the Confederate currency).[92] Dropped in at Scribner's and soon retired in disgust . . . On reaching the gun found that she had been engaged during the day. The Yanks threw three missiles through our embrasure without hurting anyone.
>
> Monday. 11th July. This dear little mocking bird treated us to a delicious concert for two hours this morning. A very quiet day along the line. Weather oppressively hot.[93]

Lieutenant Prosper Landry, while commanding the Canonnier section, was still under arrest for not returning on time from leave back in May. "A thought," for Landry, "which made the hours drag still more heavily in the trenches. . . . Finally, on the 11th of July he received his commission of captain, 'to date from Major Maurin's promotion' on the 27th of February 1864."[94] Landry later wrote his wife: "I still did not know what would become of me when out of the blue sky . . . I received the special order announcing [I] was promoted to Captain . . . so my pay as captain of the artillery ($140.00 per month) was retroactive . . . but you know that it was the least of my worries."[95]

Now under the command of "Captain" Landry, Levy continued his account of the Donaldsonville Artillery's two guns in Rives's Salient at Petersburg.

> Tuesday. 12th July. The yanks continue to increase the strength of their works by day and night. Slight shower of rain last night. Nicaud[96] was kind enough to allow me to obtain a pass in place of himself and I started to the rear at six o'clock. Bathed and paid a visit to the Keiley family at whose house I was most agreeably entertained. Some soldiers under pretext of practicing played some tolerable music on the piano and violins. In return, the Misses Keiley and Dorothy sang some popular airs quite badly. Major Jack insisted that I should remain during the night and for the first time in many weeks, I rested securely between sheets undisturbed by sounds of war.[97]
>
> Wednesday. 13th July. Rose early and went to the caisson rendezvous at Bank's Farm . . . dined with Overby[98] at the caisson camp (washed and mended my ragged clothes; then went to town for an adventure)[99] and returned to my gun before dark. Found that the enemy had turned their twenty-four pounder mortars in the direction of Rives' House and the bombs had been falling thick and fast in the direction of my gun. One shell had buried itself in the embrasure (but little harm was done, except to some of the shelters in the ditch and on the inner slope of the ramparts).[100] After dark the Yanks threw about fifty shells at us but the best shot came within twenty feet of my shanty. Thanks to a merciful Providence no one was hurt as it is quite easy to trace the course of the bombs by the lighted fuse.[101]

By visiting the town and caisson camp that day Levy missed out on the day's work of building bomb proofs along the line. Walters recorded, "Our boys are mortally opposed to work" except when the mortar shells visited. Then they were "quite willing to build." Walters added "our work is very fatiguing as the clay is almost hard as a brick, and the weather intensely hot and no air stirring."[102]

In his journal Levy continued on Thursday, July 14, "Breakfast . . . bill of fare comprised pork and beans, corn bread, with coffee. Our boys have exchanged papers with the enemy's pickets."[103] At this time a Mississippian noted, "We read each others papers in fifteen minutes after the newsboys bring them up from the offices. The boys deal considerable with them [the Yankee pickets] for various little articles such as coffee, knives, pipes, writing paper and envelopes."[104]

About their rations that July in the trenches at Rives's Salient another of the Magnolia State soldiers wrote, "At this time, we are getting tolerable good rations of flour, bacon, tea, rice, sugar and coffee. Things are very high [in price] up here. A month's wages will not get a man's dinner. Peas is selling at two dollars a quart, onions a dollar fifty and two dollars a piece, and every other thing at the same proportion."[105]

Levy continued with his entry, "William Morrison of the 12th Virginia supped with me. Rec[eive]d pay for the months of January and February, $24."[106]

The Donaldsonville Artillery diarist also recorded on July 14, "Gen[era]l Lee appeared among us for the first time since we have taken position on this line. In company with Mahone he mounted the earthwork in front of my gun and reconnoitered the enemy's position."[107] Levy noted,

> How the boys worship General Lee, whose calm, handsome face and noble mien command reverence! Always in undress uniform on these occasions, and with a couple of orderlies holding the horses near by, he looks the personification of modest dignity. He always has a pleasant word for the officers or privates near whose quarters he chances to rest, while inspecting through his field glasses the powerful siege guns of the enemy's fortifications within the sweep of his vision. A. P. Hill, pale and delicate-featured, is at the side of the great leader . . . and little "Billy" Mahone . . . they confer with great earnestness . . . and at its conclusion General Lee mounted his horse, shook hands with Hill and Mahone, bowed to the group of officers and men . . . and rode back towards the city.
>
> As Hill was about to leave . . . an irreverent Creole cried out, "Cut that curl!" alluding to a stray fragment of his ambrosial locks that straggled from his kepi down the middle of his forehead. The cry was taken up . . . and "Cut that curl!" echoed for miles along the front of the Third Corps.[108]

Levy's entries continued,

> Friday, 15th July. Heavy artillery duel on our left in direction of Chesterfield Heights, all serene in our immediate front. The pickets refused to exchange papers this morning and the inference is that the Yanks do not desire us to find out how successful Early has been.[109] Pleasant day and very cool night. Dual between the mortar batteries at sunset which produced some excitement.
>
> Saturday. 16th July. A distinguished group gathered near my shanty this morning and held a conference. The party consisted of Gen[era]ls Lee, R. H. Anderson, A. P. Hill, Fields, Mahone, and Heath.[110]

Walters recorded the "military talents" were, "just in the rear of my gun, and who were viewing the operations of the enemy and discussing their movements. I felt uncomfortable the whole time they were there, fearing that the enemy might discover the group and throw a shell into it, but this did not occur. The day passed off very quietly. The enemy are as busy as beavers in strengthening their works, though we send a few shell among them occasionally to disturb the monotony of the day."[111]

The right end gun of Prosper Landry's section and left end gun of Grandy's Battery were located next to each other. Coincidently it seems, the Canonnier diarist Levy and the Blues diarist Walters were assigned to that respective gun where the batteries connected in the entrenchments. Moore's Norfolk Battery was located on the other side of Grandy's.

Of Rives's Salient and the enemy line, Major Charles Richardson later wrote, "As from a horrid dream I wake to find 'Fort Hell' just opposite me, and 'Fort Damnation' a little to our right—goodness, what a fearful environment. The fort confronting us was named Fort Sedgwick, the one on our right Fort Mahone, but some of our facetious men applied to them those diabolic titles."[112] Levy wrote,

> A short distance to the [right] of our position, and advance of the main line of field works, is an immense seven-gun lunette, shaped like a fish hook, which is "No. 29" in official parlance, but its garrison has dubbed it by a less euphonious title. Opposite this [Confederate] salient, at a distance of about 400 feet, is a federal fort, mounting several Thirty-two-pound rifled guns, that has gained a resounding sobriquet. When one opens on working parties, or sweeps the front preparatory to a dash of our pickets the other always has a finger in the pie; then we little fellows, with light field pieces, are signaled to fire on the guns parapets on both sides; an occasional lucky shot enters an embrasure and injures or dismounts a gun, when a wild shout of triumph makes the welkin ring above the roar of big and little guns.[113]

"To day is more quiet than the other days of the week," wrote a Mississippi diarist doing picket duty on Sunday, July 17. " Both sides seem to have some regard of late for the quietude and observance of the Sabbath. Dust is still supreme."[114] Levy's attentive writings continued this day with, "The enemy continues to erect new works and strengthen his old ones by day and night. A drunken Yankee picket came down to within ten feet of our vedettes and, although ordered off, continued to harangue our men on the war question much to the

Confederate trenches at Petersburg.
Courtesy of the Library of Congress.

amusement of the spectators who crowned the ramparts on both sides."

"Monday, 18th July," Levy recorded, "There was to have been a charge made by Field's division (1st Corps) before day this morning but the design was frustrated by the desertion of some of our pickets. This is another evidence of the demoralization of our men which I take to be the natural consequence of being so long kept behind breastworks."[115] Walters added, "At early daylight we saw that the enemy had been crowding their works on our left with men during the night, and learned subsequently that four men of Field's Division had deserted to the enemy." Walters added that previously "several men belonging to the 64th Georgia Regiment, Wright's Brigade, who were on picket in our front, deserted to the enemy . . . this is getting to be somewhat of a common practice with this regiment, who are mostly of the new issue and have but lately joined the brigade."[116]

"Tuesday. 19th July," continued Levy,

> The enemy's mortar shells troubled us a good deal early this morning. One of these terrible missiles came very near to my head and fell about ten feet beyond my shanty. I had just time to throw myself on the ground when it burst tearing up the ground all around it. I experience no inconvenience except a slight nervous shock and a ringing in the ears. Rain set in at seven o'clock and continued until 5 P.M. much to the gratification of everyone for the dust had become intolerable and vegetation was suffering very much on account of the protracted drought. Went to Petersburg, slept on the portico of Jarratt's hotel (among a crowd of jolly, noisy soldiers.)[117]
>
> Wednesday. 20th July. Arose early, bathed in the Appomattox [River] and changed my clothing. Had a cup of tea made at a private house and was kindly furnished with bread to accompany the beverage . . . dined . . . at a restaurant. Steak, bread, eggs, and coffee; cost $15 . . . in the afternoon I visited Miss Helen Schribner and at dark returned to the front."[118]

While Levy was returning to the lines, Walters was going to town on a permit. For the day he documented, "Nothing was done on the line till this afternoon when the enemy opened a brisk artillery fire on our position, during which they wounded two or three of the infantry who hold our line. Our artillery opened in reply and shortly after, both sides ceased."[119]

The next day Levy wrote, "Formed an acquaintance of Capt. Rush, Lieut. and Sgt. Levy, and all of the 22nd Ga. Regt., Wright's Brigade . . . they live at Augusta, Gea.[120] (The news of the removal of General Joe Johnston from command of the Army of Tennessee has caused a very uneasy feeling in this army. When we remember his admirable conduct of the retreat from Yorktown, the battle of Williamsburg and the Battle of Seven Pines, our special wonder is evoked).[121] Ran the blockade to town at sundown in order to have the ringworm on my face painted with iodine. Spent the evening with Miss Helen Scribner and reached the front by midnight."[122] Clearly the Shakespeare book given to Levy changed his mind about Miss Scribner being of a lower class. Levy never addressed the issue again and continued to associate with the lady.

On July 22 Levy recorded, "The skirmishing on the left in front of Longstreet's Corps was continually heavy until daylight this morning."

Years later Levy, with help from his diary, would reminiscence about this day, "The rattle of musketry seldom has the effect of disturbing the repose of those of us who are not immediately interested; it is only when the dead and wounded are carried over the field works in the vicinity of our guns that sympathy is fully aroused, and the boys lend a helping hand. On these occasions our crude knowledge of surgery, gained by observation and experience on so many battlefields, rendered us helpful to our comrades."[123]

Levy's diary notes continued, "Lowenstein, his brother,[124] and Sgt. Jack Levy dined with me today. Pork and beans, corn bread, and rice with sugar constituted the bill of fare. Huge preparations on the part of the enemy and corresponding defensive tactics on our side continue to be carried on by night and day. There is a perfect calm in the immediate front of Hill's Corps while lively skirmishing designates the position of Longstreet's troops."[125]

Levy remembered too,

> On our side fatigue duty at night has become the rule, our attention being devoted mainly to adding entanglements to the abbatis in front our works. Can it be that Grant expects his legions to attempt the direct assault again?[126]
>
> Saturday. 23rd July. Forwarded my application for furlough for having furnished a recruit in the person of C. Besson[127] on the 8th of June. Hood, the successor of Joseph E. Johnston, has met with a partial success in front of Atlanta. The troops appear to be very much encouraged of this sudden and unexpected result.[128]
>
> Sunday. 24th July. Had some excellent bread prepared in town (made to order by a skillful darky)[129] and had the pleasure to entertain at dinner Capt. Rush and Lieut. Levy of the 22nd Ga. Also Lieut. Phillips[130] and Lowenstein, 12th Va. [the nearest supporting regiments to the Donaldsonville guns] the affair passed off in a very satisfactory manner. (Our guest were amused at night by the singing of French songs around the camp fire by the glee club of the (Canonnier) company).[131] Miss Helen Scribner sent me a fine home made cake which proved quite acceptable. Prices of edibles are rising daily. I was forced to pay $2.25 per [pound] for flour and $3 for a quart of cowpeas. Rain set in at 5 o'clock P.M. and continued throughout the night. As a severe wind prevailed the occupants of my shanty were soon drenched to the skin and we had no remedy but to grumble until dawn.
>
> Monday. 25th July. Arose perfectly chilled through by the cruel East wind and, after a fruitless attempt to light a fire, crouched into a dark corner of the bomb proof and dozed for half an hour. Crawled up to a comrade's fire and suffered from smoke and cold until the glorious sun shone out. Letters from the home folks . . . at Mobile, warmed the cockles of our hearts. Procured the approval of Capt. Landry and Lt. Col. Richardson to my application for furlough. My time having come around to enjoy a day of liberty I bathed and visited the Keiley family. Passed the evening at the chess board and enjoyed a comfortable bed.
>
> Tuesday. July 26 . . . Dined at a snack house, $5 for a plate of Irish stew accompanied by cold bread. After another game of chess with little Ben Keiley[132] I started for the lines, stopping on the way to see my acquaintances of the 22nd Ga. Regt. I had to promise that I would return after nightfall before Capt. Rush would allow me to proceed. Played whist[133] and euchre[134] until past midnight and decided to spend the balance of the night with the boys as it was very dark.
>
> Wednesday. 27th. The enemy opened an enfilading battery on our position and continued to annoy us throughout the day. A thirty-two pounder shell fell within six feet of my shelter after having passed through the top of the earthwork; through the grace of God (the fuse proved defective) it did not explode (or the intruder would have blown some of us to "kingdom come.")[135] In the vicinity of my gun considerable damage was done to tents and their contents. A little fellow belonging to Finnegan's [Florida] division had the top of his skull blown off (as cleanly as if cut with a knife)[136] when coming from the well and while a song quivered upon his lips. Another poor devil lost a leg and still another his arm, all within sight of my shelter. I busied myself during the morning with washing socks and composing a little "pasquinade";[137] truly this expression comprises the sublime and ridiculous. . . . Large details from the infantry work daily at strengthening the fortifications of both armies. . . . All of the Third Corps except Anderson's division has left this line. Heath's [Henry Heth] division left yesterday and its position is now occupied by Wright's brigade in single file.[138]

Levy later added, "It appears like our infantry support is reduced to one poor, starved reb every 10 feet of earthwork. Having the interior line, we can re-enforce any threatened point through the covered ways at short notice, and, again, we have supreme confidence in the ability of "Marse Bob" to do the right thing at the right time. It does seem, however, that, with all his genius and prescience, he cannot prevail much longer against the enormous mass of men and guns opposed to us. New batteries of heavy siege guns are being uncovered by the enemy."[139]

In alluding to new battery positions another combatant wrote, "The lines of fire from the several batteries were soon understood, and when we saw a puff of smoke, and an instant later heard the roar of the heavy gun, we could at least approximate the objective point of the shell. Occasionally a new battery would be placed in position, and the line of flight of its projectiles would be unknown. 'One stands with eyes and mouth open, every sense alert. Where will it drop? We soon learn, and if not too uncomfortably near, we burrow no farther on account of that battery.'"[140]

Of the casualties suffered in the trenches another Confederate remarked, "Even the death of [a] soldier is looked on as one of those inevitable results of War and a man drops out of the ranks and is scarcely spoken of, after a few minutes. I hear men talking, laughing & singing when two were killed an hour ago and they appear as unconcerned as if nothing had happened."[141]

"There must be a special Providence watching over our [Donaldsonville] battery," wrote Levy, "for, while hardly a day passes but that Grandy's or Moore's batteries, our neighbors . . . have some of their gallant men to mourn, we pass unscathed through the same dangers. Looking back through the numerous battles and skirmishes . . . we have been engaged, from the siege of Yorktown to the present time, it does appear remarkable that our loss by wounds and death has been comparatively small. 'Le bon Dieu' [the good God] and divers patron saints are supposed to exercise especial care of the men of this battery, if heaven ever intervenes in such affairs as the wholesale murder which was dignified by the name civil war."[142]

"This evening," continued Levy on July 27,

> Capt. Landry turned in his section of Richmond Parrots and received in their stead two fine Napoleon's which were immediately placed in position. (Being so close to the enemy (now about 800 feet distant as well as we can judge), the risk of a quick rush is more immanent from a vigilant foe, and these smooth-bore guns can spit canister and spherical case as fast as we can feed it to them in the event of an uninvited intrusion on the part of the Yankees).[143] I ran the block at dusk and paid a visit to Miss Helen Scribner in order to thank her for the nice cakes which she had sent, and returned by ten o'clock. A light rain fell during the night.
>
> Thursday. 28th July. News of a splendid victory by Early over Crook in the Valley has inspired me with fresh hope as to the speedy termination of the campaign.[144] The enemy had the impertinence to relieve their pickets at noon, (instead of at nightfall, as is customary. What is up?)[145] We had no orders to fire upon them. In the course of the afternoon I sauntered up to the right of the line and after visiting my friends in the 12th Va., spent the evening with Lowenstein and his messmates.
>
> Friday. 29th July. Lieut. Levy spent the morning and dined with me . . . .in the afternoon a number of friends from the Twelfth Virginia dropped in for a visit. Some brought rations with them, while we contributed soup and bread to the Lucullan feast. Strange fact that these infantrymen, seasoned veterans as they are, dodged every time a cannon ball or shell whizzed over their heads as they sat at dinner, deep down in the trenches.[146]

> The gun detachment was aroused at 2 A.M. [July 30] in anticipation of an assault as a deserter had brought the information that the Feds were clearing decks for action. Of course, every eye was strained in the direction of the opposing lines and shortly after sunrise, perceiving no indication of the charge, we were heartily cursing the Yank for having disturbed our repose. Suddenly the earth appeared to throb beneath our feet and a moment after, as if a volcano had burst from the bowls of the land (200 yards to my left) men, wheels, spades, logs, vast boulders of earth, and an indiscernible debris obscured the rising sun.[147]

Walters, next to the Donaldsonville guns, recorded, "As day brightened all eyes were strained to discover the movements in the Yankee lines, but scarcely a man could be seen there . . . in this suspense, the minutes glided by until a quarter to five o'clock when a dull noise and heavy shock of the earth caused us to look around, when a singularly horrid sight presented itself about three quarters of a mile on our left, which was no less than the going upward of a huge mass of earth, together with logs, guns, wheels, limber chest, muskets, and men."[148]

As if in unison Levy and Walters in their diaries exclaimed, "The enemy had sprung a mine on us!"[149]

Levy added,

> While we yet stood transfixed with horror at the appalling spectacle a crash of artillery came whizzing, shrieking, tearing at us. In a moment every man was at his post awaiting orders to fire and, as no orders came to the troops in the vicinity of my gun, all hands kept low down behind the works. The cheers and volley's of the assaulting column which entered the breech opened by the mine, while our infantry in the immediate vicinity were confused at the horrible accident, rose high above the combined thunders of cannon and mortars and the shrill whistle of the rifle balls. Unfortunately, the embrasure for my gun led in the opposite direction from the point of attack so that the men looked eagerly for the enemy to appear on our right.[150]

Petersburg Sunrise. The exploding of the Yankee mine on July 30, 1864.
ARW; courtesy of the Library of Congress.

When the explosion occurred, Walters's account described how, "At the moment of doing so they opened a furious cannonading all along our line, while their sharpshooters and skirmishers rained over a shower of bullets. At the same time they threw forward heavy columns of their troops on the portion that they had breached, who succeeded in taking possession of our shattered breastworks and portions immediately adjoining the opening, from which they poured an enfilading fire on our men who held the works, and who were soon forced to fall back to a second line which we had there."[151]

What Levy and Walters were writing about was the 4:44 a.m. explosion of a mine excavated and filled with explosives placed through a tunnel to and under the Confederate works. Dug by the Union's Forty-eighth Pennsylvania Infantry Regiment, which was composed largely of coal miners, it blew a crater in the Southern defensive line 170 feet long, 60 to 80 feet wide, and 30 feet deep. The exploitation by Federal troops failed, as the reaction of Confederate soldiers was exemplary.[158]

Levy later wrote,

> I was leaning carelessly against the front of the embrasure a solid shot struck the earthwork with sufficient force to give me a severe blow in the back. Ten minutes after, while I was watching the enemy, a shell burst just in front of my face forcing gravel and splinters into my face and throat, only one small fragment of the missile striking a glancing blow on my ribs just below the right breast. The shock turned me quite around and I immediately assured my companions that I was not badly hurt. A little water soon cleared my right eye sufficiently that I might discern objects, and when the fire of the enemy had slackened, I started for Petersburg accompanied by Doc [his brother].
>
> When about a mile from the front I met Gen[era]l Lee and staff and drawing up on the side of the road made the military salute. My noble commander checking his horse, remarked in a tone which indicated profound sympathy, "My friend, I hope you are not badly hurt?" This exhibition of his noble nature overcame me; I answered "No General, thank God!" and passed quickly on to avoid his beholding the tear of gratitude which coursed down my cheek. Can it be wondered at that this man has won our hearts and minds? Opposed as I am to hero worship I shall never utter the name of Robert E. Lee unless with respect and veneration.[152]

Upon entering Petersburg Levy recorded,

> A Mr. Weeks who lives at the head of Sycamore St.[153] insisted on bathing my face and would have forced me to stay at his house but that I insisted on going to the hospital. No ambulances or other conveyance presented itself so that I was forced to walk to the "Confederate Hospital" on Washington Street.[154] My appearance was such on arriving at this institution that I was immediately dubbed "Beauty" and being in fine spirits, I commenced a flirtation with the good looking Miss Winnifry,[155] matron of my ward. In less than a minute I was rendered comparatively comfortable. Doc, who had done everything to promote my ease which brotherly affection could dictate left me to return to the front. Dr. Ward,[156] who had charge of the hospital, was an acquaintance of Doc's so that I soon procured a promise to be transferred to Richmond as soon as my eyesight should be restored. As the wounded from the battle came pouring in, the immense tobacco factory was soon crowded to it's utmost capacity and it became impossible to procure proper attention. I took a little milk at supper time as the condition of my mouth would not admit of indulgence in more substantial food. Notwithstanding that night was made hideous by the sounds of sorrow and anguish, I managed to enjoy a delicious repose.[157]

During the day at Rives's Salient Walters recorded the Federals "kept up their fire on our line till nearly sunset," adding, "one of our corporals was instantly killed by a large shell striking him in the head, taking the whole top off from the tongue upward."[159] Other

Donaldsonville Artillery casualties were Private William Ely, Levy's friend and messmate, wounded seriously in the arm by the same shell that struck Levy,[160] and twenty-year-old Donaldsonville native, Corporal Arthur Comstock, who received a gunshot wound in the arm and side during the battle. His injuries were slight, and Comstock, who "served in every major engagement," remained with his comrades.[162]

The next day, July 31, Levy wrote from his hospital bed:

> Doc appeared early this morning bearing the gratifying intelligence that our old division had driven the enemy at every point and succeeded in reestablishing our line as it was before the assault of yesterday. On this occasion, for the first time, Anderson's Division (Mahone commanding) mingled black and white Yankees in a common grave. Among the prisoners were over 200 negro soldiers who we forced to go in front of the works and carry in our dead and wounded. The courteous Capt. Rush and the gallant Lieutenant Levy were numbered among many choice spirits who on the fatal Saturday "Slept the sleep that knows no waking." Peace to their ashes![163]

Donaldsonville Private Albert Schmidt visited the wounded and half-blind Levy a day after the battle and wrote in Levy's diary: "How the ministering angels, those venerated women of the Confederacy, were there, to aid the surgeons and prayerfully close the eyes of the dead heroes."[164] Levy remembered, "Ah! those dear patriotic Virginia women! What an ever-present inspiration their self-sacrifice affords!"[165]

On this "hot and oppressive,"[166] July 31, 1864, a Louisiana artillery officer wrote, "This morning Gen. Lee allowed Gen. Grant an armistice of three hours, to bury his dead, left in front of our works after the explosion of the mine. A long trench was dug equidistant between our works and the enemy's, and the negro prisoners were made to carry the dead bodies to the trench and throw them in. . . . At the expiration of the three hours a signal-gun was fired, and the armistice ended."[167]

Chapter Sixteen

Grand Événements
(Great Events)

While one section of the Donaldsonville Artillery under the command of Lieutenant Prosper Landry was marching to Spotsylvania Court House on May 15, 1864, the Donaldsonville Artillery's other section of 10-pounder Parrott rifles under Lieutenant Camille Mollere remained at Gordonsville for another week. Since the town was exposed and had been threatened by possible enemy cavalry attacks, Mollere was ordered to relocate south by train to Charlottesville, twenty-two miles away, with his section of guns, forty-three Canonniers, and fourteen horses. After leaving Gordonsville on May 24, the train carrying the Canonniers passed Lindsey's Turnout and Cobham Station and rattled along through a beautiful region composed of low mountains and hills, the tracks coming to and following Mechunk Creek into Charlottesville.

The city of Thomas Jefferson and home of the University of Virginia was situated among the red clay foothills of the Blue Ridge Mountains and was an important east-west railroad junction. The small market town had a central court square surrounded by a jail, courthouse, taverns, library, post office, small stores, and homes, and a storage depot for commissary supplies. Most of the university's buildings (one mile west of the town) were by this time used as hospitals. Temporary structures had also been built to take care of and look after Confederate wounded.

The three thousand residents of Charlottesville were "news starved" and a "community of mourning,"[1] but to artillerymen they were known to be "very hospitable and kind."[2] Soap and tobacco was liberally distributed to the soldiers, though fine seven-year-old Killickinick smoking tobacco cost $1.50 per pound.[3] Beef, bacon, sugar, vinegar, cabbage, turnips, chicken, and yeast were issued rations.[4] The patriotic young ladies of the town were known to give out treats such as "ice cream, cherries, and ice water" though a few soldiers preferred something stronger.[5] The town's pure water was "something," wrote one soldier, "that I like better."[6]

The stay of Mollere's Donaldsonville Artillery detachment no doubt was enjoyable and agreeable, what with the Charlottesville hospitality and peaceful beauty of the area, but after just one week of ease in the university town instructions were received to bring the Gunners of Donaldson section via railroad to Lynchburg, a "rendezvous point."[7] On June 1 the Canonniers, their two guns, caissons, and few horses were again loaded onto cars of the Orange and Alexandria Railroad. After boarding, the train's engine shook and coughed, groaned and creaked, and began moving southbound. It pulled away with heavy black smoke pouring forth from the locomotive, the feet of the Canonniers shuddering on the floor beneath them as the iron wheels clattered along the tracks. Traveling through the foothills of the Blue Ridge Mountains, the tracks descended into the flattened South Piedmont section of Virginia. The Louisiana artillerists took in the sights of the hills, apple orchards, and plains as the train went through meadows and fields, and passed scattered farm houses and hedges over culverts and bridges with the engine's shrill steam whistle sounding often. The engine's smokestack belched forth its dense, murky cloud of smoke and, like all trains pulling passenger, box, and flat cars, made regular stops for cords of wood set alongside the tracks and water at water tanks.

After three and a half hours covering forty-nine miles, the placid town of Amherst Court House, surrounded by farms, was reached, then a high hillside town called Monroe, with a cluster of houses. The train continued on and again descended from the foothills to the Orange Bridge across the James River at Daniel's Island. The sixty mile, four hour and fifteen minute journey[8] from Amherst ended by crossing the trestle and then paralleling the river basin and Kanawha Canal for one final mile before stopping at an end of the line rail station located in the city of Lynchburg. Here the tracks and gentle hill concluded at a chasm where the Blackwater Creek flowed into the James River.[9]

Mollere's detachment unloaded at the city of "Seven Hills" [10] that served as a major supply depot for the Confederacy and a hub to Virginia's railroads. Lynchburg was one huge medical complex, with tobacco factories and warehouses along with the Fairgrounds building converted into hospitals housing hundreds of wounded. Churches, tents, meeting halls, and homes in the city took care of the overflow patients.[11]

After detraining, Mollere reported to Lynchburg's military district commander, Brigadier General Francis T. Nicholls, a Donaldsonville native.[12] Major Victor Maurin was here too, worn out, reticent, and now aged beyond his years. Nicholls, missing an arm and a leg from battle wounds, no doubt exchanged sentimental tidings, after which he informed Mollere that he anticipated a possible enemy move on Lynchburg that was a "real threat to the town."[13] Nicholls planned to guard the approaches by having small earthworks erected on the different roads leading into the city but to man them he only had a force of 1,300 men. This outfit was made up of reserves and convalescent soldiers, and now, boasted Nicholls—"a portion of the Donaldsonville Artillery."[14]

Nicholls signed requisitions to liberally supply the Donaldsonville men and their few horses with rations and fuel and instructed them "to remain at this post until further orders."[15] At the railroad depot was an artillery park where they could secure and refit their guns and equipment.

After settling in the Canonnier detachment had "little to do."[16] They met with many people in the city who were acquaintances from Louisiana and they watched the "ladies promenading"[17] and had "a good social chat."[18] They sang the latest music, read, and enjoyed the high quality of Lynchburg's tobacco. The town still "reeked of tobacco from one end to the other."[19] The only entertainment advertised in the city newspaper was The Army Book Store at 115 Main Street, where one could purchase *Joseph II and his Court,* $7.50; *Lady Audley's Secret* (by Miss Braddon), $5.00; *Eleanor's Victory,* $5.00; *Macaria* (by Miss Evans, Mobile), $5.00; *Mrs. Lirripper's Lodgings* (by Dickens), 3.00; *No Name* (by Willie Collins), $5.00; *A Strange Story* (by Bulwer), $5.00; *The Aid-de-Camp-Romance of the War,* $3.00; *Clarimonde-Tale of New Orleans Life,* $1.50; *The Bohemian,* $1.00; *Wild Western Scenes,* $1.50; and *The Confederate,* $1.50, "together with a large lot of Miscellaneous Books and Military Works."[20]

Of Lynchburg in the summertime it was written that the "sun poured terrible heat upon the broad James River, which, opposite the network of tracks at the depot, flowed placidly at the base of an immense cliff . . . a few rafts and flatboats, steered by bared-armed and bareheaded negroes, drifted lazily on the stream . . . and, in the distance, were blue outlines of mountains, with tiny cloud-wreaths around them."[21] The city's streets, many filled with tobacco warehouses, sloped towards the river. The streets, a Confederate noted "are generally very narrow besides, many of the buildings are old and untasty in their design."[22]

On June 11 Nicholls received word that the railroad between Lynchburg and Charlottesville was cut. Two days later it was reported that 3,500 enemy cavalry were heading towards Amherst Court House, from which they could move on Lynchburg. Word was also received that the enemy's main column of 15,000 troops had already captured Lexington.[23] The fear that Lynchburg would be next prompted Nicholls to urgently send off a message to Richmond: "I earnestly request re-enforcements."[24]

In the meantime excitement prevailed in the city. The *Lynchburg Virginian* reported, "It was apprehended that an effort would be made by the enemy to reach this city, and accordingly the forces [detailed men, convalescent soldiers, reserve, second class militia and volunteers] were collected and marched to the defenses outside of the city."[25] While nearly every able bodied man was now under arms and busy making trenches,[26] Nicholls supplied Maurin with twenty-one additional horses and instructions that the two Donaldsonville guns move to the crest of Daniel's Hill and fortify. This position overlooked the Orange and Alexandria Railroad tracks on the Orange Bridge that crossed the James River at Daniel's Island, a point the enemy's cavalry, coming from Amherst, could reach by following the tracks.[27]

Forty-three Canonniers, guided by Maurin and Mollere, and eleven servants and laborers, along with thirty-five horses, and two Parrott rifles and caissons ascended the lofty hill along the farm road that enveloped them in a cloud of suffocating dust. They passed Judge Daniel's Point of Honor and Rivermont, a two-story Greek Revival manor surrounded by farmland, where one "enjoyed an unparalleled view down the valley of the James."[28] After reaching the heights near the bluffs overlooking the river and railroad bridge (northwest of Rivermont) two earthworks were constructed and the guns placed in position.[29]

For the next couple of days the Canonniers remained watchful with their only duties being the hauling of corn and hay to feed the horses and stoking their cooking fires with firewood issued by the quartermaster department.[30] The tracks from Charlottesville were repaired and open, and around one o'clock in the evening of June 17 the first of several locomotive whistles were heard. The Donaldsonville gunners on top of Daniel's

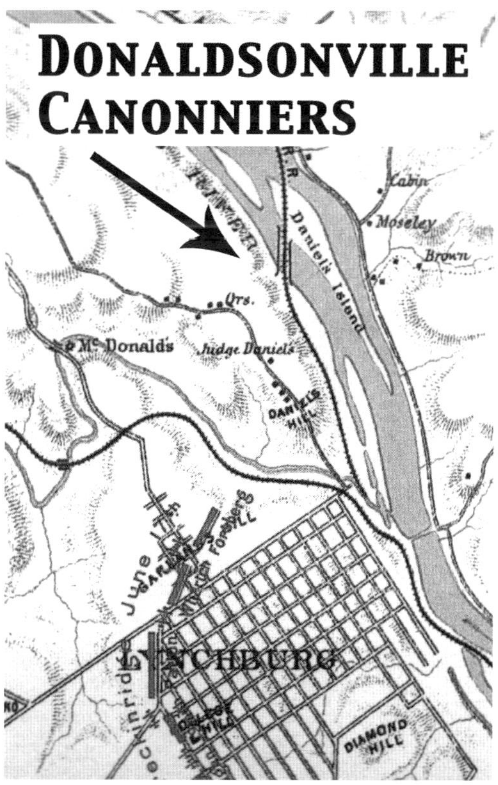

The position of the Canonnier guns and two earthwork at Lynchburg. From *Atlas of OR*.

Hill looked down upon the first of several trains coming out of the hills and crossing the trestle towards Lynchburg, their engines screeching and snorting while pulling passenger, freight, flat, and baggage cars filled with gray and butternut-clad troops who leaned out the sides and sat on top the cars. Several more trains soon followed with more the next day bringing a total of 8,000 soldiers from Lee's Army of Northern Virginia's Second Corps under Major General Jubal A. Early's command. His orders were to attack the considerably larger Yankee force threatening the city.[31]

The enemy under Major General David Hunter attacked Lynchburg on the afternoon of June 18 before all the Second Corps arrived; however, Early, with the assistance of Major General John C. Breckenridge's Division, reported the attacking Federal force "was handsomely repulsed with considerable loss to the enemy."[32] Nicholls himself commanded a small group guarding one approach to Lynchburg while Maurin and the Gunners of Donaldson remained on post overlooking and guarding the important trestle.[33]

With the threat of an attack lessened and Early's infantry pursuing the retreating Federals on June 19, Nicholls now resumed his duties as the Lynchburg Military District commander. Besides Lynchburg the other most important point in the district was near Farmville at the High Bridge, a lofty railroad trestle built in 1853 as part of the South Side Railroad that joined the cities of Petersburg and Lynchburg, with a spur of the Richmond and Danville Railroad at Burkeville Junction leading to Richmond. Previously, on May 8, 1864, Nicholls ordered ten companies of Virginia reserves from local counties to duty and organized them into a regiment (Third Virginia Reserves) under the command of Colonel Richard A. Booker.[34] These companies assisted (with slave labor) in the construction of fortifications at both ends of High Bridge, and Booker's troops remained to protect the railroad crossing.[35] On June 22 Nicholls ordered Mollere's section and their two Parrott rifles "sent to High Bridge, Prince Edward County, at which point for the protection of said High Bridge it [was to] remain."[36]

The two guns and caissons, with twenty-seven horses and the majority of Canonniers under Mollere, marched down Daniel's Hill and across the wooden bridge over Blackwater Creek into Lynchburg. There they boarded a South Side Railroad train at the Percival Island Depot and began a seventy-two mile journey that was relatively easy through pleasant and gently sloping country. About halfway along the route the train made one of its frequent stops to get water and wood at Appomattox Station not far from its courthouse. It was just another depot the Gunners of Donaldson assuredly took no notice of even though they had passed through it once before in '61.

Continuing on for another thirty-three miles, the train came to Farmville, a town alongside the Appomattox River with "the stamp of a New England town in the vivacity of it streets."[37] It now had some 1,500 inhabitants, many of whom were refugees, a long and busy main street, large tobacco warehouses, the Farmville Female College, and a 1,200-bed Confederate hospital complex located in tobacco warehouses and factories.[38]

Northeast of Farmville the tracks made a gradual incline while paralleling the Appomattox River past woods, green fields, and pasture for four miles, at which point they came to the majestic High Bridge spanning the Appomattox River valley. The span was constructed of twenty brick piers that varied in height from sixty feet at the abutment to 125 feet near the river and supported the tracks on a wooden superstructure stretching 2,400 feet from the bluff in Prince Edward County to the bluff in Cumberland County.[39]

The train stopped before crossing, and the Donaldsonville artillerists and their guns disembarked beside the western end of the bridge near the John Mottley Overton home, where passengers and freight normally unloaded. Here the Canonniers took in the scenic and broad view of the area with the Appomattox River below the span, the valley's cultivated farmlands, and the distant mountains. They were greeted by Booker's reserve troops who guarded and manned the bridge's four casemated earthworks.[40] Mollere's artillerymen set up their bivouac about a hundred yards from Overton's home, across from but within fifty yards of the tracks. The Canonniers were comfortably lodged in log cabins. With fresh water only a hundred yards away at a creek, the place was soon called by the Donaldsonville veterans "Camp Paradise."[41]

A total of nineteen Donaldsonville artillerymen (including cooks and servants) with seven horses remained with Major Maurin in Lynchburg from June 22 to July 1, ostensibly to procure artillery pieces for the High Bridge fortifications. In the city's artillery park there were a number of guns. Maurin, assuredly with Nicholls's assistance, received the "proper permit" to cut through "the red tape" of seeing "'Major So-and-So,' who would give him an order on 'Captain So-and-So.'"[42] In the end, nineteen cannons were taken, albeit some were condemned pieces and, along with a procurement of munitions, all was loaded and sent by train to the High Bridge fortifications. On July 1 Maurin, being well, was ordered to take command of the High Bridge post, thus ending his stay in Lynchburg. With the small Donaldsonville detachment Maurin rejoined Mollere's section and took command at the bridge. There the casemated works were fortified with additional guns consisting of one 20-pounder Parrott, seven 6-pounder guns, five 12-pounder howitzers, four 3-inch rifles, one Clay rifle, and one 16-pounder Blakely gun, with accompanying ammunition stored and stacked in ammunition pits or magazines dug into the ground of the forts.[43]

The Gunners of Donaldson became artillery drillmasters to Booker's reserve infantrymen, who would have to help staff the nineteen additional guns. Besides being drillmasters the short duty list of the Canonnier section included providing one man to handle the commissary department and another to guard the stable, loading and unloading corn and fodder from the forage wagon into storage and caring for the horses. The guarding of the forts and bridge were left to the reserves. Later, when "Yankee negroes" were kept nearby as prisoners, the reserves guarded them too.[44]

Leaving the recently promoted First Lieutenant Camille Mollere[45] in command, Maurin journeyed to Richmond, where on September 1 he met Henri Garidel, who worked in the War Department's Ordnance Bureau. Garidel recorded in his journal: "In the evening I had a visit from Major Maurin, one of my oldest friends from the College d'Iberville. We hadn't seen each other in thirty-two years. It gave me a great deal of pleasure to see him."[46] Maurin soon returned to command the High Bridge post, where he had his headquarters in a cabin that on occasion entertained wealthy and patriotic old citizens from the neighborhood such as Captain Thomas F. Perkinson, owner of Elmwood plantation with its mill on the Appomattox River a few miles northeast of the bridge.

Discipline at the post was not enforced and, with just a minimal amount of duties to attend to (one mess even hired "Negro convicts" to chop wood)[47] there was plenty of time for the Louisiana artillerists to go on expeditions in search of food and adventure. "After the morning and afternoon drill," remembered a Donaldsonville Canonnier, "the men of the garrison had nothing better to do than to cultivate the friendship of patriotic families in the neighborhood."[48]

A local historian wrote, "Good food is a Prince Edward [County] tradition. From breakfast of white lake fish and spoon bread, or ham and eggs, or beefsteak, or fried chicken through hearty dinners to substantial suppers, the Prince Edward resident liked to eat well. He welcomed guests . . . it was quite all right for a traveler to stop at a friend's home for a

High Bridge
Courtesy of the Library of Congress.

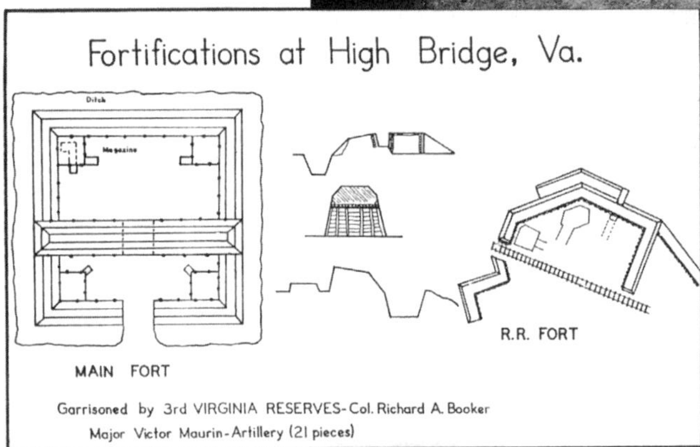

Sketch of High Bridge Fort.
From Christopher M. Calkins, *The Final Bivouac*.

High Bridge with the wagon road and bridge below crossing the Appomattox River.
Courtesy of the Library of Congress.

meal or for a night, supper, and breakfast."[49] Prosper Landry wrote, "You do not find here the aristocracy that you call the FFV (First Family of Virginia), but these are honest farmers and their families. I do not know if there is any great wealth, but there is no poverty. They are all in very comfortable conditions as far as earthly goods are concerned."[50] He also wondered how the residents could be so cheerful "when one does not drink wine? Here one drinks only milk . . . which I find delicious."[51]

The Donaldsonville boys soon made acquaintances with the "honest people,"[52] in the region. About his comrades, Prosper Landry recorded,

> Although they are threadbare, nevertheless they are from Louisiana and the chic creole . . . shines even through their poverty. And also a rare thing here and very admired—they speak French and they sing, and they often go out giving serenades. So they are pampered and feasted by everyone and they are the pets of all the ladies and all doors are open for them—a few hearts also. They even talk marriage . . . they have given several picnics in their honor and often a wagon load of beauties would come mingling in the middle of the camp. Without invitation they come to dine with our gunners, but do not believe that they lack graciousness, for each brings her dinner, and this dinner is always amply sufficient for two. What luck![53]

En visité (visiting) and *avoir amusé* (having fun) became the favorite pastimes of the Canonniers at Camp Paradise, especially at homes where a number of girls and young woman were present. Sweet music and piano performances were enjoyed, along with dances at neighboring houses and farms. Various country games usually followed the outings, and there was conversation, which, wrote a Donaldsonville artilleryman, was of "the usual quantity of stuff about sweet hearts and marriage."[54] This talk resulted in at least one Canonnier private, appropriately named Tom Love, going on furlough to be married immediately.[55] Another, twenty-nine-year-old French native and Donaldsonville resident Peter Hauplin, returned after the war to Prince Edward County, married, and lived at nearby Hampden Sydney.[56]

Soon after being stationed at High Bridge, Donaldsonville Private Ernest Monnot, a young widower, along with three other Canonnier comrades, walked three miles early one morning to a dignified looking farmhouse of two stories with a high brick basement. It was the Lockett family home. The Assumption Parish boys asked for a canteen of milk, but Mr. James S. Lockett's standing injunction to his household was to give any and all soldiers who passed a good meal. Since Mrs. Lockett was out visiting, her eighteen-year-old daughter, Miss Lelia (described by one Canonnier as a "fine looking woman" who "if dressed by a French modiste . . . would be considered handsome"),[57] was quite amicable and acted as mistress of Piney View. The tall and elegant hostess with an energetic personality gladly served the Louisianians breakfast. Monnot liked the biscuits so well he remarked to one of his comrades, "Mr. Tomplete,"[58] that he, "was going to see if he couldn't get a wife here after the war was over."[59] Monnot would return to Piney View annually after the war to visit Miss Lelia, and in 1869, with her family's blessings, he took her to Bayou Lafourche as his bride.[60] After the war Mrs. Monnot wrote that General Francis T. Nicholls would later tell her she had he to thank for her husband as he ordered the Donaldsonville Artillery "sent to the High Bridge."[61]

The most popular places besides Perkinson's Elmwood and Lockett's Piney View were Pleasant Shade of Mr. Samuel Vaughan, Sunnyside of Mr. James D. Walthall, Chatham of Major James Watson, Panola of Samuel W. Bondurant, and Longwood of Widow Venable, along with the farms of Mr. and Mrs. Madison, Stephen Farley, Widow McGehee, Widow Chambers, and the Widow Richardson.[62]

Here in Prince Edward and Comberland Counties the land was unspoiled by war. "The farms of that day," wrote the area's historian,

The Lockett house near Farmville and High Bridge, Va.
From the author's collection.

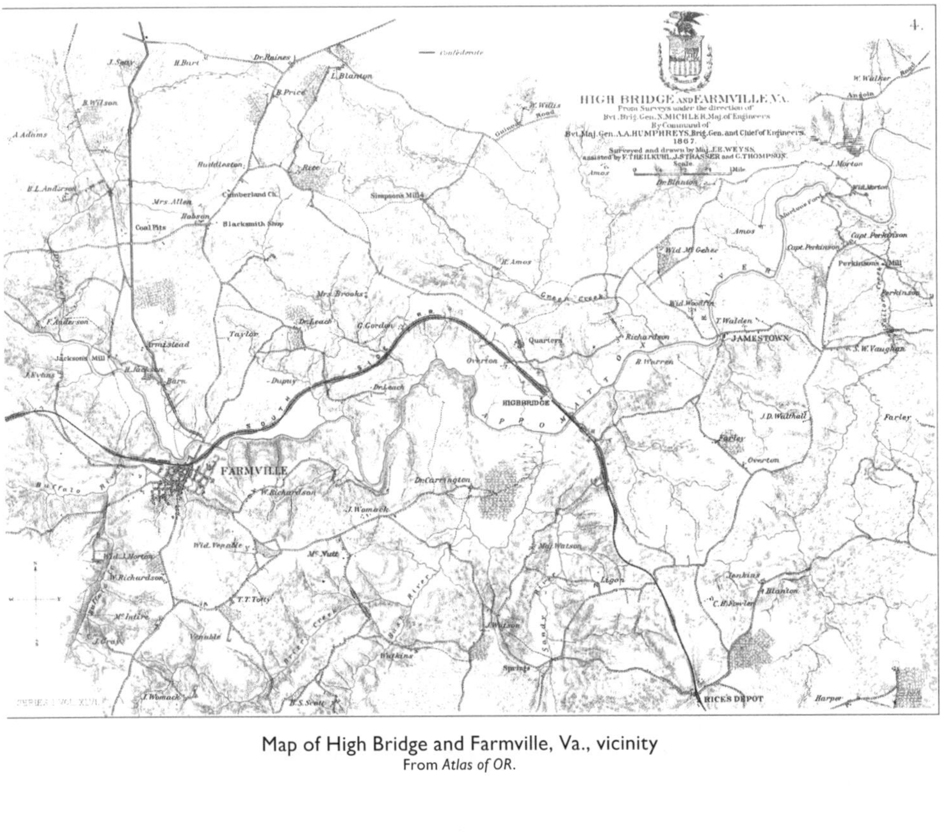

Map of High Bridge and Farmville, Va., vicinity
From *Atlas of OR*.

> had extensive orchards . . . There were a variety of fruit: apples, peaches, pears, cherries, damsons, green gage plums, sometimes apricots. Then the chestnut was found at some homes as well as the walnut, which was often found growing wild. . . . The farm through this period continued to be to a considerable extent a self-sustaining unit. Garden and orchard, cattle, sheep, and hogs provided food, and . . . the farmer also tried to provide enough flour and meal for the needs of his family and his slaves, as well as of his livestock, from his production of wheat and corn, and oats and rye were raised to provide feed for stock. . . . The typical Prince Edward farm also raised cotton for clothing.[63]

Although fishing and hunting were popular activities, on a typical day at Camp Paradise the Donaldsonville boys were absent visiting their newfound friends in the countryside. Farmville was frequented, and there the Canonniers not only bought candles, tobacco, or other needed items (horseshoes and salt were often requisitioned from Farmville by Maurin and Mollere) but they also attended concerts of the Farmville Female College.[64] Besides the local farms, Jamestown Church[65] was a gathering place on Sundays for service and a sermon. Wrote Prosper Landry while near High Bridge,

> I went to the church with Blouin. When one says "go to church," that does not mean go to Mass, which would in fact be impossible, because here there is no Catholic Church. . . . I wanted to see the good inhabitants of the countryside who have treated so well my "Gunners of Donaldson" . . . living far from church, they [the locals] have the habit to take with them a snack, which today included ham, some roast lamb, bread, biscuits and a big basket of excellent grapes. Invited to share this snack, I did not refuse and thought that I was not at church, but at a well organized picnic.[66]

In Camp Paradise food was often delivered to the Donaldsonville artillerymen from their friends in the neighborhood. The Locketts were noted for sending Monnot a quantity of provisions that included potatoes, sausage, meat, and fresh salted pork, all for the benefit of his mess. Other foods to be had were roasted chicken, eggs, butter, watermelons, apples, peaches, cookies, and cakes. Prosper Landry especially mentioned the "blackberry wine sangaree."[67] Liquid spirits were easily obtained. Levy noted that a Canonnier "used up by the nights dissipation"[68] would usually sleep it off all the next day. Chess and reading were other leisure pursuits. Despite the relaxed ambiance in camp, Maurin (as inspector and mustering officer) rated the discipline, instruction, and military appearance of Mollere's Donaldsonville Canonnier detachment "good" and their armament "in order."[69]

As the months went by the physical appearance of the Gunners of Donaldson at the High Bridge post improved. All were in good health. The obvious reason was the more than sufficient provisions and meals provided by the good neighbors, but the area was also noted for its Lithia Springs, which provided pure water noted for its curative properties.[70] The weather was relatively mild and temperate and extremely pleasant in the fall. The gray wool uniforms of Maurin's Canonniers were reported "good" (no doubt because of the donations and sewing and mending by the locals) and with the approach of winter were supplemented with blue Union overcoats and jackets.[71]

While the seasons changed, the routine did not for Maurin, Mollere, and the section of Canonniers who "remained there to protect the Bridge."[72] One adjustment that did occur at the post in early November 1864 was Booker's reserves being exchanged with ten companies of the First Virginia Reserves under Colonel Benjamin L. Farinholt.[73] With the switch of commands, the Donaldsonville boys once again had to instruct and drill the infantry reserves in the working of artillery. One Donaldsonville Canonnier private had a disdainful opinion of Farinholt's men whom he called "stupid country louts."[74]

Christmas 1864 at High Bridge found the weather quite cold, but the Creole artillerists, over "right frozen roads," visited acquaintances and celebrated with them by eating Christmas dinners of "turkey, mutton, pork, a variety of cheese, vegetables and the usual appendages of . . . desert."[75] Music topped the festivities while lucky Canonniers received gifts such as woolen socks and heart pincushions from the fairer sex. This wasn't the first time the Virginia ladies took up sewing and knitting for the Gallant Creoles. Canonnier Private "Charley" Fuhri returned to the cold Petersburg trenches and "brought from the fair dames of Cumberland County socks for his gun's crew. A special gift was sent [to Private Eugene Levy] of 2 prs. socks and 1 pr. gloves by a young lady who heard a portion of [his] letter to Charley [Furhi] read."[76]

"The new year," of 1865 wrote Levy (recently transferred from the Petersburg trenches because of his health), "opened auspiciously with a clear sky and bright sun. Old mother earth looks lovely wrapped in her virgin robe. The snow birds are darting about right merrily singing their morning hymn of praise to Him who has vouchsafed in life, and health, and a thousand earthly blessings. God grant that we may not feel another year of war!"[77]

Many in Mollere's section had mixed feelings about being posted at the High Bridge while the other two sections were fighting at Rives's Salient in Petersburg. Reports arrived daily by train, and in January 1865 the news conveyed was of "great suffering in the army on account of meager rations."[78] With the trains came passengers from Richmond and Petersburg of whom, Levy observed and noted, "Citizens are very despondent and seem willing to accept any terms of peace which might be proposed."[79]

The greatest danger at this time for the Donaldsonville artillerists at High Bridge was the frozen ground. "Walking has become difficult and dangerous," according to Levy.[80] On January 22 he wrote,

> The sleet of yesterday, which continued to fall during the night, proved to be one of the most wonderful phenomena of nature! Throughout the night the crashing of limbs in the forest as they yielded to the weight of accumulated ice fell upon the ear. Fortunately there are few trees in the vicinity of camp, and but few cabins sustained even a trifling damage. This morning a magnificent spectacle greeted the sight, a forest of ice. Every bough curved gracefully under the tension of their loads. As the wind arose the swaying of the great trees detached the ice which fell in constant showers. Woe to the unlucky fellow who is caught by one of these miniature avalanches for the blow from the sharp edged icicles, falling from a great height leaves no inconsiderable wound.[81]

With the very cold weather prevailing throughout January, Levy recorded, "As it had been decided by my comrades to get up a dramatic association I interested myself in the affair and was selected to compose a play, local in it's character and adapted to our condition and wardrobe. The plot of the play which shall be styled 'The Fortune's of War' was conceived today [January 10] and I'll start immediately into its creation."[82]

The next day Levy obtained the use of the parlor in Overton's house and worked for four hours on the play, which he finished by noon the day after. On January 13 Levy, along with Canonnier Corporal Paul Humbert,[83] went "to the house of Major Watson"[84] to see about "engaging his barn as a theatre. Found that the building was in use . . . on returning to camp found that the boys had appealed in vain to Major Maurin for the use of the fodder house as a theatre, as the old ass refused merely out of his natural spirit of contrariness."[85]

Levy had served in the battery since March 1862 and had written that he was in "the company under charge of the gallant Major Maurin."[86] Now stationed at this post for less than a month, Levy derided his commander over not being able to use the fodder house for his thespian work. Levy incidentally was placed on the duty list the next day and detailed to get corn and fodder. The hard work of loading and unloading the wagon did not stop him from reading his play and "caused the roles to be accepted."[87] Within a few days "old Major Maurin," crowed Levy, "left on furlough," and "we now have possession of the fodder barn and are fitting it up for theatrical purposes."[88]

A few days after the takeover of the fodder barn, the first readings were made of Levy's comedy, in addition to a vaudeville by Canonnier Private Eugene Jeff Hardy.[89] For the next few weeks the members labored at fixing up the barn while at night, with the "inspiring notes"[90] of cheerfull Canonnier Private Pierre "Turiaffe" Babin's violin playing, rehearsals of the songs and dances were held. There were some delays with the production when Farinholt's reserves were ordered away for a couple of days, which meant all of Mollere's section were "placed on guard. Some over the Yankee Negroes, others at the High Bridge, and the balance at the fortifications which defend the post."[91] During these days there were more interruptions of *La Dramatic Association* when orders would arrive to make ready for action whenever a reported enemy cavalry demonstration was about to occur along the railroad line. Levy bemoaned these orders, but as soon as the danger was over "forthwith the work at our theatre was continued."[92]

Improvements continued slowly on the theatre. Levy complained he was not "getting much help from the ignorant, narrow minded Acadians who suspect a sort of plot because the Americans take an interest in the affair."[93] This points to the difference and distrust between the Louisiana French and Americans present ever since the 1803 Louisiana Purchase. It was reported Acadians and French Creoles were an "honest, steady, and plodding people" and "kept themselves together with a reserve and exclusiveness almost impenetrable." Among Americans and French there was an "open distrust of one group by the other."[94] Levy's disparaging remarks along with "bad ease"[95] between he and a few of the Acadians may not have had anything to do with past social differences but, as in the case of cursing Major Maurin, might have reflected Levy's frustration over progress towards the completion of the theatre for his comedy.

Levy had a number of friends at the High Bridge detachment of Canonniers from different social groups including Sabin Braud, James Carothers, "Buck" Chase, Tom Love, Bienvenu "Cyr" Cire, Eugene Jeff Hardy, A. J. "Gotreau" Gautreaux, Achilles Dupuy, "Arthur" Echavaria, "Turiaffe" Babin, Miles Joyner, and Humbert, along with cabin mates "Philo" Viala and Monnot. Like any societal group there was aversion or indifference on a personal basis, and Levy recorded Canonnier Bugler Joseph Numa Braud and Private Octave Boudreau, both Acadians, were not very "congenial" towards him while the Irishman Timothy Boham "proved so ungrateful."[96]

On February 10, exactly one month after the introduction of *La Dramatic Association*, the Canonniers held their first performance. With the "weather still quit[e] cold," Levy wrote the participants (Hardy, Carothers, Sabin Braud, Louis Comes, "AJ" Gautreaux, and the indispensable violin player "Turiaffe" Babin) were

> busy preparing for the event of the season . . . the people commenced to arrive an hour before the appointed time in ox carts, wagons, and carriages, and the ladies soon crowded the officers' headquarters while their escorts came to the private's cabins to warm. By six-thirty o'clock the theatre was crowded and the performance commenced with a vaudeville composed by Hardy entitled, "A Frenchmen Lost at the High Bridge" which went off tolerably well. Comes never varies the intonations of his voice, hence he becomes an uninteresting actor. Sabin Braud looked and acted the women well. Jim Carothers was decidedly good in his personation, while Hardy is very good. Then came the recitation of Hood's "Song of the Shirt"[97] by myself, an effort which was not appreciated by the audience as much as the miserably sung ballad (by Comes) of "Villikens and His Dinah."[98] In conclusion was enacted my comedy of "The Fortunes

of War." This was very well-performed. No one lost his self-possession, and it was only the stupid Gautreaux who failed in rendering the text.

At nine o'clock all was over and the only fault the audience found was that the programme was too short. Everybody seemed pleased; no one more so than myself, at the success of the enterprise. Many of the guest brought refreshments which were given to the actors, but Carothers and myself did not wait for the distribution, having accepted an invitation to go home with George Vaughan's party. As the crust of the snow cut the feet of the oxen, they could not pull, so that we had to help the girls through the snow for a mile. Enjoyed a nice supper and feather bed.[99]

In less than two weeks *La Dramatic Association* (after being on guard and with more grand rehearsals) gave a second entertainment on February 22, Washington's Birthday. "The day has been bright and the weather mild," recorded Levy, "but the roads are in terrible condition and this circumstance prevented many parties from being present. The wagons commenced to arrive at an early hour of the afternoon and by six o'clock the theatre was crowded to its utmost capacity. The programme comprised 'The Lost Frenchmen at High Bridge,' then a parody on 'Woodman Spare That Tree'[100] called 'Nigger, Put down dat Jug'.[101] Sung by myself (in character) assisted by Jim Carothers. 'The Misanthrope'[102] followed afterwards, and in conclusion, 'The Fortunes of War.' The affair went off with a great deal of '<u>éclat</u>' and to the manifest delight of the assembled multitude . . . by ten o'clock all was over."[103] This was the last performance of High Bridge's *La Dramatic Association.*[104]

During March 1865 the cheerful and agreeable Canonniers passed most of their time visiting the locals and gathering in each other's cabins to sing, whistle, and tell old yarns, and read *Don Juan!*, *Byron*, *What Will He Do With It?*, and *Blair's Rhetoric*.[105] The Louisiana artillerists again had to relieve the reserves when they were ordered to Lynchburg for a time, but they continued to make local visits for good meals with the "usual gratifying results."[106] Levy also noted that with the warmer weather "a few blades of grass may be discovered in many places and the songs of the swallow cheer the ear."[107]

With April 1865 approaching the reserves were again called out and ordered this time to Richmond; the Canonniers were placed back on guard over the "negro prisoners" and stationed at the High Bridge and fortifications. While the reserves were leaving Levy recorded he believed General Lee was massing the troops in front of Richmond in anticipation of a big fight.

Being on guard made the time hang heavily, and the days seemed to get longer. On Wednesday, March 29, Levy scrawled in his diary,

Having been anxious for some time past to visit Richmond I decided to "run the block" on the sick furlough of Bienvenue Cyer,[108] and left camp at one o'clock P.M. this day. On reaching the Junction[109] the news of the approach of a heavy raiding party under "Cavalry" Sheridan which had left Grant's army early this morning. There was considerable excitement prevailing at Burkeville and it was 4 o'clock P.M. before the regular train was allowed to leave for Richmond. At ten o'clock the lights of the city became visible and ten minutes later I was in the great vortex of crime and dissipation in search of a resting place. "Was it not pitiful in a whole city full, home I had none." After an unsuccessful application at the L[ouisian]a Home[110] I went to the Gen[era]l Receiving Hospital[111] and procured a miserable pallet. The rain came soon, pattering on the roof and lulling me into a sweet slumber, notwithstanding the booming of cannon in the distance, familiar sound to the ears of the citizens of this beleaguered city.

"Thursday, 30th March," continued Levy,

Raining yet. Took breakfast at Smith's where I was well received. Collected . . . $350 net proceeds sale of [Yankee]overcoat. Bought music and books and attended to various

> commissions for the boys. Visited [various acquaintances then] having heard of terrific fighting at Petersburg, I telegraphed to Doc [his brother still with Prosper Landry's section, and] spent a sociable evening at Smith's.
>
> Friday, 31st. Still it rains. Up at six o'clock, took a light meal, and left after bidding my good friends the Smith's farewell, took the seven o'clock train for Burkeville . . . Ye gods! What a slow train I have hit upon! It occupied 8 hours in making the journey of 57 miles. Of course we missed the connection and I walked from Burkeville to the [High] Bridge, a distance of 13 miles on the cross ties. Nothing of interest had happened since my departure except the shooting of a deserter by a detachment of my comrades under Lt. Mollere. A scouting party of 5 men has been sent to report progress of Sheridan's new raid against the rail-roads, my messmate Monnot is with them.[112]

It was around this time that Levy noted, "The times are big with great events."[113] A few days after Levy returned to the High Bridge post, he and others attended the Jamestown Church on Sunday, April 2, 1865, and listened to the pastor deliver a long sermon with an execrable nasal twang. While the congregation listened, they were unaware of the great events (*grand évenéments*) about to reach Prince Edward and Cumberland County from the direction of Petersburg, Virginia.

Chapter Seventeen

La Dernier des Mohicans
(Last of the Mohicans)

In front of Petersburg, Virginia, at the end of the temporary armistice after the Crater attacks on July 30, 1864, and for the next eight months, there were no further direct attacks upon the Confederate trenches but rather a succession of efforts against the flanks. During these attacks General Robert E. Lee had to use his infantry from the entrenchments, which reduced the manpower in the works to a mere skirmish line. "Unusual vigilance and activity was enjoined upon the artillery," wrote Confederate Brigadier General Edward Porter Alexander, "lest the enemy should suspect our weakness and seek to take advantage of it."[1]

Captain Prosper Landry's section of the Donaldsonville Artillery, with its two Napoleon guns assigned to Lieutenant Colonel Charles Richardson's Battalion during the siege kept busy in the trenches changing gun positions around Rives's Salient, where they built and repaired bomb proofs of every pattern and design to protect them from enemy fire and mortar shells.[2] All along the line Confederate artillerists were engaged in strengthening and repairing the entrenchments, cutting timber for the works built of pine logs and red clay,[3] digging pits for the guns,[4] building covered ways, and arranging abatis.[5] It was reported, "Nearly the whole of the available force of the artillery is at work day and night."[6]

At Rives's Salient were infantry of Brigadier General Nathaniel H. Harris's Mississippi Brigade, composed of the Twelfth, Sixteenth, Nineteenth, and Forty-eighth regiments from Mahone's Division. The Mississippians acted as skirmishers on the picket lines and in the trenches supported the artillery by "repairing and building new entrenchments."[7] One of Harris's infantrymen simply noted, "Sharpshooters and artillery very noisy."[8]

The labor at the works was "very severe," wrote Private John Walters of Grandy's Norfolk Blues Battery of Richardson's Battalion on August 12, 1864. "Especially," he noted, "as the heat and flies prevent our sleeping enough during the day to recover from our fatigue."[9] Regarding the heat, "It seems," wrote another, "as if the perspiration runs in streams all the time and brings no relief."[10] A Louisiana artillerist noted, "One of the most singular features about Petersburg, as month after month passed on . . . was the way in which the hill-side embankments would be honeycombed into human dens and places of shelter and refuge . . . the ground . . . cut up with such a maze of alleys and streets of trench work . . . with fireplaces and cooking utensils . . . encamped inside these narrow avenues."[11]

According to one soldier, "All along the line . . . with . . . guns . . . lie the Cannoniers all day long watching enemy's lines and occasionally he jumps up, says fire, and another

Cannonier pulls a little string and bang goes the gun followed by the rush of the shot, shell or canister and the crashing . . . on the enemy's side and if it is a shell the dull report of its bursting . . . but probably do very little damage to anyone. These higher compliments are also returned at intervals by the enemy, and so the work and war goes on."[12] "It was not possible to take a constitutional 'in the open,'" wrote another combatant. For the most part life in the trenches was "very monotonous."[13] The forts, redoubts, rifle pits, bomb proofs, covered ways, and defensive obstacles were continuously improved upon with time and, noted a Confederate veteran facetiously, "After getting the breastworks in good shape, we settled down to enjoy life among the bullets."[14]

Colonel Lindsey Walker's Third Corps Artillery was responsible for and defended the works from Rives's Salient (Battery No. 25) to Battery No. 45. In making the defenses stronger, a number of heavy guns, 32-pounder Blakelys, 8-inch Columbiads, and 24-pounder and 8-inch howitzers were issued to Walker along with several Coehorn mortars. The mortars were placed in pits behind Rives's Salient with members of Grandy's Battery operating them, plus two of the 8-inch howitzers. Grandy's remaining artillerists still served their four light artillery pieces on the line next to the two Donaldsonville Napoleon guns. Captain Nathan Penick and thirty members of his Pittsylvania Battery were also assigned on August 18 to two of these heavy guns, and in consequence the Donaldsonville Canonniers received an additional two U.S. 10-pounder Parrott rifle guns.[15]

The four guns of the Donaldsonville Artillery were now repositioned from the ruins of Rives's house and defended the earthworks on the left flank of the Salient, where they now guarded not only the flank but also the left side of the whole of Walker's command.[16] The next artillery position on Landry's left was about 1,200 feet away, where three batteries of the 13th Virginia Light Artillery Battalion of the First Corps, under command of ex-Washington Artillery adjutant and now Major William M. Owen, were located.[17]

Walker's line stretched off into the other direction, with Grandy's Norfolk Blues Battery immediately to the right of the Canonniers, their end guns being but five yards apart. Next was Captain Joseph D. Moore's Norfolk Battery with four guns, then two guns from Colonel Allen S. Cutts's Sumter Georgia Battalion, followed by six guns astride the Jerusalem Plank Road of Captain George M. Patterson's Company from the Sumter Battalion. Across the road in advance of the main Confederate line of trenches was Fort Mahone, a semidetached earthen fortification casemated by guns from Captain Hugh M. Ross's Company, also of the Sumter Battalion. Next came the sixteen guns from the four companies of New Orleans's Washington Artillery (detached from the First Corps) in Batteries No. 34-38, though they were occasionally moved and at one time occupied Batteries 30-35. McIntosh's and Pegram's battalions extended Walker's defensive line to Battery No. 45.[18]

The battalion commander of the Donaldsonville Artillery later described their position in Rives's Salient:

> At irregular intervals along the defenses covering Petersburg were redans for artillery. They were designated from left to right thus, "1," "2," "3," etc. The one requiring mention here was Battery 27. It was confronted by the Union Fort Sedgwick, profanely called "Fort Hell." Its right rested on the Jerusalem Plank road, which, in prolongation of Wythe street, Petersburg, extended to the Black Water. Its left flanking traverse [Battery 25] stood on the lip of a narrow swale, whose bottom was about nine feet lower than the terreplein of the redan, and was sheltered from view of the enemy by a high epaulment stretching across its mouth. Commencing a few feet in rear of the left traverse and extending southwest, parallel with the main parapet, was a ditch six feet wide and three feet deep; the excavated earth being thrown up on the side toward the enemy, thus forming a covered way for the safe passage of troops along the line.

> This covered way was intersected immediately behind the redan by another ditch, running zig-zag out to Petersburg, and used for the same purpose as the main ditch.[19]

While Lee and Grant clashed over flanking movements, the trenches, reported an artillerist, continued to be "just infested with sharpshooting, mortar firing, and artillery practice, all day and more or less all night."[20] The reports of other battery commanders along the line were similar in content to that of Prosper Landry's, who recorded the events for the Donaldsonville Artillery: "This section has been in position in Rives' salient on S[outh] Side of Appomattox River. Nothing beyond the usual shelling incident to the close proximity of the two lines has occurred."[21] Another Confederate battery commander wrote home, "My time is passed on the lines and is often mostly employed in digging and perfecting my earth works from which to fight in safety."[22]

Concerning the protection of the artillerists, two innovations employed along the line and by the Gunners of Donaldson were reported by Canonnier Private Eugene Levy. He wrote,

> The guns have been fitted with "Gantlet's" which are semi-circular screens composed of four layers of ¼ in[ch] plank resting on the piece at its reinforce. The object of this . . . is to protect No. 4, 3, and the gunner against Minnie balls. Should a cannon shot happen to strike the affair it increased the chances of killing or wounding those behind it, so that the gun detachment has decided to dispense with it in time of action.[23] There are also funnel-shaped wooden forms inserted in the earthworks near the parapet through which a good view of the front can be had without danger from sharp-shooters. The boys style the last instrument the "Dimmock open-glass."[24]

Besides the guns in the earthworks, the batteries maintained in the rear areas a wagon and caisson yard and a camp with stables for the horses. By March of 1865 Richardson's Battalion had just fifty "good" horses available for Prosper Landry's, Grandy's, and Moore's Batteries. Typically, they required 109. In comparison, Cutts's Battalion had sixty-four horses in "poor" condition with eighty-two needed; the Washington Artillery had thirty-eight horses in "fair" condition with fifty more required; Owen's Thirteenth Virginia Battalion had sixty horses with many not good. From August 1864 to March 1865 a typical artillery battalion lost almost three-fourths of its animals; this included horses that were received as replacements. Even the best attention, with horses groomed twice a day, watered regularly by the battery drivers, and receiving full rations of hay and corn, could not prevent the reduction in horses. Many animals, some having served with their batteries since 1862, died of disease while others remained unhealthy. Period inspections condemned many horses that were ordered turned in with the hopes of getting them in a better condition. Others were deemed serviceable though worthless if required to pull a gun or caisson. To ease some of the shortage, orders were given to keep only one caisson for two guns.[25]

Duty at the wagon yard or horse camp was neither easy nor safe; a member of the First Company Washington Artillery was mortally wounded at the wagon yard when struck on his way to dinner. Duty was especially hazardous at night when the artillerymen had to carry shells from the caisson depots to the front while the mortars fired. Prosper Landry reported the Donaldsonville Artillery had one horse wounded during the winter months.[26]

A cooking yard was maintained as well with a ration wagon delivering food. In early August one of the Mississippians wrote in a letter home, "Well, let me tell you what I had for my dinner yesterday. First, sweet cakes and apples. Next, blackberry dumplings. . . . We are living very well at present on . . . cornbread, bacon, coffee, sugar, peas, and some . . . rice. Pretty good . . . in these besieging times. We drew lots of good food four days ago when seven trains of cars come into Petersburg loaded with blockade goods."[27]

Early in September 1864 Levy recorded that the Canonniers received "once or twice a little rice" that they used for breakfast to make "greased rice and bread."[28] A small slice of rancid bacon usually supplied the accrual of grease for cooking. The rations continued to decrease in quantity as time went on. Levy later reported that they were getting "flour and meat/bacon and beef alternately, and distributed regularly."[29] Still later he noted the Donaldsonville boys were day after day getting, "Corn-meal [and] bacon, both of bad quality."[30] How bad was it? "The pork caused you to hold your nose to eat it," wrote another Confederate.[31]

By January 1865 a meticulous diarist of the Louisiana artillery noted that per day he was issued, "1 lb. hard bread, 2 ounces coffee, 2 ounces rice, and 2 ounces of salt."[32] Prosper Landry's Donaldsonville gunners were clinging "to old Soda Biscuits."[33] An officer wrote, "The lack of full rations had become so common that in [their] diary the food question is for months scarcely ever mentioned."[34]

The coming of fall and winter weather along with the bad rations brought on fever and diarrhea to the artillerymen. The camp's sick and slightly wounded artillerists were treated at an artillery corps hospital of tents located on the north bank of the Appomattox River, just above the factory village of Ettrick. The severely wounded and seriously sick were sent from this field infirmary by ambulance train to Richmond or Farmville for hospitalization. In October at Louisiana Hospital, Levy noted he "visited our boys . . . and found" Henri Gamotis, John Murphy, John Suarez, Eugene Queprotte, all of whom were sick, and Charley Fuhri, with Henri Newchurch "slightly wounded."[35]

During the siege (mid-June 1864 to April 2, 1865), the Donaldsonville Artillery recorded sixteen men hospitalized with illness (one twice) with five each reporting sick in the months of October and November. Out of the sixteen cases, four remained in the field hospital or artillery corps hospital situated on the north bank of the Appomattox River until well. The others were sent on for treatment at different hospitals. Ten went to Richmond with seven receiving treatment in the Louisiana Hospital under the administration of Dr. W. C. Nichols and the Sisters of Charity. Levy favorably reported, "The affairs of this establishment are all coordinated in every department."[36] Not one of the ill Donaldsonville Canonniers became disabled from or died of sickness during the siege. Thirteen of the sixteen returned to full duty with the battery at Petersburg.[37]

In comparison, Grandy's battery had twelve men hospitalized (one twice) for sickness, with most illnesses being fever, diarrhea, or debilitas. Most of Grandy's men were treated at Chimborazo Hospital Number 1 in Richmond with two dying from sickness. Only five of Grandy's artillerists returned to duty. Moore's Norfolk Battery had twenty men hospitalized (two twice) with ten becoming ill in January 1865. Diarrhea or dysentery was the most common ailment, and most were treated in Richmond at General Hospital Number 9, though some went to Chimborazo Hospital Numbers 1 and 5. Nine of Moore's men returned to duty. The following is a breakdown of the sick in Richardson's Battalion for the Petersburg siege:[38]

	SICK	DIED	RETURNED TO DUTY
Landry's Battery . . .	16	0	13
Grandy's Battery . . .	12	2	5
Moore's Battery . . .	20	1	9

Captains of the different batteries along the siege line were kept "pretty constantly busy."[39] This also applied to the Donaldsonville Artillery captain, Prosper Landry, on whom the heavy workload took its toll. On August 31 after signing the battery's muster roll for July/August 1864, he became incapacitated by sickness. Having served the battery with valor and distinction, Landry even while sick evinced an active interest in the battery's endeavors by continuing with the necessary charge of paperwork.[40] While sick with fever he made requisitions for stationary and received three quires of letter paper and one of foolscap paper. Presumably he did not wish to overburden Lieutenant Hubert Treille, temporarily commanding the guns on the line.

Prosper Landry, ever aware of his *toilettes et apparence* (his dress and appearance), may very well have been the model of one of Richardson's *Tales of a Warrior* characters. The battalion commander wrote.

> Goodness! what a voice he had; it wasn't shrill, nor harsh, but mellow, as the notes of a saxhorn. . . . Every man . . . liked . . . I may say they loved him, though he was so strict. . . . But didn't he have an eye! goodness! I never saw such a pair of eyes in the head of any creature...He wasn't so awful big either. . . . He had a neat foot; and . . . boots . . . they always looked tidy, and never wore out. . . . He managed as well to keep his cap looking neat; he wore a red kepi with a dark blue band around it; all the men of our company had such caps when we came out into the war, but time and hard usage had made them generally so dingy that you couldn't tell what their original color was . . . he stood erect—straight as an ash tree—you could distinguish him from any other man in our battalion as far as you could see him.[41]

Prosper Landry wrote to his "*tres chers*" (very dear) wife on September 10, 1864: "The hardships of this campaign, especially at Petersburg, where it was necessary to work all night and where a very hot sun beats on you every day, made me sick enough to obtain a sick furlough. . . . I have not had any fever for more than a week, but I am still too feeble to put on the uniform again."[42] After recuperating at the home of the Madison's near High Bridge, Landry returned to the Petersburg entrenchments on October 15, 1864, to again take charge of the four Donaldsonville guns.[43] By displaying a conscientious effort to persevere with his duties while sick, "the grand old man"[44] earned the respect and esteem of all. To the Donaldsonville Canonniers he was remembered as their "beloved chieftain."[45]

It is notable that much of the time Prosper Landry was away sick Major M. B. "Buck" Miller temporarily commanded the battalion for the reason that Richardson was again under arrest. The record gives no indication why, but Richardson was relieved from arrest on September 4, 1864, and placed on detached service by Third Corps Artillery commander Lindsey Walker. Richardson again commanded the battalion's three batteries at the completion of the muster roll dated October 31, 1864.[46]

The discipline of the Gunners of Donaldson while in the Petersburg trenches always remained "good,"[47] though it was a "life of sameness and vacancy."[48] Levy in November 1864 noted the days became "characterized by nothing different from its predecesser."[49] Morale remained good in the trenches, and this was in no small part due to the leadership, engaging personality, warm heart, and sympathy of Prosper Landry, who spoke French and English fluently, the distinguished Treille, who led "with soldier feeling,"[50] and Lieutenant Antoine Sanchez, who "commanded unqualified popular esteem."[51]

Another reason the Canonniers were "in good spirits"[52] was that each man every few days received a day of recreation out of the trenches and was allowed to go to the rear and into Petersburg. Some went and bathed in the Appomattox River or searched for additional rations. Some, noted a Louisiana artillerist, "Would often slip into town and get the girls together and have a dance."[53] Another Louisiana artilleryman noted that the appealing places were "the two hotels and one or two coffee houses, the bridge and river bank." However, the favorite place was

> one of the old finely furnished saloons. The traditional coffee-house pictures, with their voluptuous and impossible beauties still hung on the walls; the glasses and bottles still glittered; and . . . during all of those long months of bombardment one man still remained behind the counter with neat cuffs and hair parted in the middle, ready to administer to the wants of his thirsty fellow-man. Nevertheless, the supply of stimulants was at a low ebb . . . and once the visitor had paid his two or three dollars, and swallowed the moderate amount of Nepenthe allowed him . . . he was expected to foot it back . . . to camp forthwith.[54]

Fresh gossip was also received from these visits to the rear and passed on to others. Naturally in camps the rumors flourished. "We get no news," wrote an artillerist, "but by rumor and papers," adding that the rumors were called "grapevine telegraphs and canteen dispatches."[55] A private in the Sixteenth Mississippi Regiment that at times supported the Donaldsonville guns in Rives's Salient noted, "We had learned from experience that the grapevine always had the news about right."[56]

Rumors were rampant and widespread. Walters of Grandy's battery wrote on August 10, "An unusual quiet has prevailed for several days along our lines and conjecture runs riot as to the probable movement which Grant will next make." The tranquility along the lines did not last long as the very next day Walters recorded, "A little artillery firing from both side relieved the monotony of the day in a slight degree. The enemy did no damage nor can I see that we did any."[57]

Not only did the rumors run wild on the slightest pretext but clash of arms did as well. A Louisiana artillery officer from the entrenchments near the Donaldsonville guns in a letter related:

> A funny thing occurred on the lines . . . which kicked up a great row. A flock of wild geese alighted between the picket lines . . . bang, bang, bang went the pickets. The men shouted, the geese squawked, fasta shot the pickets, when boom went one . . . Napoleon, followed quickly by . . . [Parrott] rifles and . . . [3-inch ordnance rifle] guns, and then the ball opened. The Yanks replied vigorously and a deafening roar and a crashing of things in general was the consequences . . . mortars shot high into the heavens. The 8 in[ch] and 24 p[ounde]r shells which falling into the enemy's lines and works stirred up things with a looseness, away goes the enemy's 8 in[ch] mortars and for an hour . . . you would have thought 'Hell was about to pop.' Shells rose in the air and crossed and recrossed each others path like so many meteors. It was a beautiful sight but rather 'dangersome' as the old lady said of the short tailed dog.[58]

Whenever a lull occurred in the telling of rumors, time was passed very pleasantly, even in the trenches. One man read to his comrades around the campfire Shakespeare and other classic works, along with poetry, or new novels, especially those from abroad that got past the blockade.[59] The most popular novel in the trenches seemed to be *Les Miserables* by Victor Hugo, and because of it, noted a Confederate, "we called ourselves Lee's Miserables."[60] The Donaldsonville veterans also enjoyed chatting over a cheery fire while smoking the abundant Virginia tobacco in their pipes. "Writing letters, getting up wood, etc., visiting other commands, playing [card] games, principally whist . . . sleeping, such were some of our pastimes," wrote a veteran who also recorded, "the men were always in good humor and ready for fun of any kind."[61]

The artillerist also spent time at night just watching shells "with their lighted fuses, crossing each other in their flight through the air." They did indeed make a beautiful sight before striking the ground with a "thud peculiar, but not pleasant if too near," discerned a Confederate.[62] "I liked to watch the flash of the guns in our front," wrote another, "as we had ample time to dodge before the shells could reach us. It was interesting to note how much time would elapse between the flash of the gun and the sound of the report. Even the whistles of the bombs as they passed over our head, was some seconds behind the streak of fire that marked the flight of the missiles showing it was some distance overhead and we had some fun out of one and another, who not having been watching, would duck down his head involuntarily at the sound of a shell that had already passed by."[63]

All the artillerymen's time on the duty watch was not spent observing the pyrotechnics as one Louisiana artillery officer explained: "I give way to idle fancies of my mind and of late meditating too." He added that he "never experienced such a monotonous career . . . a daily repetition of the day passes."[64] Yet, wrote another artillery officer, "One has but too much time in the night watches of the trenches for meditation on [the hereafter] and kindred topics. In the day and night too I have been analyzing the various sounds a minie ball has. They are sharpshooting over my work all the time and the balls vary curiously in sound."[65]

Quiet moments in the trenches were times when the soldiers and artillerymen often daydreamed, particularly of loved ones back home. Such thoughts brought to mind the antebellum sweetheart songs such as:

Ever of thee, when sad and lonely,
Wandering afar my soul joy'd to dwell,
Morn, noon, and night,
Where 'er I may be,
Fondly I'm dreaming ever of thee,
Fondly I'm dreaming ever of thee![66]

The most popular sweetheart song in the Confederate army was the melodious but melancholy strains of "Lorena" that saddened and soothed the troops in the trenches.[67] Of course the Donaldsonville Canonniers sang their French songs around the campfire, and "in fact," recorded Levy, "crowds of soldiers gather near us on these occasions to listen to these gay songs in a foreign tongue." Sentimental and emotional poetry was also composed with this abridged example written by a Confederate artilleryman in the trenches near Petersburg and appropriately titled "Dreaming In The Trenches":

Well, whether I ever march home again
To offer my love and a stainless name,
Or whether I die at the head of my men—
I'll be true to the end all the same.[68]

Invariably when not dreaming, composing, or sitting around a campfire, it was, according to a Confederate artillery private: "Dig, dig, bore, bore, is the word on both sides while Boom, boom from the mortars, and shrill whistle of Minnie balls alone break the monotony of the . . . siege."[69] Some days of the week passed very gently with an occasional shelling and "a sharp crack, crack of the skirmisher's rifles, but these [days] are so invariable that we call them quietness," wrote an artilleryman.[70] One soldier asked in a letter, "Do you know what 'quiet' means hear [*sic*]?" He answered his own question: "It simply means that the big guns and mortars are silent and you do not hear more than a doz[en] or 20 rifle shots a minute. That's quiet with a variance. Continuous [means] there is an almost continuance crackling of musketry and mortars firing on both sides."[71] Sundays were usually still and quiet and from the trenches a Southern artilleryman noticed they could hear "the church bells of the city and where the silence is broken, as it were . . . by the occasional boom of a gun or the dropping sharp crack of a skirmisher's rifle."[72]

Then there were the "hot and heavy days" with "brisk cannonading."[73] It was on one

Petersburg, September 1864.
ARW; courtesy of Library of Congress.

such day, September 3, while engaged in an artillery duel that Donaldsonville Canonnier Corporal and gunner Ygnace Rougeau was killed by a solid shot ball passing through the embrasure as he was in the act of aiming his Parrott gun.[74] The shot struck him in the head, sending scalp, skull, and pieces "flying in every direction to a distance of ten or fifteen yards."[75] Rougeau's comrades collected his remains while Prosper Landry, still ill with fever, requisitioned and procured a coffin that was received in the field and in which he was buried.[76] While recuperating, Landry wrote his wife, "My Gunners of Donaldson . . . are gathering laurels. But poor Ignace Rougeau will never wear his. . . . He was not only brave, but what is even more rare, he always faithfully fulfilled all his duties. Have someone tell his family this sad news."[77] Levy later noted he "missed Rougeau, a splendid soldier."[78]

Walters also wrote that day, "One of the men of [Moore's] Battery . . . (to the right of mine) had a portion of his left arm, involving the loss of that hand, carried away while serving vent [No. 3 position] at his gun. He was also wounded in the side, which latter may prove a mortal wound, as from the blood that he is constantly spitting, it is thought the left lung is injured."[79] Private Henry Goodsen of the Norfolk Battery was mortally wounded and died September 19, 1864, in the field infirmary.[80]

Of these artillery duels Levy remembered the singing of the Creole Canonniers, "At the invocation, 'Allons enfants de la patre,' ['Come, children of the Fatherland' the first line of the *Marseillaise*] the blood seems to course through the veins with fever heat, and the nervous feeling with which one invariably goes into the fray gives way . . . the gayety of the Creole is thus displayed."[81]

Rougeau had the sad and unfortunate distinction of being the only Donaldsonville Canonnier killed during the siege of Petersburg. The wounded of the Donaldsonville Artillery in 1864 at Petersburg were Corporal Arthur Comstock,[82] Private Eugene Levy, Private Antoine "Tony" Suarez, and the "indefatigable" William Ely,[83] all wounded on July 30, the day of the

Crater explosion. Others wounded later were Private Henry "Henri" Newchurch, wounded in the right elbow in September;[84] Private William "Bill" Newchurch (Henry's younger brother) slightly wounded while asleep in his tent during the night of November 18;[85] Private Suarez, shot through the calf on the morning of November 19 (his second wound);[86] young Private William Leresche, a debilitating wound to the hand by a bullet that pierced it on December 26;[87] and Corporal Antoine "Fortune" Sobral, wounded in the head by an exploding shell.[88]

The total casualty figures at Petersburg for Richardson's Battalion was:[89]

	KILLED	WOUNDED
Landry's Battery	1	9
Grandy's Battery	3	6
Moore's Battery	3	0

Levy returned to Petersburg on September 21 from his wound furlough, but before rejoining the battery he stopped off at Keiley's store. He related:

> Dined by invitation with Major Keiley where a true Irish welcome was accorded me. Left the house at 3 P.M. and went to my old haunt on Halifax st[reet] where I found Miss Helen Schribner at the point of death and her cousin Lizzie the same dirty, stupid, vulgar thing as before. Hastened out to the line and although the covered way protected me to a considerable extent I ran great risk from the bullets of the sharpshooters as I approached the old gun by 5 p.m. I had the pleasure to greet Doc [brother Julian] and my comrades; found all looking well and in good spirits . . . hear the boys speak cheerfully of their design to establish our dear country among the family of nations. Sat down by the campfire and related my adventures while the Minnie balls whistled over the parapets preventing anyone from assuming an erect posture while in the works. From 6 till 7 every evening a truce exists of which both armies take advantage by relieving the pickets. The display of a white flag from the Yankee's side indicates the commencement of the truce and as the signal is displayed the picket's jump from their holes with a shout of relief. Having an opportunity to look about while the quiet prevailed I found that the situation had now been materially changed since last July. Although the picket line of the enemy in front of Rives' farm had been advanced fifty yards nearer our pits . . . the Yankee line-of-battle is now farther removed from us. The semi-circular fort, which annoyed my gun so much on many occasions has been leveled and its guns removed. The extension of their line to the Weldon Railroad has caused a corresponding movement on our part. A few heavy guns have been mounted on the heights in the rear of our line, a complicated system of covered ways has been initiated, and our countermines from Battery 27 is yet in progress of construction.
>
> Doc and Eckleburg[90] occupied a small shelter tent into which I was admitted. Rain fell during the night; I found my plank bed to be rather uncomfortable and did not enjoy the night.[91]

During one of these truces Levy recorded he was

> amused at the fire of repartee which the opposing pickets are in the habit of indulging in as they sit on the edge of the pits. The Yanks have the upper hand today [September 23, 1864,] as they can boast of Sheridan's defeat of Early's army, details of which appear in the latest papers. Our boys brag of feasting on the beef which Hampton captured on Sunday. "Won't you come down and have some Hampton beef-steak, Yank?" "No, Reb, it's too early to go into the valley!" "Grey-back, how would you like to take a ride in that car?" (referring to the train running between the Appomattox and Weldon R[ailroad]). "I wouldn't mind it, Blue-Jay, if you kept a separate coach for the niggers!" Those are specimens of the badinage of the rifle-pits.[92]

Petersburg lines.
Courtesy of Library of Congress.

"In the autumn of '64," wrote Richardson,

> the skirmishers of the two sides seemed to have agreed not to fire at each other without notice; anyhow, they did not fire—they stood up in their pits and talked. 'Hello, Johnny! Hev you sent out your sassyfras detail yet?' This from 'a Nutmeg,' jestingly, to one of our hickory-nuts. We got so familiar after a while that we did not mind each other at all. . . . When there was a truce we would go over the parapet and play 'prisoners' base' on the glacis, just like school-boys. The Yanks would stand up on their parapet in their main lines and watch the game, and laugh and hurrah, and seemed delighted.[93]

"A curious ruse," reported Levy, "has been resorted to in order to draw the enemy's fire and thus secure fragments of iron to sell to the ordnance department, namely, the 'Sham charge.' The officers in command of the pickets commence giving orders: 'Attention! right dress, steady, fix bayonets, forward, double-quick, charge!' The enemy, naturally expecting an assault, opens heavily along the line, and during truce hour we gather the harvest of wasted shot and shell."[94]

On a more serious note, the Louisianian William M. Owen, commander of the Thirteenth Virginia Battalion to the left of Prosper Landry's guns, recorded, "On the 12th of October one-half of our artillery-drivers are armed with muskets, and placed on duty in 'Battery Gregg' . . . all supernumeraries are being armed, and will assist in defending the lines. Every man counts now; no one can be spared. Our strength is being lessoned [*sic*] daily, and there is no material to draw from. We are the, *'last of the Mohicans'* as it were."[95]

"General Lee is adopting the most stringent measures," reported Levy, "in order to increase the army. Negroes are being impressed as teamsters, while all supernumeraries and detailed men are being armed with muskets and sent to the front. Of our battery, John S. Mioton, [Clairville] Savoy, [Jean] Delmere and [Gustave] Charlet were ordered to Fort Gregg, a heavy earthwork . . . to form part of the garrison there."[96]

Mioton wrote,

On October 13th . . . four men from the Donaldsonville Artillery were ordered to report to [the chief of artillery] Walker . . . the writer, being one of the four. We were then sent to Fort Gregg, under the command of Captain Chew, of Maryland, with Frank McElroy, of the 3rd Company, Washington Artillery, as our lieutenant.

During our stay in the fort we were drilled as infantry by one or two officers of General Mahone's Brigade. Our winter quarters were just back of the fort—that portion protected by a stockade—the front and sides being an earthwork, with a good sized ditch in front. There was no artillery in the fort at the time, but in constructing it provisions had been made for four guns.[97]

Fort Gregg was an earthen fortification built as an outpost to guard the western approaches to Petersburg. There were a total of sixty-four[98] artillerists detailed from Walker's Third Corps artillery battalions that became known as the "Musketeers"[99] but "in vulgar parlance of soldier's as 'Walker's Mules.'"[100] They spent the winter at the earthen fort and drilled in infantry tactics. "It was something new," wrote a Musketeer,

and the boys took great interest in the manual of arms and drill evolutions. As the winter on that bleak hill was quite cold and wood scarce, we divided up into mess squads of from four to eight men and dug square pits in the ground that our tents would stretch over, about four feet deep, digging a small chimney by building a funnel above the ground with mud and sticks. And we thought we were pretty well fixed up for the winter. And while we found new associates, we missed the daily association with our old friends back in the old companies, and the stay at Fort Gregg would sometimes grow monotonous.[101]

By October 15 the weather had turned from "winterish" to "Indian summer"[102] at Rives's Salient where each gun detachment was limited to seven men and a corporal with the supernumeraries acting as infantry in support of their guns. A typical October week along the lines for the Gunners of Donaldson was recorded by Levy: "Monday Oct. 17th Heavy firing on our line in which my piece was actively engaged (a very spirited artillery duel).[103] The mortar practice of the enemy is too accurate for comfort. Two infantrymen, who were visiting us, got down in the bombproof and decided not to stay for dinner for fear of accidents."[104] He continued,

After dinner Eckleberg and myself cut wild grass for a bed and enjoyed an excellent rest after midnight for until that hour the Yankee mortar shells fell around our positions in profusion. The danger was too imminent for me to appreciate the romantic part of the exhibition.

Tuesday. 18th Oct'r. Went to town to buy salt and on returning found that one of the enemy's eleven-inch bombshells had torn the embrasure of my gun to pieces. Was detailed to cut wattling poles, but as no wagon could be found for the conveyance, the expedition was deferred until morrow. Played chess with a captain of the 16th Mississippi and was victor.

Wednesday. 19th. On detail from 8 A.M. to 4 P.M. with a large party engaged in making a covered way for the artillery (to retreat through in case of emergency. Solved the abstruse)[105] problem: "how little work can be accomplished by a certain number of cannoniers in a limited time?" was solved in soldier-like style. (Severe bombardment of our position by the siege guns and mortar batteries diagonally opposite.)[106] Intended to write in the afternoon but the falling of mortar-shells in the vicinity of my quarters prevented a grouping of ideas.

Thursday. 20th. This day was distinguished by the heavy and continuous bombardment to which the line was subjected. A gun of [Grandy's Norfolk] Blues twenty yards to the right of my piece was disabled by a mortar shell."[107]

Walters of the Blues Battery recorded in his diary, "This morning I was again sent on a detail to cut poles for the traverse which our company is building, though I think this will be about the last, as one wagon load more will be enough. . . . I returned to my gun between eleven and twelve o'clock, having waited for the moon to rise. On arriving I found that the enemy had been throwing mortar shells over in a very lively manner. One of which, striking the left wheel of my gun, knocked it to pieces, though no other damage was done, and this was soon repaired by putting up one of our spare wheels."[108]

Levy continued his journal that night,

> At 10 o'clock P.M. orders were received to prepare to repel an assault which [Yankee] deserters stated was about to take place at dawn tomorrow. Friday, 21st Oct'r, /64. Reveille at 4 o'clock; no assault made much to the disappointment of the gun detachment. Jim Phillips[109] sent the mess a few potatoes.
>
> Saturday. 22nd . On 48 hours leave of absence . . . went to town and found the place so infernally stupid that I returned to the front. A hail storm swept over the country east of the river at about four o'clock and the weather became instantly cold. Got wet by rain while on guard and retired to shiver until morning.
>
> Sunday. Being troubled with a toothache went in search of a dentist and had the fang extracted . . . returning to the gun . . . as we had been warned by last nights experience to prepare for the chill blast of winter all hands had, on getting up in the morning, commenced demolishing the chimney and clearing out the tent preparatory to making a "kennel," as it is called. The work once inaugurated had to be continued and . . . by dark the work had sufficiently progressed for us to make temporary arrangements . . . built a merry little fire in our cosy chimney place and as the weather had moderated, we managed to get along comfortably . . . an excellent camp dinner and a cup of real tea at dark.
>
> Monday, 24th. Doc went to town last night and brought cut light bread and sugar so that we were able to prepare a good breakfast . . . the mortar shells began to fall pretty briskly after breakfast . . . finishing the new habitation. It consist of a hole, about three feet below the surface of the ground; [by six in length] roofed with a shelter tent and having a [daubed] chimney in one corner. The [sleeping] bunk [for the mess] occupies two-thirds of the [elegant] "apartment," leaving a space of about two feet by six in which we stow away wood and arrange our household goods. On the whole it is a mighty snug little place and I feel intense satisfaction in sitting on the side of the bunk and contemplating the work of my hands. (We felt that it was well done. It was the custom for the member of the mess on guard to mind the fire after his two hours "vigil." Thus we kept from freezing, despite the fact that but one blanket was available for covering purposes.)[110] After dinner Eckleberg and myself bathed in a creek near town.[111]

The siege continued with the Donaldsonville guns occupying the same positions on the line in November 1864. The gun and caisson drivers had to support the guns whenever the Twelfth Virginia Regiment and Sixteenth Mississippi Regiment left the entrenchments. The other Mississippi regiments were taken from the line and placed in reserve on November 11 and 12 respectively. Around this time Levy wrote: "No matter how many of Grant's hirelings are killed or wounded, he merely makes a requisition on mankind at large for more food for powder and it is furnished. This fact is ever before us, causing the men to feel that with all of Lee's genius he cannot create soldiers to fill the gaps in our ranks."[112]

All along the front line, according to the journal keepers of the Washington Artillery, Norfolk Blues, and other writers in the artillery, the new year of 1865 brought "the very worst weather of a bad winter."[113] In the blustery days of March there was less writing of picket firing, artillery duels, and mortar battles, (though it was still death for any man who put his head above the ramparts) but continuous jottings of the elements. In the entrenchments a little fireplace kept the men warm "and in spite of the bitter cold," wrote a Confederate veteran, "we could keep comparatively comfortable if it had not been for the constant dripping of water and the numerous rats that made their holes in the walls."[114] Another gray veteran remembered, "The weather was very wet and cold all winter. The citizens told us it was the worst winter they had had for years. We were in a bad plight, half frozen, half starved, and deserters were leaving us every night."[115]

"Desertion continued to sap the man-power of the army," wrote Lee's biographer Douglas Southall Freeman, who added, "The reason for this wastage in an army that had been distinguished for nothing more than for its morale were all too apparent—hunger, delayed pay, the growing despair of the public mind, and, perhaps more than anything else, woeful letters from wives and families telling of danger and privation at home."[116] In the Petersburg entrenchments there was great suffering because of meager rations, and in the Donaldsonville Artillery there were complaints "of threaten[ed] starvation."[117] Their pay was months in arrears. A Washington Artillery diarist recorded in February 1865, "I was paid off today for the months of July, August, September, and October without the clothing allowance. Amount $76."[118] Citizens were despondent, and a woeful letter was enough to make a "gallant Confederate veteran"[119] like Major Victor Maurin take furlough and leave his post at High Bridge to render family assistance.[120]

The Donaldsonville Artillery to its credit had just two men from the Petersburg trenches go absent without leave between June 1864 to March 1865. Both were married with children back in occupied and burnt Donaldsonville. The two left for home together and both were captured by Federal authorities at the Mississippi/Louisiana State line in the railroad town of Osyka, Mississippi.[121]

A Federal report to the commander of the Army of the Potomac dated December 14, 1864, reads: "A deserter from the Donaldsonville Light Artillery, Richardson's battalion, A. P. Hill's Corps, about 1 o'clock this p.m. States that the battery is stationed near Fort 29, near the Jerusalem plank road." After questioning, this deserter was sent on December 15 to City Point, Virginia, where he took the Oath of Amnesty and was released. The deserter identified himself as James Bryan of Ascension, Louisiana, and informed the Yankees he was a private in the Donaldsonville Battery. James Bryan was never listed or mentioned as a member of the Donaldsonville Artillery in any official record, private correspondence or muster roll. He obviously knew of the Canonniers but was not quite familiar with where they were from since he gave "Ascension" as his home. Ascension is not a town but the parish (like a county) and one does not normally give the name of their county instead of town as the place they live. The deserter also did not provide, perhaps purposely, the Donaldsonville guns' exact position at Battery 25.[122]

The question is then asked, "Who was this deserter?" The Sixteenth Mississippi Regiment from late August to November provided infantry support to the batteries in Rives's Salient and on their roster, in Company K, is listed Lieutenant James H. Bryan. However, he was captured on August 21, 1864, at the Battle for the Weldon Railroad and sent to Fort Delaware as a prisoner of war until his release in June 1865. The deserter, perhaps a member of this regiment, but positively not a member of the Donaldsonville Artillery, deceitfully gave Bryan's name and the Donaldsonville Canonniers as his unit, thus hiding his true identity to this day.[123]

Near the end of 1864 a Louisiana artillerist recorded, "It is reported the citizens . . . would give the army a real Christmas dinner, we had visions of hams, turkeys, chickens and all kinds of good things for distribution, we were hungry and no doubt our wish was father to the thought. Suffice to say Christmas came true to form but that dinner failed to materialize."[124]

January 1865 passed quietly away despite the cold and stormy weather. It was disquieted living in the trenches without any significant actions or events taking place. A solemn Lee worried about lengthening lines and thinning of forces, the privations the soldiers had to meet, and the scarcity of food for them and horses. He later reported, "Unless the men and animals can be subsisted the army cannot be kept together, and our present lines must be abandoned." [125]

January 1865 arrived with Landry's Gunners of Donaldson "Well and in good spirits."[126] Then February came and went with the Canonniers remaining quietly in position, in their dens and pits along the earthworks with the blue smoke curling from the mud chimneys. They became "thoroughly benumbed"[127] during guard duty in the trench line of Rives's Salient and afterwards sat over big campfires and discussed "the merry days."[128]

Prosper Landry noted, "In spite of the weariness of this company, which is excessive, I have not yet heard a single expression of jealousy against those [in Mollere's section] who lead a so soft existence at High Bridge. 'It is not their fault,' they say, 'if they are having fun.'"[129] Neither did the patriotic spirit wane for the Gunners of Donaldson. At a meeting of officers and men in the trenches of Petersburg, they pledged their "unadultarable devotion to the cause for an unlimited period of time."[130] Landry's Canonniers wrote out their resolutions relative "to the measures best calculated to secure peace, and urging prosecution of the war" and presented the paper to Louisiana's Senator Edward Sparrow, after which the resolution (in open session) was ordered to lie upon the table in the Provisional Confederate Congress and be printed.[131]

"At the campfire the sentiments of the [Donaldsonville] boys on viewing the old flag [of stars and stripes] were discussed," recorded Levy, "and the opinion holds that it is now but the symbol of oppression and tyranny."[132] Of another campfire discussion the Canonnier diarist sarcastically wrote, "Every man announces his plan for circumventing Grant's movements. Strange how many thousands of military geniuses this war has developed?"[133]

On February 22 Grandy's four Norfolk Blues guns were withdrawn from the salient. Walters, who was on furlough recovering from rheumatic pains that day, wrote,

> This morning . . . I learned that our company was ordered to withdraw their guns from the line for the purpose of being held in readiness in case of a battle on the right, at which point Grant is expected soon to make a desperate and final effort for the possession of the Southside Railroad. As soon as I heard this, I left town and in an hour reached my gun where I had the satisfaction of being told by all that I was a fool for coming out looking as badly as I did. After considerable exertion I succeeded in getting my things together and then waited for night, under cover of which we were to take our pieces out. Towards nightfall I began to feel so bad that I deemed it advisable to remain on the lines all night, which I did, being accommodated with a good bed in the tent of the Donaldsonville Battery . . . during the night, I suffered so much with pains in my limbs that I found it impossible to sleep. At an early hour . . . I got up and left the lines, and after great exertion and much pain, reached the house at which our company had quarters at the head of [Harding] Street. On reaching there I was so much exhausted that I took to the floor where I lay all day, unable to move.[134]

Walters recovered from his illness and reported back to duty on March 14.

The beginning of March found fifty thousand men left under Lee's immediate command at Petersburg, where Prosper Landry on March 7 submitted to the Adjutant and Inspector General's Office the last muster roll of the Donaldsonville Artillery, from January 1 to February 28, 1865, which reflects:

RECAPITULATION, FOR DUTY: one Captain, two Lieutenants, two Sergeants, three Corporals, one Bugler, two Artificers, and thirty-five Privates, TOTAL: 3 Officers, 43 Enlisted;

SICK, PRESENT: one Private;

SICK, ABSENT: one Sergeant, four Privates.

MILITARY APPEARANCE: Good.

ARMS: 4 metal pieces.

CLOTHING: Fair.

RECORD OF EVENTS: Nothing of importance has occurred on this line. This section still occupies the same position in Rives' Salient (since June '64) about two miles from Petersburg. One section on detached service at High Bridge, S. S. R. Road since May 1864.

ON DETACHED SERVICE: one Lieutenant, four Sergeants, six Corporals, forty-four Privates.

TOTAL: 1 Officer, 54 Enlisted [at High Bridge- 44, Fort Gregg- 4, Treasury Department- 2, Third Corps Artillery Ordnance Train- 1, Recruiting Service- 1, Surgeon General's Office, Richmond- 1, Hospital Duty, Richmond- 1]

DISCHARGED BY ORDER [of Secretary of War]: one Private. STRENGTH-PRESENT AND ABSENT: Officers- 4, Enlisted- 121, Aggregate- 125.[135]

In March 1865 Lieutenant Colonel Henry Mortimer Favrot, on orders from Henry W. Allen, the Louisiana governor, notified Prosper Landry to complete a "succinct narrative" and roster of the battery and submit it to Favrot in Richmond. The governor previously had appointed Favrot as historian and commissioner of army records for the state of Louisiana and instructed him to obtain a record of all Louisiana troops mustered into service, noting their organization along with marches, battles, and incidents, which were to be transcribed into suitable books. On February 1, 1865, Favrot received a ninety-day pass from the Headquarters Post at Richmond and went about notifying and assisting the different Louisiana units stationed at Richmond and Petersburg regarding their *Historical Memoranda,* which the Donaldsonville Artillery and other Louisiana commands completed in the latter days of March 1865.[136]

In the Petersburg trenches on March 10 a Louisiana artillerist recorded in his diary, "We have remained quietly . . . for the past month . . . for some weeks we have been having a hard time in the eating line, and are now receiving rations of one-fourth pound of bacon and three-fourths pound of corn-meal a day; sometimes coffee and sugar, but not often."[137] Nights were no more soothing than their meals, as an artilleryman noted, "Awoke at one o'clock this morning by the rain leaking on my bunk. Tried to sleep on three small boxes before the fire. No go. Lay upon my overcoat and got a short nap. Blankets all wet."[138]

Lee's defensive line around Petersburg by this time was almost bare of men, especially after the line was stripped of infantry units to make one last offensive effort. This attack, which involved nearly half of Lee's army was concentrated against the right of Grant's line on March 25 against Fort Steadman. The assault failed and immediately following the repulse the Federals advanced along the right of Lee's positions almost to Hatcher's Run and took the entrenched picket lines.[139] To bolster the defense on the right, Grandy's guns were positioned in reserve near McGowan's Brigade at the Boisseau farm off the Boydton Plank Road in support of Fort Gregg. Here Grandy's men, along with a large detail from all the artillery, began building a large earthwork.[140]

> All Lee's Intelligence reports on the 27th indicated that the anticipated Federal movement was about to start and that it was directed against the upper stretches of Hatcher's Run. This meandering stream covered Lee's right flank. Rising some fifteen miles west and southwest of Petersburg, it was not on the watershed of the Appomattox [River], but ran roughly parallel to that stream for about seven miles from west to east, and then turned to the southwest . . . between Hatcher's run and the Appomattox [River] ran the Southside railroad, one of Lee's two essential lines of communication, via Burkeville. . . . During the forenoon of the 29th Lee received word that hostile cavalry and infantry had started a march southwestward from the Federal lines . . . and had crossed Hatcher's Run.[141]

To counter these moves Lee made new dispositions by sending McCowan's Infantry Brigade westward beyond Burgess Mill on Hatcher's Run and ordering more cavalry to the extreme right. As a further precaution, Lee ordered Walker to have Pegram's Battalion report by daylight to Lieutenant General Richard H. Anderson at Burgess Mill with twenty pieces of artillery. Richardson, the Donaldsonville Artillery's battalion commander, also received instructions: "As soon as it is dark enough . . . withdraw from the trenches."[142] Richardson was advised to relocate with Landry's and Moore's Batteries to the vicinity of Burgess Mill, thus relieving some of Pegram's guns in the entrenchments there on Heth's Division front.

With a heavy rain falling into the night of March 29 Grandy's two Napoleon guns on the line at the Boisseau Farm were again shifted and, recorded Walters, "We reached there in the midst of the rain and as soon as our guns were placed in position, the horses were sent off to bring the guns of [Moore] and Donaldsonville Batteries of our battalion out of the lines on the left of the Jerusalem Plank Road, but owing to the firing this could not be done."[143] In the darkness and rain the Federal artillery opened fire on a large part of the Petersburg front and continued it all night "as if Grant was feeling out the line in an effort to prevent the movement of troops to the right."[144]

With Grandy's horses unable to retrieve Prosper Landry's and Moore's guns, Pendleton notified Colonel H. P. Jones, chief of artillery, Anderson's Division, to "please relieve with some of your reserve guns those which Lieutenant-Colonel Richardson has in position on the line about Rives Salient, and direct Colonel Richardson to report immediately to General Walker the fact of his being relieved."[145] Upon the arrival of Jones's reserve guns they were unable to replace Richardson's because of the "most terrific bombardment of cannon & shells lighting up the entire line of the enemy."[146] The barrage subsided at eleven-thirty and at midnight the Donaldsonville Canonniers (under the interim command of Lieutenant Hubert Treille) and Moore's artillerists were able to leave their bomb proofs and entrenchments with their scanty belongings and accoutrements. Their guns stayed in place as they secured the horses and took the harnessed guns of Jones's crews. When this was done the Canonniers, along with Moore's artillerymen, were ordered "to the vicinity of Burgess Mill, which is some four miles to the right of the position occupied by [Grandy's] company."[147]

At the time the Canonniers were ordered from Rives's Salient (March 29) their commander, Prosper Landry, was in Richmond. The *Historical Memoranda* of the battery had been completed the day before and he was now delivering it to Commissioner Favrot in the city.[148]

Moore's Norfolk Battery and the Donaldsonville Artillery, with Treille and Sanchez leading the two sections of four Donaldsonville guns, traveled west from the city on the corduroyed Boydton Plank Road. Rain fell "in such torrents as to make it impossible to move a wheeled vehicle, except as corduroy roads were laid."[149] Richardson accompanied the guns as they plunged along the rough road. Though it was planked, the Canonniers still were "toiling thro deep red mud" and "very thick rain."[150] For twelve miles the artillery moved in the fearfully dark night. The horses and crews worked their way through pine forest and abandoned winter camps along the road, passing "ambulances . . . & trains of mules roped together & sutlers wagons showing that [the] army was in front, then crowds of niggers with deserted huts & all the remains of last nights bivuack, couriers on jaded horses spurring thro' the motley collection."[151] Moore and Treille at last led the guns across a plank bridge over the now-raging Hatcher's Run. Richardson's two batteries then reached the "half demolished"[152] Burgess Mill, around which Heth's infantrymen were lying in bivouac beside flaring fires.

With the drenching rains still pouring down, the guns were placed beyond the mill on the south side of Hatcher's Run on a ridge that ran parallel with the creek, along White Oak Road in "fine fortifications."[153] Moore's Norfolk guns were positioned to the right of the Donaldsonville guns, which were posted nearer the plank bridge on the Boydton Road. Three earthen forts for artillery covered the approaches to Burgess Mill and the bridge. Other strong artillery redoubts were located at short intervals along the entrenchments and were occupied by guns from Braxton's Battalion of artillery and Pegram's just-arrived battalion.[154]

The well-located and constructed works at Burgess Mill, a "highly important position,"[155] had wide slashings of timber in front and abatis covering a ditch with a large open field beyond. While the cold and wet Donaldsonville men placed their guns in the redoubts, they were informed that the enemy lines in front were concealed by a thick belt of pine trees. Once the guns were in place, the artillery horses were picketed and knotted together by their drivers in the rear. It was noted along the line there were fires made up of piled fir branches "tier over tier just like old kitchen ranges & men in every conceivable attitude drying themselves. . . . Officers on good horses & couriers on ragged jades hurry hither & thither but the line of entrenchments [are] well manned."[156] A chilled and wet soldier in the works wrote, "We piled up great heaps of brush and fired them and warmed ourselves to some sort of comfort."[157]

Soon after dawn, in the hard rain, General Lee riding his gray horse Traveller and wearing a black raincoat with a steeple white hat and gold band, along with Anderson, Pendleton, and several of his staff rode "quietly down the line to Burgess Mill placing guns on partic[ular] points and strengthening others [and] as he goes couriers come dashing up & deliver verbal messages or hand [the general's adjutant, Walter] Taylor a slip of paper to wh[ich] he replies on his horse paper & pen in his holster."[158]

The adjutant of Pegram's Battalion at Burgess Mill wrote of Lee riding among the troops this morning with a "calm face."[159] He noted, "It was touching to see the affection which lit up every dirty courageous face as he passed along the lines, and amusing to hear the homely remarks indicative of their perfect confidence in his skill. 'I wonder what "Mars" Robert is after this rainy morning?' 'Never you mind, his head's level, and he knows, and that's enough.' 'He's riding the grey, and if Mister Grant don't mind, some of his folks'll be hurt this very day.'"[160]

It continued to rain very hard throughout the morning and around twelve noon the enemy made a reconnaissance in front of Burgess Mill. While making these movements, a Federal officer reported the Confederate artillery opened fire "from some breast-works near Burgess house."[161] At two-thirty in the afternoon other Federal units made advances and reported being fired upon from the works near Burgess Mill as they "pressed as closely . . . as practicable without assaulting."[162] The Yankee skirmishers moved "close up against the . . . works,"[163] while the Gunners of Donaldson and Confederate artillery along the line "kept up a pretty constant fire."[164]

Throughout the remainder of the day the rain fell incessantly. "Very few," wrote a Confederate, "could enjoy the luxury of a sleep," even among those not working the guns or on the firing line.[165] By four o'clock in the evening Yankee pickets of Major General Gouverneur Warren's Fifth Corps were entrenched in front of the Burgess Mill works on the left of the Boydton Plank Road. On the right of the road extending out stood Major General Andrew A. Humphreys's Second Corps.[166]

The rain and firing finally stopped a short time before sunset, but because of the soaking wet ground a little sleep came only to those who were "overpowered with weariness."[167] The respite was not long, for about one o'clock on the morning of March 31 it began to rain again. It continued to fall until after daybreak.

During these early hours Lee rode down the Burgess Mill line and discovered the Federal left flank unprotected, opposite the end of his own line along White Oak Road. Lee immediately made arrangements for an assault to turn the Union flank with the only four brigades he had available.[168] Their attack in midmorning initially was successful, pushing Warren's Federal Fifth Corps back for about a mile or more until halted at the Boydton Plank Road along Gravelly Run, where strong Federal positions and support held the line. In about an hour the Federals counterattacked; Humphreys's Second Corps went to the relief of Warren's Corps.

Between one and two o'clock in the afternoon, elements of Brevet Major General Gershom Mott's Division of Humphreys's Corps also attacked toward Burgess Mill in an attempt to carry the redoubts and entrenchments covering the Boydton Road crossing. Mott reported, "The enemy [picket's] rifle-pits . . . were carried . . . but our men were unable to proceed any farther under a cross-fire of artillery sweeping our entire front, besides a brisk firing of musketry, and when ordered to fall back the retreat was found as perilous as the advance had been. The assault by the Second Brigade met with the same obstacle—heavy slashing, sweeping cross-fire of artillery, and brisk firing of musketry . . . the men being unable to reach the works of the enemy."[169] The "brisk shelling"[170] and "very heavy fire of artillery"[171] by the Donaldsonville Canonniers, Moore's Battery, and other guns along the line lasted about an hour before Mott's regiments withdrew and covered their positions with breastworks.

The Union counterattack on Mott's left pushed the four attacking Confederate brigades back past their picket line and into the entrenchments. The Federal commander of the Fifth Corps reported, "I thought we might be able to carry the enemy's breast-works at once, and thus force in their right flank and carry all their line south of Hatcher's Run. I at once commenced a personal reconnaissance . . . and superintended personally the advances of our skirmishers to gain points of observation. We thus drew a very severe fire from the line, particularly of artillery. The examination showed me that the enemy's defenses were as complete and as well located as any I had ever been opposed to."[172]

When the Yankees advanced from Gravelly Run, the Confederate commander of the four brigades, Major General Bushrod R. Johnson, reported, "The enemy's attack fell with force . . . and all our forces were then . . . drawn into the main [Burgess Mill] breast-works, where they lay during the night, with pickets well out on the White Oak road . . . the loss of the enemy were heavy, including about 470 prisoners. Our losses were about 800, including killed, wounded, and prisoners."[173]

Fortune again favored the Donaldsonville Artillery, which did not sustain a casualty during the day's fighting, but the Norfolk gunners of Moore's right section nearby suffered casualties, along with the wounding of their battalion commander Charles Richardson. Walters of Grandy's Battery, located a few miles to the left on the defensive line, recorded on

March 31,

> In the afternoon, we learned that the enemy had charged our picket lines near Burgess Mill in front of the position occupied by [Moore's] Battery, a portion of which [the picket line] they captured and from which, they annoyed our artillery greatly, almost preventing the working of the guns. A short time after, we learned that [Moore's] Battery had lost three men killed and four wounded. . . . Lt. Colonel Richardson of our battalion was also wounded, the ball entering his right side above the hip, and is supposed to have lodged in the spine, though it has not been found yet. The wound is considered dangerous. Toward dark the fighting ceased.[174]

Richardson was "most severely wounded" and transported with the other wounded of Moore's Battery to Jackson General Hospital, located in the western suburbs of Richmond. A nurse there recorded, "We feared at first that he must die, but now there is a little more hope. It is so sad that after four years . . . he should be brought to his native city . . . dangerously if not mortally wounded. . . . I love to sit by his bedside and try to cheer him; his friends seem to vie with each other in kind attentions to him."[175]

The night of March 31 was stormy, starless, and, after the moon set, intensely dark. Sleeping soldiers of both armies could only be aroused by shaking.[176] Wrote an infantry officer in the entrenchments with the Donaldsonville guns after daybreak, "We were not much disturbed this day, directly; for the enemy only ventured to sharpshoot irregularly with the picket in front . . . but the slow firing along the line between us and Petersburg gave evidence of the enemy's design to attack, and the muffled roar of artillery and musketry which reached us from the direction of Dinwiddie Court House assured us that Pickett's division was already engaged in murderous battle.[177] It was a bright, warm, idle day, I remember—just the calm that proverbially foreruns the storm."[178]

Chapter Eighteen

Tout perdu
(All Lost)

On the evening of April 1, 1865, Confederate troops along the Hatcher's Run entrenchments remained on alert. The troops were comprised of Johnson's Division of Anderson's Corps, with McGowan's South Carolina and Scales's North Carolina Brigades (from Wilcox's Division) and McRae's and Cooke's North Carolina Brigades (from Heth's Division) of Hill's Corps, along with artillery pieces from Braxton and Pegram's Battalions, and guns from Moore's Norfolk Battery and the Donaldsonville Artillery. In strong but very muddy redoubts positioned where the Boydton Plank Road led to a small plank bridge across Hatcher's Run, Lieutenant Hubert Treille commanded the battery with one section under the charge of Lieutenant Antoine Sanchez.[1] "As night approached," a Confederate in the works near the Donaldsonville guns wrote, "the enemy showed a disposition to push upon our picket, and the discharges along the two lines became far more rapid and continuous. By the time dark fell, there was an almost incessant rattle . . . not long after dark, we perceived a great stir among Johnson's division . . . we heard that they had been ordered to quit the works."[2]

Johnson's Division withdrew with a bustle at six-thirty in the evening. They headed toward the tracks of the South Side Railroad a few miles away. The movement caused firing to increase all along the line and the enemy now made and continued to make frequent demonstrations along the Confederate works. The Northerners pushed the hard-pressed Southern pickets back behind the now thinly occupied breastworks where the Donaldsonville guns and others fired repeatedly from redoubts, though nothing was discernible in the dimly lit night.

The breaking of twigs and the tramping of the enemy went on a long time, during which Confederate muskets and artillery kept up a steady fire aimed at the noise. Near midnight the enemy made an attack along the left side of the Boydton Plank Road toward Burgess Mill. Treille and Sanchez's Donaldsonville gunners and other artillery fired "heavily"[3] into the dark.[4]

A Federal along the skirmish line observed their line of battle moving forward with a yell in the dark and recorded, "They struck the slashed timber in front, received a galling fire . . . which threw them into confusion, and they fell back. The result of this was, that a brisker fire than ever was opened upon our line."[5] It was officially reported, "The pickets of the enemy were carried successfully, but the moon going down left our men in a complete darkness, under woods obstructed by slashings and unable to find their way any farther. The fire of the enemy having already sufficiently demonstrated that they were there in force the party was withdrawn and returned to the breast-works."[6] In this "unusual darkness"[7] the Yankees were heard going back through the bushes until they were out of earshot of the Confederate redoubts.

Remaining in their earthworks along the Burgess Mill/Hatcher's Run line, the Donaldsonville Canonniers and other artillerists with the remnants of the four infantry brigades remained vigilant and on alert, protecting the right flank of Lee's battle line. They waited and began looking back, away towards Petersburg where one Confederate observer wrote: "From the [Burgess] mill as far back as could be seen or heard the bombs were being passed from each line, all kinds . . . were bursting in every direction and the flashes were so fast that it kept the skies lighted up."[8]

Skirmishing along the Hatcher's Run line continued and was at times fierce. When the Gunners of Donaldson were not loading and firing their pieces, some passed the hours of the night watching and listening. Others were exhausted and laid in the works and dozed. Many were able to snatch "a few moments' repose"[9] until shortly after 4:40 a.m. when, wrote a soldier near Treille's guns, "we could hear the keen cracking of muskets away over in the direction of Petersburg. Nearer and nearer it came—a storm of thunder and lightning by shells and a hail-storm of rifle bullets."[10] An officer at Burgess Mill added,

> Several miles on our left, and rather half-way to Petersburg, the volleys of musketry were furiously fast and concentrated. They were not continuous, like our slow fire, but they would break out in an instant, with a fierce roar of small arms, accompanied by a rapid discharge of artillery, then melt away almost to complete calm, then reopen with the former violence—so alternating between two extremes as to give us assurance of no ordinary struggle . . . men listened to these discharges, and, although they said little, seemed to feel that the end was drawing near.[11]

What was heard was the Federal Sixth Army Corps breaking through with an overpowering attack that shattered the Confederate defensive line and overwhelmed its defenders.[12]

This enemy assault struck and overran Grandy's Norfolk Light Artillery Blues Battery, which put up a valiant fight at the Boisseau farm. It was recorded: "All of the infantry had been withdrawn, and the Blues fought without supports. The enemy charged in front and to the right of them. The assault in front was checked, but the works were carried on their right and the exultant foe charged down the trenches upon the battery. A portion of the guns changed front to meet this attack, and they were fought until the enemy reached their muzzles, when the battery . . . was captured. The enemy's loss was very heavy and the price paid for the battery was a dear one."[13] Grandy's casualties were forty-two captured, including their captain, one killed, and seven wounded. With the loss of their four guns the Norfolk Light Artillery Blues Battery ceased to exist, although some members avoided capture and later joined the detailed portion of their company that escaped from the mortar battery behind Rives's Salient at Petersburg.[14]

At the breakthrough the Yanks drove the survivors right and left. Those thrown to the right headed for Hatcher's Run while those driven left and to the rear rallied at Fort Gregg about two miles northeast.[15] The Virginia army's historian described its importance: "Fort Gregg . . . covered the angle of the 'L' on which the Confederates had to keep their grip until nightfall made possible an unassailed withdrawal. If the enemy took Fort Gregg and the adjoining work to the North, Fort Baldwin [also called Whitworth], he would have between him and Petersburg nothing but the old inner line on the east side of Indian Town Creek. The battle then might be in the streets of Petersburg. Gregg must be held at least until Longstreet could occupy the line from battery 45 to the Appomattox."[16]

Stationed at the semicircular Fort Gregg with its ditch twelve or fourteen feet wide and from four to six feet deep and walls six to eight feet wide at the top, on a hill at an isolated spot a little in the rear of the main trenches, were the sixty-two Third Corps artillery Musketeers that included Donaldsonville Artillery Privates Gustave Charlet, Jean Delmere, Clairville Savoy, and John Mioton.[17] One of the four Canonniers kept a diary. Years later he shared the dairy with one of his comrades, who then keenly wrote out his recollections of the affair:

> Early on that memorable Sunday morning . . . Generals A. P. Hill and Heth called and examined the fort and its garrison, and gave some instructions to our officers. About eight or nine o'clock A. M. General Walker called and we were ordered out and formed on the right of the fort, towards Hatcher's Run, the order being given to deploy as skirmishers and charge the federal pickets, which was accomplished; having driven the Yanks as far back as a farm, on which was a two-story dwelling, in which a good many United States pickets had taken shelter, and for a time the ex-artillerist tried their hands as sharpshooters. The order was then given to retreat into the fort. This was accomplished in a somewhat hasty manner, for the Yanks were getting very thick and the situation hot, to say the least.
>
> On our return to the fort we found two guns of the Third Company of Washington Artillery, two three-inch Parrot guns, which had been stationed in our front, but not having the horses, they were rolled by hand into the fort. They occupied the position looking towards Hatcher's Run. We were also reinforced by a portion of General Harris' gallant Mississippians, the 12th and 16th Regiments, about 150 men, under command of Colonel [James H.] Duncan.[18] The writer happened to be at what was considered the weakest part of the fort, in the angle where the stockade and earthworks met. He [the writer] being a small man, was ordered to go elsewhere, so he took position between the two guns.[19]

Mioton, who wrote the article, stood five feet five inches. He continued:

> The assault began on our right flank. They came in three lines of battle, one behind the other, with their flags floating in the center, but it was only after the fourth charge that they succeeded in entering the ditch in front of the fort. For some time we could hear the federal officers ordering their men on the top of the fort; the officers several times got on the parapet, with their colors in their left hand and their revolvers in their right, and demanded of us to surrender; but many of those brave officers were slain . . . it was then that the brave and gallant No. 4 on the gun nearest the stockade, which was double-shotted with canister, was ordered by the federals, who had by then swarmed the parapet, not to pull the lanyard which he held, but quick as a flash the brave Berry, of the Third Company, Washington Artillery, shouted back, "Pull and be d--d." Useless to say that all in front of that gun were swept off, and our gallant artilleryman was shot down at once, and thus the heroic Berry sold his life dearly.[20]

Another Fort Gregg defender wrote, "There was pandemonium for a good half hour, you would think all Hades had broken loose."[21] Mioton continued his narrative,

> After the garrison [by turning their musket butts up] had surrendered, the federals were so elated at our capture that they discharged their muskets in the air, which action led the Confederates on our left to believe that we were being given no quarter, and they began shelling poor and gallant Fort Gregg. After an hour's hard fighting the garrison . . . after being removed from the fort . . . were taken near Grant's observatory [near Federal Fort Fisher], where each man's name and command was taken by a federal officer, seated in an open buggy, who . . . was the biggest ruffian it was the writer's misfortune to meet. From there we were taken to City Point, and from there to Point Lookout, Md., and remained until the end of July, 1865, when we were paroled.[22]

Federal Brigadier General Robert S. Foster, who commanded a division in the attack by the Twenty-Fourth Army Corps reported, "At about 1 p.m., pursuant to orders, I directed an assault upon Fort Gregg, which was gallantly made, and resulted in the capture of the works . . . the fighting on both sides at this point was the most desperate I ever witnessed, being a hand to hand struggle for twenty-five minutes after my troops had reached the parapet."[23] The Union corps commander Major General John Gibbon reported, "The enemy made a most desperate resistance, and it was not until Fort Gregg was almost entirely surrounded and our brave men succeeded in climbing upon the parapet under a most murderous fire, that the place was finally taken by the last of several determined dashes with the bayonet . . . this assault, certainly one of the most desperate of the war, succeeded . . . but at a fearful cost."[24]

"They made a Homeric defense," wrote Freeman, adding, "The Federals had to charge themselves with 714 casualties in return for fifty-seven Confederate dead, 129 wounded prisoners and thirty [prisoners, including the four Donaldsonville artillerymen] who were worn and grimy but unhurt. The other Southerners escaped to receive the plaudits of observers and the assurances that their resistance had given 'Old Pete' [Longstreet] sufficient time in which to organize a thin but stalwart defense of the works on Indian Town Creek."[25]

Just before dawn back at the redoubts along Hatcher's Run and at Burgess Mill, Treille's and Sanchez's Donaldsonville sections and other defenders in their dirty gray or butternut-colored cotton cloth gazed but a few yards into a misty fog while "listening to the great roll of musketry that swept for miles along the lines, and was returned to [them] in horrible echoes from a hundred forests."[26]

A Confederate infantry officer near the Donaldsonville guns wrote, "When day dawned we were exhausted by waking and anxiety, and every pale face appeared to ask, 'What next?' It was difficult to tell where the enemy were. At one time our artillery was about to open [fire] on the portion of woods and abatis unpicketed in our front, from the belief that they lurked around our very works; but, after a time, we learned that they were not so near, and the action was deferred."[27]

After sunrise the fog dissipated as the spring sun shone through the new foliage. At about seven o'clock on the morning of April 2, 1865, with it bright and clear, two Yankee batteries took position in front of the redoubts protecting the Boydton Plank Road and the bridge across Hatcher's Run and opened fire on the works. The Confederate guns replied. This artillery duel lasted an hour before a Yankee regiment advanced. It was halted by the Confederate infantry and artillery, which "opened a terrific fire of musketry, shells, and canister upon [them]," after reaching their own picket line. [28]

By this time word had reached the troops at Burgess Mill that the enemy had stormed and carried the defenses of Petersburg and that Lieutenant General A. P. Hill had been killed. Major General Henry Heth reported, "As soon as I found that the enemy had possession of the Boydton Plank Road [between Hatcher's Run and Petersburg] and that he was moving down this road my position being no longer tenable I gave orders to withdraw to Sutherland's Station on the S[outh] S[ide] Rail Road."[29] The artillery caissons and baggage that could not be hauled away for lack of horses or space were then burned.

With severe skirmishing going on, the Confederate cannons from the redoubts near Burgess Mill fired very freely at the enemy's batteries and infantry. The drivers hurriedly harnessed the horses, hitched up caissons and wagons, and prepared the horses to pull out their pieces from the redoubts. Between eight-thirty and nine o'clock that morning the guns fired one last shot, after which their teams were hitched-up and withdrew the guns quickly from the embrasures "while the men filed out on the run behind the entrenchments."[30]

Just before limbering up Treille's and Sanchez's Canonniers were hailed by a messenger from a neighboring battery asking for assistance to get a gun out of a hole. Donaldsonville

Henri Michel Gamotis
Courtesy of Joseph Thomas Hardy and Beverly Gamotis Hardy of New Orleans.

Privates Henri Gamotis and Alcide Giroir volunteered and were allowed to go. After helping, they were too late to reach the plank bridge across Hatcher's Run. Gamotis plunged in and saved himself by swimming. Giroir was not heard from by his comrades and was reported missing.[31]

The Gunners of Donaldson "contributed materially" to checking the pressure on the line and the advance of the enemy. This gave other Confederate troops time to reach the bridge and the only road by which they could retreat. The Canonniers "had barely time to limber up, and were among the last to cross that memorable bridge. Corporal Arthur Comstock had failed to 'mount' and was diligently footing it behind when he came upon Sergt. L. A. Landry, who, out of breath, had given up the race. 'Come along, Tip—there's the bridge—we can make it yet.'—and they did make it, escaping unhurt despite the many bullets aimed at them."[32]

Upon leaving the redoubts Treille and Sanchez led the four Donaldsonville guns towards the Claiborne Road, which led to the railroad in the rear.[33] Describing the movement of the four brigades and guns from Burgess Mill, a Confederate officer wrote,

> We moved rapidly [back]ward, passed out of the line of works, crossed Hatcher's Run, and bore northwest, in the direction of Sutherland's Station, on the South Side Railroad. Artillery and ordnance wagons hurried along the same route with their customary noise, and with more than their customary celerity.
>
> After a march of about three miles we came in sight of the railroad. The enemy, following us with energy, now opened with artillery upon the rear of the Confederate column, and a few pieces of the latter replied to them. It was evident that we must give them battle. The trains of wagons and artillery were hurried up past us, and Gen. Heth selected a line of defense. This line ran, for nearly half its length, just on the edge of a highway, and, for its whole length, was almost parallel with the South Side Railroad. The right of the Confederate line rested by a large house on the west of the road by which we came; our left against a country church. . . . The railroad was a hundred yards in rear of the left of the line, and passed through a deep cut here. We were on the summit of a perfectly smooth, open ridge, which commanded the slope towards our enemy for six or eight hundred yards. At about that distance ran a small stream and a ravine. Beyond the ravine rose a high ridge, similar to the one we occupied, but covered partly with large oaks, partly with pine . . . our lines—Cook's, [*sic*] Scales', McRae's, McGowan's . . . were allowed a few pieces of artillery, principally on the flanks and near the center of the line.[34]

The Confederate artillery had one gun at the church, two in the center, and four guns near the tavern. Moore's Norfolk Battery and the Donaldsonville Artillery operated some of these guns to support the infantry.[35]

The Federals closely followed the retreating Confederates and at about noon found them in the above position behind a low dirt embankment that was hastily thrown up by the defenders with bayonets, tin cups, plates, or whatever else they had to move dirt, then fortified the mound with rails from the neighboring fences.

The Yankees immediately attacked with two brigades. A Confederate defender recorded,

> We were not long left in suspense. All the length of the crest of the ridge before us began . . . to glitter with arms, and then to grow blue with the long lines of the enemy swarming to the attack. Although at least half a mile from us . . . with yells . . . they rushed forward rapidly, disordering their line . . . our artillery fired upon them . . . [and] all our troops within rifle range opened on them. They replied volley to volley and shout to shout. . . . The Federals paused . . . then swayed and reeled hither and thither, and finally fled in confusion. Loud and long cheers proclaimed the result.[36]

During the battle a Confederate sharpshooter recorded,

> Within six paces of where we were was a piece of field artillery, with four horses; and the artillerist, to protect themselves from the enemy sharpshooters, lay down behind the earthworks, amongst us. But the standing horses, being plain to see, were a fair mark, and it was but a little while before one of them was struck down, then another, and presently another, and then the last. I shall never forget the piteous looks of one of them, wounded, as he lay on his side in his harness every now and then raising his head to look back at his wound, then laying his head on the ground again, without a sigh or a groan; it was indeed piteous.[37]

The Yankees made a second assault on the entrenched Confederate line with the assistance of the artillery of their division that had by this time come up. After being placed in position, the Yankee guns began a "vigorous shelling."[38] This attack, like the first, was also repulsed, "Owing to a terrific enfilading fire of artillery and musketry."[39]

After this attack the artillery of both sides maintained a "slow fire"[40] for about an hour as the Federals assembled another brigade in the woods on the flank of the Confederate line. At about 2:45 p.m. a third attack was launched that overlapped and struck the extreme right (near the church) and the railroad tracks. The Yankees double-quicked with a hearty cheer. The Confederate cannons then fired grape and canister into the attackers and though "its use was of short duration," a Federal officer reported, "the fire . . . did considerable execution."[41] Through the smoke the Northerners swept rapidly down inside the Confederate entrenchments, enveloping them into "one living cloud of blue coats."[42]

The only two guns left of Moore's Norfolk Battery were surrounded and captured, as it was later recorded: "The . . . Battery was in position . . . and . . . held its ground until further fighting became useless and impossible, and then, yielding to the inevitable, became prisoners of war."[43] Many of the forty-six members of the Norfolk Battery were captured at Sutherland Station, where the Federal Corps commander reported "Taking one flag, two guns, and 600 prisoners."[44] The captured Southerners were sent without guards towards the camps at Burgess Mill, where the Confederate wounded remained behind when the lines were evacuated.[45] Perhaps as many as twenty of Moore's artillerists escaped captivity at Sutherland Station or before the Yankees had a guard detail to watch the prisoners, though only two from the battery, First Sergeant John W. Ashe and Private Nathaniel G. Reid, managed to escape and joined with the Donaldsonville Artillery.[46]

Before the whole line collapsed and while bullets whizzed through the air, a Confederate officer recorded how a wild uproar arose among the surviving Confederates:

> Some were for resisting to the last, some advised immediate flight, some gave up the cause, and counselled unconditional surrender. It was not easy to decide in this conflict of opinions. The idea of fighting to the death was the heroic one, certainly; but there was more pride than wisdom to it. The idea of surrender was not base; because we all felt that the lines around Petersburg were gone—we could hear, even above our own battle, the roar of those last assaults which were carrying with incredible slaughter the fortresses about the beleaguered city—and Petersburg lost, the capitol was gone, and the army rent to pieces. . . . The most thorough discipline was unequal to the control of men, in these circumstances; everyone must elect for himself. So there was a Babel of tongues, a hurrying, thronging, watching, and planning—until, at last, there came a rupture, some staying behind in despair, some disputing the progress of the enemy, retiring, some fleeing for life. On came the Federal lines, like the converging currents of a storm, cheering, firing, sweeping over the whole field.[47]

While the Donaldsonville guns under Sanchez "fought"[48] in support of the infantry, the French language, the Spanish Isleños dialect, the Irish brogue, and the English and German tongues of the Donaldsonville contingent under Treille, had their own debate. Described as "all Creoles and gallant soldiers,"[49] the Louisiana artillerymen decided to remain "continuously in service on the retreat."[50] Their goal, along with other units, was "to join the main army, from which we had been cut off by the break."[51] Around forty haggard and exhausted Canonniers with their four guns and wagon that carried few supplies and the "books of the company"[52] moved off from Sutherland Station. Four privates did not make it past the station.[53]

Compelled by overwhelming numbers to give way, three of the four Confederate brigades got caught in the panic and fled the field or crouched motionless in their defenses. The Federals captured a large number of prisoners, while the others escaped in "precipitous flight" according to the Federal division commander.[54] Those going rapidly to the rear joined the most disorderly movement of wagons, troops, and guns, with only Brigadier General John R. Cooke's North Carolina Brigade and the four artillery pieces near the tavern retreating in a fairly controlled manner.

A retiring Confederate officer wrote:

> A weary, mortified, angry stream of men poured through the fields and the roads. . . The commands were mingled confusedly . . . So we wandered—strung along the [Appomattox] river bank for miles, straggling through brush and brier, floundering in the beds of small streams or in mud-holes filled by the recent heavy rains, and pressing forward to some points undetermined in our minds. Night fell upon us, but even that brought us no repose, until, at a late hour, we . . . lay down by the road side, in utter exhaustion of body and almost utter despair of mind. Some of us were so worn, that we slept like the dead—others so anxious and harassed that we could not sleep at all.[55]

Hungry and exhausted the Donaldsonville Canonniers finally stopped during the night.

The march was resumed soon after sunrise on April 3 along byroads where the horses and guns passed through mudholes filled with water and along ruts made by the wagons in front. The men on foot walked through open fields alongside the muddy road, their stomachs growling for a small parcel of rations. The column was strung out for miles and at about nine o'clock in the morning reached Deep Creek, where the infantry continued to cross during the day, but the wheeled vehicles had to cross at a ford some three miles above the muddy road. After, the wagons and artillery were collected two or three miles west of Deep Creek and halted as the scattered foot soldiers came up and rejoined with Johnson's Division and the remains of Pickett's Division. About the survivors from Sutherland Station, Freeman wrote, "That any of them got away and succeeded in reaching Lee's line of march from Petersburg was due more to the character of the individual soldier than to the persistence of the old-time discipline of the Third Corps."[56]

Mollere's Detachment at High Bridge

On the night of April 2 at High Bridge near Farmville, Virginia, the militia received marching orders. Lieutenant Camille Mollere's detachment of the Donaldsonville Artillery aroused at three o'clock in the morning with orders to again guard the bridge fortifications. Some of the Canonniers (armed with muskets from the Reserve Corps) were detailed to guard the "Negro prisoners."[57] At eight o'clock on the morning of April 3, after being relieved from guard duty, Donaldsonville Canonnier Private Eugene Levy recorded,

> Oh ever memorable day of horror! I heard of the capture of Petersburg, the evacuation of Richmond, and the retreat of Lee's army in the direction of Burkeville. Joe Walton[58] came up on the train and brought the most soul-harrowing details of the disaster. Pickett's division having been flanked [at Five Forks] and driven from the South Side Railroad allowed Sheridan to turn our right. What other military combinations combined to force us from our works could not be positively ascertained. A. P. Hill is among the slain. May God protect our noble commander, for the name of Lee will act as a talisman for the recall of the army. Overpowered, yet not beaten, our gallant men will rally around his standard, determined to do or die. All day long most cruel rumors have reached camp; all is hurry, bustle, and intense excitement. My poor brother and comrades, I tremble to think of their probable fate: death, gaping wounds, or a Northern dungeon. Yet, I must not despair. Lee will bring order out of chaos, and with [the] help [of] our heavenly Father, all will be well.[59]

Levy continued to record his and the activities of Mollere's Canonnier detachment: "Anticipating marching orders I made all the necessary preparations and having ascertained that horses would be furnished to the section to-morrow, devoted the afternoon to making calls." Levy spent the evening and the next morning returning books and bidding farewell to the "kind people" in the neighborhood of High Bridge. "The ceremonies of parting with such friends depressed my spirits, and I spend a night of watchful anxiety," he wrote.[60]

On the morning of April 4 Private Thomas B. Whiting of Grandy's Norfolk Blues Battery, who had been on furlough, found his way into the Canonnier's Camp Paradise after attempting for several days to reach the army. From one of the cabins at High Bridge, Whiting related "that all of the artillery in the first line fell into the hands of the enemy," adding, "It appears that the line in front of Petersburg was 'crushed' by the masses of Yankees at an enormous sacrifice of life." On hearing this, Levy jotted that he "wandered about like a disturbed spirit from cabin to cabin and all around the neighborhood my mind was unquiet and my heart sick."[61]

From each straggling cavalryman that arrived fresh rumors were heard and passed along. In the evening Levy recorded, "All was confusion in camp . . . it had been decided to retreat to Farmville as the latest reports indicate the advance of the enemy beyond the [Burkeville] junction. If horses arrived by midnight, which have been promised, it is proposed to move the entire section. Having procured everything for marching I threw myself on some straw and slept until 12 o'clock a.m."[62]

Mollere received the promised horses. Levy's diary continued on April 5,

> At a quarter to three the two guns without caissons and one wagon moved from Camp Paradise on the road to Farmville. At half past three we fired a train and exploded the magazine of Battery 3. Then we cut down the guns and caissons which we were forced to abandon, and traveled through the heavy rain and thick gloom away from the seat of so many innocent delights. I took the railroad being unable to walk on the slippery

> road, and reached town before dawn. Laid down for an hour in the corridor of Booker's Hotel,[63] then joined the guns as they passed up the Prince Edward C[ourt] H[ouse] Road. At seven o'clock we went into bivouac alongside of the Reserve camp on Mrs. Venable's farm[64] and an hour later were retracing our steps to town. Then we traveled westward on the Lynchburg road and went into park just outside of the town. A lying courier caused us to hitch up and remained on the 'quive vive'[65] for some time, but when the excitement ceased the boys straggled about town. I bathed and . . . dined in camp on some good cheese from Mrs. Lockett's. . . . I managed to get the glee club to serenade the young ladies at the College. The affair passed off pleasantly and the boys serenaded Miss Sturtevant,[66] the most elegant looking girl in town . . . As rain fell just after midnight, Jim [Canonnier Private James B. Carothers] and myself took refuge in a neighboring house.[67]

On April 6 Levy continued,

> Before breakfast . . . it commenced to rain . . . when the infernal cavalry scouts came dashing up the road alarming women and children with the much dreaded announcement "Yankees coming." About the time that I reached the bivouac, the pieces were ready for action. We dashed through town as rapidly as our miserable horses could trot, women crying and waving handkerchiefs, and the most intense excitement visible. With Booker's regiment[68] in advance we gained the heights a mile from town, went into battery, and the . . . piece (to the left of mine) fired a couple shots at the column of [Yankee] cavalry which had the effect of driving them from our front. Then we advanced to the next ridge while pretty brisk skirmishing went on to the left. In half an hour the enemy disappeared, retreating in the direction of High Bridge.[69]

Two regiments of Federal infantry (123rd Ohio and Fifty-fourth Pennsylvania), along with three companies of cavalry (I, L, and M of the Fourth Massachusetts), were sent in advance to burn the High Bridge over the Appomattox River. The senior cavalry officer who escaped uninjured reported,

> We proceeded quietly until, when within two miles of our destination, the advance guard was fired on by a few mounted rebels. The cavalry then pushed forward to hold a road leading to the bridge, while the infantry followed slowly. A few minutes later we came to a small stream, the bridge over which had been torn up, and on a hill just beyond were about thirty rebel cavalry who commenced firing as soon as the head of our column came in sight. The advance guard . . . dashed forward, laid the planks, charged up the hill, and drove the enemy for more than a mile until, near Farmville, they were re-enforced and made a stand. We skirmished with them for half an hour or more, when they opened on us with *artillery*, and we gradually fell back, hearing our infantry firing quite rapidly in our rear.[70]

Soon after, about midday, more Confederate cavalry from Major General Fitzhugh Lee's command and Major General Thomas L. Rosser's division arrived and attacked and defeated the Yankee cavalry and infantry. The Federals who were not casualties were for the most part captured.

Levy recorded, "I walked over with Jim [Carothers] to view the scene of action and on returning stopped at an elegant white house about a mile from Farmville the property of Widow Venable,[71] occupied by Dr. Carrington's family, which proved to be 'Longwood' the birthplace of the great Gen[eral]l Joseph E. Johnston.[72] Accepting the hospitality of the elegant Mrs. Carrington I indulged in a most sumptuous dinner served with wine in Southern style.[73] Miss Mildred Carrington is a remarkable beauty."[74] The patriotic Mrs. Carrington entertained a large party of officers and soldiers for dinner and remembered Levy years later.[75]

"By four o'clock," continued Levy, "the guns passed through Farmville on the way to the old bivouac amidst the cheering smiles of the heroic ladies. As the advance guard of the army reached town before dark there was unusual bustle on Main St. All the boys turned 'flaneurs'[76] and wandered about the streets consoling their comrades. Gen[era]l Breckinridge[77] took rooms at the Hotel and was the observed of all observers. After dark the interminable stream of wagons and ambulances passed on the Lynchburg road. The 'glee club' serenaded Rev[eran]d W. McIlvaine and returned at midnight."[78]

On the memorable Sunday morning of April 2, 1865, Donaldsonville Artillery commander Captain Prosper Landry happened to be still in Richmond after delivering the company's *Historical Memoranda* and was unable to return to Petersburg. Without a horse, Landry trekked on foot from Richmond to Farmville, and after five days of traveling over sixty miles, Landry in the evening of April 6, located and joined Mollere's Donaldsonville Canonnier detachment at High Bridge. There he assumed command of that section of the Donaldsonville Artillery.[80]

Treille's and Sanchez's Detachments

Meanwhile, on April 3, the sections of Donaldsonville Canonniers under Treille and Sanchez with Major Merritt B. "Buck" Miller and Major General Richard H. Anderson's remnants from Sutherland Station halted two or three miles west of Deep Creek, where they went into park. This being an opportune moment, the men scattered through the woods and fields "seeking food and rest."[81] Though heavy skirmishing was heard in the afternoon, the wagons and guns remained parked until midnight when they moved off. "The troops generally following them," wrote a veteran from Sutherland Station. "The depression of spirits and exhaustion of the bodies of our men increased. They fell about and slept heavily, or else wandered like persons in a dream . . . we marched slowly forward until a little after noon, when we reached Amelia Court House. There were commissary stores here, and we drew perhaps a day's rations of meat—possibly, some hard bread, but of that I am doubtful." Some bacon and bread was issued, but noted the veteran, "I had reached that pitch of hunger where food actually nauseates. I found myself greatly improved by eating a little."[82]

At Amelia Court House the troops from the Richmond lines united with those from the Petersburg lines. For those who escaped from Hatcher's Run, there was much rejoicing at rejoining Lee's main army. A Sutherland Station survivor said that it "was indeed like getting home from a distant voyage."[83] A few "were silent and depressed," but for the most part Lee's veterans "laughed" and were "cheerful as of yore."[84]

During the morning of April 4 Lee ordered Brigadier General William N. Pendleton to make arrangements for reducing the artillery with the troops to a proportionate quantity in order to not encumber the road and slow down the retreat. Accordingly, the Third Corps artillery commander Brigadier General Lindsay Walker received orders to lead all the artillery not needed with the troops, estimated at one hundred guns, on a longer route north of the road used by the rest of Lee's army. With Treille's gunners, drivers, and horses worn and wearied, the Donaldsonville guns along with Major "Buck" Miller remained all that was left of Richardson's Battalion capable of a fight. They were ordered to join the lengthy column of reserve artillery that included the Washington Artillery and "several hundred baggage wagons and a number of ambulances."[85] Years later an artillery veteran upon being asked by another about the retreat, replied, "I am very much like you, everything from Petersburg to Appomattox is mixed up with me, except at Amelia Court House, all surplus baggage & broken horses & wagons & caissons were fired, of course the broken horses were turned out."[86]

Garnering some rest but with few provisions for the horses and practically out of food, (wagons were sent out into the country side but returned almost empty) Walker's artillery train with Treille's and Sanchez's Petersburg contingent of Donaldsonville Artillery struck off in a northwesterly direction on a "wet and gloomy" April 5 morning.[87] The march was monotonous, though "rumors," wrote an artilleryman, "are plentiful," noting, "One is that Genl R. E. Lee is captured."[88]

The half-starved mules and gaunt-looking, staggering horses stalled in the mudholes and creeks. The artillerists, tramping wearisomely behind their guns and battery wagons, and many for the most part barefooted in the mud, loaned their shoulders and hands in pushing and extricating the wheels out of the slime and ruts. As the day wore on, the men and horses became, if possible, more exhausted.[89] A worn out artilleryman wrote,

> It became necessary to relieve the battery horses of some of their burden, for they, as well as the men, were suffering from the lack of food, and were jaded from the constant marching. Accordingly, one or two of the cannon . . . were dismounted and buried, the wheels of the limbers and caissons were cut down, and so much of the ammunition as could not be carried along was destroyed. Thus lightened of their labor, the horses were enabled to hold out to the end. Though foodless, footsore, and sleepy were the men, the march was continued . . . with no event or incident of importance to relate.[90]

The column stretched out as they moved over the rolling hills. The dogwoods and redbuds bloomed forth on hills and in meadows, but the surrounding country and farms had little in the way of provisions to relieve the hunger of the artillerists who subsisted on a parched-corn supply.[91] A Louisiana artillery diarist recorded, "We marched to & crossed the Appomattox river at Clementown bridge & camped."[92] In ending the day another cannoneer diarist wrote, "Many rumors are afloat of the presence of the Yankee cavalry along the route which is supposed we will take, and it is evident that our position is not altogether a safe one. We camped at 9 P. M. within five miles of Clementown Mill's Bridge over the Appomattox river."[93]

The batteries of Walker's column began moving on the morning of April 6 at four o'clock.[94] A Louisianian noted, "It rained this morning early, balance of the day clear."[95] There was a great deal of straggling. One worn artilleryman described how, "It may well be conceived that . . . was a weary procession. It was akin to a funeral march, a journey to the dead . . . the men walked on almost in silence. There was no loud or boisterous talk, no songs, no merriment. All hearts were sad, many faces despondent; few hopeful words were spoken."[96]

The Donaldsonville contingent, along with the remnants of the Washington Artillery, continued on with Walker's column, turning west at Tobaccoville then south over a hilly and rough Cumberland Court House-Farmville Road. They passed through the small town of Cumberland Court House with dwellings strung out along the road and a pleasant looking courthouse that had large chimneys and rippled panes of glass. The tired and tattered Louisiana artillerists were probably unaware that across the street from the courthouse stood the old Effingham Tavern, which had served travelers since the American Revolution.[97]

After passing Cumberland the artillery train trekked on. A Washington Artillery diarist noted that they "marched about 20 miles & stopped at 6 P.M. about 10 miles of Farmville, fighting going on at High Bridge."[98] Another diarist, a battalion adjutant with the artillery train, simply recorded, "Reached the Fork of Willes' Cr."[99]

One artilleryman would later write his wife about this march, "Without rest, or food, or sleep, how could men move on continuously, and keep their places by the guns? Men slept while walking along. The drivers slept upon their horses. Men would drop down by the wayside and be asleep in a second. Only the strongest and most resolute could keep their places and continue to march."[100] A Virginia artillerist wrote, "Such an arduous march as this caused a great deal of straggling on part of the boys, the majority of whom were completely broken down."[101] The next day a Washington artillerist recorded, "A great many of the Virginians in the army are deserting every day and are not willing to leave the state."[102]

The Donaldsonville Canonniers with Walker's artillery train broke camp again at daylight on April 7 and continued their movement over rough country roads to Curdsville, a small village located three miles south of Willis Mountain. The town had a Masonic temple, a tobacco warehouse, several mechanic shops, a small tavern, and a mill. While on the move, Walker's guns and wagons, several miles ahead of Lee's retreating army that was moving north on the Buckingham Plank Road from Farmville, met with elements of the army carrying rumors. Of the stories heard, a Louisianan noted, "A portion of our army was whipped at High Bridge."[103]

This news no doubt made the Donaldsonville Canonniers with the Petersburg sections heartsick, particularly Julian "Doc" Levy who in turn wondered about the probable fate of his brother and other comrades with Mollere's detachment. About these reports another wrote, "Several alarming rumors of the nearness of the Yankee Cavalry are prevalent, and several stories are told of their daring and successful attempts to cut off portions of our artillery and wagon trains. Most of them, however, are doubtless the creation of excited imaginations."[104]

Walker's artillery train now became *l'avant-garde* (the vanguard) of Lee's retreating army. A Louisiana artilleryman later wrote, "It was a race for life, for men who were hungry, and for gaunt-looking horses who were dropping by the road side; but we had to push on."[105] They did press on, though halting frequently during the day for rest as they passed farmhouses, ploughed fields and foot high wheat, white flowered cherry and plum trees, and blossoming peach orchards. At every opportunity the horses were grazed and hay foraged during these stops. About six miles beyond Curdsville the column passed through New Store, a stage line stop on the Richmond-Lynchburg (Cumberland) Stage Road that consisted of the Louis D. Jones house, called Keswick, a cobbler's shop, a store, and three offices,[106] and "a good view of the Blue Ridge [mountains] about forty miles distant."[107]

After traveling about thirteen and a half miles for the day, camp was made by the Louisianians at eight o'clock in the evening a mile or two past New Store. An artilleryman recorded, "Under these circumstances, the first thing done after the horses are unhitched is to find water. No one asked if the water was clear or good. It had to be drunk anyhow, and these were unnecessary questions."[108] After dark an anonymous Confederate wrote, "We turned in upon the cold ground by the roadside—supperless and hungry. Perhaps my meal may be in a few yards of me—but not knowing where it is—it might as well be in Africa."[109]

L'avant-garde took up the line of march on April 8 between one and two o'clock on a misty morning, though it turned out to be a "clear"[110] day. After moving about nine miles from New Store, Walker's batteries turned south at Rose Bower and continued their toilsome marching on a better road ascending and descending elevated ridges from which a large section of the country could be seen. "On the west," wrote one, "the Blue Ridge rose in its morning garb, and on the east a broad plain of green, here and there broken by gradual elevations, appeared under the morning mist."[111] Early in the evening the Donaldsonville guns and horses, along with Walker's hundred or so guns and around two hundred wagons, "clattered through the village" of Appomattox Court House. There the "excited villagers" of women and children looked on.[112] The column continued on about two miles past the courthouse, but before reaching the fork in the road leading to Appomattox Railroad Station and the city of Lynchburg, the guns and wagons went into park. The fields that they camped in were bordered by woods and old groves.[113]

"Halting in the field, as each piece drove up," wrote an artilleryman after the twenty mile march, "the teams were unhitched and given their scant food, or allowed to graze while the men were busied making their corn and coffee and cooking probably the remnants of an old cow, from which rations had been dealt and eaten that morning within an hour after her slaughter."[114] Some wagons brought into camp several hundred sacks of shelled corn. Another artillerist recorded, "Here at last we hoped to find rest for our weary bodies as well as sustenance, for we were told that at the [railroad] station which was a very short distance off at the foot of the hill, there was a train with commissary supplies. My haversack had long since been lightened of its load. . . . I need hardly say that the knowledge that food was obtainable in the immediate vicinity gave a new zest to life. . . . After parking [the guns], we threw ourselves on the ground to get some rest after a long day's march, soon to find relief in that sound, stupid sleep which follows fatigue and hunger."[115] Before long many were "comfortably snoozing,"[116] but others went to wash off or get drinking water at a nearby spring. A few set up the three-legged baking kettles of various sizes around several campfires.[117]

Near dusk, while most of the camp was asleep, there came the old cry, "The cavalry are coming, they are at the station and coming up the hill."[119] Another artillerist wrote,

> In this irregular bivouac so little was the nearness or approach of an enemy suspected that no sort of a guard had been set, and when the report of arms and the sight of Federal cavalry in the wood skirting the field, startled officers and men from their little mess fires and slumbers, the surprise was complete and astounding . . . but . . . in a moment quick orders sent cannoneers flying to their post. Never were guns more quickly unlimbered, loaded and brought into action, nor . . . perform a neater or more expeditious piece of work than on that field, under circumstances that might well have demoralized and stampeded them. In an incredibly short time the confusion of a surprised camp was suppressed and every gun was pouring canister into the ranks of the enemy, who had advanced to the edge of the woods, less than two hundred yards distant.[120]

Another artillerist remembered, "Suddenly a horseman dashes down, yelling out that the Federals were charging! For a moment some confusion prevailed. But we stood our ground. The infantry[121] fell into line, our guns were quickly shotted, and just as the Blue Coats burst from the cover of the wood before us, we opened on them, loading and firing as rapidly as we could. The enemy charged up almost to our guns, calling out: 'Surrender! surrender!' But we gave them canister and the infantry saluted them so warmly, that they soon retired, with the loss of several of their men."[122]

The Yankee cavalry fell back to regroup for another charge while screened by the dense woods. This gave time for Walker, who at the time of the first attack was in the process of shaving,[123] to form a defensive line with musket-carrying artillerymen in the fringe of pines. Behind this line the Donaldsonville and Washington Artillery batteries, and others, formed into what was described as "a hollow circle of some 40 feet diameter, presenting 'war's horrid brazen front' on all sides to the advancing foe."[124] In the semi-circle of artillery were parked many wagons, and they, along with a major portion of Walker's guns, attempted to move away from the area where "everything," wrote a surplus Virginian, "was pell-mell, hurry-scurry. Several horses, with harness dragging, passed me, but I could not catch them."[125]

A Confederate cavalry brigade under the command of Brigadier General Martin W. Gary[126] rode into and through Appomattox Court House just as the sun was setting. Soon after, upon hearing the incessant roar of cannons, Gary led his horsemen rapidly towards the scene. He communicated with Walker, and the brigade was dismounted and double-quicked to the batteries. Some were deployed as skirmishers with the musket-armed artillerymen.

One of the cavalrymen, a South Carolinian, remembered,

> By this time the grey of twilight was lighted up by the rising moon, and there seemed to be a lull in the attack . . . Before our men could get to the guns the enemy charged and got among them, but were driven back by the fire and our rush. . . . Our men fell between the guns, and then began one of the closest artillery fights . . . the guns were fought literally up to the muzzles. It was dark by this time, and at every discharge the cannon was ablaze from touch-hole to mouth, and there must have been six or eight pieces at work, and the small arms of some three or four hundred men packed in among the guns in a very confined space. It seemed like the very jaws of the lower regions. They made three distinct charges, precluding always with the bugle, on the right, left and center, confusing the point of attack; then, with a cheer and up they came. It was too dark to see anything under the shadow of the trees but the long dark line. They would get within thirty or forty yards of the guns and then roll back, under the deadly fire that was poured upon them from the artillery and small arms. Amid the flashing, and the roaring, and the shouting, rose the wild yell of a railroad whistle . . . sounding on the night air as if the devil himself had just come up and was about to join in what was going on.[127]

A member of the First Company Washington Artillery later noted in his diary, "The Yanks charged our camp & we opened on them with about 40 guns and continued firing until our wagons got out into the road."[128] Another artillery defender wrote, "We loaded with canister and as the enemy approached our position (which was a miserable one) we poured a fire into them which completely broke them. They returned to the charge four times and each time were similarly repulsed. This kind of reception did not seem to their liking, and they appeared to have retired . . . at this moment, and while we were waiting in expectation of a renewal of the attack, which had dwindled into firing between a few skirmishers, orders were received from General Walker . . . to withdraw our guns to an adjacent road."[129]

For three hours the Donaldsonville Canonniers and Washington Artillery held their ground with other guns of Walker's command against Brevet Major General George A. Custer's Cavalry Division's repeated assaults. Some attacks were powerful while others reckless and disorganized. It was reported that Custer was now wild with desperation as Yankee officers surmised from the silence of Walker's artillery that the Confederates were attempting to withdraw their main batteries.[130]

With the lull in fighting, a member of the Third Company Washington Artillery recorded, "Sat down on the trail [of the gun] feeling very tired and was laughing at the accounts of the big stampede when Major [Merritt B. "Buck"] M[iller] orders us to limber to the rear and move out. Took the road and passed into a confused mass of wagons."[131]

Treille too was ordered to limber up the Donaldsonville Artillery guns, and they moved off at once, it being but a few hundred yards to the main road. A South Carolina cavalryman noted,

> In passing from the old field, where the guns had been at work, into the woods that separated it from the turnpike, two men were walking just in front of me following their gun, which was on before. I heard one say, "*Tout perdu.*" I asked at once, "What battery do you belong to?" "Donaldsonville." It was the Creole company; and they might well have added the other words of the great Francis, after the battle of Pavia, "*Tout perdu fors l'honneur,*" all lost but honor; for well had they done their work from "sixty-one, when they came to Virginia, until now, when all was lost, "*Tout perdu*"—it was the motto of the occasion.[132]

> The silence of the guns soon told our friends over yonder what was going on, and they were not long in following after; our men, facing to the rear, delivered their fire steadily, moving in retreat, facing and firing every few steps, effectually keeping off a rush; they pressed us, but cautiously—the darkness concealed our numbers . . . before we got

> to the turnpike we heard the bugles of the enemy down it, and as the head of our column came into the road their cavalry charged the train some two or three hundred yards below us. Sixty pieces of cannon, at the point where we came into the road, the drivers were attempting to turn back toward the Court House, had got entangled with one another and presented a scene of utter confusion. As our regiment got into the road . . . I had but little fear of the enemy's cavalry riding into us on the road, so blocked up as it was with the routed artillery train, and there were woods on both sides just here.[133]

"Tout Perdu" (all is lost).
From R. A. Brock (editor) *Gen. Robert Edward Lee.*

Treille, Sanchez, and the highly esteemed Quartermaster Sergeant Louis Aimé Richard led the Donaldsonville Canonniers onto the turnpike road. The scene was described as an, "indiscriminate mass of guns, caissons and baggage-trains . . . the road was packed . . . in one grand inextricable confusion, some headed one way and some another, and all so thoroughly interlocked and obstructing the road, that . . . ordinarily passable for several wagons traveling abreast of each other, a single horseman could with difficulty select a bridle path."[134]

The four companies of the Washington Artillery Battalion also went into the mass of wagons. After a short distance they halted as heavy musket fire broke out in a field on the left that was separated from the road by a strip of woods with thick undergrowth. "After standing thus in column for five minutes," wrote a member of the Third Company Washington Artillery,

> the firing drew nearer and our men began to dodge into the road and strike double quick back towards the courthouse into the woods beyond. Just at this juncture General Walker dashed up from the rear and orders us in a very excited manner to come about and go back to Appomattox . . . order from him to <u>come into Battery and give them canister</u>. Halted to unlimber but found the struggling mass of wagon drivers and infantry in the way. Lead horse . . . got entangled in the brush—extricate him and dashed ahead after the pieces. Just then ahead the bugles of the Yankee cavalry sound a charge. Gave the drivers orders to push on at a gallop and shots began to come whizzing along—striking men, horses, and pieces. Then a yell burst forth and it was plain that the enemy has broken through our lines which was asunder. One and more gobbling up the train at a fast rate . . . the moon was shining brightly and one could see them trimming the train. Still the clatter of horse's feet came and went up the lane and we heard the leader say 'come on boys we've got "em on the run." The <u>rally</u> sounded and they charged on up the road capturing wagon after wagon and piece—after piece.[135]

Custer's Calvary "by a flank movement"[136] hit the trains of baggage, supplies, and artillery and advanced along the road towards Appomattox Court House. The Donaldsonville Artillery and Washington Artillery were "cut into."[137] Three batteries of the Washington Artillery were forced into the direction of the courthouse while their Second Company was "separated from the others and forced in the direction of the railroad station."[138]

Treille, Sanchez, and Richard, with the remaining Canonnier drivers and gunners, fell back to the courthouse town, where in the streets they met infantry coming to their support and who in turn drove the Yankee cavalry back.[144] The remaining Canonniers included Jacques Esprit "James" Besson, with the company for just eleven months, a former

Donaldsonville student whose father was associated with the antebellum Canonniers; Severin Blanchard, "extremely popular"[139] and considered to have no superior as a soldier though he maintained a "cheerful continence";[140] Désiré Carmouche, a "good soldier";[141] Eugene Cooley, a pious and faithful fighter; Henry Edouard Duffel, a modest, dutiful veteran from one of the leading families of Ascension Parish and nephew to Captain Prosper Landry; John "Eck" Eckleburg, looked upon favorably by his officers; Cleophas Landry, an ordnance driver, who was "popular," "noble," and "conscientious";[142] James Landry, a youthful veteran admired by his comrades who accompanied him to the end; John McCoy, five and a half feet tall with black eyes, black hair, and a dark complexion, a native of Tennessee; the valiant Morin brothers, "Edouard" and Mathieu; and Louis Armas Triche, "a good citizen"[143] and cavalry veteran. These Canonniers reached the other side of Appomattox Court House, where they observed what another described as "glimmering . . . fire-flies, on the hills just beyond the little village" that was the "camp-fires of all that remained of the Rebel host."[145]

In the mayhem of that night some of the guns of the Washington Artillery and possibly some of the Donaldsonville Artillery were captured "for want of sufficient room to maneuver."[146] Custer reported the capture of twenty-four pieces of artillery[147] in the mass of guns, caissons, and baggage-trains seized. Seven Donaldsonville Canonniers were captured in the turmoil of the battle. They were the popular Corporal Antoine "*La Fortune*" Sobral, who in later years would sit with his "Donaldsonville cronies" on the cool veranda of his Oak Alley Plantation and fight their battles over and over every Sunday afternoon with "long, tall tales which always ended in explosive laughter and: 'We gave those Yankees hell!'";[148] Charles Pidoux, who did "faithful service as a Cannoneer . . . during the whole war";[149] John "Edouard" Newchurch, the oldest of three brothers serving with the battery and "a gallant soldier";[150] John Sabastien Suarez, just five feet one inch tall but "respected";[151] Narcisse Plesencia, diminutive but plucky; François Leon Dugas, another "good and faithful soldier of [the] company";[152] and the brave bugler Edward Severin Terrio, who disregarded danger in the "strict performance of duty."[153]

Before being moved off to Farmville, where the seven Canonnier captives were paroled a few days later, they, along with many others, were marched under guard to a piece of woods where the Louisiana prisoners, about fifty in all, gathered around a campfire. Here the Washington Artillery prisoners "tried to console the rest of the captives by singing until taps."[154]

Those Gunners of Donaldson who escaped completely were the "widely known"[155] Corporal Arthur Comstock, who would later proudly say he was "never captured";[156] Emile Bergeron, with blond hair and black eyes, who "served gallantly until the end"[157] and was regarded as "a true gentleman";[158] William "Deles" Delesdernier, a veteran volunteer that remained "to the end of the war";[159] Henri Gamotis, who won "the encomiums from his comrades for the dauntless spirit and brave deportment displayed by him in action";[160] Maurice Landry, who in escaping the confusion later admitted he didn't "remember where I was";[161] Silvere Augustin "Sylvester" Landry, "a gallant soldier"[162] noted for his "sturdy virtues";[163] "Henri" Newchurch, another "good and worthy citizen";[164] and the Louisiana Tiger veteran Asbury Overby, who after the war remained in Virginia and married.

With hunger and exhaustion taking its toll, many of the men in Walker's artillery train "had fallen out of ranks the last day or two, broken down or sick and disabled."[165] The Donaldsonville Canonniers unaccounted for at the end were Ernest Lynd, a college student who enlisted in 1863 at age seventeen; Alexander McCullet, a forty-year-old Irishman who suffered for months with diarrhea; Antoine "Tony" Suarez, recently recovered from his leg wound in the Petersburg trenches; his cousin Raphael Suarez, thirty-one years old; Collins

"Colin" Sutherland, another thirty-one-year-old; and "VH" Williams, a veteran attendant with the battery since Yorktown.

At least one Donaldsonville contingent escaped with Major Miller and the three guns of the Second Company Washington Artillery that were ordered by Walker to bring up the rear. These Canonniers were led by twenty-four-year-old Sergeant Louis Aristide "Tip" Landry, the five foot eight inch, hazel-eyed son of a former Congressman who had just made it across Hatcher's Run days earlier. His crew was comprised of Privates Eugene Queprotte, a French immigrant who lived in Terrebonne Parish and was one of the first to enlist after Fort Sumter; the "kind"[166] Henry Nicaud, just seventeen years of age; and Seymore Mioton, who, along with Nicaud, was a student in New Orleans before joining the battery in June 1863. Mioton now had the added burden of grief, believing that his brother John died at Fort Gregg. With this group was also Cyrille Decoux, son of a New Orleans constable; John Murphy, a blue-eyed Irishman no doubt thinking of and wondering if he would ever see his wife Catherine and three-year-old daughter back in Donaldsonville; Julian "Doc" Levy, burdened with not knowing what had become of his brother Eugene with Mollere's High Bridge detachment; and finally J. Guggenheimer, in his forties, who latched on and marched with "Tip" Landry's gun detachment.[167]

These eight Canonniers escaped—along with fifty-four artillery pieces and many caissons, forges, and wagons—with Walker.[168] Of their night march towards Lynchburg one of the escaping artillerymen remembered it "like a confused dream. Forward and on, but whither and to what fate . . . forward and on, walking sometimes in sleep, holding on to tail of gun or wagon, as is the belief and assertion of some, who believe they remember the fact. Tired out drivers urged on poor, jaded beast, ready to drop with fatigue, hunger and thirst, but . . . on and on, through the dark hours, tired teams and men were urged on . . . the slow coming dawn found the company still trudging on . . . and the rising sun has seldom looked down on a group of men and animals more completely wearied out."[169]

"Brig. Genl Walker," wrote one member of the Washington Artillery party, "after two or three attempts to move his wagon train . . . failed and disbanded his command telling everyone to take care of himself."[170] A member of the Second Company Washington Artillery recorded, "We then proceeded up the road a short distance and disabled our guns & buried them with many misgivings, about 30, or 40 of us started down the road going to Lynchburg, and there some one suggested that we might be fired on, a flag of truce in the shape of a sheet was procured from a nearby dwelling, and tied to a pole, and carried by [Quartermaster Sergeant] Joseph DeMeza a member of our company who started the Hymn of 'Soon with Angels will be marching.' We went to Lynchburg Va and were paroled there, my parole being dated Apl 13th 1865 . . . signed by 1st Lieut. Sam Hawes."[171]

Hawes of the Second Company Washington Artillery also signed the paroles of the Donaldsonville Canonniers at Lynchburg.[172] The Zouave veteran, blacksmith, and native of France, Donaldsonville Canonnier Private Leopold Keroll, escaped and straggled into Lynchburg where he was paroled on April 14 with three other artillerists from other batteries.[173]

One of the thirty or forty reaching Lynchburg on their own was First Company Washington Artillery Private Frank Lobrano who, like Corporal Tomasso Morelli of the Donaldsonville Artillery (because of his readable handwriting) did his company's writing, i.e. printed the muster rolls and other necessary paperwork. Lobrano's diary on April 9 notes, "I lost all the [Second Company Washington Artillery] company books."[174] Like Lobrano's mishap the commander of the Gunners of Donaldson, Prosper Landry, would later make known in correspondence that "all the books and papers of the [Donaldsonville Artillery]

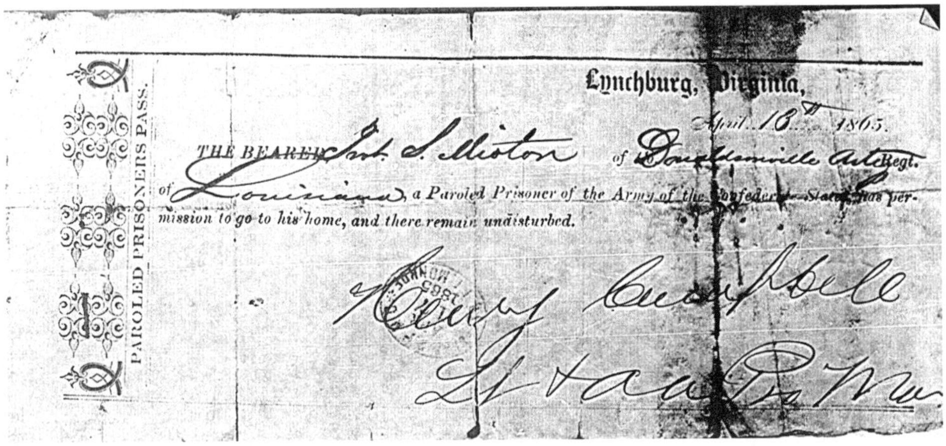

Paroled prisoner pass of Donaldsonville Canonnier Seymore Mioton, dated "Lynchburgh, Virginia, April 13th 1865."
Courtesy of the Louisiana Division of Archives, Records Management, and History (hereafter cited as LDA).

company were lost during the retreat from Petersburg to Appomattox C. H."[175]

Mollere's High Bridge Detachment

Back at Farmville on April 7 Captain Prosper Landry commanded Mollere's two-gun detachment of the Donaldsonville Artillery and received instructions to report to Colonel David McIntosh's Artillery Battalion, which back at Amelia Court House was selected to follow Lee's army along with the rear division and cover the retreat. In moving down the road from Farmville towards Cumberland Court House to join the battalion, Prosper Landry's guns entered "amidst a confused mass of men, guns, wagons, and stragglers."[176] While moving along the road Donaldsonville Artillery Private Eugene Levy recorded, "Just outside Farmville I saw the God-like Lee and in the impulse of the moment presented him with the bouquet [a souvenir] which Miss Pritchard[177] [in Farmville] had sent me. The troubled expression of his noble countenance was changed for a moment as he gave one of his sweet smiles and thanked me. God preserve him from witnessing the defeat of his fondly cherished hopes!!"[178]

The Donaldsonville guns went into park about a mile outside Farmville while the exceedingly slow wagon train of Longstreet's column passed by sometime after eleven o'clock in the morning on the Buckingham Road, heading to the Lynchburg Road and Curdsville. Near two o'clock in the afternoon, after Prosper Landry's detachment had joined the procession, "guns began growling"[179] from the Cumberland Church vicinity. "Our progress behind the wagon train," wrote Levy,

> was necessarily slow except when a charge of the Yankee cavalry caused a stampede of the wagons on which occasions we had to draw off to the right flank and prepare for action. We had no occasion to unlimber during the day. Heard of Doc's [brother Julien Levy] safety through several parties, also of the recapture of our other [Grandy and Moore's] guns . . . all along the route the wreck of the army was left and vast columns of smoke indicated but too plainly the fate of abandoned wagons. Plunder was plentiful and rations were freely distributed to all parties. The road was in horrible condition so that by dark we had made but 5 miles. Halted at 10½ o'clock on the farm of the Widow Johns, nine miles distant from Farmville on the main road to Lynchburg. We were engaged until midnight in cooking. A mule which I had picked up in the

> morning proved a good friend and I concluded to forage on joint account. I retired much exhausted, but agreeably disappointed at not having been captured by the Yanks. As the rain had ceased before dark, I enjoyed a good sleep.[180]

The march resumed at one o'clock in the morning along the red mud roads with Longstreet's command now in the rear of the army but followed by friendly cavalry. Recently assigned to McIntosh's Battalion was Lieutenant Colonel William M. Owen, former adjutant of the Washington Artillery Battalion, who recorded, "The march . . . continued without orders all night, the men falling asleep at every halt. And so the retreat rolls on. We are passing abandoned cannon, and wrecked and overturned wagons, and their now useless contents belonging to the quartermasters. Horses and mules dead or dying in the mud. At night our march is lighted by the fires of burning wagons."[181]

Around daylight on April 8 New Store was passed. After dawn it turned into a "lovely day."[182] Longstreet's column wearily tramped on all day long in their clothes that were by now tattered and covered with mud. Levy noted they "traveled at a pretty round pace until dark, by which time we had arrived at the base of the hill."[183] Levy also noted there was "considerable skirmishing in our front all the afternoon, yet the train continued to press its way towards Appomattox."[184] McIntosh's Battalion, with Mollere's two Donaldsonville guns led by Prosper Landry, went into bivouac despite the sound of artillery fire in front.

What remained of Lee's army, including sixty-one guns and thirteen caissons among the infantry, halted about nightfall and stretched six miles alongside the road before Appomattox Court House. Owen reported the artillery parked along Rocky Run, a little stream just east of the wooded hill where Lee had his headquarters and about two miles from the courthouse.[185] "Here we parked for the night," wrote Levy, "and having bathed my feet and face felt sufficiently re-freshed after the 22 miles march. Concluded to have my flour prepared at the hotel."[186]

As was his way, Levy left camp and went into Appomattox Court House to the Clover Hill Tavern kitchen[187] where he later wrote,

> I had just bargained with the buxom negro cook to bake my flour when with a terrific rush, unheralded by the noise of fighting, our cavalry came pell mell through the village closely pursued by the enemy. Hearing the ladies scream I ran to the house to comfort and advise them, induced them to be quiet, then set about seeking an avenue for escape. Having prepared for any emergency by arranging my finances, securing some bread, and stripping a bed of its blankets, I watched until the street was clear (the view from the hotel window by moonlight was quite convenient) and prepared to execute a flank movement. On appearing on the front porch I was hailed by a picket and concluded to submit gracefully as there was no other alternative.
>
> My captor, one of the 15th N[ew] Y[ork] Cavalry, Custer's Division, Sheridan's Corps, proved very kind.[188] He permitted me to pick up some clothing on the route and although he fancied my French blanket gave me two excellent ones in place of them. For four miles the road was encumbered with captured wagons and guns, the contents of the former strewn around and trodden in the dirt. At one time I was ordered to drive a team of mules attached to a wagon, but I managed to run into another train immediately on starting. I was summarily deprived of my position and continued to follow my captor until I was again pressed in to drive some broken down horses of the Washington Artillery which I also managed to get rid of. Met several of the W[ashington] A[rtillery] bragging as usual in a disgusting manner. Formed a mess with a very clever South Carolinian named Muldon[189] and as he had meat and I bread we got along famously. Having decided to cook a chicken the guard furnished us with every convenience and added sugar and coffee to our larder. We moved once during the night to a field adjoining Appomattox Depot and had the glare of the burning depot to assist us when the moon had set. Slept but a short time but so soundly that I did not hear the

Clover Hill Tavern where Canonnier Private Eugene Levy "submitted gracefully" to capture on the front porch.
Courtesy of the Library of Congress.

> reveille.[190]

Levy was eventually marched to Farmville where he was paroled a few days later.

"After we went into bivouac this evening," wrote Owen with McIntosh's Battalion and Prosper Landry's Canonniers,

> the artillery firing, we had heard in front late in the afternoon, seemed to be approaching nearer. It was not a great while before long trains of wagons came tearing down the road from the front, the driver's whipping up their mules and shouting lustily. I mounted my horse and rode forward to see what was the matter. I had not gone far before I came up to a force of infantry that were being aligned across the road and preparing for defense. Here I met some officers and men of the Washington Artillery, from whom I learned that Gen. Walker's column of artillery [met] . . . the enemy [who] advanced . . . again and again . . . the artillery that could be gotten off, fired retiring, and fell back to Appomattox Court-House, where in the streets of the town, they met infantry coming . . . who in turn drove the cavalry back with loss.[191]

Levy was not the only Donaldsonville Canonnier to leave camp. Sergeant Oscar Demesme, a native of France, went forward to reconnoiter, probably to learn what had become of Treille's Canonnier detachment. Upon reaching the village and during the "course of the melee"[192] Demesme reportedly was "killed . . . in the uniform of the Northern Army, in which, while acting as a spy, he is supposed to have been shot through mistake by his own friends."[193]

Later during the balmy evening Landry, the Canonnier captain, recorded,

> After [the] wearisome [march] . . . we were smoking our pipes round the bivouac fire, when some one remarked that a great [battle] would be fought the next day; for long before the sun had gone down we heard the distant cannon boom in front. And we knew it meant that Gen. Sheridan had got ahead and that we would [have] to cut a passage through his great cavalry while fighting Gen. Grant in our rear. Captain Williams, a friend and guest of our . . . comrade Lieut. Camille Mollere, answered

> very seriously "No! Sir! There will [be] no fight tomorrow" and continuing he said in substance: that a friend of his—an officer of high rank, had informed how that the march from Petersburg to Appomattox Court House had reduced [the army] to such a condition, that Gen. Lee might find it his duty to accept the proposal which Gen. Grant had already made—namely: to surrender.[194]

In the valley below the village of Appomattox Court House clustered around thousands of campfires, the exhausted men of the Army of Northern Virginia ended their discussions and whispers of surrender and rested on the damp ground.

Chapter Nineteen

Une Armée n'existe plus
(An Army No More)

At 5:36 a.m., April 9, 1865,—a foggy morning—Palm Sunday the sun rose over Lieutenant Camille Mollere's detachment of forty-four Donaldsonville Canonniers under command of Captain Prosper Landry in their bivouac along Rocky Run. Joining them later this morning were Lieutenants Hubert Treille and Antoine Sanchez and thirteen Canonniers, all that remained of the Donaldsonville Artillery assigned to the two sections that left the lines at Burgess Mill seven days earlier. While they were gathered around campfires, General Robert E. Lee ordered what remained of the Army of Northern Virginia's Second Corps (comprising one-half of the army's organized infantry) under command of Major General John B. Gordan to attack at daybreak on the Lynchburg Road, half a mile west of the Appomatox Court House, in an attempt to cut a way through the enemy's lines.

Prosper Landry recorded, "The . . . only section of the company present for duty [Mollere's], was ready to obey orders. In the mean time Gen. Gordon had marched forward—and he was fighting the enemy—he took prisoners who [were] conducted to the rear—he also took a cannon with its howser and its gun detachment—All this did not look like a surrender and we commenced to think that our friend [talking of surrender the night before] had been misinformed, when lo! The firing ceased and Gordon's men were seen descending the hill and returning to us."[1] By eight o'clock in the morning Gordon's Corps had failed in its breakthrough attempt and was fought "to a frazzle."[2]

Between eight-thirty and nine o'clock in the morning preparations to receive an attack in front and behind were made by Longstreet's infantry. The Donaldsonville Artillery along with McIntosh's Battalion received orders and moved out into the road where Lieutenant Colonel William M. Owen, leading the guns, wrote:

> Just as we emerged Gen. Lee was riding by, going towards the rear accompanied by . . . his staff. As I saluted him he reined up his horse and said, "Good-morning, Colonel! How are your horses this morning? Do you think you can keep up with the infantry to-day?" I replied, "I thought I could; that they had had a pretty good feed of shucks, and appeared to be in tolerable condition. But, General," I added, "I have no orders." He replied, "You will find Gen. Longstreet on the hill yonder; he will give you orders." And, touching his hat in acknowledgement of my salute, he continued his ride . . . Not seeing Col. McIntosh I moved the Battalion forwards toward the hill, where I was to find Gen. Longstreet.[3]

Lee continued to the rear and rode through Longstreet's encampments and the picket line expecting to meet Grant for an interview on the general terms of peace but was disappointed in that they did not meet. By a note, Lee again requested an interview and a suspension of hostilities pending the surrender of the army.[4]

After receiving orders, William M. Owen led the battalion with the Gunners of Donaldson over the stage road less than a mile towards the courthouse to a hill with woods on the left, past a little apple orchard with a deserted wooden house at the far edge. The guns were then turned to the right into an open broom sedge field of gray, crowded with guns and wagons. They parked near Major John C. Haskell's artillery battalion that was already there. The Canonniers stood by their guns and rested.[5]

"Then came a Federal officer," remembered Prosper Landry, "holding in front of him a white handkerchief—riding a splendid bay horse. He was slim and tall, and his long blond hairs were floating on his shoulders."[6] Owen noted the officer came down the road waving the handkerchief up and down and,

> He inquired for Gen. Lee, and was directed to Gen. Longstreet upon a hill. Upon approaching the general he dismounted and said, "Gen. Longstreet, in the name of Gen. Sheridan and myself I demand the surrender of this army. I am Gen. Custer." Gen. Longstreet replied, "I am not in command of this army. Gen. Lee is, and he has gone back to meet Gen. Grant in regard to a surrender."
>
> "Well," said Custer, "no matter about Gen. Grant; we demand the surrender be made to us. If you do not do so we will renew hostilities, and any blood shed will be upon your head!"
>
> "Oh, well!" said Longstreet, "if you do that I will do my best to meet you;" then, turning to his staff, he said, "Col. Manning, please order Gen. Johnson to move his division to the front, to the right of Gen. Gordon. Col. Latrobe,[7] please order Gen. Pickett forward, to Gen. Gordan's left. Do it at once!" Custer listened with surprise depicted on his countenance; he had not thought so many of our troops were at hand with Longstreet. He, cooling off immediately, said, "General, probably we had better wait until we hear from Grant and Lee. I will speak to Gen. Sheridan about it; don't move your troops yet." And he mounted and withdrew in a much more quiet style than in his approach.
>
> As he passed out of hearing, Longstreet said quietly, with that peculiar chuckle of his, "Ha! ha! that young man has never learned to play the game of 'Brag.'" The divisions of Johnson and Pickett were only a myth, and had no existence whatever after the fight at "Five Forks."[8]

Shortly after this Lee rode back into the lines and remained near Longstreet's position until eleven o'clock in the morning. Lee stopped in a small apple orchard at the foot of the hill, a short distance before the line of battle that had been drawn up facing westward. After sending a note through the lines, Lee stretched himself out under an apple tree on a pile of fence rails.[9]

About an hour and fifteen minutes later a Federal officer accompanied by a Confederate escort met with Lee near the apple tree and soon thereafter, wrote Landry with the remaining Donaldsonville Canonniers, "We saw the same officer returning with Gen. Lee and some officers of his staff going to Appomattox C[ourt] H[ouse]. What transpired in that historic house on that hill near the Court House—I need not tell."[10]

"By no means all the men were prepared for the surrender," chronicled Lee's biographer Douglas Southall Freeman, "the rapidity of the retreat, the failure of rations, and the dwindling of brigades to companies had spelled disaster in the minds of the intelligent. The circle of fire reflected on the clouds the night of the 8th had convinced the discerning that the army was virtually surrounded. The halt of the morning and the frequent passage of flags of truce had confirmed their fears of capitulation. Yet such was the faith of the army in itself and in its commander that many were unwilling to believe the end had come."[11]

Lee at Appomattox.
ARW; courtesy of Library of Congress.

Lee's surrender of the Army of Northern Virginia was completed at 3:45 p.m. in the parlor of Wilbur McClean's house.[12] Prosper Landry recorded, "After his meeting with Gen. Grant—when Gen. Lee was returning to the Army—his army no more—an army no more—one man started to meet him, then another—then ten—twenty—a hundred—In a few minutes he was surrounded by a thousand men. He was on horse back—holding his hat in his hand—he was speaking to those around him—and those who were near enough to hear what he [said] was weeping—and also those who [were] too far to hear a single word. And those old veterans surrounding their [beloved] old chieftain formed a picture which once beheld is never forgotten."[13]

Freeman described the scene:

> Lee came toward them down from the ridge, across the little valley, up the hillside through the pickets, and into the line. He was as erect as ever, but he was staring straight ahead of him . . . the men started to cheer him . . . but somehow their cheers froze in their throats at the sight of him. They hesitated a moment as he rode fixedly on, and then without a word they broke ranks and rushed to him.
>
> "General," they began to cry, 'are we surrendered?'
>
> He tried to go on, but they crowded about him, bareheaded. He removed his hat . . . and attempted once more to proceed. The road was too full of frenzied, famished faces. He had to halt and answer his loyal old soldiers. "Men," he said, "we have fought the war together, and I have done the best I could for you. You will all be paroled and go to your homes until exchanged." Tears came into his eyes as he spoke. He attempted to say more . . . moving his lips in a choking "good-bye," he again essayed to ride on to the orchard from which he had come.
>
> "General, we'll fight 'em yet," they answered.
>
> "General, say the word and we'll go in and fight 'em yet."
>
> Everywhere as the news spread, each soldier reacted to it in his own fashion. Some wept, openly and without abashment. Others were dazed, as though they did not understand how the Army of Northern Virginia, Lee's army, could surrender . . . it seemed incomprehensible. To others, it was as the very end of the world . . . some blasphemed and some babbled, but all who could do so crowded to say farewell to Lee. Catching hold of his hands, they looked up at him and cried the more. They touched his uniform or his bridle rein, if they could not grasped his hand, and if they could not reach him, they smootherd Traveller's flanks or patted his neck. And in a confused roar, half-sob, half-acclamation, they voiced their love for him, their faith in him, their good-bye to him as their commander.

> Passing on slowly . . . he stopped at the apple orchard [and] retired a short distance into the orchard away from the road . . . pacing up and down under a tree . . . until the Federal wagons had begun to arrive with [promised] rations . . . the sun was now nearing its setting. . . . Lee mounted Traveller and started toward his headquarters, which were under a large white oak, about a mile to the rear.[14]

As he started, "There was," wrote one Confederate,

> a general rush from each side of the road to greet him as he passed, and two solid walls of men were formed along the whole distance. Their officers followed, and behind the lines of men were groups of them, mounted and dismounted, awaiting his coming. . . . As soon as he entered this avenue of these old soldiers . . . the men who had stood to their duty through thick and thin in so many battles, wild, heartfelt cheers arose which so touched General Lee that tears filled his eyes and trickled down his cheeks as he rode his splendid charger, hat in hand, bowing his acknowledgements. This exhibition of feeling on his part found quick response from the men whose cheers changed to choking sobs as, with streaming eyes and many evidences of affection, they waived their hats as he passed. Each group began in the same way, with cheers, and ended in the same way, with sobs, all along the route to his quarters. Grim, bearded men threw themselves on the ground, covered their faces with their hands and wept like children. Officers of all ranks made no attempt to conceal their feelings, but sat on their horses and cried aloud. . . . Traveller . . . took as much pleasure in applause as a human being, and always acknowledged the cheers of the troops by tosses of his head . . . on this . . . last appearance before them, his head was tossing a return to the salutes all along the line.[15]

The Donaldsonville Artillery commander related it was a "great but sad honor to have been one of those last soldiers.[16]

Lee, wrote Owen, "Rode on to his tent and disappeared from our view, 'the Army of Northern Virginia' passed away, leaving upon the page of history a record of valor and devotion never excelled."[17] The sentiment of the Donaldsonville Canonniers was aptly expressed almost thirty-five years later in the obituary of Canonnier Private Hypolite Templet: "To have belonged to the Army of Northern Virginia to him was a pride greater than any other."[18]

"The army slept soundly last night upon the ground," noted Owen on April 10, "and obtained the much-needed rest they had been strangers to for many a long day."[19] Another artillerist, a private, wrote, "This morning, we slept as late as we pleased . . . and drew rations for two days from the Federals."[20] During the morning, rain began to fall steadily, but later Owen recorded, "In the absence of Col. McIntosh . . . I had the Battalion assembled and informed the men of the terms of the surrender, which were as follows: that each officer and man were to go to their homes after receiving a parole. The officers to retain their side-arms and private horses. The rolls were then called and but few men were found missing."[21]

The final muster rolls for government property and the troops of the Donaldsonville Artillery, Norfolk Blues Artillery, and Norfolk Battery were made out and signed by Prosper Landry. Fourteen of Grandy's "Blues" artillerymen answered the muster from Petersburg while only three of Moore's Norfolk artillerymen remained to answer their roll call. For the first time since May 15, 1864, the Donaldsonville Artillery (or what was left of it) commanded by Landry, and three sections under Mollere, Treille, and Sanchez, again were consolidated.

The following Gunners of Donaldson answered the roll at Appomattox Court House:

Captain R. Prosper Landry, with one horse.
1st Lieut. Camille Mollere, with one horse.
2nd Lieut. Hubert Treille, with one horse.
Jr. 2nd Lieut. Antoine Sanchez, with one horse.

Mollere's Section

1st Sergeant William V. Parks
2nd " Pierre T. Blouin
1st Corporal J. Philogene Viala
2nd " Arthur Echevarria
3rd " Tomasso Morelli
4th " Adolphe Grilhe
5th " William F. Chase
Bugler J. Numa Braud, one horse.
Guidon Pierre S. Braud
Artificer Olibert Hebert
" Bienvenue Cire
Private Lubin Guedry
" William Taylor
" Miles Joyner
" Camille Templet
" Hypolite Templet
" John Richard
" Jean Baptiste Gaudet
" Jules Mestayer
" R. Octave Landry
" Ernest L. Monnot
" James B. Carothers
" Pierre Caesar Rybisky
" John Schrouner
" Louis M. Comes
" Paul A. Druilhet
" William G. Hart
" Peter Hauplin
" Gabriel Kling
" Martin Heim
" Octave LeBlanc
" Octave Boudreau
" Achille D. Dupuy
" Gustave E. Aucoin
" Gontrand Dugas
" P. Turiaffe Babin
" Estevan Hildago
" Eugene Hardy
" J. Alfred Gautreaux
" Abraham Klotz
" Theophile Menson
" Numa Cure
" Thomas S. Love

Treille's and Sanchez's Sections

Artificer Louis Aimé Richard, one horse.
Private Jacques Besson
" Armas Triche
" Cleophus Landry
" John S. McCoy
" John P. Eckleburg
" Désiré Carmouche
" Severin Blanchard
" Mathieu Morin
" Edward Morin
" Henry E. Duffel
" Eugene Cooley
" James Landry

Also answering this last roll call of the battery were four servants:

Louis Lefort
H. Blum (cook)
Jno. Mampley
Jno. Semple[22]

The free man of color Louis Lefort had gone to Virginia with the Canonnier gunners

Soldiers cutting down the apple tree General Lee rested under on April 9, 1865,
ARW; courtesy of Library of Congress.

when they left Donaldsonville three years, six months, and twenty-three days earlier, and continued in the service of Major Victor Maurin until the commander left on leave for Louisiana in February 1865. Lefort remained with Mollere's section at High Bridge and "looked after all the white friends from Donaldsonville and returned wearing the 'Gray.'"[23]

While waiting and at rest on April 10 many men remembered the day before when Lee sat and rested under the apple tree before meeting with Grant. Lee had been in plain view and observed by quite a long stretch of the Confederate line. The idea occurred to many to have a piece of the apple tree as a souvenir, and consequently the tree, which had more leaves than its neighbors was cut down and its remotest roots dug up.[24] Among the many to have a fragment were the Donaldsonville Canonniers who "while passing the time . . . and waiting . . . each man took a small piece of wood from the tree as a memento of the occasion."[25] A Louisianian in his diary recorded, "Every soldier wanted a piece of that tree . . . so they took every splinter, until they had almost uprooted it. Young Laresche had a piece of it."[26]

Confederate Brigadier General Edward P. Alexander recorded, "It was arranged to give each paroled person a parole signed by one of his commanding officers, and also a copy of an order issued from Grant's headquarters referring to these papers and validating them as paroles."[27] Consequently Owen received the following note from Alexander:

Head-quarters Artillery, First Corps.

> Colonel:—I send up a sufficient number of paroles for your command, including the Thirteenth Virginia Battalion of Artillery, the Washington Artillery, and Donaldsonville Artillery. You must sign for all except your own, which will be signed by Gen. Alexander. There is a difference in the form, but they are all the same. One is to be given to each man. No duplicates are to be made. Send back any blanks you don't need, as we are very short.
>
> Yours respectfully,
> J. C. Haskell,
> A.A.Gen'l.

To Lieut. Col. W. M. Owen, Commanding Battalion Artillery.

"With the assistance of Col. Edmund Pendleton, Fifteenth Louisiana, Captains Owen and Norcom, and Liet. George Apps of the Washington Artillery," wrote Owen, "I, proceeded to parole the men of the artillery command, as directed. The paroles were slips of paper about the size of a blank check, and read as follows:—

> Appomattox Court-House, April 10, 1865.
>
> The bearer, Private, of Battery of Artillery, a paroled prisoner of war of the Army of Northern Virginia, has permission to go to his home and there remain undisturbed until exchanged.
>
> (Signed)
> W. M. Owen,
> Lieut. Col. Commanding
> Battalion of Artillery.[28]

Owen recorded, "Another night was spent sleeping soundly in the mud and rain, and this A.M. (11th), according to instructions, I had my teams hitched up and moved my . . . batteries . . . to the main road, where I turned them over to the Federal officer detailed to receive them."[29] Alexander had arranged to form all the artillery guns on the road early Tuesday morning, April 11, and did so, making a column over half a mile long. After the guns were moved to the road the artillerists remained in their camps all day with mud all around as it rained heavily.[30]

Owen added, "Officers and men of the Federal army mingled freely with our officers and men around our camp-fires, and not a harsh word was spoken on either side. . . . They sent our starving men provisions, and not a shout of exultation nor the music of a band was heard during all the time we were at Appomattox. A feeling of great and deep sadness filled the breast of our army, and a feeling of delicate sympathy pervaded the other. Brave men . . . understood and respected one another."[31] Another Confederate veteran simply recorded, "We lay huddled together, silent and sorrowful."[32]

"On the morning of April 12th," Owen recorded,

> our battalion and the remnants of other battalions to be paroled were assembled for the last time in front of our camp-fire, and I read to them the farewell address of Gen. Lee, as follows:
>
> Head-quarters Army of Northern Virginia,
> Appomattox Court-House, April 10, 1865.
>
> General Orders No. 9:—
>
> After four years of arduous service, marked by unsurpassed courage and fortitude, the Army of Northern Virginia has been compelled to yield to overwhelming numbers and resources.
>
> I need not tell the brave survivors of so many hard fought battles who have remained steadfast to the last, that I have consented to this result from no distrust of them; but feeling that valor and devotion could accomplish nothing that would compensate for the loss that must have attended a continuance of the conflict, I determined to avoid useless sacrifice of those whose past services have endeared them to their countrymen. By terms of the agreement, officers and men can go to their homes and remain until exchanged.
>
> You will take with you the satisfaction that proceeds from the consciousness of duty faithfully performed, and I earnestly pray that a merciful God will extend to you his blessing and protection.

> With an unceasing admiration of your constancy and devotion to your country, and a grateful remembrance of your kind and grateful consideration for myself, I bid you an affectionate farewell.
>
> R. E. Lee
>
> The men listened with marked attention and with moistened eyes as this grand farewell from our old chief was read, and then receiving each his parole . . . every one shook my hand warmly and bade me good-by and breaking up into parties of three and four, turned their faces homeward; some to Richmond, some to Lynchburg, and some to far-off ruined Louisiana.[33]

The Confederate veterans headed home and kept their paroles as treasured mementoes. In later years, upon request some would reveal them, such as Donaldsonville Privates John Richard and Seymore Mioton.[34] Like Ernest Monnot, they would proudly say, "Have my discharge signed by Col. Owen."[35]

After a slim breakfast of hard bread and coffee,[36] a young artillerist wrote, "Comrades wept as they gazed upon each other, and with choking voices said, farewell! And so—they parted. Little groups of two or three or four, without food, without money, but with 'the satisfaction that proceeds from the consciousness of duty faithfully performed,' were soon plodding their way homeward."[37]

The worn-down and crestfallen Louisiana artillerymen at the last roll call for the most part wore an old, seedy, brown-colored slouched hat, though a few still wore the kepi, and threadbare, ragged, dirty gray or butternut clothes. They kept no pretense to uniformity, as many had picked up castaway Yankee blankets and overcoats. With their haversacks, and canteens, and a few trifles, they headed away from Appomattox leaving their guns, caissons, and horses in the road. "It was," wrote an artillery officer, "a pitiable sight."[38]

Sixty-eight Donaldsonville Canonniers and servants, with their paroles in hand, could now "look wistfully back, with shattered hope; to their ruined and broken homes, to meet again the loved ones they had left behind."[39] In passing through Appomattox County they observed white flags all over the place and, for miles on both sides of the road, "one eternal scene of desolation & destruction . . . scattered in every direction—Broken wagons, cannon carriages, caissons all cut down or burnt and cannon balls, grape shot & shell enough for an army's supply for two great battles . . . Not a sprig of grass & not a rail [fence] left."[40] A veteran remembered, "We had a pretty hard time getting something to eat on the way to our homes, there were so many together at the start, but as we scattered out we fared better . . . the citizens

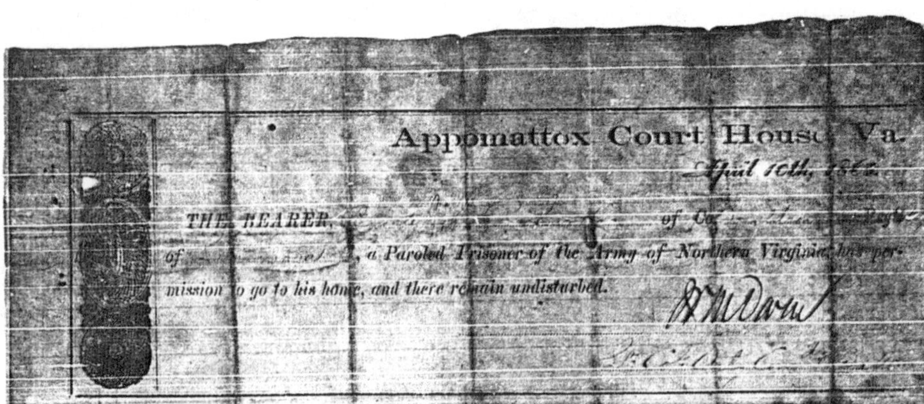
Appomattox Court House, Va.
April 10th, 1865
THE BEARER, ... of ... a Paroled Prisoner of the Army of Northern Virginia, has permission to go to his home, and there remain undisturbed.
W M Owen

Appomattox Parole of Donaldsonville Canonnier John Richard signed by "W. M. Owen."
Courtesy of LDA.

were kind to us all."[41]

Donaldsonville Corporal Antoine Sobral returned on foot to Louisiana in his tattered uniform, while Private Achilles Désiré Dupuy, after receiving his Appomattox parole, was again paroled upon arriving in Lynchburg. Alongside thousands of paroled Confederates, others headed back to Farmville where there were several trains, that were soon jammed and packed full of men. After being paroled, Levy met up with Canonniers John Eckleburg, a messmate and fellow New Orleanian, and Jim Carothers, along with Abraham Klotz, Gabriel Kling, Charles Pidoux, and Eugene Cooley. They all managed to ride on top of a boxcar on a train for Petersburg and "sat in a pelting rain until within five miles of the city, when we got off and walked."[42] Levy eventually got passage to New Orleans on the *Atlanta*, a "slow vessel"[43] carrying 600 other Louisianians. Canonnier Klotz did not worry about being paroled again, or food, because he walked "all this time in company with federal soldiers, owing to the fact that he wore a blue coat."[44] Klotz took a steamer to New Orleans.

Upon reaching the East Coast many of the Louisianans returned home by taking free passage to New Orleans provided by the Federal government on steamboats. Prosper Landry was included in this number and remembered many years later, "When I was returning home on the steamer *Ruth* there came on board the same self officer with the long blond hair [who had demanded Longstreet's surrender on April 9]. It was then I learned that he was Gen. Custer, who was killed by Sitting Bull."[45]

In Louisiana along Bayou Lafourche a Southern girl and cousin of a Donaldsonville Canonnier wrote in French,

> Thursday, April 13.—Terrible news reached us from all sides. If they are true they are disasters for the Confederacy. Petersburg, Richmond, Mobile, have fallen into the power of the Federals in the space of two weeks. The joy of the Yankees does not allow us to doubt the truth of this news. Twice since Friday they fired volleys in all the military posts. This afternoon the volleys were so incessant that our house, which is four miles from Donaldsonville, shook at each volley. While the Yankees are rejoicing our hearts are bleeding. Who would have expected such a result?
>
> "All hope is not lost," somebody has said, but what can we expect, on what help can we count? And yet if we could be reassured about the fate of our relatives who were at Petersburg and at Richmond! We have had no details about the fall of these strongholds. We know only that they were evacuated . . . Petersburg, Richmond, and Mobile in their hands! I can hardly believe it. For four years what privations did our soldiers induce! How often did they fight to defend those places! . . .
>
> It is said that we shall soon have peace . . . . Let us hope that henceforth the leaves of this little copybook will record only incidents that may be remembered pleasantly.
>
> Friday evening, April 14.—We saw today in a paper some details about the fall of Petersburg . . . where bloody battles [were] fought, terrible massacre, scenes without parallels since the beginning of the war.
>
> We are anxious about our cousins, who were at Petersburg. We have heard also of the surrender of Lee's army . . . all will be over; there will be no longer a Confederacy. If, at least, we should have the happiness of seeing again those who have gone to the war . . .
>
> April 20.—President Lincoln, sixteenth of the republic of the United States, was killed by an audacious individual named Wilkes Booth . . . on Good Friday, April 14, at 10 P.M., he was shot, and he died the next day. . . .
>
> May 14.—At last! After a month of anxiety we have had news of our soldiers. It seems to me that what I saw yesterday is a dream, for can one believe it? The Cannoneers of Donaldsonville have been released on parole; we saw several friends, but the one we

> were expecting did not come. Having taken another route in the hope of arriving here sooner he was obliged to go back, on account of the disturbances caused by the death of Lincoln. We are expecting him at any moment. . . .
>
> Thursday Evening, May 18.—According to the conditions of the surrender of Lee's army, the officers and the soldiers were to return home on parole with their baggage. But I do not know how it is that the soldiers who wish to pass through Maryland are still detained there. We have received today a letter from [Donaldsonville Lieutenant Hubert] Treille, who says he is detained in a prison at Alexandria [Virginia] with 422 other officers and soldiers from Louisiana . . . Although on parole they will not be allowed to go home before having taken the oath of allegiance to the United States.
>
> Friday, May 26,—Two of our soldier cousins arrived Saturday, the 20th. Treille arrived at Donaldsonville at 2 A.M., and Leopold by another route at noon. One may easily conceive our joy. The traces of four years of war may be seen on their faces.[46]

There was little known of the plot to murder Lincoln and "it was naturally ascribed to Confederates in general."[47] This caused a group of Louisiana artillerymen to be forced into a voluntary surrender of their paroles and to take the Oath of Allegiance to the United States government before being released from prison by Federal authorities. These men included: Treille, along with paroled Canonnier Privates William Taylor, a veteran who was wounded at Dr. Gaines's farm during the Seven Days' Battles around Richmond in June 1862; Louis Comes, son of a former mayor of Donaldsonville; Paul Druilhet, a veteran and relation to a future mayor of Jeanerette; and Gontrand Dugas, like his brother a good and faithful soldier of the battery. Treille and Taylor were set free on May 8 with Comes, Druilhet, and Dugas released the next day.[48]

While heading back to Donaldsonville after being paroled at Appomattox, Canonnier Private Charles Numa Cure related that he "went to Fortress Monroe a prisoner . . . then [was] sent to New Orleans and was released." When asked if he ever took the Oath, he replied, "I have not" and "under no circumstances."[49] Canonniers Eugene Levy, John Eckleburg, William Hart, and "Buck" Chase, after arriving by steamer in New Orleans, "wandered about the streets enjoying everything which reminded us of our old homes."[50]

Of the returning artillerists of her locality, and apropos for most of the homecomings, a woman wrote in her diary: "But their return is even sadder and amid bitter tears than their departure, for now 'we weep as they that have no hope.' Everybody is cast down and humiliated. . . . I suppose we shall be subjected to every indignity that hatred and malice can heap upon us. Till it comes, 'Let us eat, drink and be merry, for to-morrow we die.' Only, we have almost nothing to eat, and to drink, and still less to be merry about."[51]

While the Donaldsonville Canonniers were heading home, Major Victor Maurin, with his furlough over and duty again calling, said goodbye to his family at his brother's home in Assumption Parish and began the journey back to his command at High Bridge, Virginia. At Augusta, Georgia, the news of Lee's surrender reached Maurin and Captain George V. Moody,[52] who was returning to Virginia from a furlough at his home in Port Gibson, Mississippi. They, together with Moody's servant, who drove a light covered wagon, set out back to Louisiana. From Augusta they arrived in Washington, Georgia, a town of about twenty-two hundred citizens, two-thirds of which were black. It was "like most of the older towns . . . built around an open square, in the center of which stood the quaint old county courthouse . . . with the business houses of the village grouped around it."[54]

A local woman wrote of the last few months of the war, "Little Washington has gotten to be the great thoroughfare of the Confederacy . . . since . . . the only line of communication between Virginia and this part of the country . . . is through there and Abbeville."[55]

On April 24 she recorded, "The shattered remains of Lee's army are beginning to arrive. There is an endless stream passing between the transportation office and the depot, and trains are going and coming at all hours. The soldiers bring all sorts of rumors . . . our avenue leads from the principal street on which they pass, and great numbers stop to rest in the grove. . . . A great many of the soldiers camp in the grove, though . . . a public camping-ground for them [is located] further out of town."

Her diary continues the next day,

> The square is so crowded with soldiers and government wagons that it is not easy to make way through it. It is especially difficult around the government offices, where the poor, ragged, starved, and dirty remnants of Lee's heroic army are gathered day and night. The sidewalk along there is alive with vermin. . . . Poor fellows . . . there could be no more pitiful evidence of the hardships they have suffered than the lack of means to free themselves from these disgusting creatures. . . . At the spring in our grove, where the soldiers come in great numbers to wash their faces, and sometimes, their clothes, lice have been seen crawling in the grass, so that we are afraid to walk there.[56]

Thousands of people passed through Washington for days. On April 30 the wife and four children of Confederate President Jefferson Davis, plus Mrs. Davis's small escort led by the President's private secretary, Burton N. Harrison, arrived. Mrs. Davis noted the whole town of Washington was "in a state of most depressing disorder."[57] It was during this time that Maurin and Moody arrived there.

The next day, May 1, Harrison was at Haywood, the large home of Judge Garnett Andrews. "Men were coming in all day, with busy faces, to see Mr. Harrison," wrote Andrews's daughter, and later, "while we were at dinner, a brother of Mrs. Davis came in and called for Mr. Harrison, and after a hurried interview with him, Mr. Harrison came back into the dining-room and said it had been decided that Mrs. Davis would leave town to-morrow . . . but I suppose they were alarmed by some of the numerous reports that are always flying about the approach of the Yankees. Mother called on Mrs. Davis [at Dr. Fielding Ficklen's][58] this afternoon, and she really believes [the Yankees] are on their way here and may arrive at any moment."[59]

Another reason to leave town: during the afternoon a riot broke out in the streets, led by a "Texas regiment . . . about their rations." They were soon joined by all the disorderly elements among both soldiers and citizens who raided the commissary department building and then the quartermaster stores. "Negroes and children joined the mob and grabbed what they could of the plunder," wrote Andrews, adding, the "provost guard refused to interfere, saying they were too good of soldiers to fire on their comrades, and so the plundering went on unopposed. Nobody seemed to care much, as we all know the Yankees will get it in the end, any way, if our men don't."[60]

Of all those who visited the First Lady and Harrison in Washington, Georgia, it was Maurin and Moody who offered their services as "an additional escort."[61] Mrs. Davis later wrote, "Colonel Moody, a Mississippi lawyer . . . and Colonel Moran, [*sic*] of Louisiana, volunteered to accompany us and take charge of the party."[62] Accompanying her now were the President's private secretary, Burton N. Harrison, Mrs. Davis's younger brother Jefferson Howell (recently paroled at Augusta, Georgia), her sister Maggie Howell, a maid and servant, three Kentucky cavalrymen, and some paroled Confederate teamsters from southern Mississippi who would drive the four-mule-team army wagons obtained from the quartermaster's camp before the riot.[63]

"Into the wagons, [the] next morning, we put Mrs. Davis' luggage, a few muskets with ammunition, two light tents for the ladies and children, and utensils for cooking, with supplies for ourselves and feed for the animals supposed to be sufficient to take us to Madison [Florida]," wrote Harrison. "As most of the country we were to pass through had been recently devastated by Sherman's army, or was pine woods, sparsely inhabited, these things were necessary."[64]

Now "re-enforced by two gallant volunteers"[65] in Maurin and Moody, Mrs. Davis's wagon train left the Washington town square in the broad light of the forenoon on May 2 and went "toilsomely"[66] down the dirt road southward. "Our teamsters," recorded Harrison, "were instructed not to say anything, to anybody whatever, as to who we were or whence we came or whither we were going. They were all old soldiers and obeyed orders. It frequently amused me to hear their replies to the country people, during the next few days, when questioned on these matters.

'Who is that lady?'

'Mrs. Jones.'

'Where did you come from?'

'Up the road.'

'Where are you going to?'

'Down the road a bit,' etc., etc."[67]

After about ten miles, tents were pitched for the ladies and children and, wrote Mrs. Davis, "We were trying to get our tea in the awkward manner of townspeople camping out."[68]

The next day, May 3, with the weather clear and hot, the First Lady of the Confederacy recorded, "We moved on and met crowds of soldiers walking home, some very foot-sore and depressed, but generally cordial. I invited as many as we could to take a drive in one or the other of the wagons or the ambulance."[69] Their journey continued without incident on May 4 and 5.

"We made a long march, and had halted for the night in a pine grove, just after crossing a railroad track, when several visitors sauntered into our camp," recorded Harrison.

> Presently, one of the teamsters informed me that, while watering his mules near by, he had been told an attempt would be made during the night to carry off our mules and wagons, and that the visitors were of the party to make the attack. A council of war was held immediately, and we were discussing measures of resistance, when Captain Moody went off for a personal parley with the enemy. He returned to me with the news that the leader of the party was a fellow-Freemason, a Mississippian, and apparently not a bad sort of person. We agreed he had better be informed who we were, relying upon him not to allow an attack upon us after learning that Mrs. Davis and her children were of the party. Captain Moody made that communication in the confidence of Freemasonry, and the gallant Robin Hood immediately approached Mrs. Davis in all courtesy, apologized for having caused her any alarm, assured her she should not be disturbed . . . and delivered to Captain Moody a formal 'order,' entitling us to 'pass' his outposts at the cross-roads![70]

Mrs. Davis wrote of May 6,

> After many protestations of regard, they gave us a safe-conduct to pass by another party whom we met on the cross roads. I explained to them that in lieu of money I had a few groceries, my clothes, and nothing more. One of them said, "I am sorry it is not money, you could have kept it." Now we began to see branches of trees newly broken lying in the road; evidently, from the number of them, they indicated something, and it gave the gentlemen in charge [Maurin and Moody] much uneasiness. Colonel Moody communicated his suspicions to me, that we were followed by some enemy.
>
> At last, after a long day's journey, we halted about sundown, and my coachmen went

> into town for some milk. A party of men met him, took the mule that he was riding, and told him that they would have all the mules and horses that night. Our dread was great of being left helpless in the woods without transportation. Upon hearing this circumstances the gentlemen parked the wagons and tied the horses and mules inside. They divided into watches so as to meet the robbers before they had made an assault.[71]

"It was decided, of course to prepare for an effective defense," wrote Harrison. "As night came on, we turned off into a side road, and reaching a piece of high ground in the open pine woods, well adapted for our needs, halted—corralling the animals within a space enclosed by the wagons (arranged with the tongue of one wagon fastened by chains or ropes to the tail of another) and placing pickets."[72]

The day after Mrs. Davis's party left Washington, Georgia, President Davis and his escort and wagon train arrived in the town. Ironically, in this town named Washington, Davis dissolved the Confederate government (until such time that it could be reassembled) and then continued his retreat with a small escort. "On the second or third day after leaving Washington," wrote the Confederate President,

> I heard that a band of marauders, supposed to be stragglers and deserters from both armies, were in pursuit of my family, whom I had not seen since they left Richmond, but who, I heard at Washington, had gone with my private secretary and seven paroled men, who generously offered their services as an escort, to the Florida coast. I immediately changed direction and rode rapidly east across the country to overtake them.
>
> About nightfall the horses of my escort gave out, but I pressed on with [former Postmaster Gen. and now interim] Sec. [of the Treasury, John H.] Regan and my personal staff. It was a bright moonlight night; and just before day, as the moon was sinking below the tree tops, I met a party of men in the road, who answered my questions by saying they belonged to an Alabama regiment; that they were coming from a village[73] not far off, on their way homeward. Upon inquiry being made, they told me they had passed an encampment of wagons, with women and children, and asked me if we belonged to that party. Upon being answered in the affirmative, they took their leave.
>
> After a short time, I was hailed by a voice which I recognized as that of my private secretary, Burton N. Harrison, who informed me that marauders had been hanging around the camp, and that he and others were on post around it, and were expecting an assault as soon as the moon went down.[74]

Harrison remembered,

> In the middle of the night I, with two teamsters, constituted the picket on the road running north. After a while we heard the soft tread of horses in the darkness approaching over the light, sandy soil of the road. The teamsters immediately ran off to arouse the camp, having no doubt the attack was about to begin. I placed myself in the road to detain the enemy as long as possible, and, when the advancing horsemen came near enough to hear me, called "Halt." They drew rein instantly. I demanded "Who comes there?" The foremost of the horseman replied "Friends," in a voice I was astonished to recognize as that of President Davis, not suspecting he was anywhere near us.[75]

There was enjoyment in the reunion of the Davis family.

The next morning, May 7, the journey slowly continued over very sandy roads through sparsely settled pinewoods. The day was "intensely hot"[76] as Davis rode most of the time in an ambulance with his wife. The loyal but reticent Maurin continued to ride his strutting steed along in escort, but the Davis reunion and children undoubtedly made him yearn for his own family back in the bayou country.

Camp was made during the evening between Dublin and Abbeville. The president's scouts reported that Federal cavalry in the area knew about the Davis train.[77] Davis remained that night but after breakfast the next morning (May 8) he, "Bade us good-bye and rode forward with his own party, leaving us, in deference to our earnest solicitations, to pursue our journey as best we might with our wagons and encumbrances," wrote Harrison.[78]

Maurin and Moody remained with Harrison and the president's family as they traveled throughout the day. Near the rain-swollen Ocmulgee River they had difficulty getting the wagons through the bottomlands, but after crossing the river at Brown's Ferry, and with darkness coming on, they halted on its western bank, one mile and a half above Abbeville.

From there Harrison recorded, "About the middle of the night I was aroused by a courier sent back by the President with the report that the enemy was . . . near . . . and the advice that I had better move on at once to the southward. . . . I started my party promptly, in the midst of a terrible storm of thunder, lightening, and rain. As we passed through the village of Abbeville, I dismounted and had a conversation with the President in [an old deserted] house."[79] The teamsters stopped just long enough to feed their animals before being urged to move on as the President informed Harrison he would catch up with them during the night after his horses had more rest.

"We kept to the southward all night," wrote Harrison,

> the rain pouring in torrents most of the time, and the darkness such that, as we went through the woods where the road was not well marked, in a light, sandy soil, but wound about to accommodate the great pines left standing, the wagons were frequently stopped by fallen trees and other obstructions. In such a situation, we were obliged to wait until a flash of lightening enabled the drivers to see the way. In the midst of that storm and darkness the President overtook us.[80]

The rain stopped in the morning and the combined parties, except for a short time at sunrise to cook breakfast, traveled throughout the day on roads that were in good condition for marching, apart from the swollen streams that ran across the road here and there. They moved through a vast pine forest where not a human being, house, or cultivated field was seen.[81] Harrison noted the president "was still with us when, about five o'clock in the afternoon . . . I halted my party for the night, immediately after crossing the little creek just north of Irwinville, and went into camp. My teams were sadly in need of rest, and . . . we apprehended no immediate danger."[82]

Harrison immediately lay down and went into a "profound sleep"[83] as Moody afterward kindly stretched a canvas as a roof over his head and lay beside him. They were on the same side of the road as Mrs. Davis's tent, where the president slept, and the tent with the children and Miss Howell. The others, including Maurin, all slept on the west side of the road in or near the wagons amid the level pinewoods.[84]

During the early morning hours of May 10, 1865, in the darkness and deep shadows of the forest, two different commands of Yankee cavalry, the Fourth Michigan and First Wisconsin, each unaware of the other, approached the camp of the president of the Confederate States. "Just as earliest dawn appeared," wrote one commanding officer,

> I put the column in motion, and we were enabled to approach with in four or five rods of the camp undiscovered, when a dash was ordered, and in an instant the whole camp, with its inmates, was ours. A chain of mounted guards was immediately thrown around the camp and dismounted sentries placed at the tents and wagons. The surprise was so complete, and the movement so sudden in its execution, that few of the enemy were enabled to make the slightest defense, or even arouse from their slumbers in time to grasp their weapons, which were lying at their sides, before they were wholly in our power. But, at this moment . . . for we had not held possession of the camp but a few minutes . . . sharp firing was commenced between the dismounted force . . . and, what was supposed at the time to be, the rebel force guarding the train. The firing was about

> 100 rods in rear of the camp, and across a narrow swamp. I immediately ordered all my forces forward to the scene of the firing, leaving only a force sufficient to guard the camp and prisoners. On arriving on the ground I found my men engaging a force of dismounted men, who were concealed behind trees, &c. . . . I became apprehensive that we were contending with some of our own men . . . this mistake was not discovered until it had cost the loss of two men killed . . . and several [severely and] slightly wounded.[85]

Harrison recorded, "I was awakened by [the President's] coachman . . . running to me about day-break with the announcement that the enemy was at hand! I sprang to my feet, and in an instant a rattling fire of musketry commenced on the north side of the creek. Almost at the same moment [the Michigan cavalry] charged up the road from the south upon us . . . we were taken by surprise, and not one of us exchanged a shot with the enemy. . . . It was, as yet, scarcely daylight."[86]

The Michigan Cavalry commander reported,

> As soon as the firing had ceased I returned to camp and took an inventory of our capture, when I ascertain we had captured Jeff Davis and family (a wife and four children), John H. Regan, his Postmaster-General; Colonels [William P. Johnston] and [Francis R.] Lubbock, aides de-camp to Davis; Burton N. Harrison, his private secretary; Major Maurin, Captain Moody, Lieutenant Hathaway, Jeff D. Howell, midshipman in the rebel navy, and 12 private soldiers; Miss Maggie Howell, sister of Mrs. Davis; 2 waiting maids, 1 white and 1 colored, and several servants. We also captured 5 wagons, 3 ambulances, about 15 horses, and from 25 to 30 mules. The train was mostly loaded with commissary stores and private baggage of the party.[87]

"The business of plundering commenced immediately after the capture," noted Harrison, "and we were soon left with only what we had on and what we had in our pockets . . . all our horses were promptly appropriated by the officers . . . the colonel himself claimed and took the lion's share."[88] The troopers were looting the camp and wagons too "with great celerity," wrote Mrs. Davis, adding, "there was a shriek dreadful to hear, and our servants told us it came from a poor creature who, in prying up the lid of a trunk with his loaded musket, shot off his own hand."[89] Lubbock added the Federal troopers "plundered and robbed everyone of all and every article they could get hold of. They stole watches, jewelry, money, clothing, etc."[90]

"Upon returning to camp" continued the Michigan Cavalry commander,

> I was accosted by Davis from among the prisoners, who asked if I was the officer in command; and upon my answering him that I was, and asking him whom I was to call him, he replied that I might call him what or whom I pleased; when I replied to him that I would call him Davis, and after a moment's hesitation he said that was his name; when he suddenly drew himself up in true royal dignity and exclaimed, "I suppose that you consider it bravery to charge a train of defenseless women and children, but it is theft—it is vandalism!" After allowing the prisoners time to prepare breakfast, I mounted them on their own horses, taking one of the ambulances for my wounded, and one of the wagons for the dead, using the other two ambulances for the conveyance of the women and children, and started on my return by the direct route to Abbeville, where I arrived at sunset the same day.[91]

Harrison recorded, "After we had breakfast, it was arranged that each of the prisoners should ride his own horse to Macon, the captors kindly consenting to waive right of possession meantime; and that arrangement was carried out, except that Mr. Davis traveled in one of the ambulances."[92] The captured party, escorted by Yankee cavalry, at an early hour on the morning of May 11 started and continued during the daylight hours on their journey. "We marched in a column of twos and Major Maurin and I rode together," stated Harrison.

> He was very taciturn: but when, on the second or third day, we came upon a cavalry camp where a brass band, in a large wagon drawn by handsome horses, was stationed by the roadside and suddenly struck up "Yankee Doodle" as the ambulance carrying Mr. Davis came abreast of them, the silent old Creole was moved to speech. The clatter of the cymbals and the noise of the drums set our horses to prancing; when Major Maurin had composed his steed, he turned to me with a broad smile and revenged himself with: "I remember the last time I heard *that* tune; it was at the battle of Fredericksburg, where a brass band came across the pontoon bridge with the Column, and then occupied a house where they struck up "Yankee Doodle." I myself sighted a field gun at the house, missed it with the first shot, but next time hit it straight. In all your life you never heard Yankee Doodle stop so short as it did then."[93]

Between two and three o'clock in the afternoon of May 13, the prisoners were halted a short distance from Macon with Federal soldiers drawn up in line on both sides of the road. "It is needless to say," remembered Mrs. Davis, "that as the men [in line] stood at ease, they expressed in words unfit for women's ears all that malice could suggest."[94] In about an hour the captives were moved and entered Macon, where a journalist reported, "From all parts of the city, men, women, and children, soldiers, and negroes, flocked to the sidewalks and blocked up the way . . . the throng moved directly forward to Mulberry street and from thence up to the Lanier House. In front of that hotel the crowd had grown so dense that it was with difficulty the way could be clear. At last the carriages and the ambulance were stopped, and the party alighted . . . not a shout or token of exultation was manifested during the whole time by the Federal soldiery, while the citizens looked on with countenance generally expressing regret."[95]

President Davis recorded,

> When we reached Macon, I was conducted to the hotel[96] where [Brigadier] General [James H.] Wilson had his quarters. A strong guard was in front of the entrance, and when I passed in it opened ranks, facing inward and presented arms.
>
> A commodious room was assigned to myself and family. After dinner I had an interview with General Wilson. After some conversation . . . I told him that some of the men with me were on parole, that they were riding their own horses—private property—and I hoped they would be permitted to retain them. I have a distinct recollection that he promised me it should be done, but have since learned that their horses were taken; and some who were on parole, viz., Major Moran, [*sic*] Captain Moody, Lieutenant Hathaway, Midshipman Howell, and Private Messec, who had not violated their obligation of parole, but were voluntarily traveling with my family to protect them from marauders, were prisoners of war, and all incarcerated in disregard of the protection promised when they surrendered.[97]

Maurin and the president's entourage left Macon under guard by a special train at seven o'clock that evening and arrived at daylight on May 14 in Atlanta. From there they were conveyed and escorted on another train to Augusta, Georgia, arriving at sunset. Carriages brought the prisoners four miles below the city, and by eight o'clock that evening they were on board a steamer headed for Fortress Monroe, Virginia, where they arrived at noon on May 19.[98]

Having escorted and protected the Davis family, Maurin's association with the first family of the South ended when the federal chief of staff arrived on May 20 and arranged the dispersal of the prisoners to several locations. The Donaldsonville Artillery's major was transferred to Fort McHenry, Maryland, where he was confined on May 23 and allowed no communication whatsoever. In pursuance of instructions from President Andrew Johnson, Maurin remained a prisoner until he took the Oath of Allegiance and gave his parole of honor to report whenever called upon. He also was required to report his whereabouts weekly by letter to the secretary of war. After doing so he was released on July 20, 1865, and arrived in Donaldsonville in August 1865.

Maurin returned to a wife and family who had perhaps suffered more than he from fear and uncertainty in not knowing his fate as a prisoner. Upon his return, he rebuilt his old home in Donaldsonville. With his remarkable business ability as a merchant, Maurin soon recovered his losses. Along with Lise Vives Maurin, his "gentle, cultured and unselfish" wife, whose "charity knew no bounds" and "kindly spirit pervaded not only the home circle . . . but extended throughout the community, both rich and poor testifying to the loveliness and saintliness of her character,"[99] the Major raised five sons and a daughter through the trying times of Reconstruction. He was "offered many civil official positions, but never aspired to honors of that kind and always respectfully declined them, owing to the fact that his time was fully occupied in looking after his extensive business interest."[100]

Major Victor Maurin died on March 9, 1875, at the age of fifty-six, just a few months before the re-organization of his beloved *Le Compagnie d'Artillerie de Donaldson.*

President Jefferson Davis and family's arrival in a hospital wagon, along with his entourage that included Major Victor Maurin, under guard by Federal troops in front of the Lanier Hotel, Macon, Georgia, May 13, 1865. From Michael Ballard's *A Long Shadow, Jefferson Davis and the Final Days of the Confederacy.*

Chapter Twenty

La Fin
(The End)

The gallant Creole veterans were "wiser if not better men"[1] when the war ended. Upon their return they found Donaldsonville in "blight and confusion."[2] The town was under strict military rule and occupied by the Eleventh United States Colored Heavy Artillery.[3] Many sections of Donaldsonville were still in ruins, having been burned, including the courthouse, jail, and nearby farms and plantations. All along Bayou Lafourche the land was badly run down or in ruins. Sugar mills were destroyed, horses and livestock had been carried off, and many a returning Confederate soldier found his house ransacked or burned and his land overrun with weeds and grass.

In July 1865 a contemporary correspondent wrote from Ascension Parish,

> While a shade of disappointment is visible on the countenances of all, it is gratifying to observe that no feeling of despondency or resentment is manifested. All are going cheerfully to work to repair their shattered fortunes. The utmost good feeling prevails among those who were so recently arrayed in deadly strife, and all accept their changed conditions with resignation . . . the only resentment, the only animosity observable is between the regular Confederate soldier who remained at their post, and the skulking jayhawkers who, while claiming title of Confederate and wearing their uniform, were stealing from the aged fathers and mothers, the young sisters and brothers of those who were in the army. With this class the returned Confederates will not fraternize or associate.[4]

"It was a discouraging picture that lay before him," wrote a Louisiana historian, "but he set to work following the arts of peace as bravely as he had once followed the arts of war."[5] The veteran Donaldsonville Canonniers took up their civic duties and the town rebuilt, completing a courthouse and jail on April 16, 1867.[6] The Confederate veterans who suffered throughout the war learned, wrote an ex-Confederate artillery veteran,

> that life was passable and enjoyable without a roof or even a tent to shelter from the storm; that cheerfulness was compatible with cold and hunger; and that a man without money, food, or shelter need not feel utterly hopeless, but might, by employing his wits, find something to eat where he never found it before; and feel that, like a terrapin, he might make himself at home wherever he might be. Men did actually become as independent of the imaginary "necessities" as the very wild beast. And can a man learn all this and not know better than another how to economize what he has, and how to appreciate the numberless superfluities of life? Is he not made, by the knowledge he has of how little he really needs, more independent.[7]

Agriculture made slow progress for the next ten years and social life was characterized by simplicity, modesty, and a general lack of pretension and extravagance. The great majority of the people now lived in reduced circumstances, but that did not deter from an almost daily occurrence of picnics and parties, with lots of courting.[8]

In the North there was a faction that bitterly opposed any mild method of dealing with the South and thought that it ought to be severely punished for the part it had taken in the war. This group of Republicans, called Radicals, wished to do this by taking the vote away from ex-Confederates and extending it to the newly freed African Americans who they expected would vote with newcomers from the North called carpetbaggers—those that came south with high hopes of taking advantage of the confusion and turmoil. The Radicals gained control of Congress and put the southern states under strict military rule until an acceptable state government was set up and organized. In the Confederates' eyes, the eight years of dishonest and extravagant carpetbag government in Louisiana was nearly as great a trial as the four years of war that had preceded it. During the period of Reconstruction, they viewed new laws passed as unjust, considered public money wasted, and held in low regard the public improvements made. In their opinion, the people suffered under constant lawlessness and political turmoil.[9]

The war was officially declared ended in Louisiana on April 2, 1866.[10] Ascension Parish was fortunate enough to be devoid of turmoil for five years because the Radicals could never get well established. There were two main reasons for the failure of radicalism in Donaldsonville and surrounding areas. One was "every man is apt to consider his own interest and to lookout for the means of obtaining bread and butter for his family."[11] The other, and more important, was the organization in Donaldsonville of a conservative faction made up of blacks and whites, Republicans and Democrats, and ex-Confederates.

Louis Lefort, who surrendered with the Gunners of Donaldson at Appomattox, was one of the leading African American men of the town. He later wrote,

> It was my pleasure at the head of a committee . . . to introduce [African American Pierre Caliste Landry] to [former Donaldsonville Artillery officer] Judge William C. Lawes, the guardian of the free colored people of the town, for the service of his people just out of slavery. He [Pierre Landry] wisely cast his lot and usefulness with the best white people of the town and parish and became an indispensable leader in those dark days, and was so regarded and respected by all . . . against the fire-eating radical element of our people under the leadership of its organized white political interlopers who took advantage of the people just out of slavery to lead them into active violence. It was in the interest of peace and safety that under the leadership of Pierre Landry a conservative party was organized by which mob violence was avoided in the town and parish until 1870.[12]

Pierre Landry "quickly earned the respect and confidence of Donaldsonville's white population while simultaneously establishing himself as the leader of Ascension Parish's African-American community."[13] In April 1868, with the help of a biracial electoral coalition, Landry served a one-year term as mayor of Donaldsonville, thus becoming America's first African American mayor. He wrote, "I affiliated with the best class of Southern white men who composed the wealth, culture and intelligence of this State. . . . I have nothing to regret for having labored with such a people so as to better the condition of my own race by making it possible to live together in peace." Landry also wrote, "The Confederate soldiers returning from the lost cause were under fear of the effects of this radical party (and rightly so) that it was not safe for them to take issue with those radical leaders and their followers. That woeful condition appealed to my sense of justice so strongly that I brought together the thinking men of my race."[14]

They included not only Lefort, elected constable in 1868, but Prosper Conway, a member of the Donaldsonville Artillery field band who had marched off to Virginia in September 1861, and other "freemen of color under the guardianship of Judge William C. 'Billy' Lawes."[15] Together these local black leaders cooperated with white Democrats and ex-Confederates that included Major Victor Maurin and former Canonnier First Lieutenant François Lestang Fortier. Fortier commanded the Donaldsonville guns at the Battle of Williamsburg in May 1862 while sick and during Pierre Landry's term in office, he served on the parish police jury.[16]

Following Pierre Landry as mayor was "Billy" Lawes, the Democrat and ex-Confederate Canonnier officer who "was suspected of having Republican tendencies" but "was a very good conservative man, and one that everybody respected."[17] The following year Marx Schoenberg, a white Republican was elected mayor.

In November 1870, a dispute occurred over where to count Ascension Parish's election ballot boxes. The votes by law were to be counted at the Donaldsonville Courthouse, but to prevent this and seize the ballot boxes the Radical Republicans assembled several hundred black men and merged them with a larger group of black state militia (mobilized in St. James Parish) to march on Donaldsonville. This "Negro mob,"[18] as it was called, additionally planned "to kill Pierre Landry first, the white people next, and burn the town."[19] Evidently, upon hearing reports of the mob, "a little army of [Donaldsonville] citizens divided themselves into three squads, under the command of Major Maurin, Judge W. C. Lawes and J. J. Claverie, for the protection of the town and the lives of the inmates."[20]

That evening, November 9, 1870, Lawes and Schonberg went to the outskirts of Donaldsonville under a flag of truce to halt the advance of the radical mob by hand delivering an order obtained from the Radical's candidate for state senator, who happened to be a brigadier general in the militia. While parleying with the mob, Lawes and Schoenberg were murdered. Lawes's body was fearfully mutilated. The black multitude subsequently marched on Donaldsonville the next day and "apparently spent the day celebrating in the streets."[21]

Lefort recorded that it was "[Pierre] Landry's leadership which thwarted the success of this mob, and thereby saved our people from the consequences."[22] It was also reported, "Major Maurin and Dr. J. J. Claverie were most instrumental in keeping the [Radical Republican] negroes in check."[23] Though Lefort gave credit to Landry's leadership, Major Maurin's wartime servant, valet, and cook played a conspicuous part himself as many of Donaldsonville's citizens departed before the militia entered: "It was feared that if the negro militia was permitted to enter Donaldsonville rapine and murder would ensue. Lefort opposed their entrance . . . and sought by every means to deter them from marching in. This action . . . excited animosity of the . . . militia." Lefort was "'arrested,' tried by a drum head court-martial and sentenced to be shot on the public green. Here it was that Lefort . . . stood unblanched in the middle of the public square, opened his shirt and dared the negro militia to fire." Awed, they refused.[24]

The following day two companies of United States troops arrived and "found that the town of Donaldsonville had not been burned, as had been widely rumored and reported in newspapers throughout the state; in fact, the town was virtually deserted. The mob had already scattered and peace had been restored."[25] The mob purportedly "picketed the town, and helped themselves . . . to things about town and created a great deal of consternation generally," but "when the negroes heard that [United States] troops were coming, they were disbanded."[26]

After the election day incident Donaldsonville remained untroubled by violence until the end of Reconstruction, but, "Louisiana was practically in a state of civil war, with race riots and other disorders in many sections."[27] The carpetbag government continued in Louisiana with the repeated use of Federal troops to keep men in office against the will of the majority of white citizens. It was not until 1877 that Reconstruction ended in Louisiana.

On March 13, 1875, the headlines of the local newspaper read: "Another Old Citizen Gone. Death of Major Victor Maurin." The news story went on: "Early in the afternoon of [March 9] the community was shocked by the intelligence of [his] sudden death . . . which sad event occurred at his residence . . . that he dropped dead from heart disease. . . . The news of this tragic occurrence spread like wildfire, and soon a large number of sympathizing people had gathered at the house to tender their aid, and condolence to the stricken family."[28]

The funeral the next day

> was perhaps the largest ever seen in Donaldsonville, the numerous attendance indicating the universal respect and admiration felt for the estimable deceased. The cortege, as it moved from the Maurin residence to the Catholic Church was in the following order: 1. The Silver Cornet Band; 2. The honorary members of Phoenix Fire Company, followed by the active members in full uniform; 3. The St. Cecile Brass Band; 4. Honorary and active members of Ascension Hook and Ladder Company; 5. The hearse, attended by eight pall bearers; 6. Relatives of deceased; 7. Members of the Masonic order, without regalia, members of the old company of Donaldsonville Cannoneers, and a large throng of people belonging to none of the organizations. On the way to the church, and from there to the cemetery, dirges were played alternately by the two bands, and a multitude of heavy hearts beat time to the mournful music. During the beautiful and solemn services in the church . . . the spacious sanctuary was crowded to its utmost capacity, while many persons were compelled to remain outside. The procession moved to the cemetery . . . the priest and his attendants walked in the lead followed by the hearse. At the tomb an affecting scene ensued: The voice of the reverend priest as he chanted the burial service mingled sadly with the sobs of the mourners, producing a feeling of awe and commiseration in the hearts of all present, and as the crowd ebbed slowly away at the conclusion of the last sad rites, many an eye glistened and many a bosom heaved in sympathy with the suffering relatives of the good man whose loss all so deeply deplored.[29]

A few months later, on July 10, 1875, the *Donaldsonville Chief* newspaper displayed in bold letters, "Donaldsonville Cannoneers. Reorganization of the Old Company—Patriotic Celebration of the Fourth of July."[30] Prosper Landry, who signed the parole roll of the Donaldsonville Artillery at Appomattox, held a meeting on July 3, 1875, at the Hall of the Ascension Hook and Ladder (volunteer fire) Company in Donaldsonville with the purpose of reorganizing the Gunners of Donaldson. At the assemblage the roll was prepared with sixty-five volunteers, nearly equally divided between old members and new recruits. The next day, in celebration of the ninety-ninth anniversary of American Independence, the renewed company, led by the Canonnier Field Band,[31] marched to the railroad depot to greet previously invited dignitaries. From the depot the dignitaries were escorted to the St. Joseph's Academy where a stage was decorated with the United States and Louisiana flags draped in the background, and hanging between them a large portrait of "Gen. Washington" with one of "Gen. Grant" on his right and "Gen. Lee" on his left. Suspended above the stage was the inscription: "1837—Canonniers de Donaldson—1875." The paper also noted, "On either side of this . . . appeared the names of the principal battles of the late war in which the Cannoneers had taken part."[32]

Captain Prosper Landry was again chosen to lead the company, and he called the large gathering to order and introduced Francis T. Nicholls, the one-armed and one-legged Confederate veteran and native son to speak. "He congratulated the Cannoneers upon their reorganization," and "advised the cultivation of friendly feelings between North and South, a burial of all animosities, a remembrance that this is a common country and it is the duty of all good citizens to aid in its maintenance; but it must not be thought that love for the South is inconsistent with love for the Union, nor must bitterness be confounded with patriotism."[33]

Prosper Landry was then called upon, and he

> delivered an address abounding with the eloquence of thought and utterance which is characteristic of his polished oratory. Capt. Landry reviewed the history of the Cannoneers from their organization in 1837 to dissolution in 1865, and paid fervent tribute to the memory of their old commander, Major Maurin. . . . The speaker stated the objects of the reorganization of the Cannoneers to be:—to keep alive remembrance of the honorable past of the old company; to endeavor to be of service to the community, and to "fraternize in heart and spirit with the growing band of American patriots, who . . . are receiving with open arms our fellow Confederates, believing, as we do, that the bravest of soldiers are the most reconcilable of men, both North and South, and they are this day the best lovers of the Constitution and the Union." The speaker retired amid loud and prolonged applause.[34]

Le Compagnie d'Artillerie de Donaldson was again "En Avant!" and prepared to be useful to their fellow citizens. During the November 1876 election that would end the rule of the Radicals and restore government in Louisiana to Southern white men, an article in the newspaper noted, "We are pleased to record, as further evidence of the avowed policy of both parties to have peace and order on election day, that Capt. R. P. Landry of the Donaldsonville Cannoneers has tendered the command of that organization to W. G. Wilkinson, Esq., United States Deputy Marshal, pending the election. In case of threatened riot or tumult, the Cannoneers may be summoned by the marshal as a posse, and the officers give assurance that the call will be promptly obeyed. Capt. Landry is a Democrat, while Mr. Wilkinson is a Republican, and their arrangement is in keeping with the expressed intention of the leaders of the opposing parties to cooperate in the work of securing a fair, peaceable election."[35]

No trouble occurred on Election Day in Donaldsonville, and though Nicholls and the Democrats won the election, the Radical Republicans disputed it to the Federal government. In January 1877 the two parties had dual inauguration ceremonies in New Orleans. A detachment of Canonniers under command of Prosper Landry and an unusual number of Donaldsonville residents journeyed to Nicholls's ceremony.

The Donaldsonville paper recorded, "Most of those who went from here, particularly the Cannoneers, were interested only in the installation of the Nicholls' government."[36] Three months later the Federal government withdrew its troops, thus allowing Nicholls and the Democrats full control of the legislature and governorship. "The evil days of Reconstruction," wrote a Louisiana historian, "were a thing of the past."[37]

In 1877 it was reported, "We again had the right to bless providence for the return of liberty, and . . . freely indulge in the feelings of joy for our restoration to that honorable position, among our sister States to which we were entitled." For the first time in many years Donaldsonville celebrated the Fourth of July "with great *éclat*."[38] Invited to and participating in the celebration were Canonnier war veterans, the Washington Artillery with three companies led by Colonel William M. Owen, a good number of Confederate veterans and honorary members, the Continental Guards and Rex's Royal Guards from New Orleans, and the Baton Rouge Zouaves led by Captain Leon Jastremski, along with a detachment of the Baton Rouge Villies. Governor Nicholls and other public officials along with distinguished orators partook of the festivities too.

The celebration began early on the Fourth of July with the booming of cannon from the Washington Artillery's *Redemption* and *Resurrection* and the Canonnier's own gun, the *14th of*

September.[39] The boisterous artillery and muskets salutes welcomed the numerous visitors and excursionists arriving by steamboat from New Orleans, Baton Rouge, and Iberville Parish, and those coming from Assumption and St. James parishes, and along Bayou Lafourche.

"One of the earliest and most pleasant incidents of the day," according to the local newspaper,

> was the presentation of a beautiful banner to the Cannoneers, at the residence of their late lamented commander, Major Victor Maurin. The presentation was made by the ladies of Ascension, through little Miss Ella Maurin, in whose behalf Judge R. N. Simms spoke as follows . . . "In the contemplation of the glories of this occasion, the dearest among them all to you must be the regeneration of our beloved State, by means of which the angry passions of party have been dissipated and the smiles and sunshine of peace have returned to gladden and brighten the souls of our people, and the reappearance upon this scene of your noble band for the first time in many years, in all of its ancient splendor.
>
> The ladies of Ascension, catching quickly the inspiration of the hour, and holding ever the fresh remembrance the heroism of our Cannoneers on many a bloody battle field, have prepared for you this beautiful and radiant flag, and they have very appropriately selected and appointed to present it to you, little Ella Maurin, the charming and lovely daughter of your late commander, who led you safely through the perils of so many hard fought battles. It is in her name, therefore, that I now present to you this beautiful token of esteem and affection from the ladies of Ascension. On its folds is blazoned the motto of your brave company—those stirring words which have given a charm of danger, and made you forget the peril of the battle field. . . . Let it be to you the emblem of peace and good will, and whate'er betide—whether in peace or in war—may it ever inspire you with that high and ennobling sentiment which should animate every patriotic heart: Love of country and devotion to duty."
>
> Capt. R. Prosper Landry . . . replied in eloquent and appropriate terms, expressing warm gratitude and appreciation with which his soldiers received the splendid gift.[40]

"Headed by the Independent band in their neat new uniforms—gray coat, pants and cap, with red trimmings—the Cannoneers in *their* new uniforms—dark blue coat, pants and cap; trimmed with red—marched to the Catholic Church, accompanied by their military guest and a large crowd of people; where the flag was blessed with impressive ceremony,"[41] reported the *Donaldsonville Chief.*

The paper's account continued, "High Mass was then celebrated by Father Boglioli . . . who went [to] war with the Cannoneers. This good father met with a hearty welcome from the people of the community, among whom he bided many years, endearing himself to all by his gentle disposition and purity of character. Some of the meetings between Father Boglioli and friends of former days were quite affecting; more than once tears of pleasure coursed down the good father's cheeks."[42]

After Mass a meeting was called at the rear of the church, where a stage had been erected for the distinguished speakers. The Declaration of Independence was read, after which the dignitaries gave eloquent addresses and patriotic speeches to frequent and hearty plaudits. Three bands were present and entertained the large audience as well.

The newspaper reported, "At three o'clock the Cannoneers invited their military and other guests to a bountiful dinner, prepared in the St. Joseph's Academy, on the church grounds . . . fully a thousand persons partaking of the repast."[43] Another reporter wrote this feast "fully sustained the reputation of this ancient town for hospitality and good cookery."[44] It was also observed,

> The streets in all directions swarmed with people, and it is probable Donaldsonville

> never held so many souls before. A side show sprung up . . . while orators of the tooth paste, hair dye, corn medicine and Chinese grip persuasion abounded everywhere, increasing the general vivacity with their endless chin music.
>
> At six o'clock the military organizations marched to the public square, or *Place de la Louisiane,* where they were reviewed by Gov. Nicholls and staff, in the presence of an immense concourse of spectators. After the review the troops marched through the main streets. . . . The [Washington] Artillery, Cannoneers and Continentals were each preceded by a brass band, which furnished music throughout the march . . . and the evolutions of the troops were witnessed with wrapt [*sic*] attention. . . . The day's pleasures closed with a ball at the [Silver Cornet Band Hall] which was a truly brilliant affair . . . the handsome toilettes of the ladies, contrasting pleasantly with the military uniforms. . . . Gov. Nicholls was present in full dress. The crowd was almost too great for comfortable dancing . . . the festivities continued until two o'clock in the morning, at which hour the visiting organizations rendezvoused at their respective steamers and departed for home . . . given a hearty send off by the Cannoneers and townspeople.[45]

Again a uniformed company and armed with rifles and a cannon, Prosper Landry's veteran leadership prepared the company as a military unit so that it could be used for any emergency, or to keep the peace, which it did in August of 1878, when four convicted murderers were executed by Donaldsonville's sheriff. Four thousand people flocked to town to witness the hanging that took place in front of the courthouse and jail yard. The local newspaper reported, "The Cannoneers of Donaldson were drawn up in a semi-circle directly in front of the gallows, with fixed bayonets; several guards paced back and forth . . . to prevent the entrance of the crowd, and forty or fifty Sheriff's special deputies . . . were stationed in and about the Court House."[46]

In July of 1879 a mass meeting of citizens of Ascension Parish met at Donaldsonville and adopted the following resolution, "Whereas, the Cannoneers of Donaldsonville, in order more effectually to accomplish the object of their organization, which is 'to be useful to their fellow-citizens' have deemed it advisable and necessary to join the State troops; and . . . the Louisiana Field Artillery have kindly consented to accept them as a company . . . we, the people of Ascension . . . do hereby promise and agree to do all in our power to aid and assist them in the noble object they have in view."[47] *Le Compagnie d'Artillerie de Donaldson,* "So long celebrated for achievements in love and valor, are, on the third of August, to be mustered into the State Service as a company in the Louisiana Field Artillery."[48]

In Donaldsonville there was a great gathering of military men and excursionist from New Orleans to observe the Donaldsonville Cannoneers, sixty strong, under Prosper Landry, parade around town, preceded by their twelve piece band. After making the circuit, the company celebrated Mass, after which Landry "drew his men up in line . . . each officer's and man's name was called he stepped forward two paces, until the entire roll had been called . . . the company took [the oath], and was then duly declared mustered in as Company 'E' of the Louisiana Field Artillery."[49] Landry's Battery's identity was later changed from Company E to Battery Ascension Artillery, under which name it remained in the state's service through the 1880s.

On July 3, 1880, the "Cannoneers of Donaldson" received a "splendid 12-pounder, brass Napoleon gun from the Louisiana Field Artillery via the steamer *William Fagan"* which, the *Donaldsonville Chief* reported, "arrived . . . just in time to belch forth a salute in honor of the glorious fourth. The piece is a beauty and the Cannoneers are just the boys to handle it in the right style."[50]

Two months later Prosper Landry led twenty-five members[51] of the Donaldsonville Cannoneers to New Orleans, where they participated as Battery E in the Louisiana Field

Artillery Regiment, and along with the First Regiment, Louisiana National Guard, and Orleans Artillery, in a memorial to the dead from the battle of Liberty Place in New Orleans that occurred on September 14, 1874. These ceremonies and a parade celebrated the struggle to end Reconstruction in Louisiana. The artillery regiment, including the Gunners of Donaldson, formed on each side of the middle aisle of the St. Louis Cathedral while Cherubini's Mass was sung by a full choir. A New Orleans newspaper reported, "The entire ceremony was very impressive. At the moment of 'consecration' all of the soldiers knelt, one hand holding the gun, the other slightly elevating their shakos. The captains alone remained standing with heads reverently bowed in devotional attitudes. The low and measured beating of the drums, the hollow booming of the cannons coming in through the wide open portals, the swelling tones of the organ and the chanting of the priest, formed a fitting accompaniment to the solemn words, *Requiem aternam dona iis, Domine*—'Give eternal rest to them. O Lord.'"[52]

A review took place after the Mass, followed by a procession and other ceremonies and visits to the cemeteries. Prosper Landry and the Donaldsonville Cannoneers and friends visited the St. Louis Cemetery, Number 2, and paid their respects at the tomb of their veteran comrade Sabin Braud, who died three days earlier. A newspaper recorded, "Three rounds were fired by the company in [his] memory. . . . Capt. [Prosper] Landry made an eloquent address, though, as he expressed it "there was so much of his heart behind the cold marble that he could scarcely speak."[53] The newspaper also reported, "The Donaldsonville Cannoneers were well entertained by their city bretheren during their stay, and were quartered at Antoine's."[54]

In February 1885 the *Donaldsonville Chief* noted, "The Cannoneers of Donaldson were *en avant* in commemorating . . . Washington's birthday, and the occasion was one that doubtless revived many slumbering memories in the minds of the older members of this veteran command, and imbued both them and their younger comrades with new hopes for the future of the organization . . . a parade took place during the afternoon and at nightfall the soldiers assembled at the Peep-o' Day Hotel and partook of an elegant dinner."[55]

During the 1880s the martial spirit waned and many militia units in the state disbanded. The Cannoneer Company dwindled too as the war veterans resigned and joined organizations such as the Benevolent Association of the Army of Northern Virginia and the United Confederate Veterans, of which the Donaldsonville veterans had their own Major Victor Maurin Camp Number 38. Just a few months after commemorating Washington's birthday it was reported "the brass gold piece in the keeping of the Donaldsonville Cannoneers . . . for a long time past, was shipped on the steamer Assumption . . . consigned to . . . the militia organization of [Thibodaux] designated Company A, S[tate] M[ilitia]. When the Cannoneers decided to follow their regiment—the Louisiana Field Artillery—in withdrawing from the State militia, Capt. Landry signaled their readiness to return the piece, but was directed to hold it subject to the orders of the Adjutant General. The shipment was made . . . pursuant to instructions from that official."[56]

The "Sons of Veterans, C.S.A. of the parish of Ascension and the Donaldsonville Artillery" organized in 1888 under the leadership of Major Maurin's son Edmund. The organization constituted the only uniformed, armed, and equipped company of Sons of Confederate Soldiers in Louisiana with the purpose of honoring the heroes of the Donaldsonville Artillery and other gallant veterans, and firing salutes on holidays. The Cannoneers again were armed with a 12-pounder, smooth bore, bronze field piece they named the *Lady Florence* after Canonnier veteran Abraham Klotz's daughter,[57] and it did the duty of firing salutes while handled by the uniformed Donaldsonville Sons of Confederate Soldiers.[58] Each event was overseen by the now "grim old veterans" of the "old guard."[59] In July 1891 it was reported,

"The Cannoneers of Donaldsonville are taking great interest in their company and are drilling several times a week."[60] The Daughters of Veterans, led by Lieutenant Hubert Treille's daughter, Carmelite, along with the Sons, "Helped to inculcate a spirit of reverence for those brave men who struggled against overwhelming odds for Southern independence."[61] They, the sons and daughters, "Proudly waved the State flag, and a guidon, the latter a silent witness to the hero deeds of the bellum Donaldsonville Artillery."[62]

The martial spirit did not wane under Prosper Landry and Hubert Treille's tutelage, as reported in February 1893, when the Commandant of the Cadets at the Louisiana State University put the Cannoneers "through a spirited drill in infantry and artillery tactics . . . at the Armory." The drill was "extremely entertaining and beneficial." The Donaldsonville boys also reassembled a "Gatling gun . . . then took the piece to the levee . . . where a drum of cartridges was emptied in target practice and . . . rapid firing."[63]

A month after the Commandant's visit, the Donaldsonville battery's brick armory caught fire, though most of its contents were saved, "including the three cannon, forty-five Springfield rifles and other paraphernalia of the Cannoneers."[64] Unfortunately the wind driven flames consumed a number of buildings including the hall of the Major Victor Maurin United Confederate Veteran's Camp and the Sons of Veterans, along with the homes of Mrs. Victor Maurin Sr. and Victor Maurin Jr. [65]

The fire seemed to rekindle the martial spirit, and two months later Prosper Landry led the Cannoneers of Donaldsonville to Baton Rouge to participate in the "intercollegiate festival and sham battle." One newspaper reported the Donaldsonville soldiers "wore their new service uniforms for the first time, and presented a fine appearence." It was also noted, "They were accompanied by the St. Joseph Brass band, also in new uniforms."[6]

Dr. Charles E. Coates, Dean Emeritus, College of Pure and Applied Science, and first football coach of Louisiana State University, is credited with naming the football team the "Tigers" in the fall of 1893. Coates was also the son-in-law of Major Maurin's son Victor. He wrote, "The Louisiana Tigers had represented the state in the Civil War and had been known for their hard fighting. This name was applied collectively to the New Orleans Zouaves, the Donaldsonville Cannoniers, and . . . other Louisiana companies sent to Virginia, who seemed to have the faculty of getting into the hardest part of the fighting and staying there, most of them permanently."[67]

By November 1895, with an average attendance of just three men, the Donaldsonville Cannoneer Battery, still led by sixty-nine-year-old Prosper Landry, mustered out of service under a reorganization of the Louisiana Field Artillery.[68] A rebirth took place in just two years with the company reorganizing on May 25, 1897, with thirty or so members. Prosper Landry officially resigned from command on September 6, 1897, and Richard M. McCulloh[69] was elected the sixth (and last) captain and commander of *Le Compagnie d'Artillerie de Donaldson.*[70]

Exactly one year later the President of the United States authorized Louisiana to furnish three batteries of field artillery for the war with Spain that broke out after the sinking of the battleship *Maine.* The artillery organizations of the state anxiously awaited this call from Washington, and when it came on May 1, 1898, Governor Murphy Foster decided "to divide the honor between the Washington Artillery and the Louisiana Field Artillery . . . and the Donaldsonville Cannoneers."[71] The Ascension Artillery boasted an enrollment of sixty-two members under McCulloh at this time. These three batteries, designated "A" (Louisiana Field Artillery), "B" (Washington Artillery), and "C" (Donaldsonville Cannoneers)[72] each now with 106 enlisted men, were mustered into the United States service at New Orleans on July 6, 1898.

Of their departure from Donaldsonville the following lines were dedicated in a local paper:

See the Donaldson Artillery,
Drawn up in grand array,
Ready waiting for the order,
To the war to march away.

Many men are from Ascension,
And we know they're brave and true,
But don't forget Assumption boys,
Are in the Battery too.

Those boys are noble strong and brave,
As men should ever be,
They would freely fight for country,
Whate'er the cause may be.

God knows we all will miss them,
For they leave their dear ones here,
Father, mother, sister, brother,
And friends that they hold dear.

We'll offer prayers to God for them,
Who've gone so far away,
That He will bring them home unharmed,
As when they went away.

La.[73]

Expecting, like all volunteers "to get somewhere and do something"[74] the cannonneers were doomed for disappointment. After only a short time in camp at Jackson Barracks in New Orleans, the three batteries were mustered out on November 12, 1898, having been in the national service a little over four months.[75]

The mustering out of the *Canonniers* of battery "C" in November 1898 ended the history of *Le Compagnie d'Artillerie de Donaldson.* Though they had a "reputation for undaunted courage"[76] and a brilliant record for sixty-one years, "Pen and press have neglected its gallant career."[77] Until now.

Top: Sons of Veterans, Confederate States of America of the Donaldsonville Artillery and Ascension Parish, gun detachment in front the Donaldsonville Courthouse at Louisiana Square on September 18, 1891, celebrating the thirtieth anniversary of the *Canonniers de Donaldson* leaving for Richmond, Va. Bottom: a different view of the same celebration. Courtesy of the Confederate Memorial Hall, New Orleans, La.

Soldier, rest! thy warfare o'er,
Sleep the sleep that knows not breaking:
Dream of battled fields no more,
Days of danger, nights of waking.
In our isle's enchanted hall,
Hands unseen thy couch are strewing,
Fairy strains of music fall,
Every sense in slumber dewing.
Soldier, rest! thy warfare o'er,
Dream of fighting fields no more:
Sleep the sleep that knows not breaking,
Morn of toil, nor night of waking.

From "*The Lady of the Lake,*" by Sir Walter Scott, 1810.

Decoration Day at Major Victor Maurin Camp No. 38 Tomb, Ascension of Our Lord Catholic Cemetery, Donaldsonville, circa 1905.

Courtesy of the Louisiana and Lower Mississippi Valley Collections, Louisiana State University Libraries, Baton Rouge, La.

Appendix

Rosters and Biographies

This biographical roster of the officers and men of the Donaldsonville Artillery who fought during the Civil War has been assembled from a number of sources. The most important primary source is the *Compiled Service Records of Confederate Soldiers who served in Organizations from the State of Louisiana*. The *CSR* is part of Record Group Number 109 (War Department Collection of Confederate Records) in the National Archives, Washington D.C., and is available on microfilm. This microfilm publication is National Archives Microcopy Number 320 and consists of 414 rolls. The Donaldsonville Artillery is listed as Captain Landry's Company and is covered in rolls 54 and 55.

Sixteen muster rolls for the Donaldsonville Artillery have survived and are preserved in the National Archives. The rolls (each covering a two month period) from September 1861 to February 1862 and May-June 1864 are missing. Additionally, the first half of the roll covering July-August 1863 has been lost.

Another important source is the Louisiana Historical Association Collection on deposit in the Rare Books and Manuscript Section of Tulane University in New Orleans. In this collection cataloged under 55-V, Association of the Army of Northern Virginia Papers, will be found Bound Volume 11, *Record Roll of Donaldsonville Artillery 1861-1865*, which includes a *Historical Memoranda*. This record was copied and transcribed on November 14, 1885, by veteran John S. Mioton from the original completed by members of the battery in March 1865 at Petersburg, Virginia.

In this same collection are Bound Volumes 19 and 20, *Membership Applications 1875 to 1917*, which contain information relative to twenty-four Donaldsonville artillerists who applied for membership in the Benevolent Association Army of Northern Virginia, Louisiana Division. This association was organized in the autumn of 1874 by Louisiana veterans based on a similar one started in Virginia. It was later incorporated into the United Confederate Veterans and designated Camp Number 1.

The roster information is supplemented by Andrew B. Booth's *Records of Louisiana Confederate Soldiers and Louisiana Confederate Commands* (three volumes), published in 1920, and Sydney A. Marchand's *Forgotten Fighters 1861-1865*, published in 1966. A source pertaining to the Appomattox paroles comes from the *Southern Historical Society Papers*, Volume XV, pages 62 and 63.

Birth, death, and marriage records for many can be found in the multiple volumes of the *Diocese of Baton Rouge Catholic Church Records*. Information was also gleaned from the yearly New Orleans City Directories located at Tulane University's Special Collection Library, along with the U.S. Census and multiple volumes of *Louisiana Death Records Index* located in the Louisiana Division of Archives, Records Management, and History in Baton Rouge. Located there too is invaluable data obtained from applications submitted by the veterans or their spouses for Confederate pensions from the State of Louisiana. This information is preserved on microfilm and titled *Board of Pension Commissioners; Confederate Pension Applications*, Rolls 1-151.

The Louisiana Adjutant General's Office Library, Jackson Barracks, New Orleans, has original rosters of the following United Confederate Veterans camps: Louisiana Division, Army of Northern Virginia (New Orleans) Camp No. 1; Leroy Stafford (Caddo Parish) Camp No. 3; Baton Rouge (East Baton Rouge Parish) Camp No. 17; Iberville (Iberville Parish) Camp No. 18; Major Victor Maurin (Ascension Parish) Camp No. 38; Amite City (Tangipahoa Parish) Camp No. 78; General Braxton Bragg (Iberia Parish) Camp No. 196; General Fred N. Ogden (Ascension Parish) Camp No. 247; General Frank Gardner (Lafayette) Camp No. 580; and General Francis T. Nicholls (Assumption Parish) Camp No. 1142; two original bound record books on the New Orleans Camp Nicholls Soldier's Home; and a card file containing Grave Registration Forms cataloged by Louisiana parishes that list numerous veteran's internments. Photo static copies of "Landry's Battery, Donaldsonville Arty., Muster Rolls, 71 sheets," copied by the United States Government in 1903, are contained in Book No. 146 and Book No. 147 of the library's Louisiana Military Records, C.S.A. Collection, along with photographed "Individual Record Cards" of each member of the battery. Other unique sources of information along with newspaper articles and obituaries are noted with each entry.

Abbreviations

ACH	Appomattox Court House
AOL	Ascension of Our Lord Catholic Cemetery
AWOL	Absent without leave
BAANV	Benevolent Association Army of Northern Virginia, Louisiana Division
ca.	circa
Co.	Company
OR	*The War of the Rebellion: A Compilation of the Official Records of the Union and Confederate Armies*
UCV	United Confederate Veterans

ACOSTA, HYPOLITE EUGENE. Enlisted at Donaldsonville, 9/13/1861, Private, promoted to Corporal, March 1863. Born 3/5/1838 in Ascension Parish to Manuel Acosta and Margueritte Gonzales; one of nine children. Occupation unknown but lived in Donaldsonville. Appears to have escaped capture in April 1865. Returned to Donaldsonville after the war and married Antoinette Martinez with a daughter born on 8/5/1867. Daughter died at one year old and wife died almost exactly one year later. In 1880 worked as a farm laborer and lived in the 1st Ward of Assumption Parish with widowed Celestine Guilfort, a forty-year-old servant and cook, Augustine Guilfort, a ten-year-old girl boarder, and Guilfort's eight year old daughter Georgiana.

ALBA, CHARLES FELIX. Enlisted at Donaldsonville, 9/13/1861, Private. Born 6/9/1841 in Assumption Parish to Louis Alba, a "worthy, intelligent and upright citizen . . . of Plattenville" who was from Barcelona, Spain, and Marie Caballero; the second oldest son with four brothers and three sisters. Worked as a saddle maker in Plattenville, Assumption Parish. Captured by Federal Calvary, 4/21/1864 in Ascension Parish and carried AWOL on muster roll. Married Estella Montaldo in Assumption Parish, 10/25/1866 and had four sons. He was later described "as a man of large proportions" and after the war moved to New Orleans where he lived intermittently for thirty years. Engaged in steamboating on the Mississippi River for fifteen years then worked as a commercial traveler. Due to Alba's close friendship with Judge Edward D. White in New Orleans he became involved in politics, from which he was appointed to Federal positions from 1880-1883. Alba worked as a grocery clerk in the 8th Ward of Assumption Parish, then a store in St. Charles Parish and some time after his Federal service moved to Biloxi, Mississippi, and opened a store. Moved back to New Orleans in 1899 and lived with and was associated with a son's dry goods and notions store located on Magazine Street, near Napoleon Avenue. Died of heart failure at 10:15 a.m. on 7/16/1901. Interred Metairie Cemetery, New Orleans. In 1902 his wife applied for a Confederate Widow's Pension and was denied for the reason: "deserter on furlough." His photograph accompanied obituary in the *New Orleans Times Picayune,* 7/17/1901. His brother served as a private in Company H, 28th (Thomas's) Louisiana Infantry Regiment and became a POW, captured and paroled at Vicksburg, Mississippi, on 7/4/1863. Rodolphe died on 7/30/1877 and was interred in Assumption Catholic Cemetery, Plattenville. The *Donaldsonville Chief,* 8/11/1877 erroneously identified Charles as being his brother Rodolphe E. Alba in the obituary.

ALBARES, AUGUSTIN. Enlisted at Donaldsonville, 9/13/1861, Private. Born 1/22/1844 in Plattenville, Assumption Parish, to Joseph Valery Albares and Adelina Cuvilliers, one of six sons. Worked as a farm laborer living in Assumption Parish. Captured 7/20/1863 near Hedgesville, Berkley County, Virginia, during the Gettysburg Campaign. Captured with Canonnier Octave Dupas. A Federal officer recorded: "On retreat from Gettysburg he left ranks on the march in the night—returned to Hedgeville and then voluntarily surrendered."[1] Albares took Oath of Allegiance and was released from Camp Chase, Ohio, on 5/11/1865. Married Elizabeth Vining in New Iberia, Iberia Parish, 10/25/1869, and had three daughters. Lived with family and mother in the 3rd Ward of Iberia Parish. Died 10/16/1874 and interred AOL in Donaldsonville.

ARCENAUX, LAURENT DÉSIRÉ. Enlisted at Donaldsonville, 9/13/1861, Private. Born 11/18/1838 in St. James Parish to Désiré Arcenaux and Gracieuse Dicharry, the youngest and only son of three children. Worked as a cooper in Donaldsonville. Carried AWOL in March 1864, deserted while on furlough to join Confederate Trans-Mississippi Cavalry, surrendered 5/26/1865 at New Orleans and paroled 6/6/1865 at Natchitoches, Natchitoches Parish. Married Marie Estelle Theriot 1/5/66 in Donaldsonville and had three sons and three daughters. *Donaldsonville Chief*, 6/23/1883, reported, "None could know him well without feeling more than an ordinary regard for him." Died of congestive fever on 6/21/1883 in Smoke Bend, Ascension Parish, and interred at AOL.

AUCOIN, GUSTAVE EVARISTE. Enlisted at Donaldsonville, 9/13/1861, Private. Born 3/9/1843 in Assumption Parish to Firmin Aucoin and Marguerite Hebert, one of twelve children. Worked as a laborer in Assumption Parish. Hazel eyes, dark hair, light complexion, 5'0". Paroled ACH, 4/10/1865. Married widow Marie Ann Estelle Edwin Smith on 3/19/1867 in Plattenville, Assumption Parish. Confederate Pension Application states Aucoin, who was childless, derived his support as a laborer "by hard struggle." In an affidavit dated 11/19/1906 Canonnier comrades E. L. Monnot and Duffosard Mollere related his habits "are good and free from dishonor." Lived in Plattenville up to the time of his death on 9/24/1924 and believed interred in Assumption Catholic Cemetery, Plattenville.

BABIN, JOSEPH FELIX. Enlisted at Donaldsonville, 9/13/1861, Private. Born 8/28/1842 in Ascension Parish to Joseph Arsenes Babin and Marie Louise Peignie, the only son and second oldest of four children. Worked as a laborer in Donaldsonville. Wounded "slightly"[2] at Fredericksburg, Virginia, 12/13/1862. Went AWOL in March 1864, deserted while on furlough. Married first cousin Priscella Amelina Babin Rougeau (widow of Canonnier Adolph Rougeau, killed in action on 9/3/1864 at Petersburg, Virginia) in Donaldsonville on 12/21/1868 and had five daughters. Worked as a laborer until, as noted by the *Donaldsonville Chief*, 7/7/1883, elected as one of six policeman in Donaldsonville. Still living in Donaldsonville in 1890 with all daughters at home. Believed to have died on 8/19/1914 in Terrebonne Parish.

BABIN, PIERRE, "TURIAFFE." Enlisted at Donaldsonville, 9/13/1861, Private. Born 7/14/1840 in Ascension Parish to Armand Prudent Babin and Marguerite Celina Rivet, the oldest and only son of three children. Clerked in Donaldsonville. Stated on a Confederate Pension Application, 11/12/1907, witnessed by Canonnier comrades Bienvenue Cire and Antoine Sobral that he received a "wound in the calf of the leg . . . at Gaines Mill. It was but a slight flesh wound." According to *Levy Diary* (1/3/1865) he played an "inspiring" violin. Paroled ACH, 4/10/1865. Joined BAANV (Application No. 342, 8/27/1874) stated he "served up to the surrender." Member UCV, Major Victor Maurin Camp No. 38, and one of the camp's lieutenants while serving as an alternate delegate to UCV's Annual Meeting and Reunions. Married Louise Lodoviska (Lodoiska) Leblanc on 1/29/1866 at St. Francis Catholic Church in Point Coupee Parish and though childless he and his wife later raised several orphans. Lived in the 5th Ward of Ascension Parish working as a farm overseer until moving to Darrow, 7th Ward of Ascension Parish, next to Canonnier Joseph Gustave Boudreau. On 5/8/1886 established his own hack line and livery stable where passengers and freight crossing the river from

From Sydney A. Marchand, *Marchand's on the Mississippi and the St. Lawrence.*

Donaldsonville to Darrow by the ferry steamer *Ascension* were conveyed by stage line, which ran five miles along a dirt road aside the levee and made connections with the passenger trains of the Yazoo and Mississippi Valley Railroad. Also clerked and collected for the Burnside and Donaldsonville Packet Company's Mississippi River steamers *Gracie Kent* and the *Virgie.* The *Donaldsonville Chief,* 3/3/1928, paid tribute: "Captain Babin, as he was known to all, filled the responsible position with perfect satisfaction to the traveling public and the company. Old aged forced his retirement from work." Died 1/25/1918 and interred UCV, Major Victor Maurin Camp No. 38 tomb, AOL Catholic Cemetery in Donaldsonville. *Donaldsonville Chief,* 1/26/1918 reported, "Beloved citizen mourn . . . one of Ascension's oldest, most widely known and best loved citizens died at his home" and "by reason of his unfailing courtesy and cheerfulness, he made friends . . . with whom he came in contact." The news of his death, it added, "Was received with profound sorrow wherever the genial old gentleman was known."

BARRAS, LOUIS EMILE. Enlisted at Donaldsonville, 9/13/1861, Private. Born 3/18/1836 in Ascension Parish to Jacques Barras and Zoe Celestine Barraban, one of two sons with eleven sisters. A farmer living in the 1st Ward of Assumption Parish, listed his occupation as an Engineer at enlistment. According to *R. O. Landry Diary* he was wounded (slightly) at Gettysburg, Pennsylvania, on 7/2/1863. Went AWOL in March 1864, deserted while on furlough. Married before the war to Mathilda Truxillo and at time of enlistment had a five -year-old daughter, Myrtee. A son was born on 5/15/1861, with another two sons born after the war while living in the 1st Ward of Assumption Parish next to wealthy father-in-law. The household had three black servants. Barras noted his occupation in the 1870 U.S. Census as an "Engineer." Later became a sugar planter and listed in Bouchereau's *The Louisiana Sugar Report, 1870-1917.* In 1914 living in Donaldsonville and still grinding sugarcane in season. Died 2/4/1919 and interred Assumption Catholic Cemetery, Plattenville.

BERGERON, EMILE THEODULE. Enlisted at Williamsburg, Virginia, 2/28/1862, Private. Previously served as a private with Co. E, 1st Battalion (Dreux/Rightor's) Louisiana Infantry from 4/25/1861. Born 7/25/1839 in Plattenville, Assumption Parish, to Zenon Theodule Bergeron and Marie Azelie Barilleau, one of two sons with four sisters. A farmer living two miles above Labadieville in Brule Texas, Assumption Parish. Black eyes, blonde hair, and light complexion, 5'8". Appears to have escaped capture in April 1865. Joined UCV as a member of Major Victor Maurin Camp No. 38. In 1866 worked as a laborer in New Orleans, then farmed a 100-acre homestead along the Attakapas Canal in the 2nd Ward of Ascension Parish for the remainder of his life. After the war married Oceana Rogers. Widowed with no children he married in November 1869 at Paincourtville. His wife, Mathilda Blanchard, was sister to Canonnier Severan Blanchard, Claire, the wife of Canonnier Henry M. Newchurch, and Eulalie, the wife of Canonnier Joseph Alfred Gautreaux. Their marriage produced three sons and a daughter. The *Assumption Pioneer,* 1/21/1899, reported he "was a true gentleman, [who] served gallantly until the end of the war." Died of pleurisy on 1/13/1899 and interred Assumption Catholic Cemetery, Plattenville.

BESSON, JACQUES ESPRIT, "JAMES." Enlisted at Brookhaven, Mississippi, 5/20/1864, Private. Born 5/7/1846 in Ascension Parish, son of Joseph Besson (believed to have been a member of the antebellum Donaldsonville Canonniers) and Marie Celestine Richard, fourth and only son out of five children. Numa Augustin (first captain of the Donaldsonville Canonniers) was a witness at father's wedding on 2/22/1840 in Ascension Parish. Grandfather came from Marseilles, France, and settled in St. James Parish, where he married an Acadian, Françoise Dugas. James was a student at Donaldsonville before the war. Gray eyes, dark hair, dark complexion, 5'8". *Levy Diary* on 5/31/1864 near Richmond noted, "Besson, a new recruit from Donaldsonville was induced to become my substitute in order that I might procure a furlough." Paroled ACH, 4/10/1865. Joined UCV as a member of Iberville Camp No. 18. In the 1880s was a sugarcane planter living in the 4th Ward of Iberville Parish and listed in Bouchereau's *The Louisiana Sugar Report, 1870-1917.* In 1900 worked as a "canal contractor" living with two sisters and twenty-one-year-old twin nephews named Jacques Besson Landry and Joseph Amedee Landry in the 6th Ward of East Baton Rouge Parish. Died 11/24/1902 in Iberville Parish and interred St. Joseph Catholic Cemetery, Baton Rouge.

BLANCHARD, JOSEPH SEVERIN. Enlisted at Donaldsonville, 9/13/1861, Private. Born 12/4/1840 in Assumption Parish to Armand Blanchard and Clarisse Breaux, the second oldest of seven children. Worked as a farm laborer and lived five miles above Labadieville in the 9th Ward of Assumption Parish. Paroled ACH, 4/10/1865. Joined UCV as a member of Major Victor Maurin Camp No. 38, later transferred to Gen. Francis T. Nicholls Camp No. 1142. Married 11/7/1865 in Paincourtville to Lorenza Landry (who became postmaster of Paincourtville, Assumption Parish, and lived until 5/21/1937) and had one son, Henry. Sisters Mathilda, Claire, and Eulalie Blanchard married Canonniers Emile Bergeron, Henry M. Newchurch, and Joseph Alfred Gautreaux respectively. The *Assumption Pioneer* on 5/10/1879 spoke of his "cheerful countenance" and on 10/20/1900 reported, "As a soldier, [he] had no superior. His brother soldiers . . . spoke most highly of him. He was extremely popular and twice elected Sheriff of [Assumption] parish." He was a "hotel keeper" at the time of death that occurred at home in Paincourtville from a cancerous throat tumor on 10/19/1900. Interred St. Elizabeth Catholic Cemetery, Paincourtville.

BLOUIN, PIERRE THEOPHILE, "PAUL." Enlisted at Donaldsonville, 9/13/1861, 2nd Corporal, promoted 4th Sergeant, and then 2nd Sergeant. Born 5/22/1841 in Ascension Parish to Pierre Emile Blouin and Aimée Blouin, one of three children. Worked as a laborer living in the 4th Ward of Ascension Parish. Gray eyes, black hair, fair complexion, 5'11". Paroled ACH, 4/10/1865. Joined BAANV (Application No. 492, February 23, 1882) that stated at "Appomattox Court House, was promoted Sergeant in 1863." A practicing Catholic during the war he was believed to be a *spiritali amicitia* (spiritual friend) of Captain Prosper Landry.[3] After the war worked as a laborer living in Donaldsonville with youngest sister Aimée Braud and her husband. By 1890 living alone in Donaldsonville between African American neighbors James and Lucy Davis, ages forty-six and fifty-three, born in Virginia, and William Delly, age forty-five.

BLUM, MARX, "MAX." Enlisted at Donaldsonville, 9/13/1861, Private. Born ca. 1835 in Niederbronn, Alsace, France. Immigrated in 1860, by July 1860 working as a shoemaker and peddler in Donaldsonville. Believed to be the older brother and next door neighbor to Cannonier cook Henry Blum. Black eyes, black hair, dark complexion, 5'11". On Confederate Pension Application dated 1/23/1899 and witnessed by Canonnier comrades "Buck" Chase and E. L. Monnot he stated he had a wound that was "slight, in the neck, in 7 days fight." Discharged from service on Surgeon's Certificate of Disability on 4/25/1864 (Doctor C. Walker) due to heart disease (heart flutters). After discharge went to Napoleonville, Assumption Parish; moved to Shreveport, Caddo Parish, in 1866. Joined UCV as a member of General Leroy Stafford Camp No. 3. Married a German born woman by the name of

Louisa and had four sons and a daughter. A widower by 1870 he married another German-born woman named Francis (though called Fannie) and had three daughters and a son. In 1880 at Shreveport working as a grocer until 6/25/1899 when he applied for a Confederate Pension on which he stated his livelihood was: "Selling a few sausages." Died in Shreveport on 11/11/1904 and interred Hebrew Rest Cemetery, Number Two, Shreveport. Epitaph on grave obelisk reads: "Proud Confederate Soldier." The 1860 U.S. Census taker spelled his name "Bloom."

BOHAM, TIMOTHY, "TIM." Enlisted at Donaldsonville, 9/13/1861, Private. Born ca. 1831 in Ireland. Worked as a laborer in Donaldsonville. *Levy Diary* on 5/4/1864 noted Boham "was detailed to bear the letter" from Major M. B. "Buck" Miller "that horses will probably be furnished . . . when we will join the . . . battalion on the line of battle." *Levy Diary* on 6/4/1864 noted Levy "slept in Ely's tent, Boham having proved so ungrateful" but on 8/1/1864 Boham "was the first man to see me this morning [after Levy was wounded]; this act indicates more nobility of spirit than I had given him credit for." Captured 12/14/1864 while on sick furlough near Whitehall Mills, LaSalle Parish. Paroled from Camp Townsend, Vicksburg, Mississippi, 5/6/1865. Joined BAANV (Application No. 463, 12/3/1880) that stated he "was in all the engagements . . . from Yorktown, to sometime in October 1864. When on furlough I was captured and sent to prison at Ship Island." Married before the war to a woman named Susanna, with a daughter born in 1860. In 1870 living in the 3rd Ward of New Orleans with wife and daughter, two black levee workers, a mulatto woman, and a mulatto stone cutter and his family of five. Died 5/15/1884 and interred in tumulus BAANV, Metairie Cemetery, New Orleans.

BOUDREAU, JOSEPH GUSTAVE. Enlisted at New Orleans, 4/16/1862, Private. Born 11/5/1844 near Corner View on New River Bayou in 8th Ward of Ascension Parish, the third of ten children born to "popular"[4] Leufroi Boudreau (1818-1900) and Margaret Eulalie Hebert (1822-1905). Brother of Canonnier Octave Boudreau. Farmed at Cornerview, where father operated a small sugarhouse. Captured at Hatcher's Run on 4/2/1865 and released from Point Lookout, Maryland, 6/9/1865 after taking Oath of Allegiance. After the war lived in Darrow, 7th Ward of Ascension Parish, next to fellow Canonniers Pierre "Turiaffe" Babin and Lubin Guedry. Witness to sister Florentine Cecile Boudreau's marriage to Canonnier Bernard Herman Landry in April 1870.

BOUDREAU, OCTAVE CRISSE. Enlisted at Donaldsonville on 9/13/1861, Private. Born 1/27/1843 near Corner View on New River Bayou in 8th Ward of Ascension Parish, the second of ten children born to Leufroi Boudreau (1818-1900) and Margaret Eulalie Hebert (1822-1905). Brother of Canonnier Gustave Boudreau. Listed occupation as a planter in Cornerview, where father operated a small sugarhouse. Blue eyes, light hair, light complexion, 5'8". *R. O. Landry Diary* noted he was wounded at Gettysburg, 7/1/1863. *Levy Diary* on 1/27-28/1865, at the High Bridge fortifications recorded, "My position was decided to be on the Cumberland [County] side of the Appomattox [River] at a case-mated earthwork in company with Corp'l J. Braud and Octave Boudreau. Neither of these men are at all congenial to me" and, "As Boudreau spent the morning in camp, I stayed at my cabin." Paroled ACH, 4/10/1865. Returned to farming at Corner View. Married Marguerite Olivia Babin, 10/17/1865, (sister of Canonnier Pierre "Turiaffe" Babin) at New River, that was witnessed by Canonniers Felicien Hebert and brother Gustave Boudreau. Marriage produced one son and three daughters. Sister Florentine Cecile Boudreau married Canonnier Bernard Herman Landry.

BRAUD, JOSEPH NUMA. Enlisted at Donaldsonville, 9/13/1861, Bugler. Born 4/6/1843 in Donaldsonville, the oldest of six children to Severin Edouard Braud and Anna Ursula Elisca Cire. Cousin to Canonniers Edward Severin Terrio and Sabin Braud. Occupation unknown but lived in Donaldsonville. Gray eyes, black hair, light complexion, 5'7". *Levy Diary* on 1/27/1865 at the High Bridge fortifications recorded, "My position was decided to be on the Cumberland [County] side of the Appomattox [River] at a case-mated earthwork in company with Corp'l J. Braud and Octave Boudreau. Neither of these men are at all congenial to me." Paroled with one horse at ACH, 4/10/1865. Joined UCV as a member of Major Victor Maurin Camp No. 38. After the war worked as a merchant clerk for father in Darrow, Ascension Parish. Married Ellen Wall on 2/23/1876 and had one daughter that died at five years of age. Died 10/2/1902 on Cora Plantation, White Castle, Iberville Parish. Believed interred in Major Victor Maurin Camp No. 38 tomb, AOL.

BRAUD, PIERRE SABIN. Enlisted at Donaldsonville, 9/13/1861, Private; appointed Guidon during Gettysburg Campaign. Born 10/18/1840 in New Orleans to Joseph Adelard Braud, a commission merchant of marble statuary for churches and Henriette Landry, the oldest and only son of three children. Worked as a bookkeeper in Donaldsonville. *Levy Diary* on 2/10/1865 noted he "looked and acted the woman well" in *La Dramatic Association's* play "A Frenchmen Lost at the High Bridge." On 2/12/1865 he translated for Levy "Moliere's comedy of 'The Misanthrope' for the next performance." Paroled ACH, 4/10/1865. Married Eugenie Jamey of New Orleans on 6/16/1870 (her father was Charge D'Affaires of the Ursuline Convent) and had two sons and two daughters. Lived in Darrow, Ascension Parish, and ran a "bookkeeper store" in Donaldsonville. A good son, he visited his sick mother in New Orleans two days a month from Donaldsonville in the 1870s.[5] The *Donaldsonville Chief*, 10/11/1879, recorded a war-worn veteran and correspondent for the *Pointe Coupee Pelican* wrote he was fortunate to meet his friend "Sabin B.," a "distinguished" soldier and "army companion" of the Canonniers whom he described as "the Little Giant." The *Donaldsonville Chief*, 9/18/1880, reported he "was a brave and faithful soldier [who] never lost [his] buoyant spirits and genial disposition." Served as a lieutenant in the post-bellum Donaldsonville Cannoniers. The *New Orleans Daily Picayune,* 9/15/1880 reported, "The Donaldsonville Cannoneers [in New Orleans for ceremonies commemorating that cities September 14, 1874, battle of Liberty Place attended a requiem Mass at St. Louis Catherdral after which, with] a number of friends visited the St. Louis Cemetery . . . paying their respects at the tomb of Lieut. Braud who was buried last Sunday. Three rounds were fired by the company in [his] memory. . . . Capt. [Prosper] Landry made an eloquent address, though, as he expressed it, 'there was so much of his heart behind the cold marble that he could scarcely speak.'" Died 9/11/1880 at midnight in New Orleans, funeral conducted at St. Vincent de Paul's church, 3053 Dauphine Street, and interred in St. Louis Cemetery No. 2, Square 1, Tomb 14, Alley 2 LSC, New Orleans. Sabin's father died in New Orleans nine days after his son's death. After wife passed away the four children were raised by Celina "Teen" Jamey, their mother's sister, a piano teacher, in the 9th Ward, 3rd Precinct, in New Orleans.

BURNS, THOMAS. Enlisted at Williamsburg, Virginia, 3/28/1862, Private; promoted 10th Corporal 5/28/1863. Previously served as a Private with Co. E, 1st Battalion (Dreux/Rightor's) Louisiana Infantry from 4/16/1861. Born May 1841 in Ireland, immigrated in 1855. Clerked in Houma, Terrebonne Parish. Gray eyes, brown hair, light complexion, 5'8". *Levy Diary* noted on 12/10/1864 he arrived, probably sick, with "Herman" Fuhri in Richmond. In January 1865 carried AWOL on muster roll. Paroled by Federal forces on 5/11/1865 at Bayou

Sara, West Feliciana Parish. Married in 1865 to Caroline (born in Louisiana to parents of German descent) while working as a laborer in New Orleans. In 1900 still worked as a day laborer living at 740 Conti Street, New Orleans, where four other renters lived. He and wife were childless.

BYNUM, ALFRED L. Enlisted at Williamsburg, Virginia, 3/14/1862, Private. Previously served as a Private with Co. B, 1st Battalion (Dreux/Rightor's) Louisiana Infantry from 5/1/1861. Born 2/4/1839 in Barnwell, South Carolina, to Benjamin Franklin Bynum and Sarah Ann Eliza O'Bannon. His uncle and namesake was killed in the massacre at Goliad, Texas, 3/27/1836, during the Texas War for Independence. Occupation unknown but lived in New Orleans. Gray eyes, light hair, fair complexion, 5'8". Captured while detailed to the Medical Department at Frederick, Maryland, (Sharpsburg Campaign) 9/12/1862, declared exchanged on 11/10/1862. Transferred to Captain James F. Hart's Washington Light Artillery (2nd South Carolina Battery) 3/26/1864. Described as "lively . . . and a soldierly looking little man."[6] Married 1/10/1869 to wealthy widow Ann Virginia Allen Ward of Marion, Texas, who had a daughter. Was farming but by 1880, according to the U.S. Census, was "maimed, crippled, bedridden, or other wise disabled." Died 10/16/1883 and believed to be interred in Marion, Texas.

CARMOUCHE, DÉSIRÉ NUMA. Enlisted at New Orleans, 4/16/1862, Private. Born 9/29/1840 in Assumption Parish to French born father François Hypolite Carmouche and Marie Adeline Henriette Bourg, the second youngest of seven children. Younger brother Pierre was born nine days after their father's death on 9/27/1842. Clerked in Assumption Parish while living with oldest brother François (a deputy sheriff) and his wife and two children, his mother, another older brother, and younger brother. Dark eyes, dark hair, dark complexion, 5'8". Paroled ACH, 4/10/1865. The *Assumption Pioneer,* 9/13/1884, reported, "He entered Confederate Service in the famous Donaldsonville Cannoneers . . . in Virginia under Major V. Maurin." Married Marie Olimpe Bourgeois on 10/24/1866 in Lafourche Parish. Widowed, he remarried widow Francis Berthe "Bertha" Himel on 1/8/1873 in Lafourche Parish and had five children. Brother-in-law to Canonnier Charles Felix Pidoux. A grocer in Labadieville, 4th Ward of Assumption Parish in 1880, he afterwards became lessee and manager of Ricohoc Plantation in St. Mary Parish. Died of congestive chills and fever on 9/11/1884 on Ricohoc Plantation. Interred AOL. The *Donaldsonville Chief,* 9/27/1884, reported, "Another one of our good soldiers is gone."[7] Son Sergeant Charles Carmouche served with the Donaldsonville Cannoneers, Battery C, United States Federal Service in 1898.

CAROTHERS, JAMES B., "JIM." Enlisted at Williamsburg, Virginia, 2/28/1862, Private. Previously served as a Private with Co. E, 1st Battalion (Dreux/Rightor's) Louisiana Infantry from 5/5/1861. Born 2/2/1841, probably in Terrebonne Parish, to James L. Carothers (of Scottish descent and a wealthy planter in Terrebonne Parish and a native of Pennsylvania) and Aurora McIntyre. Worked as a laborer in Tigerville, Terrebonne Parish, living with maternal grandfather John McIntyre and family. Brown eyes, black hair, dark complexion, 6'1". *Levy Diary* on 12/22/1864 noted he arrived at the High Bridge fortifications and "dined with Jim Carothers's mess and slept with Hart." *Levy Diary* on 2/10/1865 recorded Carothers in *La Dramatic Association's* "A Frenchman Lost at the High Bridge" was "decidedly good in his personation." Paroled ACH, 4/10/1865. William Ely (fourteen times) and Carothers (thirteen times) were mentioned in Levy's Diary more than any other Canonniers except Levy's brother Julien "Doc" Levy. Carothers had a cousin from Ohio with the same name that enlisted in Company G, 20th Ohio Infantry Regiment.

CAZARÉ, MICHEL. Enlisted at Donaldsonville, 9/13/1861, Senior 2nd Lieutenant; promoted Junior 1st Lieutenant. Born ca. 1827 in Louisiana. Worked as a butcher in Donaldsonville. Sick in Louisiana from March 1862 until being dropped from the rolls by Special Order No. 45/8, Adjutant and Inspector General's Office, 2/23/1863. Married Marie Eugenie Edwin on 11/24/1853, had one son and three daughters. Died 3/13/1863 from a catarrh in Plattenville, Assumption Parish. Interred Assumption Catholic Cemetery, Plattenville. *O'Hara Diary* noted, "None of his friends was present at his death." His fifth child, a son, was born on 11/24/1863. Wife applied for a Confederate Widow's Pension in 1903 and lived in Plattenville until her death on 8/15/1925. Son Michel Cazaré was elected and served a number of years as Justce of Peace in the 2nd Ward of Assumption Parish.

CHARLET, GUSTAVE W. Enlisted at Donaldsonville, 9/13/61, Private. Born 11/16/1840 in Plattenville, Assumption Parish, to wealthy planter Pierre Charlet from Grenoble, France, and Françoise Estelle Landry, one of eight sons with one sister. Brothers Alphonse, 2nd Lieutenant in Company H, 29th (Thomas's) Louisiana Infantry Regiment, and Pierre Alcee, Private in Company H, 2nd Louisiana Cavalry Regiment, and nephew, Moleon (or Maulion) Macoire Charlet, Private in Company H, 2nd Louisiana Cavalry Regiment, served with Confederate forces. Charlet's father was a soldier under Napoleon Bonaparte and in all the battles from 1804 to 1814, and one of the survivors of the memorable and disastrous retreat from Moscow, Russia. Father interred in Assumption Catholic Cemetery, Plattenville, where his epitah reads: "Soldat de Napoleon I." Descendants have in their possession his father's epaulettes with their fringe of tarnished gold, shoulder straps and a bayonet, a long pistol in a box lined with purple velvet that bore a Belgian army manufacture's address and a St. Helena medal inscribed, "To my companion in glory my last thought."[8] The Charlet Plantation was sold in the spring of 1835 to William Whitmell Pugh who built Woodlawn. Gustave worked as a cooper in Paincourtville, Assumption Parish, and lived with the family of his thirty-two-year-old nephew Maulion Charlet. Hazel eyes, brown hair, light complexion, 5'3". Captured during battle of Fort Gregg, Petersburg, Virginia, 4/2/1865, released 6/10/1865 from Point Lookout, Maryland, prisoner of war camp after taking Oath of Allegiance. Joined BAANV (Application No. 608, March 1889) that stated, "I was captured . . . sent to Pt. Lookout, Md., as a prisoner of war." Joined UCV as a member of the Louisiana Division, Army of Northern Virginia Camp No. 1, later transferred to Gen. Francis T. Nicholls Camp No. 1142. Married Victorine Jolibois on 2/2/1869 in Labadieville, Assumption Parish, and had one son and three daughters. Worked as a clerk on the Bayou Lafourche steamer *Assumption* while living in Labadieville on a small tract of land. Applied for a Confederate Pension, 3/18/1911, witnessed by Canonnier comrades Evariste Aucoin, Maurice Landry, and Duffosard Mollere. Died 12/27/1928 in Labadieville and interred St. Philomena Catholic Cemetery, Labadieville.

CHASE, WILLIAM F., "BUCK." Enlisted at Williamsburg, Virginia, 3/8/1862, Private; promoted Corporal 5/8/1863 then 5th Corporal. Previously served as a Private with Co. F, 1st Battalion (Dreux/Rightor's) Louisiana Infantry from 4/11/1861. Born 2/26/1842 in New Orleans; father a native of Massachusetts. Clerked in New Orleans. *Levy Diary* on 3/8/1865 at High Bridge fortifications noted, "Had pleasant reunion at Chase's cabin where we sang, whistled, and told yarns, concluding by reading Don Juan." Paroled ACH, 4/10/1865. *Levy Diary* on 4/29/1865 noted he along with Chase, John Eckleburg, and "Willie" Hart, after arriving in New Orleans "wandered about the streets enjoying everything which reminded us of our old homes." Joined UCV as a member of General Leroy Stafford Camp No. 3. Has an entry in Biographical Chapter of *Confederate Military History, Volume XIII, Louisiana, Extended Edition* (Atlanta, Georgia, 1899) pages 378-379. After the war married Nonie M. Gamble and had one son. Worked as an accountant in Coushatta, Red River Parish. Died 6/19/1914 and interred Greenwood Cemetery, Shreveport, Caddo Parish.

CHOINIER, JEAN BAPTISTE. Enlisted at Yorktown, Virginia, 3/6/1862, Private. Previously served as a Private with Co. E, 1st Battalion (Dreux/Rightor's) Louisiana Infantry from 4/16/1861. Born 7/15/1826 in Bertrichamps, France, to Pierre Valentin Choinier and Marguerite George. Carpenter living with Mary Froisie, a fifty-one-year-old woman of color and a cook in Houma, Terrebonne Parish. Gray eyes, light hair, dark complexion, 6'0". Detailed March 1865 for hospital guard duty in Richmond and escaped capture in April 1865. Died 10/4/1865 in Terrebonne Parish and interred St. Francis de Sales Catholic Church Cemetery No. 1, Houma.

Courtesy of Lorraine Trepagnier Toerner, Baton Rouge, La.

CIRE, [ST. CYR] FRANÇOIS, "BIENVENUE." Enlisted at Donaldsonville, 9/13/1861, 4th Artificer; promoted to 3rd Artificer. Born 3/26/1838 in Donaldsonville, one of eight children to Pierre Aman St. Cire (from the "Capitol of Arkansas") and Marianne Zoraide Marous from Santo Domingo. A student in Donaldsonville. Hazel eyes, dark hair, dark complexion, 5'6". *Levy Diary* on 3/29/1865 at the High Bridge fortifications stated, "Having been anxious for some time past to visit Richmond, I decided to 'run the blockade' on the sick furlough of Bienvenue Cyr, and left camp . . . this day." Paroled ACH, 4/10/1865. Joined UCV as a member of Major Victor Maurin Camp No. 38 and served camp as an alternate delegate and later as a delegate to UCV's Annual Meeting and Reunions. Became adjutant of the camp and would be one of the camp's last members. A farm manager in the 4th Ward of Ascension Parish after the war, he lived in Donaldsonville with his wife Leonie Leblanc, whom he married on 2/14/1871. Had three sons and a daughter with all but the oldest son dying as toddlers. Ten years after becoming a widower he married Odile Trepagnier (born 2/18/1862) on 2/15/1887 in Donaldsonville. Lived in Darrow, Ascension Parish, and by second wife had a son and two daughters. Family returned to Donaldsonville, by 1911 stated he was doing "nothing."[9] Died in Donaldsonville at 626 Mississippi Street on 10/28/1915 of apoplexy. Interred AOL. Wife applied for a Confederate Widow's Pension in 1928 and died 6/29/1950, at which time daughters discovered the veteran's *Historical Memoranda* notebook.

COMES, LOUIS MARCELLIN. Enlisted at Fredericksburg, Virginia, 6/5/1863, Private. Previously served as a Private with Company H, Confederate Guards Regiment, Louisiana Volunteer State Troops from 3/8/1862 to 4/30/1862. Born 10/18/1835 in Ascension

Parish, the youngest of five children to Louis Marcellin and Marie Arthemise Braud. Father was mayor of Donaldsonville in 1826 and died nineteen days before Louis was born. Clerked in New Orleans. Dark eyes, dark hair, dark complexion, 5'8". *Levy Diary* on 2/10/1865 noted he "never varies the intonations of his voice, hence he becomes an uninteresting actor" in *La Dramatic Association's* play, "A Frenchmen Lost at the High Bridge." That night Comes also sung the ballad "Villikens and his Dinah." Paroled ACH, 4/10/1865, and again captured and imprisoned until 5/9/1865 when he surrendered his parole and took the Oath of Amnesty in Alexandria, Virginia. After the war lived in New Orleans and married Henriette Collignon, a daughter born in 1867 and a son in 1868. A second son, Jean Marie Raphael Louis Charles Comes was born four months and ten days before his father's death in New Orleans on 3/5/1871. The infant son died at seventeen months of age.

COMSTOCK, JOSEPH ARTHUR. Enlisted at Donaldsonville, 9/13/1861, Private; promoted 6th Corporal March 1863. Born 10/2/1843 in Donaldsonville to John Louis Comstock Jr. (from New Orleans and Donaldsonville Sheriff from 1846-1859) and Victorine Hortense Theriot, one of six children and nephew of Canonnier Philippe Comstock. Worked as a clerk in Donaldsonville while living with Conrad Mavor and his second wife, Comstock's sister Camilla, and her seven stepchildren that included sixteen-year-old Florence, his future wife. Appears to have escaped capture in April 1865. His Confederate Pension Application recorded, "Wounded at the Battle of the Crater, [7/30/1864] siege of Petersburg, gunshot wound in the arm and side, both." Joined BAANV (Application No. 317, 7/24/1877) that stated, "Never captured—engaged in all battles from Yorktown to the surrender at Appomattox Court House." Joined UCV as a member of the Louisiana Division, Army of Northern Virginia Camp No. 1. After the war worked as a clerk for the steamboat *Lessie Taylor* and later became a steamboat captain. Married Florence Alice Jobs Mavor. Widowed on 8/28/1875, after which he lived in Donaldsonville with his widowed sister Camilla caring for his son and two daughters born in 1866, 1868, and 1875. Moved to 2141 State Street, New Orleans in 1910 with youngest daughter's family while still working as a steamboat captain on the Mississippi River, from Cairo, Illinois, to the jetties at the mouth of the Mississippi River and the Gulf of Mexico. Board member of Camp Nicholls's Soldiers Home, New Orleans. Applied for a Confederate Pension in October 1912. Died at home of daughter, 1311 Arabella Street in New Orleans on 12/4/1930 and interred in tumulus BAANV, Metairie Cemetery, New Orleans. The *New Orleans Times Picayune,* 12/5/1930, reported the "widely known steamboat man served in every major engagement of [the Donaldsonville Artillery] until the surrender at Appomattox and was wounded." Survived by children, eight grandchildren, and seven great-grandchildren.

COMSTOCK, PHILIPPE EDOUARD. Enlisted at Donaldsonville, 9/13/1861, 1st Artificer. Born 2/6/1821 in Ascension Parish to Jean Comstock of Opelousas, St. Landry Parish, and Rosalie "Rose" Anne MacMaryman, with two sisters and a brother. Uncle of Canonnier Joseph Arthur Comstock. Carpenter in the 4th Ward of Ascension Parish. AWOL in January 1865, deserted while on furlough. Married before the war to Anna C. McGill of Kentucky and being childless, adopted a daughter, Lillie, in 1859. Returned to the 3rd Ward of Ascension Parish, working as a carpenter. In 1890 living in Donaldsonville with wife and daughter. Was interdicted and sent to East Louisiana State Hospital (one of the first mental hospitals in the South) in Jackson, East Feliciana Parish.

COOLEY, EUGENE CHARLES. Enlisted at Fredericksburg, Virginia, 6/5/1863,

Private. Previously served as a 2nd Lieutenant with Co. E, 14th Louisiana Infantry Regiment from 6/25/1861 until resignation on 12/22/1861. Born 7/20/1840 in Point Coupee Parish to Thomas Jefferson Cooley (a lawyer and wealthy planter) and Adelaide Ledoux, one of five brothers and five sisters. Clerked in Point Coupee Parish. Wounded through the right leg below the knee at the battle of Fredericksburg, 12/13/1862. *Levy Diary* on 5/7/1864 noted he went with Cooley on a "foraging expedition. Procured a quart of beans . . . ice water . . . and more beans and a fine dinner." Paroled ACH, 4/10/1865. Joined BAANV (Application No. 586, 9/20/1887) that stated "surrendered and paroled at Appomattox Court House." Joined UCV as a member of the Louisiana Division, Army of Northern Virginia Camp No. 1, later transferred to Amite City Camp No. 78 and served as a delegate to the UCV's Annual Meeting and Reunions. On 10/19/1902 the *New Orleans Times Picayune* reported he, along with comrades Prosper Landry and E. L. Monnot, were each appointed aide-de-camp with the rank of major to the commanding general of the Louisiana Division, UCV. In 1870 worked as a merchant in the 6th Ward of Point Coupee Parish, and married Alice Hancock (born in Tennessee to Louisiana parents) and had five sons and three daughters. Later moved to the 5th Ward of Point Coupee Parish and became a sugar planter. Believed to be the war-worn correspondent for the *Pointe Coupee Pelican* who in 1879 related he was fortunate to meet his friend and army companion Sabin Braud. In 1883 moved to Amite City, 3rd Ward of Tangipahoa Parish where he worked as a "Homeland Trucker." The *New Orleans Daily Picayune,* 3/31/1907, noted friends and acquaintances in Amite City recognized him as "Major" Cooley. Applied for a Confederate Pension in August of 1910. Died 12/22/1922 and interred Amite City Cemetery, Amite. The *Florida Parishes Times* (no date) reported he "had labored and fought faithfully." Epitaph reads: *U[nited] C[onfederate] V[eteran], A Friend To His Country And A Believer In Christ.*

CURE, CHARLES NUMA. Enlisted at Donaldsonville, 9/13/1861, Private. Born 3/16/1840 in St. James Parish to Charles Cure and Marie Aurore Gaudet, the only son of four children. The family later moved to Donaldsonville, five houses from Captain Victor Maurin. Worked as a cooper in Donaldsonville. Blue eyes, dark hair, fair complexion, 6'0". Paroled ACH, 4/10/1865. Joined BAANV (Application No. 525, 12/27/1883) that stated he "belonged to that section of the company which went to Lynchburg, and was after stationed at High Bridge—paroled at Appomattox Court House." On his application for a Confederate Pension he wrote, "Paroled at Appomattox, went to Fortress Monroe a prisoner . . . then sent to New Orleans and was released." Asked if he had ever taken the Oath of Allegiance he replied, "I have not" and "under no circumstances." Joined UCV as a member of Major Victor Maurin Camp No. 38. Married Affea Hebert in 1870 and had four sons and a daughter. Worked as a cooper and lived in the 9th Ward of Terrebonne Parish with his family, a nephew, a sister-in-law, and a brother-in-law who was also a cooper. By 1890 living in New Orleans still working as a cooper until moving to New Iberia, Iberia Parish (before 1900) in the same occupation. On Confederate Pension related he "served during the whole time and received no injuries" and used intoxicants but "not to excess." Died 9/15/1907 from a ladder fall in Lake Charles, Calcasieu Parish. Interred Old Catholic Cemetery, Lake Charles.

DECOUX, CYRILLE. Enlisted at Sharpsburg, Maryland, 9/18/1862, Private. Previously served as a Private with Co. A, 7th Louisiana (St. Paul's Foot Rifles) Infantry Battalion from 4/22/1861. Born ca. 1839 in Louisiana (probably at New Orleans) to Valmont Valery Decoux (a constable in New Orleans) and Marie Antoinette Bozant. Clerked in New Orleans. Paroled at Lynchburg, Virginia 4/13/1865. Died 6/16/1876 in New Orleans.

DELESDERNIER, WILLIAM GOULD, "DELES." Enlisted at Williamsburg, Virginia, 3/8/1862, Private. Previously served as a Private with Co. F, 1st Battalion (Dreux/Rightor's) Louisiana Infantry from 4/11/1861. Born ca. 1839 in Canada of British citizenship and came to the United States as a minor. Clerked in New Orleans. *Levy Diary* on 6/26/1864 at camp on Swift Run near Petersburg noted, "Rose early and went with Deles in search of milk which was procured at the very reasonable price of a dollar per quart." Levy and "Deles" went into Petersburg on 7/1 and 7/2/1864 and on the latter day they "spent a couple of hours after dark in conversation with two Misses Schribner whose acquaintance we had accidentally formed. Innocent pastime." Appears to have escaped capture in April 1865. Married on 3/6/1866 in Yazoo City, Mississippi, to Hannah Ellis of Illinois, whose parents came from England. Had six daughters and one son. His naturalization was 6/10/1868, officially changed last name to Deles. Retail merchant in Yazoo City. From November 1887-1888 served as justice of the peace, Yazoo City District 3; elected mayor of Yazoo City, April 1888 to 1892; elected Yazoo City treasurer, April 1908. As mayor contracted to have city furnished with water by the Michigan Pipe Company in 1891. Served as alternate lay delegate for Trinity Episcopal Church, Yazoo City. Secretary in 1890 of the Knights of Pythias, Yazoo City Section 441; member of the Grand Commandery, Knights Templar, in the State of Mississippi, Yazoo Commandery, No. 23. Joined BAANV (Application No. [none], 10/13/1906) that stated, "When the Battalion [Dreux/Rightor's] was disbanded . . . I joined the Donaldsonville Artillery . . . and remained with the latter company to the end of the war." Attended 1911 Confederate Reunion in New Orleans.[10] Mrs. Deles was present at the February 1898 organizational meeting and a member of the Jefferson Davis Chapter No. 216, Yazoo City, United Daughters of the Confederacy. In 1910 sold stationary at his bookstore in 1st ward of Yazoo City and lived at 301 Jefferson. Died at home, in Memphis, Tennessee, at 3:10 a.m. on 4/24/1926. Buried in Yazoo City.

DELMER[E], JEAN OLEZIPHORE, "ONIZIFOR." Enlisted at Donaldsonville, 9/13/1861, Private. Born 10/21/1835 in Donaldsonville to Andres Delmere and Melita Mingo. Witnessed sister Clementine's marriage in Donaldsonville on 8/16/1859 to brother of Canonnier Antoine Sanchez. Worked as a laborer in Donaldsonville. Hazel eyes, dark hair, light complexion, 5'2". Captured during battle of Fort Gregg, Petersburg, Virginia, 4/2/1865, and released 6/26/1865 from Point Lookout, Maryland, prisoner of war camp after taking the Oath of Allegiance. Confederate Pension noted he was "released after the surrender, sent to Washington D.C., then Cairo, Il., thence by boat to New Orleans and thence to Donaldsonville." Pension also asked if he was ever wounded and replied, "No. Received no other injury than such as naturally results from four years of service during war." Joined UCV as a member of Major Victor Maurin Camp No. 38. Never married, he worked as a laborer doing "any odd jobs" while living at Smoke Bend, Ascension Parish, in "a small room on land which does not belong to me." Entered Camp Nicholl's Soldiers Home, New Orleans, 9/16/1909, and died there at two o'clock in the morning on 3/11/1910. Friends and acquaintances attended the funeral at the Soldier's Home followed by interment in Vault 19, Soldier's Home Tomb, Greenwood Cemetery, New Orleans. The Home spelled his name "Delmar."

DEMESME, OSCAR FREDERICK. Enlisted at Donaldsonville, 9/13/1861, 1st Corporal; promoted to 3rd Sergeant, March 1863. Born ca. 1837 in St. Jermain, France. Laborer in New River, 4th Ward of Ascension Parish, living with his mother the widow G. Demesme and another older women, possibly an aunt, Aglae Melle Chiote (both women were born in France), along with an older brother, Charles Paul Demesme. The Demesme's were residents in Assumption Parish until moving (believed to be in early 1860) to Ascension Parish. Oscar was a witness to Canonnier John Suarez and Josephine Falgout's wedding on 1/13/1860 in Paincourtville, Assumption Parish. The *Assumption Pioneer*, 6/8/1851 noted the police jury appointed brother Charles Demesme as "Head of Patrols" in Assumption's Ward 1. Charles was an overseer on the Laferiere Levesque Plantation in Assumption Parish that had a real estate value of $100,000 along with seventy-seven slaves. Sophia Demesme (colored), in the *New Orleans Directories of 1890-1891* identified herself as the widow of Charles Demesme, Oscar's older brother, and it seems they were the parents of three sons born ca. 1850, 1851, and 1858. The oldest son was named Oscar, the middle Paul, and the youngest Leon. Oscar Demesme (listed by the census takers as Mesme, Mesmate, and Masino) was the Canonnier's nephew who later had seven children; his oldest son named after his grandfather, Charles. His next son was named Lord Byron and the next son, the fifth child, was named Oscar Junior. Charles's son Leon named one of his sons Frederick Oscar Demesme. The *Levy Diary* noted the Donaldsonville Canonnier Sergeant Oscar Demesme was killed "in the course of a melee'" at the battle of Appomattox Station on 4/8/1865. The *Donaldsonville Le Drapeau,* 1/26/1867, reported he was "killed and buried in the uniform of the Northern Army, in which, while acting as a spy, he is supposed to have been shot through mistake by his own friends." Buried near where he was killed, until the Ladies Memorial Association of Appomattox Court House met to provide suitable interment for Confederate soldiers whose bodies had not been deposited in some regular burying ground. After coffins for the bodies were made with donated lumber, the re-interment with religious services took place on 12/1/1866 on top of a beautiful knoll deeded to the Association about a half-mile west of the Court House. Grave No. 2 reads: "Sergt. O. F. DeMesme, Donaldsonville Art. La." Today the Appomattox Court House National Historical Park administers the cemetery, which contains nineteen graves.[11] Appomattox Chapter 11, Virginia Division, United Daughters of the Confederacy, retains ownership of the cemetery.

DRUILHET, PAUL ALEXANDRE. Enlisted at Williamsburg, Virginia, 3/8/1862, Private. Previously served as a Private with Co. F, 1st Battalion (Dreux/Rightor's) Louisiana Infantry from 4/11/1861. Born 1/25/1839 in St. James Parish to Louisiana native Narcisse Alfred Druilhet and Jamaica-born Celeste Poché, one of ten children. Clerked in New Orleans. Dark eyes, dark hair, dark complexion, 5'11". Paroled ACH, 4/10/1865. Joined UCV as a member of General Braxton Bragg Camp No. 196. Married Marie Antoinette Webre on 2/1/1869 at St. Michael Catholic Church, Convent, St. James Parish, and had six children. Moved to New Orleans after the war and worked as a clerk at 115 Decatur Street. Years later worked as an overseer with son Paul Jr. while renting a house in the 1st Ward of Terrebonne Parish. Worked in St. Mary and Iberia parishes at times. By 1911 had retired to New Orleans living in a house he bought at 6315 Magazine Street. Died 6/11/1916 of heart failure at home and interred in Jeanerette Catholic Cemetery, Iberia Parish. The *New Orleans Daily Picayune,* 6/13/1916, stated he "leaves a large family of grown children."

DUFFEL, HENRY EDOUARD, II. Enlisted at Culpeper Court House, Virginia, 11/1/1862, Private. Previously served as a Private with Co. H, Confederate Guards Regiment, Louisiana Volunteer State Troops from 3/8/1862. Born 10/29/1843 in the 1st Ward of Ascension Parish on his father's 500-acre plantation named Woodstock, the oldest of four surviving children to Henry Leonard Duffel and Ann Dunnington of Virginia. Grandfather Edward Duffel, born 7/31/1786 in Philadelphia, Pennsylvania, was a surgeon in the United

States Navy and came to Louisiana when stationed at the forts on the Mississippi River below New Orleans. Grandfather married (at New Hope Plantation, Donaldsonville) the widow Marie Celeste Landry Vives, a cousin of Canonniers Adolphe Landry, Prosper Landry, and Jean Trasimon Landry.[12] Young Duffel was a student in Ascension Parish. Paroled ACH, 4/10/1865. Joined BAANV (Application No. 588, 11/11/1887) that stated, "Surrendered . . . at Appomattox Court House." Joined UCV as a member of Louisiana Division, Army of Northern Virginia, Camp No. 1. Married cousin Bertha Rose Duffel, 11/12/1878 (whose parents were Edward Duffel Junior and Desirée Landry) with Canonniers Prosper Landry and Jean Trasimond Landry serving as witnesses. First wife died childless. Remarried Josie M. Thompson in Iberville Parish on 10/26/1882. They had two sons and one daughter. Kept a grocery store on Woodstock Plantation which produced a sugar crop until 1880, when rice was then cultivated. In 1882 it was recorded, "The first rice field from Donaldsonville is here met with, and it breaks the monotony of sugar places to the great delight of everybody around. The neighbors view with pleasure the basin of 400 acres of water held by levees as in a bowl. They admire the dartings of shrimp and fishes as they disport themselves in the limpid lake. The gyrations of cranes, grosbecs and other aquatic birds over this pellucid sheet of water in search of mud-cats and tadpoles is a never-ceasing source of amusement to the good people. They love to see the water as it spouts through crayfish holes and flows over roots of the adjacent cane and corn, which grow apace in the delicious bath. . . . What music can excel the concert of a few hundred thousand frogs, wherein the shrill demi-semi-quaverings of the green junipers unite with the sonorous and resounding deep basses of the wa-wa-wa-rons in delightful melody! And . . . the soft rustling of the tender rice plants, as they bend and sway in the gentle breezes, beneath the weight of their golden heads?"[13] Duffel lived his whole life on Woodstock Plantation with his father and family members until death overtook him on 8/9/1898 of apoplexy. Interred AOL. Wife applied for a Confederate Widow's Pension in February 1914 and moved to 520 Codifer Street, Metairie, Jefferson Parish, where she died on 9/29/1929 survived by her three children.

DUGAS, JOSEPH GONTRAN[D]. Enlisted at Donaldsonville, 9/13/1861, Private. Born 3/28/1842 in Ascension Parish to Michael Ulgere Dugas and Emeline Landry, one of seven sons. Brother to Canonnier François Leon Dugas. Clerked in Donaldsonville. Gray eyes, dark hair, dark complexion, 5'8". Paroled ACH, 4/10/1865. Captured again and imprisoned until 5/9/1865 when he surrendered his parole and took the Oath of Amnesty in Alexandria, Virginia. Married seventeen-year-old Helene Elmina Hebert on 2/19/1867 and had a son born nine months later and a daughter in 1870. Died on 1/29/1891 in Ascension Parish and believed interred (with no marker) in Cornerview Cemetery, Gonzales, Ascension Parish. Wife moved to Texas in 1898; in 1914 applied for a Widow's Pension in Texas while living with widowed daughter in Port Arthur, Jefferson County, Texas. On the application she noted her husband served with the "Cannoniers of Donaldson (Donaldsonville Artillery) . . . served 4 years . . . was a private throughout time of service." She died 10/8/ 1915.

DUGAS, FRANÇOIS LEON. Enlisted at Donaldsonville, 9/13/1861, Private. Born 1/3/1831 in Ascension Parish to Michael Ulgere Dugas and Emeline Landry, the oldest of seven sons. Brother to Canonnier Joseph Gontrand Dugas. Worked as a mason. Married the widow Delphine Richard Guilfont on 2/11/1851 and had two daughters. Wife died during son's birth in 1854. Had one surviving daughter when he remarried Marie Gertrude Landry, 12/28/1857, with a son born on 6/22/1861. Lived in Donaldsonville with second wife and daughter from deceased first wife and first wife's widowed mother and her son and daughter.

Gray eyes, black hair, dark complexion, 5'10". *Levy Diary* on 4/9/1865 recorded, "Squads of prisoners continue to be thrust in the open [fields]; among them Plesancea, Terio, and Dugas of Treile's section" who were captured at the Battle of Appomattox Station the evening before. Paroled at Farmville, Virginia, 4/14/1865. Captain Prosper Landry noted he "was a good and faithful soldier of [the] company."[14] After the war had another two sons and two daughters with the last daughter named Olive Virginie. In December 1865 bought, with money from wife's mother's estate, "a certain improvement in a tract of land measuring three and one half arpents front by fourteen in depth . . . together with six heads of cattle and twenty heads of hogs more or less"[15] on New River Bayou in the 8th Ward of Ascension Parish. Died 10/25/1885 of typhoid pneumonia at St. Amant, Ascension Parish, and interred with an upright Confederate Grave stone in Cornerview Cemetery, Gonzales, Ascension Parish.

DUPAS, OCTAVIUS "OCTAVE." Enlisted at Donaldsonville, 9/13/1861, Private. Born ca. 1843 in New Orleans to Mahturin Dupas (a native of France living in New Orleans working as a blacksmith and locksmith) and Sophie Clemence. Had two brothers in New Orleans working as blacksmiths while he worked as a blacksmith in Paincourtville, Assumption Parish. Dark eyes, florid hair, florid complexion, 5'7". Captured 7/20/1863 near Hedgesville, Berkley County, Virginia, during the Gettysburg Campaign with Canonnier Augustin Albares. A Federal officer recorded: "On retreat from Gettysburg he left ranks on the march in the night—returned to Hedgeville and then voluntarily surrendered."[16] Took Oath of Allegiance and released from Camp Chase, Ohio prison on 5/11/1865. Married the widow Pamela Crochet on 2/27/1866 in Paincourtville with a son born four months later. After being widowed married Eveline Marie Simoneaux on 6/2/1873 in Pierre Part, Assumption Parish. Worked as a locksmith and a blacksmith. In June 1884, while living in San Rafael, Marin County, California, obtained a patent (#300,056) for a horse detaching apparatus (safety release from a carriage or wagon). Also lived and worked in Virginia City, Storey County, Nevada; Grass Valley, Nevada County, California; and San Francisco. Died before 1910, possibly in San Francisco, where widowed wife and son John M. Dupas lived. Son became vice-president of the French-American Bank of Savings in San Francisco, now the French Branch of the Bank of America that is located (since 1907) in the French Bank Building that is part of the finest rows of buildings in downtown San Francisco.

DUPUY, ACHILLES DÉSIRÉ. Enlisted at Mobile, Alabama, 5/22/1863, Private. Born 2/13/1840 in Ascension Parish. Clerked in New Orleans. *Levy Diary* on 1/26/1865 at High Bridge noted he "accompanied Dupuy to visit the Lockett family." Paroled ACH, 4/10/1865 and again in Lynchburg, Virginia. On a Confederate Pension Application it was related he "served honorably . . . remaining a cannoneer to the end of the war." Returned to New Orleans and married Marie Pascal on 4/28/1866 in St. Louis Cathedral, New Orleans. They had two daughters. Died of "General debility" on 9/27/1876 in Plaquemine, Iberville Parish, and interred in St. Louis Cemetery (unknown if 1, 2, or 3) in New Orleans. Wife, a school teacher, lived at 2909 Ursulines Street, New Orleans, and applied for and received a Confederate Widow's Pension in 1915. She died 12/22/1935.

ECHEVARRIA, JEAN ARTURE, "ARTHUR." Enlisted at Donaldsonville, 9/13/1861, Private; promoted to 2nd Corporal March 1863. Born 5/20/1841 in Assumption Parish to Jean Julien "Docteur" Echevarria and Emelie Melancon. Clerked in the 1st Ward of Assumption Parish while living with widowed mother and five-year-old sister. Blue eyes, dark hair, dark complexion, 5'6". *Levy Diary* on 2/27/1865 noted near High Bridge, "Yesterday,

Echavaria and myself dined at Major Watson's and spent the night with Mrs. P. Liggen's folks." Paroled ACH, 4/10/1865. Joined UCV as a member of Major Victor Maurin Camp No. 38. Married Olivia Mollere on 7/26/1866 in Paincourtville, Assumption Parish, and had four children with only one son surviving. The *Assumption Pioneer,* 5/28/1898, reported, "He was one of the first to enlist [and] served with credit and distinction until honorably discharged after the surrender." Died after a "long sickness" on 5/22/1898 at nine o'clock in the evening in his home at Belle Rose, Assumption Parish. Victor Maurin Camp No. 38, United Confederate Veterans conducted the funeral after which, he was interred at St. Elizabeth Catholic Cemetery, Paincourtville. Survived by three grandchildren and wife who received a Confederate Widow's Pension up to the time of her death on 10/2/1944.

ECKLEBURG, JOHN P., "ECK." Enlisted at Williamsburg, Virginia, 3/8/1862, Private. Previously served as a Private with Co. A, 1st Battalion (Dreux/Rightor's) Louisiana Infantry from 7/20/1861. Born ca. 1838 in New York City. Druggist and clerk living with a doctor (with an estate value of $40,000) who was also a druggist in the 11th Ward of New Orleans. On 8/1/1864 *Levy Diary* noted Eckleburg after being wounded the day before, "sat with me [in Petersburg hospital] for a while during the morning and evening." *Levy Diary* on 9/22/1864 in Petersburg trenches recorded, "Doc and Eckleburg occupied a small shelter tent into which I was admitted." *Levy Diary* on 10/12/1864, noted "Found that John Eckleburg had drawn two pieces of Confederate shelter tent and built a nice chimney at one end of it so that my mess possesses a very comfortable establishment." On 10/17/1864 Levy wrote, "After dinner, Eckleburg and myself cut wild grass for a bed." On 10/18/1864 Levy noted, "Eckleburg received his copy of Shakespeare from Gordonsville, and I read aloud from 'Othello' for the benefit of my messmates." Paroled ACH, 4/10/1865. *Levy Diary* on 4/29/1865 noted that Eckleburg, "Willie" Hart, "Buck" Chase, and Levy, after arriving in New Orleans, "wandered about the streets enjoying everything which reminded us of our old homes." After the war married Charlotte T. in New Orleans. In April 1885 Captain Prosper Landry wrote a "favorable" letter of recommendation for him to the Camp Nicholls Soldiers Home, New Orleans. Died 8/31/1887 at 211 Julia Street in New Orleans leaving widowed wife childless.

ELY, WILLIAM H. Enlisted at New Orleans, 3/21/1862, Private. Born ca. 1842 in Lee County, Virginia. Worked as an overseer while living in Donaldsonville. Wounded at the Battle of the Crater, Petersburg, Virginia, on 7/30/1864. In the *New Orleans Times Picayune,* 7/28/1902, Levy wrote, "My friend and messmate, Ely . . . was wounded in the arm . . . by the same shell that struck me." After being examined by a Board of Surgeons at the General Hospital, Farmville, Virginia, Ely was placed on retirement (Invalid Corps, Provisional Army Confederate States) on 11/29/1864 because of his wound. It seems he stayed in Virginia as *Levy Diary* on 1/6/1865 noted Ely arrived at the High Bridge fortifications. William Ely (fifteen times) and Carothers (thirteen times) were mentioned in Levy's Diary more than any other Canonnier except Levy's brother Julien "Doc" Levy. Ely, according to Levy, served as No. 1, with himself as No. 3, on Piece No. 3 (a Parrott rifle) with Corporal Ignace Rougeau the gunner. Joined BAANV (Application No. 640, May 2, 1892) that stated, "Was wounded severely . . . and honorably retired from service." Joined UCV as a member of Louisiana Division, Army of Northern Virginia, Camp No. 1. After the war remained in Virginia and married Martha J. Dalton on 11/20/1866 in Lee County, Virginia. They had three daughters and two sons. Lived in Rocky Station, near Jonesville, Lee County, before moving to Hancock County, Tennessee, in mid-1870s. After becoming a widower he returned to Louisiana where the *New Orleans Daily City Item* on 10/10/1877 noted he was the "indefatigable manager of Poplar Grove plantation" in West Baton Rouge Parish. Married Sara Fletcher on 10/19/1880 in Madison, Madison Parish. Died at Hotel Dieu Hospital, New Orleans on 1/17/1894. Funeral attended by officers and members of Army of Northern Virginia, Camp No. 1, UCV. Interred in tumulus BAANV, Metairie Cemetery, New Orleans.

EP[P]INGER, GEORG FRIEDRICH (FREDERICK), "GEORGE." Enlisted at Yorktown, Virginia, 2/1/1862, Private. Previously served as a Corporal (teamster) with Co. F, 1[er] Louisiana Zouave (Coppen's) Infantry Battalion from 4/4/1861. Born 3/12/1812 to Christoph Philipp Eppinger and Anna Maria Margaretha in Notzingen, Donaukreis, Wuerttenberg, Germany. Emigrated from Germany on the ship *Atlantic* that sailed from Antwerp and arrived in New York City on 9/30/1851. Lived and worked as a wagoner in New Orleans. Discharged from active service 2/9/1865 by order of the Confederate Secretary of War after having served a three-year enlistment. Died 1/11/1873 in New Orleans.

FLANNIGAHN, MICHAEL, "HICK." Enlisted at Donaldsonville, 9/13/1861, Private. Born ca. 1831-1834 in Ireland. Worked as a laborer in Donaldsonville. Blue eyes, brown hair, fair complexion, 5'9". Captured at Hatcher's Run, 4/2/1865, and released from Point Lookout, Maryland, 6/26/1865, after taking the Oath of Allegiance. Returned to the 2nd Ward of Ascension Parish and lived between Duffel's Woodstock Plantation and McCall Plantation working as a "Boss Ditcher." Headed a household in the 1880s with seven other ditchers and laborers. Irish, Black, and Mulatto families all lived nearby and worked on the rice and sugar plantations.

FORTIER, FRANÇOIS LESTANG. Enlisted at Donaldsonville, 9/13/1861, Senior 1st Lieutenant. While serving in antebellum Donaldsonville Canonniers he was appointed 1st Artificer in 1850, promoted to Sergeant in 1854, and appointed Junior 1st Lieutenant on 2/12/1859, then Senior 1st Lieutenant on 4/29/1861. Born ca. 1826 in Louisiana. Worked in the mercantile business and as a collector in Donaldsonville. Wrote letter of resignation on 6/18/1862 stating, "Owing to bad health and a disinclination to serve in my present Corps I hereby tender my resignation." In accepting the resignation, Colonel J. Thompson Brown replied, "I take great pleasure in testifying to the energy and faithfulness which Lieutenant Fortier has displayed in the discharge of his duties, and would exceedingly regret to lose the services of so valuable an officer."[17] The resignation was accepted in August 1862. Married Rosalie Irma Braud on 5/15/1847 in Donaldsonville with Lawrence D. Nicholls and Canonnier Camille Leblanc witnessing. Had one daughter and five sons before the war; four of the children died at a young age. Another son was born on 2/3/1862, but died twenty-five days later. Yet another child died a few minutes after birth on 8/31/1863. A son Felix was born in 1866 and he had a son born in 1886 that was named Lestang. It has been written, "The Fortier family history in Louisiana begins with the early French colonial period of the state, only a few years after Bienville founded the city of New Orleans."[18] Died 9/7/1874, interred AOL. The *Donaldsonville Chief*, 9/12/1874, reported, "This community has lost one of its best citizens . . . upright and loyal in every action and instinct."

FOUIN, VICTOR. Enlisted at Donaldsonville, 9/13/1861, 7th Corporal. Born ca. 1826 in France. Lived in Brule St. Martin, Assumption Parish, before becoming School Master in Donaldsonville. On sick furlough in Louisiana from July to September 6, 1862, then carried AWOL on muster roll; deserted. It appears that under the name of Viron Fonin he, along with

Canonnier Sylvain Lion, were arrested by Union officials and released during the war "upon the insistent demands of New Orleans's French consulate" since "many Lafourche country men claimed French citizenship."[19]

FREDERLE, FREDERICK, "FRED." Enlisted at Yorktown, Virginia, 2/3/1862, Private. Previously served as a Private with Co. A, 1st Louisiana Zouave (Coppen's) Infantry Battalion from 3/29/1861. Born ca. 1839 in Baden, Germany. Worked as a carpenter in New Orleans. Captured 7/18/1863 near Greencastle, Pennsylvania, (Gettysburg Campaign) and sent to Fort Mifflin, Pennsylvania, as a rebel deserter. Released 10/13/1863. In 1870 living in Baltimore, Maryland, with wife Catherine and two sons and a daughter.

FUHRI, HENRY CHARLES ARMAND, "CHARLEY." Enlisted at Williamsburg, Virginia, 3/8/1862, Private. Previously served as a Private with Co. C, 1st Battalion (Dreux/Rightor's) Louisiana Infantry from 4/28/1861. Born ca. 1838 in Hague, Holland, and immigrated in 1858. A druggist in St. Landry Parish but moved to New Orleans by mid-April 1861. Gray eyes, dark hair, florid complexion, 5'4". *Levy Diary* on 5/15/1864 noted while marching twenty-three miles past Louisa Court House, "Tip Landry carried my rations, and Fuhri my blanket. Road very heavy" with "blanket and clothing wet through." *Levy Diary* on 6/12/1864 near Cold Harbor recorded, "Fuhri brought from Richmond a few cakes and herrings which were demolished for supper." *Levy Diary* on 10/5/1864 noted Fuhri was sick at Richmond's Louisiana Hospital and after a sick furlough recorded 11/14/1864, "Fuhri arrived [at Petersburg] and reported for duty. He brought from the fair dames of Cumberland County [High Bridge] socks for his gun's crew. A special gift was sent me of 2 prs. socks and 1 pr. gloves by a young lady who heard a portion of my letter to Charley read." Detailed as a corresponding clerk in Treasury Department, Richmond, from January 1865 and paroled in Charlotte, North Carolina, on 5/13/1865. After the war the *New Orleans Times Picayune,* 2/13/1867, advertised that he was working as a freight clerk at 5 Bank Street, New Orleans, which served the New York-New Orleans steamship *Lodona.* This newspaper on 9/12/1869 also reported, "AN ATTEMPTED BURGLARY—Mr. H. C. Fuhri, on returning from his office about 11 o'clock to the residence of Mrs. Leech, No. 199 Camp street, [now 817 Camp Street] where he is boarding with his family, heard a noise in the coal shed and immediately walked into the yard . . . when a large, stalwart negro man rushed out. Mr. Fuhri instantly grappled with the burglar, who was, however, too powerful a man for him to hold. After a protracted struggle, during which Mr. Fuhri received several severe injuries, the black rascal broke away and ran, escaping through a gate in the back yard. . . . This is the second burglar that has visited the premises within a week—another having stolen a cloak—and Mr. Fuhri is now amply prepared for all such visitations." The *New Orleans Daily Picayune,* 2/5/1871 reported he died in New Orleans on 2/3/1871, at three o'clock in the morning "of consumption."

GAILLARD, JOSEPH ROSEMOND. Enlisted at Donaldsonville, 9/13/1861, 2nd Sergeant. Born 8/15/1834 in Ascension Parish to Henry Gaillard (from New Orleans) and Marie Hortense Leblanc, the only son of three children. Occupation unknown but lived in Donaldsonville. Admitted into Louisiana Hospital, Richmond, on 12/11/1862 and died there of small pox on 1/4/1863. Interred under the name of R. Garlin in the Soldier's Section, Grave D-27, Hollywood Cemetery, Richmond. Lived before war with widowed mother (who died at age ninety-five on 12/25/1885) and older surviving sister Celeste Hirenee, who married in April 1864. Gaillard's grandfather Pierre owned Homeplace Plantation (constructed between

1787 and 1791) which is one of the finest and least altered examples of a large French Colonial raised cottage left standing today. It is located on the west bank of the Mississippi River in St. Charles Parish and in 1970 was designated a National Historic Landmark.

GAMOTIS, HENRI MICHEL. Enlisted at Mobile, Alabama, 6/15/1863, Private. Born 3/16/1846 to Laurent Gamotis and Jean Louise Modeste Bel, the fourth of ten children in New Orleans. Was a student in New Orleans. Joined BAANV (Application No. 358, 12/3/1877) stated, "Served from the battle of Gettysburg to the end of the war. Escaped at Appomattox Court House and surrendered at Augusta, Ga., May 3, 1865." Joined UCV as a member of Louisiana Division, Army of Northern Virginia Camp No. 1. The *New Orleans Daily City Item* on 12/12/1891 reported he "won the encomiums from his comrades for the dauntless spirit and brave deportment displayed by him in action." The *New Orleans Daily Picayune*, 12/12/1891 reported, "Though but little more than a child when the war broke out, his brave spirit chafed to bear its part in the struggle . . . he broke through the restrain imposed upon him on account of his youth, and hastening to the front, joined the Donaldsonville Artillery, with which command he participated in the battle of Gettysburg, where he received his first baptism of fire, and served until the final surrender with that historic command." The *New Orleans Times Picayune*, 12/12/1891 recorded he was "a gallant soldier, a faithful comrade and a man true to all the responsibilities of life." Married Marie Mathilde Massicot after the war and had five daughters and two sons. Worked as a bookkeeper and as the secretary of Crescent City Ice Company in New Orleans. Lived at 205 Harmony Street, New Orleans. Died 12/11/1891 in Covington, St. Tammany Parish, with his remains returned to New Orleans for interment. Cannoniers J. S. Mioton, Captain Prosper Landry, and J. A. Comstock appointed by Louisiana Division, Army of Northern Virginia Camp No. 1, to draft resolutions regarding the death of their comrade.

GAUDET, JEAN BAPTISTE. Enlisted at New Orleans, 4/16/1862, Private. Born 10/11/1838 in Assumption Parish. A farmer in Assumption Parish. *R. O. Landry Diary* recorded he was wounded slightly in the head on 7/5/1863, (Gettysburg Campaign) after being taken prisoner with the wagon train near Greencastle, Pennsylvania, and later freed (same day) by Confederate cavalry. Paroled ACH, 4/10/1865. Joined UCV as a member of Camp Francis T. Nicholls Camp No. 1142. Died 10/30/1923 in Gretna, Jefferson Parish, and interred St. Philomena Catholic Cemetery, Labadieville, Assumption Parish.

GAUTREAUX, JOSEPH ALFRED, "AJ." Enlisted at Donaldsonville, 9/13/1861, Private. Born 1/12/1841 in Ascension Parish to Joseph Gervais Gautreaux and Marie Louise Leblanc, the third oldest of seven children. Clerked in Donaldsonville. *Levy Diary* on 2/10/1865 noted he "failed in rendering the text" of "The Fortunes of War" in their *La Dramatic Association* performance. Paroled ACH, 4/10/1865. Married Eulalie Blanchard, the sister of Canonnier Severan Blanchard, Claire, wife of Canonnier Henry M. Newchurch, and Mathilda, wife of Canonnier Emile Bergeron. Died 6/23/81 in Ascension Parish.

GIROIR, ALCIBIDE LEUFROY, "ALCIDE." Enlisted at Chancellorsville, Virginia, 6/16/1863, Private. Previously served as a Private in Co. H, 2nd Louisiana Cavalry. Born 9/6/1838 in Assumption Parish to Damas Giroir and Carmelite Barillou, one of seven children. Brick mason living in Assumption Parish near Napoleonville. Captured on 4/2/1865 at Hatcher's Run[20] and imprisoned until 5/8/1865, when he surrendered his parole and took Oath of Allegiance in Alexandria, Virginia. Appears to have been paroled again on 6/4/1865 at

Alexandria, Rapides Parish. Joined UCV as a member of Camp Francis T. Nicholls No. 1142. Married Camilla Templet (sister of Cannoniers Hypolite and Camille Templet) on 5/7/1861 at Plattenville, witnessed by Canonnier Claudious Linossier, who was later killed in action on 12/13/1862 at the battle of Fredericksburg. Had one son, Camille, born on 6/1/1862. After the war engaged in farming and sugar planting about one mile above Napoleonville on the west bank of Bayou Lafourche. Listed in Bouchereau's *The Louisiana Sugar Report, 1870-1917. Assumption Pioneer*, 11/10/1923, reported, "He was a good citizen." Died 11/6/1923 in Assumption Parish and survived by wife, four sons, and four daughters. His funeral in Paincourtville, reported the *Assumption Pioneer*, 11/10/1923, "Was well attended by his relatives and numerous friends. His remains were followed to the grave by one old comrade proudly bearing his cherished flag of the Confederacy." Interred at St. Elizabeth Catholic Cemetery, Paincourtville.

GRILHE (GRILÉ), JEAN BAPTISTE ADOLPHE, "ADOLPH." Enlisted at Donaldsonville, 9/13/1861, Private; promoted to 7th Corporal then to 4th Corporal. Born 12/29/1839 in Donaldsonville to Jean Grilhe (from Garonne, France) and Marie Pauline Berthelot, one of five children. Cooper in Ascension Parish. Gray eyes, light hair, light complexion, 5'5". Wounded "severely"[21] at battle of Fredericksburg, Virginia, 12/13/1862. Paroled ACH, 4/10/1865. Married Marie 'Mary' Solar on 1/29/1872 (witnessed by Canonnier P. T. Blouin) and had two sons and three daughters. A "Fruit Seller" in 1870, The *Donaldsonville Chief*, 4/13/1878, noted he was Donaldsonville's "confectionary" and on 8/19/1883 reported he was "a good hearted Man." Died 8/17/1883 and interred AOL.

GUEDRY, JULES. Enlisted at New Orleans, 3/21/1862, Private. Born 3/7/1836 in Convent, St. James Parish, to F. Guedry and Adelaide Rodriguez. Cooper in Donaldsonville with real estate valued at $800 and personal estate at $1,500 in 1860. Roll for October 1864 shows AWOL, captured with Canonnier Sergeant Major Clement Israel on 10/7/1864 in Osyka, Mississippi. Imprisoned at Elmira, New York and paroled 2/9/1865, then sent to Camp Lee near Richmond for exchange. Married in Donaldsonville on 2/19/1857 to Victorine Melancon, the younger sister of Canonnier Alfred Melancon who was later mortally wounded in battle on 9/17/1862 at Shapsburg, Maryland. By 1860 had two daughters. The *Baton Rouge Advocate*, 5/7/1861, reported: "An ACT [No. 199] 'Be it enacted by the Senate and House of Representatives of the State of Louisiana, in General Assembly convened, that Victorine Melancon, a minor, wife of Jules Guedry, residing in Ascension . . . is hereby emancipated from all. . . . law against minors, and authorized to . . . enter into, and contract all obligations . . . as if she had attained the age of twenty-one years. Approved March 20, 1861' by Thos. O. Moore, Governor of the State of Louisiana." A son was born on 12/13/1865 and named Alfred, presumably after the deceased Canonnier with two more sons born in 1866 and 1869. On 7/11/1865 while constable at Donaldsonville, Guedry killed a freedman; a jury failed to find a True Bill.[22] Moved in 1870 to the 7th Ward of East Baton Rouge Parish and worked as an overseer on Horace P. Beckworth's Moss Side Plantation. Guedry was deceased and interred in St. Joseph's Catholic Cemetery, Baton Rouge, when daughter married at St. Theresa Catholic Church, Gonzales, Ascension Parish, in April 1875. The Widow Guedry remarried in October 1875 to Gustave Landry (uncle to Canonnier Captain Prosper Landry) who was twenty-one years older than his new wife. They had two daughters.

GUEDRY, LUBIN "PETER." Enlisted at Donaldsonville, 9/13/1861, Private. Born ca. 1837 in Louisiana. Worked as an overseer and lived in Donaldsonville. Paroled ACH,

4/10/1865. Married to Louise Luce Dugas on 5/29/1871 while working as a farm laborer. Lived next to Cannonier Gustave Boudreaux in Darrow, 7th Ward of Ascension Parish. Later bought and worked his own land. Had a daughter, Melanie, born in 1872 and a son named after him in 1874. Died 8/11/1875 in Ascension Parish and interred AOL. The *New Orleans Times Picayune*, 3/29/1876, in a public sale of property at the Donaldsonville courthouse reported the widow bid on and retained a horse, a cow and two calves, shotgun, etc., for $157 with the landed property in Ascension Parish ($13,000), a small tract of land in IbervilleParish ($167), and the other cow, along with Parish Warrants ($175) all bid by and won by a local businessman. Widow and children in 1880 were living with his brother Adam Guedry's family in Sacramento Brule, Ascension Parish. In 1892 Lubin Guedry, now an orphaned son, lived with his Uncle Prosper Guedry at Brule McCall, Ascension Parish, and, reported the *New Orleans Daily City Item*, 11/18/1892, at eighteen years of age suffered, "A Frightful Death; Crushed From Toes to Waist" in a terrible cane mill accident in Colonel J. E. St. Martin's Pelico sugar house.

HARDY, EUGENE JEFF. Enlisted at Hamilton's Crossing, Virginia, 3/15/1863, Private. Previously served as a Sergeant, then 1st Lieutenant in Co. D, 1st Louisiana Zouave (Coppen's) Infantry Battalion from 4/18/1861. While on special duty by order of the secretary of war he was captured in the Lafourche District, La., on 10/27/1862 and paroled on board a prison ship at New Orleans on 1/1/1863, confined to the city limits subject to the orders of the Provost Marshal. Born ca. 1835 in France. Clerked in New Orleans. *Levy Diary* on 2/10/1865 noted *La Dramatic Association's* first act was a vaudeville composed by Hardy entitled, 'A Frenchmen Lost at the High Bridge,' which went off tolerably well." Levy also noted Hardy's acting "is very good." Paroled ACH, 4/10/1865. Bartlett's *Military Record of Louisiana* in 1875 reported Hardy, presumably in New Orleans, was "murdered since the war."

HART, WILLIAM G., "WILLIE." Enlisted at Williamsburg, Virginia, 3/8/1862, Private. Previously served as a Private with Co. F, 1st Battalion (Dreux/Rightor's) Louisiana Infantry from 4/11/1861. Born ca. 1842 in Louisiana. Clerked in New Orleans. *Levy Diary* on 12/22/1864 noted he arrived at the High Bridge fortifications and "dined with Jim Carothers's mess and slept with Hart." Paroled ACH, 4/10/1865. *Levy Diary* on 4/29/1865 noted he along with Hart, John Eckleburg, and "Buck" Chase after arriving in New Orleans "wandered about the streets enjoying everything which reminded us of our old homes."

HAUPLIN, PETER. Enlisted at Donaldsonville, 9/13/1861, Private. Born ca. 1835 in France. Worked as a shoemaker in Donaldsonville. Paroled ACH, 4/10/1865. Remained in Prince Edward County, Virginia, at Hampden Sydney and married Virginia born Nannie. They had a daughter, Hanna, and he was still making shoes in 1880.

HEBERT, FELICITE CELESIE, "FELICIEN." Enlisted at Donaldsonville, 9/13/1861, Private. Born 4/12/1836 in Assumption Parish to Issac Hebert and Marie Landry, one of six children. Planter living in 1st Ward of Ascension Parish on father's wealthy sugar plantation. On 10/20/1862 was sick furloughed to Louisiana until carried AWOL on muster roll for January 1864. Having recovered while on sick furlough he joined the 5th Louisiana Field Battery (Pelican Artillery) and served until paroled 6/6/1865 at Natchitoches, Natchitoches Parish. Joined UCV as a member of Major Victor Maurin Camp No. 38. Married widow Emma Boudreaux Gaudin on 11/13/1867 in Donaldsonville and had two sons and a daughter. Lived in the 1st Ward of Ascension Parish working as a carpenter. Died in "indigent-circumstances" in Donaldsonville on 3/23/1904 and believed interred in UCV, Major Victor Maurin Camp No. 38 tomb, AOL.

HEBERT, JOSEPH OLIVER, "OLIBERT." Enlisted at New Orleans, 4/16/1862, Private; promoted 5th Artificer on 7/28/1862. Born 2/5/1831 in Ascension Parish to Arsene Hebert and Marguerite Cecile Judice, the youngest of seven children. Married Marie Claire Landry in August 1852 about eight miles from Donaldsonville by a Catholic priest. A planter in the 1st Ward of Ascension Parish, he owned real estate valued at $2,500. Wife's sister and her two children lived with them and next door to widowed mother's huge and prosperous sugarcane plantation. *Levy Diary* on 1/28/1865 recorded Hebert was in charge of the "Commissary Department" for Mollere's Section at the High Bridge fortifications. Paroled ACH, 4/10/1865. His comrades considered him an "engineer."[23] In a Confederate Widow's Application it was stated he "served honorably until the close of the war." The *Donaldsonville Chief,* 5/10/1884, reported he was "a most estimable gentleman." Died from a tumor of the stomach on 5/6/1884 at his home, River Bend Plantation, St. James Parish. Interred in St. James Catholic Cemetery. Wife, childless, applied for a Confederate Widow's Pension in 1910 while living at 417 Hypolite (N. 6th) Street, Baton Rouge, Louisiana.

HEBERT, VALENTIN. Enlisted at Donaldsonville, 9/13/1861, Private. Born 5/22/1842 in Ascension Parish to Valentin Hebert and Magdeleine Leblanc, one of eight children with only three living to adulthood. Occupation unknown but lived in Donaldsonville. Admitted into General Hospital, Danville, Virginia, 5/15/1862 and returned to duty for a short time. Admitted into Louisiana Hospital, Richmond, where he died of "debilitas" on 8/15/1862. Interred under the name of V. Hubert in the Soldier's Section, Grave Q-298, in Hollywood Cemetery, Richmond. Father, age fifty-two, relocated to New Orleans' 3rd Ward to live with relatives after his son's death.

HEIM (HEINE), JACOB, "JACKO." Enlisted at Donaldsonville on 9/13/1861, Private. Born ca. 1840 in Darmstadt, Germany. Worked as a tailor in Donaldsonville. Brother of Canonnier Martin Heim. Went AWOL in January 1864, deserted. Returned to Donaldsonville working as a merchant.[24] It seems in 1870 he was in Sacramento, California, making hats but returned to Assumption Parish after his brother died in 1879 and took up residence one house away from his brother's widow. Lived with a black woman by the name of Francis Black, age thirty-six, and her daughter, age eleven, in 1861. By 1880 had fathered six children, four girls and two boys. Died 3/13/1903 in Napoleonville, Assumption Parish, and interred St. Anne's Catholic Cemetery, Napoleonville.

HEIM (HEINE), MARTIN. Enlisted at Donaldsonville, 9/13/1861, Private. Born ca. 1837 in Mainz, Germany. Brother of Canonnier Jacob Heim. Worked as a shoemaker in Donaldsonville. Blue eyes, red hair, light complexion, 5'7". Paroled ACH, 4/10/1865. The *Assumption Pioneer,* 3/1/1879, reported Captain Victor Maurin ranked him "as one of the bravest of the brave." After the war married a black woman by the name of Seraphine Harris and had six children, the oldest, named Martin F., in 1880 working at age thirteen as a shoemaker. The second oldest child, born in 1870, was named Jacob. Martin Heim died 2/26/1879 in Napoleonville, Assumption Parish, and interred St. Anne's Catholic Cemetery. The widow Seraphine remained in Napoleonville and never remarried though she had a total of thirteen children with eight living.

HERNANDEZ, JEAN SILVERY, "JOHN." Enlisted at Donaldsonville, 9/13/1861, Private. Born 9/13/1828 in Assumption Parish to Esteve Hernandez and Marie Gonzales. Listed as a baker and worked as a laborer in Paincourtville, Assumption Parish. Wounded in left arm at battle of Gaines's Mill, 6/27/1862, during the Seven Days' Battles for Richmond. Sick furloughed to Woodville, Mississippi, on 12/2/1863, then carried AWOL on muster roll for January 1864. While on sick furlough joined the 5th Louisiana Field Battery (Pelican Artillery) and served until paroled, 6/6/1865, at Natchitoches, Natchitoches Parish. Joined UCV as a member of Major Victor Maurin Camp No. 38. Entered Camp Nicholls's Soldier's Home, New Orleans on 11/10/1890. Officers from both units he served with endorsed his application to the Home along with Lieutenant Colonel David Zable of the 14th Louisiana Infantry Regiment. Hernandez on his application related he was "unable to return to his command in Virginia at the end of his furlough, by reason that the roads were in possession of the enemy and so he joined and enlisted in the Pelican Battery were he served until the end of the war." Married before the war to Carmel Hernandez, with a son born in 1860 at French Settlement, Livingston Parish. Died 2/22/1893 and believed interred in UCV, Major Victor Maurin Camp No. 38 tomb, AOL.

HIDALGO, ESTEVAN ANTONIO, "ESTEVE." Enlisted at Donaldsonville, 9/13/1861, Private. Born 9/2/1842 in Ascension Parish to Manuel Hildalgo and Florencia Hernandez, one of seven sons and three daughters. A farmer in Ascension Parish. Dark eyes, dark hair, dark complexion, 5'5". Paroled ACH, 4/10/1865. Joined UCV as a member of Major Victor Maurin Camp No. 38 and served camp as an alternate delegate and later as a delegate to UCV's Annual Meeting and Reunions. Married Cornelia Pocurro on 1/29/1879 at St. Louis Catherdral, New Orleans, and had two children. Worked as a laborer living ten miles above Labadieville, Assumption Parish, and later as a sugar planter on west bank of Bayou Lafourche at Crane's Forge (six miles above Napoleonville, Assumption Parish). Listed in Bouchereau's *The Louisiana Sugar Report, 1870-1917.* In 1890 and through 1900 lived in the 2nd Ward of Ascension Parish working as a plantation overseer. In May 1910 living in Napoleonville when he applied for a Confederate Pension on which he stated, "All my life [I lived in Louisiana] except when in the A. N. V. C. S. A." Signed by "his X mark" that was witnessed by Canonnier comrades Antoine Sobral, Bienvenue Cire, and Turiaffe Babin. Received pension and in 1917 lived at Bayou Goula, Iberville Parish. Moved to Barton, Ascension Parish, where he died on 4/1/1921 of "old age—stomach trouble." Interred in UCV, Major Victor Maurin Camp No. 38 tomb, AOL. Survived by wife, son, and three grandchildren.

HUMBERT, PAUL. Enlisted at Donaldsonville, 9/13/1861, Private; promoted to 3rd Corporal, March 1863. Born ca. 1838 in Germany and worked as a jeweler in Donaldsonville until his store burned down on 6/21/1861 as reported by the *Richmond Daily Dispatch,* 7/1/1861. Escaped at Appomattox Court House and joined the 5th Company, Washington Artillery, also known as Semple's Battery Light Artillery commanded by Captain C. H. Slocomb. Surrendered with Slocomb's Company at Citronelle, Alabama, by Lieutenant General Richard Taylor, 5/4/1865, and paroled at Meridian, Mississippi, 5/10/1865. Never married. The *Assumption Pioneer,* 2/1/1879, reported he "committed suicide on [1/28/1879] at his home in Donaldsonville by taking poison. He is the last of the Humbert family on the Lafourche." Interred AOL.

ISRAEL, CLEMENT. Enlisted at Donaldsonville, 9/13/1861, Sergeant Major. Born

3/14/1840 in Ascension Parish to Jean Baptiste David Israel and Marie Ann Michelle Mollere, the oldest of four children. Father baptized in Catholic church at age twenty-eight, three days before his marriage in 1839. Sugar planter living in Donaldsonville. Cousin to Canonnier Camille Mollere. Roll for October 1864 shows AWOL, captured with Canonnier Private Jules Guedry 10/7/1864 in Osyka, Mississippi. Imprisoned at Elmira, New York, and paroled 2/9/1865, then sent to Camp Lee near Richmond for exchange. Married 5/14/1861 in Donaldsonville to Marie Sidonia Vives, a niece of Mrs. Victor Maurin nee Lisa Vives. They had a daughter born on 3/18/1862. Son David born in 1866 and another daughter, named Louisiana, born a year before his death. Died in Donaldsonville of yellow fever on 9/20/1878 and interred AOL. Sister and her husband, Canonnier Lieutenant Camille Mollere, named their youngest son, born in February 1879, Marie David Clement Mollere. Another nephew, David Israel, became mayor of Donaldsonville two years after Clement's death.

JOYNER, MILES. Enlisted at Williamsburg, Virginia, 3/3/1862, Private. Previously served as a Private with Co. C, 1st Battalion (Dreux/Rightor's) Louisiana Infantry from 4/28/1861. Born ca. 1842 in Texas. Clerked in New Orleans. Wounded by gunshot in hip (injuring bone) at battle of Williamsport, also called the Waggoner's Fight (Gettysburg Campaign), on 7/6/1863. Returned to duty in February 1864. *Levy Diary* on 2/22/1865 recorded, "Miles Joyner arrived from Petersburg and became the guest of my mess." Paroled ACH, 4/10/1865.

JUDICE, JEAN GUSTAVE. Enlisted at Mobile, Alabama, 6/3/1863, Private. Born 4/7/1836 in Ascension Parish. Clerked in New Orleans. Possibly as a result of the Mine Run Campaign, died of fever on 12/4/1863 at Pratt Hospital, Lynchburg, Virginia. Interred Row 2, No. 10, Confederate Section of Lynchburg City Cemetery.

KEENE (KEEN), WILLIAM ALONZO. Enlisted at Williamsburg, Virginia, 3/22/1862, Private; promoted to 5th Corporal September 1863. Previously served as a Private with Co. B, 1st Battalion (Dreux/Rightor's) Louisiana Infantry from 4/15/1861. Born ca. 1837 in New Orleans to Hezekiah Dodge Keen and Harriett Ditch. A seaman who received his U.S. Protection Certificate in 1856.[25] Hazel eyes, brown hair, dark complexion, 5'10". Transferred to Confederate States Navy, 11/7/1863 by Special Order 265/10. Married Louisa Patton (1844-1873) and had a son Harry Leo Keen (1871-1954). After becoming a widow lived at 210 Camp Street, New Orleans, with parents who ran a boarding house.

KELLET, JAMES. Enlisted at Donaldsonville, 9/13/1861, 11th Corporal; promoted to 4th Corporal. Born ca. 1832 in Ireland. Worked as an overseer in Donaldsonville. Sick at Louisiana Hospital, Richmond, from March to June 4, 1862, where he died (according to *O'Hara Diary*) "of 'erysipelas.'" Interred Soldier's Section M, Masonic Burial Ground, Lot 20, in Hollywood Cemetery, Richmond. Survived by three-year-old daughter Adelaide Soulant whose mother by the same name gave birth at seventeen years of age, a neighbor of Kellet who at the time worked as an overseer on the J. N. Brown Plantation that was one of the richest in Plaquemine Parish.

KEROLL, LEOPOLD A. Enlisted at Yorktown, Virginia, 4/1/1862, Private. Previously served as a Private with Co. A, 1st Louisiana Zouave (Coppen's) Infantry Battalion from 3/29/1861. Born ca. 1835 in France and immigrated to New Orleans in 1849. Worked as a blacksmith in New Orleans. Paroled at Lynchburg 4/14/1865.

KLING, GABRIEL. Enlisted at Donaldsonville, 9/13/1861, Private. Born 9/23/1836 in France. Clerked in Duchtown, Ascension Parish. Paroled ACH, 4/10/1865. Joined UCV as a member of Major Victor Maurin Camp No. 38. After the war went into a two year business partnership with Canonnier Abraham Klotz buying and selling horses, then became a retail grocer on his own. Civil marriage on 3/5/1867 in Donaldsonville to Julia Idisok. Lived in the 10th Ward of Assumption Parish with wife and one daughter (the oldest), six sons, two nephews, and two clerks. The nephews and clerks were natives of France and worked in his store. Moved to Plaquemine, Iberville Parish, where he died on 6/13/1899 of blood-poisoning and interred in Plaquemine.

KLOTZ, ABRAHAM. Enlisted at Donaldsonville, 9/13/1861, Private. Born 4/17/1836 in Uhruviller, Alsace, France, son of Solomon Klotz. Immigrated in 1851, spoke German, French, and English. Peddled goods along Bayou Lafourche while settling in Assumption Parish. Paroled ACH, 4/10/1865. Joined BAANV (Application No. 429, 3/24/1879) stated, "Was captured on the retreat from Gettysburg and rescued by General Imboden's command" and "served until the surrender at Appomattox Court House." Joined UCV as a member of Louisiana Division, Army of Northern Virginia, Camp No. 1, later transferred to Major Victor Maurin Camp No. 38, then to Gen. Francis T. Nicholls Camp No. 1142. The *New Orleans Daily Picayune,* 3/28/1907, reported, "His business prospered and when the war came . . . he joined the Donaldsonville Artillery as one of the gunners of that famous command. He was with the command through every one of the many engagements . . . time and again proving himself a fearless soldier and a faithful follower of the cause of his adopted land." The *New Orleans Daily Item,* 3/28/1907, recorded "he joined the Donaldsonville Artillery, serving that command with distinction." The *Donaldsonville Chief,* 8/5/1893 reported Klotz was "a brave veteran." After the war, clerked for a short time in New Orleans then returned to Assumption Parish and started a general merchandise business while buying and selling horses in partnership for two years with Canonnier Gabriel Kling. Highly respected for his business dealings, he became a prominent merchant and sugar planter on his own. Listed in Bouchereau's *The Louisiana Sugar Report, 1870-1917,* as owner of Star Plantation on Bayou Lafourche's west bank, Assumption Parish. *New Orleans Daily Picayune,* 3/28/1907, reported, "A town grew up around his store and this town became known as Klotzville, and Mr. Klotz became the guiding spirit of that little community which was struggling to overcome the ruin brought about by the years of strife. All along the bayou he was known for his great charity and big-heartedness. No one in trouble appealed to him in vain." Married Julia Abraham of Alsace, France, on 3/4/1868 and had two daughters. In 1871 became a

Courtesy of Chandler L. Klotz Jr,. McComb, Miss.

widower, married Pauline Abraham (deceased wife's sister) in 1874 and had two sons and three daughters. The *Donaldsonville Chief,* 6/15/1907, reported, "His soldierly bearing in camp, on the march and on the battlefield won commendation from his comrades" and after the war "he was known for his charitable dispositions towards brother-Confederates." The *Assumption Pioneer,* 8/5/1893, reported the Donaldsonville Sons of Veterans of the Artillery and Ascension Parish (organized in 1888) named their cannon *Lady Florence* after one of Klotz's daughters. Has an entry in *Biographical and Historical Memoirs of Louisiana,* Volume I, pages 516-517 (Chicago, 1892). Died 3/27/1907 at four o'clock in the morning at Asheville, North Carolina, where he had been for a week to improve his health. A funeral on 3/29/1907 was conducted at a daughter's home, 5322 Dryades Street, New Orleans, under the auspices of the Louisiana Relief Lodge No. 1, F. & A. M. (Klotz was a Master Mason member of Ascension Lodge No. 251) and Headquarters BAANV, Camp No. 1. Interred in tumulus BAANV, Metairie Cemetery, New Orleans.

KUHN, WILLIAM. Enlisted at Donaldsonville, 9/13/1861, Private. Born ca. 1842 in Louisiana. Clerked in Donaldsonville. Was mortally injured on 5/14/1864. *R. O. Landry Diary* recorded: "This morning went out a few miles with horses hitched to limbers to graze and break to harness our new horses and during the afternoon on coming back to camp the caisson of the 4th piece busted [exploded] and the tongue driver William Kuhn was mortally wounded . . . his two horses were killed." *Levy Diary* recorded, "Lingered until 10 p.m. Thus departed a brave, true hearted, amicable soldier." Buried in the field, probably behind the Exchange Hotel in Gordonsville. Soon after the war ended the soldiers buried in these fields were moved to the Confederate Soldier Section of Gordonsville's Maplewood Cemetery. Survived by father J. M. Kuhn (a tailor from Germany), mother Elizabeth (born in New York) and a brother.

LANDRY, JOSEPH PHILLIPPE ADOLPH, "ADOLPHE." Enlisted at Donaldsonville, 9/13/1861, 6th Artificer. Born 8/24/1819 in Donaldsonville, the third youngest of four sons and three daughters of Philippe Ursin Landry and Marie Clemence Leblanc. Mother died when he was eight years old and father died when he was ten years old. Cousin to Canonniers Prosper Landry and Jean Trasimon Landry, second cousin to Louis Aristide Landry and Dick Winchester. Adolphe, Jean Trasimond, and Prosper Landry's grandfather was Joseph Landry who came from Acadia in 1750 and settled four miles above Bayou Lafourche where he and his wife Ann Bujol had five sons and eight daughters with one dying in infancy. Joseph Landry was appointed governor of the province and later under American rule was the first American commandant of the region. Clerked in Donaldsonville. Hazel eyes, gray hair, dark complexion, 5'8". Received a certificate of disability for hernia and old age and discharged at Richmond on 7/14/1862. Married Marie Telcide Bergeron on 5/25/1857 at Donaldsonville and had two daughters before the war. Lived after the war in Gonzales, Ascension Parish, had a daughter on 8/20/1866 named Melanie Virginie and a son born in 1870. Apparently became a widower in September 1877 with the 1880 U.S. Census noting he was single and living with his cousin J. Aristide Landry (the father of Canonnier Louis Aristide Landry) in the 4th ward of Ascension Parish. Died 11/14/1887 in Donaldsonville and interred AOL.

LANDRY, BERNARD HERMAN. Enlisted at Donaldsonville, 9/13/1861, Private. Born 5/20/1843 in Ascension Parish to Joseph Valentin Landry and Elizabeth Landry. Nephew (by mother) of Canonnier Silvere Augustin Landry and cousin to *Cannonier* Romain Octave

The Joseph Landry Tomb (left) and Major Victor Maurin Camp No. 38, United Confederate Veterans Tomb (right) which are located in Ascension of Our Lord Cemetery, Donaldsonville.
Courtesy of Andrew Capone, Labadieville, La.

Landry. Called Herman, he listed his occupation as a planter living in Darrow, Ascension Parish. Dark eyes, dark hair, dark complexion, 5'7". Discharged 11/12/1862 at Richmond by a surgeon due to chronic diarrhea. Confederate Pension Application recorded "discharged on account of sickness, eight months later being well I joined Winchester's Battery (Pelican Artillery)." Discharged in Navarro County, Texas, and paroled 6/5/1865 in Alexandria, Rapides Parish. Joined UCV as a member of Major Victor Maurin Camp No. 38. Married Florentine Cecile Boudreau on 4/27/1870 at St. Theresa Catholic Church in Gonzales, Ascension Parish, and had six sons and one daughter. Wife was a sister of Canonniers Gustave and Octave Boudreau. Lived in Darrow, 7th Ward of Ascension Parish (across the river from Donaldsonville) where he ran a "small" livery stable and a blacksmith shop. In applying for a Confederate Pension in 1911 he was asked, "What prevents you from earning a living now?" He answered: "Life has become costlier, and my advanced age prevents me from performing any manual labor." A widower when he applied, he sent a letter to the Pension Board on 4/2/1913 : "Will you please send my original discharge and parole papers now that the board has passed favorably on my application. I wish to leave these papers to my children." The *Donaldsonville Chief*, 11/14/1931, reported he

H. B. Landry Livery, Feed and Hitch Stable at Darrow, Ascension Parish. Landry is in the doorway, with daughter Haydee and his grandchildren: Oneil, Ray, Audrey, Etta, and Norma Landry.
From a 1961 Christmas Card by Sidney O. Broussard, New Orleans, La.; courtesy of Ms. Louise "Pie" Lanoux, Gonzales, La.

was a "highly esteemed citizen of east Ascension Parish." Died 11/10/1931 in Darrow and interred AOL. His Catholic Baptismal papers listed his name as above, but all his life was known as Herman Bernard Landry.

LANDRY, JEAN DÉSIRÉ. Enlisted at Donaldsonville, 9/13/1861, Private. Born 12/27/1835 in Ascension Parish to Jean Baptiste Landry, a wealthy sugar planter, and Aspasie Adeline Braud. Brother of Canonnier Cleophas Landry and cousin to Canonnier Romain Octave Landry. Unknown occupation but living in Donaldsonville. Discharged 2/26/1862 by reason of disability from an injury to his leg. Upon recovering he joined the Confederate cavalry on 6/20/1863 at Brashear City (Morgan City) located in St. Martin and St. Mary parish. On his Confederate Pension Application in May 1904 stated, "Was wounded in Va.; furloughed home, then joined Co. [H] 2nd L[ouisian]a Cal[vary] . . . until end of war." Paroled 6/4/1865 in Alexandria, Rapides Parish. Joined UCV as a member of Major Victor Maurin Camp No. 38. Married Emma Hatkinson on 1/29/1867 in Donaldsonville (witnessed by Cannoniers "Philo" Viala and Herman Landry) and had three daughters and a son. In 1870 lived in the 2nd Ward of Ascension Parish and farmed with Canonnier John Richard. Died 10/5/1904 of heart disease in Donaldsonville and interred AOL. The *Donaldsonville Chief,* 10/8/1904, reported, "Members of Major Victor Maurin Camp, UCV, of which he was a member, attended the funeral in a body."

LANDRY, JEAN REYNAUD JACQUES PROSPER. Enlisted at Donaldsonville, 9/13/1861, elected 9/2/1861 as Junior 2nd Lieutenant; promoted Senior 2nd Lieutenant, 9/7/1862; promoted Senior 1st Lieutenant, January 1863; promoted Captain 7/11/1864 (by order of C.S.A. Secretary of War) to date from 2/27/1864. Born 3/2/1826 on father's sugar plantation two miles west of Donaldsonville to Isadore Valery (died 9/21/1863) and New Orleans-born Felicité Desirée Reynaud. Cousin to Canonniers Adolphe Landry and Jean Trasimond Landry, second cousin to Louis Aristide Landry and Dick Winchester. An 1846 graduate of Georgetown College in Washington. D.C., he afterwards spent two years traveling through Europe before graduating from the University of Louisiana at New Orleans (now Tulane University) in 1854 with a law degree. Returned to Donaldsonville practicing as an attorney and notary until appointed Ascension Parish's attorney in 1861. Married Françoise Adele Pedesclaux (his cousin by her mother, Marie Arthemise Landry) on 2/16/1855 at her home[26] in lower Ascension Parish by Rev. Charles Boglioli, C. M., which was witnessed by cousins and Canonnier comrades Adolphe Landry and Jean Trasimon Landry. "When war was declared," reported the *Donaldsonville Chief,* 4/20/1907, "he bade farewell to his young wife and two small children and enlisted as a private in the 'Canonniers de Donaldson' . . . before the battery took its departure . . . Landry was elected second lieutenant." His wife gave birth to a third child, a son

Courtesy of Confederate Memorial Hall, New Orleans, La.

named Charles, on 6/9/1862. Captain Victor Maurin in his battle report of Fredericksburg in December 1862 acclaimed Landry's "gallant conduct."[27] In September 1864 he wrote his wife Adele: "I saw enough battles to satisfy the taste of the most difficult person. I understand war and [in] learning to understand it, I learned to understand peace. Peace! Could I tell you all that this word contains, of gentleness, of poetry, of love and of happiness? For me, it is the memory of all the beautiful days that we spent together . . . and to enjoy each other to the end of our days. Alas!"[28] *Levy Diary* on 12/21/1864, a day before Levy's sick transfer to High Bridge from Petersburg recorded, "Nearly dark, called at Capt. Landry's room for a letter, and found Prosper in the act of making a most elaborate toilet. Blarneyed him a little." Levy characterized Prosper Landry as "an upright, honest gentlemen." [*sic*] Paroled ACH, 4/10/1865 and signed surrender muster roll as "Capt. Com'd'g Donaldsonville Art'y." Paroled again in May 1865.[29] After the war the family grew with the addition of two daughters, the oldest born on 4/28/1866, and another son born in 1867 with the godfather being fellow Canonnier Lieutenant Camille Mollere. Joined BAANV (Application No. 127, 3/21/1876). Joined UCV as a member of Louisiana Division, Army of Northern Virginia Camp No. 1, later transferred to Major Victor Maurin Camp No. 38 and served the camp as an alternate delegate to UCV's Annual Meeting and Reunions. On 10/19/1902 the *New Orleans Times Picayune* reported that he, along with Canonniers E. C. Cooley and E. L. Monnot were each appointed aide-de-camp with the Rank of Major to the commanding general of the Louisiana Division, United Confederate Veterans. The *Donaldsonville Chief*, 4/20/1907, recorded that Landry was, "Just and upright, warmhearted and sympathetic, a man of highest integrity and exceptionally engaging personality, he earned the regard and affection of his intimates and the respect and esteem of all who knew him, both in the business and social world, and those who knew him best loved him most." After the war Landry returned to the practice of law, and in 1875 headed a five person committee demanding state senatorial, state representative, and municipal elections, and taking the legal steps necessary to compel the opposing town authorities to order an election required by a new charter.[30] Landry would continue to serve Ascension Parish after the Reconstruction Era as a member of the parish's police jury, notary public, parish judge, tax collector, secretary of the police jury, and parish treasurer, and as a delegate to several state conventions. He reorganized the Donaldsonville Cannoneers and commanded them from 1875 to 1895. Landry's father died during the war and after his plantation sold of which, reported the *Donaldsonville Chief*, 9/2/1882, "Like many others, it was purchased by a stranger; but after a while it returned to the possession of one of its heirs, Capt. R. Prosper Landry, who named it 'Souvenir.' After a short reign over the homestead, the Captain had the mortification to see it again transferred." Landry remained active in politics and veteran affairs and addressed many political meetings, speaking in French and English with equal fluency. The *New Orleans Times Picayune*, 1/12/1900, noted he was president of the "Bryan-Stevenson-Broussard Club" made up of "enthusiastic Democrats" and a member of the Knights of Columbus. The captain, at the advanced age of seventy-nine, also testified in a 1905 pension claim on behalf of an aged and infirmed Cannonier veteran and related, "I can only depend upon my memory—which, of course, does not retain everything, but there are certain things which I remember as well as if they had happened yesterday. For instance; I can call the names of every man of the company who went wrong and the circumstances of their going wrong."[31] Landry no doubt forgave them, but he never forgot their actions. After a short illness Prosper Landry peacefully and painlessly passed away at his home on St. Patrick Street in Donaldsonville at 10:55 a.m. on 4/16/1907. Interred in the Landry Tomb, AOL where the obsequies were attended by the Knights of Columbus; the faculties and pupils of Donaldsonville High School, St. Vincent's Institute, and St. Joseph's Commercial Institute;

delegations from Major Victor Maurin Camp, UCV, Captain Victor St. Martin Camp USCV, and Hubert Treille Chapter, UDC; members of the police jury and other parochial and municipal officers, and a large number of friends and acquaintances, and family. The *Donaldsonville Chief*, 4/20/1907, reported, "It may be said that no citizen of Ascension parish stood higher in the esteem of his friends and the public generally than did R. Prosper Landry, and his demise has caused a void that only time can fill and a wound that naught but a divine Providence can heal." The *Donaldsonville Chief*, 12/21/1907, reported veterans John S. Mioton and Ernest L. Monnot presented a crayon portrait of their esteemed captain to the Army of Northern Virginia, Camp No. 1, UCV, at a December 1907 meeting in Memorial Hall, New Orleans, where it was said: "If the title of Chevaler Bayard, 'sans peur et saus reproche' is justly applied to those whose deeds of valor and lofty conception of duty deserves to place them in the front rank of their fellowmen, well may the encomium be bestowed on him whose memory we now revere. We love our chief more now, for in war we knew of his fearlessness and many deeds of bravery, but the succeeding years of peace each have added new luster to his many virtues, and his character, after all this time, stands forward in all the splendor of its immaculate spotlessness."

United Confederate Veteran Adjutant and Donaldsonville Artillery Captain Prosper Landry (top row, far right) shown here on August 8, 1902, at the Cabildo in New Orleans with officers of the Louisiana Division of the United Confederate Veterans organization and Louisiana's Governor W. W. Heard (first row, third from right.) Other prominent Confederate veterans are A. B. Booth and Leon Jatremski (first row, third and fourth from left), J. H. Tichenor (middle row, third from left), and Joseph Maurin (back row, middle), son of Donaldsonville Artillery Major Victor Maurin. Courtesy of Confederate Memorial Hall, New Orleans, La.

LANDRY, JEAN TRASIMOND "JOHN," "J.T." Enlisted at Donaldsonville, 9/13/1861, 3rd Corporal; promoted to 5th Sergeant in March 1863 and to 4th Sergeant in September 1863. Born 3/20/1831 in Ascension Parish, the eldest and one of two sons and five daughters of Jean Trasimon Landry (wealthy planter, state representative, state senator, and Louisiana's lieutenant governor in 1846, also a colonel of militia) and Modeste Braud, who died 5/31/1863. Sugar planter working for father while living at New Hope Plantation that also was called Home, built by his grandfather Joseph Landry. The *Donaldsonville Chief*, 9/2/1882, reported, "Home is a sacred and holy spot to many persons of this and other parishes. In its substantial mansion house many were brought into this world; many were there given in marriage, and many were carried from it to their last resting place." His father in 1860 owned several tracts of land under cultivation on both sides of the river and vast sections of forestlands with a total real estate value of $275,000 and personal value of $540,000. In 1907 the Canonnier veteran's wife related on a Confederate Widow's Pension Application that all she had left was "an uncultivated tract of land; value not over $600." He married Marie "Mary" Amelia Seghers on 5/1/1855 in St. John the Baptist Parish and had two boys and one girl. Before the war Landry was also in a business partnership with Canonnier Jonathan Scheuer, which was known as "Scheuer & Landry, Dealers in Hardware, Plantation Dry Goods, &c., &c., &c.; Buggies, Carriages and Philadelphia Wheel Wrights."[32] Cousin to Canonniers Adolphe Landry and Prosper Landry, and second cousin to Canonniers Louis Aristide Landry and Dick Winchester. The *Donaldsonville Chief*, 3/13/1880, recorded that the mere presence of "J. Tras." and Louis Aristide Landry and their "participation in the 'doings'" was enough to bring a *"hearty enjoyment"* to any occasion. It was noted that "he served honorably . . . at Seat of War in Virginia" and while sick was "detached for office work" in June 1864 to the Confederate States Treasury Department in Richmond. *Levy Diary* on 8/8/1864 from Louisiana Hospital, Richmond, noted, "John Landry called this morning but left without breaksfast." Returned home on furlough from Virginia during the war after which wife had a son (Robert Boyd Lee Landry) born 9/10/1863 in Ascension Parish. Escaped capture at the end of the war and had a son born on 3/3/1866 in St. John the Baptist Parish. Another son was born in 1873, along with three daughters born in between 1867 and 1872. The *New Orleans Times Picayune,* 11/22/1874 recorded he was "one of the most gallant among those who followed the fortunes of the Confederacy . . . as a man he was the soul of honor; as a soldier, fearless to a fault; as a friend, trusty and true." Thirteen months after his father passed away, he died "from a lingering sickness" on 11/10/1874 at his home in the city of Baton Rouge, East Baton Rouge Parish. Interred St. Joseph's Catholic Cemetery, Baton Rouge.

LANDRY, JOSEPH CLEOPHAS. Enlisted at Donaldsonville, 9/13/1861, Private. Born 6/22/1842 near Paincourtville in Assumption Parish to Jean Baptiste Landry, a wealthy sugar planter, and Aspasie Adeline Braud. Brother of Canonnier Jean Désiré Landry and cousin to Canonnier Romain Octave Landry. Clerked in Paincourtville, Assumption Parish. Blue eyes, light hair, fair complexion, 5'0". Paroled ACH, 4/10/1865. Joined UCV as a member of Major Victor Maurin Camp No. 38, later transferred to Gen. Francis T. Nicholls Camp No. 1142. After the war married Eugenie Hebert and had two sons while living in Paincourtville. After becoming a widower married Louise Laborde on 1/19/1874 in Paincourtville and had three sons and four daughters. Became chief engineer of an open-pan refinery with a reputation as a "faithful and conscientious engineer" and, as reported by the *Assumption Pioneer,* 2/21/1914, "as a citizen, husband and father . . . truly exemplary. He was a devout Roman Catholic." This newspaper article added that he lived a "useful and noble life . . . and served his country from the beginning to the bitter days of Appomattox." Died of an "atheromatous heart . . . following attack of acute indigestion" on 2/14/1914 in Paincourtville. Survived by seven children and his wife, who received a Confederate Widow's Pension in 1914. His funeral "was one of the largest attended . . . seen in a long time." Interred St. Elizabeth Catholic Cemetery, Paincourtville.

LANDRY, JOSEPH JAMES. Enlisted at Donaldsonville, 9/13/1861, Private. Born 2/27/1845 in Paincourtville, Assumption Parish, to Murville Baptiste Landry and Fidelie

Dugas. Stepmother was Jane Newchurch Landry, sister of the three Canonnier Newchurch brothers. She named her first twin sons born after her brothers the Canonniers Edward and William Henry. Had one sister, six brothers, five stepsisters, and four stepbrothers. Was a student in Paincourtville. Gray eyes, dark hair, light complexion, 5'10". Paroled ACH, 4/10/1865. Joined BAANV (Application No. 496, 4/23/1882), stated, "Served from Yorktown to the surrender at Appomattox Court House." Joined UCV as a member of Major Victor Maurin Camp No. 38. Married Emma Blanchard on 2/11/1868 in Paincourtville and had five daughters. Worked as an overseer and considered a "pioneer sugar Planter." Became manager of the large Magginis Brothers' Hermitage Plantation in Ascension Parish. After becoming a widower married Annie Lawrence on 1/4/1890 at St. Patrick's Cathedral, 724 Camp Street, New Orleans. In 1905 the family was living in Klotzville, Assumption Parish, when he applied for a Confederate Pension on which he stated, "With the company at Appomattox, Virginia." Died of "General debility" at home in Klotzville on 12/9/1908. The *Assumption Pioneer,* 12/12/1908, reported his "body was escorted to the grave by his comrades." Interred in UCV, Major Victor Maurin Camp No. 38 tomb, AOL. Wife received a Confederate Widow's Pension in 1924 and until her death on 3/25/1955 while living at 4221 Prytania Street, New Orleans.

LANDRY, LOUIS ARISTIDE, "TIP." Enlisted at Donaldsonville, 9/13/1861, 5th Corporal; promoted to 6th Sergeant in March 1863. Born 7/24/1840 in Donaldsonville to Aristide Joseph Landry, congressman, state representative, and president of the Ascension Parish Police Jury, and a sergeant in the antebellum Chasseurs de l'Ascension cavalry. Mother was Anne Estelle Landry. Worked as a merchant for father in Donaldsonville. Second cousin to Canonniers Adolphe Landry, Prosper Landry, and Jean Trasimond Landry, and cousin to Dick Winchester. Hazel eyes, black hair, light complexion, 5'8". *Levy Diary* on 5/15/1864 noted that while marching twenty-three miles past Louisa Court House, "Tip Landry carried my rations, and [Henry] Fuhri my blanket. Road very heavy" with "blanket and clothing wet through." Prosper Landry related the Canonnier guns "had barely time to limber up, and were among the last to cross that memorable bridge [at Hatcher's Run on 4/2/1865]. Corporal Arthur Comstock had failed to 'mount' and was diligently footing it behind when he came upon Sergt. L. A. Landry, who, out of breath, had given up the race. 'Come along, Tip—there's the bridge—we can make it yet.'—and they did make it, escaping unhurt despite the many bullets aimed at them."[33] Paroled at Lynchburg, Virginia, 4/13/1865. Joined BAANV (Application No. 495, 4/22/1882) that stated he was "promoted to Sergeant . . . and surrendered." Joined UCV as a member of Major Victor Maurin Camp No. 38. Served as a Lieutenant in the post war Donaldsonville Artillery. The *Donaldsonville Chief,* 3/13/1880, recorded he and Jean Trasimon Landry's mere presence and their "participation in the 'doings'" was enough to bring a *"hearty enjoyment"* to any occasion. Married Marie Augustine Leblanc on 6/12/1866 in Donaldsonville (witnessed by Cannoniers J. T. Landry, Philo Viala, and Camille Mollere) and had five sons and four daughters while planting in the 4th Ward of Ascension Parish. Died at home (on ninety acres of land) of "general debility" on 11/14/1909. Interred in AOL believed to be in UCV, Major Victor Maurin Camp No. 38 tomb.

LANDRY, MAURICE LUCIEN. Enlisted at New Orleans, 4/16/1862, Private. Born 9/11/1844 in Paincourtville, Assumption Parish, to Marcellin Landry and Clementine Dupre with both parents apparently dying when he was very young. A student in Assumption Parish living with Canonnier Camille Templet's family who raised him. Landry seems to have escaped capture in April 1865 though on his Confederate Pension Application in 1922 recorded: "Paroled, don't remember where I was." Joined UCV as a member of Major Victor Maurin Camp No. 38, later transferred to Gen. Francis T. Nicholls Camp No. 1142. Married Louise Veneda Aucoin on 2/20/1867 in Plattenville, Assumption Parish, and had six daughters and three sons while sugar planting and farming in the 3rd Ward of Assumption Parish next to Canonnier Armas Triche's tract near Bertie. Moved to Ascension Parish in 1906 but in 1909 returned to the 3rd Ward of Assumption Parish, where he brought a civil suit against the estate of Canonnier Camille Templet's widow who was forced to sell at auction. Landry then bought and took charge of the Templet Plantation.[34] Listed in Bouchereau's *The Louisiana Sugar Report, 1870-1917.* Wife died on 9/1/1911 from the shock of a boating accident (no one drowned) when his gasoline boat with twenty passengers overturned. Married widow Valerie Triche Rodrigue on 2/18/1915 in Paincourtville. In March 1923 living in Napoleonville, Assumption Parish, where he was allowed a Confederate Pension of $20.00 a month. His wife Valerie became the last surviving Canonnier widow and passed away at age ninety-one on 10/11/1964 at a daughter's home in Jackson, Tennessee. The *Donaldsonville Chief,* 5/11/1935, reported, "He was a man of high personal character . . . respected and esteemed by all who knew him." The *Assumption Pioneer,* 5/11/1935 reported, "Engaged in the sugar cane industry and was recognized as a successful farmer" and "one of our . . . best known citizens . . . a veteran of the Civil war." Died 5/8/1935 of "Heart Trouble" at his home; the last surviving veteran of the Donaldsonville Artillery. At the time of his death eight children, sixty-four grandchildren, and eighty-four great grandchildren survived him. Interred Assumption Catholic Cemetery, Plattenville.

LANDRY, ROMAIN OCTAVE. Enlisted at New Orleans, 3/21/1862, Private. Born August 9, 1843, in Ascension Parish to Adlard Landry, a wealthy sugar planter, and Marie Ursin Gaudin. Nephew (by father) of Canonnier Silvere Augustin Landry and cousin to Canonniers Jean Désiré Landry and Cleophus Landry. Called Octave by his parents and friends, he was attending Spring Hill College in Mobile, Alabama, when the war started. A resident of Modeste, Ascension Parish, he returned home and joined the Donaldsonville Canonniers. Paroled ACH, 4/10/1865. Joined UCV as a member of Louisiana Division, Army of Northern Virginia Camp No. 1. The *New Orleans Times Picayune,* 2/25/1908, recorded, "Young Landry's devotion to the cause made him respected by his officers and loved by his comrades." Married Georgiana Discharry on 2/12/1866 in Donaldsonville by Rev. Charles Boglioli, C. M., (witnessed by Canonniers James Besson and Herman Landry) and though they had no children they raised orphaned Marie Babin from childhood. Lived in the 1st Ward of Ascension Parish and associated with his father and brothers rebuilding their plantation for some years. He then opened and operated a country store across the river near the John Burnside Plantation, and being prosperous in that undertaking, bought the "old 'Melancon tract' (six miles up river of Donaldsonville) on which there was crevasses in 1828."[35] Canonnier officer William Lawes previously owned the land

From the *New Orleans Picayune*, February 25, 1908.

after which his brother Dr. Lawes sold it to Landry who named it Delicia Plantation. The *Donaldsonville Chief,* 8/19/1882, reported Landry as "a type of the progressive man" and when he obtained the tract "the place was unimproved; now a dwelling and store, a sugar-house with engines; cribs, stables and cabins adorn it . . . and has of late turned his attention to the making of bricks, which he bakes to a turn—a bright red one."[36] Listed in Bouchereau's *The Louisiana Sugar Report, 1870-1917.* Retired in 1905 and became one of the best-known retired sugar planters and Confederate veterans of the State. Bought a comfortable home at 1507 Prytania Street in New Orleans from where he often visited Confederate Memorial Hall, 929 Camp Street. Died at home on the morning of 2/24/1908 from a three week illness after "a severe attack of la grippe." The *Donaldsonville Chief,* 2/29/1908 reported Landry was "a devout Catholic . . . warmhearted and true friend, a man and a citizen of which any community might be justly proud." Wartime diary in possession of a great-grand niece. Interred in tumulus BAANV, Metairie Cemetery, New Orleans "where," reported the *New Orleans Times Picayune,* 2/25/1908, "lie others of the glorious heroes who wore the gray, the gallant old veteran making this as a last request."

LANDRY, SILVERE AUGUSTIN, "SYLVESTER," "SYLVANY." Enlisted at Donaldsonville, 9/13/1861, Private. Born 6/20/1840 near Philadelphia Point to "the honest old Creole"[37] Auguste Hycinthe Landry, a son of Acadian parents exiled to Maryland for ten years then to Louisiana, and Marguerite Eugenie Babin. Brother to Adlard and Elizabeth, uncle to Canonniers Romain Octave Landry and Bernard Herman Landry. Cooper in Donaldsonville living in the 1st Ward of Ascension Parish. Dark eyes, dark hair, dark complexion, 5'11". Escaped capture until paroled on 5/1/1865. On Confederate Pension Application recorded, "Paroled . . . Appomattox, then on my way home was again paroled by Yankees." Joined UCV as a member of Major Victor Maurin Camp No. 38. Married Marie Lisa Babin on 7/2/1861 in Donaldsonville; she died during the war and he remarried in Donaldsonville on 12/27/1865 to Elmire Bujol, widow of Private Numa Babin, Company K, 8th Louisiana Infantry Regiment, who was mortally wounded the day before he died on 5/4/1863 near Fredericksburg, Virginia. The Landrys had three sons and two daughters, plus a stepdaughter from his first wife. Lived his whole life in the 1st Ward of Ascension Parish as a planter on his father's plantation, though he also ran a large cooperage shop. In 1911 he had "weak eyesight and deaf" but had a real estate assessment valued at $750.[38] Working a "small truck garden" in 1911 when he applied for a Confederate Pension that he received in 1913. The *Donaldsonville Chief,* 8/19/1882, noted his "sturdy virtues" and on 12/16/1916, "He was a gallant soldier of the south . . . his whole career was characterized by energy, industry, and a sublime sense of duty." The paper also reported he was a man of "fine character and honorable . . . whose modest virtues and sterling worth will endure forever in the memories of those who knew him in life." Died 10/31/1916 at Hohen Solms in the 1st Ward of Ascension Parish and interred AOL.

LANOIX, LOUIS. Enlisted at Donaldsonville, 9/13/1865, 3rd Artificer. Born 2/17/1822 in St. James Parish. Worked as an overseer in Ascension Parish. Gray eyes, light hair, dark complexion, 5'7". Received certificate of disability for impaired motion of knee caused by fractured leg and kidney disease. Discharged at Richmond on 7/13/1862. Married Marie Olivia Braud on 8/1/1842 and had two boys and one girl. Died 8/8/1867 in Ascension Parish and interred in AOL Catholic Cemetery in Donaldsonville.

LARESCHE, WILLIAM FRANCIS. Enlisted at Gordonsville, Virginia, 8/9/1863,

Private. Born 1/29/1847 in New Orleans, one of ten children to Paul E. Leresche (a New Orleans notary and attorney) and Marin Del Carmen "Carmelite" Prados. A student in New Orleans. A month after his enlistment his family arrived as exiles in Richmond on September 8, 1863. Father served in Richmond's Company D, Local Defense, 3d Virginia, while brother Paul E. Laresche Jr. joined the 3rd Company, Battalion Washington Artillery on 1/14/1864. *Levy Diary* on 5/3/1864 recorded, "As Mr. [Paul] Leresche, father of [William] an amiable comrade, was about to leave for Richmond, I took advantage of the opportunity to send all my superfluous clothing for the year." Wounded by a bullet that pierced his hand at Petersburg, Virginia, on 12/26/1864.[39] Certificate of Disability granted by Medical Examining Board, Receiving and Wayside Hospital, Richmond on 1/17/1865. Captured 4/3/1865 and confined to Libby Prison, Richmond, until sent to Point Lookout, Maryland, prisoner of war camp. Released 6/13/1865 after taking Oath of Allegiance. After the war married Laurentine Laurent and sold cigars in New Orleans at 162 (now 710) Royal Street. Member of the Pelican Mutual Benevolent Association that was "representative . . . of the best elements of [the] old Creole population."[40] Under the headline "More Chivalry in Louisiana" it was reported on 5/3/1874 that Laresche became involved in a "private matter" dispute in a club-room resulting in a duel taking place at the Globe Ballroom, at the corner of Treme and St. Peter streets in New Orleans. The weapons chosen were colichemardes, a type of dueling sword. A correspondent reported:

> In the morning at 10:30 o'clock the two gentlemen accompanied by their seconds and surgeons, met, and after the usual preliminaries both took their positions. As they put themselves *en garde* they were calm and collected, each eyeing closely his antagonist, and ready for a response to any movement. After some advances and feints they got to work well, and the contest waxed hot. The glimmer of steel in the dim light of the room, the silent group of gentlemen about the combatants, and the rattle of the foils, made the scene dramatic in the extreme. After a number of passes the seconds threw up the swords, and it was discovered that Mr. Laresche was wounded in the stomach and Mr. Grandjean in the shoulder. A parley was held and the friends of both parties being satisfied, the wounded men left their post. The whole party then returned to the city, after the surgeons had dressed the wounds, which were pronounced not dangerous. . . . The whole affair was conducted with extreme secrecy . . . both are doing well today, and their hurts will only inconvenience them for a short time.[41]

Lareche died at two o'clock in the afternoon of 5/25/1876 at 268 (now 1110) Royal Street (his mother's home) after a "Bloody Rencontre." The *New Orleans Daily Picayune,* 5/25/1876, reported Laresche at about half past one o'clock in the afternoon was escorting a close friend from Superior Criminal Court and after walking and reaching the center of the 100 block of Bourbon Street defended his friend from an assault by identifying himself as a law officer. A shot was fired by Laresche striking the known assailant and in chasing him he was ambushed by another assailant. Shot once in the back, he fell to the ground and was shot twice more. He was taken to a drug store at the corner of Bourbon and Customhouse Streets where he gave a deathbed statement of the incident while a Catholic priest was summoned. After his confession was heard and last sacraments administered he was removed to his mother's home where he expired.

LAWES, WILLIAM CONWAY, "BILLY." Enlisted at Donaldsonville, 9/13/1861, Senior 1st Lieutenant. Born 11/11/1829 in Ascension Parish to Ascension Parish Judge Robert Lawes and Elizabeth Ana Conway who after being widowed, married Nicholas Henry Rightor. Lawes was half-brother to Major Nicholas H. Rightor who later commanded the 1st Louisiana Infantry (Dreaux/Rightor's) Battalion and the brother of Dr. Robert Lawes, who served as a Confederate surgeon in the Trans-Mississippi Department. First cousins were the mulatto brothers Prosper and Frederick August "Gus" Conway through his uncle John Conway, who bought a female slave from Virginia named Cecile (their mother) in 1819. Both cousins lived with Lawes at the northeast corner of Lessard and Iberville streets in Donaldsonville. Gus (born ca. 1827) and Prosper (born ca. 1831) also served in the Donaldsonville Canonnier field band, with Gus being the bandleader. Respected by everybody, Lawes was considered the guardian in Donaldsonville of a large population of free men of color. The *Donaldsonville Chief*, 8/19/1882, remembered he was "loved by everybody." Graduated from Wesleyan University in Middletown, Connecticut, 1848.[42] At Donaldsonville's 1849 July 4th celebration the *Le Vigilant* newspaper (7/7/1849) reported after the public reading of the Declaration of Independence, Lawes gave, in English, *"un magnifique discours"* (a magnificant speech) *"qui a ete cent fois interrompu par les bravos de l'assemblee"* (which was one hundred times interrupted by the cheers of the assembly). As an Old Line Whig he was elected in 1854 as a state senator representing Ascension, St. James, and St. John parishes, was acting judge for the Fourth Judicial District from April 2, 1860, to January 14, 1861, and a large property holder that included the old Melancon tract plantation in the 1st Ward of Ascension Parish. "In the days of succession," reported the *New Orleans Republican*, 11/28/1870, "he was known as an outspoken and unflinching Union man." Lawes resigned his commission as Major in the Ascension Regiment of Louisiana Militia to accept the First Lieutenant's position in the Donaldsonville Artillery. While on sick furlough in Louisiana he was dropped from the rolls by Special Order 45/8 dated 2/23/1863. In 1864 worked as an attorney in Ascension Parish.[43] Lawes was arrested with other Confederate officers and men near Pierre Part at Harden Burnley's Plantation in Assumption Parish in early 1865 for smuggling medicine, mail, and contraband goods through Federal lines.[44] In the latter half of 1865 served as an alderman of Donaldsonville and in 1869 a one-year term as mayor of Donaldsonville. According to the *New Orleans Times Picayune*, 3/6/1868 he was an Ascension delegate to the Democratic State Convention with Trasimon Landry, Duncan F. Kenner, and Alexander Landry. The *New Orleans Times Picayune*, 9/13/1870, reported Lawes was again one of two Ascension Parish Delegates to the Democratic State Convention. Two months later, on 11/9/1870, Lawes and Donaldsonville Mayor Marx Schoenberg were murdered when the two men, to preserve the peace, went to the outskirts of Donaldsonville (in the rear of Salsburg Plantation) under a flag of truce to meet with a mob of black militia from St. James Parish. This organized mob of Radical Republicans had threatened to burn Donaldsonville over a dispute about where to count election ballot boxes. While parleying with them, Schoenberg was shot and killed and fell out the buggy. Lawes was shot then dragged from the buggy and put against a fence where he was shot many more times before being run through with a sword and dying. It was reported while being shot Lawes entreated the mob not to kill him, that he had come on a mission of peace.[45] He was cruelly mutilated with one newspaper account noting the body "was so much disfigured that many of his intimate friends could scarcely recognize it."[46] Lawes was interred the next day in AOL. The *New Orleans Republican,* 11/28/1870, reported: "Lawes was incapable of a dishonorable act" and the "purest and most inoffensive gentleman." It also noted he was "marked for his quiet, gentle, and amicable disposition . . . was warmhearted and kind, and bore enmity to no human being . . . modest and retiring in his habits, he was beloved and esteemed by all who knew him." The Donaldsonville town counsel on 9/23/1890, twenty years after the murder, dedicated in his memory the batture lots lying below the steamboat wharf and named it *Lawes Park*. The resolution stated Lawes "sacrificed his life in defense of the people of Donaldsonville."[47]

LE BESQUE, FRANÇOIS, "FELIX." Enlisted at Richmond, 11/7/1861, Private. Previously served as a Corporal in Guyol's Company of Orleans Artillery, 1st Brigade, Louisiana Volunteer Troops and later the 5th Texas Volunteer Infantry Regiment, Co. A, Bayou City Guards. Born ca. 1831 in France. Clerked in New Orleans. On 2/5/1862 was commissioned a captain and transferred to Company B, (DeGourney's) 12th Louisiana Battalion, Heavy Artillery. Died 7/1/1863 in the Confederate General Hospital after protracted illness during the siege of Port Hudson, East Baton Rouge Parish. Married Felide Bayln in New Orleans on 7/7/1850. Childless, his wife never remarried and after the war lived the remainder of her life with niece Estelle M. Momus at 2030 Hospital Street, New Orleans. The widow died on 4/1/1911.

LEBLANC, JOSEPH CLARVILLE, "CAMILLE." Enlisted at Donaldsonville, 9/13/1861, 12th Corporal. Born 8/18/1827 in Ascension Parish to Isaac Colin Leblanc and Seraphino Landry, one of eight children. Occupation unknown but lived in Donaldsonville. Member of the antebellum Canonniers and promoted to corporal in 1850. Probably due to ill health left the company on 3/28/1862 and discharged on 5/27/1862. Married Marie Emma Cire on 1/14/1851. Died 1/5/1866 and interred in AOL.

LEBLANC, LOUIS-DERNAUD, "DERNON." Enlisted at Donaldsonville, 9/13/1861, Private. Born 5/20/1836 in Ascension Parish, the eighth of eleven children to Edward Leblanc and Marie Gertrude Mollere. Brother of Canonnier Narcisse Octave Leblanc and cousin to Canonniers Camille Mollere and Duffosard Mollere. Listed occupation as a planter in Ascension Parish. Hazel eyes, dark hair, dark complexion, 5'11". Wounded in the left foot (Achilles Heel) at battle of Fredericksburg, Virginia, on 12/13/1862. Admitted to Louisiana Hospital, Richmond (foot amputated) discharged on Surgeon's Certificate from Jackson Hospital, Richmond, 11/24/1863. Leblanc remained in Richmond after his discharge and assisted other wounded comrades. On 8/6/1864 Levy, from the Louisiana Hospital in Richmond wrote, "Dernon Leblanc called early in the morning and took lunch with Schmidt, Ely, and myself. On parting, he offered to advance me any amount of money that I might desire. I was much pleased at this indication of his gratitude for the attention I paid him when he was in a similar condition." Died 4/6/1879 and interred St. Anne Catholic Cemetery, Napoleonville, Assumption Parish.

LEBLANC, NARCISSE OCTAVE. Enlisted at Donaldsonville, 9/13/1861, Private. Born 11/18/1838 in Ascension Parish, the ninth of eleven children to Edward Leblanc and Marie Gertrude Mollere. Brother of Canonnier Dernon Leblanc and cousin to Canonniers Camille Mollere and Duffosard Mollere. A student in Ascension Parish. Gray eyes, dark hair, dark complexion, 5'0". Paroled ACH, 4/10/1865. Died 8/19/1868 and interred in AOL.

LEVY, EUGENE HENRY. Enlisted at Williamsburg, Virginia, 3/2/1862, Private. Previously served as a Private with Co. C, 1st Battalion (Dreux/Rightor's) Louisiana Infantry from 11/13/1861. Born 1/28/1840 in Grand Gulf, Claiborne County, Mississippi, to Jacob "Jack" Louis Levy and Sara Edwitha Marks, one of nine children. Brother of Canonnier Julian H. "Doc" Levy with another brother, Joseph C. Levy, a 2nd Lieutenant in the 1st Louisiana (Strawbridge's) Infantry, killed in the April 1862 battle at Shiloh, Tennessee. Father was descended from a Jamaican family that settled in Charleston and later moved to New Orleans, where he listed his occupation as an exchange broker but participated as a commission merchant in the slave-trade and manufacture of servant's clothing.[48] Graduated

Courtesy of Hebrew Union College.

with honors from the University of Louisiana then worked as a clerk-cashier in a cotton factory-mercantile house in New Orleans. The well-known Eugene on 2/8/1861 was involved in a much-publicized "affray" where after a disagreement and being struck twice by a cowhide, he shot and killed his assailant who was a long time friend and coworker, a member of Dreux's Orleans Cadets military unit. The "renconter" was over an allegation of theft by Levy against the coworker that created "not a little excitement and discussion about town." A few days later a jury of inquest rendered a verdict of manslaughter against Levy.[49] During the war Levy wrote he was No. 3 and William Ely served as No. 1 on a Parrott rifle gun, Piece No. 3, with the gunner being Corporal Ignace Rougeau. At the siege of Petersburg (Battle of the Crater) on 7/30/1864, noted he received a "flesh wound right-side" and was temporarily blinded by an enemy shell burst. Splinters had to be extracted by a surgeon from his inflamed eye. Visiting Levy in the Petersburg hospital on 8/2/1864 were Canonnier comrades Boham, Burns, Fuhri, Keroll, McCoy, and brother "Doc," and on the following day Seymour Mioton, McCullet, and Boham again. Levy transferred due to sickness and the need of "indulging in a vegetable diet" to the High Bridge fortifications on 12/22/1864. Captured at Appomattox Court House on 4/8/1865 and paroled on 4/14/1865 at Farmville, Virginia. Levy recorded on 4/18/1865 the ship *Trumpeter* conveyed him "from fair Richmond" down the James River to Old Point Comfort, "and as I passed . . . monuments of our former glory, my tears flowed freely and I thought with the noble Moor, 'farewell content, farewell the tranquil mind, the spirit spiring, the ear-piercing fife, and all the pomp, pride, and circumstance of glorious war.' Othello's occupation's gone!"[50] At Old Point Comfort, Virginia, Levy boarded and rode the ship *Atlanta* to New Orleans. On 4/29/1865 Levy recorded he, along with Canonniers John Eckleburg, "Willie" Hart, and "Buck" Chase, after arriving in New Orleans "wandered about the streets enjoying everything which reminded us of our old homes." Known by his old comrades as an enthusiastic soldier, Levy joined the UCV as a member of the Louisiana Division, Army of Northern Virginia Camp No. 1, and later became a member of the New York Camp of Confederate Veterans. Appointed by the governor of Louisiana to the committee to mark the positions (in November 1894) of Louisiana troops at Gettysburg. Simon Wolf in *The American Jew as Patriot, Soldier, and Citizen* (Philadelphia, PA 1895) gave his thanks in the book's introduction to "Captain" Eugene H. Levy for his assistance. A modern day scholar described a young Levy as an "intellectual, assimilated and secure, well-read and well-mannered, a lover of literature and music" but, "a riddle."[51] The *New York Tribune's* "Grant Memorial Supplement" of 4/28/1897 included an article by Levy titled "Reminiscences of a Soldier of the 'Lost Cause.'" In 1902 Levy contributed a series of articles (June 9, 16, 23, 30; July 14, 21, 28; August 4, 11, 18) in the *New Orleans Times Picayune,* which were "adapted from my diary" regarding "the history of the part taken by a Creole battery . . . in the defense of Petersburg." The *New York Times,* 2/28/1912, reported, "Forty members of the Confederate Veterans' Camp of New York attended a meeting . . . at the Hotel Astor . . . and Eugene H. Levy . . . read a diary which he kept during the . . . siege of Petersburg." Levy kept a diary throughout the war but only the fourth book containing entries from 5/1/1864 to 5/19/1865 with 165 pages survived.[52] The first three diary books were in Levy's trunk at Alfred Moses's

Dry Goods Store located a 63 W Main Street, Richmond, which went up in flames when the city burned in April 1865. Married Pendleton, South Carolina, native Almeria Emma "Minnie" Moses on 9/5/1866 in Sumter, South Carolina. Returned to New Orleans and had four daughters and four sons. Worked with his father in the brokerage and banking business until his father's death in 1873. Levy became known as a prominent broker with a well-known business record until the *New Orleans Times Picayune* on 4/30/1876 reported he was planning to retire "with a view of restoring his health and strength by a few years of the quiet and repose of country life." He bought and cultivated a "small" sugar plantation near Lafayette, Vermilion Parish, from 1884-1886 but "was forced by ill health to sell out." Levy then moved to New York City, where he lost everything in the stock market crash of 1886. Worked for the *New York City Record* newspaper as a correspondent and with the *New Orleans Picayune* reporting on New York literary and financial matters. A member of the New York Press Club, Levy became well-known in newspaper circles as one of the most persistent talkers in the newspaper profession. Levy was described as being adept at controversy though having a humorous side. He was more than once elected president of the Ready Punster's Club, an organization of witty, jovial fellows. Levy gained some fame by publishing a one-act comedy called, "Endowed-Beds; or, An Hour With Jolly Hospital Surgeons." Later worked as an insurance agent on the twentieth floor of the Tract Society building, New York, where his friends heard he was weeping and shedding tears. "The veteran," reported the *Butte Weekly Miner*, 1/6/1898, "who has an aquiline nose, eagle eye and a high Websterian forehead, was holding a box at arm's length, while the tears trickled down his face. His friends offered him consolation, but he said, 'No, I cannot help weeping; tears are a relief.'" After some persuasion he told what happened,

> 'While in the army . . . a beautiful boy, only 16 years of age, fought in the ranks with him. He was a manly fellow and endured hardships like the rest of us. In battle, he did not mind the whistling of the bullets and a smile would be on his face as he charged the enemy. Sometimes a lock of his curly hair would be clipped by a passing minie [bullet], but he only laughed. He seemed to bear a charmed life, and in the last great battle, just before the surrender of Gen. Lee, he was missing . . . today I received a box by express from the boy soldier, my comrade in arms. With trembling hand I opened the box, and putting my face close to it, I began to cry. I could not help it.' 'What was in the box . . ?' 'Why, red pepper, and I got it into my eyes. That boy has a fine patch of red pepper near Lake Pontchartrain. Somebody, please, pour melted vaseline into my eyes.'

Levy later owned the Dixie Book Shop in the basement of 41 Liberty Street, New York City. On 12/29/1917, the *New York Evening Mail* published an article about the "cheery young old man," Levy, and his treasure house of books. "Queer old basement," went the article, "down a flight of steps much too steep for comfort, he has his den . . . blithe and gay . . . his eye is keen, he smiles often and never frowns and he finds more happiness, more contentment, more cheer in that basement among his ponderous books" where "bankers, great lawyers, masters of industry weid their way now and then to browse in bookland." Levy also produced an annual catalog of approximately forty-eight pages: "The Dixie Book Shop—Books and Pamphlets on Railroads, Canals, Investment, Speculation, Finance, Banking, Accountancy, Economics and Business Generally." After his first wife died Levy, at age fifty-six, married Marle Melanie Simpkins of Staten Island in August 1896 with the wedding taking place in the New York City mayor's office and officiated by New York's acting mayor. They lived at 223 West 125th Street, New York, and had a daughter named Helen. In April 1921 he filed for a Confederate Pension noting he was "now suffering from senile disability, confined to the house." Died 6/1/1921 in New York City and interred in the Confederate Veterans Plot,

Mount Hope Cemetery, Hastings-On-Hudson, New York.[53]

LEVY, JULIEN HILLEL, "DOC." Enlisted at Richmond, Virginia, 5/22/1862, Private. Previously served as a Private with Co. A, 1st Battalion (Dreux/Rightor's) Louisiana Infantry from 4/15/1861 until discharged 5/31/1861. Ordered into the service of the state on 2/27/1862 as 1st Lieutenant, Co. I, 3rd Regiment, 2nd Brigade, 1st Division Louisiana Militia. Born 8/3/1843 in Louisiana to Jacob "Jack" Louis Levy and Sara Edwitha Marks, one of nine children. Brother of Canonnier Eugene H. Levy with another brother Joseph C. Levy, a 2nd Lieutenant in the 1st Louisiana (Strawbridge's) Infantry, killed in the 1862 battle at Shiloh, Tennessee. Father was descended from a Jamaican family that settled in Charleston and later moved to New Orleans, where he listed his occupation as an exchange broker, but participated as a commission merchant in slave-trade and the manufacture of servant's clothing.[54] Clerked in New Orleans. *Levy Diary* on 12/8/1864 noted, "Doc [in the trenches at Rives's Salient, Petersburg] had been hit in the head by a minnie ball, but fortunately, the missile was spent." Paroled 4/13/1865 at Lynchburg, Virginia. In 1870 worked as a clerk in Vermilionville, Lafayette Parish, returned to New Orleans by 1880, single, working as a merchant. Married Corinne A. Davis of Petersburg, Virginia, (born in 1859 and the niece of the wife of Richmond's mayor, A. M. Keiley) and had four children. Migrated between Virginia and Louisiana until 1890s when the family settled in Sumter, South Carolina, and opened a successful grocery store. Died 2/27/1916 and interred Sumter Jewish Cemetery.

LINOSSIER, CLAUDIUS AUGUSTE. Enlisted at Donaldsonville, 9/13/1861, Private. Born 4/2/1838 in Assumption Parish to French native Claudius Linossier, a well respected citizen of Plattenville, Assumption Parish, and paid secretary of the Catholic Church of the Assumption in Plattenville.[55] Mother was deceased by 1850 at which time father ran a tavern and popular cockfighting pit of which, the *Assumption Pioneer,* 4/6/1851, recorded, "Mr. Linossier's rooster, instead of fighting to the end, ran from the pit like a coward." Father died in 1861. Young Claudius clerked and worked as a "coffee housekeeper" in Plattenville. Killed in battle of Fredericksburg on 12/13/1862 of which, Prosper Landry wrote, "And they succeeded in getting that gun out; but, alas! they did not succeed in getting out between shots, for as they emerged above ground the next shot came and, bursting in their midst, killed as good and brave a man as ever lived—Claudius Linossier."[56] Captain Victor Maurin reported, "It [the gun] was scarcely out, and not yet in position, when Canonnier Linossier fell, dead, pierced to the heart by a piece of shell. The fate of their comrade seemed to inspire my men with renewed determination."[57] Linossier's burial site is unknown though many of the unknown Confederate dead buried in the area were removed after the war at private expense into two local Fredericksburg cemeteries. Linossier's brother Julien (one year older) was a member of Nicholls's Phoenix Company (Company K) 8th Louisiana Infantry Regiment and in 1862 died of illness in Virginia. They were the last of the Linossier line in Louisiana.

LION, SYLVAIN. Enlisted at Donaldsonville, 9/13/1861, 6th Corporal. Born ca. 1841 in Forbach, France, immigrated with family in 1843. Lived with family and worked in Donaldsonville for father who was a dry goods merchant specializing in cloth and styles from New Orleans and the north until the store burned down on 6/21/1861.[58] On sick furlough in Louisiana beginning in January 1862 and carried AWOL in July 1863. Married before the war to Celestine Lalande and had a daughter born on 9/29/1862. Under the name of Elie Lion he, along with Canonnier Victor Fouin, were arrested by Union officials and released during the war "upon the insistent demands of New Orleans' French consulate" since "many

Lafourche country men claimed French citizenship."[59] Lion became a United States citizen in 1863. Married second wife Victorine (a native of France) in 1867 and lived first in the 2nd Ward, then the 9th Ward of Galveston, Texas. Worked as a clerk and dry goods merchant and in 1883 associated with the Block, Oppenheimer, and Company, one of the leading wholesale dry goods and boot and shoe houses in Galveston until it failed in 1887. Had five daughters and two sons born in Galveston. Served as a trustee for the Knights of Honor, Galveston Lodge 774 and a trustee for the Independent Order of B'nai B'rith, Zacharias Frankel Lodge 242. Believed to have died in Galveston between 1910 and 1920.

LOEB, HENRY. Enlisted at Donaldsonville, 9/13/1861, Private. Born 6/25/1833 in Edenkoben (near Frankfurt) Germany. Clerked in Donaldsonville. *Levy Diary* on 9/19/1864 noted he "met . . . Loeb" in Richmond. Received Certificate of Disability for inguinal hernia dated 11/12/1863 and ordered to report to Salisbury, North Carolina, for Recruiting Service by Special Order 302/30. Paroled 6/6/1865 in Monroe, Ouachita Parish, Louisiana. After the war became a dry goods dealer in partnership with the Lemann Family of Donaldsonville, the establishment being "Grand Bazar . . . le Magnifique etablissement."[60] Married a Prussian girl by the name of Lenora. The *Donaldsonville Chief*, 5/26/1877, reported he was "rotund, smiling, and serene." Died 9/18/1878 of yellow fever in Donaldsonville and interred Bikur Shalom Cemetery, Donaldsonville.

LOVE, THOMAS S., "TOM." Enlisted at Williamsburg, Virginia, 3/8/1862, Private. Previously served as a Private (company teamster) with Co. F, 1st Battalion (Dreux/Rightor's) Louisiana Infantry from 5/18/1861. Born ca. 1838 near Brunswick, Ireland. Clerked in Darrow, Ascension Parish. *Levy Diary* noted he and Love on 1/4/1865 "went on a voyage of discovery" in the area of High Bridge and Farmville, Virginia, and that Love was furloughed on 2/19/1865 "to be married." Paroled ACH, 4/10/1865.

LYND, ERNEST P. Enlisted at Mobile, Alabama, 6/15/1863, Private. Born ca. 1846 in Louisiana, likely in New Orleans as his father, Robert Lynd, was a "Health Commisioner" for the city. Two brothers served in Company C, Orleans Light Artillery Regiment. Attended Spring Hill College in Mobile, Alabama, from 1860. Appears to have escaped capture at the end of the war. After the war worked as a clerk living with father in the 6th Ward of New Orleans. Married Alice A. Sago in 1873 and had three sons and four daughters while working as a car driver for the New Orleans and Carrollton (streetcar) Railroad. Moved to Biloxi, Mississippi, in 1895 with their six living children ages nine to twenty-three. The *Mississippi Dailey Herald*, 2/9/1901, reported Lynd was "a well-known and respected citizen." Died on 2/7/1901 at 11:55 p.m. at home on Croesus Street between Front and near Water Street in Biloxi, Mississippi. Interred in the Biloxi City Cemetery.

MARKS, WILLIAM MARTINEAU. Enlisted at New Orleans, 4/16/1862, Private. Previously served as Captain of the Hope Guards (Assumption Parish) 1st Brigade, 2nd Division, Louisiana Militia Troops from 8/24/1861. Born 4/14/1825 in Edge Hill, Liverpool, England, to John Marks and Rebecca Boyd, and arrived in the United States at thirteen years of age. School Master living in Plattenville, Assumption Parish. Captured in Jackson Hospital, Richmond, 4/3/1865 (turned over to Provost Marshal on 4/29/1865) and remained in Jackson Hospital until released in May 1865. Married to Aurela Blanchard on 11/26/1851 and had five daughters and a son born before enlistment. After the war had three more children with Robert Edward Lee Marks born on 2/20/1866. The *Assumption Pioneer*,

9/5/1880, reported he was "a teacher for many years and after retirement . . . a notary." An advertisement by Marks in English and French announced: "School, For Classical and Commercial Education. Situated one mile below Napoleonville, Parish of Assumption. W. M. Marks, Teacher. The course of instruction embraces deportment of useful and polite learning in the English, French, and Spanish languages; and parents may confidently rely on the experience, industry, and professional tact of the teacher, who is well known as an Educator throughout this district, Corporal chastisement is never applied."[61] Died 9/23/1880 in Plattenville and interred Assumption Catholic Cemetery, Plattenville. The *Assumption Pioneer,* 10/2/1880, reported he was "an upright, honorable, pure Christian gentleman." Son John served in the Louisiana House of Representatives from 1896-1908.

MAURIN, VICTOR AUGUSTE. Enlisted at Donaldsonville, 9/13/1861, Captain; promoted Major on 3/14/1864 (by order of CSA Secretary of War) to date from 2/27/1864. Born 10/2/1818 in Donaldsonville, the oldest of four sons with two sisters born to Victor Marie Maurin, a son of Baron Jacques Marie Joseph Maurin, a native of Apt, Department of Vancluse, France, and sheriff of Donaldsonville (June 1820-August 1827) and Elizabeth Anne Slattery of Johnstown, New York, daughter of Sir John Slattery of Kiltinnin, Limerick, Ireland. Went to school at the Academy of Donaldson and in Ogdeuburg, New York and the College d'Iberville.[62] A successful Donaldsonville retail and wholesale grocer with a store on Mississippi Street between Lessard and Cabahanosse and a stand on Mississippi Street opposite the Theatre.[63] He was also the steamboat agent for the New Orleans and Lafourche packet steamer *Fanny Sparhawk* in 1855.[64] In 1850 at age thirty-two Maurin was described as "a gentleman" by a "loyal Louisianian."[65] He served Donaldsonville as postmaster from 1850 to 1853, an alderman and city treasurer, mayor for two terms from 1859 until his resignation in 1861. On 11/8/1852 married Lise Vive, educated in New Orleans at the Ursulines Convent, on her father's plantation Belle Alliance in Assumption Parish, the wedding conducted by Rev. Charles Boglioli, C. M.[66] They had two sons and three daughters with two dying before the war. A third son, Eugene Charles, was born on 1/29/1862. Son Louis Auguste was born on 8/14/1866 with another son and daughter born in 1870 and 1872. Confederate Brigadier General Roger A. Pryor distinguished the officers who he "thought worthy of promotion" in July 1862 after the battles around Richmond and reported: "Capt. V. Maurin, of the Donaldsonville Artillery, attached to my brigade, exhibited himself a most courageous and capable officer."[67] The general of artillery in the Army of Northern Virginia reported Maurin was "an officer of true merit."[68] Returning to Virginia from furlough in April 1865, Maurin learned of the surrender of the army under Lee at Appomattox. He then volunteered his services as an escort to the wife and family of Confederate President Jefferson Davis and was consequently captured with the President's party at Irwinville, Georgia, on 5/10/1865. Maurin was imprisoned

Courtesy of Mr. Charles Coates, Baton Rouge, La.

at Fortress Monroe, Virginia, as a result and subsequently transferred to Fort McHenry in Baltimore, Maryland. He was released on 7/20/1865 after taking the Oath of Allegiance and giving his parole of honor to report whenever called upon and to report weekly by letter his whereabouts to the United States secretary of war. Again a retail dealer and successful merchant after the war, Maurin was an honorary member of Donaldsonville's Phoenix Fire Company and godfather of its fire engine *Katie.* Died on 3/9/1875 "suddenly at 2 p.m." of "heart disease" at home in Donaldsonville. Interred in AOL. The *Donaldsonville Chief,* 3/13/1875, reported,

> The funeral . . . was perhaps the largest ever seen in Donaldsonville, the numerous attendance indicating the universal respect and admiration felt for the estimable deceased . . . maintaining during all the long period of his life a character for the strictest integrity, benevolence, courage, public spirit, and all the attributes that go to form the exemplary citizen, successful tradesman and model man . . . of the late war . . . in the Confederate service as Captain of the Donaldsonville Cannoneers . . . became noted for heroic conduct upon the field of strife . . . promoted to Major, and would have doubtless attained still higher rank but for his modest and unassuming disposition which led him rather to shrink from notoriety than court it. As a soldier he was as brave as the bravest, a strict disciplinarian, though neither cautious or inhumane, and was beloved by all the men of his command.

Two of his sons were later elected and served as mayors of Donaldsonville, Victor (1883-1886, two terms) and Charles (1905-1911, four terms). Due to "Financial reverses" Mrs. Maurin was allowed a Confederate Widow's Pension in 1914, which she received until dying on 10/7/1916. On her application, son Edmund noted his father was mentioned in *The War of the Rebellion: A Compilation of the Official Records of the Union and Confederate Armies* (130 Volumes) in the following, Series I, Volumes 2, 11, 19, 21, 27, 29, 46, 49, 51, Series II, Volume 8.

McCOY, JOHN S. Enlisted at Williamsburg, Virginia, 3/8/1862, Private. Previously served as a Private, Co. B, 1st Regiment Louisiana Volunteer Infantry, transferred 4/28/1861 to Co. C, 1st Battalion (Dreux/Rightor's) Louisiana infantry. Born ca. 1836 in Nashville, Tennessee. Clerked in New Orleans. Black eyes, black hair, dark complexion, 5'6". Paroled ACH, 4/10/1865.

McCULLOUGH (McCULLET), ALEXANDER, "ALEX." Enlisted at Donaldsonville, 9/13/61, Private. Born ca. 1825 in Ireland. Worked as a laborer in New Orleans and presumably on Donaldsonville's riverfront. Wounded in battle at Sharpsburg, Maryland, on 9/17/1862. Appears to have escaped capture at the end of the war. Signed muster roll with 'his X mark.'

MELANCON, ALFRED PROSPER. Enlisted at Donaldsonville, 9/13/1861, Private. Born 1/5/1839 in Ascension Parish to Marcelin Melancon and Mathilde Melancon, the second youngest of four sons and a sister (two years younger) who married Canonnier Jules Guedry. Clerked in Donaldsonville. Mortally wounded in battle at Sharpsburg, Maryland, on 9/17/1862. *Landry Diary* recorded, "Alfred had his leg cut off by a shell and he died some days after." Captured and paroled by provost marshal general, Army of the Potomac on 9/30/1862. Subsequently died of wound. Before the war Alfred lived with his widowed mother, who died in Donaldsonville at "age 50 and a few years, buried 25 November 1864."[69] Jules and Victorine Melancon Guedry had a son born 12/13/1865 and named him Alfred.

MEMINGER, LOUIS. Enlisted at Yorktown, Virginia, 4/1/1862, Bugler. Possibly detached to the company on 2/1/1862 from service as a Private, Co. F, 1st Louisiana Zouave (Coppen's) Infantry Battalion from April 1861. Born ca. 1816 in Strasbourg, France. Cooper in New Orleans. Gray eyes, dark hair, dark complexion, 5'7". Slightly wounded at battle of Gaines's Mill on 6/27/1862 during the Seven Days' Battles for Richmond. Discharged on 3/25/1863 on Surgeon's Certificate due to cataracts and decay of eyesight.

MENSON, THEOPHILE. Enlisted at Donaldsonville, 9/13/1861, Private. Born ca. 1840 in Louisiana. Lived in Donaldonville and listed his occupation as a farmer. Hazel eyes, brown hair, dark complexion, 5'5". Paroled ACH, 4/10/1865. The *New Orleans Item*, 8/29/1893 reported Theophile Monson, a New Orleans butcher located on Magazine Street at the south east corner of Gaiennie Street (from 1875 to 1893) died on 8/25/1893 at his residence on 41 Gasquet (now Cleveland) Street, New Orleans. Name also spelled as Manson and Mauson in CSR.

MESTAYER, FRANÇOIS JULES. Enlisted at Mobile, Alabama, 10/22/1863, Private. Born 7/29/1844 in Iberia Parish to wealthy planter François Mestayer, who was born in 1800 in Saint Domingue, and Euphemie Ida Meyer from St. Martin Parish, the second oldest and only son of five children. A student in St. Martinsville and lived in Fausse Point, Iberia Parish. Paroled ACH, 4/10/1865. Married Philomene Corine De Cuir on 6/29/1868 and had one son. After the war lived in New Iberia, Iberia Parish. Died 2/15/1888 in New Iberia.

Courtesy of Confederate Memorial Hall.

MIOTON, JOHN STEPHEN, "JOHNEE." Enlisted at Mobile, Alabama, 6/11/1863, Private. Born 12/10/1845 in New Orleans to François Nicolas Marc Mioton and Catherine Sarah Irma Johnson, the second and last son of five siblings. Brother to Canonnier Seymore Mioton, both being students in New Orleans. Hazel eyes, brown hair, fair complexion, 5'5". Canonnier Eugene Levy described him as "Fond and Petit" and "Faithful."[70] Captured during battle of Fort Gregg, Petersburg, Virginia, on 4/2/1865 and released 6/10/1865 from Point Lookout, Maryland, prisoner of war camp after taking Oath of Allegiance. Joined BAANV (Application No. 275, 2/21/1877), stated he arrived at Gettysburg "on the 2nd day of July 1863 and served . . . up to the Siege of Petersburg. When I was attached as infantry to form part of the garrison of Fort Gregg. Was taken prisoner at Fort Gregg on the 2nd of April 1865." Joined UCV as a member of Louisiana Division, Army of Northern Virginia Camp No. 1. Served camp as a delegate to UCV's Annual Meeting and Reunions and as financial secretary, eventually elected colonel and camp commander. On 10/19/1902 the *New Orleans Times Picayune* reported he along with Canonniers Prosper Landry and E. C. Cooley were each appointed aide-de-camp with the rank of major to the commanding general of the Louisiana Division, UCV. In 1893 was one of eight pall bearers who carried the remains of Jefferson Davis, the lamented president of the Confederacy, when they were removed from the BAANV's Tomb in Metairie Cemetery, New Orleans, to reinterment in their final resting place in Hollywood

Cemetery, Richmond.[71] Mioton has an entry in the Biographical Chapter of *Confederate Military History, Volume XIII, Louisiana, Extended Edition* (Atlanta, GA 1899) pages 511-512. Returned to New Orleans after the war and married Marie Georgiana Lanaux on 6/3/1867 at Annunciation Catholic Church, New Orleans, and had four sons and two daughters. On his Confederate Pension Application in 1915 he noted his children "all married." Worked for the New Orleans Insurance Association as a clerk. Mioton's papers and relics were displayed at Confederate Memorial Hall in New Orleans[72] with the *New Orleans Daily City Item*, 4/22/1891, reporting he donated to the Historical Association, "A Confederate Haversack, canteen and mess—thin, worn in service . . . by John S. Mioton, Donaldsonville Artillery." Son John Jr. served in the Louisiana House of Representatives from 1904-1908. Died of heart disease at home, 2013 Ursulines Street, New Orleans, at 1:30 p.m. on Armistice Day, 11/11/1918. Interred St. Louis Cemetery, No. 3, New Orleans.

Removal of the remains of Jefferson Davis.
New Orleans Times Picayune, May 28, 1893

MIOTON, ETIENNE SEYMORE. Enlisted at Mobile, Alabama, 6/11/1863, Private. Born 6/3/1844 in New Orleans to François Nicolas Marc Mioton and Catherine Sarah Irma Johnson, called Seymour, he was the oldest of two sons and five sisters. Brother to Canonnier John S. Mioton, both being students in New Orleans. *Levy Diary* on 5/15/1864 noted while marching twenty-three miles past Louisa Court House and near Tolersville, Virginia: "Having no shelter, Seymour [Mioton] and myself went to the nearest house and after a long engagement were allowed to spread our blanket on the floor." Paroled 4/13/1865 at Lynchburg, Virginia. Married Marie Theodosia Ulmo on 6/13/1868 at St. Anne's Catholic Church in New Orleans. A son, Seymour, was born ca. 1869. Lived at 7 (now 1107) Columbus Street in New Orleans and employed as a cotton sampler. Suffered from dementia and committed to insane asylum at Jackson, Louisiana, on 6/22/1890. Died two months later on 8/31/1890 of "Disease of the lungs, caused from cold" and interred St. Louis Cemetery, No. 3, New Orleans. Son married Mary Velez in New Orleans on 6/29/1891. Widow received a Confederate Widow's Pension in 1902.

MOLLERE, JEAN BAPTISTE CAMILLE. Enlisted at Donaldsonville, 9/13/1861, 4th Corporal; elected 2nd Junior Lieutenant 9/7/1862, promoted (by order of C.S.A. Secretary of War) to Junior First Lieutenant 3/22/1864 effective 2/27/1864. Born 5/6/1839 in Ascension Parish to Jean Baptiste Mollere, an original member of the *Canonniers de Donaldson* and Sergeant Major in 1848, and Victoire Alsina Gaudin, the oldest of eight children. His sponsor or Godmother was father's half-sister, the mother of Canonnier Clement Israel. Paternal and maternal g g g grandfather was from New Orleans and an officer of Militia at St. Gabriel, Iberville Parish, and g g grandfather was a brother to Victor Maurin's mother-in-law. Educated at St. Mary's of the Barrens Seminary in St. Louis, Missouri, where it was thought he would be a "model priest." In December 1858 as a nineteen year old he headed one of four groups for the Catholic Church's Association for the Propagation of the Faith in Assumption Parish.[73]

Lived in the 4th Ward of Ascension Parish near New River Bayou with grandfather Edward Gaudin, father, and other family members. Probably a planter when the war began but also doing notary work. Hazel eyes, dark hair, dark complexion, 5'8". Canonnier Private Eugene Levy in the *New Orleans Times Picayune*, 8/11/1902, wrote, "Lieutenant Camille Mollere, the most popular officer of the command." *Levy Diary* on 1/3/1865 near High Bridge noted, "At dark, fifteen of us headed by Lieut. Mollere set out to respond to the invitation to pass the evening at George Vaughan's." *Levy Diary* on 3/31/1865 reported, "Nothing of interest had happen . . . except the shooting of a deserter by a detachment of my comrades under Lt. Mollere." Paroled ACH, 4/10/1865. Joined BAANV (Application No. 383, 2/17/1878) stated he "was engaged in all battles and campaigns of the company from Yorktown to Appomattox Court House where I surrendered." Captain Victor Maurin in his battle report of Fredericksburg acclaimed Mollere's "gallant conduct."[74] Joined UCV as a member of Major Victor Maurin Camp No. 38 and served Camp as a delegate to UCV's Annual Meeting and Reunions. After the war engaged in sugar planting in the 4th Ward of Ascension Parish, then filled successfully the offices of postmaster (assuming charge of the office from *Canonnier* servant Louis Lefort) and chief of police in Donaldsonville. Married Adele Michael Israel (2nd Degree Consanguinity) and the sister of Canonnier Clement Israel on 9/24/1867 in the Donaldsonville Catholic Church. Had three daughters (born 1868, 1870, and 1881) and four sons with two dying in infancy and the others, it seems, at a young age. In 1890 three daughters, two sisters, and mother lived with him and his wife. The *Donaldsonville Chief*, 9/15/1906, reported, "By faithful performance of duty and the exhibition of soldierly qualities of the highest order he earned promotion to the rank of First Lieutenant before the surrender at Appomattox." Died 9/9/1906 at nine o'clock in the evening at Donaldsonville and interred in AOL. The *New Orleans Daily Picayune*, 9/11/1906, reported, "Few citizens of this place were so well and favorably known and as universally esteemed as this gallant old Confederate soldier . . . in his passing away the community suffers the loss of one of its most loyal citizens and a gentleman in every sense of the word . . . the funeral . . . was attended by a large concourse of sorrowing relatives and friends. Major Victor Maurin Camp No. 38, U. C. V. . . . paid the last respects to the memory of their departed comrade by attending the funeral in a body."

MOLLERE, JOSEPH DEFOSSAT, "DUFFOSARD." Enlisted at New Orleans, 4/16/1862, Private. Born 9/27/1842 in Assumption Parish to Joseph François Mollere and Marie Osite Mollere, the youngest of three sons and two daughters. Mother died when he was three years old. Paternal and maternal great-grandfather was from New Orleans and an officer of Militia; paternal grandfather a captain of militia at St. Gabriel, Iberville Parish, and a brother to Victor Maurin's mother-in-law. Second youngest brother served in Company H, 2nd Louisiana Cavalry. Worked as a laborer in Assumption Parish. Hazel eyes, black hair, dark complexion, 5'6". *R. O. Landry Diary* recorded he was with the wagon train and captured on 7/5/1863 by enemy cavalry near Greencastle, Pennsylvania, during the Gettysburg Campaign. Sent to Fort Delaware, Delaware as a prisoner of war. Released 6/9/1865 after signing (by X mark) the Oath of Allegiance. Joined UCV as a member of Major Victor Maurin Camp No. 38, later transferred to Gen. Francis T. Nicholls Camp No. 1142. Sugar Planter near Bertie in Assumption Parish and listed in Bouchereau's *The Louisiana Sugar Report, 1870-1917.* Married widow Pamila Templet on 2/22/1876 at Plattenville, Assumption Parish, witnessed by Canonnier Hypolite Templet. Confederate Pension application in 1909 stated he was married with no children while living in Plattenville, where he worked at "Hard labor daily—when able." Entered Camp Nicholls Soldier's Home, New Orleans, on 10/31/1917. Died 6/19/1919 in Charity Hospital, New Orleans. The *New Orleans Times Picayune,* 6/20/1919, reported friends and acquaintances attended his funeral held at the Soldier's Home with interment following in the Soldier's Home Tomb, Greenwood Cemetery, New Orleans.

MONNOT, ERNEST L., "ED." Enlisted at New Orleans, 4/16/1862, Private. Born 4/30/1840, the second of three sons along with a sister who died in infancy to Dr. Charles Claude Monnot, a native of Besancon, France, and a physician of note. Dr. Monnot served in 1813-1814 as a sub-aide and major health officer of the 93d Regiment of the Line in Napoleon Bonaparte's army and was praised by the regimental commander for "his zeal, his talent and his devotion to duty." When Napoleon was exiled to St. Helena, Dr. Monnot came to Louisiana and in 1823 was appointed surgeon of the 7th Louisiana Militia Regiment by the governor. He married an Acadian, Josephine Bourgeois, and while practicing his profession superintended his plantation, Vaufrey, at Bertie, a mile and a half below Napoleonville, Assumption Parish. An incident in the life of Dr. Monnot was his capture by the noted smuggler and pirate Jean Lafitte, who came down Bayou Lafourche to the vicinity of Napoleonville and being in need of a physician on his vessel kidnapped the doctor. After a short and exasperating captivity, Dr. Monnot managed to return to his family. It was written of the "good doctor" that he trained his young wife "in the art of handling mortar and pestle. 'Quick, Josephine,' he would tell her, 'We need more quinine. There are five with fever at the Charlet's and six at the Boudreauxs'."[75] Dr. Monnot died in 1847. His son Ernest completed his education in New Orleans at Louisiana College and afterward (in 1858) at the Audubon College. He then returned to the family's plantation and the beautiful home on the left descending bank of Bayou Lafourche in the 3rd Ward of Assumption Parish and assumed management of the place. *Levy Diary* on 3/31/1865 at High Bridge reported, "A scouting party of 5 men . . . sent out to report the progress of Sheridan's new raid against the railroads; my messmate, Monnot, is with them." Paroled ACH, 4/10/1865. Joined BAANV (Application No. 501, 12/20/1882) stated, at "High Bridge . . . until fall of Richmond; fell in with the retreating army, was present at the surrender at Appomattox Court House. Have my discharged signed by Col. [William M.] Owen." Joined UCV as a member of Louisiana Division, Army of Northern Virginia, Camp No. 1, later transferred to Major Victor Maurin Camp No. 38, then to Gen. Francis T. Nicholls Camp No. 1142, serving Camp 1142 as a delegate to the UCV's Annual Meeting and Reunions and as adjutant. Has an entry in Biographical Chapter of *Confederate Military History, Volume XIII, Louisiana, Extended Edition* (Atlanta, GA 1899) pages 513-515. Married Emelie Webster on 1/29/1861 in Assumption Parish, her mother was Clarisse Templet (Nathan) Webster, sister of Canonniers Hypolite and Camille Templet. Had a daughter, Lila. Wife died (probably during childbirth) in September 1861. Married

From Alcée Fortier's *Louisiana, Comprising Sketches of Counties . . .*

Lelia Lockett of Prince Edward County, Virginia, on 5/20/1869 and had three daughters. In a letter dated 8/8/1927 to the Confederate Pension Board for Mrs. Monnot, Lawrence H. Pugh wrote: "Since early youth, I have heard my uncle Governor [Francis T.] Nicholls, speak of Mr. Monnot's gallant service to the Confederacy, and he also used to claim, in a jocular way, that he was responsible for the marriage." Mrs. Monnot wrote that General Nicholls would later tell her she had he to thank for her husband as he ordered the Donaldsonville Artillery "sent to the High Bridge."[76] *Levy Diary* on 1/26/1865 noted Lelia was "a tall, fine looking woman . . . quite sensible and of a lively disposition." Monnot returned to the plantation at Bertie and became a prosperous planter at what became known as Elm Field where his wife Lelia named their 500 acre sugarcane field after her husband's initials. The Monnot's were neighbors to Canonnier Armas Triche's tract of land. Listed in Bouchereau's *The Louisiana Sugar Report, 1870-1917.* The *New Orleans Times Picayune,* 4/2/1911, reported he was "looked upon as one of Assumption's best authority on cane planting and his advice was sought, which he was always ready to give to any and all." President of the Bank of Napoleonville, president of The Pioneer Publishing Company (owner and publisher of the weekly newspaper *Assumption Pioneer*), for many years holder of the office of president of the Assumption Parish School Board (to which he was originally appointed to in 1877 by Governor Nicholls), and for some time a member of the Lafourche Levee Board. He was offered the nomination of state senator but declined. The *Assumption Pioneer,* 4/1/1911, reported "he was a man of spotless character, and . . . gallant." Canonnier Eugene H. Levy, after being transferred from the Petersburg trenches to the detachment at High Bridge on December 23, 1864, recorded in his diary, "I was duly installed as an inmate [tenant] of a little hut with Philo Viala and Ernest Monnot as mess mates." Thirty years after the war, Monnot received a letter from Levy the "old war comrade" and noted, "This letter is still cherished (in 1909) by the recipient on account of the beautiful sentiment it contains." Monnot died of "Hardening of Arteries" on 4/1/1911 at one o'clock in the morning in the house where he was born at Elm Field. Interred Assumption Catholic Cemetery, Plattenville. "Monnot/Lanier Family Papers" are located at Earl K. Long Library, University of New Orleans, New Orleans, Louisiana. Has entries in *Biographical and Historical Memoirs of Louisiana,* Volume II (Chicago, IL 1892), page 262, and *Louisiana, Comprising Sketches of Counties, Towns, Events, Institutions, and Persons, Arranged in Cyclopedic Form,* Volume III, Alcee Fortier, editor (Atlanta, GA 1909) np. Lelia received a Confederate Widow's Pension in 1927 and died at home on 3/8/1940. The Monnot's Elm Field home was demolished in 1970.

MONTERO, FRANÇOIS, "FRANK." Enlisted at Donaldsonville, 9/13/1861, Private. Born 8/2/1843 in Donaldsonville to Laurentio "Laurent" Montero, a native of Grettol, Spain, and Constantia Gomez, one of five sons and two daughters. Worked as a laborer in Port Barrow, across the bayou from Donaldsonville. Deserted while on furlough in February 1864 and carried AWOL. Edmund Maurin in a letter to the Confederate Pension Board dated 9/18/1914 wrote: "His services at Gettysburg deserves recognition. All his comrades united in endorsing his application and they certainly would not have done so if they believed he was deserter." Those Canonnier Comrades were Antoine Sobral, L. A. Landry, Esteve Hidalgo, and Herman Landry. He claimed on his application that while on furlough at home he was shot at and captured, and unable to leave Federal territory after being forced to take the Oath of Allegiance. Pension was denied because "he should not have gone into the enemy's lines so as to expose himself to capture." Married Mary Carbo in a civil ceremony and later in the Donaldsonville Catholic Church on 6/11/1871. The union had seven daughters and five sons between 1868 and 1886. Farmed and worked as a caulker while living in Port Barrow. Died of "Infirmities of Age" in Port Barrow on 10/5/1927 and interred in AOL.

MORELLI, TOMASSO, aka THOMAS MOREL. Enlisted at Donaldsonville, 9/13/1861, Private; promoted to 4th Corporal in March 1863 and to 3rd Corporal before the surrender. Born ca. 1835 in Italy. A sailor living in Donaldsonville. Dark eyes, dark hair, dark complexion, 5'10". Paroled ACH, 4/10/1865. Joined BAANV (Application No. 284, 5/18/1876), stated, "Was paroled at Appomattox Court House, April 10th, 1865." Included with Morelli's application was an endorsement letter from Captain Prosper Landry that said, "Being the best 'printer' in the company his services were very valuable, he was always called upon in every battle, and he was ever ready and willing to serve." He went on to write Morelli was a "good, honest, and brave man." Captain Victor Maurin in his battle report of Fredericksburg in December 1862 wrote his "skill as a gunner cannot be too highly prized."[77] Levy said in a reminiscence printed in the *New Orleans Times Picayune*, 7/21/1902: "In battle, nothing can be more inspiriting than when Morel, the crack gunner of the battery, with rich bass voice, starts up the 'Marseillaise.'" Wounded on 12/13/1862 at the battle of Fredericksburg and sent to Richmond on 12/15/1862 where he was admitted into Louisiana Hospital for treatment of a head wound. Released on 1/2/1863 and returned to the battery on the same day. Maurin identified him as Thomas Morel in the battle report though he signed the muster roll as Tomasso Morelli. In June of 1903 Salvatore Morelli, a twenty-two-year-old laborer, listed his father as Tommaso Morelli of Italy and his mother Virginia Giani on a Marriage License Application in Probate Court, Mahonong County, Ohio.

MORIN, JOSEPH EDWARD, "EDOUARD," "ED." Enlisted at New Orleans, 3/21/1862, Private. Born 9/2/1841 near Donaldsonville to Michel Morin and Antoinette Duverney, christened on 12/13/1841 in St. Louis Cathedral, New Orleans. Worked as a carpenter living in the swamps below Acy (at Pointe Acile that is today Seles Point Road) in the 7th Ward of Ascension Parish. Joined the Canonniers with father Michel and brother Mathieu. Gray eyes, dark hair, fair complexion, 5'8". On Confederate Pension stated, "I was captured at Green Castle . . . after the Battle of Gettysburg but escaped and made my way back to our lines—I was never a prisoner again until the final surrender at Appomattox." Paroled ACH, 4/10/1865. Member UCV, Gen. Fred N. Ogden Camp No. 247 and served camp as an alternate delegate to UCVs Annual Meeting and Reunions. The *Gonzales Weekly*, 2/12/1921, reported, "Served valiantly . . . and with his father and brother . . . took a daring and conspicuous part in the Battle of Gettysburg." Married Marie Eugenie Villeneuve and between 1870 and 1893 had five sons and four daughters while working as a small farmer cultivating cotton and corn and giving half his shares as rent. Children baptized at St. Joseph's Catholic Church in French Settlement, Livingston Parish, although they lived at Couteau Brown, Livingston Parish (now Laurel Ridge, Ascension Parish). In 1911 noted he was a "'small' farmer" with real estate valued at $250.[78] Upon becoming a widower he married Eugenie Templet.

Courtesy of Sylvia Degruy and Doris Melancon, Gonzales, La.

Applied for a Confederate Pension with his brother on 2/10/1899 and stated, "My eyesight is very defective owing to age and experience to which I was subjected." Died 1/29/1921 in St. Amant, Ascension Parish, survived by three sons and four daughters and a large number of grandchildren and great-grandchildren. Interred Holy Rosary Cemetery, St. Amant, where his tombstone inscription taken from Scott's "Lady of the Lake" reads: "Rest Soldier, Rest—Thy warfare is o'er."

Courtesy of Sylvia Degruy and Doris Melancon, Gonzales, La.

MORIN, MATHIEU. Enlisted at New Orleans, 3/21/1862, Private. Born 2/20/1843 and christened in Donaldsonville to Michel Morin and Antoinette Duverney. Worked as a carpenter living in the swamps below Acy (at Pointe Acile that is today Seles Point Road) in the 7th Ward of Ascension Parish. Joined the Canonniers with father Michel and brother Edward. Gray eyes, dark hair, dark complexion, 5'4". Applied for a Confederate Pension with his brother on 2/10/1899; stated he was "continuously with the command in all engagements in which it took part" and "was in line at Appomattox when General Lee surrendered, was paroled and returned to my home." Paroled ACH, 4/10/1865. Married Camilla "Mary" Camille Louveau in 1867 and had two daughters and nine sons with the youngest born in 1896. Children baptized at St. Joseph's Catholic Church in French Settlement, Livingston Parish, though they lived at Couteau Brown in Livingston Parish (now Laurel Ridge, Ascension Parish). There he, like his brother, cultivated cotton and corn, and "owned one horse and a few head of cattle." Wife died in 1901 and interred in the French Settlement Community Cemetery, Livingston Parish. In 1911 noted he was "sickly" while working as a laborer.[79] Died 11/22/1916 in St. Amant, Ascension Parish, and interred Holy Rosary Cemetery, St. Amant.

MORIN, MICHEL CELICOUR, "CALABASSE." Enlisted at New Orleans, 3/21/1862, Private; promoted 7/28/1862 to 6th Artificer. Born 10/22/1814 in New Orleans to Jean Eduardo Morin and christened at St. Louis Cathedral, New Orleans. Worked as a house carpenter living in the swamps below Acy (at Pointe Acile that is today Seles Point Road) in the 7th Ward of Ascension Parish. Joined the Canonniers with sons Edward and Mathieu. Gray eyes, gray hair, light complexion, 5'6". Honorably discharged on 4/2/1864 by Special Order 64, dated 3/17/1864, Adjutant and Inspector General's Office due to "old age." Married Antoinette Duvernay on 3/19/1835 in New Orleans and had five daughters and three sons. Returned home and worked as a laborer. After being a widower he married a widow, Elizabeth 'Isabelle' Sanchez Bourgeois, on 7/9/1877 in St Amant, Ascension Parish, by a Justice of the Peace and had two daughters (born in 1879 and 1882) while still living at Pointe Acile. Believed to be a member of UCV, Gen. Fred N. Ogden Camp No. 247. Applied for a Confederate Pension in October 1898 with Prosper Landry and L. A. "Tip" Landry witnessing on Morin's application his "habits good and free from dishonor." Prosper Landry endorsed a letter dated 4/21/1902 in which he wrote, "I knew Michel Morin before, during and after the war. In order to follow his two young boys, he enlisted at the age of [forty-seven years] . . . he was honorably discharged—he left his two sons in the field, to return to his old wife and a daughter who needed and <u>asked</u> his protection and support—he is probably the oldest [Confederate] veteran in the state and probably one of the most deserving." It seems because of state bureaucracy his application was never approved. With old age, paralysis, and unable to earn a living, he derived his support the last years of his life "by aid furnished by old army comrades and friends—and help provided by my children." Canonnier comrades noted and assisting on his Confederate Pension Application were Prosper Landry, Camille Mollere, Antoine Sanchez, L. A. "Tip" Landry, R. Octave Landry, and John S. Mioton. At ninety-one years old Michel Morin died of "age and fever" at his Pointe Acile home on 12/8/1905. Interred in Holy Rosary Cemetery, St. Amant.

MURPHY, JOHN J. Enlisted at Donaldsonville, 9/13/1861, Private. Born ca. 1830 in Ireland. Worked as a carpenter in Donaldsonville. Blue eyes, dark hair, dark complexion, 5'6". Paroled 4/13/1865 at Lynchburg, Virginia. Married before the war to Catherine O'Brien with one daughter and another daughter born on 4/24/1862. After the war worked as a laborer in the 5th Ward of St. James Parish, then moved to New Orleans (before 1870) where he worked as a warehouse keeper at 141 Magazine Street. Living with the Murphys after the war was a fifty-five-year-old black man from Virginia named "Doc Jordan" who described himself as a "horse doctor." Murphy died between 1870 and 1880. Doc Jordan remained with the family.

NEWCHURCH, JOHN EDWARD, "EDOUARD." Enlisted at Donaldsonville, 9/13/1861, Private. Born 5/13/1835 to Henry Smith Newchurch of Virginia and Elisa McCaskey of North Carolina, baptized 4/16/1843 at Assumption Catholic Church, Plattenville. Had three sisters and four brothers, two of whom enlisted with him in the Canonniers. One brother died as a toddler while the youngest brother joined and served with Company H, 2nd Louisiana Cavalry. Carpenter in Paincourtville, Assumption Parish. Paroled between 4/11 and 4/21/1865 at Farmville, Virginia. Married Felice Tonnellier on 4/13/1869 in Plattenville (sister of Canonnier Clarville Savoy's wife) and had three sons and six daughters, the first born in 1870 and the youngest in 1883. Later as a widower he married the widow Clara Girourd. The *Assumption Pioneer*, 5/19/1894, reported he "was a gallant soldier." Died 5/16/1894 at Brule St. Vincent, Assumption Parish, and interred St. Elizabeth Catholic Cemetery, Paincourtville.

NEWCHURCH, HENRY McCASKEY, "HENRI." Enlisted at Donaldsonville, 9/13/1861, Private. Born 12/31/1838 to Henry Smith Newchurch of Virginia and Elisa McCaskey of North Carolina, baptized 4/16/1843 at Assumption Catholic Church, Plattenville. Had three sisters and four brothers, two of whom enlisted with him in the Canonniers. One brother died as a toddler while the youngest brother joined and served with Company H, 2nd Louisiana Cavalry. Carpenter in Paincourtville, Assumption Parish. Wounded September 1864 during the Siege of Petersburg "in the arm in the right elbow." *Levy Diary* on 10/5/1864 noted he was "slightly wounded" and at the Louisiana Hospital, Richmond. Appears to have escaped capture at the end of the war. Joined UCV as a member of Major Victor Maurin Camp No. 38, later transferred to Gen. Francis T. Nicholls Camp No. 1142. Married Claire Elizabeth Blanchard on 11/22/1865 in Paincourtville (sister of Canonnier Severan Blanchard; Mathilda, wife of Canonnier Emile Bergeron; and Eulalie, wife of Canonnier Joseph Alfred Gautreaux) and had seven sons and two daughters. After the war lived in Napoleonville, Assumption Parish, working as a sugar plantation overseer, engineer, and carpenter. The *Assumption Pioneer*, 5/22/1909, reported he was "a good and worthy citizen." Died at home of pneumonia on 5/21/1909 at four-thirty in the evening in Paincourtville. Interred St. Elizabeth Catholic Cemetery, Paincourtville. *The Louisiana Planter and Sugar Manufacturer*, 5/29/1909, reported he "was well known throughout the Parish. His funeral was largely attended." Wife was allowed a Confederate Widow's Pension in 1909, which she received until her death on 10/15/1936.

NEWCHURCH, JOSEPH WILLIAM, "WILLIE." Enlisted at Donaldsonville, 9/13/1861, Private. Born 2/27/1842 to Henry Smith Newchurch of Virginia and Elisa McCaskey of North Carolina, baptized 4/16/1843 at Assumption Catholic Church, Plattenville. Had three sisters and four brothers, two of whom enlisted with him in the Canonniers. One brother died as a toddler while the youngest brother, a year younger than William, joined and served with Company H, 2nd Louisiana Cavalry. Worked as an apprentice mason in Paincourtville, Assumption Parish. *Levy Diary* noted he was "slightly wounded while . . . asleep inside his tent" on the night of 11/18/1864 during the Siege of Petersburg, Virginia. A surgeon at Jackson Hospital, Richmond, on 11/25/1864 documented that the wound was serious enough that he "will not be able to resume his duties in the field in a less period than two months." After his wound furlough was carried AWOL in February 1865. Married Emelie Savoy, 3/5/1867 in Paincourtville (witnessed by the bride's brother Canonnier Clarville Savoy) and had two daughters and four sons, the youngest born two and a half months before his father's death on 12/21/1881 near Brule St. Vincent, Assumption Parish, from "stomach and kidney troubles." Interred St. Elizabeth Catholic Cemetery, Paincourtville.

NICAUD, HENRY MICHEL. Enlisted at Mobile, Alabama, 6/21/1863, Private. Born ca. 1848 in Louisiana. Was a student at New Orleans. *Levy Diary* on 7/12/1864 noted during the Siege of Petersburg, Virginia, "Nicaud was kind enough to allow me to obtain a pass in place of himself." Paroled April 1865 at Lynchburg, Virginia. Joined BAANV (Application No. 543, 5/3/1884,) stated, "Enlisted in Mobile, Al., and in battle of Williamsport." Returned to New Orleans after the war and worked as a clerk and an "enumerator census." Lived with grandmother Clara dé Maupa and Aunt Clemence del Maupa, both French natives. Died 3/29/1891.

O'HARA, JOHN. Enlisted at Donaldsonville, 9/13/1861, 10th Corporal; promoted to 9th Corporal, then to Quartermaster Sergeant in March 1863. Born ca. 1831 in Ireland. Cooper in Donaldsonville. Deserted while on furlough in February 1864 and carried AWOL. Two small diaries belonging to O'Hara were found in the Civil Court Records at the Ascension Parish Courthouse in 2000 and now are archived in the Louisiana Division of Archives, Records Management, and History in Baton Rouge, Louisiana. O'Hara wrote in his diary, "Captured on the 8th day of February in 1864. Took the Oath of Allegiance to the United States Government on this day." Remained in Donaldsonville and worked as a laborer until his death on 2/25/1867. With no known heirs in Louisiana, a public sale of his possessions (one double barrel gun at $11.00 and one gold watch and chain at $90.00) was held in Donaldsonville on 7/20/1870.

OUBRE, PIERRE JUSTINIEN. Enlisted at Donaldsonville, 9/13/1861, Private; promoted 4th Artificer on 7/28/1862. Born 1/18/1838 in St. James Parish to Pierre Oubre and Justine Guidry, the second of five children. Worked as a butcher in Donaldsonville. Deserted while on furlough in February 1864 and carried AWOL. Married Helena Theriot on 6/3/1861 in Donaldsonville and had a son born in Donaldsonville on 3/29/1862. A daughter was born 10/30/1864 in Convent, St. James Parish, with five daughters and a son following. Died

8/22/1889 and interred in AOL.

OVERBY, ASBURY A. Enlisted at Fairfax Court House, Virginia, 9/2/1862, Private. Previously served as a Sergeant with Co. C, 1st Battalion (Wheat's) Louisiana infantry from 4/27/1861. Born ca. 1837 in North Carolina. Worked as a carpenter and lived in Trinity, Catahoula Parish. *Levy Diary* on 7/14/1864 at Petersburg noted, "Dined with Overby at the caisson camp, and returned to my gun before dark." Appears to have escaped capture though later paroled in Cumberland County, Virginia, on 5/16/1865 after taking the Oath of Allegiance. Married after the war and widowed. Worked as a carpenter in Marshall, Buckingham County, Virginia, with a one year-old daughter in 1870. A brother and resident of Washington D.C. on 9/30/1882, placed an information wanted ad in the *Donaldsonville Chief* seeking any intelligence as to Asbury's whereabouts; it noted that he "belonged to a good family."

PARKS, WILLIAM VINCENT. Enlisted at Donaldsonville, 9/13/1861, 4th Sergeant; promoted 1st Sergeant March 1863. Born 8/25/1827 in Lafourche Parish to James Stenad Parks and Marie Marguerite "Mary" Conway, the oldest of two boys. Worked as a cooper and carpenter in Donaldsonville. Hazel eyes, dark hair, sandy complexion, 5'9". Paroled ACH, 4/10/1865. Joined UCV as a member of Major Victor Maurin Camp No. 38. Married Hermina Celestine "Emma" Mollere (cousin to Victor Maurin's wife) 11/15/1859 in Donaldsonville that was witnessed by Canonnier John O'Hara. One son was born in 1860 and a daughter born 3/7/1866, followed by three more sons and two daughters. Entered Camp Nicholls Soldier's Home, New Orleans, on 5/11/1896 due to "old age" but left on own accord 2/2/1897. An endorsement letter to the Camp Nicholls Soldier's Home from the UCV, Major Victor Maurin Camp No. 38 stated he was "a good soldier all through the war." Died in Donaldsonville on 2/7/1898 of paralysis, which his wife on her 1907 Confederate Widow's Pension application claimed was "caused by exposure during the war." Interred in Major Victor Maurin Camp tomb, AOL.

PEREZ, FRANÇOIS, "ADOLPH." Enlisted at Donaldsonville, 9/13/1861, Private. Born ca. 1837 in France. Stave maker in Donaldsonville. Wounded severely in three different places at the battle of Fredericksburg on 12/13/1862 and died of wounds at Henningsen Hospital, Richmond, on 5/5/1863. Left $26.50 in effects and interred under the name of F. Perry in the Soldier's Section, Grave T-529, in Hollywood Cemetery, Richmond.

PIDOUX, CHARLES FELIX. Enlisted at Donaldsonville, 9/13/1861, 9th Corporal; placed in ranks as a Private by own request in October 1862. Born 7/25/1834 in New Orleans. Clerked in Donaldsonville. Dark eyes, dark hair, fair complexion, 5'0". Paroled between 4/11 and 4/21/1865 at Farmville, Virginia. Married Antonia Martinez on 3/19/1861 in Donaldsonville. In 1880 living in the 1st Ward of Ascension Parish working as a brick mason. Brother-in-law to Canonnier Désiré Carmouche (wives were sisters) with no children, but nephew François Carmouche, after his father's death, lived with them. Entered Camp Nicholls Soldier's Home, New Orleans, on 5/3/1886. An endorsement letter to the Camp Nicholls Soldier's Home from Captain Prosper Landry stated he did "faithful service as a Cannoneer of Donaldson during the whole war." Died in Soldier's Home on 5/24/1886 and interred in Soldier's Home Tomb, Greenwood Cemetery, New Orleans.

PLESENCIA (also PLAISANCE and PLACENTIA), NARCISSE VILLENEUVE CORNELL. Enlisted at Donaldsonville, 9/13/1861, Private. Born ca. 1840 in Louisiana. Worked as a farmer and lived in Donaldsonville. Dark eyes, light hair, fair complexion, 5'3". *Levy Diary* on 4/9/1865 recorded, "Squads of prisoners continue to be thrust in the open [fields]; among them Plesancea, Terio, and Dugas of Treile's section," captured at the Battle of Appomattox Station the evening before. Paroled between 4/11 and 4/21/1865 at Farmville, Virginia. In 1880 working as a laborer living in 11th Ward of Asusmption Parish (Bruly des Olivi) married to Sifroni (born in 1851) with son Oseme, five, and daughter Virginie, one. In 1920 living with wife "Sop" in 1st Ward, 2nd Precinct ("Down Town Road") Iberville Parish, still farming and "working on own account." Died at White Castle, Iberville Parish, on 9/14/1926.

QUEPROTTE (KEYPROUT), EUGENE. Enlisted at Yorktown, Virginia, 3/6/1862, Private. Previously served as a Private with Co. E, 1st Battalion (Dreux/Rightor's) Louisiana Infantry from 4/16/1861. Born ca. 1825 in France. Carpenter living in Houma, Terrebonne Parish. Black eyes, chestnut hair, sandy complexion, 5'2". Paroled 4/13/1865 at Lynchburg, Virginia. Married Rosema Geautreaux on 5/6/1867 in New Orleans and lived at 262 St. Peter Street. The Widow Queprot died on 11/7/1879.

RAMIREZ, MATHIAS NICOLAS. Enlisted at Donaldsonville, 9/13/1865, 5th Sergeant; promoted to 2nd Sergeant March 1863. Born 9/10/1818 and baptized in New Orleans at St. Louis Cathedral. Father was Francisco "Antoine" Silvester Ramirez, a native of the Canary Islands, and Maria Morino. One of eight children and brother of Canonnier Pierre Ramirez. Lived in Donaldsonville working as a laborer. Paroled 4/13/1865 at Lynchburg, Virginia. Married Victorine Louviere on 12/10/1842 in Convent, St. James Parish, with one son, Prosper, born in 1845. Died before 1870.

RAMIREZ, PIERRE ANTOINE DOLORES, "PETER." Enlisted at Donaldsonville, 9/13/1861, 1st Sergeant. Born 1/18/1825 in Plattenville, Assumption Parish, to Francisco "Antoine" Silvester Ramirez, a native of the Canary Islands, and Maria Morino. One of eight children and brother of Canonnier Mathias Ramirez. Listed his occupation as a "trader" in Donaldsonville. Dark eyes, gray hair, dark complexion, 5'4". Discharged 12/2/1862 on Surgeon's Certificate because of chronic rheumatism. Joined BAANV (Application No. 128, 3/21/1876), stated, "Served from Yorktown to Richmond . . . and was honorably discharged on account of old age and ill health in the beginning of December 1862." Married Carmelite Vega on 5/13/1844 at Plattenville, Assumption Parish, and had four sons before the war and twin sons born on 8/26/1864. Died 12/5/1876 in Donaldsonville and interred in AOL.

RICHARD, LOUIS AIMÉ. Enlisted at Donaldsonville, 9/13/1861, 2nd Artificer; promoted to Quartermaster Sergeant 9/6/1864. Born 8/31/1839 in Ascension Parish to Theodule Richard and Marie Emelina Dubourg, the oldest of two brothers and two sisters. Carpenter living in Donaldsonville. Gray eyes, black hair, fair complexion, 5'7". Played a wooden flute that he carried throughout the war.[80] Paroled with one horse at ACH, 4/10/1865. Married Rosalie Clara Cire on 4/25/1866 in Donaldsonville that was witnessed by Canonnier Numa Braud. Wife was the sister of Canonnier François "Bienvenue" Cire. Had three sons and four daughters. Worked as a carpenter and house builder after the war in Sunset, St. Landry Parish. In 1911 he was allowed a Confederate Pension noting he suffered "from the effects of the service." The *Donaldsonville Chief*, 3/29/1930, reported, "He was endowed with

Courtesy of John S. Hilbert, Los Angeles, Ca.

a very quiet and unassuming disposition . . . and was held in the highest esteem by all who knew him." Family members described him as "quiet, gentle, intelligent, and devoutly religious" and "that on only two occasions did he ever speak . . . about the war, and on both occasions he became very emotional and cried . . . the story concerned the day he saw Robert E. Lee . . . the incident . . . taken place at Appomattox."[81] A grandson remembered, "'Papa Me' (as we called Aimée) . . . was already a very feeble old man . . . he said very little and what little he did say he said in French to Mama. Mostly I remember him to be covered by bruises caused by repeated falls. I wonder how many times I helped Mama pick him off the floor and sit him in his favorite spot—an old rocking chair near a window in his room. My most vivid memory of him was what he said (in French) a few minutes after we had seated him in this spot. Mama's eyes filled with tears and she left the room without replying to him. . . . I asked her what he said. His remark has remained to me a symbol of the indomitable spirit of everyone to hold on to life regardless of a painful present and an even bleaker looking future. He had just seen a beautiful Cardinal on a tree limb outside his window, which prompted him to remark: 'The world is too beautiful to die.'"[82] After living in New Orleans for fourteen years he died a peaceful death at 4:15 p.m. in the afternoon of 3/28/1930 surrounded by his daughter, son-in-law, and their children at 7907 Nelson Street, New Orleans. Interred in AOL.

RICHARD, JEAN MARIE MATHIEULA, "JOHN." Enlisted at Donaldsonville, 9/13/1861, Private. Born 11/9/1838 in Ascension Parish but grew up in St. James Parish, the only son (with four sisters) of John Marie Richard and Elise Braud. Cooper in Donaldsonville. Black eyes, dark hair, fair complexion, 5'10". Paroled ACH, 4/10/1865. Joined UCV as a member of Major Victor Maurin Camp No. 38. In 1870 lived in the 2nd Ward of Ascension Parish on a farm working as a carpenter with Canonnier Désiré Landry. Married Virginie Landry on 1/3/1872 in Donaldsonville, witnessed by Canonnier Gontrand Dugas. Widowed and childless he married Elizabeth Landry on 1/30/1883 at home in Donaldsonville and had four daughters and two sons. Retired as a farm manager and in 1911 was allowed a Confederate Pension, noting on his application he had half a lot near McCall Plantation and was "tenant farming—unprofitable." Died of "Heart failure" on 7/11/1922 and interred in Major Victor Maurin Camp tomb, AOL.

RODRIQUE, PIERRE ADAM. Enlisted at Donaldsonville, 9/13/1861, Private. Born 7/1/1842 in Ascension Parish to Jean Baptiste Rodrigue and Genevieve Seraphine Amirati, one of eleven sons and three daughters. Clerked in Donaldsonville. Appears to have escaped capture at the end of the war. Married Jeanne Alexandrine Vantage on 9/25/1865 in Donaldsonville. Widowed and childless he married Elydia Clara Hebert on 6/10/1868 in Donaldsonville and had a daughter. Died 4/18/1879 and interred in AOL.

ROUGEAU, ADOLPHE AUGUSTE. Enlisted at Donaldsonville, 9/13/1861, Private. Born 8/28/1836 in Assumption Parish to Pierre Barre Rougeau, a native of Paris, France, Ascension Parish's constable and a Donaldsonville proprietor of a bookbinding and book rental business, and Josephine Albares, one of thirteen children. Brother of Canonnier Ignace

Rougeau. Worked as a bricklayer in Donaldsonville. Roll for January 1864 shows AWOL. Married Elodie Leblanc on 9/30/1856 in Donaldsonville that was witnessed by Aristide Joseph Landry, former congressman, state representative, and president of the Ascension Parish Police Jury. Had a son and three daughters with another daughter born on 6/10/1862. Widowed on 3/11/1864, he married the widow Mathilde Josephine Toups Barras on 1/10/1865 in Paincourtville, Assumption Parish, and had a son born on 10/30/1865. Rougeau in June 1865 was commissioned to buy an organ for the Donaldsonville Catholic Church and "was shipwrecked and lost everything."[83] Second wife died in May 1867, and three months later he married brother Ignace's widow Priscella Amelina Babin in Donaldsonville. Died 1/5/1868 and interred in AOL. A year later the Widow Rougeau married Canonnier Felix Babin.

ROUGEAU, YGNACE LOUIS, "IGNACE." Enlisted at Donaldsonville, 9/13/1861, Private; promoted 11th Corporal March 1863. Born 2/1/1840 in Assumption Parish to Pierre Barre Rougeau, a native of Paris, France, Ascension Parish's constable and a Donaldsonville proprietor of a bookbinding and book rental business, and Josephine Albares, one of thirteen children. Brother of Canonnier Adolphe Rougeau. Married to Priscella Amelina Babin. Clerked in Donaldsonville. Killed instantly by fragments of shell during the siege of Petersburg, 9/3/1864. Captain Prosper Landry in a letter to his wife wrote that Rougeau "had his head blown off by a cannon ball while he was aiming his gun. He was not only brave, but what is even more rare, he always faithfully fulfilled all his duties. Have someone tell his family this sad news."[84] Rougeau was the gunner on Piece 3, a Parrott rifle, served by William Ely as No. 1 and Eugene Levy as No. 3, according to Levy who also noted he "missed Rougeau, a splendid soldier."[85] Unknown burial location though almost certainly interred at nearby Blandford Church Cemetery, Petersburg, where 30,000 Confederate dead are buried with only about 2,000 identified.

RYBISKI, PIERRE CAESAR, "PETER." Enlisted at Donaldsonville, 9/13/1861, Private. Born ca. 1843 in Edgard, St. John the Baptist Parish, the second oldest of five sons and one daughter born to Antoine Theodore Rybiski, a native of Poland, and Adele Hymel. His father immigrated in 1837 and owned a large sugarcane and pirique tobacco plantation called Pape Vert. Father was one of the largest slaveowners in St. James Parish and after the war many of his former slaves settled in the Hahnville area of St. Charles Parish and retained the name "Robiski." Caesar listed his employment as a sugar maker while living in Donaldsonville. Blue eyes, black hair, fair complexion, 5'8". Paroled ACH, 4/10/1865. Married Sara Lee who died seven months after the birth of a daughter, Adele "Haley" Eudoxie Rybiski, on 1/27/1878. In September 1880 married Julia Bergeron at St. Michael's Catholic Church in St. James Parish while he and his daughter were living with his mother and father and a brother in St. John the Baptist Parish. Had a daughter, Altee, born in 1882 and a son Wittfield in 1883, both baptized at St. Michael's. Died 9/6/1908 in Kenner, Jefferson Parish, and interred Carrollton Cemetery, New Orleans.[86]

SALLES, BENJAMIN ADRIEN. Enlisted at Richmond, 11/8/1861, Private. Previously served as a Private with Co. F, 5th Texas Infantry Regiment that was mustered into service on 8/7/1861. Born 12/8/1836 in St. Mary Parish to Jean Bernard Sylvain Salles, a native of la Haute Garonne, France, and Louisiana-born Hortencia Carlin, the eleventh of fifteen children. Married Marie Anna Hirsch in 1858 in Vermilionville, Lafayette Parish, and had a daughter and son born before the war and a daughter and son after. Living in Vermilionville, Lafayette Parish in 1860. Transferred 5/30/1863 by Special Order 129/11 to Medical

Department, New Iberia, Iberia Parish, as a hospital steward. *Lafayette Gazette,* 10/26/1901, recorded he had a "robust constitution" and "always of cheerful, amenable temperament." It also noted "many good deeds were recorded in his favor. He was a charitable man and gave unstintedly to the needy." Joined UCV as a member of General Frank Gardner Camp No. 580, Lafayette. Operated with his wife a family style hotel in the 900 block of Lafayette Street, Lafayette (formally Vermilionville) and worked as a salesman for the Carthage Flour Milling Company of Carthage, Missouri. The *Lafayette Advertiser,* 10/16/1901, recorded he "always possessed the confidence and respect of all who knew him" and was "a good citizen." Died after a month-long sickness in the home (512 South Buchanan Street) of his son-in-law Dr. Hypolite C. Salles (Lafayette's first dentist) in Lafayette on 10/19/1901. Dr. Salles's home and office has since been moved to the Acadian Village in Lafayette. *Lafayette Gazette,* 10/26/1901, reported the veteran's "funeral was very largely attended." Interred St. John the Evangelist Catholic Cemetery, Lafayette.

SANCHEZ, ANTONIO RAYMOND RUFIN, "ANTHONY," "ANTOINE," "TONY." Enlisted at Donaldsonville, 9/13/1861, Private; elected Junior 2nd Lieutenant, 3/26/1863. Born 7/30/1834 in Ascension Parish to Pedro 'Pierre' Sanchez and Marie Oncal, residents of Valenzuela Dans La Fourche in Assumption Parish. Grandfather was a native of Aguimes, Canary Islands. One of nine sons and three daughters. Clerked in Assumption Parish. Dark eyes, dark hair, dark complexion, 5'4". Paroled with one horse at ACH, 4/10/1865. Joined BAANV (Application No. 511, 2/17/1883) stated that as a "private . . . participated in the following engagements: Seven Pines, Mechanicsville, Gaines's Mill, Fraziers's Farm, and Fredericksburg. Was then elected lieutenant and commanded my section in the battles of Gettysburg and Petersburg. Was cut off with General [Richard H.] Anderson's Corps from Burgess Bridge on Hatcher's Run and fought with it to Amelia Court House where I joined the rest of General Lee's Army and with it surrendered at Appomattox C. H." Joined UCV as a member of Baton Rouge Camp No. 17. Married Mary Hernandez in June 1855 at the Church of the Assumption, Plattenville, Assumption Parish, and had a daughter born in 1859 and a son, Antoine, born on 6/1/1861 and baptized at the Donaldsonville Catholic Church on 6/22/1861. After the war moved to Baton Rouge, East Baton Rouge Parish, and had four sons and five daughters. A son born on 2/9/1877 was named Francis Nicholls Sanchez. Worked as a jailer, deputy sheriff, and inspector and collector of markets for the city of Baton Rouge. It was recorded "he was an influential citizen who commanded unqualified popular esteem" and "served as a gallant soldier of the Confederacy during the entire period of the . . . war."[87] The *Baton Rouge States-Times Advocate,* 4/30/1913, reported he "served with distinction in the company." In his Baton Rouge home during his lifetime hung a frame containing a *Le Canonniers de Donaldsonville* button, his parole signed by W. M. Owen, BAANV certificate of service, and a five dollar Confederate note.[88] Died of acute indigestion on 4/30/1913 at four o'clock in the morning at a son's home in Alexandria, Rapides Parish. Interred St. Joseph's Catholic Cemetery, Baton Rouge.

SAVOY, CLAIRVILLE ADRIEN. Enlisted at Donaldsonville, 9/13/1861, Private. Born 2/24/1843 in Assumption Parish to Victor Savoy and Victorine Celestine Aucoin, one of five sons and two daughters. Worked as a laborer in Assumption Parish. Brown eyes, brown hair, light complexion, 5'9". Captured during battle of Fort Gregg, Petersburg, Virginia, on 4/2/1865 and released 6/19/1865 from Point Lookout, Maryland, prisoner of war camp after taking Oath of Allegiance. Joined UCV as a member of Major Victor Maurin Camp No. 38, later transferred to Gen. Francis T. Nicholls Camp No. 1142 and served as an alternate delegate to UCV's Annual Meeting and Reunions. Married Marie Felide Tonnellier on 10/22/1868 (sister of Canonnier John Edward Newchurch's wife) and had two boys and two girls. The *Assumption Pioneer*, 11/27/1909, reported he was "one of the most prominent citizens of Paincourtville and was greatly esteemed by every one in the community. He was gentle in his manners, and courteous and friendly to every one. He held many positions of trust through out his life and he never forfeited the trust reposed in him. He was a valuable citizen and an exemplary husband and father." After the war was a grocer, conducted a mercantile business, and ran the Paincourtville Bakery. Elected justice of the peace and held that office at the time of his death at nine o'clock in the evening on 11/20/1909 at home in Paincourtville, Assumption Parish. Survived by his wife and three children. Under the auspises of the Confederate Veterans, Knights of Columbus, Woodmen of the World, and Improved Order of Red Men, Savoy's funeral "was one of the largest held in Paincourtville for many years." Interred St. Elizabeth Catholic Cemetery, Paincourtville.

SAVOIE, JULES HOMERE. Enlisted at Williamsburg, Virginia, 2/28/1862, Private. Previously served as a Private with Co. E, 1st Battalion (Dreux/Rightor's) Louisiana Infantry from 4/16/1861. Born 1/24/1840 at Thibodaux, Terrebonne Parish, to Jourdan Savoie and Clemence Richard, one of nine children. Cooper in Thibodaux. Married Elizabeth Ellender on 7/12/1859 in Houma, Terrebonne Parish. Hazel eyes, dark hair, dark complexion, 5'8". In January 1864 carried AWOL, deserted after being on thirty-day sick furlough from Louisiana Hospital, Richmond on 11/7/1863.

SCHEUER, JONATHAN. Enlisted at Donaldsonville, 9/13/1861, Quartermaster Sergeant. Born ca. 1821 in Mayence, Germany. Married German born Johanna "Josephine" Lekesch, age twenty, in 1859 at New York City.[89] Moved to Donaldsonville and worked for the Lemann Family business. With Canonnier John Landry went into partnership known as "Scheuer & Landry, Dealers in Hardware, Plantation Dry Goods, &c., &c., &c.; Buggies, Carriages and Philadelphia Wheel Wrights."[90] Died in camp near Fredericksburg, Virginia, on 12/24/1862 and interred in the third row of the Soldier's Section in Hebrew Cemetery on Shockoe Hill, Richmond. The railing around the Soldiers' Section is known for its artistic and emblematic merit and described: "The posts are furled flags and stacked muskets, surmounted by the flat soldier cap of Confederate days. The railing between the post is of crossed swords and sabers, hung with wreaths of Laurel."[91]

SCHMIDT, ALBERT JULIEN. Enlisted at Donaldsonville, 9/13/1861, Private. Born 4/21/1833 in Louisiana to Gustavus Adolphus Schmidt, a prominent New Orleans attorney, historian, linguist, and native of Mariestad, Sweden, who settled in New Orleans in 1829. Father was a "noted International lawyer . . . established (1844) the state's first law school . . . a forerunner of Tulane Law School."[92] Mother was Melanie Seghers, second oldest son, with a sister and four younger half-brothers with one being Canonnier Oscar Schmidt, one year younger. Oldest brother Charles E. Schmidt (like his father a scholar and prominent New Orleans attorney) enlisted 3/8/1862 in Company G, Crescent Regiment, Louisiana Infantry, and was discharged 7/3/1862. Sister Euphrozine Julie married Pierre F. V. de la Barre of New Orleans in 1857 and purchased and settled on a plantation in Assumption Parish. Barre served in the 2nd Louisiana Cavalry.[93] Clerked and operated a bookstore at 93 Exchange Place in the French Quarter of New Orleans. The family lived in New Orleans and on a plantation at the Mississippi River near Bayou Sara (St. Francisville) in West Feliciana Parish. The bookstore continued in business after his enlistment and after New Orleans surrendered. The *New*

Orleans Times Picayune, 11/6/1862, reported the store had for sale "superior pictures, maps, portraits, etc., which are well executed, and well worth the attention of purchasers." Among the most prominent features for sale were Yankee "Lithographic likenesses of the heroes of the war" and, "A large size lithograph of Abraham Lincoln, President of the United States." Schmidt, on picket duty near Rapidan Station, Virginia, in November 1863 wrote a letter to his father in New Orleans: "If I could receive, one good blanket, some clothes and a little money from home; I would have nothing to wish for. If you could send me those things, dear father, you would oblige me exceedingly and would probably save me from sickness, this winter."[94] Schmidt visited the wounded Levy on 7/31/1864, a day after the Crater Battle at Petersburg, and wrote in Levy's diary: "How the ministering angels, those venerated women of the Confederacy, were there, to aid the surgeons and prayerfully close the eyes of the dead heroes."[95] Blue eyes, light hair, fair complexion, 5'6". Captured in Richmond while on light duty assigned to Surgeon General's Office, paroled on 5/17/1865. Returned to New Orleans and by 1866 working again as a clerk and operating the bookstore. From 1888 to 1892 wrote in French a series of letters to brother's family in New Orleans from "Retraite, Louisianaise." In 1900 was a patient in the New Orleans Insane Asylum. Died on 6/28/1911 and interred in St. Louis Cemetery No. 2, (Vault 3 me Alle a droite S. L. 27) New Orleans.[96]

SCHMIDT, OSCAR V. Enlisted at New Orleans, 4/15/1862, Private. Born ca. 1844 in Louisiana to Gustavus Adolphus Schmidt, a prominent New Orleans attorney, historian, linguist, and native of Mariestad, Sweden, who settled in New Orleans in 1829. Father was a "noted International lawyer . . . established (1844) the state's first law school . . . a forerunner of Tulane Law School."[97] Mother was Estelle Marie Mascey with three brothers and a half-sister and half-brother, Canonnier Albert J. Schmidt, one year older. Oldest was step-brother Charles E. Schmidt (like his father a scholar and prominent New Orleans attorney) enlisted 3/8/1862 in Company G, Crescent Regiment, Louisiana Infantry, and discharged 7/3/1862. A student in New Orleans. Sister Euphrozine Julie married Pierre F. V. de la Barre of New Orleans in 1857 and purchased and settled on a plantation in Assumption Parish. Barre served in the 2nd Louisiana Cavalry.[98] The family lived in New Orleans and on a plantation at the Mississippi River near Bayou Sara (St. Francisville) in West Feliciana Parish. Absent, missing, and captured at Gettysburg, 7/2/1863, and sent to Fort Delaware, Delaware, a prisoner of war. Reported exchanged with the sick and wounded men and sent to South Carolina Hospital in Petersburg, then transferred to Louisiana Hospital, Richmond. Obtained a sick furlough to Mobile, Alabama.[99] On muster roll for January 1864 carried AWOL. After the war listed in the New Orleans City Directory without an occupation, living with his father. Died at six-thirty in the evening of 11/16/1880 at 267 S. Rampart Street, New Orleans. Probably interred in family tomb, St. Louis Cemetery No. 2, New Orleans.[100]

SCHRAMER, JOHN MARTIN. Enlisted at Yorktown, Virginia, 2/1/1862, Private. Previously served as a Private in Co. F, 1st Louisiana Zouave (Coppen's) Infantry Battalion from 4/4/1861. Born ca. 1831 in Switzerland. Emmigrated from Le Havre, France, on ship *Nuremburg* and arrived in New Orleans on 3/23/1861. Listed his occupation as a farmer. Paroled ACH, 4/10/1865. Entered Camp Nicholl's Soldier's Home, New Orleans 5/17/1886. On Home application he claimed he "broke back at 2nd Manassas," but muster rolls carry him present for duty. Died at Soldier's Home of heart disease on 1/6/1887 and interred in tumulus BAANV, Metairie Cemetery, New Orleans. The marble tablet in the tomb spelled his name "Schroner." The Appomattox Parole spelled it "Schrouner." The Soldier's Home spelled it "Schraener."

SCHRIVER, ADAM H. Enlisted at Williamsburg, Virginia, 3/8/1862, Private. Previously served as a Private with Co. D, 1st Battalion (Dreux/Rightor's) Louisiana Infantry from 4/20/1861. Born ca. 1841 in Virginia. Listed his employment as a carpenter and boatman while living in Ouachita Parish. Blue eyes, light hair, light complexion, 5'9½". Captured at Hatcher's Run, 4/2/1865 and released from Point Lookout, Maryland, 6/20/1865 after taking Oath of Allegiance. Married Mary from Indiana and lived after the war in Weitzel County, Virginia. Moved to Mississippi and had a son and a daughter. By 1880 settled on five acres near Horn Hill, Limestone County, Texas, where he had another daughter and two sons. Worked as a carpenter until applying for and receiving a State of Texas Confederate Pension in 1906. Died 11/27/1927 at daughter's home in Groesheck, Limestone County, and interred Sec. H, Faulkenberry Cemetery, Limestone County, Texas.[101] Tombstone reads "Adam H. Schrivier, Landry's Co La Art CSA."

SOBRAL, ANTONIO MARCELIN, "ANTOINE," "LA FORTUNE." Enlisted at Donaldsonville, 9/13/1861, Private; promoted to 12th Corporal March 1863. Born 6/1/1844 in Lanhelas, Caminha, Portugal, to Richardo Louis Sobral (member of the Portugese army who took part in that country's revolution of 1848) and Hortencia Desylva. "From Portugal came news that a fortune had been bequeathed to the De Alfarez ["Dalferes" of Donaldsonville] family and they quickly dispatched a member to claim the inheritance. He was gone a long time and when he returned he brought back bad news and a wide-eyed little boy of ten years—no fortune . . . the little boy's quiet, shy way, and his big brown eyes warmed the hearts of the De Alfarez clan and they began to call their little cousin . . . 'la fortune' . . . Antoine's visit lengthened into years and when his uncle finally went back to Portugal, Antoine refused to go. He loved Louisiana and here he stayed."[102] Sobral clerked for and lived with the family of J. F. Tureaud (a store keeper) in Assumption Parish before the war. On Confederate Pension Application in 1908 stated he was wounded, "In the battle at Fredericksburg and at the Siege of Petersburg. First by shells or pieces of shells, second by an exploded shell. I was both times wounded in the head." Neither wound was officially documented though noted in *Landry Diary* and *Cire Diary.* Has an entry in *Biographical and Historical Memoirs of Louisiana,* (Volume II, Chicago, IL, 1892, page 397). The night before the surrender Sobral tried to escape at Appomattox Court House to join General Johnston's army but was captured and paroled at Farmville, Virginia, between 4/11 and 4/21/1865. Joined BAANV (Application No. 381, 2/17/1878), stated, "Promoted to Corporal [and] engaged in the battles and campaigns of the battery from Yorktown to Appomattox Court House." Joined UCV as a member of Major Victor Maurin Camp No. 38 and was one of the camp's lieutenants. Married Evelina Gonzales on 8/3/1868 and had three sons and five daughters. "After the war," it was written, "his means consisted of a wornout confederate suit, but he was not at all discouraged, and went to work on Magnolia plantation in La Fourche parish . . . until 1867 . . . went to Ascension parish, and was an overseer on Union plantation nine years, when he bought St. Amelie plantation. In 1881 he sold that plantation and bought Oak Alley [where he became] very successful as a sugar planter."[103] Oak Alley is a Greek revival style antebellum home with twenty-eight massive Doric columns around the house (seven on each side) that was built in 1837-39 on the west bank of the Mississippi River in St. James Parish. It is a popular tourist attraction today and noted for its twenty-eight evenly spaced giant live oak trees that are nearly 300 years old, which form a quarter-mile canopy from the Mississippi River to the house. "The house and grounds are a thing of indescribable beauty and the sunrise, seen from the upper front gallery through the long avenue of oaks, is a sight unparalleled anywhere."[104] Sobral made a good record as a brave and faithful soldier and was always a popular figure, and his many friends often gathered on the wide, cool verandas of Oak Alley to fight again the shared battles of the war. It was recorded, "Mr. Sobral and his Donaldsonville cronies fought those battles over and over every Sunday afternoon. They told long, tall tales which always ended in explosive laughter and: 'We gave those Yankees hell!'"[105] Bouchereau's *The Louisiana Sugar Report, 1870-1917* listed Sobral as a sugar planter at St. Amelie then Oak Alley Plantation. The *New Orleans Item*, 5/19/1891, reported Sobral, "a well-known planter . . . was severely injured while assisting in taking down a sugar mill, which he purchased for transfer to his Oak Alley plantation." He was buried "under the tumbling mass, breaking his right arm and left leg, and painfully bruising his neck, back and head." He sold Oak Alley in 1905 due to poor health and advancing years and lived the remainder of his life in a house valued at $200 in Donaldsonville.[106] In 1908 noted he was "living on money saved up as overseer." Died at home on 9/27/1918 and interred in St. James Catholic Cemetery, St. James Parish.

STANLEY, JOSEPH. Enlisted at Donaldsonville, 9/13/1861, 5th Artificer. Born ca. 1820s in Ohio, possibly Madison, Guernsey County; the Ascension Parish 1850 U.S. Census list age as thirty-five while the Ascension Parish 1860 U.S. Census list age as forty-one. Worked as a laborer on New River Bayou, 5th Ward of Ascension Parish and lived with a woman named M. Savoie, age forty-five, Azede Savoie, age twenty-three, and Louisa Savoie, age nineteen, and Seymore Lanon, age seventeen. Killed in battle at Beaver Dam Creek near Mechanicsburg, Virginia, Seven Days' Battles for Richmond on 6/27/1862. *O'Hara Diary* noted he was interred in the Soldier's Section M, Masonic Burial Ground, Hollywood Cemetery, Richmond. *Levy Diary* on 6/2/1864 noted, "On reaching . . . Mechanicsville, our route lay eastward by the Gaines's Mill Road. A few minutes march brought us to Ellerson's Mill where poor Stanley was killed two years ago." On May 17, 1869, *Ascension Parish Civil Records* documented in court at Donaldsonville that Major Victor Maurin and others witnessed the Vacant Succession of Stanley's property of, "Seven Hundred Dollars in gold valued at Nine Hundred and Ninety-Four Dollars in U.S. Currency." In 1870 a Louisa Savoie was living in Ohio.

SUAREZ, ANTOINE ANDRE, "TONY," "ANTHONY." Enlisted at Donaldsonville, 9/13/1861, Private. Born 11/19/1841 in Ascension Parish to Francisco Suarez of the Canary Islands and Augustine Rodrigue, with one sister and four brothers of which two died young. Brother of Canonnier John Sebastien Suarez and cousin to Canonnier Raphael Hilaire Suarez. Farmer in Assumption Parish. Wounded twice during the siege of Petersburg. First on 9/3/1864 when he was "slightly wounded in shoulder" and again on 11/19/1864 with *Levy Diary* noting he was "shot through the calf of his leg this morning." Appears to have escaped capture at the end of the war. Joined UCV as a member of Major Victor Maurin Camp No. 38. Married Anaize Acosta on 5/7/1866, witnessed by Canonnier Augustine Albares. Had two sons and a daughter. Died on his farm in A-Bend, 4th Ward of Ascension Parish on 2/18/1916, survived by his wife. The *New Orleans Times Picayune*, 2/22/1916 reported, "Major Victor Maurin Camp U.C.V. . . . attended the funeral in a body." Interred AOL.

SUAREZ, JOHN SEBASTIEN. Enlisted at Donaldsonville, 9/13/1861, Private. Born 4/21/1843 in Assumption Parish to Francisco Suarez of the Canary Islands and Augustine Rodrigue, with one sister and four brothers, of whom two died young. Brother of Canonnier Antoine Suarez and cousin to Canonnier Raphael Hilaire Suarez. Blue eyes, black hair, dark complexion, 5'1". Cooper in Donaldsonville. Paroled between 4/11 and 4/21/1865 at Farmville,

Virginia. Married Marguerite Gonzales on 2/22/1866 in Paincourtville, Assumption Parish, witnessed by Canonnier Esteve Hildago. The *Donaldsonville Chief*, 6/2/1883, reported he was "a respected citizen." Died 6/1/1883 in Port Barrow, Ascension Parish, and interred AOL.

SUAREZ, RAPHAEL HILAIRE. Enlisted at Donaldsonville, 9/13/1861, Private. Born 2/12/1834 in Ascension Parish to Antonio Suarez of the Canary Islands and Josephea "Josephine" Gonzales, the second youngest of five sons. Cousin to Canonniers Antoine and John Sebastien Suarez. Worked as a laborer in Assumption Parish. Appears to have escaped capture at the end of the war. Married Josephine Falgout on 1/13/1860 in Paincourtville, Assumption Parish, witnessed by Canonnier Oscar F. Demesme. After the war returned to Ascension Parish where he died on 10/3/1878 at eight o'clock in the evening. Interred AOL.

SUTHERLAND, COLLINS, "COLIN." Enlisted at Donaldsonville, 9/13/1861, Private. Born ca. 1833 (of Scottish descent) in Province of Nova Scotia, Canada. Worked as an overseer on a plantation in Assumption Parish owned by Marks Kilou, a wealthy retail merchant from France. Appears to have escaped capture at the end of the war. Married Mary J. (an English woman from New Brunswick) and in 1870 lived near Egg Point, (now Greenville, the county seat) Washington County, Mississippi. A few years later moved to Nova Scotia with wife and son; two daughters were born in Nova Scotia.

SYLVIA, G. Transferred from Company E, 3rd South Carolina "Palmetto" Battalion of artillery on 8/4/1864 but never reported to the battery.

TAYLOR, WILLIAM. Enlisted at Williamsburg, Virginia, 5/2/1862, Private. Previously served as a Private with Co. C, 1st Battalion (Dreux/Rightor's) Louisiana Infantry from 4/28/1861. Born December 1837 in Ireland and immigrated in 1851. Worked as a shoemaker in New Orleans. Gray eyes, dark hair, dark complexion, 5'9". Wounded at battle of Gaines's Mill on 6/27/1862 during the Seven Days' Battles for Richmond. Paroled ACH, 4/10/1865 and captured again. Imprisoned until 5/8/1865 when he surrendered his parole and took Oath of Allegiance in Alexandria, Virginia. Married in 1856 Ellen (Ella) Elizabeth Fulton, born ca. 1838 in Ireland and had a daughter born in 1859 and a son in 1861. Returned to New Orleans after the war and had six more children. Lived at 3014 Constance Street, New Orleans, where he died of "Heart failure suddenly" at five o'clock in the evening on 4/9/1906. Interred Greenwood Cemetery, New Orleans. On Confederate Widow's Pension Application in 1906 wife stated they were married 11/28/1870 in County Carlow, Ireland. She received a pension up to the time of her death on 7/22/1922 and was survived by two sons and three daughters.

TEMPLET, CAMILLE. Enlisted at Chancellorsville, Virginia, 6/16/1863, Private. Previously served as a Corporal with Co. H, 2nd Louisiana Cavalry from 9/1/1862 until captured 4/14/1863 at Bayou Teche (Battle of Irish Bend) near Franklin, St. Mary Parish, and sent to New Orleans for exchange. Born 10/22/1835 on the Templet Plantation a little more than a mile above Napoleonville on the left descending bank of Bayou Lafourche in the 3rd Ward of Assumption Parish to Florentin Templet and Clarisse Blanchard, with five brothers and eight sisters. Brother of Canonnier Hypolite Templet and brother-in-law to Canonnier Alcide Giroir. Brick mason and planter living on father's sugar plantation. Paroled ACH, 4/10/1865. Joined UCV as a member of Major Victor Maurin Camp No. 38. Married on 5/21/1859 at Church of the Assumption, Plattenville, to Elmina Templet, a first cousin, witnessed by Canonnier Alcide Giroir. Had two daughters before the war and a son, Jean Camille, born on 2/8/1864.[107] After the war had another five sons with the oldest born on 2/28/1866. Returned to sugar planting with Bouchereau's *The Louisiana Sugar Report, 1870-1917*, recording his crop on Templet Plantation and a second crop in conjunction with his brother Canonnier Hypolite Templet on the right descending bank of Bayou Lafourche near Napoleonville. Across wife's Confederate Widow's Pension Application in 1909 was scripted, "Mr. A. Sanchez his Lieutenant says this man served to the end at Appomattox." The *Assumption Pioneer*, 5/8/1897, reported he "was not only a soldier in name but a soldier in deed" and a "worthy and esteemed comrade in arms." Died of "Kidney Trouble" on 5/7/1897 at two o'clock in the morning at his home and interred in Assumption Catholic Cemetery, Plattenville. The *Assumption Pioneer*, 5/15/1897, reported, "His funeral under direction of Major Victor Maurin Camp of Confederate Veterans, was largely attended." In March 1909 Canonnier Maurice Landry (raised by the Templet family) brought suit against the estate of Camille Templet's widow, then bought the plantation at public auction and moved in.[108] The widow Elmina Templet moved out and stayed with a granddaughter, Mrs. Charles J. Blanchard of Napoleonville, who "cared for her." In May 1909 she applied for and was allowed (in December 1910) a Confederate Widow's Pension, which she received until death on 6/16/1932 at age ninety-three. Mrs. Templet left a large number of grandchildren and great-grandchildren.

TEMPLET, HYPOLITE, "HIP." Enlisted at New Orleans, 4/16/1862, Private. Previously served as a Lieutenant in the Hope Guards (Assumption Parish) 1st Brigade, 2nd Division, Louisiana Militia Troops from 8/18/1861. Born 5/25/1832 on the Templet Plantation a little more than a mile above Napoleonville on the left descending bank of Bayou Lafourche in the 3rd Ward of Assumption Parish to Florentin Templet and Clarisse Blanchard with five brothers and eight sisters. Brother of Canonnier Camille Templet and brother-in-law to Canonnier Alcide Giroir. Overseer and clerk on father's sugar plantation. The *Assumption Pioneer*, 6/8/1851 noted the police jury appointed him "Head of Patrols" in Assumption's Ward 3. Gray eyes, light hair, light complexion, 5'7". Paroled ACH, 4/10/1865. Joined UCV as a member of Major Victor Maurin Camp No. 38, later transferred to Gen. Francis T. Nicholls Camp No. 1142. Married Irma Berthaut and had a son and three daughters before the war, with another daughter born in 1862. Returned to sugar planting on family plantation two miles above Napoleonville and had another three sons and two daughters with the oldest girl born on 1/31/1866. Listed in Bouchereau's *The Louisiana Sugar Report, 1870-1917*, that recorded his crop on Nellie Plantation and a second crop in conjunction with his brother Canonnier Camille Templet on the right descending bank of Bayou Lafourche near Napoleonville. The *Assumption Pioneer*, 12/16/1899, reported, "His genial disposition and kind heart were proverbial" and "to have belonged to the Army of Northern Virginia to him was a pride greater than any other." Died 12/16/1899 at three-thirty in the morning at his home. Interred Assumption Catholic Cemetery, Plattenville.

From the *Assumption Pioneer*, December 16, 1899.

TERRIO, EDWARD SEVERIN. Enlisted at Donaldsonville, 9/13/1861, Private; promoted Bugler 7/5/1863. Born 2/11/1833 in Ascension Parish. Cousin to Canonnier Numa Braud, who's father was his sponsor (Godfather) and cousin to Canonnier Sabin Braud, who's mother was his sponsor (Godmother). Worked as a butcher in Donaldsonville. Blue eyes, dark hair, light complexion, 5'0". *O'Hara Diary* on 9/20/1861 noted that while stopped at Vicksburg, Mississippi, on the side-wheeler steamboat *Prince of Wales*, "Edward Terrio invented a new plan for getting whiskey by the sentinels easily." *Levy Diary* on 4/9/1865 recorded, "Squads of prisoners continue to be thrust in the open [fields]; among them Plesancea, Terio, and Dugas of Treile's section," captured at the Battle of Appomattox Station the evening before. Paroled between 4/11 and 4/21/1865 at Farmville, Virginia. The *Donaldsonville Chief*, 9/6/1884, reported, "Entering the Confederate service as a private . . . he was promoted to bugler and served as such until the war ended. He was noted for his happy disposition, strict performance of duty and disregard of privations or danger." A friend wrote, "Unappreciated Edouard, he would have died without a murmur, on any of the battlefields of Virginia, in the defense of the rights and firesides of fellow citizens." Terrio, a private in the antebellum Canonniers, was acknowledged in the *New Orleans True Delta*, 1/6/1859, for his witty remarks during a toast. Never married. Before the war lived with his mother and the family of Villeor Dugas, the forty-one-year-old sheriff of Donaldsonville and lieutenant in the antebellum Canonniers. Died on 9/2/1884 in Donaldsonville and interred AOL.

THIBIDEAUX, SIMON TRESIMOND. Enlisted at Williamsburg, Virginia, 2/28/1862, Private. Previously served as a Private with Co. E, 1st Battalion (Dreux/Rightor's) Louisiana Infantry from 4/16/1861. Born 3/24/1838 in Thibodeaux, Terrebonne Parish, to Benjamin Hylaire and Madeleine Lambert, the second oldest of four sisters and a younger brother. Farmed in Assumption Parish. Gray eyes, dark hair, dark complexion, 5'6". Captured on 7/3/1863 during the battle of Gettysburg and sent to Fort Delaware, Delaware, a prisoner of war. Forwarded to City Point, Virginia, on 3/7/1865 and exchanged at Boulware's and Cox Wharf, March 10-12, 1865. Married sixteen-year-old Marcelline Euphrasie Guidry on 10/23/1871 in Montegut, Terrebonne Parish, and had four sons and four daughters. Farmed, first in Montegut and later in Theriot (Bayou Dularge) Terrebonne Parish. Died at Bayou Dularge on 2/3/1902.[109]

TREILLE, FRANÇOIS HUBERT, "POUSSE." Enlisted at Donaldsonville, 9/13/1861, 3rd Sergeant; promoted Senior 2nd Lieutenant 3/25/1863. Born 5/13/1834 in Donaldsonville to the town's sheriff (1827-1840) of the same name and Marie Carmelite Dupuy. Treille's father and Canonnier "Philo" Viala's father both were natives of Laveyron, France. Had two sisters and a brother who died at eight months. Treille's father died in 1847 and he took up farming while living in Port Barrow, Ascension Parish. Hazel eyes, black hair, dark complexion, 5'6". Confederate Brigadier General Francis T. Nicholls's father was the sitting judge for Ascension Parish when Treille's father was sheriff; wrote Treille, "When we were youngsters our fathers being employed in the courthouse, we were constant playmates . . . we were almost inseparable" and "grew up together and were very close friends." Both the boys "left Donaldsonville on the same day for school—Mr. Treille going to the Military College . . . and Mr. Nicholls to West Point."[110] Treille graduated from Tybee Springs (Tennessee) Military School.[111] Slightly wounded with a contusion to right shoulder in battle at Shepardstown (Botelor's) Ford, Sharpsburg Campaign on 9/19/1862. Paroled with one horse at ACH, 4/10/1865. Captured a second time and imprisoned until 5/8/1865 when he surrendered his parole and signed Oath of Allegiance in Alexandria, Virginia.

In an undated letter in his wife's 1903 Confederate Widow's Pension Application it was

Courtesy of Memorial Hall, New Orleans, La.

related, "A brother Lieutenant who holds his parole at Appomattox says Treille . . . made a soldier on every and all occasions." Joined UCV as a member of Major Victor Maurin Camp No. 38 and served camp as an alternate delegate to UCV's Annual Meeting and Reunions. Married Olphida Leblanc on 4/22/1856 in Assumption Parish and had three daughters with the oldest dying a year later. The youngest, born on 9/6/1861 (just two weeks before the Canonniers embarked for Richmond) was named Virginie. Treille's home was located near the intersection of Bayou Lafourche and the Mississippi River, opposite Donaldsonville, and was purportedly the only house in Port Barrow to remain standing after the bombardment and burning of Donaldsonville by Federal gunboats on 8/9/1862. Fort Butler was built by the Federals in 1863 around the Treille house that stood until sold and torn down in 1926. Mrs. Treille, in applying for a Confederate Widow's Pension in 1903, noted she still lived in the "old house and lot which has been ruined by the yanks." After the war the veteran returned to his home and had four more daughters and one son, Hubert Treille Jr. Listed in Bouchereau's *The Louisiana Sugar Report, 1870-1917* as an Ascension sugar planter at P. O. Ayraud and Company. Aid-de-camp and advisor to the Sons of Veterans, C. S. A. of the Donaldsonville Artillery and Ascension Parish, 1888-1898. The Civil War veteran died at home of heart disease on 11/6/1898 and interred in the family tomb, AOL. The Donaldsonville Chapter, No. 307 of the United Daughters of the Confederacy was named in his honor. Son was 2nd Sgt. Hubert Treille Jr. who served with the Donaldsonville Cannoneers, Battery C, United States Federal Service in 1898.[112] In 1943 from a bomber base on the Tunisian front in North Africa during World War II it was written that United States Army Air Corps Master Sergeant Hubert J. Treille (the grandson of the Canonnier) spoke excellent French and from a nearby French army unit was able to obtain much needed supplies for the Americans.[113]

TRESCHE, BENJAMIN M., "SEBASTION." Enlisted at Yorktown, Virginia, 2/1/1862, Private. Previously served as a Private with Co. A, 1st Louisiana Zouave (Coppen's) Infantry Battalion from 3/29/1861. Born ca. 1840 in Bremelau, Germany. Lived in Muensingen District and emmigrated in 1854 from Wuerttemberg, Germany. Occupation unknown but lived in New Orleans. Captured on 7/2/1863 during the battle of Gettysburg and arrived at Fort Delaware, Delaware, a prisoner of war between July 7-12, 1863. Probably died there and no record was made of his death in the chaos and confusion that reigned on Pea Patch Island prisoner-of-war camp during July and August 1863.[114]

TRICHE, LOUIS ARMAS. Enlisted at Chancellorsville, Virginia, 6/16/1863, Private. Previously served as a Private with Co. H, 2nd Louisiana Cavalry from 9/1/1862 until captured 4/14/1863 at Bayou Teche (Battle of Irish Bend) near Franklin, St. Mary Parish, sent to New Orleans for exchange. Born 4/22/1843 in Assumption Parish to Charles and Marguerite Alexandre, one of nine children. Farmed on father's plantation one mile below Napoleonville on the left descending bank of Bayou Lafourche in the 3rd Ward of Assumption Parish near Bertie. Paroled ACH, 4/10/1865. Joined UCV as a member of Gen. Francis T. Nicholls Camp No. 1142. Married Nohemie Leblanc Streck, a widow, witnessed by Canonnier Ernest Monnot. Had three sons and two daughters while living on the old Triche tract and "engaged in planting . . . for many years." Tract was located between Monnot's and *Canonnier* Maurice Landry's plantation. Listed in Bouchereau's *The Louisiana Sugar Report, 1870-1917. Assumption Pioneer*, 11/12/1921, reported, "He was a Confederate Veteran and was a good citizen." He died a widower of thirty years on 11/11/1921 at home, survived by a son and a daughter. Interred St. Anne's Catholic Cemetery, Napoleonville.

VEQUE, JULES. Joined August 1862 at Hopewell Gap, Virginia, on Second Manassas Campaign. Born ca. 1838 in Louisiana. Clerked in New Orleans. Left New Orleans for Florida when war began and entered Confederate service as a drummer boy in the 1st Louisiana (Coppen's) Infantry Battalion. Subsequently promoted to Corporal and served as such in the battles of Yorktown and around Richmond, Virginia. Upon joining the BAANV (Application No. 326, July 1876) wrote he "lost my battalion before the fight of Sharpsburg [9/17/1862] entered it with Donaldson Artillery and was wounded." After being hospitalized and recovering from the wound he returned to his command and was commissioned 1st Lieutenant in Company A, 1st Louisiana Zouave (Coppen's) Infantry Battalion. Returned to New Orleans after the war and married Estelle, worked as a painter. Died in New Orleans on 8/4/1882.

VIALA, JOSEPH PHILOGENE, "PHILO." Enlisted at Donaldsonville, 9/13/1861, 8th Corporal; promoted to 1st Corporal May 1863. Born 3/21/1842 on Raccourci (Viala) Plantation in 3rd Ward of Ascension Parish to Jean Pierre Hypolite Viala, a native of Laveyron, France. Viala's father, like Canonnier Hubert Treille's father, was a distinguished Frenchman who came to Louisiana on a visit and decided to remain. He succeeded as a "venturesome and energetic settler" and married on 1/5/1830 in Napoleonville, Assumption Parish, Euphemie Comeau, "a true and noble woman . . . kind, charitable and sympathetic, and possessed rare intellectual attainments." Sugar planter with plantation real estate valued at $55,000 and family's personal estate valued at $52,000 in 1860. Lived with widowed mother and twin brother François Theogine Viala who enlisted in Company A, 1st Louisiana Cavalry on 8/26/1861 and served until captured near Donaldsonville on 1/29/1865. Had another brother and three sisters with one, Marie Emma Euphemie, born 3/3/1833, marrying Jean Lafitte Jr., of New Orleans and believed to be the son of Jean Lafitte the famous privateer. It was said the pirate Lafitte conducted smuggling operations in Ascension Parish and used the Viala Plantation (now the River Dale Golf Course) as his base. The Viala home was a large raised Acadian cottage built in the 1790s. It was still standing in the 1950s but fell into disrepair until restored in 1974 and moved near the Sunshine (Mississippi River) Bridge where it gained fame as Lafitte's Landing Restaurant. It burned down in 1995. Canonnier Eugene H. Levy, after being transferred from the Petersburg trenches to the detachment at High Bridge on December 23, 1864, recorded in his diary, "I was duly installed as an inmate [tenant] of a little hut with Philo Viala and Ernest Monnot as mess mates." Paroled ACH, 4/10/1865. In July 1874 Philo lived in Houma, Terrebonne Parish, where he owned and and was master of the new thirty-ton schooner *Comet.* On its first sailing from Brashear (Morgan City) to New Orleans it was reported by the *New Orleans Picayune*, 7/2/1874, the vessel was "seen bottom up, and that all hands were lost. She carried a crew of four . . . J. P. Viala, H. Viala, J. F. Viala [his newphew Ferdinand and brother Hypolite's son] and one man unknown. The friends of the captain in Houma are anxious to hear from the *Comet* and learn the fate of those aboard." Having survived the sinking, Philo and his twin brother Theo in the following year were reported by the *New Orleans Picayune,* 12/1/1875, to be successful tenant sugar farmers on the "old Hanna or Ardoyne Plantation" on upper Bayou Black in Terrebonne Parish.

After the war sugar production burgeoned in Texas with the use of convict labor and Philo, with his brother Hypolite and nephew Ferdinand relocated to Brazoria County, Texas, where they managed Lake Jackson Plantation with its stately buildings and sugar mill complex. Today the site is an Archeological Landmark where Lake Jackson Historical Museum has the signature of J. P. Viala on an, "Inventory of the Property . . . under date February 28, A. D., 1878." In 1880 Philo was running the prison farm with four guards, two farm laborers, and twenty-nine convicts. Four miles north of Lake Jackson was Retrieve Plantation where the Willis family, former slaves from South Carolina, lived. In 1881 their oldest daughter, thirty-year-old Charlotte with five children gave birth to Ferdinand Viola. Philo Viala and Charlotte Willis's family grew with the birth of George Viola in 1884, Emil Viola in 1887, and W. L. Viola in 1890. With the end of convict labor at Lake Jackson Plantation in 1884; Philo with his brother Hypolite and nephew Ferdinand leased 100 acres from Asenath Jackson Groce, one of the heirs to Lake Jackson Plantation, for farming. In 1886 Philo and Charlotte began raising cattle and by 1890 had 200 head valued at $1,000 and paying a State and County Tax of $9.75. Philo Viala's mother lived to be ninty-three years old; dying on 6/12/1898 in New Orleans. The *New Orleans Daily Picayune* reported in her obituary that Philogene, "died some years ago" (possibly on 7/21/1893.) In 1910 the widow Charlotte Willis lived at 239 Retrieve Road, Brazoria County. Since 1919 and after purchasing 5,766 acres of Retrieve Plantation the Texas Department of Corrections, Wayne Scott (formerly Retrieve) Unit, of the Texas Department of Criminal Justice, Institutional Division, oversees more than 700 prisoners that raise crops and livestock. It is one of the most productive farms in the prison system and where prisoners laboring in the hot and humid Gulf Coast climate sometimes noted Retrieve was "Burnin' Hell."[115]

WAGNER, FREDERICK. Enlisted at Yorktown, Virginia, 2/1/1862, Private. Previously served as a Private with Co. A, later companies D and F, 1st Louisiana Zouave (Coppen's) Infantry Battalion from 4/18/1861; appointed and transferred 6/1/1861 as Hospital Steward. Born ca. 1838 in Germany. Worked as a butcher in New Orleans. Killed in battle at Shepardstown (Botelor's) Ford, Sharpsburg Campaign on 9/19/1862. Wagner's gravesite is unknown though the most likely place interred would be Elmwood Cemetery in Shepardstown, West Virginia.

WALFRAM, LUDWIG, "LOUIS." Enlisted at Yorktown, Virginia, 2/1/1862, Private. Previously served as a Private with Co. F, 1st Louisiana Zouave (Coppen's) Infantry Battalion from 4/4/1861. Born ca. 1837 in Germany. Worked as a baker in New Orleans. Transferred on 4/6/1864 by Special Order 95/15 to the Confederate States Navy. In 1910 lived in 1st Precint of Belmont, Middlesex County, Massachusetts, with wife Mary A. Only two of their ten children were living in 1910 though their daughter May gave them seven grandchildren.

WILLIAMS, VERLA HARVEY, "VH." Enlisted at Williamsburg, Virginia, 3/8/1862, Private. Previously served as a Private with Co. D, 1st Battalion (Dreux/Rightor's) Louisiana Infantry from 4/20/1861. Born October 1842 in Kentucky. Father G. W. Williams was a planter and recorder (plantation worth $110,000) near Trinity, Ward 10, Concordia Parish, Louisiana. At enlistment was farming in Natchez, Mississippi. Appears to have escaped capture at the end of the war. Died 6/25/1904 and interred Diamond Grove Cemetery, Jacksonville, Morgan County, Illinois.

WIEDEMERE, ARNOLD. Enlisted at Yorktown, Virginia, 2/28/1862, Private. Previously served as a private with Co. B, 1st Louisiana Zouave (Coppen's) Infantry Battalion from 4/4/1861. Born 9/19/1838 in Switzerland, immigrated in 1858. Worked as a carpenter in New Orleans. Black eyes, light hair, dark complexion, 5'4". Wounded in battle by explosion of a shell at Shepardstown (Botelor's) Ford, Sharpsburg Campaign on 9/19/1862 that caused his right arm to be amputated at the shoulder joint. Captured and paroled on 9/30/1862 and returned to duty under Brigadier General Robert B. Vance at Camp Anderson, Asheville, North Carolina. Captured near the end of the war and sent to Rock Island, Illinois, as a prisoner-of-war. After the war worked only "sometimes" for just board and clothing while living in Live Oak, Suwannee County, Florida. Joined BAANV (Application No. 562, 6/13/1885), stated that he "was wounded at Shepardstown on return of Lee's Army into Virginia, and lost my right arm from the wound." Joined UCV as a member of Louisiana Division, Army of Northern Virginia Camp No. 1. In April 1885 received a "favorable" letter from Captain Prosper Landry and admitted to Camp Nicholls Soldier's Home, New Orleans on 5/13/1885. Died at six o'clock in the morning on 3/16/1901 in Charity Hospital, New Orleans. Funeral with relatives, friends, and acquaintances held at Camp Nicholls Soldier's Home and interred in Vault 12, Soldier's Home Tomb, Greenwood Cemetery, New Orleans. His BAANV Certificate of Membership and photograph were displayed in Confederate Memorial Hall, New Orleans.[116]

WINCHESTER, FRANÇOIS "JOSEPH" RICHARD, "DICK," "J. R." Enlisted at Donaldsonville, 9/13/1861, 6th Sergeant. Born 9/4/1831 in Ascension Parish to Judge Benjamin Winchester (1790-1852) and Marguerite Carmelite Constant with Trasimond Landry (Louisiana lieutenant-governor and father of Canonnier Jean Trasimond Landry) and Elizabeth Duffel as Godparents. Had four brothers and sisters. Father was a state senator and district judge (1821-1836) living on Buena Vista Plantation in St. James Parish at the Ascension Parish line where he, as a sugar planter, managed Buena Vista.[117] Uncle was Archbishop of Cincinnati, Ohio, and was first cousin to Canonniers Louis Aristide Landry and second cousin to Adolphe Landry, Jean Trasimond Landry, and Prosper Landry. Discharged on 5/24/1862 by order of the C. S. A. Secretary of War and commissioned 1st Junior Lieutenant of the 5th Louisiana (Pelican Light Artillery) Field Battery, 10/31/1862. Married Philomene Aimée Frere after the war and had a son and three daughters. Served as judge of the Court of Appeal for the Fifth Circuit of Louisiana in New Orleans. The *Donaldsonville Chief*, 6/26/1880, described him as "able, affable, an Honorable gentleman." Died 6/22/1880 in Hendersonville, North Carolina, where he had gone because of "feeble health." The *New Orleans Daily Picayune*, 6/29/1880, reported a committee appointed by the Nineteenth Judicial Court of Louisiana recorded Winchester's "reputation as a jurist, his high character as an honest and upright gentleman . . . the great loss this circuit has sustained in his untimely death . . . this Court do now adjourn, and that these resolutions be spread upon the minutes of this Court, and a certified copy thereof be forwarded to the members of the family." Believed to be interred in AOL.[118]

Donaldsonville Canonnier Field Bands

BARRÉ, JOHN. Born ca. 1842 in Ascension Parish. "Col'd" (colored)[119] living in Ascension Parish working as a brickmason. Witnessed and signed name to Louis Lefort's marriage certificate in Donaldsonville on 12/3/1867.

BARRÉ, LANLEE

CONWAY, FREDERICK AUGUSTUS, "AUGUSTE," "GUS." Born ca. 1819-27 to John Conway and Cecile, an African American woman. Brother to Prosper Conway and a cousin to Canonnier Lieutenant William C. Lawes. The *New Orleans True Delta*, 1/6/1859, noted he had marched at the age of ten or twelve at the head of the Donaldsonville Canonniers as its first fifer since the organization of the company. The 1880 U.S. Census listed his age as sixty-one, which would make him eighteen at the time of the company's organization in 1837. Like his brother he was reported to be "a splendid musician" by the *Memphis Daily Appeal*, 9/24/1861. This newspaper also described him as a "tall yellow boy, who weighs three hundred pounds." A reporter for a New Orleans newspaper "particularize[ed]"[120] him not only for his fife playing but his singing. Lived after the war on Railroad Avenue in Donaldsonville and maintained the musical organization of the Donaldsonville Canonnier Field Band, which was known as the Conway Field Band. It was later called the St. Cecile Brass Band up to the time of his death on 12/13/1882. The "old fifer of the field band of the Cannoneers of Donaldson" worked as a tailor and left a widow, Octavia, two sons, ages twenty-four and fifteen, and two daughters, ages twenty and eleven. Interred in AOL.[121]

CONWAY, PROSPER. Born ca. 1831 to John Conway and Cecile, an African American woman. He was the band's drummer and described as a "splendid musician" by the *Memphis Daily Appeal*, 9/24/1861. Brother to Gus Conway and a cousin to *Canonnier* Lieutenant William C. Lawes. Officially married Catherine Thomas on 5/12/1869 but they had a son born in 1853, a daughter in 1857, and another daughter born on 2/7/1863 in Ascension Parish. Two more daughters were born in 1866 and 1870. In 1864 living and working in Donaldsonville as a bricklayer.[122] In 1870 working as a house servant living next to cousin "Billy" Lawes in the 2nd Ward, town of Donaldsonville.

BRAUD, SOSTHENE. Born ca. 1832 in St. James Parish to Michel Joachim Braud, a white farmer, and Marie Joseph, his slave whom he freed. In 1860, living with parents, three sisters, and younger brother (by two years) working as a sugar maker. Braud was the band's drummer. Married Celestine Blouin and had seven children. Worked as a sugar maker and laborer in St. James Parish and died 5/19/1911 in New Orleans.

Donaldsonville Canonnier Servants

Paroled Appomattox Court House, 4/10/1865:

BLUM, HENRY. Cook. Born ca. 1830 in France. Lived in Donaldsonville with wife Pauline (also born in France), had a one-year-old son in 1860. Worked as a peddler. Believed to be the younger brother and next door neighbor to Cannonier Marx Blum. The 1860 census taker spelled the name "Boom."

LEFORT, LOUIS G. Born 8/20/1835 in Haiti to Hyacine, a free woman of color. The family arrived in Thibodaux, Terrebonne Parish, in 1837 and lived in Donaldsonville by 1844. On 7/28/1860 his mother donated to him Lot #26 with all its improvement that was located in Fauburg Conway, facing Rue Attakapas. As a free man of color Lefort worked as an artistic painter by trade. He voluntarily joined the Donaldsonville Canonniers as Captain Victor Maurin's valet, cook, and servant, and departed for Virginia with the company on September

18, 1861. It was reported by the *New Orleans Times Picayune*, 11/3/1902, that Lefort "oftened participated in battle" and his "bravery and courage was well known." Surrendered and paroled with the Donaldsonville Artillery at Appomattox Court House on 4/10/1865 and returned to Donaldsonville. Married on 6/9/1861, he divorced his wife (Canonnier Lieutenant William Lawes was his attorney for the court proceedings) after she had a child in 1863 while he was away serving in Virginia. Remarried Ophelia Fobb on 12/3/1867 (witnessed by Canonnier musician John Barré) and after her death married Elizabeth Therence. With each of these wives he had eleven children. After the war the popular and respected Lefort was elected to the Ascension Parish School Board, elected as a constable in 1870, and after that, served as a deputy sheriff and jailer. The *Donaldsonville Le Drapeau*, 3/11/1871, reported Lefort was voted a $200.00 reward by the police jury and Donaldsonville mayor for arresting one of the murderers of Canonnier William Lawes and former Mayor Schoenberg. Lefort also served as an assessor in 1871, the same year he was a member of the Republican Convention in New Orleans, and appointed supervisor of voter registration in 1876 under the Republican rule and remained in the position for 1877 during the Democratic adminstration of Governor Nicholls. Member of the Ascension Parish Police Jury and President Pro-tem in 1878 and in 1880. That same year, urged by friends, he ran for the Donadlsonville treasurer's office. The local newspaper reported Lefort had good prospects of success but during the campaign he withdrew in favor of one of Major Maurin's sons who won the election. The *Donaldsonville Chief*, 5/8/1880, editorialized about the election: "Mr. Lefort's part ought to be highly appreciated by those who reaped the benefits of his self-sacrifice." On 10/31/1881 Lefort was appointed postmaster of Donaldsonville, and when his term expired on 2/15/1886 the *Donaldsonville Chief*, 2/20/1886, reported,

> Under his administration the affairs of the important office have been conducted in a manner highly satisfactory to the public and creditable in the greatest degree to the officer himself. Assuming the position under circumstances that led many of his political opponents to regard the appointment with dislike and to predict for him an unsatisfactory official career, he has so comported himself as to win confidence of the public and the government and the respect, if not the good will, of those who were most inimical to him at the outset of his term of service. . . . Mr. Lefort retires with a clean balance sheet and has faithfully accounted for all the money and property passing through his hands during the last four years, aggregating in value many thousands of dollars annually.

In all the many offices that Lefort held it was recorded by the *New Orleans Times Picayune*, 11/3/1902: "While corruption and dishonesty were epidemic around him in those days, Lefort was honest and reliable." That newspaper noted too he was "a noted chef and could prepare the best Creole dishes." The lunch stalls of the Donaldsonville Market in Crescent Park were auctioned off each year by the city government to the highest bidder, except for the first stall from which a respected and popular Lefort during the remainder of his life sold coffee, pies, biscuits, and other things for breakfast. Widowed by June 1900, Lefort still resided at 258 Houmas Street, Donaldsonville, with seven daughters, the youngest two years old, two sons, the youngest five years old, and an eight year old granddaughter. On 8/2/1902, after taking a walk on the levee, Lefort had a stroke and fell. Some men brought him to a bench and after took him across the street where he died in front of the market. A Confederate veteran wrote in his journal, "Louis Lefort Confederate and member of the Donaldsonville Cannoniers War of 61 to 65 . . . Best citizen of Ascension Parish."[123] Lefort was buried with Confederate military honors wearing the gray and interred in AOL. "The funeral of Louis Lefort, the colored valet of the late Major Victor Maurin," reported the *New*

Orleans Times Picayune on 11/4/1902, "was largely attended . . . U. C. V. Camp 38 turned out. A large delegation of Sons of Veterans, together with the sons of Major Victor Maurin, attended the funeral."[124]

MAMPLY, JNO.

SEMPLE, JNO.

TITUS. Slave and cook of Captain Prosper Landry (Not listed on Appomattox parole).

Chaplain of the Donaldsonville Artillery

Reverend Father CHARLES BOGLIOLI, C. M. Born 12/1/1814, in the Duchy of Parma, a native of Apennine Mountains, about forty miles from Genoa, Italy. Studied philosophy for three years in the College of Piancenza and theology for six years. Arrived in America at New Orleans in December 1840 as a missionary and ordained a deacon on 2/28/1841, by Bishop Antoine Blanc of New Orleans at the Church of the Ascension in Donaldsonville. Two days later the bishop raised him to the priesthood at St. Mary's Church in New Orleans. Sent to the Vincentian college at Cape Girardeau, Missouri, he served as a professor until being moved to St. Francis Seminary in Brown County, Ohio, as professor and vice-rector. In 1845 transferred for a short time to St. Louis, then sent to Louisiana and served as professor at the Diocesan Seminary at Plattenville on Bayou Lafourche and at the same time Father Superior for the Assumption Parish Church. In 1856 suffered a severe attack of yellow fever from which he recovered.[125] Conducted mission work in the vast Lafourche District territory, which included Donaldsonville's Church of the Ascension. Gave religious instructions, performed confirmations, and validated or blessed marriages of slaves on the plantations. In one instance he wrote the bishop of New Orleans seeking approval for a "dispensation from disparity of cult for John, slave of Valeri Landry (father of Captain Prosper Landry) and Elene(?), slave of Mrs. Prosper Landry, alias Adele Pedesclaux."[126] Father Boglioli was eventually assigned as Catholic administrator at the church in Donaldsonville where he was very favorably known. His good manners and polished sermons attracted the esteem of Donaldsonville's Catholic population. Associated with the antebellum *Canonniers de Donaldson*, he received permission of the bishop to join the *Compagnie d'Artillerie* and "share their hardships" while trying "to save their souls as he could not save their bodies." Left with and served as chaplain for the Donaldsonville Artillery from 9/13/1861 to 3/24/1862. From Virginia he returned to the Lafourche District and continued his priestly duties until the end of the war. In 1866 he was stationed at St. Joseph's Church in New Orleans, across the street from Charity Hospital. Thereafter the kindly priest with the erect, military bearing and shock of snowy hair, faithfully made his daily rounds among the sick and dying of the hospital's wards. One of the Daughters of Charity wrote:

> He said mass in our little chapel and, as he was most exact in the fulfillment of every duty, never did he fail in this most sacred one, coming each morning most punctually at the appointed time, never causing a moment's delay . . . to doctors and students he showed the utmost deference and was by them most highly respected. With the poor he was at home, attending most faithfully to their spiritual wants and in meeting the convalescent patients or in visiting the wards, he passed a few pleasant words, thus cheering their poor and sad hearts; he was truly a kind father to all he came in contact. He promptly answered the many calls to administer to the sick and dying, which occurred night and day.

His heroic character is described with the following deed, "In 1878, the yellow fever was spreading over Louisiana and, as might be expected, the Charity Hospital received a great many patients. Not wishing the younger priests of the parish to expose themselves to the plague, Father Boglioli made himself a voluntary prisoner in the hospital in order to attend to the plague-stricken. He succeeded in weathering the epidemic without suffering any ill effects from the dread disease." Just two years later the good Reverand was forced into retirement and a room at the hospital as it was reported, "In past years several patients suffering with leprosy received treatment at the hospital . . . these people the priest was especially attentive to, giving them much more of his care than his duties to the church required, so that even the attending physicians warned him of the danger to which he exposed himself. He paid no attention to the warning, and the result was he became infected with the dread disease, and, after a long illness, died . . . of leprosy." He suffered greatly his last few years with the effects of Oriental Leprosy, his weight at one time dropping from 205 to 157. Father Boglioli passed away peacefully at seven-thirty on the evening of 7/22/1882. A funeral was held two days later at St. Joseph's Church after a solemn high Mass with interment following at St. Vincent's Cemetery on Soniat Street in New Orleans.[127]

U. C. V. Major Victor Maurin Camp No. 38 Tomb, Ascension of Our Lord Catholic Cemetery, Donaldsonville. It was Canonnier Lieutenant and veteran Hubert Treille's "idea virtually" to erect a tomb with a statue in the Catholic Cemetery. It is believed that the tomb was completed and dedicated in April 1899. The statue, unveiled on Confederate Memorial Day, June 3, 1907, still stands surmounting the Confederate Veterans' tomb. The Hubert Treille Chapter of the United Daughters of the Confederacy purchased "the handsome and enduring work of art" statue with funds obtained by public subscription and through entertainments of various kinds given at intervals for several years. Courtesy of Andrew Capone, Labadieville, La.

Bibliography

ABBREVIATIONS

B & L Johnson, R. U. and C. C. Buel, eds. *Battles and Leaders of the Civil War.* 32 vols. and 4 vols. New York, 1884-87.

CV Confederate Veteran (Magazine) published 1893 - 1932 by United Confederate Veterans

DPL Donaldsonville, Louisiana Public Library.

FSNMP Fredericksburg and Spotsylvania National Military Park. Fredericksburg, Virginia.

HNOC Historic New Orleans Collection. New Orleans, Louisiana.

HMDLM Historical Military Data on Louisiana Militia. Library of the Adjutant General of Louisiana. Jackson Barracks. New Orleans, Louisiana.

HUC Hebrew Union College, The Jacob Rader Marcus Center of the American Jewish Archives. Hamilton County, Ohio.

LAGL Library Adjutant General of Louisiana. Jackson Barracks. New Orleans, Louisiana.

LDA Louisiana Division of Archives, Records Management, and History. Baton Rouge, Louisiana.

LSU Louisiana State University. Baton Rouge, Louisiana.

MCR The Museum of the Confederacy, Eleanor S. Brockenbrough Library. Richmond, Virginia.

NA, CSR National Archives, Compiled Service Records. Washington, D. C.

NPL Norfolk, Virginia Public Library.

OR *The War of the Rebellion: A Compilation of the Official Records of the Union and Confederate Armies.* 130 vols. Washington, D. C., 1880-1901.

PNBP Petersburg National Battlefield Park. Petersburg, Virginia.

RNBP Richmond National Battlefield Park. Richmond, Virginia.

SCHS South Carolina Historical Society. Charleston, South Carolina.

SHSP *Southern Historical Society Papers.* 52 Volumes. Southern Historical Society, Richmond, VA 1876-1959.

TU Tulane University. New Orleans, Louisiana.

UDC United Daughters of the Confederacy, Memorial Library. Richmond, Virginia.

UNCCH University of North Carolina at Chapel Hill, Southern Historical Collection. Chapel Hill, North Carolina.

UT University of Texas. Austin, Texas.

UV University of Virginia. Charlottesville, Virginia.

PRIMARY SOURCES

MANUSCRIPT COLLECTIONS

Alabama Department of Archives and History. Montgomery, Alabama.
"Eighth Alabama Regiment Infantry," Typescript.
Purifoy, John. "History of Jeff Davis Artillery."

Appomattox Court House National Historical Park. Appomattox, Virginia.
Cauble, Frank P. "The Battle of Appomattox Station April 8, 1865 and The Battle of Appomattox Court House April 9, 1865, A Narrative Study to Accompany Appomattox Court House Troop Movement Maps."

Antietam National Battlefield Visitor Center. Antietam, Maryland.
Hanson, Joseph M. "A Report on the Employment of the Artillery at the Battle of Antietam, MD."

Thomas Balch Library. Leesburg, Virginia.
Big Spring Creek File.
"Some of the Experiences of James C. Reed as a Soldier in the Army of the Confederate States." Typescript.

Bull Run Regional Library. Manassas, Virginia.
Concise History of Antioch Church from its organization in 1837 to October 1, 1862.
Virginia Historic Landmarks Commission Survey, Antioch Church.

Cincinnati Historical Society. Cincinnati, Ohio.
Roger Hannaford Diary.

Colonial Historical National Park. Yorktown, Virginia.
Minnich, J. W. "Reminiscences Relating to the, Siege of Yorktown, April - May 1862."

Donaldsonville Public Library. Donaldsonville, Louisiana.
Helene Dupuy Manuscript.
Louis Lefort File.
Romain Octave Landry Diary.

Duke University. Rare Book, Manuscript, and Special Collections Library. Durham, North Carolina.
John Richardson Porter Diary.
Henry E. Taintor Papers.
Samuel S. Biddle Papers.

Emory University. Atlanta, Georgia.
Henry Woodfin Grady Papers.

Farmville Area Chamber of Commerce. Farmville, Virginia.
Order Books in Cumberland County Clerk's Office.
Proceeding of the Committee of Safety of Cumberland and Isle of Wight County.

Fort Delaware Society. Delaware City, Delaware.
R. Hugh Simmons. Correspondence.

Fredericksburg and Spotsylvania National Military Park. Fredericksburg, Virginia.
Charles Richardson File.
National Military Park Historian Files.

Gettysburg National Military Park. Gettysburg, Pennsylvania.
John B. Bachelder Maps.
McMillan House File.
National Military Park Historian Files.

The Handley Regional Library. Winchester, Virginia.
James Bradford Diary.

Hebrew Union College-Jewish Institute of Religion. The Jacob Rader Marcus Center of the American Jewish Archives. Cincinnati, Ohio.
Bertram W. Korn Papers.

Sara Hightower Reginal Library. Rome, Georgia.
W. B. Judkins Memoir.

Historic New Orleans Collection. New Orleans, Louisiana.
Francis Dunbar Ruggles Diary.
Walton-Glenny Family Papers.

Library of the Adjutant General of Louisiana. Jackson Barracks. New Orleans, Louisiana.
A South-side History of the War Shown in the Letters of, and to General P. G. T. Beauregard of the Confederate States Army. Catalogue No. 1148, Part II.
Camp Nicholls's Soldier's Home Records.
David W. Pipes Memoirs.
Historical Military Data, 352 Bound Volumes plus Supplements. Research, typing and binding done by Works Projects Administration employees, sponsored by the Adjutant General of Louisiana.
Photographed Record Sheets (from National Archives) of Donaldsonville Artillery, Bound Volumes 145 and 146.
Photographed Record Sheets (from National Archives) of Paroles.
Report of the Adjutant General of the Louisiana Militia, 1851, 1852, 1857, 1858, 1860.
Squires, Charles W. "The Last of Lee's Battle Line." Typescript.
Washington Artillery Collection.
Washington Artillery Order Book, No. 2.

Library of Congress. Washington, D. C.
Confederate Secretary of War Letters-Sent Book, Febuary 21 - Sept. 15, 1861.
Ezra A. Carman Papers.
Given Campbell Papers.
John S. Anglin Papers.

Louisiana Division of Archives, Records Management, and History. Baton Rouge, Louisiana.
Ascension Parish Civil Records, 1803-1926
Board of Pension Commissioners, Confederate Pension Applications.
Fourth Judicial District Court Records.

Louisiana State University. Hill Memorial Library, Special Collections. Baton Rouge, Louisiana.
Andrew Jr. and George Hero Papers.
George M. Lester Collection.
Gustavus Schmidt, Correspondences.
John C. Burruss and Family Papers.
Leon Jastremski Family Papers.
Landry-Pedesclaux Family Papers.
W. W. Pugh Family Papers.

Mississippi Department of Archives and History. Jackson, Mississippi.
J. J. Wilson Papers.
McWillie-Compton Family Papers.
Oscar J. E. Stuart Letters.

The Museum of the Confederacy, Eleanor S. Brockenbrough Library. Richmond, Virginia.
Capt. Victor Maurin, Reports, Returns, and Letters.
John O'Farrell Diary.
John Thompson Brown Collection.

R. H. Anderson, Letters-sent Book.
Thomas Holley Letter.
W. N. Pendleton, Order Book.

National Archives. Washington, D. C.
Record Group 109, War Department Collection of Confederate Records.
Record Group 359, Records of the Louisiana State Government.
United States Civil War Draft Registrations Records, 1863-1865.

New Orleans Public Library. Louisiana Division/City Archives. New Orleans, Louisiana.
Enumeration of Ex-Confederate Soldiers. 1911 Louisiana Census.

Norfolk Public Library. Sargent Memorial Room. Norfolk, Virginia.
John Walters Diary.

North Carolina Department of Archives and History. Raleigh, North Carolina.
James W. Albright Diary.
John Willis Council Diary.

Petersburg National Battlefield Park. Petersburg, Virginia.
J. J. Purcuval Reminiscences.
Keiley, W. S. "A Wartime Story of a Battery's Last Days" in *Historical Stories about Petersburg*.
Natioanal Battlefield Park Historian Files.

Richmond National Battlefield Park. Richmond, Virginia.
"Inventory of Early Architecture and Historic Sites: County of Henrico, Virginia. December, 1976."
National Battlefield Park Historian Files.

South Carolina Historical Society. Charleston, South Carolina.
J. H. A. Wagener Diary.

University of South Carolina. South Carolinian Library. Columbia, South Carolina.
Eugene Whitefield Dabbs Papers.

Texas State Library and Archives. Austin, Texas.
Texas Confederate Pension Applications.

Tulane University, Special Collections. New Orleans, Louisiana.
Favrot Papers.
Gaudet Family Papers.
Nicholls Family Papers.
Rosemonde and Emile Kuntz Collection.
Schmidt Family Papers.

Tulane University, Amistad Research Center. New Orleans, Louisiana.
Dunn-Landry Family Papers.

Tulane University, Louisiana Historical Association Collection. New Orleans, Louisiana.
Association of the Army of Northern Virginia Papers.
Civil War Papers.
Historical Memoranda.
Muster Rolls and Records.

United Daughters of the Confederacy. Memorial Library. Richmond, Virginia.
François Bienvenu Cire Memorandum Book (copy).

University of Georgia. Florence Hodgson Heidler Collection. Athens, Georgia.
Francis M. Coker Letters.

University of New Orleans. Louisiana and Special Collections. New Orleans, Louisiana.
Monnot/Lanier Family Papers.

University of North Carolina at Chapel Hill. The Wilson Library. Southern Historical Collection. Chapel Hill, North Carolina.
Andrew McCollam Papers.
Augustus Osborne Papers.
Edwin I. Kursheedt Papers.
H. L. P. King Diary.
J. A. Lineback Papers.
Thomas Ware Diary.
Westwood A. Todd Papers.
William N. Pendleton Papers.
William Beavens Papers.

University of Notre Dame. Archives. Notre Dame, Indiana.
Archdiocese of New Orleans Collection.

University of Texas. Briscoe Center for American History. Austin, Texas.
James K. Kirkpatrick Diary.
O. T. Hanks Manuscript.
Yates, Jerome B. Confederate States of America Records, 1856-1915.

University of Virginia. Albert and Shirley Small Special Collections Library. Charlottesville, Virginia.
Jean Reynaud Jaques Prosper Landry Letter.
Michael Wise Papers.
William Anderson Letters.

Virginia Historical Society. Richmond, Virginia.
David G. McIntosh Reminiscences.
Keiley Family Papers.
Osman Latrobe Diary.
Pegram-Johnson-McIntosh Collection.
Richmond C. Price Papers.
Robert Edward Lee, Headquarters Papers.
Watkins Kearn Diary.

Virginia Military Institute. Archives. Lexington, Virginia.
Isaac N. Baker Memoirs.
John H. Cameron Memoirs.

Virginia State Library. Richmond, Virginia.
Tredegar Gun Foundry Book.

Wardlaw-Hartridge School. Edison, New Jersey.
Alumni and Developmental Office, Correspondence.

Washington-Wilkes Historical Foundation.
Josephus E. Strother Journal.
"Operations of Company (C) Irvin Artillery from May 5th, 1864." Report of Capt. John T. Wingfield.
Wilkes Guard and Survivors Association of the Irvin Guard Record 1860-1893. Washington, Georgia.

The Western Reserve Historical Society. William P. Palmer Collection of Civil War Manuscripts. Cleveland, Ohio.
Victor Maurin Letter.

PUBLISHED DOCUMENTS AND BOOKS

Acts of Louisiana, 1839. Louisiana State Supreme Court Library, New Orleans, Louisiana.
Acts of Louisiana, 1848. Louisiana State Supreme Court Library, New Orleans, Louisiana.
Annual Report of the Board of Health to the General Assembly of Louisiana for the year 1880. New Orleans, 1881.
The Atlas to Accompany the Official Records of the Union and Confederate Armies. Washington, D. C., 1891-1895.
Biographical and Historical Memoirs of Louisiana. 3 vols. Chicago, 1892.
The Civil War: The Bloodiest Day, Battle of Antietam, 1862. Time-Life Books. Alexandria, VA, 1984.
Diocese of Baton Rouge Catholic Church Records, 22 vols. Baton Rouge.
Historic Culpeper. Culpeper, VA, 1974.
History and Directory of the Boroughs of Adams County, 1880.
History of Cumberland and Adams County . Chicago, 1886.
A History of the Proceedings in the City of New Orleans, on the occasion of the Funeral Ceremonies in Honor of James Abram Garfield, Late President of the United States, which took place on Monday, September 26th, 1881. New Orleans, Louisiana 1881. *Journals of the Congress of the Confederate States of America, 1861-1865.* 7 vols. Washington, D. C., 1904-1905.
Louisiana: A Guide to the State, Compiled by Workers of the Writers' Program of the Work Projects Administration in the state of Louisiana. New York, 1941.
Louisiana Historical Association Catalogue, Memorial Hall. New Orleans, 1917.
Minutes of the Third Annual Meeting and Reunion of the United Confederate Veterans Held in the City of New Orleans, La., April 8th and 9th, 1892. New Orleans, 1892.
Old Homes of Hanover County, Virginia. Hanover, VA, 1983.
Register of the Confederate Dead, Interred in Hollywood Cemetery, Richmond, Va. Richmond, 1869.
Reports of Committees of The House of Representatives for the Second Session of the Forty-third Congress, 1874-'75. Washington D. C., 1875.
Virginia: A Guide to the Old Dominion, Compiled by workers' of the Writer's Program of the Work Projects Administration in the State of Virginia. New York, 1940.
The War of the Rebellion: A Compilation of the Official Records of the Union and Confederate Armies. 130 Volumes. Washington, D. C., 1880-1901.
West Virginia: A Guide to the Mountain State, Compiled by worker's of the Writer's Program of the Work Project Administration in the State of West Virginia. New York, 1941.
Williamsport and Vicinity Reminiscences, Early Part of the 18th Centuary to the Early Part of 1933, Inclusive; Compiled by the Williamsport Chamber of Commerce. Hagerstown, MD.

MEMOIRS AND REMINISCENCES

Adams, John G. *Reminiscences of the Nineteenth Massachusetts Regiment.* Boston, 1899.
Alexander, E. P. *Military Memoirs of a Confederate.* New York, 1907.
Allen, Randall and Keith S. Bohannon, eds. *Campaigning with Old Stonewall, Confederate Captain Ujanirtus Allen's Letters to His Wife.* Baton Rouge, 1998.
An English Combatant [pseud.]. *Battle-Fields of the South, from Bull Run to Fredericksburg, with Sketches of Confederate Commanders, and Gossip of the Camps.* New York, 1864.
Andrews, Eliza F. *The War-Time Journal of a Georgia Girl, 1861-1865.* New York, 1908.
Andrews, W. H. *Footprints of a Regiment, A Recollection of the 1st Georgia Regulars, 1861-1865.* Atlanta, 1992.
Ashby, Thomas A. *The Valley Campaigns Being the Reminiscences of a Non-combatant While Between the Lines in the Shenandoah Valley During the War of the States.* New York, 1914.
Avary, Myrta L. *A Virginia Girl in the Civil War, 1861-1865; Being a Record of the Actual Experiences of the Wife of a Confederate Officer.* New York, 1903.
Axford, Faye A. *The Journals of Thomas Hobbs.* University, AL, 1976.
Baer, Elizabeth R., ed. *Shadows on My Heart, The Civil War Diary of Lucy Rebecca Buck of Virginia.* Athens, GA, 1997.
Baker, Henry H. *A Reminiscent Story of the Great Civil War, Second Paper, A Personal Experience.* New

Orleans, 1911.
Barrett, John G. *Yankee Rebel, The Civil War Journal of Edmund DeWitt Patterson.* Chapel Hill, 1966.
Bartlett, Napier. *Military Record of Louisiana.* Baton Rouge, 1875.
———. *Clarimonde: A Tale of New Orleans Life, and of the Present War.* Richmond, 1863.
Bennett, A. J. *The Story of the First Massachusetts Light Battery, Attached to the Sixth Army Corps.* Boston, 1886.
Benson, Berry G. *Berry Benson's Civil War Book: Memoirs of a Confederate Scout and Sharpshooter.* Athens, GA, 1962.
Billings, John D. *Hardtack and Coffee.* Boston, 1887.
———. *The History of the Tenth Massachusetts Battery of Light Artillery in the War of the Rebellion 1862-1865.* Boston, 1909.
Blight, David W., ed. *When This Cruel War Is Over.* Amherst, MA, 1992.
Borcke, Heros Von. *Memoirs of the Confederate War for Independence.* 2 vols. New York, 1938.
Boykin, Edward M. *The Falling Flag. Evacuation of Richmond, Retreat and Surrender at Appomattox.* New York, 1874.
Brent, Joseph L. *Memoirs of the War Between the States.* New Orleans, 1940.
Brock, R. A., ed. *Gen. Robert Edward Lee; Soldier, Citizen, and Christian Patriot.* Atlanta, 1897.
Brunson, J. W. *Historical Sketch of the Pee Dee Light Artillery by Orderly Sgt. J. W. Brunson, Together with a Roll of McIntosh's Battalion Artillery.* Winston-Salem, NC, 1927.
Caldwell, J. F. J. *The History of a Brigade of South Carolinians.* Philadelphia, 1866.
Callaway, Felix R. *The Bloody Links.* Shreveport, LA, 1907.
Chamberlayne, C. G., ed. *Ham Chamberlayne-Virginian, Letters and Papers of an Artillery Officer.* Richmond, 1932.
Chamberlaine, William W. *Memoirs of the Civil War.* Washington, D. C., 1912.
Chesson, Michael B. and Leslie J. Roberts, eds. *Exile in Richmond, The Confederate Journal of Henri Garidel.* Charlottesville, VA, 2001.
Clark, Walter, ed. *Histories of the Several Regiments and Battalions from North Carolina in the Great War 1861-'65.* 5 vols. Goldsboro, NC, 1901.
Cockrell, Monroe F., ed. *Gunner with Stonewall, Reminiscences of William Thomas Poague.* Jackson, TN, 1957.
Cockrell, Thomas D. and Michael B. Ballard, eds. *A Mississippi Rebel in the Army of Northern Virginia, The Civil War Memoirs of Private David Holt.* Baton Rouge, 1995.
Couture, Richard T., ed. *Charlie's Letters, The Civil War Correspondence of Charles E. Denoon.* Collingswood, NJ, 1989.
Cutrer, Thomas W. and T. Michael Parrish, eds. *Brothers in Gray, The Civil War Letters of the Pierson Family.* Baton Rouge, 1997.
Dame, William M. *From the Rapidan to Richmond and the Spotsylvania Campaign.* Baltimore, 1920.
Dawson, Francis W. *Reminiscences of Confederate Service, 1861-1865.* Baton Rouge, 1980.
Davis, Archie K. *Boy Colonel of the Confederacy, The Life And Times of Henry King Burgwyn, Jr.* Chapel Hill, 1985.
Davis, Varina. *Jefferson Davis, Ex-President of the Confederate States of America: A Memoir by His Wife in Two Volumes.* New York, 1890.
DeFontaine, Felix G. *Marginalia; or, Gleanings from an Army Note-book.* Columbia, SC, 1864.
De Peyster, J. Watts. *Sailor' Creek to Appomattox Court House, 7th, 8th, 9th April 1865; or, The Last Hours of Sheridan's Cavalry. War-Memoranda of Henry Edwin Tremain.* New York, 1885.
De Trobriand, Regis. *Four Years with the Army of the Potomac.* Boston, 1889.
Dinkins, James. *1861-1865 By an Old Johnnie.* Cincinnati, 1897.
Dunaway, Wayland F. *Reminiscences of a Rebel.* New York, 1913.
Dunlop, William S. *Lee's Sharpshooters; or, The Forefront of Battle. A Story of Southern Valor That Never Has Been Told.* Little Rock, 1899.
Durkin, Joseph T., ed. *Confederate Chaplain, A War Journal, of Rev. James B. Sheeran, c.ss.r., 14th Louisiana, C. S. A.* Milwaukee, 1960.
Early, Ruth H. *Lieutenant General Jubal Anderson Early C. S. A. Autobiographical Sketch and Narrative of the War Between the States.* Philadelphia, 1912.
Ellis, Billy. *Tithes of Blood, A Confederate Soldier's Story.* Murfreesboro, TN, 1997.
Everson, Guy R., and Edward H. Simpson Jr., eds. *Far, Far From Home, The Wartime Letters of Dick*

and Tally Simpson, 3rd South Carolina Volunteers. New York, 1994.
Figg, Royal W. *"Where Men Only Dare To Go!" or the Story Of A Boy Company.* Richmond, 1885.
Fleming, Francis P. *Memoir of Capt. C. Seton Fleming.* Jacksonville, FL, 1884.
Folsom, James M. *Heroes and Martyrs of Georgia, Georgia Record in the Revolution of 1861.* Macon, GA, 1864.
Forbes, Edwin. *Thirty Years After, An Artist's Story of the Great War.* New York, 1890.
Gallagher, Gary W., ed. *Fighting for the Confederacy, The Personal Recollections of General Edward Porter Alexander.* Chapel Hill, 1989.
Gordon, Armistead C. *Memories and Memorials of William Gordon McCabe,* Two Volumes. Richmond, 1925.
Grant, Ulyssess S. *Personal Memoirs of U. S. Grant in Two Volumes, II.* New York, 1886.
Graves, Joseph A. *The History of the Bedford Light Artillery.* Bedford City, VA, 1903.
Hamilton, J. G. deRoulhac, ed. *The Papers of Randolph Albert Shotwell.* 2 vols. Raleigh, NC, 1936.
Handerson, Henry E. *Yankee in Gray: The Civil War Memoirs of Henry E. Handerson with a Selection of His Wartime Letters.* Cleveland, 1962.
Harrison, Mrs. Burton. *Recollections Grave and Gay.* New York, 1911.
Hassler, William W. *The General to His Lady: The Civil War Letters of William Dorsey Pender to Fanny Pender.* Chapel Hill, 1965.
Harwell, Richard B., ed, *A Confederate Diary of the Retreat from Petersburg April 2-20, 1865.* Atlanta, 1953.
Hewitt John H. *War: A Poem, with Copious Notes, Founded on the Revolution of 1861-1862.* Richmond, 1862.
Hoke, J. *Reminiscences of The War; or, Incidents Which Transpired in and about Chambersburg, During the War of the Rebellion.* Chambersburg, PA, 1884.
Houghton W. R. and M. B. Houghton. *Two Boys in the Civil War and After.* Montgomery, AL, 1912.
Hurst, M. B. *History of the Fourteenth Regiment Alabama Volunteers.* Richmond, 1863.
Jacobs, M. *Notes on the Rebel Invasion of Maryland and Pennsylvania and the Battle of Gettysburg July 1st, 2d and 3d, 1863.* Philadelphia, 1864.
Johnson, R. U. and C. C. Buel, eds. *Battles and Leaders of the Civil War.* 4 vols. New York, 1884-87.
Jones, Benjamin W. *Under the Stars and Bars: A History of the Surry Light Artillery; Recollections of a Private Soldier in the War Between the States.* Richmond, 1909.
Jones, Terry L., ed. *The Civil War Memoirs of Captain William J. Seymour,*
———. *Reminiscences of a Louisiana Tiger.* Baton Rouge, 1991.
Kent, Arthur A., ed. *Three Years with Company K, Sergt. Austin C. Stearns, Company K, 13th Mass. Infantry (Deceased).* Cranbury, NJ, 1976.
Kirk, Hyland C. *History of the 4th New York Heavy Artillery.* New York, 1890.
Lankford, Nelson D., ed. *An Irishman in Dixie, Thomas Conolly's Diary of the Fall of the Confederacy.* Columbia, SC, 1988.
Lasswell, Mary, ed. *Rags and Hope: The Memoirs of Val C. Giles.* New York, 1961.
Lee, Laura E. *For-Get-Me-Nots of the Civil War, A Romance containing Reminiscences and Original Letters of Two Confederate Soldiers.* St. Louis, MO, 1909.
Lee, Susan P. *Memoirs of William Nelson Pendleton.* Philadelphia, 1893.
Leon, L. *Diary of a Tar Heel Confederate Soldier.* Charlotte, NC 1913.
Livermore, Thomas L. *Days and Events, 1860-1866.* Boston, 1920.
Longstreet, James. *From Manassas to Appomattox.* Philadelphia, 1896.
Lord, Walter, ed. *The Freemantle Diary.* Boston, 1954.
Maurice, Frederick, ed. *An Aide-De-Camp of Lee Being the Papers of Colonel Charles Marshall.* Boston, 1927.
McCarthy, Carlton, ed. *Contributions to a History of the Richmond Howitzers.* 4 Pamphlets. Richmond, 1884.
———. *Detailed Minutiae of Soldier Life in the Army of Northern Virginia, 1861-1865.* Richmond, 1882.
McClendon, William A. *Recollections of War Times.* Montgomery, AL, 1909.
McDonald, Archie P., ed. *Make Me A Map of the Valley, The Civil War Journal of Stonewall Jackson's Topographer Jedediah Hotchkiss.* Dallas, 1973.
McGuire, Judith. *Diary of a Southern Refugee.* New York, 1867.

Moore, Edward A. *The Story of a Cannoneer Under Stonewall Jackson.* New York, 1907.
Moore, Frank, ed. *The Rebellion Record.* 12 vols. New York, 1861-1868.
Morgan, James M. *Midshipman in Gray.* Boston, 1917.
Neese, George M. *Three years in the Confederate Horse Artillery.* Boston, 1911.
Owen, William M. *In Camp and Battle with the Washington Artillery.* Boston, 1885.
Park, Robert E. *Sketch of the Twelfth Alabama Infantry of Battle's Brigade, Rhodes' Division, Early's Corps, of the Army of Northern Virginia.* Richmond, 1906.
Polley, J. B. *Hood's Texas Brigade.* New York, 1910.
Pratt, Fletcher, ed. *My Diary North and South, William Howard Russell.* New York, 1954.
Pryor, Mrs. Roger A. *Reminiscences of Peace and War.* New York, 1904.
Putnam, Sallie B. *Richmond During the War, Four Years of Personal Observation.* New York, 1867.
Reid, J. W. *History of the Fourth Regiment of S. C. Volunteers.* Greenville, SC, 1891.
Richardson, Charles. *Tales of a Warrior, Sanguine but Not Sanguinary For Old-time People.* New York, 1907.
Roberson, Elizabeth W. *Weep Not for Me Dear Mother.* Gretna, LA, 1996.
Robson, John S. *How a One-legged Rebel Lives, Reminiscences of the Civil War.* Durham, NC, 1898.
Roe, Alfred S. *The Tenth Regiment Massachusetts Volunteer Infantry 1861-1864, A Western Massachusetts Regiment.* Springfield, MA, 1909.
Roman, Alfred. *Military Operations of General Beauregard in the War Between the States, 1861 to 1865.* 2 vols. New York, 1884.
Rourke, Norman E., ed. *I saw the Elephant: The Civil War Experiences of Baily George McClelen, Company D, 10th Alabama Infantry Regiment.* Shippensburg, PA, 1995.
Rowland, Dunbar, ed. *Jefferson Davis, Constitutionalist, His Letters, Papers and Speeches.* 10 vols. Jackson, MS, 1923.
———. *Official and Statistical Register of the State of Mississippi,* Vol. 5, *Military History of Mississippi, 1803-1898.* Nashville, 1908.
Rozier, John. *The Granite Farm Letters, The Civil War Correspondences of Edgeworth & Sallie Bird* Athens, GA, 1988.
Runge, William H., ed. *Four Years in the Confederate Artillery: The Diary of Private Henry Robinson Berkely.* Chapel Hill, 1961.
Russell, William H. *Pictures of Southern Life, Social, Political, and Military Written for the Londen Times.* New York, 1861.
Scheibert, Justus. *Seven Months in the Rebel States During the North American War, 1863* Tuscaloosa, AL, 1958.
Shoemaker, John J. *Shoemaker's Battery, Stuart's Horse Artillery, Pelham's Battalion, Army of Northern Virginia.* Memphis, 1908.
Silver, James W., ed. *A Life For the Confederacy, From the War Diary of Robert A. Moore, Pvt. C. S. A."* Wilmington, NC, 1987.
Steiner, Lewis H. *Report of Lewis H. Steiner, M. D., Inspector of the Sanitary Commission, containing a Diary kept during the Rebel Occupation of Frederick, Md.* New York, 1862.
Stewart, William H. *A Pair of Blankets.* New York, 1911.
Stiles, Robert. *Four Years Under Marse Robert.* New York, 1903.
Taylor, F. Jay, ed. *Reluctant Rebel, The Secret Diary of Robert Patrick, 1861-1865.* Baton Rouge, 1959.
Thomson, R. Howard and William H. Rauch, eds. *History of the "Bucktails": Kane Rifle Regiment of the Pennsylvania Reserve Corps, 42nd Infantry.* Philadelphia, 1906.
Tower, R. Lockwood, ed. *Lee's Adjutant, The Wartime Letters of Colonel Walter Herron Taylor, 1862-1865.* Columbia, SC, 1995.
Tyler, Mason W. *Recollections of the Civil War with Many Original Diary Entries and Letters Written from the Seat of War, and with Annotated References.* New York, 1912.
United Daughters of the Confederacy, John K. McIver Chapter. *Treasured Reminiscences Collected by the John K. McIver Chapter, United Daughters of the Confederacy.* Columbia, SC 1911.
Valentine, Herbert E. *Story of Co. F, 23d Massachusetts Volunteers in the War for the Union 1861-1865.* Boston, 1896.
Walcott, Charles F. *History of the Twenty-First Regiment Massachusetts Volunteers in the War for the Preservation of the Union 1861-1865 with Statistics of the War and of Rebel Prisons.* Boston, 1882.
Walker, C. Irvine. *Life of Lt. Gen. Richard Heron Anderson.* Charleston, SC, 1917.

Watson, William. *Life in the Confederate Army Being the Observations and Experiences of An Alien in the South During the American Civil War.* New York, 1888.
Welch, Spencer G. *A Confederate Surgeon's Letters To His Wife.* New York, 1911.
White, Henry A. *Memoirs of the Confederate War for Independence.* Philadelphia, 1867.
Wiley, Bell I., ed. *Recollections of a Confederate Staff Officer.* Jackson, TN, 1959.
———. *Reminiscences of Big I by Lieut. William Nathaniel Wood.* Jackson, TN, 1956.
Williams, Evelyn C., ed. *Letters of James Peter Williams, 1861-1865.* Lynchburg, VA, 1937.
Wilson, Legrand J. *The Confederate Soldier.* Memphis, TN, 1973.
Wright, Stuart T., ed. *The Confederate Letters of Benjamin H. Freeman.* Hicksville, NY, 1974.

PRIMARY SOURCE JOURNALS AND ARTICLES

Alexander, Edward "The Battle of Fredericksburg. Paper No. 1." *Southern Historical Society Papers* X.
———. "The Battle of Fredericksburg. Paper No. 2." *Southern Historical Society Papers* X.
Andrews, W. H. "Tige Anderson's Brigade at Sharpsburg." *Confederate Veteran* XVI (1908).
Bouve, Edward T. "The Battle at High Bridge." *The New England Magazine* 10, no. 5 (July 1891).
Bradwell, I. G. "From Gettysburg to the Potomac."*Confederate Veteran* XXX (1922).
———. "General Lee at Sharpsburg, 1862." *Confederate Veteran* XXVIV (1921).
———. "On Picket Duty in Front of Fort Steadman, 1865." *Confedertae Veteran* XXV (1917).
———. "On Picket Duty in Front of Fort Steadman." *Confederate Veteran* XXXVIII (1930).
———. "Soldier Life in the Confederate Army." *Confederate Veteran* XXIV (1916).
Brunson, James A. "Cannoneers As Cavalrymen." *Confederate Veteran* XXIII (1915).
Butler, H. A. "Fredericksburg—Personal Reminiscences." *Confederate Veteran* XIV (1906).
Caffey, Thomas. "Letters From the Front." *Confederate Veteran* XXVI (1918).
Clark, George. "Wilcox's Alabama Brigade at Gettysburg." *Confederate Veteran* XXVII (1909).
Conerly, Buxton R. "How Fort Gregg Was Defended." *Confederate Veteran* XV (1907).
Conner, Forrest P., ed. "Letters of Lieutenant Robert H. Miller to His Family, 1861-1862." *The Virginia Magazine of History and Biography* 70, no. 1 (1962).
Cottrell, E. C. "The Fight at Fort Gregg." *Confederate Veteran* VII (1899).
Cummings, C. C. "Battle of Fredericksburg, December 13, 1862." *Confederate Veteran* XXIII (1915).
Cummings, J. D. "The Last Sad Days." *Southern Historical Society Papers* XXXV.
Day, W. A. "Life Among Bullets—In the Rifle Pits." *Confederate Veteran* XXIX (1929).
"D'Gournay's Battalion of Artillery." *Confederate Veteran* XIII (1905).
Easley, D. B. "Experiences at Seven Pines." *Confederate Veteran* XXXVII (1929).
Goolsby, J. C. "Crenshaw Battery, Pegram's Battalion, Confederate States Artillery." *Southern Historical Society Papers* XXVIII (1900).
Groene, Bertram H., ed. "Civil War Letters of Colonel David Lang." *The Florida Historical Quarterly* 14 (1976).
Gomer, A. P. "Service of Third Virginia Infantry." *Confederate Veteran* XVIII (1910).
Halstead, E. "The First Day at the Battle of Gettysburg." *The Gettysburg Papers, Washington D. C. MOLLUS* 1-2 (1887).
Hamilton, Vol. II, 31, 32; Berkeley Minor. "The Night After Gettysburg."*Confederate Veteran* XXXIII (1925).
Harrison, Burton N. "The Capture of Jefferson Davis." *The Century Illustrated Monthly Magazine* 27 (November 1883 - April 1884).
Hawes, Percy G. "Last Days of the Army of Northern Virginia, A Courier's Recollections of the Last Ten days of War." *Confederate Veteran* XVII (1919).
Hebert, Hilary A. "History of the Eighth Alabama Volunteer Regiment, C. S. A." *Alabama Historical Quarterly* 39 (1977).
Hicks, E. M. "Stories of Service in Virginia." *Confederate Veteran* XX (1912).
Hogan, N. B. "Gaines's Mill—Pickett and Hood." *Confederate Veteran* V (1898).
Hoole, Stanley, ed. "The Letters of Captain Joab Goodson, 1862-1864." *The Alabama Review* X (1957).
Hunter, Alexander. "A High Private's Account of the Battle of Sharpsburg, Paper No. 1." *Southern Historical Society Papers* X.

Irvine, H. I. "Getting Out of It." *Confederate Veteran* XXXIV (1926).
Kimble, June. "Tennesseeans at Gettysburg—The Retreat." *Confederate Veteran* XXVIII (1910).
"The Last Roll." *Confederate Veteran*, X (1902).
"The Last Roll." *Confederate Veteran*, XXXIII (1925).
"The Last Roll." *Confederate Veteran*, XXXIV (1926).
Landry, R. Prosper. "The Donaldsonville Artillery at the Battle of Fredericksburg." *Southern Historical Society Papers* XXIII.
Leech, John W. T. "The Battle of Frazier's Farm." *Southern Historical Society Papers* XXI.
Levy, Eugene H. "The Donaldsonville Artillery." *Southern Bivouac* III (March 1885).
"Lutheran Theological Seminary." *Confederate Veteran* XXI (1913).
Marye, John L. "The First Gun at Gettysburg." *The American Historical Register* (July 1895).
Maury, Richard L. "The Battle of Williamsburg, Va." *Southern Historical Society Papers* XXII.
McCabe, William G. "Annual Reunion of Pegram Battalion Association." *Southern Historical Society Papers* XIV (1886).
Mellon, Knox, Jr. "A Florida Soldier in the Army of Northern Virginia: The Hosford Letters." *The Florida Historical Quarterly* XLVI, no. 3 (1968).
Minnich, J. W. "Incidents of the Peninsular Campaign." *Confederate Veteran* XXX (1922).
———. "Picturesque Soldiery." *Confederate Veteran* XXXI (1923).
Mitchell, Mary B. "In the Wake of Battle (A Woman's Recollection of Shepherdstown During Antietam Week)." *The Century; A Popular Quarterly* 32, no. 3 (1886).
Moncure, E. C. "Reminiscences of the Civil War." *Bulletin of the Virginia State Library*, XVI, no. 2-3 (July 1927).
Moon, W. H. "Beginning of the Battle at Gettysburg." *Confederate Veteran* XXXIII (1925).
Moore, J. B. "Description of the Battle of Sharpsburg." *Southern Historical Society Papers* XXVII.
Morrison, James L., Jr., ed. "The Memoirs of Henry Heth, Part II." *Civil War History* 8 (September 1962).
Osborne, Hampden. "The Struggle for Fort Mahone." *Confederate Veteran* XXV (1917).
Park, Robert E. "Sketch of the Twelfth Alabama Infantry...Army of Northern Virginia." *Southern Historical Society Papers* XXXIII.
"Paroles of the Army of Northern Virginia, R. E. Lee, Gen., C. S. A. command, surrendered at Appomattox C. H., Va., April 9, 1865, to Lieutenant-General U.S. Grant, commanding Armies of the U.S." *Southern Historical Society Papers* XV.
Plecker, A. H. "Who Saved Lynchburg From Hunter's Raid?" *Confederate Veteran* XXX (1922).
Poindexter, Charles. "Richmond Howitzers. Facts about the battery during the Appomattox Campaign." *Southern Historical Society Papers* XXVI.
Popkins, W. A. "Imboden's Brigade at Gettysburg."*Confederate Veteran* XXII (1914).
Purifoy, John. "Concerning Battle of Gettysburg."*Confederate Veteran* XIX (1911).
———. "In Battle Array at Williamsport and Hagerstown." *Confederate Veteran* XXXIII (1925).
———. "The Retreat From Gettysburg." *Confederate Veteran* XXXIII (1925).
Robinson, W. F. "Last Battle Before Surrender." *Confederate Veteran* XXII (1924).
Shewmaker, Kenneth E. and Andrew K. Prinz, eds. "A Yankee in Louisiana: Selections from the Diary and Correspondences of Henry R. Gardner, 1862-1866." *Louisiana History* V, no. 3 (1964).
Slack, A. L. "After the Battle of Frazier's Farm." *Confederate Veteran* II (1894).
Snead, C. G. "Another Unwritten Artillery Duel." *Confederate Veteran* XXIX (1921).
Stewart, William H. "Appomattox." *Tales of the Civil War* (1896).
Strother, A. E. "Battle and Capture of Fort Gregg." *Confederate Veteran* XXIX (1921).
Townsend, Harry C. "Townsend's Diary—January-May, 1865; From Petersburg to Appomattox, Thence to North Carolina to Join Johnston's Army." *Southern Historical Society Papers* XXXIV.
Tucker, John S. "The Diary of John S. Tucker." *Alabama Historical Quarterly* 43 (1981).
Unidentified. "The Battle at Fort Gregg, Louisiana Survivors Tell the Story of the Fight." *Southern Historical Society Papers* XXVIII.
Welsh, George P. "Civil War Letters from Two Brothers." *The Yale Review* XVIII (1929).
Winder, J. R. "Reminiscences of J. R. Winder." *Confederate Veteran* VIII (1901).
Wright, Gilbert, ed. "Some letters to His Parents By a Floridian in the Confederate Army." *Florida Historical Quarterly* XXXVI (1958).

NEWSPAPERS

Adams (Gettysburg, Pennsylvania) *Sentinel,* 1837.
Amite City (Louisiana) *Times,* 1984.
Amite (Louisiana) *News Digest,* 1984.
Assumption (Napoleonville, Louisiana) *Pioneer,* 1851, 1879, 1880, 1893, 1894, 1887-1900, 1907-1909, 1911, 1914, 1921, 1923, 1935.
Atlanta (Georgia) *Constitution,* 1882, 1914.
Baltimore (Maryland) *Sun, 1904.*
Baton Rouge (Louisiana) *Gazette and Comet,* 1860.
Baton Rouge (Louisiana) *States-Times Advocate,* 1913.
Baton Rouge (Louisiana) *Advocate,* 1861.
Baton Rouge (Louisiana) *True Advocate,* 1891, 1893.
Butte (Montana) *Weekly Miner,* 1898.
Charleston (South Carolina) *Daily Courier,* 1861, 1862.
Charleston (South Carolina) *Mercury,* 1861, 1862.
Cincinnati (Ohio) *Daily Inquirer,* 1870, 1874.
Charlottesville (Virginia) *Daily Chronicle,* 1864.
The Civil War News (Tunbridge, Vermont), 2004.
The (False River, Louisiana) *Democrat,* 1861.
The (Fredericksburg, Virginia) *Free Lance,* 1885
Donaldsonville (Louisiana) *Chief,* 1874, 1875, 1877, 1878, 1880, 1882-1884, 1886, 1893, 1904, 1906-1909, 1913, 1915, 1916, 1918, 1928, 1930, 1931, 1935.
Donaldsonville (Louisiana) *Daily Times,* 1896-1898.
Donaldsonville (Louisiana) *Gazette,* 1826.
Donaldsonville (Louisiana) *Le Drapeau,* 1867, 1868, 1871.
Donaldsonville (Louisiana) *Le Vigilant,* 1846, 1847, 1849, 1850-1852, 1854.
Flake's Bulletin (Galveston, Texas), 1870.
Florida Parishes (Amite City, Louisiana) *Times,* 1922.
The Galveston (Texas) *Daily News,* 1879, 1883.
The Gettysburg (Pennsylvania) *Compiler,* 1894.
Gettysburg (Pennsylvania) *Star and Sentinel,* 1894.
Gonzales (Louisiana) *Weekly,* 1921.
Lafayette (Louisiana) *Advertiser,* 1901.
Lafayette (Louisiana) *Gazette,* 1901.
Lynchburg (Virginia) *Virginian,* 1864.
The Louisiana Planter and Sugar Manufacturer (New Orleans, Louisiana) *A Weekly Newspaper,* 1909.
The Macon (Georgia) *Daily Telegraph,* 1850, 1865.
The Macon (Georgia) *Weekly Telegraph,* 1862.
Memphis (Tennessee) *Daily Appeal,* 1861.
Memphis (Tennessee) *Daily Avalanche,* 1861.
Mississippi (Biloxi) *Daily Herald,* 1901.
New Orleans (Louisiana) *Bee,* 1837, 1841.
New Orleans (Louisiana) *Courier,* 1830.
New Orleans (Louisiana) *Dailey City Item, 1879,* 1880, 1891, 1892, 1907.
New Orleans (Louisiana) *Daily Crescent,* 1861, 1866.
New Orleans (Louisiana) *Daily Delta,* 1861.
New Orleans (Louisiana) *Daily Picayune,* 1861, 1872, 1882, 1899.
New Orleans (Louisiana) *Daily True Delta,* 1859, 1861.
New Orleans (Louisiana) *Item,* 1891.
New Orleans (Louisiana) *L'Abeille,* 1837, 1861.
New Orleans (Louisiana) *Republican,* 1870, 1871.
New Orleans (Louisiana) *Times-Democrat,* 1877, 1892, 1905.
New Orleans (Louisiana) *Times Picayune,* 1837, 1847, 1850-1852, 1861, 1862, 1865, 1867-1872, 1874-1876, 1876,1880, 1882, 1885, 1887, 1891, 1893, 1896, 1898-1903, 1906-1908, 1911, 1914, 1916, 1918, 1919, 1930.

New York Evening Mail, 1917.
New York (New York) *Herald,* 1861, 1862, 1871, 1886, 1892.
New York (New York) *Times,* 1862, 1887, 1890, 1912.
New York (New York) *Tribune,* 1897.
Ouachita (Louisiana) *Telegraph,* 1877.
The Petersburg (Virginia) *Index,* 1860, 1867, 1869, 1870.
Philadelphia (Pennsylvania) *Inquire,* 1862.
Philadelphia (Pennsylvania) *Weekly Times,* 1879.
Richmond Daily (Virginia) *Whig,* 1861
Richmond Daily (Virginia) *Dispatch,* 1861, 1862, 1902.
Daily Richmond (Virginia) *Examiner,* 1862, 1864.
Daily Richmond (Virginia) *Enquirer,* 1861, 1862.
Richmond (Virginia) *Sentinel,* 1864.
Richmond (Virginia) *Times Dispatch,* 1905, 1934.
Rome (Georgia) *Courier,* 1862, 1863.
The Winchester (Virginia) *Star,* 1991.
Washington (Pennsylvania) *Reporter,* 1848.
West Baton Rouge (Louisiana) *Sugar Planter,* 1860.

SECONDARY SOURCES

BOOKS

Abel, E. Lawrence. *Singing the New Nation, How Music Shaped the Confederacy, 1861-1865.* Mechanicsburg, PA, 2000.
Aleman, Snyder and Hilda M. Lovett. *A Brief History of Trinity Evangelical Lutheran Church, Stephens City, Virginia 1765-1990.* Stephens City, VA, 1990.
Alvarez, Eugene. *Travel on Southern Antebellum Railroads, 1828-1860.* University, AL, 1974.
Andrews, J. Cutler. *The South Reports the Civil War.* Princeton, NJ, 1970.
Baber, Lucy H. M. and Evelyn L. Moore, *Behind the Old Brick Wall, A Cemetery Story.* Lynchburg, VA, 1968.
Ballard, Michael B. *A Long Shadow, Jefferson Davis and the Final Days of the Confederacy.* Athens, GA, 1997.
Baudier, Roger. *The Catholic Church in Louisiana.* New Orleans, 1939.
Beers, Henry. *The Confederacy, A Guide to the Archives of the Government of the Confederate States of America.* Washington, D. C., 1986
Bill, Alfred H. *The Beleaguered City Richmond, 1861-1865.* New York, 1946.
Black, Robert C., III. *The Railroads of the Confederacy.* Chapel Hill, 1952.
Boatner, Mark M. *The Civil War Dictionary.* New York, 1959.
Bouchereau, Louis. "The Louisiana Sugar Report, 1870-1917." In *Statement of the Sugar and Rice Crops, Made in Louisiana.* New Orleans, 1870-1917.
Bourgeois, Lillian C. *Cabanocey: The History, Customs, and Folklore of St. James Parish.* Gretna, LA, 1957.
Bradshaw, Hebert C. *History of Prince Edward County, Virginia, From Its Earliest Settlements Through Its Establishment in 1754, To Its Bicentennial Year.* Richmond, 1955.
Brasseaux, Carl A. *Acadian to Cajun, Transformation of a People, 1803-1877.* Jackson, MS, 1992.
Brock, Sallie A., ed. *The Southern Amaranth.* New York, 1869.
Burrell, Charles E. *History of Prince Edward County, Virginia, From Its Formation in 1753, to the Present.* Richmond, 1922.
Calkins, Christopher M. *The Appomattox Campaign, March 29-April 9, 1865.* Conshohocken, PA, 1997.
———. *The Battles of Appomattox Station and Appomattox Court House, April 8-9, 1865.* Lynchburg, VA, 1987.
———. *From Petersburg to Appomattox.* Farmville, VA, 1983.
———. *The Final Bivouac: The Surrender Parade at Appomattox and the Disbanding of the Armies,*

April 1 to May 20,1865. Lynchburg, VA, 1988.

Cartmell, T. K. *Shenandoah Valley Pioneers and Their Descendants: A History of Frederick County, Virginia From its Formation in 1738 to 1908*. Bowie, MD, 1908.

Chambers, Allan S., Jr. *Lynchburg, An Architectural History*. Charlottesville, VA, 1981.

Chambers, Henry E. *A History of Louisiana, Wilderness—Colony—Province—Territory—State—People*. 3 vols. Chicago and New York, 1925.

Chandler, David G. *The Campaigns of Napoleon*. New York, 1966.

Conrad, Glenn R., ed. *A Dictionary of Louisiana Biography*, 2 vols. Lafayette, LA, 1998.

———., ed. *Readings in Louisiana History*. New Orleans, 1978.

Cooke, John Esten. *The Life of Stonewall Jackson*. Richmond, 1863.

Dabney, Thomas E. *100 Years of the Canal Bank and Trust Company*. New Orleans, 1931.

Daigle, Jules O. *Cajun Self-taught*. Ville Platte, LA, 1992.

Daniel, Frederick S. *Richmond Howitzers in the War*. Richmond, 1891.

Davis, Edwin Adam. *Louisiana, A Narrative History*. Baton Rouge, 1971.

Dicharry, Warren, C. M. "Father Charles Boglioli (1814-1882): Leper Priest of Charity Hospital."In *Religious Pioneers, Building the Faith in the Archdiocese of New Orleans*, edited by Dorothy Dawes and Charles Nolan. New Orleans, 2004.

Day, Yvonne L. *Gathering Home: The Cemeteries of Amite City, La*. Baton Rouge, 2002.

De la Souchere, Simon. *Napoleon's Soldiers in America*. New Orleans, 1972.

Din, Gilbert C. *The Canary Islanders of Louisiana*. Baton Rouge, 1988.

Driver, Robert J. *The 1st and 2nd Rockbridge Artillery*. Lynchburg, VA, 1987.

Evans, Clement A., ed. *Confederate Military History, Extended Edition*. 17 vols. Atlanta, 1899.

Ezekiel, Herbert T. and Gaston Lichtenstein. *The History of the Jews Of Richmond from 1769 to 1917*. Richmond, 1917.

Farrar, Emmie F. *Old Virginia Houses Along the James*. New York, 1957.

Foote, Shelby. *The Civil War: A Narrative*. 3 vols. New York, 1958-1974.

Forrest, Mary. *Women of the South Distinguished in Literature*. New York, 1866.

Fortier, Alceé. *Louisiana: Comprising Sketches of Parishes, Towns, Events, Institutions, and Persons, Arranged in Cyclopedic Form*. 3 vols. 1914.

Fox, John J., III. *Red Clay to Richmond, Trail of the 35th Georgia Infantry Regiment, CSA*. Winchester, VA, 2004.

Freeman, Douglas S., ed. *Lee's Dispatches* New York, 1915.

———. *Lee's Lieutenant's, A Study in Command*. 3 vols. New York, 1942.

———. *R. E. Lee, A Biography*. 4 vols. New York, 1934.

———. *The South to Posterity*. New York, 1951.

Gallagher, Gary W., ed. *Antietam, Essays on the 1862 Maryland Campaign*. Kent, OH, 1989.

———., ed. *The Antietam Campaign*. Chapel Hill, NC, 1999.

Gandolfo, Henri A. *Metairie Cemetery, An Historical Memoir, Tales of Its Statesman, Soldiers and Great Families*. New Orleans, 1981

Gayarré, Charles. *History of Louisiana*, 4 vols. New Orleans, 1885.

Geary, Patrick J., ed. *Celine, Remembering Louisiana, 1850-1871, Celine Fremaux Garcia*. Athens, GA, 1987.

Geier, Clarence R. and Stephen R. Potter. *Archaeological Perspectives on the American Civil War*. Gainesville, FL, 2000.

General, Foy. *History of the War in the Peninsula, Under Napoleon; to which is prefixed A View of the Political and Military State of the Four Belligerent Powers*. Vol. 2, bk. 1. London, 1827.

Gibbon, John. *The Artillerist's Manuel*. New York, 1863.

Gills, Mary L. *It Happened at Appomattox, The Story of an Historic Virginia Village*. Richmond, 1948.

Gordon, Armistead C. *In the Picturesque Shenandoah Valley*. Richmond, 1930.

Greene, A. Wilson. *Civil War Petersburg: Confederate City in the Crucible of War*. Charlottesville, VA, 2006.

Griffin, William E., Jr. *One Hundred Fifty Years of History Along The Richmond, Fredericksburg and Potomac Railroad*. Richmond, 1984.

Hearn, Lafcadio. *Gombo Zhebes, Little Dictionary of Creole Proverbs*. New York, 1885.

Heinel, Robert Debs, Jr. and Nancy Gordon Heinel. *Written in Blood, The Story of the Haitian People 1492-1971*. Boston, 1978.

Henderson, William D. *12th Virginia Infantry.* Lynchburg, VA, 1984.
Hite, Mary E. *My Rappahannock Story Book.* Richmond, 1950.
Huddle, W. P. *History of the Hebron Lutheran Church, Madison County, Virginia, from 1717 to 1907.* Madison, VA, 1908.
Hurst, Patricia J. *The History and People of Clark Mountain, Orange County, Virginia.* Rapidan, VA, 1988.
———. *Soldiers, Stories, Sites and Fights, Orange County, Virginia 1861-1865 and the Aftermath.* Rapidan, VA, 1998.
Johnson, Elizabeth B. and C. E. Johnson, Jr. *Rappahannock County, Va., A History Fact, Fiction, Foolishness and the Fairfax Story.* Orange, VA, 1981.
Johnston, Angus J., II. *Virginia Railroads in the Civil War.* Chapel Hill, NC, 1961.
Johnson, C. E., Jr. *Rappahannock County, Va., A History Fact, Fiction, Foolishness and the Fairfax Story.* Orange, VA, 1981.
Jones, J. William. *The Davis Memorial Volume or Our Dead President, Jefferson Davis and the World's Tribute To His Memory.* Richmond, 1890.
Jordan, Ervin L., Jr. *Charlottesville and the University of Virginia in the Civil War.* Lynchburg, VA, 1988.
Kalbian, Maral S. *Frederick County, Virginia: History Through Architecture.* Winchester, VA, 1999.
Kane, Harnett T. *The Bayous of Louisiana.* New York, 1944.
Kendall, John S. *A History of New Orleans.* 3 vols. Chicago, 1922.
Klorer, John D. *The New Louisiana, The Story of the Greatest State of the Nation.* New Orleans, n.d.
Korn, Betram W. *Jews and Negro Slavery in the Old South 1789-1865.* Elkins Park, PA, 1961.
Landry, Kirk P. *Postcards from the Past.* Donaldsonville, LA, 2004.
Lanoux, Louise "Pie." *We have met Our Neighbors.* Gonzales, LA, n.d.
Lemann, Bernard. *The Lemann Family of Louisiana.* Donaldsonville, LA, 1965.
Longfellow, Henry Wadsworth. *Evangeline.* New York, 1892.
Lonn, Ella. *Foreigners In the Confederacy.* Chapel Hill, 1940
Marchand, Sidney A. *Acadian Exiles in the Golden Coast of Louisiana.* Donaldsonville, LA, 1943.
———. *The Chief in the Land of the Chetimaches.* Donaldsonville, LA, 1959.
———. *The Flight of a Century (1800-1900) in Ascension Parish, Louisiana.* Donaldsonville, LA, 1936.
———. *Marchands on the Mississippi and the St. Lawrence.* Donaldsonville, LA, 1968.
———. *The Story of Ascension Parish Louisiana.* Donaldsonville, LA, 1931.
Martin, David G. *Confederate Monuments at Gettysburg.* Hightstown, NJ, 1986.
———. *Gettysburg July 1.* Conshohocken, PA, 1995.
Martin, François-Xavier and John F. Condon. *The History of Louisiana From the Earliest Period, to which is appended Annals of Louisiana.* New Orleans, 1882.
McElfresh, Earl B. *Maps and Mapmakers of the Civil War.* New York, 1999.
Miller, Francis T., ed. *The Photographic History of the Civil War in Ten Volumes; Volume Nine, "Poetry and Eloquence of Blue and Gray."* New York, 1911.
Miller, J. Michael. *The North Anna Campaign, "Even to Hell Itself" May 21-26, 1864.* Lynchburg, VA 1989.
Niles, Blair. *The James.* New York, 1939.
Palfrey, Francis W. *The Antietam and Fredericksburg.* New York, 1882.
Pena, Christopher G. *Touched By War, Battles Fought in the Lafourche District.* Thibodaux, LA, 1998.
Porter, John W. H. *A Record of Events in Norfolk County, Virginia, From April 19th, 1861, to May 10th, 1862, With a History of the Soldiers and Sailors of Norfolk County, Norfolk City and Portsmouth Who Served in the Confederate States Army or Navy.* Portsmouth, VA, 1892.
Priest, Lyman W. *The Penick Family; Descendants of Edward Penick, Penix, Pinix of St. Peter's Parish, New Kent County, Virginia.* Verona, VA, 1982.
Prucha, John J. and Norman A. Foss. *Kinnickinnic Years.* DeWitt, NY, 1993.
Quarles, Garland R. *Some Old Homes in Frederick County, Virginia.* Winchester, VA, 1999.
Ramey, Emily G. and John K. Gott, eds. *The Years of Anguish, Faquier County, Virginia, 1861-1865.* Bowie, MD, 1998.
Rhea, Gordon C. *To the North Anna River, Grant and Lee, May 13-25, 1864.* Baton Rouge, 2000.
Ripley, Warren. *Artillery and Ammunition of the Civil War.* New York, 1970.

Roland, Charles P. *Louisiana Sugar Plantations During the American Civil War.* Leiden, Netherlands, 1957.
Saunders, James. *Early Settlers of Alabama With Notes and Genealogies.* Bowie, MD, 1899.
Saxon, Lyle, Edward Dreyer, and Robert Tallant, eds. *Gumbo Ya-Ya, A Collection of Louisiana Folk Tales.* New York, 1945
Shugg, Roger W. *Origins of Class Struggle in Louisiana, A Social History of White Farmers and Laborers during Slavery and After, 1840-1875.* Baton Rouge, 1939.
Simonhoff, Harry. *Jewish Participation in the Civil War.* New York, 1963.
Sommers, Richard. *Richmond Redeemed, The Siege at Petersburg.* Garden City, NY, 1981.
Smith, Jo D. *A History of High Bridge.* Richmond, 1987.
Stanley, Vara Smith. *A History of Appomattox County.* Appomattox, VA, 1965.
Swayze, J. C. *Hill and Swayze's Confederate States Rail-road and Steam-boat Guide.* Griffin, GA, 1862.
Sylvia, Stephen W. and Michael J. O'Donnell. *The Illustrated History of American Civil War Relics.* Orange, VA, 1978.
Thomas, William H. B. *Gordonsville, Virginia Historic Crossroads Town.* Orange, VA, 1971.
Tinker, Edward L. *Les Ecrits de Langue Francaise en Louisiane au XIX Siecle: Essais Biographies et Bibliographiques.* Paris, 1932.
Todd, Frederick P. *American Military Equipage, 1851-1872.* 2 vols. Providence, RI, 1977.
Verret, Celine B. *The Church of the Assumption Through the Years.* Plattenville, LA, 1995.
Waitt, Robert W., Jr. *Confederate Military Hospitals in Richmond.* Richmond, 1964.
Walker, C. Irvine. *Life of Lt. Gen. Richard Heron Anderson.* Charleston, SC, 1917.
Ward, James A. *Railroads and the Character of America, 1820-1887.* Knoxville, TN, 1986.
Warner, Ezra J. *Generals in Gray.* Baton Rouge, 1959.
Warren, Cary R. *Grimes Battery.* Portsmouth, VA, 1927.
Wheeler, Richard. *Witness to Gettysburg.* Edison, NJ, 1994.
Wiley, Bell I. *The Life of Johnny Reb.* Indianapolis, 1943.
Williams, T. J. C. and Folger McKinsey, eds. *History of Frederick County Maryland.* 2 vols. Salem, MA, 1910.
Wilson James D. and Louise E. Wilson. *Edinburg, 1861 to 1865, Civil War Incidents & Anecdotes.* Woodstock, VA, 1982
Winters, John D. *The Civil War in Louisiana.* Baton Rouge, 1963.
Wise, Jennings C. *The Long Arm of Lee or The History of the Artillery of the Army of Northern Virginia.* 2 vols. Richmond, VA, 1915.
Yancey, Rosa F. *Lynchburg and Its Neighbors.* Richmond, 1935.

JOURNALS, ARTICLES, AND CORRESPONDENCES

Adams, William H. "The Louisiana Whigs." *Louisiana History* XV, no. 3 (1974).
Alexander, Ted. "Ten days in July, The Pursuit to the Potomac." *North and South* 2, no. 6 (June 1999).
Anonymous, "The Light Artillery!" *Southern Historical Society Papers* XXXI.
Cable, George W. "New Orleans Before the Capture." *The Century: A Popular Quarterly* 29, no. 6 (April 1885).
Casey, Powell A. "Artillery in the Battle of New Orleans." Library Adjutant General of Louisiana. Jackson Barracks. New Orleans, Louisiana.
Coates, Charles E. "How the Tigers Got Their Name." *LSU Alumni News* (October 1937).
Daniels, R. L. *Scribners Monthly, An Illustrated Magazine For the People* 20, no. 4 (August 1880).
Durel, Lionel C. "Creole Civilization in Donaldsonville, 1850, According to 'Le Vigilant'." *The Louisiana Historical Quarterly* 31 (1948).
"Edmund Maurin." *The "Lost Cause"* (November 1899).
Greer, James K. "Louisiana Politics, 1845-1861." *The Louisiana Historical Quarterly* 12 (1929).
———. "Louisiana Politics, 1845-1861 Fourth Installment." *The Louisiana Historical Quarterly* 13 (1930).
———. "Louisiana Politics, 1845-1861 Fifth Installment." *The Louisiana Historical Quarterly* 13 (1930).

———. "Louisiana Politics, 1845-1861 Sixth and Last Installment." *The Louisiana Historical Quarterly* 13 (1930).

Hoegerl, Carl. "Two Redemptorist Accounts During the American Civil War." *Redemptorist North American Historical Bulletin* 19 (2003).

Jefferson Davis Memorial Historic Site. "Brief History Jefferson Davis Memorial Historic Site." Fitzgerald, GA.

Jensen, Leslie D. "A Survey of Confederate Central Government Quartermaster Issue Jackets, Part I," *Military Collector & Historian, Journal of the Company of Military Collectors & Historians* (Rutland, MA) 41 (Fall 1989).

Jones, Mildred and Mary Stevens Jones. "The History of Stevensburg Baptist Church, 1833-1983." *Stevensburg Baptist Church 150th Year Celebration, Pictorial Directory.* Stevensburg, VA.

Kajencki Francis C. "The Louisiana Tiger." *Louisiana History*, Volume XV, No. 1, 1974.

Kay, William K. "Mementoes of the Donaldsonville Artillery." *Military Collector & Historian, Journal of the Company of Military Collectors & Historians* VIII (Spring 1956).

Kendall, Lane C. "The Interregnum in Louisiana in 1861, I." *The Louisiana Historical Quarterly* 16 (1933).

King, Edward. "The Great South: A Ramble in Virginia." *Schribner's Monthly* 7, no. 6 (1874).

Lathrop, Barnes F., ed. "An Autobiography of Francis T. Nicholls, 1834-1881." *The Louisiana Historical Quarterly* 17 (1934).

———."The Lafourche District in 1861-1862: A Problem in Local Defense." *Louisiana History* 1, no. 2 (1960).

———. "The Lafourche District in 1862: Militia and Partisan Rangers." *Louisiana History* 1, no. 3, (1960.

Lawler, Peter A. "Orestes Brownson and the Truth About America." *First Things,* 128 (December 2002.)

Machar, A. M. "The Whip-Poor-Will." *Scribners Monthly, An Illustrated Magazine for the People* 20, no. 4 (August 1880).

Malgee, David G. "A Brief History of Ellerslie." Colonial Heights Historical Society (1996).

———. "A Brief History of Fort Clifton, 1864-1865." Colonial Heights Historical Society (1995).

Monroe, William H. "The Battle of Antietam: A Military Study." *Journal of the Military Service Institution of the United States* (New York) XLIX (1911).

Moore, John H. "Appomattox, Profile of a Mid-Nineteenth-Century Community." *The Virginia Magazine of History and Biography* 88 (1980).

Nichols, C. Howard. "Some Notes on the Military Career of Francis T. Nicholls." *Louisiana History* 3, no. 4 (1962).

Pace, Robert F. "'It Was Bedlam Let Loose: The Louisiana Sugar Country and the Civil War." *Louisiana History* XXXIX, no. 4 (1998).

"Powhite and Selwyn." *Hanover County Historical Society Bulletin*, no. 23 (November 1980).

Prichard, Walter, ed. "A Tourist's Description of Louisiana in 1860." *The Louisiana Historical Quarterly* 21 (1938).

Reed, Merl. "Boom or Bust—Louisiana's Economy During The 1830s." *Louisiana History* 4, no. 1 (1963).

Reinders, Robert C. "Militia in New Orleans, 1853-1861." *Louisiana History* 3, no. 1 (1962).

Roth, Dave. "Day of Decision at Petersburg." *Blue and Gray Magazine* XVIII, no. 3 (Winter 2001).

Smalley, Eugene V. "The New Orleans Exposition." *The Century: A Popular Quarterly* 30, no. 2 (June 1885).

Slipek, Edward. "The Story of Richmond's Forgotten Mayor." *Style Weekly* (November 2005).

Weller, Jac. "The Field Artillery of the Civil War, Part 1." *Military Collector & Historian, Journal of the Company of Military Collectors & Historians* V (Summer 1953).

Whitt, Walter Carr. "A Short History of Pioneer Baptist Church from 1843 to 1976." n.d.

Wilson Jr., James D. "The Donaldsonville Incident of 1870: A Study of Local Party Dissension and Republican Infighting in Reconstruction Louisiana." *Louisiana History* 38 (1997).

Wise, Jennings C. "The Boy Gunners of Lee." *Southern Historical Society Papers* XLII.

THESIS

Lathrop, Barnes F. "The Pugh Plantation, 1860-1865, A Study of Life in Lower Louisiana." PhD diss., University of Texas, 1945.

Leland, Edwin A. "Organization and Administration of the Louisiana Army During the Civil War." Tulane University, 1938.

Notes

CHAPTER ONE

1 Henry Wadsworth Longfellow, *Evangeline* (New York, 1892), 62.

2 Isleños was the way Spanish immigrants from the Canary Islands referred to themselves. Gilbert C. Din. *The Canary Islanders of Louisiana* (Baton Rouge, 1988), 12, 14, 28, 64, 88.

3 John D. Klorer, *The New Louisiana, The Story of the Greatest State of the Nation* (New Orleans, n.d.), 41

4 Father Revillagodos served Ascension Parish until his death on December 16, 1784. Sidney A. Marchand, *The Story of Ascension Parish Louisiana* (Donaldsonville, La., 1931), 20, 49; ibid., *Acadian Exiles in the Golden Coast of Louisiana* (Donaldsonville, La., 1943), 47.

5 *The New York Times*, August 25, 1862.

6 *New Orleans Republican*, September 27, 1871.

7 *Times-Picayune*, hereafter cited as *Times-Picayune*, June 11, 1837. The *New Orleans Daily Picayune* in 1914 absorbed the *New Orleans Daily Times* and became the *New Orleans Times Picayune*. The newspaper is often recognized througout its history as the *Times Picayune*.

8 Harnett T. Kane, *The Bayous of Louisiana* (New York, 1944), 155.

9 "Creole" refers to the descendants of European parents in French or Spanish colonies. A nineteenth-century reporter wrote, "The Creole Louisianian (by which term, let it be explained for the hundredth time for the benefit of persistent ignorance, is meant, not a mulatto, but a native white of French or Spanish ancestry), is short of stature, slight of frame, with a curious mixture of languor and vivacity in manner, carefully dressed, very polite, and with small interest in the doings of the world outside his own state." Eugene V. Smalley, "The New Orleans Exposition," *The Century*, 30:2 (June 1885), 195. "No true Creole ever had colored blood. This erroneous belief, still common among Americans in other sections of the country, is probably due to the Creoles' own habit of calling their slaves 'Creole slaves' and often simply 'Creole.'" Lyle Saxon, Edward Dreyer, Robert Tallant, ed., *Gumbo Ya-Ya, A Collection of Louisiana Folk Tales* (New York, 1945), 139; Sidney A. Marchand, *The Chief in the Land of the Chetimaches* (Donaldsonville, La., 1959), 188; Marchand, *Acadian Exiles*, 100; Marchand, *Story of Ascension*, 35, 120, 131; Lionel C. Durel, "Creole Civilization in Donaldsonville, 1850, According to 'Le Vigilant,'" *The Louisiana Historical Quarterly* 31 (1948), 994; Walter Prichard, ed., "A Tourist's Description of Louisiana in 1860," *The Louisiana Historical Quarterly* 31 (1938), 1123; *New Orleans Courier*, November 11, 1830.

10 Merl Reed, "Boom or Bust—Louisiana's Economy During The 1830's," *Louisiana History* 4 (1963), 35, 36; Carl A. Brasseaux, *Acadian to Cajun, Transformation of a People, 1803-1877* (Jackson, Miss., 1992), 8, 10; Roger W. Shugg, *Origins of Class Struggle in Louisiana, A Social History of White Farmers and Laborers during Slavery and After, 1840-1875* (Baton Rouge, La., 1939), 17, 324.

11 "Cajun" was the soubriquet of Louisiana Acadians exiled from Nova Scotia. Louisiana Acadians called themselves "Creole Français." Acadian, pronounced "Cajun," was a corruption implying contempt and used by many as an "objectionable epithet." R. L. Daniels, *Scribners Monthly, An Illustrated Magazine For the People*, August 1880, 383.

12 Charles Roland, *Louisiana Sugar Plantations During the American Civil War* (Leiden, Netherlands, 1957), 1. Though there remained many small Acadian farms, by 1860 half the real estate in Ascension Parish was owned by nineteen Anglo-American households. Only 35% of the parish's potential voters owned slaves.

13 Charles Gayarre, *History of Louisiana*, Vol. III (New Orleans, 1885), 658, 659; François-Xavier Martin and John F. Condon, *The History of Louisiana From the Earliest Period, to which is appended Annals of Louisiana* (New Orleans, 1882), 440, 441.

14 *New Orleans Bee*, hereafter cited as *Bee*, August 22, 1837

15 *Adams Sentinel*, September 11, 1837. The "Horrid" incident was reported in this paper published in a place that twenty-six years later was known to all: Gettysburg, Pennsylvania.

16 *New Orleans L'Abeille*, August 22, 1837.

17 Ibid. Translated from French. The English version, the *Bee*, on August 22, 1837, reported the name of the Donaldsonville paper as the *Advocate.* The overseer was murdered on land near Paincourtville owned by Augustin Franklin Pugh that at times was called Bellvue, Whitmell, and Highland Plantation. It is today named Westfield. Correspondence of Robert Pugh, May 2, 2012.

18 Glenn R. Conrad, ed., *Readings in Louisiana History* (New Orleans, 1978), 127, 133.

19 *Donaldsonville Chief*, August 30, 1884.

20 *Canonniers de Donaldson* file in Gaudet Family Papers, TU.

21 Ibid. Article 9 of the regulations disposed that a committee of *Commissaires*, chosen by the captain and consisting of one officer, one sergeant, the chief artificer, two corporals, and four soldiers, would enforce regulations; administer finances; judge validity of absences; and decide on request for admission. To join, a citizen applied in writing and proclaimed in writing to submit to the *Canonniers de Donaldson* regulations.

22 The Canal Bank branch in Donaldsonville was located on Mississippi Street, between Chetimaches Street and Crescent Place.

23 *Bee*, May 20, 1837; *New Orleans Times-Democrat*, April 17, 1892; John S. Kendall, *A History of New Orleans*, Vol. I (Chicago, 1922), 143; Thomas E. Dabney, *100 Years of the Canal Bank and Trust Company* (New Orleans, 1931), 9, 13; Sidney A. Marchand, *The Flight of a Century (1800-1900), in Ascension Parish, Louisiana* (Donaldsonville, La., 1936), 116; Pugh (Col. W. W. and Family), Papers, Scrapbook Number 7 (1860-1877), LSU. Inside the scrapbook is a program pamphlet on the occasion of the reorganization of the Donaldsonville Artillery in July 1875; Conrad, ed., *Readings in Louisiana History*, 101; Edwin Adam Davis, *Louisiana, A Narrative History*, 3d ed. (Baton Rouge, 1971), 216.

24 *Donaldsonville Chief*, September 18, 1915.

25 General Foy, *History of the War in the Peninsula, Under Napoleon; to which is prefixed A View of the Political and Military State of the Four Belligerent Powers.* Vol. II, Part I (London, 1827), 30, 92, 450.

26 Robert Debs Heinel Jr. and Nancy Gordon Heinel, *Written in Blood, The Story of the Haitian People 1492-1971* (Boston, 1978), 121, 125-129.

27 Pamphlet in Pugh Papers, LSU; *Biographical and Historical Memoirs of Louisiana*, Vol. II (Chicago, 1892), 244; Marchand, *The Flight,* 106.

28 *Louisiana Legion, 1847-1860*, Supplement (LAGL, 1943), 103.

29 Pamphlet in Pugh Papers, LSU. "En Avant" means, "Forward, to the front" and was part of the battle cry of Napoleon's army as they charged, the soldiers constantly repeating, "En avant! En avant! Vive la Republique!" David G. Chandler, *The Campaigns of Napoleon* (New York, 1966), 68.

30 Pamphlet in Pugh Papers, LSU.

31 Ibid.

32 *New Orleans L'Abeille*, August 22, 1837.

33 Pamphlet in Pugh Papers, LSU.

34 Marchand, *Story of Ascension*, 146. *Governor's Messages, Legislative Proceedings, Militia Appointments, 1806-1908*, Vol. 351 (LAGL, 1941), 64.

35 Father Gautier to Bishop Anthony Blanc, November 28, 1837, Archdiocese of New Orleans Collection, University of Notre Dame Archives, Notre Dame, Ind. *Te Deum Laudamus* is a centuries old rhythmical prose sung by Catholics in thanksgiving to God for a special blessing. The historic nature of the prayer is documented in the journals of the explorers De Soto, 1541; Hennepin, 1680; La Salle, 1682; and Iberville, 1699. Every significant event in their explorations, from finding a simple point of safety to the founding of the Louisiana colony, resulted in the praying of the *Te Deum.*

36 Tinker, Edward L. *Les Ecrits de Langue Française en Louisiane au XIX Siecle: Essais Biographies et Bibliographiques* (Paris, 1932), 266. No further information has been located on Hinkley.

37 *Governor's Messages, Legislative Proceedings, Militia Appointments, 1806-1908*, Vol. 351 (LAGL, 1941), 65.

38 Ibid. 7, 49, 65-67; *Parishes of Louisiana, 1823-1885*, Vol. 352 (LAGL, 1941), 31.

39 *Historical Military Data on Louisiana Militia, July 1-August 31, 1877*, Vol. 204 (LAGL, no date), 10.

40 *Donaldsonville Le Vigilant*, January 12, 1850.

41 *Donaldsonville Chief*, July 7, 1877. The uniforms were similar to the pre-1851 United States artillery full dress uniform. The *Reglemens de la Compagnie des Canonniers de Donaldson* prescribed the uniform.
42 *Acts of Louisiana, 1839* (Louisiana State Supreme Court Library, New Orleans), 70-72.
43 *Bee*, December 31, 1841; Marchand, *Ascension Parish*, 146. Gaudet Family Papers, The appropriation continued by *An Act*, Number 56.
44 The orders were published in local newspapers such as the Donaldsonville *Le Vigilant*, which was printed in French and published semi-weekly, Wednesday and Saturday, from 1845 to 1856. The Howard-Tilton Library, Tulane University, New Orleans, has an extensive collection of the tabloid. Numbered orders by the Canonnier Captain to its members were issued in this local newspaper approximately eighteen times each year with the reissuing of Order No. 1 in most years beginning each August, the anniversary date of the founding of the *Canonniers de Donaldson*. There were exceptions as some years Order No. 1 was issued in January.
45 *Esprit d'corps* is the selfless and often enthusiastic and jealous devotion of the members of a group or association of persons to the group or to its purposes.
46 This replaced their original "well-worn flag" that they still possessed a decade later. *New Orleans True Delta*, January 6, 1859. Aimé Bercegeay was born September 8, 1813, in Ghent, France. He settled in Donaldsonville in 1838 and joined the *Compagnie d'Artillerie*. Bercegeay not only presented but also donated this flag. As one of Ascension's oldest citizens, Bercegeay died in Donaldsonville in May 1887. *Assumption Pioneer*, May 21, 1887. Marchand, *The Flight*, 96.
47 The Donaldsonville town square was at different times called Crescent Square, Place d'Armes, Place de la Louisiane, and Government Square.
48 *Parishes*, Vol. 352, (LAGL, 1941), 24-29.
49 Ibid.
50 Ibid.
51 *Memphis Daily Appeal*, September 24, 1861.
52 Ibid. This Field Band had been associated with the *Canonniers de Donaldson* since at least 1847 and probably longer. *Donaldsonville Chief*, May 18, 1878, and December 23, 1882.
53 *Parishes*, Vol. 352, (LAGL, 1941), 14, 15, 31, 35-37, 40. *Donaldsonville Le Vigilant*, April 26, 1854.
54 *HMDLM, 1844-1845*, Vol. 69 (LAGL, 1937), 86-89.
55 *HMDLM, 1846*, Vol. 75 (LAGL, 1938), 20, 21.
56 *HMDLM*, Vol. 69. (LAGL, 1937), 90.
57 *HMDLM, 1843-45*. Vol. 330 (LAGL, 1940), 100.
58 In five months Augustin was promoted to Major and assigned the position of Brigade Inspector in the Legion. *Louisiana Legion*, Vol. 66 (LAGL, 1938), 201, 202; ibid., Vol. 77 (LAGL, 1937), 46, 47; ibid., *1854-1859*, Vol. 89 (LAGL, 1938), 136. *Le Vigilant*, March 15, 1846.
59 *Le Vigilant*, September 7, 1850.
60 Ibid. April 10, 1849.
61 Ibid. March 21, 1849.
62 The birth place of Francis T. Nicholls, Confederate Brigadier General, two-time (1877-1880 and 1888-1892), Louisiana governor, and Chief Justice of the Louisiana Supreme Court.
63 *Times-Picayune*, December 6, 1847. The *Washington Reporter*, January 1, 1848, copy expanded the article. Taylor's Baton Rouge estate and home were located on the present-day State Capitol Garden and Grounds near the Huey Long monument.
64 Marchand, *The Flight*, 134, 135. *Mexican War, January-July 1847*, Vol. 78 (LAGL, 1938), 138. Robert Nicholls died at thirty-four years of age in 1849. Dr. Edward Nicholls died at thirty-one years old in 1851 when his horse slipped on ice in Donaldsonville while responding to a medical call.
65 *Governor's Messages*, Vol. 351 (LAGL, 1941), 100.
66 *Acts of Louisiana, 1848* (Louisiana State Supreme Court Library, New Orleans), 117.
67 The Louisiana Constitution of 1845, Article 96, limited militia commissions to four years.
68 *Le Vigilant*, March 21, 1849.
69 *HMDLM*, Vol. 75 (LAGL, 1938), 29.
70 *Le Vigilant*, March 21, 1849. Vidal died in Donaldsonville on February 12, 1858, survived by his wife Carmelite Landry, six sons, and twin daughters. *Diocese of Baton Rouge Catholic Church Records*, Vol. 9, 1858-1862 (Baton Rouge, 1989).

71 *Assumption Pioneer,* October 12, 1851.
72 *Le Vigilant,* April 19, 1852.
73 *Assumption Pioneer,* October 12, 1851; *Le Vigilant,* September 26, 1849, June 1, 1850, and October 29, 1851; *Parishes,* Vol. 352 (LAGL, 1941), 24. Report of the Adjutant General of the Louisiana Militia, 1857, LAGL.
74 *Times-Picayune,* December 7, 1850.
75 *Le Vigilant,* December 29, 1849, and June 1, 1850.
76 Ibid., July 2, 1846. Both Lawes and Maurin were secretaries of the "Whigs for the Parish of Ascension."
77 Ibid., August 6, 1851.
78 Ibid., August 25, October 12, 30, November 8, 1851; Marchand, *The Flight,* 126, 130, 132.
The returns were 313 votes for Powell and 307 votes for his Democratic opponent Oscar S. Ayraud, the parish assessor. Powell received the majority of the Donaldsonville vote, 142-85. Democrats at this time were largely described as "Americans" while their political opponents were Whigs, who advocated public education, interior improvements at Federal expense, and tariff protection, which the sugar planters needed. James K. Greer, "Louisiana Politics, 1845-1861," *The Louisiana Historical Quarterly* 12 (1929), 392, 393.
79 Report of the Adjutant General of the Louisiana Militia, 1851, LAGL.
80 William H. Adams, "The Louisiana Whigs," *Louisiana History* 15 (1974), 221. Report of the Adjutant General of the Louisiana Militia, 1852, LAGL.
81 *Le Vigilant,* April 17, 1852.
82 Ibid.
83 Marchand, *Story of Ascension,* 146.
84 William K. Kay, "Mementoes of the Donaldsonville Artillery," *Military Collector and Historian* 8 (1956), 21. Translation: "Honor" and "Fidelity."
85 *Le Vigilant,* April 28, 1852.
86 Ibid.
87 *Times-Picayune,* December 9, 1851.
88 Robert C. Reinders, "Militia in New Orleans, 1853-1861," *Louisiana History* 3 (1962), 38.
89 *Times-Picayune,* December 9, 1851. A law was passed in 1853 on the composition of Louisiana militia units, which officially ended Powell's *Campagnie d'Artillerie's* official association with the Orleans Artillery Battalion. The *Canonniers de Donaldson* were again an independent volunteer company.
90 *Robert the Devil* by Giacomo Meyerbeer premiered in Paris in 1831.
91 *Daughter of the Regiment* by Gaetano Donizetti premiered in Paris in 1840.
92 *The Barber of Seville* by Pierre Beaumaechais was first performed in 1775 in the Tuileries.
93 *The Black Domino* by Daniel Auber premiered in Paris in 1837.
94 Durel, 981-994.
95 Ibid., 994.
96 All current or future officers of the *Canonniers de Donaldson.*
97 *Le Vigilant,* September 13, 1856. Filmore, the former 13th United States President, finished third in this hotly contested election won by James Buchanan, who carried the South and Louisiana.
98 Edwin A. Leland, "Organization and Administration of the Louisiana Army During the Civil War" (M.A. Thesis, Tulane University, 1938), 13.
99 Ibid., 17.
100 Report of the Adjutant General of the Louisiana Militia, 1857, LAGL.
101 *Legislative ACTS on Louisiana, 1850 to 1858,* Vol. 310 (LAGL, 1940), 26, 46, 72, 80, 81; *Legislative ACTS on Louisiana, 1857 to 1865,* Vol. 312 (LAGL, no date), 4; The Nicholls Family Papers, L. D. Nicholls notebook, TU. Lawrence D. Nicholls was clerk of court, eight-term mayor of Donaldsonville for most of the 1850s, and a sergeant in the *Canonniers de Donaldson.* Nicholls recorded the town council's accounts and warrants of reimbursements. Promoted to Second Lieutenant, he married, on June 4, 1856, Elisa Maurin, sister of Canonnier First Lieutenant Victor Maurin, who officially witness the wedding alongside William C. Lawes.
102 *Le Vigilant,* April 19, 1852.
103 Ibid., December 29, 1849.
104 Report of the Adjutant General of the Louisiana Militia, LAGL, 1860.
105 *HMDLM,* May 1-18, 1861, Vol. 104 (LAGL, 1938), 25. The .54 caliber 1841 percussion rifles

were produced at Harpers Ferry and earned the name "Mississippi rifle" when the First Mississippi Volunteers, led by Colonel Jefferson Davis, used them at the 1847 Battle of Buena Vista in the Mexican War.

106 Report of the Adjutant General of the Louisiana Militia, LAGL, 1860. There were only twelve other cannons in possession of various state units. Report of the Adjutant General of the Louisiana Militia, LAGL, 1858.

107 *Parishes*, Vol. 352, (LAGL, 1941), 28.

108 *Le Vigilant*, September 1, 1850.

109 Ibid., March 23, 1850. The creator of the insect cake topping was Leon J. Fremaux, a French immigrant whose family originally boarded with the family of former Canonnier Aimé Bercegeay. In the April 8, 1847 *Le Vigilant* Fremaux advertised himself as a stone and metal worker, and he later worked with Powell, until 1853, in the state land office in Donaldsonville. He then moved with his family to New Orleans. When war came in 1861 Fremaux was elected Captain of the Creole Guards, Company A, 8th Louisiana Infantry Regiment, Confederate States of America, and in March 1862 transferred to General P. G. T. Beauregard's staff as an engineering officer. The very artistic Fremaux is today considered one of the war's "great topographical engineers" because of his maps and drawings. Earl B. McElfresh. *Maps and Mapmakers of the Civil War* (New York, 1999), 25, 26, 106; Patrick J. Geary, ed. *Celine, Remembering Louisiana, 1850-1871, Celine Fremaux Garcia* (Athens, Ga., 1987), xii, 8-10.

110 *New Orleans True Delta*, January 6, 1859.

111 Ibid.

112 Elisa Maurin Nicholls to Ellen McCollam, February 4, 1859, Andrew McCollam Papers, Southern Historical Collection, UNCCH. Powell later worked as an appraiser, land agent, and plantation broker in New Orleans, where he was commissioned in the First Division of Louisiana Volunteer Troops as Quartermaster with the rank of Lieutenant Colonel. In February 1862 he was promoted to Brigadier General and commanded the Third Brigade, Louisiana Militia Troops. Powell died on May 12, 1867, it being said his death was brought on by the loss of his only son, Major Thomas N. Powell, 10th Louisiana Infantry, CSA, killed on April 2, 1865, in Petersburg, Virginia. *HMDLM*, April 21-30, 1861, Vol. 103 (LAGL, 1938), 112; *New Orleans Crescent*, May 14, 1867; Napier Bartlett, *Military Record of Louisiana* (Baton Rouge, 1875), 55.

113 Maurin served as a First Lieutenant in the company for twelve years. He was promoted after former First Lieutenant R. W. Nicholls became Brigade Major in the Louisiana State Militia, recruiting volunteers for the Mexican War. Report of the Adjutant General of the Louisiana Militia, LAGL, 1860; Records of the Louisiana State Government, M359, Roll No. 19, NA; *Parishes*, Vol. 352 (LAGL, 1941), 14; *Biographical and Historical Memoirs of Louisiana*, Vol. II, 245. *Donaldsonville Gazette*, March 4, 1826.

114 *West Baton Rouge Sugar Planter*, March 24, 1860.

115 Ibid., May 5, 1860. One of the band's leading members was Frederick August "Gus" Conway, who maintained the musical organization (also called the Conway Field Band), up to the time of his death in 1882. *Donaldsonville Chief*, May 18, 1878, and December 23, 1882.

116 Ibid., July 31, 1875. Organized in 1859 after the John Brown raid at Harper's Ferry, the Pelican Rifles later became Company K of the 3rd Louisiana Infantry Regiment, CSA.

117 *Baton Rouge Gazette and Comet*, March 13, 1860; William Watson, *Life in the Confederate Army Being the Observations and Experiences of An Alien in the South During the American Civil War* (New York, 1888), 60, 61; *HMDLM, 1860*, Vol. 94 (LAGL, no date), 34, 43.

118 Douglas tallied 356 votes in Ascension Parish to John Bell's 279 and John C. Breckinridge's 144. James K. Greer, "Louisiana Politics, 1845-1861 Fourth Installment," *The Louisiana Historical Quarterly* 13 (1930), 278; ibid., "Louisiana Politics, 1845-1861 Fifth Installment," *The Louisiana Historical Quarterly* 13 (1930), 472, 473, 476, 481; ibid., "Louisiana Politics, 1845-1861 Sixth and Last Installment," *The Louisiana Historical Quarterly* 13 (1930), 641.

119 Greer, "Louisiana Politics, 1845-1861 Sixth and Last Installment," 621-623; Lane C. Kendall, "The Interregnum in Louisiana in 1861, I" *The Louisiana Historical Quarterly* 16 (1933), 179, 180, 182, 193, 206.

120 John D. Winters, *The Civil War in Louisiana* (Baton Rouge, 1963), 3. Ascension's delegates split their vote with Duffel being for the ordnance and Cottman's vote one of the seventeen nays.

CHAPTER TWO

1 *New Orleans Daily True Delta,* January 11, 1861; William M. Owen, *In Camp and Battle with the Washington Artillery* (Boston, 1885), 3, 4; Watson, 76-78.
2 "A South-side History of the War Shown in the Letters of, and to General P. G. T. Beauregard of the Confederate States Army," Catalogue No. 1148, Part II, (LAGL), 29.
3 Barnes F. Lathrop, "The Pugh Plantation, 1860-1865. A Study of Life in Lower Louisiana" (M.A. Thesis, University of Texas, 1945), 90.
4 Watson, 122.
5 Ibid. 123.
6 *New Orleans Daily Picayune,* November 27, 1872.
7 Colonel Augustin later served as a Volunteer Aide-de-Camp to Beauregard during the April 6-7, 1862 Battle of Shiloh in which Augustin "almost reproved" Beauregard for seizing the colors of the 18th Louisiana Regiment and leading them into a heavy fire. Augustin told Beauregard, "The order must now be 'follow,' not 'go!'" and took the flagstaff from Beauregard and led the troops. Joseph Numa Augustin died in New Orleans on November 26, 1872, at age sixty and was interred in St. Louis Cemetery, Number Two. *Alfred Roman, Military Operations of General Beauregard in the War Between the States, 1861 to 1865* Vol. 1 (New York, 1884), 16, 317, 528, 529. *HMDLM,* May 19-31, 1861. Vol. 105 (LAGL, 1938), 159.
8 *HMDLM,* April 1-20, 1861, Vol. 102 (LAGL, no date), 67.
9 Ibid., June 1-December 31, 1891, Vol. 172 (LAGL, 1938), 3. The British correspondent described it as "that undefinable region called 'the seat of war.'" William H. Russell, *Pictures of Southern Life, Social, Political, and Military Written for the London* Times (New York, 1861), 89.
10 *New Orleans Daily Crescent,* April 15, 1861.
11 *OR* (Washington, D. C., 1880-1901),Series IV, Vol. I, 748. Unless otherwise indicated, all citations are to Series I.
12 Watson, 123.
13 Russell, 12. The British newspaper correspondent Russell journeyed across the South, which included a visit to Donaldsonville.
14 Ibid. 13.
15 Carl Hoegerl, "Two Redemptorist Accounts During the American Civil War," *Redemptorist North American Historical Bulletin,* June 2003, 9, 10.
16 Albert Schmidt to Gustavus Schmidt, September 13, 1861, letter (translated from French). Gustavus Schmidt Correspondences, LSU.
17 Watson, 118. Watson, who joined a Louisiana company also noted, "Of the thousands who at this time rushed to arms, I believe very few had in their minds the question of slavery."
18 Russell, 13.
19 The inscription on the reverse of one veteran's button was "*TW & W*" indicating it was made by the French firm *Trelon, Welon et Weil* in Paris. William K. Kay, "Mementoes of the Donaldsonville Artillery," *Military Collector & Historian, Journal of the Company of Military Collectors & Historians,* 8 (Spring 1956), 22.
20 Since Confederate Army uniform regulations did not appear until June 6, 1861, (designating gray as the official color of the upper garment), the Donaldsonville Canonniers headed for New Orleans dressed in their dark blue antebellum uniforms. *Times-Picayune,* December 9, 1851.
21 *HMDLM* Vol. 104, (LAGL, 1938), 14, 25; *New Orleans Crescent,* May 4 and 21, 1861; F. Jay Taylor, ed. *Reluctant Rebel, The Secret Diary of Robert Patrick, 1861-1865* (Baton Rouge, 1959), 29; Watson, 126; *New Orleans Daily Picayune,* May 3, 1861; Russell, 69.
22 *HMDLM,* Vol. 104, 25.
23 Ibid., 14.
24 George W. Cable, "New Orleans Before the Capture," *The Century: A Popular Quarterly,* 29:6, April 1885, 918.
25 Creoles of the Lafourche district habitually called the city of Donaldsonville, "Donaldson," and the most conspicuous and revered organization of the locality the "*Canonniers de Donaldson.*" *Times-Picayune,* June 10, 1914.
26 Tayor, 30; Fletcher Pratt, ed., *My Diary North and South, William Howard Russell* (New York, 1954), 138, 139; *New Orleans Daily Picayune,* May 3 and 5, 1861; *New Orleans Daily Crescent,* May 2, 1861. The racecourse operated from 1838 until the beginning of the Civil War. From 1865 to

1872 it reopened under the auspices of the Metairie Jockey Club, but due to financial difficulties, it sold its interest to the Metairie Cemetery Association, which turned it into a burial ground. The most impressive monument in the well-known cemetery is the mausoleum or tumulus of the Association Army of Northern Virginia, Louisiana Division, which has fifty-seven vaults (and the remains of six Donaldsonville Artillery veterans), in the tomb chamber that is covered by grass, except for the entrance, and surmounted by an approximate thity-eight-feet high granite column with a statue of General Thomas Jonathan 'Stonewall' Jackson at the top. Henri A. Gandolfo, *Metairie Cemetery, An Historical Memoir, Tales of Its Statesman, Soldiers and Great Families* (New Orleans, 1981), 13, 15, 27.

27 Watson, 141, 142, 144. *New Orleans Daily Crescent*, May 2 and 7, 1861.

28 *Baton Rouge Daily Advocate*, May 7, 1861.

29 *OR*, Series IV, Vol. I, 276.

30 *HMDLM*, Vol. 104, 40.

31 *New Orleans Le 'Abeille,* September 23, 1861.

32 *New Orleans Daily Crescent*, May 4, 1861.

33 NAMP, M359, Roll 19, Order 307.

34 *HMDLM,* August 1-31, 1861, Vol. 113 (LAGL, 1938), 115.

35 *OR*, IV, Vol. I, 685. The telegraph was sent May 17, 1861.

36 Ibid. 686.

37 Francis T. Nicholls to Trasimon Landry, May 24, 1861, Nicholls Papers, TU.

38 The Phoenix Company was designated Company K of the 8th Louisiana Infantry Regiment and left for Virginia from Camp Moore in two groups on June 22 and 24, 1861. *HMDLM,* Vol. 113, 115; *New Orleans Le 'Abeille*, September 23, 1861; Barnes F. Lathrop, ed., "An Autobiography of Francis T. Nicholls, 1834-1881," *The Louisiana Historical Quarterly* 17 (1934), 248, 249.

39 Lathrop thesis, 93.

40 *HMDLM*, Vol. 113, 115.

41 Scrapbook, 29, 30 in Pugh Papers, LSU.

42 Ibid.

43 There is no evidence that Edmonson successfully raised a battalion or had one accepted into Confederate service.

44 Scrapbook, 29, 30 in Pugh Papers, LSU.

45 The Fortier family history in Louisiana dates back to the early French colonial period; they distinguished themselves in the public and the professional life of New Orleans and the state. Alcée Fortier, *Louisiana: Comprising Sketches of Parishes, Towns, Events, Institutions, and Persons, Arranged in Cyclopedic Form*, Vol. 3 (Madison, Wisconsin 1914), 169, 170.

46 *Historical Military Data on Washington Artillery, 1861.* (LAGL, 1937), 26.

47 *HMDLM*, Vol. 113, 115; *New Orleans Le 'Abeille*, September 23, 1861.

48 L. D. Nicholls to wife, August [no date] 1861, Nicholls Papers, TU.

49 *HMDLM,* Vol. 113, 115.

50 NAMP, M359, Roll 19, Order 835; Francis T. Nicholls to Trasimon Landry, May 24, 1861, Nicholls Papers, TU.

51 A. Franklin Pugh Diary, August 26 and 29, 1861; Pugh Papers, LSU.

52 *HMDLM*, Vol. 113, 115. L. D. Nicholls to wife, September 8, 1861, Nicholls Papers; *Memphis Daily Avalanche*, September 24, 1861. In 1866 the greater portion of Donaldsonville's debt was incurred as a result of buying equipment for the Donaldsonville Artillery five years previously. Marchand, *The Flight*, 173. John Clark's New Orleans Foundry manufactured furnaces, railway car axles, and cotton presses until the outbreak of the war, when it began casting cannon tubes by private contract. The Clark foundry building stood as a converted residence at the corner of Race and Tchoupitoulas streets in New Orleans until Hurricane Katrina, after which it was torn down. The foundry seems to have specialized in the engraving of many of its guns. A Clark 6-pounder engraved "Jeff Davis" is today located at the military academy in West Point, New York. Another engraved Clark cannon, a 12-pounder howitzer smooth bore, is located at Shiloh National Battlefield Park. Cannon carriages made of white oak and other war appliances for the cannon tubes were made in New Orleans by the firm of Mulliken and Luster. Winters, 61.

53 Confederate Secretary of War Letters-Sent Book, Library of Congress, Washington, D. C.

54 Ibid.

55 The officer promotions were signed by Governor Moore on September 11, 1861.

56 *Donaldsonville Chief,* April 20, 1907.
57 Ibid.
58 Eugene H. Levy, Diary, Bertram W. Korn Papers, HUC. "Toilet" meaning the act of dressing and grooming oneself.
59 *Biographical and Historical Memoirs of Louisiana,* Vol. I, 531, 532. *Donaldsonville Chief,* June 15, 1907.
60 *New Orleans Republican*, November 28, 1870.
61 Pierre Landry Manuscript, Dunn-Landry Family Papers, Amistad Research Center, TU. Lawes, a bachelor, age thirty, lived at the corner of Lassard and Iberville streets in Donaldsonville with two mulatto first cousins. One, Prosper Conway, was a bachelor and house servant; the other, Frederick "Gus" Conway, was married with five children. Both cousins were musicians in the Donaldsonville Canonnier field band.
62 *New Orleans Republican*, November 28, 1870.
63 NAMP, M359, Roll 19, Register of Commissions Officers Louisiana Militia, Order 1006 & 1007.
64 Bernard Lemann *The Lemann Family of Louisiana.* (Donaldsonville, La., 1965), 28, 29; *New Orleans Daily Crescent*, May 1, 1861; *New Orleans The Daily True Delta*, September 17, 1861.
65 Illsley was unanimously elected lieutenant and "acted as drillmaster of the company from the day of its arrival to its departure [for the war], and is a most excellent permanent acquisition." *The* (False River, La.)*, Democrat*, August 17, 1861.
66 Dorothy Dawes and Charles Nolan, ed. "Father Charles Boglioli (1814-1882): Leper Priest of Charity Hospital," by Warren Dicharry, C.M., in *Religious Pioneers, Building the Faith in the Archdiocese of New Orleans* (New Orleans, 2004), 65-75. For more on the noble and laudable life of Father Boglioli see the "Roster and Biographies" addendum.
67 *HMDLM*, Vol. 104, 14, 25; *Donaldsonville Chief,* July 7, 1877. Jean Trasimon Landry was born December 16, 1795, and served as an officer in the Louisiana militia during the War of 1812. He was elected state representative in 1824, state senator 1832, and lieutenant-governor in 1846. He owned several sugar plantations on both sides of the river, and when war came in 1861 he organized the Landry Guards in Donaldsonville while serving as a Colonel of Militia. This renowned citizen died October 1, 1873.
68 *Donaldsonville Chief,* September 2, 1882.
69 *Donaldsonville Chief,* March 13, 1880.
70 Ella Lonn, *Foreigners In the Confederacy* (Chapel Hill, N.C., 1940), 453.
71 *Donaldsonville Chief,* September 18, 1880.
72 Ibid., November 14, 1931.
73 NA, CSR.
74 *Assumption Pioneer*, May 10, 1879.
75 Ibid., October 20, 1900.
76 Ibid.
77 Confederate Pension Application, Louisiana Division of Archives, Records Management, and History.
78 *Assumption Pioneer*, November 27, 1909.
79 Ibid., February 21, 1914.
80 Prosper Landry, *Southern Historical Society Papers,* Vol. 23, 200.
81 Celine B. Verret, *The Church of the Assumption Through the Years.* (Plattenville, La., 1995). The Linossiers lived a couple of houses from the church rectory. His father was a well-respected citizen of Plattenville and a paid secretary of the Church of the Assumption before his death in 1861.
82 *Assumption Pioneer*, May 28, 1898.
83 *Donaldsonville Chief,* June 2, 1883.
84 Levy Diary, HUC.
85 *Assumption Pioneer*, March 1, 1879.
86 Lonn, 453.
87 Benevolent Association of the Army of Northern Virginia application of J. A. Comstock, dated July 24, 1877. LHAC.
88 *Assumption Pioneer*, May 19, 1894.
89 Ibid., May 22, 1909.
90 NA, CSR.

91 *Richmond Daily Dispatch*, July 1, 1861.
92 Lonn, 100.
93 Donaldsonville Artillery Roster and 1860 United States Census. Six occupation are unknown.
94 *Memphis Daily Appeal*, September 24, 1861.
95 *Donaldsonville The Daily Times,* September 19, 1896. After the war the band became the *Conway Field Band* and continued to play for the postbellum Donaldsonville Artillery. *Donaldsonville Chief*, May 18, 1878.
96 Louis Lefort, unaddressed letter, December 10, 1884, TU; Clerk of Court's Office, Ascension Parish Courthouse, Fourth Judicial District Court, November 11, 1867, Case Number 1546; NA, Maurin File.
97 Jean Reynaud Jacques Prosper Landry to Adele Pedesclaux Landry, September 1864, UV.
98 *Donaldsonville Chief*, August 30, 1884.
99 *HMDLM*, Vol. 172, 95. The only description of the Canonnier flag is that of a guidon, which is usually a forked flag carried by cavalry and light artillery. On March 3, 1861, New Orleans received notification by telegraph of the first national Confederate flag, known as the Stars and Bars. It can only be speculated that this was the pattern of the Donaldsonville Canonnier flag. Confederate flag historian Ken Legendre noted: "Remaking pre-war militia stars and stripes into Confederate first nationals [stars and bars] appears to have been a common practice in the Southern States." It was also noted that the Confederate national flag would have mottoes commonly painted on the center (white), bar, and at times elsewhere. In a post war speech Prosper Landry made allusion to "En Avant" being inscribed on the flag. Frederick Todd, *American Military Equipage, 1851-1872* Vol. II (Providence, R. I., 1977), 475, 479; *New Orleans Daily Crescent,* March 3, 1861.
100 *New Orleans Daily Crescent*, May 15, 1861.
101 *Baton Rouge Weekly Advocate*, September 22, 1861.
102 The market building was constructed in 1853 in the middle of Crescent Park (or Place), on Mississippi Street that parallels the levee and river. Although damaged, it survived the war whereupon the city leased out its stalls for use each year. In 1918 the old market, in disrepair, was torn down. Kirk Landry, *Postcards from the Past* (Donaldsonville, La., 2004), 25.
103 *Donaldsonville Chief*, June 3, 1909.
104 There is no documentation on the uniform, blue or gray, the Donaldsonville Canonniers wore at the time of their departure. Two days after their departure the New Orleans newspaper *Daily Delta* published an article reporting the "blue uniforms in extensive use in this state are objectionable" particularly as "all the troops from the other states are uniformed in gray cloth." *HMDLM*, Vol. 115 (LAGL, 1938), 39; Record Roll of the Donaldsonville Artillery, Louisiana Historical Association Collection, TU; *Memphis Daily Avalanche*, September 21, 1861; *New York Herald*, November 12, 1861; *New Orleans L'Abeille*, September 23, 1861.
105 *Donaldsonville The Daily Times*, September 19, 1896.
106 *New Orleans L'Abeille*, September 23, 1861.
107 John O'Hara Diary, Ascension Parish Civil Records, 1803-1926, LDA.
108 Ibid.
109 Ibid.
110 *New Orleans True Delta*, January 6, 1859.
111 *Donaldsonville Chief*, September 6, 1884.
112 John O'Hara Diary, LDA.
113 *Memphis Daily Avalanche*, September 24, 1861.
114 Russell, 110, 112, 115. This is Russell's description on taking the same trip on the *Mary T* in June 1862.
115 *HMD*, Vol. 172, 96. François Bienvenu Cire, Memorandum Book, courtesy Mrs. Lorraine Trepagnier Toerner of Baton Rouge, La., Cire's granddaughter. Copy donated to United Daughters of the Confederacy, Memorial Library, Richmond, Va. Hereafter cited as Cire Memorandum, UDC. The book was found by the family when handling the succession of Odile Cire, Cire's wife, after her death in Donaldsonville on June 29, 1950. The original is in possession of her daughter, Karen Dodds of Chatom, Alabama. Lorraine Toerner, letter to author, March 11, 2001.
116 O'Hara Diary, LDA.
117 *New Orleans The Daily True Delta*, September 24, 1861.
118 *Memphis Daily Avalanche*, September 24, 1861.
119 Ibid. September 23, 1861.

120 *Memphis Daily Appeal,* September 26, 1861.
121 Ibid. September 24, 1861.
122 *Memphis Daily Avalanche,* September 23, 1861.
123 Ibid.
124 Ibid.
125 *Memphis Daily Appeal,* September 24, 1861.
126 In the 1814-15 campaign for New Orleans the British lost fourteen cannons, all were 18 and 24-pounder guns which were spiked and abandoned because of their size when they retreated after the January 8, 1815, Battle of New Orleans. Powell A. Casey, "Artillery in the Battle of New Orleans," LAGL.
127 Legrand J. Wilson, *The Confederate Soldier* (Memphis, Tenn., 1973), 206, 207.
128 Albert Schmidt to Gustavus Schmidt, October [no date] 1861, Schmidt Correspondences, LSU.
129 O'Hara Diary, LDA.
130 Saxon, 182.
131 Eugene Alvarez, *Travel on Southern Antebellum Railroads, 1828-1860* (Tuscaloosa, Ala., 1974), 51, 56, 57, 122; James A. Ward, *Railroads and the Character of America, 1820-1887* (Knoxville, Tenn., 1986), 31; Angus J. Johnston II, *Virginia Railroads in the Civil War* (Chapel Hill, N. C., 1961), 14.
132 O'Hara Diary, LDA.
133 Cire Memorandum, UDC.
134 Albert Schmidt to Gustavus Schmidt, October [no date] 1861. Schmidt Correspondences, LSU.
135 Norman E. Rourke, ed. *I Saw the Elephant: The Civil War Experiences of Baily George McClelen, Company D, 10th Alabama Infantry Regiment* (Shippensburg, Pa., 1995), 10.
136 O'Hara Diary, LDA.
137 *HMDLM, October 1-11, 1861,* Vol. 116 (LAGL), 36.
138 O. T. Hanks, "Account of Civil War Experiences," Manuscript, 6. UT.
139 Albert Schmidt to Gustavus Schmidt, October [no date] 1861, Schmidt Correspondences, LSU.
140 Edward King, "The Great South: A Ramble in Virginia," *Scribner's Monthly,* 7:6 (New York), 663.
141 Ibid.
142 Blair Niles, *The James* (New York, 1939), 238.
143 King, "The Great South," 663.
144 Jo D. Smith, *A History of High Bridge* (Richmond, Va., 1987), 5-11.
145 J. C. Swayze, *Hill and Swayze's Confederate States Rail-road and Steam-boat Guide* (Griffin, Ga., 1862), 25, 34, 35; *Charleston Mercury,* August 16, 1861; Alvarez, *Travel,* 67.
146 Albert Schmidt to Gustavus Schmidt, October [no date] 1861, Schmidt Correspondences, LSU.

CHAPTER THREE

1 *Charleston Mercury,* August 16, 1861; *New York Herald,* July 28, 1862; Hanks, 6; Alfred H. Bill, *The Beleaguered City Richmond, 1861-1865* (New York, 1946), 296.
2 *Richmond Dispatch,* October 7, 1861.
3 *HMDLM,* Vol. 172, 96; *Richmond Inquirer,* September 17, 1861.
4 J. W. Minnich, "Picturesque Soldiery," *Confederate Veteran* 31 (1923), 296.
5 The Blakely had a range of 1,760 yards compared to the 6-pounder smoothbore gun's range of 1,523 yards. George M. Neese, *Three Years in the Confederate Horse Artillery* (Dayton, Ohio, 1988), xii; Warren Ripley, *Artillery and Ammunition of the Civil War* (New York, 1970), 366, 372; Douglas S. Freeman, *Lee's Lieutenant's, A Study in Command, Vol. 1* (New York, 1942), 310.
6 Cire Memorandum, UDC. The subject of the Donaldsonville Artillery's uniform after arriving in Richmond is not broached in any located sources. However, the photograph of Canonnier Pvt. Antoine Sanchez and an unidentified comrade indicates that in the Fall of 1861, the Confederate quartermaster issued Maurin's gunners gray jackets that appear to be Richmond Depot Type I. These probably replaced their antebellum dark blue uniform coats. Sanchez and his comrade each wore the cross cannon emblem on their kepi caps and Pelican (state seal type) belt buckles (See William K. Kay, "Mementoes of the Donaldsonville Artillery," *Military Collector & Historian, Journal of the Company of Military Collectors & Historians* 8 (Spring 1956). At the battle of First

Manassas in July 1861, the Washington Artillery of New Orleans wore blue uniforms similar to the Donaldsonville Canonniers. The Washington Artillery did not get gray uniforms until September 1861. Owen, 54.

7 *Richmond Dispatch*, October 10, 1861.

8 NA, Maurin File.

9 John Walters Diary, October 13, 1862, Norfolk Public Library, Sargeant Memorial Room. Norfolk, Va.; *Richmond Daily Whig*, May 22, 1861; Sallie B. Putnam, *Richmond During the War, Four Years of Personal Observation* (New York, 1867), 87; Bill, 3.

10 Russell, 108. The British correspondent also recorded that Donaldsonville was a "remarkable city."

11 *Richmond Dispatch*, July 1, 1861.

12 Bill, 103; *New Orleans Daily Crescent*, December 2, 1861; *Charleston Daily Courier*, September 4, 1861; *Richmond Dispatch*, June 8, 1861. Charles R. Rees's photo gallery was located at 145 Main Street, above West and Johnson's Bookstore. The building burned in the April 1865 evacuation fire. In taking photographic portraits, Rees usually posed the soldier sitting with one leg across the other, resting the left arm on a cushion. For similar portraits by Rees see Leslie D. Jensen, "A Survey of Confederate Central Government Quartermaster Issue Jackets, Part I," *Military Collector & Historian, Journal of the Company of Military Collectors & Historians* 41 (Fall 1989). Pvt. Henry R. Berkley had his photograph taken in the same pose and a similar uniform (though that of a private) as Maurin's. William H. Runge, ed. *Four Years in the Confederate Artillery: The Diary of Private Henry Robinson Berkely* (Chapel Hill, N.C., 1961), 5.

13 Michael B. Chesson and Leslie J. Roberts, eds., *Exile in Richmond, The Confederate Journal of Henri Garidel* (Charlottesville, Va., 2001), 46.

14 Ibid.

15 The Columbian Hotel stood at the southeast corner of Twelfth and Cary Streets near the Danville and Petersburg railroad depots. It did not survive the fires of April 1865. Richard Irby of the 18th Virginia Infantry wrote that before the war the hotel "was the favorite of the country people though plain in its outfit. The fare was plentiful and well served." A State Department bureaucrat by the name of Littleton Q. Washington recorded in his diary in January of 1862 about the comfort and good food at the Columbian. Thanks to Robert E. L. Krick, Richmond National Battlefield Park historian, for this information in correspondence of September 24, 2003. See also *New Orleans Daily Picayune*, January 18, 1899.

16 *Charleston Daily Courier*, December 6, 1861.

17 James M. Morgan, *Midshipman in Gray* (Boston, 1917), 63.

18 *Richmond Daily Whig*, May 22, 1861; W. R. Houghton and M. B. Houghton, *Two Boys in the Civil War and After* (Montgomery, Ala., 1912), 58, 60.

19 Napier Bartlett, *Clarimonde: A Tale of New Orleans Life, and of the Present War* (Richmond, Va. 1863), 5.

20 Brasseaux, 31.

21 *New Orleans Republican*, November 28, 1870.

22 *New Orleans Daily Picayune*, July 23, 1882. Brownson (1803-1876), a native of Vermont, was almost certainly the greatest American Catholic thinker of the nineteenth century. He wrote the classic political volume, *The American Republic: Its Constitution, Tendencies, and Destiny* in 1866 and asserted, "He who dies on the battlefield fighting for his country ranks with him who dies at the stake for his faith." Peter A. Lawler, "Orestes Brownson and the Truth About America," *First Things* 128 (December 2002), 23-28. Father Boglioli presided over the marriages of Maurin in 1852 and Prosper Landry in 1855.

23 *Times-Picayune*, November 3, 1902.

24 Lillian C. Bourgeois, *Cabonocey—The History, Customs and Folklore of St. James Parish* (Gretna, La., 1957), 116, 134, 135.

25 Lonn, 453.

26 Ibid. 29.

27 Levy Diary, HUC.

28 *Donaldsonville Chief*, January 26, 1918.

29 *Times-Picayune*, July 21, 1902.

30 Charles Moore Jr. Diary, LHAC.

31 *Donaldsonville Chief*, March 13, 1880.

32 John D. Billings, *Hardtack and Coffee* (Chicago, Ill., 1960), 196, 197.
33 *HMDWA*, Vol. 112, 112; *HMDLM*, Vol. 172, 96.
34 *OR* LI:2, 370.
35 Eugene H. Levy, "The Donaldsonville Artillery," *Southern Bivouac* 3 (March 1885), 302.
36 Chesson, 83, 113.
37 Kursheedt to Miss Sallie letter, no date, Edwin I. Kursheedt Papers, UNCCH.
38 The remnants of Kingsmill wharf, also known as Allen's, still remain.
39 C. S. Irwin, "The Army Wagon," *The Century: A Popular Quarterly* 29 (April 1885).
40 The aggregate number of personnel was now 105 rank and file, with nine band members and servants. In Richmond on November 7 and 8, 1861, Felix Le Besque and Benjamin Salles enlisted as privates. NA, Maurin File.
41 Minnich, 296.
42 Carlton McCarthy, *Detailed Minutiae of Soldier Life in the Army of Northern Virginia, 1861-1865* (Richmond, Va. 1882), 65.
43 *OR* IV, 697, 698.
44 McCarthy, 79.
45 Houghton, 57.
46 O'Hara Diary, LDA. Charles Alba, "Numa" Cure, Gontrand Dugas, "Sabin" Braud, "Arthur" Comstock, "Désiré" Arceneaux, Augustin Albares, and "Octave" Dupas comprised one mess with the other made up of "Frank" Montero, Narcisse Plesencia, "Désiré" Carmouche, "Willie" Newchurch, Adolphe Rougeau, "Alex" McCullet, "Tom" Love, William Keen, William "Buck" Chase, and William "Deles" Delesdernier.
47 McCarthy, 37.
48 NA, Maurin File. A cord equals 128 cubic feet of cut wood or a 4x4x8 foot stack.
49 John H. Hewitt, *War: A Poem, with Copious Notes, Founded on the Revolution of 1861-1862.* (Richmond, Va. 1862), 18.
50 Jennings C. Wise, *The Long Arm of Lee*, Vol.I (Richmond, Va. 1915), 423.
51 John Gibbon, *The Artillerist's Manuel* (New York, 1863), 352.
52 Donaldsonville Artillery Historical Memoranda, LHAC.
53 R. U. Johnson and C. C. Buel, eds. *Battles and Leaders of the Civil War,* Vol. II (New York, 1884-87), 190. Hereafter cited as *B & L.*
54 *Times-Picayune,* July 5, 1902.
55 Leon Jastremski to brother, December 9, 1861, letter, (translated from French), Leon Jastremski Family Papers, LSU.
56 Regis De Trobriand, *Four Years with the Army of the Potomac* (Boston, 1889), 164.
57 Levy, 302.
58 Leon Jastremski to brother, December 9, 1861, letter, (translated from French), Leon Jastremski Family Papers, LSU.
59 Cire Memorandum, UDC.
60 Gary W. Gallagher, ed. *Fighting for the Confederacy, The Personal Recollections of General Edward Porter Alexander* (Chapel Hill, N. C., 1989), 74.
61 *OR* IV, 703.
62 Moore Diary, LHAC.
63 In December 1861 forty-four of the sixty-two pieces of field artillery in Magruder's army were located at Yorktown. *OR* IV, 716.
64 Cire Memorandum, UDC. The camp was likely named after James R. Randall, the admired Southern poet and author of the spirited and inspirational song, "My Maryland." Randall wrote the song at Poydras College in Pointe Coupee, La. It was first published in the *New Orleans Daily Delta* on April 26, 1861. E. Lawrence Abel, *Singing the New Nation, How Music Shaped the Confederacy, 1861-1865* (Mechanicsburg, Pa., 2000), 68, 69, 72.
65 *Richmond Daily Dispatch*, November 13, 1861.
66 NA, Maurin File.
67 Saxon, 164.
68 Faye A. Axford, *The Journals of Thomas Hobbs* (Tuscaloosa, Ala., 1976), 250.
69 *OR* IV, 715.
70 Moore Diary, LHAC.
71 Putnam, 90, 92; NA, Maurin File. The requisition issued was 3,000 feet of 1-inch board, 10 kegs

of nails, 6 hatchets, 3 hand saws, 2 cross cut saw files, 2 cross cut saws, 1 frow, 6 sash, 3 augers, 1 saw square, 5 pounds of chalk, 4 door locks, plus twelve camp kettles for the battery to replace unusable ones.

72 An artificer is a military mechanic, such as a carpenter, blacksmith, or mason.

73 *Donaldsonville Chief,* March 29, 1930.

74 Fred A. Ober, "The Campaign of the Peninsula," Civil War Papers, LHAC.

75 "Order Number 580," Civil War Papers, LHAC; Francis C. Kajencki, "The Louisiana Tiger," *Louisiana History* 15 (1974), 52, 53.

76 "Order Number 580," Civil War Papers, LHAC.

77 Billings, 187, 188.

78 Guy R. Everson and Edward H. Simpson Jr., eds. *Far, Far From Home* (New York, 1994), 121.

79 Oscar Stuart to Aunt, April 29, 1862, letter, Oscar J. E. Stuart Letters., Mississippi Department of Archives and History, Jackson, Miss.

80 Hilary A. Hebert, "History of the Eighth Alabama Volunteer Regiment, C. S. A.," *Alabama Historical Quarterly* 39 (1977), 45, 48, 49.

81 NA, CSR.

82 "D'Gournay's Battalion of Artillery," *CV,* XIII (1905), 31.

83 NA, CSR; Cire Memorandum, UDC.

84 Maurin to Capt. Henry Bryan, March 24, 1862, letter, MCR.

85 Other commanders evidently made similar complaints. Five days after Maurin's letter it was noted the Secretary of War gave no further authorizations to the numerous permits by individuals to raise companies. *OR* XI:3, 411.

86 Levy, 303.

87 The cosmopolitan make up of the Donaldsonville Artillery continued. The nationalities of the new enlistees were: English-9, German-5, French-5, Creole/Cajun-4, Irish-4, Switzerland-2, Scottish-2, Dutch-1, Canadian-1. They came from the following units: Rightor's 1st Louisiana Battalion, Company "A"-2, "B"-2, "C"-4, "D"-2, "E"-7, "F"-6, and Coppen's Zouave Battalion, Company "A"-2, "B"-1, "D"-1, "F"-4.

88 *Times-Picayune,* February 25, 1908.

89 *Gonzales Weekly,* February 12, 1921.

90 NA, CSR. Cire Memorandum, UDC; "Board of Pension Commissioners, Confederate Pension Applications" with April 21, 1902 letter of Capt. Prosper Landry to Pension Board, LDA; Chesson, 94.

91 *Assumption Pioneer,* December 16, 1899.

92 *Donaldsonville Chief,* September 27, 1884.

93 Ibid. May 10, 1884.

94 *New Orleans Daily City Item,* October 10, 1877.

95 National Archives, Record of Events (Donaldsonville Art'y), March & April 1862 NA.

96 *New York Tribune,* April 28, 1897.

97 Cire Memorandum, UDC. Author's italics.

98 Putnam, 93.

99 Cire Memorandum, UDC.

100 Record of Events (March/April 1862). The Record of Events are from the bi-monthly Muster Roll and can also be found on the Photographic Record Sheets of the Donaldsonville Artillery (Landry's Battery), Bound Vols. 145 and 146, LAGL. Jones, a physician from Pinhook, La., assumed command of the 14th Louisiana when Colonel Sulakowski resigned on February 15, 1862, on account of Howell Cobb of Georgia being appointed brigadier general instead of himself.

101 *OR* IX, 60.

102 Cire Memorandum, UDC.

103 Forrest Conner, ed. "Letters of Lieutenant Robert H. Miller to His Family, 1861-1862," *The Virginia Magazine of History and Biography* 70 (1962), 77.

104 Cire Memorandum, UDC.

105 Conner, 77.

106 NA, Record of Events (Donaldsonville Art'y), March & April 1862.

107 Conner, 77.

108 *Amite News Digest,* August 29, 1984; Richmond C. Price to Sister, August 16, 1861, letter,

Richmond C. Price Papers, Virginia Historical Society, Richmond, Va.; Conner, 71, 72, 77.
109 Cire Memorandum, UDC.
110 Cire Memorandum, UDC; *Donaldsonville Chief*, July 7, 1877; *New Orleans Daily Picayune*, July 23, 1882. The Vincentian Father returned to Donaldsonville and from there conducted mass throughout the Lafourche region where he was a good friend to the poor while comforting the sick through the trying times. In May 1864 he even completed the first communion for forty-three of Ascension's children. Boglioli to Archbishop [Odin], May 17, 1864, letter, Archdiocese of New Orleans Collection, University of Notre Dame.
111 NA, Maurin File. Average per horse was fourteen pounds of hay and twelve pounds of oats, barley, or corn each day. The exact number lost was seven horses and one mule. Maurin's forage requisitions during this time listed the number of horses at eighty-two.
112 Maurin to Maj. Brown, March 26, 1862, letter, MCR. Using six horses at each piece was a rarity in the Confederate artillery, four was the norm.
113 *OR* XI:3, 426.
114 NA, Maurin File.
115 *OR* XI:3, 410.
116 Ibid. Pt. 3, 422.
117 Redoubt No. 4 at times was called Fort Magruder or White Redoubt and was located about half a mile southwest of the main Yorktown defenses and connected with earthworks. Redoubt No. 5 was called Fort Rains or Red Redoubt and was southwest of the other redoubt, connected by a curtain. The redoubts and curtain in between no longer stand though the location is in Colonial Historical National Park, Yorktown Battlefield. Redoubt 4 was northeast of the present day intersection of State Route 238 (Goosely Road) and 17 (George Washington Memorial Highway), between Highway 17 and CHNP's Historical Tour Drive. Redoubt 5 was located on what is now Highway 17, southwest of the rebuilt Revolutionary War "Pigeon Hill Redoubt" and south of 17's intersection with 238. *OR* Atlas, Plate XIV, Number 1 and Plate XV, No. 3 show the redoubts. J. W. Minnich, "Reminiscences Relating to the, Siege of Yorktown, April – May 1862," Typescript in Colonial Historical National Park (Yorktown), 2, herafter cited as Minnich Typescript. Ruth H. Early *Lieutenant General Jubal Anderson Early C. S. A. Autobiographical Sketch and Narrative of the War Between the States* (Philadelphia, 1912), 59; Consolidated Morning Report of Artillery in and between Redoubts No. 4 & 5, April 13, 1862, and Return Of Capt. Victor Maurin's Company, April 1862. MCR. *OR* XI:1, 403.
118 Minnich Typescript, 5.
119 *OR* XI:1, 286, 297, 298, 303, 304, 403; NA, Record of Events (Donaldsonville Art'y), March & April 1862. Canister shot was used primarily in defense and had a range of 400 yards. It consisted of a tin can filled with small cast-iron or lead balls that scattered immediately upon leaving the cannon's muzzle.
120 O'Hara Diary, LDA. This was the beginning of McClellan's siege operations by the Army of the Potomac.
121 *OR* XI:1, 403.
122 NA, Record of Events (March/April 1862).
123 *OR* XI:1, 303.
124 Cire Memorandum, UDC.
125 O'Hara Diary, LDA.
126 NA, Record of Events (Donaldsonville Art'y), March & April 1862.
127 Minnich Typescript, 11, 12.
128 Conner, 80.
129 Orders for Regulations of Redoubts No. 4 and 5, April 8, 1862, MCR.
130 *OR* XI:1, 406, XI:3, 437; Early, 61, 62.
131 Joseph L. Brent, *Memoirs of the War Between the States* (New Orleans, 1940), 113.
132 Cire Memorandum, UDC.
133 Miller, 181.
134 *OR* XI:3, 448.
135 Thomas Holley to Father (James R. Holley), April 18, 1862, letter, MCR.
136 Houghton, 61.
137 William Anderson to wife, April 26 and May 1, 1862, letters, UV.
138 Cire Memorandum, UDC.

139 William Anderson to wife, April 18, 1862, letter, UV.
140 John G. Barrett, *Yankee Rebel, The Civil War Journal of Edmund DeWitt Patterson* (Chapel Hill, N.C., 1966), 18.
141 Hebert, 54.
142 Miller, 181.
143 Cire Memorandum, UDC.
144 Runge, 15.
145 Return of Captain Victor Maurin's Company of the Donaldsonville Artillery, May 1, 1862, MCR.
146 Putnam, 125.
147 Cire Memorandum, UDC.
148 "Eighth Alabama Regiment Infantry," typescript, Alabama Department of Archives and History, 3.
149 Cire Memorandum, UDC.
150 NA, Maurin File, *OR* XI:1, 602, 606.
151 Cire Memorandum, UDC.
152 Ibid.
153 Early, 67.
154 Richard L. Maury, "The Battle of Williamsburg, Va." *SHSP*, Vol. 22, 109.
155 Gallagher, *Fighting*, 78, 79.
156 John S. Tucker, "The Diary of John S. Tucker," *Alabama Historical Quarterly* 43 (1981), 10.
157 Maury, 109.
158 Cire Memorandum, UDC.
159 *OR*, XI:1, 602, 606; OR, XI:3, 482; J. G. deRoulhac Hamilton, ed. *The Papers of Randolph Albert Shotwell*, Vol. 1 (Raleigh, N.C., 1936), 192.
160 Maury, 110.
161 Ibid.
162 Ibid., 112.
163 James Dinkins, *1861-1865 By an Old Johnnie* (Cincinnati, 1897), 32.
164 Hamilton, Vol. 1, 194.
165 *Donaldsonville Chief*, September 12, 1874.
166 Cire Memorandum, UDC.
167 De Trobriand, 198.
168 *OR* XI:1, 583.
169 *OR* LI:1, 86. The NA, Record of Events (Donaldsonville Art'y), May/June 1862 (dated August 16, 1862), states the guns at Williamsburg fired "two hundred rounds without cessation."
170 *OR* LI:1, 90.
171 *Ibid.* 87.
172 Emily G. Ramey and John K. Gott, ed. *The Years of Anguish, Faquier County, Virginia, 1861-1865* (Bowie, Maryland 1998), 186.
173 *OR* XI:1, 583.
174 *OR* LI:1, 86. Fort Magruder is located two miles east of Williamsburg in a small, enclosed city park. Only segments of the west and south walls remain, and they are overgrown with trees and underbrush.
175 NA, CSR of Lestang Fortier. Brown was apparently well respected by the Donaldsonville officers. He later became Chief of Artillery in the Second Corps, A. N. V. and was killed by a sharpshooter while seeking a position for his guns at the Battle of the Wilderness on May 6, 1864. Prosper Landry in going to the front that day wrote, "Here was a horse with saddle and bridle which was being led behind an ambulance that advanced at a slow walk, but I knew well this horse—'Col. Brown is therefore wounded?' 'He is dead.' I approach to see him once more—I had known him since Yorktown—and I continued on my way in thinking of his poor wife." Jean Reynaud Jacques Prosper Landry to Adele Pedesclaux Landry, September 1864, letter, UV.
176 Carlton McCarthy, ed., *Contributions to a History of the Richmond Howitzers*, Pamphlet No. 3 (Richmond, Va., 1884), 38.
177 Hamilton, Vol. 1, 199.
178 Ibid.
179 Levy, 303.

180 *OR* XI:1, 604, 605.
181 Tucker, 11.
182 Hamilton, Vol. 1, 200, 201.
183 Levy, 303.
184 Barrett, 23.
185 Tucker, 11.
186 Cire Memorandum, UDC.
187 Hebert, 58.
188 Cire Memorandum, UDC.
189 William Anderson to wife, May 10, 1862, letter, UV.
190 James M. Folsom, *Heroes and Martyrs of Georgia, Georgia's Record in the Revolution of 1861* (Macon, Ga., 1864), 53; *OR* XI:3, 503.

CHAPTER FOUR

1 Dinkins, 33.
2 J. W. Minnich, "Incidents of the Peninsular Campaign," *CV*, 30 (1922), 56.
3 Houghton, 61.
4 *B & L*, Vol. II, 223; Everson, 123. Five Federal naval vessels moved up the James River toward Richmond; after a four-hour duel with Confederate shore batteries at Drewry's Bluff, the Federal squadron withdrew. The troops along the Chickahominey River were also aware of Beauregard's victory claim at Shiloh, Tennessee on April 6-7, 1862.
5 Cire Memorandum, UDC.
6 Tucker, 11.
7 Ibid.
8 Cire Memorandum, UDC. Franklin Stearns, Esq., a liberal-hearted, enterprising, and prominent Richmond merchant was known for distilling whiskey from which he reaped "a golden harvest." Stearns was exonerated in April 1862 after being charged as a disloyal citizen. His farm, called Tree Hill, is located three miles southeast of the state capitol along the bluffs of the James River overlooking with a majestic view fields and the city of Richmond. The two-story house (still standing as a private home), was built circa 1775 and is located on an expansive lawn shaded by beautiful trees. Later during the war the land surrounding the mansion was used for grazing livestock belonging to Chimborazo Hospital. It was the site of the surrender of Richmond by the mayor in 1865. *Richmond Examiner*, March 4, 1862; *Richmond Dispatch*, April 23, 1862; *Richmond Enquirer*, April 26, 1862; Emmie F. Farrar, *Old Virginia Houses Along the James* (New York, 1957), 55, 56; "Inventory of Early Architecture and Historic Sites: County of Henrico, Va. December, 1976" in files, RNB
9 Cire Memorandum, UDC.
10 Tucker, 12.
11 Levy, 303.
12 Owen, 80.
13 NA, Maurin File.
14 Folsom, 35.
15 *Donaldsonville Chief*, June 26, 1880.
16 Cire Memorandum, UDC.
17 Ibid.
18 *Richmond Dispatch*, May 27, 1862. Its unknown if Maurin got his horses back. The Louisiana General Hospital building was rented from the Baptist College and is still standing at the northeast corner of N. Lombardy and W. Grace Streets (one block from General Robert E. Lee's statue on Monument Avenue). The University of Richmond had used the building with an annex wing that was later attached. It is now abandoned and (in 2010) for sale. During the war there was a long one storied wooden building near the main brick building and connected by a narrow covered way on the first floor. The united capacity of the wards was 210 patients served by 3 surgeons and 20 nurses. The hospital was highly praised for its order and cleanliness. Robert W. Waitt Jr., *Confederate Military Hospitals in Richmond* (Richmond, Va., 1964), 21; NA, M331; Inspection Report dated November 15, 1862, in CSR of William A. Carrington.

19 Cire Memorandum, UDC. The New Bridge Road was a turnout from the Nine Mile Road to New Bridge over the Chickahominy River.
20 NA, Maurin File; Photographed Record Sheets of Donaldsonville Artillery Muster Roll for May/June 1862, Bound Vols. 145 and 146, LAGL.
21 War Diary of Francis Dunbar Ruggles, typescript, HNOC, 1.
22 Robert E. Park, *Sketch of the Twelfth Alabama Infantry of Battle's Brigade, Rhodes' Division, Early's Corps, of the Army of Northern Virginia* (Richmond, Va., 1906), 28.
23 James Longstreet, *From Manassas to Appomattox* (Philadelphia, 1896), 91.
24 Frank Moore, ed., *The Rebellion Record*, Vol. 5 (New York, 1866), 98.
25 *OR* XI:1, 940, 943; Longstreet, 101; *Charleston Mercury*, June 2, 1862.
26 O'Hara Diary, LDA.
27 Moore, Vol. 5, 103.
28 Ibid. *99.* Also moving up the Williamsburg Road from the Charles City Road at 5:00 p.m. was Longstreet's remaining three infantry brigades, followed by two brigades from Huger's Division.
29 Levy, 303.
30 Casey's headquarters were in a large tent just beside the famous Twin Houses and Casey's redoubt and rifle pits, about three-fourths of a mile west from the crossroads at Seven Pines and just south of the Williamsburg Road. *OR* XI:1, 913. Today there are interpretive markers in the area, but no historic homes, earthworks, or even any vistas or view sheds. The ground where the redoubt and Twin Houses were are now covered with high density 1930s housing. Robert E. L. Krick correspondence, March 23, 2004, RNB
31 Evelyn C. Williams, ed. *Letters of James Peter Williams, 1861-1865* (Lynchburg, Va., 1937), 17.
32 L. D. Nicholls to wife, June 2, 1862 letter, TU.
33 Cire Memorandum, UDC.
34 *Amite City Times*, September 5, 1984.
35 Conner, 82, 83.
36 E. C. Williams, 17.
37 Tucker, 13.
38 *OR* XI:1, 944.
39 E. C. Williams, 19.
40 Moore, Vol. 5, 99.
41 D. B. Easley, "Experiences at Seven Pines" *CV* 37 (1929), 131.
42 *OR* XI:1, 945.
43 E. C. Williams, 19.
44 Cire Memorandum, UDC.
45 L.D. Nicholls to wife, June 2, 1862, letter, TU. Nicholls, now Captain of Ascension Parish's Phoenix Company (Co. K, 8th Louisiana Infantry Regiment), was on sick leave at the Louisiana Hospital in Richmond. With two other Louisiana officers he left the hospital early in the morning of Sunday, June 1, 1862, and participated in the battle of Seven Pines with the 14th Louisiana Infantry Regiment.
46 Cire Memorandum, UDC.
47 O'Hara Diary, LDA.
48 *OR* XI:1, 945.
49 L. D. Nicholls to wife, June 2, 1862 letter, TU.
50 Ibid. Their guns were fired at Yorktown, Williamsburg, and Seven Pines.
51 NA, Record of Events (Donaldsonville Art'y), May & June 1862.
52 *OR* XI:1, 945.
53 E. C. Williams, 19.
54 Freeman, *Lieutenants,* Vol.1, 225, 262; Douglas S. Freeman, *R. E. Lee, A Biography*, Vol. II (New York, 1934), 74, 77. Fair Oaks Station was located about 1,600 yards to the west of Seven Pines along the Nine Mile Road.
55 *OR* XI:1, 945.
56 Cire Memorandum, UDC.
57 Ibid.
58 Freeman, *Lee*, Vol. II, 80, 81.
59 Ruggles, HNOC, 2.
60 Cire Memorandum, UDC.

61 Most of the army's artillery camped around Oakwood Cemetery and Blakely's Millpond, less than a mile north of Harrison's House located on the Williamsburg Road at the junction with the Charles City Road. There is an abandoned mall on the site today. Robert E. L. Krick correspondence, March 23, 2004, RNBP; Douglas S. Freeman, *A Calendar of Confederate Papers* (Richmond, Va., 1908), 408.

62 Levy, 303.

63 *Donaldsonville Chief*, October 4, 1913.

64 Ibid.

65 William Pegram to Mary Evans Pegram Anderson, Febuary 11, 1864, letter, Pegram-Johnson-McIntosh Collection, Virginia Historical Society.

66 The Bellville Garden was also called Schad's Garden. Ernest T. Walthall, *Hidden Things Brought to Light* (Richmond, Va., 1908), 37.

67 Chesson, 56, 57.

68 L. D. Nicholls to wife, June 9, 1862, letter, TU.

69 Saxon, 64.

70 NA, CSR; O'Hara Diary, LDA. Kellet in 1860 was an overseer on one of the richest sugar plantations in Plaquemines Parish. A three-year-old daughter survived him. The Masonic Burial Grounds in Hollywood Cemetery is located at Section M of the Confederate Soldiers Section, in the northwest quadrant of the cemetery. The Soldier's Section has the landmark pyramid-shaped Confederate monument built of granite that was erected in 1869.

71 Mattie to brother [L. D. Nicholls], May 5, 1862, letter, TU.

72 Ibid.

73 Conner, 82.

74 Richmond's newest, finest, and most popular hotel was six stories tall, including the basement where the city's post office was located. Built in 1859, it stood at the southeast corner of Main and 8th streets. It survived the April 1865 fire only to burn on Christmas morning, 1870. Today the location is the heart of Richmond's financial district and contains a variety of commercial, retail, and office buildings.

75 Conner, 84.

76 L. D. Nicholls to wife, June 9, 1862, letter, TU.

77 Ibid.

78 L. D. Nicholls to wife, June 2, 1862, letter, TU.

79 Mattie to brother [L. D. Nicholls], May 5, 1862, letter, TU.

80 Cire Memorandum, UDC.

81 J. Cutler Andrews, *The South Reports the Civil War* (Princeton, N.J., 1970), 184.

82 Ed. M. Burruss to Mother, June 14, 1862, letter, John C. Burruss Papers, LSU

83 Bell I. Wiley, ed. *Reminiscences of Big I by Lieut. William Nathaniel Wood* (Jackson, Tenn.,1956), 21; Susan Lee, *Memoirs of William Nelson Pendleton* (Philadelphia, 1893), 189. *OR* XI:3, 577; Freeman, *Lee*, Vol. II, 107.

84 Ed. M. Burruss to Papa, June 25, 1862, letter, John C. Buruss Papers, LSU.

85 Cire Memorandum, UDC.

86 *OR* XI:2, 816, 817. On June 25, 1862, McClellan ordered his Third Corps to move forward on the Williamsburg Road as part of the Union Army's advance against Richmond. This was the first of the Seven Days' Battles and was known as the battle of King's School House or Oak Grove.

87 Cire Memorandum, UDC.

88 *OR* XI:3, 612, 613.

89 Conner, 87.

90 Mark M. Boatner, *The Civil War Dictionary* (New York, 1959), 674.

91 Niles, 240.

92 Pryor's Brigade was composed of the 14th Alabama, 2nd Florida, 14th Louisiana, and 3rd Virginia regiments, and St. Paul's 7th Louisiana Battalion and Coppens' 1st Louisiana Zouave Battalion, consolidated. *OR* XI:2, 486. Ezra J. Warner, *Generals in Gray* (Baton Rouge, 1959), 247, 248.

93 Mrs. Roger A. Pryor, *Reminiscences of Peace and War* (New York, 1904), 174.

94 Jean Reynaud Jacques Prosper Landry to Adele Pedesclaux Landry, September 1864 letter, UV.

95 Pryor, 174, 175.

96 *OR* XI:3, 616.

97 Pryor, 176.

98 Billings, 195.
99 *OR* XI:2, 756.
100 Wiley, *Reminiscences,* 22.
101 Owen, 86, 87.
102 Mechanicsville was an important crossroads made up of half-dozen frame houses, a two-story house, stores and a saloon. Wiley, 22; *OR* XI:2, 756; Freeman, *Lee*, Vol. II, 123, 124, 129; David G. McIntosh, "Reminiscences, 1911," Virginia Historical Society, 3; An English Combatant [pseud.]. *Battle-Fields of the South, from Bull Run to Fredericksburg, with Sketches of Confederate Commanders, and Gossip of the Camps* (New York, 1864), 325.
103 David Zable Reminiscences, LHAC. Zable, a New Orleanian, was born in 1832. He was captain of the Hope Baseball Club of New Orleans and "when war broke out the baseball club evolved into a military company . . . known as the Lafayette Rifle Cadets. The captain of the baseball nine was elected Captain of the company [Company K] . . . and became Colonel of the regiment." *Times-Picayune*, May 30, 1903.
104 *OR* XI:2, 780.
105 *OR* XI:2, 780, 782; Zable Reminiscences, LHAC; Gallagher, 62; Moore, Vol. 5, 249.
106 Zable Reminiscences, LHAC.
107 The Catlin house, "Hoary with age," still stands though it and the nearby trees were "cut to pieces by cannon and minnie-balls" during the battle. Located on Cold Harbor Road in Mechanicsville, the house has been remodeled and serves as a private home today. It is surrounded by a subdivision named Beaverdam Park that overlooks the Beaver Dam Creek unit of the Richmond National Battlefield Park. *Old Homes of Hanover County, Virginia* (Hanover, Va., 1983), 10.
108 An English Combatant, 334.
109 Andrews Battery was assigned to Brigadier General William D. Pender's Brigade, A. Hill's Division.
110 *OR* XI:2, 782, 783; McCarthy, Pamphlet No. 2, 118, 119; *An English Combatant*, 329, 385; R. Howard Thomson and William H. Rauch, *History of the "Bucktails": Kane Rifle Regiment of the Pennsylvania Reserve Corps, 42nd Infantry* (Philadelphia, 1906), 113.
111 *Richmond Daily Dispatch,* June 30, 1862.
112 *An English Combatant,* 386.
113 *OR* XI:2, 783.
114 *Richmond Daily Dispatch*, June 30, 1862.
115 *An English Combatant,* 386.
116 McCarthy, Pamphlet No. 2, 119.
117 *OR* XI:2, 899, 900.
118 McCarthy, Pamphlet No. 2, 119.
119 *OR* XI:2, 770, 771. The Federal Third Division (Pennsylvania Reserves), of the Fifth Corps were ordered to fall back. In casualties their commander reported "but slight loss" because of their prepared earthworks and the clearing of the ground in front. *OR* XI:2, 400.
120 McCarthy, Pamphlet No. 2, 119.
121 *OR* XI:2, 783.
122 Ibid. 780.
123 Levy, 304. It can be presumed he was killed by a sharpshooter's bullet. Stanely, who had no heirs, was buried near Kellet in the Masonic Burying Grounds (Section M of the Confederate Soldiers Section), of Hollywood Cemetery in Richmond. O'Hara Diary. LDA. The 1850 U. S. Census of Ascension Parish listed Stanely's age at thirty-five, but the 1860 census had him as a forty-one-year-old laborer. On May 17, 1869, at the Ascension Parish Courthouse in Donaldsonville, Victor Maurin and others witnessed the Vacant Succession of Stanely's property of "Seven Hundred Dollars in gold valued at Nine Hundred and Ninety four Dollars in U. S. Currency." Ascension Parish Civil Records, 1803-1926, LDA.
124 M. B. Hurst, *History of the Fourteenth Regiment Alabama Volunteers* (Richmond, Va., 1863), 11. *Macon* (Georgia), *Weekly Telegraph,* July 14, 1862
125 David G. McIntosh Reminiscences, "Notes concerning a tour of Civil War battlefields around Richmond, Va. (1911), Virginia Historical Society, 3. Many of the fallen men were from Ripley's Brigade made up of the 1st and 3rd North Carolina and 44th and 48th Georgia regiments.
126 *OR* XI:2, 756, 771, 780, 783; Hurst, 11; McCarthy, Pamphlet No. 2, 120; Frederick Maurice, ed. *An Aide-De-Camp of Lee Being the Papers of Colonel Charles Marshall* (Boston, 1927), 97.

127 McIntosh Reminiscenses, 1911, 4, VHS.
128 N. B. Hogan, "Gaines's Mill—Pickett and Hood" *CV*, 5 (1898), 567.
129 Barrett, 31.
130 *An English Combatant*, 332.
131 McCarthy, Pamphlet No. 2, 120.
132 Selwyn was the home of Walker Hogan and is still today a private home and in excellent condition. The outer houses bore every appearance of having been used for hospitals with numerous mounds of earth covering the dead nearby. "Powhite and Selwyn," *Hanover County Historical Society Bulletin*, No. 23, November 1980.
133 *An English Combatant*, 334.
134 Ibid.
135 *OR* XI:2, 780.
136 Hogan, 567. The Federal defensive position was behind Boatswain's Swamp, a stream with its adjacent overflowed land, on a long hill with steep grades that at times was called Turkey Hill. The Federal position is part of the Gaines' Mill battlefield of Richmond National Battlefield Park. The Civil War Trust organization in 2012 is attempting to buy a 285-acre tract for preservation by the RNBP where Longstreet's division attacked. This land includes the position of the Donaldsonville Artillery near Dr. Gaines's House.
137 Powhite was the home of William Fleming Gaines, M. D. (b. 1804 - d. 1874). The original home was still standing in 1937, but later destroyed. The bricks from the four massive chimneys were used in the construction of the present house. The old house, called an "elegant Mansion" by one of the Donaldsonville Canonniers was fifty feet wide and twenty-eight feet deep, with a front and back porch across the entire house, eight feet wide. "Powhite and Selwyn," *Henrico County Historical Society Bulletin,* No. 23, November 1980; *New York Times*, May 28, 1862; Levy Diary, HUC.
138 Brent, 170.
139 *OR* XI:2, 318, 772, 780.
140 Ibid. 307.
141 Ibid. 304.
142 Levy, 304.
143 *OR* XI:2, 237, 264. The 20-pounder's range was 2,100 yards at five degrees.
144 C. Irvine Walker, *Life of Lt. Gen. Richard Heron Anderson* (Charleston, S.C., 1917), 88.
145 *OR* XI:2, 772.
146 McCarthy, Pamphlet No. 2, 120.
147 Hogan, 568.
148 J. W. Brunson, *Historical Sketch of the Pee Dee Light Artillery by Orderly Sgt. J. W. Brunson, Together with a Roll of McIntosh's Battalion Artillery* (Winston-Salem, N.C., 1927), 4.
149 *B & L,* Vol. II, 398, 399.
150 McCarthy, Pamphlet No. 2, 120.
151 *OR* XI:2, 780.
152 Levy, 304.
153 *OR* XI:2, 301.
154 *An English Combatant*, 341.
155 James Bradford Diary, Handley Regional Library, Winchester, Va., 5.
156 Levy, 304.
157 McCarthy, Pamphlet No. 2, 121.
158 *Minutes of the Third Annual Meeting and Reunion of the United Confederate Veterans Held in the City of New Orleans, La., April 8th and 9th, 1892* (New Orleans, 1892), 39.
159 Confederate Pension Application of Pierre "Turiaffe" Babin, November 12, 1907, witnessed by comrades Bienvenue Cire and Antoine Sobral, LDA.
160 Barrett, 33, 34.
161 McCarthy, Pamphlet No. 2, 123, 124.
162 Zable Reminiscences, LHAC.
163 *An English Combatant*, 342.
164 Levy, 304.
165 Brent, 177.
166 Barrett, 35.

167 Hamilton, Vol. 1, 248.
168 J. W. Reid, *History of the Fourth Regiment of S. C. Volunteers* (Greenville, S.C., 1891), 99.
169 Bradford Diary, 5.
170 I. G. Bradwell, "Soldier Life in the Confederate Army," *CV* 23 (1916), 24.
171 *OR* XI:2, 345.
172 Ibid. 297.
173 Ibid. 305.
174 Cire Memorandum, UDC.
175 Ruggles Typescript, 5.
176 Hamilton, Vol. 1, 248.
177 Moore, Vol. 5, 252.
178 John G. Adams, *Reminiscences of the Nineteenth Massachusetts Regiment* (Boston, 1899), 34, 35.
179 *Richmond Whig*, July 3, 1862.
180 Ibid.
181 *OR* XI:2, 759, 775.
182 Cire Memorandum, UDC.
183 John W. T. Leech, "The Battle of Frazier's Farm," *SHSP*, Vol. XXI, 162.
184 Barrett, 36.
185 The chapel was burned to the ground later in the war. All that was left was the communion pitcher and two matching cups found by a teenager sifting through the ashes. The youth took the set home and stored it away until his descendants presented the communion set to the church in 1993 during the church's 150th anniversary. The chapel was not rebuilt until 1897 and remained in use until torn down in 1960 to make room for the present church building. Completed in 1966, it is located at 3140 Darbytown Road, the site of the original church. Walter Carr Whitt, "A Short History of Pioneer Baptist Church from 1843 to 1976," in Office of Pioneer Baptist Church; Judy Stell to author, October 15, 2003, letter.
186 Ruggles Typescript, 5; Leech, 162; *OR* XI:2, 77; Freeman, *Lee*, Vol. II, 179; Owen, 91.
187 Barrett, 45.
188 Leech, 162.
189 Barrett, 46.
190 *OR* XI:2, 775. Pryor's Brigade was positioned on Wilcox's left with Featherston's Brigade in reserve behind Pryor's. The other three brigades of Longstreet's Division were located on the right of the road.
191 Hamilton, Vol. 1, 251.
192 Levy, 304.
193 Hamilton, Vol. 1, 251.
194 Cire Memorandum, UDC.
195 *OR* XI:2, 781.
196 Cire Memorandum, UDC.
197 Leech, 164.
198 Thomas L. Livermore, *Days and Events, 1860-1866* (Boston, 1920), 92. Pryor's Brigade was to have gone into action on the left of Wilcox and simultaneously, but the brigade met with delays in the woods and did not reach the front until after Wilcox had been driven back from his advanced position. Pryor's troops charged four hundred yards over a clear field before reaching the Union line protected by a slight barricade of wooden fence rails. They made it to within one hundred yards of the Federal guns.
199 *OR* XI:2, 785.
200 J. F. J. Caldwell, *The History of a Brigade of South Carolinians* (Philadelphia, 1866), 47, 48.
201 Levy, 304.
202 The Federal units are believed to have been Captain James Thompson's Battery G, 2nd United States Artillery, whose left piece was near and a little in the rear of Lieutenant Alanson M. Randol's right piece, Battery E, First United States Artillery. Supports for Thompson's guns were Brigadier General John C. Robinson's First Brigade of Brigadier General Philip Kearny's Third Division, Third Corps. During the battle, regiments from Birney's, Berry's, and Caldwell's brigades also came up in support. Brigadier General George A. McCall's Division supported Randol's Battery. Thompson's Battery retired at about 7:30 p.m. after having exhausted their ammunition. They lost one gun and three caissons. A two-gun section of Battery E, 1st Rhode Island Artillery

came on the field as Thompson's was leaving and lost one of its guns. Randol's Battery, overrun by Wilcox's Brigade, lost all six of their 12-pounder Napoleon guns, plus four caissons and two limbers. Freeman, *Lee*, Vol. II, 191; *OR* XI:2, 168, 170-178, 255.
203 *OR* XI:2, 781.
204 A. L. Slack, "After the Battle of Frazier's Farm," *CV* 2 (1894), 20.
205 McCarthy, Pamphlet No. 2, 124.
206 Cire Memorandum, UDC.
207 Moore, Vol. 5, 267.
208 Levy, 304.
209 *OR* XI:2, 781.
210 Frederick S. Daniel, *Richmond Howitzers in the War* (Richmond, Va., 1891), 62, 63.

CHAPTER FIVE

1 A. J. Bennett, *The Story of the First Massachusetts Light Battery, Attached to the Sixth Army Corps* (Boston, 1886), 62.
2 Cire Memorandum, UDC.
3 Ruggles Typescript, 6.
4 Moore, Vol. 5, 267.
5 Alfred S. Roe, *The Tenth Regiment Massachusetts Volunteer Infantry 1861-1864, A Western Massachusetts Regiment* (Springfield, Mass., 1909), 123.
6 Brent, 236.
7 O'Hara Diary, LDA.
8 McCarthy, Pamphlet No. 2, 124.
9 *OR* XI:2, 500, 501.
10 Freeman, *Lee,* Vol. II, 245.
11 Wood, 26.
12 Levy, 303.
13 Cire Memorandum, UDC.
14 Moore, Vol. 5, 267.
15 On July 7, 1862, Lincoln met with General McClellan at Harrison's Landing.
16 Walton, the Washington Artillery's commander, was placed in charge of the camp and Longstreet's artillery. Washington Artillery Order Book, No. 2, Order 13, LAGL.
17 By "Special Requisition" Maurin received at Camp Longstreet three wall tents "to replace the same number . . . which was left standing at Yorktown, per order of General Commanding." NA, Maurin File.
18 Ruggles Typescript, 8.
19 *Amite City Times,* September 5, 1984.
20 Lewis, 42.
21 James J. Kirkpatrick Diary, 1861-1864, UT.
22 A. C. Jones Diary, LHAC.
23 Charles Moore, Jr. Diary, September 1, 1861- October 23, 1865, Civil War Papers, LHAC.
24 Owen, 95.
25 Barnes F. Lathrop, "The Lafourche District in 1861-1862: A Problem in Local Defense," *Lousiana History* 1 (1960), 129.
26 Mattie Nicholls to Lisa Nicholls, August 13, 1862, letter, TU.
27 Ibid.
28 *New Orleans Republican,* September 27, 1871.
29 Barnes F. Lathrop, "The Lafourche District in 1862: Militia and Partisan Rangers," *Lousiana History* 1 (1960), 235, 236.
30 *Brule* meaning a place with a small cluster of houses with maybe a store. It usually was located on the backside of planted fields and near where the swamps began.
31 Sister M. Clara to Father [Francis Burlando] July 15, 1863, letter, Archdiocese of New Orleans Collection, University of Notre Dame.
32 *Donaldsonville Chief,* October 4, 1916.
33 Roland, 123.

34 Lewis, 42.
35 According to Lieutenant Prosper Landry the gun was captured in the Battle of Frayser's Farm on June 30, 1862, where McCall was taken prisoner. The 3-inch Ordnance Rifle, M-1861, was a much-admired wrought iron field piece and especially valued. During the war it became the favorite field piece of Confederate artillerymen. The gun had a range of 2,788 yards, which was 1,028 yards farther than the Blakely and 1,265 yards more than the 6-pounder. R. Prosper Landry, "The Donaldsonville Artillery at the Battle of Fredericksburg," *SHSP*, Vol. 23, 198; Ripley, 161, 163, 374.
36 Capt. C. McRaeSelph, A. Q. M., to Col. J. B.Walton, Chief of Artillery, Right Wing, July 14, 1862, letter, Washington Artillery Collection, Box 23, LAGL.
37 NA, Maurin File.
38 *New Orleans Republican*, November 28, 1870.
39 NA, CSR. He later received a discharge and was officially dropped from the Donaldsonville Artillery rolls.
40 *OR* XI:3, 647. The New Market Road was the shortest advance to Richmond for McClellen's army.
41 Bennett, 63.
42 James J. Kirkpatrick Diary, 1861-1864, UT.
43 W. H. Andrews, *Footprints of a Regiment, A Recollection of the 1st Georgia Regulars, 1861-1865* (Atlanta, 1992), 53.
44 NA, Record of Events (Donaldsonville Art'y), July & August 1862; *OR*, LI:2, 595, 596, 600.
45 Ramey, 188, 189; Longstreet, 154.
46 Jones Diary, LHAC; Ruggles Typescript, 9. Unbeknownst to the Canonniers this was the day Donaldsonville was bombarded and burned.
47 *Donaldsonville Chief*, May 26, 1877. Prosper Landry in a letter to his wife in September 1864 noted he had his night shirt and slippers in his trunk. The great fire that accompanied the evacuation of Richmond in April 1865 destroyed their baggage trunks and other possessions. Levy Diary, HUC.
48 Ruggles Typescript, 9.
49 *OR* LI:2, 604, 606.
50 Ruggles Typescript, 10.
51 Garnett's artillery column moved from Almond Creek onto present day Old Osborne Turnpike (State Primary Route 5), to East Main Street, which turns into West Main Street. The column likely turned at Adams Street going about three and one-half blocks to Brook Road (where Azeala Avenue becomes U. S. Highway 1), on which, they moved northeast to Mountain Road (State Primary Route 625), to U. S. 33 that was followed to Gordonsville. Garnett's route was the same as Walton's column that left the day before.
52 Gibbons, 348-350.
53 Cire Memorandum, UDC.
54 Charles F. Walcott, *History of the Twenty-First Regiment Massachusetts Volunteers in the War for the Preservation of the Union 1861-1865 with Statistics of the War and of Rebel Prisons* (Boston, 1882), 126.
55 The twenty-year-old Hebert was the son of Valentin Hebert, a storekeeper in Donaldsonville. He was buried in Richmond's Hollywood Cemetery in the Soldier's Section, Grave Q-298.
56 Cire Memorandum, UDC.
57 Ibid.
58 Louisa Court House was established in 1742 and today has about 1500 inhabitants.
59 Cire Memorandum, UDC.
60 Donaldsonville Artillery *Historical Memoranda*, LHAC.
61 This Gordonsville landmark, a galleried railroad hotel built in 1860, is today the Exchange Hotel Civil War Museum, 400 South Main Street.
62 George Wise, *History of the Seventeenth Virginia Infantry, C.S.A.* (Baltimore, 1870), 39.
63 Jones Diary, LHAC.
64 Ruggles Typescript, 10.
65 William H. B. Thomas, *Gordonsville, Virginia Historic Crossroads Town* (Orange, Va., 1971), 44.
66 Joseph T. Durkin, ed., *Confederate Chaplain, A War Journal* (Milwaukee, 1960), 6.
67 Wood, 27.

68 Wire, 2.
69 Freeman, *Lee* Vol. II, 283.
70 Orange had a population at this time of about 3,000 people. Today's population is 4,100. Originally called Orange Court House, it has served as the Orange County seat of government since 1749. The present courthouse was constructed in 1859. The eastern half of the town was consumed by fire in 1908, but buildings from its earliest days remain in its western half.
71 For the movements between August 16-18, 1862 see: Cire Memorandum, UDC; Ruggles Typescript, 10, 11; Lobrano Diary, LHAC; and Jones Diary, LHAC.
72 There were changes in Pryor's Brigade since the battles around Richmond. The 14th Louisiana Regiment and Coppen's Louisiana Battalion were transferred and replaced with the 5th and 8th Florida Regiments. The 2nd Florida, 14th Alabama, and 3rd Virginia remained. Longstreet's "Right Wing" was composed of five divisions with Longstreet's old division now split into two temporary and informal commands of three brigades. Brigadier General Cadmus Wilcox led his own, plus Featherston and Pryor's brigades, while Brigadier General James Kemper led the other three brigades.
73 Charles J. Lewis, Reminiscences, "Campaign of Second Manassas," Civil War Papers, LHAC.
74 Houghton, 31.
75 Walcott, 133.
76 Cire Memorandum, UDC.
77 C. G. Chamberlayne, ed. *Ham Chamberlayne-Virginian, Letters and Papers of an Artillery Officer* (Richmond, 1932), 95.
78 *Charleston Daily Courier*, August 30, 1862. The ford was located a short distance up river from the hamlet. Today there are just a few residents as the village was deserted when the highway bridge, built in 1888, washed out in 1942. *Historic Culpeper* (Culpeper, Va., 1974), 133.
79 Wise, 79.
80 Andrews, 50-52.
81 Ruggles Typescript, 15.
82 *Charleston Daily Courier*, August 30, 1862.
83 Ibid.
84 Jennings Place was built circa 1800 and is located on State Route 610 at 647. *Historic Culpeper*, 120.
85 *OR* XII:2, 596. The road to Kelly's Ford crosses Mountain Run and continues up a hill for one-half mile before gradually descending two miles to the Rappahannock River ford.
86 Thomas D. Cockrell and Michael B. Ballard, ed. *A Mississippi Rebel in the Army of Northern Virginia, The Civil War Memoirs of Private David Holt* (Baton Rouge, 1995), 100.
87 *Charleston Daily Courier*, August 30, 1862.
88 Cockrell, 101.
89 *Charleston Daily Courier*, August 30, 1862. The Federal Cavalry brigade was composed of the 1st Michigan, 5th New York, 1st Vermont, and 1st West Virginia regiments under the command of Brigadier General John Buford.
90 *OR* XII:2, 596, 597.
91 *OR* XII:2, 597. The enemy camp at Kelly's Ford was that of Major General J. L. Reno's 1st and 2nd Divisions of the Ninth Army Corps. Of the cavalry charge Reno sent notes to headquarters reporting, "Buford had a lively little skirmish. His loss small." Reno added in a second note, "A very successful skirmish, compelling their whole force to retire." *OR* XII:3, 609, 610.
92 *Charleston Daily Courier*, August 30, 1862. The Federal battery was either the Eighth Battery of Massachusetts Light Artillery or the Second U. S. Artillery, Battery E, both assigned to Reno's Ninth Corps. *OR* XII:3, 609.
93 Jones Diary, LHAC.
94 Cire Memorandum, UDC.
95 Donaldsonville Artillery *Historical Memoranda*, LHAC. Longstreet chronicled, "At Kelly's Ford it seemed possible to force a crossing. As we were preparing for it, an order came . . . to march . . . as we were leaving Kelley's the enemy made a dash to cross, and engaged . . . in a sharp fight . . . but the main column marched on, while the affair was still in progress." Longstreet, 163. Though Maurin's Canonniers and Mississippians believed the wrong road was taken because of the spy's fictitious order, it was given to Major General David R. Jones to halt or reverse his division. Apprehended, the spy fit the description of a rider who on the previous night shot one

of Longstreet's couriers. The spy and murderer was given a drumhead court-martial and hung. Continuing its march, Longstreet's troops with Wilcox's command and Maurin's Battery passed almost under the tree where he was left swinging. Owen, 101, 102; Bell I. Wiley, *Recollections of a Confederate Staff Officer* (Jackson, Tennessee, 1959), 89, 90.

96 Ruggles Typescript, 11.

97 *OR* XII:2, 597.

98 *Charleston Daily Courier*, August 30, 1862. Incorporated in 1782, Stevensburg was originally called York. It is the oldest and for many years was the largest town in Culpeper County. *Historical Culpeper*, 134.

99 Ruggles Typescript, 11. On the eastern edge of town on top of an overlooking hill is Stevensburg Baptist Church. Founded in 1833, a meeting house measuring 40 x 50 feet "well finished and well furnished" was built in 1858 and used for a hospital by Southern soldiers during the winter of 1862–1863. The church building caught fire and burned to the ground that winter and a new meetinghouse, built on the foundation of the old church was erected in 1874. Through the years the church has expanded and is thriving today. Mildred Jones and Mary Stevens Jones, "The History of Stevensburg Baptist Church, 1833-1983," *Stevensburg Baptist Church 150th Year Celebration, Pictorial Directory* (1983).

100 *Charleston Daily Courier*, August 30, 1862.

101 Cire Memorandum, UDC.

102 Longstreet ordered the Washington Artillery's Colonel J. B. Walton to place batteries in position at Rappahannock Station (now the town of Remington), and drive the enemy from his position on both sides of the Rappahannock River. Walton's Third Company under command of Captain Merritt B. "Buck" Miller opened the cannonade between 6:00 and 6:30 in the morning.

103 Squires' guns in line from right to left were the First Company Washington Artillery, four 3-inch rifle guns; Dixie Artillery, Captain W. H. Chapman, one Napoleon gun and one 3-inch rifle; and Stribling's Battery, three Napoleons and one 3-inch rifle. Some distance to Squires' left, near the road to Beverly Ford, were other Confederate guns under Miller. The Federal batteries near the bridge were Captain Ezra W. Matthews' 1st Pennsylvania Light Artillery, Battery F (entrenched on the south side); Captain James Thompson's 1st Pennsylvania Light Artillery, Battery C; Captain George F. Leppien's Maine Light Artillery, 5th Battery (E); and Captain James A. Hall's Maine Light Artillery, 2d Battery (B).

104 *OR* XII:2, 573, 574.

105 *Charleston Daily Courier*, August 30, 1862.

106 Ruggles Typescript, 12.

107 *OR* XII:2, 564.

108 Ruggles Typescript, 12.

109 *OR* XII:2, 575.

110 Ibid. 569, 570.

111 Landry, 201.

112 James J. Kirkpatrick Diary, 1861-1864, UT.

113 North Cliff c. 1848 also known as the Coons after its builder, is located about three miles east of Rixeyville on North Cliff Lane near the Hazel River. The T-shape 2-story red brick house of Federal design has eleven large rooms, a dwarf Greek portico, and three brick chimneys along with the brick kitchen, stone dairy house, log corncrib, and log slave house. All are still standing. *Historic Culpeper*, 61. Ruggles Typescript, 14.

114 James J. Kirkpatrick Diary, 1861-1864, UT.

115 Jones Diary, LHAC. The Little Fork Episcopal Church building at Rixeyville was completed in 1776. During the war Union soldiers tore out all the wood, leaving only the shell of the building and the reredos on the east wall. Church services were infrequent until 1976, when restoration of the building was undertaken.

116 Mrs. Burton Harrison, *Recollections Grave and Gay* (New York, 1911), 103.

117 Named Jeffersonton in 1799 it had been a bustling town situated on the Piedmont State Route from Washington to Milledgeville, Ga. *Historical Culpeper*, 132.

118 Cire Memorandum, UDC.

119 *Charleston Daily Courier*, September 3, 1862.

120 Ibid. September 10, 1862.

121 Cire Memorandum, UDC.

122 Jones Diary, LHAC. For the Bayou Lafourche Acadians shoes were a luxury and when worn, they had sabots (wooden shoes). Being barefoot was natural for many of the rural Ascension and Assumption Canonniers, but not on long marches over rough and rocky roads.
123 Cire Memorandum, UDC.
124 The river was called Hedgeman's until a little farther downstream where Carter Run joined it near Waterloo Bridge. From there it was called the Rappahannock River.
125 The approach to Henson's Ford originally ran parallel to and on the west side of the current road. The old roadbed is still visible. Only the mill's foundation and Henson cemetery remain while the road leading up the other side from the river is today called Bear's Den Road.
126 J. B. Polley, *Hood's Texas Brigade* (New York, 1910), 76.
127 Thomas Ware Diary, UNCCH.
128 Ibid.
129 Cire Memorandum, UDC.
130 James J. Kirkpatrick Diary, 1861-1864, UT.
131 *Charleston Daily Courier,* September 10, 1862.
132 Ibid., September 3, 1862.
133 Ibid.
134 *An English Combatant*, 447.
135 *Charleston Daily Courier,* September 10, 1862.
136 Jones Diary, LHAC. Salem has since been renamed Marshall.
137 *OR* XII:2, 564. Wilcox's Brigade had assigned to it the Thomas (Va.), Artillery, Featherston's Brigade had Captain W. H. Chapman's Dixie (Va.), Artillery, and Pryor's Brigade had the Donaldsonville Artillery. Additional batteries were temporarily assigned for the march through Hopewell. Wilcox's brigade added the Third Company Washington Artillery, and Featherston added the First Company Washington Artillery and Captain Greenlee Davidson's Letcher (Va.), Artillery. No additional batteries were temporarily attached to Pryor's Brigade.
138 *OR* XII:2, 597, 598. Hopewell Gap has an altitude of 804 feet. Antioch Baptist Church was organized in 1837 and met in a small log building that survives today. A stone church was built circa 1840 and was demolished about 1900 with the present frame building erected in 1901. Regular church services ceased in 1962, though an occasional wedding or funeral and an annual homecoming is held each August. The cemetery contains 110 marked graves. "Virginia Historic Landmarks Commission Survey," and "Concise History of Antioch Church from its organization in 1837 to October 1, 1862," source unknown, Bull Run Regional Library, Manassas, Va.
139 Benevolent Association of the Army of Northern Virginia Application of Jules Veque, July 1876, LHAC.
140 Charles W. Squires, "The Last of Lee's Battle Line," 59, 60, LAGL.
141 *An English Combatant*, 443.
142 Owen, 114.
143 Ibid. 116.
144 Squires, 60, LAGL.
145 The Brawner House is today located in Manassas National Battlefield Park, where much of the landscape still retains its wartime character.
146 Kursheedt to Sarah, August 25, 1862, letter, Kursheedt Papers, UNCCH.
147 Mary Lasswell, ed. *Rags and Hope: The Memoirs of Val C. Giles* (New York, 1961), 132.
148 The blowing out of the bushing of the vent disabled one of Squires' guns, which was sent from the field after firing only one round.
149 Clark, ed., Vol. I, 572. Ruggles reported his gun of the First Company, Washington Artillery fired 101 rounds. Ruggles Typescript, 15, HNOC.
150 *Charleston Daily Courier*, September 17, 1862.
151 J. H.A. Wagener's Diary, South Carolina Historical Society, Charleston, S.C.
152 *Charleston Daily Courier*, September 11, 1862.
153 McClellen, 26.
154 Owen, 118.
155 Ibid., 117.
156 *Charleston Daily Courier*, September 6, 11, 1862; *OR* LI:2, 613; Longstreet, 186-188.
157 *B & L*, Vol. II, 521.
158 Owen, 120.

159 Donaldsonville Artillery *Historical Memoranda*, LHAC.
160 Wiley, *Recollections*, 91, 92.
161 *Charleston Daily Courier*, September 11, 1862.
162 Cire Memorandum, UDC.
163 *Charleston Daily Courier*, September 11, 1862.
164 Alexander Hunter, "A High Private's Account of the Battle of Sharpsburg, Paper No. 1," *SHSP*, Vol. 10, 505.
165 *An English Combatant*, 452, 453. Federal dead, wounded, and missing were estimated at 16,054; Confederate at 9,197.
166 Cire Memorandum, UDC. Maurin's guns did picket duty between Bull Run and Cub Run near present day Cedar Spring. In going back over Bull Run they followed Sudley Road north to Sudley Springs, where they rejoined the army that had taken the Groveton-Sudley Road.
167 Archie McDonald, *Make Me a Map of the Valley, The Civil War Journal of Stonewall Jackson's Topographer Jedediah Hotchkiss* (Dallas, 1973), 77.
168 Cire Memorandum, UDC.
169 Hunter, *SHSP*, Vol. 10, 506.
170 Ibid.
171 *OR* XII:2, 558.

CHAPTER SIX

1 *OR* XIX:2, 144.
2 Ibid.
3 Freeman, *Lee*, Vol. II, 351.
4 Ibid., 353.
5 Alexander, 139.
6 *Assumption Pioneer*, December 16, 1899.
7 Hunter, *SHSP*, Vol. X, 507. Frying Pan Meeting House (Primitive Baptist Church), was built in 1791 in the community of Frying Pan, now Floris, Virginia. It still stands today. The building and park are designated a Virginia Landmark on the National Register of Historic Places. In 1964 the last surviving Trustee of the Meeting House deeded the property to the Fairfax County Park Authority. Located on the Centreville Road (SSR 657), three miles from Chantilly, the building and grounds are preserved near the bustle of Washington's Dulles International Airport.
8 Cire Memorandum, UDC. Freeman, *Lee*, Vol. II, 354.
9 Wagener's Diary, SCHS.
10 Lobrano Diary, LHAC; Ruggles Typescript, 16. The population of Dranesville in 1940 was still only 100 people; the reported population of unincorporated Dranesville in 2010 was 11,921.
11 O'Hara Diary, LDA.
12 Cire Memorandum, UDC.
13 Neese, 111. Goose Creek is just under four miles from Leesburg.
14 Cire Memorandum, UDC.
15 Longstreet, 199.
16 Heros Von Borcke, *Memoirs of the Confederate War for Independence*, Vol. 1 (New York, 1938), 185.
17 Major Gen. Lafayette McLaws, Major Gen. Richard H. Anderson, Major Gen. David R. Jones, Brigadier Gen. John G. Walker, and Brigadier Gen. John B. Hood commanded Longstreet's five divisions. The three brigades (including Pryor's), previously commanded by Brigadier Gen. Cadmus Wilcox were now attached to Anderson's Division composed of Armistead's, Mahone's, and Wright's brigades. Anderson's artillery battalion was commanded by Major John S. Saunders and had Capt. Frank Huger's Norfolk (Va.), Battery, Capt. Marcellus Moorman's Lynchburg (Va.), Beauregard Artillery, and Capt. Gary F. Grimes' Portsmouth (Va.), Light Artillery
18 Jones Diary, LHAC. Leesburg's population today is 42, 616.
19 Ruggles Typescript, 17.
20 Morven Park or "Big Spring" as it was known is the largest of many limestone springs feeding Big Spring Creek. The Virginia State Water Control Board in 1975 classified the creek from Big Spring to the Potomac River a natural trout stream. It has also been labeled a "Natural Wonder."

Thomas Balch Library, Leesburg.

21 Hamilton, Vol. I, 309.

22 *OR* XIX:2, 195.

23 G. M. Sorrel, AAG, to Col. J. B. Walton, Chief of Artillery, September 5, 1862, letter, Civil War Papers, LHAC.

24 Photographed Record Sheets of Donaldsonville Artillery, bound vols. 145 and 146, containing Muster Roll for July/August 1862, LAGL. Cire Memorandum, UDC. Ripley, 109, 110, 370. Lack of ammunition for the English Blakely's was probably the main factor for the exchange, though the Parrott (having a range of 1,900 yards at 5 degrees elevation), outshot the Blakely. The depleted Confederate battery has not been determined, but one and most likely the other Parrott gun issued to the Donaldsonville Artillery were Federal pieces captured at the first battle of Bull Run. See *OR* XIX:1, 350; *OR* II, 346. Francis W. Palfrey, *The Antietam and Fredericksburg* (New York, 1882), 128.

25 John Esten Cooke, *The Life of Stonewall Jackson* (Richmond, Va., 1863), 341.

26 PRS of Donaldsonville Artillery Muster Roll for July/August 1862, LAGL.

27 Freeman, *Lee,* Vol. II, 354.

28 Hunter, 508; PRS of Donaldsonville Artillery Muster Roll for July/August 1862, LAGL;

29 *Donaldsonville Chief,* September 15, 1906.

30 NA, CSR. The vacancy was from the resignation of Lieut. Lestang Fortier. Mollere's commission was backdated to August 4, 1862. The other officers, Lieut. Michel Cazare', since February 1862, and Lieut. William Lawes from the start of the Manassas Campaign, were still on sick leave in Louisiana.

31 *B&L,* Vol. II, 607.

32 Cire Memorandum, UDC. A good view of the large bend in the river, where White's Ford is the shallowest and narrowest portion of the river, can be obtained from Dickerson Regional Park on the Maryland side.

33 Freeman, *Lee,* Vol. II, 354.

34 *OR* XIX:2, 592.

35 Hamilton, Vol. I, 310.

36 Cire Memorandum, UDC.

37 David G. McIntosh, "Reminiscences, 1910," Virginia Historical Society, Richmond. The C. & O. Canal is 184.5 miles long from Washington, D. C. (Georgetown), to Cumberland, Maryland, and is today a National Historical Park. The seven-arched Monocacy Aqueduct made of white and pink quartz sandstone and completed in 1833 still stands and is a beautiful picnic site and recreation area near Dickerson, Maryland.

38 T. J. C. Williams and Folger McKinsey, *History of Frederick County Maryland,* Vol. 1 (Salem, Mass., 1910), 376.

39 Hunter, 508.

40 Henry Alexander White, *Memoirs of the Confederate War for Independence* (Philadelphia, 1867), 199.

41 Cire Memorandum, UDC.

42 George B. Shinn, "Recollections of the Late War," Augustus Osborne Papers, UNCCH.

43 NA, Maurin File; McDonald, 79.

44 H. L. King Diary, 31, UNCCH.

45 Hunter, 508.

46 Owen, 133, 134.

47 Longstreet, 205.

48 Andrews, 72.

49 Dickert, 151, 152.

50 Author's italics. The diarist estimated there were "over 3,000" African-Confederates with Lee's army passing through Frederick, an average of about one servant per twenty soldiers. Donaldsonville's free man of color Louis Lefort was there along with three or four other servants with the Canonniers, which equaled the army's average. Lewis H. Steiner, *Report of Lewis H. Steiner, M. D., Inspector of the Sanitary Commission, containing a Diary kept during the Rebel Occupation of Frederick, Md.* (New York, 1862), 19.

51 H. L. King Diary, 31, UNCCH.

52 Jones Diary, LHAC.

53 James J. Kirkpatrick Diary, 1861-1864, UT.
54 Walcott, 193.
55 Osman Latrobe Diary, Virginia Historical Society.
56 McLaws' Division was composed of Kershaw's, Cobb's, Semmes', and Barksdale's brigades with Col. Henry C. Cabell commanding an artillery battalion consisting of Capt. Henry H. Carlton's Troup (Ga.) Battery, Capt. Miles C. Macon's Richmond (Va.) Fayette Battery, Capt. Basil C. Manly's Ellis (N. C.) Light Artillery, Capt. Edward S. McCarthy's First Company, Richmond (Va.), Howitzers, and Capt. John W. Read's Pulaski (Ga.) Battery.
57 *OR* XIX:1, 852.
58 Freeman, *Lieutenants,* Vol. II, 184.
59 King Diary, 31, UNCCH. Burkittsville, at the foot of South Mountain is today virtually unchanged from its nineteenth century setting with the same houses, barns, and two churches built in 1829 and 1859. The steeple can still be seen above the trees as one approaches on the road. The population today is 158. The most distinctive quality of the village is its setting among the fields with open vistas to the rolling hills.
60 Landry Diary, DPL. When a portion of the Federal army moved through Burkittsville following McLaws' command a Yankee artilleryman noted, "The farms seem not to have been plundered. Indeed, except the wear and tear of the roads, there is little to denote that an army has recently passed through." Bennett, 76.
61 Saxon, 202.
62 Ibid.
63 Hunter, 507.
64 Ibid. 509-511.
65 Squires, 65, LAGL.
66 Francis Fleming, *Memoir of Capt. C. Seton Fleming* (Jacksonville, Florida 1884), Appendix I, October 24, 1862, letter. The Appalachian Trail is laid out north-south along the top of South Mountain. The dirt road at Brownsville Gap used to connect Burkittsville, east of the ridge, with Brownsville on the west side but is no longer passable by vehicle. You can still cross by vehicle 1.5 miles to the north at Crampton Gap (the location of Gathland State Park), by Gapland Road from West Main Street, Burkittsville.
67 Cire Memorandum, UDC.
68 Bennett, 74.
69 McClelen, 28.
70 This main road was the Baltimore and Winchester Turnpike. McLaws, with just ten brigades, attacked Maryland Heights and Elk Ridge overlooking Harpers Ferry, guarded two passes (Brownsville Gap and Solomon's Gap on Elk Ridge), and defended three passes at Weverton, Crampton's Gap, and Sandy Hook, where the road from Harpers Ferry leads to Pleasant Valley.
71 Weverton, nearly three miles east of Harpers Ferry, was situated in the pass between South Mountain and the Potomac River where the Baltimore & Ohio Railroad, Chesapeake & Ohio Canal, and the Baltimore and Winchester Turnpike passed through. Scattered homes, a Lutheran Church, a canal lock house, an industrial center embracing a marble works, a steel and file manufacturing company, a cotton mill, and three large shale buildings for workmen and their families comprised the place that today has disappeared with scarcely a trace.
72 Cire Memorandom, UDC.
73 Williams, Vol. 1, 274.
74 Cire Memorandom. UDC.
75 Hunter, 511.
76 W. B. Judkins, "Memoir," 37, Sara Hightower Regional Library. Rome, Georgia.
77 *Ibid.*
78 *Ibid.*
79 John D. Billings, *The History of the Tenth Massachusetts Battery of Light Artillery in the War of the Rebellion 1862-1865* (Boston, Massachusetts 1909), 91.
80 King Diary, 37. UNCCH.
81 E. Alexander, *Military Memoirs of a Confederate* (New York, 1907), 234.
82 Hebert, 75.
83 A New England Yankee not so far off noted the cold. Arthur A. Kent, ed. *Three Years with Company K, Sergt. Austin C. Stearns, Company K, 13th Mass. Infantry (Deceased),* (Cranbury, N.J.,

1976), 121.
84 Hebert, 75, 76.
85 Elizabeth W. Roberson, *Weep Not for Me Dear Mother* (Gretna, La., 1996), 88.
86 *OR* XIX:2, 855.
87 Ibid.
88 Cire Memorandum, UDC.
89 Ibid.
90 King, 39, UNCCH.
91 Caldwell, 72.
92 Freeman, *Lieutenants*, Vol. II, 201; Dickert, 150.
93 Halltown today is an unincorporated community in Jefferson County located off of US 340 on West Virginia Route 230 (Shepardstown Pike).
94 *OR* XIX:2, 857.
95 Landry Diary, DPL.
96 Lewis, 53; Dickert, 151.
97 King Diary, 39, UNCCH.
98 Hebert, 76.
99 Dinkins, 57.
100 A. Gomer, "Service of Third Virginia Infantry," *CV* 18 (1910), 227, 228.
101 Hebert, 77.
102 *The Rome* (Ga.), *Courier*, September 30, 1862.
103 William W. Chamberlaine, *Memoirs of the Civil War* (Washington, D. C., 1912), 32.
104 Freeman, *Lee*, Vol. II, 387.
105 Dinkins, 57.
106 Ibid.
107 Donaldsonville Artillery *Historical Memoranda*, LHAC.
108 NA, CSR. Decoux's official enlistment date with the Donaldsonville Artillery is September 18, 1862.
109 Also known as Packhorse, Shepherdstown, or Blackford's Ford.
110 McClelen, 29.
111 Hurst, 14.
112 Landry Diary, DPL.
113 Levy to Carman, letter, March 17, 1900, Ezra A. Carman Papers, Library of Congress, Washington, D. C. Levy wrote "east" either mistakenly or to conform with D. H. Hill's report misidentifying the Donaldsonville Artillery in action with A. P. Hill's command at Burnside's Bridge later in the day. Levy erroneously marked a map for Carman, which Prosper Landry received and corrected. Of Levy's location for the battery Prosper Landry noted: "All this is wrong. The Battery was on the left of Sharpsburg [west of the Turnpike] facing one of the Federal Batteries on the other side of the Antietam. Signed: R. Prosper Landry." Copy of map with notes in Louisiana Historical Association Collection, Civil War Papers, TU.
114 Freeman, *Lee*, Vol. II, 393. Numerous references erroneously list the Donaldsonville Artillery as being part of Anderson's divisional artillery battalion under Major John S. Saunder's at this time. Maurin's Battery was still assigned to Pryor's Brigade.
115 Ezra A. Carman Papers, draft manuscript, "Maryland Campaign," Chapter XVIII, 21, Library of Congress, Washington, D. C.
116 Antietam Battlefield Marker at Antietam National Battlefield; Cary R. Warren, *Grimes Battery* (Portsmouth, Va., 1927), 10-12, 15; Joseph M. Hanson, "A Report on the Employment of the Artillery at the Battle of Antietam, MD.," Antietam National Battlefield File, ANB Visitor Center.
117 Carman, Chapter XVIII, 54.
118 Chamberlaine, 35.
119 Levy to Carman letter, March 17, 1900, Ezra A. Carman Papers, Library of Congress. The Donaldsonville Artillery's initial targets were probably the 14th Indiana Infantry Regiment facing the Sunken Road and Battery A (Tompkin's Battery), Rhode Island 1st Light Artillery.
120 Carman Manuscript, Chapter XVIII, 36-40.
121 The Federal regiments entering the cornfield were the 7th New York, 81st Pennsylvania, and 5th New Hampshire, followed by the 2nd Delaware and the 52nd New York, with the 61st New York

and 64th New York advancing on the previous units' flank.
122 Bartlett, 138.
123 Carman Manuscript, Chapter XVIII, 49.
124 Ibid. 60.
125 *OR* XIX:1, 290.
126 *Times-Picayune,* July 21, 1902. The *Marseillaise* was composed by the Frenchman Claude-Joseph Rouget de Lisle. The invocation translation is: "Let us go children of the Fatherland." Levy is referring to Canonnier Corporal Tomasso Morelli, also known as Thomas Morel.
127 *The Charleston Daily Courier*, September 29, 1862.
128 W. H. Andrews, "Tige Anderson's Brigade at Sharpsburg," *CV* 16 (1908), 578. For the day's battle Hardaway's Battery reported nine men wounded while Peyton's had eight wounded.
129 *B & L*, Vol. II, 677.
130 Hurst, 14.
131 I. G. Bradwell, "General Lee at Sharpsburg, 1862," *CV* 29 (1921), 379.
132 *OR* XIX:1, 343.
133 Captain Jefferson Peyton's Richmond "Orange" (Va.), Battery from Major Hilary Jones' Battalion with one 3-inch Rifle, one 12-pounder howitzer, and three 6-pounder Smoothbores, joined Maurin, Hardaway, and Macon's guns on the ridge.
134 *OR* XIX:1, 1030, 1031.
135 Carman Manuscript, Chapter XVIII, 64. Graham's loss was 4 men killed, 5 severely wounded, 17 horses killed, and 6 horses severely wounded. *OR* XIX:1, 344.
136 Robert Krick, "It Appeared As Though Mutual Extermination Would Put a Stop to the Awful Carnage, Confederates in Sharpsburg's Bloody Lane," in Gary W. Gallagher, ed., *The Antietam Campaign* (Chapel Hill, N.C., 1999), 246.
137 *The Charleston Daily Courier*, September 29, 1862.
138 William H. Monroe, "The Battle of Antietam: A Military Study," *Journal of the Military Service Institution of the United States* 49 (New York, 1911), 275. A systematic metal detector survey was implemented in the Piper Orchard where the presence of 6-pounder explosive ordnance fragments collected was probably "related to the charge and hasty retreat of the 7th Maine. Only Confederate batteries were equipped with 6-pounder guns, and the men of the 7th Maine were the only Union targets to move through this area." Many of the recovered 6-pounder ordnance fragments no doubt were fired by the Donaldsonville Artillery's *Honoré, Fidelité,* and *Libértié et Égalité,* under the command of newly elected Lieut. Camille Mollere. Clarence R. Geier and Stephen R. Potter, *Archaeological Perspectives on the American Civil War* (Gainesville, Fla., 2000), 319, 358.
139 Carman Manuscript, Chapter XVIII, 66, 67.
140 *Charleston Daily Courier*, September 29, 1862.
141 Hebert and Vegue both received sick furloughs on October 20, 1862. Hebert returned home to Louisiana where he joined the 5th Louisiana Field Battery (Pelican Artillery), until paroled at Natchitoches, Louisiana, on June 6, 1865. After his recovery Vegue returned to his command where he had enlisted in 1861 as a drummer boy. He was, after his wounding and return, commissioned a First Lieutenant in Company A of the First Louisiana Zouave Battalion. Benevolent Association of the Army of Northern Virginia Application of Jules Veque, July 1876, LHAC; NA, CSR. Melancon was twenty-three years old and a clerk from Ascension's New River community (across the Mississippi River from Donaldsonville), where before the war he lived with his widowed mother and next door to his sister and brother-in-law, Canonnier Pvt. Jules Guedry
142 King Diary, 42, UNCCH.
143 *An English Combatant*, 491.
144 *B & L*, Vol. II, 681.
145 *An English Combatant*, 491
146 *Charleston Daily Courier,* September 29, 1862.
147 *An English Combatant*, 491.
148 Mary B. Mitchell, "In the Wake of Battle. (A woman's recollection of Shepherdstown During Antietam Week.)," *The Century* 32:3 (New York, 1886), 439.
149 *OR* XIX:1, 151.
150 Ibid. 840.
151 Hurst, 14.
152 Owen, 159.

153 NA, CSR; *Diocese of Baton Rouge Catholic Church Records*, Vol. 10 (1863-1867), (Baton Rouge, 1990), 407. Alfred Melancon's gravesite is unknown. Confederate remains around Sharpsburg were re-interred after the war to Washington Confederate Cemetery in Hagerstown, Maryland; Mount Olivet Cemetery in Frederick, Maryland; and Elmwood Cemetery in Shepardstown, West Virginia. Approximately 2,800 Southerners are buried in the three cemeteries; the majority are unknown. Melancon's sister and brother-in-law (Canonnier Pvt. Jules Guedry), had a son born in 1865 that they named Alfred, who became a farmer in Ascension Parish, married, and had three sons and a daughter.
154 Moore, 146.
155 Bartlett, 143.
156 Owen, 60, 61.
157 Ibid.
158 Ibid.
159 Donaldsonville Artillery *Historical Memoranda*, LHAC.
160 *OR* XIX:1, 831. On the left of the Donaldsonville guns on the heights, to the right of the ford was one gun under Lieut. Thomas A. Maddox, Company D, Cutt's (Ga.) Battalion, then five guns of Capt. John Milledge's (Ga.) Artillery and two guns from Captain W. H. Chapman's Dixie (Va.) Artillery. Pendleton had a total of forty-four guns, with thirty-three over looking the river and eleven in reserve.
161 Cire Memorandom, UDC.
162 The Federal batteries during the morning were Capt. John C. Tidball's 2d U. S., Battery A, Capt. James M. Robertson's 2d U. S., Batteries B and L, and Capt. Horatio G. Gibbon's 3d U. S., Batteries C and G. Carmen Manuscript, Chapter XXII, 9.
163 Nick J. Hoey to Gen. Munford, letter, November 17, 1890, Army of Northern Virginia Artillery, Civil War Papers, LHAC.
164 Benevolent Association of the Army of Northern Virginia Application of E. L. Monnot, December 20, 1882, LHAC.
165 Thomas T. Munford to Nick J. Hoey letter, November 19, 1890. Army of Northern Virginia Artillery, Civil War Papers, LHAC. Munford (1831-1918), an 1854 Virginia Military Institute graduate, related the above twenty-eight years later at an annual Confederate Veterans reunion. Nick J. Hoey of Captain Louis E. D'Aquin's Louisiana Guard Artillery upon hearing Munford remark about "a little Louisiana Battery" fighting at Shepardstown (Boteler's Ford), mistakenly believed and informed Munford the battery was the Louisiana Guard Artillery. The guns Munford unknowingly described belonged to the Donaldsonville Artillery with the captain spoken of being Victor Maurin. Two details confirm this:

The first being Maurin's two Parrott guns were on the right flank on the heights overlooking the crossing, while D'Aquin's two Parrott guns were on the left flank nearer to the river and to the left of another battery sweeping the road on the opposite shore. Munford stated his command was "stationed on the right flank watching the fords" and he "wanted . . . to see what was going on to the left of our lines." Maurin's Battery and the two guns in action on the extreme right flank were left of Munford's command.

The second and most compelling detail is the language used by the artillerist and Munford's courier describing them as "Frenchmen." The Donaldsonville Canonniers and their descendants, although bilingual, primarily spoke French. They not only spoke French throughout the war but into the 1920s. The vast majority of the Louisiana Guard Artillery, eighty percent, was composed of English and Irishmen from New Orleans, with the remainder having Spanish, German, and Italian surnames. Only 3 out of 123 members assigned to D'Aquin's Battery were French, signifying that neither they nor any other battery along Pendleton's line on this day spoke French except for *Le Compagnie d'artillerie de Donaldson*. The British correspondent Russell also noted, "The customary language of the Creoles is French . . . but they speak English fluently." Russell, 97.
166 *Times-Picayune*, July 21, 1902.
167 C. G. Snead, "Another Unwritten Artillery Duel," *CV* 29 (1921), 63.
168 J. B. Moore, "Description of the Battle of Sharpsburg," *SHSP*, Vol. 27, 213.
169 Ibid.
170 Snead, 64. The Federal batteries joining in the artillery combat in the afternoon were Lieut. William E. Van Reed's Battery K, 5th United States Artillery, one gun each from Lieut. Alanson

M. Randol's batteries E and G, 1st United States Artillery, Capt. Charles Kusserow's Battery D, 1st Battalion New York Light, Capt. Robert Langner's Battery C, 1st Battalion New York Light, and Capt. Stephen H. Weed's Battery I, Fifth United States Artillery with four 20-pounder Parrott guns near the ford. *OR* XIX:1, 207, 353, 354; Carman Manuscript, Chapter XXII, 9.

171 NA, CSR. Federal surgeons evidently amputated Wiedemere's arm and released him upon his recovery to Confederate authorities who then admitted him to Richmond's Chimborazo Hospital No. 1 on November 21, 1862. From there he was transferred on March 12, 1863, to General Hospital No. 2 in Danville, Virginia. The one-armed Wiedemere returned to duty on April 20, 1863, collecting his $12.00 a month pay while stationed at Camp Anderson in Asheville, North Carolina, under Brigadier Gen. Robert B. Vance. Near the end of the war Wiedemere was captured and sent as a prisoner to Rock Island, Illinois, where he was released. After the war he worked only "sometimes" for board and clothing while living in Live Oak, Florida. In April 1885 he received a favorable letter from Prosper Landry and the following month was admitted into the Camp Nicholl's Soldiers Home in New Orleans where he remained a resident until his death at New Orleans Charity Hospital on March 16, 1901. Benevolent Association of the Army of Northern Virginia Application of Arnold Wiedemere, June 13, 1885, LHAC; Camp Nicholl's Soldiers Home Records, LAGL.

172 *OR* XIX:1, 848; NA, CSR. Wagner's final resting place, like Melancon's, is unknown.

173 Snead, 63.

174 *OR* XIX:1, 832.

175 Cire Memorandum, UDC.

176 *OR* XIX:1, 848.

177 Moore, 214.

178 Ibid., 215.

179 Levy to Carman, letter, March 17, 1900, Ezra A. Carman Papers, Library of Congress.

180 Col. Stephen D. Lee a couple of months after the battle would remark, "Sharpsburg was Artillery Hell." Alexander, 247.

CHAPTER SEVEN

1 Cire Memorandum, UDC.

2 *OR* XIX:1, 848.

3 *OR* XIX:1, 350; *OR* II, 346; Palfrey, 128.

4 Lobrano Diary, LHAC.

5 Caldwell, 85.

6 Hebert, 85.

7 Caldwell, 86, 87.

8 W. B. Judkins, "Memoir," 39, Sara Hightower Reginal Library, Rome, Ga.; O'Hara Diary, LDA; NA, Maurin File.

9 Battalion Washington Artillery, Order Book Number 2, LAGL.

10 Washington Artillery File, LAGL.

11 Landry, *SHSP*, Vol. 23, 201.

12 John Purifoy, "History of Jeff Davis Artillery," 35, Alabama Department of Archives and History.

13 Everson, 146.

14 Ruggles Typescript, 22, HNOC.

15 Everson, 152.

16 Durkin, 34.

17 Jones Diary, LHAC.

18 *New York Times*, August 25, 1862. Union Rear Admiral David G. Farragut commanded the naval forces on the Mississippi River and ordered the destruction of Donaldsonville because Confederate Partisan Rangers near the town fired upon passing Union transport ships.

19 Mattie Nicholls Pugh to Lisa Maurin Nicholls letter, dated August 13, 1862, Nicholls Family Papers, TU.

20 Kenneth E. Shewmaker and Andrew K. Prinz, ed., "A Yankee in Louisiana: Selections from the Diary and Correspondences of Henry R. Gardner, 1862-1866," *Louisiana History*, 5 (1965), 289.

21 O'Hara Diary. LDA.
22 *Donaldsonville Chief,* October 4, 1916.
23 James J. Kirkpatrick Diary, 1861-1864, UT.
24 Ruggles Typescript, 22, HNOC.
25 Ibid.
26 NA, Maurin File.
27 Wilcox was not with his brigade at Sharpsburg because of illness. Upon his return, he assumed temporary command of the division while Anderson recovered from his wound received at Sharpsburg.
28 *OR* LI:2, 627.
29 Ruggles Typescript, 22, HNOC.
30 Cire Memorandum, UDC.
31 T. K. Cartmell, *Shenandoah Valley Pioneers and Their Descendants: A History of Frederick County, Virginia From its Formation in 1738 to 1908* (Bowie, Md., 1908), 56.
32 William A. McClendon, *Recollections of War Times* (Montgomery, Ala., 1909), 155. Bunker Hill was midway between Martinsburg and Winchester, at the intersection of the Valley Turnpike and the road to Charlestown and Harpers Ferry.
33 Cire Memorandum, UDC.
34 Owen, 168.
35 Gallagher, *Fighting,* 155. The Opecquon Creek forms a crescent around Winchester "from whence all of her great roads leading out in every direction, except due west, must, within six miles, cross this historic stream."
36 J. Q. Dabbs letter, October 4, 1862, Eugene Whitefield Dabbs Papers, South Carolinian Library, University of South Carolina.
37 Polley, 137.
38 R. Lockwood Tower, ed. *Lee's Adjutant, The Wartime Letters of Colonel Walter Herron Taylor, 1862-1865* (Columbia, S.C., 1995), 47.
39 Borcke, 202.
40 James J. Kirkpatrick Diary, 1861-1864, UT.
41 Borcke, 201.
42 Bartlett, 160.
43 Purifoy, 36.
44 Freeman, *Lee*, Vol. II, 415-418.
45 *OR* Vol. XIX:1, 151.
46 Ibid., Pt. 2, 647-654.
47 *OR* Vol. LI:2, 639.
48 *OR* Vol. XIX:1, 834.
49 Freeman, *Lee,* Vol. II, 415.
50 *OR* Vol. XIX:2, 644.
51 Ibid., 645.
52 Walton-Glenny Papers, LHAC.
53 Owen, 169.
54 Polley, 137.
55 Lewis, 56, 57.
56 Clark, Vol. III, 68.
57 Ruggles Manuscript, 23, HNOC.
58 Walton-Glenny Papers, LHAC.
59 Cire Memorandum, UDC.
60 F. M. Coker to wife, October 5, 1862, Florence Hodgson Heidler Collection, University of Georgia Libraries.
61 *OR* Vol. XIX:2, 642.
62 Ibid.
63 Ibid.
64 Cire Memorandum, UDC.
65 Owen, 169.
66 Ibid.
67 Jones Diary, LHAC.

68 Owen, 169. Wolseley later became commander in chief of English military forces.
69 Ibid 170.
70 Ibid.
71 Ruggles Typescript, 25, 26, HNOC; Jones Diary, LHAC; Lobrano Diary, LHAC.
72 The replacement gun likely came from the Winchester Depot and was one of the seventy-three field pieces captured at Harpers Ferry or from the disbanded batteries that turned in forty surplus guns. The animals came from the disbanded batteries or from six-hundred and fifty horses captured during a cavalry raid to Chambersburg, Pennsylvania (October 10-12, 1862), by Major General J.E.B. Stuart's command.
73 Cire Memorandum, UDC.
74 Lewis, 56, 57.
75 Battalion Washington Artillery, Order Book Number 2, LAGL; Ruggles Typescript, 24, HNOC; Jones Diary, LHAC.
76 PRS of Donaldsonville Artillery Muster Roll for September/October 1862, LAGL.
77 Cire Memorandum, UDC.
78 The column reached Winchester some time around 3:00 p.m. The city is the oldest Virginia city west of the Blue Ridge Mountains and located near the northern entrance to the Shenandoah Valley. It is the seat of Frederick County with a handsome courthouse, one of the few Revival style courthouses in Virginia. It was used until 1984 and today is home to a Civil War museum. During the war the city had a market place, fifty stores, and a dozen churches, along with the three-story historic Taylor Hotel located in the center of town, which was described as having a neat compactness about it with the houses built flush against the streets. During the five weeks following the Sharpsburg battle, Winchester was also a turbulent city with thousands of wounded men lodged in every available building. Wives, relatives, and visitors teemed there. It was also the primary depot for supplies to Lee's nearby army.
79 Thomas Ware Diary, UNCCH.
80 Cire Memorandum, UDC.
81 Ed. M. Burruss to Kate, November 10, 1862, John C. Burruss Papers, LSU.
82 Walters Diary, NPL.
83 Borcke, 229. Chester Gap, elevation 1,670 feet, was originally called Happy Creek Gap from the stream that rises there and flows through Front Royal. There were two settlements of a few houses on each side of the gap. Elizabeth B. Johnson and C. E. Johnson Jr. *Rappahannock County, Va., A History Fact, Fiction, Foolishness and the Fairfax Story* (Orange, Va., 1981), 114.
84 Cire Memorandum, UDC. Flint Hill was a small village on a hill named after the white flint rocks found there. Its elevation is 620 feet. It was described by an artilleryman as "rather a poor looking place." Walters Diary, NPL.
85 Thomas Ware Diary, UNCCH.
86 Jones Diary, LHAC. Picturesque Washington is the county seat of Rappahannock in the foothills of the Blue Ridge Mountains, the Piedmont section. The county has more than fifty ridges and mountains with individual names.
87 McDonald, 92.
88 Cire Memorandum, UDC. From Winchester to Front Royal was twenty miles, to Flint Hill thirteen miles, to Ben Venue (Gaines Cross Roads) four miles, to Washington six miles, to Sperryville five miles, and finally to Culpeper Court House twenty miles, a total of sixty-eight miles.
89 Lewis, 61.
90 Richard T. Couture, ed. *Charlie's Letters, The Civil War Correspondence of Charles E. Denoon* (Collingswood, N.J., 1989), 31.
91 James J. Kirkpatrick Diary, 1861-1864, UT.
92 Roe, 223.
93 Ibid. 31.
94 Walters Diary, NPL.
95 Jones Diary, LHAC.
96 *OR* LI:2, 642.
97 Cire Memorandum, UDC.
98 James W. Biddle to Rosa Biddle, January 27 and February 3, 1863, Samuel S. Biddle Papers, Perkins Library, Duke University.

99 James W. Silver, ed. *A Life For the Confederacy, From the War Diary of Robert A. Moore, Private, C. S. A.*(Wilmington, N.C., 1987), 115.
100 Everson, 158.
101 W. N. Pendleton Order Book, June 17, 1862-April 2, 1865, MCR.
102 Jones Diary, LHAC.
103 Battalion Washington Artillery, Order Book Number 2, LAGL.
104 *Florida Parishes* (Amite City, La.) *Times*, (no date in December, 1922), LSU.
105 Yvonne L. Day, *Gathering Home: The Cemeteries of Amite City, La.* (Baton Rouge, 2002), 20.
106 Barnes F. Lathrop, "The Pugh Plantations 1860-1865: A Study of Life in Lower Louisiana," Ph.D. Dissertation, 1945, 203, 204, UT.
107 Ibid.
108 Sister M. Clara to Father, August 1863, Archdiocese of New Orleans Collection, University of Notre Dame Archives.
109 Helene Dupuy, "Diary of a Southern Girl During the War Between the States," typed manuscript copy translated by Alcee Fortier, 1912, Donaldsonville Public Library.
110 Ruggles Typescript, 27, HNOC. The Federal advance had reached Warrenton and was halted not because of a repulse, but due to the Army of the Potomac changing commanders.
111 Gilbert Wright, ed. "Some letters to His Parents By a Floridian in the Confederate Army," *Florida Historical Quarterly*, 36 (1958), 362. Perry was a native of Massachusetts practicing law at Pensacola, Florida in 1861. He joined the Confederate Army as a captain in the 2nd Florida Regiment of which he later became colonel because members "admired him for his affability of manner, his gallantry, his thorough strict discipline" and being "an honest, upright man." Fleming, 68, 71. Longstreet reassigned the two other regiments of the brigade. The 3rd Virginia Regiment went to Kemper's Virginia Brigade, Pickett's Division, and the 14th Alabama Regiment went to Wilcox's Alabama Brigade, Anderson's Division.
112 Gary W. Gallagher, ed., *Antietam, Essays on the 1862 Maryland Campaign* (Kent, Ohio, 1989), 50.
113 Freeman, *Lieutenants*, Vol. 2, 141, 211, 232, 265, 266. Unable to regain another command, Pryor resigned on August 26, 1863, and immediately enlisted as a private in the Third Virginia Cavalry.
114 R. H. Anderson Letters-sent Book, May 29, 1861-August 23, 1863, MCR. The Donaldsonville Artillery in effect replaced Thompson's (formerly Grimes'), Portsmouth Light Artillery, which was disbanded with the reduction of artillery on October 4, 1862. The men of that battery were distributed between Huger's and Mooreman's. On November 18, 1862, Mooreman's Battery was transferred to Stuart's Horse artillery.
115 *OR* XXV:2, 640.
116 Ibid.
117 R. Lockwood Tower, ed., *Lee's Adjutant, The Wartime Letters of Colonel Walter Herron Taylor, 1862-1865* (Columbia, S.C., 1995), 52.
118 James M. Folsom, *Heroes and Martyrs of Georgia, Georgia Record in the Revolution of 1861* (Macon, Ga., 1864), 112.
119 *Donaldsonville Daily Times*, January 23, 1897.
120 *OR* XIX:2, 124.
121 NA, Record of Events (Donaldsonville Art'y), November & December 1862.
122 Ibid.
123 Silver, 116.
124 *OR* Pt. 2, 645, 646.
125 Pendleton Order Book, MCR.
126 Cire Memorandum, UDC.
127 Ed. M. Burruss to Kate letter, November 23, 1862, John C. Buress Papers, LSU.
128 Ruggles Typescript, 28, HNOC.
129 Ed. M. Burruss to Kate letter, November 23, 1862, John C. Burruss Papers, LSU.
130 Ibid.
131 Ibid.
132 Ruggles Typescript, 28, HNOC.
133 Owen, 174.
134 Freeman, *Lee,* Vol. II, 432.

135 Edwin Forbes, "Marching Through the Rain," *Thirty Years After, An Artist's Story of the Great War* (New York, 1890), 53, 54.
136 Couture, 34.
137 Freeman, *Lee*, Vol. II, 434.
138 Stanley Hoole, ed., "The Letters of Captain Joab Goodson, 1862-1864," *The Alabama Review*, 10 (1957), 131.
139 Ruggles Typescript, 31, HNOC.
140 *Donaldsonville Chief*, September 6, 1884.
141 Silver, 117.
142 Ed. M. Burruss to Kate letter, November 23, 1862, John C. Burruss Papers, LSU.
143 Jones Diary, LHAC.
144 Chamberlayne, 141.
145 Ed. M. Burruss to Kate letter, November 23, 1862, John C. Burruss Papers, LSU.
146 R.A. Pierson to Father, December 9, 1862, Rosemonde and Emile Kuntz Collection, TU.
147 Ibid.
148 Hoole, 131.
149 In the *OR Atlas* XXXIII, Map 1, "Fredericksburg" the farm is located between the River Road and Orange C. H. Turnpike (present US 3 or Germanna Highway, Plank Road), and identified as "Downman." There still is a home and farm on the site today, between a few homes at the end of Briscoe Lane, next to Interstate 95, and nearby Cowan Boulevard and the large Central Park Shopping Complex. The entrance to the farm begins at the intersection of Fall Hill Avenue (old River Road) and Carl D. Silver Parkway.
150 *OR* XXI, 569.
151 W. B. Judkins, "Memoir," 41., Sara Hightower Regional Library, Rome, Ga.
152 Ibid.
153 Dinkins, 65.
154 Runge, 35.
155 Alexander was acting in place of the Washington Artillery's commander Colonel J. B. Walton who was out on a leave since October 11, 1862. Walton returned on December 9, 1862.
156 *OR* LI:2, 653, 654.
157 The French term of *bastion,* i.e., a fortified position, was used by Maurin in his report. The pits dug out for the artillery along Marye's Heights were identified by names such as redoubt, which is a small temporary defensive work, or parapet, a defensive position used to shelter from fire while affording the defender a sweeping fire over the opponent's line of approach. Epaulement was used in place of parapet, although an epaulement was intended simply as a screen or cover. In actuality the pits were mud lunettes, field works consisting of a face projecting towards the enemy and two flanks making the whole shaped like a crescent moon. The Canonnier lunette nearest the Orange Plank Road (modern day William Street), still stands as an ivy-covered mound on the University of Mary Washington campus, the only lunette now extant on campus. The other Donaldsonville Artillery lunettes along with many others were over the years leveled down by the plow.
158 Owen, 175.
159 Landry, *SHSP*, Vol. 23, 198. The four lunettes of the Donaldsonville Artillery extended from South Hall next to William Street to Trinkle Hall, on the campus of the University of Mary Washington.
160 *OR* LI:2, 654.
161 *OR* XXI, 1046.
162 Couture, 36; Wise, Vol. I, 374.
163 Henry H. Baker, *A Reminiscent Story of the Great Civil War, Second Paper, A Personal Experience* (New Orleans, 1911), 59.
164 Ruggles Typescript, 29, HNOC.
165 Silver, 120.
166 Couture, 37.
167 Silver, 120.
168 Couture, 36.
169 Freeman, *Lee,* Vol. II, 442.
170 Ibid.
171 Couture, 38.

172 Billings, 195.
173 Landry, *SHSP*, Vol. 23, 198.
174 *OR* XXI, 620.
175 Walcott, 237.
176 Ibid.
177 Baker, 45, 46.
178 Barrett, 88.
179 Ibid.
180 McIntosh Reminiscenses, 1910. 27, Virginia Historical Society.
181 An English Combatant, 506.
182 Edward Alexander, "The Battle of Fredericksburg. Paper No. 1," *SHSP*, Vol. 10, 389.
183 Gallagher, *Fighting*, 171. The enemy's three-mile line consisted of 147 guns across the heights from Falmouth to Pollack's Mill, with thirty-six additional guns posted on the banks of the river near the upper and middle bridges.
184 Ibid.
185 *OR* XXI, 586.
186 Ibid., 620.
187 Walters Diary, NPL.
188 On this day, December 11, 1862, the Canonniers suffered no battle casualties but lost Sergeant Joseph Rosemond Gaillard after he was admitted to the Louisiana Hospital in Richmond, suffering from small pox. The 28-year-old Donaldsonville resident who before the war lived with his widowed mother and sister died at the hospital on January 4, 1863. Gaillard was interred the next day in Richmond's Hollywood Cemetery, Soldier Section D, Grave No. 27. *Register of the Confederated Dead*, 41. Gaillard's older sister Celeste married in April 1864.
189 Baker, 40, 41.
190 *OR* LI:2, 661, 662.
191 Ruggles Typescript, 31, HNOC.
192 *OR* XXI, 620.
193 Ruggles Typescript, 31, HNOC.
194 *OR* XXI, 574.
195 Landry, *SHSP* Vol. 10, 391, 392.
196 *OR* XXI, 620.
197 Walcott, 240. The Lacy house, also known as Chatham, was built about 1750 on high ground overlooking the river and the town directly across from Maurin's position. During the battle it was headquarters for Major General Edwin V. Sumner, commander of the Army of the Potomac's Right Grand Division made up of the 2nd and 9th Corps.
198 Butler, H. A., "Fredericksburg—Personal Reminiscences" *CV*, 14 (1906), 181.
199 *OR* XXI, 612.
200 *B & L*, Vol. III, 97.
201 *OR* XXI, 565.
202 *B & L*, Vol. III, 97.
203 Landry, *SHSP*, Vol. 23, 198.
204 *OR* XXI, 553.
205 Freeman, *Lee*, Vol. II, 456.
206 *OR* XXI, 620.
207 McIntosh Reminiscenses, 1910, 28, Virginia Historical Society.
208 Lobrano Diary, LHAC.
209 Tower, 146.
210 Dunbar Rowland, ed., *Jefferson Davis, Constitutionalist, His Letters, Papers and Speeches*, Vol. VII (Jackson, Miss., 1923), 19.
211 *OR* XXI, 620.
212 Landry, *SHSP*, Vol. 23, 199.
213 Edward Alexander, "The Battle of Fredericksburg. Paper No. 2—(Conclusion.)" *SHSP*, Vol. 10, 450.
214 *B & L*, Vol. III, 98.
215 Ibid.
216 Freeman, *Lee*, Vol. II, 460.

217 *OR* XXI, 620.
218 Landry, *SHSP*, Vol. 23, 199.
219 Alexander, *SHSP,* Vol. 10, 450.
220 Landry, *SHSP*, Vol. 23, 199.
221 Brigadier General Thomas R. R. Cobb's Georgia Brigade of McLaw's Division was located along the sunken road while Brigadier General John R. Cooke's North Carolina Brigade of Ransom's Division fired from the crest. During later attacks Kershaw's North Carolina Brigade, also of McLaw's Division, and two of Ransom's brigades reinforced the battle line in the sunken road. Freeman, *Lieutenants*, Vol. II, 362.
222 Walcott, 241, 242. The writer was with the 21st Massachusetts Infantry Regiment.
223 Landry, *SHSP*, Vol. 23, 199, 200.
224 Freeman, *Lee,* Vol. II, 461.
225 *OR* XXI, 620.
226 *Landry*, SHSP, Vol. 23, 199.
227 *OR* XXI, 621.
228 *Donaldsonville Chief,* August 19, 1882.
229 NA, CSR.
230 Ibid.
231 Cockrell, 146, 147.
232 Ibid., 146. The Donaldsonville Artillery was mistaken for the Washington Artillery by the Mississippi soldier who also misidentified Washington's mother to be Martha Washington. George Washington's mother Mary died on August 25, 1789, and was interred in an unmarked grave until 1833 when President Andrew Jackson laid a corner stone to a monument in her memory. In 1862 the pedestal remained unfinished and the marble shaft lay beside it. The pieces, damaged during the war, were removed in 1893 and the present 131-feet obelisk monument stands there, having been dedicated in 1894.
233 *OR* XXI, 620.
234 Freeman, *Lieutenants,* Vol. II, 363.
235 NA, Record of Events (Donaldsonville Art'y), November & December 1862; Donaldsonville Artillery *Historical Memoranda*, LHAC.
236 Bourgeois, 58; NA, CSR.
237 NA, CSR. He was also treated for diarrhea; it was noted he "is improving slowly."
238 Osman Latrobe Diary, Typescript, 14, Virginia Historical Society, Richmond, Va.
239 Owen, 190, 191.
240 Landry, *SHSP*, Vol. 23, 199.
241 Ibid., 200.
242 *OR* XXI, 620. Linossier's burial site is unknown and his name does not appear on any of the identified Confederate dead buried in Fredericksburg and Spotsylvania Confederate Cemeteries. Many soldiers killed in this battle had wooden headboards to mark their graves, but other soldiers seeking firewood during the long winter of 1862-1863 removed these. Many of the unknown Confederate soldiers who died in the area were removed after the war at private expense and placed into two local cemeteries.
243 *OR* XXI, 620, 621.
244 Landry, *SHSP*, Vol. 23, 201.
245 George and Philip Welsh. "Civil War Letters from Two Brothers," *The Yale Review*, 18 (1930), 155.
246 *OR* XXI, 439.
247 *The Yale Review*, 18 (1930), 157, 158.
248 Ibid., 158. Both Pennsylvania Regiments were assigned to Brigadier General Erastus B. Tyler's First Brigade of Brigadier General Andrew A. Humphrey's Third Division in Brigadier General Daniel Butterfield's Fifth Corps, Center Grand Division, Army of the Potomac. The Federal casualties resulting from the Gunners of Donaldson's action was one major, George W. Todd, age thirty-six, a Mexican War veteran, with a shattered leg that was later amputated (died of wounds on December 19, 1862), one lieutenant, George W. Murphy, age twenty-seven, of Company I (mortally wounded), and nine men killed, with several others wounded. The brigade commander reported, "The position first assigned us on the right of the Plank road subjected us to an enfilading fire from the enemy's batteries...of our loss there I am unable to give an accurate account...the

loss there is principally accounted for among the missing." Thirty-four men were listed missing in the 91st and 126th Pennsylvania regiments. *OR* XXI, 137, 437, 439, 440. Photographs of Todd and Murphy are posted at freepages.military.rootsweb.ancestry.com/-PA91. On December 19, 1862, the *Philadelphia Inquirer* published the following story of another casualty from Landry's gun: "Single Fidelity of a Dog on the Battlefield: On Monday last, as Hon. John Covode, in company with a number of officers, was passing over the battle-field beyond Fredericksburg, their attention was called to a small dog lying by a corpse. Mr. Covode halted . . . to see if life was extinct. Raising the coat from the man's face, he found him dead. The dog, looking wistfully up, ran to the dead man's face and kissed his silent lips. Such devotion in a small dog was so singular that Mr. Covode examined some papers upon the body, and found it to be that of Sergeant W. H. Brown, Company C, Ninety-first Pennsylvania. The dog was shivering with the cold, but refused to leave his master's body, and as the coat was thrown over his face again he seemed very uneasy, and tried to get under it to the man's face. He had, it seems, followed the regiment into battle, and stuck to his master, and when he fell remained with him, refusing to leave him or to eat anything. As the party returned an ambulance was carrying the corpse to a little grove of trees for interment, and the little dog following, the only mourner at that funeral, as the hero's comrades had been called to some other point." In a letter dated December 23, 1862, Sgt. William H. Brown's captain wrote his widow relating he "was mortally wounded . . . and died from the effects of his wounds on the morning of the 16th . . . had his leg amputated . . . he was struck by a shell which injured both legs and tore off parts of his thigh." NA, Widow's Pension File of Sarah Brown.

249 Landry, *SHSP*, Vol. 23, 201.
250 *OR* XXI, 621.
251 Ibid.
252 Landry, *SHSP*, Vol. 23, 201.
253 R. Prosper Landry to E. D. Willet, May 18, 1876, endorsement letter with Benevolent Association of the Army of Northern Virginia Application of T. Morelli, LHAC.
254 OR *XXI*, 621.
255 *Times-Picayune*, July 21, 1902.
256 Benevolent Association of the Army of Northern Virginia Application of T. Morelli, May 18, 1876, LHAC.
257 NA, CSR; *OR* XXI, 621; Levy Diary, August 5, 1864, HUC.
258 NA, CSR. A stave maker is one who placed narrow strips of wood or narrow iron plates edge to edge to form sides, covering, or lining of a barrel or structure. The Globe Hospital was formerly a tobacco factory with a capacity of 150 patients. The Receiving Hospital or General Hospital Number 9 was a public warehouse near the Virginia Central Railroad Depot and had a capacity of 900 patients. Henningsen was a private hospital under the direction of Mrs. Henningsen and had an average of 75 patients under Dr. D. J. Watson, Surgeon-in-charge. Waitt, 7, 13, 14. Perez was interred in Richmond's Hollywood Cemetery, Soldier Section T, Grave No. 529. *Register of the Confederated Dead*, 80.
259 Landry, *SHSP*, Vol. 23, 202.
260 *OR* XXI, 621.
261 Donaldsonville Artillery *Historical Memoranda*, LHAC.
262 Wise, Vol. I, 389.
263 Jennings C. Wise, "The Boy Gunners of Lee," *SHSP*, Vol. 42, 159.

CHAPTER EIGHT

1 Alexander, *SHSP*, Vol. 10, 456.
2 Hoole, 136.
3 Freeman, *Lee,* Vol. II, 466; Freeman, *Lieutenants*, Vol. II, 373, 374.
4 Alexander, *SHSP*, Vol. 10, 460.
5 Walters Diary, NPL.
6 *OR* XXI, 621.
7 Ibid., 555.
8 Walters Diary. NPL.
9 *OR* XXI, 613.

10 Cire Memorandum, UDC.
11 Lobrano Diary, LHAC.
12 *New York Herald*, December 16, 1862. Italics by author signifying the chapter title.
13 Hoole, 136.
14 Walters Diary, NPL.
15 C. C. Cummings, "Battle of Fredericksburg, December 13, 1862," *CV*, 23 (1915), 358.
16 *B & L*, Vol. III, 118.
17 Bartlett, 166.
18 Hamilton, Vol. I, 442.
19 William H. Stewart. *A Pair of Blankets* (New York, 1911), 77, 78.
20 Freeman, Douglas S. *The South to Posterity* (New York, 1951), 3.
21 Brock, Sallie A., ed., *The Southern Amaranth* (New York, 1869), Mrs. Margret J. Preston, "Song of the Snow," 342.
22 Figg, Royal W., *"Where Men Only Dare To Go!" or the Story Of A Boy Company* (Richmond, 1885), 95.
23 Donaldsonville Artillery *Historical Memoranda*, LHAC. Scheuer's body was taken to Richmond where he was buried in the third row of the Soldiers' Section of the Hebrew Cemetery on Shockoe Hill. See his biography for a description of this beautiful section of the cemetery. Cire's Memorandum recorded Scheuer died on December 22, 1862.
24 *OR* XXI, 620, 21.
25 Ibid., XXI, 618.
26 Ibid., XXI, 609.
27 Ibid., XXI, 628.
28 Ibid., LI:2, 663.
29 Ibid., XXI, 555.
30 Ibid., XXI, 556.
31 Alexander, *SHSP*, Vol. 10, 464.
32 Wise, Vol. I, 406, 407.
33 Ibid., 389.
34 *OR* XXI, 1,077.
35 Everson, 168.
36 Walters Diary, NPL.
37 Cockrell, 155.
38 Lt. William McWillie to wife, January 3, 1863, McWillie-Compton Family Papers, Mississippi Department of Archives and History. Jackson, Miss.
39 Barrett, 91.
40 Hoole, 136, 137.
41 Lobrano Diary, LHAC.
42 Miller, Francis T., ed., *The Photographic History of the Civil War in Ten Volumes; Vol. Nine, "Poetry and Eloquence of Blue and Gray* (New York, 1911), 148. William G. McGabe, "Christmas Night of '62."
43 Walters Diary, NPL. The road taken was known as the Potomac Path or King's Highway, and Telegraph Road during the war. It is now designated United States Route 1. Captain John W. Lewis' Virginia Battery was retained on the front line at Fredericksburg while Maurin, Grandy, and Huger's batteries of Anderson's Division moved to the rear. Major Charles Richardson was appointed chief of artillery of the division after its arrival at Fredericksburg, though the batteries still answered to their brigade commanders.
44 NA, Maurin File; Cire Memorandum, UDC; Walters Diary, NPL.
45 Owen, 201.
46 *Donaldsonville Chief*, May 10, 1884.
47 Donaldsonville Artillery *Historical Memoranda*, LHAC.
48 Bartlett, 175.
49 NA, Maurin File; William E. Griffin, Jr. *One Hundred Fifty Years of History Along The Richmond, Fredericksburg and Potomac Railroad* (Richmond, 1984), 90. After the war the name was changed from Chesterfield Station to Ruther Glen. The station, the first in Caroline County, no longer exists, but it was located near the intersection of Chesterfield Road (State Route 620) and Ruther Glen Road (State Route 652). There are a few houses still about the R. F. & P. Railroad tracks that

are used by the CSX Transportation System. The camp location is still in a quiet, pastoral setting, just a stone's throw from a busy I-95 Interstate Highway.

50 Lobrano Diary, LHAC.

51 Joseph A. Graves, *The History of the Bedford Light Artillery* (Bedford City, Va., 1903), 27.

52 *OR* XXV:2, 597; Wiley, *Recollections,* 97; Jules O. Daigle, *Cajun Self-taught* (Ville Platte, La., 1992), 12A.

53 *Donaldsonille Chief,* March 13, 1880.

54 Figg, 97.

55 Dan Emmett's "Jordan is a Hard Road to Travel" was parodied by John R. Thompson, editor of the *Southern Literary Messenger* into "Richmond is a Hard Road to Travel," which contained eight versus with a chorus. The first verse goes:

"Would you like to hear my song, I'm afraid it's rather long,
Of the famous 'on to Richmond' double trouble;
Of the half a dozen trips, and half a dozen slips,
And the very latest bursting of the bubble.
'Tis pretty hard to sing and, like a round, round ring,
'Tis a dreadful knotty puzzle to unravel;
Though all the papers swore, when we touched Virginia's shore,
That Richmond was a hard road to travel.
CHORUS: Then pull off your overcoat and roll up your sleeve,
For Richmond is a hard road to travel.
Then pull off your overcoat and roll up your sleeve,
For Richmond is a hard road to travel, I believe."

56 In Euchre each player is dealt five cards and trump requires three tricks to win a hand.

57 Gallagher, *Fighting,* 188.

58 Walters Diary, NPL.

59 Cire Memorandum, UDC.

60 Founded in 1788 the Massaponax Baptist Church is a rectangular brick structure built in 1859. An addition was added in 1949, and today it is still a ministering church. Located in Spotsylvania County, the building during the war served as a headquarters for both armies, a stable, and a hospital, and the walls were filled with graffiti of stories, crude battle scenes, messages of love, and the names of soldiers and companies. After the war members cleaned and whitewashed the walls, but some writings were preserved and are still visible today in the balcony.

61 Cire Memorandum, UDC.

62 Bennett, 102.

63 Ibid.

64 *The Rome* (Ga.) *Courier,* March 19, 1863. The United States Mine Ford is located about eight miles west of Fredericksburg, although it is thirteen miles by the Orange Plank Road to Spotswood Road, to U. S. Ford Road. It was a primary crossing of the Rappahannock River in the nineteenth century. A trace of the old ford road remains from Spotswood Road. Present-day Riverview Drive incorporates another part of the old road and from its southern cul-de-sac (at 8100 Riverview Drive) a dirt road on private property continues on that leads to the old crossing that drew its name from the United States Gold Mine in the area known as Mineral Springs. "We saw traces of the 'diggins,'" wrote a Confederate soldier during the war. Westwood A. Todd Reminiscences, 88, Westwood A. Todd Papers, UNCCH. These traces can still be discerned today, along with remnants of the Confederate breastworks. Conversation by author with Eugene Zimmerman, Fredericksburg, Va., September 18, 1994.

65 Cire Memorandum, UDC.

66 Gallagher, *Fighting,* 189.

67 R. H. Anderson Letters-sent Book, May 29, 1861-August 23, 1863, MCR.

68 Westwood A. Todd Reminiscences, 88, Westwood A. Todd Papers, UNCCH.

69 Cire Memorandum, UDC.

70 Walters Diary, NPL.

71 W. B. Judkins, "Memoir," 43, 44, Sara Hightower Regional Library.

72 Ibid., 43.

73 Walters Diary, NPL.

74 Cire Memorandum, UDC. In front of the Canonnier earthworks were built "an infantry

breastwork of good proportion" with traverses from which the infantry could pour a fire onto the ford and "render the crossing of the river a rather difficult business." Walters Diary, NPL.

75 Westwood A. Todd Reminiscences, 88, Westwood A. Todd Papers, UNCCH.

76 Stewart, 79.

77 Cockrell, 161.

78 NA, Record of Events (Donaldsonville Art'y), January & February 1863.

79 Folsom, 17, 90.

80 *The Rome* (Georgia) *Courier*, March 19, 1863.

81 Cire Memorandum, UDC.

82 Ibid. Located 5.4 miles south of Fredericksburg where the Old Mine Road crossed the Richmond, Fredericksburg, and Potomac Railroad, Hamilton's Crossing became a Confederate railhead in the winter of 1862-63 and a village of tents and huts.

83 Terry L. Jones, ed., *The Civil War Memoirs of Captain William J. Seymour, Reminiscences of a Louisiana Tiger* (Baton Rouge, 1991), 44.

84 Cutrer, 176.

85 Edward A. Moore, *The Story of a Cannoneer Under Stonewall Jackson* (New York, 1907), 175.

86 Randall Allen and Keith S. Bohannon, ed. *Campaigning with Old Stonewall, Confederate Captain Ujanirtus Allen's Letters to His Wife* (Baton Rouge, 1998), 228.

87 Couture, 176; PRS of Donaldsonville Artillery Muster Roll for January/February 1863, LAGL. Distributed on March 12, 1863, the payroll of the Donaldsonville Artillery totaled $2,872.53.

88 Billings, *Hardtack*, 312. The nervousness of the mule under fire made it unfit for the artillery, and so it was used, usually in a six-mule team, to pull the ammunition and forage wagons.

89 De la Souchere, Simon, *Napoleon's Soldiers in America* (New Orleans, 1972), 110

90 Monnot/Lanier Family Papers, University of New Orleans. Simaruba (Susera S. or "Gumbo-Limbo"), its resin is used as a treatment for gout with anti- flamatory properties; Buckhorn is a bush were the bark is used and has choleric effects over the bile, and can relax the intestinal muscles;"Carb. of Iron" or Calcium carbonate is used as an antacid.

91 PRS of Donaldsonville Artillery Muster Roll for January/February 1863 and "Batteries" Tabulation, April 1863, Washington Artillery Papers, LAGL.

92 Thomas Caffey, "Letters From the Front," *CV*, 26 (1918), 198.

93 Cire Memorandum, UDC.

94 Jones, 44.

95 Couture , 177.

96 Cire Memorandum, UDC; "Batteries" Tabulation, April 1863 in Washington Artillery Papers, LAGL; NA, Maurin File; Gallagher, *Fighting*, 188. Chesterfield Station (now Ruther Glen) and Carmel Baptist Church lie less than a mile apart. Caroline County's oldest church was organized in 1773. The congregation still meets today in the third church building (built in 1874) on the site.

97 NA, M331, John J. Garnett File.

98 NA, Record of Events (Donaldsonville Art'y), March & April 1863.

99 *OR* XXV:2, 614, 728, 729. The common practice was to recognize the battalions by their commander's name as opposed to the letter designation assigned.

100 Eliza F. Andrews, *The War-Time Journal of a Georgia Girl 1864-1865* (New York, 1908), 189.

101 *OR* XXV:2, 615; Ibid., LI, 645; Owen, 16; *Richmond Times Dispatch*, June 25, 1905; Walters, NPL. The Second National Confederate flag was known as the "Stainless Banner." This one was supposedly made by Garnett's sister or sister-in-law out of a portion of her wedding dress. John James Garnett (born March 30, 1839), was the seventh child of Henry T. Garnett, justice of the peace and a large landowner in Westmoreland County, Virginia. They lived in a magnificent home on Ingleside Plantation (a little over five miles from George Washington's birthplace), that still stands and is today the home of Ingleside Estate Vineyards and Winery. Garnett's older brother Lieutenant Colonel Thomas S. Garnett commanded the 48th Virginia Infantry Regiment while another older brother, Dr. Alernon S. Garnett, was a navy veteran that served on the ironclad C. S. S. Merrimac at the time it dueled with the Monitor. Allyne G. Pearce, *You Must Give Something Back, Descendants of John Garnett, Gloucester County, Virginia* (Abilene, Tex., 2000), 29.

102 Walters Diary, NPL.

103 "'Memorandum of Clothing for Issue,' Memo of Clothing, April 11, 1863, for B. W. Arty., Maurin-Anderson Div., Manly-McLaws Div.," and "Required for 3rd Company Battalion

Washington Artillery, April 14th, 1863," Washington Artillery Papers, LAGL.

104 Wise, Vol. I, 440, 441.

105 *The Daily Times* (Donaldsonville), March 5, 1898.

106 *Baton Rouge States-Times Advocate,* April 30, 1913.

107 Chambers, Henry E. *A History of Louisiana: Wilderness, Colony, Province, Territory, State, People.* Vol. III (Chicago and New York, 1925), 72.

108 Jean Reynaud Jacques Prosper Landry to Adele Pedesclaux Landry, September 1864 letter, UV.

109 Levy Diary, May 15, 1864, HUC.

110 NA, CSR. The openings came about when six Corporals were promoted, one died, one went on sick furlough, one was discharged, one was reduced to private at his own request, and one was absent without leave.

111 Clement A. Evans, ed., *Confederate Military History Extended Edition, Vol. XIII Louisiana* (Atlanta, 1899), 379.

112 *Times-Picayune,* December 5, 1930.

113 *Assumption Pioneer,* May 28, 1898.

114 *Donaldsonville Chief,* August 19, 1883.

115 *Times-Picayune,* July 21, 1902.

116 *Assumption Pioneer,* February 1, 1879.

117 Jean Reynaud Jacques Prosper Landry to Adele Pedesclaux Landry, September 1864, UV.

118 Bourgeois, 58.

119 NA, Maurin file; PRS of Donaldsonville Artillery Muster Roll for March/April 1863;

120 Jac Weller, "The Field Artillery of the Civil War, Part 1," *Military Collector & Historian, Journal of the Company of Military Collectors & Historians,* 5:2 (1953), 29, 30. Named after Emperor Louis Napoleon, the gun was developed in France and introduced to American service as the Model 1857. It had a range of shot of 1,680 feet at 5 degrees elevation, greater than the obsolete 6-pounder and more accurate. Against attacking infantry the Napoleon was downright vicious at a quarter mile. Ripley, 27, 366.

121 *OR* XXV:2, 749. This correspondence to Pendleton was dated April 25, 1863. Delivery of the 6-pounders from the First Corps batteries began in February 1863. *OR* XXV:2, 651; "J. R. Anderson & Company, Papers Relating to Citizens or Business Firms," National Archives Record Group 109; Tredegar Gun Foundry Book, Virginia State Library; NA, Record of Events (Donaldsonville Art'y), May & June 1863.

122 E. C. Moncure, "Reminiscences of the Civil War," *Bulletin of the Virginia State Library,* Vol. XVI (July 1927), No. 2 & 3, 57.

123 Griffin, 90.

124 William N. Pendleton Order Book, June 17, 1862 to April 2, 1865, MCR.

125 Jones Diary, LHAC.

126 Ibid. Father Sheeran celebrated Easter with the Louisiana Brigade on April 5, 1863, and was now visiting different portions of Lee's army so others could make their Easter communion.

127 David W. Pipes Memoirs, LAGL.

128 Landry Diary, DPL.

129 *OR* LI:2, 698; "Tabulation of Artillery, May 13, 1863" in William N. Pendleton Papers, UNCCH.

130 Lobrano Diary, LHAC.

131 *OR* LI:2, 698. Grandy's other section was on picket duty at United States Ford and later took part in the battle on May 1 and 2.

132 "Batteries" Tabulation, April 1863, Washington Artillery Papers, LAGL; Lobrano Diary, LHAC; Jones Diary, LHAC.

133 Lobrano Diary, LHAC. The Washington Artillery's Adjutant, William Owen, reported forty-five men were lost with the six guns at Marye's Heights after "they were put in exposed positions, with meager infantry support, and were run over by mere weight of numbers, after repulsing again and again the enemy's attacks." Owen, 225, 226.

134 Cire Memorandum, UDC.

135 NA, Record of Events (Donaldsonville Art'y), May & June 1863.

136 *OR* XXV:2, 776, 780; ibid., XXV:1, 884. Hanover Junction, today called Doswell, is about two and one-half miles south of the river crossing. It is where the Richmond, Fredericksburg & Potomac and the Virginia Central (today the Chesapeake and Ohio), railroad tracks cross each

other. The 11th North Carolina Regiment was stationed at the North Anna River bridges, the 26th and 47th North Carolina regiments were at Hanover Junction, and the 52nd North Carolina Regiment had five companies at the South Anna River bridges. Walter Clark, ed. *Histories of the Several Regiments and Battalions from North Carolina in the Great War 1861-'65* (Goldsboro, N.C., 1901), Vol. 1, 588; Vol. 2, 341; Vol. 3, 88; 234, 235.

137 *OR* XXV:2, 846, 885.
138 Cire Memorandum, UDC.
139 Ibid.
140 Boatner, 138.
141 *OR* XXV:2, 793.
142 NA, Record of Events (Donaldsonville Art'), May & June 1863.
143 John Richardson Porter Diary, May 18 June 14, 1863, Duke University.
144 Lobrano Diary, LHAC.
145 Couture, 193.
146 J. Q. Dabbs letter, June 1863, Eugene Whitefield Dabbs Papers, University of South Carolina.
147 Ibid.
148 Lobrano Diary, LHAC.
149 Walters Diary, NPL.
150 John Richardson Porter Diary, May 18-June 14, 1863, Duke University.
151 Ibid.
152 Jones Diary, LHAC.
153 *OR* XXXIX:2, 654; NA, Maurin File; ibid., Garnett's Artillery File.
154 Jones Diary, LHAC. Nathaniel Banks assumed command of the Department of the Gulf at occupied New Orleans from Major General Benjamin "Beast" Butler in December 1862.
155 Comes was born on October 18, 1835, nineteen days after his father Marcelin's death.
156 Couture, 68.
157 *OR* XXV:2, 840, 850; "Asking for Battn. To be Supplied with Guns, May 29, 1863, with Reply, May 30, 1863," Washington Artillery Papers, LAGL.
158 Freeman, *Lieutenants*, Vol. 2, 706, 707.
159 Lobrano Diary, LHAC.
160 Cire Memorandum, UDC.
161 Walters Diary, NPL.

CHAPTER NINE

1 *OR* XXV:2, 739.
2 NA, CSR; Donaldsonville Artillery *Historical Memoranda*, LHAC.
3 Lineback Papers, 45, UNCCH.
4 Cire Memorandum, UDC.
5 Walters Diary, NPL.
6 Ibid. This eminence, now in the Fredericksburg and Spotsylvania National Military Park, is located about a mile and a half southwest of the lower end of Fredericksburg. Its name, Lee's Hill, came from the day the Army of Northern Virginia's commander rode Traveller up it to direct the battle on December 11, 1863. Today two cannon on the hill represent the Confederate artillery positions.
7 Walters Diary, NPL.
8 Caldwell, 130.
9 Cire Memorandum, UDC.
10 Walters Diary, NPL.
11 *OR* XXVII:2, 652. At the start of the war Walker commanded the Purcell (Va.), Battery. He then served as chief of artillery in A. P. Hill's Division and subsequently commanded Hill's Third Corps artillery. A Virginian of high connections and graduate of the Virginia Military Institute, he was described as a skillful leader, careful and free of recklessness, and knew when the artillery could afford to be bold." Freeman, *Lieutenants*, Vol. 2, 707, 708. It was also said that Walker had "The highest virtues both as a man and as a soldier." Wise, Vol. II, 572. A civil engineer after the war, Walker died in 1888 at his home Point of Forks on the James River in Fluvanna County,

Virginia.

12 Garnett's Battalion of seventeen guns was assigned to Heth's Division. Walker ordered Major William T. Poague's Battalion of sixteen guns to Major General William D. Pender's Division and Lieutenant Colonel Allen S. Cutt's Battalion of seventeen guns under command of Major John Lane to Major General Richard H. Anderson's Division. The battalions of Major David G. McIntosh (sixteen guns) and Major William J. Pegram (twenty guns), were assigned as Corps Reserve.

13 Heth was a West Point graduate of 1847 and highly rated and solidly endorsed by Gen. Robert E. Lee. One of the few generals whom Lee called by his first name, "Harry" was described as truthful and socially charming, with the finest elements of character, and though he proved himself capable in war, he was unlucky. Freeman, *Lieutenants*, Vol. II, 507. Heth's four brigades were commanded by Brig. Gen. James J. Pettigrew, Col. John M. Brockenbrough, Brig. Gen. James J. Archer, and Brig. Gen. Joseph R. Davis, the Confederate President's nephew.

14 Walter Lord, (ed.). *The Freemantle Diary* (Boston, 1954), 186, 187. Not all the African-Confederates were slaves, as can be attested to by the honorable service of the Donaldsonville Artillery's Louis Lefort.

15 Cire Memorandum, UDC. The order of march normally for an artillery battalion was one battery taking the advance one day, then falling to the rear the next, thereby changing the advance company each day.

16 Lineback Papers, 45, UNCCH.

17 Walters Diary, NPL.

18 Knox Mellon Jr. (ed.), "A Florida Soldier in the Army of Northern Virginia: The Hosford Letters," *Florida Historical Quarterly*, 46 (1968), 261.

19 Landry Diary, DPL.

20 *Assumption Pioneer*, May 8, 1897.

21 Ibid., November 12, 1921, and November 10, 1923.

22 Mellon, 261.

23 Landry Diary, DPL.

24 Walters Diary, NPL. Walters uses the word packed throughout his diary, evidently meaning parked.

25 Landry Diary, DPL.

26 Clark, Vol. II, 341. Pettigrew's Brigade recently joined the Army of Northern Virginia from North Carolina.

27 Billy Ellis, *Tithes of Blood, A Confederate Soldier's Story* (Murfreesboro, Tenn., 1997), 99.

28 Archie K. Davis, *Boy Colonel of the Confederacy, The Life And Times of Henry King Burgwyn, Jr.* (Chapel Hill, N.C., 1985), 272.

29 Ibid.

30 Walters Diary, NPL.

31 Davis, 272.

32 Lineback Papers, 49, UNCCH.

33 E. Taylor to H. K. Burgwyn, August 2, 1863, Burgwyn Family Papers, UNCCH.

34 Walters Diary, NPL.

35 Ibid.

36 Lineback Papers, 49, UNCCH.

37 Ibid.

38 Cire Memorandum, UDC.

39 Walters Diary, NPL.

40 *OR* XXVII:2, 611.

41 Lineback Papers, 49, UNCCH.

42 John J. Fox III, *Red Clay to Richmond, Trail of the 35th Georgia Infantry Regiment, CSA.* (Winchester, Va., 2004), 180.

43 Walters Diary, NPL.

44 Stewart, 91.

45 Fox, 180.

46 Walters Diary, NPL. The road through Chester Gap is today Virginia State Route 522.

47 Elizabeth R. Baer, ed., *Shadows on My Heart, The Civil War Diary of Lucy Rebecca Buck of Virginia* (Athens, Ga., 1997), 221.

48 Spencer G. Welch. *A Confederate Surgeon's Letters To His Wife* (New York, 1911), 55.
49 Lineback Papers, 49, UNCCH.
50 Walters Diary, NPL.
51 Thomas A. Ashby, *The Valley Campaigns Being the Reminiscences of a Non-combatant While Between the Lines in the Shenandoah Valley During the War of the States* (New York, 1914), 240, 241.
52 Cire Memorandum, UDC.
53 Lineback Papers, 49, UNCCH.
54 Walters Diary, NPL.
55 Cire Memorandum, UDC.
56 Welch, 55.
57 Lineback Papers, 49, UNCCH. The tall white post and lantern duplicates one erected by Lord Fairfax about the year 1760 marking the route to his Greenway Court estate. There have been a few replacements since the invention of the automobile, but a white post with lantern still stands in the intersection's center.
58 *Philadelphia Weekly Times,* May 31, 1879.
59 Lineback Papers, 49, UNCCH. It seems the Donaldsonville Canonnier field band was no longer with the battery. It may be deduced that one member, the drummer Prosper Conway, had returned to Louisiana in May 1862 in that his fiancee' Catherine Thomas gave birth to a baby girl in Ascension Parish on February 7, 1863. *Diocese of Baton Rouge Church Records*, Vol. 10, 1863-1867 (Baton Rouge, 1990), 144.
60 Lord, 179.
61 Lineback Papers, 49, UNCCH.
62 Cire Memorandum, UDC.
63 Chamberlayne, 188.
64 *OR* XXVII:2, 654.
65 Lineback Papers, 49, UNCCH.
66 Wright, 363.
67 Couture, 69.
68 Reminiscences Army Northern Virginia, July 1-4, 1863, Civil War Papers, LHAC.
69 Walters Diary, NPL.
70 Lineback Papers, 49, UNCCH. Before the war Berryville, Virginia, was a flourishing community in an area of country estates producing wheat, horses, and cattle. The red-brick, rectangle Clarke County Courthouse with its portico in the Roman Doric style was built in 1840 and still stands. The population today is almost 3,200.
71 Walters Diary, NPL.
72 James J. Kirkpatrick Diary, 1861-1864, UT.
73 William D. Alexander Diary, UNCCH.
74 Stewart, 92. The order given refered to General Order No. 72, dated June 21, 1863, "governing the seizure of supplies for the army while in the enemy's country . . . by formal requisition . . . or by purchase and payment in Confederate money." Freeman, *Lee,* Vol. III, 55; *OR* XXVII:3, 912, 913.
75 Barrett, 110.
76 Lineback Papers, 49, UNCCH.
77 Ibid.
78 Hamilton, Vol. I, 484.
79 Westwood A. Todd Diary, UNCCH.
80 Walters Diary, NPL. Charles Town is named for its founder, Colonel Charles Washington, youngest brother of George. With a population today of a little over 2,900 it is a contiguous city with Ranson. Charles Town before the war was an educational and social center, a tranquil southern town, steeped in tradition and with many taverns. Situated in the midst of a fertile agricultural section it was the seat of Jefferson County, Virginia (today West Virginia), with the nucleus of the Jefferson County Courthouse built in 1836. The red brick Georgian Colonial building is set on a high stone foundation and has a tall portico with four Doric columns across its front and a clock in a square-dome tower. It was the scene of John Brown's treason trial in 1859. In October 1863 the building was badly damaged by shellfire; it was neglected until 1871-2 when it was extensively remodeled. "By the middle of the war not an adult male was left in the

community," states the *WPA West Virginia Guide*, 200.
81 Lineback Papers, 49, UNCCH.
82 Cire Memorandum, UDC.
83 Ibid.
84 Walters Diary, NPL. Shepardstown claims the distinction of being the oldest continuously settled community in the state. The compact town occupies about a square mile on the Potomac River.
85 Lineback Papers, 49, UNCCH.
86 Walters Diary, NPL.
87 Welch, 56.
88 James Saunders, *Early Settlers of Alabama With Notes and Genealogies* (Bowie, Md., 1899), 148.
89 Cire Memorandum, UDC.
90 Walters Diary, NPL.
91 Chamberlayne, 188.
92 Walters Diary, NPL. Jones Crossroads today is named Lappans.
93 Barrett, 109, 110.
94 Wiley, 165.
95 Cockkrell, 192.
96 Walters Diary, NPL.
97 Barrett, 110.
98 Caldwell, 132.
99 Lineback Papers, 49, 55, UNCCH.
100 Cire Memorandum, UDC.
101 Walters Diary, NPL.
102 Stewart, 93.
103 William W. Hassler, *The General to His Lady: The Civil War Letters of William Dorsey Pender to Fanny Pender* (Chapel Hill, N.C., 1965), 254, 255.
104 Shelby Foote, *The Civil War: A Narrative, Fredericksburg to Meridian*, Vol. II (New York, 1963), 443.
105 Walters Diary, NPL. Just northwest of and along the old pike was the schoolhouse and a tollhouse; both are still standing and used as private dwellings. The double wooden covered bridge was called "Twin Bridges." In the 1930s it was replaced by two metal structures named "The Iron Bridges." One of them is gone, replaced by a concrete bridge on the main highway but the second iron bridge is still in use on the now secondary by-pass to the west. John H. McClellan to author, May 24, 2004.
106 Caldwell, 132.
107 Walters Diary, NPL.
108 Welch, 57.
109 Walters Diary, NPL.
110 Caldwell, 133.
111 Westwood A. Todd Diary, UNCCH.
112 Ibid.
113 Lineback, 55, UNCCH.
114 Caldwell, 133.
115 R. A. Brock, ed., *Gen. Robert Edward Lee, Soldier, Citizen, and Christian Patriot* (Atlanta, 1897), 260, 261.
116 Lineback, 55, UNCCH.
117 Richard B. Harwell, ed. *Cities and Camps of the Confederate States by Fitzgerald Ross* (Urbana, Ill., 1958), 35.
118 Wiley, 170.
119 E. M. Hicks, "Stories of Service in Virginia," *CV*, 20 (1912), 561.
120 McCarthy, Pamphlet No. 2, 200.
121 John R. Porter Diary, Duke University.
122 Ibid.
123 Westwood A. Todd Diary, UNCCH.
124 James A. Brunson, "Cannoneers As Cavalrymen," *CV*, 23 (1915), 259; OR XXVII:2, 611.
125 Westwood A. Todd Diary, UNCCH.
126 Harwell, 39.

127 *Louisiana, A Guide to the State*, 94.
128 Ibid., 92.
129 Robert Stiles, *Four Years Under Marse Robert* (New York, 1903), 201. After the passing of seventy-eight years the Writer's Program of the Works Projects Administration in the state of Louisiana for the American Guide Series still noted, "Dancing is the most popular pastime" of the "Cajuns" and "dances are called 'Fais-do-do' literally 'go to sleep'—or an all night party." *Louisiana, A Guide to the State*, 93.
130 Walters Diary, NPL.
131 John O'Farrell Diary, MCR.
132 Cire Memorandum, UDC.
133 Brunson, 611.
134 Walters Diary, NPL.
135 John L. Marye, "The First Gun at Gettysburg," *The American Historical Register* (July 1895), 1228.
136 Welch, 61.
137 Erected in 1837, the splendid iron factory recently had been burned by Jubal Early's troops of Ewell's Second Corps. It remained a mass of crumbling masonry into the next century. The only visible reminders of the early ironworks on the site today are the reconstructed stack and blacksmith shop that are in Caledonia State Park. Thaddeus Stevens was a leader of the Radical Republicans and noted for his extreme abolition views and his intense hatred for slaveholders.
138 Walters Diary, NPL. The mountain and agricultural hamlet nestles at the foot of Rock Top, which rises almost perpendicularly to a height 410 feet above. The Cashtown Tavern, a two-and-a-half-story red brick building dating from 1797 is still standing and open as a bed and breakfast. *History of Cumberland and Adams County* (Chicago, 1886), 255.
139 M. Jacobs, *Notes on the Rebel Invasion of Maryland and Pennsylvania and the Battle of Gettysburg July 1st, 2d and 3d, 1863* (Philadelphia, 1864), 18, 21.
140 Lineback, 55, UNCCH.
141 Jacobs, 121.
142 W. H. Moon, "Beginning of the Battle at Gettysburg," *CV*, Vol. XXXIII (1925), 449.
143 Thomas Ware Diary, UNCCH.
144 *OR* XXVII:2, 637.
145 Clark, Vol. V, 115.
146 Flohr's (Lutheran), Union Church, its cornerstone laid in 1822, stood next to the cemetery. The congregation erected a new building on the site in 1875 that still stands. *History and Directory of the Boroughs of Adams County* (1880), 148, 149.
147 Clark, Vol. II, 343; Vol. III, 88; Vol. V, 115, 116; Lineback, 55.
148 Cire Memorandum, UDC.
149 Sarah M. Broadhead, *The Diary of a Lady of Gettysburg, Pennsylvania, from June 15 to July 15, 1863.* (unpublished), 11, Gettysburg National Military Park Library.
150 Clark, Vol. III, 88, 89.
151 Cire Memorandum, UDC.
152 Wayland F. Dunaway, *Reminiscences of a Rebel* (New York, 1913), 83, 84.
153 Clark, Vol. V, 115, 116; *OR* XXVII:2, 317.
154 James L. Morrison, Jr. (ed.). "The Memoirs of Henry Heth, Part II," *Civil War History*, 8 (September 1962), 303.
155 Freeman, *Lieutenants*, Vol. 3, 78.

CHAPTER TEN

1 Brock, 264.
2 Walters Diary, NPL.
3 NA, Record of Events (Donaldsonville Art'y), July & August, 1863.
4 *OR* XXVII:2, 652.
5 William G. McCabe, "Annual Reunion of Pegram Battalion Association," *SHSP*, Vol. 14 (1886), 15-17.
6 Clipping from "The American Register," 97, in GNMP Pegram File, Gettysburg National Military Park.

7 Morrison, 320, 321.
8 Brunson, 15.
9 Brock, 260, 261.
10 Jennings C. Wise, "The Boy Gunners of Lee," *SHSP*, 42 (1917), 166.
11 Monroe F. Cockrell, (ed.). *Gunner with Stonewall, Reminiscences of William Thomas Poague* (Jackson, Tenn., 1957), 70.
12 Brock, 266, 267.
13 Walters Diary, NPL.
14 Map of the Battle Field of Gettysburg, July 1st, 2nd, 3rd, 1863, New Edition (Washington, D.C., 1883), GNM. The maps are referred to as the John B. Bachelder Maps.
15 OR XXVII:2, 652. The six pieces were the Donaldsonville Artillery's two 10-pounder Parrott guns and one 3-inch Ordnance Rifle, one 10-pounder Parrott from Lewis's Pittsylvania Artillery, one 10-pounder Parrott and one 3-inch Ordnance Rifle from Moore's Norfolk Battery. The current battlefield markers for the above batteries mistakenly list the time for relieving Pegram's guns at "about 3:30 p.m." See John B. Bachelder, July 1, 1863, Map, Gettysburg National Military Park, for the location of Wierman's farm and position of Garnett's Battalion.
16 *Gettysburg Star and Sentinel,* November 20, 1894. *The Gettysburg Compiler*, November 20, 1894, recorded it was "300 yards south of Herr's tavern, on the crest of the ridge."
17 *OR* XXVII:2, 678. McIntosh's guns extended Pegram's line on the right side of the pike where their fire was "occasionally brisk, but deliberate." *OR* XXVII:2, 675. Built in 1815, Herr Tavern is located on the south side of the Chambersburg Pike. During the battle the Tavern was utilized as a Confederate hospital. In the early 1900s the building was used as a dairy farm and in 1977 restoration took place returning it to a restaurant and bed and breakfast. Though it has been heavily altered both on the inside and outside with a substantial addition, the original portion of the two-story brick house remains today. Most of the area on Herr Ridge where the artillery deployed now has private homes and modern tree growth.
18 Anonymous, "The Light Artillery!," *SHSP,* Vol. XXXI, 97.
19 *OR* XXVII:2, 652.
20 Caldwell, 138.
21 The Yankee infantry belonged to Colonel Roy Stone's Second Brigade, composed of the 143rd, 149th, and 150th regiments of Pennsylvania Infantry from the Third Division of Maj. Gen. Oliver O. Howard's Eleventh Army Corps. Stone's men were located on the McPherson farm area along the Chambersburg Turnpike.
22 *OR* XXVII:2, 675.
23 Ibid., Pt. 1, 341. This was the 149th Pennsylvania infantry.
24 Ibid., Pt. 1, 347. This was the 150th Pennsylvania infantry.
25 Ibid., Pt. 1, 362. The batteries were Lieutenant John H. Calef's 2d U. S. Horse Artillery, Battery A, Captain Gilbert H. Reynolds' 1st New York, Battery L, and Captain James H. Cooper's 1st Pennsylvania, Battery B.
26 David G. Martin, *Gettysburg July 1* (Conshohocken, Pa., 1995), 207.
27 *OR* XXVII:2, 675.
28 Ibid., Pt. 2, 610.
29 Ibid., Pt. 2, 349.
30 Freeman, *Lee,* Vol. III, 71.
31 Welch, 64.
32 Brock, 271. Garnett recorded, "Heth's division had suffered severely." Brock, 272. The 26th North Carolina Regiment of Pettigrew's Brigade, with which Garnett's Battalion marched on the campaign, went into the battle with eight hundred men and came out with 216 unhurt. *OR* XXVII:2, 645.
33 Cire Memorandum, UDC.
34 Freeman, *Lee*, Vol. III, 71.
35 OR XXVII:2, 675, 678.
36 Cire Memorandum, UDC.
37 NA, Record of Events (Donaldsonville Art'y), July & August, 1863. The seminary was built in 1832 and still functions today as the Lutheran Theological Seminary that was founded in 1826. At the close of the first day's battle this building was used as a hospital by the Confederates with about five hundred wounded placed in the library and recitation rooms. The cupola was said to be

the choice observation point during the battle. "Lutheran Theological Seminary," *CV,* 21 (1913), 389.

38 *OR* XXVII:2, 652.
39 Brock, 268, 269.
40 E. Halstead, "The First Day at the Battle of Gettysburg," *The Gettysburg Papers,* Vol. 1, (D. C. MOLLUS, Vol. 2, 1887), 157.
41 Brock, 269.
42 *OR* XXVII:2, 349.
43 Ibid.
44 Brock, 273. Brig. Gen. Stephen D. Ramseur, age 26, was one of Lee's youngest generals and commanded a North Carolina brigade in Maj. Gen. Robert E. Rhodes Division of the 2nd Corps.
45 *OR* XXVII:2, 349.
46 Ibid., Pt. 2, 652.
47 McCarthy, Pamphlet No. 2, 202.
48 Martin, 463
49 Richard Wheeler, *Witness to Gettysburg* (Edison, N.J.,1994), 159.
50 Caldwell, 140, 141.
51 McCarthy, Pamphlet No. 2, 203.
52 Walters Diary, NPL.
53 *OR* XXVII:2, 652.
54 The McMillan House was called "Wildwood." In 1894 a large addition was built to it with the rear of the house made the front and now facing West Confederate Avenue in Gettysburg National Military Park. It still stands as a private home. McMillan House File, Gettysburg National Military Park Library. The positions of Garnett's batteries are marked today with Iron tablets located along Seminary Ridge on West Confederate Avenue. Their locations south from the Fairfield Road for Maurin's two 10-pounder Parrott and one 3-inch Ordnance rifles is .25 mile, for Lewis's two 3-inch Ordnance rifles .3 mile, Moore's 3-inch Ordnance rifle and 10-pounder Parrott rifle .47 mile, and Grandy's two 3-inch Ordnance rifles .5 mile. To the left of Maurin's guns was McIntosh's Battalion. Pegram's Battalion extended the line north of Grandy's battery. *Richmond Times-Dispatch,* June 25, 1905; David G. Martin, *Confederate Monuments at Gettysburg* (Hightstown, N.J., 1986), 69, 70, 100, 101, 105-108, 193, 194, and attached map.
55 Brock, 276.
56 Wheeler, 170.
57 Ibid.
58 McCarthy, Pamphlet No. 2, 204.
59 NA, CSR.
60 McCarthy, *Minutiae*, 200, 201.
61 *New Orleans Daily City Item,* December 12, 1891.
62 *Louisiana Historical Association Catalogue, Memorial Hall, September 1, 1917,* Book 2, LHAC.
63 Evans, Vol. XIII, 511, 512.
64 NA, CSR.
65 McCarthy, Pamphlet No. 2, 204.
66 McMillan House File, Gettysburg National Military Park.
67 McCarthy, Pamphlet No. 2, 204.
68 Harwell, 50; Bartlett, 193; Runge, 50; *OR* XXVII:2, 354; McMillan House File, GNM. David McMillan in 1882 made a claim to the Federal government seeking compensation for damages made by the rebel army involved in taking 1,225 rails and 16 posts from his fences.
69 Richardson, 218.
70 NA, CSR. Schmidt was half-brother to Canonnier Pvt. Albert J. Schmidt who later wrote their father, "Oscar was taken prisoner…and was exchanged with the sick and wounded men; he went then to the South Carolina Hospital in Petersburg, from there he was transferred to the Louisiana hospital in Richmond and while there he obtained a furlough to Mobile. His intention was to go home. Has he not succeeded?" Albert Schmidt to Father, November 21, 1863, Gustavus Schmidt Correspondences, LSU. No record or trace of Treshe has been located after he arrived at the prisoner of war camp located on Pea Patch Island, Fort Delaware, where he probably died. No record was likely made of his death in the chaos and confusion that reigned at the camp during

July and August 1863. R. Hugh Simmons, Fort Delaware Society, to author, April 8, 2008, correspondence.

71 Walters Diary, NPL.
72 *OR* XXVII:2, 352.
73 McCarthy, Pamphlet No. 2, 204, 205.
74 Walters Diary, NPL.
75 Donaldsonville Artillery *Historical Memoranda*, LHAC.
76 Cire Memorandum, UDC.
77 Landry Diary, DPL.
78 Walters Diary, NPL.
79 *OR* XXVII:1, 749.
80 Ibid. 457.
81 Brock, 291.
82 Landry Diary, DPL.
83 *OR* XXVII:2, 652.
84 Runge, 51.
85 Cire Memorandum, UDC.
86 Richardson, 217.
87 Gallagher, *Fighting,* 243.
88 Bartlett, 192.
89 *B & L*, Vol. III, 360.
90 McCarthy, Pamphlet No. 2, 206.
91 *OR* XXVII:2, 351.
92 Ibid.
93 Owen, 248. Owen recorded the total guns as one hundred and thirty-seven, but nine guns from Capt. Willis J. Dance's First Virginia Reserve Battalion of Ewell's Corps were placed in Walker's line making the total, according to Pendleton, "nearly one hundred and fifty." *OR* XXVII:2, 352.
94 Walters Diary, NPL.
95 Brock, 286.
96 McMillan House File, GNMP.
97 Kent, 199, 200.
98 Brock, 285, 286.
99 *OR* XXVII:2, 653.
100 Gallagher, *Fighting,* 247.
101 *OR* XXVII:2, 652.
102 Never reported or stated, the identity of the guns was deduced by identifying those available in the Third Corps. Sixty-three pieces were engaged on July 3rd with two disabled and unable to be used. In reserve were six 12-pounder howitzers of Pogue's Battalion, Patterson's six guns with Ross' piece "detailed," and Garnett's eight smoothbore guns. Pogue's six howitzers remained under his command, leaving Patterson's seven guns plus the two Donaldsonville Napoleons available to make up the detachment as Garnett reported his "remaining six guns bore no part in these actions." Throughout Garnett's report he failed to mention that Maurin's two 12-pounder Napoleons were part of his command and because of this, the cast iron tablets on the battlefield erroneously list the Donaldsonville Artillery as having only three rifle guns for their armament. *OR* XXVII:2, 635, 653, 674; Gallagher, *Fighting,* 249; Owen, 249.
103 Gallagher, *Fighting,* 247, 248.
104 Stewart, 99.
105 Gallagher, *Fighting,* 250, 251.
106 Ibid. 249. Alexander later reported "it all" to Pendleton and Longstreet, and "felt quite like preferring charges" against Richardson. Later circumstances sent Longstreet's Corps and Alexander "out west," and that was the end of it.
107 Richardson, 214.
108 NA, Record of Events (Donaldsonville Art'y), July & August 1863.
109 Brock, 289, 290. The Federal guns on and near Cemetery Hill are listed in *OR* XXVII:1, 238.
110 McCarthy, Pamphlet No. 2, 207.
111 Wilson, 120.

112 Stewart, 99.
113 George Clark, "Wilcox's Alabama Brigade at Gettysburg," *CV*, 17 (1909), 230.
114 Linebrink, p.59. UNCCH.
115 June Kimble, "Tennesseeans at Gettysburg---The Retreat," *CV*, 18 (1910), 460.
116 Cockrell, 197.
117 Felix R. Callaway, *The Bloody Links* (Shreveport, La., 1907), 34.
118 Brock, 291.
119 McMillan House File, GNM. Years later the McMillan family was offered money for this tree by Union veterans who wanted to have the section containing the shell splintered hole for their Grand Army Post room. The McMillan family refused the offer believing the tree was too much a part of the battlefield to be removed from the place where it received its wound.
120 McCarthy, Pamphlet No. 2, 208, 209.
121 Francis W. Dawson, *Reminiscences of Confederate Service, 1861-1865* (Baton Rouge, 1980), 95.
122 *OR* XXVII:1, 750.
123 *OR* XXVII:1, 240; McMillan House File, GNMA. A piece of oral history passed down from generation to generation in the author's family was a story told by Donaldsonville Canonnier Pvt. Camille Templet to his children. He never named the battle but related how he and his comrades shamelessly exited a house in a hurry when Yankee shells came flying through. One round that came "flying through" the McMillan house, which had a center hall, struck the panel of one of its doors. It had traveled over a mile in flight from the Union line on Cemetery Hill and remained lodged in the door for over ninety years.
124 *OR* XXVII:2, 610.
125 Brock, 291.
126 John W. H. Porter, *A Record of Events in Norfolk County* (Portsmouth, Va., 1892), 256, 258.
127 *OR* XXVII:1, 749.
128 McCarthy, Pamphlet No. 2, 208, 209.
129 *OR* XXVII:2, 321.
130 Ibid., Pt. 1, 239.
131 John Purifoy, "The Retreat From Gettysburg," *CV*, 33 (1925), 338.
132 Brock, 299.
133 Lord, 216.
134 Ibid., 214.

CHAPTER ELEVEN

1 Owen, 254.
2 John Purifoy, "The Retreat From Gettysburg," *CV*, Vol. 33 (1925), 338.
3 Walters Diary, NPL.
4 *OR* XXVII:2, 654. Imbodin's command consisted of the 18th Virginia Cavalry, 62nd Virginia (mounted infantry), Capt. John H. McNeil's Virginia Partisan Rangers, and Capt. J. H. McClanahan's (mounted) Virginia Battery.
5 *B & L*, Vol. III, 423.
6 *OR* XXVII:2, 654, 655.
7 Stewart, 113.
8 *B & L*, Vol. III, 423.
9 *OR* XXVII:2, 655. W. A. Popkins, "Imboden's Brigade at Gettysburg," *CV*, 22 (1914), 552. J. Hoke, *Reminiscences of The War; or Incidents Which Transpired in and about Chambersburg, During the War of the Rebellion* (Chambersburg, Pa., 1884), 84-86. "The vastness of this train, and the aggregate of woe, suffering and anguish it contained, it seems has never been understood by the country," wrote Hoke.
10 Hamilton, Vol. II, 31.
11 Cire Memorandum, UDC.
12 *B & L*, Vol. III, 424.
13 Landry Diary, DPL.
14 Hamilton, Vol. II, 31, 32; Berkeley Minor, "The Night After Gettysburg," *CV*, 33 (1925), 140.
15 Bartlett, 195.

16 *B & L,* Vol. III, 425.
17 Hoke, *Reminiscences*, 88.
18 Ibid. The battery of black field pieces were Parrott guns or 3-inch Ordnance Rifles whose tubes were black as opposed to the Napoleon's bronze.
19 Ibid.
20 Ibid., 89.
21 Ibid., 89, 90.
22 Landry Diary, DPL. Gaudet, a 24-year-old farmer from Assumption Parish was not hospitalized from the slight wound. The 20-year-old Mollere, also from Assumption Parish, was sent to the prisoner of war camp at Fort Delaware, Delaware, and finally released on June 9, 1865, after signing (by "X" mark), an Oath of Allegiance.
23 *Biographical and Historical Memoirs*, Vol. I, 517.
24 *Donaldsonville Chief,* June 15, 1907.
25 Benevolent Association of the Army of Northern Virginia Application of Abraham Klotz, March 24, 1879, LHAC.
26 *Donaldsonville Chief,* June 15, 1907.
27 Cunningham's Crossroads is today the unincorporated community of Cearfuss. The Greencastle Pike that they traveled on is now Maryland State Route 63.
28 *B & L,* Vol. III, 425.
29 W. A. Popkins, "Imboden's Brigade at Gettysburg," *CV,* 22 (1914), 552.
30 John H. Cameron, "Memoirs," 19, Virginia Military Institute, Lexington, Va.
31 NA, CSR.
32 *Gonzales Weekly*, February 12, 1921.
33 Tombstone of Joseph Edward Morin, died January 29, 1921, in Holy Rosary Cemetery, St. Amant, Ascension Parish, La.
34 *OR* XXVII:2, 655.
35 Landry Diary, DPL.
36 *B & L,* Vol. III, 425.
37 *OR* XXVII:2, 655.
38 John H. Cameron, "Memoirs," 20, Virginia Military Institute.
39 *B & L,* Vol. III, 426.
40 *OR* XXVII:2, 655. Laid out in 1787 Williamsport, Maryland, is beautifully and picturesquely located on high ground at the confluence of the Potomac River and Conococheague Creek. The town is noted for the grandeur of the surrounding scenery with the verdure of fields, woodlands, and nearby mountain ranges. Having unusually wide streets lined with substantial brick and stone houses, it was a junction of important early trails and a busy shipping point along the river and the C. & O. Canal. The town was converted into a great hospital for the thousands of Confederate wounded who occupied churches, public buildings, and homes at this time. *Williamsport and Vicinity Reminiscences, Early Part of the 18th Century to the Early Part of 1933, Inclusive; Compiled by the Williamsport Chamber of Commerce* (Hagerstown, Md., n.d.) Historic and vibrant Williamsport has over 2,200 residents today.
41 *B & L,* Vol. III, 426, 427. In Hoke's *Reminiscences* (page 86), Imboden recorded he armed about five hundred men by ordering three out of every four "wagoners" to be mustered and armed.
42 Durkin, 49.
43 Hoke, *Reminiscences*, 88.
44 Jones Diary, LHAC.
45 *OR* XXVII:2, 437, 655; Hoke, *Reminiscences,* 89. The colonel of the 16th Pennsylvania Cavalry engaged in pursuing the wagon train on the pike reported the road was filled with broken-down wagons, abandoned limbers and caissons filled with ammunition ready for instant use. *OR* XXVII:1, 977, 978.
46 Bartlett, 195.
47 D. W. Pipes to Mr. Reily, November 23, 1928, Washington Artillery File, LAGL.
48 Donaldsonville Artillery *Historical Memoranda*, LHAC. The Donaldsonville battery had three enlisted men unaccounted for. One of these privates was captured near Greencastle, the Federals reporting he, while on the march, stopped and hid in a barn and upon approach of Yankee cavalry surrendered as a rebel deserter. The other two were captured at or near Hedgeville, west of Williamsport, with the Federals reporting they left the ranks on the march during the night and

went to Hedgeville and voluntarily surrendered. NA, CSR.
49 *OR* XXVII:2, 655.
50 Hoke, *Reminiscences*, 87.
51 Besides Landry's Donaldsonville gun on the Greencastle Road, four guns of the Washington Artillery were posted on the Boonsboro Road and another four of their guns on the Hagerstown Road. Between the roads was Captain James F. Hart's Company A, Washington (S.C.), Artillery of Hampton's Legion with two guns, along with Moore's two guns. A few guns of Captain J. H. McClanahan's (Va.) Battery of six guns occupied positions between the Greencastle Road and the Conocoheague Creek on the left, with their remaining guns between the Boonsboro Road and the Potomac River on the right. The Courtney (Va.) Battery under Capt. William A. Tanner had two guns on the left of the Hagerstown Road and two on the far right of the defensive line. *OR* XXVII:2, 437, 499.
52 *B & L*, Vol. III, 427.
53 *OR* XXVII:2, 655.
54 Isaac N. Baker, "Memoirs." Virginia Military Institute.
55 Wilson, 130
56 I. G. Bradwell, "From Gettysburg to the Potomac," *CV*, 30 (1922), 429.
57 *OR* XXVII:1, 928.
58 Durkin, 49.
59 *B & L*, Vol. III, 427.
60 *OR* XXVII:2, 655.
61 Landry Diary, DPL. Joyner, a 22 year old Texan was working as a clerk in New Orleans at the outbreak of war. He joined Dreux's 1st Louisiana Infantry Battalion in April 1861 and at the expiration of his one-year enlistment joined with the Donaldsonville Artillery during the Peninsula Campaign. During the battle at Williamsport he received a gunshot wound to the hip, injuring the bone, and was sent to General Hospital in Staunton, Va. On October 3, 1863, he was transferred to Louisiana Hospital in Richmond until returning to duty with the battery in January 1864.
62 The Federal commander Brig. Gen. John Buford reported Confederate casualties as being "more than quadruple mine." Union losses for the Williamsport battle are believed to be: 14 killed, 37 wounded, and 69 captured or missing. *OR* XXVII:1, 928. Ted Alexander, "Ten days in July, The Pursuit to the Potomac," *North and South*, 2:6 (June 1999), 20.
63 *B & L*, Vol. III, 428.
64 Isaac N. Baker, "Memoirs," Virginia Military Institute.
65 Walters Diary, NPL.
66 John Purifoy, "The Retreat From Gettysburg," *CV*, Vol. 33 (1925), 338. Wheeler, 255.
67 Brock, 300.
68 Westwood A. Todd, 135, UNCCH.
69 Walters Diary, NPL.
70 Brock, 300.
71 McCarthy, Pamphlet No. 2, 211. See *OR* XXVII:2, 353 for the order in which the army moved.
72 Walters Diary, NPL.
73 Bartlett, 194.
74 Cockrell, 200.
75 Westwood A. Todd, 135, UNCCH.
76 McCarthy, Pamphlet No. 2, 211.
77 Welch, 69.
78 Cockrell, 204.
79 *OR* XXVII:2, 309.
80 John Purifoy, "The Retreat From Gettysburg," *CV*, 33 (1925), 339.
81 Cockrell, 203.
82 NA, M331, Garnett file.
83 Ibid.
84 A short distance past Fairfield the road forked to the right toward the tiny hamlet of Iron Springs. This was nothing more than a group of company houses that originally sheltered workers at the nearby ruined Maria Iron Furnace that was established in 1830 but destroyed by fire in 1842. The Iron Springs Road taken by Lee's army was a haul road affording access for bog ore transporters

to the old iron furnace and was not heavily traveled at the time of the withdrawal. Today Iron Springs Road is a narrow two-lane paved road and still not heavily traveled.

85 Gallagher, *Fighting,* 267.

86 Bartlett, 194.

87 Walters Diary, NPL.

88 Clark, Vol. II, 587. Fairfield Gap was called Monterey Gap in the dispatches and official reports of both armies. Lee's army turned south where Iron Springs Road crossed Toms Creek. This mountain road continues on across the Adams-Franklin County line, west of Pine Mountain, and over extremely steep terrain until it reaches the narrow gap at the crest and foot of Monterey Peak. Today it is still a lightly traveled mountain road until one reaches the top, where it exists as a foot trail. From here the route continued straight for about a mile to the Mercersburg, Greencastle, and Waynesboro Turnpike tollhouse, located at the present day intersection of Pennsylvania Route 16 and Old Route 16. A local historian, John McClellan, noted "old timers" who lived nearby "claimed that into the early 1900s, you could walk the sides of the turnpike and find all sorts of harness and tack, wagon wheel hubs and rims, buckles and metal" from Lee's army. Just recently off the gap route a hunter found a musket barrel sticking up, as a stake would, out of some leaves and found a skeleton, cap and coat devices, buttons, belt buckle and shoe nails, the remains of a soldier from a Georgia unit. John H. McClellan to author, May 23, June 28, and July 6, 2004, correspondences.

89 Walters, NPL. The turnpike is Old Route 16. Frogtown was an early colloquial name for Pikesville, which in 1873 became Rouzerville. The marsh was a flood plain of Red Run, a tributary of the East Branch of Antietam Creek that has since been drained by the lowering of the water table. It is now commercially and residentially developed. John H. McClellan to author, May 22, 2004.

90 Walters, NPL. Brigadier General William "Extra Billy" Smith took office January 1, 1864, as Virginia's governor after resigning from the army. He served in the army from the Peninsular to the Gettysburg Campaigns and had been wounded five times.

91 Walters Diary, NPL.

92 James J. Kirkpatrick Diary, 1861-1864, UT.

93 Walters Diary, NPL.

94 James J. Kirkpatrick Diary, 1861-1864, UT.

95 Donaldsonville Artillery *Historical Memoranda*, LHAC.

96 *OR* XXVII:2, 653.

97 Landry Diary, DPL.

98 *OR* XXVII:1, 940.

99 Landry Diary, DPL.

100 Robert J. Driver, *The 1st and 2nd Rockbridge Artillery* (Lynchburg, Va., 1987), 45.

101 Laura E. Lee, *For-Get-Me-Nots of the Civil War, A Romance containing Reminiscences and Original Letters of Two Confederate Soldiers* (St. Louis, Mo., 1909), 88.

102 Henry C. Carter to brother, July 8, 1863, letter, GNMP.

103 Gallagher, *Fighting,* 270.

104 McCarthy, Pamphlet No. 2, 214.

105 NA, CSR of Prosper Landry.

106 Ibid.

107 James J. Kirkpatrick Diary, 1861-1864, UT.

108 Owen, 258.

109 Linebrink, 63, UNCCH.

110 *OR* XXVII:2, 322, 323.

111 Cire Memorandum, UDC.

112 Lineback, 63, UNCCH.

113 Isaac N. Baker, "Memoirs," Virginia Military Institute.

114 NA, Record Group 109, Garnett's Artillery Battalion file.

115 John Rozier, *The Granite Farm Letters, The Civil War Correspondences of Edgeworth & Sallie Bird* (Athens, Ga., 1988), 122.

116 Landry Diary, DPL. Captain Scott was apparently assigned to the Third Corps quartermaster department.

117 Rozier, 122.

118 *Donaldsonville Chief,* April 20, 1907.

119 NA, Record Group 109, Garnett's Artillery Battalion file. Hewitt was again absent sick in October 1863 and finally dropped from the rolls on February 29, 1864, with nephritis. His replacement as A. Q. M. was Capt. E. Williams who served in this capacity until the end.

120 "Batteries" Tabulation, April 1863 in Washington Artillery Papers, LAGL; *OR* XXVII:2, 356; NA, Garnett's Artillery File.

121 "'Home, Sweet Home' was probably the most popular of all songs sung by wearers of the gray," wrote a preeminent Civil War historian, adding, "Lorena," "All Quiet Along the Potomac Tonight," "Annie Laurie," "Juanita," "Annie of the Vale," "Sweet Evelina," "Lilly Dale," "The Girl I Left Behind Me," "Bell Brandon," "Her Bright Eyes Haunt Me Still," "Listen to the Mocking Bird," and "Just Before the Battle, Mother," (the last borrowed from the Yankees), were ranked very high in Confederate soldier esteem and frequently heard about the campfire. Bell I. Wiley, *The Life of Johnny Reb* (Indianapolis, 1943), 152.

122 Clark, Vol. II, 399.

123 McCarthy, Pamphlet No. 2, 213.

124 Rozier, 119.

125 Foote, Vol. II, 443, 444.

126 Everson, 264. A Confederate soldier arriving at Williamsport a day after the "wagoners' fight" later suggested the "negroes" also participated in the defense against the "Blue Coats." Hamilton, Vol. 2, 35.

127 *Times-Picayune*, November 3, 1902.

128 *OR* XXVII:2, 301.

129 McCarthy, Pamphlet No. 2, 214.

130 Walters Diary, NPL.

131 NA, Record of Events (Donaldsonville Art'y), July & August 1863.

132 Walters Diary, NPL.

133 St. James is located five miles southwest of Hagerstown. It is the oldest Episcopal boarding school in the United States, having opened in 1842 as an upper secondary school and college. The construction of the original building (a magnificent mansion called Fountain Rock), was started in 1792 and was bought for the school by the Episcopal Church. The Georgian-style campus, located on serene rolling farmland that contains a natural spring, fields, and streams, has added many new buildings conforming to the manor house. The school was forced to close its doors in 1864 due to the decimation caused by the war and reopened in 1869 after extensive repairs as a secondary school only. It today has 215 students.

134 Hill's Corps and Heth's Division was the center of Lee's defensive line. Anderson's Division was positioned on the right (south), and Pender's Division on the left (north). Longstreet's Corps extended the line south through Downsville, almost to the Potomac River. The northern flank was just west of Hagerstown and held by Ewell's Corps. This line was built in three days (between July 7-10) by laborers working around-the-clock. Freeman noted it was "an admirable defensive line." Freeman, *Lee* Vol. III, 138.

135 *OR* XXVII:2, 610; NA, Record of Events (Donaldsonville Art'y), July & August 1863.

136 Stewart, 113.

137 McCarthy, Pamphlet No. 2, 215.

138 Landry Diary, DPL.

139 McCarthy, Pamphlet No. 2, 215.

140 John Purifoy, "In Battle Array at Williamsport and Hagerstown," *CV*, 33 (1925), 372.

141 Walters Diary, NPL.

142 John Purifoy, "In Battle Array at Williamsport and Hagerstown," *CV*, Vol. 33 (1925), 372.

143 Ibid.

144 L. Leon, *Diary of a Tar Heel Confederate Soldier* (Charlotte, N.C., 1913), 41.

145 Driver, 45.

146 *OR* XXVII:2, 611.

147 *OR* XXVII:2, 653.

148 Longstreet, 429; Walters Diary, N.; Freeman, *Lee*, Vol. III, 143; Bartlett, 196.

149 *OR* XXVII:2, 653.

150 *OR* XXVII:2, 667. Located at a bend in the Potomac River, the tiny hamlet of Falling Waters was established in 1815. Named for a small spring-fed stream that cascades into the river, it is still a small residential community with numerous historic homes. In a rural setting it has a local

population of 7,000.

151 The four batteries of Carter's Battalion were Capt. William J. Reese's Jeff. Davis (Ala.) Artillery, Capt. William Carter's King William (Va.) Artillery, Capt. C. W. Fry's Orange (Va.) Artillery, and Capt. Richard C. M. Page's Morris (Va.) Artillery.

152 *OR* XXVII:2, 353. Of the four unidentified guns assigned from Garnett's Battalion, a portion were from Grandy's Norfolk Light Artillery Blues with another one or two guns probably being from Moore's Norfolk Battery.

153 John Purifoy, "In Battle Array at Williamsport and Hagerstown," *CV*, 33 (1925), 373.

154 Ibid.

155 *OR* XXVII:2, 653.

156 Ibid. 603.

157 John Purifoy, "Concerning Battle of Gettysburg," *CV*, 19 (1911), 77.

158 *OR* XXVII:2, 323; Clark, Vol. II, 378.

159 NA, Record of Events (Donaldsonville Art'y), July & August 1863.

160 *OR* XXVII:2, 653.

161 Walters Diary, NPL.

162 Cire Memorandum, UDC.

163 Leon, 41.

164 Fox, 192.

CHAPTER TWELVE

1 McCarthy, Pamphlet No. 2, 217.

2 Ibid.

3 Ibid.

4 Walters Diary, NPL.

5 Westwood A. Todd, 140, UNCCH. Martinsburg, West Virginia, founded in 1778, is the seat of Berkeley County. The B.&O. Railroad roundhouse and station were built in 1849 and burned by "Stonewall" Jackson's troops in October 1862. The present roundhouse complex was rebuilt after the war and is a National Historic Landmark. The city's population is now over 17,000.

6 Walters Diary, NPL.

7 NA, Garnett's Artillery File. It was here that the sick quartermaster, Capt. Thomas M. Hewitt, turned over to Landry $400 in "QM" funds for the purchase of food and forage. Darkesville was established in 1791 along the turnpike and was known by a number of names (Darkes, Darkville, James Town, Locke, and five variations of Buckellstown). Originally Bucklesville, it was renamed Darkesville in honor of Gen. William Darke, a frontier hero at the time of its incorporation. Today it is an unincorporated historic district located on the Winchester Pike (U. S. Highway 11) that parallels Interstate 81.

8 Walters Diary, NPL.

9 An early western Virginia settlement located 2.7 miles south of Darkesville on the Winchester Pike, Bunker Hill today is an unincorporated town of 5,000. It has a historic district that includes Christ Episcopal Church or Morgan's Chapel, built in 1851, and the Presbyterian Church, built in 1854.

10 Stewart, 117.

11 Lineback, 67, UNCCH.

12 James J. Kirkpatrick Diary, 1861-1864, UT.

13 Leon, 41.

14 *OR* XXVII:3, 1111.

15 Walters Diary, NPL.

16 Everson, 257.

17 NA, Garnett's Battalion Artillery File. A pair of army shoes (brogans), cost $6.00 while the more expensive shoe, ankle boots, was likely necessary for the drivers who also wore spurs. *OR* IV:1, 371. *OR* IV:2, 230.

18 *OR* XXVII:2, 356, 612. PRS of Donaldsonville Artillery Muster Roll for July/August 1863, LAGL.

19 OR XXVII:2, 343-345.

20 Ibid. Pt. 2, 343.
21 Tower, 70.
22 Walters Diary, NPL.
23 Freeman, *Lee,* Vol. III, 144.
24 Walters Diary, NPL. The last eight days being July 13 to July 20, 1863.
25 The root bark of the 30 to 40 foot tall Sassafras tree makes a spicy tea, but one Confederate soldier reported the tea proved to be debilitating as a steady diet. Houghton, 60.
26 Westwood A. Todd, 140, UNCCH; Cockrell, 208, 209.
27 Welch, 75.
28 J. C. Goolsby, "Crenshaw Battery, Pegram's Battalion, Confederate States Artillery." *SHSP*, 28 (1900), 358.
29 Ibid.
30 Walters Diary, NPL. Everson, 257. Port Hudson, located about twenty-five miles north of Baton Rouge, was once a thriving little river port. In 1862 it became a Confederate stronghold guarding the Mississippi River, and after a forty-eight-day siege (the longest in American military history) and thousands of casualties, it surrendered to Union forces on July 9, 1863. One of the Confederate casualties was Captain François "Felix" LeBesque, commander of Company B, Twelfth Louisiana Battalion, Heavy Artillery. LeBesque had been a Donaldsonville Canonnier private from November 7, 1861, to February 5, 1862, when he obtained his discharge after appealing to the Secretary of War and received a Captain's commission. Sent from Virginia to Port Hudson, LeBesque died during the siege on July 1, 1863, in the general hospital after a protracted illness. Married with no children, his widow Felide never remarried and lived to an old age with her niece in New Orleans. NA, CSR; Confederate Pension Applications of Felide LeBesque, October 5, 1898, LSA.
31 Couture, 72.
32 Everson, 257.
33 W. R. Houghton and M. B. Houghton, *Two Boys in the Civil War and After* (Montgomery, Ala., 1912), 63.
34 McCarthy, Pamphlet No. 2, 217; Lineback, 67, UNCCH.
35 Justus Scheibert, *Seven Months in the Rebel States During the North American War, 1863* (Tuscaloosa, Ala., 1958), 124.
36 Walters Diary, NPL. Chartered in 1758, Newton today is called Stephens City with a population of 1,800 or so. The Stephens City United Methodist Church was located on the west side of the turnpike at the upper end of town. The sanctuary in 1863 was the second built and located on the foundation of the original log church constructed in 1789. The church was used as a hospital to treat wounded soldiers during the war, and though Federal troops burnt the parsonage when occupying the town, the sanctuary survived until 1882. It was then torn down and a third church built on the same site. The present Stephens City United Methodist Church was built in 1913 on a corner lot less than 100 feet to the south of the old building. SCUMC information provided by the church administration.

The Lutheran Church was Trinity Evangelical. It was built in 1812 with the brick building for the greater part taken down and a new, enlarged, neat, and handsome structure of brick and stone built in 1851. The bell from the former church hung in the new steeple. During the war the church was also used as a hospital and though mutilated in many ways survived until 1906 when a new church was built across the street. A brick auditorium was built on the site with the north wall being from the old church. Snyder Aleman and Hilda M. Lovett, *A Brief History of Trinity Evangelical Lutheran Church, Stephens City, Virginia 1765-1990.* (Stephens City, Va., 1990), 1-5. The hotel was The Tavern, a two-story, Flemish-bond brick, Federal-style dwelling with two interior gable-end chimneys, jack arches over the windows, and a gable roof of slate shingles. The first floor's north side was the parlor with the bar and liquor stock on the south side; the cooking was done in the basement kitchen in a huge fireplace and food carried to the upper level by servants. Four large bedrooms were located on the second floor. Constructed in 1819, it still stands at the town's main intersection and after extensive restoration, remains much the same as when it was built. It is home to the Newtown Historical Center (Museum), and maintained by the Stone House Foundation. Garland R. Quarles, *Some Old Homes in Frederick County, Virginia* (Winchester, Va., 1999), 200-202.

37 Tradition has it that Grand View, with its barn (the original barn was burned during the war),

and outbuildings that sat on a 285-acre tract of land, was built in 1848. It still stands as a private home. Nearby is the Family Drive-In Theater that opened in 1956 and is still in operation during the summer months. *The Winchester Star,* The Frederick County Edition, June 5, 1991; Maral S. Kalbian, *Frederick County, Virginia: History Through Architecture* (Winchester, Va., 1999), 169.

38 Cire Memorandum, UDC. The Valley Turnpike was a macadamized road constructed in 1838 from Winchester to Staunton. It became "the traffic way between the Lower and Upper Valley" and follows today's U. S. Route 11, though the configuration has changed some in certain locations with the straightening out of the road or turns, etc. Armistead C. Gordon, *In the Picturesque Shenandoah Valley* (Richmond, Va., 1930), 37.

39 Lineback, 67, UNCCH.

40 Walters Diary, NPL.

41 Cire Memorandum, UDC.

42 Walters Diary, NPL.

43 Ibid.

44 NA, Record of Events (Grandy's Battery), July & August 1863.

45 Walters Diary, NPL.

46 Jones Diary, LHAC.

47 Cire Memorandum, UDC.

48 Nestled in the valley on the North Fork of the Shenandoah River, the Strasburg settlement before 1761 developed primarily due to it being a crossroads of major routes of travel. Nicknamed "Pot Town" for its potteries, the industry had vanished by 1908. Massanutten Mountain terminates between Strasburg and Front Royal, which is located about sixteen miles to the southeast. Strasburg's population today is over 4,000. The Hotel Spengler, built about 1807, contained much fine woodwork. It was later renamed the Colonial Inn. It still stands today with the outside looking much the same as in 1863, though the first floor consist of retail space and the second floor with apartments. The Valley Pike follows the same route here as it did in 1863 although the appearance has changed with pavement, automobiles, signs, and numerous overhead wires.

49 Forbes, "The Moving Column," 45.

50 The courthouse in the center of Woodstock (seat of Shenandoah County), is today the oldest courthouse still in use west of the Blue Ridge. The town, with a population today of more than 4,500, was established in 1761 by an Act in Virginia's House of Burgesses that was sponsored by George Washington.

51 Walters Diary, NPL.

52 Cire Memorandum, UDC.

53 McCarthy, 52.

54 James D. Wilson and Louise E. Wilson, *Edinburg, 1861 to 1865, Civil War Incidents & Anecdotes* (Woodstock, Va., 1982), 27.

55 Walters Diary, NPL. Edinburg today has over 900 inhabitants, and the town still retains much of its nineteenth-century charm. The three-story Edinburg Mill on Stony Creek along the pike was built in 1848 and was in continuous operation as a gristmill until 1978. It was then converted into a home and restaurant. The town eventually bought the mill, and it is today a museum highlighting the Valley Pike and surrounding area.

56 McCarthy, 52, 53.

57 Walters Diary, NPL. Originally called Mount Pleasant, the name was changed to honor the hero of New Orleans. During the war Mount Jackson was a hospital town where even the Union Church, a little brick building built about 1825 and surrounded by trees and tombstones, was used as a hospital. The Confederate Cemetery contains graves of five hundred soldiers, 112 of them unknown. Population today is a little over 2,000.

58 Cire Memorandum, UDC.

59 New Market then and still today is one of the most attractive looking towns in the valley and has a population over 1,800.

60 U. S. Route 211 (Lee Highway), goes through Massanutten Pass, though it is now called New Market Gap and located amidst the George Washington National Forest. Massanutten Mountain is forty miles long and stands between the Shenandoah River's North and South Fork.

61 Cire Memorandum, UDC.

62 McCarthy, Pamphlet No. 2, 219.

63 Forbes, "Roadside Refreshment," 102.

64 Luray was established in 1812 and today has a population of nearly 5,000 people. The Luray Caverns system (discovered in 1878) is one of the largest in the country and is a major tourist attraction. Near Pumpkin Hill, Route 11 enters Shenandoah National Park, which stretches out along the crest of the Blue Ridge Mountains.
65 A. M. Machar, "The Whip-Poor-Will," *Scribners Monthly, An Illustrated Magazine for the People*, 20:4 (August 1880), 493.
66 Cire Memorandum, UDC.
67 Landry Diary, DPL.
68 Walters Diary, NPL.
69 Mary E. Hite. *My Rappahannock Story Book* (Richmond, Va., 1950), 272.
70 Walters Diary, NPL. It seems the battalion camped in the same fields that Stonewall Jackson's Corps did on the way to join Lee's army at Fredericksburg on November 25, 1862. See Virginia Historical Marker, Madison County: Rte. 612, 1 mile north of Criglersville. From Pumpkin Hill and up and through the mountain gap, down to Estes Mill on the other side is a little over twelve miles, about the same distance to the campsite on the Robinson River. The day's march totaled about twenty-four miles.
71 Walters Diary, NPL.
72 McCarthy, Pamphlet No. 2, 219, 220.
73 Dickert, 228.
74 Walters Diary, NPL. The red brick, gabled-roof court house building has an arcade front and octagonal cupola. Built in 1829, it is still in use. Even today the county is thinly settled with the population of Madison, the county seat, being nearly 300.
75 Cire Memorandum, UDC.
76 Ibid.
77 Lee, 90.
78 *OR* XXVII:2, 653, 654.
79 *OR* XXIX:2, 665.
80 Victor Maurin Letter, William Palmer Civil War Collection. The Western Reserve Historical Society.
81 Taylor, 149.
82 Welch, 75.
83 Walters Diary, NPL.
84 NA, Maurin file. The total amount signed for by Maurin was 6,000 pounds of corn, 375 pounds of sheaf, 12,312 pounds of hay, and 1,914 pounds of fodder. This equaled out to a daily average for each horse of 5 pounds of corn, 1/3 pound of sheaf, 10 pounds of hay, and 1 1/2 pounds of fodder. The amount was still under the normal prescribed ration of 14 pounds of hay and 12 pounds of oats, barley, or corn.
85 Runge, 56.
86 Jones Diary, LHAC.
87 Lobrano Diary, LHAC.
88 Tucker, 26.
89 Lobrano Diary, LHAC.
90 Cockrell, 214.
91 Wiley, *The Life of Johnny Reb*, 151, 168, 172, 347.
92 Jedehia Hotchkiss to wife, August 30, 1863, Jedehia Hotchkiss Papers, Library of Congress.
93 Henry E. Handerson, *Yankee in Gray: The Civil War Memoirs of Henry E. Handerson with a Selection of His Wartime Letters* (Cleveland, Ohio, 1962), 65.
94 Freeman, *Lee*, Vol. III, 162, 163.
95 Caldwell, 156
96 Landry Diary, DPL. "The cornmeal," wrote a veteran, "was harder to manage than flour." Houghton, 82.
97 *OR* LI:2, 754, 755.
98 Ibid.
99 NA, CSR; Chesson, 272. The Secession Club in Richmond was located on Main Street between 13th & 14th Streets.
100 NA, Maurin file. The Muster Roll was dated August 11, 1863. PRS of Donaldsonville Artillery Muster Roll for May/June 1863, LAGL.

101 Cire Memorandum, UDC.
102 Walters Diary, NPL. Walters identified the farm as owned by "a Mr. McMullon." It can be found in the OR Atlas, Plate LXXXIV, No. 8, and was located about half a mile northeast of Gordonsville between the Rockingham Turnpike and Orange Turnpike.
103 Thomas, 47.
104 Jones Diary, LHAC.
105 Josephus E. Strother Journal, Washington-Wilkes Historical Foundation.
106 Tucker, 26.
107 Born in Eindhoven, Holland, on September 1, 1815, he was one of two Redemptorist (the other was Father James Sheeran), who served as chaplains for the Confederacy. After a petition begging for a Catholic priest as chaplain by officers of the 8th Louisiana Infantry Regiment, Smulders was appointed by the Archbishop and the President of the Confederate States. He ministered to the troops all during the war. Father Smulders died on May 25, 1900, at the Rock Church, St. Louis. Hoegerl, 8, 10, 12.
108 Hoegerl, 12.
109 Cutrer, 209; Caldwell, 157.
110 *Times-Picayune,* June 30, 1902.
111 NA, Maurin file; PRS of Donaldsonville Artillery Muster Roll for July/August 1863, LAGL. The cost of the clothing taken out of the uniform allowance was: Pants-$11.00, Shirts-$2.50, Drawers-$2.50, Socks-$1.25, Shoes-$6.00.
112 NA, Maurin file; Cockrell, 210; Caldwell, 156.
113 Cockrell, 209.
114 John S. Robson, *How a One-legged Rebel Lives, Reminiscences of the Civil War* (Durham, N.C., 1898), 13.
115 Thomas, 47.
116 Stuart T. Wright, ed. *The Confederate Letters of Benjamin H. Freeman* (Hicksville, N.Y., 1974), 26, 27, 29.
117 Cockrell, 219.
118 NA, Maurin file. The rations for the animals signed for by Maurin in the beginning of September were 10,338 pounds of corn, 8,649 pounds of new corn, 4,330 pounds of hay, and 11,874 pounds of fodder. This equaled out to a daily average for 60 horses of 10 ½ pounds of corn, almost 2 ½ pounds of hay, and 6 ½ pounds of fodder, which was a little more than the previous month's daily ration though it remained under the norm of 26 pounds per horse per day.
119 Forbes, "A Wagoner's Camp," 198.
120 NA, Garnett's Battalion file, M-258.
121 Billings, *Hardtack,* 177
122 Walters Diary, NPL.
123 Bertram H. Groene, ed., "Civil War Letters of Colonel David Lang," *The Florida Historical Quarterly* 14 (1976), 358.
124 NA, CSR; Ibid., Record of Events (Donaldsonville Art'y), September & October 1863. Of the remaining original members, 4 were detailed, 10 had resigned or were discharged, 4 were killed in battle, 5 had died from sickness, 4 were in the hospital, 2 were in the hands of the enemy, and 3 were absent without leave.
125 Cire Memorandum, UDC.
126 NA, Record of Events for September & October 1863 of Moore and Penick's batteries respectively. Lee's Army of Northern Virginia at this time was minus Longstreet's First Corps with three artillery battalions that were in mid-September sent to General Braxton Bragg's Army of Tennessee. Longstreet's command would later return.
127 Rapid Ann Station is now called Rapidan Station. The banks of the Rapidan River have changed radically since 1863-64 because of floods. The River Road as traveled by the soldiers washed away in the flood of 1937. There followed more damaging floods but the worst one was in June 1995 when the river was thirty-two feet high and so rampant the last public steel truss bridge in Orange County, the 195-foot span Willis Bridge (built in 1906), was swept off its columns and twisted to the Culpeper County bank. This bridge was a little down river from the old Willis Ford or Horse Ford. Patricia J. Hurst, *The History and People of Clark Mountain, Orange County, Virginia* (Rapidan, Va., 1988), 126, 127, 131.
128 Wilson, 137, 138. The twin peaks today are known as Buzzard's Mountain. See *OR* Atlas, Plate

XLIV, No. 3 and Plate XLV, No. 1.
129 James J. Kirkpatrick Diary, 1861-1864, UT.
130 Ibid.
131 Ibid.
132 Powell was in the area visiting his son Capt. Thomas N. Powell in the 10th Louisiana Infantry Regiment.
133 Bartlett, 55.
134 Landry Diary, DPL; Christopher G. Pena, *Touched By War, Battles Fought in the Lafourche District* (Thibodaux, La., 1998), 334, 397. On June 28, 1863, a force of Texas cavalry attacked Fort Butler at Donaldsonville and were repulsed with the aid of Union gunboats. See *OR* Vol. XXVI:1.
135 A. F. Rightor to Andrew McCollam, December 3, 1864, Andrew McCollam Papers, UNCCH.
136 Charles Batchelor to Father, August 12, 1863, Batchelor Papers, LSU.
137 Ibid.
138 NA, Record of Events (Donaldsonville Art'y), September & October 1863; Walters Diary, NPL.
139 Cockrell, 215, 216.
140 Ibid.
141 *New Orleans Times-Democrat,* July 14, 1877.
142 Ibid.
143 *Fais do-do* is the French equivalent of a shindig, a social gathering with dancing. Not far from the Donaldsonville Artillery camp along the Old Fredericksburg Road, today's Clark Mountain Road, stood Mount Pisgah Baptist Church or the New Brick Church (built in 1853), and across the road on the northside the all denomination Old Mount Pisgah Meeting House or Orange Chapel, made of wood sometime before 1839. They were the likely gathering places for the dances. Both buildings have since been torn down. Patricia J. Hurst, *Soldiers, Stories, Sites and Fights, Orange County, Virginia 1861-1865 and the Aftermath* (Rapidan, Va., 1998), 284.
144 *OR* Atlas, Plate LXXXVII, No. 4. Madison Mills was named in 1792 for the family of James Madison, fourth President of the United States, who operated the mill located on the Rapidan River that constituted the boundary for Orange and Madison County. The Lee farm was located on the Orange County side. Just north of Madison Mill in Madison County is Hebron Lutheran Church (built in 1740); it is today the oldest continuously operated Lutheran Church in the United States and one of a handful of wooden Virginia churches that predate the Revolutionary War. Renovated in 1962, it still today has in use its circa 1800 Tanneburg organ, unmodified, and the only one remaining where it was erected. W. Huddle, *History of the Hebron Lutheran Church, Madison County, Virginia, from 1717 to 1907* (Madison, Va., 1908).
145 Cire Memorandum, UDC; Wise, Vol. II, 717; Caldwell, 157.
146 NA, Garnett Battalion file, M258; NA, Maurin file. The other batteries received as follows: Grandy's 66 horses- 9,378 lbs. corn, 536 lbs. oats, 7,168 lbs. fodder; Moore's 57 horses- 11,170 ½ lbs. corn, 456 lbs. oats, 8,778 lbs. fodder; Penick's 62 horses- 12,888 ½ lbs. corn, 496 oats, 10,416 fodder. NA, Capt. Charles R. Grandy file; Capt. Joseph D. Moore file; Capt. Nathan Penick file.
147 NA, Maurin file. The gun with serial number "1814" was made by the Anderson Company at the Tredegar Iron Works in Richmond and stamped with "J. R. A. & Co." The gun weighed 1,255 pounds. Tredegar Gun Foundry Book, Virginia State Library. The implements received were 2 sponges & covers, 1 water bucket, 2 gunner's haversacks, 2 tube pouches, 1 vent cover, 1 vent punch, 1 gunner's gimlet, 2 priming wires, 2 lanyards, 2 thumbstalls, 1 fuse cutter, 1 harness.
Capt. John W. Lewis resigned as commander of the Pittsylvania Artillery on July 29, 1863, and Lt. Nathan Penick, a teacher and Baptist preacher, pious and Christian, and 32 years of age, was promoted on July 31, 1863. Remaining assigned to Garnett's Battalion, Lewis' Battery from then on was known as Penick's Battery. Lyman W. Priest, *The Penick Family; Descendants of Edward Penick, Penix, Pinix of St. Peter's Parish, New Kent County, Virginia* (Verona, Va., 1982), 110, 111.
148 There is nothing in the record that signifies exactly when the Donaldsonville Artillery obtained the two rifle guns. The circumstantial evidence suggest it was at this time. When Maurin wrote the letter to Pendleton in August seeking the return of their two guns the battery had just 44 horses, enough to pull three guns and their caissons. At this time, the first week in October, the battery had seventy-three horses, enough for a full six-gun contingent. Additionally, Maurin on

October 8, 1863, received six sets of artillery harness.

149 McCarthy, Pamphlet No. 2, 224.

150 NA, Maurin file. The invoice of the Captain's unserviceable equipment was 4 sets of artillery harness, 10 pairs of tracer, 18 bridles, 10 pairs harness, 4 officer horse saddles, 3 drivers saddles, and 280 feet of picket rope.

151 Nearby in the Madison Cemetery a monolith marks his grave.

152 Cire Memorandum, UDC.

153 Lineback, 83, UNCCH.

154 Freeman, *Lee,* Vol. III, 174; *OR* XXVIV:2, 426.

155 Cire Memorandum, UDC.

156 Lineback, 83, UNCCH; Mellon, 257; Leon, 49.

157 Cire Memorandum, UDC. Cire wrote "Robertson" river.

158 James J. Kirkpatrick Diary, 1861-1864, UT.

159 Caldwell, 159.

160 Cire Memorandum, UDC. Cire wrote "Hews" river.

161 Leon, 49.

162 Mellon, 257. The march turned east near present day Revercombs Corner.

163 Caldwell, 159.

164 Cire Memorandum, UDC. From the Waterloo Turnpike the column headed north on Dulin's Ford Road, crossed the river at Glen Mill to Palmer's Crossroads, then turned east towards Warrenton. Glen Woolen Mills was located in a Rappahannock River hollow known as The Glen, about two miles from Waterloo. All that remains of the woolen factory today is a chimney in a field.

165 Couture, 80.

166 Walters Diary, NPL.

167 Caldwell, 160. George G. Meade commanded the northern Army of the Potomac.

168 Cire Memorandum, UDC.

169 Mellon, 257, 258.

170 Bennett, 137.

171 Walters Diary, NPL.

172 Ibid.

173 Landry Diary, DPL.

174 Caldwell, 160.

175 Poague, 80; Westwood A. Todd Papers, UNCCH; NA, Record of Events (Donaldsonville Art'y), September & October 1863.

176 Cockrell, 214.

177 *OR* XXVIV:2, 427, 436-38. The Battle of Bristoe Station cost Lee about 1,900 casualties with Federal losses in the II Corps at 548.

178 Cire Memorandum, UDC.

179 Landry Diary, DPL.

180 Cire Memorandum, UDC.

181 Landry Diary, DPL.

182 Cire Memorandum, UDC. Warrenton Junction at Calverton is nine miles southeast of Warrenton, where a branch line left the Orange & Alexandria Railroad.

183 Walters Diary, NPL.

184 Welch, 81.

185 Walters Diary, NPL.

186 Ibid.

187 Cire Memorandum, UDC.

188 Lineback, 87, UNCCH.

189 Watkins Kearn Diary, Virginia Historical Society.

190 Lineback, 87, UNCCH.

191 Walters Diary, NPL.

192 Cire Memorandum, UDC.

193 Mellon, 255.

194 Watkins Kearn Diary, Virginia Historical Society.

195 McCarthy, Pamphlet No. 2, 229.

196 NA, CSR. Capt. Thomas Hewitt was the battalion's quartermaster and went to Richmond sick. He was later dropped from the rolls on the recommendation of a medical examining board in February 1864.

197 NA, Garnett, Richardson, and Maurin files. The clothing allowance cost for the articles was $25.00 for an overcoat, $9.00 per blanket, $12.00 per jacket, and now $8.00 for a pair of shoes.

198 Landry Diary, DPL.

199 PRS of Donldsonville Artillery Muster Roll for September/October 1863, LAGL.

200 Couture, 83. The Donaldsonville Artillery listed just five men in camp sick and eight men absent sick. Italics are the authors with the French translation being *en toutes circonstances,* the chapter's title.

CHAPTER THIRTEEN

1 Walters Diary, NPL.

2 Freeman, *Lieutenants*, Vol. 3, 265-269.

3 Cire Memorandum, UDC.

4 Lineback, 91, UNCCH.

5 Walters Diary, NPL.

6 Ibid.

7 Ibid.

8 Cire Memorandum, UDC.

9 Landry Diary, DPL.

10 Wilson, 143.

11 Walters Diary, NPL.

12 James J. Kirkpatrick Diary, 1861-1864, UT.

13 Wilson, 143.

14 Landry Diary, DPL; Wilson, 143.

15 Cire Memorandum, UDC.

16 Lineback, 91, UNCCH.

17 Ibid.

18 Cire Memorandum, UDC.

19 James J. Kirkpatrick Diary, 1861-1864, UT. The campsite is believed to have been located between present day River Dale Lane and Spring Hill Lane near Virginia Secondary State Route 689 (Willis Bridge Road). SSR 736 (Willis Ford Road), is across the river. Both routes dead end near the river as there is no bridge across since the Willis Bridge washed away in 1995.

20 Cockrell, 214.

21 Albert Schmidt to Father, November 21, 1863, Gustavus Schmidt Correspondences, LSU.

22 Twenty-two pieces of equipage were received by the Maurin's Battery: 1 sponge & rammer, 3 sponge covers, 1 sponge bucket, 1 worm & staff, 2 spare poles, 20 halters, 1 ½ lbs. of dubbin (oil and tallow for leather), 2 harness awls, 1 paper of harness needles, 1 lb. of iron tacks, 6 cavalry bridles, 12 collars, 20 collar pads, 3 pair of spurs and straps, 1 lb. shoe thread, 1 paper of tacks, a tar bucket, 4 (fur), water buckets, 1 lb. black ware, 60 pounds of axle grease, 1 pintle hook key, and 1 battery lantern. NA, Maurin file.

23 Cire Memorandum, UDC.

24 Ibid.

25 NA, Record of Events (Donaldsonville Art'y), November & December 1863; Couture, 87; Lineback, 95, UNCCH; Walters, NPL.

26 *OR* LI:2, 788. On November 25, 1863, Grandy and probably Moore and Penick's guns were assigned from the artillery camp to the defensive line between the Rapidan and Robinson rivers.

27 NA, Record of Events (Donaldsonville Art'y), Record of Events November & December 1863.

28 Tower, 94.

29 Cire Memorandum, UDC.

30 Orange Springs, near present day Danton and the intersection of the Pamunky and the Old Fredericksburg Road, was a well-known resort from the 1790s with three mineral springs near Terry's Run. The seventh generation of the Coleman family still lives in the house that was originally the hotel for the springs. Orange County Historical Society, Map of Orange, Jeremy

Francis Gilmore Collection, Virginia Historical Society.

31 James J. Kirkpatrick Diary, 1861-1864, UT.

32 Cire Memorandum, UDC.

33 The present and second church was built in 1853 and has retained its original, historic architecture with two front doors and an inside gallery.

34 Jones, *The Civil War Memoirs of Captain William J. Seymour*, 101.

35 McCarthy, Pamphlet No. 2, 233. Like Cire's memorandum, many contemporary accounts simply refer to Verdiersville without indicating whether it was the new or old hamlet. New Verdiersville on the newer Orange Plank Road consisted of just three or four buildings. It was one and one-half mile south of Old Verdiersville with its four structures. Then as now a road connects them. Lee made his headquarters during part of the campaign at the Catlett Rhoades' house (a small frame structure on side of the road), in New Verdiersville. The house stood near the intersection of the Orange Plank Road (SSR 621), and State Route 20, where now stands a more recent house with a beauty shop and auto repair shop. Route 20 follows the original Orange Turnpike, or very close to it, but it is significantly further south of the turnpike in the area of the two Verdiersville. Greg Mertz to author, November 16, 2004, correspondence, FSNM.

36 Freeman, *Lieutenants*, Vol. III, 275.

37 McCarthy, Pamphlet No. 2, 234.

38 Tower, 94.

39 Cire Memorandum, UDC.

40 Many of the Mine Run built earthworks still exist, although none are on public property and very few are visible from public roads. These entrenchments and other fortifications on privately owned land are about as well preserved as any Civil War sites. Greg Mertz to author, November 16, 2004, correspondence, FSNM.

41 Ibid.

42 Walters, NPL.

43 McCarthy, Pamphlet No. 2, 235; Caldwell, 166.

44 Walters, NPL.

45 Clark, Vol. II, 588.

46 Cockrell, 217.

47 Cire Memorandum, UDC.

48 Freeman, *Lee,* Vol. III, 201, 202.

49 Walters, NPL.

50 Ibid.

51 *OR* XXIX:1, 829.

52 Record Roll of Donaldsonville Artillery, 1861-1865, LHAC.

53 NA, CSR. Judice is buried in Row 2, Number 10, Confederate Section, Lynchburg City Cemetery. In this section lie 2,701 Confederate soldiers with each grave marked with the soldier's initials, company, regiment and state. Lucy H. M. Baber and Evelyn L. Moore, *Behind the Old Brick Wall, A Cemetery Story* (Lynchburg, Va., 1968), 233.

54 Hurst, *Soldiers*, 114.

55 Wilson, 143, 144.

56 Cire Memorandum, UDC.

57 Lineback, 99, UNCCH.

58 Tower, 95.

59 Lee, 308.

60 Cire Memorandum, UDC.

61 Cockrell, 231.

62 James J. Kirkpatrick Diary, 1861-1864, UT.

63 Freeman, *Lee,* Vol. III, 251, 252.

64 Cire Memorandum, UDC.

65 McCarthy, 80.

66 *Biographical and Historical Memoirs of Louisiana,* Vol. II, 245.

67 NA, Maurin file. The "Fuel requisition for January 1864" listed the number present in the battery.

68 Walters, NPL. Pegram and Pougue's battalions also camped near Lindsay's Turnout while Haskell's (of Longstreet's Corps) and apparently McIntosh's made camp near Cobham Station,

about three miles further south on the railroad line. Cutt's Battalion was the only Third Corps artillery battalion that remained on the picket line near Rapidan Station.

69 NA, Garnett's Battalion file. Grandy, Moore, and Penick had 67, 61, and 61 horses in their batteries after turning in 3, 8, and 7 unserviceable horses at the end of the year.

70 Landry Diary, DPL.

71 McCarthy, 80, 81.

72 Cire Memorandum, UDC.

73 McCarthy, 81, 83-85.

74 William Pegram to Sister, December 16, 1863, Pegram-Johnson-McIntosh Collection, Virginia Historical Society.

75 McCarthy, 87.

76 Driver, 47; J. B. A. Dabbs, December 16, 1863, J. B. A. Dabbs Letters. University South Carolina.

77 Cire Memorandum, UDC.

78 Cockrell, 221.

79 Lineback, 103, UNCCH.

80 *Donaldsonville Chief,* December 30, 1876.

81 Landry Diary, DPL.

82 PRS of Donaldsonville Artillery Muster Roll for November & December 1863, LAGL.

83 PRS of Donaldsonville Artillery Muster Roll for January & February 1864, LAGL.

84 NA, Maurin file. That many of the Donaldsonville Canonniers wore Yankee uniforms is established in that three, Sgt. Oscar Demesme, Pvt. Abraham Klotz, and Pvt. Eugene Levy were chronicled from scant written sources of wearing the blue in 1864 and 1865. Additional corroboration that the Gunners of Donaldson of Garnett's Battalion wore Federal jackets and long coats at Camp Taylor in the winter of 1863-64 was revealed to the author during a research trip in September 1994. Upon meeting a prolific Civil War artifact metal detector, Raymond Shaw of Inglewood Farm near Gordonsville, Virginia, he brought the author and his father Robert "Bob" Marshall on September 24, 1994, to an isolated woods near Lindsey's. There he pointed out where he had previously detected, dug, and recovered artillery implements and numerous horse shoes, along with one Louisiana State seal (Pelican) jacket button, five Virginia State seal buttons, and a "few" Confederate "A" artillery buttons. Garnett's Battalion consisted of three Virginia batteries and the Donaldsonville Artillery, the only Louisiana battery that camped in this area near Lindsey's Turnout. According to Shaw there is no evidence to suggest that at any time during the war other units from either side camped at this location. The relative component of Shaw's find in conjunction with the wearing of United States blue army jackets and coats by Garnett's artillerymen was the recovery of "at least a dozen" Federal "Eagle with I" infantry coat buttons found throughout the campsite.

85 Freeman, *Lee,* Vol. III, 246, 247.

86 Couture, 92.

87 Caldwell, 168.

88 *OR* XXXIII, 1076.

89 Ibid., 1114.

90 Ibid., 1117.

91 Benevolent Association of the Army of Northern Virginia Application of L. A. Landry, April 22, 1882, LHAC.

92 *OR* LI:2, 755. Pvt. Laurent Desire Arcenaux joined the cavalry and served honorably until paroled at Natchitoches, Louisiana, on June 6, 1865. NA, CSR.

93 Adam Shriver Confederate Pension Application, Texas State Library and Archives.

94 Robert F. Pace, "'It was Bedlam Let Loose': The Louisiana Sugar Country and the Civil War," *Louisiana History*, 39 (1998), 398.

95 *Biographical and Historical Memoirs of Louisiana,* II: 244, 245; NA, Maurin file; *Donaldsonville Daily Times*, January 23, 1897; *Donaldsonville Chief,* October 16, 1916.

96 "Board of Pension Commissioners, Confederate Pension Applications," Microfilm; Capt. Prosper Landry to Pension Board, April 21, 1902, LDA.

97 Cockrell, 226.

98 Freeman, *Lee,* Vol. III, 252. NA, Maurin and Garnett Battalion files. In January, Grandy's Battery lost another six horses, Moore's lost seven, and Penick's lost thirteen.

99 William Pegram to Sister, February 11, 1864, Pegram-Johnson-McIntosh Collection, Virginia Historical Society.
100 NA, CSR of Richardson.
101 Donaldsonville Canonnier Pvt. Ernest Monnot in a "Miscellaneous Accounts Book" kept a cure for "Colic in Horses" that read: "The following remedy never fails to give relief in this disease if promptly administered in good time. Sulphuric ether, one pint aromatic spirits of ammonia, one pint sweet spirits of nitre, two pints of opium, one fourth of assafoetidappav. [asafoetida] one pint camphor 1/4 pound. mix. Let stand 14 days before using. dose one oz. or less according to size of animal every thirty minutes until relieved. The above is efficient for a farm having 40 to 50 mules." Monnot/Lanier Family Papers, University of New Orleans.
102 Cire Memorandum, UDC.
103 Ibid.
104 Walters, NPL. Grandy sent two guns to Cobham Station, about three miles down the Virginia Central Railroad tracks.
105 Landry Diary, DPL.
106 Walters, NPL. The advance was a demonstration made at Morton's Ford by Meade's Second Corps, Army of the Potomac. *OR* XXXIII, 114.
107 *OR* XXXVI:2, 946.
108 *OR* XXXIII, 1269.
109 NA, Garnett Battalion files.
110 McCarthy, Pamphlet No. 2, 238.
111 M. Cockrell, 81.
112 *OR* XXXIII, 1144.
113 Douglas S. Freeman, ed. *Lee's Dispatches* (New York, 1915), 138, 139. A footnote by the editor states, "The 'Louisiana' battery was either Moody's, 1st Corps, or Landry's, 3rd Corps, sometimes called respectively the 'Madison' and the Donaldsonville batteries. The Washington Artillery may possibly be meant." Lee absolutely was signifying Captain Victor Maurin's Donaldsonville Artillery. At the time Moody's Battery was with Longstreet's Corps in Tennessee and the four batteries of the Battalion Washington Artillery were spending their winter detached at Petersburg, Virginia. The only other Louisiana battery to serve in the Army of Northern Virginia was the Louisiana Guard Battery with Ewell's Second Corps. They were captured on November 7, 1863, with Hay's Brigade at Rappahannock Station and the remnants sent to Richmond for reorganization. Text made "Bold" by author.
114 *OR* XXXIII, 1173.
115 *OR* XXIX:2, 840, 841.
116 NA, M331, A. & I. G. records.
117 Freeman, *Lee,* Vol. III, 224, 225.
118 Trower, 111; Order No. 47, HQ ANV; William N. Pendleton Papers, MCR.
119 NA, Garnett's file; William N. Pendleton to Maj. David G. McIntosh, February 20, 1864, William N. Pendleton Papers, UNCCH.
120 Landry Diary, DPL.
121 Walters, NPL.
122 Ibid.
123 Ibid.
124 The person making the charges most assuredly was Third Corps Artillery Chief Rueben Lindsey Walker. Garnett eventually became Inspector of Artillery in the Army of Tennessee. Garnett never faulted Lee for his dismissal and in July 1896 wrote about Lee at Gettysburg in Frank Leslie's *Popular Monthly* magazine. A year later he expanded that article and contributed another for an adulatory biography about the general in *Robert Edward Lee, Soldier, Citizen and Christian Patriot.* The above articles were similar versions of his book, *Gettysburg, A Complete Historical Narrative of the Battle of Gettysburg, and the Campaign Preceeding It*; published in 1888 by New York's J. M. Hill. Garnett was a native of Wakefield, Westmoreland County, Virginia, and at 68 years of age took his own life on September 12, 1902, in New York City, where he was president of the St. James Publishing Company. Following the war and up to 1872 he directed the Weston Military Institute at Weston, Fairfield County, Connecticut. Afterward Garnett lived in New York for thirty years where he held public office, worked as a city editor of a daily newspaper, and had interests in several theatrical enterprises. He had a country home in Baldwin, Staten Island,

where his wife survived him. Garnett was a friend of Pres. Theodore Roosevelt, a prominent member of the Southern Society and of the Confederate Camp of Veterans in New York City. In ceremonies at General Lee's Richmond Monument unveiling, Garnett, on behalf of the camp, received a banner and in a speech stated: "When we enrolled ourselves beneath that [Confederate] banner we believed that we were right and that belief was vital in our heart." Of New York social interest, Garnett in December 1886 "created great enthusiasm by toasting Miss [Winnie] Davis [former Confederate President Jefferson Davis' daughter] as 'A Nation's queen, born in a Nation's anguish.' Afterwards . . . several solos were sung by Colonel Garnett . . . the entire company joined in singing 'Dixie's Land,' 'God Save the Queen' and the 'Star Spangled Banner,' Miss Davis taking part in the latter song with great enthusiasm." Garnett was well known on upper Broadway (New York's Tenderloin District, an entertainment and red-light area in the heart of Manhattan), where, in July 1892, a newspaper reported: "The Colonel was the hero of an adventure . . . which created considerable comment." The story relates how the fifty-eight-year-old Garnett, after being confronted, landed with one blow a knockout punch to his much younger antagonist. *New York Times*, September 13, 1902, May 30, 1890; *Richmond Daily Times*, September 13, 1902; *Richmond Dispatch*, September 13, 1902; *New York Herald*, December 24, 1886, July 2, 1892.

125 NA, Richardson CSR. The disparaging remarks by Richardson were most likely directed at Walker.

126 NA, Garnett Battalion file. Landry signed for: Five quires fools cap paper, five steel pens, one pen holder, twenty-five letter envelopes, twenty-five official envelopes, one led pencil, and one blank book.

127 Cire Memorandum, UDC.

128 NA, Maurin and Garnett battalion files.

129 S. A. Poche to Members of the Board of Directors of Camp Nicholls, May 7, 1896, Camp Nicholls Soldier's Home File, LAGL.

130 McCarthy, 41.

131 Walters, NPL. The orders for deployment was a result of Brig. Gen. George A. Custer's cavalry division making a diversionary raid to Charlottesville, Virginia, in support of the Kilpatrick-Dahlgren raid on Richmond from February 28 to March 4, 1864.

132 Walters, NPL.

133 Ibid.

134 Cire Memorandum, UDC.

135 Walters, NPL.

136 Ibid.

137 Ibid.

138 Cire Memorandum, UDC.

139 J. Q. Dabbs letter, March 5, 1864, Eugene Whitefield Dabbs Papers, University of South Carolina.

140 Lafcadio Hearn, *Gombo Zhebes, Little Dictionary of Creole Proverbs* (New York, 1885), 3.

141 McCarthy, 86.

142 Ibid., 75, 76.

143 Jean Reynaud Jacques Prosper Landry to Adele Pedesclaux Landry, September 1864 letter, UV.

144 PRS of Donaldsonville Artillery Muster Roll for January/February 1864, LAGL.

145 NA, CSR.

146 Landry Diary, DPL.

147 *OR* XXXVI:2, 945.

148 NA, Garnett's Battalion file.

149 Landry Diary, DPL.

150 NA, CSR. The only other "In arrest or Confinement" listed (with one man), on a Donaldsonville Artillery Muster Roll occurred in July/August 1863, LAGL.

151 Freeman, *Lee*, Vol. III, 240.

152 *OR* XXXIII, 1150.

153 Freeman, *Lee*, Vol. III, 241; Pougue, 81, 82.

154 Hoegerl, 12, 11.

155 Cockrell, 231.

156 William N. Pendleton to Gen. R. E. Lee (report draft), UNCCH. The final version can be found in *OR* XXIX:2, 839-842; NA, Richardson's CSR; Frederickburg and Spotsylvania National

Battlefield Park, Charles Richardson file. Regarding promotions in the artillery see Freeman, *Lee*, Vol. III, 222, 223.

157 Landry Diary, DPL.

158 NA, Maurin file; *OR* Series IV, III, 178; *OR* XXIX:2, 853, 854.

159 *OR* XLII:3, 1341.

160 There is no documentation that Maurin was hospitalized, but the only explanation can be that he was sick and unable to command. It appears that he went to Lynchburg, Virginia, to recover in the beginning of April 1864. The last requesition Maurin signed for his battery, Company "B," during this time was on March 31, 1864, for two camp kettles and seventy pounds of salt for the horses.

161 Confederate Pension Application of Michel Morin. Capt. Prosper Landry to Pension Board, April 21, 1902, LDA.

162 Report of Artillery Companies, Third Corps at Camp Taylor, April 9, 1864, William N. Pendleton Papers, UNCCH.

163 Landry Diary, DPL.

164 Walters Diary, NPL.

165 William M. Dame, *From the Rapidan to Richmond and the Spotsylvania Campaign* (Baltimore, 1920), 62. Italics are the author's and the translation in French is the chapter's title, "Notre travail, notre loisir."

CHAPTER FOURTEEN

1 Levy Diary, HUC. Unfortunately, Levy's other three journals were kept in a trunk in storage at Richmond. When the capital was partially burned in April 1865, the trunk went up in flames. The diaries were particularly rich in detail, and if they had survived the inferno the history of the Donaldsonville Artillery from 1861 through 1865 quite possibly would have been published due to Levy's literary skill and love of books.

2 Cobham Station information from Martha Smith of Cobham, Virginia, letter to author, April 3, 2003. The depot building was moved in 1907 to Bracketts Farm near Trevilians in Louisa County and still stands as a private home. A new depot was built at Cobham and lasted until 1966, when it was sold for $1.00 and torn down. A few homes remain near the railroad tracks at Cobham Station Lane (County Road 640).

3 Walters, NPL. Richardson's promotion from Major was effective April 30, 1864, though he took rank from February 27, 1864. NA, Richardson file.

4 Lineback, 115, UNCCH.

5 Levy Diary, HUC.

6 Ibid.

7 Ibid.

8 Mr. Arthur M. Colomb of San Francisco, Maurin's grandson, has the original commission presented to Victor Maurin in his possession. Mr. Colomb graciously photocopied a copy for the author on April 3, 1997. The appointment date is March 14, 1864, "to rank as such from" February 27, 1864. Maurin was believed to be in Lynchburg at this time due to sickness.

9 Cire Memorandum, UDC.

10 Walters, NPL. In the interchange of guns the Donaldsonville Artillery received Moore's three Richmond made 10-pounder Parrott's for their three Napoleons. Grandy swapped a 3-inch ordnance rifle for Penick's Napoleon.

11 Levy Diary, HUC.

12 Landry Diary, DPL.

13 This was the beginning of the Wilderness Campaign. Anticipating the movement of the Federal army now led by General Ulysses S. Grant, Lee moved the Army of Northern Virginia's Second Corps on the Orange Turnpike and Hill's Third Corps (minus Anderson's Division and Cutt's Artillery Battalion) on the Plank Road toward Chancellorsville. Lee hoped to strike the Federals moving through the difficult terrain. Longstreet's First Corps, now back with the army, and Stuart's cavalry moved to join the attack while Anderson and Cutt's artillery guarded the rear near Orange Court House. Boatner, 919.

14 Levy Diary, HUC. It was noted that Levy's bunk mate, Canonnier Pvt. Tim Boham, a thirty-

two-year-old Louisiana native and Donaldsonville resident who left his wife when embarking in September 1861 with the battery, was "detailed to bear the letter" to headquarters requesting more horses on May 4, 1864.

15 Jean Reynaud Jaques Prosper Landry to Adele Pedesclaux Landry, September 1864, UV.

16 Ibid.

17 *New Orleans Daily City Item,* February 27, 1880.

18 Ibid., February 28, 1880.

19 Miller died in New Orleans on February 26, 1880. "In respect to the memory of Capt. M. Buck Miller" the post-war Donaldsonville Artillery fired, under direction of Prosper Landry, a series of minute-guns. *Donaldsonville Chief,* March 6, 1880.

20 *Biographical and Historical Memoirs of Louisiana,* I:532.

21 Jean Reynaud Jacques Prosper Landry to Adele Pedesclaux Landry, September 1864, UV.

22 Ibid.

23 Levy Diary, HUC.

24 Landry Diary, DPL. The dates are May 5, 6, and 7. Octave Landry made no entries for May 8 and 9, 1864.

25 Levy Diary, HUC. Beans were usually given to the hungry artilleryman by local residents.

26 Ibid. The battalion had forty-two unserviceable horses remaining. Report of Artillery Companies, Third Corps at Camp Taylor, April 9, 1864, William N. Pendleton Papers, UNCCH.

27 Cire Memorandum, UDC.

28 Landry Diary, DPL.

29 Levy Diary, HUC.

30 Brig. Gen. George A. Custer's cavalry brigade attacked Beaver Dam Station on May 9-10 and caused serious damage to the Virginia Central Railroad running between Richmond and Gordonsville.

31 Levy Diary, HUC.

32 Ibid.

33 *Biographical and Historical Memoirs of Louisiana,* I:532.

34 Jean Reynard Jaques Prosper Landry to Adele Pedesclaux Landry, September 1864, UV.

35 Landry Diary, DPL. The seventy-four horses were for both batteries and would not be enough to outfit them.

36 Levy Diary, HUC. Sergeant Ruffin B. Walker of the 7th Louisiana Regiment was, like Levy, a clerk in New Orleans before the war. Ruffin was captured on November 7, 1863, at Rappahannock Station and imprisoned at Point Lookout, Maryland, until exchanged on March 15, 1864. Now guarding prisoners, Walker soon returned to his command and was again captured after being wounded in the right thigh at Monocacy, Maryland, on Early's Washington raid in July 1864. Walker was again exchanged from Point Lookout on September 28, 1864. NA, CSR.

37 Levy Diary, HUC.

38 Landry Diary, DPL.

39 Levy Diary, HUC.

40 Kuhn was probably buried with a wooden headboard in burial fields behind the Exchange Hotel near camp. Soon after the war ended the soldiers buried in these fields were moved to the Confederate Soldier Section of Gordonsville's Maplewood Cemetery. Hurst, *Soldiers,* 275-279.

41 Jean Reynaud Jaque Prosper Landry to Adele Pedesclaux Landry, September 1864, UV.

42 Ibid.

43 *Donaldsonville Chief,* June 15, 1907.

44 Levy Diary, HUC. Levy had no shelter because he "left my tent with Mrs. Mann who keeps the hotel at Gordonsville." The road taken from Gordonsville parallels the Virginia Central Railroad and passed through Louisa Courthouse, then six miles beyond Tolersville. There, with Richmond forty-seven miles further east, Miller's command turned off and headed northeast at the depot town of Tolersville now known as Mineral. The United States Post Office changed the name in 1899. Before it was called Mineral City because of the discovery and mining of several mineral deposits after the war.

45 Ibid. No information has been located regarding Dr. Gibson's farm.

46 The McKenney farm is found in *O. R. Atlas,* Plate XCVI, Map 3, "Map of the Battle-field of Spotsylvania Court House, Va." Today there are some scattered houses along the road and a driveway that leads back to a house that stands in the area of where the old McKenney house

would have been. The property is well outside the Fredericksburg and Spotsylvania National Military Park—about two miles south of the park's nearest boundary. "As it is in Spotsylvania County the farm site could become a subdivision at anytime" wrote historian Don Pfanz to author, November 3, 2004, correspondence, FSNMP.

47 Levy Diary, HUC; John W. H. Porter, *A Record of Events in Norfolk County, Virginia, From April 19th, 1861, to May 10th, 1862, With a History of the Soldiers and Sailors of Norfolk County, Norfolk City and Portsmouth Who Served in the Confederate States Army or Navy* (Portsmouth, Va., 1892), 253, 257, 258. Porter listed one man wounded in Grandy's Battery and one wounded and two killed in Moore's Battery in fighting at Spotsylvania Court House during this time.

48 Spotsylvania Court House was a modest settlement of three churches, a hotel, a store, and a few county buildings.

49 Levy Diary, HUC.

50 *OR* XXXVI:1, 1019.

51 Levy Diary, HUC.

52 Ibid.

53 Walters Diary, NPL.

54 *OR* XXXVI:1, 1046.

55 Wilcox's old brigade was assigned to Mahone's Division and included the 8th, 9th, 10th, 11th, and 14th Alabama regiments commanded by Colonel John C. C. Sanders.

56 The 55th North Carolina Regiment and band of eight musicians was assigned to Brig. Gen. Joseph R. Davis's Brigade of Heth's Division, which included the 2nd, 11th, 26th, and 42nd Mississippi regiments.

57 Levy Diary, HUC. Lanes's and Scales's North Carolina brigades of Wilcox's Division were sent forward to feel the enemy out and see what they were doing.

58 Freeman, *Lee,* Vol. III, 340, 341, 344.

59 J. T. Wingfield, "Report of the Operations of Company C Irvin Artillery from May 5th 1864 to July 31, 1864," Washington-Wilkes Historical Foundation.

60 Levy Diary, HUC. The Herndon farm is marked in the *O. R. Atlas*, Plate XLV, Map No. 1, "Map of Orange County, etc., Va." and Plate XCI, Map 1, "Map of Spotsylvania County." The location is near modern day Duerson Store, about a mile southwest of Mount Pleasant, Spotsylvania County, Virginia.

61 William D. Henderson, *12th Virginia Infantry, The Virginia Regimental Histories Series* (Lynchburg, Va., 1984), 74.

62 Freeman, *Lee,* Vol. III, 344, 349.

63 Gordon C. Rhea, *To the North Anna River, Grant and Lee, May 13-25, 1864* (Baton Rouge, 2000), 251.

64 Ibid., 255.

65 Levy Diary, HUC.

66 *OR* XXXVI:1, 1046.

67 J. Michael Miller, *The North Anna Campaign, "Even to Hell Itself" May 21-26, 1864* (Lynchburg, Va., 1989), 40, 41. The North Anna River crossings from west to east with corresponding railroad junctions that were generally located about a mile south of the river were: Anderson's Ford/Beaver Dam Station, four miles east was Butler's Bridge and Island Ford/Hewlett's Station, another three miles was Jericho Mills/Noel's Station, then two miles to Ox Ford/Anderson's Station that was also called Verdon, then three miles to Fox's Bridge/Hanover Junction where the Telegraph Road from Richmond crossed the river. One half mile east of the Telegraph Road bridge was the Richmond, Fredericksburg and Potomac Railroad Bridge that the Donaldsonville Artillery guarded for a few days in May 1863.

68 Freeman *Lee,* Vol. III, 352; Stewart, 135.

69 Levy Diary, HUC. Levy identified the matron as Mrs. Tweed.

70 Walters Diary, NPL.

71 The location of E. M. Anderson's farm is found in the *OR Atlas,* Plate LV, Map 4, "Map of the Battle-fields of North Anna" and Plate XCVI, Map 2, "Map of the Battle-field of North Anna, Va."

72 Freeman, *Lee,* Vol. III, 353-355.

73 Levy Diary, HUC.

74 Lineback, 119. UNCCH. The wagon train stopped at the South Anna River.

75 Rhea, 325.
76 Levy Diary, HUC.
77 Ibid.
78 Weisiger's Brigade was composed of the 6th, 12th, 16th, 41st, and 61st Virginia regiments.
79 Stewart, 136.
80 Rhea, 338, 441. Today in North Anna Battlefield Park in Hanover County, Virginia, a historical marker identifies the still existing breastworks of the two Donaldsonville Artillery 10-pounder Parrott guns. It is still possible to walk along Mahone's entrenchments past Prosper Landry's Canonnier positions and see the variation in construction from regiment to regiment.
81 Freeman, *Lee,* Vol. III, 356, 357.
82 *OR* XXXVI:1, 1047.
83 Meaning infantry rifle fire. "Minies," short for Minie Ball, refers to the rifled bullet fired by the foot soldiers.
84 Levy Diary, HUC.
85 Miller, 101-105.
86 Ibid., 132.
87 Levy Diary, HUC.
88 Hyland C. Kirk, *Heavy Guns and Light: A History of the 4th New York Heavy Artillery* (New York, 1890), 246.
89 Levy Diary, HUC.
90 Miller, 128.
91 Walters Diary, NPL.
92 Levy Diary, HUC.
93 Ibid.
94 Boatner, 597, 598.
95 Levy Diary, HUC.
96 The Hanover Academy School was established in 1849 and closed in 1890. It is now a private home and farm with only two of the old buildings remaining. One is the remodeled two-story main residence, with its spacious porch on a hill overlooking sowed fields, still surrounded by old oaks.
97 Levy Diary, HUC.
98 Ibid.
99 Freeman, *Lee,* Vol. III, 362.
100 Levy Diary, HUC. Lee ordered a forced reconnaissance by cavalry in the direction of Haw's Shop, where a vigorous fight occurred. The Canonniers observed the wounded of that fight in passing.
101 Ibid.
102 Walters Diary, NPL.
103 Freeman, *Lee,* Vol. III, 366.
104 Carter's house, Laurel Grove, still stands in the midst of a suburban Mechanicsville neighborhood named, fittingly, Laurel Grove. A piece of timber found in the lovely old home when it was being remodeled had the date 1761 carved thereon, and it was stated that there were hundreds of wild laurel trees through the avenues and approaches to the house that gives it its name. *Old Homes of Hanover County, Virginia* (Hanover, Va., 1983), 88, 89. For its location see *OR Atlas*, Plate XCVI, Map 6, "The Battle of Totopotomoy, Va."
105 Brig. Gen. William W. Kirkland's North Carolina Brigade, formerly Pettigrew's, of Heth's Division, was composed of the 11th, 26th, 44th, 47th, and 52nd regiments, the same regiments the Donaldsonville Artillery accompanied on the march to Gettysburg.
106 John R. Cooke's regiments were the 15th, 27th, 46th, and 48th North Carolina, also of Heth's Division.
107 Levy Diary, HUC.
108 Boatner, 842, 843.
109 Levy Diary, HUC.
110 Ibid.
111 Ibid.
112 This lovely old two-story frame house over a brick English type basement with its original doors and woodwork still stands with the scars of war. Located near Shady Grove Road, it is now nearly

surrounded by the Avondale subdivision. It is the home of Charles and Barbara Bourne who were gracious enough to give the author a tour in May 2003. *Old Homes of Hanover County, Virginia.* (Hanover, Va.), 1983, 11. It too can be found in *OR Atlas*, Plate XCVI, Map 6, "The Battle of Totopotomoy, Va.," though it is identified as the R. E. Ganiner house. The present address is 7305 Cranwell Circle, Mechanicsville.

113 Levy Diary, HUC.
114 Freeman, *Lee,* Vol. III, 383.
115 Gallagher, *Fighting,* 404.
116 Levy Diary, HUC.
117 Freeman, *Lee,* Vol. III, 395.
118 Ibid.
119 Levy Diary, HUC.
120 *OR* XXXVI:1, 1032.
121 Boatner, 163.
122 Walters Diary, NPL.
123 Levy Diary, HUC.
124 *Macaria; or, Atlas of Sacrifice* was published in 1864. It was a wartime best seller by Augusta Jane Evans, one of the leading women writers of nineteenth-century domestic fiction.
125 Dr. Gaines's and McGhee's locations can be found in *OR Atlas*, Plate XIX, Map 1, "Campaign... Map 3, White House to Harrison's Landing." The map identifies two McGhee farms (incorrectly spelled McGee's), a mile or so east of Gaines's house. The southern most McGhee house sat on Turkey Hill and belonged to Joseph Foster McGhee, who lived circa 1819 to 1896. The house no longer stands, and a physical description has not been found.
126 Lane's Brigade was composed of the 7th, 18th, 28th, 33rd, and 37th North Carolina regiments.
127 There were six or eight McGhee's in the greater Cold Harbor area, and this house was the second of the two east of Dr. Gaines's. It belonged to the family matriarch, Sally McGhee, who was about eighty-two years old in 1864. It was described as a substantial brick structure resting on brick pilings with a nearby orchard and small grove of trees. Apparently it stood until the 1930s. Harris and Weisiger's brigades of Mahone's Division occupied the Confederate line at and north of the house with Richardson's Napoleon guns located along the line about 500 yards north. Robert E. L. Krick to author, February 3, 2003, and September 7, 2004. Richmond National Battlefield Park.
128 Capt. George M. Cayce's Purcell (Va.) Battery was part of Lt. Col. William J. Pegram's Battalion. It was originally captained by the Third Corps artillery commander Colonel Lindsey Walker.
129 Levy Diary, HUC. Canonnier Pvt. Henry Fuhri.
130 Driver, 49.
131 Bennett, 156.
132 No information has been found regarding the Williams farm. Williams was probably some sort of tenant or renter, which was a very common thing around Richmond during the war years. Robert E. L. Krick to author, September 8, 2004. Richmond National Battlefield Park.
133 Levy Diary, HUC.
134 Ed. M. Burruss to Ned, June 15, 1864, John C. Burruss Papers, LSU.
135 Freeman, *Lee,* Vol. III, 407.

CHAPTER FIFTEEN

1 Freeman, *Lee,* Vol. III, 404.
2 Ibid., 405.
3 Cutts was assigned command of the two battalions to be used as a reserve on June 5, 1864. Maj. John Lane at that time took command of the Sumter (Ga.) Battalion. Folsom, 112.
4 The J. S. Atlee farm can be found in *OR Atlas*, Plate XIX, Map 1, on the western side of the Darbytown or Central Road near where Cornelius Creek crosses the road. The farm was a landmark along the Darbytown Road as it was mentioned with some frequency in the diaries and journals of veterans, but never in any substantial way. The farm does not exist today and was located in an area that is now being developed at a frenzied pace. Robert E. L. Krick to author, November 1, 2004. Richmond National Battlefield Park.

5 Levy Diary, HUC.
6 Josephus E. Strother Journal, Washington-Wilkes Historical Foundation.
7 Caldwell, 213.
8 Freeman, *Lee,* Vol. III, 420, 421.
9 *Times-Picayune,* June 9, 1902. Levy published a series of newspaper articles in which he expanded on his diary. The *Times-Picayune* citations identify Levy's added or exchanged words.
10 W. Knight was an old-time planter, usually called Colonel Knight. He was an acquaintance of that ancient and ardent secessionist Edmund Ruffin. The farm was just opposite Drewry's Bluff on the Henrico County side of the river. Robert E. L. Krick to author, November 1, 2004. Richmond Natioanl Battlefield Park.
11 Drewry's Bluff rose ninety feet above the water and commanded a sharp bend in the James River. The defensive work was an integral part of Richmond's defense and a key to the river defenses. Fort Drewry is now a unit of the Richmond National Battlefield Park.
12 The obstructions were both rock laden sunken vessels and pilings that zigzagged and stretched across the river just beneath Fort Drewry. They were placed to stall any Union warships coming up the river so that guns in the fort could bombard them. Robert E. L. Krick to author, November 1, 2004. Richmond National Battlefield Park.
13 The Watkins family lived there during the war. William O. Watkins (born in 1847 and died on March 20, 1912), is buried in the Ampthill Plantation Cemetery. Col. Archibald Cary, an American Revolutionary leader, was the original owner of the impressive Ampthill, which dates from 1730. The house was disassembled and moved to Richmond in 1929, and the land tract, about seven miles from Richmond, was bought in 1927 by the Du Pont De Nemours and Company who built an enormous industrial complex there. Today it is the Spruance Plant Industrial Site and nearby Port of Richmond. Robert E. L. Krick to author, November 1, 2004. Richmond National Battlefield Park.
14 Gen. Pierre Gustave Toutant Beauregard was a native of St. Bernard Parish, Louisiana, and the "Hero of Fort Sumter." His small command at Petersburg fought off the Army of the Potomac's assaults of June 15-18, 1864. Lee's biographer wrote, "Beauregard's troops made a splendid fight in front of Petersburg, and were handled by him with great skill and boldness." With the arrival of the Army of Northern Virginia, Beauregard's command acted under Lee's direction. Freeman, *Lee,* Vol. III, 443.
15 The city of Petersburg's nickname came from the rosette the men wore on their caps for the cause of 1812. Its 1860 population was 18,266, of which half were black and nearly a third of them free. The city's population in 2010 was 32,420.
16 Levy Diary, HUC. Archer's Hill, a designation that originally applied to the whole of the long bluff on the north side of the Appomattox River opposite Petersburg is now embraced by the city of Colonial Heights. The hill with its elevation provided the best view of Petersburg and derived its name from George Archer, a seventeenth-century land magnate. It was also called Oak, Hector's, Dunn's, or Pleasant Hill. The side of the commanding heights now goes practically straight down to Archer Avenue, having been mostly dug out for fill used in the washed out railroad tracks after the Big Flood of Petersburg. During the war it was a gentle slope to the river where cows had once grazed. Author conversation on May 30, 2003, with long time Carroll Avenue (Archer's Hill), resident William B. Gates, III.
17 Freeman, *Lee,* Vol. III, 449.
18 Levy Diary, HUC. Three 10-pounder Parrott guns came from the batteries of Cutts's Sumter (Ga.), Battalion, Company A, Capt. Hugh M. Ross and Company B, Capt. George M. Patterson, and two 20-pounder and two 3-inch Ordnance rifles from Company C, Capt. John T. Wingfield. Lt. Col. Allen Sherrod Cutts was a thirty-six-year-old Americus, Georgia, planter and Mexican War veteran who continued to command his own and Richardson's Battalion. He served after the war as a state legislator, a mayor, and law officer before dying in November 1896.
19 Folsom, 114. The Archer house or Oak Hill, built 1825 (see *OR Atlas*, Plate LVI, Map 1), belonged to eighty-six-year-old Jane Archer, who during the war lived in Petersburg with John T. Phillips, the thirty-year-old editor of a Petersburg newspaper, and his wife and four children.The Archer house is two one-story clapboard structures connected by a deep inside porch that extended to an uncovered section. From the long bluff and lawn of this house that overlooks Petersburg and the Appomattox River, French troops of General LaFayette in May 1781 set up artillery behind a boxwood hedge and shelled the British occupying Petersburg. Some historians though insist that

Lafayette's guns were near the Violet Bank, the name of the portion of old Archer's Hill that lies east of the Petersburg-Richmond Highway. The 151 Carroll Avenue house, located in Colonial Heights, Chesterfield County, remains today a private home, but with additions. The area around the house was developed from 1910 onwards. *Petersburg The Progress-Index*, May 24, 1970.

20 *Times-Picayune*, June 16, 1902.

21 Ibid.

22 Levy Diary, HUC. Number 3 holds his thumb on the vent during reloading, then moves to the trail and moves it right or left with the trailspike as directed by the gunner aiming. The No. 3 position then punctures the cartridge bag after it is seated with the vent pick.

23 "Operations of Company (C), Irvin Artillery from May 5th 1864 to July 31, 1864," Report of Capt. John T. Wingfield, Washington-Wilkes Historical Foundation.

24 Herbert E. Valentine, *Story of Co. F, 23rd Massachusetts Volunteers in the War For The Union, 1861-1865* (Boston, 1896), 131.

25 *OR* XL:1, 757.

26 *OR* XL:1, 519, 520.

27 Pryor, 282.

28 Levy Diary, HUC.

29 *Times-Picayune*, June 16, 1902.

30 Levy Diary, HUC.

31 *OR* XL:1, 757.

32 *OR* XL:1, 655-671. For the Federal positions see *OR Atlas*, Plate LXVII, Map 9, "Sketch Showing the Positions of the Redoubts and Batteries of the Lines of the U. S. Forces in front of Petersburg, Va."

33 The Beasley house was described as "commodious" and was taken down. Puddledock Road (SSR 645), or old River Road went from Beasley's to the river. The area is now an industrial park and landfill. "J. J. Purcuval Reminisciences" and Chris Caulkins to Author, November 15, 2004, PNM.

34 Houses near Battery 4 (identified as Battery 5 "Dictator" by Petersburg National Battlefield Park), are the Friend or Whitehill house and the Jourdan house, the former standing until 1923 while the latter was pulled down during the war. Only their foundations remain and are located inside the park's boundaries. "J. J. Purcuval Reminisciences" and Chris Caulkins to Author, November 15, 2004, PNM.

35 Levy Diary, HUC. This was the Weldon Railroad Operations of June 22-23, in which Hill's Third Corps moved to counter a Union threat to seize the railroad. With Wilcox's Division blocking one Federal Corps, Mahone and Johnson's divisions attacked the exposed flank of another Federal corps pushing them back. Mahone's Division took 1,600 prisoners.

36 *Times-Picayune,* June 16, 1902.

37 The wheel is composed of a nave into which the axle-tree enters of a certain number of spokes fastened in the nave and the circumference of the wheel, which is composed of a number of felloes equal to half the number of spokes.

38 Levy Diary, HUC.

39 *Times-Picayune,* June 16, 1902.

40 Fishing in the Appomattox River at Petersburg is still popular today. Man-made improvements and changes to the river's course have occurred since the war. Chris Caulkins to author, November 15, 2004, PNBP.

41 The Federals designated it Battery 5.

42 Levy Diary, HUC.

43 *Times-Picayune,* June 16, 1902.

44 Donaldsonville Artillery Pvt. William H. Ely.

45 *Times-Picayune,* June 16, 1902.

46 According to an officer from the Georgia battalion in a letter dated July 4, 1864, "Lt. [Bryan] James [from Ross' Battery] had his right arm torn off by a shell. It was amputated at the shoulder joint, and I am very glad to say that he is doing well with every prospect of recovering." James survived and was retired from service by a Board of Surgeons on October 31, 1864. NA, CSR. F. M. Coker to wife, July 4, 1864, Florence Hodgson Heidler Collection, University of Georgia.

47 Fort Clifton was a formidable defensive work built during the winter of 1863-64 around the Clifton house. It was located on a high elevation near the junction of the Appomattox River and

Swift Creek. The fort was north of Archer's or Pleasant Hill. David G. Malgee, "A Brief History of Fort Clifton, 1864-1865," (1995), Colonial Heights Historical Society. Also see *OR Atlas*, Plate LXXVII, Map 3.

48 Folsom, 114.

49 *Times-Picayune,* June 16, 1902.

50 Donaldsonville Artillery Pvt. William G. Delesdernier.

51 *Times-Picayune,* June 23, 1902.

52 Sydney Smith, 1771-1845, an English clergyman, writer, and master of wit and satire.

53 Petersburg tobacconist David Dunlop bought two hundred acres of land north of modern Colonial Heights and Petersburg along Swift Creek and built Ellerslie, a palatial country home, in 1858. The Italian Villa-style home with a trademark tower had a picturesque view, a green lawn, a trimmed and groomed glade, a grove, and numerous single trees scattered about. In 1864 it stood in the center of the Swift Creek defensive line with rifle pits dug on the property. Beauregard made his headquarters at Ellerslie in May 1864, and Confederate troops with plenty of shade and water bivouacked nearby. On the southern border of the estate was Dunlop's Station on the Richmond and Petersburg Railroad, which had a commissary depot for supplies. Ellerslie still stands as a private home though it had extensive renovations in 1909 that gave it a modern appearance. Today it is surrounded by a residential subdivision and urban sprawl. David G. Malgee, "A Brief History of Ellerslie," (1996), Colonial Heights Historical Society.

54 *Times-Picayune,* June 23, 1902.

55 Campbell's Bridge across the Appomattox River connects Petersburg with Ettrick (west of Archer's Hill, Colonial Heights), with the current modern bridge, near the base of Fleet's Hill, at the same spot of the original one built in 1810.

56 Levy Diary, HUC. The A. P. Hill Public Library is located a block away from Halifax Street and Baylors Lane intersection.

57 Walters Diary, NPL.

58 Levy Diary, HUC.

59 Walters Diary, NPL.

60 Levy Diary, HUC.

61 Ibid.

62 Ezra A. Carman Papers, Levy letter dated April 21, 1900, Library of Congress.

63 *Times-Picayune,* June 23, 1902.

64 Helena Scribner, age 23, and her cousin Eliza Scribner, age twenty-six, lived with Helen's parents Isaac and Caroline Scribner in the Petersburg Heights section of the city with lots and buildings numbered 347, 350, 351-353 St. Mathews Street. Their dwelling was less than a half mile from the Halifax/Baylor intersection. Census records indicate the family originally were from New Jersey. In 1860 Issac, a brick layer and manufacturer, and his wife lived in Petersburg with the two women and a son, Sylvester B. Scribner. He served in the 3rd Virginia Infantry of Pryor's Brigade that had the Donaldsonville Canonniers as their support in 1862. Young Scribner later transferred to the Signal Corps, which for the most part took well educated men with high social standing.

Helena was well educated. Eliza or Lizzie came to her uncle's from Brooklyn, New York. In May 1860 she was involved in an incident that "had created a profound sensation in the fashionable circles" of that city. A gentleman used a towel saturated with chloroform on her and "intended to commit an outrage" but being unsuccessful shot her in the cheek, finger, and arm. Miss Lizzie Scribner testified, "I cannot imagine why [he] should thus attempt to take my life; my relationships and associations with him have been of a friendly character, but not intimate." After shooting her, the rejected lover came to his death "by shooting himself in the head with a pistol." *Petersburg Index,* May 17, 1860. After the war Eliza married Charles A. Meyer, a consulate fifteen years her elder. Her second husband was William M. Yager. She died June 2, 1913, and is buried at Maplewood Cemetery in Jewett, New York.

Helena was still living with her parents when they lost their house in 1868 for nonpayment of taxes. After that, they left Petersburg for Somerset, New Jersey. *Petersburg Index,* January 1, 1870. Helena married John Randolph, a farmer twenty-six years her elder, and lived in Hartwood, Stafford County, Virginia. They had two children, but only a daughter born in 1879, Florence, survived. Helena became a widow and moved to Plainfield, New Jersey with her daughter. There she was asked by a neighbor to teach their "delicate child" and soon was teaching the daughters of many of the best families. In 1884 she founded The Misses Scribner and Newton School for Girls. This became the Miss Scribner and Miss Green's School for Girls in 1889. In 1903 it became The Hartridge School named after the new owner. Today the school continues to educate pre-kindergarten through grade twelve as The Wardlaw-Hartridge School in Edison, New Jersey. Helena Schribner Randolph later ran a boarding house at 115 Church Street in Plainfield. She died in her eighties sometime between 1920 and 1930. Carrie Bennett, Alumni and Developmental Office, Wardlaw-Hartridge School (Edison, N.J.), correspondence, May 19, 2006. In Levy's *Times-Picayune* newspaper series for June 23, 1902, he omitted this July 2, 1864, diary entry and made no comment.

65 William S. Keiley (1845-1925), was employed by the Quartermaster Department as a clerk from 1862 to 1864. He enlisted as a private on June 15, 1864, in Capt. S. Taylor Martin's (Va.) Battery or Battery B, 12th Virginia Light Artillery Battalion. Willie was described as "unselfish" and after the war became an attorney in New York City, where he was one of the original founding and prominent members of the Confederate Veterans Camp of New York. He later became commander of the camp. Included in the camp's membership were Roger Pryor, John J. Garnett, and Eugene H. Levy. Keiley died on May 9, 1925. "The Last Roll," *CV* 34 (1926), 24.

66 Ellen Keiley never married and at the age of seventy-nine died in Richmond of burns after a dreadful accident while stirring a fire in her sitting room. Hot coals fell upon the skirt of her dressing gown and she strove in vain to remove them. A "negro maid" found her semi-conscious on a blazing rug. *Atlanta Constitution*, February 26, 1914.

67 John Denis "Jack" Keiley Jr. (1839-1901) was quartermaster of Walker's Brigade and described as a "chivalrous and gallant gentleman, and successful young merchant." He also "gained the reputation of being the 'best quartermaster in the Confederate Army.'" Acting as Chief of the Quartermaster Department, he was captured in April 1865 at the Petersburg railroad depot "in the active discharge of his duties." A Petersburg resident, Keiley owned a store during the war that afforded his family to have a set dinner party in November 1864 when food was scarce. The Keiley fare was turkey, corn beef, fine vegetables, and desserts of fruitcake, tarts, almonds, and raisins. After the war he was a successful businessman, and after marrying he moved to Brooklyn, New York, where he became the city treasurer and a prominent player in politics. *The Petersburg Index*, October 30, 1868; "The Last Roll," *CV* 10 (1902), 37; Keiley Family Papers in Virginia Historical Society.

68 An older brother, Anthony Michael Keiley (1835-1905), was a lieutenant in the "Petersburg Riflemen," Company E, 12th Virginia Infantry; he was seriously wounded July 1, 1862, at Malvern Hill. Upon returning to duty he saw action at Gettysburg but, because of his previous wound, was discharged and elected to the Virginia House of Delegates. Called back into the army, he twas captured serving with the militia at Petersburg on June 9, 1864, during what became known as the Battle of Old Men and Young Boys by Petersburg residents. Levy noted in November 1864 that he visited his "esteemed friend Anthony Keiley" (after his release as an exchanged prisoner) in Petersburg and partook of the aforementioned dinner party. Keiley later wrote a book of his captivity, *In Vinculis: or, The Prisoner of War,* which was published in New York in 1866. He later served one term (1871-1876), as Richmond's first elected post-Reconstruction mayor and ten years as the city attorney. He and his wife lived at 707 E. Franklin Street, the dwelling of Robert E. Lee's family during the war. Canonnier Pvt. Julian "Doc" Levy would years later marry Corrine A. Davis (born in 1859), a niece of Keiley's wife, Rebbeca Davis (who's father was probably the wealthiest man in Petersburg), and whom "Doc" Levy called his aunt-in-law. Before moving to Richmond, Mrs. A. M. Keiley was treasurer of the Petersburg Ladies' Memorial Association. General Lee asked of her: "'Mrs. A. M. Keiley: Will you do me the favor to place [$25.] to the credit of the Ladies'Association of Petersburg, in aid of their pious work for the preservation and protection of the graves of the Confederate Dead, and believe me to be, with great respect, Your obedient servant, R. E. Lee.' In the breast of the great leader of the lost cause the fire of affectionate respect for the heroes who followed his banner and fell in its defense suffers no diminution with the lapse of years," reported *The Petersburg Index,* April 2, 1867, Keiley Family Papers, Virginia Historical Society; Edward Slipek, "The Story of Richmond's Forgotten Mayer," *Style Weekly* (Richmond, Va.), 23:44 (November 5, 2005), 14-16, 18-19.

69 The Dimmock line defense was a ring of fifty-five earthen fortifications numbered consecutively from east to west and connected by trench lines. Started in late 1862, it extended for ten miles and was completed the next year under the supervision of Capt. Charles H. Dimmock. The guns commanded by Prosper Landry in Rives's Salient were located at Battery 25 on the old

Dimmock defensive line. In 1907 a Confederate veteran of the Petersburg entrenchments wrote, "I visited . . . and found that all the breastworks had been leveled, the shell holes made by mortars had disappeared, and the young corn was growing peacefully where war had done its worst." I. G. Bradwell, "On Picket Duty In Front of Fort Steadman," *CV*, 38 (1930), 307. Due to a misunderstanding between the landowner and the administration of what would become Petersburg National Battlefield Park, the remains of Rives's Salient and the Donaldsonville Artillery's position was leveled while the park was being created. The Salient land was sold to Pine Garden Real Estate and there remain no traces of the Donaldsonville Artillery gun positions, which are now located in a residential neighborhood about the intersection of South Boulevard and Colston Street, less than a block from Walnut Hill Plaza Shopping Center, PNBP.

70 Levy Diary, HUC.

71 Walters Diary, NPL.

72 James J. Kirkpatrick Diary, 1861-1864, UT.

73 Brig. Gen. Ambrose R. "Rans" Wright's distinguished brigade had the 2nd and 10th battalions, 3rd, 22nd, 48th, and 64th regiments of Georgia Infantry.

74 Levy Diary, HUC.

75 *Times-Picayune,* June 23, 1902.

76 Levy Diary, HUC.

77 James J. Kirkpatrick Diary, 1861-1864, UT.

78 *Times-Picayune,* June 30, 1902.

79 Levy Diary, HUC.

80 Valentine, 130.

81 Capt. Prosper Landry, in a letter dated December 1886, wrote, "All I remember now of our position is that we occupied Reeves Salient, where an old well was the only thing left to mark the spot where Reeves home had once been." *Times-Picayune,* January 17, 1887. Timothy Rives (pronounced Reeves), was born in 1807 and lived with his wife, sister, seven daughters, and one son on a large plantation that the defensive salient took its name after. In 1860 Rives's land was valued at $210,000 dollars. He was a delegate to the Virginia Succession Convention in 1861 and enlisted as a Captain in Pryor's 3rd Virginia Infantry in November 1861. He resigned seven months later. He was captured serving with the militia during the battle of June 9, 1864, at Petersburg; Federal cavalry burned his mansion down the day he was captured. After imprisonment at Point Lookout, Maryland, he later died in Petersburg on October 29, 1865.

82 Henry "Harry" H. Marks was twenty-two years old when he enlisted in the First Company Washington Artillery in June 1863. He was a clerk in New Orleans before the war. The four companies of the Washington Artillery were positioned about two thousand feet to the right of Battery 25 (Rives's Salient), in the Petersburg line at Batteries 34 through 38.

83 Levy Diary, HUC.

84 Walters Diary, NPL.

85 Ibid.

86 Ibid.

87 Levy Diary, HUC.

88 Walters Diary, NPL.

89 James J. Kirkpatrick Diary, 1861-1864, UT.

90 Jarratt's Hotel was located at the southwest corner of Washington and Union streets. It served passengers on the Petersburg and Weldon Railroad that ran down the center of Washington Street to connect with the other rail lines in the area. It advertised as "The Largest And Best House In The City," but a woman during this time described it as "an ugly old hotel in the heart of the town." Myrta L. Avary, *A Virginia Girl in the Civil War, 1861-1865; Being a Record of the Actual Experiences of the Wife of a Confederate Officer* (New York, 1903), 288. Jarratt's stood until 1902, when it was razed. Chris Calkins to author, November 15, 2004, PNBP.

91 Bragg lost Lookout Mountain and the seemingly impregnable position on Missionary Ridge during the Chattanooga, Tennessee, campaign in November 1863. Pres. Jefferson Davis reluctantly concluded Bragg was not qualified to command the Army of Tennessee and assigned him to his office, where he held responsibilities similar to a modern chief of the general staff.

92 *Times-Picayune,* July 14, 1902.

93 Levy Diary, HUC.

94 *Biographical and Historical Memoirs of Louisiana*, II:532.

95 Jean Reynard Jaques Prosper Landry to Adele Pedesclaux Landry, September 1864, UV.
96 Donaldsonville Artillery Pvt. Henry Nicaud, sixteen years old, was a student from New Orleans when he joined the battery in June 1863.
97 Presumably Ellen. Dorothy or Dora was still single at age thirty-two in 1870.
98 Donaldsonville Artillery Pvt. Asbury A. Overby.
99 *Times-Picayune,* July 14, 1902.
100 Ibid.
101 Levy Diary, HUC.
102 Walters Diary, NPL.
103 Levy Diary, HUC.
104 Jerome B. Yates to Marie Yates Swanson, July 19, 1864, UT.
105 J. J. Wilson to James E. Wilson, July 24, 1864, J. J. Wilson Papers, Mississippi Department of Archives and History.
106 William H. Morrison, born 1841, was a corporal and soon would be promoted to sergeant for the second time in Company "B." A native of Petersburg, he was quite wealthy in 1860 as a result of his family-owned furniture business. William D. Henderson, *12th Virginia Infantry* (Lynchburg, Va., 1984), 144.
107 Levy Diary, HUC.
108 *Times-Picayune,* June 30, 1902.
109 Lt. Gen. Jubal A. Early led what was later called the Washington Raid, June 27-August 7, 1864. Following the relief of Lynchburg, Lee ordered Early to the Shenandoah Valley to divert strength from the besieging Federal army at Petersburg. On July 9, Early, with four divisions of infantry and one of cavalry, defeated the Federal forces at Monocacy, Maryland, and he reached the outskirts of Washington (Silver Springs, Maryland) on July 11. Finding the capitol reinforced, the Confederates withdrew and crossed the Potomoc River at Leesburg, Virginia, on July 14, 1864. "Before General Early was detached with his command," wrote Levy, "he rode along the line with a black feather in his felt hat, and as the gay boys were reminded by the ornament of a duck's tail, the 'Quack, quack!' from hundreds of throats betokened the approach of the most profane general officer of the army." *Times-Picayune,* June 30, 1902.
110 Gen. Robert E. Lee commanded the Army of Northern Virginia; Lt. Gen. Richard H. "Dick" Anderson was acting commander of Longstreet's First Corps while that general recovered from wounds; Lt. Gen. A. P. Hill commanded the Third Corps; Maj. Gen. Charles W. Field commanded Hood's old division in the First Corps; and Brig. Gen. William Mahone and Maj. Gen. Henry Heth both commanded divisions in Hill's Third Corps.
111 Levy Diary, HUC.
112 Charles Richardson, *Tales of a Warrior, Sanguine but Not Sanguinary For Old-time People* (New York, 1907), 219. This description was taken from "First Sergeant Ball, Co. B," one of nine fictional short stories (most having Confederate themes), written by the Donaldsonville Artillery's battalion commander. About one thousand feet along the earthworks to the west stood Battery 27 at the Jerusalem Plank Road (U. S. Route 301 and now named Crater Road), and a further thousand feet was Fort Mahone along with its opponent Fort Sedgewick. Both forts were bulldozed down in the 1960s "and now the shopping malls that took their place are almost empty. Where Fort Mahone stood there's an empty K Mart." *The Civil War News,* September 2004, 28, PNBP.
113 *Times-Picayune,* July 14, 1902.
114 James J. Kirkpatrick Diary, 1861-1864, UT.
115 Levy Diary, HUC.
116 Walters Diary, NPL.
117 *Times-Picayune,* July 14, 1902.
118 Levy Diary, HUC.
119 Walters Diary, NPL.
120 George W. Rush was elected captain of Company "A" on June 2, 1862. Nathaniel Elean Levy was elected second lieutenant of the same company on December 8, 1862, and his brother, Sergeant Jacob R. "Jack" Levy would be promoted to lieutenant on July 30, 1864. NA, CSR. Eugene was not related to the brothers.
121 *Times-Picayune,* July 14, 1902.
122 Levy Diary, HUC.
123 *Times-Picayune,* July 21, 1902.

124 Isadore Lovenstein was a private and would later be captured on the retreat to Appomattox. Henderson, 138, 148. His brother was William Lovenstein..
125 Levy Diary, HUC.
126 *Times-Picayune,* July 21, 1902.
127 Jacques Esprit Besson officially enlisted in Brookhaven, Mississippi, in May 1864. Joseph Numa Augustin, the first captain of *Le Canonniers de Donaldsonville,* served as a witness at the wedding of Besson's father in 1840. *Diocese of Baton Rouge Catholic Church Records,* Vol. 6, 66.
128 Recently placed in charge of the Army of Tennessee by Pres. Jefferson Davis, Lt. Gen. John B. Hood launched four major offenses in July in an attempt to break the siege of Atlanta, Georgia. All failed and resulted in significant Confederate casualties.
129 *Times-Picayune,* July 21, 1902
130 James Eldred Phillips was a master tinner for a Richmond building contractor before the war. After March 1864 he commanded Company "G" until paroled at Appomattox. He died December 1, 1905. Henderson, 138, 148.
131 *Times-Picayune,* July 21, 1902.
132 Benjamin Joseph Keiley (1847-1925), was "a man of profound learning and of great strength as well as gentleness of character" who served as a private "with marked heroism and valor" after entering Confederate service in 1864. "The Last Roll," *CV* 33 (1925), 302. "Ben" Keiley went to Rome in 1869. He was ordained a priest in 1873 and appointed pastor in Newcastle, Delaware. In 1900 he was named Seventh Bishop of Savannah, Georgia, and twenty years later Pope Pius XI appointed him Titular Bishop of Scillium. While in Italy Keiley was allowed an audience and met the Holy Father in person. James Longstreet often visited Keiley when he lived in Atlanta. "We," wrote the Bishop, "often talked of the war and its sequel. I recall . . . one day . . . I said: 'Well, General, you and I are both glad to-day that we have a united country, and perhaps in God's providence it is well that we were defeated even though we were clearly in the right.' 'I do not believe in placing the blame on the Lord,' said Longstreet. 'We ought to have whipped the Yankees, restored the Union and settled the negro question ourselves, but we had a big load to carry in some of our own leaders.'" Keiley Family Papers, Virginia Historical Society.
133 Whist was widely played in the eighteenth and nineteenth centuries. The classic game is a plain-trick game with simple rules. Four players in fixed partnership are dealt every card with the last being turned face up to indicate the trump suit. Each player in turn plays a card with the highest trump—or if it contains no trump, the highest card, which wins the trick. When all thirteen tricks have been played the side that won more tricks scores 1 point for each trick in exceeding 6. The partnership that first reaches 5 points wins the game.
134 Euchre reached America in the early nineteenth century. It too is a plain-trick game for four players but has just five cards dealt to each player from twenty-five cards, consisting of A, K, Q, J, 10, 9, and the jokers. It was the original game in which the Joker was introduced into the playing-card pack in the 1850s (to serve as the highest trump), making the rank of the cards different. The process in making trump is also more complicated.
135 *Times-Picayune,* July 21, 1902.
136 Ibid.
137 *Pasquinade* is a composition that imitates somebody's style in a humorous way.
138 Levy Diary, HUC.
139 *Times-Picayune,* July 24, 1902.
140 Valentine, 130.
141 W. S. Grady to wife, July 12, 1864, Henry Woodfin Grady Papers, Emory University.
142 *Times-Picayune,* July 14, 1902.
143 Ibid., July 21, 1902.
144 Returning from the Washington raid on July 23-24, 1864, Early again defeated Hunter's old command now under Brig. Gen. George Cook at Kernstown, Virginia. Early's forces then went on to capture and burn Chambersburg, Pennsylvania, on July 30 in reprisal for Hunter destroying private property in Virginia on the Lynchburg Campaign.
145 *Times-Picayune,* July 21, 1902.
146 Ibid. Lucious Licinius Lucullus was a Roman statesman and general known for his luxurious feast. The name Lucullus came to be used as an adjective for lavishness or sumptuousness, especially with regard to a banquet or party.
147 Levy Diary, HUC.

148 Walters Diary, NPL.

149 Ibid. The only difference in the diary entry by both artillerists was that Levy omitted the words "on us" in his sentence. For the location regarding the guns at Rives's Salient near the Jerusalem Plank Road see *OR Atlas,* Plate 78, No. 5, "Petersburg Mine Explosion, July 30, 1864."

150 Levy Diary, HUC.

151 Walters Diary, NPL.

152 Levy Diary, HUC. Lee arrived at the Gee house on the Jerusalem Plank Road, within five hundred yards of the Crater, soon after 6:00 a.m. Brig. Gen. Edward Alexander wrote, "From the windows of this house a view could be had of the whole field, & Gen. Beauregard was already there...Genls. Lee & Beauregard viewed the fighting from this near point during its whole progress." Gallagher, *Fighting,* 464.

153 Sycamore Street was the leading commercial street in Petersburg.

154 Confederate States Hospital had 400 beds. It opened in 1862 in the Dunn and Beasley Tobacco Factory at West Washington and Jones Street. A. Wilson Greene, *Civil War Petersburg: Confederate City in the Crucible of War* (Charlottesville, Va., 2006), 87.

155 Mary Winfree, twenty-one-year-old Petersburg native and resident of the city's West Ward.

156 Dr. John R. Ward (1840-1884), of Campbell County, Virginia, received his medical degree from the University of Virginia Medical Department in 1860. He was appointed confederate surgeon on June 22, 1863. He moved to Austin, Texas, in 1871 and worked as a dentist until becoming a farmer and successful land speculator. Texas State Cemetery website at www.cemetery.state.texas.us, John R. Ward [accessed November 23, 2011]. Information courtesy Denise "DeeDee" DiBenedetto Sanders.

157 Levy Diary, HUC.

158 Mahone's infantry received orders at 6:00 a.m. to stop the Union advance. Weisiger's (including the 12th Virginia Regiment), and Wright's brigades moved at 6:30 a.m. to counter attack. Saunder's Brigade of Mahone's Division launched a final attack shortly after 1:00 p.m. and cleared the crater of Northern troops while "forcing those still alive to surrender." Henderson, 83, 84. The Federals had 20,708 men engaged and lost 3,798, while the Confederates had about 1,500 casualties from an estimated 11,466 combatants. Boatner, 647-649.

159 Walters Diary, NPL. The corporal's name was Robert Butler.

160 *Times-Picayune,* July 28, 1902.

161 Ibid., December 5, 1930.

162 Association of the Army of Northern Virginia Papers, "Comstock Application, July 24, 1877," LHAC.

163 Levy Diary, HUC. From the hospital in Petersburg, Eugene Levy added, "Poor Jacob [Levy] came to see me in the course of the day. He seems absolutely broken hearted . . . sobbed at my bedside, his arm in a sling, shot through by a minie ball, as he related the death of his brother and brother-in-law in yesterday's fight; so of the four who played whist at his campfire a few nights ago, two are wounded and two are at the bivouac of heroes." Jacob R. Levy would later be killed in battle at Hatcher's Run on February 6, 1865. *Times-Picayune,* July 28, 1902.

164 *Times-Picayune,* July 28, 1902. Levy's left eye was "still very much inflamed" after a splinter was pulled out of the lid. Donaldsonville Canonniers that visited Levy in the following days were Tim Boham ("the first man to see me this [August 1st] morning") Thomas Burns, John "Eck" Eckleburg, who "sat with me for a while during the morning and evening," Henry Fuhri, Leopold Keroll, brother Julien "Doc" Levy, John McCoy, Alexander McCullet, and Seymore Mioton. Others who visited were Maj. "Jack" Keiley, Maj. "Buck" Miller, and Washington Artillery Lt. Edwin I. Kursheedt and Adjutant "Harry" Marks. Levy Diary, HUC.

165 *Times-Picayune,* June 9, 1902. On August 1, Levy, still in the hospital, recorded, "Miss Keiley sent me a basket of ice and other ingredients for lemonade" and "Good Mrs. Keiley sent me some bread and ice."

166 Henderson, 84.

167 Owen, 346, 347.

CHAPTER SIXTEEN

1 Ervin L. Jordan, Jr. *Charlottesville and the University of Virginia in the Civil War* (Lynchburg, Va., 1988), 38.

2 John J. Shoemaker, *Shoemaker's Battery, Stuart's Horse Artillery, Pelham's Battalion, Army of Northern Virginia* (Memphis, 1908), 65.

3 *Charlottesville Daily Chronicle*, June 3 and 19, 1864. Killickinick is an American Indian word meaning "that which is mixed" and refers to a 3:1 smoking mixture of the inner bark of willow or dogwood trees and tobacco. The mixture when smoked has a pleasant taste and aroma far more agreeable than the undiluted strong, harsh leaves of the tobacco plant. John H. Prucha and Norman A. Foss, *Kinnickinnic Years* (DeWitt, New York, 1993), 1, 2.

4 Jordan, 56.

5 J. S. Anglin to his parents, June 28, 1864, John S. Anglin Papers, Library of Congress; William Beavens Diary, William Beavens Papers, Southern Historical Collection, UNCCH.

6 John Wise to A. D. Trotter, June 21, 1862, Papers of Michael Wise, UV.

7 C. Howard Nichols, "Some Notes on the Military Career of Francis T. Nicholls," *Louisiana History*, 3(1962), 312.

8 Swayze, 33.

9 Daniel's Hill was named for Judge William Daniel Jr. (1806-1873), owner of the nine hundred-plus acre tract. Point of Honor, built in 1815, is located near the base of the hill and is probably Lynchburg's best known and finest dwelling. The two-story extremely articulate and refined Federal style mansion is now part of the Lynchburg Museum system.

10 The hills of Lynchburg include Daniel's, annexed after being developed in the 1870s and connected by a modern bridge across Blackwater Creek, College, Garland, Federal, Diamond, White Rock, and Franklin. The city's 2010 population is 75,568. S. Allen Chambers, Jr. *Lynchburg, An Architectural History* (Charlottesville, Va., 1981), 66-72.

11 Henry Beers, *The Confederacy, A Guide to the Archives of the Government of the Confederate States of America* (Washington D. C., 1986), 168, 194.

12 Three Nicholls brothers served in the antebellum *Canonniers de Donaldsonville*, Edward, Robert, and the lamented Lawrence that married Maurin's sister and was killed in battle on June 27, 1862, at Gaines' Mill during the Seven Days' Battles.

13 Nichols, 312.

14 Barnes F. Lathrop, ed. "An Autobiography of Francis T. Nicholls, 1834-1881," *The Louisiana Historical Quarterly*, 17 (1934), 252.

15 NA, Maurin File.

16 Nichols, 312.

17 Allen, ed., 153.

18 Ibid.

19 Rosa F. Yancey, *Lynchburg and Its Neighbors* (Richmond, Va., 1935), 19.

20 *Lynchburg Virginian,* June 9, 1864.

21 Edward King, "The Great South: A Ramble in Virginia," *Schribner's Monthly*, 7:6 (1874), 646.

22 Allen, ed. 153.

23 *OR,* XXXVII:1, 156.

24 Ibid., Pt. 1, 760.

25 *Lynchburg Virginian*, June 13, 1864.

26 Ibid., June 22, 1864.

27 NA, Maurin file.

28 Chambers, Jr., 176-178. Judge Daniel built Rivermont in 1852 for his second wife, Elizabeth Hannah Cabell (1811-1892). The home still stands, although it is crowded by lesser houses on three sides. The farm road is now Cabell Street.

29 NA, Maurin File. Following present day Cabell Street to Willow Street leads you to Battery Street and a two-story stone house called Battery Place on the James. The street to the inhabited house gives credence to the fact that the two Donaldsonville Artillery redoubts were located there and stood until the house was built in 1928. The overlook of the river from the yard of Battery Place is outstanding, dominant, and overlooked the Orange Railroad Bridge below. The bridge, completed in 1861, connected the Orange and Alexandria Railroad from points northward with Lynchburg. The O. & A. became the Southern Railway in 1894 and in 1912 construction was

completed on a new trestle over the James River thus creating a new Southern main line through Lynchburg after which the Orange Bridge was taken out of service. Only its stone piers and abutments remain. Chambers, Jr., 73, 74, 436. The two redoubts are marked at Battery Place on an 1860s "Amherst County Map" in the Lynchburg Museum's collection.

30 NA, Maurin File.

31 Early, 373-376.

32 Ibid., 375.

33 Nichols, 312.

34 The forty-seven-year-old Booker was formally captain of Company F, Farmville Guard, 18th Virginia Infantry Regiment, but resigned after being wounded at Second Manassas in August 1862. After recovering, he organized a reserve company from Prince Edward County made up of men too old or incapacitated for active service and boys too young. He subsequently was elected colonel of the 3rd Virginia Reserve Regiment. Booker was a tobacconist and the proprietor of the Randolph House hotel in Farmville; he was described as one of the towns "foremost and most respected citizens, a character in many regards unique and . . . as a soldier . . . chivalric and courageous . . . loyal and true . . . he always had some cheerful greeting . . . and some word of inspiration." *Farmville Herald,* May 6, 1904; Hebert C. Bradshaw, *History of Prince Edward County, Virginia, From Its Earliest Settlements Through Its Establishment in 1754, To Its Bicentennial Year* (Richmond, Va., 1955), 382; ibid., *History of Farmville Virginia, 1798-1948* (Fredericksburg, Va., 1994), 27, 28.

35 Jo D. Smith, *A History of High Bridge* (Richmond, Va., 1987), 5; NA, Record of Events (Third Virginia Reserves), November & December 1864.

36 Donaldsonville Artillery *Historical Memoranda*, LHAC.

37 Edward King, "The Great South: A Ramble in Virginia," *Schribner's Monthly,* 7:6 (1874), 663.

38 Farmville in 2010 has a population of almost 9,000 people. In the nineteenth century it was an important tobacco market. The Farmville Female College is now Longwood University. John H. Moore, "Appomattox, Profile of a Mid-Nineteenth Century Community," *Virginia Magazine of History and Biography*, 88 (1980), 479, 483; Bradshaw, *Prince Edward*, 392.

39 The height of High Bridge deterred many people from traveling on the South Side Railroad. It was written, "Timid passengers who have passed over this lofty bridge, in a train of cars, have involuntarily closed their eyes, and committed themselves to the care of providence." *Richmond Whig,* January 28, 1862. In the valley below there was also a common wagon-road bridge a few hundred yards on the side of the railroad bridge that crossed the one hundred foot wide Appomattox River. Though High Bridge underwent changes in design and structural materials, it remained in use until June 22, 1914, when it was replaced by a steel bridge alongside it. After 1914 the old bridge's superstructure was dismantled and its brick piers left as the only reminders of the old South Side Railroad. Clear of trees a century ago, the piers today are enveloped in regrowth and overshadowed by their steel counterparts. Smith, 8-11. The Norfolk Southern Railroad officially abandoned the line that passed over High Bridge when the last train crossed in 2004. The rail line has been donated to the state of Virginia and is now part of the High Bridge Trail State Park.

40 Two fortifications, one on each side of the tracks, were located at each end of the bridge.

41 Levy Diary, HUC. In September 1864 Prosper Landry recorded, "Horses being so rare, it is probable that [Mollere's section] will stay [at High Bridge] longer still. He has enough horses now, but apparently they belong to the department of Lynchburg and [Mollere] can not keep them if he does not stay here. It is because of this circumstance that the gunners of this section are here." Jean Reynaud Jacques Prosper Landry to Adele Pedesclaux Landry, September 1864, UV.

42 A. H. Plecker, "Who Saved Lynchburg From Hunter's Raid?" *CV* 30 (1922), 373.

43 *OR* XLII:3, 1322, 1323. Stephen W. Sylvia and Michael J. O'Donnell, *The Illustrated History of American Civil War Relics* (Orange, Va., 1978), 243. Relic hunters in 1960 sunk deep shafts into the remains of a High Bridge fortification and recovered eight hundred artillery projectiles, found just as they had been stacked.

44 "The Morning Report of Artillery Defenses, R & D R Road," Pendleton Papers, UNCCH. Presumably these prisoners were United States Colored Troops from Grant's one division of black troops in the Army of the Potomac captured at the Battle of the Crater, Petersburg, on July 30, 1864. Between 1,101 and 1,910 captured Yankees, with "over 200 negroe soldiers," were transported on the South Side Railroad. "The free Negroes of the North are held in strict confinement . . . but . . . are treated very much in the same manner as our other captives," reported

Confederate Sec. of War James Seddon. As such the "Yankee negroes" likely held near High Bridge were war prisoners not recognized or identified as recaptured slaves who would have been returned to their owners. The white prisoners were sent to Lynchburg, then on to Andersonville, Georgia, for imprisonment. Levy Diary, HUC; *OR* Series II, VII, 704.

45 On July 11, 1864, by "Special Order No. 24, in accordance with General Orders No. 43, Adjutant and Inspector General's Office...the following promotions are announced"—Mollere to First Lieutenant and R. Prosper Landry to Captain—"to date from that of Major Maurin's" on February 27, 1864." William N. Pendleton, Order Book, MCR.

46 Chesson, 204.

47 Levy Diary, HUC.

48 *Times-Picayune,* August 11, 1902.

49 Bradshaw, *Prince Edward*, 666.

50 Jean Reynaud Jacques Prosper Landry to Adele Pedesclaux, September 1864, UV. While commanding the Donaldsonville Artillery at Petersburg in September 1864, Prosper Landry became feeble and ill with fever; his condition was serious enough to receive a sick furlough, of which he wrote, "Knowing how the good inhabitants of this country [near High Bridge] treated our men from Louisiana, when I received my leave, I wrote to Mollere asking him to find me a good house where they would be willing to receive me . . . Mr. and Mrs. Madison received me as if I were an old acquaintance they had been waiting for."

51 Ibid.

52 Levy Diary, HUC.

53 Jean Reynaud Jacques Prosper Landry to Adele Pedesclaux Landry, September 1864, UV.

54 Ibid.

55 NA, CSR.

56 United States Census, 1880.

57 Levy Diary, HUC. *Modiste* meaning dress maker.

58 Lelia Lockett was referring to Hypolite or Camille Templet, brothers and Canonnier privates. The Acadian pronunciation is "Tomp-play." Hypolite and Camille's sugar cane plantations were near Monnot's along the descending east bank of Bayou Lafourche near Napoleonville in Assumption Parish.

59 *Richmond Times-Dispatch*, December 5, 1948.

60 *Assumption Pioneer*, April 1, 1911.

61 Letter to the Editor of the *Richmond Times-Dispatch* dated May 21, 1934, from (Mrs.), E. L. Monnot.

62 Levy Diary, HUC. The houses and farms around High Bridge can be located in *OR Atlas*, Plate LXXVIII, Map 4 (High Bridge and Farmville, Va.) and Plate LXXVII, Map 4 (Jetersville and Sailor's Creek, Va.), Some still stand today, including Lockett's Piney View. Others like Chatham Plantation, built in 1858-59, eventually fell into disrepair and were torn down.

63 Bradshaw, *Prince Edward*, 339, 350. Men from Booker's command were detailed from the service to farm. NA, Muster Roll for Third Virginia Reserves in November & December 1864.

64 The Farmville Female Seminary was erected in 1839-42 and occupied the site of the Longwood College Rotunda administrative building that was destroyed by fire in 2001.

65 Jamestown was chartered in 1796 and became an important trading point along the Appomattox River. After the construction of the South Side Railroad, the town was abandoned except for the old church and a few residents. Built as a free church open to all denominations, the building stood until 1953 when it was taken down. Bradshaw, *Prince Edward,* 839, 840.

66 Jean Reynaud Jacques Prosper Landry to Adele Pedesclaux Landry, September 1864, UV. Canonnier Sergeant Pierre Theophile Blouin was Prosper Landry's companion to church.

67 Ibid.

68 Levy Diary, HUC.

69 PRS Mollere's Section of Company B, Richardson's Battalion Artillery, Muster Roll for November/ December 1864, LAGL.

70 Charles E. Burrell, *A History of Prince Edward County Virginia, From Its Formation in 1753, To The Present* (Richmond, Va., 1922), 47.

71 PRS Mollere's Section of Company B, Richardson's Battalion Artillery, Muster Roll for November/ December 1864, LAGL.

72 Cire Memorandum, UDC.

73 Farinholt was a young soldier whose military career was described as "one gallant adventure." The 1st Virginia Reserves were previously stationed at the Staunton River Bridge. On November 10, 1864, Booker's companies (33 officers and 280 men) and Farinholt's companies (17 officers and 206 men) exchanged post. No explanation is given in the *Official Records* for the switch. Both commands were assigned to Brig. Gen. James A. Walker's Brigade of Brig. Gen. Henry A. Wise's First Military District, Department of North Carolina and Southern Virginia. Interestingly, Lt. Col. John J. Garnett at Hicksford, Virginia, commanded another brigade in the district. Freeman, *Lee,* Vol. III, 455; *OR* XLII:2, 1267, 1268; *OR* XLVI:2, 1262.

74 Levy Diary, HUC. After returning from his wound furlough Levy rejoined Prosper Landry's section in Petersburg. After taking sick in November 1864, Levy was ordered to the High Bridge detachment the following month for health reasons.

75 Ibid.

76 Ibid. Dated November 14, 1864, from Rives's Salient.

77 Ibid.

78 Ibid.

79 Ibid.

80 Ibid.

81 Ibid. Usually the snowfall in this area is infrequent and generally of overnight duration.

82 Ibid.

83 The German born Humbert was a twenty-six-year-old resident of Donaldsonville who enlisted in September 1861. He was promoted early in 1863. Fourteen years later it was reported he "committed suicide . . . at his residence in Donaldsonville by taking poison. He is the last of the Humbert family on the Lafourche." *Assumption Pioneer,* February 1, 1879.

84 Levy described the forty-nine-year-old Watson as, "A jolly and simple fellow who knows how to live comfortably."

85 Levy Diary, HUC. *Contravenes* meaning to go or act contrary to, to oppose in argument.

86 Levy, Eugene H. "The Donaldsonville Artillery." *Southern Bivouac,* 3 (1885), 302.

87 Levy Diary, HUC.

88 Ibid.

89 Hardy was a twenty-nine-year-old French native who worked as a clerk in New Orleans before joining the Donaldsonville Artillery in March 1863. In 1875 it was reported he was "murdered since the war." Bartlett, 66.

90 Levy Diary, HUC.

91 Ibid.

92 Ibid.

93 Ibid.

94 James K. Greer, "Louisiana Politics, 1845-1861," *The Louisiana Historical Quarterly,* 12 (1929), 387, 388. The political maneuvering of the French and American groups is what caused the 1830 removal of the state capitol to Donaldsonville from New Orleans for one year. Greer, 393.

95 Levy Diary, HUC.

96 Ibid.

97 The popular "The Song of the Shirt" was written by London born Thomas Hood and published anonymously in 1843. The first of twelve stanzas went:

With fingers weary and worn,
With eyelids heavy and red,
A woman sat, in unwomanly rags,
Plying her needle and thread—
Stitch! stitch! stitch!
In poverty, hunger, and dirt,
And still with a voice of dolorous pitch
She sang the "Song of the Shirt."

98 "Vilikins Avd His Dinah! Or The Cup of Cold Pison" was a printed song sheet published by H. De Marsan of New York. It also made its way into a couple of Confederate songbooks, though the usual chorus of, "Singing, to la lol la rol lall to ral lal la" was omitted. The words went:

'Tis of a rich merchant who in London did dwell,
He had but one daughter, an unkimmon nice young gal,
Her name—it was Dinah, scarce sixteen years old;
With a very large fortune in silver and gold.

As Dinah was a valiking the garden one day,
Her papa he came to her, and thus he did say,
"Go dress yourself, Dinah, in gorgeous array,
And take yourself a husband, both galliant and gay.

"Oh papa, oh papa, I've not made up my mind,
And to marry just yet, why I don't feel inclined;
To you may large fortune I'll gladly give o'er,
If you'll let me live single a year or two more.

"Go, go, boldest daughter," the parent replied,
"If you won't consent to be this here young man's bride,
I'll give your large fortune to the nearest of kin,
And you shant reap the benefit of one single pin.

As Vilikins was valiking the garden ground,
He spied his dear Dinah laying dead upon the ground,
And the cup of cold pison, it lay by her side,
With a billet-doux a stating 'twas by pison she died.

He kissed her cold corpus a thousand time o'er,
And called her his Dinah though she was no more,
Then swallowed the pison like a lovyer so brave,
And Vilikins and his Dinah lie both in one grave,

MORAL

Now all you young maidens take warning by her,
Never not by no means disobey your governor;
And all you young fellows, mind who you claps eyes on,
Think of Vilikins and Dinah and the cup of cold pison."

99 Levy Diary, HUC.

100 "Woodman! Spare That Tree!," a ballad of four stanzas published in 1837 with words by George Pope Morris and music by Henry Russell.

101 In 1868 Beadle and Company of New York published a series of ten *Beadle's One Cent Song Book* of which, No. 5 was titled "Nigger, Put Down Dat Jug" and four other songs. The four stanza title song went:

1. Nigger put down that jug.
Touch not a single drop;
I'd gin it many a hug,
And dar you lef it stop;
'Twas dis ole nigger's hand
Dat fust did place it dar,
An dar you lef it stand
Or else dis nigger swar.

2. Dat ole familiar jug,
Chock full ob nigger rum,
Lord how I lub to hug
Because de drunk soon come;
Dar nigger lef it lay,

3. When but a nigger boy,
A hoeing massa's corn,
Lord how it gub me joy
To take from dat a horn;
I kiss it two tree time,
An den I suck him dry;
Dat jug he name but mine
So dar yu's lef him be.

4. My moufh around he cling
Close as de rum ole friend,
I kiss he an I sing
Dat rum may nebber end;
Nigger put down dat jug,

Touch not a single taste;--
Golly I cum dat way
Your back wid ropes I haste.

Touch not a single drop;
I'd gin it many a hug,
An dar you lef it sto

102 Moliere wrote *Le Misanthrope* in 1666. It is a French tragic comedy in which the main character always tells the truth in spite of what others may want to hear. Sabin Braud translated the play from French to English for Levy.

103 Levy Diary, HUC.

104 Levy evidently had some talent as a playwright. After the war he gained some fame by publishing a one-act comedy in New York City called "Endowed-Beds; or, An Hour With Jolley Hospital Surgeons." *Times-Picayune,* August 5, 1896.

105 *Don Juan* was another of Moliere's tragic comedy's written in 1665. About a graceless brigand of hearts who defies all warnings to mend his ways, it was very popular in America. *Don Juan* and *Le Misantrope* were known for their beauty and style. The Englishman George Gordon, Lord Byron (1788-1824), was as famous in his lifetime for his personality cult as for his romantic poetry. He wrote (from 1819-24), a long satiric narrative poem called *Don Juan.* Never completed, modern critics consider it Byron's masterpiece.

What Will He Do with It (1858), originally ran as a serial in England's Blackwood's *Edinburg Magazine* from June 1857 through January 1859 prior to volume publication. Written by Baron Edward G. D. Bulwer-Lytton (1803-1873), Charles Dickens reportedly supplied the title. The English novelist is best remembered for his historical novels *The Last Days of Pompeii* (1834) and *Rienzi* (1835). *Blair's Rhetoric* was titled *Lectures on Rhetoric and Belles Lettres,* first published in Edinburgh, England (1783), in two volumes. It was written by Hugh Blair (1718-1800), a famous English preacher and lecturer.

106 Levy Diary, HUC.

107 Ibid.

108 Canonnier Artificer François "Bienvenue" Cire had a sixty-day sick furlough for January & February 1865. Cire had quit writing in his memorandum book upon arriving at High Bridge on June 22, 1864.

109 Burkeville village developed at the junction where the Richmond and Danville and the South Side Railroads intersected. Nearby Burke's Tavern was built in 1800 and still stands. Bradshaw, *Prince Edward,* 841.

110 The Louisiana Home in Richmond was established by John Perkins Jr., a New Orleans attorney, District Judge, Somerset (cotton) Plantation owner in Ashwood, Madison Parish, and former United States and now Confederate States member of Congress. Half of the old Exchange Hotel located at the southeast corner of Fourteenth and Franklin streets was used for the convenience of Louisiana soldiers passing through the city, providing a place where "the weary may find rest and comfort and entertainment, among the soldiers of his own state." Levy noted the bill of fare was beef, bread, potatoes, and beans, all well prepared and nicely served. *Richmond Sentinel,* September 1, 1864.

111 This was General Hospital #9, with a capacity of 900 patients and located on the north side of Grace Street, between Seventeenth and Eighteenth Streets. It was built in 1810 as a tobacco warehouse and became a municipal-owned public warehouse called Seabrook. It was known as "the billboard of Richmond" because it was always well "papered" with show and circus sheets, announcements, and political placards. The City's Seabrook Playground is on the site today. Waitt, 13.

112 Levy Diary, HUC.

113 Ibid.

CHAPTER SEVENTEEN

1 Gallagher, *Fighting,* 473.

2 I. G. Bradwell, "On Picket Duty in Front of Fort Steadman," *CV,* 38 (1930), 303.

3 Hampden Osborne, "The Struggle for Fort Mahone," *CV,* 25 (1917), 226.

4 Walters, NPL.

5 Chamberlayne, 256.

6 *OR* XLII:II, 1,168.
7 Dunbar Rowland, *Official and Statistical Register of the State of Mississippi,* Vol. 5, "Military History of Mississippi, 1803-1898" (Nashville, 1908), 80.
8 James J. Kirkpatrick Diary, 1861-1864, UT.
9 Walters, NPL.
10 Mason W. Tyler, *Recollections of the Civil War with Many Original Diary Entries and Letters Written from the Seat of War, and with Annotated References* (New York, 1912), 233.
11 Bartlett, 202.
12 David W. Blight, ed. *When This Cruel War Is Over* (Amherst, Mass., 1992), 315.
13 Herbert E. Valentine, *Story of Co. F, 23d Massachusetts Volunteers in the War for the Union 1861-1865* (Boston, 1896), 129.
14 W. A. Day, "Life Among Bullets—In the Rifle Pits," *CV* 29 (1921), 173.
15 *OR* XLII:II, 1,184, 1,208:III, 1,355; PRS of Donaldsonville Artillery Muster Roll for July/August 1864, LAGL.
16 "Sketch of Rives's Salient," Andrew and George Hero Papers, LSU
17 William M. Owen to Col. John B. Walton, October 13, 1864, Walton-Glenny Family Papers, HNOC.
18 Richard Sommers, *Richmond Redeemed, The Siege at Petersburg* (Garden City, N.Y., 1981), 211, 212.
19 Richardson, 179, 180. This was taken from Richardson's fictional short story "The Conscript" and seems to be an accurate description of Rives's Salient and left redan (Battery 25), where Prosper Landry's four Donaldsonville Artillery guns were positioned.
20 Gallagher, *Fighting,* 469.
21 NA, Record of Events (Donaldsonville Art'y), November & December 1864.
22 Chamberlayne, 264.
23 Levy Diary, HUC. The piece rested on the cannon's barrel protecting Cannoneer Number 4 who stood near the rear of the left wheel and pulled the lanyard to fire the cannon. Cannoneer Number 3 thumbed the vent after firing and while the gun was loaded, then punctured the cartridge bag with the vent pick before standing near the rear of the right wheel. The gunner was chief of the piece and aimed the gun while it is loaded. He stood to the rear of Cannoneer Number 4 and gave the command to fire.
24 Levy Diary, HUC. The forms were made of heavy oak and had a hole cut through them. Tacked over the hole in the block on the side toward the enemy was a piece of sheet iron about one inch thick with a small hole about an inch in diameter to look through. I. G. Bradwell, "On Picket Duty in Front of Fort Steadman, 1865," *CV* 25 (1917), 408.
25 Pendleton Papers, UNCCH; *OR* XLVI:2, 1305.
26 Jones Diary, LHAC; James W. Albright Diary, North Carolina State Archives; NA Record of Events (Donaldsonville Art'y), November & December 1864.
27 Jerome B. Yates to Marie Yates Swanson, August 2, 1864, UT.
28 Levy Diary, HUC.
29 Ibid.
30 Ibid.
31 "Some of the Experiences of James C. Reed as a Soldier in the Army of the Confederate States," Typescript, Thomas Balch Library, 27.
32 Jones Diary, LHAC.
33 Levy Diary, HUC.
34 Hilary A. Hebert, "History of the Eighth Alabama Volunteer Regiment, C. S. A." *Alabama Historical Quarterly*, 39 (1977), 143.
35 Levy Diary, HUC. At the beginning of the war Ettrick had about 830 residents with Campbell's Bridge being the only direct thoroughfare across the Appomattox River into Petersburg, as it is today. In 1882 Virginia State University was founded at Ettrick, the first fully supported institution for higher learning for African-Americans. Today's campus has 5,600 students while the population of Ettrick in 2010 is 5,313.
36 Levy, HUC. The Catholic sisterhoods included the Sisters of Charity, the Sisters of Mercy, the Sisters of St. Joseph, and the Sisters of the Holy Cross. Soldiers and civilians alike made no distinction between the orders, and all the dark robed angels of mercy were called "Sisters of Charity."

37 NA, Compiled Service Records of the Donaldsonville Artillery. Others no doubt were hospitalized without documentation or had their records lost, making the statistics higher than the number recorded.
38 NA, Compiled Service Records of Grandy's Battery and Moore's Battery.
39 Chamberlanye, 287.
40 NA, Landry File; *Biographical and Historical Memoirs of Louisiana*. Vol. I (Chicago, 1892), 531, 532; *Donaldsonville Chief*, June 20, 1907.
41 Richardson, 207-209.
42 Jean Reynaud Jacques Prosper Landry to Adele Pedesclaux Landry, September 1864, UV.
43 Levy Diary, HUC.
44 *Donaldsonville Chief*, June 15, 1907.
45 Ibid., December 21, 1907.
46 NA, Richardson File.
47 PRS of Donaldsonville Artillery Muster Rolls, July through December 1864, LAGL.
48 Chamberlayne, 282.
49 Levy Diary, HUC.
50 *The Daily Times* (Donaldsonville, La.), April 27, 1898.
51 Chambers, 72.
52 Levy Diary, HUC.
53 Owen, 354.
54 Bartlett, 199, 201, 202.
55 Chamberlayne, 255, 266.
56 Holt, 300.
57 Walters, NPL.
58 William M. Owen to J. B. Walton, October 13, 1864, Walton-Glenny Family Papers, HNOC.
59 Armistead C. Gordon, *Memories and Memorials of William Gordon McCabe*, I (Richmond, Va., 1925), 178. On October 28, 1864, Levy noted Canonnier Pvt. John Eckleburg "recieved his copy of Shakespeare from Gordonsville and I read aloud from 'Othello' for the benefit of my messmates" and "to a crowd of the boys" in the trenches. Levy Diary, HUC; *Times-Picayune,* August 11, 1902.
60 Lineback Papers, 147, UNCCH.
61 Ibid.
62 James W. Albright Diary, 11. North Carolina Department of Archives and History.
63 Lineback Papers, 151, UNCCH.
64 Andrew Hero, September 25, 1864, Andrew Jr. and George Hero Papers, LSU.
65 Chamberlayne, 260.
66 Abell, 208, 209, 339. "Ever of Thee" was so popular several songwriters claimed authorship. Confederate publishers issued nine editions of the song and reprinted it in eight different songsters.
67 Ibid., 213.
68 Gordon, Vol. I, 183.
69 James W. Albright Diary, North Carolina Department of Archives and History, 11.
70 Chamberlayne, 282.
71 Henry E. Taintor to Mother, July 22, 1864, Duke University.
72 Chamberlayne, 282.
73 Walters, NPL.
74 Levy Diary, HUC.
75 Walters, NPL.
76 NA, M258 Records on Artillery Battalions. Rougeau was almost certainly buried at nearby Blandford Church Cemetery, where 30,000 Confederate dead are interred and only about 2,000 are identified.
77 Jean Reynaud Jacques Prosper Landry to Adele Pedesclaux Landry, September 1864 letter, UV.
78 Levy Diary, HUC.
79 Walters, NPL.
80 NA, CSR.
81 *Times-Picayune,* July 21, 1902.
82 Comstock received gunshot wounds to the arm and side, both probably superficial for there is

no record of him being admitted into a hospital. Most likely he was treated at the artillery corps hospital or field hospital at Ettrick before returning to duty.

83 *New Orleans City Item,* October 10, 1877. Ely was sent to Louisiana Hospital where, on August 3, he was issued clothing. He received a thirty-day sick furlough and traveled to Mobile, Alabama, with Levy. They left Richmond by train on August 9 with Ely continuing on to Woodville, Mississippi. His sick furlough was renewed through November 1864. He reported to the General Hospital in Farmville, Virginia, where a Board of Surgeons examined and honorably retired him to the Invalid Corps, Provisional Army, Confederate States on November 29, 1864. He remained with the High Bridge section, according to Levy Diary, in December 1864 and January 1865.

84 "Henri" Newchurch was admitted and treated at the Louisiana Hospital in Richmond; he received a sick furlough before returning to duty in January 1865.

85 "Bill" Newchurch was probably treated at the field hospital and received a furlough in December. He didn't return and on the January/February 1865 Muster Roll was noted as "Absent without leave."

86 Eugene Levy, HUC. "Tony" Suarez was treated at the field hospital and returned to duty within a month.

87 Chesson, 271.

88 On his application to the Benevolent Association of the Army of Virginia Sobral related that an exploding shell wounded him in the head at Petersburg. The application was endorsed by Maj. M. B. "Buck" Miller and Cpl. J. A. Comstock, dated February 17, 1878. There is no record of Sobral being admitted to a hospital, although he probably received aid at the field hospital. LHAC.

89 NA, CSR of Landry's, Grandy's, and Moore's batteries; Porter, 253, 254, 257, 258.

90 Donaldsonville Artillery Pvt. John "Eck" Eckleburg.

91 Levy Diary, HUC.

92 Ibid.

93 Richardson, 220. Glacis was the slope extending down from the fortifications while Prisoner's Base was a game in which two teams capture opposing players by tagging them and taking them to their own base.

94 *Times-Picayune,* August 4, 1902.

95 *La Dernier Des Mohicans,* or "Last of the Mohicans," refers to James Fenimore Cooper's historical romance novel, the second book of five so-called Leather Stocking Tales published in 1826. It ends with the tragic death of the last warrior of the race of the Mohicans. Italics are the author's.

96 *Times-Picayune,* August 4, 1902.

97 "The Battle at Fort Gregg, Louisiana Survivors Tell the Story of the Fight," Unidentified author, *SHSP,* 28, 265. Donaldsonville Artillery Pvt. "Johnee" Mioton, is believed to be the anonymous writer of the account.

98 Bartlett, 218.

99 Walters, NPL.

100 E. C. Cottrell, "The Fight at Fort Gregg," *CV,* 7 (1899), 308.

101 A. E. Strother, "Battle and Capture of Fort Gregg," *CV,* 29 (1921), 425.

102 Levy Diary, HUC.

103 Ibid.

104 *Times-Picayune,* August 4, 1902. Levy's diary noted the two soldiers were Jake Levy and one of the Lovenstein brothers.

105 Ibid.

106 Ibid.

107 Levy Diary, HUC.

108 Walters Diary, NPL.

109 No information on Phillips has been uncovered

110 *Times-Picayune,* August 11, 1902. Remarks in parentheses in this paragraph are additions Levy made in the newspaper article that were not in his diary.

111 Levy Diary, HUC.

112 *Times-Picayune,* August 11, 1902.

113 Freeman, *Lee* Vol. III, 535.

114 I. G. Bradwell, "On Picket Duty in Front of Fort Steadman," *CV,* 38 (1930), 303.

115 W. A. Day, "Life Among Bullets—In the Rifle Pits," *CV,* 39(1921), 217.

116 Freeman, *Lee* Vol. III, 541.

117 Levy Diary, HUC.
118 Jones Diary, LHAC.
119 *Donaldsonville Chief,* March 13, 1875.
120 Levy Diary, HUC.
121 NA, CSR.
122 *OR* XLII:3, 995.
123 NA, CSR.
124 "Memoirs of David Washington Pipes," LAGL.
125 Freeman, *Lee* Vol. III, 537.
126 Levy Diary, HUC.
127 Ibid.
128 *Times-Picayune,* June 23, 1902.
129 Jean Reynaud Jacques Prosper Landry to Adele Pedesclaux Landry, September 1864, UV.
130 Levy Diary, HUC.
131 *Journals of the Congress of the Confederate States of America, 1861-1865* (Vol. 4), Washington, D. C., 1904-1905. At High Bridge on February 16, 1865, Levy noted, "The Richmond [news]papers contain a series of patriotic resolutions adopted at a meeting of the [Donaldsonville] section at Petersburg."
132 *Times-Picayune,* June 23, 1902.
133 Ibid., July 14, 1902.
134 Walters Diary, NPL.
135 NA, Record of Events (Donaldsonville Art'y), January & February 1865.
136 After receiving the records from the different commands, Favrot preserved all of them in a trunk, including the Donaldsonville Artillery's, and returned to Louisiana. He safe guarded them until he turned over the documents on April 21, 1879, to the Adjt. Gen. of Louisiana, P. G. T. Beauregard. The twelve bound volumes of the Army of Northern Virginia's ten Louisiana regiments, along with three of its battalions, and the Donaldsonville and Louisiana Guard batteries and Battalion Washington Artillery are today located in the Louisiana Historical Association Collection on deposit in the Howard-Tilton Memorial Library, Tulane University, New Orleans, Louisiana. The Donaldsonville Artillery's bound volume in the collection was "copied and transcribed from the original" on November 14, 1885, by Donaldsonville Canonnier veteran John S. Mioton.
137 Owen, 364.
138 John Willis Council Diary, North Carolina Department of Archives and History.
139 Freeman, *Lee,* Vol. IV, 16, 22.
140 Walters Diary, NPL.
141 Freeman, *Lee,* Vol. IV, 22, 27-29.
142 *Richmond Times Dispatch,* June 25, 1905.
143 Walters Diary, NPL.
144 Freeman, *Lee,* Vol. IV, 30.
145 *OR* XLI:III, 1,315.
146 Nelson D. Lankford, ed. *An Irishman in Dixie, Thomas Conolly's Diary of the Fall of the Confederacy* (Columbia, S. C., 1988), 73.
147 Walters Diary, NPL. Documentation on the type of guns taken over from Jones has not been located.
148 Favrot Papers, TU.
149 *OR* XLVI:I, 53.
150 Lankford, 74.
151 Ibid.
152 Chamberlayne, 314.
153 De Trobriand, 728.
154 Clark, Vol. I, 683; *Richmond Times Dispatch,* June 25, 1905; BAANV Application of A. R. Sanchez dated February 17, 1883, LHAC; Gordon, Vol. I, 171, 172; *OR* XLVI:I, 788 (Federal reports that include maps of the position are located on pages 810, 814, 819). Also see *OR Atlas* LXVI, Map 9. The millpond has been expanded and is today man-made Jordan Lake. Lt. Col. Carter M. Braxton's Second Corps Battalion included the Lee (Va.) Battery, Capt. William W. Hardwicke; Stafford (Va.) Light Artillery, Capt. Raleigh L. Cooper; and the Alleghany (Va.) Artillery, Capt. John C. Carpenter. Col. W. J. Pegram's Battalion was composed of Capt. Thomas Ellett's (Va.)

Battery (formerly Crenshaw's); Fredericksburg (Va.) Artillery, Capt. Edward A. Marye; Letcher (Va.) Artillery, Capt. Thomas A. Brander; Purcell (Va.) Artillery, Capt. George M. Cayce; and McQueen Light Artillery or Company C, 18th (S. C.) Battalion, Capt. Thomas E. Gregg.

155 Freeman, *Lee,* Vol. IV, 43.

156 Lankford, 74.

157 Caldwell, 269.

158 Lankford, 77. Walter Taylor was Lee's Assistant Adjutant-General.

159 Gordon, Vol. I, 173.

160 Ibid., 172.

161 *OR* XLVI:I, 808.

162 Ibid., 676.

163 Ibid.

164 Ibid.

165 Caldwell, 269.

166 *OR* XLVI:1, 686, 810. Warren reported four men killed and nine wounded, while Humphreys's loss for the day's operation was three killed, fifty-eight wounded, and four missing.

167 *OR* XLVI:1, 827.

168 The four brigades led by Maj. Gen. Bushrod R. Johnson were from three different divisions, Moody's Alabama and Wise's Virginia of Johnson's Division, Anderson's Corps; McGowan's South Carolina of Wilcox's Division, Hill's Corps; and Hunton's Virginia of Pickett's Division, Longstreet's Corps. Because of the terrain and rain it was impractical for artillery and none was attached.

169 *OR* XLVI:1, 686, 776, 777. Regiments from the Second Brigade that attacked were the 5th Michigan and 1st Massachusetts Heavy Artillery (serving as infantry), and from the Third Brigade, 11th Massachusetts Volunteers, 120th New York, and the left wing of the 8th New Jersey supported by the 11th New Jersey Regiment. Mott reported six killed, fifty-nine wounded, and forty-four missing.

170 *OR* XLVI:1, 781.

171 Ibid., 724.

172 Ibid., 816.

173 Ibid., 686, 819, 1288. Warren's Fifth Corps sustained the brunt of the Confederate attack and suffered 126 killed, 811 wounded, and 470 missing. Humphreys's Second Corps, minus Mott's casualties, lost 45 killed, 260 wounded, and 42 missing.

174 Walters Diary, NPL. Moore's casualties according to Walters and matched by the NA, CSR, listed Sgt. Edward E. Beaton, and Privates Richard M. Boutwell and William O. White, killed, Cpl. Richard D. Brown and Privates Henry W. Hebert, Richard Rye, and William Oscar Edwards White wounded. A post-war source incorrectly lists different dates for their wounds.

175 Judith McGuire, *Diary of a Southern Refugee* (New York, 1867), 350, 351. Richardson recovered from his wound and was paroled as a prisoner of war on May 8, 1865. Interestingly, during the war he invented a "War-Chess, Game of Battle" which, in December 1866 he patented (#60,247). It was described: "One of the most attractive and ingenious Games of strategy . . . of the highest interest and merit . . . played by two persons with figures representing Soldiers (Cavalry, Artillery, and Infantry), forming two antagonistic armies, operating on a board." Charles C. Richardson was born at Richmond in 1831 to John and Lavania Washington Dandridge, whose grandfather was the brother of Martha Dandridge that married George Washington. A year after marrying (on June 8, 1869), fellow Virginian Charlotte Blaine, daughter of a wealthy Presbyterian minister, the Richardson's moved to New York City, where he worked as a bookkeeper. Richardson's widowed aunt Eleanor Julianna Dandridge (Charles was named after his uncle, her husband), remarried Lawrence W. Willis, owner of Willis Hill Plantation and a pickle factory in Fredericksburg. In 1875 the Richardsons moved to Fredericksburg, where Charles began putting up pickles at the large and commodious pickle plant on the corner of Frederick Street and Prince Edward Street. It was named Windsor Manor Pickle Factory and was known by its motto, "Quality Before Quantity." The company manufactured, canned, and bottled pickles and preserves. In no small part due to the Colonel's marketing skills, it became nationally and internationally known. Richardson's pickles, beginning with the Centennial Exhibition in 1876, won medals and diplomas at every international exposition, including the 1889 Universal Exposition in Paris, France. It is believed that Richardson became a widower on June 30, 1878, and raised his three children, William

Dorrington, born 1871 (and in 1902 named secretary and treasurer of the Richardson Pickling Company), Samuel Blaine, born 1873, and Lavinia Dandridge, born 1875. By 1907 Richardson was retired at his Willis Hill home on Marye's Heights, where in 1885 he had built the house currently standing on the property that is owned by the Fredericksburg and Spotsylvania National Military Park. Richardson wrote two books in 1907, *The Chancellorsville Campaign, Fredericksburg to Salem Church* and *Tales of a Warrior; Sanguine but not Sanguinary, For Old-time People.* Richardson died at home on September 6, 1913, and is buried (without a gravestone), in the Fredericksburg Confederate Cemetery. He was survived by his three children and one grandchild, Dortothea Richardson. FSNMP, Richardson File; *The Free Lance* (Fredericksburg, Va.), February 6, 1885; *Richmond Dispatch,* July 8, 1902; "War-Chest, Game of Battle" advertisement in: Forrest, Mary, *Women of the South Distinguished in Literature* (New York, 1866).

176 *OR* XLVI:1, 822.

177 Gordon, Vol. I, 163. Pickett's infantry, with cavalry, and Col. William J. Pegram commanding four guns from Ellett's Battery and two of Hardwicke's Battery (of Braxton's Battalion) were engaged in the Battle of Five Forks.

178 Caldwell, 278.

CHAPTER EIGHTEEN

1 Benevolent Association of the Army of Virginia application of A. R. Sanchez dated February 17, 1883, LHAC.

2 Caldwell, 278.

3 *OR* XLVI:1, 678.

4 Ibid., 678, 711, 902; Benson, 187.

5 Hyland C. Kirk, *History of the 4th New York Heavy Artillery* (New York, 1890), 379. The attacking force was made up of regiments from the 73rd New York, 124th New York, and 110th Pennsylvania of the First Brigade commanded by Brig. Gen. Regis de Trobriand of the Third Division, Maj. Gen. Gershom Mott commanding, from Maj. Gen. Andrew A. Humphreys' Second Army Corps.

6 *OR* XLVI:1, 686, 777. Casualties reported in the Third Division were 2 killed, 18 wounded, and 6 men missing.

7 Ibid., 902.

8 Clark, Vol. I, 684.

9 Caldwell, 280.

10 Clark, Vol. I, 684.

11 Caldwell, 280.

12 Freeman, *Lee,* Vol. IV, 48; Freeman, *Lieutenants,* Vol. 3, 680.

13 Porter, 250.

14 At least thirty-three of Grandy's artillerists rejoined Lee's army on the retreat. It appears four of them made it to Hatcher's Run and marched with the Donaldsonville Artillery. NA, CSR.

15 Freeman, *Lee,* Vol. IV, 48; Freeman, *Lieutenants,* Vol. 3, 680.

16 Freeman, *Lieutenants*, Vol. 3, 682.

17 Buxton R. Conerly, "How Fort Gregg Was Defended," *CV,* 15 (1907), 505.

18 Also entering to defend the fort were fragments of Thomas and Lane's North Carolina brigades, thus making the number of infantry entering about two hundred in all. Owens, 371.

19 Unidentified, "The Battle at Fort Gregg, Louisiana Survivors Tell the Story of the Fight," *SHSP*, Vol. XXVIII, 265, 266.

20 Ibid. The "brave Berry" was Lawrence Berry.

21 Washington Artillery Collection, Civil War Papers, LHAC.

22 Ibid.

23 *OR* XLVI:1, 1179.

24 Ibid., 1174.

25 Freeman, *Lieutenants*, Vol. 3, 682, 683. All that remains today of Fort Gregg is an earthen mound in a field near Interstate 85. Stop 14 of the *Siege Line Tour of Petersburg National Battlefield Park.*

26 Caldwell, 280.

27 Ibid.

28 *OR* XLVI:1, 789. The regiment was the 8th New Jersey. The two Federal batteries were the 10th Massachusetts and Battery M, 1st New Hampshire Artillery. *OR* XLVI:1, 792.
29 H. Heth to O. Latrobe [11 April 1865], Report of Operations since 2 April, Robert Edward Lee Headquarters Papers, 1850-1876, Virginia Historical Society.
30 De Trobriand, 728.
31 Giroir was captured and imprisoned until May 8, 1865. He then surrendered his parole and took the Oath of Allegiance in Alexandria, Virginia, before being released and returning home to Napoleonville.
32 *Times-Picayune,* January 17, 1887.
33 *OR* XLVI:1, 679, 734, 777. The entrenchments from the Boydton Plank Road ran parallel to the White Oak Road (Secondary State Route 613), approximately 1.7 miles to the intersection of the Claiborne Road (Secondary State Route 631). This road, traveling north about one mile, crosses Hatcher's Run and between two and three miles further reaches Sutherland Station. See map in *OR* XLVI:1, 819.
34 Caldwell, 281, 282. The Claiborne Road from White Oak Road and the entrenchments led to the Fendell C. Sutherland house and tavern known as Fork Inn at Sutherland Station. The fourteen-room affair built in 1803 served as a stagecoach stop, tavern, and post office in the early nineteenth century. It later served rail passengers on the nearby South Side Railroad, giving the family name to the railway station. The refurbished inn still stands. Dave Roth, "Day of Decision at Petersburg," *Blue and Gray Magazine,* 18:3, 60, 62. The country church is Ocran Methodist Church, built around 1854. The congregation still worships there, though only sections of the wartime church are original. Christopher M. Calkins, *From Petersburg to Appomattox* (Farmville, Va., 1983), 19.
35 Christopher M. Calkins, *The Appomattox Campaign, March 29-April 9, 1865* (Conshohocken, Pa., 1997), 48; Porter, 257; BAANV Application of A. R. Sanchez dated February 17, 1883, LHAC.
36 Caldwell, 282, 283. The first attack was by the Second Brigade, the second attack by the Third Brigade of Brevet Maj. Gen. Nelson A. Miles's First Division, Second Army Corps. *OR* XLVI:1, 711.
37 Benson, 190.
38 *OR* XLVI:1, 711.
39 Ibid., 725.
40 Caldwell, 284.
41 *OR* XLVI:1, 746.
42 William S. Dunlop, *Lee's Sharpshooters; or, The Forefront of Battle. A Story of Southern Valor That Never Has Been Told* (Little Rock, 1899), 276.
43 Porter, 257. Published twenty-seven years after the war, it was erroneously recorded the capture took place, "On the 1st of April, 1865, the [Norfolk] Battery was in position on Hatcher's Run." Brevet Major General Miles commanded the attacking division at Sutherland Station and reported the capture of "2 pieces of artillery." Three regiments, the 69th New York, 4th New York Heavy Artillery (infantry), and 8th New Jersey claimed the capture of both pieces while the 64th New York, 145th Pennsylvania, and 148th Pennsylvania claimed the capture of one of the pieces. See *OR* XLVI:1, 712, 724, 733, 746, 748, 754, 755.
44 *OR* XLVI:1, 680.
45 This may explain why members of the Norfolk artillerymen, including Captain Joseph D. Moore, were listed as captured at Petersburg or Hatcher's Run instead of Sutherland Station.
46 *OR* XLVI:1, 737; NA, CSR. Ashe and Reid were later joined by Sergeant John E. Wadsworth, acting Commissary Sergeant for the battalion. The three were the only members of Moore's Norfolk Battery to reach Appomattox Court House, where they surrendered with the Donaldsonville Artillery.
47 Caldwell, 286.
48 BAANV Application of A. R. Sanchez dated February 17, 1883, LHAC.
49 *B & L,* Vol. III, 97.
50 Donaldsonville Artillery *Historical Memoranda,* LHAC.
51 Clark, Vol. II, 455.
52 R. Prosper Landry to F. A. Ober, April 4, 1885, Camp Nicholls Soldiers Home Papers, LHAC. The books contained copies of the muster rolls and records of the battery.

53 The four were Giroir, as already noted, Gustave Boudreau, Adam Shriver, and Michael "Hick" Flannighan. The names of the latter three Canonniers were hurriedly recorded by a Federal registration officer on the same list with fifteen of Moore's Norfolk artillerist and documented as captured at Petersburg and Hatcher's Run. The three Donaldsonville men were sent to prison at Point Lookout, Maryland, by way of City Point, Virginia, and were made to take the Oath of Allegiance before being released on June 9, 20, and 26, 1865. NA, CSR. No record of Giroir's capture as been located, which is not surprising in that his name is pronounced Shee-wa, and with his Bayou Lafourche Cajun accent, his name was probably grossly misspelled on a list by Federal authorities.

54 *OR* XLVI:1, 711.

55 Caldwell, 287, 288.

56 Freeman, *Lieutenants*, Vol. III, 688.

57 Levy Diary, HUC.

58 Joseph F. L. "Joe" Walton, about twenty-four years of age, was a native of Farmville, Virginia.

59 Levy Diary, HUC.

60 Ibid.

61 Ibid. Whiting, from Norfolk, surrendered at Appomattox with the Donaldsonville Artillery.

62 Ibid. Since High Bridge was in the Lynchburg Military District and the city of Lynchburg was a collection point and supply depot, it can be presumed that Brig. Gen. Raleigh E. Colston commanding (he replaced Donaldsonville's Brig. Gen. Francis T. Nicholls), promised the horses. Nicholls was ordered in December 1864 to command the Conscriptive Service in the Trans-Mississippi Department. *OR* XLI:4, 1122.

63 Originally known as Randolph House, it was located at the northeast corner of N. Main and E. Second streets. The proprietor was tobacconist and commander of the reserves Col. Richard Booker. On April 7 Federal troops along with Gen. U. S. Grant entered Farmville, the Union general spending the night at Randolph House. Grant noted the hotel was almost destitute of furniture and wrote, "The next morning when I came out I found a Confederate Colonel there, who reported to me and said that he was the proprietor of that house, and that he was a colonel of a regiment that had been raised in that neighborhood. He said that when he came along past home, he found that he was the only man of the regiment remaining with Lee's army, so he just dropped out, and now wanted to surrender himself." The hotel underwent renovations in 1907 after which it was renamed the Prince Edward Hotel. The building stood until it collapsed under going renovations in 1964. Booker was also the proprietor of the *Farmville News* newspaper. The Colonel died in 1904. Ulysess S. Grant, *Personal Memoirs of U. S. Grant in Two Volumes*, II (New York, 1886), 480; *Petersburg Daily Index,* January 28, 1870.

64 Evidently Mrs. Mary Priscilla Venable ran the farm while her husband Col. Thomas F. Venable was away. Venable had a "high reputation for his Snuff and Tobacco" and his *Scott-Greene Plantation* contained fifty-five slaves in 1860. The farm was still worth $10,000 in 1870. The Venables had twelve children with two serving the Confederacy, 2nd Lt. Clement Reade Venable of the 1st Confederate States Engineers, wounded and captured on April 7 at High Bridge, and Matthew Walton Venable who celebrated his eighteenth birthday with the Confederate Army at Appomattox on April 9, 1865. *The Petersburg Index*, March 20, 1867.

65 The correct French spelling is *qui vive* meaning "on alert."

66 Unmarried Sarah A. Sturdivant, about twenty-seven years old, was from Petersburg. Her brother was Maj. Nathaniel A. Sturdivant, captain of the Albermarle (Va.), Light Artillery that was captured at Petersburg on June 15, 1864. He was later exchanged and while commanding a battalion of artillery promoted to major on March 17, 1865. Soon after the war Sturdivant was elected Mayor of Richmond but was not allowed to take office by the Federal government. He was a business associate of A. M. Keiley who gave a flattering eulogy for Sturdivant at the time of his death in 1869. *The Petersburg Index*, August 9, 1869.

67 Levy Diary, HUC.

68 Evidently Booker's 3rd Virginia Reserve Regiment returned from guarding the Staunton River Bridge and on the retreat disbanded.

69 Levy Diary, HUC.

70 *OR* XLVI:1, 1169. Italics are the author's for the artillery was Mollere's section of the Donaldsonville Artillery. Maj. Gen. Edward O. C. Ord commanding the Army of the James sent the Federal force to High Bridge with instructions "if not too well guarded, to burn it." Years later it was

believed and recorded that spies informed Ord the High Bridge fortifications were abandoned, but the Massachusetts's cavalry reportedly found the bridge "well defended, a redoubt mounting several guns being near its head." *OR* XLVI:1, 1161. Mollere's detachment had "cut down" the guns in the redoubts when they left High Bridge. It was also reported, "The enemy's numbers were such, and their artillery fire so heavy, however, that they could not be driven." Edward T. Bouve, "The Battle at High Bridge," *The New England Magazine,* 10 (July, 1891), 631. Evidently the Donaldsonville Artillery gun firing "a couple of shots" from a hilltop made the impression of severe artillery fire.

71 Mary Embra Scott Venable's husband Nathaniel E. Venable (1793-1865), had recently passed away. Their son was Col. Charles Scott Venable, the principal staff officer to General Lee.

72 Johnston was born at the location, but Nathaniel E. Venable bought the land from the Johnstons and built the present Longwood House in 1815. It is one of the grand old houses of Prince Edward County, a beautiful two and one-half story, Greek Revival style with a Doric front porch that is currently home of the president of Longwood University. The school was chartered in 1839 as the Farmville Female Academy, a preparatory school.

73 "Southern style" or as Prosper Landry wrote, "American style, everything at once on the same small plate." The Creoles of Louisiana and New Orleanians took their meals from the French Table Serving style in which, the table is neatly set with different plates and silverware. The food is presented and one decides, with proper plate and utensils, what one would like. The meal is usually multi-course. Jean Reynaud Jaques Prosper Landry to Adele Pedesclaux Landry, September 1864, UV.

74 In 1860 Dr. William F. Carrington, 41, was stationed at Escambia, Florida while serving in the U. S. Navy. He and his wife, 37, had four children with the oldest being nineteen year-old Mildred.

75 *Times-Picayune,* August 18, 1902.

76 *Flaneur* meaning idler, dawdler, or stroller.

77 Maj. Gen. John C. Breckinridge, on February 4, 1865, became Confederate Secretary of War.

78 William McIlvaine was one of three chaplains serving at the Farmville General Hospital. Burrell, 184.

79 *Donaldsonville Chief,* December 21, 1907. "Without fear and without reproach," quote by William Gilmore Simms (1806-1870), in his *The Life of the Chevalier Bayard (1848)* about Pierre de Bayard of France, 1476-1524, who gained renown both for skill in combat and for his knightly virtues.

80 Levy Diary, HUC.

81 Caldwell, 290.

82 Ibid., 291.

83 Clark, Vol. II, 456, 457.

84 Freeman, *Lee*, Vol. IV, 68.

85 *OR* XLVI:1, 1281. Frank Cauble, "The Battle of Appomattox Station April 8, 1865 and The Battle of Appomattox Court House April 9, 1865, A Narrative Study to Accompany Appomattox Court House Troop Movement Maps" (January 1961), Appomattox Court House National Historical Park, 5, 6, ii, iii. . Other battalions assigned to Walker train included Lightfoot's, Coit's, Cabell's, Walker's, Leydens', Hardaway's, Lane's, Huger's, and Owen's. Chris M. Calkins, *The Battles of Appomattox Station and Appomattox Court House April 8-9, 1865* (Lynchburg, Va., 1987), 266.

86 G. W. Koontz to D. G. McIntosh letter of May 11, 1907, Pegram-Johnson-McIntosh Collection, Virginia Historical Society.

87 Freeman, *Lee*, Vol. IV, 71.

88 Council Diary, North Carolina Department of Archives and History.

89 Bartlett, 222; Percy G. Hawes, "Last Days of the Army of Northern Virginia, A Courier's Recollections of the Last Ten days of War," *CV,* 17 (1919), 34; W. F. Robinson, "Last Battle Before Surrender," *CV,* 22 (1924), 470.

90 Benjamin W. Jones *Under the Stars and Bars: A History of the Surry Light Artillery; Recollections of a Private Soldier in the War Between the States* (Richmond, Va., 1909), 256.

91 J. R. Winder, "Reminiscences of J. R. Winder," *CV,* 8(1901), 411.

92 Lobrano Diary, LHAC. The route from Amelia follows nearby Virginia Secondary Route 681 north across the Appomattox River at Clementown Bridge, where camp was made before reaching Tobbaccoville.

93 Harry C. Townsend, "Townsend's Diary—January-May, 1865; From Petersburg to Appomattox,

Thence to North Carolina to Join Johnston's Army," *SHSP* Vol. XXXIV, 103. The corn and flour mill on the Appomattox River was built about 1760 and burned around 1930.

94 Ibid.

95 Lobrano Diary, LHAC.

96 Jones, Benjamin W., 258.

97 The first positive call for a completely independent American nation issued by a governmental body was made on April 22, 1776, from the balcony of the Effingham Tavern. There Carter H. Harrison read Cumberland County's committee instructions to their delegates to the State convention: "We therefore, your constituents, instruct you positively to declare for an Independency, that you solemnly abjure any allegiance to His Britannic Majesty and bid him a good night forever." The Virginia Convention decided to follow Cumberland's lead resulting in the Virginia Resolutions, which were presented to the Continental Congress and embodied in the Declaration of Independence. Unfortunately the inn, which served so many travelers on the early road to western Virginia burned in 1933. "Proceeding of the Committee of Safety of Cumberland and Isle of Wight County" and "Order Books in Cumberland County Clerk's Office," Farmville Area Chamber of Commerce.

98 Lobrano Diary, LHAC.

99 Gordon, Vol. I, 166. Though many of the modern roads continue to follow the original roadbeds of that period, others do not. A number of these byways remain merely dirt paths traversing the natural terrain and consequently there has been much speculation and some confusion in the actual route taken by the artillery train. After reaching Tobbaccoville the column headed west on Virginia Primary Route 13 to U. S. Route 60, then south through Cumberland Court House until it beared off to the left on Virginia Primary Route 45, the Cumberland Court House-Farmville Road. This was followed to near modern day Brown's Store where, according to the *OR Atlas,* Plate C, a road that does not exist today as it did then branched off to the west and crossed the Little Willis River near its fork with Willis River (where the artillery train bivouacked for the night), then continued on between the two rivers to Curdsville.

100 Jones, Benjamin W., 258.

101 Townsend, 103, 104.

102 Lobrano Diary, LHAC.

103 Ibid.

104 Townsend, 104.

105 Bartlett, 222.

106 Calkins, *From Petersburg*, 35; Calkins, *The Battles*, 13-16.

107 Council Diary, North Carolina Department of Archives and History.

108 Figg, 250.

109 Richard B. Harwell, ed. *A Confederate Diary of the Retreat from Petersburg April 2-20, 1865* (Atlanta, 1953), 15. The day's march started from the river's fork to Curdsville, where it continued west along today's Virginia Secondary Route 633 to 635, then Route 609 into New Store.

110 Lobrano Diary, LHAC.

111 William H. Stewart, "Appomattox." *Tales of the Civil War* (Boston, 1896), 470.

112 Mary L. Gills, *It Happened at Appomattox, The Story of An Historic Virginia Village* (Richmond, Va., 1948), 13.

113 From New Store the march continued west on State Secondary Route 636 to the Appomattox-Buckingham State Forest Headquarters where a left turn was made onto SSR 2307 (Richmond Forest Road), that runs into SSR 626 (Old Richmond Road), to Primary Route 24 through Rose Bower (area of 24 and SSR 618 intersection, about six miles from Appomattox Court House), south on PR 24 (the original road turned off for a short distance on SSR 697 and returns to 24 near New Hope Church), and continues on PR 24 through Appomattox Court House (now Appomattox Court House National Historic Park), to PSR 131 (the Old Courthouse Road). The artillery campsite off the Old Courthouse Road is in an area bordered by present day Jones Street (SSR 1012), SSR1040, and SSR1009. The Civil War Trust (devoted to preservation of Civil War battlefields), in 2010 purchased 45 acres of the Battle of Appomattox Station and Walker's camp site.

114 Charles Poindexter, "Richmond Howitzers. Facts about the battery During the Appomattox Campaign." *SHSP*, Vol. XXVI, 327.

115 W. S. Keiley, "A Wartime Story of a Battery's Last Days" in *Historical Stories about Petersburg.*

Petersburg National Battlefield Park. This is "Willie" Keiley who befriended Eugene Levy in Petersburg.

116 *New Orleans Daily Crescent,* January 26, 1866.

117 Diary of Roger Hannaford, April 2-14, 1865, written in March 1870, Cincinnati Historical Society.

118 Lobrano Diary, LHAC.

119 Keiley, "A Wartime Story of a Battery's Last Days," Petersburg National Battlefield Park.

120 Poindexter, 327, 328.

121 The Confederate infantry referred to numbered less than one hundred artillerymen armed with muskets and rifles from Capt. David N. Walker's Otey and Capt. Crispin Dickeson's Ringgold Virginia batteries. The Federal Cavalry commander, Brevet Maj. Gen. George A. Custer declared they were "about two divisions of infantry, in addition to over thirty pieces of artillery." Poindexter, 328, 329.

122 Jones, Benjamin W., 259.

123 Walker, while shaving, was talking to Brig. Gen. Pendleton who had rode up from the head of the column of Lee's army now moving near Appomattox Court House. During the attack that seemed "entirely remedied" to Pendleton, he reported he "received by courier a note requesting my presence with the commanding general." Pendleton immediately departed but did not meet up with Lee until about one o'clock in the morning; he recorded the general "briefly expressed to me his views" and "desired me, worn and weary, to get some rest, and closed by directing me,—'In the morning be governed by circumstances.'" Lee, 403, 404.

124 Townsend, 104.

125 H. R. Irvine, "Getting Out of It," *CV,* 34 (1926), 383.

126 Cauble, 8, 9. Gary's Brigade was composed of the 7th South Carolina Cavalry Regiment, 420 men, the South Carolina Hampton Legion Cavalry Battalion, 239 men, 7th Georgia Cavalry Regiment, 42 men, and the 24th Virginia Cavalry Regiment, 163 men. This is the number of men indicated surrendered at Appomattox so it is presumed there were more during the battle. *OR* XLVI:1, 1275; "Paroles . . . " *SHSP,* Vol. XV.

127 Edward M. Boykin, *The Falling Flag. Evacuation of Richmond, Retreat and Surrender at Appomattox* (New York, 1874), 49-51.

128 Lobrano Diary, LHAC.

129 Townsend, 104.

130 Cauble, 13.

131 John Richardson Porter Diary, Duke University.

132 Boykin, 52. In 1525 in a decisive battle at Pavia (Italy), during the Franco-Spanish war the French army was smashed, its nobility slaughtered, and King Francis I (1494-1547) was captured. A military catastrophe for France, this battle was hailed as the first modern battle in which firearms defeated men-at-arms.

133 Ibid., 51, 52.

134 J. Watts De Peyster, *Sailor' Creek to Appomattox Court House, 7th, 8th, 9th April 1865; or, The Last Hours of Sheridan's Cavalry. War-Memoranda of Henry Edwin Tremain* (New York, 1885), 30.

135 John Richardson Porter Diary, Duke University.

136 Lobrano Diary, LHAC.

137 *New Orleans The Times-Democrat,* October 5, 1905.

138 Ibid.

139 *Assumption Pioneer,* October 20, 1900.

140 Ibid., May 10, 1879.

141 *Donaldsonville Chief,* September 27, 1884.

142 *Assumption Pioneer,* February 21, 1914.

143 Ibid., November 12, 1921.

144 Owen, 381.

145 De Peyster, 30.

146 B. Lynch, "Retreat from Petersburg Va of the Army of N. Va.," Civil War Papers, LHAC.

147 *OR* XLVI:1, 1132.

148 Bourgeois, 58.

149 Camp Nicholl's Soldiers Home Records, LAGL.

150 *Assumption Pioneer,* May 19, 1894.

151 *Donaldsonville Chief*, June 2, 1883.
152 Camp Nicholl's Soldiers Home Records, LAGL.
153 *Donaldsonville Chief*, September 6, 1884. Levy recorded on April 9 in his diary he saw Plesencia, Dugas, and Terrio with a "squad of prisoners . . . moved to headquarters of provost marshal on George Abbet's farm."
154 Levy Diary, HUC.
155 *Times-Picayune,* December 5, 1930.
156 BAANV Application of J. A. Comstock dated July 24, 1877, LHAC.
157 *Assumption Pioneer*, January 21, 1899.
158 Ibid.
159 BAANV Application of William G. Delesdernier dated October 13, 1906, LHAC.
160 *New Orleans Daily City Item*, December 12, 1891.
161 Confederate Pension Application of Maurice Landry, LDA. Landry was born September 11, 1844, and lived to 90, dying May 8, 1935, the last Donaldsonville Artillery veteran.
162 *Donaldsonville Chief*, December 16, 1916.
163 Ibid., August 19, 1882.
164 *Assumption Pioneer,* May 22, 1909.
165 Jones, Benjamin W., 259.
166 Levy Diary, HUC.
167 Guggenheimer appears to be Joseph Gugenheim, a native of Bavaria who on the 1860 U. S. Census in New Orleans was about forty years old and a dry goods merchant. He is also listed on a muster roll dated April 2, 1861, for Company C, 4th Regiment, European Brigade, La. Militia, but does not appear on any other muster rolls for the war. He may have been one of a number of exiled New Orleanians in Richmond, but how and when he joined the Donaldsonville Canonniers to surrender at Lynchburg is a mystery. CSR.
168 *OR* XLVI:1, 1257.
169 Poindexter, 330-332.
170 Lobrano Diary, LHAC.
171 B. Lynch, "Retreat from Petersburg Va of the Army of N. Va.," Civil War Papers, LHAC.
172 Photographed Record Sheets (from National Archives), Book of Paroles-Lynchburg, Va., LAGL. Paroled also at this time in Lynchburg was forty-six year old Canonnier Sergeant Mathias Ramirez who, according to the muster rolls, had been sick in Lynchburg's Hospital Number 3 since April of 1863.
173 Ibid. Two were from the Louisiana Guard Battery, the other from Capt. William Marshall's Faquier Virginia Artillery.
174 Lobrano Diary, LHAC. He also recorded in his diary on March 27, 1865, "I went down to get Lt. [John R.] McGaughy to sign the historical Memoranda." Evidently it was delivered to Favrot in Richmond and is, like the Donaldsonville Artillery's *Historical Memoranda*, in the Louisiana Historical Association Collection at Tulane University, New Orleans.
175 Adam Shriver Confederate Pension Application, Texas State Library and Archives. A similar statement by Landry is documented in R. Prosper Landry to F. A. Ober, April 4, 1885, letter, Association of the Army of Northern Virginia Papers, LHAC.
176 Levy Diary, HUC.
177 Elizabeth Pritchard, eighteen years old, of Petersburg was probably attending the Farmville Female Academy. In 1870 she was still living at home with her parents who had a total of twelve children. Four brothers served in the Confederate army: William B., 23, who attended the Virginia Military Institute and became a captain in the 38th Virginia Infantry Regiment; John H., 21, private in the 12th Virginia Infantry Regiment; Charles E., 20, also a private in the 12th Virginia; and Nathan B., who in 1864, at 16, enlisted in the Petersburg Local Defense Regiment and in January 1865 transferred to Martin's Battery, Company B, 12th Virginia Light Artillery Battalion. This was the same artillery unit William S. Keiley was in. The 12th Virginia Infantry with John and Charles (six of the ten companies of the regiment were from Petersburg), was the same unit the Donaldsonville Artillery entrenched with during the North Anna Campaign (May 23-May 27, 1864), and again in the Petersburg trenches. No doubt information was exchanged about the 12th Virginia by Miss Pritchard and Levy who remembered the Virginians were "an intelligent set of men." All but John is listed as having surrendered at Appomattox Court House. After the war William taught at the Virginia Military Institute until moving to California where,

in 1876 at San Francisco, he married Margaret S., the fourth child of Confederate Gen. Albert S. Johnston.

178 Levy Diary, HUC. Lee was probably at his temporary headquarters (most likely the R. D. Thaxton house), just outside Farmville north of the Appomattox River in the fork of the road. Freeman, *Lee,* Vol. IV, 97.

179 Levy Diary, HUC.

180 Ibid.

181 Owen, 379.

182 Levy Diary, HUC.

183 Ibid.

184 Ibid.

185 Owen, 380; J. D. Cummings, "The Last Sad Days," *SHSP*, 36 (1908), 261-65; Freeman, *Lee*, Vol. IV, 113, 114, 119.

186 Levy Diary, HUC.

187 Clover Hill Tavern was built in 1819 and restored in 1954. Behind the tavern is the kitchen, now a bookstore, part of the Appomattox Court House National Historical Park.

188 The 15th New York Cavalry in attacking Walker's artillery train pushed on towards the courthouse. A dozen troopers led by their commander moved ahead of the column and charged through the town where they met Confederate skirmishers. They received a volley in front of the courthouse that killed their commander and instantly drove them back. In a moment all was confusion as the rest of the 15th New York ran into Confederate pickets, causing them to fall back through the village. Along the way one captured Levy. Calkins, *Battles,* 41.

189 Robert M. Muldron, 31, (1833-1912), from Sumter, South Carolina, was Assistant Surgeon of Holcombe's Legion. The Legion's four cavalry companies were consolidated with five independent companies to form the 7th South Carolina Cavalry Regiment in March 1864. The 7th was part of Gary's Brigade that went to the aid of Walker's artillery at the Battle of Appomattox Station.

190 Levy Diary, HUC.

191 Owen, 381.

192 Levy Diary, HUC.

193 Donaldsonville *Le Drapeau*, January 26, 1867, TU.

194 R. Prosper Landry Address, Landry-Pedesclaux Family Papers, LSU. The first message by Grant requesting Lee to surrender was received on April 7th at about half-past nine o'clock in the evening. Coincidently, Grant's note was written and sent from the Booker Hotel (Randolph House), in Farmville. In the afternoon of April 8th Pendleton approached Lee and told him that a number of officers had met the previous evening and concluded they "ought to stop the fighting and open negotiations for the surrender of the army." Lee's response was, "Surrender? I have too many good fighting men for that!" Freeman, *Lee,* Vol. IV, 103, 109.

CHAPTER NINETEEN

1 R. Prosper Landry Address, Landry-Pedesclaux Family Papers, LSU.

2 Freeman, *Lieutenants*, Vol. III, 729.

3 Owen, 382. Owen had de facto command when McIntosh, along with several companions, determined that morning to "Effect our escape, and quietly rode off before any orders had been promulgated. We lay in the swamp of the Appomattox all the day and escaped through the enemy's lines the following night." United Daughters of the Confederacy, John K. McIver Chapter, *Reminiscences Collected by the John K. McIver Chapter, United Daughters of the Confederacy* (Columbia, S. C., 1911), 52.

4 Freeman, *Lee,* Vol. IV, 128.

5 Owen, 380; Gallagher, *Fighting,* 530, 537, 538; Graves, 63.

6 R. Prosper Landry Address, Landry-Pedesclaux Family Papers, LSU.

7 This is the same Osman Latrobe who came to "play the deuce with the enemy" with Prosper Landry's gun at the battle of Fredericksburg on December 13, 1862. Osman Latrobe Diary, Typescript, 14, Virginia Historical Society.

8 Owen, 384, 385.

9 Freeman, *Lee,* Vol. IV, 129-131.

10 R. Prosper Landry Address, Landry-Pedesclaux Family Papers, LSU.
11 Freeman, *Lee,* Vol. IV, 143, 144.
12 Ibid., 142.
13 R. Prosper Landry Address, Landry-Pedesclaux Family Papers, LSU.
14 Freeman, *Lee,* Vol. IV, 144-146.
15 Ibid., 146, 147.
16 R. Prosper Landry Address, Landry-Pedesclaux Family Papers, LSU.
17 Owen, 387.
18 *Assumption Pioneer,* December 16, 1899.
19 Owen, 387.
20 Graves, 63.
21 Owen, 388, 389. Only three Donaldsonville Canonniers from the High Bridge detachment did not answer the roll. They were Sgt. Oscar Demesme, killed in action, Pvt. Eugene Levy, captured, and Cpl. Paul Humbert, who escaped on his own and on April 14, 1865, joined the Fifth Company, Washington Artillery, commanded by Capt. C. H. Slocumb. Humbert surrendered with Lt. General Richard Taylor's command at Citronelle, Alabama, on May 4, 1865, and was paroled at Meridian, Mississippi, on May 10, 1865.
22 *Southern Historical Society Papers,* 15 (1887), 62, 63. Prosper Landry also listed the following four men on the Appomattox Roll of the Donaldsonville Artillery to be paroled: Ernest A. Delahaye, a lieutenant in St. Paul's Foot Rifles, 7th Louisiana Zouave Infantry Battalion that was later merged into the 15th Louisiana Infantry Regiment; Joseph Prados, a private in Captain Charles A. Green's Louisiana Guard Battery; and A. Bormare or Boiuare and H. Thing or Thery, of whom there is no definite information on.
23 "To Whom It May Concern" from Louis Lefort, December 10, 1884, Dunn-Landry Family Papers, Amistad Research Center, TU.
24 Gallagher, *Fighting,* 537, 538.
25 Chandler L. Klotz Jr. to the author, January 19, 1999, letter. Donaldsonville Pvt. Abraham Klotz's little piece of wood was encased in "some kind of metal" along with his certificate from the Benevolent Association of the Army of Northern Virginia and remains in possession of his descendants.
26 Chesson, 380. Paul E. Laresche was the brother of Donaldsonville Canonnier William. On January 14, 1864, he enlisted at sixteen years of age as a private in the 3rd Company, Battalion Washington Artillery, and surrendered at Appomattox Court House with his command.
27 Gallagher, *Fighting,* 541.
28 Owen, 389, 390.
29 Ibid., 390, 391.
30 Gallagher, *Fighting,* 541.
31 Owen, 391.
32 Caldwell, 308.
33 Owen, 392, 393.
34 Confederate Pension Applications, LDA. Both included their parole with their application. Mioton was paroled at Lynchburg on April 13, 1865.
35 Benevolent Association of the Army of Virginia application of E. L. Monnot, December 20, 1882. LHAC.
36 John Richardson Porter Diary, Duke University.
37 McCarthy, *Detailed Minutiae,* 157, 158.
38 Gallagher, *Fighting,* 541.
39 *Donaldsonville Chief,* June 3, 1909.
40 John H. Moore, "Appomattox, Profile of a Mid-Nineteenth-Century Community." *The Virginia Magazine of History and Biography,* 88 (1980), 490, 491.
41 W. B. Judkins Memoir, Sara Hightower Regional Library.
42 Levy Diary, HUC.
43 Ibid.
44 *Biographical and Historical Memoirs of Louisiana,* Vol. I, 517.
45 R. Prosper Landry Address, Landry-Pedesclaux Family Papers, LSU.
46 Helene Dupuy Diary, DPL. Pvt. William Leopold served in the 22nd Louisiana Infantry Regiment and was captured and paroled at Vicksburg, Mississippi on July 4, 1863. He was exchanged and

served as an artilleryman with the 22nd Louisiana Infantry Regiment Consolidated but was again captured at Spanish Fort, Mobile, Alabama, on April 8, 1865 and again paroled at Vicksburg on May 6, 1865.

47 Gallagher, *Fighting,* 547.

48 NA, CSR.

49 Confederate Pension Application of Charles Numa Cure, LDA.

50 Levy Diary, HUC.

51 Andrews, *The War-Time Journal,* 184, 185.

52 Moody was the commander of the Madison (La.) Light Artillery of Lt. Col. Frank Huger's Battalion, formally Alexander's in the Army of Northern Virginia. Moody was described as straight and muscular, over six feet tall and weighing two hundred pounds by Brig. Gen. Edward Alexander, who also wrote that Moody "always dressed well and . . . rather prided himself in a carriage and general appearance not unlike Gen. Lee's. He was a good soldier and disciplinarian . . . but he was not an easy man to get along with generally." Gallagher, *Fighting,* 160, 161.

53 *New York Herald,* July 4, 1865.

54 Andrews, *The War-Time Journal,* 175. The town of Washington today describes itself as an elegant and graceful town of Southern hospitality with tree-lined streets and historic sites. The population is around 4,000.

55 Ibid., 92.

56 Ibid., 181-184.

57 Varina Davis, *Jefferson Davis, Ex-President of the Confederate States of America: A Memoir by His Wife in Two Volumes* (New York, 1890), II:616.

58 Ficklen's beautiful home "Holly Court" today operates as a Bed & Breakfast located on Liberty Street between South Alexander and Jefferson Streets in Washington, Georgia.

59 Andrews, *The War-Time Journal,* 192, 193. Eliza Francis Andrews (1840-1931) became a well-known teacher, writer, and botanist. She wrote several novels, a textbook on botany, and published her diary of her experiences during the War Between the States. Visiting Haywood after being transferred to Washington, Georgia, in February 1865 was one of Eliza's "far-off Virginia cousins" Lt. Col. John J. Garnett, Maurin's former battalion commander. Of the "charming Creole accent" Eliza made note in her diary that it is "a pleasure to listen to." Andrews, 92, 137, 192.

60 Ibid., 193.

61 Burton N. Harrison, "The Capture of Jefferson Davis," *The Century Illustrated Monthly Magazine,* 27 (November 1883 to April 1884), 139.

62 Davis, Vol. II, 617.

63 Harrison, 138, 139. Harrison, an 1859 Yale University graduate, was born in New Orleans.

64 Ibid., 139. Harrison recruited a driver for each team plus several supernumeraries, friends of the drivers, with the promise that the wagons and mules should be divided between them when at the journey's end.

65 Mrs. Burton Harrison, *Recollections Grave and Gay* (New York, 1911), 225.

66 Ibid.

67 Harrison, "The Capture of Jefferson Davis," 140.

68 Davis, II:617, 618.

69 Ibid.

70 Harrison, "The Capture of Jefferson Davis," 140.

71 Davis, II:618, 619.

72 Harrison, "The Capture of Jefferson Davis," 140.

73 This was in the evening of May 6th near Dublin, described as a "miserable little village." *The Macon Daily Telegraph,* May 14, 1865.

74 Davis, II:636, 637.

75 Harrison, "The Capture of Jefferson Davis," 140, 141.

76 *OR* XLIX:1, 520.

77 Given Campbell Papers: "Memorandum of a Journal, Kept Daily during the Last March of Jefferson Davis," Library of Congress; John Taylor Wood Diary, Southern Historical Collection, UNCCH.

78 Harrison, "The Capture of Jefferson Davis," 141.

79 Ibid. At this time Abbeville had only three families living there. *OR* XLIX:1, 521.

80 Ibid.

81 *OR* XLIX:1, 539, 540.

82 Harrison, "The Capture of Jefferson Davis," 141. Just six or so houses comprised Irwinville that today is still rural, with a population of 297.

83 Ibid., 142.

84 Ibid., 143. Videttes were posted on the road, but they too, from utter exhaustion, went to sleep. *The Macon Daily Telegraph,* May 14, 1865.

85 *OR* XLIX:1, 536.

86 Harrison, "The Capture of Jefferson Davis," 142.

87 *OR* XLIX:1, 536, 537.

88 Harrison, "The Capture of Jefferson Davis," 144.

89 Davis, Vol. II, 640.

90 J. William Jones, *The Davis Memorial Volume; or our Dead President, Jefferson Davis and the World's Tribute to His Memory* (Richmond, Va., 1890), 408.

91 *OR* XLIX:1, 537.

92 Harrison, "The Capture of Jefferson Davis," 144. Several days after the capture, Reuben Walton Clements, a thoroughly unreconstructed rebel and Confederate soldier, visited the site. He vowed that when God would allow him the strength and health to rebuild his fortunes he would buy the land so that it would always remain in the hands of the southern people. In a short time he managed to do just that. In July of 1920 Clements's son, the Honorable J. B. Clements, successfully deeded to the state of Georgia four acres of land containing the capture site. Today the Jefferson Davis Memorial State Historic Site is a 12.6-acre park with a monument and museum. The site is listed on the National Register of Historic Places. The capture location is 178 miles southwest of Washington, Georgia. "Brief History Jefferson Davis Memorial Historic Site," Jefferson Davis Memorial Historic Site, Fitzgerald, Georgia.

93 Dunbar Rowland, ed. *Jefferson Davis Constitutionalist, His Letters, Papers and Speeches*, Vol. VII (Jackson, Miss. 1923), 19. This is from a pencil memorandum, apparently in Harrison's hand in the Burton N. Harrison Collection, Library of Congress. In an 1884 *Century Magazine* article Harrison wrote about the incident but changed his punctuation, two words, and two sentences. Instead of "The clatter of the cymbals and the noise of the drums . . ." he rephrased it: "The startling burst of Music . . . " and, "then occupied a house where they struck up 'Yankee Doodle'" he rewrote, "occupied a house within range of my guns, where they began 'Yankee Doodle.'" Harrison, "The Capture of Jefferson Davis," 144, 145.

94 Davis, II:642.

95 *Macon Daily Telegraph*, May 14, 1865.

96 The commodious Lanier House Hotel, four stories high with an observatory turret on top, was opened in 1850 after being elegantly and tastefully built. In downtown Macon, it was torn down in 1975 to build a parking garage. *Macon Daily Telegraph*, June 25, 1850.

97 Davis, II:644, 645.

98 *OR* XLIX:1, 537. The steamer *Standish* brought them to Savannah, Georgia, where they boarded the *Emilie* to Hilton Head, South Carolina. There they transferred to the *Clyde* and under convoy of the steam sloop-of-war *Tuscarora*, arrived off the coast of Virginia at Fortress Monroe.

99 *Donaldsonville Chief*, October 4, 1916.

100 *Biographical and Historical Memoirs of Louisiana,* Vol. II, 245.

CHAPTER TWENTY

1 *Times-Picayune,* July 18, 1865.

2 Marchand, *Flight*, 165.

3 NA, CSR.

4 *Times-Picayune,* July 18, 1865.

5 William O. Scroggs, *The Story of Louisiana* (New York, 1936), 273.

6 Marchand, *Flight*, 165.

7 McCarthy, 215.

8 It would be several decades before agricultural production equaled that of 1860-61. Edwin A. Davis, *Louisiana, A Narrative History* (Baton Rouge, 1961), 275, 278.

9 Scroggs, 274-278; Davis, *Louisiana, A Narrative History*, 271.

10 Marchand, *Flight*, 165.
11 James D. Wilson Jr., "The Donaldsonville Incident of 1870: A Study of Local Party Dissension and Republican Infighting in Reconstruction Louisiana." *Louisiana History*, 38 (1997), 333.
12 "To Whom It May Concern" from Louis Lefort, December 10, 1884, letter, Dunn-Landry Family Papers, Amistad Research Center, Tulane University. Pierre Caliste Landry was born on April 19, 1841, on a plantation across the Mississippi River from Donaldsonville and sold into slavery at age thirteen to M. S. Bringier, owner of several large sugar plantations in Ascension Parish. Having been school educated at an early age, he was subsequently appointed superintendent of the yard and its servants on the Houmas Plantation. He was also allowed to form a commercial partnership with the chief butler, and they operated a prosperous store on the plantation until 1863. Landry remained on Houmas Plantation until 1866 when he moved across the river and settled in Donaldsonville.
13 Wilson Jr., 332.
14 Pierre Landry, untitled manuscript, Dunn-Landry Family Papers, Amistad Research Center, TU.
15 Ibid.
16 Marchand, *Flight*, 166. Fortier also headed the committee to supervise the construction of the new courthouse and jail in 1867.
17 *Index to Reports of Committees of The House of Representatives for the Second Session of the Forty-third Congress, 1874-'75* (Washington, D. C., 1875), 640. The report is in "Conditions of the South, February 23, 1875, Report No. 261," 639-641. The mayor's term of office was for one year.
18 Wilson Jr., 340.
19 "To Whom It May Concern" from Louis Lefort, December 10, 1884, letter, Dunn-Landry Family Papers, Amistad Research Center, TU.
20 *Cincinnati Daily Enquirer,* November 17, 1870.
21 Wilson Jr., 342.
22 "To Whom It May Concern" from Louis Lefort, December 10, 1884, letter, Dunn-Landry Family Papers, Amistad research Center, TU. Three murderers of Lawes and Schoenberg were acquitted when a Legislative Act changed the venue to Jefferson Parish, and after a short deliberation the jury rendered a verdict of not guilty. Despite the acquittal, other Republicans were determined to prosecute and the three were re-arrested by Lefort, who at the time was a Deputy Sheriff. Corrupt Reconstruction politicians had the murderers again released.
23 *Flake's* [Galveston, Texas] *Bulletin*, November 19, 1870.
24 *Times-Picayune,* November 3, 1902.
25 Ibid.
26 *Index to Reports of Committees of The House of Representatives for the Second Session of the Forty-third Congress, 1874-'75* (Washington D. C., 1875), 640.
27 Davis, 270.
28 *Donaldsonville Chief,* March 13, 1875.
29 Ibid.
30 *Donaldsonville Chief,* July 10, 1875.
31 This is the same band of black men that went to Virginia with the Donaldsonville Artillery in September 1861.
32 *Donaldsonville Chief,* July 10, 1875.
33 Ibid.
34 Ibid.
35 Ibid., November 4, 1876.
36 Ibid., January 13, 1877.
37 Scroggs, 282.
38 *Assumption Pioneer,* July 7, 1877.
39 Five 12-pounder brass howitzers were seized during the battle of Liberty Place at the foot of Canal Street in New Orleans by the Democratic militia forces that defeated the Republican Reconstruction government forces of the Metropolitan Police and black militia under former Confederate Gen. James Longstreet. Two guns named *Redemption* and *Resurrection* where taken for the use of the Washington Artillery. The *14th of September,* the date of the Battle of Liberty Place in 1874, is believed to be one that was brought from the state arsenal by the Washington

Artillery to Donaldsonville for use by the Canonniers.

40 *Donaldsonville Chief*, July 7, 1877. The flag was made "of costly blue silk, edged with gold fringe. On one side is the inscription: Cannoneers of Donaldson./En Avant. In the center is the device of the State seal—a pelican feeding its young, encircled with the motto, 'Union, Justice and Confidence.' On the reverse of the banner is inscribed: Presented by the Ladies/of the/Parish of Ascension./July 4th, 1877. Beneath the inscription appears the familiar representation of two cannon crossed, over three cannon balls."

41 *Donaldsonville Chief*, July 7, 1877, and December 23, 1882. The Canonnier Field Band was also called the Conway Field Band under the leadership of Frederick "Gus" Conway, and it continued to furnish music for *Le Compagnie d'Artillerie. Donaldsonville Chief*, May 18, 1878. This was the Donaldsonville Canonniers first reappearance in their blue antebellum uniform since they wore Confederate gray.

42 *Donaldsonville Chief*, July 7, 1877.

43 Ibid.

44 *Assumption Pioneer*, July 7, 1877.

45 *Donaldsonville Chief*, July 7, 1877.

46 Ibid., August 14, 1878.

47 *New Orleans Daily Picayune*, July 22, 1879.

48 Ibid. Veteran Confederate soldiers organized the Louisiana Field Artillery about 1869. Two noteworthy members were Lt. Col. Merritt B. "Buck" Miller, second in command, the same position held when during the last year of the war he was assigned to Richardson's artillery battalion that included the Donaldsonville Artillery. The commander of the Field Artillery's Battery "A" was New Orleanian Joseph Numa Augustin, the son of *Le Compagnie d'Artillerie de Donaldson's* first captain of the same name.

49 *New Orleans Daily Picayune*, August 5, 1879.

50 *Donaldsonville Chief*, July 10, 1880.

51 *New Orleans Daily Item*, September 16, 1880.

52 *New Orleans Daily Picayune*, September 14, 1880.

53 Ibid., September 15, 1880.

54 Ibid. World-renowned Antoine's Restaurant opened in 1840 and moved to its present location at 713 Rue St. Louis in the French Quarter in 1868. It is still serving French-Creole cuisine from the 1868 location and can hold upwards of 700 guest.

55 *Donaldsonville Chief*, February 28, 1885.

56 *Times-Picayune*, April 27, 1885.

57 *Assumption Pioneer*, August 5, 1893.

58 HMDLM, June 26-July15, 1898, Vol. 234 (LAGL, 1938), 113.

59 *New Orleans Daily City Item*, June 9, 1891.

60 *Baton Rouge True Advocate*, July 18, 1891.

61 "Edmund Maurin," The "Lost Cause," (November 1899), 69.

62 HMDLM, June 1-December 31, 1891, Vol. 172 (LAGL, 1938), 12, 95.

63 *Baton Rouge True Advocate*, February 14, 1893.

64 *Assumption Pioneer*, March 18, 1893.

65 Ibid.

66 *Times-Picayune*, May 14, 1893.

67 Charles E. Coates, "How the Tigers Got Their Name," *LSU Alumni News*, October 1937.

68 *New Orleans Times Democrat*, November 16, 1895; Report of the Adjutant General, 1895, 61, LAGL.

69 Born February 17, 1860, in Donaldsonville, McCulloh became Ascension Parish's District Attorney in 1888. It was recorded "through his [father's] interposition that the records of the parish were not burned during the war." *Biographical and Historical Memoirs of Louisiana*, Vol. II, 221.

70 Prosper Landry was also serving as Quartermaster of the United Confederate Veteran's Victor Maurin Camp No. 38.

71 *New Orleans Daily Picayune*, June 22, 1898.

72 Donaldsonville's Battery C was recruited from Ascension, Assumption, Lafayette, St. Martin, East Baton Rouge, West Baton Rouge, West Feliciana, and St. James parishes. Sergeant Hubert Treille Jr. was the only son of former Canonnier Lt. Hubert Treille and Sgt. Charles Carmouche

the son of the late Canonnier Pvt. Desire Carmouche. They were the only ones in the battery who were sons of veterans that served in the Donaldsonville Artillery with the Army of Northern Virginia.

73 *Assumption Pioneer,* July 2, 1898.
74 HMDLM, 1898, Vol. 237 (LAGL, 1938), 26.
75 General Orders No. 6, State of Louisiana, Adjutant General's Office, April 2, 1898, LAGL.
76 *New Orleans Daily City Item,* August 4, 1879.
77 *Baton Rouge Daily Advocate,* January 25, 1895.

ROSTERS and BIOGRAPHIES

1 NA, CSR.
2 OR, XXI, 620.
3 Jean Reynaud Jacques Prosper Landry to Adele Pedesclaux Landry, September 1864, UV.
4 Louise "Pie" Lanoux correspondence with author dated May 13, 2008.
5 Eugenie Braud, New Orleans, to Archbishop Perche in Lourdes, France, June 10, 1876, Archdiocese of New Orleans Collection, Notre Dame Archives.
6 Cutrer, 177.
7 Katherine Kerne, a granddaughter from Thibodeaux, related that some of the children were sent to relatives to be raised (see Pidoux entry). Carmouche's war mementos were destroyed by a fire at Mrs. Kerne's mother's home. Author's correspondence with Katherine Kerne, March 1, 1997.
8 Simone de la Souchere, *Napoleon's Soldiers in America* (New Orleans, 1972), and *Louisiana: Comprising Sketches of Parishes, Towns, Events, Institutions, and Persons, Arranged in Cyclopedic Form,* Vol. 3, 601-602, Alcée Fortier, ed., published in 1914 by Century Historical Association.
9 Enumeration of ex-Confederate Soldiers, 1911 census, New Orleans Public Library, New Orleans.
10 LHAC.
11 Vara Smith Stanley, *A History of Appomattox County* (Appomattox, Va., 1965), 33, 34.
12 *Biographical and Historical Memoirs of Louisiana,* Vol. 1, 398.
13 Marchand, *Flight*, 206.
14 Louise "Pie" Lanoux, Pie, *We Have Met Our Neighbors* (Gonzales, La., n.d.), 39.
15 Ibid.
16 NA, CSR.
17 NA, CSR.
18 Alcée Fortier, ed., *Louisiana: Comprising Sketches of Parishes, Towns, Events, Institutions, and Persons, Arranged in Cyclopedic Form,* Vol. 3, (Century Historical Association, n.d.), 169-170.
19 *Louisiana History* 38 (Spring 1997), 167, 168.
20 *Times-Picayune,* January 17, 1887.
21 *OR,* XXI, 620.
22 NA, Records of the Assistant Commissioner for the State of Louisiana, Bureau of Refugees, Freedman and Abandoned Lands, 1865-1869, microfilm M1027, Roll 34, Records Relating to Murders and Outrages.
23 Donaldsonville Artillery *Historical Memoranda*, LHAC.
24 NA, *U. S. Civil War Draft Registrations Records, 1863-1865.*
25 NA, United States Seaman's Protection Certificates, 1792-1868.
26 The Widow Pedesclaux's Plantation, formerly known as Point Pleasant, was sold in 1871 to Jacob Lemann. He had the magnificent antebellum plantation dwelling taken down and rebuilt across from the Donaldsonville Courthouse in 1881. Lemann lived in the large and elegant mansion located at 218 Houmas Street. Still standing, it has been modernized with extensive renovations and bricked. *Times-Picayune,* January 24, 1852, January 23, 1870, November 20, 1901.
27 *OR,* XXI 620.
28 Jean Reynaud Jaques Prosper Landry to Adele Pedesclaux Landry, September 1864 letter, UV.
29 *Louisiana Historical Association Catalogue, Memorial Hall,* September 17, 1917, Book 2. Landry's parole was displayed in the North Hall Annex.
30 *Donaldsonville Chief,* April 17, 1875.
31 Adam Shriver Confederate Pension Application, Texas State Library and Archives.

32 Ascension Parish Probate Records, 1812-1897, LDA.
33 *Times-Picayune,* January 17, 1887.
34 *The Louisiana Planter and Sugar Manufacturer* (New Orleans Weekly), January 22 and March 6, 1909, 53, 148.
35 Marchand, *Flight,* 209.
36 Ibid.
37 Ibid., 208.
38 Enumeration of ex-Confederate Soldiers, 1911 census, New Orleans Public Library.
39 Chesson, 271.
40 The M. B. A. Hall was located at 51 (now 611), Bienville Street, New Orleans, and its motto was: *Non Sibi Seds Suis* ("Not for Ourselves but for Others"). *A History of the Proceedings in the City of New Orleans, on the occasion of the Funeral Ceremonies in Honor of James Abram Garfield, Late President of the United States, which took place on Monday, September 26th, 1881* (New Orleans, 1881), 98, 207.
41 *Cincinnati Daily Enquirer,* May 7, 1874.
42 *New York Herald,* July 21, 1871.
43 NA, *U. S. Civil War Draft Registrations Records, 1863-1864.*
44 *OR* IIL, I:176.
45 *Reports of Committees of the House of Representatives for the Second Session of the Forty-third Congress, 1874-'75,* 640. The report is in "Conditions of the South, February 23, 1875, Report No. 261," 639-641.
46 *Flakes Bulletin* (Galveston, Texas), November 19, 1870.
47 Marchand, *Flight,* 224.
48 Betram W. Korn, *Jews and Negro Slavery in the Old South, 1789-1865* (Elkins Park, Pa., 1961), 42.
49 *New Orleans Daily Crescent,* February 9, 1861; *New Orleans Daily Delta*, February 9, 1861; *New Orleans Daily True Delta*, February 9, February 12, 1861.
50 From Shakespeare's *Othello,* Levy's favorite play. He is quoting from Othello's well-known and moving farewell speech in Act III, scene iii.
51 Simonhoff, Harry. *Jewish Participants in the Civil War* (New York, 1963), 249.
52 *New York Times*, February 28, 1912.
53 *Times-Picayune*, October 21, 1891, August 5, 1896, January 13, 1918.
54 Korn, *Jews and Negro Slavery in the Old South,* 42.
55 Celine B. Verret, *The Church of the Assumption Through the Years* (Plattenville, La., 1995), 38.
56 Prosper Landry, *Southern Historical Society Papers*, Vol. 23, 200.
57 *OR*, Vol. XXI, 620.
58 *Richmond Daily Dispatch*, July 1, 1861.
59 *Louisiana History* 38 (1997), 167, 168.
60 *Donaldsonville Le Drapeau,* February 1868.
61 Located in "Monnot/Lanier Family Papers," University of New Orleans.
62 *Times-Picayune*, March 19, 1902.
63 *Le Vigilant*, November 29, 1846. An advertisement noted Maurin's Groceries had in stock: "Bordeaux and Marseilles Wine in cask; Claret in boxes, Chateau-Margaux, Hautbrion, Lafitte, Latour, St. Estephe and St. Julien; Madeira, Muscat, Malaga, Champague and white wine; Anisette in barrels and baskets; Maraschino, Curacao, Dantzick Brandy, Absynthe, Guignolet, Kirsh Wasser, Cordials assorted in boxes; Orange Flower water; French and American Brandy; Holland and American Gin; Old Bourbon and common Whiskey; Jamaica and Louisiana Rhum; Olive, Lard and Sperm oil; Sperm and Star candles; French, Boston, Western and New Orleans Soap; Olives, Pickles, capers, Sardines, Pickled shad, Salmon and Lobsters; Sugar cured hams, smoked shoulders; Lard and Butter; Crashed, Loaf and brown sugar; Powder in kegs and canisters; Shot all sizes; Percussion Caps; Demijohn and bottled corks; Vermicelles; Tea, Gunpowder and Imperial; Havana and Rio coffee; Letter Foolscap and wrapping paper; Raisons, Prunes and almonds; matches, nails all sizes; chocolate, codfish, herrings and mackerel, ginger, pepper, nutmegs, cloves, pearlash, American and French mustard; chewing, smoking leaf tobacco and snuff. Always on hand a general assortment of Havanna, melees and common segars and other articles too numerous to mention. Victor Maurin."
64 *Times-Picayune*, January 31, 1855.

65 Durel, 988.
66 She was the daughter of Hypolite Vives and Eulalie Mollere Vives, sister of Canonnier Camille Mollere's grandfather and Canonnier Duffossard Mollere's grandfather.
67 *OR* XI:2, 781.
68 *OR* XIX:1, 834.
69 *Diocese of Baton Rouge Catholic Church Records*, Vol. 10, 407.
70 *Louisiana Historical Association Collection, Memorial Hall, September 1, 1917*, Book 2, LHAC.
71 *Times-Picayune*, May 28, 1893.
72 *Louisiana Historical Association Catalogue, Memorial Hall, September 1, 1917*, Book 2, LHAC.
73 University of Norte Dame Archives: Camille Mollere to Archbishop, March 9, 1857 letter; J. D. Porres to Archbishop, September 6, 1857 letter; Father Bertail to Father, December 6, 1858 letter.
74 *OR* XXI, 620.
75 De la Souchere, 110, 183.
76 Letter to the Editor of the *Richmond Times-Dispatch*, May 21, 1934, from (Mrs.) E. L. Monnot.
77 *OR* XXI, 620.
78 Enumeration of ex-Confederate Soldiers, 1911 census, New Orleans Public Library.
79 Ibid.
80 A descendent noted Aimé's flute survived the war but was broken by great-great grand "kids" playing with it. Denise "DeeDee" Sanders correspondence with author, October 17, 2010.
81 John S. Hilbert to author, February 26, 2001, letter.
82 Milton F. Hilbert Jr. to John S. Hilbert, December 28, 2000 (copy of letter in possession of the author).
83 Letters of Rougeau, June 12, 1865 and October 16, 1865, Archdiocese of New Orleans Collection, University of Notre Dame.
84 Jean Reynaud Jaques Prosper Landry letter to Adele Pedesclaux Landry, 1864, UV.
85 *Times-Picayune*, August 4, 1902.
86 John A. Rybiski letters to author, August 16, 1995, and February 9, 1996.
87 Chambers, 72.
88 William K. Kay, "Mementoes of the Donaldsonville Artillery," *Military Collector & Historian, Journal of the Company of Military Collectors & Historians,* 8 (Spring 1956), 21, 22.
89 *The Lemann Family of Louisiana: An Account Compiled by Bernard Lemann from Diaries, Correspondence and Personal Reminiscenses* (Donaldsonville, La., 1965).
90 LDA: Ascension Parish Probate Records, 1812-1897.
91 Herbert T. Ezekiel and Gaston Lichrnstein, *The History of the Jews Of Richmond from 1769 to 1917* (Richmond, Va., 1917), 194, 195.
92 Glen R. Conrad, ed., *A Dictionary of Louisiana Biography*, Vol. II (New Orleans, La., 1998), 722-723.
93 *Assumption Pioneer*, April 20, 1907.
94 Albert Schmidt to Father, Noevember 21, 1863 letter, Gustavus Schmidt Correspondences, LSU.
95 *Times-Picayune*, July 28, 1902.
96 *Schmidt Family Papers, 1816-1916,* located in Special Collections, TU.
97 Conrad, 722-723.
98 *Assumption Pioneer*, April 20, 1907.
99 Albert Schmidt to Father, November 21, 1863, Gustavus Schmidt Correspondences, LSU.
100 *Schmidt Family Papers, 1816-1916* .
101 Adam Shriver Confederate Pension Application, Texas State Library and Archives.
102 Bourgeois, 58.
103 Sobral File, Oak Alley, Louisiana, Courtesy Andre Jacobs, Lutcher, Louisiana.
104 Bourgeois, 32.
105 Ibid., 58.
106 Enumeration of ex-Confederate Soldiers, 1911 census, New Orleans Public Library.
107 *Archdiocese of Baton Rouge Records.*
108 *The Louisiana Planter and Sugar Manufacturer, A Weekly Newspaper,* January 22, 1909, and March 6, 1909.
109 Marie Dugas (Thibideaux's great-granddaughter), letter to the author, October 17, 2005.

110 *The Daily Times* (Donaldsonville), May 13, 1896.
111 Francis T. Nicholls to Lawrence D. Nicholls, November 5, 1854, letter, Nicholl's Family Papers, TU.
112 *Times-Picayune*, July 9, 1898.
113 Gordon H. Coe, "Get the Job Done," *Air Force*, July 1943.
114 R. Hugh Simmons, Fort Delaware Society, to author, April 8, 2008, correspondence.
115 On Ferdinand Viola's Death Certificate dated November 11, 1961, father listed as "Joe P. Viola of Louisiana." Comptroller's Office, "Texas County Tax Rolls, 1846-1910." Texas State Archives, Austin, Texas. Lucko, Paul M. "Retrieve Plantation," Handbook of Texas Online. Accessed on July 4, 2012. Texas State Historical Association.
116 *Louisiana Historical Association Catalogue, Memorial Hall, September 1, 1917,* Book 2, LHAC.
117 Bourgeois, 76. Buena Vista was bequeathed in 1943 to the American Red Cross.
118 Marchand, *Flight*, 220. Buena Vista Road today leads to the cemetery, all that is left of the plantation except for the fields of sugar cane still under cultivation.
119 NA, *U.S. Civil War Draft Registrations Records, 1863-1865.*
120 *New Orleans Daily True Delta*, January 6, 1859.
121 *Donaldsonville Chief,* December 23, 1882, June 2, 1883.
122 NA, *U. S. Civil War Draft Registrations Records, 1863-1864.*
123 East Ascension Genealogical and Historical Society, *Ascension Roots*, XVI:4 (December 1996).
124 DPL
125 *Annual Report of the Board of Health to the General Assembly of Louisiana for the year 1880* (New Orleans, 1881), 213, 214.
126 April 10, 1856, letter, Archdiocese of New Orleans Collection, University of Notre Dame. A marriage between a Catholic and non-Catholic should not be. Therefore one of the slaves in this instance was a Catholic and the other was not. Father Boglioli was seeking permission to validate (or bless), their marriage. Louise "Pie Lanoux" correspondence to author, September 30, 2010.
127 Dorothy Dawes and Charles Nolan, ed. "Father Charles Boglioli (1814-1882): Leper Priest of Charity Hospital," by Warren Dicharry, CM. *Religious Pioneers, Building the Faith in the Archdiocese of New Orleans* (New Orleans, 2004), 65-75; *New Orleans Daily Picayune*, July 23, 1882; *The Atlanta Constitution,* July 27, 1882.

INDEX

(Does not include the "Rosters and Biographies" Section)